Glory of the Logos in the Flesh

Glory of the Logos in the Flesh

ST. JOHN PAUL'S THEOLOGY OF THE BODY

Michael Maria Waldstein

SAPIENTIA PRESS
of Ave Maria University

Sapientia Press
of Ave Maria University
5050 Ave Maria Blvd.
Ave Maria, FL 34142
800-537-5487

Distributed by:
The Catholic University of America Press
c/o HFS
P.O. Box 50370
Baltimore, MD 21211
800-537-5487

Text and Cover Design: Kachergis Book Design
Cover Image: *Bacchus and Ariadne*, by Titian. Used by permission of the
National Gallery, London.

Printed in the United States of America.

Library of Congress Control Number: 2015955270

ISBN: 978-1-932589-76-4

For Scott Hahn

CONTENTS

PART III. MAP

Introduction 675

Part One, Chapter One. Christ Appeals to the Beginning (TOB 1–23) 684

Part One, Chapter Two. Christ Appeals to the Human Heart (TOB 24–63) 703

Part One, Chapter Three. Christ Appeals to the Resurrection (TOB 64–86) 729

NOTE ON THE COVER ART

Titian, *Bacchus and Ariadne* (1523),

copyright National Gallery London

The story of Dionysus (Bacchus) and Ariadne is part of the founding myth of Athens. Titian's *Bacchus and Ariadne* shows the first encounter between the god and Ariadne.

King Minos of Crete had compelled Athens to send seven young men and seven young women at regular intervals to Crete to be devoured by the monster Minotaur. Theseus, the son of King Aegeus of Athens, volunteered to be one of them. He fell in love with Ariadne, daughter of King Minos, and she with him. With Ariadne's help, he killed the Minotaur and fled with her. According to one version of the myth, Dionysus appeared to him, demanding Ariadne for himself to marry her and raise her to Mt. Olympus as an immortal goddess. Theseus abandoned her on the island of Naxos in the middle of their first night together.

When Ariadne wakes up in the morning, she sees Theseus's ship far out to sea, visible in Titian's painting to the left of Ariadne's shoulder. In despair, she rushes to the edge of the cliff overlooking the ocean to throw herself down to her death. At this moment, captured by Titian, she hears the arrival of Dionysus and turns to look at him, her right arm still stretched out toward Theseus's ship. The god is leaping from his chariot, his right foot still in midair, his eyes full of intense desire. His engagement ring for Ariadne appears in the sky above her, a ring of eight stars, the constellation *Corona Borealis* (Northern Crown).

The encounter is set in a vast space of land, sea, and the heavens. Between Ariadne and the god, in the far distance, at a point to which the eye is guided by the landscape, Titian placed a building that is out of place in a Greek setting. It has a characteristically upward pointing tower, the tower of a Christian Church, one of the many details in Titian's reshaping of the myth in his Christian imagination.

When Socrates had been condemned to death by the Athenian assembly, his execution had to be postponed for several weeks because the ship of Theseus had been consecrated to reenact the mythical voyage portrayed by Titian. It was a sacred time of peace for Athens. No executions were allowed. Violence against philosophy had to wait.

Introduction

1. Questions

The purpose of this volume is to help readers enter the wonder of St. John Paul's *Theology of the Body* (TOB).[1] To enter, one needs to ask questions, sharpen them, and follow through with them. Questions are the lifeblood of reason, the darlings of the intellect.

What is the main thesis of TOB? Responding to the debate about *Humanae vitae*, TOB argues that the human body in its masculinity and femininity is an image of the Trinity. "It has been created to transfer into the visible reality of the world the mystery hidden from eternity in God" (TOB 19:4; Ephesians 3:9). In the sacrament of marriage, it signifies and communicates the union of Christ and the Church (Ephesians 5:29–32) and the ultimate root of that union, the communion of the divine persons. "And I, the glory you have given me I have given to them, that they may be one as we are one" (John 17:22). This thesis is the core of an "integral vision" of the human person and the conjugal act on which *Humanae vitae* is based.

> It is precisely by moving from "an integral vision of man and of his vocation, not only his natural and earthly, but also his supernatural and eternal vocation" (*Humanae Vitae*, 7), that Paul VI affirmed that the teaching of the Church "is founded upon the inseparable connection, willed by God and unable to be broken by man on his own initiative, between the two meanings of the conjugal act: the unitive meaning and the procreative meaning." (*Familiaris consortio* 32)

1. This volume is a more developed version of the introduction to my translation of TOB. See John Paul II, *Man and Woman He Created Them: A Theology of the Body*, introduction and trans. Michael Waldstein (Boston: Pauline Books and Media, 2006), 1–128. Earlier sketches of parts of the argument: Michael Waldstein, "John Paul II and St. Thomas on Love and the Trinity," *Anthropotes* 18 (2002): 113–38; 269–86; "John Paul II: A Thomist Rooted in St. John of the Cross," *Faith and Reason* 30 (2005): 195–218.

Why does John Paul see Humanae vitae as important? He sees contraception not simply as one among other moral issues but as a tight knot in which two central questions of our age come together. How can man and woman love each other authentically? What is a reasonable practice of reason in an age of science and technology shaped by the ambition for "the empire of man over things" (Bacon) in which "we make ourselves masters and possessors of nature" (Descartes).[2]

Is the main thesis new? It is fresh in approach and language and at the same time deeply rooted in Scripture and the theological tradition, especially Paul, John, John of the Cross, and Thomas Aquinas. "An authentic interpretation of this 'theology of the body' relies on an appreciation of the intersection of the thought of St. John Paul and Thomas Aquinas."[3] TOB also shows the fruits of an intense triangular dialogue between mutually opposed visions of the human person: John Paul's Trinitarian personalism of self-gift, Kant's anti-Trinitarian personalism of autonomy, and Scheler's theomorphic personalism of solidarity.

What is the logical and literary structure of TOB? Navigating TOB can be like sailing on the open ocean in the fog without a compass. Part III of this volume is a map of TOB that summarizes each numbered paragraph in a sentence or two and explains the order of the argument.

How can TOB contribute to dialogue between faith, reason, and science in our Post-Reformation culture? Both John Paul and Luther develop a spousal theology anchored in the prophets, Paul, and the Gospel of John. Both have a powerful grasp of the total gift of self in spousal union. In contrast to John Paul, however, Luther was formed in the nominalist and voluntarist Scholasticism of William of Ockham (1288–1348).[4] "There I lost Christ," he says.[5] Finding Christ again through Paul meant rejecting Ockham's violently voluntarist practice of reason. It is not clear, however, whether Luther's rejection of Ockham was thorough

2. "If someone strives to renew and increase the empire of humanity itself over the whole universe of things, then that ambition (if that is what we must call it) is no doubt more sober and majestic than the others. Now the empire of man over things lies in the arts and sciences alone." Francis Bacon, New Organon 1.129. "It is possible to reach knowledge that will be powerfully useful to life and instead of the theoretical philosophy ... we can find a practical one by which ... we make ourselves masters and possessors of nature." René Descartes, *Discourse on Method*, 6. See part I, chap. 3, for a discussion of these pivotal texts.

3. Thomas Petri, OP, *Aquinas and the Theology of the Body: The Thomistic Foundations of John Paul II's Anthropology* (Washington, DC: Catholic University of America Press, 2016), xi.

4. *Voluntarism:* will and power have primacy over reason. *Nominalism:* the human mind is incapable of understanding natures. The term *tree* does not have an intelligible content applicable to all instances. It is universal only as a name, Latin *nomen*, hence *nominalism*. Since English *tree* and Latin *arbor* are distinct names but the same term, *termism* would be a more precise label than *nominalism*.

5. Martin Luther, *Resolutiones Lutheranae super propositionibus suis Lipsiae disputatis*, in Martin Luther, *Martin Luthers Werke: Kritische Gesamtausgabe*, 120 vols. (Weimar: Böhlau, 1883–2009), 2:414.

enough to make room for a more biblical, receptive understanding of reason. Through Luther, Ockham contributed to the violent practice of reason heralded by Bacon and Descartes.

What is John Paul's understanding of reason? He follows the open and receptive practice of reason exemplified by Socrates, Plato, Aristotle, Plotinus, and the intellectual tradition indebted to them. Tertullian (ca. 155–240) asked the famous rhetorical question, "What does Athens have to do with Jerusalem, what the Academy with the Church?"[6] The short answer highlighted by John Paul in *Fides et ratio* is, "In the beginning was the *Logos* [reason, discourse, word] . . . and the *Logos* became flesh" (John 1:1, 1:14; see *Fides et ratio* 11 and 34). Reason does not lie outside of faith but within it. The impression of opposition between faith and reason in contemporary culture is in large measure due to the violent and irrational choice of power over nature as the purpose of knowledge and the consequent choice of mechanics as the master science of nature.

What is John Paul's understanding of faith? He relies on Scripture as the written word (*logos*) of God. He unfolds Scripture in often surprising ways with the help of ordinary human experience, philosophical reflection, contemporary exegetical tools, and the theological resources of the tradition. Following John of the Cross, he reads texts on marriage as illumined by the mystery of the Trinity.

In his *Regensburg Lecture*, Benedict XVI reflects about the breadth of reason.

> I am reminded of something Socrates said to Phaedo. In their earlier conversations, many false philosophical opinions had been raised, and so Socrates says: "It would be easily understandable if someone became so annoyed at all these false notions that for the rest of his life he hated and mocked all talk about being—but in this way he would be robbed of the truth of beings and would suffer a great loss." The West has long been endangered by this aversion against the fundamental questions of its rationality and could thereby suffer a great loss.
>
> Courage for the breadth of reason, not denial of its greatness—this is the program with which a theology grounded in Biblical faith enters the debate of our time. "Not to act reasonably, not to act with *logos*, is contrary to the nature of God," said Manuel II, according to his Christian understanding of God, in response to his Persian interlocutor. It is into this great *logos*, into this breadth of reason, that we invite our partners in the dialogue of cultures. To rediscover it constantly is the great task of the university.[7]

6. Tertullian, *De praescriptionibus adversus haereticos* 7.
7. Benedict XVI, *Regensburg Lecture*, December 12, 2006, conclusion.

2. Rejection and Attraction

When *Humanae vitae* was published in 1968, the year of a decisive step in the sexual revolution, a wave of rejection had already been prepared to overwhelm it. Contraception—the majority argued—is simply part of progress in the modern age. It is self-evident like antibiotics. The encyclical repeats the Church's mistake in the Galileo affair. It is a throwback to medieval obscurantism, motivated by clerical power interests.

TOB reaffirms *Humanae vitae* in a manner that has attracted and fascinated many men and women. They find an unexpected beauty and freedom in its vision of the sexual body. "What is at stake here is an authentically 'humanistic' meaning of the development and progress of human civilization" (TOB 129:2). Is contraception part of fully *human* progress? Or is it part of a narrow and violent practice of reason that has colonized progress?

What comes first in the teaching of Jesus is not the law of the body but the gospel of the body, redemption. The *Logos* made flesh gives himself to men and women and by this gift speaks to them from deeply within themselves, as the *Logos* (reason, discourse, word) by which "the creator created them male and female" (Matthew 19:4).

In a short story by Vladimir Solovyov, the Antichrist calls an ecumenical council to persuade Christians to support him as emperor of the United States of the World. He offers gifts, any gift dear to them. "What is dearest to you?" he asks. They discuss the question but do not come to an agreement. In a tone of irony the emperor suggests that what is dearest may differ according to the divisions among Christians. To Catholics he offers worldwide moral authority for the common good of peace and justice, to Protestants a richly endowed university for free inquiry into the Scriptures, and to the Orthodox the restoration of sacred customs and a museum of Christian archeology. Many accept the good news joyfully and join the emperor on the platform. Pope Peter II, Professor Pauli, and the Elder John stay behind, abandoned by the majority, drawing closer to each other.

> In a grieved voice, the Emperor addressed them, "What more can I do for you? You strange people! What do you want from me? I cannot understand. Tell me yourselves, you Christians, deserted by most of your peers and leaders, condemned by popular sentiment. What is dearest to you in Christianity?"
>
> At this, the Elder John rose up like a white candle and answered quietly, "Great emperor! Dearest to us in Christianity is Christ himself—in his person. Everything rests on him, for we know that 'in him dwells all the fullness of the Godhead bodily'" (Colossians 2:9).[8]

8. Vladimir Solovyov, *War, Progress and the End of History* (Hudson, NY: Lindisfarne Press, 1990), 183–84.

The gift of the one in whom the Godhead dwells bodily completes the gift of creation beyond all desire and hope. The gift calls for an answer. The inner order of this answer, the *logos* of Christian morality, is Dilige et quod vis fac. "Love! And do what you will!"[9] When they celebrate the sacrament of marriage in the eucharistic liturgy "in remembrance of me" (Luke 22:19), when they consummate their vows, and when they renew them in their conjugal life, men and women "announce the death of the Lord until he comes" (1 Corinthians 11:26). In remembrance they answer the gift by loving God and by loving each other radically according to the unitive and procreative meaning of their bodies. Pope Francis underlines this fundamental order, in which God's gifts come first and moral norms second.

> We cannot insist only on issues related to abortion, gay marriage and the use of contraceptive methods.... I have not spoken much about these things, and I was reprimanded for that. But when we speak about these issues, we have to talk about them in a context.... This is also what fascinates and attracts more, what makes the heart burn, as it did for the disciples at Emmaus.... Otherwise even the moral edifice of the church is likely to fall like a house of cards, losing the freshness and fragrance of the Gospel. The proposal of the Gospel must be more simple, profound, radiant. It is from this proposition that the moral consequences then flow.... The proclamation of the saving love of God comes before moral and religious imperatives.[10]

In September 1939, Hitler invaded Poland. His military government arrested the majority of Polish priests and put them in concentration camps. Laypeople had to shoulder the pastoral burden. Karol Wojtyła, then a first-year student in Polish literature at the Jagiellonian University in Kraków, came under the pastoral care of a tailor, Jan Tyranowski.[11] "He was an apostle of God's greatness, God's beauty, and God's transcendence. This he learned from his spiritual guide, St. John of the Cross."[12] The encounter with Tyranowski gave Wojtyła a living entry into the writings of St. John of the Cross. In 1942 he asked to be admitted as a novice in the Carmelites, John of the Cross's order. The Nazi occupation made such a step impossible.[13]

9. Augustine, *In Epistolam Ioannis Tractatus* 7.8. See Marie-François Berrouard, "Dilege et quod uis fac," in *Augustinus-Lexikon*, edited by Robert Dodaro and Cornelius Mayer (Basel: Schwabe, 1999), 2:453–55.

10. Pope Francis, "Interview with Antonio Spadaro," *America Magazine*, September 30, 2013, 15–38, at 26.

11. Adam Boniecki, *The Making of the Pope of the Millennium: Kalendarium of the Life of Karol Wojtyła* (Stockbridge, MA: Marian Press, 2000), 65.

12. Karol Wojtyła, "The Apostle," in Boniecki, *Kalendarium*, 66–70, at 69.

13. See Boniecki, *Kalendarium*, 90.

The poetry and theological commentaries of John of the Cross, especially the *Spiritual Canticle* and the *Living Flame of Love*, are filled with the imagery and atmosphere of the Song of Songs. They contain a rich implicit theology of the body. TOB can be understood in large measure as making this implicit theology of the body explicit (see part II, chap. 6, in this volume). Other sources such as Scheler's Phenomenology came to play an enriching role as well, but John of the Cross is the first and most important source.

In his theological commentaries on his poems, John of the Cross develops the Pauline spousal analogy of Christ's relation to the Church (Ephesians 5:31–32) by connecting it with the Trinity, often by appeal to the Gospel of John. He points to a likeness between the union of man and woman in marriage and the union of the divine persons, a likeness affirmed on a more general level for all disciples by Jesus's prayer, "that they may be one as we are one" (John 17:11, 17:21–23). A concept central for John Paul plays the key role in John of the Cross's account of this unity; namely, the gift of self.[14]

John Paul sees the nucleus of insights expressed by John of the Cross reflected in a passage of Vatican II's pastoral constitution *Gaudium et spes*, which he quotes more than twenty times in TOB. This text, he claims, expresses "the whole truth about man and woman" (*Mulieris dignitatem* 7).

> The Lord Jesus,
> when he prays to the Father, "that all may be one . . . as we are one"
> (John 17:11, 17:21–22)
> thus offering vistas closed to human reason,
> indicates a certain likeness
> between the union of the divine Persons
> and the union of God's sons in Truth and Love.
> This likeness shows that man,
> who is the only creature on earth God willed for itself,
> cannot fully find himself except through a sincere gift of self.
> Cf. Luke 17:33 ["Whoever seeks to make his life secure
> loses it and whoever loses will make it live"]. (*Gaudium et spes* 24)

A particularly important parallel to this text is John of the Cross's commentary in *Living Flame of Love* on the line "give both warmth and light to its beloved" *calor y luz dan junto a su querido.*

14. See the excellent presentation and discussion of John of the Cross's Trinitarian theology in J. Mario Faraone, *La inhabitación trinitaria según San Juan de la Cruz* (Rome: Gregorian University Press, 2002), esp. 425–55.

> [The soul] is conscious there that God is indeed its own and that it possesses him . . . through *the grace of his gift of himself.* Having him for its own, it can *give him* and *communicate him* to whomever it wishes. Thus, it *gives him* to its Beloved, who is the very God who *gave himself to it.* By this donation it repays God for all it owes him, since it willingly *gives as much as it receives* from him.
>
> Because the soul in this gift to God *offers him the Holy Spirit, with voluntary surrender, as something of its own* (so that God loves himself in the Holy Spirit as he deserves), it enjoys inestimable delight and fruition, seeing that it gives God something of its own that is suited to him according to his infinite being. . . .
>
> A reciprocal love between God and the soul is thus actually formed, *in conformity with the marriage union and surrender,* in which the goods of both (the divine essence that each possesses freely by reason of the voluntary surrender between them) are possessed by both together. They say to each other what the Son of God spoke to the Father through John: *All that is mine is yours and yours is mine* (John 17:10).[15]

In this text one can glimpse an important reason for the attractive power of TOB. John of the Cross's writings sharpened Wojtyła's sense for the beauty of love, including its Trinitarian depth. They also schooled him in sustained attention to consciously lived experience. The young student of Polish literature was so fascinated that he immediately learned Spanish to read the poems and commentaries of the *Doctor Mysticus* in the original. In 1946, Wojtyła submitted a master's thesis to the Jagiellonian University on "The Means of Union with God According to Saint John of the Cross." Two years later, he completed a doctoral thesis on faith as the proportionate means of union with the Trinity, directed by the professor of dogmatic and spiritual theology at the Angelicum, Réginald Garrigou-Lagrange, OP.[16]

After his return from Rome to Kraków, Wojtyła served as student chaplain in a parish near the university. He formed bonds of friendship with students and accompanied many of them as they came to love each other, married, and had children and eventually grandchildren. They called the resulting loosely organized community Środowisko, that is, Habitat or Environment. The intellectual level of some of its shared activities was high. "Wojtyła formed a study

15. John of the Cross, *The Living Flame of Love*, B 78–80; emphasis added. Some of John of the Cross's writings are attested in two versions, cited as A and B. See Kieran Kavanaugh, ed., *The Collected Works of St. John of the Cross*, trans. Kieran Kavanaugh and Ottilio Rodriguez, rev. ed. (Washington, DC: Institute of Carmelite Studies, 2017), 467.

16. Karol Wojtyła, *Faith According to St. John of the Cross* (San Francisco: Ignatius, 1981); *La dottrina della fede in S. Giovanni della Croce* [Doctrina de fide apud S. Joannem a Cruce], Latin text with facing Italian translation, ed. Massimo Bettetini (Milan: Bompiani, 2003).

group that read its way through the *Summa Theologiae* of St. Thomas Aquinas in the original Latin."[17] When my wife and I served as members of the Pontifical Council for the Family (2003–2009), we came to know couples on the Council who had been formed in Środowisko by this student chaplain. They called him Wujek (Uncle), so as not to alert the secret police to the activities of a Catholic priest but also to express a deep sense of familiarity. They were impressed by Wojtyła's sensitivity to their experience, by his willingness to learn from them, and by his surprising capacity to help them understand their experience, not only in times of joy but also in times of darkness and suffering.[18] Looking back in 1994, more than half a century after the beginning of Środowisko, John Paul wrote,

> As a young priest I learned to love human love. This has been one of the fundamental themes of my priesthood—my ministry in the pulpit, in the confessional and also in my writing. If one loves human love, there naturally arises the need to commit oneself completely to the service of fair love, because love is fair, it is beautiful. After all, young people are always searching for beauty in love. They want their love to be beautiful.[19]

This text points to Wojtyła's formative experience, the experience that set its seal on his whole life. "I learned to love human love because love is beautiful." Tota pulchra es Maria. "You are all-beautiful, Mary." Wojtyła wrote these words as the motto of TOB in the top right corner of the first page of his manuscript, probably the first words of TOB to be written. They are based on the cry of joy in the Song of Songs addressed by the man to the woman. "You are all-beautiful, my friend, and there is no stain in you." Tota pulchra es, amica mea, et macula non est in te (Song of Songs 4:7, Vulgate). In the form quoted by John Paul, with *Maria* replacing *amica*, they serve as the antiphon for the Feast of the Immaculate Conception. "You are all-beautiful, Mary and there is no stain, no *macula* in you." You are immaculate. Next to this motto, Wojtyła wrote the date of the first page, December 8, 1974, Feast of the Immaculate Conception.

In Wojtyła's experience the beauty of love is particularly tied to Mary. The

17. George Weigel, *Witness to Hope: The Biography of Pope John Paul II* (New York: HarperCollins, 1999), 95.

18. Wojtyła's sharing in the experience of men and women seems to be unknown to some critics who see TOB as disembodied, out of touch with the reality of sex in all its earthiness, complexity, humor, suffering, and ambiguity. "He seems to have paid little attention to actual human experience." Luke Timothy Johnson, *The Revelatory Body: Theology as Inductive Art* (Grand Rapids, MI: Eerdmans, 2015), 24. For an earlier version of the same criticism, see Luke Timothy Johnson, "A Disembodied 'Theology of the Body': John Paul II on Love, Sex & Pleasure," *Commonweal*, January 26, 2001.

19. John Paul II, *Crossing the Threshold of Hope*, ed. Vittorio Messori (New York: A. A. Knopf, 1994), 123.

words "commit oneself *completely* to the service of fair love" are closely related to his episcopal and papal motto: *totus tuus*, all yours. John Paul explains that *totus tuus* recalls the events at Golgotha in the Gospel of John. "When Jesus saw the mother and the disciple, whom he loved, standing beside her, he said to the mother, 'Woman, here is your son.' Then he said to the disciple, 'Here is your mother.' And from that hour the disciple took her into his own" (John 19:25–27). John Paul comments,

> Throughout its history, the people of God has experienced this gift of the crucified Jesus: the gift of his Mother.... As is well known, my episcopal coat of arms symbolically illustrates the Gospel text quoted above; the motto *Totus tuus* is inspired by the teaching of St. Louis Marie Grignion de Montfort (cf. *Gift and Mystery*, 42–43; *Rosarium Virginis Mariae*, 15). These two words express total belonging to Jesus through Mary: Tuus totus ego sum, et omnia mea tua sunt. "I am all yours, and all that is mine is yours" St. Louis Marie wrote.[20]

Louis de Montfort quotes the phrase *tuus totus* from the *Psalterium Beatae Mariae Virginis*, a text that circulated under the name of St. Bonaventure.[21] The immediate context in Pseudo-Bonaventure is the Song of Moses and Miriam (Exodus 15–16) recast to address the Virgin Mary.

> I am all yours, *Tuus totus ego sum,* and all that is mine is yours
> (cf. John 17:10),
> glorious Virgin, blessed above all (cf. Luke 1:42, 45, 48–49).
> Let me set you as a seal on my heart (cf. Song of Songs 8:6a),
> because your love is strong as death (cf. Song of Songs 8:6b).[22]

The words *commit oneself completely to the service of beautiful love* also echo the self-praise of personified Wisdom as the mother of beautiful or fair love in Sirach, applied to Mary in the liturgy. "I am the Mother of fair love" ἐγὼ μήτηρ

20. John Paul II, *Letter to the Montfort Religious Family*, Feast of the Immaculate Conception, December 8, 2003.

21. Louis-Marie Grignon de Montfort, *Traité de la vraie dévotion à la Sainte Vierge* (Paris: Oberthur, 1906), 190; Frederick W. Faber, trans., *Treatise on True Devotion to Mary* (London: Burns and Lambert, 1863), 152; in editions with continuous paragraph numbering, the phrase is at par. 233. See Étienne Richer, *Suivre Jésus avec Marie—Un secret de sainteté de Montfort à Jean-Paul II*, preface by François-Marie Léthel (Nouan-Le-Fuzelier: Éditions des Béatitudes, 2006), 281n53. Early manuscripts and lists of Bonaventure's works do not contain the *Psalterium*. It is printed among Bonaventure's works in *Bonaventurae opera omnia* (Rome: Typographia Vaticana, 1596), *tuus totus* at 515. The Quaracchi critical edition of Bonaventure's works does not contain the *Psalterium* but lists it among spurious works.

22. [Pseudo-]Bonaventura, *Psalterium maius beatae Mariae virginis* (Basel: Flach, between 1473 and 1475), unnumbered pages, at 77.

τῆς ἀγαπήσεως τῆς καλῆς (Sirach 24:24).[23] John Paul's acute sensibility for the beauty of love, combined with attention to experience, is clear in a text that expresses the spiritual center of TOB. Here one comes close to the source of the mysteriously attractive and transformative power of TOB.

> Although keeping one's own body "with holiness and reverence" (1 Thessalonians 4:4) is formed *by abstaining from "lustful passion"*—and this way is indispensable—nevertheless it always bears fruit in the deeper experience of the love that has from the "beginning" been inscribed in the whole essence of man and thus also in his body according to the image and likeness of God himself. For this reason, Paul ends his argument in 1 Corinthians 6:13–20 with a significant exhortation: "Therefore glorify God in your body" (v. 20).
>
> Purity as a virtue or ability of "keeping one's own body with holiness and reverence," allied with the gift of piety as a fruit of the Holy Spirit's dwelling in the "temple" of the body, causes in the body such a fullness of dignity in interpersonal relations that *God himself is thereby glorified.* Purity is the glory of the human body before God. It is the glory of God in the human body, through which masculinity and femininity are shown.
>
> From purity springs that singular beauty that permeates every sphere of reciprocal common life between people and allows them to express in it the simplicity and depth, the cordiality and unrepeatable authenticity of personal trust.[24] (TOB 57:3; emphasis original)

The title of this volume, *Glory of the Logos in the Flesh*, is taken from this text combined with the prologue of John. "And the *Logos* became flesh and pitched his tent among us, and we have seen his glory, a glory as of an only-begotten from the Father, full of gift and truth" (John 1:14). In Polish, the word for *body* and for *flesh* is the same, *ciało. Teologia ciała* can be understood both as *theology of the body* and as *theology of the flesh.*

Beauty and experience combine in John Paul's method. It is difficult to run on one leg alone. Beauty alone would be quite a strong leg to stand on. Yet it is the pairing of beauty with experience that gives to the argument of TOB its intellectual and pastoral power. A detached beauty seen from afar as an object of admiration and longing, out of reach of experience, can stir nostalgia, but it can-

23. The Rahlfs edition of the *Septuagint* (Stuttgart: Deutsche Bibelgesellschaft, 1935) prints this passage only as a variant in the apparatus. Based on better manuscript evidence, the *Göttingen Septuagint* (Ziegler, 1980) prints the passage in the main text and notes its absence from a few manuscripts in the apparatus.

24. A revised version of the text of TOB is used in this volume. Thanks are due to Grzegorz Ignatik for going through the English translation of the Italian with me to compare it with his understanding of the original Polish. For the relation between the Italian and the Polish, see the introduction to, Part III, sections 3–4, in this volume.

not change lives. Beauty understood as realizable in the body and as connected with daily experience in all its complexity, humor, obscurity, and suffering—this has great power to change lives. TOB invites readers to test this beauty in their own experience.

By coincidence, the abbreviation TOB can be read as a more general way of expressing John Paul's main thesis about the human body. Hebrew *ṭôḇ* (pronounced *tove*) means *good, merry, pleasing, desirable, beautiful.* Despite sin, sickness, and death, the human body is in its own being *ṭôḇ*, even very *ṭôḇ*, very good and beautiful, Genesis repeats six times and then adds very *ṭôḇ*:

It was *ṭôḇ* (1:4)
It was *ṭôḇ* (1:10)
It was *ṭôḇ* (1:12)
It was *ṭôḇ* (1:18)
It was *ṭôḇ* (1:21)
It was *ṭôḇ* (1:25)
And indeed, it was very *ṭôḇ* (1:31)

The human body is good and beautiful above all in view of the incarnation of the *Logos*, where body/flesh reveals "a glory ... full of gift and truth" (John 1:14). It is no secret that many Catholics, especially academics, reject the Catholic understanding of sex. John Paul's argument shows a positive way forward beyond entrenched battle lines. It extends an invitation that is difficult to resist. "Your desire for the beauty of love will lead you. Try out this path. Judge for yourself by your own lived experience." Benedict XVI underlines the importance of beauty on such a path of verification.

> I believe these two things go hand in hand: reason, precision, honesty in reflection on the truth—and beauty. A reason that would, so to speak, strip off beauty would be cut in half, it would be a blinded reason. Only both together form the whole, and precisely for faith this union is important....
>
> "Always be prepared to give a defense [Greek: *apologia*] to anyone who asks you for the reason [Greek: *logos*] of the hope that is in you" (1 Peter 3:15), an *apologia* of the *logos* of hope: to turn the *logos*, the reason of hope, into an *apologia*, into an answer to human beings. He was thus evidently convinced that faith is *logos*, that it is a reason, in fact, a light from creative reason itself, and not some pretty concoction that we thought up for ourselves. This is why the faith is universal, this is why it is communicable to all.
>
> This creative *logos* is precisely not a merely technical *logos* ... but it is broad, for it is after all a *logos* of love, and thus a *logos* that expresses itself in beauty and in goodness.... When we fight for the reasonableness of faith, in this epoch, then we fight precisely for the insight that reason does not end

> where experimental discoveries end. . . . We are fighting for the broadening of reason, and hence for a reason that, precisely, is also open to the beautiful and does not need to set it aside as something quite different and irrational.[25]

3. After *Amoris laetitia*

An Alleged Paradigm Shift

Amoris laetitia indicates a shift from a premodern paradigm of sexual love to a postmodern paradigm, according to Stephan Goertz.[26] The shift will finally enable the Catholic Church to keep the promise made at Vatican II, reconceiving Catholic life in a pastorally effective way as an attractive and realistic option in the modern world. In agreement with Goertz, Magnus Striet argues that the attractive option consists at its core of protecting human freedom and autonomy from power.

> Church may see itself ever so much as guided by God himself, by his Holy Spirit, but in the first place it too is a social system. And what dominates social systems is always power. One might think that such a view of Church is not legitimate. . . . I am soberer at this point. The reason is that sober reflection—which does not always "know it all" right away but remains critical in relation to the assemblage of notions that have sprung up—is and remains the only way to wake up from the dogmatic slumber that prevents us from being Church in the world of today . . .
>
> Kant merely destroyed a kind of knowledge that was no knowledge at all—BUT he made room for a liberal faith. Whatever we then claim as knowledge is only relatively certain. . . .
>
> When Pope Francis wants the Church's face to change, when the ambiguities and ambivalences of real life are given room to exist within the Church because the Church cares for human beings, this means a change of doctrine. . . .
>
> When one hears today that *Amoris laetitia* did not change the Church's doctrine but merely understood it more deeply, it is really quite astonishing. This is simply not true. One should say so without any compulsive attempt to look for support in the tradition.[27]

25. Benedict XVI, *Address to the Clergy of South Tirol*, Brixen, August 6, 2008.

26. See Stephan Goertz and Caroline Witting, eds., *Amoris Laetitia: Wendepunket für die Moraltheologie, Katholizismus im Umbruch* [Amoris laetitia: Turning point for Moral Theology, Catholicism in Transition], vol. 4 (Freiburg: Herder, 2016).

27. Magnus Striet, "Katholische Kirche, willkommen in der Moderne. Wunderbar, man streitet

The alternate tradition in which Striet and Goertz look for support is Kant's personalism of autonomy (see part II, chap. 2, in this volume) and (behind Kant) William of Ockham's voluntarist and nominalist philosophy (see part I, chap. 2, sections 6 and 7, in this volume). Striet describes the new paradigm as "constructivist." Any statement claiming to be true is a contingent "construct" subject to change.

> If God is truly ... free in his will, then the tight order of the world begins to wobble. Nothing needs to remain as it is. And above all: the factually existing world does not allow any sure inferences that lead back to God....
>
> Theological nominalism is celebrating its presence in knowledge generating discourses that understand themselves from a constructivist point of view. Modernity that has become reflexive for itself is the prolongation of the nominalist God. With this exception: the almighty God once believed in is now reflexively raised to awareness as a construct of thought. And constructs of thought don't come with any guarantee about being.[28]

Ockham is still caught in a premodern mindset, according to this view. He sees a real world and a real God that do not depend on human thought or language. We live after the linguistic turn and do not hold his naïve view. Still, Ockham points in the right direction. In Ockham, the meaning of each being is what God happens to impose on it by will. By his ordained power (*potentia ordinata*), God has commanded us to love him and each other. By his absolute power (*potentia absoluta*), he could command us to hate instead. While in Ockham, the choice is God's, in the constructivist paradigm, it is ours. God's will is a human construct. The human will is alone in its autonomy. This nominalist vision is liberating inasmuch as it denies intelligibility. To affirm intelligibility is to impose limits on freedom. Striet and Goertz present this constructivist paradigm as the most up-to-date version of modernity. Our age does not want old answers to new questions.

Speaking of old, Ockham was born in 1287, only thirteen years after the death of St. Thomas Aquinas. Even in the high middle ages, his view was already old. The primacy of will over reason and the consequent rejection of intelligibility was vigorously proposed in ancient Greece by rhetoricians such as

---

sich" ["Catholic Church, welcome to modernity. Wonderful! There is a fight"], *Herder Korrespondenz* 71 (2017): 13–16.

28. Magnus Striet, "*Ius divinum*: Freiheitsrechte, Nominalistische Denkkonstruktionen in konstruktivistischer Absicht" ["Divine law: rights to freedom, nominalist constructs of thought in constructivist intent"], in *Nach dem Gesetz Gottes: Autonomie als christliches Prinzip*, Katholizismus im Umbruch 2 [According to God's law: autonomy as a Christian principle, Catholicism in radical transition 2], ed. Stephan Goertz and Magnus Striet (Freiburg: Herder, 2014), 91–128, at 112.

Thrasymachus, Socrates's opponent in Plato's *Republic* (see part I, chap. 5, in this volume). In Ockham, as in Thrasymachus before him, the good and its causality disappear in favor of a primacy of will. What is first in the order of causes is the imposition of will, not the good known by reason as good.[29] Ockham's voluntarist and nominalist thought resembles the dominant Cartesian philosophy that often settles parasitically on the unquestionable authority of natural science. The only thing that is real in nature, according to that philosophy, is matter moved by forces understood in mathematical terms. Goodness and beauty, male and female—all such notions of our ordinary experience do not disclose anything real. They are socially constructed or personally chosen preferences.

If the material world does not have its own goodness, if it consists only of particles in motion, the only characteristics of which are those that can be measured and expressed in mathematical equations, we are thrown back on ourselves to construct meaning. As a construct, such meaning can only have relative truth. It can only be true for me right now. Other constructs can replace it. No one has the right to impose their construct on anyone else. We are free in the degree to which we ourselves give meaning.

In his brilliant critique of Goertz and Striet, Karl-Heinz Menke puts the main question in a nutshell. *Does Truth Make Free or Freedom True?*[30] It depends on whether these words are a construct or not. "Indeed, it was very good" (Genesis 1:31). A good initial description of being free is being able to do what one wants. Experience shows that the word *really* needs to be added to the word *wants*. To be free is to be able to do what one *really* wants. Being deceived about the good can make it impossible to do what one really wants. Striking a friend in a spasm of anger may seem a good thing to do at the time, but regret often begins as soon as anger cools. "This is not really what I wanted." The path of becoming free by knowing the truth about the good is closed if the universe is a value-free machine. In that case, goodness and beauty are like the overlay projected by digital glasses to augment reality. In the most radical proposals shaped by the linguistic turn, even the neutral mechanism of nature is a construct of our language. All reality is virtual. Virtual reality *does* come alive with color and action, but its meaning lasts as long as we—or those who have power over us—keep the movie running.

29. See Stephen F. Brown, "Ockham and Final Causality," in *Studies in Medieval Philosophy*, ed. John F. Wippel (Washington, DC: Catholic University of America Press, 1987), 249–72 at 269–71.

30. Karl-Heinz Menke, *Macht die Wahrheit frei oder die Freiheit wahr? Eine Streitschrift* [Does truth make free or freedom true: A dispute] (Regensburg: Pustet, 2017).

Goertz on *Humanae vitae*

An association of German Catholic moral theologians published a collection of essays for the fiftieth anniversary of *Humanae vitae* with the subtitle *The Scandalous Encyclical.*[31] The contributors share a mindset (with variations) that has many attractive features: openness to the modern age without resentments, eagerness to embrace scientific discoveries, commitment to freedom, empathy with the joys and difficulties experienced by couples, and distaste for the aggressive tribalism found (not exclusively) among some defenders of *Humanae vitae.* A comparable British volume edited by Alana Harris of King's College London also locates itself in the cultural mainstream but with less angry defensiveness. It is even open to "yearnings for the experience of 'a love which is total.'"[32]

Goertz contributed an essay with the title "Moral Truth and Biological Laws: How *Humanae vitae* Prevented the Reception of its Conjugal Morality."[33] Like other essays in the volume, it applies a template developed in the immediate aftermath of *Humanae vitae* by Franz Böckle: *Humanae vitae* uses new personalist arguments to buttress the old naturalistic conclusions about marriage. It cannot remain faithful to personalism, however, because it subjects the person to biological nature.[34] Going a step beyond Böckle but reinforcing his template, Goertz claims that *Humanae vitae* was decisively influenced by Wojtyła, who supplied an idiosyncratic form of personalism from outside the academic mainstream to buttress the naturalistic conclusions (not arguments) of the discredited neo-Thomist natural law theory. Another essay in the volume expresses the template in its very title, "An Indissoluble Connection: *Humanae vitae* and the Theology of the Body."[35]

Gilfredo Marengo has definitively refuted this template in his groundbreaking study, *The Birth of an Encyclical: Humanae vitae in Light of the Vatican Archives.*[36] The documentation on *Humanae vitae* in the archives, excerpts of

31. Konrad Hilpert and Sigrid Müller, eds., *Humanae vitae: Die anstößige Enzyklika* (Freiburg: Herder, 2018).

32. Dagmar Herzog, "Afterword—Looking for Love," in *The Schism of '68: Catholicism, Contraception and "Humanae Vitae" in Europe, 1945–1975*, ed. Alana Harris (London: Palgrave Macmillan, 2018), 349–63, at 350.

33. See Stephan Goertz, "Moralische Wahrheit und biologische Gesetze: Wie die Enzyklika *Humanae vitae* die Rezeption ihrer Ehemoral verhindert hat," in Hilpert and Müller, *Die anstößige Enzyklika*, 38–60.

34. Franz Böckle, "Nachwort," in *Die Enzyklika in der Diskussion: Eine orientierende Dokumentation zu "Humanae vitae,"* ed. Franz Böckle and Carl Holenstein (Zürich: Benziger, 1968), 195–206.

35. Gerhard Marschütz, "Eine unlösbare Verknüpfung: *Humanae vitae* und die Theologie des Leibes," in Hilpert and Müller, *Die anstößige Enzyklika*, 127–46.

36. Gilfredo Marengo, *La nascita di un'enciclica: Humanae vitae alle luce degli Archivi Vaticani* (Rome: Liberia Editrice Vaticana, 2018).

which Marengo reproduces in the second half of his volume, shows a more complex picture. Gustave Martelet, SJ, wrote the first draft, Cardinal Giovanni Colombo of Milan the substantially new second draft. The Colombo draft was sent out in several waves of consultation to a committee of theologians assembled for this purpose (including Martelet, Colombo, and Josef Fuchs, SJ), to the Vatican Secretariat of State, to the Congregation for the Faith, and to participants in the 1967 Synod of Bishops (among the respondents are Döpfner, Legér, Lorscheider, Shehan, Suenens, and Wojtyła).[37] Marengo pays particular attention to the documentation of Wojtyła's involvement, including the role played by the Kraków memorandum sent by Wojtyła and other Polish bishops to Paul VI.[38] He concludes that Wojtyła's influence was, relatively speaking, minor. "Some scholars [Marengo mentions Joseph A. Selling] have constructed the hypothesis of an important influence of this text on the final redaction of the encyclical. This thesis does not seem to be confirmed by the sources."[39]

Goertz claims that the personalist arguments of *Humanae vitae* remythologize the biological reality of sexual reproduction. They attribute a sacred objective inviolability to the inseparability of the procreative and unitive meaning. In the infertile period of the woman's cycle, God and natural processes regularly separate the two meanings, he claims. They remove the procreative meaning and leave the unitive meaning intact. Husband and wife, by contrast, somehow violate the sacred inviolability if they separate the meanings by artificial means. The encyclical, as Goertz reads it, does not give reasons why such an artificial separation is prohibited while natural and divine separation is allowed. Rationality, he concludes, is a façade in *Humanae vitae*. What stands behind the façade is not reason but clerical power interest.

> The suspicion inevitably arises that all objections from the point of view of anthropology, medicine, and moral theology simply bounce off from the con-

37. These consultations are discussed by Marengo, *La nascita*, 69–74 (Martelet draft), 74–78 (Colombo draft), 78–88 (Secretariat of State and Congregation for the Doctrine of the Faith), 88–98 (Synod of Bishops).

38. See Karol Wojtyła et al., "The Foundations of the Church's Doctrine Concerning the Principles of Conjugal Life: A Memorandum Composed by a Group of Moral Theologians from Kraków," *Nova et Vetera* 10 (2012): 321–59; Janet Smith, "The Kraków Document," *Nova et Vetera* 10 (2012): 361–81. Paweł Stanisław Gałuszka, who inclines toward maximizing Wojtyła's contribution, observes that there are points of difference as well as likeness between the memorandum and *Humanae vitae*. "In his document, Paul VI did not fully take up the rich personalistic context suggested by the group from Kraków." *Karol Wojtyła e Humanae vitae: Il contributo dell'Archivescovo di Cracovia e del gruppo di teologi polacchi all'encyclica di Paolo VI* (Siena: Cantagalli, 2017), 262.

39. Marengo, *La nascita*, 97. See Michael J. Barberi and Joseph A. Selling, "The Origin of *Humanae Vitae* and the Impasse in Fundamental Theological Ethics," *Louvain Studies* 37 (2013): 364–89.

> jugal morality of *Humanae vitae* because Paul VI's main concern was the loyal conservation of the teaching of his predecessors.... When the defense of a particular conjugal morality is at root motivated by the profession of loyalty to tradition, practical reason, that is, human freedom, always arrives too late.[40]

Despite his high level of sensitivity to questions of power, Goertz seems unaware of the Baconian-Cartesian power interests that shape the dominant way of thinking (see part I, chap. 3, in this volume). He reads the text of *Humanae vitae* through the glasses of dualism between value-free extended thing (*res extensa*) and value-generating thinking thing (*res cogitans*). It is not surprising, then, that he fails to represent the encyclical's concept of *inseparability* and its concept of *conjugal act*.

1. Inseparability

Goertz understands the *inseparability* of the two meanings in *Humanae vitae* as a *norm* rather than a *fact*. He can hardly do otherwise, because he equates procreative *meaning* and procreative *outcome*.[41] If husband and wife know that a particular conjugal act cannot have a procreative *outcome*, it cannot have a procreative *meaning*. The unitive meaning, separated from the procreative meaning, can remain intact. Husband and wife *can* separate the meanings but *should* not.

> The two meanings, loving union and procreation, can obviously be separated without a problem, provided only that the biological laws of the divine plan of creation are the cause of this separation. Every other form of separation intentionally brought about "artificially" by human intervention is not allowed.[42]

Dietrich von Hildebrand reads *Humanae vitae* in exactly the same way (see part I, chap. 4, in this volume), apparently for the same reason; namely, projection of Cartesian presuppositions into a text that does not share them.

Humanae vitae sees the inseparability of the two meanings as a *fact*, not as a *norm*. The moral problem does not arise from spouses *separating* the meanings but from their inability to do so. The two meanings exist not only *together with* each other but "*through* each other" (TOB 123:6; see part I, chap. 1, section 1, in this volume). The conjugal act is unitive *through* being procreative and procreative *through* being unitive. To remove one of the two meanings is thus to remove the other as well. If a husband violently imposes sex on his wife, conception can take place, but the procreative meaning is destroyed. *Procreation* is not equivalent to *reproduction*. The word *procreation* refers to a human act with

40. Goertz, "Moralische Wahrheit," 60.

41. See Goertz, "Moralische Wahrheit," 51–52.

42. Goertz, "Moralische Wahrheit," 45.

a specific moral profile. Cows grazing on a meadow eat, but they do not dine. Dining is eating with a specifically human moral profile.

Eating is to *dining*
as *sex* is to *conjugal act*
as *reproduction* is to *procreation.*

Conversely, removal of the procreative meaning removes the act's conjugally unitive meaning. An act that has a procreative meaning can express and realize the specific form of union between a man and a woman called conjugal. This procreative form of unitive meaning is not destroyed if conception is not achieved. It *does* disappear when husband and wife contracept. An act can remain specifically the same if something outside one's own control prevents the specifying end. Looking to see something in a dark room remains looking even when one cannot see anything. Closing one's eyes, however, excludes the intention to look. Although the effect is the same—one cannot see anything—what one does is different in the two cases. As Elizabeth Anscombe lucidly shows, contraception makes it impossible to intend the conjugal act as conjugal.[43]

2. Conjugal Act

Goertz splits human bodily acts in accord with the Cartesian split between objective event in the *res extensa* and subjective intention in the *res cogitans* and projects this understanding into *Humanae vitae. Humanae vitae*, by contrast, understands the conjugal act as *one act* from the point of view of the man and woman who perform it. As *Humanae vitae* describes it, the conjugal act takes up the natural teleology of generation as part of *what man and woman do* (see part I, chap. 6, section 6, in this volume). Walking is one human act, even though one can distinguish an inner and an outer aspect of the act. From the point of view of the agent, walking takes up the natural teleology of locomotion—from here to there—as *what* the person *does. From here to there* does not run its course outside the human act as the mere objective consequence of an interior intention and choice.

Goertz's misreading of *Humanae vitae* is not an exception in the volume. Not one of the essays in *Humanae vitae: The Scandalous Encyclical* manages to present what *Humanae vitae* says. It is difficult to imagine a more disqualifying testimony about the academic competence of professors of Catholic moral the-

43. See Elizabeth Anscombe, "On *Humanae Vitae*," in *Faith in a Hard Ground: Essays on Religion, Philosophy, and Ethics by G.E.M. Anscombe*, ed. Mary Geach and Luke Gormally (Charlottesville, VA: Imprint Academic, 2008), 192–98.

ology than the rejection of a Catholic teaching coupled with the inability to state accurately what that teaching is.

Laudato si' and *Amoris laetitia*

It is equally difficult to see the merit of Goertz's attempt to enlist Pope Francis as support for a shift to constructivism. The encyclical *Laudato si'* begins with a line from St. Francis's *Canticle of Creatures,* "Praise be to you, my Lord, through our Sister, Mother Earth, who sustains and governs us." Pope Francis comments, "Our common home is like a sister with whom we share our life and a beautiful mother who opens her arms to embrace us" (*Laudato si'* 1). Here and elsewhere, *Laudato si'* shows a vivid grasp of the beauty and goodness of the earth and a correspondingly vivid grasp of its fragility. It sees creatures as witnesses to the wisdom and love of the Creator. It also sees them as witnesses to his power, but power only by way of wisdom and love, not in Ockham's voluntarist isolation of power from reason and love. One does not need to flee from this power to be free.

> God's infinite power does not lead us to flee his fatherly tenderness, because in him affection and strength are joined. Indeed, all sound spirituality entails both welcoming divine love and adoration, confident in the Lord because of his infinite power. In the Bible, the God who liberates and saves is the same God who created the universe, and these two divine ways of acting are intimately and inseparably connected. (*Laudato si'* 73)

On this background, Pope Francis rejects "the claim to absolute dominion over the earth" (*Laudato si'* 75). The goodness of the earth and of the bodily beings on it challenges us to find "intelligent ways of directing, developing and *limiting* our power" (*Laudato si'* 78; emphasis added). *Limiting* power sounds strange to the scientific-technological mindset of our age. We are accustomed to seeing any increase of scientific knowledge and technological power as progress. The call to limit power may sound like nostalgia for a preindustrial, rural society, but nostalgia is not Pope Francis's way.

> How can we not feel gratitude and appreciation for this progress, especially in the fields of medicine, engineering and communications? How could we not acknowledge the work of many scientists and engineers who have provided alternatives to make development sustainable? (*Laudato si'* 102)

The roots of Pope Francis's thinking about technological power go back to studies for his doctoral dissertation on Romano Guardini at the Jesuit School of Theology Sankt Georgen in Frankfurt. Although he was called back to Argentina before he completed the dissertation, these studies formed his thinking. Guardini gives one of the most penetrating philosophical and theological analyses of scientific-technological power in modernity.[44] Many passages in *Laudato si'* reflect this analysis.[45] Francis draws attention, for example, to a paradox discussed in detail by Guardini.

> Human beings are not completely autonomous. Our freedom fades when it is handed over to the blind forces of the unconscious, of immediate needs, of self-interest, and of violence. In this sense, we stand naked and exposed in the face of our ever-increasing power, lacking the wherewithal to control it. (*Laudato si'* 105)

St. Augustine saw the same paradox in Rome's military ambition for worldwide power. "The very lust for domination dominates it."[46] Lust for domination gave rise to the Roman structures of power, such as the Praetorian Guard with its enforced emperor worship. Instead of being instruments that serve human life, these structures became oppressively dehumanizing for the very people who built and sustained them.

The concerns expressed in *Laudato si'* can be seen also in *Amoris laetitia*. Pope Francis has a clear sense of the great good family life is called to realize. It is a goodness that reflects the wisdom of the Creator, who is goodness itself. When one compares Francis with John Paul, one difference is immediately clear. John Paul has a special sensibility and love for the couple and its experience of love, Francis for the larger community, for children, the family, the city, the nation, the planet. The distinctive focus of each does not exclude the other. John Paul has much to say about larger communities and Francis much about the couple.

Many of the theses of TOB are present in *Amoris laetitia* in fresh formulations. Francis finds simple ways of showing the specifying goods of marriage and the family, at times more direct and forceful than *Humanae vitae* or TOB.

44. See *Laudato si'* 105n83, which cites Guardini's seminal works on power in modernity, *Das Ende der Neuzeit: Ein Versuch zur Orientierung*, 3rd ed. (Würzburg: Werkbund-Verlag, 1951); *The End of the Modern World* (Wilmington, DE: ISI Books, 1996); *Die Macht: Versuch einer Wegweisung* (Würzburg: Werkbund-Verlag, 1951); *Power and Responsibility: A Course of Action for the New Age* (Chicago: Regnery, 1961).

45. See the discussion of Guardini as a source of inspiration in *Laudato si'* by Fernando Chica Arellano, "'Ecología humana' (LS 155) y 'conversión ecológica' (LS 216–221): En los cimientos de Laudato si,'" in *Laudato si': El cuidado de la casa común, una conversión necesaria a la ecología humana*, ed. Federico Lombardi and Fernando F. Sánchez Campos (Madrid: Biblioteca de Autores Cristianos, 2018), 69–96, at 83–88.

46. Augustine, *De civitate dei*, prol.

> The child who is born "does not come from outside as something added on to the mutual love of the spouses, but springs from the very heart of that mutual giving, as its fruit and fulfilment" (Catechism, no. 2360). He or she does not appear at the end of a process but is present from the beginning of love as an essential feature, one that cannot be denied without disfiguring that love itself. From the outset, love refuses every impulse to close in on itself; it is open to a fruitfulness that draws it beyond itself. Hence no genital act of husband and wife can refuse this meaning, *Humanae vitae* 11–12. (*Amoris laetitia* 80)

In this restatement of the main argument of *Humanae vitae*, Francis expresses simply and directly how specific goods give rise to what genital acts are in their full human meaning as acts of husband and wife. From the beginning, the child is present as an essential feature, a feature that gives to the love of husband and wife its specific nature as the love of spouses.

A particularly important thesis in *Amoris laetitia*, most directly contrary to nominalist constructivism and closest to Jesus's saying, "the truth will make you free" (John 8:31), is the image of the Trinity in man and woman.

> With a gaze of faith and love, grace and fidelity, we have contemplated the relationship between human families and the divine Trinity. The word of God tells us that the family is entrusted to a man, a woman and their children, so that they may become a communion of persons in the image of the union of the Father, the Son and the Holy Spirit. Begetting and raising children, for its part, mirrors God's creative work. (*Amoris laetitia* 29)

4. More Questions

Man and Woman as an Image of the Trinity

Among questions raised about TOB, the most important addresses the image of the Trinity. "*Man became the 'image and likeness' of God not only through his own humanity but also through the communion of persons,* which man and woman form from the very beginning" (TOB 9:3; emphasis original). A Thomist friend took me aside in 1998 to warn me with greatest earnestness against this thesis. "*Don't go down that path! It leads nowhere!* Augustine and Thomas refuted this image of the Trinity.[47] Follow their account of the image of the Trinity

47. See Augustine, *De trinitate* 12.2.5–6. Thomas, *Summa* I, q. 93, a. 6, obj. 2 and ad 2. Quotes of Thomas follow the Leonine edition, *Sancti Thomae Aquinatis, doctoris angelici, opera omnia iussu Leonis XIII. P.M. edita* (Rome: Propaganda Fide; Paris: Cerf, 1884–2014). Updated texts not yet published by the Leonine commission are quoted from Enrique Alarcón, *Opera omnia S. Thomae*; see www.corpusthomisticum.org. Numbers at the end of citations preceded by "no." are paragraph numbers in the Marietti editions. Translations from Latin are my own.

in the procession of the inner word. The analogy of the word, not the analogy of mutual love, is the heart of Trinitarian theology." The questions raised by this warning, a warning repeated by other scholars, have been foremost in my mind for the past two decades as I studied TOB and Trinitarian theology.

Augustine and Thomas object to an image that consists of bodily relations of origin on the generic level of body. In the view criticized by Augustine, Adam is an image of the Father because he is the origin of his children. Adam's children are images of the Son. Eve is an image of the Holy Spirit because she comes from Adam without being his daughter, just as the Spirit proceeds from the Father without being his Son. John Paul does not posit such a structural correspondence between the Trinity and the father-mother-child triad. He sees the image of the Trinity in the communion of persons shaped by the two meanings of marriage and the conjugal act, union and procreation in their inseparable connection.

Unitive Meaning: In his commentary on the words of Jesus, "that they may be one as we are one" (John 17:11, 17:21–22), Thomas points to the likeness between the union of divine persons and the union of human beings.

> There is a *twofold unity* in God, the *unity of nature and the unity of love* in the Father and the Son which is the unity of the Spirit. … They are *one by a love* that is not derived from the gift of someone else but that proceeds from them. For the Father and the Son love each other by the Holy Spirit but we by a love in which we participate as derived from a higher source.[48]

What is required for an image is a specific likeness, that is, a likeness in rational life. The unity of the Spirit communicated to human beings meets this requirement. Thomas does not explicitly conclude that this is an image of the Trinity. The conclusion follows, however, from what he does say about what constitutes an image.

Procreative Meaning: Thomas argues that "man is from man as God is from God." In this respect, human procreation is an image of the Trinity, not only *per accidens* but *per se.*

> In these and similar [respects] *the image of God is more perfect in man* than in an angel. But in this respect the account of the divine image is not found *per se* in man, except if the first imitation is presupposed, which is according to the intellectual nature. Otherwise even brute animals would be to the image of God.[49]

48. Thomas, *Super Ioannem*, cap. 17, lect. 3, no. 2214; emphasis added.

49. Thomas, *Summa* I, p. 93, a. 3, corp.; emphasis added. Cf. *Super I sent.*, d. 3, q. 3, ad 4; *Super II sent.*, d. 16, a. 3.

The double negative "not found *per se* except if" can be converted into the equivalent positive. The divine image is found *per se* in human procreation if one presupposes that it is procreation of persons by persons (see part II, chap. 7, section 1, in this volume).

John Galvin and Joseph Selling on Personalism

Some critics argue that personalism has been definitively refuted by Charles De Koninck in *The Primacy of the Common Good: Against the Personalists* (see part I, chap. 7, in this volume).[50] John Paul describes himself as a personalist.

In response, *personalism* can signify various sorts of emphases on the person, some of them in agreement with De Koninck, others opposed. Pius XII speaks about "healthy personalism" as a necessary ingredient of the political order.[51] John Paul sees Ephesians 5:31–32 as "personalistic in the full meaning of the word" (TOB 117:3). He is aware of different directions in which modern thinkers have developed the concept of *person*, particularly in the two radically opposite forms of personalism proposed by Kant and Scheler (see part II, chaps. 2–3, in this volume). At times, he uses *personalist* in a negative sense.

> A personalist conception based on pure subjectivism and, as such, unmindful of the nature of the human person—obviously taking the word "nature" in the metaphysical sense—would lend itself to every sort of ambiguity, even in the canonical domain.[52]

Yet *pure subjectivism* is precisely what some critics attribute to John Paul's personalism. In an essay on *Humanae vitae* under the heading "Reliance on Personalist Phenomenology," John Galvin raises the following objection.

> [When it] speaks of an "inseparable connection" between "the unitive meaning and the procreative meaning," *Humanae vitae* is creating out of thin air a concept that has never before existed in any form of Catholic doctrine.... The substitution of the new concept "meaning" in place of the traditional language of "end" or "purpose" represents a radical restructuring.... How did the mag-

50. See Charles De Koninck, "The Primacy of the Common Good: Against the Personalists," *Aquinas Review* 4 (1997): 1–71.

51. Pius XII, *Address to the Italian Section of the Council of European Communities*, December 6, 1957.

52. John Paul II, *Address to the Tribunal of the Roman Rota*, January 27, 1997. "Egotistical personalism," *Discourse to Religious*, Quito (Ecuador), January 30, 1985. "Pseudo-liturgical personalisms," *Discourse to the Center of Liturgical Action*, November 30, 1984. "You are stronger than all egotistical and personalistic ambitions." *Prayer to Mary*, Vaduz (Liechtenstein), September 8, 1985, *Insegnamenti* 8, no. 2 (1985): 638–40.

> isterium come to discard the natural law explanation of such a fundamental institution as marriage and replace it with a novel and untried philosophy? The answer, in a word, is "Personalism." ... It is apparent that *Humanae vitae* acted as a springboard by which personalism could launch its new philosophy of marriage, displacing the traditional teaching ... with an impenetrable philosophy of interpersonal relationships that has proven disastrous in practice.[53]

From another place on the theological spectrum, Joseph Selling sees a similar break with the tradition in "the novel teaching of HV no. 12 on what has come to be known as the inseparability principle.... There is no foundation in the tradition for ... an inseparability principle."[54] Selling reports that his extensive research about an inseparable connection of unitive and procreative meaning in the Catholic tradition came up empty-handed. He attributes the novel teaching of *Humanae vitae* to the peculiar Polish personalism developed by Wojtyła.[55]

According to Galvin, John Paul replaces the objective terms *nature*, *good*, and *end* by the vague subjective notion of *meaning*. He overlooks that John Paul clarifies *meaning* in relation to the more traditional terms *nature*, *good*, and *end*.

> The *"essence"* (*or nature*) of the conjugal act constitutes *the basis* for an adequate rereading of the meanings that must correspond to the conjugal act in the consciousness and the decisions of the acting persons.... What is at stake here is the truth, *first in the ontological dimension*, "innermost structure," and then—as a consequence—in the subjective and psychological dimension, "meaning" (TOB 118:6; emphasis added).

According to this text, *nature*, *good*, and *end* signify what belongs to the order of being. *Meaning* does not exclude this order. It does not signify *only* what is subjective or psychological in contrast to being. It differs from *good* and *end* by addition, not subtraction. It signifies the whole reality of *good* and of *end* but adds conscious appreciation of them in human knowledge and love. The *Oxford English Dictionary* defines the first sense of *meaning* as "the significance, purpose, underlying truth of something." Examples for *meaning* in the sense of *purpose* go back to 1603. In current English, certain questions—such as What is the *meaning* of this act? and What is the *meaning* of life?—can be understood as questions about the *good* or *purpose*.

53. John Galvin, "*Humanae vitae:* Heroic, Deficient—or Both," *Latin Mass* 11 (2002): 7–17.

54. Joseph A. Selling, "The Recovery of Aquinas's Action Theory: A Reply to William Murphy," *Theological Studies* 73 (2012): 139–50, at 141n8.

55. See Michael J. Barberi and Joseph A. Selling, "The Origin of *Humanae Vitae* and the Impasse in Fundamental Theological Ethics," *Louvain Studies* 37 (2013): 364–89; and in popular form Joseph Selling, "Overwriting Tradition: *Humanae vitae* Replaced Real Church Teaching," *National Catholic Reporter* 54, no. 16 (May 18, 2018): 12–13.

A second aspect of *meaning* pointed out by both *Humanae vitae* and TOB is close to the *signification* of words. Man and woman say definite words of the body to each other. These words correspond to the two meanings of the conjugal act. "I am yours and you are mine" and "It is with you that I want to have children."

Selling is correct in claiming that the phrase *inseparable meanings* is new. It is new on the level of the words, but old on the level of their meaning. Augustine distinguishes three goods of marriage. "All of these are good and because of them marriage is a good: faithful union, offspring, and the sacrament."[56] *Faithful union* and *offspring* correspond to the unitive and procreative meanings. *Sacrament* does not add a third good on the same level but raises marriage as a whole to be an effective sign of grace. The word inseparability is not used, but it is clear that the two goods of marriage are not isolated from each other.

More than a century before Augustine, the Roman Jurist Modestinus defined marriage as "a joining of male and female and a shared lot of life as a whole, granting divine and human right."[57] "Joining (*coniunctio*)" highlights the bond of union between the spouses. *Shared lot* (*consortium*) *of life as a whole* points to the total extent of this union. The phrase *of male and female* indicates that the joining and shared lot is of a specific kind, the kind shaped by procreation.

Thomas understands Modestinus's term *joining* (*coniunctio*) as the genus of marriage and the ordering to procreation as its specific difference.[58] Genus and specific difference do not stand side by side as two separable items in a nature. They are conceptually distinguishable but ontologically inseparable in each specific nature. Marital union is procreative, and procreation is maritally unitive. Patrick Lee and Robert P. George give a profound and clear account of this inseparability. In the following text they do not use the phrase *inseparable connection*, but they explain the reality to which it points.

> The common good that defines marriage—and so its fundamental distinguishing nature—is the bodily, emotional, and spiritual unity that finds its fruition in bearing and rearing children together.... There is an intrinsic link between these two aspects of the community; the multileveled (and intrinsically sexual) relationship is fulfilled by, and is not merely incidental to, the conceiving and rearing of children. Hence marriage is fundamentally distinct

56. Haec omnia bona sunt, propter quae nuptiae bonum sunt, proles fides sacramentum. Augustine, *De bono coniugali* 32.

57. Nuptiae sunt coniunctio maris et feminae et consortium omnis vitae, divini et humani iuris communicatio. Modestinus in *Codex iuris civilis, Digesta* 23.2.1.

58. See Thomas, *Super IV sent.*, d. 27, a. 1; cf. *Summa* II-II, q. 154, a. 2; *Summa* III, q. 29 a. 2 corp.; *Contra gentiles* III, cap. 25.

> from a relationship of cohabitation combined with regular sex, and it is not merely an alliance formed to raise children. Rather, it is the union of a man and a woman, formed by their commitment to sharing their lives together, on all levels of their being—bodily-sexual as well as emotional and spiritual—in the kind of community that would be naturally fulfilled by begetting and rearing children together. This community is by its nature between a man and a woman and demands exclusivity and the sincere pledge of permanence.[59]

Tadeusz Styczeń on Wojtyła's Breakthrough

In his introduction to the Italian translation of *Person and Act*, Tadeusz Styczeń, Wojtyła's assistant and successor in the chair of theological ethics in Lublin, claims that Wojtyła developed a radically new philosophical approach. It breaks through the limits of classical philosophy inasmuch as it pays attention to consciously lived experience. Classical philosophy, Styczeń argues, begins with the ready-made definition of man as *rational animal* without attention to this kind of experience.

> In his anthropology, Wojtyła *does not begin with a philosophical system that is already ready* but with the human person's look into itself, with human experience. ... It is *a reversal* in the whole tradition of anthropology *in the framework of so called classical philosophy*, which is oriented above all to being as such, its structures and categories, and consequently searches for the place that belongs to man in reality as a whole, looking for his proximate genus among the beings that surround him to show on this background, at the end, the distinctive specific feature that distinguishes him from them.[60]

If classical philosophy begins with ready-made definitions, it is neither classical nor philosophy. Aristotle sees experience as the source of all knowledge. "Knowledge and skill come to human beings from experience (ἐμπειρία).... Experience made skill, lack of experience luck."[61] An inexperienced doctor may hit on a cure by luck. An experienced doctor can find a cure in many cases. Examining a patient is an experience in the sense of conscious looking, listening, touching, asking, and so on. To express this first sense of *experience*, Wojtyła uses Polish *przeżycie* (from życie = life and *prze* = through), which signifies consciously living through such acts. German has a close etymological equivalent

59. Patrick Lee and Robert P. George, *Conjugal Union: What Marriage Is and Why It Matters* (Cambridge: Cambridge University Press, 2014), 67.

60. Tadeusz Styczeń, "Introduzione," in Karol Wojtyła, *Metafisica della persona: Tutte le opere filosofiche e saggi integrativi*, ed. Giovanni Reale and Tadeusz Styczeń (Milan: Bompiani, 2003), 805; emphasis added.

61. Aristotle, *Metaphysics* 1.1.981a.1–5.

often used by Scheler; namely, *Erleben* (er- = a prefix that expresses successful completion of an act's purpose; -leben = to live). English and Italian lack such a word. As a makeshift, the Italian translation of *Person and Act* uses *esperienza vissuta, lived experience.* A contrast can help clarify the meaning of this phrase. When one says about a doctor that she has much experience, one speaks about *experience* in the sense of *the cumulative effect of many lived experiences.*

John Paul gives a brilliant example of the interplay between definition and the two senses of *experience* (lived and cumulative) in his reading of the creation of Eve. After saying "It is not good for the man to be alone" (Genesis 2:18), God does not solve the problem right away by forming a woman. He forms *all* the animals of the field and *all* the birds of the air—twice the word *all.* He brings them to the man to name them *all*—a third time *all.* The man then names "*all* cattle and birds, and *all* animals of the field"—a fourth and fifth time *all*, an extraordinary accumulated emphasis on *all.* How long did it take the man to examine a specimen of each of the roughly 10,000 species of birds and 5,500 species of mammals, not to speak of reptiles and insects, so as to name them all? In each of these encounters, the man had to answer the question, Am I still alone? Each disappointment intensified the man's lived experience of being alone. The cumulative effect of these encounters was the man's self-understanding by the proximate genus *animal* and the specific difference *rational.*

> The observation that the man cannot identify himself essentially with the visible world of the animals has . . . a positive aspect for this primary search. Even if this observation is not yet a complete definition, it nevertheless constitutes one of its elements. If we accept the Aristotelian tradition in logic and anthropology, one would have to define this element as the "proximate genus." . . . With this knowledge, which makes him go in some way outside of his own being, man at the same time reveals himself to himself in all the distinctiveness of his essence. . . . That process of seeking a definition of himself, sketched so incisively in Genesis 2:19–20, leads—attaching ourselves again to the Aristotelian tradition—to indicating not only the proximate genus . . . [but also] the specific difference, which according to Aristotle's definition is *nous* [reason], *zoon noetikon* [rational animal]. (TOB 5:5–6)

John Paul's reading of Genesis focuses in a fresh manner on an old experience and an old definition that flows from it. It shows how the man's lived experience of being alone, even though he had the company of irrational animals, leads him toward the definition *rational animal.* Genesis does not start with the Aristotelian definition ready-made. It does not even arrive at it explicitly, but it describes the experience, both lived and cumulative, that is needed for the definition. When the classical definition is the fruit of such lived and cumulative experience, it holds within itself a grasp of human personhood and subjectivity, that is, of "I" and "you" as distinctive features of a rational animal. The world did not have to wait for phenomenology to arrive at such a personalist understanding. According to Wojtyła, personalism is present in Genesis and in Aristotle.

Thomas Petri on Thomism and Phenomenology

Thomas Petri's important work on SS. John Paul and Thomas shows that their thought is "more connected than is often suggested."[62] He concludes "that an authentic interpretation of this 'theology of the body' relies on an appreciation of the intersection of the thought of St. John Paul and Thomas Aquinas."[63]

Petri accepts the hypothesis (suggested by some interpreters and seemingly confirmed by the "Author's Preface" to Wojtyła's main philosophical work, *The Acting Person*) that in the sixties Wojtyła shifted away from his Thomistic roots toward the Phenomenology of Max Scheler. Petri could have more easily made his argument about the connection between TOB and Thomas Aquinas if he had questioned this widely accepted hypothesis. His acceptance of it, of course, also lends strength to his argument. One cannot accuse him of being violently irenic. He sees the shift hypothesis as a difficulty but does not brush it aside. He still succeeds brilliantly in showing that TOB and Thomas are so closely connected that one should read TOB in light of Thomas and (less commonly affirmed by Thomists) vice versa.

George Weigel's biography of John Paul II suggests one version of the shift hypothesis.

> That he [Wojtyła] looked to Scheler as a possible guide, and that he put himself through the backbreaking work of translation so that he could analyze Scheler in his own language, suggests that Wojtyła had become convinced that the answers were not to be found in the neo-scholasticism of Father Reginald Garrigou-Lagrange.[64]

Buttiglione argues for another version of the hypothesis. Wojtyła, he claims, combined Thomism and Phenomenology into a new philosophical system that reconciles the Catholic tradition with modernity as understood by Descartes, Kant, and Scheler.

62. Thomas Petri, OP, *Aquinas and the Theology of the Body: The Thomistic Foundations of John Paul II's Anthropology* (Washington, DC: Catholic University of America Press, 2016), xi.

63. Petri, *Aquinas and the Theology of the Body*, i; cf. 195–96.

64. Weigel, *Witness to Hope*, 128.

> It is a matter of a new synthesis in which modern elements and traditional elements are harmoniously fused and the tradition shows itself capable of developing out of itself those aspects which it was criticized for neglecting. The philosophy of consciousness ceases to be thought of as another philosophy which is situated beyond the philosophy of being and becomes one of the articulations of a more complete and wiser philosophy of being, which is purified of the deviations which had made it a mere philosophy of entity. At the same time, the contrast between modernity and Christianity disappears.[65]

Wojtyła occasionally expresses dissatisfaction with Thomas's objectivist way of speaking. Petri seems to agree with this judgment. He puts it quite sharply.

> Aquinas did not offer a full view of the experience of human consciousness or a full explanation of human personhood . . . Consciousness and human personhood did not become overriding issues until the modern period.[66] Wojtyła believes that in Aquinas's "objectivistic view" of reality, there is no place to examine the subject.[67]

Therese Cory has shown, contrary to the judgment "no place," that Thomas has a profound and penetrating account of consciousness.[68] No doubt, there is a difference of degree in the attention paid to consciousness. Reflection on consciously lived experience occupies more of the foreground of interest in Wojtyła, but the same can be said already about John of the Cross. The relative increase is not a shift away from Thomas toward Descartes, Scheler, and Kant, but a more extensive exploration of what Thomas affirms.

David Schindler on Constitutive Relations

David Schindler makes fruitful use of Ratzinger's discussion of *anamnesis*, remembrance. "Do this in *anamnesis* of me" (Luke 22:19; 1 Corinthians 11:24–25). He shows that John Paul understands the spousal meaning of the body as an inner and constitutive characteristic of our being, first received in a filial manner before it is enacted. Human acts arise in an *anamnesis* of filial reception that shapes human interiority from its very roots. Only in this way can one do justice to the depth at which the spousal meaning of the body is found.

65. Rocco Buttiglione, *Karol Wojtyła: The Thought of the Man Who Became Pope John Paul II* (Grand Rapids, MI: Eerdmans, 1997), 184.

66. Petri, *Aquinas and the Theology of the Body*, 311.

67. Petri, *Aquinas and the Theology of the Body*, 115.

68. Therese Scarpelli Cory, *Aquinas on Human Self-Knowledge* (Cambridge: Cambridge University Press, 2014).

> John Paul II's theology of the body, in a word, is about God and being as love, and about the body and the sexual difference insofar as these are a sign and expression of the theologically-ontologically-anthropologically prior love, even as the body precisely in its sexual difference provides a new and just so far enriched and deepened understanding of this prior love.[69]

Schindler argues that there is a tension between this thesis and Thomas, at least a Thomas understood as agreeing with Aristotle about substance and accident. My Aristotelian-Thomistic reading of TOB in the introduction to the translation of TOB falls short.

> Waldstein rightly emphasizes John Paul's rejection of a Cartesian in favor of an Aristotelian-Thomistic understanding: "the purpose of TOB as a whole," he says, "is to defend the spousal meaning of the body against the alienation between person and body in the Cartesian vision of nature." My question, however, is whether his argument suffices to give us more than Aristotle's human-organic body: in other words, whether what this line of argument gives us in the end is truly a filial-spousal body or indeed person: a body or person understood as gift or love already in its constitutive order *qua body and qua person.*[70]

The failure to understand the person and body as gift and love in its constitutive order, Schindler holds, is a necessary consequence of agreeing with Aristotle's thesis that relations are accidents (*symbebēkota*) said about a substance (*ousia*).[71] Aristotle's thesis, he argues, implies that relations enter only on a secondary level of being, too late to save substance from being nonrelational. Aristotelian substance is, as such, free of all accidents. Consequently, when they are understood as accidents, relations cannot be understood as internal and constitutive.

> There is *no order of relation built into* the very structure of the human being as created *ex nihilo*.... Lacking this original inscription of love, the (sexual) body in its original constitution becomes simply the bearer of biological finalities that can so far, *even on an Aristotelian-Thomistic account of the organic body*, be only instrumentalized expressions of the spouses in their personal exchanges of love.[72]

Schindler is right. If the Aristotelian account of substance and accident implies that there is no order of relation built into the very structure of the person,

69. David L. Schindler, "The Embodied Person as Gift and the Cultural Task in America: *Status Quaestionis*," *Communio* 35 (2008): 397–431, at 410.

70. Schindler, "Embodied Person as Gift," 417–18.

71. See Michael Waldstein, "Constitutive Relations: A Response to David L. Schindler," *Communio* 37 (2010): 495–518.

72. David L. Schindler, "Being, Gift, Self-Gift: A Reply to Waldstein on Relationality and John Paul II's Theology of the Body (Part One)," *Communio* 42 (2015): 221–51; emphasis added.

then that account must be false. If the conditional clause is true, the main clause must be true. The question is whether the conditional clause is true.

Schindler's reading of Aristotle can perhaps be understood in light of his early writings as a doctoral student at Claremont Graduate School.[73] Under the leadership of John Cobb, Schindler's thesis advisor, Claremont was a center of Process Thought inspired by Whitehead.[74] Schindler does not simply align himself with Whitehead in his early writings but criticizes aspects of Process Thought with strength and courage, injecting the voices of Thomas and Aristotle into the debate, voices not always welcome in Process circles.

In line with Process Thought, however, Schindler criticizes Aristotle as static, essentialist, and substantialist, lacking an understanding of the act of being (*esse*), of interiority, and of relation. Thomas achieved a partial breakthrough to *esse*, he argues, but did not free himself fully enough from Aristotle. If one strips away the Aristotelian layer of essentialism and substantialism, the result is a Thomas who can enter fruitful dialogue and even synthesis with Process Thought. Schindler follows Gerald Phelan in his evaluation of Aristotle and Thomas.

> Gerald Phelan, while pinpointing the metaphysics of *esse* as Aquinas's distinct contribution to philosophy, nonetheless argues that Aquinas couched his insights in the vocabulary of Aristotle, with the result that those insights "still bore the stamp of the essentialism or substantialism of that great Greek thinker." . . .
>
> Phelan's article . . . [suggests] an interesting historical situation for the continuing discussion between Thomists and Whiteheadian process philosophers. For is it not the case that much of this discussion has presupposed in Aquinas just the essentialistic, substantialistic, or formalistic horizon of Greek philosophical literature to which Phelan refers? What exactly would result from a Thomism rethought in terms of a metaphysics of *esse* disengaged from such a horizon?[75]

73. In chronological order: David L. Schindler, "Creativity as Ultimate: Reflections on Actuality in Whitehead, Aristotle, Aquinas," *International Philosophical Quarterly* 13 (1973): 161–71; "Knowing as Synthesis: A Metaphysical Prolegomenon to a Critical Christian Philosophy," PhD diss., dir. John B. Cobb Jr. (Claremont Graduate University Faculty in Religion, 1976); "Whitehead's Challenge to Thomism on God and Creation: The Metaphysical Issues," *International Philosophical Quarterly* 19 (1979): 285–99; "Critical Studies and Reviews: W. Norris Clarke, S.J., The Philosophical Approach to God," *Process Studies* 11 (1981): 40–46; "Whitehead's Inability to Affirm a Universe of Value," *Process Studies* 13 (1983): 117–31.

74. See John B. Cobb Jr. and David Ray Griffin, *Process Theology: An Introductory Exposition* (Philadelphia: Westminster Press, 1976).

75. Schindler, "Critical Studies and Reviews: W. Norris Clarke, SJ, The Philosophical Approach to God," 40; cf. Gerald B. Phelan, "The Being of Creatures," *Proceedings of the American Catholic Philosophical Association* 31 (1957): 118–25.

What such a Thomas disengaged from the Philosopher might look like can be seen, at least in part, in Schindler's earliest published essay (1973), which reaches the following conclusions.

> In summary, then, I have attempted to argue three points in this paper:
>
> first, that creativity is a distinct and fundamentally important principle of being in Whitehead's metaphysics, that it is functionally equivalent to (prime) matter in Aristotle and the act of existence (*esse*) in Aquinas;
>
> secondly, that creativity goes a long way toward resolving the problem of universals, of the One and the many, because "it" is not a thing and hence adds "no-thing" to particulars but merely gives them actuality, similar to Aquinas' *esse*;
>
> and lastly, that creativity is finally inadequate as ultimate in Whitehead's metaphysics because, not being itself actual, it cannot ground the actuality of actual entities, in contrast with *esse* in Aquinas, which is concretized in a single Source that is supremely actual, God as *ipsum esse subsistens*.[76]

It is a surprising conclusion, to say the least, that Aristotle's prime matter, Thomas's *esse*, and Whitehead's creativity are functional equivalents. How can the principle of pure potency (prime matter) and the principle of the actuality of all acts (*esse*) be functionally equivalent?

Two of Whitehead's main theses are at work in Schindler's early writings. The first is the critique of Aristotelian substance. Whitehead writes,

> The simple notion of an enduring substance sustaining persistent qualities, either essentially or accidentally, expresses a useful abstract for many purposes of life. But whenever we try to use it as a fundamental statement of the nature of things, it proves itself mistaken. It arose from a mistake and has never succeeded in any of its applications.[77]

The second thesis is the positive counterpart of this rejection of substance. Individual beings are bundles of distinct entities in what Whitehead calls *concrescence*, the process of growing together. Concrescence takes the place of Aristotelian substance.

> In their natures, entities are disjunctively "many" in process of passage into conjunctive unity. This Category of the Ultimate replaces Aristotle's category of "primary substance." Thus the "production of novel togetherness" is the ultimate notion embodied in the term "concrescence."[78]

76. Schindler, "Creativity as Ultimate," 171.

77. Alfred North Whitehead, *Process and Reality: An Essay in Cosmology*, corrected ed., David Griffin and Donald Sherburne (New York: Free Press, 1978), 113.

78. Whitehead, *Process and Reality*, 54–55. *Concrescence* comes from Latin *con* = together and *cresco* = grow.

The concept *concrescence of many entities* brings out a pervasive pattern of thought in Whitehead's philosophy; namely, seeing conceptually distinct aspects of being as distinct in being. A similar tendency can be seen in Plato. Aristotle resists this tendency by arguing that whatever is received is received according to the mode of the recipient. Part of the mode of the recipient in human knowledge is the use of many distinct concepts to grasp what is one in being. In the absence of this correction, entities multiply. The multiplication is evident in the many levels of universality on which Plato posits forms or ideas (εἴδη) as distinct in reality.[79] Whitehead reads Aristotle himself in his own un-Aristotelian pattern as proposing substance as one such entity among others, distinct from other entities such as relation. Aristotelian accidents, however, are not entities. They do not exist. They are the being of substance, not its being at all rather than not at all, but its being in this place or that, hot or cold, and so on (see part I, chap. 6, sections 3–5, in this volume).

That Schindler's present views about substance and relation are rooted in Whitehead is a tentative hypothesis. The name Whitehead is frequent in Schindler's early writings. In later writings, Hans Urs von Balthasar occupies more of the foreground. Balthasar rarely refers to Process Thought, and when he does, he tends to distance himself from it.[80] Schindler may well have heeded Balthasar's caution since the publication of his early writings.

Aude Suramy on Wojtyła, Garrigou-Lagrange, and Waldstein

Aude Suramy published a deeply insightful reading of Wojtyła's main philosophical work, *Person and Act*.[81] In light of this reading, she finds my introduction to TOB not Thomistic enough.

> Waldstein studies the influence of John of the Cross on Wojtyła. He is the first to underline the Sanjuanist character of Wojtyła's concept of love and to speak of Wojtyła's "Carmelite personalism." Waldstein also studies the con-

79. The root difference between Plato and Aristotle is discussed in Thomas, *De spiritualibus creaturis*, a. 3, corp.; see part I, chap. 5, section 5, in this volume.

80. Balthasar mentions Whitehead only once in his trilogy but briefly discusses Process Thought in other places. See Hans Urs von Balthasar, *Herrlichkeit: Eine theologische Ästhetik*, 7 vols. (Einsiedeln: Johannes, 1961–69), 3/1/2:556; *The Glory of the Lord: A Theological Aesthetics*, 7 vols. (San Francisco: Ignatius Press, 1982–89), 5:209; *Theodramatik*, 5 vols. (Einsiedeln: Johannes, 1973–83), 3:299, with explicit mention of Whitehead; *Theodrama: Theological Dramatic Theory*, 5 vols. (San Francisco: Ignatius Press, 1988–98), 4:322; *Theologik*, 3 vols. (Einsiedeln: Johannes, 1985–87), 51n91; *Theo-Logic: Theological Logical Theory* (San Francisco: Ignatius Press, 1985–87), 3:59n91.

81. See Aude Suramy, *La voie d'amour: Une interprétation de Personne et acte de Karol Wojtyła, lecteur de Thomas d'Aquin* (Rome: Cattedra Karol Wojtyła, Istituto Giovanni Paolo II per Studi su Matrimonio e Famiglia, 2014).

> tributions of Scheler and Kant to Wojtyła's thought to reach a better grasp of his theology.
>
> Waldstein's study is limpid but unfortunately fails to present the influence of Thomas Aquinas, which seems to us essential for grasping the foundations of the thought of "one who" in working out his most fundamental philosophical work was clearly "a reader of St. Thomas." Waldstein's "Introduction" remains a help; at the same time, it is a motivation for our work.[82]

Granted, it is only half a step to point to John of the Cross. That John Paul's thesis on the image of the Trinity in man and woman has its roots in John of the Cross seemed to me a valid first line of defense against Thomist attacks on TOB. When the introduction was published (2006), I did not see clearly how to respond more directly. In the present volume I attempt to complete the step by analyzing the principles of Thomas's Trinitarian theology with special attention to his understanding of the analogy of the inner word in the human mind and the analogy of love between distinct persons (see part II, chap. 7, in this volume).

Suramy convincingly shows Wojtyła's closeness to Thomas. She also argues, however, that there is a substantial disagreement between Wojtyła and his thesis director, Réginald Garrigou-Lagrange, about intentionality, closely intertwined with the controversy about nature and grace surrounding Henri de Lubac's *Surnaturel*.[83] Garrigou-Lagrange, she points out, graded Wojtyła's thesis *summa cum laude*.[84] Nevertheless, his evaluation includes the following critical remarks.

> Instead of the often repeated expression, "Divine form in an intentional way" *forma Divina modo intentionali* or "a form intentionally unlimited" *forma intentionaliter illimitata* one should simply speak of the Divine Object. The notion of form suggests the possibility of interpreting it in the sense of an intentional species while we know that in the [beatific] vision the Divine Essence is reached with an immediate knowledge without a species. It itself functions as the species.[85]

Suramy reads this passage as showing Garrigou-Lagrange's resistance against the experiential side of Christian life as a participation in God's life. The reason for the resistance, she argues, is the concern to keep the natural order clearly distinct from the supernatural. On this basis she goes on to raise the following critical questions.

82. Suramy, *La voie d'amour*, 31.

83. See Suramy, *La voie d'amour*, 238–39.

84. See Suramy, *La voie d'amour*, 239.

85. See Garrigou-Lagrange's notes on Wojtyła's dissertation, reproduced in facsimile and transcription in Suramy, *La voie d'amour*, 240. For the thesis that God himself will take the place of the intelligible species, see Thomas, *Summa* I, q. 12, a. 9.

> Garrigou-Lagrange's rejection of the expression *intentional* is far from inconsequential. Could it be the rejection of one of the most fundamental contributions of Wojtyła's thesis? By the mystical expression "intentionality" and in conformity with the etymology of that expression [in-tendo = stretch into], Wojtyła shows the greatness of human nature. In all the weakness of its being, human nature tends toward the Other so as to participate. Could it be this intentional participation that arrests Garrigou-Lagrange somewhat in the fear that he will see the supernatural reduced to the natural?[86]

If Wojtyła had accepted Garrigou-Lagrange's suggestions, "they would have annihilated his work and categorically opposed his thought."[87]

Suramy places the emphasis on the word *intentional* in Garrigou-Lagrange's phrase "divine form *in an intentional way*." One should perhaps emphasize the word *form* in the first part of the phrase, "divine *form* in an intentional way." Garrigou-Lagrange's point, as Suramy herself recognizes, is that *no created form* can mediate the presence of God in the beatific vision. Speaking of *divine form in an intentional way* about the knowledge of God in our present state should not lead one to suppose that such a form distinct from God will be present in the beatific vision.

Garrigou-Lagrange explicitly affirms intentionality while rejecting a created species. "By the beatific vision, the mind of the blessed *in some way*, namely, *intentionally*, becomes God, as Cajetan says, and this cannot happen by any created species."[88] In the bibliography of his dissertation, Wojtyła lists two works by Ambroise Gardeil, OP, Garrigou-Lagrange's teacher in mystical theology, who argues that mystical experience in our present life involves a created form and is intentional.[89]

Still, Suramy's critical questions have a point. On the one hand, Garrigou-Lagrange counteracts a widespread tendency to sideline St. John of the Cross as irrelevant for ordinary Christian life.[90] On the other hand, his account of mystical language as opposed to Thomistic scientific language tends to form a barrier against the theological relevance of John of the Cross, especially in Trinitarian

86. Suramy, *La voie d'amour*, 243.

87. Suramy, *La voie d'amour*, 253.

88. Réginald Garrigou-Lagrange, *De Deo Uno: Commentarium in Primam Partem Summae S. Thomae* (Turin: Marietti, 1938), 274, emphasis original; *The One God: Commentary on the First Part of St. Thomas' Theological Summa* (St. Louis, MO: Herder, 1943), 345, emphasis added.

89. See Ambroise Gardeil, "La contemplation mystique est-elle intentionelle?," *Revue Thomiste* 32 (1932): 228–50; 279–393, esp. 249–50. This essay takes up theses developed more fully in Gardeil's earlier two-volume treatment, *La structure de l'ame et l'experiénce mystique* (Paris: Gabalda, 1927).

90. See the chapters on infused contemplation in Réginald Garrigou-Lagrange, OP, *The Three Ages of the Interior Life: Prelude of Eternal Life*, 2 vols. (Rockford, IL: Tan, 1989), 2:309–41.

theology.[91] This barrier is evident in his resistance against the analogy of mutual love and the exclusive identification of the analogy of the word with the heart of Trinitarian theology. He does not criticize John of the Cross's statements about the Trinity directly, but his critique of Richard of St. Victor's Trinitarian theology makes clear where he stands.[92] The unintended consequence of such an exclusive emphasis on the analogy of the word is the tendency toward collapsing the supernatural mystery of the Trinity into the natural order and reducing the Church's faith in the Trinity to private philosophical conviction (see part II, chap. 7, section 9, in this volume).

Garrigou-Lagrange is a complex figure.[93] De Koninck identifies him as a representative of the personalism against which he wrote *The Primacy of the Common Good: Against the Personalists.* In a letter to Maritain, Yves Simon gives a report of the discussion at Notre Dame immediately after a lecture by De Koninck.

> After the lecture there was a party at my house. I had told W[aldemar Gurian] to open fire. He didn't delay. Hardly had De Koninck sat down when he got the fatal question right in the solar plexus: Who are these personalists? De K[oninck] hesitated visibly and showed a little less Belgian good nature and a little more reserve. He mentioned a Californian review (do you remember, *The Personalist*, which Mounier discovered four or five years after launching *Esprit*); Adler and Farrel; Garrigou-Lagrange, with insistence.[94]

5. The Practice of Reason

What Thomism?

Josef Pieper met Cardinal Wojtyła at the 1974 Thomistic Congress held in Rome and Naples for the 700th anniversary of St. Thomas's death.

> More than a thousand "Thomists" from all over the world attended the Conference ... Without any doubt, [Cardinal Wojtyła] was the only ecclesiastic of such high rank who was able to contribute with competence to the discussion. We had an immediate good understanding for each other. It became clear that

91. See the chapter "The Language of Spiritual Writers Compared with That of Theologians," in Garrigou-Lagrange, *Three Ages of the Interior Life,* 2:3–20.

92. See Reginald Garrigou-Lagrange, *De deo trino et creatore: Commentarium in Summam theologicam S. Thomae, Ia q. XXVII–CXIX* (Milan: Marietti, 1943), 47–49; *The Trinity and God the Creator: A Commentary on St. Thomas' Theological Summa, Ia, q. 27–119* (St. Louis, MO: Herder, 1952), 69–72.

93. See Richard Peddicord, OP, *The Sacred Monster of Thomism: An Introduction to the Life and Legacy of Réginald Garrigou-Lagrange, O.P.* (South Bend, IN: St. Augustine Press, 2005).

94. Letter of Yves Simon to Jacques Maritain, September 8, 1944, Yves Simon Archives, Maritain Center, University of Notre Dame.

> I was not unknown to the former professor of philosophy at Lublin. It was in equal measure welcome and unexpected to hear him say what he repeated several times in the next few days. "You absolutely must come to Poland."[95]

Pieper told his friend Joseph Ratzinger, then Archbishop of Munich, to take note of the name Wojtyła. Ratzinger did.

> My first encounter with Cardinal Wojtyła of Kraków—the future Pope John Paul II—was indirect. A friend of mine, the Philosopher at Münster, Josef Pieper, had participated in an international philosophical conference in [Rome and] Naples. He told me that the real event of those days had been the talk by the Archbishop of Kraków. He had finally encountered a real philosopher again who, with fresh energy and the intuition of a genius, asked the essential questions anew, not entangled in academic theories but animated by the passion of knowing and the will for truth. One should remember this name. I remembered it, but at first, I could not find any of Wojtyła's works in a language accessible to me.[96]

For Pieper, being a philosopher means looking at things themselves in openness for whatever may show itself. Wojtyła first encountered Thomas not in Scholastic manuals prepared for the convenience and limits of seminarians, but in St. John of the Cross. From the very beginning, he saw a fuller and more living Thomas than the one offered by the manuals.

One of the most striking features of Wojtyła as a thinker is his suppleness, a trait he shares with Pieper. He disagrees with Kant and Scheler on many fundamental questions. Yet he shows no trace of antagonism, polarization, or defensive narrowness. His loyalty to Thomas goes hand in hand with attentive openness to any truth that comes to him from other authors and from his own reflection on experience. Balthasar sees this quality of supple openness as an essential aspect of the greatness of St. Thomas himself. He adds a warning.

> In the truly supernatural serenity, which remains the mystery of this great Saint, what opens before one's ever newly astonished eyes is a heavenly world of wisdom, as it were, in which all that seems confused and hopeless on this dark earth dissolves like clouds into a radiant blue. Yet, when one cannot assume that such unique holiness comes together with such unique circumspection, when the supernatural gift of grace is only imitated externally as if it were a technique one can pick up, this special charism of the Angel of the Schools,

95. Josef Pieper, *Werke*, 10 vols., ed. Berthold Wald (Hamburg: Felix Meiner Verlag, 2000–2012), 10:604–5.

96. Joseph Ratzinger, "Begegnungen mit Papst Johannes Paul II," in *Die Kraft des Augenblicks: Begegnungen mit Papst Johannes Paul II*, ed. Wladyslaw Bartoszewski (Freiburg: Herder, 2005), 44–58, at 44.

> the gift of clarifying, smoothing, and calming, which somehow lives from the grace of the risen Lord that gives to the heart a peace beyond all understanding (Philippians 4:7), can be the ruin of thought. The limits of school purposes can give rise to attempts of bringing everything one examines to a solution as simply, quickly, and univocally as possible. The logic that almost inescapably develops in service to this end is not only the logic of bringing to rest but not seldom the strange art of evasion and reductionism.[97]

The first sentence of Domingo Báñez's commentary on the *Summa* expresses what being a learner in relation to St. Thomas means to me. "Having turned over in my mind the learning and teaching of the Angelic Doctor by rather steady reading for many years, I see myself as just now beginning. All the more vehemently do I desire to be again a learner (*discipulus*) in relation to him."[98] The word *beginning* is striking. Having spent many years turning over in his mind the learning and teaching of the Doctor Angelicus, Báñez says, he sees himself as beginning. *Beginning* may refer, of course, to starting his commentary, but it seems to mean more than that, as evidenced by the vehement desire to learn. However much time and thought Báñez may have spent, he remains a beginner with a vehement desire to learn. That is the condition of every theologian, including Thomas. The vehement desire to learn is distinct from the desire to repeat what someone else says. It implies taking full responsibility for one's own learning as its principal cause. Marcus Berquist points out the difference.

> A human teacher is not the principal cause of learning but only an assisting cause. The principal causes are within the learner: first the natural power of his own understanding; and second, the premises, which he already knows.... [The teacher] only assists the principal cause by putting the objects of thought in order, which objects are already within the mind of the learner. He is like an assistant who aids an artisan by holding firm that upon which the artisan operates. He does not impart the form or quality, but he does make it possible for the artisan to do so by holding things in such a way that the power of the principal agent can be effective.[99]

97. Hans Urs von Balthasar, *Von den Aufgaben der Katholischen Philosophie in der Zeit* (Freiburg: Johannes Verlag, 1998), 52.

98. "Huius Angelici doctoris eruditionem, doctrinamque per multos annos continua fere lectione versans nunc mihi incipere videor, cuiusque denuo discipulus fieri vehementius desidero." Domingo Báñez, *Scholastica commentaria in primam partem Angelici Doctoris D. Thomae* (Salamanca: S. Stephanus, 1585), 3.

99. Marcus Berquist, "Learning and Discipleship," in *Learning and Discipleship: The Collected Papers of Marcus R. Berquist*, ed. Anne S. Forsyth (Santa Paula, CA: Thomas Aquinas College, 2019), 5–50, at 15.

I apply Báñez's words not only to Thomas but also to four others whose writings I have turned over in my mind for years: John Paul II, Benedict XVI, Hans Urs von Balthasar, and Charles De Koninck. Of particular help and encouragement on this path have been the writings of Pascal Ide, who has for many years turned over the writings of the same five teachers in his mind.[100]

Can anyone turn seriously to Thomas as the *Doctor Communis* and at the same time to the other four? Isn't only one of them a Thomist? Don't the other four disagree about important matters with Thomas and each other? When one learns from such different teachers, will the outcome not be confusion and eclecticism?[101] One can respond that the alternative is another form of ec-lecticism; namely, picking out (*ek-legein*) a mere part from a whole. It is a hallmark of the Catholic tradition that it embraces the whole. If theology is to be Catholic, it needs the whole tradition, from Scripture through the Fathers, both Greek and Latin, all the way to theologians of our own age. This is how Thomas himself understood the task of theologians.

Pascal Ide shows that De Koninck connects on a deep level; namely, in the category *gift* with John Paul, Ratzinger, and Balthasar. De Koninck takes up an axiom of self-communication stated by Aristotle as a tangent in his *Meteorology*. In the context of discussing weather, Aristotle considers the impact of weather on the ripening of fruit. He goes on a tangent to ask, "When is fruit ripe?" He answers, "The ripening is completed when the seeds in fruit are able to produce another like themselves." He then goes on a second tangent to formulate a far-reaching metaphysical axiom. "For in *all* other cases as well *this is what we call perfect*."[102] De Koninck reformulates the axiom and points out its importance as an axiom that crosses the boundaries between all realms of being: the material world both as created and redeemed, spiritual creatures, and the Trinity itself (see part I, chap. 6, sect. 7, in this volume).

100. See Pascal Ide, "Une théologie du don: Les occurrences de *Gaudium et spes* 24:3 chez Jean-Paul II," *Anthropotes* 17 (2001): 149–78, 313–44; *Le Christ donne tout: Benoît XVI, une théologie de l'amour* (Paris: L'Emmanuel, 2007); "La philosophie de la nature de Charles De Koninck," *Laval théologique et philosophique* 66 (2010): 459–501; *Une théologie de l'amour: L'amour, centre de la Trilogie de Hans Urs von Balthasar* (Brussels: Lessius, 2012); *Une théo-logique du don: Le don dans la Trilogie de Hans Urs von Balthasar* (Louvain: Peeters, 2013). Perhaps the final section of Ide's second book on Balthasar could have given more importance to the music of Mozart, which Balthasar loved for its overflowing joy; see Daniela Mohr, *Existenz im Herzen der Kirche: Zur Theologie der Säkularinstitute in Leben und Werk Hans Urs von Balthasars* (Würzburg: Echter, 2000), 16–39.

101. See Berquist, "Learning and Discipleship," 34.

102. Aristotle, *Meteorology*, 4.3.380a.13–15; emphasis added.

> The *essence of nature is communication of itself.* (See the splendid article in Q. *de Potentia*, q. 2, a. 1.) The more this communication is necessary the more perfect it is. That is the case in the Trinity.... Paradoxically: the more a *suppositum* is incommunicable, the more it is a principle of communication. This throws overboard the false implications drawn from the distinction between individuality and personality. Authors such as Maritain claim that man as a person is above society, for instance; and that he is a member of society as an individual. This is purely and simply false. Man is a member of society because he is a person. That is why ants are not members of a society. *This principle is true transcendentally:* in the Trinity, in the Church, in angelic universes.[103]

Roots of Reason in Childhood

Báñez's programmatic sentence *I see myself as just now beginning* can serve as an antidote against the abuse of any author. In an essay on the first and lasting roots of reason, De Koninck emphasizes common notions (*notiones communes*), which Thomas, following Aristotle, distinguishes from notions that are fruits of deliberate effort (*notiones propriae*).[104] Notions such as *mother, brother, food, water, light* arise from shared human experience of the world. They first express one's understanding as a child. In their indistinctness, richness, and depth, such shared notions resist attempts to reduce them to what Descartes calls clear and distinct ideas.[105] They are like the sense of touch, which is not as clear as sight but quite certain. *Sedeo ergo sum.* I sit, therefore I am.[106]

A good example of a notion not shared by children but formed by deliberate effort is Kant's *transcendental synthetic unity of apperception*, the first principle of thought and of being in his *Critique of Pure Reason*. One cannot understand what Kant means without having followed him through a long argument that constructs this notion.

The starting point of philosophy, De Koninck argues, lies in pre-philosophical notions shared by all, first shared by any person in childhood. It is not a starting point one can leave behind, as one might kick off a ladder after reaching the roof.

103. Charles De Koninck, *Letter to Mortimer Adler*, Quebec, June 15, 1938, De Koninck Archives, University of Notre Dame; emphasis added.

104. Charles De Koninck, "Three Sources of Philosophy," *Proceedings of the American Catholic Philosophical Association* 38 (1964): 13–22, at 13–19. A more detailed argument is presented by Marcus Berquist, "Common Conceptions and Proper Conceptions," in *Learning and Discipleship*, 243–67.

105. Descartes, *Principia philosophiae* 1.45, AT 8:21–22. Citations of Descartes will be by AT (Adam and Tannery) from René Descartes, *Oeuvres*, 13 vols., ed. Charles Adam and Paul Tannery (Paris: Vrin, 1897–1910).

106. See Charles De Koninck, "*Sedeo ergo sum*: Considerations on the Touchstone of Certitude," *Laval Théologique et Philosophique* 6 (1950): 343–48.

One needs to stay connected with these concepts. St. John Henry Newman finds Aristotle's attention to such concepts exemplary.

> While the world lasts, will Aristotle's doctrine on these matters last, for he is the oracle of nature and of truth. While we are men, we cannot help, to a great extent, being Aristotelians, for the great Master does but analyze the thoughts, feelings, views, and opinions of human kind. He has told us the meaning of our own words and ideas, before we were born. In many subject-matters, to think correctly, is to think like Aristotle; and we are his disciples whether we will or no, though we may not know it.[107]

Balthasar's warning should immediately be repeated after such high praise for Aristotle. If one learns the distinct notions developed by Aristotle without personally going through the difficult labor of reflecting on the indistinct notions formed in childhood and of returning to them over and over again, one turns him into an obstacle to knowledge. Aristotle warns against this shortcut.

> Lack of experience (ἀπειρία) diminishes our ability to see the recognized facts together (συνορᾶν). Hence those who have come to dwell more among natural things (ἐνῳκήκασι) are more capable of laying down beginnings that can speak as one about much, while those whom many words have kept from looking at the existing things are rather too ready to pronounce by looking at a few.[108]

The advice to dwell among natural things is close to an argument by Aristotle quoted by John Paul (see TOB 66:6, note 76). Since knowledge of the world comes through sense experience, our bodies must be part of what we are as human beings. As a sentient body, I cannot identify myself as a soul trapped in a body. What am I? I am a body, a living body, a sentient body, a rational body. "Man is a body, a body among bodies," John Paul repeats more than twenty times in TOB.[109] He is fully aware that to Cartesian ears this is a scandalous statement. How can the person, the *res cogitans*, the thinking thing, be identified with a body, a mere *res extensa*, an extended thing?[110] Are soul and body not of entirely different orders, spiritual as opposed to material? Is Aristotle unaware of the mind-body problem that is occupying the ingenuity of analytic philosophers?

107. John Henry Newman, *The Idea of a University Defined and Illustrated* (London: Basil Montagu Pickering, 1873), 109–10.

108. Aristotle, *On Generation and Corruption* 1.2.316a5–10.

109. See TOB 5:5–6, 6:3–4, 8:1, 10:1–4, 19:4, 21:3, 29:4, 44:6, 45:1, 55:2, 60:1–2, 69:2–4, 72:5, 85:9, 86:4, 99:4, 102:5, 119:4.

110. Descartes, *Principia philosophiae*, II.2, AT 8:41.

We grasp our own existence not primarily in nonbodily self-awareness, *Cogito, ergo sum*, I think, therefore I am.[111] If a touchstone of certainty were needed, it would be *sedeo, ergo sum*. I sit, therefore I am. *I sit* is a fascinating statement. It looks unremarkable at first glance, but it implies two truths that can hardly be overestimated in their importance. *First*, I identify myself fully with my body as I feel myself sitting on a rock, its hardness pressing against me. Consciousness cannot sit. Only a conscious and personal body can. I can, because I am a body. *Second*, the statement implies that this body is not just some body but *somebody*. It differs in kind from other bodies. It is a personal body. This truth of bodily personhood has the deep certainty of unclear and indistinct ideas. We preserve this truth from childhood into adult life, and it inevitably clings to us even when we think we can reject it, as Descartes and Kant believe they can.

6. A Violent Practice of Reason

Descartes uses radical doubt as an artificial means to sideline or disqualify the shared concepts of ordinary experience, in order to rebuild the whole of human knowledge on a new foundation of clear and distinct mathematical ideas. What leads him to take this step—a violent one for a rational animal who once was a child—is the ambition for technological power over nature. He uses a similarly artificial rescue from doubt by the *cogito* and the ontological argument for the existence of God to conclude what the artifice of doubt intended to conclude from the outset; namely, that the clear and distinct ideas of mathematical mechanics are the only certain and objective ideas we can form about nature. Although theoretical truth still interests him, his reform of knowledge aims at making us masters and possessors of nature. In this respect, he follows the lead of Bacon (see part I, chap. 3, in this volume).

> BACON: Human knowledge and power come to the same thing, for ignorance of the cause puts the effect beyond reach. For nature is not conquered save by obeying it; and that which in thought is equivalent to a cause, is in operation equivalent to a rule.[112]
>
> DESCARTES: It is possible to reach knowledge that will be powerfully useful to life and instead of the theoretical philosophy, which is now taught in the schools [Aristotelian philosophy], we can find a practical one, by which,

111. Descartes, *Principia philosophiae* I.7, AT 8:7.

112. Francis Bacon, New Organon 1.3, in *The Instauratio magna Part II: Novum organum and Associated Texts*, The Oxford Francis Bacon (Oxford: Clarendon Press, 2004), 64–65.

> knowing the force and the actions of fire, water, air, stars, the heavens, and all the other bodies that surround us as distinctly as we know the various skills of our artisans, we can employ them in the same way for all the uses for which they are fit, and so make ourselves masters and possessors of nature.[113]

The choice of power as the goal of knowledge leads inevitably to the choice of mechanics as the master science of nature. Mechanics gives a precise mathematical account of how force needs to be applied to control the behavior of bodies. Since the method of mechanics is mathematical, it shares the limits of mathematics. Mathematics deals only with quantity and with more abstract items that can be set in quantitative relations. Goodness, beauty, life, consciousness, knowledge, love, male, and female—all of these cannot be grasped by mathematics. In the degree to which mechanics becomes the master science of nature, what cannot be grasped mathematically fades into insignificance, mere subjective impression, and eventually nothing. What can be grasped mathematically stands out as significant, clearly known, and objectively real.

In this way the choice of power as the goal of knowledge automatically leads to the root dogmas of Descartes. On the one side stands the thinking thing (*res cogitans*), the only attribute of which is nonbodily consciousness; on the other stands matter, understood as extended thing (*res extensa*), the only attributes of which are those grasped by mathematical mechanics. The result is a deep alienation of the person from the body. The body is emptied of all qualitative richness, life, interiority, goodness, and beauty. Cartesian matter is the perfectly suited counterpart of mechanics. It stands in a one-to-one correspondence with mechanics across the whole breadth of being. The correspondence is artificial. It is what Descartes intends to arrive at from the very beginning. He reconfigures the natural world so that it lies ready at hand as an object of mechanical power.

America, de Tocqueville observes in his chapter "Philosophical Method of the Americans," is the country "where the precepts of Descartes are least studied and are best applied.... The Americans do not read the works of Descartes ... but they follow his maxims."[114] Since 1840, when de Tocqueville's text was first published, globalization has spread the Cartesian creed everywhere on the planet.

Facts measured by experiments are one thing, the dominant Cartesian orthodoxy tells us; values are another. Reason concerns itself with measured facts, not with values. Values are social constructs or chosen preferences connected with personal feelings rather than reason. Religious faith is a way of encoding and enforcing such preferences. Faith, therefore, has no right to speak on the

113. Descartes, *Discourse on Method*, 6, AT 6.61–62.

114. Alexis de Tocqueville, *Democracy in America*, 2 vols., ed. Phillips Bradley (New York: Vintage Books, 1945), 2.4.

stage of public reason. Conversely, one cannot argue from facts to values. Everyone is entitled to choose their own values, not their own scientific facts. As long as we respect each other's rights, it does not matter what we do with each other's bodies.

For John Paul, by contrast, the human body can have "a singular beauty that flows through every sphere of common life" (TOB 57:3). It reflects God's glory, not as a foreign light of goodness and beauty imposed on it from the outside, like a colorful movie reflected on an indifferent silver screen, but as a light that is constitutive of its very being, the being of *some-body*, a human person.

The first effect of the *Logos* becoming flesh to which the Gospel of John draws attention is the expression of his glory. "The Word (*Logos*) became flesh and pitched his tent among us and we have seen his glory, a glory as of an only-begotten from the Father, full of gift and truth" (John 1:14). The incarnate *Logos* communicates this glory to those for whom he suffers and dies. "And I, the glory you have given to me, I have given to them, that they may be one as we are one" (John 17:22). What must be the nature and breadth of human reason (*logos*), if it is to grasp the logic of this *Logos* and its glory in the flesh?

The Baconian-Cartesian confidence that increase of power always means progress has been increasingly questioned. The author of the following text should remain anonymous for a moment.

> The Cartesian approach to the human story allows us to believe that we are separate from the earth, entitled to view it as nothing more than an inanimate collection of resources that we can exploit however we like; and this fundamental misperception has led us to our current crisis.... We have assumed that our lives need have no real connection to the natural world, that our minds are separate from our bodies, and that as disembodied intellects we can manipulate the world in any way we choose. Precisely because we feel no connection to the physical world, we trivialize the consequences of our actions. And because this linkage seems abstract, we are slow to understand what it means to destroy those parts of the environment that are crucial to our survival. We are, in effect, bulldozing the Gardens of Eden.

This text sounds like John Paul, Benedict, or Pope Francis. It was written by former Vice President Al Gore.[115] Gore focuses on bulldozing the trees of Eden understood as endangering our food supply. He does not apply his penetrating critique of the Cartesian story to contraception. Still, he shows that the truly important problem is deeper and more urgent than the problem of food. The

115. Al Gore, *Earth in the Balance: Ecology and the Human Spirit* (New York: Houghton and Mifflin, 2000), 144, 218.

problem is the violent practice of Cartesian reason rooted in the will to power over nature. This practice of reason cuts us off from our sexual bodies. The paradigm shift from classical physics to quantum mechanics has done nothing to change this situation. It has given us another form of mathematical mechanics, still dominated by the choices made by Bacon and Descartes. Unaware of these historical roots, many of our contemporaries simply take them for granted as self-evident.

Like Al Gore, John Paul is concerned about bulldozing Eden, especially in the form of bulldozing human hearts and sexual bodies. We can connect with the natural world around us, he argues, only if we connect with our bodies as women and men (see TOB 27:3–4). Our great challenge in the technological age is to find the roots of reason and, as a consequence, the right relation between reason (*logos*) and science, science and faith, love and freedom, nature and technological power. Only in this way can we identify more fully with our bodies and their rich meaning.

7. The Structure of This Volume

TOB is a difficult text, even for seasoned theologians. For twenty years, I have been teaching it in undergraduate and graduate courses and in nonacademic settings as well. The experience has taught me that readers wrestle with three main difficulties. The three parts of this volume address them one by one, in three concentric circles, on three levels of difficulty, for beginners, intermediate, and advanced readers.

The first difficulty is finding one's sense of direction in reading TOB. Part III provides a map that summarizes each paragraph of TOB in one sentence (if possible) and adds some remarks or headings about the order of the argument. This is the innermost circle, designed for beginners but perhaps useful also for the more advanced.

The second difficulty is understanding the roots of TOB in Wojtyła's earlier writings. Part II sketches these roots. This is the intermediate circle.

The third difficulty is understanding Wojtyła's relation to the philosophical and theological tradition. TOB joins a conversation that has been going on for a long time. Many readers find it difficult to pick up the thread. Part I sketches important moments in that conversation—Plato, Aristotle, Thomas Aquinas, William of Ockham, Luther, Bacon, and Descartes. This is the outermost circle.

For those who are new to TOB, it is best to begin with Part III as a companion in reading TOB itself and then turn to the other parts.

Part I: Debate about the Breadth of Reason

TOB contributes to a debate about the nature and scope of reason in relation to will and power that is documented already in the first major texts of Greek myth and philosophy. The debate has become more urgent since the scientific revolution. An artificially narrowed understanding of rationality focused on mechanics has become so habitual that it appears to many self-evident as the one and only reasonable practice of reason. Part I addresses this narrowing and sketches the greater breadth of reason presupposed by TOB.

The Point of Departure

Chapter 1: Humanae vitae in Context. The chapter presents the argument of *Humanae vitae* and its further development in TOB. It examines the reasons why *Humanae vitae* was rejected with such bitterness by many theologians. As Cardinal Suenens put the problem in a nutshell during the Council, "We do not want another Galileo case." Contraception is simply part of scientific-technological progress (see TOB 123:1).

Two triads of chapters build on this point of departure. Chapters 2–4 offer a critical genealogy of the narrowing of reason that stands behind the rejection of *Humanae vitae.* Chapters 5–7 present an argument for the full breadth of reason.

Critical Triad: Chapters 2–4

Chapter 2: The Logos of Scripture in Luther and John Paul. Luther develops a spousal theology rooted in the Song of Songs, Hosea 2, and other marital texts of Scripture that has many points of contact with TOB. Luther's understanding of reason was shaped by Ockham's nominalism and voluntarism, in which will and power have primacy over reason. He has a vivid understanding of the gift of self in the love between man and woman. Yet his rejection of Scholastic theology in its Ockhamist form remained incomplete and did not lead to a more scriptural understanding of reason. The problem comes to a head in Trinitarian theology, which Luther sees as contradicting reason.

Chapter 3: Reason as an Instrument of Power in Bacon and Descartes. Bacon and Descartes were heralds of a technological narrowing of reason. They transfer Ockham's primacy of will and power to the human level by choosing power over nature as the goal of knowledge. This choice leads to the promotion of mathematical mechanics to queen of sciences and to the neglect and eventual denial of nonmechanical aspects of nature.

Chapter 4: Loss of the Logos of Marriage in Hildebrand and Doms. The narrow understanding of nature leads to a loss of a full account (*logos*) of marriage.

Hildebrand exemplifies an early and partial form of this loss, Doms a more consistent and radical one.

Constructive Triad: Chapters 5–7

Chapter 5: The Nature of Logos in Plato's Republic. The *Republic* is a good test case for John Paul's appeal to Greek philosophy. Socrates reflects deeply about the relation between power, reason, and the good. He seems to make violent proposals for the sexual politics of the city constructed in speech (*logos*). Instead of living together in marriage, men and women hold each other and their children in common. Sexual intercourse is regulated by the city in breeding episodes planned according to mathematical eugenic principles. Sexual partners change each time. Children do not know their parents and vice versa. If these violent proposals count as rational, Greek philosophy may not be a good place to turn to. Yet, according to Socrates's own argument, it would be a mistake to consider the city formed by such laws a good city. These laws are based on the spirited part of the soul, not yet on reason. Socrates calls his own violent sexual politics into question when he finally introduces reason (*logos*). Most characteristic of human reason, he argues, is a completely universal love and openness. The love specific to the spirited part of the soul is a love for one's own with hatred for the foreigner. The love characteristic of reason, by contrast, is a love for all of being. "Those who welcome each being itself should be called lovers of wisdom (philosophers) rather than lovers of opinion" (*Republic*, 480a). In its openness to being without any narrowing, human reason is marked by a desire for happiness that cannot rest in anything finite.

Chapter 6: The Logos of Nature in Aristotle's Physics. The account of nature in Aristotle's *Physics* complements Socrates's argument about the good. Three points in the *Physics* are especially important for TOB. The *logos* (both in the sense of intelligibility and of nature) of anything flows from its specifying good. Second, the principle of individuation of human persons is "the underlying nature" or "first material" (*materia prima*). Third, the human person is one being with one nature, not two. It is a substance (*ousia*) that belongs to the genus *body*, with the specific difference *rational*. It is not enough to repeat these theses. One needs to reflect on them as rooted in the common notions of ordinary experience.

Chapter 7: The Common Good as the Logos of Reason. Reflection on the primacy of the common good affirmed by Plato, Aristotle, the Greek Fathers, and Thomas Aquinas completes the analysis of goodness and nature in chapter 6. Human reason orders each person to the common good as each person's greatest good. Marriage is an example of such ordering. The intrinsic common good of marriage is the union of husband and wife. Its extrinsic common good are their children. The intrinsic common good receives its specific nature from the extrinsic common good. This is why the unitive meaning is inseparable from the procreative meaning.

Part II: The Breadth of Reason in John Paul

The Point of Departure

Chapter 1: Wojtyła's Trinitarian Personalism of Self-Gift. This chapter summarizes Wojtyła's book on Vatican II, an excellent compendium of his theology. The Council, Wojtyła argues, has its center in the Trinitarian personalism of self-gift (*Gaudium et spes* 22 and 24). Two triads of chapters build on it, one of them critical (chapters 2–4), the other constructive (chapters 5–7).

Critical Triad: Chapters 2–4

Chapter 2: Kant's Anti-Trinitarian Personalism of Autonomy. The two laws of the life of persons in *Gaudium et spes* 24 are helpful for understanding the triangular relation between three opposite forms of personalism: Kant, Scheler, and Wojtyła. Kant's guiding principle is akin to the first law, "Man is the only creature on earth God willed for itself." Every person, Kant argues, must be treated as an end, never as a mere means. The reason lies in the autonomy of the person. Assent to my own autonomy as a person demands respect for the autonomy of every other person. Every person must be treated as *being* an end. According to Wojtyła (explicitly correcting Kant), every person must be treated as *having* an end.

Chapter 3: Scheler's Theomorphic Personalism of Solidarity. Scheler's guiding principle is akin to the law of the gift. "Man cannot fully find himself except through a sincere gift of self." He emphasizes the solidarity of persons in which each person carries responsibility for all others.

Chapter 4: Wojtyła's Critique of Scheler. Wojtyła's book on Scheler is structured according to the Aristotelian causes: form, efficient cause, and end. It critiques Scheler's Phenomenological account of ethics in three chapters from the point of view of each of the causes, most decisively from that of the final cause.

Constructive Triad: Chapters 5–7

Chapter 5: Wojtyła's Person and Act. The chapter sketches the argument of Wojtyła's main philosophical work *Person and Act* with particular attention to its understanding of reason and will in comparison with Kant, Scheler, and Thomas.

Chapter 6: John Paul and John of the Cross. The chapter discusses John of the Cross's Trinitarian theology and his implicit theology of marriage. It traces the manner in which John Paul builds on and expands this foundation.

Chapter 7: Image of the Trinity. With particular attention to the Gospel of John and the Trinitarian theology of Thomas Aquinas, the chapter continues the reflection on Trinitarian theology begun in chapters 1 and 6. It discusses the main thesis of TOB, man and woman as an image of the Trinity. The chapter argues that John Paul and Thomas agree much more broadly on Trinitarian theology than is often supposed.

Part III: Map

While Parts I and II sketch the intellectual context of TOB in two concentric circles, Part III focuses on the center, the text of TOB itself. Readers of TOB often feel disoriented. They find themselves sailing on the open sea in a fog without GPS. Luke Timothy Johnson, a learned and sensitive New Testament scholar, finds TOB "exceptionally difficult to read and almost mind-numbingly repetitious."[116] Others turn the impression into a compliment by describing the argument of TOB as Slavic or spiraling, meditative or mystical. The impression is mistaken in either case. It is partly due to the absence of John Paul's own headings from all early editions of TOB except the Polish. TOB has a clear structure. Part III of this volume summarizes each numbered paragraph of TOB and explains the division and order of chapters and sections. It pays attention not only to the logical steps of the argument but also to the literary artistry invested in it by John Paul.

116. In his 2015 book *Revelatory Body*, 23, Johnson still uses the first English edition, *Theology of the Body: Human Love in the Divine Plan* (Boston: Pauline Books and Media, 1997). This edition does not contain the original headings that indicate the structure of the argument. The edition of TOB with the original headings had been published nine years before Johnson's book, in 2006. Securing a critical text is a basic demand for responsible work, particularly when it is work by a New Testament scholar.

PART I

Debate about the Breadth of Reason

CHAPTER 1

Humanae vitae in Context

1. Two Inseparable Meanings

Humanae vitae does not propose a new thesis on contraception. It points to what the Church already teaches. "*The Church ... teaches* that every conjugal act must remain through itself directed to the procreation of human life."[1] The authentic Latin text behind *through itself directed to* is *per se destinatus ad. Destinatus* is not one of the frequent terms in discussions of teleology. St. Thomas does not use it to express finality. St. Paul VI's choice of the word suggests that in summarizing the already existing teaching, he draws on *Casti connubii*, which uses this rare word. "Since the conjugal act is *by its own nature directed* (*destinatus*) to generating a child, those who in performing it deprive it on purpose of this natural strength and power act against nature."[2]

In this context, the word *destinatus* does not, of course, mean destiny as an inescapably realized outcome. According to Thomas, "*Destinare* signifies directing somebody, such as a messenger, to something."[3] "*Destinare* is to send."[4] In *Casti connubii* and *Humanae vitae*, *destinatus* is close in meaning to the more usual term *ordinatus, ordered.* It expresses the act's essential inner order to its defining end. It expresses the causality of the goods of marriage as giving rise to the nature of the conjugal act as a chosen human act.

1. *Ecclesia ... id docet* necessarium esse, ut quilibet matrimonii usus ad vitam humanam procreandam per se destinatus permaneat. Paul VI, *Humanae vitae* 11; emphasis added.

2. Cum autem actus coniugii suapte natura proli generandae sit *destinatus*, qui, in eo exercendo, naturali hac eum vi atque virtute de industria destituunt, contra naturam agunt. Pius XI, *Casti connubii* 54; *Acta Apostolicae Sedis* 22 (1930): 539–98, at 559; emphasis added.

3. Thomas, *Super I sent.*, d. 40, q. 2, a. 1, corp.

4. Thomas, *Summa* I, q. 23, a. 1, corp.

Paul VI qualifies *destinatus* by the phrase *per se*. One possible translation of *per se* is *through itself*. It belongs to the conjugal act through itself, through what it is as a freely chosen act of a rational animal, to be directed or ordered to procreation. This meaning is close to the parallel text in *Casti connubii* 54, "*by its own nature* directed." Paul VI's *per se* can also be read together with the phrase *must remain*. *Per se*—that is, as far as the conjugal act itself is concerned—it must remain directed to procreation rather than being deprived of this direction. Being *directed* to procreation is not the same, of course, as *resulting* in procreation. The nature of the act is more stable than its outcome.

The Frequently Misunderstood Phrase "Open To"

The most widely used English translation of *Humanae vitae* 11 differs from the one used above. It reads "*open to* the transmission of life" rather than "*through itself directed to*." It is based on the Italian text *aperto a* rather than the normative Latin *per se destinatus ad*. At least in Italy and the English-speaking world, *open to* is the main phrase in the debate about contraception. One frequent misunderstanding is to overlook that *open to the transmission of life* qualifies *every conjugal act*, and thus to understand *open to* as a general attitude of welcoming children. Read in this way, *open to* can look like an argument against natural family planning. The purpose of abstaining from sex at fertile times is to close the door against conception. Can closing the door, or at least abstaining from walking through it, be described as open to the transmission of life?

Some defenders of *Humanae vitae* respond that abstaining does not actively slam the door in the face of conception as contraception does. Still, abstaining from the transmission of life can hardly be described as being open to transmitting it. Some argue in response that couples cannot be completely certain about the reliability of natural family planning. Realizing that a child might be conceived, they can resolve to be open if a child happens to be conceived despite their efforts. The fact remains, however, that abstaining is the most effective way of avoiding the transmission of life. It is absolutely effective. In this perspective, Boyd's argument has some plausibility.

> Theology of the Body and Natural Family Planning will, one day, be viewed from their rightful home in the trash bin of theological fads that did great harm to the Church and Her faithful.... It seems silly to claim that one is "open to children" when one is organizing one's life around having sex not likely to be fruitful![5]

5. Jay Boyd, *Natural Family Planning: Trojan Horse in the Catholic Bedroom?* (self-pub., 2013), 19 and 250.

Boyd interprets *open to* as the general attitude of welcoming children. What *Humanae vitae* 11 says instead is that every conjugal act must remain through itself and as far as it itself is concerned ordered to the end of procreation. What it excludes is imposing infertility on an act that would otherwise be fertile. For obvious reasons, one cannot impose infertility on an act from which one abstains. Abstaining raises important moral questions, but different ones. Do husband and wife harm their relationship by neglecting sex (unitive meaning)? Are they generous enough in their desire for children (procreative meaning)? *Humanae vitae* 3 and 17 mentions the principle of totality, which is related to the general attitude of openness.

The Good as the Cause of What a Thing Is

At the center of the argument, expressed by the word *destinatus* both in *Humanae vitae* and *Casti connubii*, stands a link between *what* something is and the good it aims at from within itself. When one asks *What is it?* about any natural being or human act, the deepest answer flows from *for the sake of a specific good, due to its goodness*. For example, seeing is the act that belongs to human eyes as eyes. It is impossible to understand *what* eyes are without pointing to this act, which is their good and end. It is also impossible to understand *what* the act of seeing is without pointing to its good and end; namely, the objects of sight as possessed in the act of seeing. The end allows one to understand from within *what* the act and the organ of sight are. The intelligibility flows from the goodness of the end to the nature. The good is what is most intimate to the eye and to the act of seeing, more intimate than they are to themselves. Eyes are most themselves in seeing; seeing is most itself in reaching the object of sight.

The case of the human mind is similar. It is impossible to understand *what* the mind is without pointing to the act of thinking, which is the good the mind is directed toward. It is, in turn, impossible to understand the act of thinking without pointing to its good; namely, truth. When we say about what is, *It is*, and about what is not, *It is not*, the statements are true. If this correspondence between thought and being were impossible, if there were no truth to be known, thought would be impossible from its very root. Its nature as an activity flows from the goodness of truth. The goodness of truth is most interior to thought, more interior than thought is to itself. Thought is most itself in raising the question of truth and in reaching truth. Likewise, the nature of marriage and of the conjugal act flows from the goodness of union and procreation. Marriage is most itself in the presence of these goods. They are more intimate to marriage than it is to itself.

The Inseparability Principle

The reason *Humanae vitae* gives for "must remain through itself directed to the procreation of human life" is the indissoluble link between the two meanings of the conjugal act, the unitive and the procreative meaning.

> This teaching ... rests on *the indissoluble link* established by God, which man on his own initiative may not break, *between the unitive meaning and the procreative meaning*, both of which are inherent in the conjugal act.
>
> The reason is that due to its innermost account (*ratio*), the conjugal act, when it unites husband and wife by a very close bond, also makes them capable of generating new life, *according to laws written into the very nature of man and woman*. If each of these essential accounts (*ratio*), namely of unity and of procreation, is preserved, the marriage act fully keeps the sense of mutual and true love and its order to the very high mission of parenthood (*Humanae vitae* 12; emphasis added).

TOB rephrases the argument, bringing out some points more explicitly.

> In the conjugal act, it is not licit to separate artificially the meaning of love from the meaning (that is, a sign) of potential parenthood, because the one as well as the other belongs to the innermost truth of the conjugal act. The one is realized together with the other and, in a certain way, *the one through the other*. This is what the encyclical teaches (see *Humanae vitae* 12). Thus, in such a case, when the conjugal act is *deprived of its inner truth*, because it is deprived artificially of its potential parenthood, it also *ceases to be an act of love*. The meaning of the act of love—"unitive meaning" as we read in *Humanae vitae* 12—is due to it in the "indissoluble union" with the other meaning, namely, of the potential parenthood.
>
> One can say that in the case of an artificial separation of these two meanings, a real bodily union is brought about in the conjugal act, but it does not correspond to the inner truth and dignity of personal union, "*communio personarum*." This union demands, in fact, that the "speech of the body" be expressed reciprocally in the integral truth of its meaning. If this truth is lacking, one can speak neither of the truth of possessing oneself nor of the truth of the reciprocal gift of self and of the reciprocal acceptance of oneself by the persons. Such a violation of the inner order of conjugal union, a union that plunges its roots into the very order of the person, *constitutes the essential evil of contraception*. (TOB 123:6–7; first emphasis added)

The word *through* is helpful. Each meaning is realized not only *together with* the other but *the one through the other*. The indissolubility of the two meanings is a matter of fact, not of ought. The point is not that the connection *should* not be dissolved. It *cannot*. The two meanings or ends depend on each other in such a way that they stand or fall together. One cannot take one away and leave the other standing. Just as each comes to be through the other, so each is destroyed when the other is destroyed. "When the conjugal act is deprived ... artificially of potential parenthood, *it also ceases to be an act of love*" (TOB 123:6; emphasis added). The conjugal act is by its nature, by *what* it is as a human act, procreative because it is unitive and unitive because it is procreative. It is unitively procreative and procreatively unitive.

An objection raised by Luke Timothy Johnson is helpful for clarifying this argument.

> John Paul II recognizes, from one side of his mouth, two ends of sexual love, namely unitive intimacy and procreation. But from the other side of the mouth, he declares that if, in an act of intercourse, procreation is blocked, not only that end has been cancelled but the end of unitive intimacy has as well. He has thereby, despite his protestations to the contrary, simply reduced the two ends to one.
>
> This can be demonstrated by applying his logic in reverse: Would we insist that an act of sexual intercourse that did not manifest unitive intimacy also cancel the procreative end of the act? The papal position could actually be read as approving as moral an act of intercourse within marriage that was coerced, even violently, so long as a contraceptive was not used.[6]

One can leave aside Johnson's suggestion, hardly worthy of a careful scholar, that John Paul can be read as approving rape in marriage. In its logical form, Johnson's argument is a reduction to the absurd. He examines John Paul's statement about the indissoluble link to see whether a false consequence necessarily follows from it. If it does, one can conclude that there is no indissoluble link. According to John Paul, the link is indissoluble from both sides. If removing the procreative meaning removes the unitive meaning, then removing the unitive meaning must also remove the procreative meaning. Yet, Johnson argues, when a man destroys the unitive meaning by raping his wife, the procreative meaning can still remain. A child can still be conceived. The procreative meaning, therefore, is separable.

Procreative through Being Unitive

As Paul VI and John Paul use it, the word *procreation* does not simply mean *reproduction*. It means specifically human reproduction. Animals *eat* but do not

6. Luke Timothy Johnson, *The Revelatory Body: Theology as Inductive Art* (Grand Rapids, MI: Eerdmans, 2015), 32.

dine. Dining signifies a distinctively human or personal way of eating. In a similar way, animals *reproduce* but do not *procreate. Procreation* signifies the distinctively human or personal way of reproduction.[7] There is a similar difference between the terms *sex* and *conjugal act. Conjugal act* is not an antiquated way of saying *sex* or a polite euphemism for it. It is the name of sex in its fully human form as a personal act between spouses. *Sex* is to *conjugal act* as *reproduction* to *procreation* and both are as *eating* to *dining.*

Homer's *Odyssey*, a text at the roots of Western culture (eighth century BC), shows the fully human and personal nature of the union between husband and wife that is the basis for procreation. Odysseus, King of Ithaca, has come back from the Trojan War after twenty years. He finds his wife Penelope faithful to him despite a crowd of suitors who were pressing her to marry one of them. Her faithfulness reaches a paradoxical extreme when she refuses to recognize him despite strong proofs of his identity. It is late at night. They finally stand at the door of their bedroom. Then and there Penelope applies the final test. He has her permission, she tells him, to sleep in the marriage bed but alone, outside the bedroom, in the hall. She will sleep on the floor in the bedroom. She instructs the servants to carry out the bed. Odysseus responds angrily.

> Oh woman, this word you speak stings my heart. Who has moved my bed? Hard it would be for anyone, even very skilled, unless a god were to come, who might easily put it elsewhere if he wanted. But of men there is none living, however strong in his youth, who could force it with a crowbar, for a great sign (μέγα σῆμα) is wrought in the well-fashioned bed. It was I who made it and nobody else.
>
> A bushy olive with thick foliage was growing in the inner court, mature and thriving, the trunk massive as a pillar. Around this I built the wedding chamber with close-fitting stones until I reached the end [the Greek verb *etelessa* used here is based on the noun *telos*, end or purpose], covered it well with a roof, setting firmly glued doors, closing tight, then sheared off the rich-leafed olive branches, shortened the trunk above the roots, worked all around it with a plane, smooth and exact, straight to the plumb-line, fashioning it into a bedpost, and drilled it all with a drill. Beginning with this, I built the bed until I reached the end [again *etelessa* from *telos*, end], decorating it beautifully with inlaid gold and silver and ivory. Then I fastened a web of ox hide strips, shining purple.
>
> I show you this sign (τόδε σῆμα). I know nothing whether the bed is still

7. See Donald Asci, *The Conjugal Act as Personal Act: A Study of the Catholic Concept of the Conjugal Act in the Light of Christian Anthropology* (San Francisco: Ignatius, 2002), 52–53. Asci's book is the best study of these questions known to me, singular in depth and clarity.

> firmly set in the ground, woman, or some man has cut away the trunk of the olive and moved the bed elsewhere.[8]

There are fascinating parallels between this passage and John Paul's account of the conjugal act as a sacramental sign. The phrase "great sign" μέγα σῆμα in Homer's Odyssey is the exact equivalent of the phrase "great sign" (TOB 95b:7, 97:2), which John Paul uses to bring out an aspect of the Pauline phrase "great mystery" μυστήριον . . . μέγα (Ephesians 5:32) of marriage.

Odysseus did not touch the living olive tree, ancient symbol of fruitfulness, until he had reached the end (*etelessa*) of building the wedding chamber around it, including the roof and the tightly fitting doors. Only then did he cut off the tree's branches and shape its trunk into a bedpost. It is part of the archetypal power of this scene that the marriage bed serves as the great sign of recognition between husband and wife after their long separation, just as it had been the great sign of their union twenty years earlier. Odysseus built the bed secretly, with his own hands. Its center post has roots still anchored in the earth, expressing the stability of the intimate space created by the love of husband and wife.

The wedding chamber in the *Odyssey* is part of a large house, the royal palace of Ithaca, which has room for many guests. The good of hospitality, a great and central good in Homer and the whole tradition of the West, belongs to the nature of spousal love. By its innermost energy, the space of love is not a space the spouses want to occupy alone. From the center of the intimate space, from the marriage bed, a larger space is shaped, in which there is room for guests, above all for the best of guests, children.

The power of the conjugal act in shaping a space of love may be the reason for a curious way of speaking. "The end which nature intends from within the conjugal act is the procreation and education of children."[9] One might grant the point about procreation but wonder how the conjugal act is ordered to the education of children. It is not an audiovisual display to which the children are invited. Its importance for education lies in building an intimate and private space reserved for husband and wife. This intimate space shapes the larger space of the house so that it is not only a house but also a home with an atmosphere of love in which children can flourish.

From this perspective, one can understand how the conjugal act is unitively procreative, that is, procreative through being unitive. The union it produces is an open union that leads of itself to hospitality for children. One can see the indissoluble link both from the side of the children and from the side of the

8. Homer, *Odyssey* 23.183–202.

9. Thomas, *Super IV sent.*, d. 33, q. 1, a. 3, qc. 1, corp.

parents. From the side of the children, the wider space of a home that flows from the more intimate space created by the love of their parents is the space they need as children. God, who is love, gives being to a child out of love and for love. Correspondingly, a child ought to be conceived in a space of love. The gift of children completes and fulfills the union of love between the spouses. The pain of couples who are unable to have children is a testimony to the greatness of this fulfillment.

The coming to be of the procreative meaning through the unitive meaning (unitively procreative) is the basis on which one can see the moral problem of in vitro fertilization and embryo transfer. "The act of conjugal love is to be considered the only place worthy of human procreation" *unicum locum dignum procreationis humanae.*[10] In vitro fertilization is one side of the coin. It compromises the act's *unitively procreative* meaning. Contraception is the other side. It compromises the act's *procreatively unitive* meaning.[11]

Unitive through Being Procreative

The unitive meaning comes to be through the procreative meaning. The conjugal act is procreatively unitive. John Paul formulates this point sharply. "When the conjugal act is *deprived of its inner truth* because it is deprived artificially of its potential parenthood, it also *ceases to be an act of love*" (TOB 123:6).

The argument seems outrageously unjust. Johnson's anger is understandable. He is right to insist that contraception does not stop all affective bonds between husband and wife as the collapse of a bridge across a river stops of the flow of all traffic or the flick of the main electrical switch turns off all lights in a house. On the contrary, the reason why couples use contraceptives is to express their love for each other sexually even when the conception of a child should for various reasons be avoided. Contraception gives more room to their union of love.

In thinking through this objection, one needs to focus on the specific form of unity that arises from the procreative meaning. It is the unity of those who do what men and women do to become parents.[12] This form of unity between a man and a woman can be realized only by an act that is by its nature procreative. It cannot be achieved by holding hands or by mutual masturbation. It is the specifically conjugal form of the union of love. Other forms of unitive meaning,

10. Congregation for the Doctrine of the Faith, *Donum Vitae,* section II, subsection B 5.

11. On the consistency of this logic, see Paul F. deLadurantaye, "From *Humanae vitae* to *Donum Vitae*: Symmetry and Consistency in Catholic Biomedical Teaching," *Linacre Quarterly* 66 (1999): 9–20.

12. See Asci, *Conjugal Act,* 212–13.

such as those expressed by caressing or kissing, can still exist. They will not remain unaffected if the specifically spousal meaning is excluded.

In this perspective, one can see the importance of a correct understanding of the phrase "through itself directed to procreating human life" *ad vitam humanam procreandam per se destinatus*. Just as human sexual organs are by their nature generative at all times, even when they are not being used for generation, so a conjugal act is procreative by its nature, even when no child is conceived. The nature, which is a specific nature by its inner ordering to a good, remains the same on a deep level, whatever the effect of the act may turn out to be.

It is a Cartesian intellectual custom to dismisses the causality of the good in shaping stable natures. From the Cartesian perspective, it is impossible to answer the question "What is it?" about any human act involving the body. One needs to ask two separate questions. First, what is the deliberate intention of the thinking thing? Second, what event takes place in the extended thing, and what are its consequences? Cartesian ethical thinking splits into intentionalism (when the focus is on interior acts) and consequentialism (when the focus is on exterior acts). This split is contrary to our ordinary experience of bodily acts. In the act of walking, for example, the bodily nature of locomotion is an essential constituent of the human act called *walking*. Just as the body is truly personal, so the act of walking is inseparably bodily and spiritual. The objective natural teleology of locomotion (from here to there) is an essential component of the personal act, inevitably taken up into it.

By performing an act that is shaped in its very nature by the good of children, spouses say to each other, and say it "according to laws written into the very nature of man and woman" (*Humanae vitae* 12), "You are the one with whom I want to have children. I want our children to be both from you and from me, from us together, to be formed by our bodies and minds together, because I love you." It is in this way that the conjugal act is unitive by being procreative in its nature. It establishes or reenacts a particular kind of union between a man and a woman, the union called marriage.

This inseparable whole is what John Paul has in mind when he writes, "When the conjugal act is *deprived of its inner truth* because it is deprived artificially of potential parenthood, it also *ceases to be an act of love*" (TOB 123:6). It ceases to be an act of specifically conjugal love. Contracepted sex can remain lovemaking in the sense of expressing and fulfilling a couple's feelings of emotional closeness, joy, and pleasure in each other. What such sex cannot be, however, is *conjugal* lovemaking, and this defect deeply undermines the other elements of unitive meaning that can still be present.

The two meanings are closely linked, not only by their mutual dependence on each other but also by the logic of gift that runs through both. By its nature, the conjugal act expresses and accomplishes a radical gift of self—I am yours, you are mine—the kind of gift "through which alone one can find oneself" (*Gaudium et spes* 24). The ordering of this sexual gift of self to the good of procreation, which shapes its very nature, completes the trajectory of the gift.

> In its most profound reality, love is essentially a gift; and conjugal love, while leading the spouses to the reciprocal "knowledge," which makes them "one flesh," does not end with the couple, because it makes them capable of the greatest possible gift, the gift by which they become cooperators with God for giving life to a new human person. Thus, the couple, while giving themselves to one another, give not just themselves but also the reality of children, who are a living reflection of their love, a permanent sign of conjugal unity and a living and inseparable synthesis of their being a father and a mother. (John Paul II, *Familiaris consortio* 14)

2. The Dominance of Mechanism

When Erwin Schrödinger received the 1933 Nobel Prize for his work on quantum mechanics, the Austrian ambassador to Sweden sat next to him at the traditional Nobel banquet. "Herr Professor Schrödinger," the ambassador said when the main course had been served and the guests were eager to begin eating. "I am shortsighted. Can you recognize the embroidery in the middle of the tablecloth?" "It is too far away," Schrödinger answered. "I wonder what it is." He stood up, bent over, stretched his arms to the middle of the table, pinched the embroidery between two fingers, took firmer hold of the cloth with both fists, and pulled sharply. Glasses, platters, and plates flew.

"Ah," Schrödinger said quietly. "Here it is." "Remarkable," replied the ambassador. "It is the coat of arms of Queen Christina of Sweden. Her father, Gustavus Adolphus, came close to winning a total military victory for the Lutheran Reformation in Europe. His brilliant daughter Christina invited Descartes to live here in Stockholm to build up his scientific research. She became a Catholic under the influence of Jesuits close to Descartes. It caused an uproar." Schrödinger then turned to the guests, who were still sitting in polite silence. "We had to resolve an important question. Evidence is the basis for knowledge. What does our dinner celebrate, if not the relentless pursuit of evidence?"

The story is probably apocryphal. Still, it can illustrate two points. One of them can be seen in the flying of plates. Nothing in the universe of being is simply itself, detached, and unrelated. Everything is connected, like a great tablecloth. The cultural fabric that surrounds us is likewise woven from tightly interlocking threads with fiercely defended interests. Pulling one part of the cloth nearer to one's eyes to examine it means moving the whole cloth and everything on it, whatever the guests at the banquet may think. The unity of the cloth calls for what Hamlet calls a "large discourse, looking before and after."

> Sure he that made us with such large discourse,
> Looking before and after, gave us not
> That capability and god-like reason
> To fust in us unus'd. (*Hamlet*, act 4, sc. 4; *fust* = grow moldy)

Hamlet's description of reason as looking before and after echoes a text of Plutarch. "Should the one who presides over oaths and treaties of peace be, in the words of Homer, one *looking before and after*? Such, above all others, would be one who has *a child to plan for and a parent to plan with*."[13]

The anecdote of the tablecloth serves to illustrate another point. Neither Schrödinger nor the ambassador was anywhere near impolite enough to interrupt the celebration of scientific progress at the Nobel Prize dinner by pulling away the plates from guests eager to begin eating. Yet this is not far from the impression *Humanae vitae* made when it was published. The guests at that banquet did not sit in silence. Arguing against contraception is socially and intellectually outside the boundaries of good breeding in our society. The pill is an obvious example of progress achieved by scientific discovery. One might as well question antibiotics. Cardinal Suenens eloquently expressed this impression in a speech at Vatican II.

> Who does not see that in this way [i.e., is, by looking again at the question of contraception after the scientific discovery of the pill] we are perhaps led to further tracking down what is "according to nature or contrary to nature"? Let us follow the progress of science. I adjure you, brothers. Let us avoid a new "Galileo trial." One is enough for the Church.[14]

The name of Galileo together with the word *science* functions in the Cardinal's words as a shorthand for philosophical views and intellectual customs that

13. Plutarch, *Quaestiones Romanae* 62; emphasis added; Plutarch's reference to Homer is to *Odyssey* 24.50, where the father of one of the suitors killed by Odysseus reflects about not having given enough thought together with his son to *before and after*.

14. Intervention of Cardinal Suenens in the Conciliar Aula, October 29, 1964. "Quisnam non videt quod sic forsan ducimur ad ulteriorem investigationem illius quod est 'secundum naturam vel contra naturam?' Sequamur progressum scientiae. Adiuro vos, Fratres. Vitemus novum 'processum Galilei.' Unus enim sufficit pro Ecclesia." *Acta Synodalia Sacrosancti Concilii Oecumenici Vaticani II*, 35 vols., in 6 parts and three appended volumes (Rome: Typis Polyglottis Vaticanis, 1975), part 3, 6:58. See Leo Declerck, "Le cardinal Suenens et la question du contrôle des naissances au Concile Vatican II," *Revue théologique de Louvain* 41 (2010): 499–518.

are not themselves scientific. These views nonetheless attempt to clothe themselves in the golden mantle of science. The origin of our intellectual customs, the choice of power, is usually forgotten. The further choice of mechanics as the queen of sciences is no longer seen as a choice. Yet it is a choice, not a discovery, that accounts for the privileged place given to mechanics. The choices have been passed down as an inheritance to us in the twenty-first century, and they have shaped the intellectual customs of our culture.

The Aristotelian *Mechanics*, generally thought to be by one of Aristotle's students, was unknown to the Middle Ages, discovered only in the Renaissance. It understands mechanics as a skill that combines mathematics with physical observation to allow an increase of human power. Mathematical calculation was used, for example, in the design of oars to maximize the effectiveness of trireme galleys in a sea battle. Bacon appeals to this Aristotelian treatise. "*Aristotle said it best*, Physics and Mathematics beget Practice and Mechanics."[15]

We began with great optimism on the path laid out by Bacon. It is only recently that optimism has been giving way to a soberer judgment. Leon Kass puts his finger with precision on the issue.

> Our views of the meaning of our humanity have been so transformed by the scientific-technological approach to the world and to life that we are in danger of forgetting what we have to lose, humanly speaking.... We shall have little chance of protecting ourselves against the dangers of runaway biotechnology if we do not adequately understand what is at stake, if we do not recognize which human goods are in danger and worth defending. The first thing needful is a correction and deepening of our thinking.[16]

If St. John Paul writes a long and difficult book to make the case against contraception, and if other long books (such as this one) are published to help readers understand it, the argument must be long and difficult. It must be like climbing Mt. Everest. There are few, it would seem, who can arrive at the top, in the death zone above 26,000 feet. No wonder there is so little agreement about contraception.

The impression is mistaken. The argument of TOB is simple. Part One of TOB presents the teaching of Jesus about the spousal meaning of the body. Part Two looks at the act in which this meaning is expressed and realized: "I am yours, you are mine." It concludes that *Humanae vitae* calls men and women to

15. "*Optime Aristoteles*, Physicam et Mathematicam generare Practicam sive Mechanicam." Francis Bacon, *The Advancement of Knowledge* 3.6, in *The Works of Bacon*, 14 vols., ed. James Spedding (London: Longman, 1857–74), 1:576; emphasis original.

16. Leon Kass, *Life, Liberty and the Defense of Dignity: The Challenge for Bioethics* (New York: Perseus Group, 2002), 8.

perform this act wholeheartedly, according to the full meaning that lies in it. The argument is drawn together in two short paragraphs on the indissoluble link of the procreative and unitive meaning of the conjugal act (see TOB 123:6–7).

Less than a century ago, most people intuitively understood these reasons and were convinced. They may not have been able to express them as John Paul does, but their assent was in large measure certain. It was rooted in an understanding of love and of marriage attested in Western culture for more than three millennia. The Catholic Church still treasures this ancient ecological wisdom as a heritage from pre-Christian times. It was only when the predominant scientific-technological culture (and most Christian communities following in its wake) abandoned it less than a century ago that this wisdom became, in appearance, a typically Catholic curiosity.

It was without any doubt one of the merits of the Obama administration to stimulate public debate about contraception. The mandate requiring all employers to pay for contraceptives as part of employee health benefits was sure to be such a stimulus. Nevertheless, the debate proved to be sterile. The only realistic way to resist the mandate in the US court system was the appeal to religious liberty. Substantive grounds had to be excluded. From the point of view of practical success, the exclusion was necessary. From the point of view of intellectual and cultural impact, it was a disaster. It reinforced the impression that the Catholic position on contraception is not a matter of public reason but of private religious practice like abstaining from meat (but not fish) on Ash Wednesday and Good Friday. The appeal to religious liberty sidesteps the main question. Does contraception contribute to genuine human freedom and development or not?

Of course, no degree of ideological blockheadedness could ever have induced the Obama administration to go on from Obamacare to Obamaair. Obamaair (contrary to fact, of course) includes the Only Breathable Air Mandate, which protects the right of every citizen to breathe only clean air. If air pollution rises above the limit set by the Environmental Protection Agency, the mandate calls for citizens to stop the flow of air. If they are unable to stop on their own, government agents will slip a tightly fitting latex tube over their heads to enforce their right to clean air.

In response to Obamaair, Catholics appeal to their religious liberty. The Council of Trent (*Respiratio spiritus*, par. 7) binds Catholics in conscience, they argue before the US Supreme Court, to breathe twenty-four hours a day, seven days a week, regardless of air quality. In a 5–4 split decision, the US Supreme Court decides that Catholics shall be exempt from the mandate, provided they can give credible evidence that they feel bound in conscience by Trent.

Even to the most radical opponents of natural law, it is obvious that protecting the right to clean air by suffocating citizens is not only stupid but criminal.

A great good is at stake, the good of human life. The problems with the contraception mandate were less obvious. Yet what was at stake was also a great good, the good called marriage. We love the freedom of choice made possible by scientific and technological progress. Descartes understood this technologically driven pursuit of freedom.

> Now freewill is in itself the noblest thing we can have because it makes us in a certain manner equal to God and exempts us from being his subjects; and so, its good use is the greatest of all the goods we possess, and further there is nothing that is more our own or that matters more to us. From all this it follows that nothing but freewill can produce our greatest contentments.[17]

The contraceptive pill is good because it broadens our freedom of choice. It frees us from biological constraint. It humanizes nature, subjecting it to our will. The right to religious freedom must not trump this broadening of our more fundamental freedom of choice.

3. The Narrowing of Reason

Erwin Schrödinger offers a trenchant critique of the dominant intellectual habits that stand behind this mindset.

> I actually do cut out my mind when I construct the real world around me. And I am not aware of this cutting out. And then I am very astonished that the scientific picture of the world around me is very deficient. It gives a lot of factual information, puts all our experience in a magnificently consistent order, but it is ghastly silent about all and sundry that is really near to our heart, that really matters to us. It cannot tell us a word about red and blue, bitter and sweet, physical pain and physical delight; it knows nothing of beautiful and ugly, good or bad, God and eternity. Science sometimes pretends to answer questions in these domains, but the answers are often so silly that we are not inclined to take them seriously.

17. Descartes, *Letter to Christina of Sweden*, AT 5:85; Translation following Charles Taylor, *Sources of the Self: The Making of the Modern Identity* (Cambridge, MA: Harvard University Press, 1989), 147. One can soften the astonishing statement that freedom exempts us from being God's subjects by giving more emphasis to Descartes's use of the word *semble* (it seems). He writes, semble nous exempter de luy estre suiets. Still, he argues in another place that all human powers are finite except for choice. The freedom of indifference experienced in choice is infinite like God. It is omnipotent for all options. Descartes uses a formulation close to Anselm's *that that which nothing greater can be thought*. "It is only the will or free choice that I experience in myself as so great that I will not grasp a greater idea." *Meditations* 4.8, AT 5:57.

> So, in brief, we do not belong to this material world that science constructs for us. We are not in it, we are outside.[18]

The clarity of Schrödinger's argument is breathtaking. We do not belong to this material world. We are not in it, we are outside. What happens to a rational animal, to a body among bodies, if it ends up outside the bodily universe and therefore outside of itself? Schrödinger calls the Cartesian picture of the world into question at a fundamental level. Yet he shows its great power in the very way he calls it into question. He focuses on the mind alone. I cut out my mind, he says. Why only my mind? Why only the Cartesian thinking thing? Don't I cut out myself as a whole, as a body that is not just some body but *somebody*?

The Cartesian image of nature lifts mechanics to the level of exclusive, comprehensive, and undisputed objectivity. This violently skewed way of seeing then obscures our vision for the order of living nature in all its richness, including the richness of the erotic and sexual bodies of man and woman. Wojtyła addresses the problem along the same lines as Schrödinger but more fully.

> The expression "order of nature" cannot be confused nor identified with the expression "biological order," as the latter, even though also signifying the order of nature, denotes it *only inasmuch as it is accessible for the empirical-descriptive methods of natural sciences*, and not as a specific order of existence with a clear relation to the first cause, to God the Creator.
>
> *Confusing the order of existence with the "biological order" in this way*, or rather obscuring the former with the latter—which, together with all the empiricism, seems to loom greatly over the mentality of modern man, especially the modern intellectual—*causes particular difficulties in understanding Catholic sexual ethics on the basis of its very presuppositions.* According to these presuppositions, *sexus*, sex, and the sexual drive are not only and exclusively a specific sphere of man's psycho-physiology. The sexual drive has its objective greatness precisely because of this link with the divine work of creation, a greatness that *almost completely disappears in the field of vision of a mentality influenced by the "biological order" alone.* In relation to that order, the sexual drive is only a sum of functions, which from the biological point of view undoubtedly tend to a biological end, to reproduction.
>
> So, since man is the master of nature, should he not mold these functions—even in an artificial way, with the help of an appropriate technique—in a way that he deems fitting, that suits him? *The "biological order," as a work of the human mind separating some elements of this order from what really exists, has man as its immediate author.* From here it is easy to leap into autonomism

18. Erwin Schrödinger, *Nature and the Greeks* (Cambridge: Cambridge University Press, 1954), 93–94.

> in ethical views. The case is different with the "order of nature." It constitutes a group of cosmic relations that occur among beings that really exist. It is thus the order of existence, and the whole order present in existence finds its basis in the one who is the unceasing source of this existence, in God the Creator.[19]

Wojtyła identifies a way of thinking and seeing that is hammered into the minds of children in school and reinforced daily in adults by the cultural mainstream—the way of thinking and seeing defined by a mechanistic form of natural science, comfortably settled in the unreflective position of being customarily and therefore self-evidently true. The biological order, as a product of the human intellect, has man for its immediate author. Wojtyła does not mean, of course, that we are the authors of nature in its mechanical aspects. He means that what we call *biological order* is an abstraction, a partial representation of a fuller and richer reality.

Wojtyła underlines the need to be inside our sexual bodies. "Man can remain faithful to the person in the order of love proper to him insofar as he is faithful to nature. When he violates nature, he also 'violates' the person."[20] Violence to nature is violence to the person because the physical body and the principle of spiritual life, by which we grasp ourselves as persons, are not separate beings in us. It is in virtue of our one nature, that of rational animals, that we are persons. "The natural law thus understood does not allow for any division between freedom and nature. Indeed, these two realities are harmoniously bound together, and each is intimately linked to the other" (John Paul II, *Veritatis splendor* 50).

Because we constructed the Baconian-Cartesian biological order on the basis of our ambition for the empire of man over things, it is not surprising that we think we can assume the role of masters of the machine without any questions, except perhaps environmental ones. To this way of thinking, contraception and its mirror image, in vitro fertilization, seem self-evident. The Catholic theologian and sexologist Francoeur is a striking representative of this mindset.

> Man is a maker and a selector and a designer, and the more rationally contrived and deliberate anything is, the more human it is. Any attempt to set up an antinomy between natural and biologic reproduction on the one hand, and artificial or designed reproduction on the other, is absurd. The real difference is between accidental or random reproduction and rationally willed or chosen reproduction. . . .

19. Karol Wojtyła, *Love and Responsibility*, trans. Grzegorz Ignatik (Boston: Pauline, 2013), 40–41. Ignatik's translation is the one cited in this book. It is a significant improvement over the older translation by H. T. Willets, which is elegant but often vague and at times inaccurate. *Love and Responsibility*, trans. H. T. Willets (London: Collins, 1981; reprint, San Francisco: Ignatius Press, 1993).

20. Wojtyła, *Love and Responsibility*, 216.

> If it [artificial reproduction] is "unnatural" it can be so only in the sense that all medicine is. It seems to me that laboratory reproduction is radically human compared to conception by ordinary heterosexual intercourse. It is willed, chosen, purposed and controlled, and surely these are among the traits that distinguish Homo sapiens from others in the animal genus, from the primates down.
>
> Coital reproduction is, therefore, less human than laboratory reproduction—more fun, to be sure, but with our separation of baby making from love making, both become more human because they are matters of choice, and not chance.[21]

Francoeur's hymn to Baconian-Cartesian instrumental reason calls to mind C. S. Lewis's remarks on a scene in *Pride and Prejudice*.[22] Caroline Bingley attempts to impress Mr. Darcy by her rational thoughts about dancing. She turns to her brother Charles.

> "By the bye, Charles, are you really serious in meditating a dance at Netherfield?" . . .
>
> "As for the ball [answered Charles], it is quite a settled thing; and as soon as Nicholls has made white soup enough, I shall send round my cards."
>
> "I should like balls infinitely better," she replied, "if they were carried on in a different manner; but there is something insufferably tedious in the usual process of such a meeting. It would surely be much more rational if conversation instead of dancing were made the order of the day."
>
> "Much more rational, my dear Caroline, I dare say, but it would not be near so much like a ball." (*Pride and Prejudice*, vol. 1, chap. 11)

Caroline's proposal is not more rational.[23] It is more rational for a ball to be like a ball. The same point holds for Francoeur. As he sees it, reproduction by lovemaking is "more fun" but less human than laboratory reproduction. It is less human only if the distinctively human trait is instrumental reason narrowly conceived. Sexual reproduction is, in fact, more rational for a rational animal than laboratory reproduction. Francoeur shows how irrational it is to limit reason to scientific-technological reason.

The main question in the debate about contraception is the question of a reasonable practice of reason that allows us to be inside our bodies. If human reason is not an openness to being in all its breadth, including goodness and beauty, its practice becomes violent and irrational. The response to the narrow-

21. Robert T. Francoeur, "We Can—We Must: Reflections on the Technological Imperative," *Theological Studies* 33 (1972): 428–39, at 438.

22. See C. S. Lewis, "Priestesses in the Church," in *God in the Dock*, ed. Walter Hooper (Grand Rapids, MI: Eerdmans, 1994), 242–48.

23. See Lewis, "Priestesses in the Church," 243.

ing of reason is to defend the freedom and openness of reason. All discoveries in mathematical physics remain discoveries, of course, but they need to be seen as parts of a larger whole.

4. Intellectual Custom

Intellectual customs tend to take on the appearance of self-evidence. When limited ways of knowing have become habitual, they push fuller ways of knowing aside. Aristotle lists religious myth and mathematics as the first two intellectual customs to show the unreasonable power they can exercise over reason.

> Listening to lectures happens according to customs (κατὰ ἔθη), for as we are accustomed, so we judge it right to speak, and what follows a different way does not seem to fit. It looks contrary to knowledge and strange because it is not customary. The customary gives the impression of fitting what is known. The excessive power of custom is shown by the laws, in which—due to custom—myths and childish tales (τὰ μυθώδη καὶ παιδαριώδη) have more power than knowledge about these things. Some people do not accept what is said unless one speaks mathematically, others unless one gives instances, while others expect one to cite a poet as witness.[24]

Aristotle's first example of unreasonable custom is the fabric of religious myths imposed by Athenian custom and law. These myths are more powerful than knowledge because they are customary. Athens condemned Socrates to death because "he does not hold by custom the gods the city holds by custom."[25] Aristotle was accused of the same crime but left the city. "I will not allow the Athenians," he is reported to have said, "to sin against philosophy twice."[26]

Aristotle's second example is the custom of those who will not accept an argument unless it is expressed mathematically. Ever since natural science has run along the path of mathematical mechanics, its success has been spectacular. The wave of discoveries has been breathtaking. The success shows that mathematical patterns play an important role in nature. It does not show that these mathematical patterns are the only aspect one needs to consider. The claim that mathematics is enough is not itself a scientific claim but an unreflective philosophy that dresses up in the mantle of science.

Galileo's exaltation of mathematics in *The Assayer* (1623) is partly a result of his by then well-established intellectual custom as a mathematician, partly to

24. Aristotle, *Metaphysics* 2.3.994b32–995a7.

25. θεοὺς οὓς ἡ πόλις νομίζει ου νομίζοντα. Plato, *Apology* 24b–c.

26. Οὐ συγχωρήσω Ἀθηναίοις δὶς ἁμαρτεῖν εἰς φιλοσοφίαν. *Aristotelis Vita Marciana* 41.1.

his Pythagorean and Platonic natural philosophy, but also to his interest in the power of mechanics.[27]

> Philosophy is written in this greatest book, which stands continually open before our eyes (I am speaking about the universe), but one cannot understand unless one learns first to understand the language and recognize the characters in which it is written. It is written in mathematical language, and its characters are triangles, circles, and other geometric figures, without which means it is humanly impossible to understand a single word of it; without these, one is vainly walking in circles through a dark labyrinth.[28]

To an astonishing degree, Galileo has turned out to be right. The starting point of contemporary science is the assumption that some mathematical structure will help us to make sense of new data. It has been a highly successful assumption. The universe is not an unintelligible jumble of brute facts. Why is it mathematically intelligible? Why is mathematical order so pervasive? The success of Galileo's approach has blunted our sense of wonder about the surprising fact of mathematical order. Mathematical order has become so customary that wonder about it disappears.

Mathematical custom acts as a distortion field on Galileo's perceptions. When he claims that it is humanly impossible to understand a single word in the book of nature without mathematics, he overlooks that children read the book of nature. Adults do not leave behind what they learned as children. Children know that there are people, animals, and things. They can deal in appropriate ways with them. Yet they have little or no ability for mathematics. If scientists in their interactions with each other and their machines did not rely on the knowledge of the book of nature they gained as children, they could not take a single step in pursuing their work. Arriving at their office, they could not distinguish between their machines and the people they work with. How does one recognize a living person? Children have no difficulty. They do not need to learn mathematics to read these letters in the book of nature.

The "Life of Newton" by Chittenden, included in the first American edition of Newton's *Principia*, begins with a passage that makes seven points *in crescendo* to evoke the golden glow of emotion about Newton's discoveries.

27. See Plato, *Timaeus*, 53a–57d, and the commentary in Francis Macdonald Cornford, *Plato's Cosmology: The Timaeus of Plato* (London: Routledge, 1935), 210–39.

28. Galileo Galilei, *Il Saggiatore* (Rome: Giacomo Mascardi, 1623), 25. English translation: "The Assayer," in *The Controversy on the Comets of 1618: Galileo Galilei, Horatio Grassi, Mario Guiducci, Johann Kepler*, trans. Stillman Drake and C. D. O'Malley (Philadelphia: University of Pennsylvania Press: 1960), 163–336, at 184–85.

1. From the thick darkness of the middle ages man's struggling spirit emerged as in new birth;
2. breaking out of the iron control of that period;
3. growing strong and confident in the tug and din of succeeding conflict and revolution, it bounded forwards and upwards with resistless vigor to the investigation of physical and moral truth;
4. ascending height after height;
5. sweeping afar over the earth, penetrating afar up into the heavens;
6. increasing in endeavor, enlarging in endowment;
7. everywhere boldly, earnestly out-stretching, till, in the AUTHOR of the PRINCIPIA, one arose, who, grasping the master-key of the universe and treading its celestial paths, opened up to the human intellect the stupendous realities of the material world.[29]

The observation about a master key is particularly interesting. In the first edition of the *Principia*, Newton makes an astonishing claim. It has all the appearance of grasping for the master key. "Every body can be transformed into any other kind of body and it can take on, one after the other, all the intermediate degrees of qualities."[30] If this hypothesis were true, we could turn anything into anything whatsoever. It is a postulate for a practically unlimited scope of power. In later editions, Newton drew back from this dizzying vision. He simply states that we need to rely on experiments to find out what qualities bodies can take on. Nevertheless, he left the preface of the *Principia* in place.

> Since the Ancients, as Pappus says, thought the science of mechanics of the greatest importance in the investigation of natural things, and the more recent, dismissing substantial forms and hidden qualities, have begun to call back the phenomena of nature to mathematical laws, it seemed in this treatise one should work out mathematics so far as it regards philosophy.[31]

Newton misquotes Pappus. Pappus does not say that mechanical knowledge is important for understanding nature. He says it is important for training architects. The context is the curriculum suited to training architects.

29. Nathaniel Walter Chittenden, "Life of Sir Isaac Newton," in *Newton: Mathematical Principles of Natural Philosophy*, trans. Andrew Motte (New York: Daniel Ader, 1845), 9–61, at 9.

30. Hypothesis 3: Corpus omne in alterius cujuscunque generis corpus transformari posse, & qualitatum gradus omnes intermedios successive induere. Isaac Newton, *Philosophiae naturalis principia mathematica*, 1st ed. (London: Joseph Streater, 1687), 402.

31. "Cum Veteres Mechanicam (uti Author est Pappus) in rerum Naturalium investigatione maximi fecerint, & recentiores, missis formis substantialibus & qualitatibus occultis, Phænomena Naturæ ad leges Mathematicas revocare aggressi sint: Visum est in hoc Tractatu Mathesin excolere quatenus ea ad Philosophiam spectat." Newton, *Principia*, preface to the reader.

> Mechanical knowledge, my son Hermodorus, *since it is useful for many and great things in life*, has rightly been judged by philosophers as worthy of very great honor and is eagerly pursued by all mathematicians because it is in the first place concerned with the natural account (φυσιολογία) about the matter of the elements present in the cosmos.[32]

Newton leaves out the clause "since it is useful for many and great things in life." In Book VIII of his *Synagoge*, from which Newton's quote is taken, Pappus discusses the study of architecture, not the study of nature.[33] According to Pappus, "Mechanical knowledge . . . has rightly been judged by philosophers as worthy of very great (πλείστης) honor." The superlative πλείστης is used without the article and therefore means "very great."[34] Newton's Latin equivalent *maximi* is ambiguous because Latin does not have articles. Most translations take it to mean *greatest*, but it could mean "very great." Pappus's Greek is clearer. He does not say that mechanics is of the greatest importance but only in very high honor because of its usefulness for life, in particular for architecture.

A few paragraphs later, Pappus points to Archimedes, who had a deep understanding of mechanics. He emphasizes that Archimedes was not primarily interested in mechanics, even though he achieved popular fame for his mechanical knowledge. He was interested in geometry and arithmetic themselves, unmixed with practical purposes.

> The cause and *logos* of all these [mechanical arts], people say, was recognized by Archimedes the Syracusan . . . and yet he published only one book on mechanics. . . . Nevertheless, he became famous (δοξασθεὶς) among the many for mechanics. . . . He wrote very diligently about geometry and arithmetic . . . for it seems *he loved these sciences so much that he would not let anything external to them enter into them.*[35]

Pappus's remarks about Archimedes fit with what Plutarch says in his Life of Marcellus, the Roman general who conquered Syracuse. Plutarch describes the powerful machines by which Archimedes was able to hold off the Roman attack for a long time. He praises the mechanical power harnessed by Archimedes but even more his refusal to leave behind any documentation that would make such power generally available for military or industrial purposes.

> Huge beams were suddenly projected over the ships from the walls. . . . Ships were seized at the prow by iron claws, or beaks like the beaks of cranes, drawn

32. Pappus of Alexandria, *Synagoge* 8.1022.3–10.
33. See Glanville Downey, "Pappus of Alexandria on Architectural Studies," *Isis* 38 (1948): 197–200.
34. See Herbert Weir Smyth, *A Greek Grammar* (New York: American Book Co., 1916), §747.
35. Pappus, *Synagoge* 8.1026.5–19; emphasis added.

> straight up into the air, and then ... dashed against the steep cliffs that jutted out beneath the wall of the city.... All the rest of the Syracusans were only a body for the plans of Archimedes, and his was the one soul moving and managing everything; for all other weapons lay idle, and his alone were then employed by the city both in offence and defense....
>
> And yet Archimedes had such thoughtfulness and depth of soul, such a wealth of theorems, that although he had won a name and fame for an understanding more than human, in fact divine, he did not want to leave behind him any treatise on this subject, but considering the effort of mechanics (τὴν περὶ τὰ μηχανικὰ πραγματείαν) and every art imposed by need ignoble and vulgar (ἀγεννῆ καὶ βάναυσον), he devoted his love of what is worthy of honor only to those studies the beauty and excellence of which is not mixed with necessity.[36]

From the vantage point of a modern sensibility, one might criticize Archimedes as an elitist opposed to technological progress for the benefit of the human race. From a Christian vantage point shaped by the same sensibility, one might condemn him for being opposed to the divine command, "subdue the earth" (Genesis 1:28). Be that as it may, Pappus and Plutarch confirm how new Newton's devotion to mechanics truly was. Newton mistakenly projects his own intellectual custom into the ancients.

5. The Eclipse of Being

In the views of Stephen Hawking, one of Newton's successors in the Lucasian Chair of Mathematics at the University of Cambridge, one can observe a more radical form of the same intellectual custom.

> What is the nature of reality? Where did all this come from? Did the universe need a Creator? ... Traditionally these are questions for philosophy, but philosophy is dead. Philosophy has not kept up with modern developments in science, particularly physics. Scientists have become the bearers of the torch of discovery in our quest for knowledge.[37]

"Philosophy is dead" is neither a scientific discovery nor a mathematical law but a strangely self-contradictory thesis proposed by philosophy about herself. Hawking believes that we need to look no further than mathematical laws to account for the being of things. He easily recognizes the falseness of religious myths as explanations, but he does not critically examine his own intellectual custom.

36. Plutarch, *Life of Marcellus* 15:2, 17:3–4.

37. Stephen Hawking and Leonard Mlodinov, *The Grand Design* (New York: Bantam Books, 2010), 5.

> In Viking mythology, Skoll and Hati chase the sun and the moon. When the wolves catch either one, there is an eclipse. When this happens, the people on earth rush to rescue the sun or moon by making as much noise as they can in hopes of scaring off the wolves. There are similar myths in other cultures....
>
> Ignorance of nature's ways led people in ancient times to invent gods to lord it over every aspect of human life.... Since the connection of cause and effect in nature was invisible to their eyes, these gods appeared inscrutable, and people at their mercy. But with Thales of Miletus (ca. 624 BC–ca. 546 BC) about 2,600 years ago, that began to change. The idea arose that nature follows consistent principles that could be deciphered. And so began the long process of replacing the notion of the reign of gods with the concept of a universe that is governed by laws of nature, and created according to a blueprint we could someday learn to read.[38]

The idea of *governing* by laws is sensible when an existing government makes and enforces laws for existing subjects. *Governing* turns into a metaphor when what is supposed to do the governing is a mathematical law, that is, a generalized description of quantitative regularity after the observed facts, not a cause that comes before them. It turns from metaphor into myth when that same mathematical law begins to play the role of creator. M-theory, which attempts to unite five separate string theories into a single eleven-dimension theory, may be the long-sought explanation of the very existence of our universe, Hawking suggests.

> We will describe how M-theory may offer answers to the question of creation. According to M-theory, ours is not the only universe. Instead, M-theory predicts that a great many universes were created out of nothing. Their creation does not require the intervention of some supernatural being or god. Rather, these multiple universes arise naturally from physical law. They are a prediction of science.[39]

What relation to being and nonbeing do these laws have? How do universes arise naturally from them? Are the laws descriptions of the quantitative aspects of something that exists? If so, then it is already a universe within which beings act according to these patterns. If not, are the laws descriptions of nothing? Do they themselves exist as laws before any universe, at least in the logical and nontemporal sense of *before*? Are they a universe of immaterial Platonic ideas hovering over nothingness to govern the sudden emergence of material universes from nothing? If they are a prediction of science, is an act of prediction going on in the mind of some scientist? If not, why should one call it prediction?

38. Hawking and Mlodinov, *Grand Design*, 15–17.
39. Hawking and Mlodinov, *Grand Design*, 8.

Nonexistent physical laws, understood as predictions without anyone predicting, governing absolutely nothing in such a way that multiple universes arise naturally from nothing—this way of telling the story does not get far in plausibility beyond Skoll and Hati, except if mathematical custom has taken such a hold of the mind that one only looks for what is said mathematically. Hawking continues:

> M-theory is the most general supersymmetric theory of gravity. For these reasons M-theory is the only candidate for a complete theory of the universe. If it is finite—and this has yet to be proved—it will be a model of a universe that creates itself. We must be part of this universe, because there is no other consistent model.[40]

A consistent mathematical model—that is all we need. Hawking seems to have forgotten Hamlet's words. *To be or not to be. That is the question.* Because mathematics deals with quantity as quantity, or with even more abstract objects, many of them symbolic constructions of the mind, a mathematician does not and need not ask, Why is there something rather than nothing? The loss of being in Hawking's thinking is not surprising. It is predictable by real observers as a regular pattern of mind caused by the force of custom in frequent mathematical thought.

Physicists are likely to wave these points aside. Richard Feynman sees philosophers always as the others, never as himself. "These philosophers are always with us, struggling in the periphery to try to tell us something, but they never really understand the subtleties and depths of the problem."[41] Feynman's lack of reflection is massive. He may be right in not classifying himself as a professional philosopher and in faulting professional philosophers for not understanding scientific questions. Yet philosophy is a human activity without academic boundaries. It is as inescapable as thinking. Feynman philosophizes in the very denial of philosophizing.

Hawking and Feynman can teach an important lesson. One way to tell whether a particular claim is scientific or a popular philosophical thesis dressed up in the golden mantle of science is to ask, "Could this claim be a conclusion of the science itself, tested by experiment?" If not, then it is held on other grounds, which may be good grounds or not.

The discoveries made in mathematical physics are stupendous. John Paul is open to them without a trace of suspicion. The problem does not lie in the sciences themselves, though sciences do not enjoy immunity from error, but in the

40. Hawking and Mlodinov, *Grand Design*, 182.

41. Richard P. Feynman, *The Feynman Lectures on Physics*, vol. 1, *Mainly Mechanics, Radiation, and Heat* (New York: Basic Books, 2011), 16–17.

popular philosophical claim that some form of mechanics is the master key that alone opens all doors.

Natural science would be impossible without ways of knowing that are not scientific. An individual physicist can perform only a limited number of experiments in the course of her career. Let us assume one important experiment every day for forty years, a total of 14,600 experiments—an impossibly high number, of course. Yet her field has been built up by millions of experiments. She must take more than 99 percent of experimental data on faith. It is not religious faith, of course, but an ordinary human faith based on trusting the testimony of reliable witnesses. How does she know whom to believe? There are codes of professional practice for experimental physics. Individual scientists and their laboratories are judged according to them. How can one arrive at formulating these codes and applying them? They imply a form of knowledge that cannot be reduced to natural science itself. Yet natural science would be impossible without it. To limit reason to the scientific method is to destroy that method.

The famous watchmaker argument for the existence of God has come in for trenchant criticism by scientists. The hypothesis of God as first cause of the cosmic machine is not needed, they argue. One only needs to explore the laws of mechanics to account for any event. One does not need to appeal to any other cause. By the same argument, a real human watchmaker should not be able to know that he is the maker of his watches. Scientific investigation of the watches can only appeal to mechanical laws that have resulted in these watches. And yet what could be more obviously known to a watchmaker than making watches? It is a different form of knowledge, but if scientific intellectual customs exclude this form of knowledge, they should be unmasked as engaged in a violent and irrational practice of reason.

6. The Eclipse of Goodness

If the heavy blanket of mathematical custom extinguishes the question "To be or not to be?" its effect is even worse in the more burning question "Good or bad?" Mathematics does not deal with *good* and *bad* in its arguments. This is not a matter of personal preference by mathematicians but a matter of principle. Mathematics focuses on quantity, such as lines or numbers, or on derivatives of quantity conceived even more abstractly. Goodness does not enter the picture, nor does life, or thought—or, for that matter, most of what makes up our ordinary experience. Given these constitutive limits of mathematics, the intellectual custom formed by mathematics tends to be fertile ground for reductionist philosophies. To replace the bewildering richness of ordinary experience by clear and distinct mathematical ideas—this was Descartes's project, a project the foundations of which he attempted to spell out in his *Meditations*.

The *first step* in Descartes's *Mediations* is to establish universal doubt as the point of departure, which suspends the confusing world of ordinary experience in one blow. The *second step* is to reintroduce reality by clear and distinct ideas, beginning with the *cogito*, in which consciousness and existence are grasped as one (*res cogitans*). The *third step*, which involves (among other substeps) the ontological argument for the existence of God, is to reintroduce matter in a thoroughly cleaned condition. The only characteristics allowed are quantitative. The end product is a material world of purely extended things, *res extensae*. Power no longer needs to reckon with what is disturbingly extraneous to its own concerns, such as goodness or humanity.

Full submission of intellect and will to the dictates of Cartesian philosophy can be found at times also among Catholic theologians (see the discussion of Goertz's essay on *Humanae vitae* in section 3 of the introduction to this volume). Salzman and Lawler begin the foundational section of their book *The Sexual Person: Toward a Renewed Catholic Anthropology* with Hume's fact-value distinction, which follows readily from the Baconian-Cartesian understanding of matter and science.

> Because there will be much talk of "nature" in this and following chapters, we must first confront a difficulty with any argument from "nature." This difficulty was highlighted initially by David Hume, who asked whether we can deduce moral obligations from what exists in "nature" and answered that we cannot. We cannot draw conclusions from what is to what ought to be, from the presumed biological structure of the sexual act—for example, to moral obligation—for even after determining what is, we still have to determine whether it is right or wrong. To draw such a conclusion is a logical fallacy—a "naturalistic fallacy," Moore calls it, or a "theological fallacy," Frankena calls it. All we can understand from "nature" is the naked facticity of a reality, sexuality and sexual intercourse for instance; nothing else.[42]

The charge of the naturalistic fallacy is difficult to sustain for a Christian, one would think. "Indeed, it was very good" (Genesis 1:31). If "very good" is more than a subjective value judgment on God's part, if it is true about things, as children are inclined to agree, then the move from *is* to *ought* is reasonable. The good contains the evidence that it is to be pursued and done.

To illustrate their judgment about the neutrality of nature, its reduction to

42. Todd A. Salzman and Michael G. Lawler, *The Sexual Person: Toward a Renewed Catholic Anthropology* (Washington, DC: Georgetown University Press, 2008), 48–49.

naked facticity and nothing else, Salzman and Lawler choose an example that shows the highest degree of courage. They could hardly have chosen a better worst-case scenario for their argument.

> If the decisive criterion for the meaning of any action, including any moral action, is the meaning assigned to it by social actors, an immediate question arises. Different social actors in different social groups may define the meaning of an action in radically different ways and then, a question arises as to which definition is true. Common sense suggests that something is the "same" for each and every social and individual actor, but common sense cannot determine how that sameness is to be understood. Only critical research, interpretation, history, and dialectic can do that.
>
> The entire world watched Nazis herd gypsies, homosexuals, and Jews into gas chambers. Committed Nazis interpreted the action as purification of the race; the rest of the world interpreted it as murder of innocent people; and we can only guess how the people waiting for the gas interpreted it. For all three groups the action was naturally the "same," the herding of people into gas chambers. For each group, however, the meaning of the action was far from the same. It was radically different, and it is utterly futile to point out to committed actors the "objective" meaning of the act, for the objective meaning is the meaning assigned to the act by social actors, not the naked, uninterpreted facticity of the act.[43]

One needs to let this text sink in. One needs to ask naïve questions to let it reveal its radicalism.

NAÏVE QUESTION: Do you really think that facts are value-free? Do you think Auschwitz was value free as a fact?

SALZMAN AND LAWLER: As an event in the world of matter, Auschwitz was neutral. It was matter, motion, and electro-magnetic forces acting according to mathematical laws. A scientist studying the event will not discover values by measurements.

NAÏVE: Doesn't *Shoah* mean *catastrophe*? That's the opposite of neutral. Exactly by being a fact, a catastrophe is really bad. It ought not to have been inflicted on the Jewish people. Isn't it obvious that you can move from *really bad* to *ought not to be done*? Where is the lack of logic?

SALZMAN AND LAWLER: The value judgment expressed by *bad* doesn't tell us anything about matter as studied by science.

NAÏVE: You may well be right about natural science, which is limited by its mathematical method and attention to mechanism. You aren't saying that this

43. Salzman-Lawler, *Sexual Person*, 49–50.

is the whole picture, are you? Have you seen Auschwitz? What about the people who suffered there? Was the suffering not real as an event in the physical world?

SALZMAN AND LAWLER: The facts are governed by mathematical laws. Psychological states like suffering are subjective.

NAÏVE: What about the Nazi torturers and executioners? Didn't they govern the facts by their decisions? Didn't they turn themselves into monsters by their acts?

SALZMAN AND LAWLER: You are always confusing facts and values.

NAÏVE: God seems to have the same problem in Genesis 1:31? "God saw everything he had made and, indeed, it was very good." Is God not allowed to make such judgments about the physical world in public because they are unscientific?

SALZMAN AND LAWLER: You are talking about private religious values, socially constructed, not about objective facts available to public reason. It would be pointless to talk to a convinced Nazi about God and the goodness of creation.

NAÏVE: Have you tried? Haven't some of them turned away from what they did, horrified by themselves?

In a follow-up to their book, Salzman and Lawler protest that they are simply applying generally accepted norms of scientific understanding.[44] The Shoah is not, of course, the main subject of *The Sexual Person*. Saltzman and Lawler use the Shoah as an *a fortiori* argument. It is a mighty *a fortiori* indeed. If the Shoah, considered as an objective event of nature, is neutral, then *a fortiori* (a mighty *fortiori* indeed) the use of contraceptives is neutral. Nothing about the moral quality of contraception can be gathered from the nature and goodness of men, women, sex, or children. Moral judgments are exclusively a matter of socially constructed values. Catholics living today construct these values differently than Catholics did in the past.

Salzman and Lawler do not seem to realize that their argument is highly effective in quite another direction. It shows the bankruptcy of Cartesian rationality. Descartes's value-free world of matter may be successful within a limited range of technological know-how, exemplified by Eichmann's advanced killing machine, but it is intellectually and morally bankrupt.

44. See Todd Salzman and Michael Lawler, "Theology, Science, and Sexual Anthropology: A Methodological Investigation," *Journal of Religion and Society, Supplement Series* 11 (2015): 46–72.

7. The Geography of the Debate

The ambition of power over nature and the consequent dimming of the guiding light of goodness in nature leads to conflict with any tradition of moral wisdom based on such a light.[45] Supposed wisdom comes under immediate suspicion as an ideology shaped by power interests—an ironic reversal of the role of power in the scientific revolution. In his 1963 inaugural lecture at the University of Münster, Joseph Ratzinger described this cultural development with penetrating insight.

> We must see right through traditional value systems and expose them. In technical rationality we become our own Creators and the Creators of a world built with our own inventions. We construct ourselves and reality anew in the unconditional transparence of our rationality. This commitment finds philosophical expression in the idea that there is no pre-given human nature, so that we are free and in fact compelled by our freedom to invent ourselves, to determine what a human being will be in the future. The strongest form of this detachment from the earth, from the given that carries us, is the complete power over life and death and the abolition of the difference between man and woman.[46]

One can see such a detachment from the earth, from the human body, in the final report submitted to St. Paul VI by Henri de Riedmatten, OP, the secretary of the Papal birth control commission and a decided supporter of contraception. The report contains a draft encyclical for Paul VI called *Schema for a Document on Responsible Parenthood*. In 1967, some members of the commission leaked the schema to the press with the more media-savvy title *Majority Report*. It was an attempt to put pressure on Paul VI.[47] The *schema* emphatically embraces the Baconian-Cartesian program.

> The story of God and of man should be seen as a shared work. And it should be seen that man's tremendous progress in control of matter by technical means and the universal and total "intercommunication" that has been achieved, correspond entirely (*omnino*) to the divine decrees.[48]

45. See C. S. Lewis, *The Abolition of Man: Reflections on Education with Special Reference to the Teaching of English in the Upper Forms of Schools* (San Francisco: Harper-Collins, 2001).

46. Joseph Ratzinger, *Theologische Prinzipienlehre: Bausteine zur Fundamentaltheologie* (Munich: Erich Wewel Verlag, 1982), 96–97; *Principles of Catholic Theology: Building Stones for a Fundamental Theology* (San Francisco: Ignatius, 1987), 93.

47. For a narrative of the Special Commission's work and copies of its documents, see the dossier published by Germain Grisez, accessed April 20, 2019, www.twotlj.org/Ford.html. For a commentary on the documents, see Janet Smith, "The Beginnings of the Debate," in *Humanae Vitae: A Generation Later* (Washington, DC: Catholic University of America Press, 1991), 1–35.

48. *Majority Report*, in *The Catholic Case for Contraception*, ed. Daniel Callahan (New York: Macmillan, 1969), 150. Original Latin: *Schema documenti de responsabili paternitate*, in *Contrôle des*

It would be difficult to express a more unqualified allegiance to the Baconian-Cartesian program. Technical mastery over nature corresponds *omnino* (altogether, entirely) to the will of God. Compare this optimism with St. John Paul's warning in *Evangelium vitae.*

> Nature itself, from being *mater* (mother), is now reduced to being *matter*, and is subjected to every kind of manipulation. This is the direction in which a certain technical and scientific way of thinking, prevalent in present-day culture, appears to be leading when it rejects the very idea that there is a truth of creation which must be acknowledged, or a plan of God for life which must be respected. (*Evangelium vitae* 22)

John Paul penetrates to the core of "a certain technical and scientific thinking" and identifies the blindness of such thinking to any aspect that goes beyond mechanism. He shows that the subjection of matter is not only a moral problem. It is a problem of seeing and understanding. Among the various reasons given by the Majority Report for affirming the legitimacy of contraception, the foremost is the legitimacy of power over nature.

> The reasons in favor of this affirmation are of several kinds: social changes in marriage and the family, especially in the role of the woman; lowering of the infant mortality rate; new bodies of knowledge in biology, psychology, sexuality and demography; a changed estimation of the value and meaning of human sexuality and of conjugal relations; *but most of all* (*maxime*), a better grasp of *the duty of man to humanize what is given in nature and to bring it to greater perfection for the life of man.*[49]

The superlative *but most of all* deserves attention. Among all the reasons for the moral legitimacy of contraception, the foremost reason, the reason that is most of all a reason, is not the liberation of women from excessive pregnancies, not the threat of a population explosion, not a personalist understanding of sex, but the duty of humanizing what is given in nature. Humanizing is achieved through "tremendous progress in the control of matter by technical means."

The concept of *humanizing* comes into clearer focus when one considers the state of the question on contraception between *Gaudium et spes* (1965) and *Humanae vitae* (1968). The Council is clear in its rejection of certain forms of contraception such as sterilization and the condom. The famous footnote on contraception in *Gaudium et spes* 51:3 first excludes these older forms of contra-

---

naissances et théologie: Le dossier de Rome, Traduction, présentation et notes de Jean-Marie Paupert, ed. Jean-Marie Paupert (Paris: Seuil, 1967), 179–89, at 179.

49. *Majority Report*, 161. Latin, 183; emphasis added.

ception. Then it mentions "certain questions" that will be addressed by a special commission. It is clear that the questions are those raised by the pill.

There is an important difference between the pill and earlier forms of contraception such as the condom. A condom interferes with the conjugal act in an obvious manner by blocking the act's completion. It is like looking with one's eyes shut. The pill is different. It seems to leave the conjugal act intact. With the help of her doctor, the woman gains mastery over the internal operation of her body. During pregnancy and nursing, nature prevents or reduces conceptions, which protects the life of the growing child, safeguards the woman's health, and spaces children for the good of the family. Science helps nature provide for temporary infertility. It supplies means like those of nature to regulate fertility. The pill is a form of medicine, like an antibiotic. Would the Church say that one must not use this form of medicine? Wouldn't that be like banning antibiotics?

The pill was a new phenomenon connected with science and technology. Those aligned with the *Majority Report*, it seems, saw the pill as a question of *aggiornamento*, of bringing the Church up-to-date by embracing a new loyalty to the Baconian-Cartesian program. The Church's openness to modernity, her willingness to participate constructively in the modern program of scientific and technological progress, depended in significant measure on this loyalty, that is, on swallowing the pill.

One can understand the bitterness of many Catholics against *Humanae vitae*, a bitterness found especially among clerics and theologians. The main problem with *Humanae vitae* is not the failure to accept egalitarian relations between men and women, not the lack of awareness and concern about the population explosion, not reductive biologism and naturalism, not blindness to the personalistic dimension of sex. The main problem is the betrayal of newly found harmony with the modern age in its Baconian-Cartesian form at a point that interests everyone—sex.

Humanae vitae, published one year after the *Majority Report* in the historically pivotal year 1968, emphasizes the importance of this issue. Paul VI follows the *Majority Report* in mentioning it last in a list of reasons for reconsidering contraception and qualifies it with an adverb close to the superlative, *praesertim* above all.

> Finally, one should take note above all (*praesertim*) that man has made such stupendous progress in the domination and rational organization of the forces of nature that he tends to extend this domination to his own total life: that is, to the body, to the powers of his soul, to social life and even to the laws which regulate the transmission of life.[50]

50. Paul VI, *Humanae vitae* 2.

John Paul highlights the issue of power over nature in a similar way as the essence of the Catholic teaching on contraception.

> What is the essence of the teaching of the Church about the transmission of life in the conjugal community, the essence of the teaching recalled for us by the Council's pastoral constitution *Gaudium et spes and the* encyclical *Humanae vitae* by Pope Paul VI? The problem lies in maintaining *the proper proportion* between that which is defined as "*domination … of the forces of nature*" (HV 2) and "*self-mastery*" (HV 21), which is indispensable for the human person. Contemporary man shows the tendency of transferring the methods proper to the first sphere to those of the second. "Finally, and above all, man has made stupendous progress in the domination and rational organization of the forces of nature," we read in the encyclical, "such that he tends to extend this domination to his own total being: to the body, to psychical life, to social life and even to the laws which regulate the transmission of life" (HV 2).
>
> This extension of the sphere of the means of "the domination … of the forces of nature" threatens the human person for whom the method of "self-mastery" is and remains specific. It—that is, self-mastery—corresponds in fact to the fundamental constitution of the person: it is a perfectly "natural" method. The extension of "artificial means," by contrast, *violates* the constitutive dimension of the person, deprives man of the subjectivity that belongs to action, and turns him into *an object of manipulation …*
>
> *The essential problem* the encyclical presents is the viewpoint of the *authentic development of the human person*; such development should be measured, as a matter of principle, by the measure of ethics and not only of "technology." (TOB 123:1–3; emphasis original)

What is at issue in the question of the pill is not simply the moral goodness or evil of one act among others but the scientific culture of modernity and its practice of reason. One can hardly overestimate the importance of this deeper issue. Assent to the pill was above all an expression of the intense desire of many Catholics to emerge from medieval obscurantism by embracing the Baconian-Cartesian program. Approval of the pill would bring the governmental stamp of approval on the Church's long-desired Green Card in the land of modernity.

In his *Regensburg Lecture*, Pope Benedict uses the contrast between voluntarism (the primacy of will and power) and intellectualism (the primacy of reason, *logos*) to outline the geography of cultural debate. His proposal radically reconfigures the conventional geography. The conventional geography distinguishes two continents at odds with each other. One of them is the continent of faith, allied with rightwing repressive politics, which relies on power to achieve its ends. Traditional forms of religion, such as Christianity and Islam, inhabit this continent. The other is the continent of scientific rationality (*logos*) and of the politics of emancipation from power to achieve equality and maximize free choice. The dominant culture of the West, propagated by the school system, the universities, and mass media, occupies this continent.

The *Regensburg Lecture* points out a parallel between Islam and Western voluntarism as developed by Scotus and fully unfolded in the nominalism of William of Ockham. Voluntarism, which asserts the primacy of will and thus of power, stands at the origins of the self-limitation of reason in modern natural science. The resulting geography differs strikingly from the conventional map. One of the continents is the continent of reason (*logos*) as understood by Greek philosophy, especially Socrates, Plato, and Aristotle. From the beginning, Christianity has resolutely chosen this continent as its home. It has understood faith as a light that comes from the *Logos*, from Reason in person. The other is the continent of voluntarism, of the primacy of will and power over reason. Islam, medieval nominalism or voluntarism (Ockham, Luther, and Calvin), modern natural science, and the politics of individual rights are close neighbors on that continent.

Several decades before Benedict XVI, Hans Urs von Balthasar argued in detail for the same configuration, beginning with his early work *Apokalypse der deutschen Seele* (especially the chapters on Kant and Scheler), then in his mature trilogy *Aesthetics*, *Dramatics*, and *Logic*. He shows that voluntarism and nominalism drive a deep wedge into the Western tradition.

> After a period in which the ancient *logos*-philosophy exercised a calming influence, voluntarist radicalism burst into philosophy and theology in the work of Duns Scotus. . . .
>
> More important is its late medieval form, fully developed in Ockham. The way Ockham alternates between intra-mundane empiricism and theological positivism (or a-apriorism) represents the original form of all variations of "modern" thought. Here, divine freedom has absorbed all rationality into itself. The *potentia Dei ordinata* [actually ordered or implemented power of God] is his *potentia absoluta* [absolute power]: *Deus autem ad nullum actum potest obligari, ideo eo ipso quod Deus vult, hoc est justum fieri* [God, however, cannot be bound to any act, and therefore, by the very fact that God wills it, it is just for this to be done].
>
> This could be understood in a correct sense if external *obligation* were excluded and the divine will were irradiated to its very foundations by the divine rationality. It is clear, however, that Ockham means more than this when he says, for instance, that God could have destined us for hatred instead of love

of God. The nominalist legacy survives in the two founders of modern times, diametrically opposed though they may be, Descartes and Luther.[51]

The *Regensburg Lecture* unfolds the argument that Scripture calls for Greek *logos*. The springboard it uses is the argument of the Byzantine emperor Manuel II Paleologus against the practice of religious conversion by violence.

> Violence is incompatible with the nature of God and the nature of the soul. "God," [Manuel Paleologus] says, "is not pleased by blood—not acting reasonably (with *logos*) is contrary to God's nature. Faith is born of the soul, not the body. . . . To convince a reasonable soul, one does not need a strong arm, or weapons of any kind, or any other means of threatening a person with death." . . . The decisive statement in this argument against violent conversion is this: not to act in accordance with reason is contrary to God's nature.[52]

Using the emperor's remarks on *logos* as a point of departure, Benedict XVI argues that Greek *logos* is not external to Scripture.

> Is the conviction that acting unreasonably contradicts God's nature merely a Greek idea, or is it always and intrinsically true? I believe that here we can see the profound harmony between what is Greek in the best sense of the word and the Biblical understanding of faith in God.
>
> Modifying the first verse of the Book of Genesis, the first verse of the whole Bible, John began the prologue of his Gospel with the words: "In the beginning was the *Logos*." This is the very word used by the emperor: God acts with *logos*. *Logos* means both reason and word—a reason which is creative and capable of self-communication, precisely as reason. In this manner, John spoke the final word on the Biblical concept of God, and in this word all the often toilsome and tortuous threads of Biblical faith find their culmination and synthesis. In the beginning was the *Logos*, and the *Logos* is God, says the Evangelist.
>
> The encounter between the Biblical message and Greek thought did not happen by chance. The vision of Saint Paul, who saw the roads to Asia barred and, in a dream, saw a Macedonian man plead with him: "Come over to Macedonia and help us!" (cf. Acts 16:6–10)—this vision can be interpreted as a "distillation" of the intrinsic necessity of a rapprochement between Biblical faith and Greek inquiry. . . .
>
> The New Testament was written in Greek and bears the imprint of the Greek spirit. . . . The fundamental decisions made about the relationship between faith and the use of human reason [in the New Testament and the early

51. Balthasar, *Theodramatik*, 2:222–23; *Theodrama*, 2:245–46.

52. Benedict XVI, *Regensburg Lecture*.

Church] are part of the faith itself; they are developments consonant with the nature of faith itself.[53]

When he wrote TOB (between 1974 and 1978) and delivered it as catecheses, John Paul II was aware of this broad context. In the works immediately preceding TOB, he enters into intense discussion with Kant and Scheler. He was especially fascinated by Kant, who proposed the most consistent and stringent alternative to Greek *Logos*. Balthasar's and Benedict XVI's analysis of modernity suggests that Luther (together with Ockham) is the first thinker one should examine to understand these developments.

53. Benedict XVI, *Regensburg Lecture*.

CHAPTER 2

The *Logos* of Scripture in Luther and John Paul

1. The Spousal Reading of Scripture in Luther and John Paul

Luther's Spousal Reading

Luther has a vivid grasp of spousal love and of its importance in Scripture as an image for the relation between God and his people.

> Married love, that is, spousal love, burns like fire and seeks nothing but the spouse. It says, "I do not want what is yours; I want neither your silver nor your gold, neither this nor that; I want to have you yourself; I want to have you totally or nothing." All other loves seek something other than the beloved: this one alone wants to have the beloved's own self totally. . . .
>
> This is truly, Paul says, a great sacrament, that is, the married state signifies something truly great. Is it not something great that God is made man, that he gives himself to be man's own and wants to be his, just as the man gives himself to the woman and is hers? But if God is ours, then everything is ours. (Sermon on the Estate of Marriage, LW 44:9, WA 2:167–68)[1]

This text sounds as if it were lifted from the pages of TOB. The reason for the likeness lies in common roots. Luther's language is deeply traditional. It echoes important Scripture passages, especially Hosea and the Song of Songs, "My beloved is mine and I am his" (Song of Songs 2:16, 6:3, 7:10). In the Gospel of John,

1. Citations of Luther by LW (= *Luther's Works*) and WA (= Weimarer Ausgabe) refer to *Luther's Works*, 83 vols., ed. Jaroslav Pelikan (St. Louis, MO: Concordia, 1958–2017); *Martin Luthers Werke: Kritische Gesamtausgabe*, 120 vols. (Weimar: Böhlau, 1883–2009), translations modified.

Jesus says to the Father, "All that is mine is yours and yours mine" (John 17:10). St. Bernard, one of Luther's favorite authors, seems to have played a role as well. When Paul says, "this mystery is great" (Ephesians 5:32), St. John Paul II argues, what he has in mind is the total gift of the person (see TOB 93–95b). Luther uses similar language.

> "I will take you as my wife" (Hos 2:19). These are wonderful words. He does not say, "I will make a covenant," as he said to the fathers but, "I will take you as my wife." There is on earth no love more burning (*ardentior*) than that between bridegroom and bride. The bridegroom hands over to the bride, not a gift but himself (*non munus sed seipsum tradit sponsae*), the innermost affection of his heart and all that is his. He anticipates his bride and searches her out. (*Lectures on Hosea*; LW 18:13; WA 13:11)

It is in these terms that Luther interprets Scripture. The metaphor of marriage, he points out, signifies that God gives not only created goods but also himself. He makes the same point in a text about faith as spousal union.

> The third incomparable grace of faith is this, that it joins (*copulat*) the soul with Christ as the bride with the bridegroom. By this sacrament (*sacramento*), as the Apostle teaches, Christ and the soul are made into one flesh (Ephesians 5:31–32). And if they are one flesh and a true marriage is consummated by them—indeed by far the most perfect of all marriages, since human marriages are but weak figures of this one true marriage—it follows that everything they have they hold in common, the good as well as the bad, so that, whatever Christ has this the faithful soul can claim and glory in as its own (*tanquam suis*), and whatever the soul has, this Christ claims for himself as his own (*tanquam sua*)....
>
> For if Christ is the bridegroom, he must take upon himself also what his bride has and give to the bride what is his. If he gives her his body and himself, how shall he not give all that is his? And if he takes the body of the bride, how shall he not take all that is hers? ...
>
> In this way he takes to himself a glorious bride, "without spot or wrinkle, cleansing her by the washing of water with the word" (Ephesians 5:26–27) of life, that is, by faith in the Word of life, righteousness, and salvation. In this way he marries her in faith, steadfast love, and in mercies, righteousness, and justice, as Hosea 2:19–20 says.
>
> Who then can fully appreciate this royal marriage? Who can comprehend the riches of the glory of this gift? Here this rich and divine bridegroom Christ marries this little pauper, this impious little whore (*meretriculam*), redeems her from all her evil, and adorns her with all his goods. She can say, "Even though I sinned, yet my Christ, in whom I believe, has not sinned" and "all that is his is mine and all that is mine is his" (cf. John 17:10; Luke 15:31), as in

> the Song of Songs 2:16, "My beloved is mine and I am his." (*Freedom of the Christian*; LW 31:351–52; WA 7:54–55)

In the marriage vows, man and woman say to each other, I *take you* as my wife. I *take you* as my husband. One can take by such a vow only what is given in the form of a vow. Each can say, *I take you*, only because the other says, at least implicitly, *I give myself to you*. The form of the marriage vow known to Luther was "I am yours and you are mine" (*Estate of Marriage*; LW 44:11; WA 2:169).

I take you, you are mine. I give myself to you, I am yours. This is what John Paul calls *the language of the body*, that is, the concrete bodily words by which the spousal meaning of the body is enacted in the sacrament of marriage (see TOB 103–105). Luther understands the great power and beauty of these words. "If he gives her his body and himself, how shall he not give all that is his? And if he takes the body of the bride, how shall he not take all that is hers?" Here lies the core of the mystery of the sinner's gratuitous justification by grace alone without works of the law.

In the text quoted above, Luther focuses on the individual person's relation to Christ, but in the text about to be quoted, he speaks the language of participation in Christ and the whole Church. Ephesians sees the whole Church as the bride of Christ. Being part of the bride, participating in her reception of the bridegroom's gift, here lies the created person's highest dignity.

> "At your right hand stands the queen, all in gold" (Ps 45:9). "Queen" he calls the bride, his wife. She stands as though all in gold. This bride is the Church and the entire body....
>
> The bride is one, gathered from all these members of kings and princes, the weak and the poor, virgins and married people—and from all of these is formed one bride, the church. This is common usage, that Christ is called the bridegroom and the Church, the bride, as in Ephesians 5:23*ff*. and other passages. He calls her through Holy Baptism and the Word of the Gospel, and adorns and clothes her with mercy, grace, and the remission of sins. That is what he means when he says, "She stands at your right hand." It is a glorious (*herlich, magnifica*) commendation, and it is also appropriate that no one be nearer the bridegroom than the bride herself.
>
> But the main thing is that the Church has everything that is Christ's and that two bodies have become one, so that what is the Church's is Christ's and in the same way what is Christ's is the church's.
>
> These things are greater than human speech can present, or our heart comprehend. Still it is represented faintly in marriage, where the supreme love of the bridegroom is for the bride, one faith, one body, and one mind. Between Christ and the Church, the reality is true, whereas in physical marriage we find only mirror images and figures (*spectacula et figurae*) of these spiritual

nuptials (*nupciarum*), where Christ is the bridegroom and everything he has he gives to the Church....

She says of all the gifts of her bridegroom, "These are mine." If sin roars against her, she grasps the justice of Christ, her Bridegroom (*apprehendit Christi sui sponsi iusticiam*), and says: "I have the justice of the Bridegroom. It is mine (*illa mea est*)." ... And when sorrow plagues her, she says: "In my Bridegroom is life, grace, peace, joy, salvation. These things are mine because Christ is mine." ... As a queen she possesses with fullest right (*plenissimo iure*) life, justice, grace, and salvation in Christ....

And this I know too, that he has become the Bridegroom and has communicated (*communicavit*) to his bride, the Church, all that he has. I am a part of his Church (*eius Ecclesiae ego sum pars*). For I have sure signs and pledges, namely, Baptism, the Gospel, the Eucharist, that witness to the fact that I am a member (*membrum*) of Christ. (Psalm 45; LW 12:259–62; WA 4.2:555–59)

These texts show that Luther's scriptural hermeneutics is one of spousal gift closely akin to John Paul's "hermeneutics of the gift" (TOB 13:2). In this respect, he stands in the unbroken Catholic tradition, as he intends to. Balthasar comments on this tradition as follows.

The theological aesthetics of the commentaries on the Song of Songs—with an indissoluble union of *agapê* and *erôs*, of the glory of God and the beauty from the soul—affords an almost inexhaustibly variable treasury of themes.... An unbroken procession of these commentaries stretches through the monasteries and universities of the Middle Ages to Luther and into the Baroque period.

The biblical *erôs*-motif, expounded in relation to Christ and his Bride (Church-Mary-the soul), leads both to the heart of the distinctively Christian mysteries (for the sake of which alone the whole external theology of the coun cils and the schools is worth studying) and also to the deepest justification of the *spoliatio Aegyptiorum*, that is, *Platonicorum*.

To put it another way: the glowing heart of the mystery of Christ is pure beauty, if it is true that all revelation, all faith, all suffering and death, takes place for the sake of the wedding feast of the Lamb. It is in that wedding that creaturely and Christian truth and goodness is transfigured in the final glory.[2]

It is a common image of Luther among Catholics that he moved from *inside* the Church to the *outside*. There is some truth in this image, but in important respects the opposite is true. From far outside, from the Scholasticism of William of Ockham, Luther moved into the Catholic mainstream. The question remains whether he was sufficiently radical in rejecting Ockham.

Thomas Aquinas says (and interprets Aristotle as saying) that the reason

2. Balthasar, *Herrlichkeit*, 3/1/1:290; *Glory*, 4:322.

why something is an end is that it is good. Ockham says (and interprets Aristotle as saying) that the reason why something is an end is that it happens to be willed. Having the character of an end arises from the free initiative of the will in setting something as an end, though emotion can play a role in the form of desire. As Ockham puts it, "The causality of the end is nothing but being effectively loved and desired by the agent."[3] The opposition between these two views is the greatest possible opposition. It reaches into the very roots of philosophy and theology. Both views speak about goodness, reason, and will but in opposite ways. In Thomas, reason guides the will because it can understand the good in its goodness. In Ockham, sheer willing determines the end. If one uses the labels *Scholasticism* and *Aristotelian* to cover both Thomas and Ockham and then goes on to say, "Luther opposed Scholasticism and Aristotle," one has not yet come to the main point. Which Scholasticism and which Aristotle? There are two of them, and the distance between them is the greatest possible distance.

Luther studied Ockham closely and extensively, as attested by his marginal notes in a copy of Ockham's *Quodlibeta Septem* found in Erfurt.[4] He also steeped himself in the much less radical summaries of Ockham by Gabriel Biel and Peter d'Ailly.[5] Melanchthon highlights Luther's admiration for Ockham as the most brilliant Scholastic, more brilliant even than Thomas and Scotus.

> He did not neglect the *Sentences* commentators, Gabriel [Biel] and Cammeracensis [Pierre d'Ailly, Cardinal of Cambrai]. He often spent much time reading the writings of Occam, whose sharpness of mind (*acumen*) he preferred to that of Thomas and Scotus.[6]

Luther's discussions of Thomas show that his knowledge of Thomas was mostly indirect, based on the summaries in Biel's commentary on the *Sentences*. These summaries are for the most part fair, but they are occupied with particular questions and do not address the root questions about the good, causality,

3. William of Ockham, *Quodlibetum* 4, q. 1, a. 1, conclusio 1, *Opera Theologica*, 9:293. Citations of Ockham are from *Guillelmi de Ockham Opera Philosophica*, 7 vols.; *Opera Theologica*, 10 vols. (St. Bonaventure: St. Bonaventure University, 1967–86); *Guillelmi de Ockham Opera Politica*, 4 vols. (Manchester: Manchester University Press and Oxford University Press, 1940–94).

4. See Heinz Endermann, "Martin Luther in Erfurt: Student, Mönch und Wissenschaftler," *Luther* 72 (2001): 83–95, at 93.

5. See Gabriel Biel, *Collectorium circa quattuor libros Sententiarum*, ed. Wilfrid Werbeck and Udo Hofmann (Tübingen: J. C. B. Mohr, 1973); Pierre d'Ailly, *Questiones super primum, tertium et quartum librum Sententiarum*, ed. Monica Brinzei (Turnhout: Brepols, 2013). A useful overview of the text, listing the titles of all *quaestiones* and *articuli*, is given by Monica Calma, "Pierre d'Ailly: Le commentaire sur les Sentences de Pierre Lombard," *Bulletin de Philosophie Medievale* 49 (2007): 139–94.

6. Philipp Melanchthon, *Historia de vita et actis reverendiss. Viri D. Mart. Lutheri verae Theologiae Doctoris, bona fide conscripta* (Erfurt: G. Stürmer, 1548), 6–7.

and reason.[7] In *The Harvest of Medieval Theology*, Heiko Oberman portrays Ockham as a theologian in the Christian mainstream.[8] Luther disagrees. "I lost Christ there."

> They [the Scholastics] left the sacred letters behind and began to speak about these divine things in a human way (an easier way, they think) and so, little by little, they lost the sense of Scripture. . . .
>
> I know and confess that I learned nothing except ignorance about sin, justice, Baptism, and the whole of Christian life. I did not learn what the power of God is, what the work of God is, what the grace of God is, what faith, hope, and love are. To bring it to a point, not only did I not learn anything (which would still be tolerable), but I learned only what had to be unlearned, only what was completely contrary to the divine letters. . . . I lost Christ there. (not in LW; WA 2:414)

Luther rightly experienced the Scholasticism shaped by Ockham as *far outside* the Christian mainstream, so far that he lost Christ. Of the intense personal relation to Christ in both Luther and John Paul, one finds little evidence in Ockham. God's plan of salvation as revealed in Scripture does occupy Ockham's mind. Yet a survey of his *Ordinatio* and *Reportatio* on the *Sentences* of Peter Lombard and of his own *Quodlibeta* and *Quaestiones Variae* shows that his primary interest is not a deeper understanding of the divine plan as it was actually carried out. He is interested in thinking through with much technical brilliance how by God's absolute power this or that element of the plan could have been different. He asks, for example, whether someone who does not love God could enter eternal happiness with God.[9] He answers yes, by God's absolute power, because God does not depend on secondary causes such as love disposing a person for union. Could a woman be happily married to a man she does not love? Would she not experience this union as violent, as rape and torture? It is not surprising that Ockham shows little interest in the spousal mystery of Christ and the Church (Ephesians 5:31–32).

On this background, one needs to raise several questions. How thorough was Luther in unlearning what he thought he needed to unlearn? Did he continue to hold some of Ockham's theses that he would have unlearned had he examined them more closely? Did he react against some of Ockham's theses so

7. See John L. Farthing, *Thomas Aquinas and Gabriel Biel: Interpretations of St. Thomas Aquinas in German Nominalism on the Eve of the Reformation* (Durham, NC: Duke University, 1988).

8. See Heiko Oberman, *The Harvest of Medieval Theology: Gabriel Biel and Late Medieval Nominalism* (Cambridge, MA: Harvard University Press, 1963).

9. William of Ockham, *Quodlibetum* 6, q. 1, a. 2, conclusion 1; *Opera Theologica*, 9:587.

vehemently that he lost balance? In sum, did he submit his Scholastic education to a sufficiently critical and thorough reformation?

John Paul's Spousal Reading

John Paul's reading of Scripture follows what he calls a "hermeneutics of the gift" (TOB 13:2), that is, a systematic interpretation of the meaning of Scripture and the human body in light of the notion of *gift*. The hermeneutics of the gift is scriptural, not only in the sense that it is applied to Scripture, but more importantly in the sense that it is derived from Scripture. John Paul explains it by two passages: Matthew 19:4–6 and Ephesians 5:31–32.

Matthew 19:4–6

> The Creator created them male and female and said, "For this reason a man will leave his father and his mother and unite with his wife, and the two shall be one flesh." So it is that they are no longer two but one flesh. Therefore, what God has joined let man not separate. (Matthew 19:4–6)
>
> For this reason, a man will leave his father and his mother and unite with his wife, and the two shall be one flesh. This mystery is great. I say this with reference to Christ and the Church. (Ephesians 5:31–32)

The teaching of Jesus in Matthew 19:4–6 is the main root of TOB. The title of the book is a slightly modified quote of it, *Man and Woman He Created Them*. The speaker in this teaching is Jesus, the *Logos* through whom all things were created (John 1:1–3). The living and personal *Logos* quotes Scripture, the written *logos* of God, and repeats the creator's words by which he institutes the sacrament of marriage, "The two shall be one flesh" (Genesis 2:24).

The phrase *and said* is easily overlooked. "The Creator created them ... and said" (Matthew 19:5). The living Word in person quotes the written word of God, which in turn reports that the Creator spoke a word of wisdom, love, and power in creating man and woman. The words "The two shall be one flesh" are usually taken to be words of the narrator. Jesus attributes them directly to the Creator. The Creator's eternal Word, the *Logos* in person, is well qualified to testify about what the Creator said in the beginning, long before any written word. The Creator said by his eternal *Logos*, "The two shall be one flesh." These words are partial reflections, precontained in the fullness of the *Logos*.

Because the living *Logos* is present in "they shall be one flesh," these words of institution are not imposed on the bodies of men and women from the outside as if their bodies were artifacts. The purpose of a car is imposed on the materials from the outside, which is the case in all artifacts. By contrast, the words "they shall be one flesh" stand at the very source of the gift of being to man and woman. The meaning of these words is already present in the gift of being. Man and woman receive this meaning in receiving being. The spousal meaning is present most deeply within their bodies as man and woman. It is present before man and woman speak that meaning in conjugal acts. The meaning does not spring first into being by human activity or intention. It shapes the human body's very nature from within.

When the meaning of the human body is consciously experienced, therefore, an act of remembrance (*anamnesis*) takes place, as Schindler rightly argues following Ratzinger, a remembrance of what is already deeply present in their being.[10] The words "they shall be one flesh," spoken by the creator in the Word by which all things are created, accomplish what they signify. "As a result (ὥστε), they are no longer two but one flesh." The final sentence draws the logical consequence. "Therefore, what God has joined let man not separate" (Matthew 19:6).

"The two shall be one flesh" are thus the words of institution of marriage as the primordial sacrament, as the first effective sign of grace, given in view of Christ's future Cross and Resurrection (see TOB 96:6). The same words are also the words of the reinstitution of marriage as a sacrament of the Church when Christ quotes them in answer to the question of divorce (see TOB 98:6–99:3). John Paul draws the reader's attention to the repetition in the words, "the Creator created."

> We should now turn anew to those fundamental words that Christ used—"created" and the subject, "Creator"—introducing into the considerations carried out so far a new dimension, a new criterion of understanding and of interpretation that we will call "hermeneutics of the gift."
>
> The dimension of gift is decisive for the essential truth and depth of the meaning of original solitude-unity-nakedness. It stands also at the heart of the mystery of creation, which allows us to build the theology of the body "from the beginning" but at the same time demands that we build it in precisely this way. (TOB 13:2)

Gift and reception do not first arise on the level of creation. They have deeper roots within God himself, even if in a different manner, not as a chosen gift that could also not be given. The Creator is in himself an eternal Trinitarian exchange of gift, reception of gift, and answering gift. "As the Father has Life in himself, so he has given to the Son to have Life in himself" (John 5:26). "That they may see the glory you have given me because you loved me before the foundation of the world" (John 17:24). From these and similar texts, John Paul con-

10. See Schindler, "The Embodied Person as Gift and the Cultural Task in America: Status Quaestionis," *Communio* 35 (2008): 397–431, at 410.

cludes, "A total gift, an uncreated gift, is shared ... by God himself in the Trinitarian communion of persons" (TOB 95b:4). "Love, an uncreated Gift, is part of the inner mystery of God and is the very nucleus of Theology."[11] Because it is the nucleus of theology, this "Love, an uncreated Gift," is also the nucleus of John Paul's hermeneutics of the gift: "we have seen his glory, a glory ... full of gift and truth" (John 1:14).

The Trinitarian God creates out of love; out of love he gives the gift of being, sees that it is "very *ṭôḇ*, very good, beautiful, pleasing," and rests on the seventh day (Genesis 1:31–2:3), "rejoicing with the truth" about the good (1 Corinthians 13:6; see TOB 13:3).

Three steps are implicit in these statements. John Paul refers to them as *the mystery of creation*: (1) God who *is love* as an eternal exchange of gift in the Trinity, (2) freely creates *out of love*, (3) *for love* as the vocation of every person (see TOB 13:4–14:1; *Familiaris consortio* 11).

In his analysis of Genesis 1–2, which focuses on original solitude, unity (one flesh), and nakedness free of shame, John Paul concludes accordingly that the original meaning of the body as willed by the Creator is *spousal.*

> Seeing each other reciprocally, as if with the sight of the very mystery of creation, the man and the woman see each other all the more fully and clearly through the sense of sight itself, that is, through the eyes of the body. They see and embrace each other, in fact, with all the peace of the interior gaze, which creates precisely the fullness of personal intimacy.... At the same time, they "communicate" based on the communion of persons in which they become a mutual gift for each other, through their femininity and masculinity.
>
> In reciprocity, they reach in this way a particular understanding of the meaning of their own bodies. The original meaning of nakedness corresponds to such a simplicity and fullness of seeing in which the understanding of the meaning of the body is born in the very heart, as it were, of their community-communion. We will call this meaning "spousal." (TOB 13:1)

Owing to its femininity and masculinity, the human body has the power to express (signify) and effect the communion of persons in the unitive and procreative bodily gift of man and woman to each other. This mutual gift is an effective sign of grace through which the Trinitarian life of Gift enters the visible world (see TOB 19:3–4).

Ephesians 5:31–32

Ephesians quotes the same words about "one flesh" (Genesis 2:24) that were spoken by the Creator at the beginning and then quoted by Christ, the *Logos*

11. Karol Wojtyła, *Sign of Contradiction* (New York: Seabury Press, 1979), 55.

himself. It uses these words to draw a connection between "one flesh" and Christ's relation with the Church. "For this reason a man will leave his father and his mother and unite with his wife, and the two shall be one flesh. This mystery is great. I say this with reference to Christ and the Church" (Ephesians 5:31–32). John Paul sees the main message of Scripture as a whole in this spousal mystery.

> Given its importance, the mystery is "great" indeed: as God's salvific plan for humanity, that mystery is in some sense the central theme of the whole of revelation, its central reality. It is what God as Creator and Father wishes above all to transmit to mankind in his Word. (TOB 93:2)

The image of the Church drawn by John Paul on the basis of his hermeneutics of the gift centered in Ephesians is thoroughly spousal.

> Our thoughts turn to the words of the Apostle Paul, who traces the Church's features in a very intense passage in the Letter to the Ephesians: "glorious, without spot or wrinkle or any such thing but holy and without blemish," loved by Christ and the model of all Christian married life (cf. Ephesians 5:25–32)....
>
> To be loved by Christ and to love him with spousal love is constitutive of the Church's mystery. At its source is a free act of love which the Father pours out through Christ and the Holy Spirit. This love forms the Church and is radiated to all creatures. In this light we can say that the Church is a sign raised among the nations to bear witness to the intensity of divine love revealed in Christ, especially in the gift he made of his own life (cf. John 10:11–15). Therefore, "all human beings—both women and men—are called through the Church to be the Bride of Christ, the Redeemer of the world."[12]

John Paul's hermeneutics of the gift is thus rooted in the divine words of institution of marriage (Genesis 2:24; Matthew 19:5), which are part of the "great mystery," the "single great sign" (TOB 95:7), in which Ephesians 5:31–32 unites marriage and the love of Christ for the Church.

The ultimate source and exemplar of this "great mystery" is the Trinity. "Love, an uncreated Gift, is part of the inner mystery of God and is the very nucleus of Theology."[13] Compare Scheeben's statement. "The Trinity of persons is the highest and most characteristic object of theology, the center and the very nucleus of Theology."[14] The same light shines through all the other areas of theology.

12. John Paul II, *General Audience*, February 7, 2001, quoting *Mulieris dignitatem* 25.

13. Wojtyła, *Sign of Contradiction*, 55.

14. Matthias Joseph Scheeben, *Die Mysterien des Christentums*, ed. Josef Höfer (Freiburg: Herder, 1958), 110; *The Mysteries of Christianity* (St. Louis, MO: Herder, 1946), 131.

When one compares Luther's and John Paul's scriptural hermeneutics, one can see two main differences. The first is that Luther sees spousal union as a sacrament only in the sense of *sign of something sacred*; namely, as pointing to the relation between Christ and the Church. John Paul, by contrast, sees marriage as a sacrament in a fuller sense of participation in Christ's life, an efficacious sign.

The main difference between John Paul and Luther, however, lies in Trinitarian theology. John Paul explicitly locates the source and exemplar of the spousal relation and of Christ's relation to the Church in the Trinity, in the eternal communion of persons in God, while Luther does not. Sections 6 and 7 of this chapter will address the question, Why not?

Despite this difference, there is much common ground between them. Both develop a spousal theology derived from Scripture to grasp the meaning of Scripture as a whole. In both, the hermeneutic principle for interpreting Scripture is itself derived from Scripture. The common ground is in this double sense Scripture alone, *sola Scriptura.*

2. Scripture Alone and Accompanied

On the basis of this first point, the agreement in spousal theology, let us analyze Luther's view at six further points: (2) *sola Scriptura*, (3) conscience and reason, (4) justification, (5) the goodness of sex, (6) zero-sum logic, and (7) the Trinity. Points two and three concern the order of knowledge, the remaining four the order of love.

Luther's most famous and dramatic words about *sola Scriptura* were spoken at the Diet of Worms (April 18, 1521).

> As your Most Sacred Majesty [Charles V] and your Lordships asked for a simple response I will answer without horns or teeth as follows. Unless I am convinced by the testimonies of the Scriptures or by clear reason (*ratione evidente*)—for I do not trust either the Pope or Councils alone, since it is a fact (*constat*) that they have often erred and contradicted themselves—I am bound by the Scriptures I have quoted, and my conscience is captive in the words of God. I cannot and will not retract anything, since it is neither safe nor upright (*integrum*) to act against conscience. [I cannot do otherwise, here I stand.] May God help me, Amen. (LW 32:112, WA 7:838)[15]

15. The sentence "I cannot do otherwise, here I stand" is not attested in the official transcript or in the early printed versions of the speech published in Wittenberg under Luther's supervision. It seems to be a later hagiographical addition.

Among all texts, Scripture alone, *sola Scriptura*, can be called the word (*logos*) of God. It stands alone as the basis of faith and theology, towering above everything else.[16]

> We believe the prophets and apostles.... But we do not believe their successors except inasmuch as they declare to us what the former left behind in writings.[17]
>
> Since the starting-points from which this teaching goes forward is what is received from the Holy Spirit's revelation and possessed (*habentur*) in the Sacred Scriptures, this is what he [Dionysius Areopagita] concludes, namely, that in no way should anyone dare to say anything ... "except what has been divinely expressed to us out of the holy sayings," that is, expressed by the holy sayings. It is significant, however, that he does not say, "in the holy sayings," but "out of the holy sayings," because whatever can be drawn from what is contained in Sacred Scripture is not foreign to this teaching, even if it itself is not [explicitly] contained in Sacred Scripture.[18]
>
> In the place of self-evident principles, this teaching has the rules and articles of faith, which are passed on in the canonical Scriptures.... Only (*sola*) what pertains to the rules of faith and is passed on in the canonical Scripture brings necessity to faith.[19]

The author of these texts is not Luther but Thomas Aquinas. Pope Benedict's address at the 2008 Scripture Synod echoes the same traditional Catholic teaching. "When Theology is not essentially the interpretation of Scripture in the Church, this Theology has no foundation anymore."[20] *Sola Scriptura* understood in this way is common ground between Thomas, Luther, and John Paul.

It is also common ground that Scripture is not absolutely alone. When a mother gives birth, one can say, *sola mater*. She alone gives birth. Yet she is not alone. A man is involved as father, a child is involved, also perhaps a doctor, a midwife, and so on. Luther knows many ways in which Scripture is not absolutely alone.

Scripture Is with the Logos in Person: As a Christian, one does not give first place to a book that stands by itself. The book is part of the bridegroom's gift of himself. Luther's primary orientation to Christ himself in person is overwhelm-

16. Jesus himself applies "Word of God" to the Old Testament (e.g., Mark 7:13; Matt 15:6) and to his own teaching (e.g., Luke 8:11; cf. Mark 1:14 and Luke 5:1). The content of the Church's living proclamation was also called "word of God." "When you received the word of God by hearing from us, you accepted it not as a word of human beings but as it truly is, the word of God" (1 Thessalonians 2:13). Once the New Testament was assembled and joined to the Old Testament, it was integrated into this organically growing whole. Together with the Old Testament, it is the only text which the tradition calls "word of God."

17. Thomas, *De veritate*, q. 14, a. 10, ad 11.

18. Thomas, *Super De divinis nominibus* 1, lect. 1, par. 11.

19. Thomas, *Lectura Romana in primum Sententiarum*, prol., q. 4, a. 3, corp.

20. Benedict XVI, *Address to the Synod of Bishops on Scripture*, October 14, 2008.

ingly clear in his writings. "By faith the soul is joined to God, for by faith the Christian soul enters into marriage with God. 'I will take you as my wife in faith' (Hos 2:20)."[21] It follows that "the Christian faith is not a 'religion of the book.' Christianity is the religion of the 'Word' of God, a word which is not a written and mute word, but the Word is incarnate and living."[22]

Scripture Is with the Tradition: The Bible of the first generations of Christians was the Old Testament alone. Luther knows this. He also knows that the New Testament canon resulted from the choice of texts to be read in parallel with the Old Testament in the eucharistic liturgy. The New Testament canon is a liturgical product. Scripture as a whole is in this way part of a more comprehensive tradition received and passed on by the Church. "Sacred Tradition and Sacred Scripture constitute one sacred deposit (*depositum*) of the Word of God entrusted to the Church" (Vatican II, *Dei verbum* 10). Scripture has a uniquely normative place within the tradition. "Everything that the inspired authors or sacred writers affirm must be regarded as affirmed by the Holy Spirit" (*Dei verbum* 11).[23] The bridegroom himself speaks through these words. "God, who spoke in times past, speaks without any interruption with the bride of his beloved Son" (*Dei verbum* 8).[24] It follows that "the Magisterium is not superior to the Word of God but is its servant" (*Dei verbum* 10). The spousal principle asserted by all three—Thomas, Luther, and John Paul—shows the deepest reasons for *sola Scriptura* in this contextualized sense of *alone.*

Scripture Is with the Church's Faith: The Church as a whole receives the bridegroom in her faith as a public community. Individual persons share in the faith of the one Church as a part of the one bride. "I am a part of his Church" (*eius Ecclesiae ego sum pars*), Luther says in his comments (quoted above) on the queen dressed in gold. Thomas agrees. "This wedding was made public when he joined the Church to himself by faith, 'I will take you as my wife in faith' (Hos 2:20)."[25] Pope Benedict's words during the Scripture Synod, quoted above, underline the same point. "When Theology is not essentially the interpretation of Scripture *in the Church*, this Theology has no foundation anymore."[26] How *part* is to be understood exactly when a person is part of a social body is thus a decisive question (see part I, chap. 7, in this volume).

Scripture Is with Reason: Another context of Scripture can be seen in Luther's appeal to *clear reason* and *conscience* at the Diet of Worms. Neither of

21. Thomas, *Super Symbolum Apostolorum*, prol.

22. *Catechism of the Catholic Church* 108, quoting Bernard of Clairvaux.

23. For a detailed discussion of this text, see Michael Maria Waldstein, "*Analogia Verbi:* The Truth of Scripture in Rudolf Bultmann and Raymond Brown," *Letter and Spirit* 6 (2010): 93–140.

24. Vatican II, *Dei verbum* 8.

25. Thomas, *Super Ioannem*, cap. 2, lect. 1, no. 338.

26. Benedict XVI, *Address to the Synod of Bishops on Scripture*, October 14, 2008; emphasis added.

these is identical with Scripture, but Luther knows that one cannot read Scripture without them.

It is not easy to reconcile Luther's appeal to reason with his famous identification of reason as the apocalyptic whore who kills all the prophets and cannot do otherwise.

> [The] Gospel teaches us what obstinate things the natural light, pride, and reason are. Where reason gets mixed up with works and with the commandments, it refuses to hear anybody.... It does no good to preach to reason: no matter how much one preaches to it, no matter how many prophets God sends to it, everything that is against reason must be persecuted and killed. John portrays her as the scarlet murderess in Revelation 17:3–5. "Her name is the great whore, Babylon; she is arrayed in a scarlet and purple robe, sits on a beast which is also scarlet and has in her hand a golden drinking vessel filled with the filth and abomination of her whoredom," that is, teachings of men wherewith she leads the pure and believing souls away from the faith and ruins them. She strangles all who resist her. (Sermon for St. Stephen's Day, LW 52:89; WA 10.1:271)

In his spousal texts, Luther emphasizes union, transformation, and participation, rooted in the power of the bridegroom's love. In this text on reason as the great whore, he seems to give little room to that transforming and unitive power of love. For the mutual gift of self to take place in fully radical self-abandonment, everything in the bride, including her reason, needs to be united to the bridegroom by his power to join all things to himself. Clear reason becomes clearer reason in this joining and transformation, not less.

The following passage from Luther's last sermon preached in Wittenberg (January 17, 1546) is angrier than the one just quoted. Yet despite its vehement attack on reason, it mentions at least a possible obedience of reason.

> The devil's bride, reason, the lovely whore, comes in and wants to be wise, and what she says, she thinks, is the Holy Spirit. Who can be of any help then? Neither jurist, physician, nor king, nor emperor; for she is the foremost whore the devil has. The other gross sins can be seen, but nobody can control reason....
>
> Reason is by essence and nature (*Art und Natur*) a harmful whore. But she shall not harm me, if only I resist her. Ah, but she is so beautiful and glittering....
>
> "Don't you hear, you mangy, leprous whore, you holy reason, what the Scripture says?" ...
>
> See to it that you hold reason in check and do not follow her beautiful thoughts. Throw shit in her face and make her ugly.[27] ...

27. The English edition of *Luther's works* translates Luther's *Dreck* as "dirt." In modern German,

> "Off to the toilet with you and your pride. Shut up, you cursed whore, do you think you are master over faith, which declares that the true body and the true blood is in the Lord's Supper, and that Baptism is not merely water but the water of the Father, the Son, and the Holy Spirit?"
>
> Reason must be subject and obedient to this faith. (LW 51:374–79; WA 51:126–33)

The final sentence, which speaks of a reason obedient to faith, conceives the relation between faith and reason still in somewhat violent terms, but it seems to contain a positive, nonviolent kernel. Without such a positive, nonviolent kernel of reason, conscience would not be able to stand as a normative principle. Luther unfolds the positivity of reason more fully in one of his *Table Talks*. He even appeals to his favorite enemy, Aristotle, to make the key point.

> Reason is subject to vanity, as all of God's creatures are subject to vanity, that is, to folly. But faith separates the vanity from the substance.... The body of a whore is just as much God's creation as the body of an honorable matron. So, vanity is to be put aside, not substance (vanitas reicienda, non substantia).... Unless the good existed, the bad cannot exist, as Aristotle said (Nam nisi bonum esset, malum esse non potest, ut Aristoteles dicit); for the bad cannot exist in itself but is destroyed in itself (nam malum non potest esse in se ipso, sed destruitur in se ipso). So, vanities exist in good substances. Reason, speech, and all gifts and created things are therefore different in believers and Christians than in unbelievers. (LW 54:183; WA *Tischreden* 3:106)

This essential goodness of reason (*logos*) and its nonviolent relation to faith is implicit in Luther's insistence on *clear arguments from reason* and *conscience* at the Diet of Worms. It is important to insist on Luther's assent to the goodness of *logos* despite his angry words about Greek philosophy elsewhere. The inviolability of conscience arises from this goodness of reason and from the claim which God's *Logos* has on it precisely as *logos*, as reason.

3. Conscience and Reason

The third point to be examined is Luther's view of conscience. Luther is right to insist that one must always follow one's conscience. Eichmann followed his conscience when he carried out Hitler's orders in organizing the extermination camps on a grand industrial scale. Following one's conscience is a necessary

---

Dreck is slang for the standard word for dirt, *Schmutz*. In Luther's older German, by contrast, *Dreck* is *excrementum*. See Philipp Dietz, *Wörterbuch zu Dr. Martin Luthers deutschen Schriften* (Leipzig: Vogel, 1870), 2:452.

condition for acting well but is not sufficient (see part II, chap. 5, sect. 4, in this volume). Conscience can be wrong. For this reason one needs to examine and form one's conscience critically and responsibly. One can fail in this task and this failure can be one's own fault. If one follows one's erroneous conscience into an act contrary to reason and God's *Logos*, if the norm in question could and should have been known, one does not escape being at fault, even when one acts in accord with one's conscience.

Are Scripture and clear reason the only lights by which one needs to form one's conscience? Luther knows that the table of contents of a Bible is not part of the word of God. The list of books that make up Scripture, which is necessary for the very existence of Scripture, is not contained anywhere in Scripture. Why precisely these and no other writings from roughly the same time?

Luther accepts the Church's judgment about the canon of the New Testament, despite his misgivings about the letter of James. St. Augustine's famous dictum is objectively true about him, whether he subjectively acknowledges it or not. "I would not believe in the Gospel, if the authority of the Catholic Church did not move me."[28] In the matter of the canon, Luther forms his conscience according to the authoritative faith of the Church, leaving aside the complex issue of the deuterocanonical writings of the Old Testament.

TOB can help to understand the dynamics of this formation of conscience. In giving himself to the Church as bridegroom, Christ enters into a union that is deeply real. It includes a reliable response of faith by which God's words are passed on. As God's word, Scripture stands above the tradition as the norm of tradition. At the same time, it is part of the tradition, formed, interpreted, and passed on within it.

By assenting to the canon of Scripture, Luther agrees in principle with Vatican II: "The Church draws its certainty about all that is revealed not through Sacred Scripture alone (*non per solam Sacram Scripturam*)."[29] This statement does not endanger *sola Scriptura*, properly contextualized, because "the Magisterium is not above the word of God but serves it."[30] Scripture alone stands above all human words. Yet Scripture is not alone.

What endangers *sola Scriptura* is not the teaching authority of the Church but its denial. One cannot sustain *sola Scriptura* together with denial of that teaching authority. If the canon of Scripture is to stand, the Church's faith about it must be a reliable guide, even though no teaching of the Church, not even its list of books in the Bible, is the word of God. The theory of a self-authenticating

28. Ego vero Evangelio non crederem, nisi me catholicae Ecclesiae commoveret auctoritas. Augustine, *Contra epistulam Manichaei quam vocant Fundamenti* 5.

29. Vatican II, *Dei verbum* 9.

30. Vatican II, *Dei verbum* 10.

word of God that shows its own warrant to each individual person separately by an inward sense of the Holy Spirit is contrary to the historical fact of the gradual development of the canon of Scripture in the early Church and its corporate, social acceptance by the Church. If the rule of the Church's faith about the canon of Scripture falls, Scripture falls as well. Does one want the Church to be replaced by King James, whose authority gives its name to the Authorized Version? Scripture comes first, as God's own word, but the teaching authority of the Church is inseparable from it.

Should such a formation of conscience apply to other questions as well, or only to the canon of Scripture? Luther's answer is clear. He accepts the Creed. SS. John Paul and Thomas agree with him that the Creed is not the word of God. Nevertheless, it is a reliable guide for reading Scripture because it expresses the bride's faith. This conclusion is consistent with Luther's spousal principle: "The supreme love of the bridegroom is for the bride, one faith, one body, and one mind."

Trust in the effectiveness of the bridegroom's gift of himself is the definitive reason for letting the Creed guide one's conscience in reading Scripture. Thomas continues the text quoted above. At least concerning the Creed, Luther holds the same view.

> The one who assents to the teaching of the Church as to an infallible rule assents to everything the Church teaches. Otherwise, if he holds whatever he wants among the teachings of the Church, and refuses to hold whatever he wishes, he no longer assents to the teaching of the Church as an infallible rule but clings to his own will.[31]

Does Luther agree with this principle only in the case of the Creed? Does he draw a line in the sand somewhere else? If so, where and why? At the end of his *Disputation against Scholastic Theology and the Pelagians*, he writes, "In these statements we wanted to say nothing, and we believe we have said nothing, that does not agree with the Catholic Church and the teachers of the Church" (LW 31:16; WA 1:228). In this early text (1517), which already contains the heart of his later elaborated theology, there is no line drawn in the sand. Almost twenty years later, Luther still says in commenting on Psalm 45, "And this I know too, that he has become the Bridegroom and has communicated to the Church, all that He has. Of his Church I am a part. Eius Ecclesiae ego sum pars" (LW 12:262; WA 4.2:559). The second sentence follows strictly from the first. It is because of Christ's spousal gift to the Church that her faith can be normative for individuals. The highest dignity and personal good of individual persons are to be parts

31. Thomas, *Summa* II-II, q. 5, a. 3, corp.

of the one bride who embraces the one bridegroom. An account of the common good is important for understanding this dignity and personal good (see part I, chap. 7, in this volume).

4. Justification

The fourth point to be examined is Luther's understanding of justification by faith, which he considers decisive for breaking communion. Luther has a deep grasp of the *communio sanctorum*. In his *Sermons on John*, he comments on "one as we are one" (John 17:11.20–23), the text on which *Gaudium et spes* 24 is based.

> It clearly says, *ut sint unum, una res*, that they may be one, one thing, which in Latin or Greek is not a usual way of speaking about mere equality or agreement.... We must, therefore, translate it in this way, as we say, "One thing or one body and loaf (*kuche*)." I say this, so that we do not allow this text to be overturned or weakened by such inventions of reason and unsuitable philosophy. For, there is a mighty great consolation in this ... that we are all members of one single body as one flesh and blood.
>
> And we have the benefit that what concerns one member concerns all, which does not necessarily happen in mere equality and agreement. For even if many have one intention and will, one is not concerned for the other as in one body. Due to this oneness, Christendom (*die Christenheit*) is called the communion of saints, *Communio sanctorum*. (LW 69:77–78, WA 28:149)

> How could anyone wish anything more blessed than to be able to enter into this communion or fraternity to become a member of this body, which is called Christendom. She [*Christendom* is feminine in German] is a body to which God has given himself as her own with all his goods. In sum, she is a mighty woman and empress in heaven and on earth.... For God linked everything he has with the Lord Christ but Christ with his bride, and so every Christian is linked to the same bride as a member, and everything is linked into each other as one chain and makes an entirely round circle, indeed a lovely and beautiful wreath, *ja einen lieblichen schönen krantz*. (LW 69:104–6; WA 28:182–84)

When one meditates Luther's spousal texts and shares his love for the bride, it is difficult to read texts in which he lets his anger burn freely and fiercely, apparently without solidarity with the sinful bride. When he received news of the Council of Trent, he wrote a little tract, *Against the Roman Papacy: An Institution of the Devil*, of which the following quote is a fair sample.

> We should take him—the Pope, the cardinals, and whatever riffraff belongs to his Idolatrous and Papal Holiness—and, as blasphemers, rip out their tongues from the back of their throats, and nail them on the gallows in a row, just as they hang their seals on official documents in a row, even though everything of this sort is mild compared to their blasphemy and idolatry. After that one could allow them to hold a council, or as many as they wanted, on the gallows, or in hell among all the devils. (LW 41:308; WA 54:243)

Luther even takes joy in such flames of anger and congratulates the pope and bishops for their evil because it stirs up a mighty and infectious anger that assures him of victory over them. The following text from his tract *The Councils and the Church* begins with three or four words of humility, but anger takes the lead right after them.

> We poor, weak Christians, who must endure being dubbed heretics by such saints, ought to be happy and of good cheer. We ought to praise and thank God, the Father of all mercy, with great joy for taking such heartfelt care of us and for smiting our murderers and bloodhounds with such Egyptian blindness and such Jewish madness that they are determined to yield on no point and to let Christendom perish rather than to allow the most trifling idolatry, with which they are stuffed full and overfull, to be reformed. Of this they boast, and this they do.
>
> Cheerful, I say, we ought to be; for thus they make our case better than we could ever have desired and make theirs worse than they now might think. They know and admit that they are wrong on many points and on top of it they have Scripture and God against them, and yet they want to butt their heads against God, and knowingly defend wrong as right....
>
> So, since the Pope, with his following, simply refuses to convoke a council and reform the church, or offer any advice or assistance toward that end but boastfully defends his tyranny with crimes, preferring to let the church go to ruin, we, who have been so shamefully forsaken by the Pope, cannot go on but must seek counsel and help elsewhere.
>
> First of all, we must seek and ask our Lord Jesus Christ for a reformation. These desperate tyrants, whose evil forces us to despair of a council and of a reformation, must not drive us also to despair of Christ or to leave the church without counsel and help; we must instead do what we can, and let them go to the devil as they wish. (LW 41.10; WA 54:511–12)

An intense flame of anger meets the reader in these texts. Luther had reasons for anger, certainly. The corruption of parts of the early Renaissance Church was acute. But it is also an acute corruption to cultivate anger, cheering with triumph about corruption, offering prayers of joyful gratitude to God for it because it inflames anger, which is effective in battle. Anger and hatred, of course, were mutual in the conflict.

There are at least two sides to Luther. There is the Luther of the spousal texts and their hermeneutics of the gift. He understands and follows the spousal logic of Christ's gift of self to the Church and understands himself as part of the bride, of the queen arrayed in gold, of which he is a member. And there is the Luther consumed by an anti-spousal and individualistic logic of anger, which can be heard already in his words at the Diet of Worms. It gives a new meaning, a narrower and polemical one, to the traditional truth *sola Scriptura*.

The first Luther shows the theological foundation of an ecclesial reading of Scripture and the right way of understanding *sola Scriptura*. He is not far from St. John Paul's ecclesial hermeneutics of the gift, in which Scripture is part of Christ's spousal gift of himself to the Church.

Luther did not foresee that his hope of establishing the unity of the Church on Scripture alone would be dashed. He did not intend his reformation to be splintered into denominations, not a good testimony to the authority of Scripture.[32] Had he foreseen this result, he might well have ended up closer to John Paul's words.

> [Let us] not entertain the individualist illusion leading to the belief that one can better understand the biblical texts outside the community of believers. The contrary is true, for these texts ... have been entrusted to the community of believers, to the Church of Christ, to nourish faith and guide the life of charity.
>
> Respect for this purpose conditions the validity of the interpretation.... Far from hampering biblical research, respect for this fact fosters its authentic progress. It is comforting to note that recent studies in hermeneutical philosophy have confirmed this point of view and that exegetes of various confessions have worked from similar perspectives by stressing, for example, the need to interpret each biblical text as a part of the scriptural canon recognized by the Church, or by being more attentive to the contributions of patristic exegesis.[33]

Justification is the all-decisive issue for Luther in breaking communion. On this article of faith, he holds, the Church stands or falls. "As long as this teaching stands, the church stands; when it falls, she herself falls too" Stante enim hac doctrina stat Ecclesia, ruente autem ruit ipsa quoque (WA 40.3.351). "On this

32. These and other unintended consequences are described by Brad S. Gregory, *The Unintended Reformation: How a Religious Revolution Secularized Society* (Cambridge, MA: Harvard University, 2012). Particularly illuminating is the last chapter, which explains the background of contemporary academic life.

33. John Paul II, *Address to the Pontifical Biblical Commission*, April 23, 1993.

article stands everything we teach and live against the Pope, the devil, and the world (*Smalcald Articles*, 2.1; WA 50.199–200).

When Luther measures the Church's tradition by his judgment about justification, he finds that it has abandoned the very heart of Scripture: justification by grace alone (*sola gratia*), through faith alone (*sola fide*), relying on Christ alone (*solum Christum*) without any works of the law (*sine operibus*).

What are the points of agreement and disagreement about this article in the perspective of TOB? Justification occurs *sola Scriptura*, in accord with Scripture alone, BUT Scripture read within the community of believers with a living and continuous history from Jesus to the present and an authoritative corporate judgment by the *sensus fidei* of all members and the apostolic teaching office. It occurs *sola fide*, by faith alone, BUT by a faith that grasps and appropriates the gift of justification out of love. It grasps *solum Christum*, Christ alone, BUT a Christ who gives his bride a true and real share in his being and activity. Justification is a sheer gift without preceding works, *sola gratia*, BUT a grace that is truly a gift and therefore posits a good that is real in the creature as a "new creation" (2 Corinthians 5:17).[34]

The deepest point of agreement is the understanding of justification within a comprehensive spousal logic of total mutual gift.

> Faith produces four goods. The first is that by faith the soul is joined to God, for by faith the Christian soul contracts a certain marriage, as it were, with God. "I will take you as my wife in faith" (Hos 2:20).[35]

Faith is the foundation of all spiritual goods because it brings us into spousal union with Christ.

> Faith is the foundation of all spiritual goods, as the Apostle says, "Faith is the substance (foundation) of things to be hoped for" (Hebrews 11:1). Faith is also that by which the soul is given life through grace, according to the words of the Apostle, "The life I live now in the flesh I life in the faith of the Son of God" (Galatians 2:20); and Habakkuk, "The just shall live on account of his faith" (Habakkuk 2:4). Faith is that by which the soul is cleansed of sin. "They purify their hearts through faith" (Acts 15:9). Faith is that by which the soul is adorned with justice. "The justice of God, however, is through the faith of Jesus Christ" (Romans 3:22). Faith is that through which the soul is united in marriage to God, "I will take you as my wife in faith" (Hosea 2:20).[36]

34. See Thomas, *Summa* I-II, q. 113.
35. Thomas, *In Symbolum Apostolorum*, prol.
36. Thomas, *Super Decretales*, no. 1.

In agreement with Luther, not only the individual but also the Church is the bride who receives this spousal gift. "This wedding was publicly celebrated when he joined the Church to himself by faith, I will take you as my wife in faith" (Hosea 2:20).[37] Agreement about the essential role of love would seem to follow from agreement on this spousal logic of justification. Thomas writes,

> The soul lives the life of grace through God. *First, God dwells in the soul through faith:* "That Christ may dwell in your hearts through faith" (Ephesians 3:17); but this indwelling is not complete, unless faith is formed by love, which by "the bond of perfection" unites us to God, as Colossians 3:14 says. Consequently, "lives by faith" must be understood of formed faith.[38]

Luther, by contrast, denies that love plays any role in justification. In a striking text in his *Lectures on Galatians* about the wedding night of justifying faith, he compares the bride's love for the bridegroom to one of the family members and servants who must leave the bedroom before bride and bridegroom consummate their union. Faith alone, not love, can remain in lovemaking.

> When we are involved in a discussion of justification, there is no room for speaking about the Law. The question is what Christ is and what blessing he has brought us. Christ is not the law; he is not my work or that of the law; *he is not my love* or that of the law; he is ... the Redeemer of those who are under the law. By faith we are in him, and he is in us (John 6:56).
>
> This bridegroom, Christ, must be alone with his bride in his bed chamber (*solum cum sponsa in sua quiete*), and all the family and household must be shunted away. But later on, when the bridegroom opens the door and comes out, then let the servants return to take care of them and serve them food and drink. *There and then works and love begin, ibi tum incipiunt opera et charitas.* (LW 26.137; WA 40.1:240–41; emphasis added)

The consummation of spousal union is a deeply traditional image of justification. It is also a deeply traditional teaching that this union takes place in faith. The novelty in Luther is that he excludes love from this union. The bridegroom chases away the bride's love before he takes her into his arms in a union of faith alone. He allows her love to enter only after their lovemaking is completed and only as a servant who serves food and drink to the joyful couple. The final sentence makes the point clear: "There and then works and love begin." Love begins when the lovemaking of faith has been completed.

One might suppose that Luther means *love* in the sense of outward works of love, such as generosity toward the poor. Love performs the service of offering

37. Thomas, *Super Ioannem*, cap. 2, lect. 1, no. 338.
38. Thomas, *Super ad Romanos* 1, lect. 5, no. 108; emphasis added.

the couple food and drink. Outward works come after the union with Christ, after justification. They are not part of it. By contrast, the inner act of love for Christ, it would seem, is present as part of God's gift of justification. Otherwise, the union could hardly be described as spousal lovemaking. Luther, nevertheless, excludes the bride's inner act of love from justification.

> Do not let yourself be swayed here by the wicked gloss of the sophists [Scholastics], who say that faith justifies only when love ... [is] added to it. With this pernicious gloss they have darkened and distorted some of the finest texts....
>
> If faith does not justify without love, then faith is vain and useless, and love alone justifies; or unless faith is formed and adorned by love, it is nothing.... This gloss is to be avoided as a hellish poison, and we must conclude with Paul: By faith alone, not by faith formed by love, are we justified.
>
> We must not attribute the power of justifying to a "form" that makes a man pleasing to God; we must attribute it to faith, which takes hold of Christ the Savior Himself and possesses Him in the heart. *This faith justifies without love and before love. Haec fides sine et ante charitatem iustificat.* (LW 26.136–37; WA 40.1:239–40; emphasis added)

It is impossible to suppose that Luther thinks of spousal union as taking place without love and before love. His spousal texts clearly and powerfully express the bodily speech of love in the total mutual gift of self. Let us return to the text from *Estate of Marriage*, the first of the four texts quoted above.

> Married love, that is, spousal love, burns like fire and seeks nothing but the spouse. It says, "I do not want what is yours; I want neither your silver nor your gold, neither this nor that; I want to have you yourself; I want to have you totally or nothing." All other loves seek something other than the beloved: this one alone wants to have the beloved's own self totally....
>
> This is truly, Paul says, a great sacrament, that is, the married state signifies something truly great. Is it not something great that God is made man, that he gives himself to be man's own and wants to be his, just as the man gives himself to the woman and is hers? But if God is ours, then everything is ours. (LW 44:9–10; WA 2:167–68)

Luther expresses the heart of his theology in this passage. Yet he agrees less deeply and consistently with that heart than John Paul and Thomas do. Melanchthon's later systematic reduction of Lutheran doctrine to forensic justification alone, to acquittal of the sinner by a divine judicial decree (such a decree is certainly part of the truth), fails to do justice to the full and authentic Luther and his spousal theology.

At least on the bridegroom's side, love is present, and it is essential. Luther is clear on this point. When the bridegroom takes the bride's body to become one flesh with her, and takes her sins on himself, this *taking*, as Luther himself understands it, is a deeply real participation in her sins, far beyond any counterfactual forensic judgment. Christ's suffering is real because he loves his bride and takes what belongs to his bride as his own. On this point, there is agreement between him and Thomas, who writes about Christ's suffering in a passage to be analyzed in Part II, chapter 3, section 4, which discusses Dostoevsky's and Scheler's understanding of solidarity.

> Christ's suffering was the greatest suffering of all ... because the cause of interior pain was all the sins of the human race, for which he satisfied by suffering. This is why *he ascribed them to himself, as it were* (*quasi*), by quoting the Psalm, "[My God, my God ... why have you forsaken me? Far from my salvation are] the words of my crimes" (Ps 22:1, Vulgate).[39]

Christ can say "my crimes" even though he is innocent. In his love as bridegroom, he identifies himself with his bride, not in the sense of mistaken identity, even less in the sense of becoming a sinner himself but by the mysterious union that is an effect of love. Only in this way—that is, *quasi*—does he ascribe her sins to himself. One wishes for *Quaestiones disputatae de quasi* from Thomas's pen. Conversely, Luther sees the bride's taking of the body of the bridegroom as a real participation and transformation of the bride, who is cleansed and enriched by Christ's gift of himself.

What is it, then, that compels him, despite his affirmation of these truths, to allow only the bride's faith in the bridal chamber? What is it that compels him to exclude her love?

He seems to fear that love, which is clearly a human act, will compete with the exclusive divine causality. It will introduce works of the law into the very heart of justification. He sees no escape from the dilemma. Either the bride will boast about her own love as a work of the law, or she will consume herself in an agony of conscience, uncertain whether she loves her spouse sufficiently, uncertain whether she will escape damnation. The only solution is the denial that love plays any role in justification. In his *Lectures on Galatians*, Luther sees a strange competition between Christ and love.

> If love is the form of faith, then I am immediately obliged to say that love is the most important and the largest part in the Christian religion. And so, I lose Christ, his blood, his wounds, and all his blessings, and *I cling to love, so that I love, and I come to a moral kind of "doing," just as the Pope*, a heathen philosopher, and the Turk do. (LW 26:268; WA 40:422–23; emphasis added)
>
> What the Scholastics have taught about justifying faith "formed by love"

39. Thomas, *Summa* III, q. 46, a. 6, corp.; emphasis added.

> is an empty dream. For the faith that takes hold of Christ, the Son of God, and is adorned by Him is the faith that justifies, *not a faith that includes love*. For if faith is to be certain and firm, *it must take hold of nothing but Christ alone*; and in the agony and terror of conscience it has nothing else to lean on than this pearl of great value (Matthew 13:45–46). . . . Our opponents fail to understand this. Therefore, they reject Christ, this jewel; and *in His place they put their love, which they say is a jewel*. If they do not know, however, what faith is, it is impossible for them to have faith, much less to teach it to others; and as for what they claim to have, this is nothing but a dream, an opinion, and natural reason but not faith. (LW 26:88, WA 40.1:165; emphasis added)

The primacy of faith is not destroyed by the insistence on love. It is precisely as faith, not as love, that faith grasps justification and can therefore be called God's first gift to the sinner. It is by faith that justification is ratified and appropriated as one's own. Faith is not replaced by love. Justification is not appropriated by the merit of love but by the assent of faith.

Steven Chester criticizes my interpretation of Luther on the grounds that I do not see justification clearly enough as an apocalyptic event that breaks into our world. The absolute primacy of initiative belongs to God. No upward movement toward God by the creature is presupposed to God's act and its effect in us. Love of God and of neighbor, Chester goes on to argue, is an act performed by us that pleases God. Nothing done by us, he insists, no act of love performed by us and ascribed to us, can bring about union with Christ and achieve justification.

> It is precisely this apocalyptic context of Luther's use of marital imagery for justification, with its insistence that the believer's love flows from union with Christ rather than constituting part of its basis, that goes unrecognized by Michael Waldstein. Waldstein sees Luther's use of marital imagery for justification as inconsistent with his rejection of faith formed by love, arguing that such marital imagery ought to imply a role for love in justification: "Does not the . . . primary meaning of spousal love lie precisely in taking hold of the beloved?"[40]

I agree with Chester's main point. A divine initiative breaks into our world *without our doing* and as *the source of our doing*. Love *begins* on God's side and *creates* love on our side. "There is only love *before marriage* on the divine side of

40. Steven Chester, "Apocalyptic Union: Martin Luther's Account of Faith in Christ," in *"In Christ" in Paul: Explorations in Paul's Theology of Union and Participation*, ed. Michael J. Thate, Kevin J. Vanhoozer, and Constantine R. Campbell (Tübingen: Mohr Siebeck, 2014), 375–98, at 390n55, quoting Michael Waldstein, "The Trinitarian, Spousal, and Ecclesial Logic of Justification," in *Reading Romans with St. Thomas Aquinas*, ed. Matthew Levering and Michael Dauphinais (Washington, DC: Catholic University of America Press, 2012), 274–87, at 284.

the relationship. For the believer, love results from being united with Christ."[41] The claim is not that love is an ascent by us to God to bring God down to us by our own merit but that love is an effect of God's descent to us; not an embrace that brings Christ near but an embrace in which he warms what *before the marriage* was cold. The effect of the apocalyptic event can hardly be called marital union, if love is excluded from that effect.

When one admits love as part of the effect, one is not thereby forced to give up the primacy of faith as Luther fears. The summary of the Gospel in Romans 5:24–25 remains standing. "Justified as a gift [or gratuitously, δωρεὰν] by his grace through the redemption in Christ Jesus, whom God put forward as atonement through faith in his blood," or as some interpretations prefer, "atonement by his blood received in faith." Thomas affirms this primacy of faith.

> "The justice of God" is "*by the faith of Jesus Christ*" (Romans 3:22), not as if by faith we merited to be justified, as if faith existed from us and by it we merited God's justice, as the Pelagians said, but because in the very justification by which we are justified by God, the first movement of the mind into God is by faith. "The one who approaches God must believe" (Hebrews 11:6)....[The Apostle] indicates *how the effect of redemption reached us*, when he says, *by faith in his blood* (Romans 3:24).... "Christ died for sins once for all" (1 Peter 3:18). This death of Christ is *applied to us through faith*, by which we believe that the world has been redeemed by His death: "I live by faith in the Son of God, who loved me and gave himself for me" (Galatians 2:20). For even among men, payment made by one *does not benefit another, unless he ratifies it.*[42]

There is agreement that justification is "by the faith of Jesus ... by faith in his blood ... by faith without works of the law" (Romans 3:22, 3:24, 3:28). If faith is not formed by love, it cannot be assent to the Gospel as good news. It can only be a grudging assent to hated news. In marital terms, it can only be grudging submission to an embrace one hates, an embrace one experiences as violent. Clearly, Luther does not hold that faith is such a grudging submission.

Why, then, does he think that one overturns the Gospel if one insists on formed faith? Reflecting on zero-sum logic offers some help as one wrestles with this question. According to zero-sum logic, whatever is added to one side is taken away from the other. Whatever one attributes to God must be taken away from the creature and vice versa. Zero-sum logic is relentlessly competitive. Noncompetitive would mean that God causes us to act in such a way that our acting is truly and responsibly ours, not ours as opposed to God's. It is a gift received. "What do you have that you have not received?" (1 Corinthians 4:7).

41. Chester, "Apocalyptic Union," 390; emphasis added.

42. Thomas, *Super ad Romanos* 8, lectio 3, no. 302 and 309; emphasis added.

Not all modes of God's causality can be understood as noncompetitive. Some modes, such as creating and redeeming, belong to God alone, never to the creature. Faith and love, by contrast, are our own acts received as gifts in such a way that they are truly our acts.

What would happen if one applied zero-sum logic even to such acts? If one excludes love because it is a human act, should one exclude faith as well? Or should one say that faith is not a human act? Why see competition with the apocalyptic event in the case of love but not in the case of faith?

The inner meaning of believing is receiving the Word of the Gospel, assenting to it, ratifying it, and appropriating it. If one focuses only on this inner meaning of the act of faith, one might think one has escaped the problem of competition between human and divine agency. One might think that one has finally found a way to give all glory to God and take all glory away from the creature. Yet if one denies that faith is a human act, one also denies this meaning of faith. In a noncompetitive understanding of divine causality, there is no need to bring human agency as close to zero as possible. "If anyone is in Christ, there is a new creation, καινὴ κτίσις" (2 Corinthians 5:17). One is not first in Christ and then a new creation. God's justifying act is itself creative. It is prior to its effect in the order of causality, but among its effects there are genuine human acts for which we are responsible. St. Augustine lucidly explains this point.

> Without your will, the justice of God will not be in you. The will is your own; justice is God's own. God's justice can exist without your will, but it cannot exist in you apart from your will. … You will be the work of God, not only in being human but in being just. … God made you without you. For you did not consent to his making you. How could you have consented, since you did not exist? Yet, he who made you without you does not justify you without you. He made one who was unknowing; he justifies one who is willing.[43]

Lewis Ayres puts his finger on the import of the statement "he justifies one who is willing." Augustine does not say that the assent of faith, our acceptance of Christ as savior, is a human act independent of God's justifying act. It is the effect of God's justifying act.

> The hardest thing for the modern reader to grasp in the account … is how Augustine thinks that grace and human freedom intertwine. … Here we find what I want to highlight as one of the fundamental principles of Augustine's theology of grace: our willing, our delight in appropriate objects of desire, is given us in grace. Grace should be understood as the gift of what is most deeply our own, our own true will. … All that we have we should now receive as

43. Augustine, *Sermo* 169, 13.

> divine gift, even what is most our own. Augustine is able to use this principle as a hermeneutical key to the whole of the Pauline corpus.[44]

Luther implicitly follows Augustine's account when he exhorts his listeners to seize Christ by faith. Exhortation would be pointless if faith were not a human act of consent. Although it is a human act of seizing Christ, faith is God's gift and not an achievement of the creature that gives the creature any grounds for boasting. The same point applies to love. Sections six (zero-sum logic) and seven (Trinity) will pursue these issues further.

5. The Goodness of Sex

The fifth point to be examined is the goodness of sex. Forcefully negative judgments about sex are frequent in Luther's writings. They have had a broad impact on Western culture, particularly through Puritanism. St. Augustine is often blamed for bringing such negative judgments about sex into Christianity as a remnant of his long adherence to the Manichaean condemnation of sex as diabolical. Yet he clearly says that sex can be good, if it is shaped by love for one's spouse and love for the three goods of marriage: faithful union, children, and sacrament. "Because of all these [three goods], marriage is honorable in all things, and the marriage bed is unstained (*immaculatus*)."[45] Augustine uses the indicative rather than the imperative in this application of Hebrews 13:4. The original Greek has no verb: Τίμιος ὁ γάμος ἐν πᾶσιν καὶ ἡ κοίτη ἀμίαντος. The context makes clear that an imperative is meant. Augustine, who is doubtless aware of this context, transforms the imperative into a statement of fact. The order of the goods of marriage, when it is embraced by husband and wife, allows marriage, as a matter of fact, to be honorable.[46] Luther charges that the pope hates marriage and dirties himself with acts of lust.

> All false religion is dirtied by acts of lust (*Omnis religio falsa contaminata est libidinibus*). Just keep an eye on the dick.[47] What were pilgrimages except be-

44. Lewis Ayres, "Augustine," in *The Blackwell Companion to Paul*, ed. Stephen Westerholm (Malden, MA: Wiley-Blackwell, 2011), 345–60, at 350–351. See John A. Kincaid, "New Covenant Justification by Cardiac Righteousness: An Augustinian Perspective on Pauline Justification," *Letter and Spirit* 12 (1917): 37–58, at 41.

45. Augustine, *De gratia Christi et de peccato originali* 2:39. Augustine's account of the shame connected with sex is not a counterargument against this clear text. He explains shame by concupiscence as an inherited lack of integration, not in the sense of personal sin. See Augustine, *De civitate dei* 14:18.

46. But see Thomas, *Summa* III, q. 27, a. 2, ad 4; III, q. 28, a.1, corp., third reason.

47. "An eye on the dick," i.e., the penis. The English translation in LW 54:422 is less graphic, "an eye on sex." The manuscript as described in the Weimar edition (*Tischreden* 5:151n2) has only a vertical

> ing able to get together? What does the Pope do now but dirty himself with lust without pausing (*se libidinibus contaminet indesinenter*)? To suit their pilgrimages, people looked for well-situated places, beautiful fountains, trees, hills, and rivers, to fill themselves up with lust (*libido*). The heathen held marriage in more honor than the Pope and the Turk. The Pope hates it. (*Table Talk* 5435; WA *Tischreden* 5:151)

The charge would be difficult to sustain against John Paul, Benedict, or Francis. What is clear, at any rate, is that Luther's relation to sex is filled with tensions. Guilt about sexual thoughts imposed on him by the negative Papist judgment about sex, he says in his *Lectures on Genesis*, pushed him to enter religious life and become a celibate.

> When I was a boy, the wicked and impure practice of celibacy had made marriage so disreputable (*infames*) that I believed I could not even think about the life of married people without committing a sin. Everybody was fully convinced that anyone who intended to lead a holy life acceptable to God could not get married but had to live as a celibate and take the vow of celibacy. (LW 1:135; WA 42:101)

Luther's charge that the vow of celibacy disparages sex leads one to suppose that he himself affirms the goodness of sex in marriage. Augustine affirms this goodness when he calls the marriage bed unstained. Luther's spousal texts show that he has a deep grasp of the goodness of the mutual gift of self in sex. "All other loves seek something other than the beloved: this one alone wants to have the beloved's own self totally" (LW 44:9–10; WA 2:167–68). Nevertheless, he holds that a poison inescapably corrupts the conjugal act at its deepest point. One can appreciate the depth of this point when one reflects about one of Luther's arguments for the virgin birth. If Jesus had been conceived in the normal human way, that is, if Joseph and Mary had experienced sexual pleasure, this pleasure would have stained Jesus so horribly that he would have been conceived as a child of wrath like everyone else.

> [Scripture teaches] that she is his true natural mother and nevertheless conceived and bore supernaturally, by God, without a man, in order that her child may be a different man without sin yet having ordinary flesh and blood like other men.
>
> This could not have happened if he had been begotten by a man like other men, because the flesh is scorched and corrupted by evil *libido*, so that its natural act of begetting cannot occur without sin, and whatever receives seed and

---

stroke, which the editors take to be a phallic symbol, standing for some strong colloquial word for penis in either Latin or German.

> conceives through an act of the flesh produces also a carnal and sinful fruit. This is why St. Paul says in Ephesians 2:3 that we are all by nature children of wrath. (*That Jesus Was Born as a Jew*, LW 45:202; WA 11:317)

Sex "cannot occur without sin." "There came that poison of the Devil, the itch of the flesh and foul *libido*" accessit illud venenum Diaboli, pruritus carnis et foeda libido (LW 1:135; WA 42:101). The contrast with Thomas Aquinas's understanding of original sin is striking. Thomas holds that original sin is not passed on by lust in the act of begetting, but by the coming to be of a person as a member of the human race, in the same way that original justice was to be passed on.

> Human beings can be viewed in two ways: in one way as individual persons, in another as parts of a social whole (*collegium*). In both ways, an act can belong (*pertinere*) to them. As individual persons, the acts they perform by their own choice (*arbitrio*) and through themselves belong to them. Yet, inasmuch as they are parts of a social whole, acts can belong to them which they do not perform through themselves nor by their own choice. They are performed by the whole or by the ruler of the whole. What the ruler of a city does, we say, the city does. . . .
>
> Such a social whole made up of human beings can be seen (*reputatur*) as one human being, as it were (*quasi*), so that different people to whom different tasks are given are, as it were, different members in a natural body, as Paul says about the members of the Church (1 Corinthians 12:12). In this way, the whole multitude of human beings, considered as recipients of human nature from the first parent, are, as it were, one social whole (*collegium*). . . .
>
> At his creation, the first man received a supernatural gift, namely original justice. . . . This gift was not given to the first man only as an individual person but as the origin of the whole human nature, so that it would flow from him by origin to those after him. When the first man sinned by his free will, he lost the gift in the very sense in which it was given to him, namely, for him and for his whole posterity. For this reason, this defect is passed on from him to those after him in the very way in which human nature is passed on.[48]

The logic of original sin is the same as the logic of original justice would have been. The thesis of the essential sinfulness of sex, which Luther angrily castigates as one of the Papacy's errors, is a thesis he himself holds in disagreement with the Catholic mainstream. Without any doubt, Luther is a strong champion

48. Thomas, *De Malo*, 4.1, corp. This is Augustine's account as well, though there is some debate about the role of sexual *libido* in the child's immediate parents. For an overview of the debate, and arguments that Augustine's view differs from Luther's, see Paul Rigby, "Original Sin," in *Augustine Through the Ages: An Encyclopedia*, ed. Allan Fitzgerald (Grand Rapids, MI: Eerdmans, 1999), 607–14, at 608–9.

of marriage as a divine institution, but he is an equally strong champion of the sinfulness of all sexual acts in marriage. How can he be both?

Passages that express Luther's grasp of the beauty of spousal love often stand immediately next to sharply negative passages. Let us return to the passage from *Estate of Marriage* quoted above to see its continuation.

> All other loves seek something other than the beloved: this one alone wants to have the beloved's own self totally.... Is it not a wonderful thing that God is made man and that he gives himself to man and will be his, just as the husband gives himself to his wife and is hers? But if God is ours, then everything is ours. Consider this matter with the honor it deserves. Because the union of man and woman signifies such a great mystery, the estate of marriage must have this special significance. *This means that the wicked lust of the flesh, which nobody is without, is a conjugal obligation* and is not reprehensible when carried out within marriage, but in all other cases outside the bond of marriage, it is mortal sin. In a similar way, the holy manhood of God covers the disgrace of the wicked lust of the flesh. (LW 44:9–10; WA 2:167–68; emphasis added)

The wicked lust of the flesh a conjugal obligation? How could it be an obligation? Or is it a mistake even to raise this question? Is it a question in which reason strives for consistency where no consistency is to be found? Is moral good and evil simply determined by the will of God? Is sex in marriage not reprehensible simply because God decrees it is not, while in fact it is? There are passages in Ockham that go in this direction.

> Every will can conform itself to the divine command. But God can command the created will to hate him. Therefore, the created will can do this. Further, everything that is right during our pilgrimage (*in via*) is also right in heaven (*in patria*) but hating God can be a right act *in via*, therefore also *in patria*.[49]
>
> God cannot be bound (*obligari*) to any act, and therefore by the very fact that God wills this (*eo ipso quod Deus vult hoc*) it is right for it to be done (*iustum est fieri*).... Therefore, if God caused hatred in someone's will as the complete cause, as he always causes as a partial cause, neither [God nor the creature] would sin. God would not, because he is bound to nothing (*ad nihil obligatur*), nor the other, because that act would not be in his power.[50]

Leaving aside the voluntarism expressed in Luther's arguments, let us focus on the rejection of what is fleshly. Augustine is often accused of exaggerated spiritualizing sentiments that played a disastrous role among many Christians.

49. Ockham, *Reportatio* IV, *Opera Theologica*, 7:352.
50. Ockham, *Reportatio* IV, 7:198.

Yet he vigorously rejects spiritualizing as fleshly in the Pauline sense. "Anyone who praises the soul as the highest good, and accuses the nature of flesh as evil, is fleshly in wanting soul and fleshly in fleeing from flesh."[51]

Luther understands this metaphorical use of *flesh* and *fleshly* in Paul as Augustine does. He is not derailed by false spiritualizing. Nevertheless, he holds that flesh remains corrupt even in a holy marriage. Already in his *Lectures on Romans* (1515–16) he embraces the thesis that we are at the same time sinners and just.

> The saints are just at the same time that they are sinners; just because they believe in Christ, and his justice covers them and is imputed to them (*eos tegit et eis imputatur*) but sinners because they do not fulfill the law. (LW 25:336; WA 56:347)
>
> Simultaneously sinner and just *simul peccator et Iustus*. A sinner by true reality, *peccator re vera*, but just by reputation and by reliable promise from God *sed Iustus ex reputatione et promissione Dei certa*. (LW 25:260; WA 56:272)

Given this dialectic, Luther can say that wicked lust of the flesh is a conjugal obligation. Wicked lust is part of the divinely instituted state of marriage. To be married is to live in sin. It is to live in sanctioned sin but still in sin.

> Blessed are those who are pleased with marriage. Although it is a sin as far as the act itself is concerned, that is, having unchaste intercourse with a woman or deflowering a virgin, and is natural and human, because man is corrupted by original sin, still, to believe that God has instituted marriage, this is an article of faith. (*Table Talk*, 6929; WA *Tischreden*, 6:275)

The only difference between the *libido* of extramarital sex and the *libido* of the conjugal act of Christians is that in the latter case the defilement of sexual pleasure is covered by the snow-white purity of Christ. It remains the same defilement beneath. The spouses themselves cannot reach purity. The sheet of Christ covering the marriage bed may be white, but under the sheet there is diabolical blackness.

> By the purity that we have in spirit and faith from Christ and from the Sacraments that he instituted, the Christian is rightly said to be purer than snow, purer than the sun and the stars, even though the defilements (*inquinamenta*) of spirit and flesh cling to him. These are covered and buried under (*tecta et obruta*) by the cleanness and purity of Christ, which we obtain by hearing the Word and by faith.
>
> We should note carefully that this purity is an alien purity (*aliena puritas*), for Christ adorns and clothes us with his justice.

51. Animam carnaliter appetit et carnem carnaliter fugit. Augustine, *De civitate dei* 14.5.

> If you look at a Christian without the justice and purity of Christ, as he is in himself, even though he is most holy, you will find not only no purity but—I would say—diabolical blackness, *diabolicam nigredinem*. (LW 12:366–67; WA 40.2:407)

It seems right to conclude with Balthasar that Luther reduces human *eros* to the form it has in Dante's hell, where it lacks any inner ordering to the divine good, any transparence to the divine glory.

> Nothing can happen in Dante's Hell because what is absent is love, which—as Dante, the ancients, Augustine, and Thomas understand it—moves all things from within.... No matter how much feeling and imaginative power Dante imparts to the dramatization of the scenes, they take place entirely within the powerful grip of damnation and second death; from the existential point of view, they demonstrate total meaninglessness....
>
> This affirmation becomes fundamental for subsequent ages. For Luther and thorough-going Protestantism, as well as for Jansenism, the sinful world in its entirety is removed from the light of divine *Eros* and has fallen into a state of all-enncompassing damnation.... Here then [i.e., in Luther and Jansenism] Dante's infernal confines are generalized; they have become the limits of the world itself. Within them, of course, there may well be all the degrees of value, of true and false, good and evil, beautiful and ugly, and so on. None of these, however, is absolute as in ancient philosophy because none is animated by the *Eros* of divine truth. In damnation, philosophy is an impossibility. Within its confines, there are only dead items, only material, only facts. Even philosophical thought itself becomes "fact," a filing cabinet for facts....
>
> As a consequence, theology is deprived of the world because it is deprived of an authentic relation to the transcendence of human reason.[52]

Evil does not arise from desire or love, Augustine argues, nor from the object of love, but from deficient love for a good, whether bodily or spiritual. In integral love, each good is loved in its place in an order of goods centered on the divine good, which gives unity to the whole order.

> Avarice is not something wrong with gold
> but with someone wrongly loving gold
> to the neglect of justice, which is without comparison preferable to gold.
> Lust is not something wrong with beautiful and delicious bodies,
> but with someone wrongly loving bodily pleasures
> to the neglect of the moderation that makes us suited
> for what is more spiritually beautiful and more incorruptibly delicious.

52. Balthasar, *Herrlichkeit*, 2/2:448–49; *Glory*, 3:90–91.

Boasting is not something wrong with human praise
but with someone wrongly loving praise
without concern for the witness of conscience.
Pride is not something wrong with using power, or with power itself
but with someone wrongly loving his own power,
with contempt for the greater justice of the omnipotent.
In short, anyone who wrongly loves the good of any nature,
even if he gains it,
becomes evil in the good and wretchedly deprived of the better.[53]

Luther seems to know this passage, to judge from an echo of it in an early commentary on the Psalms. "Gold is not evil, but the love of gold is evil; the flesh is not evil, but the *libido* of flesh is evil" (LW 14:326; WA 5:57). Augustine's text can serve as a point of departure for thinking through how the mainstream Christian tradition judges the moral quality of sex, particularly sexual pleasure. Augustine's experience of addiction to sexual pleasure seems to have left a scar in the form of suspicion. Thomas argues forcefully against taking suspicion to the level of first principle.

> The end of any member of the body is its use.... The end of some members of the body is sex (*carnalis commixtio*).... That which is the end of some bodily members cannot be in itself bad because what exists by nature is ordered to its end by divine providence....
>
> Further, natural inclinations are present in beings from God, who moves all beings. It is thus impossible that the natural inclination of some species aims at what is in itself bad. All mature animals have a natural inclination for sex. It is, therefore, impossible that sex is in itself bad.[54]

"Every pleasure, inasmuch as it is of this kind [that is, pleasure] is good."[55] Without original sin, Thomas adds, sexual pleasure would have been more intense than it is now. "Sense pleasure would have been more intense in the measure in which nature was purer."[56]

Sex, including its pleasure, is a natural good. Couples should and can reach the balance of virtue in sex, even though the objective consequences of original sin remain, including concupiscence in the sense of a tendency to sin. Thomas sees three possible moral conditions of the conjugal act. They cover the whole spectrum from mortal sin through venial sin to full goodness that merits eternal life.[57]

53. Augustine, *De civitate dei* 12.8.
54. Thomas, *Contra gentiles* III, cap. 126, par. 3–6.
55. Thomas, *Super IV sent.*, d. 31, q. 2, a. 3, corp.
56. Thomas, *Summa* I, q. 98, a. 2, ad 3.
57. See *Super IV sent.*, d. 26, q. 1, a. 3, corp.

Mortal sin: If pleasure is what a man or woman seeks in the act and if they are ready to use others to gain it—so that it makes little difference if it happens to be their spouse or not—then sex with one's spouse is a mortal sin. The violence is not as open as in adultery or rape, but the cases are in many respects alike. Love, both spousal love and love for God, is dead in this condition.

Venial sin: If there is an imbalance in love for the goods of marriage but without the readiness to perform the act with someone other than one's spouse, the act is a venial sin. A remnant of love for one's spouse and God remains, even if it is in various degrees deficient.

Meriting eternal life: If spouses love God, each other, and the goodness of children, then their conjugal act is meritorious. It prepares them for eternal life.[58]

What exactly is the problem Luther sees in sexual pleasure? At what point and in what way does sin enter? A section of his *Sermon on the Estate of Marriage* seems to give an answer.

> [After the fall of Adam and Eve] this love is not pure, for although one spouse wants to have the other, nevertheless each also seeks his pleasure from the other (ßo sucht doch auch eyn yglich seyne lust an dem andern) and it falsifies this love (felscht diße liebe). Therefore, the married state is no longer pure now and without sin. The temptation of the flesh has become so strong and furious that marriage is like a hospital for incurables that prevents them from falling into graver sin. (LW 44:9–10; WA 167–68)

Luther says nothing in this text about the relation between pleasure and other goods. The only point he focuses on to explain the sin is the desire for getting one's own pleasure from the other. He sees this reflexive form of desire as a case of "seeking one's own," which is contrary to love because "love does not seek its own" (1 Corinthians 13:5).

In a monograph on the early Luther and Aristotle, Theodor Dieter shows the architectonic power of this Pauline text for Luther. Aristotle holds that by nature each being seeks its own perfection. True love *does not* seek its own. Aristotelian nature *does* seek its own. Therefore Aristotelian nature is the same as sin. Aristotle is the philosopher of the devil.[59]

58. See *Super IV sent.*, d. 26, q. 1, a. 4.

59. See Theodor Dieter, *Der junge Luther und Aristoteles: Eine historisch-systematische Untersuchung zum Verhältnis von Theologie und Philosophie* (Berlin: de Gruyter, 2001), esp. chap. 1, "Luther's Critique of Aristotle's Teleological Understanding of the Soul." Dieter does not consider that there are opposite ways of reading Aristotle. Like Ockham and Luther, he turns Aristotelian teleology on its head, even though he quotes texts that explicitly say the opposite.

Let us suppose (*per impossibile*) that a man or a woman has successfully eliminated the desire and enjoyment of erotic pleasure from sex. What will they say to each other? It is for your sake only, not at all for mine, that I do what I do. I am completely pure and selfless. The pleasure you might give me—I do not want it. I have successfully eliminated from my heart all erotic desire for you, all enjoyment of you. Your attractiveness has stopped working on me. You leave me cold.

Such altruism would not be love. It would be an insult behind the appearance of high-mindedness. Sexual desire and enjoyment play an integral part in the authentic mutual gift of self in the conjugal act. John Paul emphasizes this point.

> Man and woman are called to express the mysterious "speech" of their bodies in all the truth that properly belongs to it. Through gestures and reactions, *through the whole reciprocally conditioned dynamism of tension and enjoyment*—whose direct source and subject is the body in its masculinity and femininity, the body in its action and interaction—through all this man, *the person, "speaks."* (TOB 123:4; emphasis added)

John Paul's discussion of adultery in the heart (Matthew 5:27–28) identifies a dangerous lie that arises especially in men. In this lie, a man's heart turns first against his own defective desire to condemn it. He then transfers evil from his desire to the object of desire, the woman, whom he casts in the role of temptress.

> One must detach oneself only from the evil of the act ... and never transfer the negativity of this act to its object....
>
> This victory must go hand in hand with an effort to discover the authentic value of the object, in order that the Manichaean "anti-value" may not take root in man, in his consciousness and will. In fact, it is one of the fruits of evil ... that the object to which the act of desire turns is for the human subject "a value not sufficiently appreciated." ... The human heart ... is called to discover the full value of that which, in the act of [defective] desire, constitutes for it "a value not sufficiently appreciated." ...
>
> "Adultery committed in the heart" can and should be understood as a "devaluation" or removal of the value that belongs [to the sexual body], as an intentional privation of that dignity to which the integral value of her femininity corresponds in the person in question. The words of Matthew 5:27–28 contain a call to discover this value and this dignity and to reaffirm it. (TOB 45:4–5)

One can observe this transfer in some gnostic texts. Secret John, a gnostic text summarized in part by St. Irenaeus at the end of the second century, tells the story of sex as a plan designed by the devil, who is the creator and chief ruler of the material world.

> And the chief ruler saw the virgin who stood by Adam.... And the chief ruler defiled her, and begot in her two sons; the first and the second, Eloim and Yave.... Now up to the present day sexual intercourse continued due to the chief ruler. And he planted sexual desire in her who belongs to Adam. And he produced through intercourse the copies of the bodies, and he inspired them with his counterfeit spirit.[60]

Closer to Luther's own time, Salvo Burci's *Liber supra stella* (1235) reports a similar story told by Cathars.

> And when he says, "Let us make man," why does he speak in the plural? They interpret it to mean that Lucifer spoke in the name of his associates.... The fruit they understand in this way, that the serpent inserted its *cauda* [tail or penis] into the nature of Eve and she conceived Cain. And when Eve was joined to the serpent, that is, when she ate the fruit, then she knew the pleasure of this world. And she gave Adam to eat, that is, she joined him with herself for both to eat.[61]

Both Secret John and the Cathar story in the *Liber supra stella* transfer the evil from the man's desire to the woman. Evil enters human life by the devil arousing sexual pleasure in the woman; it then passes from the woman-temptress to the man-victim. This is the transfer to which John Paul draws attention. Against this transfer, he argues that in concupiscence the sexual attractiveness of the human body is not appreciated enough. Its beauty, depth, and meaning is reduced.

Puritanism has been the favorite whipping boy of proponents of the sexual revolution. Some scholars have come to the defense of Puritan attitudes toward sex against these attacks.[62] Still, the Calvinist thesis of the total depravity of our nature is a bedrock truth for Puritanism.[63] It inevitably implies the isolation of sexual pleasure from its full human integration in spousal love.

A particularly influential Puritan, impeccably orthodox in this isolation of sexual pleasure, though not in its evaluation, is the founder of Playboy Enterprises, Hugh Hefner. He was raised as a Puritan and turned vehemently against

60. Michael Waldstein and Frederik Wisse, *The Apocryphon of John: Synopsis of Nag Hammadi Codices II,1 III,1 and IV,1 with BG 8502,2*, Nag Hammadi Studies 33 (Leiden: Brill, 1995), Codex II, p. 24, lect. 8–17.

61. *Liber supra stella*, Latin text in Ignaz Döllinger, *Beiträge zur Sektengeschichte des Mittelalters*, 2 vols. (Munich: C. H. Beck, 1890), 2:60.

62. See Edmund S. Morgan, "The Puritans and Sex," *New England Quarterly* 15 (1942): 591–607; William Haller and Malleville Haller, "The Puritan Art of Love," *Huntington Library Quarterly* 5 (1942): 235–72; Edmund Leites, "The Duty to Desire: Love, Friendship, and Sexuality in Some Puritan Theories of Marriage," *Journal of Social History* 15 (1982): 383–408.

63. See Kathleen Verduin, "Our Cursed Natures: Sexuality and the Puritan Conscience," *New England Quarterly* 56 (1983): 220–37.

the Puritan condemnation of erotic pleasure. Finding himself unhappy in the Puritan car, he threw the car into reverse instead of getting out. He kept the isolation of sexual pleasure from personal love. He failed to find a fuller and more integrated way of experiencing and living sex. In a fascinating interview with Cathleen Falsani, he explains the religious roots of his sexual crusade.

> "I have strong feelings about the way organized religion—with the codification of all the rules related to sexuality—became law and played havoc with people's lives. And I think that—dare I say it?—is very un-Christian," Hef says at the beginning of our conversation.
>
> We are sitting next to each other on a comfy couch in the mansion's library, not far from where an original Matisse, with a burn mark where a tipsy John Lennon once left a lit cigarette, hangs. Behind the couch is a life-size bust of a topless woman. (Someone later tells me it is Hef's former girlfriend Barbi Benton—the bust, not the Matisse.)
>
> "I think that there are great unanswered questions that I don't have the answers for, and I think it is presumptuous for some people not only to suggest that they do have the answers but to codify them and establish them as a set of rules, some of which are wonderful and some of which are hurtful, in the name of the Almighty. . . .
>
> Religion was a very important part of my upbringing. I saw in it a quality, in terms of ideals and morality, that I embraced. I also saw part of it, the part related to human sexuality and other things, as hypocritical and hurtful. And I think that is the origin of who I am. The heart of who I am is a result of trying to make some sense of all of that."
>
> "Sex is there for procreation and a good deal more," Hef continues. "I was raised in a setting in which it was for procreation only and the rest was sin, and that included not only a whole lot of behavior but also a whole lot of people. That's abominable."
>
> Hef, who is dressed in his usual uniform—red-and-black-satin smoking jacket, pajamas, and slippers—is charming, disarmingly so for a man in his late seventies. He is also incredibly literate, introspective, and kind in a grandfatherly way. . . .
>
> Despite what he calls a "typical Midwestern Puritan" upbringing—and Hefner, a tenth-generation direct descendant of the Mayflower passenger William Bradford, uses the term Puritan quite specifically—the Playboy baron's own spirituality is decidedly unconventional.
>
> Call it The Playboy Theology. Hef doesn't believe in a "biblical God," but he is fairly adamant about the existence of a "Creator." . . . He says he worships on a regular basis while walking the grounds of his own backyard. . . .
>
> "Our family was Prohibitionist, Puritan in a very real sense. Never smoked, swore, drank, danced—all the good stuff. Never hugged. Oh, no. There was absolutely no hugging or kissing in my family.

> There was a point in time when my mother, later in life, apologized to me for not being able to show affection. That was, of course, the way I'd been raised. I said to her, Mom, you couldn't have done it any better. And because of the things you weren't able to do, it set me on a course that changed my life and the world.
>
> When I talk about the hurt and the hypocrisy in some of our values—our sexual values—it comes from the fact that I didn't get hugged a lot as a kid, and I understand that....
>
> I went to Catholic church on a number of occasions with my first wife [Millie] because she was Catholic.... Millie got very upset when she went to the doctor for birth control information and the doctor turned out to be Catholic and started singing, Rhythm is my business. She was so affronted," Hefner says. That was the end of Hef's connection, tenuous as it was, to the Catholic Church—or to any organized religion.[64]

Would it have made a difference if Hefner had come to know John Paul's theology of the body? He did embrace and enjoy the beauty of women but a cut-down beauty like kitsch, such as sentimental garden dwarves and other artificially sweet or perfumed toys. The garden dwarfs suffer no harm from the enjoyment of their defective beauty. It is different for women. Hefner's porn makes women objects of defective love, suppressing a depth of beauty that deserves to be the object of a greater love.

6. Zero-Sum Logic

One and the same question runs through the five points examined above—the spousal reading of Scripture, *sola Scriptura*, conscience and reason, justification, and the goodness of sex. Is created and redeemed human nature good? In the first three points this question regards the order of knowledge; in the other two the order of love, the role of love in justification and the nature of sexual love. The underlying zero-sum logic that governs Luther's views needs to be examined next. Why must any good attributed to human beings be subtracted from God and vice versa?

Charles Morerod argues that the answer lies in a philosophical understanding of divine and human causality as competitive, which Luther inherited from William of Ockham.[65] Michael Root argues to the contrary that Luther's reasons are theological.

64. Cathleen Falsani, *The God Factor: Inside the Spiritual Lives of Public People* (New York: Farrar, Straus and Giroux, 2006), 20–28; at 22, 25–46.

65. Charles Morerod, *Ecumenism and Philosophy: Philosophical Questions for a Renewal of Dialogue*, trans. Therese C. Scarpelli (Ann Arbor, MI: Sapientia Press of Ave Maria University, 2006).

> Luther's language does not imply the "philosophical theory of causality" that Morerod asserts.
>
> According to Morerod, Luther's alleged systematic denial of divine agency working within human agency is that which accounts for Luther's understanding of justification. If that were the case, then it would follow that a different understanding of the interrelation of divine and human agency would dissolve or essentially transform Luther's doctrine of justification.
>
> Here lies the most decisive of Morerod's misunderstandings of Luther. The center of Luther's understanding of justification is the insistence that the righteousness of Christ, in which the Christian participates by faith, is the only righteousness that avails before the judgment of God.... Morerod's assertion of a philosophical fundamental difference makes him miss the soteriological concern that drives Luther. To say that Luther was committed to a particular understanding of causality and thus he insisted that Christ is our righteousness is to get matters precisely backwards.[66]

Root is right to insist that Luther's theological concerns need to be given their due weight. The *Catechism of the Catholic Church* concludes its section on justification, grace, and merit with a text of St. Thérèse of Lisieux.

> After earth's exile, I hope to go and enjoy you in the fatherland, but I do not want to lay up merits for heaven. I want to work for your love alone.... In the evening of this life, I shall appear before you with empty hands, for I do not ask you, Lord, to count my works. *All our justice is blemished* in your eyes. I wish, then, *to be clothed in your own justice* and to receive from your love the eternal possession of yourself.[67]

Not wanting to lay up merits, not asking God to count works, coming with empty hands to be clothed by Christ's own justice, a justice infinitely superior to our own—all these flow from one single point. "I want to work for your love alone ... to receive from your love the eternal possession of yourself." Such love, spousal in character, implies looking away from oneself instead of examining one's own excellence for display before the beloved as a basis for being justly rewarded. The desire "to receive from your love the eternal possession of yourself" implies self-expropriation and self-forgetfulness as openness for God's gift. Luther's spousal texts show that he understands this logic of spousal love.

St. Thérèse sharpens the same logic and the convergence with Luther when she adds, "All our justice is blemished. I wish, then, to be clothed in your own

66. Michael Root, "Review of Charles Morerod, *Ecumenism and Philosophy*," *Modern Theology* 24 (2008): 505–8.

67. *CCC* 2011. Thérèse of Lisieux, "Act of Offering," in *Story of a Soul*, trans. John Clarke (Washington, DC: Institute of Carmelite Studies, 1981), 277; emphasis added.

justice." Thomas throws this point into relief when he addresses the question whether human acts can be meritorious *ex condigno*, that is, *from equal worth* before God.

> If the act is taken with respect to the substance of the work as it comes forth from free choice, there cannot be equality of worth (*condignitas*), because there is the greatest inequality.... If, however, we speak about the meritorious work inasmuch as it comes from the grace of the Holy Spirit, in this way it merits eternal life by equal worth (*ex condigno*), for in this way the *valor* (strength, value, worth) of the act is reckoned (*attenditur*) according to the power of the Holy Spirit moving us into eternal life, as it says in John 4:14, "This water ... will become in him a fountain of water springing up into eternal life."[68]

How exactly can merit from equal worth be present in human acts? One cannot understand *attenditur* as *is reckoned* in the sense of *is imputed* to us by God contrary to fact. In comparison with imputation, the *dignitas-valor* of God's act is both more within and more outside the human act than forensic imputation allows. It is more within, because it is present in the act as a cause; and it is more outside, because an infinite *dignitas* cannot be present in acts as they come from a finite agent. "All worth (*dignitas*) of a work must be traced back to the dignity of the person."[69] In this way, St. Thérèse's statement "I wish to be clothed in your own justice" converges with the theological concerns Root points to.

In *Quodlibet 6*, Ockham argues that someone can reach salvation without a created act of love, *caritas creata*.

> Nothing is meritorious except what is in our power (*in potestate nostra*). This love (*caritas*) is not in our power. Therefore, the act is not primarily meritorious because of that grace but because of the will freely causing (*propter voluntatem libere causantem*). Therefore, God could accept an act elicited by the will without such a grace.[70]

The statement sounds Pelagian, which is the charge Ockham had to face at the Papal court in Avignon. A few sentences later, Ockham responds to the charge.

68. Thomas, *Summa* I-II, q. 114, a. 3, corp.

69. Omnis autem dignitas operis a dignitate personae derivari debet. John of St. Thomas, commenting on Thomas's discussion of merit *ex condigno* in *Cursus Theologicus, In Primam Secundae*, vol. 2 (Lyons: Borde, 1663), 352, par. 5.

70. Ockham, *Quodlibetum 6*, q. 1, a. 2; *Opera Theologica*, 9:588.

> If you say that the first conclusion contains the error of Pelagius, I respond no. Pelagius holds that grace is *de facto* not needed for having eternal life. An act elicited from what is purely natural can merit eternal life from equal worth, *de condigno*. I, on the contrary, hold that such an act is meritorious only because God's absolute power accepts it as such.[71]

The logic of spousal love is absent from this understanding of justification. Ockham affirms God's absolute power as a power that is not subject to the logic of this love but only to the decisions of his will. As he appears in this text and others like it, Ockham is far from Luther in his theological concerns, far from the spousal logic of redemption. Nevertheless, Luther is still shaped by him on three important points, by agreement as well as excessive disagreement.

First, both Ockham and Luther hold that the human act of love is not needed. According to Ockham, it would not be needed if God were to decree by his *potentia absoluta*, his absolute power, that it is not needed. In Luther the act of love is simply not needed.

Second, both Ockham and Luther hold that acts are free in the degree to which they are in our power *rather than* in God's power. While Ockham affirms the existence of free acts in relation to God, Luther denies it because he sees this affirmation as boasting. Here one can observe an excessive disagreement with Ockham, still based on Ockham's premises.

Third, both Ockham and Luther give an important role to counterfactual imputation. Ockham's God could decree by *potentia absoluta* that merit from equal worth be imputed to a natural act without grace. Luther's God factually imputes the justice of Christ to the believer as someone else's justice, as *iustitia aliena*.

Root points to the following passage in Luther's *De servo arbitrio* to argue that Luther did not share Ockham's competitive view of divine causality.

> [God] does not work in us without us, because it is for this he has created and preserved us, that he might work in us and we might cooperate with him, whether outside his Kingdom through his general omnipotence, or inside his Kingdom by the special virtue of his Spirit. (LW 33:243; WA 18:754)[72]

In this passage, cooperation does look noncompetitive. Both God and human beings are the cause. Shortly after this passage, however, Luther clarifies what cooperation can and cannot mean.

> Thus, it is through us that he preaches, shows mercy to the poor, comforts the afflicted. But what is attributed to free choice in all this? Or rather, what is there left for it but nothing? And really nothing. (LW 33:243; WA 18:754)

71. Ockham, *Quodlibetum 6*, q. 1, a. 2, *Opera Theologica*, 9:588–89.
72. See Root, "Review of Charles Morerod," 506.

When God works in us to give rise to the human agency of preaching, helping the poor, and comforting the afflicted, why is there no place for agency in the full sense? Why does God's agency exclude human freedom? Luther's reasoning directly expresses a competitive relation between divine causality and human freedom. Given Luther's formation in Ockham, which is historically certain, Morerod's thesis about the influence of Ockham's philosophical zero-sum logic is plausible, at least as a partial explanation of the competitive relation between human and divine causality. One of Luther's most formal statements about his theological concerns is found in his *Lectures on Galatians*. It touches on the issue of justice highlighted by Root but covers *everything* besides.

> This teaching on grace attributes all glory and everything to God alone and nothing to human beings (*totam gloriam et omnia soli Deo tribuit, hominibus nihil*). The teaching of the Gospel, therefore, takes away all glory, wisdom, justice, and so on, from man and gives it to the Creator alone.... My doctrine is one that preaches and worships God alone, and it condemns the justice and the wisdom of all human beings. (LW 26:66; WA 40:131)

Ockham's view on competing causality can be seen in his rejection of philosophical arguments for God as the first efficient cause. "If it could be shown that God is the cause of anything, it could also be shown that he is the sufficient cause of everything, in which case other causes would be in vain."[73] The only way for other causes not to be in vain is for God to let them act out of themselves. When created causes are truly at work, God is not.

Luther says, "I am of the Ockhamist faction" (WA 6:600). Balthasar wonders "whether serious or in jest."[74] On the deep theological level, Luther is a radical opponent of Ockham. He takes Ockham as standing for reason, *logos* at its best. "By his intelligence Ockham vanquished all and refuted all other ways" (LW 54:392; WA *Tischreden*, 4:679). "Ockham my dear master.... These two [Scotus and Ockham] are the best. What are the others supposed to do?" (LW 34:27; WA 30.2:300). Reason at its best, however, is still the great whore of Babylon. Balthasar gathers the evidence as follows.

> Luther's voluntarism ... is based on Ockham ... The absoluteness of the divine will appears in the paradoxical justification of the sinner—which transcends all the philosophizing of human reason. But Luther so concentrates on this one and only significant plane of action that created freedom is limited to purely intra-mundane operations; it operates downward, as it were but not upward, toward God. Ultimately only God is free.

73. Ockham, *Quodlibetum* 2, q. 1, *Opera Theologica* 9:107–8.
74. Balthasar, *Theodramatik*, 2/1:224; *Theodrama*, 2:247.

"It follows that now free choice is plainly a divine name and cannot belong to anyone except the Divine Majesty alone." It would be sacrilegious to attribute choice to man.

"We know that man has been made master of what is below him, in which he has right and free choice, so that these things might obey and do what he wants and thinks. But our question is whether he has free choice in relation to God, so that God might obey and do what man wants."

Similarly, in the *Disputatio de homine* (1536), where Luther can actually describe human *ratio* as "something divine" (*divinum quiddam*) and "a certain divine power" (*Numen quoddam*) but only "to administer these things in this life."

As for the relationship with God, which is shaped and created solely by God, all man's greatness in this world is "almost nothing" (*paene nihil*). As the giver of grace, God is such only if, in the face of his gift, all our gifts become as nothing. "To do good to another is divine. But our God cannot give also to us what is his unless he first teaches that he does not want what is ours and that what is ours is nothing to him. . . . He wants that we only receive and that he alone gives, that he might be true God."[75]

7. The Trinity

The seventh and final point to be touched on is Luther's Trinitarian theology. Zero-sum logic seems to leave only two possibilities. Either the generation of the Son by the Father is the Father's death as he makes room for the Son who inherits divinity. Or the Son is not truly other than the Father but a mere appearance of the Father. One of the two must be nothing. Zero-sum cannot uphold the testimony of Jesus. "As the Father has life in himself, so he has given to the Son also to have life in himself" (John 5:26). "All that is mine is yours and yours is mine" (John 17:10). The creed's chain of *from* statements echoes these Johannine texts. "God *from* God, Light *from* Light, true God *from* true God." This chain is impossible in zero-sum logic. The Trinity presupposes another logic, the logic of radical gift.

The logic of gift within God is reflected in creation and in the spousal mystery of redemption. St. John Paul's theology is Trinitarian in this manner. "A total gift (an uncreated gift) is shared . . . by God himself in the Trinitarian communion of persons" (TOB 95b:4). "Love, an uncreated Gift, is part of the inner mystery of God and is the very nucleus of Theology."[76]

75. Balthasar, *Theodramatik*, 2/1:224–25; *Theodrama*, 2:247–48.
76. Wojtyła, *Sign of Contradiction*, 55.

Luther builds a wall of defense around Trinitarian theology to defend it against the attacks of reason. One can see the wall rise in the first formal disputation of the newly established University of Wittenberg for which Luther personally chose John 1:14, "The Word became flesh" ("Disputatio theologica an haec propositio sit vera in Philosophia: Verbum caro factum est," LW 38.239–77; WA 39.2.3–33). Luther interprets "The Word became flesh" as contradicting all human *logos*. As his opponent, he chooses the most prominent center of theological learning at the time, the University of Paris. The main error of Paris, he charges, is that the truths of philosophy and theology must agree. There is only one truth, the Parisian theologians claim. The Father's *Logos* expresses all of it and human speech participates in it both in philosophy and in theology. Luther's opening statement disagrees.

> In theology, it is true that the Word was made flesh; in philosophy, the statement is simply impossible and absurd. The declaration, "God is man," is not less but even more contradictory than if you would say, "Man is an ass." The Sorbonne, the mother of errors, has very incorrectly defined that truth is the same in philosophy and theology. And has impiously condemned those who have argued to the contrary. For by this abominable statement it taught that the articles of faith are taken captive under the judgment of human reason. (Theses 2–6; LW 38.239; WA 39.2.3)

After this opening salvo, Luther addresses the doctrine of the Trinity as a doctrine that is even more absurd for philosophy than the Incarnation.

> This expository syllogism is good: The Father generates in divine things; the Father is the divine essence; therefore, the divine essence generates. Although the premises are true, the conclusion is false; so, what is false follows from what is true; this is contrary to philosophy.
>
> This common syllogism is good: The Father is the entire divine essence; the Son is the divine essence; therefore, the Son is the Father. Again, the premises are true, and the conclusion is false; and this is not a case of truth agreeing with truth.
>
> This is indeed not because of the defect of the syllogistic form but because of the lofty character and majesty of the matter which cannot be enclosed in the narrow confines of reason or syllogisms. (Theses 16–20; LW 38:240–41; WA 39.2:4)

In this text, Luther takes up classical objections gathered and resolved by Peter Lombard in his *Sentences*, commented by many theologians in the four centuries between Lombard and Luther. Luther is not interested in resolving the objections. He uses them as Kant uses the antinomies, to show that human reason is completely incompetent in such matters. By banishing Trinitarian theology to the realm of the philosophically absurd, Luther deprives it of its form-giving role by which it provides light for all areas of theology. Just as the Father does not compete against the Son as his origin, so, by analogy, God's transcendent causality as the first and comprehensive cause of all the creature's being and activity does not compete against the creature. It sets the creature into its own being and activity.

A locomotive has its limited place in a chain of causes at the front of a train. It pulls the first wagon, so that the first wagon can in turn pull the second, and so on, all the way to the last. The last wagon is most distant from the locomotive and receives the locomotive's power most indirectly. It is immediately drawn only by the next-to-last wagon. Zero-sum logic governs the whole chain. God does not occupy such a limited place in the chain of causes. He is the cause of being as being. He is therefore the cause of the being of all members in the chain as well as of their causality. God's role is the opposite of competitive. The more the creator is at work, the more the creature has its own being and activity. For this reason, the first cause is most immediate and intimate to the final effect, more immediate and intimate than any of the secondary causes, including the most immediate.[77] In Augustine's famous words, the first cause is "more interior than my innermost" *interior intimo meo* (*Confessions* 3.6).

> God, as the first [cause], which moves without being in motion, is the origin of all movements, as the first being (*primum ens*) is the origin of all *to be* (*esse*). In causes that are through themselves ordered, a cause is in the same measure more a cause the earlier it is in the order of causes, because it gives being a cause to the other causes. God is therefore even more strongly a cause of all motions than the singular moving causes.[78]

This noncompetitive logic presupposes an account of participation, in which God is the fullness of *to be* (*ipsum esse*) while creatures participate in being. Each creature is one among other beings (*ens*). It *has* being (*esse habens*) rather than *being* the fullness. This form of all-encompassing causality is exclusively God's own, but far from excluding secondary causes, it posits them in their own being and activity. Affirming human nature and action as good does not subtract from the divine goodness but glorifies it. The relation between the divine persons as portrayed in Scripture is the root and exemplar of this noncompetitive relation.

77. See Thomas, *Super Librum de causis*, lect. 1.
78. Thomas, *De substantiis separatis*, 15.

CHAPTER 3

Reason as an Instrument of Power in Bacon and Descartes

1. A Reformation of Reason

One of the first to herald a rigorously technological practice of reason was Francis Bacon.[1] A devoted public servant of realistic power under Elizabeth I and her successor James I, Bacon rose to become Lord Chancellor. He ended in disgrace and poverty after signing a confession that he had taken bribes in lawsuits under his jurisdiction.[2] Thomas Hobbes, Bacon's secretary for many years, reports that his master died from pneumonia contracted while experimenting with snow to refrigerate chicken meat.[3]

Thomas Jefferson gives Bacon first place in what he calls "my trinity of the three greatest men the world had ever produced."[4] "Bacon, Locke, and Newton. . . . I consider them as the three greatest men that have ever lived, without any exception, and as having laid the foundation of those superstructures which have been raised in the Physical and Moral sciences."[5] John Paul's list of the

1. Citations of Bacon by OxfBac (= *The Oxford Francis Bacon*) and SpedBac (= Spedding's nineteenth-century edition of Bacon) refer to *The Oxford Francis Bacon*, 7 vols., ed. British Academy (Oxford: Clarendon Press, 1996–); James Spedding, *The Works of Bacon*, 14 vols., (London: Longman, 1857–74), translations occasionally modified.

2. The justice of the conviction has been intensely debated. See Nieves Mathews, *Francis Bacon: The History of a Character Assassination* (New Haven, CT: Yale University Press, 1996).

3. See John Aubrey, *Brief Lives, Chiefly of Contemporaries, Set Down in the Years 1669 and 1696*, 2 vols., ed. Andrew Clark (Oxford: Clarendon Press, 1898), 1:75.

4. Thomas Jefferson, Letter to Benjamin Rush, January 16, 1811, in *The Works of Thomas Jefferson*, ed. Paul Leicester Ford, 12 vols. (New York: G. P. Putnam's Sons, 1904–5), 11:168. The order could be primarily chronological. If so, it would still underline the preeminent greatness of Bacon.

5. Jefferson, Letter to John Trumbull, February 15, 1789, in Julian Parks Boyd, *The Papers of Thomas Jefferson* (Princeton, NJ: Princeton University Press, 1950), 14:561.

three greatest would contain only Jews and the second one would certainly be a woman. Still, Jefferson is correct in seeing Bacon as a herald of the future.

Bacon and the Death of God

Benedict XVI agrees with Jefferson, to a point.

> We must look at the foundations of the modern age. These appear with particular clarity in the thought of Francis Bacon. That a new era emerged—through the discovery of America and the new technical achievements that had made this development possible—is undeniable. But what is the basis of this new era? It is the new correlation of experiment and method that enables man to arrive at an interpretation of nature in conformity with its laws and thus finally to achieve "the triumph of art over nature" *victoria cursus artis super naturam* [Bacon, *New Organon* 1.117].
>
> The novelty—according to Bacon's vision—lies in a new correlation between science and praxis. This is also given a theological application: the new correlation between science and praxis would mean that the dominion over creation—given to man by God and lost through original sin—would be reestablished.
>
> Anyone who attentively reads and reflects on these statements will recognize that a disturbing step has been taken: up to that time, the recovery of what man had lost through the expulsion from Paradise was expected from faith in Jesus Christ: herein lay "redemption." Now, this "redemption," the restoration of the lost "Paradise," is no longer expected from faith but from the newly discovered link between science and *praxis*. It is not that faith is simply denied; rather, it is displaced to another level—that of purely private and other-worldly affairs—and at the same time it becomes somehow irrelevant for the world.
>
> This programmatic vision has determined the trajectory of modern times, and it also shapes the present-day crisis of faith, which is essentially a crisis of Christian hope. Thus hope, too, in Bacon, acquires a new form. Now it is called faith in progress.
>
> For Bacon, the recent spate of discoveries and inventions is just the beginning; through the interplay of science and *praxis*, totally new discoveries will follow, and a totally new world will emerge: the empire of man. He even put forward a vision of foreseeable inventions, including the airplane and the submarine. As the ideology of progress developed further, joy at visible advances in human potential remained a continuing confirmation of faith in progress as such.[6]

6. Benedict XVI, *Spe Salvi* 16–17.

As Benedict reads Bacon's proposal, it is radically opposed to Christian faith. Instead of placing its hope in a redemption it does not control, humanity takes its own destiny into its own hand as progress by means of power over nature. Newton still kept a deist divinity that engineered the cosmos at the beginning. The cosmos then runs by itself and only needs occasional adjustments from the chief mechanic.

While Newton's God has retired from his work as engineer (except for these adjustments), he is very much involved as an agent of apocalyptic events. Newton's writings on the Book of Revelation are more voluminous than his writings on the mechanical world system. His mechanical account, however, has little use for causal input from God. Mechanics is a mathematical science based on mathematical regularity. It does not consider what cannot be grasped mathematically.

As technological power increased and the certainty of progress grew, the deist God wandered off into increasing irrelevance. With his vehement clarity, Nietzsche tells the story of the madman who lights a lantern in the bright morning and runs through the market yelling, "I'm looking for God. I'm looking for God." People laugh.

> "Has he gotten lost?" one of them said. "Has he run off like a child?" another said. "Or has he gone into hiding? Is he afraid of us? Has he gone to sea? Gone to another country?" they cried and laughed....
>
> The madman jumped into their midst and pierced them with his eyes. "Where has God gone?" he yelled. "I want to tell you.... God is dead. God stays dead. And we have killed him. How can we console ourselves, the murderers of all murderers? The holiest and most powerful thing the world had—it has bled to death under our knives.... Must not we ourselves become gods merely to seem worthy of this deed? There never has been a greater deed. Whoever is born after us—because of this deed he belongs to a higher history than all history until now."[7]

Christian Apologetics

In a recent study of Bacon's theology, Stephen Matthews has challenged the image of Bacon as a destroyer of Christian faith.[8] Behind the Bacon of atheism, whom he sees as a construct of rationalist hagiographers, he attempts to uncover

7. Nietzsche, *The Cheerful Science* 125; KSA 3:480–81. Nietzsche's writings are cited by title and section number followed by a reference to KSA = Kritische Studienausgabe. Friedrich Nietzsche, *Sämtliche Werke: Kritische Studienausgabe*, 2nd ed., 15 vols., ed. Giorgio Colli and Mazzino Montinari (Berlin: Walter de Gruyter, 1988).

8. See Stephen Matthews, *Theology and Science in the Thought of Francis Bacon* (Aldershot: Ashgate, 2008).

the Bacon of history as a sophisticated theologian whose motives as a herald of modern natural science were specifically Christian. Matthews presents much detailed evidence.

Bacon's mother, Anne Cook, was highly educated and committed to the education of her children. Her father, Sir Anthony Cooke, was the Calvinist tutor of Edward VI, son of Henry VIII. When Edward's Catholic half sister Mary became queen in 1553 after Edward's untimely death, she attempted to reestablish the Catholic faith. Among other measures, she imprisoned Sir Anthony but eventually released him. He and his family joined the more than eight hundred prominent and wealthy Calvinist families who went into exile on the continent. Many chose Calvin's own city, Geneva, the model of a truly purified and reformed Christian commonwealth. The Marian exiles returned in triumph when Queen Mary died five years later and the Protestant Elizabeth I began her long reign of forty-four years (1558–1603). "The roots of the Puritan movement are to be found among the families of the Geneva exiles and this can certainly be seen in the convictions of Anne Bacon."[9]

Anne gave her son a thorough training in Calvinist theology. To his mother's distress, he strayed from Calvin's path under the influence of Bishop Lancelot Andrewes.[10] He regularly sent drafts of his books to Andrewes for suggestions and corrections, calling him "my inquisitor" (SpedBac 10:256). The theology of Andrewes, Matthews points out, was not primarily based on Luther and Calvin but on the Greek Fathers.[11]

> Andrewes has come to be known as one of the "fathers" of Anglo-Catholicism. His Theology ... is marked by a concern for the authority of tradition, an emphasis on ritual prayer (liturgy) ... and a concern for maintaining the Apostolic Succession.... Andrewes' reverence for the Church Fathers ... led him to develop his own theological system which, though far from unique, was fundamentally Patristic, with a decidedly Eastern turn. Our image of Andrewes should be dominated by his affinity for tradition and the Fathers, rather than an association with any of the contemporary flavors of Protestantism.[12]

Matthews's judgment about Andrewes is confirmed by John Henry Newman in his Anglican period. Newman summarizes the Oxford Movement as "inquiring minds ... following the paths of Hooker, Andrewes and Bull, or of their mas-

9. Matthews, *Theology and Science*, 1.

10. Matthews, *Theology and Science*, 28–29.

11. See Nicholas Lossky, *Lancelot Andrewes, the Preacher (1555–1626): The Origins of the Mystical Theology of the Church of England* (Oxford: Clarendon Press, 1991).

12. Matthews, *Theology and Science*, 29–30.

ters, Irenaeus or Cyprian."[13] He praises "our wisest doctors and rulers, such as Bishop Andrewes"[14] and holds up "Anglo-Catholicism, the religion of Andrewes, Laud, Hammond, Butler, and Wilson"[15] as the *via media*, the middle way between Protestantism and Popery. Newman shared the understanding of "the Mass all but Transubstantiation with Andrewes"[16] and translated Andrewes's *Private Prayers* from the original Greek into English.[17]

Matthews argues that two theses characteristic of Andrewes's Anglo-Catholicism played a pivotal role in Bacon's *Instauratio magna, The Great Instauration* or *Recovery* of human power over nature. Following the Greek Fathers, Andrewes was convinced that the fall did not imply the total depravity of reason and will posited by Luther and Calvin.

> Bacon's vision of recovery would be seriously impeded if the fall into sin meant that the human mind and soul had become so corrupt that they were prone to failure and wickedness. This point marks what is perhaps the most significant departure from Calvinism in Bacon's Theology. For Calvin and his adherents, human knowledge still existed after the fall, but it was corrupt and always untrustworthy.... Attempts to improve earthly conditions through arts and actions are ultimately vain.... As there is no hope of transformation here, the hope of the believer must focus on transcending this world by passing to the next.... The possibility of any actual recovery from the effects of the fall in this world is proscribed by the pervasiveness of the corruption it brought about.[18]

The second pivotal thesis, still according to Matthews, was the division of the history of salvation by the principle of recapitulation. Irenaeus developed this principle on the basis of Ephesians 1:10, "to recapitulate all things in Christ, those in the heavens and those on earth." The Greek translated as *recapitulate* is ἀνακεφαλαιώσασθαι, which can mean bring under a head again, bring to the beginning again, sum up, recover, restore. The Vulgate translates it as *instaurare omnia in Christo*, "to renew all things in Christ." Although the concept of *instauratio*, which appears in the title of Bacon's main work (*Instauratio Magna*), has other biblical and Patristic echoes as well, it is Irenaeus's millenarian interpretation mediated by Andrewes, Matthews argues, that stands behind Bacon's

13. John Henry Newman, "Notices of Books," *British Critic* 24 (1838): 230–38, at 232.

14. John Henry Newman, *Tracts for the Times*, 71, "On the Mode of Conducting the Controversy with Rome (No. I, Against Romanism)," in *The Via Media of the Anglican Church*, 2 vols. (London: Longmans, 1891), 2:136.

15. John Henry Newman, *Apologia pro vita sua* (Oxford: Oxford University Press, 1914), 168.

16. Newman, *Apologia pro vita sua*, 192.

17. John Henry Newman, *Tracts for the Times*, 88, "The Greek Devotions of Bishop Andrews," *Tracts for the Times*, vol. 5, *1838–40* (London: Rivington, 1840).

18. Matthews, *Theology and Science*, 70–71.

understanding of the great age of instauration, of the renewal or recovery of human power over nature lost in the fall.[19] Andrewes was convinced that in the state of innocence, human beings had a power close to omnipotence over both animate and inanimate nature. They were plenipotentiary vice regents of God with a comprehensive causal influence on the whole material world. This power, Bacon holds, they can now regain.

Suicidal Apologetics

The likeness between Bacon and Irenaeus posited by Matthews fails at a decisive point. In continuity with Plato and Aristotle, the Greek Fathers see human reason as a power receptive for being in all its extent. Bacon sees it more narrowly as an instrument for power over nature. Such a technological reason, defined by the limits of mechanics, can comfortably coexist with the total depravity of nature. Since its method is mathematical, it cannot concern itself directly with good or bad, beautiful or ugly.

Even if Bacon was influenced in some respects by Irenaeus's millenarian reading of Revelation 20:1–4, he did not follow Irenaeus in seeing the presence of Christ as the central event of the millennium. For Bacon, the center of the millennium belongs to the restoration of power over nature by science. In contrast to Irenaeus, Bacon does not focus on the divine wisdom reflected in the goodness of creatures but on the divine power—with man as the vicar of God's power on earth.

Matthews's argument is a form of apologetics. It takes the high standing of natural science in our culture as a simple given. It then uses this high standing to shed some of its glory on Christian faith by showing that faith assisted in the birth of modern science.

Although this form of apologetics may have some historical validity, it is deadly for Christianity.[20] It does not give enough critical attention to philosophical premises that pose as scientific. These premises, first articulated clearly by Bacon and Descartes, lead to a narrowing of reason to mechanical and thus mathematical aspects of the cosmos. Benedict XVI's argument in *Spe salvi* 16–17 still stands. When the practice of reason is limited by the ambition for power, limited to the method of mechanics imposed by that ambition for power, the disappearance of nonmathematical aspects of the cosmos is inevitable. The counter-proposal should be a fuller and more reasonable practice of reason.

19. Matthews, *Theology and Science*, 31, 79, and 99–102.

20. Stanley Jaki proposed a similarly suicidal form of apologetics in many books and articles. See Stanley Jaki, *The Road of Science and the Ways to God* (Chicago: University of Chicago Press, 1978).

2. The Primacy of Will and Power

However far Bacon may have moved from Calvin, he still maintained the philosophical and theological nominalism of the Reformers, which gives primacy to the divine will and power over the divine wisdom. The choice of power as the end of human knowledge transfers this primacy of power from the divine to the human level. In the preface of his *Great Instauration*, Bacon describes himself as rebuilding the whole edifice of knowledge on this new foundation.

> The only course left was to try to do everything again with better assistance, and undertake a wholesale Instauration of the sciences, arts and all human learning, raised on proper foundations. (OxfBac 11:2–3)

The most widespread narrative claims that modern natural science arose from the close observation of nature, which shook off the yoke of religious belief and Aristotelian philosophy imposed by ecclesiastical power. This narrative fails to grasp Bacon's proposal as he understands it. It fails to grasp the formative influence of the ambition for power.

Universal power over nature, Bacon believes, originally belonged to the human race before the fall. His ambition is the *Instauratio*, the restoration of this power by means of knowledge. The form in which Bacon understands both the premise and the ambition is shaped by the primacy of will developed by Duns Scotus and radicalized by Ockham. In his *Regensburg Lecture*, Benedict XVI describes this development from Scotus to Ockham as breaking the deep unity between Greek *logos* and Christian faith.

> In the late Middle Ages, we find trends in Theology which would sunder this synthesis between the Greek spirit and the Christian spirit. In contrast with the so-called intellectualism of Augustine and Thomas, there arose with Duns Scotus a voluntarism which, in its later developments [in the nominalism of William of Ockham], led to the claim that we can only know God's *voluntas ordinata*. Beyond this is the realm of God's freedom, in virtue of which he could have done the opposite of everything he has actually done. This gives rise ... to the image of a capricious God, who is not even bound to truth and goodness. God's transcendence and otherness are so exalted that our reason, our sense of the true and good, are no longer an authentic mirror of God, whose deepest possibilities remain eternally unattainable and hidden behind his actual decisions.
>
> As opposed to this, the faith of the Church has always insisted that between God and us, between his eternal Creator Spirit and our created reason there exists a real analogy, in which—as the Fourth Lateran Council in 1215 stated—unlikeness remains infinitely greater than likeness, yet not to the point of abolishing analogy and its language. God does not become more di-

vine when we push him away from us in a sheer, impenetrable voluntarism; rather, the truly divine God is the God who has revealed himself as *Logos*.[21]

By emphasizing God's arbitrary power, radical voluntarism obscures the interior goodness of created beings. It sees their order as one God happens to have imposed on them from the outside, one among many he could have imposed by his absolute power (*potentia absoluta*), though he did impose a specific order by his ordained power (*potentia ordinata*). Radical voluntarism regards natural beings as artifacts, not as natural beings. It is blind for their interior ordering toward the good. Natural beings reflect the free divine power, not the divine wisdom. For this reason, Ockham's voluntarism is closely connected with nominalism, which denies the intelligibility of natures. Taylor points out, "This line of thought even contributed in the end to the rise of mechanism: the ideal universe from this point of view is a mechanical one."[22]

Ockham died in 1348, Bacon died 278 years later in 1626, and Popper again 368 later in 1994, a total span of six and a half centuries. Popper defines himself as a nominalist. He sees the main difference between nominalism and the *essentialism* of Greek *logos* as follows.

> Methodological essentialism [exemplified by Plato and Aristotle], that is the theory that it is the aim of science to reveal essences and to describe them by means of definitions, can be better understood when contrasted with its opposite, methodological nominalism. Instead of aiming at finding out what a thing really is, and at defining its true nature, methodological nominalism aims at describing how a thing behaves in various circumstances, and especially, whether there are any regularities in its behavior. In other words, methodological nominalism sees the aim of science in the description of the things and events of our experience, and in an "explanation" of these events, that is their description with the help of universal laws....
>
> The methodological Nominalist will never think that a question like "What is energy?" or "What is movement?" or "What is an atom?" is an important question for physics; but he will attach importance to a question like: "How can the energy of the sun be made useful?" ... And to those philosophers who tell him that before having answered the "what is" question he cannot hope to give exact answers to any of the "how" questions, he will reply, if at all, by pointing out that he much prefers that modest degree of exactness which he can achieve by his methods to the pretentious muddle which they have achieved by theirs.[23]

21. Benedict XVI, *Regensburg Lecture*, December 12, 2006.

22. Charles Taylor, *Sources of the Self: The Making of the Modern Identity* (Cambridge, MA: Harvard University Press, 1989), 82.

23. Popper, *The Open Society and Its Enemies*, 2 vols. (London: Routledge and Kegan Paul, 1978), 1:32.

Popper did not write this text as a statement about Bacon. He wrote it to express his own conviction about the reasonable practice of reason in the twentieth century. That it applies remarkably well to Bacon in the sixteenth and seventeenth centuries and pinpoints Bacon's nominalist roots is not a coincidence. Popper adds, "Methodological nominalism is nowadays fairly generally accepted in the natural sciences."[24]

For Greek *logos*, Popper has only disdain. When one asks the classical Socratic question "What is it?" Popper answers, *if at all*, that he prefers exact and useful results to the pretentious muddle of Greek reason. The same tone of disdain is already found in Francis Bacon. The *wisdom* of the Greeks, he claims, is that of boys prattling *logos* in *theoria*, impotent when it comes to generating life. His own wisdom, Bacon claims, is that of mature men who generate life by establishing the empire of man over things.

> And as for its utility, I must openly declare that this wisdom, derived mainly from the Greeks, is what might be called the boyhood of science and, as with boys, it is all prattle and no procreation. For productive of controversies, it is barren in works. (OxfBac 11:2–3)

3. The Choice of Power as End

Knowledge and Power

The first principle of Bacon's philosophy is not a discovery but the choice to do a specific work.

> I keep silent concerning myself, but for the business in hand I ask men to think of it not as a question of opinion but as a job to be done (*Opus*), and to know for certain that I am not laying foundations of a sect or dogma but of utility and human greatness, *vtilitatis et amplitudinis humanae fundamenta*. (OxfBac 11:22–25)

"Human knowledge and power come to the same thing." Scientia et potentia humana in idem coincidunt. "For nature is not conquered save by obeying it" *non nisi parendo vincitur* (*New Organon* 1.3, OxfBac 11:64–65). The phrase "not conquered save by obeying it" shows that, contrary to a widespread opinion, Bacon does not simply identify knowledge and power.[25] Knowledge and power

24. Popper, *The Open Society and Its Enemies*, 1:32.

25. "Knowledge is power" serves as the title of an accessible survey of Bacon's work, a sustained apologia for the scientific revolution: John Henry, *Knowledge Is Power: How Magic, the Government and an Apocalyptic Vision Inspired Francis Bacon to Create Modern Science* (Cambridge: Icon Books,

are opposites, as are obeying and conquering. They come to the same thing only because the purpose of obeying is to conquer. "And so those twin objectives, human Knowledge and Power, do in fact come together in the same" *vere in idem coincidunt* (OxfBac 11:44–45). On this point, Bacon's secretary Thomas Hobbes agrees with his employer.

> The end or target of philosophy is that we are able to use previously seen effects for our benefit; or that by the industry of men, through the application of bodies to bodies, we may produce effects like those we conceive in our mind, as far as human power and the matter of things will allow, for the use of human life. For the inward glory and triumph of mind that a man may have for the mastering of some difficult and doubtful matter, or for the discovery of some hidden truth, is not worth as much effort as the study of Philosophy requires; nor need any man care much to teach another what he knows himself, if he think that will be the only benefit of his labor. Knowledge is for the sake of power. Scientia propter potentiam. Theorems, which serve among geometricians to find properties, are for the sake of problems, that is, for the sake of the art of construction. In short, all speculation is undertaken for some action or work.[26]
>
> I put for a generall inclination of all mankind, a perpetuall and restlesse desire of Power after power, that ceaseth onely in Death.[27]

Some passages in Bacon appear to support knowledge for its own sake.

> Just as we love light because by it we can travel, practice our arts, read, and recognize each other, and yet actually seeing the light is still more excellent and beautiful than all its various uses, so surely is the very contemplation of things as they are without superstition or imposture, error or confusion, intrinsically more worthy than all the fruits of discoveries. (*New Organon* 1.129, OxfBac 11:196–97)

Spedding comments, "This is one of the passages which show how far Bacon was from what is now called a utilitarian" (SpedBac 1:337n1). How far? It

---

2003). The phrase goes back to Bacon's statement *scientia potestas est*, which Spedding translates as "knowledge is power." In its original context, this statement does not simply identify knowledge and power. Bacon reports the opinion of some who hold that God does not have power over everything but nevertheless knows everything. "They hold that, in its extent, the knowledge of God goes beyond his power or rather (since knowledge itself is a power, *nam et ipsa scientia potestas est*) that the power by which he knows goes beyond the power by which he moves and acts." Bacon, *Sacred Meditations: Heresies*, SpedBac Latin 14:79, English 14:95. Given the context, the indefinite article should be used in the English translation, "Knowledge is a power." The power Bacon has in mind is not power in the sense of that which "moves and acts," but a power like the power of sight.

26. Thomas Hobbes, *Elementa Philosophiae* 1.1, *De Philosophia*, par. 6; *Opera Philosophica*, ed. William Molesworth, 5 vols. (London: John Bohn, 1839), 1.6; *The English Works of Thomas Hobbes*, trans. William Molesworth, 11 vols. (London: John Bohn, 1839), 1.7 (translation revised).

27. Thomas Hobbes, *Leviathan* (Cambridge: Cambridge University Press, 1996), 70.

is difficult to deny the nature of reason and the goodness of truth altogether. Bacon is one of the most resolute in making the attempt, though Kant outruns him by far. The sentence immediately before the one quoted suggests that what Bacon praises is the universal utilitarian power of knowledge in contrast to specific utility. In aphorism 117, which contains the phrase quoted by Benedict XVI ("the triumph of art over nature"), Bacon alludes to the story of Atalanta, the fastest runner of ancient Greece, who was tricked into defeat when a competitor dropped a golden ball each time she caught up with him. She stopped each time, picked up the balls, and lost the race.

> If therefore a man is fitter and handier for the mechanical arts, and is good at hunting out works solely as a consequence of being conversant with experiments, I allow and leave to him the job of culling from my history and tables the many things that lie as by the wayside, and of applying them to works, and as it were acquiring interest for a time, until the capital can be had. But I, striving for greater prizes, renounce all precipitate and premature delays in this matter as if (as I generally say) they were Atalanta's apples. For I do not chase like a child after golden apples but stake everything on a victory for art in its race against nature. (*New Organon* 1.117, OxfBac 11:176–77)

Bacon sees knowledge for its own sake not only as frivolous but as immoral. He compares it to enjoying the beauty of a prostitute. "So the end ought to bee … whatsoeuer is solide and fruitful: that knowledge may not bee as a Curtezan for pleasure & vanetie only… but as a Spouse, for generation, fruit and comfort" (*Advancement of Learning*, OxfBac 4:32). *Curtezan* is an upscale prostitute. The Latin has a much rougher word for prostitute: *scortum*, a skin.

The extent of the power sought by Bacon is vast. It is "power over nature" *potestas super naturam*, not over a limited piece of nature (*New Organon* 2.52, OxfBac 11:446–47). It is "the <power and>[28] empire of the human race itself over the whole universe of things" *humani generis ipsius potentiam et imperium in rerum Vniuersitatem* (*New Organon* 1.129, OxfBac 11:194–95).

Appeal to Scripture

In pursuing this end, Bacon sees himself as overturning the supposed knowledge inherited from pagan antiquity and the Middle Ages to reestablish the biblical truth announced in Genesis 2–3 that an authority over nature belonged by right to man but was lost through sin.

28. The Oxford Bacon omits the phrase "power and" in the English translation although it prints the Latin *potestas et* on the facing page.

> Concerning the condition of the sciences, that it is unprosperous, nor much improved, and that a way completely different from the one known before should be opened for the human intellect, and other helps devised to let the mind exert its own authority over the nature of things, *ius in rerum naturam.* (OxfBac 11:10–11)

This right or authority over things, he argues, has biblical foundations.

> At last (like a tried and trusted guardian) I can, when men have *come of age* with an *intellect beholden to none*, hand over their fortunes to them; and from this an *improvement in man's lot* is bound to follow, and an enlargement of his power over nature. For by his fall man lost both his state of innocence and his command over created things. However, both of these losses can to some extent be made good even in this life, the former by religion and faith, the latter by the arts and sciences. For the curse did not quite put creation into a state of unremitting rebellion, but by virtue of that injunction *In the sweat of thy face shalt thou eat thy bread*, it [i.e., creation] is now by various labours (not for sure by disputations and the idle ceremonies of magic) at length and to some degree conquered to allow man his bread or, in other words, for the use of human life. (*New Organon* 2.52, *OxfBac*, 11:446–47; emphasis added; translation altered)

The translation by Rees in *The Oxford Bacon* takes *curse* to be the subject, "the curse … is mitigated." The Latin rendered as *mitigated* by Rees is *subigitur*, from *subigo*, *sub-ago*, to drive under, conquer, subjugate, compel. *Subigitur* is quite close to *subicitur*, from *subicio*, *sub-iacio*, to throw under, place under, make subject. *Subicio* is the word used in the Vulgate of Genesis 1:28, subdue the earth, *subicite.* It seems likely that Bacon understands *subigitur* as fulfilling the commandment given in Genesis 1:28. The grammatical subject of *subigitur* is thus not the curse as in Rees's translation but *creation*, continuing the subject of the preceding sentence. Creation is not in unremitting rebellion, but in accord with the divine command to subdue the earth, it can still be conquered.[29]

Subigitur is the very last word of the *New Organon*. In the original publication, imitated by the *Oxford Bacon*, the last lines are shorter and shorter, forming a triangle. The very last line contains only one word, *subigitur.* Bacon is a careful writer and knows Latin well. If he consciously used *subigitur* to replace *subicitur* corresponding to the commandment *subicite*, it can be understood as an intensification. *Subigo* suggests more strength and violence than *subicio.*

Pierre Hadot draws a contrast between two ways of approaching nature, epitomized by Prometheus and Orpheus.

29. This construction of the Latin is adopted in Francis Bacon, *The New Organon*, ed. Lisa Jardine and Michael Silverthorne (Cambridge: Cambridge University Press, 2000), 221.

> In Francis Bacon, at the dawn of modern science, Prometheus was to appear as the founder of experimental science. Promethean man demands the right of domination over nature, and in the Christian era, the story of Genesis, as we have seen, confirmed him in his certainty of having rights over nature.[30]

Hadot's claim about "having rights over nature" can be read in two ways. (1) The Promethean man of technological power was a new arrival on the stage of history and secondarily justified his arrival by appeal to Genesis 1:28. (2) The Promethean man grew organically from Genesis 1:28 in the Christian era. The first of these two readings is more accurate. A millennium and a half of the Christian era passed before Bacon in which nobody proposed the primacy of mechanical power over nature. In that millennium and a half, Genesis 1:28 was read quite differently. Focus on moral self-control was the most prominent, as Harrison points out.

> A common patristic reading of "dominion over the beasts," for example, relies upon the ancient conception of the human being as a microcosm of the world and internalizes the idea of dominion, directing it inward to the faculties of the human soul.[31]

The focus, Harrison shows further, tended to be on prudence and self-mastery as distinctive of human reason, owing to reason's capacity to understand the good in its goodness.[32] The reading of Genesis 1:28 as affirming the human right to universal technological power over nature is new. Bacon is clearly conscious of the newness of his proposal. He locates himself on the cusp of a decisive turn of the ages. The turn is marked by the birth of a new generation of scientists whom Bacon describes as masculine as opposed to feminine. In Bacon's early work, *Temporis partus masculus, sive de interpretation naturae, The Masculine Offspring of Time: On the Interpretation of Nature*, an experienced scientist cast in the role of father instructs a novice scientist cast in the role of son. The father tells the son that he will bring him the most fruitful woman, nature herself, "to make her your slave" so that the son can take her "in chaste, holy, and legal marriage."

> I am come in very truth leading to you nature with all her children to bind her to your service and make her your slave.... My dear, dear boy, what I purpose is to unite you with things themselves in a chaste, holy, and legal marriage;

30. Pierre Hadot, *The Veil of Isis: An Essay on the History of the Idea of Nature* (Cambridge, MA: Belknap Press of Harvard University Press, 2006), 95.

31. Peter Harrison, "Subduing the Earth: Genesis 1, Early Modern Science, and the Exploitation of Nature," *Journal of Religion* 79 (1999): 86–109, at 90.

32. Representative examples: John Chrysostom, *Sermons on Genesis* 9; Augustine, *De Genesi ad litteram* 9.14.24–25; Thomas, *Summa* I, q. 96, aa. 1–2.

> and from this association you will secure an increase beyond all the hopes and prayers of ordinary marriages, to wit, a blessed race of Heroes or Supermen who will overcome the immeasurable helplessness and poverty of the human race, which cause it more destruction than all giants, monsters, or tyrants, and will make you peaceful, happy, prosperous, and secure.... Trust, my son, and give yourself to me that I might give you back to yourself, da te mihi, ut te tibi reddam.[33]

The reconfiguration of central Christian notions in this text is astonishing. The father promises to give the son back to himself. The state of helplessness and poverty has deprived the son of self-possession. He is unable to be happy, prosperous, and secure. Happiness, prosperity, and security are restored by the masculine power of the father, passed on to the son, and from the son to the future race of scientists. They exercise their masculine power in a cosmic marriage with the most fruitful wife, nature herself, the most useful slave.

The new age belonging to this masculine offspring has been announced beforehand by apocalyptic texts such as Daniel 12:4, "Very many shall travel through and across and knowledge will be manifold." This text joins two signs to each other: the great voyages of discovery or conquest in the New World and the growth of science.

> And this Proficience in Nauigation, and discoueries, may plant also an expectation of the furder proficience, and augmentation of all Scyences, because it may seeme they are ordained by God to be *Coevalls*, that is, to meete in one Age. For so the Prophet *Daniel* speaking of the latter times foretelleth: *Plurimi pertransibunt, et Multiplex erit Scientia* [Very many shall travel through and across and knowledge will be manifold] (Daniel 12:4), as if the opennesse and through passage of the world, and the encrease of knowledge were appointed to be in the same ages, as we see it is already performed in great part, the learning of these later times. (OxfBac 4:71)

4. Effects of the Choice of Power

Laws of Nature

The choice of power as the end of knowledge leads Bacon to see the main object of knowledge in what he calls *laws of nature* understood as descriptions of

33. Translation following Benjamin Farrington, *The Philosophy of Francis Bacon: An Essay on Its Development from 1603 to 1609 with New Translations of Fundamental Texts* (Chicago: University of Chicago Press, 1966), 62 and 72. Farrington's phrase of *Heroes and Supermen* translates the single Latin term, *Heroum*. See the Latin in Spedding, *Works of Bacon*, 3:527–41, at 541.

regularity in natural events. The use of *laws* in this sense is not completely new. Thomas defines *law* as "a certain ordering of reason for the common good by the one who has care of the community, promulgated."[34] By analogy, he extends the term to the effects of law.

> Since law is a certain rule and measure, there are two ways in which one speaks of it as being present in something. In one way it is present in what measures and rules, and since this belongs to reason alone, law in this sense exists only in reason. In another way it is present in what is measured and ruled, and in this way law is in everything that has an inclination toward something due to some law, so that every inclination that flows from a law can be called law, not essentially but by participation.[35]

English jurisprudence, with which Bacon was thoroughly familiar, frequently uses a pair of concepts, *lex et consuetudo*, law and custom. The term *law* can be used for both: law as *lex* is prescriptive; law as *consuetudo* is descriptive.[36] Like Thomas, Bacon extends law in the second sense to the whole of nature. Contrary to Thomas's understanding of such laws, however, Bacon's nominalist premises lead him to see these laws not as inclinations within things toward an end but as merely factual regularity. Factual regularity is useful if one wishes to gain power. It allows one to predict what will happen when one acts in specific ways on bodies.

Because such laws are most useful, Bacon concludes, they are most true. "What is most useful in operating is most true in knowing." Quod in operando utilissimum, id in sciendo verissimum (*New Organon* 2.4, OxfBac 11:204–5). This axiom is justified in cases when *most true* is the opposite of *false*. It is not justified when *most true* is the opposite of *not useful*. Some truths are not useful, but they remain true. In the case of useless truths, Bacon's axiom functions as a noncognitive filter for eliminating truths, not because they are not true but because they are not useful. Since they are irrelevant, they are set aside by decision or fade away by neglect.

Final Cause

The four causes investigated by the Aristotelian philosophy of nature suffer in different ways from this imposition of will. The Final Cause, the cause consid-

34. Quaedam rationis ordinatio ad bonum commune, ab eo, qui curam communitatis habet, promulgata. *Summa* I-II, q. 90, a. 4, corp.

35. Thomas, *Summa* I-II, q. 90, a. 1, ad 1.

36. Frederick Pollock and Frederic W. Maitland, *The History of English Law before the Time of Edward I*, 2 vols., 2nd ed. (Cambridge: Cambridge University Press, 1898), 175.

ered most important by Aristotle, suffers the most. It should simply be set aside in natural science.

> Just how ill-starred is the current condition of human knowledge can be seen from common assertions. Rightly do they say that *to know truly is to know by causes*. And they are not wrong when they establish four causes: the material, formal, efficient, and final. But of these the final is so far from being beneficial that it actually corrupts the sciences, except insofar as it relates to the actions of man. (*New Organon* 2.2, OxfBac, 11:200–201)

There is an unbridgeable gap between human nature, in which intention plays a role, and the universe, in which only facts play a role. "Final causes ... obviously come from the nature of man rather than of the universe." [Causae] finales ... sunt plane ex natura hominis potius quam universi (*New Organon* 1.48, OxfBac 86–87).

More important yet, giving attention to the final cause is irrelevant to the concerns of power because power is concerned with subduing a thing as material to a superimposed purpose. It is useless to understand preexisting purposes. "Inquiry into final causes is barren, and like a virgin consecrated to God gives birth to nothing" (*De augmentis* 3.5, SpedBac 2:298).

Bacon still uses the concept of final cause, but he follows Ockham in emptying it of all its causal content. Common experience suggests (and Aristotle draws it out explicitly) that the causality of the final cause arises from goodness. Ends are ends because they are good. The good is thus first in the order of causality. Ockham turns this relation on its head. Ends are ends because they happen to be intended by some will. To call something an end is to name it from outside itself, from being intended.

Bacon assigns final causes to a particular discipline, completely separated from other kinds of knowledge; namely, *Metaphysics* (see *De augmentis* 3.4, SpedBac 2:264–97). Bacon's *Metaphysics* determines what happens to be, as a matter of fact, intended and realized by divine providence. God's purposes are usually hidden from us. If God chooses to tell us, we can know the intention beforehand, as in the birth of a masculine generation of scientists. The ends are not intelligible as ends. They do not shape the natures of things.

One can see the primacy of will and power in Bacon's understanding of final causality on three parallel levels: God, technology, and politics. Bacon studied Machiavelli, to judge from numerous references and from one of his interventions in Parliament (see SpedBac 7:40). He expresses his admiration for a Machiavellian form of politics in which the ruler uses subordinates as tools of power that do not know his plans. In a masterfully balanced Latin sentence, Bacon draws out the parallels between the three levels.

As in civil actions, political prudence is much higher and more amazing
if someone can turn to use (*abuti*) the works of others for his ends and desires
and yet share nothing of his own plan with them
(so that all the while they will do what he wills
and yet not know that they are doing it)
than if he shares his plans
with those who serve his will,
so the wisdom of God shines out more amazingly
if nature does one thing
while Providence draws forth another,
than if the characters of his providence
had been impressed on all patterns and natural movements.
(*De augmentis* 3.4, SpedBac 2:296; cf. *Advancement*, OxfBac 4:87)

Three levels run parallel in this text. The most fundamental level is a voluntarist-nominalist concept of divine government. The nature of this government is reflected in a Machiavellian understanding of politics as the exercise of raw unpredictable power. The new mechanist science of nature extends the same understanding to the empire of man over things. On each level, choice and power impose an order from the outside, subjecting material to an external end.

Formal Cause

The Formal Cause, understood as the intrinsic principle by which a specific nature is actual rather than merely potential, suffers as well. Bacon continues to use the words *formal cause*, but as a label for the laws of nature. Artifacts are no less natural for him than natural things. Conversely, natural things are divine artifacts, not natural. Like artifacts, they are brought about by an extrinsic imposition of purposes. "The work and aim of human power is to generate and superimpose a new nature or new natures on a given body" (*New Organon* 2.1, OxfBac 11:200–201). What is of interest in the given body is its material capacity for receiving the pattern of behavior superimposed on it.

From the axiom "What is most useful in operating is most true in knowing," it follows readily that knowledge about matter as material is most true. Form enters the argument as a help for understanding how one might impose forms on material.

> We should rather focus on matter, its schematisms and metaschematisms, and the pure act and the law of that act or motion. For forms are fictions of the human soul, except when you want to call those laws of the act forms. (*New Organon* 1.51, OxfBac, 11:88–89)

> For although nothing really exists in nature besides individual bodies, carrying out pure, individual acts according to law, yet in the sphere of doctrine, this very law, and the investigation, discovery and explanation of it, is the very foundation of knowing as it is of operating. It is this law then, and its clauses, that I understand by the name of forms, especially as this term is current coin and crops up all the time. (*New Organon* 2.2, OxfBac 11:202–3)

5. Mechanics as the Queen of Sciences

Mechanics and Mathematics

The setting of Galileo's most famous work, *Discourses and Mathematical Demonstrations Concerning Two New Sciences Pertaining to Mechanics and Locomotion*, is the Arsenal in Venice, the place where the Venetians constructed, stored, and repaired military machines. The first sentence of the work reflects a choice close to Bacon's. "[There is] a large field for *speculative intellects to philosophize*, it seems to me, which the frequent practice of your arsenal offers, Venetian gentlemen, particularly in that part that is called *mechanics*."[37]

The word *mechanics* is derived from the Greek *mechanē*, which signifies *means*. Mechanics is the systematic study of means by which one can gain one's ends. The Aristotelian *Mechanics* had not yet been discovered and studied in the Middle Ages. It entered public discourse in the early Renaissance. Scholars in a variety of fields were interested in it: classicists, mathematicians, inventors of machines, military engineers, and philosophers of nature. The roots of Galileo's mathematical account of nature lie in these discussions of the Aristotelian *Mechanics*. Galileo lectured on the text and wrote a commentary on it (now lost) before formulating his own new mathematical science.[38]

In the prologue to the Aristotelian *Mechanics*, the author (probably one of Aristotle's students) explains the nature of a systematic *technē* that provides power. *Technē* is often translated as *art* or *skill*. Since the *Mechanics* conceives of it as a systematic form of practical knowledge based on a combination of mathematics and physical observation, the translation *technology* seems appropriate.[39]

37. Galileo, "Discorsi e dimostrazioni matematiche intorno à due nuove scienze Attenenti alla Mecanica e i Movimenti Locali," in *Le opere di Galileo Galilei: Edizione nazionale*, 20 vols. (Florence: Tipografia di G. Barbèra, 1890–1909), 49; emphasis added.

38. See Lawrence Rose and Stillman Drake, "The Pseudo-Aristotelian Questions of Mechanics in Renaissance Culture," *Studies in the Renaissance* 18 (1971): 65–104, at 66.

39. The *Shorter Oxford English Dictionary* defines *technology* as "The branch of knowledge that deals with the mechanical arts or applied sciences."

> We wonder about ... what comes to be by technology (διὰ τέχνην) contrary to nature (παρὰ φύσιν) for the benefit of human beings. Nature often does the contrary of what is useful for us ... When, therefore, we have to do something contrary to nature, the difficulty of it presents a perplexity (ἀπορίαν) and calls for technology. This is why we call the technology that helps us in such perplexities mechanics (μηχανή).
>
> The words of the poet Antiphon are quite true: "By *technē* we are powerful (κρατοῦμεν) even where nature would defeat us." Instances of this are those cases in which the less has power (κρατεῖ) over the greater, and where what has small weight moves great weights—in fact, practically all the problems which we call mechanical problems.
>
> They are not quite identical nor yet entirely unconnected with physical problems. They have something in common both with mathematical and with physical theorems; for while mathematics shows the how (τὸ ὥς), physics shows the concerning what (τὸ περὶ ὅ).[40]

When one wants to lift a heavy stone, a lever can help. Mechanics uses mathematics to show "the how" (τὸ ὥς) by calculating the needed length of the lever and the amount of force. It uses physics (in the Aristotelian sense of sense-based observation of nature) to grasp the stone and the lever as mobile beings with certain properties of hardness, flexibility, and the like.

Because mechanics is the systematic means of power over nature, mathematical laws of motion came to be seen as the path to true knowledge. Some commentators argue that Bacon failed to recognize the essential role of mathematics in the new science.[41] The contrary is true. In a passage already quoted above, he explicitly highlights mathematics as the way to Mechanics. "Aristotle [said it] BEST: Physics and Mathematics give rise to Practical Science and Mechanics." OPTIME Aristoteles, Physicam et Mathematicam generare Practicam sive Mechanicam (*De augmentis* 3.6, SpedBac 1:576). Whenever possible, Bacon argues, the laws of nature should be expressed mathematically in accord with precise measurements made in experiments. "Investigation of nature turns out best when physics is given definition in the mathematical" *quando physicum terminatur in mathematico* (*New Organon* 2.8, OxfBac 11:212–13).

> I demand that every thing to do with natural phenomena, be they bodies or virtues, should (as far as possible) be set down, counted, weighed, measured and defined. For we are after works not speculations, and, indeed, a good marriage of Physics and Mathematics begets Practice *Physica autem et Mathematica bene commistae, generant Practicam.* (*Parasceve* 7.7, OxfBac 11:465)

40. Aristotle, *Mechanics* 847a10–28.

41. See Peter Urbach, "Francis Bacon as a Precursor to Popper," *British Journal for the Philosophy of Science* 33 (1982): 113–32, at 125.

Bacon was not himself an accomplished mathematician. Mathematical laws of mechanics are a postulate for him, based on Aristotle's authority. In this limited sense, Bacon is an orthodox Aristotelian. Descartes prepared the metaphysical and mathematical ground more thoroughly and came considerably closer to grasping the basic mathematical laws of nature. Newton was the first to succeed, if succeed is the right word. His laws were considered the universally true laws of motion until the theory of relativity and quantum mechanics widened the perspective.

The Place of Mechanics in Aristotle

If the school of Aristotle had such a clear grasp of mechanics, why did it produce only a short treatise on this subject? Why did Aristotle himself not invest time and energy in mechanical research? Why did he privilege empirical research on animals, the record of which is about one-third of his literary output?

Of the three kinds of theoretical philosophy, "mathematical, physical, and theological,"[42] Aristotle says, the third is dearest to him because it investigates the movers of the stars, particularly the first mover among them, who stands uniquely outside the whole universe as its separated common good.

> One must also examine in which way the nature of the universe has the good or the highest good, as something separate and itself by itself, or as the order. In both ways, it seems, as an army does. For the good is found both in the order and the leader, and more the latter; for he is not through the order, but it is through him.[43]

We do not know the divine leader and the other movers of the stars directly but only through their effects, the visible motions of the stars. The stars are so far away that our perception of them is poor. The divine origins are reflected more dimly in living beings here on earth, but at least these beings are nearer. Our perception of them is richer and more certain.

> Of beings that exist by nature, some are ungenerated and forever imperishable, while others share in generation and perishing. Although the former are of great value (τιμίας) and divine (θείας), due to our circumstances we have less contemplation (θεωρία) of them (indeed, to the senses very little is apparent from which one might investigate them, though we long to know about them), while about perishable plants and animals we are richly prepared for

42. Aristotle, *Metaphysics* 6.1.1026a19.
43. See Aristotle, *Metaphysics* 12.10.1075a11–1075a24.

> knowledge because we live with them. One would gather much about each kind among existing beings if one investigated them thoroughly.
>
> Each of the two has beauty (χάριν). Although we grasp the former only a little, they give us more joy—due to the value of the knowledge—more than all the things near us, just as seeing only a little of those whom we love gives more joy than clearly seeing other things, even if they are many and great.
>
> The latter, on the other hand, have an outstanding place in knowledge because we know them better and more fully. In addition, due to their nearness to us and our kinship, they have more weight when compared to the philosophy about the divine (τὴν περὶ τὰ θεῖα φιλοσοφίαν).
>
> Since we already went through the former, at least by saying how it appeared to us, what is left is to speak about the animal nature, leaving out nothing as far as we are able, neither the less noble nor the more noble. For although some do not appear beautiful to sense perception, the fashioning nature (ἡ δημιουργήσασα φύσις) gives unmanageable joys (ἀμηχάνους ἡδονὰς) in their study to those who can come to know causes and are by nature philosophers....
>
> We therefore must not recoil with childish aversion from the examination of the humbler animals. In all that is natural there is something wonderful (τι θαυμαστόν), and as Heraclitus, when the strangers who came to visit him found him warming himself at the furnace in the kitchen and hesitated to go in, is reported to have asked them not to be afraid to enter, because even in that kitchen gods were present, so we should venture on the study of every kind of animal without distaste; for *in all there is something of the natural and beautiful* (καλοῦ).... Absence of haphazard and being for the sake of something—these are in nature's works, and in the highest degree. That for the sake of which they come together and come to be *holds the place of the beautiful* (τὴν τοῦ καλοῦ χώραν εἴληφεν).[44]

While Bacon condemns delight in knowledge for its own sake as dishonorable, Aristotle pursues such knowledge because he sees great beauty. Convinced with Heraclitus that gods are present even in the kitchen, he is more interested in looking than cooking. The adjective used by Plato and Plotinus in similar contexts appears here; *amēchanon, without means to get at it, unmechanicable, unmanageable.* He finds unmanageable joys (ἀμηχάνους ἡδονὰς) in pursuing the presence of divine reason in living beings.

44. Aristotle, *Parts of Animals* 1.5.644b22–645a25; emphasis added.

The Closing of the Scientific Mind

The *Mechanics* produced in the Peripatetic school suggests that Aristotle was aware of the usefulness of mechanical knowledge. The text from *Parts of Animals* explains why he was not particularly interested in it. He loved something else more because it is better. In this love, Aristotle follows the openness of reason to all of being. Bacon, by contrast, closes reason, limiting it by subjecting it to a specific purpose outside of itself. This closure is the inevitable consequence of subordinating *theoria* to the ambition for power.

The usual narrative of the origin of modern science is that critical thinkers began to open their eyes and to observe facts instead of following Aristotle who deduced facts from general principles. By having a mind open to facts, they freed themselves from the power of the Catholic Church, which imposed a particular and parochial religious faith and used Aristotle to buttress it. The historical origin of science as documented by Bacon and Descartes is the almost direct opposite. Openness to discovery did not disappear, but it became narrowly focused. Kant understood the Baconian program without wishful thinking about universally open eyes.

> Natural science took much longer [than mathematics] to hit upon the high road of science. For only about a century and a half have passed since the ingenious Bacon, Baron Verulam, made the proposal that partly prompted this road's discovery, and partly—insofar as some were already on the trail of this discovery—invigorated it further....
>
> When approaching nature, reason holds in one hand its principles, in terms of which alone concordant appearances can count as laws, and in the other the experiment that it has devised in terms of those principles. Thus, reason must indeed approach nature to be instructed by it; yet it must not do so in the role of *a pupil who lets the teacher tell him whatever the teacher wants but* in the role of *an appointed judge who compels the witnesses to answer the questions* that he puts to them.[45]

Judges must come to a verdict of guilty or innocent and deliberate about the appropriate sentence. They do not sit down with the accused to come to know them as persons. They dismiss what the accused say if it does not serve their limited task and its practical outcome. In the same manner, Kant states, Bacon is not interested in knowing nature as it is. He is interested in finding the mathematical laws of nature that can serve instrumental reason. Baconian reason

45. Kant, *Critique of Pure Reason*, B XII–XIII; emphasis added. See Kant's *gesammelte Schriften*, ed. Prussian Academy of Sciences, 29 vols. (Berlin: Georg Reimer, Walter de Gruyter, 1902–38), cited as AK. The *Critique of Pure Reason* is traditionally cited as A (1st ed.) or B (2nd ed.).

is not open to all of being. It is selectively open and selectively closed. It limits itself to what can serve human power. De Koninck points out how massive this exclusion turns out to be.

> The world of physics is as a shadow of the world of being. Thus the statistical laws of experimental science reveal in an oblique fashion the nature which tends toward determination, toward one. In them should be seen a measurable projection of the tendency of nature. Here the myth of the cave is true. Only, what is reflected comes from within the thing, and not from without as in Platonism. The statistical laws which are shadows are not recognized as signs of nature except when one already knows nature. A philosophic knowledge never awakens in shadow, at least formally. . . .
>
> The experimental image which is made in the sciences, when one separates it, and when one considers it in itself, leads toward pure disintegration, toward destruction, and universal collapse. It cannot be other than pessimistic. It leads toward night. But this image is only such when it is separated, and when it is given directly the sense of being.[46]

Kant does not raise such critical questions about the limitation of reason to mathematical laws. He is content with night in the *external* world. He simply takes for granted that Bacon's road, perfected by Newton, is the highway of knowing nature. He lacks critical distance, striking in a thinker who is famous for writing three *Critiques*, which have given him the reputation of being *the* critical thinker par excellence.

6. Wisdom and Virtue

Practical knowledge, Aristotle argues, would be the best kind of knowledge if, and only if, human beings were by nature highest in value.

> It would be strange to think that politics or prudence (τὴν πολιτικὴν ἢ τὴν φρόνησιν) is the most advantageous (σπουδαιοτάτην), since man is not the best (τὸ ἄριστον) in the cosmos. . . .
>
> But if the argument is that man is the best (βέλτιστον) of the animals, this makes no difference; for there are other [beings] much more divine in nature (θειότερα τὴν φύσιν) than man, most conspicuously the [movers of the heavenly spheres] of which the cosmos is framed.
>
> From what has been said it is plain, then, that wisdom is understanding and knowledge of what is by nature highest in value (τῶν τιμιωτάτων τῇ φύσει).[47]

46. Charles De Koninck, Manuscript, Folder on Natural Philosophy, De Koninck Archives, University of Notre Dame.

47. Aristotle, *Nicomachean Ethics* 6.7.1141a.20–1141b.3.

In this text, Aristotle focuses on prudence (φρόνησις), which is a form of moral excellence or virtue as opposed to art/technology. Art bears on making, not on doing. All making is also a form of doing, of course. Yet art/technology does not itself answer the question, Can this instance of making be called good rather than merely skillful?

Is there a place for moral virtue and prudence in Bacon? Technological power, he argues, stands in the service of charity.

> Lastly, I desire every last one of us be admonished to think on the true ends of knowledge; that we seek it not for personal gratification, or for contention, or to look down on others, or for convenience, reputation, or power, or any such inferior motive but for the benefit and use of life, and that it be perfected and regulated in charity. For from desire for power the angels fell, and from desire for knowledge men; but there is no excess of charity, and neither angel nor man was ever imperiled by it. (*Great Instauration*, preface, OxfBac 11:23)

While there can be no excess of charity, there can be a defect of it. Bacon is aware of the possible problem of an abuse of power but dismisses it.

> Lastly if anyone complains that the sciences and arts have been corruptly given over to vice, extravagance and the like, no one should take any notice. For the same can be said of all worldly goods: of brains, bravery, brawn, grace, wealth, light itself, and the rest. Let the human race only be given the chance to regain its God-given authority over nature, then indeed will right reason and true religion (*recta ratio et sana religio*) govern the way we exert it. (*New Organon* 1.129, OxfBac, 196–97)

It is chilling to read this statement about the automatically self-governing goodness of human power by right reason and true religion next to a statement about human ambition found only a few sentences earlier.

> It would not be beside the point to identify three kinds and (so to speak) grades of human ambition.
>
> The first kind belongs to those who want to increase their own power in their mother country, and this kind is vulgar and degenerate, *vulgare et degener.*
>
> The second kind belongs to those who strive to increase the authority and influence of the fatherland among men; this kind has [some measure] of dignity but no less of greed, habet dignitatis, haud minus cupiditatis.
>
> But if someone strives to restore and increase the power and empire of the human race itself over the whole universe of things, potentiam & imperium in rerum Vniuersitatem, then that ambition (if that is what we must call it) is no doubt more reasonable and venerable, sanior et augustior, than the others. Now the empire of man over things, Hominis autem imperium in Res, lies in the arts and sciences alone. For one cannot govern nature save by complying

with her, non imperatur nisi parendo. (*New Organon* 1.129, *OxfBac*, 11:194–95, translation altered)

Bacon's confident leap to *sanus* (healthy, sane, sound, reasonable) and *augustus* (noble, venerable, worthy of honor, majestic) in the third grade of ambition is frightening. The human heart is vulgar, degenerate, and covetous in the first two grades of ambition. In the third grade, the power and empire of man over things, which is simply an ambition for greater and more encompassing power possessed by the whole human race (or rather, in fact, by its technocrats) over the whole universe, the human heart is suddenly no longer contemptible, vulgar, and greedy but *sanus* and *augustus*. What is the reason for the sudden improvement?

The adjective *augustus* claimed by the emperor Augustus seems to fit Bacon's phrase *the empire of man over things*. To judge this venerable nobility, one should take a look at the list of ends Bacon proposes. He calls the items on this list *magnalia*, great works, an allusion to the *magnalia Domini*, the great works of God in the liberation of Israel from Egypt (see Vulgate of Exodus 14:13; Deuteronomy 10:21, 11:2; 2 Kings 7:21–24; Psalms 70:19, 105:21, etc.).

- The prolongation of life. The restitution of youth in some degree. The retardation of age.
- The curing of diseases counted incurable. The mitigation of pain....
- The increasing of strength and activity. The increasing of ability to suffer torture or pain.
- The altering of complexions, and fatness and leanness. The altering of statures. The altering of features.
- The increasing and exalting of the intellectual parts....
- Making of new species. Transplanting of one species into another.
- Instruments of destruction, as of war and poison.
- Exhilaration of the spirits, and putting them in good disposition....
- Making rich composts for the earth.
- Impressions of the air, and raising of tempests....
- Drawing of new foods out of substances not now in use.
- Making new threads for apparel; and new stuffs, such as paper, glass, &c.
- Natural divinations. Deceptions of the senses. Greater pleasures of the senses.
- Artificial minerals and cements (SpedBac 5:415–16).[48]

Bacon usually speaks in rather blanket terms about improving the human condition and rarely offers as much detail. Some items on the list have stature,

48. This list corresponds closely to the more detailed list of "Preparations and Instruments" and their purposes given by one of the Fathers of "Salomon's House," the research institute of the island of Bensalem, in Bacon's *New Atlantis*. See SpedBac 3:156–64.

particularly curing diseases and instruments of destruction as of war and poison, though one might wonder whether the latter improve the human condition. Conversely, cures against aging, pain killers, cosmetics, diet, fat burning pills, antidepressants, tranquillizers, erotic stimulants, fashion, and visual entertainment occupy a large part of the list. The empire of man over things and the demonstration of that empire's glory in the *magnalia* of technology turns out to serve the kinds of ends advertised on magazine covers at checkout counters in supermarkets. The words *sanus, augustus,* and *magnalia* are not the first to come to mind. Bacon is, of course, completely unaware of the ecological destruction inflicted on the planet by an affluent and heedless consumer society in pursuit of the ends he lists.

7. Descartes: Masters and Possessors of Nature

Descartes carried Bacon's proposals further.[49] He studied Bacon early in his career as documented in several letters, the first dating from 1630, before he began his first major work in natural philosophy, *Le Monde* (written 1630–33), almost a decade before his *Meditations on First Philosophy* (1641).[50]

A Practical Philosophy

Already in his *Discourse on Method* (1637), he explicitly lays down the fundamental premise of his philosophy in agreement with Bacon.

> It is possible to reach knowledge that will be very useful to life and instead of the speculative philosophy which is now taught in the schools [i.e., Aristotelian philosophy] we can find a practical one, by which, knowing the force and the actions of fire, water, air, stars, the heavens, and all the other bodies that surround us as distinctly as we know the various skills of our artisans we can employ them in the same way for all the uses for which they are fit, and so make ourselves masters and possessors of nature.[51]

Descartes is explicit. Speculative or theoretical philosophy must be replaced by a practical—that is, technological philosophy—which must decide what is, and what is not, a relevant pursuit of philosophy and its eventual offshoot, natural science. It is a fundamental misconception, though a widely accepted one,

49. Citations of Descartes by AT refer to René Descartes, *Oeuvres*, ed. Charles Adam and Paul Tannery, 13 vols. (Paris: Vrin, 1897–1910). Translations are my own.

50. See Descartes, *Letters*, AT 12:479, footnote a.

51. Descartes, *Discourse on Method* 6, AT 6:61–62.

to suppose that Descartes examined Aristotelian natural philosophy, checked it by reason and experiment, and found it lacking as a theoretical account. He set it aside as a whole to propose an altogether different program, consciously built on the primacy of power over *logos*.

In Goethe's *Faust*, the scientist-magician Faust attempts to translate *In the beginning was the Logos* into his beloved German. He chooses *Im Anfang war die Tat. In the beginning was the deed.* Goethe knows, of course, that when one retranslates Faust's German into Greek, one gets *In the beginning was praxis*, not *logos*. In the beginning was the imposition of will. Marx is a consistent follower of Descartes in making the same choice.

> The philosophers have only interpreted the world in various ways; the point is to change it.[52]
>
> The question whether objective truth belongs to human thinking—*is not a question of theory but is a practical question*. It is in *praxis* that man must prove the truth, that is, the reality and power, the this-sidedness of his thinking. The dispute over the reality or non-reality of thinking that is isolated from *praxis* is a merely scholastic question.[53]

Descartes's *Meditations on First Philosophy* are often studied as metaphysical reasoning rising to great heights. Yet the overall shape of the argument leads one to see the goal of becoming masters and possessors of nature as the guiding hand from the beginning. The argument begins with radical doubt about every certainty of ordinary experience, clearing away the old houses from the building site. It continues with a grand metaphysical flight from the unassailable fortress of self-consciousness (*cogito, ergo sum*) up into the highest reaches of metaphysics, the ontological argument for the existence of God. Many readers see the arrival at God as the goal of the *Meditations*. What comes after this arrival is then a descent into lower regions, a kind of epilogue to the main argument. Descartes's decided option for a practical/technological philosophy in contrast to theoretical philosophy shows that this reading is mistaken. The true end is reached in Meditation Six, which concludes that the only real or objective properties of natural beings are mathematically expressible properties, such as extension, shape, number, movement, and force. All other sensible and intelligible attributes are mere appearances rooted in human subjectivity. Leon Kass shows the underlying logic of this selective vision and its effects.

> Seek knowledge, and knowledge will give you power. But ... it would be more accurate to say that the new science sought first power over nature, and deriv-

52. Karl Marx, "Theses on Feuerbach," Thesis 11.
53. Marx, "Theses on Feuerbach," Thesis 2; emphasis added.

> atively, found a way to reconceive nature that yielded the empowering kind of knowledge: Seek power, and you will devise a way of knowing that gives it to you. The result can be simply put: knowledge permitting prediction and (some) control over biological events has been purchased at the cost of deep ignorance, not to say misunderstanding, of living beings, ourselves included.[54]

Descartes's *cogito ergo sum* is in some respects like St. Augustine's argument against radical doubt, *Si enim fallor, sum. If I err, I am.*[55] Augustine argues from within the position of the skeptics that at least certainty about one's own existence is inescapable, even if one is wrong about everything else. He does not embrace the doubt of the skeptics as his own. Descartes, by contrast, makes use of universal doubt as his starting point, not because he sees good theoretical reasons for such doubt, but because it is effective in the imposition of the will to power. He uses it to strip away from nature all that stands in the way of the ambition for power. His return to truth after universal doubt by way of consciousness and the subject's clear and distinct ideas about nature—that is, its mathematical ideas—concludes with the reduction of all properties of nature to the properties considered by the art of mechanics. This nonphilosophical use of doubt for the ends of power distinguishes Descartes from Augustine. Descartes's turn toward the subject is anti-Augustinian. What most separates the two is Augustine's commitment to *logos* and Descartes's commitment to *praxis*, that is, to the primacy of will and power over *logos*.

The same point holds for Descartes's exclusion of goodness from real being. "I think that in physical things I can get no use from the whole kind of causes which people usually seek from the end, because I do not think I can investigate the ends of God without temerity."[56] Descartes's pious protestation that he does not dare to investigate God's intentions shows that he conceives teleology as Ockham does, as based on the intention of some will rather than on goodness. Goodness is not an objective property of bodies discoverable in them. It cannot be measured and expressed in mathematical terms.

A way of thinking formed in this Cartesian manner will have fundamental difficulties with TOB's account of sex and marriage in terms of *ends* and *meanings.* Even worse, it will experience the normative proposal of ends and meanings as a violent imposition of will by religious leaders, depriving others of due freedom. (See, e.g., the discussion of Goertz on *Humanae vitae*, introduction, sect. 3, in this volume.)

54. Leon Kass, "The Permanent Limitations of Biology," in *The Ambiguous Legacy of the Enlightenment*, ed. William A. Rusher (Lanham, MD: University Press of America: 1995), 125.

55. Augustine, *De civitate dei* 11.26.

56. Descartes, *Meditations* 4, AT 7:55.

The shoe is on the other foot. Irrational imposition of will is the first step in Descartes. In the pursuit of power, Descartes and those who follow him (usually less consciously) do not begin with a theoretical judgment based on evidence. They begin with a choice that acts as a noncognitive selective principle to exclude many forms of knowledge. Descartes rarely draws attention to the moral character of this first foundation of his philosophy. The first foundation has no cognitive value, even though it proves to be fruitful in the development of mechanics.

This self-concealment from its own noncognitive nature still gives to the supposedly *objective* Cartesian view of nature its strength as a quasi-self-evident theoretical starting point. To its proponents, the *objective* view is so self-evidently the only true one that they can dismiss any critique of it as unfounded subjective opinion, romanticism, religious prejudice, motivated by power interests, and so on. In fact, however, the objective view is an imposition of will. It is not a discovery of reason. Descartes's philosophy is often described as rationalistic, but in its first principle, the choice of power as the end, it is antirational.

> The so-called objective view of nature is not nature's own, but one imposed on nature, imposed by none other than the interested subject.... The interested subject's demand for clear and distinct and certain "knowledge" leads him to re-present the given world before his mind, in an act of deliberate projection, through concepts (invented for that purpose) that allow him to operate on it with utmost (usually quantitative) precision. What cannot be grasped through such conceptual re-presentation drops from view. Only those aspects of the world that can be "objectified" become objects of scientific study. The given, visible world of our experience is banished into the shadows; the shadowy world of concepts gains the limelight and reconfigures everything in sight.[57]

It is impossible to overlook the similarity between Descartes and the Sophists with whom Socrates dialogues in the *Gorgias* and the *Republic*. Like the Sophists, Descartes renounces reason by a choice on the most fundamental level. He does not respect reason as a universal openness to being but uses it as an instrument of power. He differs from the Sophists because he does not propose a use of reason for personal power but for the power of science, by which we, the human race, can make ourselves masters and possessors of nature. The love that animates his philosophy is not as overtly militaristic as the love that builds the military city in the *Republic*. Still, it is not the love proper to *logos*. Since he does not aim primarily at military or political power, Descartes is able to conceal the totalitarian and violent nature of his practice of reason. It appears to be an

57. Kass, "Permanent Limitations of Biology," 131–32.

altruistic and beneficent practice committed to making a better world for the human race.

Developments after Descartes

There are many in the scientific community, of course, who are committed to reason, animated by a love of truth, ready to follow their search wherever it might take them, even if the allowable questions and answers are narrowly circumscribed ahead of time. In some cases, expressions of a universally open commitment to truth may be attempts to occupy the intellectual and moral high ground. Still, Benedict XVI is right to point to an authentically rational orientation in his *Regensburg Lecture*, echoing the introductory words by the university's rector. "The scientific *ethos* ... is ... the will to be obedient to the truth, and, as such, it embodies an attitude which belongs to the essential decisions of the Christian spirit."[58] Even in Descartes, there is fascination with truth, particularly with mathematical truth. It is impossible to extinguish the desire for truth. It took many generations for the most radical Cartesians to emerge—first Kant, then Marx.

Although their commitment to truth should not be doubted, one does not often find members of the scientific community who are aware of the choices they inherited from Bacon and Descartes and who have critically resisted the distorting influence of these choices on our way of understanding nature. Even in the paradigm shift from Newtonian physics to relativity and quantum mechanics, natural science left the key elements of the Baconian-Cartesian choices in place, above all the primacy of mathematical mechanics in the study of nature.

The corruption of reason even reaches into mathematics. Greek mathematicians such as Euclid and Apollonius of Perga focus on seeing and understanding forms, while Descartes developed methods of calculation that allow an expansion of mechanics.

> Descartes's Geometry is not a book of theorems and their demonstration. By homogenizing what is studied [i.e., by absorbing geometry into the calculations made possible by symbolic algebra], and by making the central activity the manipulative working of the mind, rather than its visualizing of form and its insight into what informs the act of vision, Descartes transformed Mathematics into a tool with which physics can master nature....
>
> Among the questions that readers will consider, as they study Apollonius in a world transformed by Descartes, are the following:

58. Benedict XVI, *Regensburg Lecture*, December 12, 2006.

What is the relation between the demonstration of theorems and the solving of problems?

What separates the notions of "how-much" and "how-many"?

Why try to overcome that separation by the notion of quantity as represented by a number line?

What is the difference between a Mathematics of proportions which arises to provide images for viewing being, and a Mathematics of equations which arises to provide tools for mastering nature?

How does Mathematics get transformed into what can be taken as a system of signs referring to signs—as a symbolism which is meaningless until applied, when it becomes a source of immense power?

What is Mathematics and why study it?

What is learning and what promotes it?[59]

The focus on calculation eventually leads to the most widely accepted contemporary view of mathematics as a human construct built on axioms adopted by choice. Mathematics understood in this manner can neither be true nor, strictly speaking, false. Even so, the scientific *ethos* highlighted by Benedict XVI is indomitable. It draws mathematicians into their discipline with a freedom of thought that on many occasions breaks the bonds of slavery created by the demands of technology.

Similar transformations can be seen in other disciplines. Cartesian principles inflicted a deadly wound on philosophy itself, which is especially clear in Kant (see part II, chap. 2, in this volume). Unlike Aristotle's *Metaphysics*, Descartes's *Meditations on First Philosophy* are not directed toward the first cause as the supreme object of contemplation. God enters the argument as a necessary step on the way to the true goal; namely, reconfiguring the natural world to be the perfect object of technological ambition.[60] Balthasar observes,

> [One can observe] ... the emergence of an hegemony of instrumental reason which seeks above all manipulative power over nature and which can do without the personal pole of indebtedness/gratitude and goodness since it reduces nature to the level of brute fact. It sees itself simply as an instrument of power and operates as such.... For Descartes, "there is no need to speak of God except in connection with the need for an absolute guarantee for human knowing, that is, in order to secure man's domination of the world." Despite the similarity between Descartes' conception of truth and that of Augustine, he is doing something profoundly different.[61]

59. Apollonius of Perga, *Conics, Books I-III*, rev. ed., with an introduction by Harvey Flaumenhaft (Santa Fe, NM: Green Lion Press, 2000), xxiii–xxiv.

60. See esp. *Meditation* 6, AT 7:78–80.

61. Balthasar, *Theodramatik*, 3:142–43; *Theodrama*, 4:156. Balthasar quotes Ulrich Hommes,

Marginalization quickly overtook the Cartesian God. In the minds of many early modern scientists, God continued to live on in weakened form as the intelligent designer and engineer who can leave his world running by its laws, as designers and engineers generally do. Newton had a robust faith in divine intervention as encoded in the Book of Revelation, but this preoccupation could be dropped and was dropped without any damage to mechanics.[62]

In Kant, God becomes a mere practical postulate without theoretical value. One can say neither *God exists* nor *God does not exist.* God is a decent and moral thought without factual content. The momentum toward divine irrelevance slowly tipped the scales, proclaimed by Nietzsche as the death of God. In contemporary academic theology, many dominant streams follow Kant's solution by reducing God to an existential challenge (Bultmann) or a symbol of liberation, social justice, and peace. Again, only science is concerned with facts. Religion is concerned with values and commitments. This is the Kantian peace between science and religion. It is a peace created by the fact-value distinction, a violent and disastrous peace for both facts and values.

Free will, understood as the freedom of indifference, as sheer self-determination independent of any cause, is the greatest human good, Descartes claims.

> Now freewill is in itself the noblest thing we can have because it makes us in a certain manner equal to God and exempts us from being his subjects; and so, its good use is the greatest of all the goods we possess, and further there is nothing that is more our own or that matters more to us. From all this it follows that nothing but freewill can produce our greatest contentments.[63]

This apotheosis of the freedom of indifference as the greatest human good already anticipates the core of Kant's philosophy of freedom and autonomy (see part II, chap. 2, in this volume). What Descartes proposes in this text is the hard core of a technological exaltation of freedom, technological before it is metaphysical, political, and moral. There is a mutual harmonic reinforcement between this exaltation of free choice and the Baconian program. What distinguishes the master of nature above all is that he can decide freely what to do

---

Transzendenz und Personalität (Frankfurt: Klostermann, 1972), 63. For a similar reading of Descartes, see Robert Spaemann, *Das Natürliche und das Vernünftige: Essays zur Anthropologie* (Munich: Piper, 1987), 101.

62. For Newton's commentary on the Book of Revelation, see the Newton Project website www.newtonproject.sussex.ac.uk.

63. Descartes, Letter to Christina of Sweden, AT 5:85. Translation following Taylor, *Sources of the Self*, 147. One can perhaps temper the astonishing statement that freedom exempts us from being God's subjects by adding the word *seems*. Descartes writes *semble nous exempter de luy estre suiets*. A parallel text is found in *Meditation* 4, where Descartes argues that all our powers are finite, except for free choice, which gives us an infinity of options and therefore makes us most like God. See AT 7:57.

with her. He is not bound by any of her preexisting purposes but sets his own over hers.

Free choice is an act of great dignity, and Wojtyła highlights it, particularly in his main philosophical work, *Person and Act*. Yet free choice is subordinate to love. On this point Wojtyła directly opposes Descartes.

> Love consists in a commitment of freedom because, after all, love is self-giving, and to give oneself means precisely to limit one's freedom on account of the other person. The limitation of one's own freedom would be something negative and unpleasant, but love makes it something positive, joyful, and creative. Freedom is for love.... Man longs for love more than for freedom—freedom is the means, whereas love is the end.[64]

The development of a mechanistic science of nature and the exaltation of freedom of choice as an ultimate value had profound effects on the understanding of the place of the human person in the cosmos. Descartes took the path of a rigorous dualism. On the one side stands the mechanical cosmos of extended things (*res extensae*). Their only attributes are extension, force, and movement. They make up an objective world of pure externality without any interiority. Animals are machines. Their apparent sensory awareness is precisely this, merely apparent. On the other side stands the "thinking thing" (*res cogitans*). Its only attribute is rational consciousness, that is, knowledge and free will. It does not have any roots in a living sentient body. Human beings are not rational animals but ghosts in machines.[65]

Others followed more narrowly reductionist paths. For bishop George Berkeley, a vigorous defender of the spiritual values of the Christian tradition, there is no independently existing material world, but every *material* thing is a mere perception of the soul (*esse est percipi*). The material world exists only as an object of personal consciousness.[66] According to Julien de La Mettrie, by contrast, there is no thinking thing at all, but man is simply "machine man," a material mechanism.[67] In each case, the tension between the person and the

64. Karol Wojtyła, *Love and Responsibility*, trans. Gregorz Ignatik (Boston: Pauline Books and Media, 2013), 117.

65. This characterization of Descartes became well known though the critique by Gilbert Ryle, *The Concept of Mind* (London: Hutchinson, 1949), which dismisses the ghost but keeps the machine. A reading of Descartes in greater continuity with classical philosophy and Christianity, relativizing the ambition for power and the primacy of free choice, is proposed by Gary Steiner, *Descartes as a Moral Thinker: Christianity, Technology, Nihilism* (Amherst, NY: Humanity Books, 2004), esp. chap. 4. Even if Descartes's own position is more complex than the sketch offered above, the effect of his writings in the growth of the modern program corresponds to the sketch.

66. See George Berkeley, *A Treatise Concerning the Principles of Human Knowledge*, ed. Colin Murray Turbayne (Indianapolis: Bobbs-Merrill, 1970).

67. See Julien Offray de La Mettrie, *Machine Man and Other Writings*, ed. Ann Thomson

material world of nature is the crucial issue, even in proposals that apparently abolish the person altogether in favor of mechanism. Even in de La Mettrie's machine man, *someone* is thinking about the machine and freely harnessing it to his own ends, however the word *someone* is to be understood.

John Paul points out a close relation between the predominant scientific picture of the world and a particular form of ethics; namely, utilitarianism.

> The development of contemporary civilization is linked to a scientific and technological progress which is often achieved in a one-sided way and thus appears purely positivistic. Positivism, as we know results in agnosticism in theory and utilitarianism in practice and in ethics. In our own day history is in a way repeating itself. Utilitarianism is a civilization of production and of use, a civilization of things and not of persons, a civilization in which persons are used in the same way as things are used. (*Letter to Families* 13)

Utilitarianism, first in practice and then also as a theory, is a natural consequence of the Baconian-Cartesian program. Persons are seen as parts of the great machine of nature, and they are treated like all other parts of the machine; namely, as things to be harnessed for progress by technology.

The decisive breakthrough, without which Descartes's call for a mathematical science could not have been so universally triumphant, was achieved by Newton about half a century after the publication of Descartes's main works. Michael Hart's book *The 100: A Ranking of the Most Influential Persons in History* places six persons at the top of the list in the following order: (1) Mohammed, (2) Newton, (3) Jesus, (4) Buddha, (5) Confucius, and (6) Paul.[68] It is a group of religious leaders. Newton is the only exception, and he yields first place only to Mohammed. He is historically more significant than Jesus.

Hart is not alone. It is difficult to imagine the intoxicating thrill experienced by many who studied Newton's *Philosophiae Naturalis Principia Mathematica* (*Natural Philosophy's Mathematical Starting Points*) when it was published in 1687. Halley's *Ode to Newton*, included in the prefatory materials of the first edition, expresses the wildly intoxicated mood.

(Cambridge: Cambridge University Press, 1996). The French original *L'homme machine* appeared in 1748, and the first English translation in 1749; the second edition (1750) has an extended subtitle: "Man a Machine: Wherein the several systems of philosophers, in respect to the soul of man, are examin'd, the different states of the soul are shewn to be co-relative to those of the body, the diversity between men and other animals, is proved to arise from the different quantity and quality of brains, the law of nature is explained, as relative to the whole animal creation, the immateriality of an inward principle is by experiments and observations exploded, and a full detail is given of the several springs which move the human machine."

68. See Michael H. Hart, *The 100: A Ranking of the Most Influential Persons in History*, 2nd ed. (New York: Citadel Press, 1992).

> But now, behold,
> Admitted to the banquets of the gods,
> We contemplate the polities of heaven;
> And spelling out the secrets of the earth,
> Discern the changeless order of the world
> And *all the eons of its history.*
> Then ye who now on heavenly nectar fare,
> Come celebrate with me in song the name
> Of Newton, to the Muses dear; for he
> Unlocked the hidden treasuries of Truth:
> So richly through his mind had Phoebus cast
> The radiance of his own divinity.
> *Nearer the gods no mortal may approach.*[69]

Nearest to the divine is the natural philosopher in possession of mathematical equations that allow prediction of movements. One begins to appreciate the vast hope Halley placed in Newton when one asks how Newton allows one to grasp not only the changeless order of the world but also all the eons *of the world's history.* Halley supposes that once we grasp the position of all atoms and then calculate their movement, mathematical physics will replace the study of history and predict future events. It will achieve the most divine wisdom of which human beings are capable. It will exhaustively explain what happened in the lives of the other five men at the top of Hart's list. Newton explains Mohammed and Jesus, not the other way around. Halley, it seems, would move Newton to the top of the list.[70]

What Halley does not draw out is the overall effect such a hope has on human life. Mathematical physics can be conceived as a closed system that needs no other mode of knowing, no causal input other than mechanical forces. The habits of thought created by continuous immersion in this one mode of knowing lead almost inevitably to the supposition that all human choices and emotions can be exhaustively explained by the movement of particles. The banquets of the gods and Apollo with the radiance of his own divinity turn out to be the clatter of a mechanism. Halley's hope turns the universe into a place without life, goodness, and beauty, an alien place, uninhabitable by rational animals.

69. Edmund Halley, *Ode to Newton*, in Isaac Newton, *Principia*, ed. Florian Cajori (Berkeley: University of California Press, 1934), xv; emphasis added.

70. Halley's hope of reconstructing history has turned out to be an illusion. Mathematical chaos theory shows that, even on the supposition of deterministic mathematical laws of motion, immeasurably small differences in the initial condition of a dynamical system can have dramatic effects. The motion of a double pendulum (made of two rigid pieces, the second of which swings freely at the lower end of the first) cannot be predicted because differences in the starting position too small to measure cause major differences in the movement. See Cathleen Alligood, Tim Sauer, and James Yorke, *Chaos: An Introduction to Dynamical Systems* (New York: Springer, 1996).

CHAPTER 4

Loss of the *Logos* of Marriage in Hildebrand and Doms

1. Sexual Physics

Sigmund Freud placed his hope for the future of humanity in the dictatorship of the Cartesian scientific spirit.

> The prohibition of thinking (*Denkverbot*), which religion has decreed in order to keep itself in existence, is by no means without danger for individuals as well as human society....
>
> Our best hope for the future is that the intellect (*der Intellekt*)—the scientific spirit (*der wissenschaftliche Geist*), reason (*die Vernunft*)—will in due course win the dictatorship (*Diktatur*) in the life of the human soul. The essence of reason guarantees that it will then give due place to human emotions and what is determined by them. The universal coercion (*Zwang*) of such a lordship of reason (*Herrschaft der Vernunft*) will turn out to be the strongest unifying bond among human beings and prepare further unifications. Whatever resists such a development—for example, religion prohibiting thought is a danger for the future of humanity.[1]

A similar passage appears in Freud's letter about war to Einstein (September 1932) with a less hopeful reference to emotions.

> One would need to invest more care in educating an upper class (*Oberschicht*) of human beings immune to intimidation, engaged in the quest for truth, who

1. Sigmund Freud, "Neue Folge der Vorlesungen zur Einführung in die Psychoanalyse," in *Gesammelte Werke chronologisch geordnet*, 17 vols., ed. Anna Freud (London: Imago, 1940–50), 15:185; James Strachey, trans. and ed., *New Introductory Lectures on Psycho-Analysis* (New York: W. W. Norton, 1964), 211–12.

> would have the task of steering (*Lenkung*) the non-autonomous masses. That the influences of political powers and the Church's prohibition of thought (*Denkverbot*) are not favorable to such breeding needs no proof. The ideal condition, of course, would be a community of human beings who have subjected their drive-life (*Triebleben*) to the dictatorship of reason (*Diktatur der Vernunft*). Nothing else could bring into being such a complete and stable unification of human beings, even if it means giving up the bonds of feeling between them. But this is most probably a utopian hope.[2]

One side of the great cultural divide posited by Freud is religion, which prohibits thinking. Religion is a matter of irrational faith artificially propped up by ecclesiastical power. It is threatened in its very existence by thinking. On the other side is science, which is simply the right exercise of reason. It is right thinking and therefore does not need to prohibit thinking. All thinking will unfailingly confirm it. Science will have the wisdom to give human emotions their due place, even if (according to Freud's letter to Einstein) we may need to give up the bonds of feeling between human beings. Freud does not elaborate what a society without bonds of feeling would look like.

There is something disturbing about these texts. Their political language is violent. *Dictatorship* and *universal coercion* were charged terms at the time of writing. Hitler achieved full dictatorship by 1933, the year after Freud published the two texts. The violent ambitions and methods of the Nazi party were already known. In this context, *dictatorship* and *universal coercion* are not idle words.

When Freud proposes the scientific spirit as the universally coercive dictator, he does not aim, of course, at any private advantage for himself such as being the dictator or the dictator's scientific advisor. Yet what does it mean for the scientific spirit to achieve dictatorship and universal coercion if not that real persons exercise dictatorship and coercion? Freud proposes an upper class of scientists who will tell the nonautonomous masses what to think and do. Since the nonautonomous masses do not understand science itself, the means of persuasion can only be various forms of pressure, in their most benign form the cultural prestige of scientists and their control over the institutions of learning.

What happens if some among the masses (or stray members of the scientific ruling class) do not agree with this practice of reason? Will the leaders of the ruling class be willing to listen to criticism? Or will they respond with ridicule or (in the case of academics) with refusal of publication, denial of promotion or tenure, and other forms of coercion at the disposal of academic institutions? These forms of coercion are not evil, of course. How could they, since they are simply the expression of a reasonable practice of reason? The *Denkverbot* decreed

2. Sigmund Freud, "Letter to Einstein," *Psychoanalytic Quarterly* 2 (1933): 3–4.

by science will only be the prohibition of wrong thinking, not of right thinking.

To judge from the reassurances he offers, Freud senses that his talk of dictatorship and coercion might cause alarm. Yet the only thing he has to offer is an inexpensive bromide. Scientific reason will eventually understand sex and love. It will give due place to human emotions and guide them, even if it means giving up all emotional bonds between people.

Is the scientific spirit as Freud conceives it open to everyting? Is it open to all of being without any exclusion? Does it have the courage to examine itself and its own history critically? Is it aware of the roots of that history in the choice of power heralded by Bacon and Descartes? As a mere choice, the Baconian-Cartesian project has no legitimate voice before the critical tribunal of reason.

Freud shows little awareness of these questions. His mind is closed by default. The choices made at the beginning of the scientific revolution determine his way of thinking at a level deeply hidden in his scientific unconscious. Would he seriously listen to Scheler's brilliant critique?

> [Mechanist psychology] results from the same illusion that led to the adoption of the world view of classical mechanics, which supposedly presented a picture of absolutely real nature.... It failed to recognize what it means to make technical purposes the starting point. For psychology, these are educational purposes, political purposes, medical purposes, and the like.
>
> Modern man, in his ravenous hunger to control, wanted to recognize as real only what could be controlled, first in the outer world of nature, then in psychological life.... Owing to his technological mind-set, he was interested only in what is dependent on the body and what is both calculable and changeable by influence from the outside.[3]

Wilhelm Reich, one of Freud's students, coined the phrase *The Sexual Revolution* as the title of a book he published in 1945.[4] The book might have been overlooked if it had not become a best-seller in 1968, the year of *Humanae vitae*. Pirated copies were mass produced and eagerly discussed by the students who spearheaded the 1968 revolutions.[5] The book's cultural impact was far-reaching. The sexual revolution received its name and suddenly picked up force.

3. Max Scheler, *Formalism in Ethics and Non-Formal Ethics of Values: A New Attempt toward the Foundation of an Ethical Personalism*, trans. Manfred Frings, 5th ed. (Evanston, IL: Northwestern University Press, 1973), 423–24; *Der Formalismus in der Ethik und die materiale Wertethik: Neuer Versuch der Grundlegung eines ethischen Personalismus*, 7th ed. (Bonn: Bouvier, 2000), 420.

4. Wilhelm Reich, *The Sexual Revolution: Toward a Self-Regulating Character Structure* (New York: Farrar, Straus and Giroux, 1945).

5. See the data for pirated reprints of *The Sexual Revolution* in 1968 and subsequent years in Albrecht Götz von Olenhausen and Christa Gnirss, *Handbuch der Raubdrucke*, vol. 2, *Theorie und Klassenkampf: Sozialisierte Drucke und proletarische Reprints, Eine Bibliographie* (Pullach: Verlag Dokumentation, 1973), 335–53.

Reich conceives sexual love, particularly its highpoint in orgasm, as a form of energy like electricity, to be studied by physics like other forms of energy.

> Sexual energy is *the* biological energy which, in the psyche, determines the character of human feeling and thinking. "Sexuality" (physiologically, the parasympathetic function) is *the* productive life energy as such. Its suppression results not only in psychic and somatic disorders but in a general disturbance of social functioning manifested in the most purposeless actions, mysticism, readiness for war, and so on.[6]

For Reich and for the 1968 revolutionaries, "Make love, not war" is not a flippant slogan but a serious proposal for saving the human race. The suppression of sexual energy, Reich believes, is responsible for the greatest human evils such as religion and war. The solution is simple. Do not suppress sexual energy. Act it out freely. Promiscuity will save the human race.

The form of energy experienced in orgasm, Reich argues, is in many ways similar to but still distinct from gravity and electromagnetic force. He calls it Orgone.

> Orgone is the bioenergetic function of orgasmic convulsion. Biological emotions, which determine psychic processes, are as such the immediate expression of an energy known to physics as cosmic Orgone....
>
> Orgone can be detected by its visual appearance, temperature, and electromagnetic effects in the ground, the atmosphere, and plant as well as animal organisms. The shimmering of the sky, which is attributed by some Physicists to the earth's magnetism, and the glistening of stars in clear, dry nights, are an immediate expression of the movement of Orgone in the atmosphere....
>
> The color of Orgone energy is blue or grey-blue.[7]

Reich corresponded with Einstein, who graciously accepted Reich's request to check his experiments to detect and measure Orgone. Einstein was unable to detect it and concluded that Reich's experiments and theories were mistaken.[8]

This episode in the history of sexual physics is instructive. It shows the damage inflicted by physics envy on other fields of knowledge, in this case psychology. Reich was confident that physics would unlock the mysteries of sexual love. He had found the key in a force field analogous to the fields already accepted by physics. What is sexual love? It is a blue or gray-blue force field, eventually to be described mathematically and then engineered technologically.

6. Reich, *Sexual Revolution*, xvii.

7. Wilhelm Reich, *Die Entdeckung des Orgons: Die Funktion des Orgasmus* (Cologne: Kiepenheuer & Witsch, 1942), 11, 289.

8. The extensive correspondence between Reich and Einstein is published in Wilhelm Reich, *American Odyssey: Letters and Journals 1940–1947* (New York: Farrar, Straus and Giroux, 1999).

For Reich, the guiding paradigm of rationality is mathematical physics. If one wants to know anything, one needs to go about it in the manner of the one and only science that is indisputably scientific; namely, mathematical physics. One needs to talk about particles, force fields, and the like.

Can such an account ever come to understand the experience of sexual love as an experience of persons? Can it understand *eros* as moved by goodness and beauty, by the attractiveness of man and woman? Can it grasp the goodness of children? Can it unfold what it means to receive a gift, in the first place the gift of one's own being. Can it bring out the inner intelligibility of the gift of self to another?

On a general level, the answer to these questions is obvious. Reich shows how disastrous the effects of physics envy can be. No force field will ever be an account of personal sexual love. Mathematical physics does not, and cannot, reach the most basic categories needed to approach an understanding of such love. This is one way in which Reich's sexual physics is instructive. It shows that, at least in the work of one of Freud's most devoted students, the reassurance Freud gives about the dictatorship and universal coercion of the scientific spirit is not reassuring at all.

Reich's sexual physics is instructive in yet another way. The failure of his effort to convince Einstein about Orgone shows that, at least in some circumstances, physics has the resources to correct excesses produced by physics envy. If experiments are flawed, a competent physicist can show that they are flawed. The achievements of physics are formidable, as Alvin Plantinga rightly emphasizes.

> Taken naively but (so I say) accurately, modern science is an enormously impressive attempt to come to know something about ourselves and our world. (Think, for example, of the development of physics from Newton's day to ours: surely an unexcelled display of cooperative intellectual power and depth.) Modern science is therefore a most impressive way in which humankind communally reflects the divine nature, a striking development of the image of God in humanity.
>
> Accordingly, it is to be prized by Christians and other theists; but then conflict between religion and science, from that perspective, is initially anomalous, disturbing, perplexing.[9]

The word *initially* should be emphasized. The conflict is only initially anomalous because the root impulses of both faith and science are rational. Yet there are good reasons to pause before one grants to physics, or to any other mechanist account patterned after it, the dictatorship proposed by Freud. There is a

9. Alvin Plantinga, *Where the Conflict Really Lies: Science, Religion, and Naturalism* (Oxford: Oxford University Press, 2011), 5.

richer and broader intellectual tradition that has come down from the Greeks. It has been sifted and unfolded for more than two millennia. Its roots reach into an ancient ecological wisdom about man and woman. This wisdom is a shared human heritage, older than Christianity. Nevertheless, the pressure of natural science has led many to abandon it.

2. Hildebrand on Marriage

Dietrich von Hildebrand is a determined opponent of the anti-personal mindset of mechanist psychology. He presents a rich vision of sex and marriage, in many ways close to TOB. Nevertheless, he is deeply influenced by Cartesian premises.[10] Hildebrand argues that procreation is the primary *end* of marriage, while the union of persons is its primary *meaning*. "Love is the primary created *meaning, Schöpfungssinn*, in marriage just as the birth of new human beings is the primary created *end, Schöpfungszweck*" (EH 7, MA 7; emphasis added).

> It seems very important to stress again the spiritual significance of marriage—and to explain not only its primary end (procreation) but also its primary meaning as the intimate union of two persons in love. (MA xxv)

The Meaning of Spousal Love

In this stress on *spiritual significance* or *meaning*, as opposed to *end* or *purpose*, Hildebrand intends to correct two tendencies he sees as mistaken. One of them is the reductive tendency among Catholic theologians to give an account of marriage primarily through its physical outcome, children. The other is the tendency of the dominant scientific culture toward "a terrible anti-personalism, a progressive blindness toward the nature and dignity of the spiritual person" (MA xxv). This anti-personalism is present, Hildebrand argues, above all in biological materialism, which considers man as a more highly developed animal, his whole personality determined by physiological processes alone. Freud's and Reich's account of sex exemplifies this vision. There is a clear convergence between Hildebrand and TOB in these concerns.

10. Citations of Hildebrand as RJ (= *Reinheit und Junfräulichkeit*), DP (= *In Defense of Purity*), EH (= *Die Ehe*), MA (= *Marriage*), and HV (= *Die Enzyklika Humanae vitae*) refer to Dietrich von Hildebrand, *Reinheit und Junfräulichkeit*, 3rd ed. (Einsiedeln: Benziger, 1950); *In Defense of Purity: An Analysis of the Catholic Ideals of Purity and Virginity* (London: Sheed & Ward, 1931); *Die Ehe* (Munich: Josef Müller, 1929); *Marriage: The Mystery of Faithful Love*, trans. by the author with a new preface (Manchester, NH: Sophia Institute, 1997); *Die Enzyklika "Humanae vitae"—Ein Zeichen des Widerspruchs* (Regensburg: Josef Habbel, 1968).

Hildebrand analyzes "the essence and meaning of marriage" both "in the realm of nature" and that of grace (EH 5, MA 4). His point of entry into the argument is the Song of Songs and its traditional interpretation as an image of the union of love between Christ and the soul. It is the same door through which Wojtyła entered the subject. Why is the relationship between man and woman chosen as the preferred image of this union of love?

> It is chosen because marriage is the closest and most intimate of all earthly unions in which more than in any other, one person gives himself to another without reserve, where the other in his complete personality is the object of love, and where mutual love is in a specific way the theme (that is to say the core) of the relationship. (EH 56, MA 4–5)

The unreserved gift of self stands thus at the center of Hildebrand's understanding of marriage. The similarity with St. John Paul II is striking. Lily von Hildebrand testifies that her husband spent five years after his conversion in 1914 reading the Fathers of the Church and the great mystics, including St. John of the Cross. One fruit of this immersive reading is what many of his students consider Hildebrand's most important work, *Transformation in Christ*.[11] The final chapter of his book is dedicated to the saying of Jesus, "The one who finds his life will lose it, and the one who loses his life for my sake will find it." Hildebrand unfolds this saying in terms of "giving oneself" unreservedly to God.

The foundations of Hildebrand's understanding of marriage are laid in the more extensive analysis of love and sexuality offered by *In Defense of Purity*, published two years before *Marriage*. In the bodily sphere, sexual union has a unique place, the book argues. While the pleasure of a good meal can be relatively peripheral, sex is always "essentially deep" (RJ 15; DP 13). It always touches and grasps the core of the person. The specific character of sexual sin testifies to this deep power and centrality of sex.

> Surrender to sexual pleasure for its own sake defiles a man in a way that gluttony, for example, can never do. It wounds him to the core of his being, and he becomes in an absolutely different and novel fashion guilty of sin. And even as compared with many other domains of experience which are not physical, sex occupies a central position in the person.... Sex can indeed keep silence, but when it speaks it is no mere aside, an *obiter dictum*, but a voice from the depths, the utterance of something central and of the utmost significance. In and with sex, man, in a special sense, gives himself. (RJ 16, DP 14)

11. Dietrich von Hildebrand, *Die Umgestaltung in Christus* (Ottilien: EOS, 1988); *Transformation in Christ: Your Path to Salvation* (Manchester, NH: Sophia Institute, 1990).

Hildebrand illustrates this central position of sex in the person by the phenomenon of shame. The sexual sphere is intimate, it touches the person's innermost, it contains in a unique way *the* mystery of the person *par excellence*. The shame connected with this intimacy is not a fear of revealing something ugly or disgusting but a protection of the intimate sphere.

This intimate character is a further proof of the special depth and central position of sex as contrasted with all other bodily functions. Since it is "the mystery of every individual, the revelation and gift of sex signifies (*bedeutet*) in a unique way a gift of self, *Selbsthingabe*" (RJ 16, DP 14).

In this account of shame or reverence, Hildebrand adds an aspect to St. Augustine's analysis of sexual shame in the *City of God*. Augustine sees the origin of shame in the fall, in accord with Genesis 2:25. He writes,

> The [sexual] act itself, which is performed with such desire (*libido*) ... avoids the public gaze.... When it is lawful and honorable, why does it call for a room hidden from judgments (*arbitriis*)? Does not the bridegroom before he begins to caress his bride, send out all the servants, and even his groomsmen, and all the others who had been allowed to enter because of some ties of kinship.... Who does not know what the spouses do between themselves for procreating children? ... And nevertheless, when the spouses do what children are born from, not even the children who were already born from this act are allowed to become witnesses of it....
>
> What is the origin of this if not that what is naturally decent is done in such a way that one is ashamed of what accompanies it as a punishment? ... Ashamed of this desire (*libido*)—this is without any doubt what human nature is, and rightly so. For in the disobedience of this [desire], which subjected the genitals only to its own movements and removed them from the power of the will, shows well enough what man's punishment is for that first disobedience.[12]

In this text, Augustine does not focus on the positive side of shame motivated by reverence for the depth and interiority of sex in the couple.

The true *meaning and essence* (*Sinn und Wesen*) of sexual union as the conjugal act can only be understood, Hildebrand argues, if one sees it *from above*, from spousal love, which is not reducible to either sexual instinct or the need to procreate (RJ 20, DP 19). Love on the level of spirit (*Geist*) expresses itself in the conjugal act and finds fulfillment in it.

> In virtue of its *quality*, the sexual sphere is an expression and a specifically important field of fulfillment for spousal love. The act of spousal communion (*Gemeinschaft*) is a unique expression of spousal love and its specific fulfill-

12. Augustine, *De civitate dei* 14.18 and 14.20.

> ment, because the two spouses, according to the words of our Lord and Savior Jesus Christ, become one flesh in it, and thus form an ultimate (*letzte*) union which is in a special way the intended end (*abzielt*) of spousal love. (RJ 27, DP 24)

One can distinguish two interconnected levels in this text.

1. *The Level of Sex in the Narrow Sense.* Sex between human beings is never a mere animal function, but it touches the core of the person. The attempt to engage in a form of sex that has been freed from everything except pleasure is bound to fail. More is necessarily present in this act. The person inevitably gives himself or herself.

2. *The Level of Spousal Love.* The meaning of self-gift that is inevitably present in sexual union only reaches its own true nature when it is an expression and fulfillment of a gift in spousal love. It is in this way that the act of sexual union becomes, properly speaking, the conjugal act, the act of the spouses as spouses with all the levels of meaning implied in these words.

A text from *Familiaris consortio* can illustrate how strikingly these two theses anticipate the teaching of John Paul II, which distinguishes the same two levels.

> Sexuality, by means of which man and woman give themselves to one another through the acts which are proper and exclusive to spouses, is by no means something purely biological but concerns the innermost being of the human person as such. It is realized in a truly human way only if it is an integral part of the love by which a man and a woman commit themselves totally to one another until death. The total physical self-giving would be a lie if it were not the sign and fruit of a total personal self-giving, in which the whole person, including the temporal dimension, is present: if the person were to withhold something or reserve the possibility of deciding otherwise in the future, by this very fact he or she would not be giving totally. (*Familiaris consortio* 11)

Two levels are again at stake.

1. *The Level of Sex.* Sexual union carries within itself a definite meaning that reaches inescapably and profoundly into the innermost experience of those who engage in it. That meaning is the gift of self.

2. *The Level of Spousal Love.* The natural language of sexual gift reaches its truly human quality only if it is "the sign and fruit of a total personal self-giving" in the conjugal act.

Hildebrand unfolds the two levels and their interrelation further in his book on purity.

> The sexual sphere and especially the act of conjugal communion contains many aspects that return analogously in higher spiritual spheres, for example, the aspect of an unreserved attention and self-gift to the other, of a certain melting, ecstasy, disclosure and self-revelation. This objective qualitative analogy does not as such imply an objective causal relation between a purely spiritual unreserved gift of self and the gift that lies in the act of conjugal communion.
>
> Even less does it imply that every gift of self, all melting, ecstasy and so on, wherever they occur, are sublimations of sexuality. This position not only replaces a qualitative analogy with a real connection but it portrays that which is a derivative image as the archetype, in fact, as the only real thing. In this view, higher forms are mere derivates of lower forms, merely dressed-up and veiled forms of sexuality....
>
> In fact, the qualitative analogy is a condition for the expression and fulfillment of a certain form of love, in which the qualitative analogy goes far beyond these formal features. As soon as the act of conjugal communion is realized in this function, there is a completely new real relation between spousal love and the sexual sphere which is based on the qualitative analogy between the former and the latter, yet in such a way that love is the point of departure and the actuating (*aktuierende*) principle. (RJ 19n2, DP 6n1)

There is a qualitative analogy between the bodily gift of self in sexual intercourse and the spiritual gift of self in spousal love. This analogy is a basis, though not the only one, for the authentic relation between the two levels. The spousal gift takes up the sexual gift to find expression and fulfillment in it. This concurrence of the two levels, Hildebrand argues, constitutes the conjugal act in the full sense of *conjugal*.

Various aspects of spousal love need to be seen in their unity, he goes on to argue. The core of spousal love is the mutual self-gift of man and woman, a gift that is "complete and ultimate" (EH 8, MA 8). To clarify this core, Hildebrand makes a distinction between *we* relations and *I-you* relations.[13] Two human beings can stand side by side to regard a common interest or goal in which they share. In this form of relation, they consciously experience each other as *we*.

But two human beings can also turn to face one another, and in touching one another in an interpenetrating glance give birth to a mysterious union of their souls. They become conscious of one another, and making the other the object of their contemplation and responses, each can spiritually immerse himself in the other. This is the *I-you* relationship, in which the partners are not side

13. See Hildebrand's social philosophy published one year after *Marriage*. Dietrich von Hildebrand, *Metaphysik der Gemeinschaft: Untersuchungen über Wesen und Wert der Gemeinschaft* (Regensburg: Josef Habbel, 1955), 34–39.

by side but *face-to-face* (see EH 9, MA 9). This form of relation is present most expressly in spousal love.

> Of all terrestrial communions, conjugal love is the most pronounced form of an *I-you* relationship. The beloved person is the object of our thoughts, sentiments, will, hope, and longing. She becomes the center of our life (as far as created goods are concerned). He whose heart is filled with such conjugal love lives not only *with* his beloved but *for* his beloved. Certainly, such an *I-you* relationship in its purest form exists only between the human soul and its heavenly Bridegroom, Jesus. In the last analysis we must live only for Him, and in marriage, too, the two partners live together for Him. But in the realm of created goods, conjugal love means living *for* one another. Compared with all other human relationships, the two partners live in a definite *I-you* communion. (EH 9, MA 9–10)

The character of the I-you communion that arises out of spousal love, Hildebrand continues, is deeply shaped by an element of decision in the declaration of spousal love, *I love you*. When this sentence functions as a declaration of spousal love, it expresses primarily the absolute decision for the other (see EH 9–10, MA 10–11).

A revelation of the beloved person as a complete unity in qualitative uniqueness is implicit in spousal love. Spousal love penetrates to "the innermost, mysterious essence of the other person," an individual and unique essence. This thesis closely resembles Scheler's concept of *individual-personal value-essence* (see part II, chap. 3, in this volume).

> Our eyes are able to penetrate the other much more deeply than in the ordinary way when our glance is distracted by innumerable trifling objects and dulled by a grey everyday atmosphere. This never goes beyond the outer aspects. Just as in supernatural love of our neighbor we penetrate at one glance to that innermost, mysterious essence of the other person in which, through all his imperfections, pettiness, arrogance, and triviality he reflects God, so in natural conjugal love the real individuality of the partner is mysteriously revealed. The deep, secret meaning which permeates all his gifts and talents, the whole rhythm of his being, is disclosed at one glance through all his imperfections. One understands, so to speak, the divine plan underlying the creation of this particular *individuality*, just as in love of neighbor one understands the general meaning of a free, spiritual person, created by God after His own image in a particular *individual*. (EH 10–11, MA 11–12)

Conjugal love is founded on the difference between man and woman, which is not merely bodily and biological but spiritual as well. For this reason, man and woman "can, purely as spiritual persons, form a unity in which they reciprocally complement one another" (EH 12, MA 15). This point is important to Hildebrand's overall argument, particularly in his understanding of the place of procreation in marriage. Procreation is an end that concerns the sexual aspect of spousal love. There is a sexual complementarity of man and woman with respect to procreation in the sense that both man and woman are needed for procreation. Yet, above this bodily level, there is a purely spiritual complementarity that cannot be connected in the same way with procreation.

Hildebrand offers a spirited apologia for being in love. Being in love is not a mere state of infatuation but the climax of seeing the revelation of the other person in his or her unique individuality, "in which the charm of the other being is completely unfolded, the full bliss of the *I-you* community realized" (EH 13, MA 15). There can be a superficial way of being in love, in which one is impressed by the exterior qualities of the other. This way of being in love involves self-deception and ends in disillusionment. True being in love is deep and grasps the true qualities of the other person. Yet even the more superficial kind is not without its merit.

> Above all, real *being in love*, even in its superficial form, must never be confused with sensual desire. Being in love always implies a respectful, chivalrous attitude toward the beloved—a certain element of humility even, a melting of the soul, of the rigidity of the ego. A person truly in love becomes tender and even pure. (EH 14, MA 17)

This condition of being in love is an essential part of spousal love, not in the sense that it must continue in the same form and the same degree of intensity throughout married life, "but this being in love must be re-actualized at specific moments" (EH 14, MA 18). It is a condition for an authentic realization of conjugal sexual intercourse.

> Only in conjugal love, where man and woman are united in a unique communion, where they give themselves to one another in the deepest sense of the word and belong to each other in an ultimate interpenetration of their souls, does this relation to the sexual sphere become intelligible. Only in this order can the sublime meaning of the sexual sphere be realized, in the union of two beings in a complete spiritual-sensual union according to the words of our Lord and Savior Jesus Christ: "And they shall be two in one flesh." (EH 15, MA 19)

Of its very nature, spousal love is exclusive. Its exclusivity is not a function of possessiveness but an outgrowth of the unreserved gift of self and of the revelation of the unique individuality of the other person, of his or her innermost, mysterious essence (see EH 15–16, MA 20–21).

The Meaning of Marriage

What is marriage? Hildebrand draws on his analysis of the meaning of the conjugal act and of spousal love to answer this question. Marriage goes beyond spousal love, but spousal love anticipates its meaning. Marriage is constituted by a solemn act in which both spouses give themselves to each other for life as a whole. In this act, the two create an objectively existing bond. This bond is fully actualized when the spouses consummate their marriage in the conjugal act. Hildebrand accordingly offers the following formulations to define marriage.

> The act of voluntary surrender of one's own person to another with the intention of forming a permanent and intimate union of love, creates an objective bond which, once established, is withdrawn from the sphere of arbitrary decision of the persons concerned.... The union desired in conjugal love becomes by this act objectively real in its fullest sense, and no other earthly communion of love can become objective to such a degree. Both partners now belong wholly to each other. An objective bond unites them: they are no longer *two* but *one*. (EH 17–18, MA 23)
>
> Marriage as such ... [exists] to unite two human beings in boundless love into a complete union and thus, in the most sublime way, to reflect the union between Jesus and the soul. (EH 26, MA 37–38)
>
> Marriage is, in its nature, principally a communion of love. (EH 19, MA 25)
>
> Great as is the natural tie originated by the solemn conclusion of marriage, which expresses the will to belong to one another in a permanent communion, nevertheless the decision consciously realized in God creates here a tie of an infinitely higher dignity and reality. (EH 31, MA 49)

Hildebrand further clarifies what marriage is by explaining how sexual intercourse is related to the marriage bond.

> An extraordinary decision is inherent in the act of getting married (*Eheschluss*) [i.e., the solemn public act]. Unlike conjugal love, it does not spring into being of itself, but it is a free act like an act of will (in the stricter sense of the term). It marks, as with religious vows, the beginning of a new *state of life*....
>
> This decisive character of marriage, on the strength of which a change takes place which removes it beyond the range of our influence, also has a qualitative analogy in bodily surrender. The physical union of husband and wife constitutes such an ultimate intimacy between them that of its essence it is a surrender valid once and for all. It is not merely a passing intimacy which establishes no objective relationship. (EH 18, MA 24)

According to these passages, marriage is an objective bond by which husband and wife belong to each other permanently and exclusively for the sake of a communion of love. This communion is expressed and consummated in the conjugal act. Marriage is in this way by its essence and meaning an outgrowth and full realization of the gift of self that takes place in spousal love.

If this is truly Hildebrand's answer to the question *What is marriage?*, one must conclude that he does not consider procreation relevant for the definition. Yet it is clear that, for Hildebrand, procreation is the *primary end* of marriage. What, then, *does* he say exactly about the relation between procreation and *the essence and meaning* of marriage?

The distinction between *meaning* and *end* is the basis of his answer to this question. What Hildebrand typically has in mind when he speaks about *end* is the relation between instrumental means and the result caused by them in the order of efficient causality, for example, medicine as a means for health, surgical instruments as means for performing a surgery, and so on. The goodness or value of the means is a purely borrowed goodness. The end is something strictly outside the means. *Meaning*, by contrast, refers to the intrinsic goodness of something, a goodness it possesses in virtue of what it itself is. The conjugal act and marriage have both kinds of goodness. They have a borrowed goodness as means for an external purpose—children—and they have an intrinsic goodness that consists of the union of love between man and woman. Among all external purposes of marriage, procreation is the first and most important, and among all aspects of intrinsic goodness, the union of love is the first and most important.

> As marriage is, in its nature, principally a communion of love, so the meaning of physical consummation is not restricted to its function as a means of procreation. Certainly, there is no greater mystery in the natural order of things than the fact that this closest of all unions procreates a human being....
>
> But this primary *end* is not the only *meaning* of the physical act. Subjectively speaking it is not even its primary meaning. Its *meaning* is primarily the realization of the sublime communion of love. (EH 19, MA 25–26)

God decided to join the purpose of the conjugal act and marriage with their intrinsic meaning and thereby confirmed the greatness of this intrinsic meaning. Hildebrand has great reverence for the joining of procreation with the union of love, which explains his rejection of contraception already in *Marriage*, published a year before *Casti connubii.*

> In order to preserve the reverent attitude of the spouses toward the mystery of this union, this general connection between procreation and the communion of love must always be maintained even subjectively, at least as a general possibility of this act.
>
> It is difficult to imagine a greater lack of reverence toward God than in-

terfering with this mystery with desecrating hands in order to frustrate this mystery. (EH 20, MA 27–28)

Although God has joined procreation and union of love, they remain outside of each other as meaning and end. They are not connected by their essence in such a way that one implies the other. The meaning of loving union is, as such, complete and sufficient without reference to children. A marriage in which husband and wife know that medical reasons beyond their control make it impossible for them to have children can "have its full, divinely-appointed meaning simply as the highest communion of love" (EH 21, MA 29).

In his book on *Humanae vitae*, Hildebrand further develops this understanding of the relation between meaning and purpose. The purpose of marriage, he argues, is a case of *superabundant* finality that differs from *instrumental* finality. In the case of instrumental finality, the purpose is "the exclusive meaning of the existence (*Daseinssinn*) of something" (HV 17). A surgical instrument, for example, has a "meaning and value ... that depends completely on its purpose." In the case of superabundant finality, by contrast, the being has its meaning and value already independently from the purpose to which it leads. In a footnote, Hildebrand uses a Scholastic distinction to clarify this point. "In the case of instrumental purpose the *causa finalis* determines the *causa formalis* while in the principle of superabundant finality the *causa formalis* departs from the *causa finalis*" (HV 18n9, cf. 36).

The phrase *departs from* can be understood in different degrees of radicalism. The most radical reading would be that the formal cause of marriage is already complete before the superabundant finality of procreation is added. Because the formal cause determines *what* something is, the essence of marriage in this radical reading would be wholly independent of procreation. In this reading, the absence of procreation in Hildebrand's account of marriage would contain an implicit denial: procreation is not part of the nature and meaning of marriage. This conclusion is unavoidable if the passage about *causa finalis* and *causa formalis* quoted above is to be understood in its full Scholastic rigor.

Perhaps, however, one should not press Hildebrand on categories in which he is not at home. His own term *superabundance* suggests a more moderate reading in greater harmony with the theological tradition. The image conveyed by this term is the overflowing of liquid from within a container. The image establishes a certain continuity, an intrinsic link between what is within the container and what overflows from it. The good of procreation emerges from the good of loving union as something intrinsically connected with it.

Hildebrand does not clearly exclude the more radical reading, nor does he explicitly develop the more moderate reading. For the most part, he focuses on counteracting a perceived overemphasis in the tradition on the good of procreation. Because he sees a competition between procreation and loving union in the traditional account—that is, a reduction of marriage to a mere means that serves the purpose of procreation—the main thrust of his thought is to create room for the primary meaning of marriage.

> Is conjugal love in itself not sublime enough to sanctify and justify this [sexual] union? . . . Can a childless marriage be regarded as a failure, as something that did not fulfill its meaning? Can we justly assert that it would have been better if such a marriage had not been brought to pass? Can it not have its full, divinely-appointed meaning simply as the highest communion of love, and glorify God by this very fact?
>
> When both partners, even though childless, belong to each other in the most perfect conjugal love, in unchangeable loyalty to one another, in imitation of the union of the soul with God, is not the ideal of marriage fulfilled to an even higher degree than in the case of a marriage with perhaps many children, where the partners are unfaithful to each other and desecrate the sacred tie by a lack of love and loyalty? Need marriage become celibate because of the knowledge that there cannot be any children? Is this not a clear indication that marriage is a symbol of the union of the soul with God, that it possesses, as such, a sublime importance and that it exists in the first place for its own sake and not exclusively for the sake of any result that it produces? (EH 21, MA 28–29)

3. Strengths and Defects

Unitive Meaning

In continuity with streams in the theological tradition on which Wojtyła draws as well, Hildebrand offers penetrating insight into spousal love and its expression in the sexual sphere. He has a vivid grasp of the gift of self that takes place on these two levels, on the latter as an expression of the former. He can give powerful and clear philosophical expression to this vivid grasp. In this area he enriches the tradition and anticipates some of the essential elements of St. John Paul II's understanding of the spousal meaning of the body.

Hildebrand is not the first in the early twentieth century to propose an understanding of marriage in terms of the unreserved gift of self, though his contribution is important. In 1928, one year before the publication of Hildebrand's *Marriage*, Émile Mersch, the great master of the theology of the mystical body, published an article on marriage that goes in a similar direction. One can see the convergence with Hildebrand particularly in a passage in which Mersch argues that marriage is indissoluble because the totality of the gift of self in spousal love implies indissolubility.

> Love, we repeat, is a union. It is impossible without a reciprocal donation of self, by which each partner renounces his life as an isolated individual, to become one with the other. But for a man to give "himself" is not a momentary thing. He is not, in fact, restricted, as animals are, to having only a vague and fugitive sensation of himself, only an obscure apprehension which is effaced with the present perception. He thinks and judges in function of the past and of the future and, when he reflects on himself, it is of all his life that there is question. This manner of knowing himself, of "possessing himself," indicates the manner in which he ought to give himself, under pain of self-contradiction: he ought to give himself for his entire life. If he wished the conjugal union but pretended not to renounce by the same act the right of taking himself back, he would give himself while refusing himself, and would therefore go contrary to the essential requirement of love.[14]

The affinity between Hildebrand and Mersch and their common affinity with Wojtyła are clear. All three have a place in a broader movement of Catholic thought in which *gift*, both the reception and the giving of a gift, was developed as a key notion for understanding love. Mersch's sources are probably French spiritual writings of the late nineteenth and early twentieth centuries, which are particularly rich in the use of *gift of self*.

Procreative Meaning

Hildebrand's view on children as the primary end of spousal love and marriage is not developed as extensively. He limits himself to calling them the primary end without unfolding the implications. He would probably have more to say about the way children are desired and loved by a couple in the best circumstances, but in his struggle against a perceived overemphasis on procreation, he leaves this side of his thought undeveloped.

One could develop an understanding of procreation in a Hildebrandian spirit along the following lines. The child is intimately connected with the mutual love of husband and wife. It is a profound affirmation of another person and of one's spousal union with that person to desire and propose that the other's life be communicated in unity with one's own life to a child who is a fruit of the love of both and bears the traces of the personal characteristics of both. This affirma-

14. Émile Mersch, *Morality and the Mystical Body* (New York: P. J. Kenedy & Sons, 1939), 217. The chapter in which this text is found goes back to Émile Mersch, "Amour, Mariage, Chasteté," *Nouvelle Revue Théologique* 50 (1928): 5–30.

tion occurs not only on the level of physical life but also on that of spiritual and cultural life. In this latter form of communication, the personal characteristics of one's spouse are even more decisive: "I want our children to be formed in their spiritual, intellectual and cultural life by you." This desire is a natural and organic part of the gift of self in marriage. As John Paul II puts it, the procreative meaning grows organically out of the spousal meaning of the body (see TOB 39:5).

When conceived, the child slowly makes its presence felt within the woman, not outside of her. Conception of a child is an intimate and transforming mystery for the woman and, by participation, for her husband. Even after its birth, the child remains within the family as within a second womb. The child lives in a personal space created and formed above all by the love between husband and wife. Precisely in their love for each other, the parents experience the child in its value, as a great good for them.

The spouses are attracted to each other by the goodness and beauty in the personal *face* of the other. Their love is, for this reason, partly directed toward each other as "that for the sake of which." In a similar way, the child enters the original relationship with its own beauty and goodness and opens that relationship to be sheltered by it. The child will leave father and mother to enter new bonds. Yet, both in the time of its presence in the family and in the time of its new life outside this womb, the child is a gift for the parents. The goodness of this gift is a cause of joy.

As such a presence, the child is also a gift of the two spouses to each other. It is part of the comprehensive logic of gift that shapes the relationship between husband and wife. It brings their mutual reception and gift of self to its inner completion. John Paul II shows the essential place of the child in this comprehensive logic of gift.

> In its most profound reality, love is essentially a gift; and conjugal love, while leading the spouses to the reciprocal "knowledge" which makes them "one flesh," does not end with the couple, because it makes them capable of the greatest possible gift, the gift by which they become cooperators with God for giving life to a new human person. Thus the couple, while giving themselves to one another, give not just themselves but also the reality of children, who are a living reflection of their love, a permanent sign of conjugal unity and a living and inseparable synthesis of their being a father and a mother. (*Familiaris consortio* 14)

Hildebrand does not explicitly draw these connections between the loving unity of husband and wife and children, but they fit with his account of procreation as a *superabundant* fruit of love, a fruit that emerges from within that love and has an intrinsic connection with it.[15]

Absence of the Common Good

The Catholic tradition understands procreation as a common good of the spouses and of the whole of humanity. Without any sense of tension between his account of self-gift and procreation, Mersch gives a central place to this common good in his reflection about love and marriage. He sees the commonness of the common good of children reflected in the very nature of love between man and woman.

> Love . . . has its reason for being, its energies, and thence its requirements, not from the individual but from the species. The individual is the carrier and the agent of it, not the master. Love is an act of the species, in this sense, that it is destined to perpetuate the species, and that, in it, the species realizes itself and acts in the measure in which it can be realized and can act. . . . Incarnating the unity of humanity, love is august and venerable with all the nobility of our race. . . .
>
> We are at the corner-stone of social morality. To disturb the position of this stone, is to imperil the whole structure. Respect for the lives of our fellow-men, for their reputations, for their goods, is only the consequence of a more fundamental obligation: "Remember to respect humanity." To insult it at its source and in the very center of its unity, and to take as a toy the august function which alone assures its existence, is to sin grievously against the first principle of all society and against the essential subordination of the individual to the species. . . .
>
> Precisely because it is an act of the species, this love profoundly affects the individual. It perfects him and exalts him to the point of making him coincide, in some way, with humanity itself, and of constituting him principle of man.[16]

This text shows Mersch's strong awareness of the common good of humanity. Much of his writing on the mystical body unfolds the importance of this perspective. A central feature of fully common goods needs to be underlined to understand Mersch's position, a feature underlined also by St. John Paul II. The common good is primarily the good of persons. It is not the good of a collective, understood as standing over against persons and possibly competing with

15. See the excellent overview in Kevin Schemenauer, *Marriage and Procreation: Dietrich von Hildebrand's Superabundant Integration* (Lanham MD: Lexington Books, 2011).

16. Mersch, *Morality and the Mystical Body*, 210–11.

them. Such goods of collectives do exist (e.g., money owned by the state), but they are only imperfectly common. They are more truly the private good of the collective. It is not in this sense that Mersch sees love as having its power and duties from the species. Nor is it in this way that he sees a subordination of the individual to the species. The common good of the species is itself the person's good. It is for the person that the common good of the species is a greater good than the individual good. It is for the person that the mystical body of Christ in all its greatness is a greater good than the good of the family. These points are unfolded in part I, chapter 7, on the common good, in this volume.

The love between husband and wife takes its form from this common good. Their love is not a merely private matter; it is a function of the mystical body. Scheeben unfolds this connection in the same direction as Mersch, half a century earlier.

> They [i.e., husband and wife] must cooperate precisely as members of the body of Christ in his Church, and hence as organs of the whole, and therefore they must unite with each other as organs of Christ's body, as organs of the whole that was brought into being by the union of Christ with the Church. Thus their union, their covenant, becomes an organic member in the great and richly articulated covenant between Christ and His Church, a member which is encompassed, pervaded, and sustained by this mystical covenant, which participates in the lofty, supernatural, and sacred character of the whole and in its innermost essence represents and reflects that whole.[17]

One searches Hildebrand in vain for an account of this common good. What one does find is the apparent opposite. Hildebrand compares marriage to other forms of community, such as the state, and finds marriage superior. His criterion for establishing a hierarchy is the depth of personal union that is achieved by a community.

> Every community of love has its specific value. A value is inherent not only in the love of the lovers but also in the union of love in which both persons are united: "Behold how good and how pleasant it is for brethren to dwell in unity." The deeper and more central this union of love, the greater is the value of this community. Now, as we have seen, the most intimate community of love among persons is marriage. Thus, even as a merely natural community, it surpasses any other (such as the family, state, or nation).... It is characteristic of the pagan errors of our epoch to believe that the nation and state rank higher than the family and higher even than marriage, and, above all, to consider

17. Matthias Joseph Scheeben, *Die Mysterien des Christentums*, 3rd ed., ed. Josef Höfer (Freiburg: Herder, 1958), 496–97; *The Mysteries of Christianity*, trans. Cyril Vollert, SJ (St. Louis, MO: Herder, 1946), 602–3.

interest in the nation or in the state as something more unselfish than the surrender of self to the family or to the marriage relationship. These communities are believed superior only because they are numerically vaster and have a longer life than marriage. In reality they are much inferior. The most perfect state or nation cannot glorify God as much as a perfect marriage. (EH 42–44, MA 70–73)

Is Hildebrand setting the private good of a couple above the common good of the state? In his *Metaphysics of Community* he argues that the traditional axiom that the part is subordinated to the whole cannot be applied to the relation between marriage and the state.[18] Marriage and the state are each constituted by a distinct domain of meaning (*Sinnbereich*). The domain of meaning proper to marriage—namely, the union of love between man and woman—lies outside the domain of meaning of the state. The domain of meaning proper to the state is the public arena and, above all, the realm of law and justice.[19] In this perspective, the marriages in a state are obviously not parts of the greater whole.

Yet whether one wishes to use the term *state* for it or not, there clearly is a whole that consists of all the forms of community and their domains of meaning in a particular place. A city, for example, is a whole composed of all persons and all communities that live in it. The good of the couple and the family is not outside such a city but in it. That there are happy families in the city is an essential part of that city's common good. Again, to say *its good*—that is, the city's good—is not to contrast the city's good with that of the persons who live in it. It is for each person in the city a great good to live in a city with happy families.

In this perspective, one can see a hierarchy in which the good of the city stands above the good of marriage and the family. To preserve the common good of a city, it is reasonable to sacrifice one's life and thereby one's marriage and membership in a family. Such a sacrifice would be irrational if the city and its common good were not superior to marriage and the family. A similar point is applicable, a fortiori, to the Church.

This political or ecclesial aspect of love and marriage, which is so central for Scheeben, Mersch, and John Paul II together with the mainstream of the theological tradition from the Fathers on, is not present in Hildebrand. Hildebrand does not deny the common good of the city, of the human race, and of the mystical body that is served by procreation and education, but it plays no role in his account of love and marriage. His account is thus *personalistic* in a restrictive or limiting sense. He views marriage as essentially a private institution to which the spouses and God alone are privy. In fact, the tradition is clear on the nature

18. See Hildebrand, *Metaphysik der Gemeinschaft*, 324–27.
19. See Hildebrand, *Metaphysik der Gemeinschaft*, 226–51.

of marriage as a public institution. It is a publicly established covenant before witnesses who represent the state and the church.

The Specifying End

A deeper defect in Hildebrand's account of marriage and the conjugal love is his failure to recognize that the goodness of specific ends gives to each being its specific nature. The same point applies to its powers and acts. Josef Fuchs rightly emphasizes this point in his review of Hildebrand.

> D. von Hildebrand ... has provided an excellent phenomenology of love as the meaning of marriage and of the conjugal act. Still, he could have set forth more fully the interior link between love and procreation as purposes, and thus the full meaning of the former and the specifying power of the latter. Although the assertion that God has linked both purposes in the same act is correct, this assertion does not yet show the interior character of the link (not even in the statement that procreation is a purpose in the manner of superabundance out of the act of love).[20]

The most important point made by Fuchs in this text is that the end of procreation has a *specifying power* in the conjugal act. It determines the specific nature of the act. By the same token, procreation has a specifying power in marriage. It makes marriage be *what* marriage is.

Hildebrand holds that a marriage in which husband and wife know that they cannot have children can "have its full, divinely-appointed meaning simply as the highest communion of love" (EH 21, MA 29). That a childless marriage can have a deep meaning is beyond doubt, though one might ask whether it is the full divinely appointed meaning of marriage in general. The suffering of many couples who cannot have children speaks against the unqualified adjective *full.*

There is a closely related case Hildebrand does not mention, though it would have clarified his position at a decisive point. If a man and a woman plan to marry with the intention of forming only a communion of love, if they deny the ordering of their love to children, their union would not be marriage but concubinage. However lofty and spiritual their sexual acts may be in their unitive meaning, they would not be conjugal acts.[21] Lack of openness to children is

20. Josef Fuchs, "Biologie und Ehemoral," *Gregorianum* 43 (1962): 244n19.

21. *Code of Canon Law* §1055: "The matrimonial covenant, by which a man and a woman establish between themselves a partnership of the whole of life and which is ordered by its nature to the good of the spouses and the procreation and education of offspring, has been raised by Christ the Lord to the dignity of a sacrament between the baptized." §1101 "If ... either or both of the parties by a positive act of the will exclude marriage itself, some essential element of marriage, or some essential property of marriage, the party contracts invalidly."

not simply a moral fault in a couple with such plans, but it prevents their being married. This case illustrates that procreation belongs more intimately and immediately to marriage than Hildebrand thinks. A definition of marriage without the explicit inclusion of procreation as the specifying end is not a definition of marriage but of concubinage.

Humanae vitae

The defects of Hildebrand's understanding of the nature of marriage are particularly evident in his book on *Humanae vitae*. He interprets the indissoluble link of the two meanings, the unitive meaning and the procreative meaning, as a moral link. The link can be dissolved but it should not. The Creator links them only for a short time during the woman's cycle.

> It is not always but only on a few days ... that God connects the conjugal act with the creation of a new human being. For this reason, the connection which it is a sin to separate exists only for a short time in the order determined by God himself. Sin consists in this alone, that man separates what God has united, that he realizes the mystery of bodily union while actively separating it from that act of creation with which it is connected at that time. (HV 26)

John Paul II understands the indissoluble link of the two meanings in a much stronger sense (see part I, chap. 1, in this volume). It is a form of inseparability by mutual essential implication. If one of the two meanings is removed, it draws the other along with itself. Deprived of its unitive meaning, the act ceases to be procreative in the full human sense, which is not mere biological causation but the begetting of a child in a human manner. There is a certain occasionalism in Hildebrand's understanding of the link between loving union and procreation. He has a strong sense of reverence for this link because it has been established by God. He admires its deep meaning. He has a correspondingly strong sense that husband and wife should be aware of the possibility of procreation during the conjugal act, but he does not see the indissoluble link as mutual essential implication.

Meaning and End

The root of the difficulty is that Hildebrand does not recognize the specifying power of procreation. He tends to equate *end* with *external effect*, for the most part the effect of efficient causes, the goodness of which reflects on the means only secondarily. He translates the Latin *finis* consistently by the German *Zweck* rather than *Ziel* or *Bestimmung*. The end of health in relation to the means of surgical instruments is his classic example of means and end.

It is here, in this understanding of *end*, that one can find at least part of the reason for the sense of competition between the intrinsic meaning and the external purpose of marriage that plays such a decisive role in Hildebrand's overall argument. Hildebrand seems to assume that the meaning of *end* in the theological tradition is the same as his *Zweck*. It is not surprising that he finds fault with a definition of marriage in terms of its primary end, procreation. This definition, combined with a positivist sense of *end*, would indeed be a utilitarian understanding of marriage in which persons and their experienced union of love are used as mere instruments for a purpose external to them. It may well be that some of the neo-Scholastic authors considered by Hildebrand shared his understanding of *end*. It is the dominant understanding of end projected in the Cartesian picture of the world. The meaning of *end* in the tradition is much wider and fuller. The end is *that for the sake of which*. It immediately includes what Hildebrand calls *meaning*. Hildebrand uses the following example to illustrate meaning and end.

> Without any doubt, it is one of the ends of knowledge to enable the human person to act. Our entire practical life, from the simplest to the most complex activities presupposes knowledge. Beyond this end, it has the higher end of enabling us to reach the moral perfection and holiness which our eternal salvation requires. Although both of these are rightly called ends of knowledge, to which knowledge is ordered, knowledge has without doubt a meaning and value in itself. The relation to the purposes which it serves has the character of overflowing fullness. Here we have a typical example of finality in which the purpose is not the exclusive meaning of the existence (*Daseinssinn*) of something. (HV 17)

In the traditional way of speaking formed by Aristotle the activity of knowledge as well as the object of knowledge can be called *ends* inasmuch as they are good. They are not ends as a mere *Zweck*, because some means leads to them or produces them as external effects. The act of knowing is an end for the human person because knowing is good. Truth is the end of the act of knowing because truth is the good reached and held by this act. Using *end* in this more universal sense as *that for the sake of which*, one can translate Hildebrand's statement *The primary meaning of marriage is union of love* into *The primary end of marriage is the union of love.*

In Hildebrand's own use of terms, the boundaries between *end* and *meaning* are not clear. At times he uses the language of finality for *meaning*. "The act of spousal communion is a unique expression of spousal love and its specific fulfillment because the two spouses … form an ultimate union which is in a special way the intended end (*abzielt*) of spousal love" (RJ 27, DP 24). In the phrase translated as "the intended end," Hildebrand does not say *das angestrebte Ziel*, but he uses the verb *abzielen*, in which the noun *Ziel* (*end*) is present. Another passage that uses the language of finality for *meaning* is clearer in the German than the English, here translated close to its phrasing.

> In marriage, mutual love is subjectively the true content—and, in addition, this communion, in mysterious connection with the procreation of new human beings, exists for the sake of the wonderful union of two persons in love and by love. (EH 7)

The phrase "exists for the sake of the … union" (*ist … um der Vereinigung … willen da*) is the classical language of finality. Aristotle often calls the end simply *that for the sake of which*. Hildebrand expresses *meaning* in terms that belong to *end*. Conversely, Hildebrand also applies the term *meaning* to the end and to the borrowed goodness of the means, a goodness derived from the end.

> Here we have a typical example of finality in which the purpose is not the exclusive meaning of the existence (*Daseinssinn*) of something" (HV 17).
>
> But this primary end [i.e., procreation] is not the only meaning of the physical act. Subjectively speaking it is not even its primary meaning. Its meaning is primarily the realization of the sublime communion of love. (EH 19, MA 26)

These examples show that Hildebrand applies the term *meaning* also to *end*. The purpose of something can be one of its meanings. Procreation is not the only meaning of the conjugal act. The communion of love is also one of its meanings (see also EH 22, MA 31). *Humanae vitae* uses the term *meaning* in the same way when it speaks in parallel terms of the unitive meaning and the procreative meaning of the conjugal act. It does not assign *meaning* to union and *end* to procreation but *meaning* to both.

In the usual way of stating his position, Hildebrand applies the term *primary* both to the *meaning* and to the *end* of marriage. This application to both suggests a certain degree of incommensurability between them. Neither of them is secondary. Both are primary, each in its irreducible and incommensurable way. In the text quoted above, however, Hildebrand removes this incommensurability by calling both procreation and union *meanings*, as *Humanae vitae* does. The meaning of the conjugal act as a union of love is primary; its meaning as a means for procreation is not primary but, by implication, secondary.

4. Lonergan on Hildebrand

Because Hildebrand speaks differently about *end* and *meaning* than the mainstream of the theological tradition, it is not surprising that even a reader as astute as Bernard Lonergan was puzzled by his book on marriage.

> Von Hildebrand's affirmation is this: while the primary end of marriage is the procreation and education of children, the primary meaning of marriage is love, the natural love intended by Christ when he raised marriage into the sacrament that showed forth his own love for his spouse, the church. The difficulty is the studied vagueness of this position.... What is a primary meaning, what would be a secondary meaning, are so many questions conveniently left without an answer. So far is such lack of precision from Catholic philosophy and theology that it reminds one rather of Anglican comprehensiveness.[22]

Lonergan's impression of Hildebrand's intention as "studied vagueness" and "Anglican comprehensiveness" does not fit Hildebrand's character. He was far from adopting political compromise by intentional vagueness about philosophical or theological truth. To understand Lonergan's charge of Anglican comprehensiveness, one must understand the context in which he considered the English translation of Hildebrand's book. Between the publication of the German original *Die Ehe* in 1929 and the publication of the English translation in 1942, Doms had published his *On the Meaning and End of Marriage* (1935), which is explicitly built on Hildebrand's main thesis. Doms knows the traditional way of speaking formed by Aristotle and St. Thomas and formulates his own thesis derived from Hildebrand as a clear and sharp antithesis to the traditional understanding of marriage. The book caused an intense debate, which reached a high point in 1944 when the Holy Office, with the approval of Pius XII, rejected several of its theses. In 1942, when the English translation of *Marriage* was published, this debate had already unfolded to the point of a first rebuke from the Holy Office. Lonergan reads Hildebrand in this context.

> From the preface and from repeated remarks in the course of the exposition, one can gather that the author considers these pages to be an original contribution to the philosophy and theology of marriage. In this claim there is this much truth that the movement originating with von Hildebrand not only has not been condemned but, in the opinion of perhaps all writers in theological reviews, contains elements that are destined to enrich Catholic thought. On the other hand, the most downright member of this school, Dr. Hubert [*sic*] Doms whose *Von Sinn und Zweck der Ehe* was published incompletely in

22. Bernard Lonergan, review of Dietrich von Hildebrand, "Christian Marriage: Values Sound—Doctrine Vague," *Canadian Register* 13 (1942): 5.

> English as *The Meaning of Marriage* (Sheed and Ward), received a very deliberate though unofficial rebuke from the Master of the Holy Office; and while Hildebrand carefully avoids not only the venturesome formulae but even the very name of Doms, it remains that he shares in the latter's fundamental outlook.[23]

Expecting a clarification by Hildebrand of his own position vis-à-vis Doms and the Holy Office, Lonergan finds only studied vagueness and Anglican comprehensiveness. Let us look at the summary of Doms's position in the later formal condemnation by the Holy Office to see how Hildebrand's position compares.

> [Some writings assert] that the primary end (*finem*) of marriage is not the procreation of offspring or that the secondary ends are not subordinate to the primary end but independent from it. In these works, the primary end of marriage is variously described, for example, the complementarity and personal perfection of man and woman through a comprehensive communion of life and action; the mutual love and union fostered by a gift of one's own person (*propriae personae traditionem*) in soul and body; and many things of this sort.[24]

Does this summary fit Hildebrand's position? One can give arguments for both sides.

FOR: The censure of Doms does not affect Hildebrand because Hildebrand says that the primary end of marriage is procreation.

AGAINST: Granted, but the Holy Office applies the term *end* to precisely the same reality to which Hildebrand applies the term *meaning*; namely, to the mutual union of love fostered by the gift of self in soul and body. What it means by *end* in this instance is precisely what Hildebrand means by *meaning*.

FOR: The fact remains that, according to Hildebrand, the primary end of marriage is procreation.

AGAINST: But if what Hildebrand means by *meaning* corresponds to what the Holy Office calls *end*, then it would be studied vagueness and Anglican comprehensiveness to give the title *primary* both to union of love and to procreation.

FOR: This is not what Hildebrand intends. He does not contradict traditional Catholic teaching.

In response to a letter that criticizes his review of Hildebrand's *Marriage*,

23. Lonergan, Review of Hildebrand, 5. Herbert Doms is mistakenly called "Hubert" on the dust jacket of the English edition.

24. Decree of the Holy Office, March 29, 1944, in *Enchiridion symbolorum definitionum et declarartionum de rebus fidei et morum*, 42nd ed., ed. Heinrich Denzinger and Peter Hünermann (Freiburg: Herder, 2009), 3838; cited as Denzinger.

Lonergan seems to agree with this final response. "Dr. von Hildebrand is in full agreement with Canon Law on the primary end of marriage, nor can your correspondent fairly say that I implied or suggested the contrary."[25]

5. Pius XII on Hildebrand

Seven years after the censure of Doms by the Holy Office, Pius XII addressed the same issue in more detail. It is not as easy to find Hildebrand in agreement with this later text.

> "Personal values" and the need to respect them are a theme which, over the last two decades, has been considered more and more by writers. In many of their works, even the specifically sexual act has its place assigned, that of serving the "person" of the spouses. The proper and most profound meaning (*senso*) of the exercise of the conjugal right should consist in this, that the union of bodies is the expression and the realization of personal and affective union. . . .
>
> If from the complete reciprocal gift of the spouses there results a new life, it is a result which remains outside, or, at the most, on the border of "personal values"; a result which is not denied but neither is it desired as the center of marital relations. . . .
>
> Now, if this relative evaluation were merely to place the emphasis on the personal values of husband and wife rather than on that of the offspring, it would be possible, strictly speaking, to put such a problem aside, but here we are dealing with a grave inversion of the order of values and of the ends established by the Creator Himself. We find ourselves faced with the propagation of a number of ideas and sentiments directly opposed to the clarity, depth and seriousness of Christian thought. . . .
>
> Now, the truth is that matrimony, as a natural institution, in virtue of the Creator's will, does not have as the primary and most interior end the personal perfection of the married couple but the procreation and upbringing of a new life. The other ends, inasmuch as they are intended by nature, are not found on the same level as the first, much less are they superior to it, but they are essentially subordinated to it. . . .
>
> Would one thereby want to deny or diminish what is good and just in personal values resulting from matrimony and its realization? Certainly not, because for the procreation of new life in marriage the Creator has destined human beings made of flesh and blood, gifted with spirit and heart, and they are called as human beings, and not as animals deprived of reason, to be the authors of their descendants. It is for this end that the Lord desires the union of husband and wife. Indeed, Sacred Scripture says of God that He created

25. Bernard Lonergan, follow-up to Review of Hildebrand, *Canadian Register* 15 (1942).

man to His image and He created him male and female, and willed—as is repeatedly affirmed in Scripture—that "a man shall leave mother and father, and shall cleave to his wife: and they shall be two in one flesh."

All this is therefore true and willed by God, but it must not be divorced from the primary function of marriage, that is, from the service for new life. Not only the common work of external life, but even all personal enrichment—intellectual and spiritual—all that in married love as such is most spiritual and profound has been placed by the will of nature and the Creator at the service of posterity. By its very nature, perfect married life also means the total devotion of parents to the well-being of their children, and married love in its power and tenderness is itself a condition of the sincerest care of the offspring and the guarantee of its realization....

The conjugal act, in its natural structure, is a personal action, a simultaneous and immediate cooperation of the spouses which, by the very nature of the agents and the proper character of the act, is the expression of the mutual gift that brings about the union "in one flesh," as Scripture says....

These personal values, whether in the sphere of the body or the senses or in the spiritual sphere, are really genuine, but they have been placed by the Creator not in the first place but in the second place on the scale of values....

If nature had intended exclusively, or at least in the first place, a reciprocal gift and possession of the spouses in joy and in delight, and if it had ordered that act only for the sake of making their personal experience happy in the highest degree possible and not for the sake of stimulating them to the service of life, then the Creator would have adopted another plan in the formation and constitution of the natural act. Now, instead, this act as a whole is subordinated and ordered to that one and only great law of "the generation and education of offspring," that is to say to the achievement of the primary end of marriage as origin and source of life.[26]

It is clear from this text that Pius XII shares Hildebrand's esteem for values of the person and applauds his contribution in this direction, particularly in the direction of the gift of self. This applause reportedly goes back to 1922, when Eugenio Pacelli was Nuncio in Germany and a friendship arose between him and Hildebrand. The friendship is particularly associated with Hildebrand's book *Marriage*, according to Alice von Hildebrand.

In 1922, Prelate Münch invited Dietrich to give a talk on marriage at a conference the Association of Catholic Intellectuals was sponsoring in Ulm....

Conscious that he was breaking new ground, and anxious never to say anything that was not in perfect harmony with the teachings of the Church,

26. Pius XII, "Allocution to Midwives," October 29, 1951, *Acta Apostolicae Sedis* 43 (1951): 835–54, at 848–52.

> Dietrich decided to expound his views to his friend Nuncio Pacelli. He often later recalled the pleasant long walks he had taken with him along the Isar River in Munich, discussing his ideas. To his delight, Msgr. Pacelli endorsed his views and encouraged him to publish them.
>
> Thanks to Pacelli's encouragement, he worked intensely on the text of his talk, which was a resounding success. Soon afterward, he enlarged and deepened his lecture and later published it under the title *Marriage*.[27]

It is impossible to reconcile Pacelli's reported unqualified support and encouragement with his later words as Pius XII. Would Hildebrand feel his position addressed in the phrases "a grave inversion of the order of values and of the ends established by the Creator Himself" and "ideas and sentiments directly opposed to the clarity, depth and seriousness of Christian thought"? Would he agree with the key statements of his friend, that the child is to be "desired as the center of marital relations" and "All that in married love as such is most spiritual and profound has been placed by the will of nature and the Creator at the service of posterity"?

In contrast to the 1944 decree of the Holy Office, Pius XII uses not only the term *end* where Hildebrand and Doms speak about *meaning* but also adopts Hildebrand's and Doms's own language of *meaning*. He describes the position he criticizes as holding "The proper and most profound meaning (*senso*)" of the conjugal act that is "the expression and the realization of personal and affective union." The Italian *senso* is a precise translation of the German *Sinn*. It is strange and uncharacteristic that Hildebrand never clarified his position vis-à-vis this pointedly clear critique of his position by Pius XII, even though he refers to this text.[28] The otherwise careful and insightful analysis of Hildebrand's understanding of procreation by Schemenauer does not address this difficulty.[29]

The root of the difficulties in Hildebrand's understanding of marriage seems to be his understanding of the relation between person and nature, particularly the subrational aspects of nature, which are at the same time truly aspects of the person. He does not see the conjugal act as by its very nature an act of the generative power of the human person. He understands it in its essence as an act of personal love. On a certain level, it is obvious that the conjugal act employs the generative organs. It leads to semen being deposited inside the woman. It can be understood as one act extended and completed in time in light of its procreative purpose.

27. Alice von Hildebrand, *The Soul of a Lion: Dietrich von Hildebrand. A Biography* (San Francisco: Ignatius, 2000), 212.

28. Hildebrand refers to the allocution in support of his own approach without mentioning any of its critical points; see Hildebrand, *Die Enzyklika*, 35n5.

29. Schemenauer, *Marriage and Procreation*.

Yet these facts of human animal nature seem to fade into the background for Hildebrand when he speaks about the personal meaning and essence of the conjugal act. Like an overwhelmingly strong light, the personal meaning of the act outshines its nature as an act ordered to generation. So strong is this light that it makes nature invisible or irrelevant, except in the degree to which there is an actual possibility of conception. It is only for a brief span of time in a woman's cycle that the procreative meaning of the conjugal act is added and linked by God to its unitive meaning. As Hildebrand views it, the conjugal act stops being a generative act when it cannot be actually fertile.

While Hildebrand sees the unitive meaning as intimately connected with the person, he sees the procreative meaning as more detachable. In response to the argument against *Humanae vitae* that procreation is merely a biological fact and therefore subject to human power, Hildebrand argues, "This objection overlooks the deep connection between person and nature" (HV 24). The deep connection to which he then points is that human procreation is the procreation of a person. Yet, in contrast to Wojtyła, Hildebrand does not unfold the connection between person and nature across the whole breadth of the question.

Hildebrand is a great defender of the spiritual person against collectivism and materialism, and he shares this honor with Wojtyła. Yet, in contrast to Wojtyła, he is not a defender of the person's nature as a rational animal against the hollowing of nature in the popular Cartesianism that accompanied the scientific revolution.

A key principle of St. John Paul II's thought, in sharp contrast to Descartes and Kant, is the Aristotelian thesis that *body* is a true genus of all bodily beings, including the human person. Rather than merely having a body, the human person is a body.[30] Members of the Hildebrand school are consistently scandalized by this claim. In Descartes, the person is a thinking thing, distinct in substance from the extended thing. The person is not an extended thing, and the extended thing is not personal.

The human person is a sentient living body, an animal. Conversely, the human animal, including its reproductive power, is personal. A human act of generation is therefore directly an act of the person. The entire dignity of the person as person is present in its acts of generation. Generation does not occur outside the sphere of personal meaning in the sphere of biology, a sphere distinct from the person. It is the person and not a separate physical reality that is ordered to procreation in sexual acts. For this reason, a truly personalistic account of the conjugal act cannot ignore the nature of that act as generative. Hildebrand's account of conjugal love and marriage is in this respect not sufficiently personalistic.

30. See, e.g., TOB 2:4, 6:3, 10:4, 99:4.

John Paul II fully integrates the person's animal nature into his personalistic account of the conjugal act. He argues that the personal gift of self of husband and wife cannot be limited to a distinct personal sphere that leaves out the ordination to the end of procreation.

> The inseparable connection about which the encyclical [*Humanae vitae*] speaks between the unitive and the procreative meaning inscribed in the conjugal act makes us understand that the body is a constitutive part of man, that it belongs to the being of the person and not to its having. In the act that expresses their conjugal love, the spouses are called to give themselves to each other. Nothing of that which constitutes their being person can be excluded from this gift.[31]

Being a sexually differentiated body is part of what constitutes a human person. Here lies the root of one of the fundamental principles of Wojtyła's sexual ethics. "Man can remain faithful to the person in the order of love proper to him insofar as he is faithful to nature. When he violates nature, he also 'violates' the person."[32]

6. Herbert Doms

Herbert Doms was strategically placed in German academic theology to become the foremost expert on sex and marriage.[33] Already the title of his first major work reflects his reliance on Hildebrand's main thesis: *On the Meaning and End of Marriage*. Doms acknowledges his dependence on Hildebrand's meaning-end distinction (see SZ 7, MM xvi, SZ 31n9 at 189, not in MM). At the same time, he is a highly original thinker. He advances the understanding of married love in many ways not found in Hildebrand. For example, he works out a personalistic argument against contraception.

31. John Paul II, *Discourse to a Conference on Responsible Procreation: Scientific, Philosophical and Theological Foundations*, September 17, 1983, 2.

32. Karol Wojtyła, *Love and Responsibility*, trans. Grzegorz Ignatik (Boston: Pauline, 2013), 216.

33. Citations of Doms by SZ (= *Sinn und Zweck der Ehe*), MM (= *Meaning of Marriage*), and GN (= *Gatteneinheit und Nachkommenschaft*) refer to Herbert Doms, *Vom Sinn und Zweck der Ehe: Eine systematische Studie* (Breslau: Ostdeutsche Verlagsanstalt, 1935); *The Meaning of Marriage*, trans. George Sayer (New York: Sheed and Ward, 1939), an incomplete and softened translation; *Gatteneinheit und Nachkommenschaft* (Mainz: Matthias-Grünewald, 1965).

For a wide-ranging description of Doms's work, see Konrad Glombik, *"Zweieinigkeit": Herbert Doms (1890–1977) und sein Beitrag zum personalistischen Eheverständnis* (Berlin: Lit Verlag, 2016). Glombik examined much of Doms's correspondence and documentation from archives. Doms, he shows, was an active member of several academic associations of the Nazi Party. Glombik argues that Doms avoided pressure to become a full member of the party.

> The personality of a human being gives itself to the spouse in the conjugal act with its [i.e., the personality's] divinely fashioned mysterious completeness, without reservations. If these persons mutilate the biological event anatomically or physiologically before, during or after the act, they give themselves with an arbitrary reservation, which is against the unchangeable nature of the sexual act and the deepest metaphysical meaning of the intention of conjugal love.... A sexual act that has been intentionally mutilated or hindered in its biological effects no longer has the meaning of a bodily realization of conjugal two-in-oneness (*Zweieinigkeit*) and accordingly it no longer has the expressive value of the gift of the whole person. (SZ 154; MM 168)

This text strikingly anticipates an argument against contraception in *Familiaris consortio.*

> When couples, by means of recourse to contraception, separate these two meanings that God the Creator has inscribed in the being of man and woman and in the dynamism of their sexual communion, they act as "arbiters" of the divine plan and they "manipulate" and degrade human sexuality—and with it themselves and their married partner [Latin: "their own person and the person of their spouse"]—by altering its value of "total" self-giving. Thus the innate language [Latin: "natural word"] that expresses the total reciprocal self-giving of husband and wife is overlaid [Latin: "opposed"], through contraception, by an objectively contradictory language [Latin: "a word of objective contradiction"], namely, that of not giving oneself totally to the other. This leads not only to a positive refusal to be open to life but also to a falsification of the inner truth of conjugal love, which is called upon to give itself in personal totality. (*Familiaris consortio* 32)

Matthias Joseph Scheeben (1835–88) argues that the family is an image of the Trinity inasmuch as it realizes a communion of persons.[34] In comparison with the father of a family, the mother has (for the most part) particular strength and skill in fostering the affective bonds between family members. In this respect, she carries a special likeness with the hypostatic mode of the Holy Spirit, who is the bond of love between the Father and the Son.[35] Doms accepts both theses from Scheeben and develops them in insightful ways (see SZ 24–27; MM 16–20). The image of the Trinity is discussed in part II, chapter 7, in this volume.

34. See Matthias Joseph Scheeben, *Handbuch der katholischen Dogmatik*, ed. Josef Höfer (Freiburg: Herder, 1948–57), 3:370–76. Scheeben's *Dogmatik* is traditionally cited by book and paragraph. Compare the corresponding passage in the much-shortened English adaptation of Scheeben's *Dogmatik:* Joseph Wilhelm and Thomas Scannell, *A Manual of Catholic Theology Based on Scheeben's "Dogmatik,"* 2 vols. (New York: Benziger, 1908), 1:395–96.

35. See Scheeben, *Mysterien*, 154–60; *Mysteries*, 181–89; *Dogmatik*, 2:1019–26; cf. Wilhelm and Scannell, *Manual of Catholic Theology*, 1:334–36.

While Doms acknowledges his debt to Hildebrand, he sees himself as taking a decisive step beyond Hildebrand's phenomenology into natural philosophy and metaphysics.

> Although we gratefully recognize the stimulus that Phenomenologically oriented authors have given to the discussion of marriage in the past few years, it was nevertheless in conscious contrast our intention to achieve the decisive understanding on the basis of a metaphysical vision in the traditional Scholastic sense. (SZ 13, not in MM)

One can see Doms's metaphysical vision in the manner in which he formulates what he sees as the main question. "What is the conjugal act? How does its object (*finis operis*) specify the nature of the act?" Hildebrand does not thematically raise this question. The traditional answer, Doms claims, is false.

> From a biological-metaphysical point of view one can and must without hesitation see the child as the *finis operis* of the conjugal act and of marriage, if one accepts Thomas's ideas about generation as a premise, but this judgment is no longer necessary if one proceeds from the results of modern biology. (SZ 81, not in MM)

Doms completed a doctorate in zoology before he began to study theology. Lonergan correctly highlights Doms's biological theses as the main novelty in his account of marriage. The decisive issue in the debate surrounding Doms is not, in Lonergan's judgment, the development of a personalistic understanding of the conjugal act as a total gift of self but a closely related question: "What is the nature of sexual union from the scientific biological point of view?"

> In the recent fermentation of Catholic thought on the meaning and ends of marriage, the basic component of novelty would seem to be a development in biological science. Quite other factors, no doubt, account for the intense and widespread interest aroused; but the ground of the intellectual problem must be placed, I think, in a new scientific insight. To this Dr H. Doms has given full prominence.[36]

In agreement with Lonergan, the following discussion of Doms will be limited to this one question. What is the nature of the conjugal act as a moral act, taken particularly from the biological-metaphysical point of view? Doms answers that conjugal union is a copulative act, not a generative act. The *finis operis* that defines it in its specific nature is not generation but copulation. Sexual

36. Bernard Lonergan, "Finality, Love, Marriage," in *Collected Works of Bernard Lonergan*, ed. Frederick E. Crowe and Robert M. Doran (Toronto: Lonergan Research Institute, University of Toronto, 1988), 4:17.

intercourse is in its essence a gift of self. Procreation is a further and relatively infrequent effect that need not be included in answering the question, "What is this act?"

7. Loss of the *Logos* of Marriage

The Disappearance of the Specifying End

Doms proposes his position on the copulative nature of the conjugal union in his first book on marriage (1935). He unfolds it more fully in a memo he wrote twenty-six years later in the preparatory phase of Vatican II and circulated among the Council Fathers.

The memo attacks the traditional account of marriage given by the Jesuit Josef Fuchs in his lectures at the Gregorian University. Doms quotes Fuchs as arguing that the primary and specifying end of sexual intercourse is procreation. Without mentioning Doms by name, Fuchs replied in a long article published in *Gregorianum*.[37] In response, Doms wrote another extensive memo to the Council Fathers to support his position by a more detailed analysis of the medieval and modern biological understanding of procreation.[38] Fuchs, Doms claims, bases his stance in part on *Casti connubii*, which points out that conjugal intercourse is morally unobjectionable at times when conception is impossible "as long as the intrinsic nature of that act and thus its due ordination to the primary end is preserved." The terms "intrinsic nature" and the correlative *primary end* are key notions on which Fuchs builds his response.

> The nature according to which the rightness of the act is shown is the very essence of the sexual faculty and act, grasped by the understanding.... Sexual activity is of itself ordered to the generation of offspring; the generation of offspring, therefore, is its natural end.[39]

One proof of the thesis that the conjugal act is essentially a generative act lies in the anatomy of man and woman, Fuchs claims. The sexual organs are designed to bring ovum and sperm together for conception. Fuchs concedes that sexual intercourse is not completely proportionate as a cause to the effect of procreation, because many natural processes must concur with this human act. It should therefore be defined more precisely as "the act suited for the gen-

37. Josef Fuchs, "Biologie und Ehemoral," *Gregorianum* 43 (1962): 225–53.

38. Revised versions of these memos are reprinted in Doms, *Gatteneinheit*.

39. Joseph Fuchs, *De castitate et ordine sexuali* [lecture notes for use by students] (Rome: Gregorian University, 1959), quoted according to *Gatteneinheit* 2.

eration of offspring" *actus aptus ad generationem prolis* (Fuchs in Doms, GN 2). In addition to the end of generation, which determines the essence of conjugal intercourse, there is another end *per se*, but it is subordinate to procreation in constituting the nature of the act.

> Sexual activity is, further, of itself ordered to the intimate expression of love between persons of different sex who are joined. This expression is, therefore, also the end of the act of sexual intercourse.... Note that sexual intercourse is through itself an act suited and ordered to the expression of personal love. This is true even when the united persons in fact express no love but only seek the "use of the body" or if they perform the act alone by themselves. (GN 3)

These two ends, Fuchs adds, do not stand next to each other without a deeper connection.

> Between the two ends of the act indicated above, there is a relative order. The generation of offspring is the primary end; the expression of love (the "personal" end) is the secondary end. This order must not be inverted; nor should the two ends be coordinated as if they were equal, but the secondary end is essentially subordinate to the primary end. (GN 3)

Fuchs explains that by "essential subordination" he means that generation is the specifying end. It gives to sexual union its specific nature, just as the object of sight gives to the act of seeing its specific nature. Among various expressions of love, sexual union is not incidentally but essentially a generative expression.

Rhonheimer, who has examined Fuchs's position from its beginnings to its most recent form, argues that one can detect signs of trouble to come in the early Fuchs's view on the ends of marriage. The later Fuchs embraced consequentialism in his ethics, which leads to a denial that any human acts are immoral in kind. The judgments about good and bad depend on evaluating the consequences of human acts. As events in the physical world, human acts are in themselves neutral. They are good or bad given the agent's intention in weighing their consequences. The early Fuchs, Rhonheimer argues, already limits himself to the neutral, objective description of the natural order and immediately reads off the laws of behavior from that order. He does not make evident how the moral judgment arises as a work of reason from the perspective of the acting person. Fuchs's natural law argument, Rhonheimer claims, is too objectivist or physicalist.

> The counterpoising of objective "nature" (the "natural order") on the one side, and subjective "reason" ("moral knowledge") on the other, favors a "physicalist" understanding of the natural law. In a physicalist notion of the natural

law, this "law" is identified with the merely natural structures and ends upon which a moral normativeness is conferred in an immediate way.[40]

One can point out in defense of Fuchs that the natural structures and ends of an act are taken up into that act's moral nature. An act that is by its objective nature (*species naturae*) an act of running will inescapably remain an act of locomotion when it is chosen by a person. The natural teleology of the act enters as a constitutive factor into the rationally chosen act of running. An act that is by its objective nature (*species naturae*) a generative act of the person will, when chosen by the person, remain inescapably generative, either as the conjugal act or as an act of fornication or adultery (*species moris*). It seems clear throughout that Fuchs considers the conjugal act in relation to reason, in its rational desirability, and thus in its moral essence (*species moris*), not only in its natural essence (*species naturae*), which it shares to some degree with the generative acts of all animals.

The Impact of Bacon and Descartes

An argument from biology stands at the center of Doms's view. The progress of natural science—this is his main objection against Fuchs—has invalidated the traditional understanding of the nature of the conjugal act as an act of generation. The same refrain still runs through the attacks on *Humanae vitae* recently published by German-speaking moral theologians (see section 3 of the introduction to this volume). Aristotle and his medieval followers thought that sexual intercourse was immediately and by its own inherent power the generative act. Sexual arousal in the male was directly behind the causative power of the human soul. It gave to its instrument, the male semen, the power to dispose the material offered by the female for the reception of the new substantial form. The high point, ejaculation, was the end point of this process and thus an efficaciously generative act. Although the semen did not act by command of the soul, but by a certain transfusion of power from it, it acted immediately at the high point of the sexual act. Everything needed for generation was contained in sexual intercourse itself. The intellectual soul was infused immediately by God, but the generative act supplied the necessary disposition.

> According to Thomas's biological-metaphysical understanding of the act of copulation, this act has as its *finis operis* (object) the generation of a human being.... According to Thomas, generation is the object "about which the ten-

40. Martin Rhonheimer, "The Cognitive Structure of the Natural Law and the Truth of Subjectivity," *Thomist* 67 (2003): 4.

> dency of the will of the spouses in the conjugal act is proximately and primarily concerned, *circa quod tendentia maritorum in actu coniugali proxime et primario versatur*."... Today we know with certainty that there is no generative act of man in copulation. (GN 16)

According to Doms, fertilization rather than sexual union is the cause of generation. Fertilization is a work of nature (*opus naturae*), not a work of man (*opus hominis*). It occurs through the natural fertilizing activity of sperm reaching the ovum inside the woman. It is only the sperm and ovum together that have, properly speaking, generative power. Apart from a transfer of semen into the woman, the male sexual act has no generative power, nor does the female act apart from receiving semen. Sexual intercourse is relatively incidental to fertilization. Doms sets forth these propositions with the confidence of a trained natural scientist.

> Thomas's ideas about generation among animals have been definitively refuted by numerous careful observations in the last half century. It is certain that the mature reproductive cells possess in themselves the powers needed either for a parthenogenetic development or fecundation; and copulation, when it is present at all, serves biologically only to bring about an external approach of the male and female gametes, often in the body of the female. In animals, there is no "act of generation," no "*actus generativus vel generationis*" of sexually mature males and females but only acts of mating and of copulation.
>
> In the human species, there are parthenogenetic steps of division of mature ova and there is the possibility, not merely of artificial insemination, even after transporting the semen thousands of kilometers by airplane, but also of in vitro fertilization with suitable fluid, in which the fertilized ovum performs several divisions.... The male and female gametes, which are modified and become independent ... have in themselves the power of uniting in pairs to become a zygote in the event of fertilization. Of course, for this event to be possible, the sperm must be transported into the female body in the act of copulation between man and woman. This is the only biological meaning of copulation for reproduction. Among human beings, too, copulation is not an "act of generation," in which a special generative causality is exercised that has a somehow formative influence on the gametes and gives them the power of fertilization. (GN 97–98)

The precise biological understanding of the beginning of new life achieved by modern science is Doms's basis for arguing that sexual intercourse is a gift of self and not an act of generation. He offers three further supporting arguments.

1. In most cases, copulation does not result in fertilization. Fertilization cannot, therefore, be its *finis operis* (GN 10–11). A woman is fertile only for about 3

hours during her cycle, according to Doms. Multiplied by the number of cycles per year (thirteen), the total is 39 hours. A year has 8,448 hours. Sexual intercourse can take place in any one of these hours (see GN 22). While other animals copulate only when the female is in heat, men and women can be sexually interested at any moment, even when the woman is pregnant (see GN 26).

2. The sexual organs of man and woman are ordered to the other person. Sexual union has the other person as its object. Male and female gametes, by contrast, are ordered to each other as gametes. The sperm seeks the ovum to unite with while a person seeks another person to unite with (see GN 7). This relation of sexual activity to the other person is evident in the fact that human beings are the only animals who perform the act face-to-face (see GN 26).

3. When husband and wife know that one or both of them cannot produce the necessary gametes, their conjugal act as a human act cannot be ordered to procreation. It cannot be an act that is *per se aptus ad procreationem*, or "through itself suited to procreation." If procreation were the primary end of the conjugal act, then an act known to be sterile would be immoral. Man and woman would not be able to order it to its primary end (see GN 19–20).

> I thus conclude that the *finis operis* (end of the act) of the natural conjugal act is the *expressio amoris* (expression of love) or, as I would prefer to call it, the display of conjugal two-in-oneness (*Zweieinigkeit*) in the act specific to marriage, rather than *generatio prolis*, generation of offspring. (GN 25)

Although in this statement Doms directly rejects the traditional understanding of the conjugal act and of marriage, he attempts to retrieve in some way what he sees as valid in the tradition. "Nevertheless, in a certain sense one can say that the conjugal act is subordinated to the purpose of procreation" (GN 31). It is subordinated, not in the sense that procreation specifies *what this act is* but that procreation is under some circumstances one further important purpose achieved through it. Doms adds, from the perspective of a community as expressed in its laws, that this further purpose can be considered primary by the law even if it is not primary from the perspective of the couple.

To illustrate how the conjugal act can have multiple ends not strictly related to each other, Doms gives an example that reveals the pattern of his thinking; namely, an infantry assault rifle. In its whole "nature," as Doms puts it, such a rifle is ordered to wounding or killing enemy soldiers, not to hunting or target shooting. Other kinds of rifles are designed for such purposes.

> A shot fired with live ammunition at an enemy in a war is certainly an *actus per se aptus ad vulnerandum hostem* (an act through itself suited to wounding the enemy). But this does not mean that every act of shooting with an infantry

> rifle has neutralizing the enemy as its *finis operis* (end of the act). For example, one can shoot with live ammunition in target practice, but one can also shoot with blank cartridges in military exercises or in an honorary salute at the graveside of a fallen soldier. The *finis operis* of the rifle remains without any change shooting with live ammunition in war, but the *actus humanus* of shooting is completely different in the two cases and is subject in each case to an entirely different moral evaluation. A shot with a blank cartridge at the graveside is not an *actus per se aptus ad vulnerandum hostem*, even though it is a genuine shot with an infantry rifle. (GN 31–32)

The loss of nature is strikingly evident in this example. Whatever the precise manner of generation or fertilization may be, an obvious fact remains. Husband and wife are the responsible origins of their conjugal act. They know that this kind of act can lead to conception. They know that conception will certainly not occur if they hold hands, not even if they kiss. Their act is the cause of conception in an obvious commonsense manner, regardless of the precise causative details involved. Whether the process should be called generation or fertilization, whether there is a formative generative power in sexual union as such or only in the cells transported by it, all these points placed by Doms's scientific knowledge in the foreground are beside the point. Sex and baby have something to do with each other. The spouses know this. They do not need Aristotle to tell them. Fuchs's stinging refutation of Doms has lost none of its power, even though Fuchs himself yielded to the pressure of the dominant mentality later in his career.

> When one believes that only the biology of the past few decades has allowed human beings to understand the fundamental meaning, that is, the *finis operis*, of the conjugal act as an act that stands at the center of human self-realization, one should not be surprised if this opinion is received with skepticism.... It remains difficult to see why the understanding of the conjugal act as an act "that has something to do with procreation" and the corresponding "metaphysics of nature"—this understanding has, one must admit, existed for millennia until the present day—should simply be proved false by modern biology. It seems as a matter of principle rather risky to put one's trust so easily in an interpretation of new biological data opposed to millennia of knowledge about the fundamental meaning of the conjugal act.[41]

Fuchs puts his finger on the decisive point; namely, Doms's trust in the revolutionary significance of scientific discoveries or, rather, of philosophical interpretations of such discoveries along the lines of Bacon and Descartes. Doms's appeal to science may not be a powerful argument, but it documents the pow-

41. Fuchs, "Biologie und Ehemoral," 230–31.

erful impression natural science made as a revolutionary force. One can hardly overestimate the power of this force in bringing about an obedient submission of mind and will. Doms describes it eloquently.

> I have participated in countless medical congresses and experienced again and again that even the most respected theologians were unable to present convincing arguments. The other participants were no match for them in the discussion and were silent—for this reason or out of politeness—until the theologians left.
>
> The theses of the *finis primarius* (primary end) and the conjugal act as an act of generation, which are treated as if they were *principia per se nota*, self-evident principles, no longer convince many circles of medical doctors and spouses, or at least no longer convince fully. For this reason, many demands of the Church that place a heavy burden on doctors and spouses do not seem truly meaningful. The consequence is that these demands fail to provide strong motives for actual moral conduct.
>
> It is only for a few modern persons that Thomas's basis of the distinction between primary and secondary ends of marriage will be convincing. We just know too much about the natural laws governing infertile intercourse. (GN 45–46)

The power of the social sea change described in this text was and still is immense. In the 1960s, confidence in the victorious power of the scientific-technological revolution was at its height. It seemed to sweep everything before it. The conviction grew that the Catholic Church had a bad start in its encounter with the scientific revolution and urgently needed *aggiornamento*. The name of Galileo was enough to paint the picture of a community unable to break out of medieval obscurantism into the clear light of knowledge. The clear duty of *aggiornamento* was to embrace the progress of science wholeheartedly. With his doctorate in zoology, Doms seemed well prepared for such *aggiornamento*.

It is easier now, in the postmodern period with its suspicions about power, to raise critical questions about the scientific revolution, especially about its ambition for power over nature as a noncognitive influence that established the primacy of mechanism. That a theologian of the quality of Fuchs eventually became a prey of the overwhelmingly dominant intellectual custom is to be lamented, but it is understandable. The tidal wave of progress seems to have felt irresistible to him, as it did to many in the late sixties. The collection of essays *Humanae vitae: The Offensive Encyclical* by German Catholic moral theologians still reflects this mindset (see introduction, sect. 3, in this volume).

CHAPTER 5

The Nature of *Logos* in Plato's *Republic*

The practice of reason proposed by Bacon and Descartes is new in the history of humanity, at least in the form of the sustained development of scientific knowledge and technological power. The consequent loss of the *logos* of marriage is also new, at least in the breadth and depth documented, for example, by the US Supreme Court's recognition of same-sex marriage. Nevertheless, the questions of modernity are not completely new. They are taken up in antiquity, at times in surprisingly different contexts and configurations.

De rerum natura by the Roman poet-philosopher Lucretius (about 99–55 BC) is a fascinating example. The book's purpose is to offer relief from religion and its fear of punishment after death. A mechanist science of nature is the means to achieve this calming of anxiety.

> Fear of death brings hate of life and light,
> and so burdened by sadness humans destroy themselves,
> unaware that this fear is the source of all their woes. . . .
> These terrors and darknesses of mind must be dispelled,
> not by rays of sun or shafts of bright day,
> but by reason looking at nature.[1]

The main step in Lucretius's reasonable look at nature is to posit that the only thing that exists is space and atoms. The choice to see the cosmos as a such a mechanism strips it of goodness, of final causality, and of the terrifying presence of gods.[2]

1. Lucretius, *De rerum natura* 3.80–93.
2. See Lucretius, *De rerum natura* 4.822–57 and 5.416–48.

Originally, all atoms in the limitless universe were falling straight down without colliding, but a small random swerve took place, in scale and vehemence the opposite of a big bang, but equally momentous. This swerve brought about a random reordering of atoms in the order we observe.[3] Animals came to be by chance, and the fittest survived.[4]

On this foundation, Lucretius builds an extensive theology of the sexual body. Use many sexual partners, he advises, so that you can enjoy the pleasure of sex while avoiding the anxieties and pains of intense love for one person.

> Take all nourishment away from love.
> Turn your mind to another.
> Spray your body juices to whatever body.
> Do not keep them for converse with one love.
> One love—anxious worry and sure pain is the only outcome.[5]

The triad of religion as an anxiety disorder, mechanist science as a sedative against this anxiety, and a sex life that finds calm and safety in numbers is well described by Stephen Greenblatt in *The Swerve*. Across two millennia, Greenblatt embraces Lucretius as a kindred spirit, as a true modern. The discovery of Lucretius in the Renaissance, he argues, was the main stimulus for the rise of modernity. *De rerum natura* narrowly escaped being destroyed by the great oppressor of freedom and scientific truth, the Catholic Church with its negative image of sex.[6]

Lucretius may well have played some role in the rise of modernity. Yet Bacon and Descartes show that the main stimulus for the triumph of mechanism came from the ambition for power. Lucretius, by contrast, chose mechanist science as a means for calming religious fear: his science is the Valium of the people. That such different historical circumstances led to a similar governing triad of cultural factors seems not to be mere coincidence.

1. Approach to the *Republic*

Plato's *Republic* presents an extensive theology of the body, spelled out in detailed laws for the ordering of sex. The *Republic* is widely seen as one of the

3. See Lucretius, *De rerum natura* 2.216–93.

4. See Lucretius, *De rerum natura* 5.855–77.

5. Lucretius, *De rerum natura* 4.1063–72. Passages directly relevant to Lucretius's theology of the body: dedication of the poem to Venus, 1.1–43; love and sex, 4.1030–1287; the origin of the family and of tribes, 5.1011–27.

6. See Stephen Greenblatt, *The Swerve: How the World Became Modern* (New York: W. W. Norton, 2011).

supreme achievements of Greek reason (*logos*).[7] It contains a critique of the primacy of will and power and an account of the reasonable practice of reason.

In his *Regensburg Lecture*, Benedict XVI argues that Greek reason (*logos*) and Christian faith are closely united, not only by accidental historical circumstances but also by an inner necessity.

> Is the conviction that acting unreasonably contradicts God's nature merely a Greek idea, or is it always and intrinsically true? I believe that here we can see the profound harmony between what is Greek in the best sense of the word and the biblical understanding of faith in God.
>
> Modifying the first verse of the Book of Genesis, the first verse of the whole Bible, John began the prologue of his Gospel with the words: "In the beginning was the *Logos*." This is the very word used by the emperor: God acts, σὺν λόγω, with *logos*. *Logos* means both reason and word—a reason which is creative and capable of self-communication, precisely as reason. John thus spoke the concluding word of the biblical concept of God, and in this word all the often toilsome and tortuous paths of biblical faith reach their goal and find their synthesis. In the beginning was the *Logos*, and the *Logos* is God, says the Evangelist. The encounter between the Biblical message and Greek thought did not happen by chance.[8]

How to Read the Republic

When Socrates builds the city in speech (*logos*), he seems to propose a violent theology of the body.

- Men and women differ no more than bald people do from those with hair (454c).
- Just as female and male dogs hunt together, both men and women must train as warriors and fight side by side in war (451d–452a).
- They must wrestle naked with each other in the gymnasia (452a–b).
- A lasting bond between one man and one woman is forbidden. Sexual relations, temporary and variable, are arranged by the government. Just as dog breeders take control of copulations to improve the breed, so the government takes control of sex to strengthen the military (457c–460a).
- Breeding encounters are scheduled in accord with a scientific

7. Citations of the *Republic* in this chapter, given in the text rather than the footnotes, are by Stephanus number. Translations are based with modifications on Allan Bloom, trans., *The Republic* (New York: Basic Books, 1968).

8. Benedict XVI, *Regensburg Lecture*, December 12, 2006.

mathematical formula of immense complexity. Only the rulers understand this formula and its eugenic purpose (546b–c).
- Sex between men and woman apart from government organized breeding encounters is severely punished. If conception has taken place, the government aborts the fetus or kills the baby after birth (461a–c).
- Babies conceived in the government's program but from parents judged inferior are killed, likewise any who at birth turn out to be less than desired (459d–460c).
- The eugenic program of making the herd fit for its military purpose by such selective killing takes place under a blanket of government secrecy and lies to avoid resentment (459e).
- Newborns are immediately taken away from their parents (460d).
- Neither father nor mother know who their children are, nor do the children know their parents (461d–e).
- Government-appointed nurses and educators raise the children in public facilities. Women are thereby liberated from childcare and can be used for military purposes (460c–d).

Karl Popper reads these violent proposals with wooden literalism. All proposals are equally Plato's philosophy. They are imposed by Plato's will to power to build the ideal city. Greek *logos*, as expressed in the *Republic*, he concludes, is violently totalitarian.

> Although I admire much in Plato's philosophy, far beyond those parts which I believe to be Socratic, I do not take it as my task to add to the countless tributes to his genius. I am, rather, bent on destroying what is in my opinion mischievous in this philosophy. It is the totalitarian tendency of Plato's political philosophy which I shall try to analyze, and to criticize....
>
> What a monument of human smallness is this idea of the philosopher king. What a contrast between it and the simplicity of humaneness of Socrates, who warned the statesman against the danger of being dazzled by his own power, excellence, and wisdom, and who tried to teach him what matters most—that we are all frail human beings. What a decline from this world of irony and reason and truthfulness down to Plato's kingdom of the sage whose magical powers raise him high above ordinary men; although not quite high enough to forgo the use of lies, or to neglect the sorry trade of every shaman—the selling of spells, of breeding spells, in exchange for power over his fellow-men....
>
> True happiness, Plato insists, is achieved only by justice, that is by keeping one's place. The ruler must find happiness in ruling, the warrior in warring; and, we may infer, the slave in slaving. Apart from that, Plato says frequently

> that what he is aiming at is neither the happiness of individuals nor that of any particular class in the state but only the happiness of the whole, and this, he argues, is nothing but the outcome of that rule of justice which I have shown to be totalitarian in character. That only this justice can lead to any true happiness is one of the main theses of the *Republic*.[9]

The reading proposed below concludes that, on the contrary, the *Republic* critiques the violent practice of reason at the root of the military city. Socrates distinguishes three parts of the soul:

the desiring part (*epithymia*) aims at bodily pleasure;
the irascible part (*thymos*) is characterized by love of one's own with hatred for the foreigner; it prizes military victory and honor;
reason (*logos*) implies a universal love for every being.

Following these three parts of the soul, Socrates builds three cities. After an initial simple city that combines all three parts of the soul in a primitive synthesis, he builds three cities incompatible with each other. He gives detailed descriptions of the first two, a luxurious city built on the desire for pleasure (*epithymia*) and a military city based on the irascible part (*thymos*). He does not give a similarly detailed description of a city built on reason (*logos*). Still, his discussion of *logos* suggests some outlines of such a city.

Defenders of a literalist reading of the *Republic* can appeal to Aristotle, who certainly knew Plato better than we do. Aristotle takes Socrates's violent proposals at face value rather than as reductions to the absurd.[10] It is doubtful, however, how much weight one should give to Aristotle's testimony. In his reading of Plato's account of the soul in *De anima*, he argues doggedly and at length against Plato's alleged teaching that the soul is circular in shape.[11] Thomas warns against assuming that Aristotle presents his own understanding of Plato.

> Often when Aristotle refutes the opinions of Plato, he does not refute them according to Plato's intention, but according to the sound of his words.... Plato says things figuratively and teaches through symbols, intending something else by the words than the words themselves sound, such as when he says that the soul is a circle.[12]

9. Karl Popper, *The Open Society and Its Enemies: The Spell of Plato*, 5th ed. (Princeton, NJ: Princeton University Press, 1966), 34, 156, and 169. "The idea of freedom is the core of Popper's philosophy." Stefano Gattei, *Karl Popper's Philosophy of Science: Rationality without Foundations* (New York: Routledge, 2009), 52.

10. See Aristotle, *Politics* 2.1–6.

11. See Aristotle, *De anima* 1.3.406b26–407b13.

12. Thomas, *Sententia de anima* I, lect. 7, no. 102.

Unpublished teachings passed on in the inner circle of Plato's Academy are attested in several independent ancient sources. A case has been made that these unpublished teachings contained a systematic account of first principles (*Prinzipienlehre*).[13] However one judges the success or failure of this case, it is clear that Plato's published writings speak in a less direct way.

In comparison with Popper, Heidegger is more sensitive to the *Republic's* complexity. In the end, however, he comes to an understanding of Platonic *logos* akin to Popper but on a deeper level. He sees Plato as the beginning of metaphysics, that is, of the violent imposition of conceptual meaning by human reason on the mystery of being. A direct line, Heidegger argues, goes from Plato stamping ideas on being to Descartes stamping human projects on matter to master and possess nature. From Descartes, the line continues to the high point and crisis of metaphysics in Nietzsche's will to power.[14]

The reason why Heidegger denies that Plato is receptive to intelligible truth, it appears, is because he himself is convinced that there is no such intelligible truth to be received. Since reception is impossible, Plato's motive for imposing the mere appearance of intelligibility can only be his will to power. Nietzsche formulated the hermeneutics of suspicion that underlies Heidegger's reading of the *Republic*.

> All values . . . when they are recalculated psychologically, are the result of certain perspectives of usefulness for holding on to and increasing human power constructs (*menschliche Herrschafts-Gebilde*). Values are projected into the nature of things as mere falsehoods. It is still man's excessive naïveté to set himself up as the measure of the meaning and value of things.[15]

According to Leo Strauss, the *Republic* is an aporetic dialogue that shows the incompatibility of the philosophical life with political life and the precarious place of philosophers in the city (execution of Socrates).[16] The Republic, he argues, shows that a rigorously philosophical political order should not even be

13. See Hans Joachim Krämer, *Der Urprung der Geistmetphysik: Untersuchungen zur Geschichte des Platonismus zwischen Platon und Plotin* (Amsterdam: P. Schippers, 1964); Hans Joachim Krämer and John R. Catan, *Plato and the Foundations of Metaphysics: A Work on the Theory of the Principles and Unwritten Doctrines of Plato with a Collection of the Fundamental Documents* (Albany: State University of New York Press, 1990); Konrad Gaiser, *Platons ungeschriebene Lehre* (Stuttgart: Klett, 1968); Giovanni Reale, *Toward a New Interpretation of Plato* (Washington, DC: Catholic University of America Press, 1997).

14. See Martin Heidegger, *Nietzsche*, 2 vols. (Frankfurt: Klostermann, 1996–97).

15. Nietzsche, *Critique of Nihilism*; KSA 13:48.

16. See Leo Strauss, "On Plato's Republic," in Strauss, *The City and Man* (Chicago: University of Chicago Press, 1978), 50–138, at 138. "Persecution and the Art of Writing," *Social Research* 8 (1941): 488–504.

attempted. Bloom and Bruell, among others, follow in Strauss's footsteps and develop the argument further.[17]

An Important Clue

A important clue for reading the *Republic* is the contradiction between the beginning of Book 5 and the beginning of Book 8. In Book 5, Socrates looks back at the city he has just founded and at the account of justice that emerges from that founding. He concludes, "Good and right I call such a city and regime, and likewise a man of this sort, but the others bad and mistaken" (449a). Immediately after this unqualified approval of the military city, he takes up the next point in logical order; namely, the ways in which this supposedly ideal city and the man like it can fall into corruption. He explicitly returns to the same point at the beginning of Book 8.

> SOCRATES: Let's recall where we took the detour that brought us here so that we can go back to the same way.
>
> GLAUCON: That's not hard. You were presenting your arguments pretty much as you are doing now, as though you had completed your description of what concerns the city, saying that you would set down a city such as you then described, and the man like it, as good (ἀγαθός). And you did this, as it seems, *despite having a still more beautiful* [*or noble*] (καλός) *city and man to tell of.* (543c–544a; emphasis added)

Glaucon is right. The city built in words up to the beginning of Book 5 is not yet the simply good city. It is not yet fully human. It is built on the first two parts of the soul without introducing the full breadth of the third. Socrates does have a better city and man to tell of.

Socrates's Purpose

Why does Socrates build a defective city and call it *good and right*? He seems to act like a physician who applies different medicines at different times in a definite order, suited to the diagnosis and progress of the patient. The incompleteness and outright falsity of some of his words, especially of the judgment that the military city is *good and right*, fit the image of the cave (458d–460a). The prisoners, who have lived in the cave with mere shadows of unsteady light cast

17. See Bloom, "Interpretive Essay," in Bloom, trans., *Republic of Plato*, 307–426. Christopher Bruell, "On Plato's Political Philosophy," *Review of Politics* 56 (1994): 261–82.

by a fire, make their way step by step out into the steady light of day, in which they can see real things, and finally the sun itself, the idea of the good.

The prisoner in the cave to whom Socrates attends in the *Republic* is Plato's older brother Glaucon and to a somewhat lesser extent their younger brother Adeimantus. In contrast to the main characters of the *Phaedrus* and the *Symposium*, Glaucon is by his own testimony not primarily an erotic man, dominated by the desiring part of the soul (see 475a). He is not a man without *eros*, of course. He has (or had) a lover (see 368a), and at the high point of the dialogue, he exclaims in language characteristic of *eros*, "An unmanageable beauty you speak of, Socrates" (509a). He is primarily a spirited man, a man of *thymos*. He breeds "hunting dogs and quite a throng of noble cocks" (459a). Like these animals, he is "always most courageous" (357a), a lover of victory, honor, and justice. He resembles the timocratic man (see 548c–e). According to Xenophon, Glaucon was not yet twenty when he wanted to become ruler of Athens. Socrates had to intervene to convince him not to make a fool of himself.[18]

Excess of *thymos* and defect of *logos* is Glaucon's diagnosis. Socrates applies a remedy that differs from the erotic remedies in the *Symposium* and the *Phaedrus*. On the way up from the cave, when the darkness begins mixing with some light, he constructs a military city based on *thymos* with a corresponding form of justice as the supposed greatest good of that city and the soul like it. Later in the ascent, when more light from the sun has become visible, he critiques it.

> ADEIMANTUS: So these [virtues] aren't the greatest, but there is something yet greater than justice and the other things we went through?
>
> SOCRATES: There is something greater and even for these very virtues it won't do to look at a sketch, as we did a while ago.... You have many times heard that the idea of the good is the greatest study and that it is by availing oneself of it along with just things and the rest that they become useful and beneficial. (504d–505a)

Socrates's critique of his own earlier view is radical. Without knowing the idea of the good, one cannot judge whether the justice that defines the military city is beneficial. The city was constructed without such knowledge, in the absence of the idea of the good. Step by step, most fully in his account of the philosopher and the orientation toward the idea of the good, Socrates shows the limits of the military city. He leads his listener to a threshold from which one can glimpse a city of *logos*. He refutes his own positive judgment about the mili-

18. See Xenophon, *Memorabilia*, 3.6. The reliability of this report is doubted by many. See Debra Nails, *The People of Plato: A Prosopography of Plato and Other Socratics* (Indianapolis: Hackett, 2002), 154–56. At the very least, the story must have had some verisimilitude, which is sufficient for a testimony about Glaucon's character.

tary city but does not work out in detail what the laws of a city of *logos* would be.

The glimpse of a city of *logos* begins with pointed irony as a digression at the beginning of Book 5.[19] Socrates has just concluded his account of justice in the city and in the individual soul, as if such an account were complete without the idea of the good. Glaucon shows at the beginning of Book 8 that he has recognized the falseness of the earlier judgment about its goodness. "You set down a city such as you then described, and the man like it, as good. And you did this, as it seems, despite having a still more beautiful city and man to tell of" (543d–544a). The military city, to which Glaucon gave his unqualified assent further down in the cave without any objections, was not the ideal city. There is a better city.

One would expect Glaucon to ask how the regime of that better city differs from the military regime. What laws would need to change? What difference would the idea of the good make for each citizen as well as for the regime? He does not ask these questions, and at the beginning of Book 8 the discussion descends back into the cave along the route laid out at the end of Book 4. Whether Glaucon has been cured of his sickness remains unclear.

In some of its literary features, the *Republic* is like the *Apology*. Both are monologues by Socrates. The audience of the *Apology* is the assembly of Athens, which will pass judgment on Socrates. No audience is mentioned in the *Republic*, though the *Timaeus* supplies the missing information.[20] As published works, of course, both the *Apology* and the *Republic* address Athens and beyond. According to Socrates's diagnosis, Athens suffers from a disease that is in some ways like Glaucon's but more severe. Athens is enslaved to its own desire (*epithymia*) for wealth and pleasure. It is the luxurious city. For this reason, Athens is also enslaved to its own will to power. It is the military city of *thymos*. It needs to free itself by *logos* from this double slavery.

The Greatest Good

The main topic pursued by Socrates in the *Republic* is *the greatest good* for human beings. The first word is Κατέβην (I went down), a highly symbolic word that anticipates the image of the cave. Having gone down to the harbor earlier, he is now on the way up again to the city when Polemarchus (the name means "War Lord," the title of the highest military officer in Athens) sees him from afar

19. In his summary of the *Republic* in the *Timaeus*, Socrates leaves out the discussion of *logos*, the main topic until the end of Book 7 (see *Timaeus*, 1719b).

20. At the beginning of the *Timaeus*, Socrates says, "One, two, three. The fourth for us, friend Timaeus, where is he? He was among the guests yesterday, who are the hosts today" (17a). The three are named: Timaeus, Critias, and Hermocrates. The fourth remains unnamed.

and sends a slave boy to arrest him. When Polemarchus finally reaches Socrates, he points to the friends with him and threatens half-jokingly, "Either prove stronger than these men or stay here." Socrates answers, "Isn't there another possibility . . . our persuading you to let us go?" Yet persuasion by *logos* is powerless when a war lord refuses to listen and simply imposes his will. "Could you really persuade if we don't listen?" (327c).

This opening scene can be read as a symbolic sketch of the city's relation to Socrates. At Socrates's trial in 399 BC, many of the five hundred Athenian assemblymen refused to listen to his defense speech and did not let him go. They found him guilty of introducing new gods and thereby corrupting the young. Socrates seems to have expected this verdict (see *Apology* 36a). The law required him to propose his own sentence. He proposed the honor given to Olympic victors, dining daily in the city government's mess hall, where the sacred fire of the goddess Hestia was kept burning all day, symbol of the city's life. "That is much more appropriate for me," Socrates says to the assembly, "than for any of you who has won a race at the Olympic games. . . . For he makes you seem to be happy, whereas I make you be happy" (*Apology* 36d).

The proposed punishment is a grimly ironic joke but serious in its claim to justice. It stirred up such a storm of anger (*thymos*) in the assembly that at least eighty of the jurors who had voted *innocent* switched sides and sentenced Socrates to death.[21] This dramatic clash shows Socrates's commitment to a life of *logos* as a service to the city, his fearlessness in the face of the city's anger, and his unwillingness to enter into any compromise for private advantage. Consciously stripping himself of power by stirring up the city's *thymos* against himself, he proposes powerless *logos*, according to which it is better to suffer than to do injustice. He seems to have embraced his own death as his final and most urgent word to the city in serving its happiness.

The main question of the *Republic* is already present in the opening scene. Socrates raises it openly when he asks Polemarchus's father, Cephalus (the Head), "What is the greatest good μέγιστον ἀγαθόν that you have enjoyed from possessing much wealth" (330d)? The greatest good, Cephalus answers, is "not having to cheat or lie to any man against one's will" and "not having to depart for that other place frightened because one owes sacrifices to a god or money to a man" (331b). Cephalus has good reasons to be afraid of that other place because wrongdoing will be punished justly by the impartial judges of the underworld.

Socrates immediately fastens on the question of justice. "As to this very thing, justice δικαιοσύνη, shall we so simply assert that it is truthfulness and giving back what one has taken from another" (331c). The question of justice, im-

21. See Diogenes Laertius, *Lives of Eminent Philosophers*, 2.5.42.

plicit in Cephalus's answer, is related to the question of the greatest good. It focuses on human life as one single whole, face-to-face with the judges in the underworld. As the measure of "how one should live," justice is closely connected with "living well" εὖ βιοῦν, εὖ ζῆν, and therefore with "being blessed μακάριος or happy εὐδαίμων" (353e–354a), even though, by itself, it is not sufficient for happiness. There is something greater than justice. Aristotle understands the word *eudaimonia* (happiness) in the same way. It names a life about which one can say, It is good. It is lived well. "Living well εὖ ζῆν and acting well εὖ πράττειν mean the same thing as being happy εὐδαιμονεῖν."[22] The universality of *well* is important. The word *all* is implicit in the unqualified or absolute use of the word *well.* When one says about a life that it is lived well, without adding any qualification or reservation, one implies that it is all good. It is or reaches the greatest good.

What Greek speakers disagree about, still following Aristotle, is not "What does the word happiness mean?" but "What is happiness?"[23] What is the life about which one can say, "This life is lived well; it is all-good; it has reached the greatest good"? People disagree about this second question, not about the first.

Aristotle outlines their disagreement in accord with Plato's distinction between the three parts of the soul, the main structuring device of Socrates's argument in the *Republic.* Some say the life of pleasure is best, others prefer the life of military victory and political honor, and others say that the best life is the *theoretical* life, in which the object attained is the divine origin and end of all things.[24]

In Book 2, still far down in the cave, Socrates says, "Justice is the greatest good" (366e). A life lived justly is the good life par excellence. Justice is happiness. Nota bene: It *is* happiness, not *makes* someone happy. A life lived justly is identical with the human life of which one can say, "It is a good life." At the center of the dialogue (Book 6), by contrast, Socrates argues in the greater fullness of light near the entrance to the cave that there is "something greater than justice" τι μεῖζον δικαιοσύνης (504d). Living justly is not the greatest good, even if it is not an optional good but a necessary part of happiness.[25]

22. Aristotle, *Nicomachean Ethics* 1.4.1095a19–20.

23. Aristotle, *Nicomachean Ethics* 1.4.1095a21–22.

24. See Aristotle, *Nicomachean Ethics* 1.5.1095b13–1096a10 and 10.7.1177a11–1178a8, together with *Metaphysics* 2.1.993b20–30 and 12.10.1075a11–24.

25. The aim of the *Republic* is set too low by the claim that "Plato undertakes to do no more, and no less, than to show Glaucon and Adeimantus, and others relevantly like them, how justice can be a . . . component of happiness." C. D. C. Reeve, *Philosopher-Kings: The Argument of Plato's Republic* (Princeton, NJ: Princeton University Press, 1988; reprint, Indianapolis: Hackett, 2006), 41. Reeve draws attention to Socrates's claim that the idea of the good is the end of all human striving. He undercuts this claim when he writes, "When Plato talks about being (*to on*), or complete being (*to pantelos on*), or

Glaucon, dominated by *thymos*, is not inclined to accept pleasure as the greatest good. He is willing, however, to give that place to justice. When Socrates describes a good that is even greater than justice, he replies in amazement, "You speak of an overwhelming beauty ἀμήχανον κάλλος.... You surely don't mean it is pleasure" (509a).

The main question of the *Republic* is thus not "What is justice?" but "About what life can one say, it is a good life? What is the greatest good a human life can attain?" Justice is a necessary part of the answer, suited particularly to Glaucon, the timocratic man, but it is not the full answer.

2. The City of the Irascible Part (*Thymos*)

Thrasymachus as an Image of the Irascible Part

After Cephalus's departure, Polemarchus proposes the definition "Justice is helping one's friends and injuring enemies" (334b). Socrates refutes this definition and concludes, "It is never just to injure anyone" (335e).

Enraged by this conclusion, Thrasymachus (= Bold in Battle, close to the meaning of *thymos*) throws himself into the debate with a great outbreak of anger (*thymos*). "When we paused and I said this, he could no longer keep quiet; hunched up like a wild beast, he flung himself at us as if to tear us to pieces" (336b). The violence with which Thrasymachus comes into the dialogue corresponds to the violence of his thesis. The best way to live is to impose one's will by sheer power, ideally as the tyrant of the city, who can do whatever he wants. "The just is the advantage of the stronger" (338c).

Socrates asks a clever series of questions, by which Thrasymachus's own answers lead him step by step to the conclusion that justice means ruling for the good of the ruled. Thrasymachus avoids the conclusion by simply switching from *just* to *unjust*. Even if one calls it unjust, the tyrant's power is free and masterful, and therefore most of all true happiness.

> Turn to the most perfect injustice, which makes the one who does injustice happiest and those who suffer it and who would not be willing to do injustice, most wretched. And that is tyranny.... Injustice, when it comes into being on a sufficient scale, is mightier, freer, and more masterful than justice. (344a–c)

---

about the being (*to einai*) of something, he is referring to what we call *predicative* being, not to *existential* being, or existence" (92). Human thought has a demiurgic power in Reeve. "The world around us and its contents, viewed from the undistorting perspective of dialectical-thought, are our attempts to make a really good world (505a5–9), a world that instantiates the good itself, and whose contents instantiate forms" (94). Reeve does not present an argument that Plato himself held this post-Kantian view.

The complete irrelevance of the contrast between *just* and *unjust* reflects the politics of Athens during the Peloponnesian War. When Athens invaded the island of Melos in 416 BC, the Athenian ambassadors attempted to persuade the Melians to surrender unconditionally.

> We will not use beautiful names (ὀνομάτων καλῶν)—either about how we are acting justly because we overthrew the Persians or are now attacking you because of injustice that you have done to us—and make a long *logos* that would not be believed . . . since you know as well as we do that justice in human *logos* is judged from equal strength (ἀπὸ τῆς ἴσης ἀνάγκης). The strong do what they can and the weak suffer what they must.[26]

The Melians decided to resist. Athens besieged the city but did not need to break through the walls.

> Some treachery took place in the city and so the Melians surrendered unconditionally. The Athenians killed all the grown men they took prisoner and sold the women and children as slaves. Later they sent five hundred colonists and inhabited the place themselves.[27]

What the Athenians formulated and then executed with straightforward brutality is a consistent voluntarism, a primacy of will over reason. This voluntarism of realistic politics corresponds to the traditional myths of divine combat. In this respect, Thrasymachus and other Sophists are in line with traditional Greek religion.

Three Cities Corresponding to Three Parts of the Soul

When Socrates catches Thrasymachus in a web of self-contradictions (see 339c), another striking scene follows. "I saw what I had not seen before—Thrasymachus blushing" (350d). Thrasymachus gives up, and nodding assent to the arguments by which Socrates eventually concludes, "The just man is happy and the unjust man wretched" (354a).

Thrasymachus's collapse disappoints Glaucon, who wants to know more fully what the good of justice is for the one who lives justly, leaving aside all rewards and punishments. He proposes the thought experiment of a perfectly just man who looks unjust and as a consequence lacks all advantages that normally flow from looking just.

26. Thucydides, *Peloponnesian War* 5.89.
27. Thucydides, *Peloponnesian War* 5.116.

> The just man ... will be whipped; he'll be racked; he'll be bound; he'll have both his eyes burned out; and, at the end, when he has undergone every sort of evil, he'll be crucified and know that one shouldn't wish to be but to seem to be, just. (353e–354a)[28]

Socrates takes up the challenge of this thought experiment, at first by arguing that the just man is still happier but eventually by bringing to light something *even greater than justice*; namely, the idea of the good (504d). The method he proposes is to build a city in speech and observe the coming to be of justice and injustice.

The order in which Socrates builds a city, or rather three cities, becomes clear only in retrospect, through his discussion of the three parts of the soul (436a–441c). After sketching a minimal city in which all three parts of soul are united in an embryonic harmony, he builds three cities by the successive unfolding of the loves that arise from the three parts of the soul: the luxurious city from the love rooted in the desiring part of the soul (*epithymia*), which is oriented toward pleasure and money; the military city from the love rooted in the irascible, spirited part (*thymos*), which is oriented toward military victory and honor; and the city of *logos* from the love rooted in the third part of the soul, *logos*. Although he sets out the principles for building this third city, Socrates does not work out its regime in detail. He only makes the paradoxical claim that lovers of wisdom should rule but does not draw out the consequences of such a rule.

By this expression of three kinds of love in three forms of cities, Socrates shows that a truly human life must be shaped above all by the love that flows from *logos*. The loves based on the desiring part and the spirited part of the soul are not enough as foundations for a happy life. They need to be integrated and ordered by the love that flows from *logos*.

The overall argument of the *Republic* thus unfolds the programmatic statement in the *Apology*, "The unexamined life is not livable for a human being" (38a). Only the life lived in agreement with *logos* is truly livable. The truth about the good, known in a receptive look (*theoria*), has absolute primacy over *praxis*. This is what Pope Benedict calls *intellectualism* in his Regensburg Lecture. In *Person and Act*, Wojtyła calls it *trueness* (see part II, chap. 5, sect. 4, in this volume).

28. The verb translated as *crucify* (following Bloom) is ἀνασχινδυλεύω, a rare equivalent of ἀνασκολοπίζω. It can be translated as "fix on a pole or stake, impale." According to Liddell-Scott, *Greek Lexicon*, "it is used convertibly with ἀνασταυρόω," the specific term for "crucify." Crucifixion was a mode of punishment practiced by the Persians and thus known to the Athenians.

The Luxurious City Gives Birth to the Military City

Socrates begins with a minimal city that "comes into being because each of us is not self-sufficient but needs much" (369b). The city lives on bread and wine, peacefully and moderately. Not limited to bodily needs, it includes festive singing of the gods.

> Setting out noble loaves of barley and wheat on some reeds or clean leaves, they will stretch out on rushes strewn with yew and myrtle and feast themselves and their children. Afterwards they will drink wine and, crowned with wreathes, sing of the gods. So they will have sweet intercourse with one another and not produce children beyond their means, keeping an eye out against poverty or war. (372b)

Socrates calls this city "the true [or truthful, ἀληθινή] city" and "a healthy one" (372e). Glaucon, however, is not satisfied with vegetarianism and lying on the ground. He wants to add *relishes* (in Athens usually fish) as well as desserts, tables, and couches (see 372c–d). When Socrates grants some relishes but keeps the diet vegetarian, Glaucon dismisses the improved city as "a city for sows." He demands what Athenians are used to: meat, couches, tables, and desserts (372d–e). Socrates calls the resulting city luxurious and feverish (372e). He follows the expansive logic of desires by adding cakes, perfume, incense, money, gold, ivory, prostitutes, rhapsodists, dancers, cosmeticians, swineherds, and therefore doctors and lawyers (373a–d).

What creates the luxurious city beyond the "healthy city" is the expansion of desire (*epithymia*). This expansion is in some respects truer to human nature than the moderate desires of the true city. The restlessness of sensual loves in human beings is not simply a result of a lack of moderation by reason. It is partly a result of reason because reason grasps the universal. Mozart's Don Giovanni defends his actions with sharp irony: "It is all love. If you are faithful to one woman, you are cruel to the others. I sense in myself such an expansive feeling that I love them all."[29] Don Giovanni's use of *all* is both rational and irrational. It is a shadowy and unsteady image of the universal reach of *logos*.

The luxurious city gives birth to a military class when its territory is no longer large enough to support its expanding desires. It must make war on its neighbors to conquer their land. The reason the military city, the city of *thymos*, comes into being is the need for an act of violent injustice to serve the lowest appetites. Socrates observes laconically, "We have found the origin of war—in those things whose presence in cities most of all produces evils both private

29. Lorenzo da Ponte, libretto for Mozart, *Don Giovanni*, Act 2, Scene 1.

and public" (373e). Even though he had said that his purpose in building a city in speech was to observe the origin of justice and injustice, he does not draw attention to this injustice. Still, for the reader, it must have been clear that he was addressing the *realist* politics of Athens in the Peloponnesian War.

War cannot be left to amateurs. The city needs professional warriors (373d–374e). Socrates euphemistically calls them *guardians* (φύλακες) (374d) even though their original purpose is conquest. If it were Socrates's purpose to construct an ideal city, would he begin with a pleasure-loving class and a military class that serves the pleasure-loving class by conquering enough land to allow it to satisfy its feverish appetites?

Philosophic Dogs and Their Theology

As he unfolds the role of the guardians, Socrates often compares them to dogs. "Do you suppose that for guarding there is any difference between the nature of a noble dog and that of a well-born young man" (375a). The likeness between dogs and members of the military class returns at key points. It serves as a premise in many important arguments. Dogs are driven by *thymos*. What they lack is *logos*.

> Will horse or dog—or any other animal—be willing to be courageous if it's not of irascible kind (θυμοειδής)? Haven't you noticed how irresistible and unbeatable *thymos* is, so that its presence makes every soul fearless and invincible in the face of everything? (375a–b)

There is a problem. The *thymos* of the military class could be dangerous for the city. How can one give the fighters two opposite attributes at the same time, being "gentle to their own and cruel to enemies" (375c)? These two attributes correspond to the false definition of justice proposed by Polemarchus. "Justice is helping one's friends and injuring enemies" (334b). Socrates already refuted this definition by arguing, "It is never just to injure anyone" (335e). Now he builds precisely this injustice into the very foundations of the military city. It follows necessarily that the military city cannot be the ideal city, despite Socrates's explicit statements to the contrary.

Socrates and Glaucon confess that they are at a loss about how to bring gentleness together with cruelty. At last, Socrates solves the paradox—by the dog.

> The dog ... is truly philosophic ... in that it distinguishes friendly from hostile looks by nothing other than a lover of learning since it defines what is its own and what is foreign by knowledge and ignorance. (376a–b)

At this point in the argument, at the very latest, it is difficult to overlook Socrates's irony. The dog is truly philosophic? That Glaucon does not object makes the irony more striking. It highlights the difference between the love characteristic of *thymos* and the love characteristic of *logos*. The former is a love for one's own coupled with hatred and cruelty toward the stranger. This is the love that shaped the politics of Athens in the Peloponnesian War. The love rooted in *logos*, by contrast, is universal. "Those who welcome each being itself should be called lovers of wisdom, philosophers" (480a). In contrast to *thymos*, *logos* is at home in all of being without exclusion. The love that arises from it is a love, not only for what is already known but even for what is not yet known. It is, in fact, more a love for what is still unknown, because human knowledge is small in comparison with the wealth of being. The opposite is true of dogs. Dogs love what they already know and hate what they do not know.

How can the city educate these dogs so that they become both gentle and cruel, gentle toward their own and cruel toward strangers? This is the subject of the remainder of Book 2 and almost the whole of Book 3 (376c–412a). The goal of educating the military class is to foster and at the same time to moderate *thymos* in them by "gymnastics for the body and music for the soul" (376e).

Socrates focuses on the military class alone. He makes no educational proposals for the original inhabitants, who continue their pursuit of wealth and pleasure as before and form their children to live in the same way. It is only much later in the *Republic* that he critiques their way of life when he discusses the two corrupt regimes that flow from the desiring part of the soul: democracy (see 555–562a) and tyranny (562–578b). Democracy and tyranny may seem to be opposites on the political spectrum, but they have the same origin; namely, the dominance of desire, *epithymia*.

In proposing the proper music for the soul, Socrates's first step is to establish "paradigms for theology, for *logos* about the divine" (τύποι περὶ θεολογίας) (379a). He does not allow the stories told by Homer and Hesiod to be told, "not even if they were true" (378a), because they portray the gods as fighting against their own, which would set a bad example for the city's military dogs.

The qualification "not even if they were true" is significant. Socrates anticipates Kant's reduction of religion to the practical order. The truth of religion in the theoretical order is irrelevant. For Kant, this reduction of religion to decent (rather than true or false) statements about the divine is demanded by the very nature of reason; for Socrates, it belongs to subrational *thymos*, which human beings share with dogs.

Some light from the sun filters into the cave when Socrates specifies the positive content of the standard of theology. Fluctuating between the plural *gods* and the singular "the god" or "a god" or "god" with eventual preference for the singular, he argues as Xenophanes did that in the divine there is no evil at all, no change, and no deception, only goodness, unity, and truthfulness.

This theological standard seems to subvert the purpose of educating the military class. It cannot nourish the required hatred and cruelty toward foreigners. Local deities who fight against the deities of foreigners would serve better as the civic religion of the military class.

The whole discussion of education is filled with such ambiguous interplay between light and shadow. It thereby calls the reader to examine carefully, in each case, where the genuine light of *logos* becomes visible. The call is insistent because Glaucon is a disappointing interlocutor after shining so splendidly in Book 2. There he presented powerful arguments, vigorously challenging Socrates with the perfectly just man who is crucified. Now he simply nods assent to whatever Socrates says. It seems to be Plato's purpose to disappoint the reader. The reader should become impatient and irritated with Glaucon, and insist on carrying out a more critical inquiry.

Lying about the Noble

Who should rule the military city and how? This is the question Socrates takes up after the section on education (see 412a–e). The word he uses for the ruler is presider (ἐπιστάτης), the title of the Athenian head of government, the office Glaucon thought he should have, according to Xenophon, when he was only nineteen years old, filled as he was with *thymos* but short on *logos*.

The topic of the ruler would be a good transition from the first two parts of the soul to *logos*, but Socrates remains within the boundaries of *thymos*, at times mixed with the light of *logos*, almost to the end of Book 5, including the first two waves of the ridiculous that structure the great digression of Books 5 through 7. In these first two waves he continues his diagnosis of Glaucon and of the Athenians driven by *epithymia* and *thymos*. It is only when the consequences of a regime built on these two lower parts of the soul have become most explicit in the account of male and female that he makes the transition to *logos*, beginning with the thesis of the philosopher-king (see 473c).

The purpose of the presider is "for the regime (*politeia*) of the city to be preserved" (412b). The same purpose is assigned later to the philosopher king. Only philosophers can preserve the military city. One wishes that Glaucon would ask Socrates whether it is good to preserve a city based on *epithymia* and *thymos* alone, without *logos*. It may be better than a city for swine, but only by being a city for dogs.

The only way in which the military regime can be preserved, Socrates argues, is by a lie about human nature and education. "By lying about one noble thing [the lawgiver must] persuade the rulers themselves most of all, or if not, at least [the rest of] the city" (414c). The lie consists in the claim that the birth and education of each of the classes was a dream. The god (Apollo) forms each citizen under the city's land from one of three metals: the rulers from gold, the military class from silver, and the rest from bronze. The founding generation of the city leaves the hands of the god as adults fully equipped for their class and task. The city's land then opens its womb and gives birth not to children but to these adults. They are in every way ready to take their place in the city as rulers, soldiers, farmers, artisans, tradesmen, and the like. The purpose of the story is clear. It ties all citizens with bonds of loyalty to their mother, the land, and it sanctions their division into classes with specific roles as divinely appointed. Custom and rearing are transformed into nature. Education can be changed; divinely appointed nature cannot.

Does Socrates propose the noble lie seriously as the foundation of an ideal city? Or is he speaking ironically, as in the case of the philosophical dogs? Would it be possible to persuade a city to accept the lie? Glaucon is skeptical. Later generations, he says, might believe the lie, but the founding generation will not (415d). The difficulties are enormous. Adults in the founding generation must be convinced that they did not live above ground as children, that they did not grow up in a household with a father and mother. They must dismiss the rich memory of waking life, which is consistent with and confirmed by the memory of their parents, siblings, and friends. As an adult generation, they have their own children, and these children are not a mere dream. The coup de grâce to the noble lie would be the question, "If these children are real and not a dream, wasn't our childhood also more than a dream?"

If the founding generation of the city does not accept the noble lie, how can it become the city's accepted narrative of self-understanding? It is astonishing to see a commentator as astute as James Adam overlook the difficulty.

> Grote justly observes that "Plato has fair reason for his confident assertion that if such legends could once be imprinted on the minds of his citizens, as portions of an established creed, they would maintain themselves for a long time in unimpaired force and credit." The first generation of citizens would remain incredulous, but the γενναῖον ψεῦδος (noble lie) would be impressed upon their children, and soon be universally believed. It would require but little effort for a Greek city like Plato's (470e) to entertain in course of time a view which has so many points of contact with Greek tradition.[30]

30. James Adam, *The Republic of Plato*, 2 vols. (Cambridge: Cambridge University Press, 1902), 1:196.

The lie's most serious problem, however, is not the certainty of its failure but the lawgiver's power over truth. The lawgiver is free to make use of both falsehood and truth as indifferent means for political ends. This primacy of will and power is incompatible with Socrates's claim later in the *Republic* that the lovers of wisdom, who are to rule the city, are "never willing to accept lying or falsehood but hate it, loving truth" (485c).

Morality and Religion

Without drawing much attention to it, Socrates proposes a revolutionary change shortly after the noble lie. He extends the prohibition of wealth from the military class to the money-making class (see 420d–422a). *Thymos* thus bends back to tame *epithymia*. The founding of the city began from below, from feverish appetites. The prohibition of wealth frees the military class from being a mere servant of the appetites of the lower class. Now the relation turns around. The military class becomes an exemplar for change in the lower class.

This first revolution raises the question whether a second revolution will follow, one in which *thymos* leaves its dominance behind and allows itself to be governed by *logos*. Socrates proposes no detailed laws for this second revolution, but the need for it becomes clear in the argument.

Marriage and the family appear in passing after the property revolution as "other matters that we are leaving aside, such as finding a spouse, marriage, and having children, which must follow as far as possible the proverb, among friends all things are held in common" (424a). The tangential claim "all things in common" serves as the literary hook for the great digression, the true heart of the *Republic*, from the beginning of Book 5 to the beginning of Book 8.

Religious laws are the last laws to be given. They are "the greatest, the most beautiful, and the first of laws to be given"— that is, first in the order of importance, not of development. They govern "the founding of temples, sacrifices, and the services to gods, daimons, and heroes" (427b). Socrates remarks that he and his interlocutors "know nothing" in this area. Apollo must draw up these laws and promulgate them through his inspired priestess, the Pythia at Delphi.

> We will obey nobody else, if we have a rational mind (*nous*), for we surely don't need any exegete other than the one we received from our fathers. For about such things, this god exegetes for all human beings as the exegete received from their fathers, sitting in the middle of the earth on the navel. (427b–c)

Particularism and universalism are curiously combined in these words of appeal to ancestral custom. If he were merely an ancestral custom, Apollo at

Delphi could not claim to exegete, to interpret events for all human beings. Only *logos* has this competence.

Here is one of the strongest objections against a literalist reading of Books 3 and 4 of the *Republic*. Socrates draws back from formulating the greatest and most beautiful laws, first in importance for the city to be founded. How can this city be ideal if the most important laws are left hanging until a message arrives from Delphi in cryptic hexameter? Some proposals relevant to religion are, in fact, implicit in Socrates's presentation of the idea of the good in three great images: the sun (505a–509d), the divided line (509d–511e), and the cave (514a–518b).

A False Greatest Good

Once the founding of the city is complete, Socrates returns to the question of justice, both in the city and in each person. The whole argument up to this point has prepared the reader to expect an account of the greatest good of the city and of each individual man. This good, the reader thinks, will now make its appearance.

Plato disappoints this expectation. He has Socrates define justice as the fixed determination of all citizens to remain in their own class and to do the work assigned to them as appropriate to that class. In an individual human being, justice is the harmonious working of the three powers of soul. Toward what object or end are these powers directed? Toward what end or good is reason itself directed? Socrates does not raise these questions here. These are the decisive questions about "the greatest good."

What evaluation of the military city and its justice could Plato expect from Athenian readers? The regime he sketches in Books 3 and 4 is in many respects like the militaristic regime of Sparta. The likeness extends even to details of the laws on men, women, and children. Some Athenians admired Sparta.[31] Xenophon was exiled by the Athenian assembly for his pro-Spartan convictions not long before the end of the Peloponnesian War. The War ended in 404 BC when Sparta crushed Athens. If the most widely accepted dating is correct, the *Republic* was published about two decades after this defeat. Could Athenians be expected to embrace a hyper-Spartan regime? Polemarchus had by then been killed by the pro-Spartan oligarchic regime of the Thirty. They confiscated the

31. Xenophon provides much firsthand testimony about Sparta in *The Politeia of the Lacedaemonians* and *Agesilaus*; see also Aristotle, *Politics*, 2.9–12.1269a29–1274a22; Plutarch, *Life of Lycurgus*; *Comparison of Lycurgus and Numa*; *Sayings of the Spartans*; *Comparison of Agesilaus and Pompey*; *Customs of the Spartans*; *Sayings of Spartan Women*. These testimonies diverge somewhat, but it is quite clear that Sparta and the *Republic*'s military city would have been seen as very much like each other.

wealth he inherited from Cephalus.[32] When the *Republic* was published, the democratic regime had returned to power.

Can one interpret the hyper-Spartan character of the *Republic* as evidence that the text was written to produce a negative response in its intended audience? Even if a case can be made, it remains circumstantial.

3. Transition to *Logos*

The Detour

One can find more direct evidence in the interruption of the dialogue at the beginning of Book 5 and in the discussion that follows it.

> SOCRATES: Good, then, I call such a city and regime, and right . . . but bad the others, and mistaken. . . . There are four forms of badness.
>
> ADEIMANTUS: What are these?
>
> SOCRATES: And I was going to speak of them in the order that each appeared to me to pass from one to the other. But Polemarchus—he was sitting at a little distance from Adeimantus—stretching out his hand and taking hold of his cloak from above by the shoulder began to draw him toward himself and, as he stooped over, said some things in his ear, of which we overheard nothing except,
>
> POLEMARCHUS: Shall we let [him] go or what shall we do?
>
> ADEIMANTUS: Not in the least.
>
> SOCRATES: What most particularly is it that you are not letting go?
>
> POLEMARCHUS: You. (449a–b)

The elaborate description of taking hold, drawing toward oneself, and not letting go recalls the opening scene of the *Republic* (327a–c). The parallel underlines the importance of this dramatic scene. Socrates has gone up part of the way out of the cave toward the daylight. Construction of the city, which had begun on the level of sense-desire (*epithymia*), has reached only the level of the irascible (*thymos*). Granted, some daylight of *logos* has penetrated now and then into the shadows of the cave. If Socrates continued from this point, as he says he intends to, with a discussion of defective regimes, he would turn around and again walk down into the cave. He would fail to take the final step, the step toward *logos*.

Taking this final step is not the reason why Polemarchus arrests Socrates. His motive is fascination with the thesis "about women and children, it is evident to everyone that what belongs to friends is common" (449c). Socrates gives

32. See Nails, *People of Plato*, at entry "Polemarchus."

him much more than he asked for, namely, all of Books 5, 6, and 7, which contain the *Republic*'s account of reason (*logos*). Socrates ends his long detour and returns to the beginning of Book 5 only at the beginning of Book 8. The pivotal exchange between Socrates and Glaucon was already quoted above.

> SOCRATES: Let's recall where we took the detour that brought us here so that we can go on the same way again.
>
> GLAUCON: That's not hard. You were presenting your arguments pretty much as you are doing now, as though you had completed your description of what concerns the city, saying that you would set down a city such as you then described, and the man like it, as good. And you did this, as it seems, *despite having a still more beautiful* (*or noble*) *city and man to tell of*. (543c–544a; emphasis added

That Books 5, 6, and 7 are a detour is the height of irony. These three books are the summit toward which the whole *Republic* tends. It may seem strange that what triggers this summit is Socrates's remark "about women and children, it is evident to everyone that what belongs to friends is common" (449c). Polemarchus finds this the most important question to be settled in the city's regime. "We think it matters much, indeed everything, for the regime (*politeia*), whether [this relation between men, women, and children] comes about in the right way or not" (449d). Socrates seems to agree. "What a huge *logos* have you set in motion about the regime, again from the very beginning" (450a).

Reduction to the Absurd

Why does the question of marriage and the family compel Socrates to go back to the roots of the discussion and start the argument all over again? The answer may be that the violence of *thymos* becomes particularly evident in Socrates's theology of the body, or rather in Socrates's failure to take bodily sexual life into account according to its actual nature. Put positively, the reason is that the nature of a rational animal expresses itself with unique intensity in erotic love, as the *Symposium* and the *Phaedrus* show.

The use to which Socrates puts Polemarchus's question about friends having all things in common becomes clearer when one notices that he gives three answers, only the second of which corresponds directly to Polemarchus's question. The implicit questions behind the other two answers differ.

1. *Not explicitly asked, but implicit in "all things common"*: Should there be the same education for men and women in the warrior class?
2. *Asked:* How will women and children be common?

3. *Not asked:* How can the military city be realized and preserved?

1. *The same education and role for men and women* (*not asked*):

We attempted in speech (*logos*) to set up the men as guardians of a herd.... Do we believe the females of the guardian dogs must guard the things the males guard along with them and hunt with them, and do the rest in common, or must they stay indoors as though they were incapacitated as a result of bearing and rearing the puppies, while the males work and have all the care of the flock? ... If, then, we use the women for the same things as the men, they must also be taught the same things.... Music and gymnastic ... these two arts, and what has to do with war, must be assigned to the women also, and they must be used in the same ways. (451c–452a; discussion 451c–457c)

2. *Sharing of wives and children* (*asked*):

All these women are to belong to all these men in common, and no woman is to live privately with any man. And the children, in their turn, will be in common, and neither will a parent know his own offspring, nor a child his parent. (457c–d; discussion 457c–471e)

3. *Setting up and keeping the city* (*not asked*):

Unless philosophers rule as kings or those now called kings and chiefs genuinely and adequately philosophize, and political power and philosophy coincide in the same ... the regime we have now described in speech (*logos*) will never be born. (473c–d; discussion 472a–543c, the remainder of Book 5 and Books 6 and 7 as a whole)

All three answers, especially the answers to the questions not asked, are part of an argument by reduction to the absurd. All three look down toward *thymos* and up toward *logos*. They show that a city ruled by a military class according to *thymos* alone cannot be the good city, however much shadowy truth it may contain. There is "a better city" (543d), one more beautiful or noble than the city sketched in Books 3 and 4 on the foundation of *thymos*.

The reduction to the absurd, is clearest in the third answer: "Philosophers should be kings or kings philosophers" (473c–e). That this answer looks up toward *logos* is clear. The life of philosophy is a life devoted to *logos*. That the answer also looks down toward *thymos* becomes clear when one pays close attention to the question it addresses.

The question is whether the city outlined in Books 3 and 4, the city of the irascible part (*thymos*), can be established and preserved exactly as described (see 472b–473c). Socrates emphasizes repeatedly that precisely this and nothing else is the question addressed by the thesis of the philosopher-king. The laws of the military regime will remain in place without any change (see 407b). Granted, as he discusses the love of wisdom in detail, he implicitly expands the function of the philosopher-king. Yet exactly the inevitability of this expansion shows that the philosopher king is not a reasonable way of answering the question how to establish and preserve a regime based on *thymos*. One cannot expect the philosopher to accept this task without asking critical questions about the greatest good of the military regime and about the primacy of *thymos*. Socrates leads the way, contrary to his assertion that the regime will not be changed (see 407b), by raising these critical questions both indirectly and directly.

Socrates compares his three answers to three waves of the ridiculous, likely to be greeted by laughter or worse (see esp. 473c), and rightly so. As Bloom observes, Socrates proves in practice that he is a more excellent comedian than Aristophanes, whose comedy *Ecclesiazousae* (*The Assembly Women*) contains similar ideas.[33]

> [Socrates produces] a comedy which is more fantastic, more innovative, more comic, and more profound than any work of Aristophanes. Socrates with an air of utmost seriousness undertakes absurd considerations; in this he is already comic. If what he appears to teach is impossible, as will prove to be the case, Socrates' comedy will be akin to the *Ecclesiazousae*.[34]

Two examples can illustrate Bloom's point, one taken from each of the first two answers. It is surprising that many commentators, even the acute James Adam, do not see them as ridiculous but as quite serious and rational proposals. Equality, Socrates argues, implies that men and women must wrestle naked with each other in the gymnasia (see 451a–d and 457a). About complications likely to arise in this practice, he remarks with hilarious dryness, seconded by Glaucon, who finally rises to the level of comedy himself.

> SOCRATES: Mixed together in naked exercise and the rest of the training, [men and women] will be led by an inner natural necessity to sexual mixing with one another, I suppose. Or am I not, in your opinion, speaking of necessities?
>
> GLAUCON: Not geometrical but erotic necessities, which are likely to be more stinging. (458c–d)

The second example is more serious but still funny. It is the problem of incest. In the military city, no citizens (except perhaps the rulers) know who their

33. The *Republic* was probably published after the *Ecclesiazousae*, though an earlier version may have been in circulation. For a detailed discussion of this question, see Adam, *Republic*, 1.345–55.

34. Bloom, "Interpretive Essay," 381.

fathers and mothers are. How can one avoid sexual relations with one's own brothers or sisters, fathers or mothers? The answer is complex.

> Of all the children born in the tenth month, and in the seventh, from the day a man becomes a bridegroom, he will call the males sons and the females daughters; and they will call him father; and in the same way, he will call their offspring grandchildren, and they in their turn will call his group grandfathers and grandmothers; and those who were born at the same time their mothers and fathers were procreating they will call sisters and brothers. Thus, as we were just saying, they won't touch one another. (461d–e)

The attempt to work out who will not touch whom under this rule runs into puzzles. Socrates points to the root problem a little later without any remark about its disastrous impact on his laws. "With everyone he happens to meet, he'll hold that he's meeting a brother, or a sister, or a father, or a mother, or a son, or a daughter or their descendants or ancestors" (463c). But if all are brothers, sisters, mothers, and fathers, then no one can touch anyone—except by special and exceptional permission of the Pythia at Delphi (see 461e). No rational eugenic regime can be built on this foundation.

4. The Greatest Good

The Question of Happiness

Socrates's proposals hold a serious kernel. The kernel is easiest to see in the thesis of the philosopher-king. If philosophers become rulers of the city, they will undoubtedly ask critical questions about the military regime. The most important is the one Socrates asked at the very beginning of the *Republic* in Cephalus's house. It is the question of happiness. What is the greatest good to be reached by human beings? For the military city, the answer is justice. Justice consists in each class of citizens keeping its place, doing its own task, and, at least for the guardians, having everything in common so as to reach the greatest degree of unity. Socrates claims that this is the greatest good for a city, a claim he rejects later in the argument.

> SOCRATES: Won't our citizens more than others have the same in common, precisely what they call "mine"? And when they have this in common, won't they more than others have pleasure and pain in common?
>
> GLAUCON: Very much so!
>
> SOCRATES: Is the cause of this—apart from the rest of the regime—the communion of women and children among the guardians?

> GLAUCON: Very much so, the most important cause!
>
> Socrates: But we agreed that *this is the greatest good for a city*—and we compared it to a body, how it relates to a part with respect to pleasure and pain.
>
> GLAUCON: And we were right to agree.
>
> SOCRATES: The cause of *the greatest good of the city* has shown itself to be the communion of children and women among the helpers. (464a–b; emphasis added)

Socrates shows the absurdity of this statement by formulating one of the most obvious truths about the body a few sentences later. "They will possess nothing private except the body (μηδὲν ἴδιον ἐκτῆσθαι πλὴν τὸ σῶμα), while the rest is common" (464d). Yet the private body threatens to unravel much of Socrates's argument in the first two waves. Bodies cannot all be in the same place. Some will be more distant, others near, even in a relatively small city. There will inevitably be concentric circles, near the center, less near, and far from the center, more private and less private. Close and intensive private relations are possible in a house, a small space in which a man and a woman live a shared life with their own children, offspring of their own bodies. The law forbids such closeness, at least for the military class.

Homer shows how intensely the Greek mainstream loved and honored the closeness of a house. The Trojan War, of which the *Iliad* tells one episode, was fought for Helen, wife of Menelaus, abducted by Paris to Troy. It was fought to preserve the close relations of husband and wife in a house. The *Odyssey* tells the story of Odysseus's journey home from that war to his wife, Penelope, and their royal house. He himself built the marriage bed with his own hands as a "great secret sign" between husband and wife. The story of Telemachus, offspring of Penelope's body together with his own, is woven into this fabric of bodily closeness. These are all matters of reason, not mere animal nature. Granted, they involve the bodily and sentient aspect of the human animal, but there is only one human nature, rational animal.

It is astonishing that Glaucon follows Socrates without any critical resistance into destroying this fabric of bodily closeness. At the very beginning of the *Republic*, Socrates identifies Glaucon as a son of Ariston, brother of Adeimantus and Plato. Later, he quotes a line from a poem. "Sons of Ariston, god-like offspring of an honorable man" (368a). He also says to Glaucon, "I see hunting dogs and quite a throng of noble cocks at your house" (459a). Is Glaucon willing to drop his closeness to Ariston, Adeimantus, and Plato? Is he willing to call everyone father and brother, even men quite distant? Is he willing to give up his house, cocks, dogs, and all? Is he willing to move into shared military barracks?

Bloom draws the right conclusion. "Socrates forgets the body in order to make clear its importance."[35]

Aristotle's Critique Is the Same as Socrates's

Aristotle attacks the *Republic*'s proposals for the military city from two opposite sides, *one* and *many*. From the side of *many*, he points out that everyone being everyone's father, mother, brother, sister, and so on, will mean little. "How much better is it to be the private cousin of somebody than to be a son in this way!"[36] From the side of *one*, he shows that the logic of Socrates's proposals makes it difficult to understand why there should be many people in a city at all. If the greatest good of a city is its unity, is it not better to cut the city down to a house, and then the house down to one individual?

> But which is better, that a well (καλῶς) settled city has all things in common as far as possible, or only some and not others? One possibility is for citizens to share women, children, and property with each other, as in Plato's *Republic*. Socrates says there that children, women, and property should be common. Which is better, as it is now, or following the law written in the *Republic*? ...
>
> The reason why Socrates says the law should be drawn up in this way does not come together clearly from his arguments. What he says ought to be the city's end is impossible as he puts it now, and how one should interpret it is not at all made clear. I mean the city being one, that it is best for all of it to be as one as possible. For this is the hypothesis Socrates adopts.
>
> And yet, it seems that by going along this way and becoming more one, it will not even be a city. For a city is by nature a multitude and by becoming more one, a city will turn into a house, and a house into an individual man, because a house is obviously more one than a city, and one man more than a house. Even if somebody could do this, it should not be done, because it will destroy the city.[37]

Aristotle's two-pronged attack (the one weakened by the many; the many negated by the one) shows that Socrates's proposal is unsuited to both aspects of the rational animal: the *logos* of the private body and the *logos* of the common good. The common good mediates between the one and the many among persons, especially bodily persons (see the discussion of the common good in part I, chap. 7, in this volume).

35. Bloom, "Interpretive Essay," 387.
36. Aristotle, *Politics* 2.2.1262a13–14.
37. Aristotle, *Politics* 2.1–2.1261a2–22.

Marriage brings two personal bodies together by two great common goods: the union of the spouses, both bodily and spiritual, which is the intrinsic common good of marriage, and children, who are the extrinsic common good. In this manner the laws on marriage and procreation are a privileged place for showing by *reductio ad absurdum* that the military city constructed by Socrates is not yet a city for rational animals.

Aristotle's forceful critique of the *Republic*'s military city turns on raising the question of the good. Is unity as conceived in the military city truly the greatest good of rational beings? Is it a true common good, one that constitutes the happiness of each without competition or violence? Socrates's own critique of the military city is no less forceful. It turns on raising the same question. The unity of the military city, Socrates says, is not the greatest good. There is a greater good. He introduces it first as an object of learning, "the greatest and most fitting *mathema*" (504d).

> ADEIMANTUS: So these [i.e., the virtues on which the military city is built] aren't the greatest, but there is something yet greater than justice and whatever else we went through?
>
> SOCRATES: There is both something greater and even for these it won't do to look at a sketch, as we did a while ago, but their most perfect elaboration must not be passed over. Or isn't it ridiculous to make every effort that other things of little worth be as precise and pure as can be, while not judging the greatest things worth the greatest precision?
>
> ADEIMANTUS: That's a very worthy thought. However, as to what you mean by the greatest object of study and what it concerns, do you think anyone is going to let you go without asking what it is?
>
> SOCRATES: Certainly not. Just ask.... You have many times heard that the idea of the good is the greatest object of study and that it's by availing oneself of it along with just things and the rest that they become useful and beneficial.... We don't have sufficient knowledge of it. And, if we don't know it without this, you know that it's no profit to us, just as there would be none in possessing something in the absence of the good. Or do you suppose it's of any advantage to possess everything except what's good? Or to be prudent about everything else in the absence of the good, while being prudent about nothing beautiful and good? (504d–505b)

One cannot bring a more devastating critique against the military city. The idea of the Good played no role in building it. Therefore the city has not yet "become useful and beneficial." It brings "no profit" because there is no profit "in possessing something in the absence of the good." It is a case of "possessing everything except what's good." The reduction to the absurd is complete.

5. The Order of Knowledge

Reason and Universality

The logical next step in Socrates's argument is to turn toward this highest object of knowledge and love, the idea of the good, in a manner suited to the capacity of Glaucon (see 435d and 503d–504d). Socrates begins his approach by pointing to the universality present in human love. This universality inevitably follows from the predicable universal *good* formed by all human beings. All human beings love and choose whatever they love and choose under the aspect of this universal notion. "When we say, someone loves (φιλεῖν) something, if it is rightly said, it must be evident that he does not love (φιλοῦντα) this of it yes, and that of it no, but loves all (πᾶν στέργοντα)" (474c). Socrates then applies this universality of the defining object of reason to the love of wisdom, which most immediately springs from the nature of reason.

> SOCRATES: When we say, someone is desirous (ἐπιθυμητικὸν) of something, will we say that he desires (ἐπιθυμεῖν) all of this kind (εἶδος, *eidos*), or this of it yes, and that of it no?
>
> GLAUCON: All.
>
> SOCRATES: Won't we also then assert that the philosopher is a desirer (ἐπιθυμητὴν) of wisdom, not of this yes, and of that no, but of all? (475b)

The first sentence contains the term *eidos*, which soon becomes central in the argument together with its close cognate *idea*. *Eidos* and *idea* are often translated as English *idea*, which is highly misleading. English *idea* usually refers to a notion in the mind. An alternate translation is English *form*, which is more objective but does not explicitly bring in the act of seeing. The verb *see* is the root of both *eidos* and *idea*. Both words signify *what is seen:* the shape or form of something, its beauty, and so on. They do not signify a notion in the mind but the object of human thought, particularly the essence or nature of a being. When the human mind raises its characteristic question, "What is it?" it looks for the answer in the *eidos* or *idea* of a being, however imperfect its grasp may be.

Socrates begins with the *desire* for wisdom, not with wisdom itself. *Wise* is too much to say about any human being, he argues in the *Phaedrus*. "At least to me, Phaedrus, calling someone wise seems a great thing, suited only to a god. Love of wisdom (*philo-sophia*) or something of this sort seems to fit and match better" (*Phaedrus*, 278d). To be a rational animal is to be on a journey toward grasping the *eidos* and *idea* of beings. We begin with an imperfect and confused but rich grasp of what things are, for the most part formed already in childhood and later developed by more distinct notions. Wisdom is the good of human reason, but it cannot be fully achieved in this human life. It is what reason by its nature tends toward.

The Universal Said about Many

The universality of the love that arises from reason implicitly contains all that Socrates goes on to say about the nature of reason. Love and desire are directed toward instances of good under the predicable universal notion *good*. They depend on the human ability to see goodness in many instances and to call each of them *good*. "The object of the will, which is the human power of love, is the universal good (*bonum universale*), just as the object of the mind is the universal true (*universale verum*)."[38] The predicable universals true and good, which are universal in the sense of being said (predicated) about many instances, give to human reason its nature, as color gives to sight the nature of sight. This is not to say that what rational desire aims at is the predicable universal as such, that is, inasmuch as it is formed by the human mind. Love goes out to things themselves in their own reality. It is to say that rational desire goes out to things themselves under the aspect of their goodness.

As Socrates's argument unfolds, it becomes clear that the predicable universal is not the only kind of universal. He closely intertwines it with another universal, the universal in causation.[39] The first kind is found in thought and speech when we think or say one thing about many. This is good and that is good. The second is found in being and causes, when one cause extends its causality to many effects. The good of victory in a battle, for example, extends its causality as purpose to the many actions taken in the battle. It is the universal cause of these actions.

Formulated in terms of the one and the many, the first kind of universal is *one after the many and said about the many*; the second is *one before the many, shared in by the many, but not said about the many*. The first kind plays an important role in several Platonic dialogues. In the *Meno*, for example, the question is raised, "Can virtue be taught?" Socrates argues that one should approach this question by first asking, "What is virtue?" In the *Republic*, at the end of his dramatic clash with Thrasymachus, he makes the same point.

> I have not had a fine banquet, but it's my own fault, not yours. For in my opinion, I am just like the gluttons who grab at whatever is set before them to get a taste of it, before they have in proper measure enjoyed what went before.

38. Thomas, *Summa* I-II, q. 2, a. 8, corp.

39. On this distinction, see the brilliant essay by Ronald P. McArthur, "Universal *in praedicando*, Universal *in causando*," *Laval théologique et philosophique* 18 (1962): 59–95.

> Before finding out what we were considering at first—what the just is—I let go of that and pursued the consideration of whether it is vice and lack of learning, or wisdom and virtue. And later, when in its turn an argument that injustice is more profitable than justice fell in my way, I could not restrain myself from leaving the other one and going after this one, so that now as a result of the discussion I know nothing.
>
> So long as I do not know what the just is, I shall hardly know whether it is a virtue or not and whether the one who has it is unhappy or happy. (354a–b)

Human reason is by its nature oriented toward the question, What is it? "The understanding's own object [i.e., the object that gives it its nature] is what something is, *quod quid est*."[40] The nature of reason is shaped above all by this form of the universal, the one that corresponds to the question, What is it?

Once it grasps what a triangle is—namely, a three-sided rectilinear plain figure—reason can understand the proof that the sum of interior angles in a triangle must be equal to two right angles. It can grasp the necessity of the conclusion. The equality of the angles is not merely a statistical fact but flows necessarily from the nature of a triangle. Reason understands this inner necessity.

The Platonic dialogues are filled with the joy of discovery in pursuit of such understanding. They are dramatic events in which readers are not to remain outside as mere observers. Plato invites them to let themselves be drawn into the argument as active participants who think through the questions and experience discovery.[41]

The receptive character of such discovery needs to be emphasized against Heidegger's charge that Plato imposes the forms on being by a sheer act of the will to power. Granted, the assent given by the mind is voluntary. Yet it is voluntary not in the sense of a self-initiated choice of the human will to impose or construct but in the sense of a free submission to evidence. Reason is truly free in the degree to which it rests on evidence and not on the will to power. The will to power does violence to reason by forcing it into an unreasonable practice.

Universal Cause

The second kind of universal is found in the order of being and causing. In this case, universal means full, perfect, extending causality to many. One can call it a one before the many because, as cause or source in which many participate, it is before them, if not in time, at least in dependence. It can also be called a one

40. Thomas, *Contra gentiles* I, cap. 58, par. 5.

41. See Jacob Klein, *A Commentary on Plato's Meno* (Chapel Hill: University of North Carolina Press, 1965; reprint, Chicago: University of Chicago Press, 1989), esp. 1–31.

shared in by the many but not said about the many. It is not said about them even though they share in it because it is distinct from the many as their source. One can say *good* about an instance of goodness, but one cannot say *goodness itself* about that instance. As one instance of goodness among others, it does not exhaust the whole fullness of goodness.

In the *Republic*, Socrates calls the foremost among these universal causes the idea (*idea*, ἰδέα) of the good. He introduces it by analogy to the sun, the light of which gives us the power to see things and make true statements about them. The idea of the good has a similar causal role, not limited, however, to the visible world but extending over the whole realm of being.

> SOCRATES: Say that what provides the truth to the things known and gives the power to the one who knows is the idea (ἰδέα) of the good. And, as the cause (αἰτία, *causa*) of the knowledge and truth, you can understand it as something known; but, as beautiful as these two are—knowledge and truth—if you consider it as something different from them and still more beautiful than they, you will consider it rightly. As for knowledge and truth, just as there [in the visible world] it is right to hold that light and sight are of the sun's kind (helio-eidetic, ἡλιοειδῆ) but to believe them to be the sun is not right; so, too, here, to hold that these two are of the Good's kind (agatho-eidetic, ἀγαθοειδῆ) is right, but to believe that either of them is the Good is not right, but one must honor the condition (ἕξις) of the Good still more.
>
> GLAUCON: You speak of an unmanageable beauty (ἀμήχανον κάλλος), if it provides (παρέχει) knowledge and truth but is itself above them in beauty. You surely don't mean it is pleasure.
>
> SOCRATES: Don't blaspheme. (508e–509a)

Glaucon's obtuse remark "Surely you don't mean pleasure" shows that his understanding of the idea of the good is, to say the least, confused. He does, however, realize that Socrates is speaking about an unmanageable beauty. The Greek word for unmanageable is *a-mechanon*, nonmechanicable. The noun *mechane* is close to power. It signifies any means by which one can reliably get a result. Glaucon's mention of pleasure causes Socrates to respond sharply with the abrupt imperative εὐφήμει, or "don't blaspheme, be silent." This imperative is found most often in sacred contexts. Taken negatively, it means "avoid all unlucky words during sacred rites: hence, as the surest mode of avoiding them, keep a religious silence." Taken positively, it means "shout in triumph, honour by praise."[42] The *Epinomis*, transmitted as part of the Platonic corpus but generally considered inauthentic, contains a passage that clearly uses the word in the second sense, "praising the gods and goddesses."[43]

42. Liddell-Scott, *Greek-English Lexicon*, at εὐφημέω.
43. *Epinomis* 992d.

In the first part of his account, Socrates focuses on the idea of the good under the aspect of knowledge and truth. In the second part, he takes the step from truth to being. The idea of the good, he says, is the universal cause, not only of knowledge and truth but also of *to be* (εἶναι, *esse*) and being (οὐσία, *substantia, essentia*).

> But consider its image still further in this way.... I suppose you'll say the sun not only provides what is seen with the power of being seen but also with generation, growth, and nourishment although it itself isn't generation.... Therefore, say that not only being known is present in the things known due to the Good, but both *to be* and "being" (τὸ εἶναί τε καὶ τὴν οὐσίαν, *et esse et substantia*) are in them besides due to it, although the good isn't being (οὐσία) but is still beyond being (ἐπέκεινα τῆς οὐσίας), exceeding it in dignity and power.
>
> And Glaucon very comically said, "O Apollo of divinely super-darting" (508e–509c).

Among Apollo's epithets, the most frequent is Shining (*Phoebus*) and, closely related, the Sun (*Helios*), Source of Splendor (*Aigletes*), and Bringer of Light (*Phanaeus*). He carries the most powerful bow and arrows and is called Shooter (*Aphetor*) and Far-Shooter (*Hekatebolos*) or Skilled-Shooter (*Hekebolos*). Glaucon's reference to Apollo fits the image of the sun. Gabrièle Wersinger-Taylor shows that Glaucon's response, *Apollon daimonias hyperboles*, follows a regular pattern of invocation in which a god's name in the vocative is followed by an attribute in the genitive of exclamation.

> A possible translation of Plato's passage reflecting the adnominal genitive would be "Apollo of divinely super-darting." We would then be at the beginning of a hymn to Apollo qualified by an epithet, an epiclesis: δαιμονίας ὑπερβολῆς, which shifted formulation would suit Glaucon's irony as imitating what may be called the *hupsēlē* style (*Euthydemus* 289e4).... But then the correct interpretation of the whole passage would be that the principle of the Good is praised as in a hymn, and it would be an indication that, as a principle, it is considered as having a sacred significance.[44]

The portrayal of the idea of the good as a universal cause of *to be* of all beings is close to a passage in Aristotle's *Metaphysics*, similar even in the move of the argument from truth to being.

> What is most true is the cause (αἴτιον, *causa*) of the others being true. For this reason, the beginnings (ἀρχὰς, *principia*) of [things] that exist always are

44. Gabrièle Wersinger-Taylor, "The Meaning of 'Ἄπολλον ... δαιμονίας ὑπερβολῆς' in Plato's *Republic* 6,509b6–c4: A New Hypothesis," in *Second Sailing: Alternative Perspectives on Plato*, ed. Debra Nails and Harold Tarrant (Helsinki: Finnish Society of Sciences and Letters, 2015), 298–303; at 302.

> most true, for they are not only sometimes true, nor do they have some cause of their *to be* (αἴτιόν … τοῦ εἶναι, cause of *esse*) but they [are the cause of *esse*] for others, so that each, as it has of *to be* (τοῦ εἶναι, of *esse*), so also of truth.[45]

One might question the likeness between this text and the *Republic*, because for Aristotle a fullness of *to be* (τοῦ εἶναι, *esse*) is present in the first cause, while Socrates says that the idea of the good is "beyond being" (ἐπέκεινα τῆς οὐσίας). Much discussion has surrounded the exact meaning of "beyond being." It is unlikely that Socrates simply excludes *to be* (εἶναι, *esse*). He calls the idea of the good "of being the most radiant" (τοῦ ὄντος τὸ φανότατον) (518c), "the happiest of being" (τὸ εὐδαιμονέστατον τοῦ ὄντος) (526e). One must, he says, turn toward the vision of the Good as "toward the contemplation of the best among the existing [things]" (πρὸς τὴν τοῦ ἀρίστου ἐν τοῖς οὖσι θέαν) (532c). These texts suggest that "beyond being" (ἐπέκεινα τῆς οὐσίας) should be taken in a more specific sense: the idea of the good is not one among other beings.

Plato and Aristotle seem to share much common ground about the universal cause of being and goodness. Both see it as an actual fullness of being. Thomas interprets their texts in this sense. "Plato, Aristotle, and their followers reached the understanding of universal to be itself (*ipsius esse universalis*), and thus they alone posited a universal cause from which all other things proceed into to be (*in esse*)."[46]

The Human Order of Knowledge

Aristotle distinguishes between universal causes and predicable universals, while the *Republic* and other Platonic writings tend to conflate them. This disagreement goes back to an even deeper disagreement about the order of knowledge in a rational animal. In quite different historical circumstances, Scheler and Wojtyła disagree in a similar way. In the context of a discussion of body and soul in Plato and Aristotle, Thomas describes the two starting points as follows.

> The reason for the difference between these two views is this: in pursuing the truth about the nature of things, some started from intelligible accounts (*ex rationibus intelligibilibus*), which was characteristic of the Platonists, others from sensible things, which was characteristic of Aristotle's philosophy, as Simplicius says in his commentary on the Categories.
>
> The Platonists noticed an order of genera and species and observed that the higher can always be understood without the lower, such as man without

45. Aristotle, *Metaphysics* 2.1.993b.25–31.
46. Thomas, *De potentia*, q. 3, a. 5, corp.

this man and animal without man, and so on. They also thought that whatever is drawn away (*abstrahitur*) in the mind is really (*in re*) drawn away, for it seemed that otherwise the mind would be wrong or pointless when it draws something away (*abstrahens*), if a thing drawn away (*res abstracta*) did not correspond to it.

For this reason, they also believed that mathematical objects had their own being, drawn away from (*abstracta*) sensible things, since they can be understood without them. For the same reason, they held there was man drawn away from these men, and so forth, all the way to being, one, and good, which they held to be the highest power of things.

For they saw that the lower is always more particular than what is above it and that the nature of the higher is shared in the lower. That which shares in something, however, is related as material to what it shares in. They held, therefore, that among things drawn away (*abstracta*) the more universal are the more formal.[47]

An objection can help bring out the meaning of this text. We cannot start with sensible things. We know sensible things by intelligible notions (*rationes intelligibiles*). Without such notions, there is only perception, no knowledge in the sense of understanding. We must therefore start with intelligible notions. In fact, we must start with the most universal notions, because less universal notions cannot be conceived without the more universal ones. There is much truth in this objection.

Something is earlier by its account (*prius ratione*) if it falls earlier in the understanding. What the understanding grasps earlier is being itself; in a secondary way, it grasps that it understands being; third, it grasps that it desires being. The notion of being, therefore, is first, the notion of truth second, and the notion of good third, although the good is in things.[48]

If the more universal notions are earlier, how can sensible things themselves be the starting point of understanding? A first response can point out that human reason depends on sensation. Sensation is earlier. More needs to be said, however, because the point from which to start (as understood by St. Thomas) is sensible things themselves, not sensation. How is this possible?

To see how it is possible, one can turn to a point that applies to all knowledge, both sensory and intellectual, although Aristotle makes it in a discussion of sensation and of the *eide*, the forms received in sensation.

47. Thomas, *De spiritualibus creaturis*, a. 3, corp.

48. Thomas, *Summa* I, q. 16, a. 4, ad 2; among many other passages, see esp. I-II, q. 94, a. 2, corp.

> Quite in general one must hold about all sensation that it is what is receptive for the sensible *eide* without matter, just as the wax receives the sign of the seal ring without the iron or gold, for it receives the gold or metal sign but not as gold or metal. Sensation likewise undergoes (πάσχει) something from each, from what has color, flavor, or sound but not as each of these is called that but as it is of this sort and according to the *logos* (κατὰ τὸν λόγον).[49]

I do not see red by being red, taste sour by being sour, or hear noise by being noisy. "As each one is called," these do not need to exist in me but as what I perceive. What exists in me is color, flavor, and sound as my attention is stretched into (*in-tentio*) an instance of red, sour, and loud. I perceive them as an *eidos*, something seen, tasted, and heard, according to its own *logos*.

The example of the seal and the wax may contain several levels of meaning. On the most immediate level, Aristotle may be thinking of the difference between gold and wax. Gold has the shape in a more lasting way and as the cause of the impression on wax. Yet he might place the emphasis not so much on the material but on the impressed shape as a sign. One presses the ring against the wax as a sign that points back to the ring and to its bearer. This reference to the bearer is close to the way the objects of knowledge are present in the person who knows. Here one encounters one of Aristotle's most important observations, which Thomas formulates as follows.

> Everything is received in another according to the mode of the recipient.... In sensation, the form has *to be* in a different way (*esse alterius modi*) than the sensible thing. For in the sensible thing it has natural *to be* (*esse naturale*) but in sensation, it has intentional *to be* (*esse intentionale*).[50]

It is possible to observe what belongs to the intentional mode and what belongs to the real mode. For example, a figure approaching in the fog may look so indistinct that one cannot tell whether it is a horse or man or something else. This indistinctness clearly belongs to the approaching figure only in its intentional being. In its real being, it is not indistinct. As it really exists, it is more knowable than a vague shape in the fog. For the one seeing it approach, it is not (yet) knowable in the same way.

We often make judgments of this sort. We distinguish what belongs to something in its presence to us as knowers and not in its real being. The example of the figure approaching in a fog shows that we can make such judgments with great accuracy and certainty based on the complex interlocking fabric of our ordinary experience. We do not need to set out on a quest to make sensible things

49. Aristotle, *De Anima* 2.12.424a.17–24.
50. Thomas, *Sententia de anima* 2, lect. 24, no. 553.

the starting point of our knowledge. They have been our constant point of reference since childhood.

Jacob Klein sees a similar account of ordinary experience in the image of the divided line (509d–511e). He approaches the line from the lowest of the four forms of knowledge, *eikasia*, which consists of distinguishing mere images of things (e.g., reflections in a mirror, on the surface of water) from things themselves. What allows this recourse to things themselves is the solidity of ordinary experience.

> Our relation to all the animate and inanimate things around us is one of unfathomable familiarity. Even things and surroundings with which we happen to be, as we say, "unfamiliar," have an index of familiarity on them that does not make it too difficult for us to deal with them, to respond to them. We are indeed "at home" among all the familiar and unfamiliar things and faces of the visible world. Our basic attitude towards them is one of unquestionable trust (*pistis*) which extends far beyond any distrust or suspicion we might feel on occasion. Overwhelmingly, we trust that all the familiar features of the visible world are here to stay, that things are as we see them. The usual and the unusual, the expected and the unexpected, routine and novelty, are labels put on things and events within the frame of our all-embracing, all-familiar common experience.[51]

When a physicist walks into her laboratory, she has no difficulty distinguishing her colleague from her colleague's reflection on the shiny surface of an instrument. She also has no difficulty distinguishing him from the instruments themselves. Her judgments on these matters are quite certain. As Klein reads the divided line, Socrates relies on this solidity of ordinary experience to anchor *eikasia* in sensible things themselves. Klein then reads the other parts of the divided line as connected with these observations. On this reading, there is more common ground between Plato and Aristotle, even if Aristotle makes different use of this common ground in understanding the predicable universal.

To approach the predicable universal, one can set up a proportion. As the vague appearance of a figure is to the actual being that is approaching, so the predicable universal is to the individuals about which it is predicated. The proportion should not be pressed. The indistinctness of the predicable universal differs in kind from the indistinctness of a figure approaching in the fog. The dim appearance in the fog is simply a defective form of the appearance. It becomes less defective when the figure comes closer. The predicable universal, by contrast, is not a defective object of sensation. On the contrary, it has in some respects a higher mode of being than the objects of sense. It allows the knower

51. Klein, *Commentary on Plato's Meno*, 114.

to understand what something is and whether attributes belong necessarily and always to a being of this nature, or only contingently, while sensation is limited to what happens to be a fact at a particular time. This superiority of the predicable universal plays a prominent role among the reasons that led Plato to posit the separate existence and the actual fullness of the predicable universal as a universal in causation.

The limits of the proportion illustrate the general principle that everything is received in the mode of the recipient. When one says, "This is a being," it is in some way the very least one can say about it. To say more, one must use more specific notions, such as *horse* or *man*. The same point can be formulated in a opposite way. When one says, "This is a being," this is in some way all there is to say about it. All that one will ever say with more specific notions will still be being in some sense. As a predicable universal, *being* refers to the whole richness of being. But it does not refer to it as an actually expressed wealth. The lack of actual expression in the notion of *being* belongs to being as received in the human mind. It does not belong to being itself.

The two universals could hardly be more different. As a predicable universal said about many, *good* has a merely potential fullness. The potentiality of this fullness arises from the intentional mode *good* has in an imperfect knower. As a universal not said about many but causing many, the universal good is the actual fullness of good. If one claims that the two universals coincide, problems arise. Directly contradictory statements will be the result.

Since the predicable universal is poor in actual content, one might be tempted to think the same of universal causes. One might conceive the One of Plato's unwritten doctrine as a principle of unity of a general sort, poor in content and therefore vast in extension. In that case the idea of the good would not contain the fullness of goodness, being, life, and understanding. It would not be universal in causation.

In working out the Platonic doctrine of principles, Krämer carries the defects of the universal in predication over into the universal in causation. On this basis, he claims that Plato's idea of the good "prefigures ... the unity of transcendental apperception in Kant,"[52] which is, as such, empty. Krämer does not take into account what Socrates says about *eros*, especially the *Symposium*, the *Phaedrus*, and the *Republic*: "Now this is what every soul pursues and for the sake of which it does everything" (505d). Krämer's hypothesis would be suited to souls without longing.

52. Krämer and Catan, *Plato and the Foundations of Metaphysics*, 180. Krämer rejects a merely mathematical account of the principles (82) as well as the "demetaphysicalization" of the principles (184). For his own account of Plato's principles, see 77–91.

6. The Order of Love

Love and Universality

Although the two universals diverge in the order of being and knowledge, they come together in the order of *eros*. *Eros* is not content with predicable universals. It goes out to things themselves. Nevertheless, it goes out to them under the predicable universal *good*, which gives it a universal scope. "When we say, someone loves (φιλεῖν) something, if it is rightly said, it must be evident that he does not love (φιλοῦντα) this of it yes, and that of it no but loves all (πᾶν στέργοντα)" (474c). Socrates goes on to argue that this universality of human love implies that the idea of the good is the target or goal of all human desires and acts.

> Now this is what every soul pursues and for the sake of which it does everything. Divining that it is something but at a loss about it, and unable to get a sufficient grasp of just what it is, or to have a stable trust such as it has about other things, it loses any profit there might have been in the rest. (505d–e)

St. Thomas makes a similar argument.

> It is impossible for man's happiness to lie in any created good. Happiness is the complete good, which brings desire wholly to rest. Otherwise it would not be the last end, if anything remained to be desired. Now, the object of the will, which is the human faculty of desire, is the universal good. Hence it is clear that nothing can bring man's will to rest except the universal good, which is not found in anything created but only in God, because every creature has participated goodness. Only God, therefore, can fill the human will, as Psalm 102 says, "who fills your desire with good" (Ps 102:13, Vulgate). Therefore, man's happiness can only lie in God.[53]

One could object that the argument equivocates on the middle term *universal good*. In its first use, *universal good* refers to the universal in predication. In its second use, it refers to the universal in causation. The only way to understand the argument as valid, it seems, is to equate the two meanings. In whatever way one resolves the question, Thomas's argument implies a close relation between the two universals in the order of love.

To get a clearer grasp of this close relation, one can begin with Socrates's claim that all human beings pursue the idea of the good in all they do. The claim seems contradictory and, at any rate, contrary to fact. How can the idea of the good be that for the sake of which all human beings do all they do, if it is so

53. Thomas, *Summa* I-II, q. 2, a. 8, corp.

vague and general that most people do not reflect about it? The actual motives for which they act are always concrete.

This objection overlooks an important fact. Human love and desire are directed toward real instances of good under the predicable universal *good*. There is a close relation between this predicable universal and the desire for happiness. What human beings desire is a life about which they can use the predicable universal *good* without further qualification.

If Xenophon's story about Glaucon is accurate, Glaucon may well have had the impression that, *if only* he were head of the government of Athens, he would be living a life about which he could say, It is good. Such impressions about *if only* are deceptive. When one arrives at what one thought would be an end point, it turns out not to be an end point at all but only another intermediate point, a means for happiness in the sense of a part of happiness, not happiness itself. One sees that *good* reaches far beyond this instance. In this way, the predicable universal *good* deeply shapes the desire for happiness. By its presence, it unmasks any good that poses as the definitive object of desire, anything, that is, short of the universal cause of goodness. Whatever may occupy the foreground of motivation in a person's awareness, the experience of this deep natural structure of desire remains. Given the nature of human reason, the journey toward happiness will necessarily be restless and open-ended, reaching out for an indefinite fullness.

Rational Love and the City

What is the impact of these truths on the city built in speech? The luxurious city was built on the love that arises from human sensory powers (*epithymia*); the military city on the love that arises from the spirited part (*thymos*). Is there a city built on the love that arises from the rational part (*logos*)?

The division of the city into classes that correspond in each case to only one of three levels of soul (*epithymia*, *thymos*, and *logos*) is obviously false. Every human being experiences love in all three forms. A class that consistently wants pleasure and nothing else, followed by a class that is consistently driven by *thymos* and nothing else, both in a merely exterior and problematic relation to the rare breed called *philosophers*—this can only be a heuristic device. Taken as a thesis, it is so obviously false that the burden of proof lies with those who read it as a serious proposal.

In the transition from the luxurious city (*epithymia*) to the military city (*thymos*), Socrates introduces new laws for the military class. He even transforms the life of the pleasure-loving class by principles taken from the military class, most clearly by extending the prohibition of wealth to the whole city (see 420d–422a). Why does he not go through similar steps in the transition to *logos*? He does have much to say in Book 7 about the education that fits reason. He describes it as an education to be given only to the future philosopher-kings, not to other members of the city. It differs from military education by devotion to truth rather than utility. If each member of the city has *logos* within, will the city not have a shared life of *logos*? How would this life differ from that of the military city? What laws would need to be added? Which laws would need to be rejected?

Socrates's silence about these questions is one of the most striking features of the *Republic*. The function of silence in the *Republic* seems to be similar to the function of *aporia* in other dialogues. It increases the urgency of the questions, provided one asks them and does not remain outside the argument as a spectator. By not describing the city of *logos* in detail but showing the insufficiency of a city not built on *logos*, Plato leads the reader to ask questions more forcefully and insistently. His student Aristotle learned this lesson and repeats it.

> For those who wish to get clear of difficulties it is advantageous to state the difficulties well. . . . People who inquire without first stating the difficulties are like those who do not know where they have to go; besides, one does not otherwise know even whether one has found what one is looking for or not.[54]

Should one go one step further and see a skeptical thesis in the *Republic*'s silence? Should one say that the absurdities built into the city by Socrates simply belong to political life, because the tensions in a rational animal are irresolvable? This seems to be how Strauss reads the *Republic*. He sees it as a proof that the city of *logos* is impossible. Philosophical life will always be at odds with political life. The best one can do is carve out a limited space for some philosophers in a political environment bent ultimately on killing philosophers.

> Socrates makes clear in the *Republic* of what character the city would have to be in order to satisfy the highest need of man. By letting us see that the city constructed in accordance with this requirement is not possible, he lets us see the essential limits, the nature, of the city.[55]

Strauss may be more pessimistic than Plato, perhaps by reading some of the *reductio ad absurdum* arguments as applying to any city rather than to a city based only on *epithymia* and *thymos* without *logos*. The presence of *logos* in all human beings shows that one needs to think about a city of *logos*.

54. Aristotle, *Metaphysics* 3.1.994a27–995b3.
55. Strauss, *City and Man*, 138.

The Object of Happiness

In the *Phaedo*, immediately before his execution, Socrates defines philosophy as a preparation for death.

> It seems to me that a man who has rightly and really spent his life in the love of wisdom ought to be confident to die, full of hope that there he will gain the greatest goods (μέγιστα ... ἀγαθὰ).... Those who rightly take hold of the love of wisdom do nothing other than prepare for death and for being dead. (6364a)

Should one understand this text as implying that a city of *logos* can only be other-worldly? When he describes the upward journey from the cave into the light of day, Socrates says nothing about death as necessary for the journey. On the contrary, the lover of wisdom is sent down again into the cave to stir up the prisoners. This is how Socrates understood his role in Athens. The present life is the focus of the *Republic*. Granted, Socrates ends with a mythical portrayal of the soul's afterlife and the cycles of reincarnation (614b–621b), but this passage serves to round off an argument about the present life. It does not construct a city of souls liberated from the body.

The Platonic tradition developed ways of understanding the journey to wisdom as taking place in this life, even if only imperfectly. Plotinus, for example, proposes the path of ascent from the visible world to solitary contemplation of the Good.

> One must go up again to the good, which every soul pursues [cf. *Republic* 505d: This is what every soul pursues and for the sake of which it does everything] ... until, passing in the ascent all that is alien to god, one sees with oneself alone the alone one itself, simple, single, and pure, from which all depends and to which all look and are and live and think: for it is the cause of life and mind and being. If anyone saw it, what loves would he feel, what thirsts, wishing to be mingled together with it, how struck outside himself with joy! ...
>
> Here the greatest, the last contest is set before souls, all toil being for the sake of this, not to be left without a share in the best vision, which, if one attains it, one is blessed in seeing that blessed sight, and, if one fails to attain it, one fails. One does not fail if one fails to win beauty of colors or bodies, or power or office or kingship even but if one fails to win this and only this, for which one should give up reaching kingship and rule over all earth and sea and sky, if only by leaving and overlooking them one may turn to that and see.
>
> But what is the way? What is the means? How can one see the unmanageable beauty (ἀμήχανον κάλλος), which stays within holy temples and does not

go forth to the outside for everyone, even for the profane, to see? Let him go and follow along into the inside—the one who can.[56]

On first reading, this text looks anti-cosmic and anti-political. Other texts in Plotinus, especially the treatise *Against the Gnostics*, give a fuller picture. The Gnostics, Plotinus says, hate the body "because they have heard how Plato often reproaches the body for the ways it is an obstacle to the soul and calls all bodily nature inferior."[57] Plotinus resists this hatred on both cosmic and anthropological grounds. His cosmic grounds echo the conclusion of the *Timaeus* (92c).

> It is not right to blame the care for the house (διοίκησιν) of the All, first because [the All] shows the greatness of the intelligible nature.... It hangs together and is radiant (ἐναργὴς). Much life exists everywhere and shows an unmanageable (ἀμήχανον) wisdom. How could anyone refuse to call it a radiant image (ἄγαλμα ἐναργὲς) of the intelligible gods?[58]

Plotinus resists the Gnostic hatred of the body also on anthropological grounds by appeal to Socrates's account of *eros* in the *Phaedrus* (251a). The characteristically human way of knowing is to see the invisible expressed in visible images and symbols. This is the nature of human *logos*.

> Those who recognize in a perceptible image the portrait of someone treasured in their mind are thrilled when they come to this remembrance of truth. From this experience (*pathos*), loves are set in motion. If someone who sees beauty well represented in a face is carried there, will he be inert in mind? Will he not be moved to anything else when he sees all that is beautiful in the world of sense, all commensurability, this great order, and the visible form (*eidos*) apparent in the stars, though they are so far away? Will he not be moved from there to deep thought? Will awe not grip him? How? Whence?[59]

Whatever a city of *logos* may look like, its integration must come from the radical openness of human reason to being and to the whole cosmic order. At

56. Plotinus, *Enneads* 1.6.7–8.

57. Plotinus, *Against the Gnostics*; *Enneads*, 2.9.17. Plotinus does not use the term "Gnostics." Porphyry testifies that he introduced it. See Porphyry, *Life of Plotinus*, 16. The view Plotinus opposes is consistent, however, with texts produced by self-designated Gnostics, such as *Secret John*. See Michael Waldstein, "The Primal Triad in the Apocryphon of John," in *The Nag Hammadi Library after Fifty Years: Proceedings of the 1995 Society of Biblical Literature Commemoration*, ed. John D. Turner and Anne McGuire (Leiden: Brill, 1997), 154–87. For the historical and systematic problems of the concept "Gnosticism" as influenced by Hans Jonas, see Michael Waldstein, "Hans Jonas' Construct 'Gnosticism': Analysis and Critique," *Journal of Early Christian Studies* 8 (2000): 341–72.

58. Plotinus, *Enneads* 2.9.8.

59. Plotinus, *Enneads* 2.9.16.

the root of this openness lies a longing for the infinite, a longing that Luigi Giussani calls "the religious sense."

> What is the formula for the journey to the ultimate meaning of reality? Living the real. There is an experience, hidden yet implied, of that arcane, mysterious presence to be found within the opening of the eye, within the attraction reawakened by things, within the beauty of things, within an amazement, full of gratitude, comfort, and hope . . .
>
> Now the question is this: How can this complex, yet simple, this enormously rich experience of the human heart . . . become vivid, how can it come alive? How can it become powerful? In the "impact" with the real. The only condition for being truly and faithfully religious, the formula for the journey to the meaning of reality, is to live always the real intensely, without preclusion, without negating or forgetting anything.[60]

In this openness, human *logos* finds itself oriented by *eros* toward the most universal cause, the idea of the good, "This is what every soul pursues and for the sake of which it does everything" (505d).

7. Four Features of Reason

The *Republic* highlights four features of human reason. All four play an important role in Wojtyła in agreement with Socrates, Plato, and Aristotle, in contrast to Descartes, Kant, and Scheler. The most important fault lines in the argument of TOB lie here, in these features that belong to the full breadth of reason.

1. *Love for All of Being:* "Those who welcome each being itself (αὐτὸ . . . ἕκαστον τὸ ὄν) one should call lovers of wisdom (philosophers) rather than lovers of opinion" (480a). To be rational (to have *logos*) means to face each being itself, and therefore all being. It means to raise questions about the meaning, goodness, and source of each being and of being as a whole. It means placing no limits on one's love for being.

Thrasymachus shows the opposite of such a universal love. The purpose of reason is not to apprehend and express being. It is to gain power, to win whatever prize one desires, victory over one's enemies and, best of all, tyrannical rule over one's city. In Plato's *Gorgias*, when Socrates challenges Gorgias's reduction of *logos* to such an instrument of power, he hesitates.

> I'm afraid to pursue my examination of you, [Gorgias,] for fear that you should take me to be speaking with eagerness to win against you, rather than to have

60. Luigi Giussani, *The Religious Sense* (Montreal: McGill-Queens University Press), 108.

> our subject become clear. For my part, I'd be pleased to continue questioning you if you're the same kind of man I am, otherwise I would drop it.
>
> And what kind of man am I? One of those who would be pleased to be refuted if I say anything untrue, and who would be pleased to refute anyone who says anything untrue; one who, however, wouldn't be any less pleased to be refuted than to refute. For I count being refuted a greater good, insofar as it is a greater good to be rid of the greatest evil from oneself than to rid someone else from it.[61]

The display of power in winning an argument is not what attracts Socrates. It stands in the way of what attracts him most. When one is refuted, one may have the impression of defeat, of a loss of power, but the impression dissolves on a deeper level. The admission that one has been mistaken brings to light a human dignity and beauty greater than power.

2. *The Primacy of Theoretical Truth:* In the *Apology*, Socrates gives an account of his activity for the city. Living in a fully human way is possible, he argues, only if one examines one's life. "The unexamined life is not livable (βιωτὸς) for man."[62] What needs to be applied to human life in this examination is above all the truth about the good. In this examination of the good, the theoretical or contemplative order has radical primacy. Of course, acts of *theoria* are themselves acts willed and performed by a human being at some time, in some place, in some circumstances. The life of *theoria* does not lie outside the moral and political order but is measured by it.

The primacy of theoretical truth does not lessen the importance of practical truth. While theoretical truth is the conformity of one's thought with being, practical truth is the conformity of a practical judgment (I shall do this now) with right desire. The absolute primacy of theoretical truth can be seen on two levels. On the root level, it can be seen in the question that aims at theoretical knowledge. "Does what I think and say fit what is the case?" Given the very nature of the question, I must answer it on its own terms. I cannot legitimately allow myself to determine the answer by my will or anybody else's will. The facts themselves—exactly as they are, not as I want them to be—must decide the answer, even if I know them only dimly and imperfectly, influenced in various ways by external power and inner desire. This demand arises from the very nature of knowing, from its aim to think or say *It is* when it is, and *It is not* when it is not.

On a second level, once I grasp the truth about the good in an act of *theoria*,

61. Plato, *Gorgias*, 457e–458a.

62. Plato, *Apology*, 38a. This sentence is often translated "The unexamined life is not *worth* living." An unexamined life may well be *worth* living, but it is not livable *in a human way*. To suffocate questions about being and the good is to live less than a fully *human* life.

this theoretical truth becomes the measure for my acting (*praxis*). I cannot legitimately go against the judgment of my own reason by submitting to external or even internal pressure. Once *theoria* has grasped the truth about the good, it binds *praxis* to that truth.

Thrasymachus lionizes the man with strong appetites and the power to satisfy them. Such a man, he believes, is free. He can do what he wants. In the *Gorgias*, Socrates grants that *doing what one wants* is a good starting point for understanding freedom. Yet when one is deceived about the good, one might do what one does not really want. The inability to uncover and overcome deception about the good destroys the possibility of doing what one really wants. Socrates's interlocutors grant the argument step by step, but when the conclusion is reached, they find it absurd. It goes directly against their impatient will to power. They ask Socrates in astonishment, "You say it is better to suffer injustice than to do it. Do you want to suffer?" Socrates answers, "I certainly would not want either, but if it had to be one or the other, I would choose suffering over doing what is unjust."[63] The radical commitment to *logos* as the rule of life, the primacy of *theoria* over *praxis*, could hardly be expressed more forcefully. Socrates did suffer when Athens executed him for denying the gods of the city and corrupting the young.

3. *Primal Wonder about Beauty:* At the high point of the *Republic*, when Socrates sketches the Idea of the Good, Glaucon exclaims, "You speak of an unmanageable beauty (*amechanon kallos*), if it provides knowledge and truth but is itself above them in beauty" (509a). The Idea of the Beautiful in the *Phaedrus* and *Symposium* is close to the Idea of the Good. *Eros* stirred by beauty permeates Plato's writings, not as a foreign element but as the innermost energy that propels a rational animal. A similar *eros* moved by beauty can be seen in the text from Aristotle's *Parts of Animals*, quoted above as a contrast with Bacon's ordering of knowledge to power. It is to the point in the present argument as well. Aristotle uses the same adjective, *amechanos*, unmanageable, unmechanicable, to describe the beauty of nature.

> What is left is to speak about the animal nature, leaving out nothing as far as we are able, neither less noble nor more noble. For although some have not been graced with respect to sense perception, the fashioning nature gives *unmanageable joys* (ἀμηχάνους ἡδονὰς) in their study to those who can come to know causes and are by nature lovers of wisdom ... for *in all there is something natural and beautiful*.... Absence of haphazard and being for the sake of are in

63. Plato, *Gorgias*, 469b–c.

> nature's works, and in the highest degree. That for the sake of which they come together and come to be *holds the place of the beautiful.*[64]

4. *Journey toward a Definitive Good:* The openness of reason to all being, its primacy as a measure of human acts, and the primal awareness of the beauty of being are closely related to the desire for happiness, the desire for a life that can be called *good* without qualification or reservation, a life that is not merely good in one way but not in another way but simply good. The presence of predicable universals in human knowledge implies that this longing cannot be satisfied by anything finite. By its primordial natural desire, human reason reaches out toward an indefinite *more*, in which the whole fullness of good is found. The building of a truly human city must reckon, above all, with the common good that is the object of this longing.

64. Aristotle, *Parts of Animals* 1.5.645a.5–26; emphasis added.

CHAPTER 6

The *Logos* of Nature in Aristotle's *Physics*

1. Aristotle's Variation on Plato's Cave

Aristotle recasts the image of the cave in Plato's *Republic* in a fragment of one of his dialogues preserved in Latin translation by Cicero.[1]

> Most gloriously Aristotle says,
> If there were [people]
>
> who had always lived underground
>   in good dwellings filled with light
>   that were adorned with statues and pictures,
>   and furnished with everything in which those abound
>   who are thought supremely happy (*beati*),
> who had nevertheless never gone out above ground,
> who had, however, heard and received a report
>   that there was some governance (*numen*)[2] and power (*vis*) of the gods,
> and who had then at some time, when the jaws of the earth opened, been able
>   to escape from these hidden dwellings
>   and come out into these places which we inhabit,

1. Cicero, *De natura deorum* 2.95.

2. *Numen* often refers to a divine being, but here it is parallel to "power (*vis*) of gods." Varro confirms this reading. "They say that *numen* means governance (*imperium*) derived from nodding (*ab nutu*), because governance belongs most of all to the one by whose nodding all things are, as in the case of Jupiter." Varro, *De lingua latina* 7.85.

when suddenly they saw the earth, the seas, and the sky,
  understood the greatness of clouds and the power of winds,
  and looked at the sun and understood its greatness and beauty
  but especially its causal power (*efficientiam*),
  that it makes the day with light poured out over the whole sky,
and when, by contrast, night darkened the earth they saw the whole sky
  spangled and adorned with stars,
  and the changing phases of the moon's light waxing and waning,
  and the rising and setting of all these,
  and their paths fixed in all eternity and unchangeable,
when they saw this,

most certainly would they have judged
that there are gods
and that these great works are works of gods (*haec tanta opera deorum esse*).

The cave fragment opens with the shortest possible conditional clause: *si essent*, if there were. The subject is understood. It is described in the immediately following four relative clauses:

who had always lived underground
who never went above ground
who had heard a story about gods
who, finally, escaped from their caves

Having introduced the *dramatis personae*, Aristotle continues with three clauses introduced by *when* (*cum*) that describe their experience. The three temporal clauses added to the four relative clauses bring the total to seven. The temporal clauses describe the experience of the cave dwellers above ground:

when they saw . . . and looked at the sun
when night darkened, they saw . . . the stars
when they saw this

The first temporal clause focuses on the day, the second on the night, while the third resumes both (when they saw *this*) and leads immediately to the main clause, the outcome of these experiences. The cave dwellers, who had heard a story, now recognize by sight what they heard. In the *Metaphysics*, Aristotle reflects briefly about the role of traditional religious stories in preparing the mind.

A tradition in the form of myth has come down from the ancients and extremely remote ancients as an inheritance for those who are later: that these [heavenly bodies] are gods and that the divine surrounds the whole of nature. The rest was then added mythically for the persuasion of the many. . . . They

> say the gods have human shape or are like some other animals and things that follow from or accompany those mentioned. If one took only the first point, that they thought the first beings (οὐσίας, substances) were gods, one would consider it divinely spoken (θείως ... εἰρῆσθαι).[3]

According to this text, Philosophy takes up a truth that comes to it as an inheritance from the mythical tradition. It is not clear whether Aristotle understands "divinely spoken" in the maximal sense as an "inspired utterance" (as Ross translates the passage in the Oxford Aristotle) or, in a minimal sense, "spoken excellently" (as suggested by Liddell-Scott, *Greek Lexicon*).

Light, Beauty, Intelligence, and Power form a cluster of themes that appears twice in the cave fragment, both before and after the escape of the prisoners. The caves in which the prisoners live before their escape are filled with bright artificial light and beautiful artifacts. Much human intelligence and power went into furnishing the caves, but the text does not directly mention this fact. It mentions two details. First, most people believe that those who own such precious artifacts are happy in the highest degree. The people in the caves, however, hear about a much greater intelligence and power; namely, "a governance and power of gods." After their escape, when they come face-to-face with the beauty, power, and light of the natural world, they see the intelligence and power they had merely heard about in their caves.

The repetition of these themes, once before and once after the escape, brings out a striking difference. Human artifacts are beautiful. It is not false to think that those who own them are happy, at least in some degree. Yet the artificial environment produced by human intelligence and power in underground caves is far less beautiful and good than the natural world. The natural world is overwhelmingly greater and more beautiful. It is so much greater that it must be the fruit of a divine intelligence and power. It spreads out in the open air, under the huge illumined sky. The fugitives are not miserable after their escape into nature—quite the opposite. Nature is not only beautiful, one might say, but glorious.

In the *Republic*, the escape from the cave to the surface of the earth symbolizes the ascent from the visible universe into the sphere of true being, a purely intelligible rather than sensible world. Aristotle's cave fragment transposes Plato's cave down to earth, from symbol to reality. Nevertheless, the cave fragment expresses the same *eros* for the divine that one finds in Plato's cave. It is when they see the natural world that the fugitives encounter a divine presence that remains mysterious and only indirectly visible. A similar experience is expressed in Plato's *Phaedrus*.

3. Aristotle, *Metaphysics* 12.8.1074a38–1074b.

> Concerning beauty, as we said, it shone when it was among those [ideas], and when we came here we grasped it, splendid and brightest, through the brightest of our senses. For sight is the sharpest of the perceptions that come to us through the body. Prudence (φρόνησις) is not seen by it—it would cause marvelous loves if it caused such a bright image (εἴδωλον) of itself by entering sight—nor are the other beloved (ἐραστά) [ideas]. But now, for beauty alone has it been ordained to be most expressive (ἐκφανέστατον) and most beloved (ἐρασμιώτατον).[4]

This passage describes an interpenetration of sensible and supra-sensual being not unlike the image of nature in the cave fragment. The *Phaedrus* expresses the interpenetration partly by the myth of remembrance, but it describes an actual expression of the divine in material being.

The cave fragment has a paradoxical twist. The world discovered by the fugitives is the world with which we are familiar—too familiar, perhaps, to see it for what it is. At the very beginning of *Orthodoxy*, Chesterton tells the story of an English sailor who miscalculates his course and discovers South Wales under the impression that it is an island in the South Seas.

> If you imagine that he felt a fool, or at any rate that the sense of folly was his sole or his dominant emotion, then you have not studied with sufficient delicacy the rich romantic nature of the hero of this tale. His mistake was really the most enviable mistake; and he knew it, if he was the man I take him for. What could be more delightful than to have in the same few minutes all the fascinating terrors of going abroad combined with all the humane security of coming home again? . . . What could be more glorious than to brace one's self up to discover New South Wales and then realize, with a gush of happy tears, that it was really old South Wales.[5]

Chesterton goes on to draw a far-reaching conclusion about philosophy. "This . . . seems to me the main problem for philosophers. . . . How can we contrive to be at once astonished at the world and yet at home in it?" In his cave fragment, Aristotle suggests such a coincidence of opposites. With intense love he looks toward nature, because a divine presence is expressed in it.

We who live in the twenty-first century do not need to dig caves to perform Aristotle's experiment. His thought experiment has gained strength above ground. Life in a modern city takes place largely in an artificial or even virtual environment. An important exception is contact with other human beings, particularly in the sexual relation between man and woman, which rises with great

4. Plato, *Phaedrus*, 250c–d.
5. Gilbert Keith Chesterton, *Orthodoxy* (New York: John Lane, 1908), 14–15.

power in our nature. It is an intense point of contact with nature. Ecological wisdom is particularly needed in this contact.

Ratzinger shows that our technological age reverses the experience of the cave fragment and therefore leads to another conclusion. It leads to the conclusion stated by Nietzsche: "God is dead—and we have killed him."

> The oppressive sense of the absence of God, which has left its mark on us all today ... is the human distress in today's technological age. Man has total power over the world. He analyzes its functions completely. He is familiar with the laws that govern its functioning. His knowledge is power. He can, so to speak, dissect the world and put it back together again; he regards the world as a functioning system that he uses and that he compels to serve him. In a world that is completely analyzed in this way, there is no longer any place for an intervention by God. Man can find help only in man, since it is only man who has power over the world. But since a God without power is no God, there is no longer any God where man alone possesses power....
>
> The problem of power is only one aspect; on a deeper level, this depends on prior decisions taken in the relationship to one's own "I," to "you," and to "us"—in the experience of being loved or being rejected. The fundamental experiences and decisions in this interplay between "I," "you," and "we" determine how a man sees the presence with him, and antecedent to him, of the One who is utterly other: Is he a competitor, a danger, or a reason for confidence? And this in turn determines whether man in the long run is compelled to contradict this Witness or to say Yes to him in reverence and thankfulness.
>
> This reflection leads us to the real starting point of the question of God, which is much more basic than the dispute about proofs of God's existence.[6]

The experience of our technological age is a complex challenge. One of its most important intellectual facets is the need to think through the very foundations of natural philosophy. Aristotle's *Physics* offers many helpful avenues.

2. Nature

Aristotle approaches an understanding of nature (φύσις) as he often approaches questions. He focuses on a common notion, a shared way of speaking that reflects ordinary human experience possessed by both adults and children.

6. Joseph Ratzinger, *The God of Jesus Christ: Meditations on the Triune God* (San Francisco: Ignatius Press, 2008), 15–17.

> Some things are by nature, others through other causes. By nature are animals and their parts and plants and simple bodies, such as earth and fire and air and water, *for we say* that these things and such things are by nature.[7]

The pronoun *we* in the phrase *for we say that* refers to Greek speakers in general. Ordinary human discourse contains a wealth of implicit meaning, without which philosophy would lose contact with real being. Aristotle asks what these things have in common over against those that are "through other causes" and are "not brought into being by nature."[8] This focus on bringing into being is not incidental. The Greek noun *physis* comes from the verb *phyo*, to bring forth, beget, just as the Latin *natura* comes from *natus*, born. This origin of the word leads one to expect a particularly close relation between nature and begetting.

Artifacts are brought into being by deliberate human intention and power; chance events come about by coincidence. By contrast, the common trait of the beings that come to be by nature, Aristotle remarks, is that "each of these things ... has in itself a beginning of moving and resting."[9] A key term in this observation is "in itself" as opposed to "outside itself." Artifacts come to be when human art, executed by human power, imposes some end and form on materials from the outside. For example, the movement of an arrow from a bow is not natural but artificial. It does not originate from within the arrow but from the string drawn by the bowman. The arrow is not directed to the target by itself but by the person who shoots it.

A mechanistic view of matter consists in the denial that there are any principles of movement and rest truly within things. External causal influence, such as attraction and repulsion, are the only modes of causality. As Cartesian extended things, natural beings are pure externality.

Perhaps a mechanistic account would grant that forces such as gravity or electromagnetic force take their origin in some sense from within material beings. It would insist, however, that there are only a few such internally directed movements, while all complex structures are superimposed from the outside on elementary particles and their movements or emerge from them as epiphenomena. Human beings are biochemical machines produced by the chance survival of the fittest.

From its root meaning in begetting and being born, Greek *physis* was extended to all interior principles of movement, especially in living beings. Aristotle therefore defines it as follows: "*Physis* is a certain beginning or cause of movement and of rest in that in which it exists, first, through itself, and not by

7. Aristotle, *Physics* 2.1.192b8–12; emphasis added.
8. Aristotle, *Physics* 2.1.192b13.
9. Aristotle, *Physics* 2.1.192b.13–14.

accident."[10] The four qualifications in this definition are helpful for focusing more clearly on *nature*.

1. The qualification "in that in which it exists" emphasizes the interiority of nature. The nature of a being is not something imposed on that being from outside, as human art or chance impose various characteristics on things, but it is present and at work in what that being is.

2. The qualification *first* draws attention to specific natures in relation to specific activities. For example, the movement of an animal falling down a cliff does not belong *first* to the animal as an animal but as composed of heavy materials. Reproduction does not belong to animals first as animals but to animals in the genus they share with plants. By contrast, sensation belongs to animals *first* as animals. In this way, *nature* is related to the full specific perfection of a being, though without excluding levels of perfection it shares generically with others.

3 and 4. Aristotle explains the qualification *through itself* and its negative counterpart *not by accident* with the example of a doctor who heals himself. Since the doctor heals *himself*, one might suppose that the medical movement toward healing is natural. Yet medicine is a skill or art (*techne*) as opposed to nature. Aristotle resolves the puzzle by pointing out that having the art of healing does not belong to a human being through itself or according to itself καθ' αὑτὸ but by συμβεβηκός, by what it has come together with, by *accident*. The healing that is the body's own effort of reestablishing health is natural. It belongs to a living being through itself and not by the medical skill present in the doctor.

Analogical extensions of the word *nature* soon developed from this origin. St. Thomas reviews this development in the millennium between Aristotle (384–322 BC) and Boethius (AD 480–524) as follows.

> The word "nature" is said or taken from being born. Hence this word is first applied to signify the generation of living beings, called nativity or springing forth, so that "*natura*" is, as it were, *na(sci)tura*, about to be born.
>
> From here, the word "nature" was carried over to signify the beginning of this generation.
>
> And since the beginning of generation in living beings is inside them, the word "nature" was further drawn from here to signify any inner beginning of movement. Accordingly, the Philosopher says in *Physics* 2 that nature is a beginning of movement and of rest in that in which it exists first, through itself, and not by accident.
>
> Now, this beginning is either form or some material. Therefore, at times material and at times form is called nature.

10. Aristotle, *Physics* 2.1.192b.20–23.

> And because the end of natural coming to be in that which comes to be is the essence of the species, which the definition signifies, such an essence of the species was consequently also called nature. This is the way in which Boethius defines nature in *De duabus naturis* when he says, that nature is the specific difference that informs each thing and completes the definition of the species.[11]

Not all of these meanings of *natura* are still present in modern English. We do not call the birth of a baby its *nature.* Even *nativity* is rarely used, except for Jesus. The English *nature* gravitates toward the last meaning, specific difference or essence, and toward the meaning *the totality of natural beings.* The question of human nature is usually taken to be the question about what we are.

3. Substance

If nature is a beginning that acts from *inside* a being as opposed to coming from the outside, there is a close relation between *nature* and *substance.* "Whatever has a beginning of this kind has a nature. All these are a substance (*ousia*); for [substance] is a subject, and nature is always in a subject."[12]

Substance is the conventional English translation of Greek *ousia* (οὐσία). It is not a good translation because *ousia* is a common notion while *substance* is a technical term imported into English from Latin. *Ousia* is a noun formed from the participle of the verb *to be.* The suffix *-ia* transforms the participle into a noun of action or an abstract noun. *Ousia* can thus be translated as that which is (a being) or as what it is (*beingness*).[13] It has a broad range of meanings that extend by analogy from these root meanings. It can mean *property, wealth*, conceived as an extension of one's being. "If I had laid my hands on wealth (*ousian*), I would be riding a saddled mule."[14] Most frequently, *ousia* refers to a concrete being. "They confidently maintain that the only thing that exists is what offers resistance and touch, defining *body* and *a being* (*ousian*) as the same."[15] It can also refer to the *to be* (Latin *esse*) of a being. "You mean *to be* (*ousian*) and *not to be* (τὸ μὴ εἶναι)."[16] The contrast with *not to be* shows that in this text *ousia* means *to be, esse.*

11. Thomas, *Summa,* III, q. 2, a. 1, corp.; see also I q. 29, a. 1, ad 4 and *Super III sent.*, d. 5, q. 1, a. 2, corp.

12. Aristotle, *Physics* 2.1.192b33–192b34.

13. Smyth, *Greek Grammar*, §840.

14. Lysias, *On the Refusal of a Pension* 11.

15. Plato, *Sophist* 246b–c.

16. Plato, *Theaetetus* 185c.

As the abstract *beingness*, *ousia* can have the sense of *essence*. In this use, *ousia* is the target of the question, "What is it?" Aristotle often places *ousia* in parallel with *what something is*. "How will the one who defines show the substance (*ousian*), the what-it-is (τὸ τί ἐστιν)?"[17] "Empedocles says that a bone exists by the account (*logos*) in it. This is *the what-it-was-to-be* (τὸ τί ἦν εἶναι) or the essence (*ousia*) of a thing."[18] The remark on Empedocles is particularly interesting: it equates *ousia* and *logos*.

For Aristotle, the primary sense of *ousia* is the concrete existing being, a human being, a horse, a tree—in short, anything of which it is true to say, *It exists*. In the *Physics*, he introduces *ousia* (substance) by pointing out that we speak about change in two ways. "Things are said to come to be in different ways. In some cases, we do not use the expression come-to-be but come-to-be-so-and-so. Only *ousiai*, we say, simply come to be."[19] These ways of speaking lead Aristotle to the more distinct notion of *ousia* as *that-which-is*, taking this phrase simply, absolutely, without any further qualification such as *here* or *warm* and so on. "For something to come to be, simply speaking, it is necessary that before then it simply was not."[20]

One misses the sense of *simply*, Greek ἁπλῶς, Latin *simpliciter* or *absolute*, when one takes it as equivalent to, or at least open to, *only*, Greek μόνον, Latin *tantum* or *tantummodo*. *Only to be* is close to *mere fact*.[21]

One can illustrate the meaning of *simply speaking* by an example unrelated to substance and accident. When she is sitting in her living room in New York, Sally may have her heart in San Francisco. Sally is in New York, *simply speaking*. She is in San Francisco, *in a certain respect*. *In New York, simply speaking* does not mean *only in New York* in the sense that this is her *only* attribute. In a similar way, to say, *Substance is that which exists, simply speaking* does not imply a notion of *esse* as mere fact.

The counterpart of *ousia* is accident, τὸ συμβεβηκός, *that which has come together with* substance or *inheres* in a substance. Accidents do not come together with substance in the way distinct beings come together. There is only one being, the substance. In this context, *accident* has thus a narrow technical meaning. Many meanings usually associated with English *accident* are either irrelevant or misleading. To call being in New York an *accident* is to say that being in New York does not account for the woman's being, simply speaking, but for her being

17. Aristotle, *Posterior Analytics* 2.7.92a34–35; cf. Plato, *Phaedo* 92d.

18. Aristotle, *Metaphysics* 1.10.993a17–18; emphasis added.

19. Aristotle, *Physics* 1.7.190a32–190a33.

20. Thomas, *In libros Physicorum* 1, lect. 12, no 107.

21. For an example of this misunderstanding, see David L. Schindler, "Being, Gift, Self-Gift (Part Two)," *Communio* 43 (2016): 409–83, at 417n16.

in a certain respect. She can be in various places, first in New York, then in San Francisco. Her being in any one of these places is not that by which she exists at all rather than not at all.

She is alive may seem like *She is in New York*. In grammatical form, it is a case of *being, not simply speaking but in a certain respect*. In content, however, *She is alive* is a case of being at all rather than not at all. "To live is for living things to be" τὸ δὲ ζῆν τοῖς ζῶσι τὸ εἶναί ἐστιν.[22] *She is alive* is therefore an example of *She is* in the absolute or unqualified sense. The same point holds for being human. For a human being, *to be human* and *to be* are the same, because *human* is what a human being is. For a human being to stop being human is to stop being. *This being is human* is for this reason to be included under *this being exists* without any further qualification.

That *to be* and *to live* are the same for a living being shows that *to be* (εἶναι, *esse*) is not an empty notion that functions as a mere logical on-off switch without content. In his attempt to refute all arguments for the existence of God, Kant famously claims that *to be* is not a real predicate. On the face of it, this thesis is paradoxical. If any predicate deserves the adjective *real*, it would seem to be *being real* or, in the case of living beings, *being alive*.

> Being (*Sein*) is evidently no real predicate, that is, a concept of some item that could come by addition to the concept of a thing. It is merely the positing of a thing or certain determinations in themselves. In its logical use, it is simply the copula of a judgment. The sentence, God is almighty, contains two concepts that have their objects, namely, God and almighty. The little word *is* is not an additional predicate but only that which posits the predicate in relation to the subject. When, therefore, I take the subject God together with all his predicates (to which almighty belongs among others) and say, *God is*, or *there is a God*, I do not add a new predicate to the concept of God but only the subject itself with all his predicates or, more precisely, the object in relation to my concept.... And so, the real (*das Wirkliche*) contains nothing more than the possible. One hundred real Dollars (*Thaler*) contain nothing more than one hundred possible ones.[23]

The example of one hundred dollars shows how completely Kant has removed *esse* from his mind and replaced it with a conceptual apparatus. One hundred real dollars do contain more than one hundred possible ones; namely, one hundred dollars. The possible ones do not contain a single dollar. For a human being, *to be* contains the whole wealth of human life.

22. Aristotle, *De anima* 3.14.415b13.
23. Kant, *Critique of Pure Reason*, B 626–27.

> What is most perfect in all effects is to be (*esse*). For any nature or form is perfected by this, that it is in act. It is compared to *to be* (*esse*) in act as potency is to act.[24]
>
> What I call to be (*esse*) is among all the most perfect, because act is always more perfect than potency. Any form one might point to is not understood as in act unless one posits to be (*esse*).[25]
>
> To be (*esse*) is itself the most perfect of all because it compares to all as act. For, nothing has actuality except inasmuch as it is. To be is itself the actuality of all things, even of forms themselves.[26]
>
> By [the very meaning] of the word, to be (*esse*) signifies something complete and simple but not subsisting; substance by contrast signifies something subsisting and lying underneath (*subiectum*) something else. We therefore posit in God both substance and to be (*esse*) but substance on account of subsistence, not on account of standing under, and *esse* on account of simplicity and completeness, not on account of inherence.[27]

By its very meaning, *to be* is encompassing, not in the manner of a genus that can be divided by specific differences. Specific differences fall outside the genus. Three sided, four sided, and the like fall outside *plane figure* and add to it. If four sided fell within *plane figure*, all plane figures would have to be four sided. The case of *to be* is different. No perfection can fall outside of *to be* (*esse*) or *being* (*ens*), which shows that neither of these terms is a genus.

Schindler's way of conceiving Aristotle's account of substance and accident seems to follow Whitehead's pattern of thought (see section 4 of the introduction to this volume). Whitehead maps distinct concepts rather quickly on correspondingly distinct entities, which leads to a multiplication of entities. The need then arises for this multiplicity to grow together into unity, as suggested by Whitehead's key concept *concrescence*. What gets lost in this reading of Aristotle is his insistence that each being is *one*.

One way to clarify the unity of one being is to say that accidents do not exist at all. Only the one being exists. Accidents are not entities. They are a substance's ways of being.

> To say *a being* (*ens*) is equivalent to saying *that which has being* (*esse habens*). This is only substance, which subsists. Accidents are called beings, *not because they are* (*or exist*), but rather because something is (or exists) in these [accidental ways] themselves, *non quia sunt, sed quia magis ipsis aliquid est.*[28]

24. Thomas, *Contra gentiles* III, cap. 66, par. 5.
25. Thomas, *De potentia*, q. 7, a. 2, ad 9.
26. Thomas, *Summa* I, q. 4, a. 1, ad 3.
27. Thomas, *De potentia*, q. 1, a. 1, corp.
28. Thomas, *Sententia metaphysicae* 12, lect. 1, no. 2419; emphasis added.

When Sally is in New York, her being in New York is not an entity distinct from her. It is a mode of her being. It is not the mode of being that directly corresponds to the question, *Does she exist at all?* but the mode corresponding to the question, *Where is she?* Only one entity is at stake, she herself. To say that place is an accident is not to say that she is in any way free of being in New York. She is totally in New York. Nothing of her being falls outside of being in New York.

4. Rational Animal

Starting with Living Beings

Since *nature* is so deeply connected with substance, one of the main questions in understanding *nature* is on what level each of the beings we encounter in our experience is truly *one being*. Is the unity of substance—that is, the unity of that which exists, speaking absolutely—to be found on the level of small particles or on the level of more complex beings, such as animals?

Ordinary experience would suggest the latter. The dominant mechanistic worldview opts without hesitation for the former. What exists, simply speaking, are the elementary particles. Everything else is a composite of them. Newton was sure he had found the *uncuttable* (Greek *atomon*) unit that truly *exists*, absolutely speaking. The Newtonian atoms are infinitely hard and completely definite in their form. The evidence gathered more recently has destroyed this excessively actual and mathematicised picture. When one approaches the inner constituents of atoms (now definitely considered cuttable, despite their inherited name), one finds indefiniteness, indeterminacy, and potentiality. Quantum physics does not favor the view that atoms or more elementary particles are the true substances in nature. Nevertheless, the atomist tendency still runs deep in contemporary natural science.

If the human person is simply a complex biochemical machine composed of separate particles as the true substances, it cannot have a nature in the full sense, because it is not one being in the full sense. There is nothing one, simply speaking, from within which there could be a beginning of movement and of rest. According to John Paul, the Catholic faith holds that the human person is a substantial whole, not an accidental composite (see TOB 66:6 with note 76). Against the denial of an intrinsic substantial unity of the person, *Veritatis splendor* 48 insists on

> the Church's teachings on the unity of the human person, whose rational soul is *per se et essentialiter* [through itself and essentially] the form of his body. The spiritual and immortal soul is the principle [beginning] of unity of the

human being, whereby it exists as a whole—*corpore et anima unus* [one in body and soul]—as a person.

This statement combats the excessive separation between body and soul in Cartesian dualism, which posits extended things somehow connected with thinking things. It also applies to the material parts of the human person. If each of these parts is a complete substance, the soul cannot be *per se et essentialiter* the form of the body and the unity of the person will be denied. The human person's existence as one substance—which allows a single answer to the question, What is it?—is at the same time a unified and thus intelligible beginning of moving and resting, a nature.

The distinctive feature of Cartesian dualism is not so much the thesis that there is a thinking thing distinct from the body but rather that the body is already a reality (or a collection of realities) that exists in its own right. Consciousness supervenes and influences the body in various ways, but the body has its own being quite apart from such influence. According to John Paul, by contrast, the soul is the principle whereby a human being exists as a whole. The whole has one being (*esse*), one actuality, and this one actuality is due to the soul. The body's principle of being at all is the soul.

First Material (*materia prima*)

By thinking through the points made above, Aristotle develops the concept of a first underlying stuff or material in all bodily beings. He names it in various ways:

the underlying τὸ ὑποκείμενον, *Physics* 1.7.190b24
the underlying nature ἡ ὑποκειμένη φύσις, *Physics* 1.7.191a7–8
the first underlying τὸ πρῶτον ὑποκείμενον, *Physics* 1.9.192a31
the first beginning τὸ πρῶτον ἐνυπάρχον, *Physics* 2.1.193a10
the first wood (building material) τὸ πρῶτον ξύλον, *Metaphysics* 9.7.1049a24
the first wood or timber ἡ πρώτη ὕλη, *Metaphysics* 5.4.1014b32–1015a7, 5.6.1017a5, and 8.4.1044a23
the first wood underlying each ἡ πρώτη ἑκάστῳ ὑποκειμένη ὕλη, *Physics* 193a29

First wood or simply *wood* seems to be Aristotle's preferred term. The standard medieval Latin translation is *materia prima*. The Blackfriars *Summa* falls into the etymological trap, as it often does, and unfortunately translates *materia prima* as *prime matter*, contrary to Thomas's understanding of the order of knowledge in which the vague but certain notions of common and ordinary experience are the starting point of understanding.[29] While *prima* and *materia* are common notions in Latin, *prime matter* is an obscure technical expression, out of touch with ordinary experience. *First stuff* or *first material* would be better.[30] *Stuff* and *material* express the potential character of *materia* more clearly, in agreement with Aristotle's preferred word *wood*, understood as building material, the stuff houses are made of.

First stuff is one of the most distinctive concepts of Aristotle's philosophy of nature in contrast to its pre-Socratic and Cartesian counterparts. It is difficult to think through this concept responsibly. It has not been proposed by the Church as a matter of faith, but it is needed to do justice to two truths, one of which is an obvious fact while the other is grasped by ordinary experience as well as proposed by the Church as a matter of faith.

That the human person is one being is a truth grasped by ordinary experience. I am aware of myself as *I* and of others as *you*, as one person, one being. It is also proposed as a matter of faith, rooted in the clarification of the meaning of *person* and *hypostasis* in the Christological controversies of the early Church. The other truth is the obvious fact that human persons come to be from something (ovum, sperm, nourishment) and pass away into something (corpse). Aristotle approaches the underlying nature from these two truths.

> We say in different ways that things come to be. In some cases, we do not use the expression "come to be," but "come to be so-and-so." Only substances, we say, come to be, simply speaking.
>
> In all cases other than substance, clearly there must be something underlying; namely, that which becomes. For when a thing comes to be of such a quantity or quality or in such a relation, time, or place, a subject is always presupposed, since substance alone is not predicated of something underlying but everything else of substance.
>
> But that substances too, and anything that can be said to "be" without qualification, come to be from something underlying, will appear on examination. For we find in every case something that underlies from which that which comes to be comes to be; for instance, animals and plants from seed.[31]

29. See Charles De Koninck, "Three Sources of Philosophy," *Proceedings of the American Catholic Philosophical Association* 38 (1964): 13–22, at 13–17.

30. Glen Coughlin's excellent translation of the *Physics* chooses *material* in many cases. See Aristotle, *Physics, Or Natural Hearing*, trans. Glen Coughlin, William of Moerbeke Translation Series (South Bend, IN: St. Augustine's Press, 2005).

31. Aristotle, *Physics* 1.7.190a.31–190b.5.

Aristotle's claim that some natural beings come to be, simply or absolutely speaking, is closely connected with his thesis that each plant, animal, or human being is one being, absolutely speaking. The dominant popular philosophy, by contrast, holds that atoms or more elementary particles are the true beings, each by itself.

If a human person is one being, then what endures in its coming to be and passing away cannot itself be an actual being. If it were an actual being, the change would be a change in quality, quantity, relation, and so on—that is, a change in accidents—in characteristics that do not account for being at all. The conclusion of this argument is extremely difficult. Particular care is needed to avoid losing contact with ordinary experience and shared ways of speaking.

One of the principles of a human being must be able to be a substance while not itself being a substance. It cannot be called *body* because *body* is a generic name for actual bodily substances. Nor can it be called matter, if by matter one means what most people mean in contemporary English; namely, *actual extended substance* as a genus.

Aristotle approaches the underlying nature by analogy with the subject of accidental change.

> The underlying nature can be known by analogy (κατ' ἀναλογίαν). For as the bronze is to the statue, the wood to the bed, or the material and the formless before receiving form to anything that has form, so is the underlying nature to substance, that is, the this or existent. (*Physics* 1.7.191a.7–12)

It is easy to grasp the first pair of concepts in this analogy, but the second pair is so radically different that the very attempt of setting up a proportion between the two pairs is almost inevitably misleading. The mind tends to fall back to the first pair when it attempts to think the second.

The first pair consists of an actually existing material such as bronze or wood that *can* have some shape and that same material that *does* have that shape. Both members of the pair are an actually existing substance, one and the same substance: bronze and the bronze statue, first considered *as able to have* this form and then *as actually having* the form. When the statute is given its form, the bronze does not come to be, simply speaking; it only comes to have the form of the statue.

The second pair consists of the underlying nature or first material and actually existing substance. When human persons are born or die, they come to be or pass away, simply speaking. If each of them is truly one on the level of substance, they are not merely composites of preexisting substances with a new quality or arrangement. The underlying nature is only potentially a substance. It can be a substance. If it were already a substance, the first and the second pair in the proportion would not differ.

In the first pair, Thomas points out, the form is *in* an actually existing subject, while in the second pair the form cannot be *in* a subject because there is as yet no subject for it to be in. In the first pair, being comes from the subject to the form; in the second pair, it comes from the form to the whole.

> Speaking properly, what is in potency to accidental being is called subject, but what is in potency to substantial being is properly called material (*materia*). It is significant that what is in potency to accidental being is called subject because one says "accidents are in a subject" but not "the substantial form is in a subject."
>
> Material (*materia*) differs from a subject in the following way. A subject is that which does not have its being (*esse*) from what comes to it but has complete being through itself, as a man does not have being from whiteness. Material, by contrast, has being from that which comes to it, because of itself it has incomplete being. Simply speaking, therefore, form gives being to material but a subject gives being to its accident.[32]

In the Cartesian account of the human person, the body is a fully real substance already before being joined to the conscious self. Consciousness supervenes to qualify that body in many ways, but consciousness does not give being to the body. In the Aristotelian account, there are only two principles in the human person: the underlying nature (first material) and the substantial form (in this case called soul, because "soul" refers to whatever accounts for something being alive). The soul, while remaining one and the same form, gives unity and existence to the whole person, including the body.

> There is this difference between a substantial form and an accidental form, namely, that an accidental form does not make a being simply in act (*ens actu simpliciter*) but a being actually of such quality or quantity, for example, big or white or something else of this sort. The substantial form, on the other hand, makes *to be* simply in act (*esse actu simpliciter*). For this reason, an accidental form comes to a subject that already actually exists beforehand (*iam praeexistenti actu*). A substantial form, by contrast, does not come to a subject that already actually exists beforehand but to that which exists only potentially, namely, to first material (*materia prima*).
>
> It is clear from this that one thing cannot have many substantial forms, because the first would make a being that actually exists, simply speaking, and all other forms would come to a subject that actually exists already so that

32. Thomas, *De principiis naturae*, 1.

> they would come accidentally to a subject that actually exists already. Thus they would not make a being that is actual, simply speaking, but in a certain respect....
>
> One and the same substantial form is that through which this individual is this something, or a substance, and through which it is a body, an ensouled body, and likewise the other [genera and species]. For the more perfect form gives to material what the less perfect form gives, and still more. [33]

There is only one substantial form of the whole human being, and that is the soul. This one form is responsible for all levels of perfection of the human person, from purely bodily perfections through vegetative and sensory perfections all the way to the perfection of rational nature. The body exists as what it is, as a body, on account of the soul. The contrast with Descartes could not be more extreme.

Body and Soul

A difficult question needs to be thought through. If the underlying nature and the soul are the only two principles of a human person, why should one speak about *body and soul* rather than *first material and soul*? At the beginning of his account of human nature in the *Summa*, Thomas even says, "man who is composed from a spiritual and a bodily substance."[34] This way of speaking sounds much like the Cartesian view in which the body is already a substance in its own right.

To open up the question, one needs to distinguish aspects that belong to the order of logic from aspects that belong to the order of being and nature. A definition corresponds to the demands of logic when it focuses on what is specific to what is to be defined.

What is specific to the soul among all substantial forms is that it accounts for the life of a bodily being. The definition of the soul as "the form of first material" would be too generic. It would not focus on that form's specific difference among all other forms. "Form of first material" applies just as much to the substantial form of lifeless beings. "Organic body" is the material that belongs to the soul as soul, because *soul* refers to what accounts for the difference between living and nonliving. "In the definition of forms one places the material belonging to each in the place of differences, as when one says that the soul is the act of a natural organic body."[35]

33. Thomas, *Sententia de anima* 2, lect. 2, no. 224–25.

34. Thomas, *Summa* I, q. 75, prologue.

35. Thomas, *De potentia*, q. 7, a. 2, ad 9. See Lawrence Dewan, "Thomas and the Causality of God's Goodness," *Laval Théologique et Philosophique* 34 (1978): 299n37.

Specific difference in relation to genus belongs to the order of logic that arises from our mode of knowing. The distinction between them does not immediately correspond to a distinction of beings in the real order. The question *What is man?* can be answered at various levels of universality: man is a body, a living being, an animal, rational. One and the same nature corresponds to these concepts, known less universally and thus more perfectly in *animal*, more universally and thus less perfectly in *body*. In the same way, the definition of the soul as "form of the body" does not imply a split of the human person in the real order into a substance called body and another one called soul. In the real order, there are only two principles: soul and the underlying nature, first material, which is not in itself a substance.

5. Individual and Person

The uniqueness of every person is a topic particularly dear to Scheler.[36] Wojtyła's clear affirmation of the Aristotelian account of material and form, including the difficult doctrine of *first material*, raises the question of whether his strong emphasis on personal uniqueness is compatible with the Aristotelian account of material as the principle of individuation. Is Wojtyła closer to Scheler than to Aristotle on this point?

Scheler on Personal Uniqueness

Scheler rejects the definition of the person as *an individual substance of a rational nature*. He attempts to understand the individuality of the person, not as an underlying subject but as an essence given in consciousness, using *essence* in a wider sense, not restricted to the target of the question *What is it?* Each person's essence is distinct precisely on the level of essence; that is, it is qualitatively unique in each person.

In unfolding Scheler's concept of personal individuality, John Crosby distinguishes the question *What is individuality?* from *What is the principle of individ-*

36. Citations of Scheler by FormEng (= *Formalism* English), FormGer (= *Formalism* German), and GW (= *Gesammelte Werke*) refer to Max Scheler, *Formalism in Ethics and Non-Formal Ethics of Values: A New Attempt toward the Foundation of an Ethical Personalism*, 5th ed., trans. Manfred Frings (Evanston, IL: Northwestern University Press, 1973); *Der Formalismus in der Ethik und die materiale Wertethik: Neuer Versuch der Grundlegung eines ethischen Personalismus*, 7th ed. (Bonn: Bouvier, 2000); *Gesammelte Werke*, ed. Maria Scheler and Manfred Frings (Bern: Francke Verlag, 1954–86; Munich: Bouvier Verlag, 1986–97). Translations modified or my own.

uation?[37] In answering the first question, he shows that, according to Scheler, the individuality of a person is simply the individuality of its irreducibly individual essence.

There are both universal and individual essences, Scheler holds. "Scheler deliberately breaks with the Greek idea that essence is always only something general or universal."[38] The individual essences of persons are unutterable in general terms. They differ from uniquely individual descriptions such as *the last soldier killed in the Civil War*, in which the unique can be completely defined by a conjunction of terms, each of which is, as such, applicable to many. In contrast to such accidental and *thin* uniqueness, each person's essence, Scheler holds, has unique qualitative strength and richness of contents.

The first copy of the *New York Times* printed each day is individual on an imperfect level. One can easily replace it by another copy. A person, by contrast, is individual in a higher and more perfect way. It is individual by being unrepeatably unique in its essential content. Scheler explains,

> It is necessary to give a more precise definition of what we understand by individual personal value-essence. Essence, as we mentioned earlier, has nothing to do with universality. An essence of an intuitive nature is the foundation of both general concepts and intentions directed to particulars.... There are essences that are given only in one particular individual. And for this reason, it makes sense to speak of an individual essence and also the individual value-essence of a person. (FormEng 489, FormGer 481)

This text indicates that Scheler's unique essences of persons belong to the order of values rather than being. They are above all *value-essences, Wertwesen*. Because values, according to Scheler, are essences given only in feeling, the person's individual value-essence is something *felt* in the feeling of love. Only love can grasp the point of goodness from which all of a person's actions spring. In this respect, love is similar to the creative intuition of the artist (see FormEng 488, FormGer 480).

The converse is true as well. Not only is love required to understand the individual value-essence, but the principal motive of love is also that same value-essence. The right way to love is not to love a person primarily because

37. See John F. Crosby, *Personalist Papers* (Washington, DC: Catholic University of America Press, 2004), 155. Crosby builds on the discussion of individuation by Jorge J. E. Gracia, *Introduction to the Problem of Individuation in the Early Middle Ages* (Washington, DC: Catholic University of America Press, 1984); *Individuality: An Essay on the Foundations of Metaphysics* (Albany: State University of New York, 1988).

38. Crosby, *Personalist Papers*, 149. Following Scheler, Crosby uses the term *essence* in a wide sense.

of the attributes that person shares with others but because of his or her unique value-essence.

> Thus Scheler says that "the love which has moral value is not that which pays loving regard to a person for having such and such qualities, pursuing such and such objectives, or for possessing talents, beauty or virtue; it is that love which incorporates these qualities, activities and gifts into its object because they belong to that individual person." The qualities appear in their full individuality only on the basis of being rooted in the person. We can say that it is this person that in a certain sense communicates full individuality to the qualities.[39]

Crosby's point that the individual essence communicates full individuality to a person's qualities provides a transition from the first question, "What is personal individuality?," to the second question, "What is the principle of individuation? What is the source of individuality?" Individuation implies, according to Scheler and Crosby, that individuality is communicated from its primary *locus* to other aspects or parts of a being. These aspects or parts are made fully individual by in some way receiving the individuality of the principle of individuation. In the individuation of human beings, individuality belongs primarily to the person's individual essence and is communicated from there to other aspects or parts of the person. In its essential core, the person is intrinsically individuated. The various layers of a person's being that are less individuated in themselves—for example, the body—are individuated by the personal core.

> The unique personal essence of each person not only serves to individualize the whole human being, marking it off against other human beings; it also serves to individualize those levels in a human being that are in a sense common to other human beings. Thus the body, the voice, the hands, the handwriting of a person are imbued with the mystery of the person's individuality and so are lifted beyond the limited individuality that they have when considered in themselves.[40]

Crosby claims that the advantage of Scheler's understanding of individuation in comparison with Aristotle's and Thomas's is that it sees persons as intrinsically individuated. They are individuated precisely as persons. In Aristotle and Thomas, he charges, human persons are extrinsically individuated. The principle of individuation is not the spiritual core of the person but *materia prima*, first material.

39. Crosby, *Personalist Papers*, 152. Crosby quotes Scheler, *Wesen und Formen der Sympathie*, GW 7:508.

40. Crosby, *Personalist Papers*, 156.

> It is also interesting to set Scheler's account of personal individuation in relation to the Aristotelian theory of matter as the principle of individuation. It is clear that he does not hold this theory and in one place he contradicts it, saying: "the ultimate and authentic principium individuationis in man (and not in angels only as Thomas supposed), lies in his spiritual soul (that is, the real substratum of his personal center)." ... Thus for Scheler we do not need one theory of individuation for human beings and an entirely different one for angels; all persons, whether human or angelic, are individual through their unique personal essence, which is always a spiritual and never, not even with human beings, a material principle of individuation.[41]

A material principle of individuation, this is Crosby's point, locates the individual unity of the person too low on the ladder of being. Persons are individuals in a higher way than a bar of gold. They are individuals precisely as unique persons. To derive their individuality from purely material individuality is to reduce the higher to the lower.

Definitions of Person

Stephen Brock has responded thoroughly to Scheler and Crosby.[42] In the present context it is enough to point out that Thomas's method in clarifying the meaning of the word "person" is precisely to distinguish lower and higher modes of individuality. He does not reduce the higher to the lower. "Person" names an individual that has the highest mode of individuality. To focus on this highest mode, he uses the same method adopted by Wojtyła in *Person and Act*; namely, moral acts, which reveal the lordship of the person over itself.

In his discussion of the Trinity in the *Summa*, Thomas devotes an article to "the meaning of this word person."[43] He begins by considering various ways (*modi*) in which something can be individual. He mentions three such ways. Each is more specific and more perfect than the one before it. On the lowest level, there is the way of being individual found in accidents, such as color. Color is not individuated through itself but through the subject in which it inheres. This is not to say that color, as such, is general or universal. It is to say that all color is the color of an individual substance and that this "being of" is the reason why

41. Crosby, *Personalist Papers*, 157. Crosby quotes from Max Scheler, *The Nature of Sympathy* (New Haven, CT: Yale University Press, 1954 [orig. 1912]), 123.

42. Stephen Louis Brock, "Is Uniqueness at the Root of Personal Dignity? John Crosby and Thomas Aquinas," *Thomist* 69 (2005): 173–201.

43. Thomas, *Summa* I, q. 29, a. 1; cf. *Super I sent.*, d. 25, a. 1; *De potentia*, q. 9, a. 2; *De unione verbi*, a. 1.

it is this or that instance of color rather than another. The individuality of color derives from the substance in which it is found.

Substances, by contrast, "are individuated through themselves."[44] In virtue of itself, each is one being, undivided in itself, distinct from others. Owing to this way of being individual, substances carry the name *hypostasis*, "that which stands under," a key term in the Christological debates of the early Church.[45]

Rational beings are individuals "in a still more specific and perfect way" (*adhuc quodam specialiori et perfectiori modo*), which is why they have the name *person*. *Person* expresses the more perfect mode of individuality that arises from rational nature. Like Wojtyła, Thomas uses moral acts to bring this special perfection of individuality to light. That persons have lordship over their acts, that they therefore act through themselves in relation to particular circumstances, shows that they are more perfectly individual than other beings.

> Just as an individual substance has *existing through itself* as its own mark, so it has *acting through itself* as its own mark . . . But to act through oneself belongs in a more outstanding way to substances of rational nature than to others. For only substances of rational nature have lordship (*dominium*) over their own acts, in such a way that they can act or not act. Other substances, by contrast, are more acted than acting (*magis aguntur quam agant*). And so it was fitting that the individual substance of rational nature has a special name.[46]

In this text, Thomas draws a parallel between being and acting. As something is in its being, so it is in its acting and conversely. Free rational acts are supremely acts performed through oneself because they imply lordship of oneself over oneself in one's own actions. To such "acting through oneself" there must correspond a parallel "being through oneself" (*esse per se*). The word *person* is used to signify an individual inasmuch as it has this most perfect mode of individual being or existence.[47]

Thomas considers four definitions of *person* (1.29). Each brings out another aspect of the more perfect individuality proper to the person.

The first definition is the one given by Boethius: "The person is an individual

44. The phrase "through themselves" is important. The principles of individuation of a substance cannot be extrinsic because all substances are individuated through themselves. Individuation must be a matter of the inner principles of a being.

45. On the level of etymology, "hypostasis" is the Greek equivalent of Latin *substantia: hypo* = *sub*; *stasis* = *stantia*.

46. Thomas, *De potentia*, q. 9, a. 1, ad 3.

47. Between substance in general and human persons in particular, Thomas could have located two major degrees of perfection in individuality—namely, plants and animals—with many gradations of individuality within each of these, e.g., higher and lower animals.

substance of rational nature," Persona est rationalis naturae individua substantia.[48] This definition should be read in light of the argument about degrees of perfection in being an individual. The phrase *rationalis naturae* adds a specific difference to the more general and, as such, less perfect *individua substantia.*

> "Individual substance" is placed in [Boethius's] definition of the person mentioned earlier, inasmuch as it signifies a singular in the genus of substance, but "of rational nature" is added inasmuch as it signifies the singular among rational substances.[49]

Again, rational nature implies a more special and perfect mode of individuality, a way visible above all in the person's having lordship over his or her own acts. An alternate way in which Thomas formulates Boethius's definition is "Person means the distinct subsisting in an intellectual nature."[50] Both *substance* and *subsists* express the idea of that which has being (*esse*) simply speaking or through itself. *Substantia* is here to be understood, following the Trinitarian and Christological controversies of the early Church, as the *suppositum*, not as the genus substance. The genus substance is the most general way of answering the question *What is it?* about any bodily being, the most general way of naming its essence.[51]

The second definition of person is given by Thomas's contemporaries among the Magistri: "The person is a *hypostasis* distinct by a property bearing on dignity."[52] Thomas formulates this definition also in terms of nobility rather than dignity. "The person is a *hypostasis* distinct by a property bearing on nobility."[53] This definition, he argues, can be understood as converging with Boethius's. "Since it is of great dignity to subsist in a rational nature, every individual of a rational nature is called person."[54]

As in the case of Boethius's definition, one must read the definition of the

48. Thomas, *Summa* I, q. 29, obj. 1. Boethius formulates the definition slightly differently. "Since, therefore, the person is found only among substances and of these among those capable of reason (*rationabilibus*) and since every substance is a nature and exists, not among universals, but among individuals, the definition of the person has been found: *naturae rationabilis individua substantia*, an individual substance of a nature capable of reason." *Liber contra Eutychen et Nestorium*, 3. The differences lie in word order and in the use of *rationabilis*, or "possessing the power of reason," instead of *rationalis*, or "rational." Loeb edition, 74:84.

49. Thomas, *Summa* I, q. 29, a. 1, corp.

50. Thomas, *Super I sent.*, d. 23, q. 1, a. 3, ad 5; cf. *Contra gentiles* I, cap. 30, par. 4.

51. See Thomas, *Summa* I, q. 30, a. 1, ad 1 (Trinity); III, q. 2, a. 2, corp. (Christ).

52. Thomas, *Summa* I, q. 29, a. 3, ad 2. Thomas attributes the definition to the *magistri* in *Super I sent.*, d. 25, q. 1, a. 1, ad 8. The definition is not yet present in the *Sentences* of the Magister par excellence, Peter Lombard.

53. Thomas, *Super I sent.*, d. 25, q. 1, a. 1, ad 8.

54. Thomas, *Summa* I, q. 29, a. 3, ad 2.

Magistri as specifying a more general and imperfect term, here *hypostasis*. The person is a *hypostasis* in a more noble way that possesses greater dignity. In fact, being a person is the highest way of being an individual inasmuch as there is no life higher than the life of knowing and loving. "Person signifies what is most perfect in the whole of nature, namely, what subsists in a rational nature."[55]

The third definition of person is the alliterative pun, Persona dicitur quasi per se una, or "through itself one."[56] The point of the pun is that the person has a specific mode of being one; namely, being one through itself. Oneness through itself is an aspect of individuality through itself. According to *Summa Theologiae* I, q. 29, a. 1, and parallels, this greater unity of the person is visible above all in the lordship of the person in freely performed human acts.

The fourth definition is Richard of St. Victor's. At least in one way of reading it, Thomas points out in agreement with Richard, Boethius's definition of the person cannot be applied to the divine persons but only to human persons. *Rational* is usually used in a sense opposed to *intellectual* to express the discursive character of thought found in rational animals. If one understands rational in this sense, God is not "of rational nature." God is also not an *individual* substance in the sense in which material substances are individual, nor does he belong to the genus substance.[57] Thomas clarifies Boethius's definition by arguing that *rational* as well as *individual* can be understood in a more universal sense that allows for the greater perfection of rationality and individuality of the divine being. Still, he approvingly quotes Richard's definition, which replaces *rational nature* by *divine nature* and *individual substance* by *incommunicable existence*. "Person as said about God is an incommunicable existence of the divine nature."[58] As Richard and Thomas understand it, this definition is applicable to the divine persons alone. Still, because *person* is an analogous term, divine personhood must also shed light on human persons.[59]

The Individuation of the Human Person

How does this account of the meaning of *person* fit with the thesis that first material is the principle of individuation? Individuality, Thomas points out, has two aspects. "An individual is what is not distinct in itself but distinct from oth-

55. Thomas, *Summa* I, q. 29, a. 3, corp.

56. Thomas, *Summa* I, q. 29 a. 4, corp., *Super I sent.*, d. 23. q. 1, a. 2 sed contra 1; d. 23, q. 1, a. 3, obj. 5 and ad 5; *De potentia*, q. 9, a. 4, obj. 14; q. 9, a. 6, obj. 3.

57. See Thomas, *Summa* I, q. 29, a. 3, obj. 4.

58. Thomas, *Summa* I, q. 29, a. 3, ad 4.

59. See *Super I sent.*, d. 25, q. 1, a. 1, ad 6.

ers."[60] A group of persons is not an individual. It consists of several individuals divided from each other. The human hand is only part of an individual, not the whole. It is not an individual because it is not divided over against other parts but forms one individual together with them.

The two aspects of individuality (undivided in itself and divided from others) correspond to two necessary aspects of being and unity in general, which is not surprising, since individuality is a necessary aspect of real being. "Something is a being in the way in which it is also one; but one is what is undivided in itself and divided from others."[61]

The thesis that first material (*materia prima*) is the principle of individuation can be understood correctly based on this understanding of individuality and its highest mode, personhood. Given the close connection between individuality, being, and unity, the principle from which the individuality of a human person stems must be what constitutes that person as a being and as one. It must be what constitutes it as undivided rather than divided. Of the two essential principles in a natural being—first material (*materia prima*) and substantial form—the principle of individuality par excellence must thus be form, because form is the principle of actual being and unity. Material is, as such, a principle of potency, not of actuality, a principle of dispersion in extension, not of unity. Something is one and a being and thus an individual primarily by its form, not by its material.

One can see a similar point by looking at "to be," *esse*. It is in virtue of being at all, rather than not at all, that something is an individual.[62] According to Crosby, Scheler would object to this thesis.

> For Gracia a being is individual only through its existence (*esse*). Scheler would remark that this existential theory of individuation is in any case no extrinsic theory, since the existence of a being is entirely intrinsic to it; but he would have a reservation about it, at least if it were meant as an exhaustive account of the source of personal individuality. He would say that with persons it does not suffice to invoke only existence; essence, too, is a *principium individuationis*. For there is an essential core in each person that establishes nothing at all in common with other beings; it establishes only the incommunicable person.[63]

60. Thomas, *Summa* I, q. 29, a. 4, corp.

61. Thomas, *In libros Physicorum* 7, lect. 9, no. 960.

62. See Gracia, *Introduction to the Problem of Individuation*, 170–78. "Principle" has a different meaning in this context since "to be," *esse*, is not a principle in the same way as form since it is the effect of form. It is a principle of actuality whose counterpart as a principle of potency is not "material" but "essence."

63. Crosby, *Personalist Papers*, 156.

In this view, in which Scheler seems to follow Kant's notion of existence as a qualitatively indifferent on-and-off switch, essence contributes qualitative features, while existence posits these qualitative features without containing the qualitative wealth of the essence. If one takes the word *esse* more concretely, one sees that it signifies all the qualitative wealth of the essence. Aristotle puts the point as follows. "To live is for living beings to be" (τὸ δὲ ζῆν τοῖς ζῶσι τὸ εἶναί ἐστιν).[64] By the same token, for human beings, *to be* is the same as "to be human."

Thomas unfolds Aristotle's principle in the context of a discussion in what sense the soul is "the life of the body."

> The *life* of a living being is its very *to live*, signified in a certain abstractness, just as *a run* is in reality not something other than *to run*. Now the *to live* of living beings is their very *to be* (*esse*), as Aristotle says in *De anima*. Since one calls an animal *living* due to its having a soul according to which it has *to be* (*esse*) in accord with its own form, it is necessary that *to live* is nothing other than such a *to be* (*esse*) as comes forth from such a form.[65]

This text makes clear that *to be* (*esse*) signifies the entire qualitative content of a being's essence. Essence is related to *esse* as the potential to the actual, as *the run* to *actual running*. Humanity is related to *actually being human* in precisely this way. *Actually being human* is the *esse* of a human being.[66] Gracia's account of individuality can thus be sustained against Scheler's objection. There is no essential or qualitative determination that would fall outside of *esse*. The appeal to *esse* is not an alternate account of individuation.

To conclude, form—and, in a different perspective, *esse*—is the primary principle of individuality in a being. Form is what accounts for a being's inner unity, its being undivided in itself, and thus also for its being divided from others. Why is a dog an individual and not simply a continuation of the meadow on which it happens to be standing? It is because of the form—that is, the soul—which gives to the dog its own being and its own unity as an animal. The rational soul gives to a human being the most perfect way (*modus*) of individuality, which is signified by the word *person*.

Why, then, does Thomas call first material (*materia prima*) the principle of individuation par excellence? Why does he not say that form is the principle of individuation? He holds, after all, that forms not received in material are not universal in the sense of predication (one said of many). They are rather individuated by themselves.[67]

64. Aristotle, *De anima* 2.4.415b13.
65. Thomas, *Contra gentiles* I, cap. 98, par. 2.
66. See Thomas, *Summa* I, q. 3, a. 4, corp.; cf. I, q. 54, a. 3, corp.
67. See Thomas, *Summa* I, q. 3, a. 2, ad 3.

It is in a precise and limited way that material is the principle of individuation, a way that takes nothing away from the form's primary role as the principle of unity and therefore of individuality. The material out of which something comes to be is in a fundamental way that which cannot be received in another. For this reason, it has an immediate connection with individuality.

To say that material is the principle of individuation is not to say that material is that which primarily possesses individuality in itself and then communicates or lends its own individuality to the rest of a being. If this were the case, there could be no hierarchy of modes of individuality, but all beings of the visible world would be individual in the same way; namely, by the individuality of *materia prima*. Thomas takes the opposite route in explaining the notion of person.

A more fundamental point leads to the same conclusion. First material is as such only potentially a substance and therefore only potentially an individual. It is not as such already individual, even though it cannot be received in another. In this respect, substance as the principle of individuation of accidents differs from first material. Substance exists as an individual in various modes of individuality and communicates this individuality to its accidents. First material cannot communicate individuality in this way, because it does not have it in the first place.

First material is a principle of individuation, not on the side of being and unity, but on the side of diversity, distinction, division, and therefore multiplicity. Quantity (length, breadth, depth) is closely connected with the divisibility and multiplicity of material.

> Determinate quantity is called the principle of individuation, not because it causes in some way its subject, which is first substance but because it inseparably accompanies substance and determines it to here and now.[68]

In virtue of quantity, distinct substances can be divided from each other in such a way that one of them is here, another there. It is in this way that "material one points to" (*materia signata*)—that is, material under definite dimensions here and now—is the principle of individuation.

> Since material is not in itself distinct, it cannot individuate a received form except inasmuch as it is distinguishable. For the form is individuated by being received in material only in this way: it is received in this material that is dis-

68. Thomas, *De principio individuationis*. This *opusculum* is attributed in some editions to Thomas, but Torrell argues that it is probably inauthentic. See Jean-Pierre Torrell, *Saint Thomas Aquinas*, vol. 1, *The Person and His Work*, rev. ed., trans. Robert Royal (Washington, DC: Catholic University of America Press, 2005), 360–61.

> tinct and determined to here and now. Material, however, is divisible only due to quantity. Hence Aristotle says in *Physics* 1 that if quantity were removed, substance would be indivisible. Material is rendered this, and pointed out, inasmuch as it is under dimensions.[69]

By itself, quantity is not a sufficient basis of individuality in the full sense. It is a basis of individuality primarily in the sense of allowing division and thereby allowing distinct individuals of the same nature, one here and the other there. "Here and now" provide a first and necessary basis for individuality among material beings. They do not provide full individuality itself. What is here and now can have a low mode (*modus*) of individuality. Perfection of individuality is primarily a positive aspect of being that arises together with unity from the form, not from the material.

The decisive question about the issue of the individuation of the human person is a question of the philosophy of nature. It can be formulated from two directions. *First*, from the direction of the form, "Is the soul through itself (*per se*) a substantial form by which first material receives all levels of perfections of a living human being, from being a body to being vegetative, sentient and intelligent?" *Second*, from the direction of the material, "Is the material that the soul informs radically first material or an already actual body—that is, the body as a substance in its own right—as it is in Descartes?"

The distinctive character of Aristotle's and Thomas's understanding of soul and body lies in affirming that the soul is indeed through itself a substantial form that gives all perfections to first material from the lowest to the highest, all the way from *body* to *somebody*. Wojtyła explicitly agrees with this way of understanding the relation between body and soul.

> In the metaphysical sense, the soul is the *form* and its relation to the body is of the kind which, according to Aristotle and also according to Thomas, the *form* has to *matter*. (One needs to add that what is at stake here is first material, *materia prima*).[70]

69. Thomas, *Super Boetium De trinitate*, pars 2, q. 4, a. 2, corp.; see also ad 3. One finds extensive discussions of these issues in two texts in which Thomas discusses the quantity of the Eucharist: *Super IV sent.*, dist. 12, q. 1, a. 1C, ad 3; *Contra gentiles* III, cap. 77, par. 2.

70. Karol Wojtyła, *Persona e atto*, ed. Giovanni Reale and Tadeusz Styczeń (Milan: Bompiani, 2001), 607. This passage is omitted in the English translation, *The Acting Person*, trans. Andrzej Potocki (Dordrecht: D. Reidel, 1979), 257.

Person and Nature

The question of person and nature can be approached in this light. Based on the distinction between natural and voluntary causes, there is a common use of *nature* and *natural* for the subrational part of the cosmos as opposed to the realm of reason and choice. Framing the question of "person and nature" often implies this use of *nature* limited to the sub-personal. Yet it would be a mistake to infer that natures belong only to the lowest orders of being. In the Trinitarian controversies of the early Church, *nature* was applied to God. Boethius's definition of the person as individual substance of rational nature implies that it is precisely because of its rational nature that a human being is a person in the first place.

Thomas unfolds the order between natural and voluntary agents in the context of an argument that God has life.[71] The argument shows that nature dominates both the lowest and the highest step in the scale of being. To live, Thomas begins the argument, is to act or operate[72] out of oneself rather than being set in movement (in a wide sense of *movement* that includes all kinds of activity, including thought) by another. In this respect, the concept of *life* is close to *nature* because nature is a principle in a being by which it acts or operates out of itself.

> Plants act out of themselves with respect to the execution of movements like growth and reproduction but the end and the form by which they act is determined for them by nature. They are not active but passive with respect to this form.
>
> Animals act out of themselves not only with respect to the execution of movements but also in virtue of forms they themselves acquire by sensation rather than by nature. Still, they cannot propose to themselves the goal of their action but pursue the end by natural instinct, which still involves a certain passivity rather than activity.
>
> Only in the highest animal, the human person, does one find a mind that can grasp the goodness of the end (in virtue of which it is the end) and propose it to itself as the basis of a voluntary action. In this way, human beings are more perfectly self-moving and alive. Yet, some aspects of the life of reason are given to them by nature, for example, the first self-evident principles of knowledge and the final end of human life, which one cannot fail to will. In this manner, the human person falls short of self-movement and is not perfectly alive.
>
> In the case of God, finally, what he is and has naturally is not determined by another. He is his own nature, his understanding, and love. In this way he

71. Thomas, *Summa* I, q. 18, a. 3, corp.

72. *Actio* is divided into less perfect actions in the manner of movement and more perfect actions in the manner of *operatio*, i.e., without necessarily involving movement. See Thomas, *Super I sent., dist.* 7, q. 1, a. 1, ad 3.

is most perfectly self-moving or self-operating and therefore most perfectly alive.

In another text, Thomas further clarifies the relation between natural and voluntary in God's own life.

> His relation to himself is necessary and natural, but his relation to other beings is according to a certain fittingness, not necessary and natural, nor violent and unnatural but voluntary, for what is voluntary is necessarily neither natural nor violent.[73]

Nature thus dominates the metaphysical ladder both at the beginning and at the end, though in a different manner. The lowest beings act only from a nature given to them by another. Within himself, God also acts only from nature, not from a nature given to him but one with which he is identical. God's voluntary actions by way of contingent choice are limited to his relation to creatures.

Nature is not insignificant on the intermediate steps of the ladder. The rational nature of created persons is decisive. It is that by which they are persons. Even choice is not intelligible without a natural movement of the will, as Wojtyła argues in *Person and Act*.

6. Marriage

Procreation as the Primary End

The causality of goodness in relation to natures can be thrown into relief by reflection about Aristotle's concept of *the underlying nature*, Thomas's concept of first material. This concept has a profound impact on the understanding of natures. In mechanistic accounts of nature before the theory of relativity, the sum of substantial beings in the world—that is, the sum of atoms—was thought to be constant. There is no coming to be and no passing away but only a reconfiguration of the building blocks. Life is only one configuration of the atomic machine.

By contrast, if one of the principles of nature is a principle of radical substantial potency, of being able to be a substance, then the generation of a living being is a momentous event. Through generation, a being of essentially greater dignity, goodness, and beauty than lifeless bodies enters the scene as something truly new. By the same token, if there is an underlying nature that is a principle of substantial potency, then that underlying nature is ordered to being the most perfect, that is, to being alive, to having rational life. The underlying nature has

73. Thomas, *Contra gentiles* I, cap. 82.

a natural inclination for and tendency toward living forms, especially an inclination for the highest living form, the human soul. It is not an active inclination, because an active inclination presupposes an actual nature.

The common notion that "some things are by nature, others through other causes" implies that nature is a cause. This causal sense attaches to the word *nature* from its origin in the verb "beget, generate, be born." It is not surprising, therefore, that among all the works of living beings, Aristotle sees begetting as the most natural.

> The most natural of the works belonging to living beings ... is to produce another like itself, an animal an animal, a plant a plant, to participate in the eternal and divine as far as they can, because all things strive for that and do for the sake of it whatever they do according to nature.[74]

In explaining why generation is the most natural work, Aristotle highlights the end of the generation of living beings, sharing in life. That for the sake of which all living beings do everything they do according to nature is to gain a share in life as a good that is primarily eternal and divine. "All things strive for that" πάντα ἐκείνου ὀρέγεται. In particular, the underlying nature (first material) and all nonliving substances have this inclination toward life. In the striving of all things for a share in what is eternal and divine, one can see a deeper reason for the close connection between nature and sexuality. For human beings, inasmuch as they are animals, sexuality and giving birth are the most natural work because in all nature, beginning with the underlying nature (first material), there is a striving for eternal and divine life.

Most people in our age are likely to be puzzled by the claim that nature "is such as to act for the sake of something."[75] Our age is unaccustomed to thinking in these terms and easily confuses opposite ways of understanding them. Two confusions are particularly common and destructive, the confusion between natural beings and artifacts and the confusion between objective ordering to an end and the rational intention of an agent.

When one shoots an arrow at a target, the movement (taken as a whole from the bow to the target) is objectively for the sake of arriving at the target. The whole movement is a movement to the target rather than elsewhere. The arrow, of course, is not aware of its directedness to that goal. It is a case of objective teleology, not merely of the archer's intention. This objective teleology would be natural if it arose from within the arrow rather than being violently impressed on it from the outside by the one who shoots the arrow.

74. Aristotle, *De Anima* 2.4.415a.26–415b.2.
75. Aristotle, *Physics* 2.1.199b.32–33.

God's creative art differs deeply from the external relation of human art to its artifacts. As the Creator, God stands at the inner origin of what is most intrinsic and most immediate to creatures. He does not impose a direction on them from the outside, which would make them artifacts, but together with their own being he gives them their own interior ordination to their end or good.

According to St. Thomas, "Nature is nothing else than the order of some art, namely the divine art, placed within (*indita*) things, by which things move to a determinate end."[76] The key term in this text is not so much *art* but *placed within*. It pinpoints the reason why the products of divine creative art are natural and not artificial, even though they are a product of what can analogously be called art.

In this order of divine art, which is most inside things, the good holds the absolutely first place. It is the cause of causes.

> Since the good has the *ratio* of being desirable, it implies the relation of final cause, the causality of which is first, because the agent does not act except for the sake of the end, and material is moved to form by the agent. For this reason, the end is called the cause of causes. And thus in causing, the good is before being, as the end is before form. For this reason, among the names that signify the causality of God [Dionysius], places the good before being.[77]

It is difficult to overestimate the weight of these truths. The good is before being in the order of causality, not only in the order of efficient cause but also in that of form, both with respect to *what* a being is and its *act* of being (*esse*). Wherever there are causes, the good is involved as the first and thus also as the most intrinsic cause, the cause that most deeply penetrates and shapes everything. This vision of the causality of the good is difficult to grasp for us who are so deeply formed in our thinking by the Baconian-Cartesian program, which has eliminated the good as a cause from nature in favor of ends imposed by human power on a nature without natures. Because our thinking is shaped by this program, we tend to suppose that material and efficient causes are sufficient as explanations. And yet the very causality of these causes depends on the good.

> The end is the cause of the causality of the efficient cause, because it makes the efficient cause to be efficient. In a similar way it makes the material be material and the form be form, since material does not receive form except through the end and the form does not perfect material except through the end. This is why one says that the end is the cause of causes, because it is the cause of the causality in all causes.[78]

76. Thomas, *In libros Physicorum* 2, lect. 14, no. 268.
77. Thomas, *Summa* I, q. 5, a. 2, ad 1; cf. *In libros Physicorum* 2, lect 5, no. 186.
78. Thomas, *De principiis naturae*, 4.

> Although the end is last in being in some things, nevertheless it is always first in causality. This is why it is called the cause of causes, because it is the cause of the causality in all causes. For it is the cause of the causality of the efficient cause, as said above. The efficient cause is in turn the cause of the causality of both material and form. For by its movement it makes material be receptive to the form and makes the form be in material. It follows also that the end is the cause of the causality of both material and form. This is the reason why in all things in which something is done for the sake of an end, such as in natural things, in moral acts and in art, the strongest demonstrations are taken from the end.[79]

Applied to sex, it is impossible to understand the male and female sex without the sexual faculty; it is impossible to understand the nature of that faculty without the act of sexual intercourse to which it is ordered; it is impossible to understand the act of sexual intercourse without its end, procreation; and it is impossible to understand procreation without the goodness of children and, through children, the good of the existence of the human species as a good that imperfectly imitates divine life. The goodness of union and the goodness of children is the cause that shapes the whole, both in the objective order of being and in our understanding.

From these starting points, one can gain a fuller understanding of the discussion between Doms and Fuchs (see part I, chap. 4, sect. 6, in this volume). Among the goods of marriage and of the conjugal act, the good of procreation is *primary* in the sense of being the *specifying* good, the good that gives to the conjugal act its specific nature as this and no other kind of act. For the same reason, the good of procreation accounts for *what* marriage is.

In What Sense Is the Union of Love the Secondary End?

Hildebrand and Doms are certainly right to insist that downplaying the importance of love between husband and wife harms the understanding of marriage. Love is the comprehensive moving and informing cause of their life together, a point underlined in *Gaudium et spes* 49.

> This love (*amor*), which is eminently human since it is directed from person to person through affection of the will, embraces the good of the whole person and can therefore enrich the expressions of body and mind with a unique dignity and ennoble them as elements and signs specific to conjugal friendship (*amicitia*). This love (*amor*) God has seen fit to heal, perfect, and raise

79. Thomas, *Sententia metaphysicae* 5, lect. 3, no. 782..

> by a special gift of grace and love (*caritas*). This kind of love (*amor*), which brings together human and divine, leads the spouses to a free and mutual gift of themselves (*liberum et mutuum sui ipsius donum*), proved by tender affection and deed, and runs through their whole life.

What gives to this kind of love and to the common life created by it its spousal character is the end of procreation. This does not mean that love is a means for producing children but that children are the natural fulfillment of specifically spousal love. Nor does it mean that the good of children is the only good present in the common life of spouses or that children are the greatest good of marriage. Thomas argues that the good of sacrament is greatest among the goods of marriage, because it is a participation in divine life.[80] To say that the good of children is the primary end does not contradict this ranking. It is to say that this end gives to the common life of man and woman its specifically sexual and spousal nature. In this context, *primary* does not mean *foremost* or *greatest* but *specifying*.

The example of the human eyes and their act of looking can show how a power together with its act can receive its nature from a specifying end (primary end) and nevertheless have another end (secondary end) that is not merely accidental.

Inasmuch as they have the power to see, the eyes are an effective place of expression. To look into another person's eyes is in a direct way to look at and into that person. The eyes have this power through themselves, not accidentally. Intense hatred or warmth of love can be present in a look, and it can be communicated in such a way that the other person can feel the attack of hatred or the warmth of love.

In some circumstances, the communication of love by a look may be a more important end than the immediate good of seeing. "You have ravished my heart, my sister, my bride, you have ravished my heart with a glance of your eyes" (Song of Songs 4:9). Nevertheless, what gives to the eyes and to the act of looking their nature is the end of sight, the visible appearance of things as possessed in sight. The question *What kind of act is this glance?* cannot be answered most specifically by *It is an expression of love*. This particular expression of love receives its specific essence from the end of sight. It is *looking with love*, where *looking* refers to the specific essence of the act while *with love* refers to one of its additional per se powers. In a similar way, the goodness of the child is the most intrinsic specifying cause of the conjugal act. The conjugal act is *procreative with love*, where *procreative* refers to the essence of the act, *with love* to one of its additional per se powers.

80. See Thomas, *Super IV sent.*, d. 31, q. 1, a. 3.

To say that procreation is the primary end of sex and of marriage means thus that it provides the essence of the act and of the institution. The other end—the expression and realization of a union of love—takes its place within the context provided by this essence. The union of love is an end essentially qualified by generation. Among the many forms of the union of love, the union of love in sex has an essentially procreative nature.

When a man and a woman come to love each other, union is often uppermost in their minds and intentions while the possibility of having children tends to remain in the background. Union may also at times occupy the foreground in the intentions of a married couple, for example, when they are past the age of fertility. Nevertheless, the union remains a union essentially ordered to procreation and in this precise sense subordinate to it.

Serenading is in its essence an act of music making. It can also be an expression and realization of a union of love, but it does not receive its nature as an act of music from love or from procreation. The example of *singing with love* differs, of course, from *procreating with love*. The expression of love flows more immediately from the nature of sex than from the nature of singing. One can sing without expressing love. Singing remains intact. Sexual union by its very nature creates "one flesh" (Genesis 2:24; Ephesians 5:31), "one body" (1 Corinthians 6:16). It is love making. If the union of love is damaged, the act does not remain intact.

Human walking is inescapably an act of locomotion. One cannot voluntarily walk without taking up the natural teleology of locomotion (from here to there) into the act as voluntarily performed (the act's essence in the order of morality, *species moris*). Similarly, eating is inescapably an act of nourishment. This end resides deeply in what this act is in the order of nature. The emperor Claudius, according to Suetonius, often stuffed himself to the point that his slaves had to "thrust a feather down his throat to relieve his stomach of the burden."[81] Cassius Dio says the same about the emperor Vitellius. "He was insatiable in gorging himself and immediately threw it all up so that he was nourished by the passing by of meals."[82] Eating cannot be stripped of its nature as an act of nourishment. One cannot oppose the nature of the act by vomiting on purpose and still preserve the act in its moral integrity and dignity. In a similar way, sexual organs cannot be used indifferently for this or that. They are by nature generative. Of course, once one has allowed mechanist ways of thinking to undermine the concepts of good, end, and nature, one cannot understand this truth any longer.

81. Suetonius, *Life of Claudius* 33.
82. Dio Cassius, *Roman History* 64.2.

Doms argues that Thomas's understanding of marriage and the conjugal act over-systematizes Aristotelian teleology.

> Thomas's theory is an attempt to bring systematic unity to the practice of Catholic marriage with the help of the concepts of his philosophy, essentially the Aristotelian philosophy. This is evident particularly in the dominant role of the concept of purpose (*Zweck*).
>
> The solutions that were reached in this process may be *neat and tidy*, but the reality created by God is *considerably deeper* than any theory, and the changes that took place in the course of centuries in the experience of life ... and the new results and methods of the scientific penetration of the object necessarily change and deepen the theoretical understanding.[83]
>
> The art of the divine Creator by which he ensures the harmonious functioning of life is much *more noble and grand than the Scholastic schemata of single- tipped subordinate finalities*.[84]

The opposite is true. The loss of nature in the so-called scientific picture of the world is above all due to the loss of the good as the final and definitive explanation of any nature and of its causes. The flattening of the wealth of being into neat and tidy formulae is the work of the positivist natural science in which Doms was formed, not of the ancient teleological vision of nature.

The Unity of Inner and Outer in the Conjugal Act

That husband and wife inevitably take up the procreative nature of the conjugal act (*species naturae*) when they choose to perform it becomes clearer when one examines the relation between the inner and the outer side of the act. From the perspective of those who perform the act, the outer act and the inner act of intention and choice make up a single whole, a single voluntary human act. Nevertheless, one can distinguish inner and outer act.

The concept *object of the act* is a key notion in St. Thomas's account of moral acts.

> In a voluntary act there is a twofold act, namely, the inner act of the will and the outer act, and *both of these have their object.*
>
> The end is properly the object of the internal act of the will while that which the external act is about is its object.
>
> As the external act receives its specific nature from the object about which it is, so the internal act of the will receives its specific nature from the end as

83. Doms, *Sinn* 79; emphasis added.

84. Doms, *Gatteneinheit und Nachkommenschaft*, 127; emphasis added.

> from its own object. What comes from the side of the will is like a form in relation to what comes from the side of the external act, because the will uses the members of the body as instruments to act. The external acts do not have a moral nature except inasmuch as they are voluntary.
>
> And therefore, the specific nature of human acts is formally considered according to the end but materially according to the object of the external act. This is why Aristotle says that one who secretly breaks into [a house] to commit adultery is, speaking per se, more an adulterer than a housebreaker.[85]

The two aspects of the conjugal act thus play a different role in establishing its moral nature as the conjugal act. The external act receives its nature from the end that belongs to it as an act of the generative power of the rational animal (*species naturae*). The inner act receives its nature from the end that belongs to it precisely as a voluntary act; namely, sexual intercourse as a rationally ordered good that is known as good and freely performed for this reason (*species moris*). Both of these are called object of the act, but in different ways.

The object of the external act of sexual union (*species naturae*) is, at least on one level, the same whether it is performed by husband and wife in the conjugal act or by a man and woman outside of marriage. The specific essence in the order of morality (*species moris*), by contrast, is different.

> It is ... possible that an act which is one in accord with its specific essence in the order of nature is ordered to different ends of the will. Killing a man, for example, which is the same act according to its specific essence in the order of nature, can be ordered to the end of preserving justice or to satisfying one's anger. And for this reason, there will be diverse acts according to their specific essence in the order of morality, because one of them is an act of virtue, the other an act of vice.[86]

While the inner act and the outer act are in some way distinct, one cannot separate them and assert that the inner act belongs to the order of persons while the outer act belongs to the order of nature.

> To be able to grasp the object of an act which specifies that act morally, it is therefore necessary to place oneself in the perspective of the acting person. The object of the act of willing is in fact a freely chosen kind of behavior.... By the object of a given moral act, then, one cannot mean [Latin: *nefas*, it is nonsense] a process or an event of the merely physical order, to be assessed on the basis of its ability to bring about a given state of affairs in the outside world. Rather, that object is the proximate end of a deliberate decision which

85. Thomas, *Summa* I-II, q. 18, a. 6.
86. Thomas, *Summa* I-II, q. 1, a. 3, ad 3.

determines the act of willing on the part of the acting person. (John Paul, *Veritatis splendor* 78)

The dominant Cartesian way of thinking sees the inner act alone as an act of the thinking thing (*res cogitans*). It pushes the outer act into exile away from the person into the separate world of extended things as if it were not the person's act. Against this alienation, TOB affirms the unity of the human person. *The human person is a body, a body among bodies.*[87]

7. Two Axioms of Self-Communication

The Aristotelian Axiom from Perfection

De Koninck summarizes the import of Aristotle's understanding of nature in the axiom "The essence of nature is communication of itself."[88] Book IV of Ar istotle's *Meteorology* raises the question how we can tell when fruit is ripe. "The ripening is complete when the seeds in fruit are able to produce ἀποτελεῖν [a word that contains the notion of *end*] another such as itself; for in all other cases as well this is what we call perfect τέλεον [again, *end*]."[89] St. Thomas recognizes in this apparently incidental remark a metaphysical axiom of great importance. He expresses it with several verbs in addition to *produce* (*producere*). Something is perfect or fully in act when it can make (*facere*) or generate (*generare*) another like itself, when it can communicate itself (*seipsum communicare*). "To pour out (*diffundere*) into others the perfection it has belongs to the account of the perfect as perfect."[90]

Self-communication is not a secondary consequence that flows from actuality, something additional to perfection but, as Aristotle puts it, "this is what we mean by perfect also in all other cases." De Koninck expresses the axiom by using the word *essence* in the sense of what belongs to the innermost character of a perfect nature. "The essence of nature is communication of itself."[91] The resting of perfect being in itself and its power to communicate itself to another are not two separate items in being, but they strictly coincide.

87. See TOB 5:5–6, 6:3–4, 8:1, 10:1–4, 19:4, 21:3, 29:4, 44:6, 45:1, 55:2, 60:1–2, 69:2–4, 72:5, 85:9, 86:4, 99:4, 102:5, 119:4.

88. Charles De Koninck, Letter to Mortimer Adler, Quebec, June 15, 1938.

89. τότε ἡ πέπανσις τελέα ἐστὶν ὅταν τὰ ἐν τῷ περικαρπίῳ σπέρματα δύνηται ἀποτελεῖν τοιοῦτον ἕτερον οἷον αὐτό· καὶ γὰρ ἐπὶ τῶν ἄλλων τὸ τέλεον οὕτω λέγομεν. Aristotle, *Meteorology*, 4.3, 380a.13–15.

90. Thomas, *Summa* I, q. 62, a. 9, ad 2.

91. De Koninck, *Letter to Mortimer Adler*, Quebec, June 15, 1938.

This Aristotelian axiom can even serve as a philosophical starting point for making the Father's generative power in the Trinity somewhat clearer to faith.

> It is the nature of every act that it communicates itself as much as possible. Therefore, everything acts according as it is in act. For acting is nothing other than communicating that through which the agent is in act, as much as this is possible.
>
> Now, the divine nature is most of all and most purely act. Therefore, it also communicates itself as much as possible. It communicates itself through mere likeness to creatures, which is clear to all, for any creature is a being in accord with likeness to it [i.e., to the divine nature].
>
> But the Catholic faith also lays down another way of communication of itself, inasmuch as it communicates itself by a natural communication, as it were, so that, just as the one to whom humanity is communicated is a human being, so the one to whom divinity is communicated is not only similar to God but is truly God.[92]

Given Thomas's account of the role of philosophy in theology, one cannot interpret this text as proving the Trinity from Aristotle's ripe fruit (see part II, chap. 7, sect. 5, in this volume). Still, the argument is suggestive because it focuses on the coincidence between perfect being and self-communication. One cannot separate the resting of the perfect within itself from its self-communication. One cannot locate perfection either in the first alone or in the second alone. In the infinite ocean of perfect being, of *ipsum esse*,[93] the resting of *ipsum esse* in its fullness and unity strictly coincides with its total self-communication to another.

Light is one of the images for the Trinity in the Creed: "light from light." The image is rooted in Scripture, "God ... has spoken to us in his Son ... who is the bright radiance from his glory (ἀπαύγασμα τῆς δόξης)" (Hebrews 1:1–3). "This is the message we have heard from him and proclaim to you, that God is light and there is in him no darkness at all" (1 John 1:5). Being perfect light and communicating light coincide.

The Platonic Axiom from Goodness

A metaphysical principle of the Platonic tradition resembles Aristotle's observation about ripe fruit. "The good pours itself out" (*Bonum diffusivum sui*). Thomas cites Dionysius (*De divinis nominibus*) as the origin of this axiom, even

92. Thomas, *De potentia*, 2.1, corp.
93. See Thomas, *Summa* I, q. 3, a. 4.

though Dionysius does not use this exact phrase. In the passage that comes closest to *bonum diffusivum sui*, Dionysius writes,

> The good is called spiritual *light, because ... it gives a share* (μεταδιδόναι), at first in a measure of splendor (αἴγλης). Then to those who taste the light and desire it more, *it gives itself* into [them] (ἑαυτὴν ἐνδιδόναι) and shines more abundantly, "because they loved much" (cf. Luke 7:47), and always stretches them up and onward in proportion to their upward look. The good above all light is called intellectual light as the fountain-like ray and hyper-outpouring flow of light (ὑπερβλύζουσα φωτοχυσία).[94]

In his commentary on this passage, Thomas focuses particularly on the image of pouring out. "In order that the fountain not be understood as standing in itself alone, Dionysius adds that it is an outpouring of light flowing from above, *effusio luminis desuper manans*."[95]

In accord with Dionysius's reference to *splendor*, Thomas connects the self-diffusion of the good with the glory of God. Commenting on the cry of the Seraphim, "Holy, holy, holy is the Lord, the God of armies; the whole earth is full of his glory" (Isaiah 6:3), he writes,

> And they praise the three, the Trinity of persons, "Holy, holy, holy"; the majesty of unity, "the Lord, the God of armies," who is before all. "Holy, holy, holy, Lord God Almighty, who is and who was and who is to come" (Rev 4:8); and the liberality of provision, "all the earth is full of his glory," because he extends the diffusion of his goodness to the very last creatures, who are referred to as "earth," "Do I not fill heaven and earth, says the Lord" (Jer 23:24). And this according to Dionysius.[96]

Thomas explains the point in more detail in his commentary on Ephesians.

> In no way does God need goods outside himself. "You have no need of my goods" (Ps 15:2). And therefore when it is said that God wills and does all things for his goodness, it is not to be understood that he does something to communicate goodness to himself, but for diffusing goodness to others. The divine goodness is communicated in the full sense to the rational creature that the rational creature might itself know it. And in this way, all things that God does among rational creatures he creates for the praise of his glory, according to Isaiah 43,7, "Everyone who invokes my name, I created him for my glory," that he might know goodness and when he knows it praise it. And therefore,

94. Dionysius the Areopagite, *De divinis nominibus*, 4.5–6; emphasis added.
95. Thomas, *Super De divinis nominibus* 4, lect. 4, no. 331.
96. Thomas, *Super Isaiam* 6, lect. 3.

> the apostle adds, "to the praise of the glory of his grace," that is that he might know how much God is to be praised and glorified.[97]

Dionysius sees the diffusive and self-giving nature of the good reflected in the diffusive and self-giving nature of love.

> And the divine love (*eros*) [all verbs and nouns are from the root *eros* unless noted otherwise] also brings ecstasy, not allowing those who are touched by it to belong to themselves but only to the objects of their love....
>
> And hence the great Paul, constrained by the divine love, and having received a share in its ecstatic power, says, with inspired utterance, "I live, and yet no longer I, but Christ lives in me." These are the words of a true erotic and ecstatic toward God, as he himself says, not living his own life but the life of his beloved as ardently loved [verb with the same root as *agape*].
>
> And we must dare to affirm, for this is the truth, that the Creator of the universe himself, in his beautiful and good *eros* towards the universe, is, through his excessive erotic goodness, transported outside of himself, in his providential activities towards all things that have being, and is overcome by the sweet spell of goodness, love and *eros*. In this manner, he is drawn from his transcendent throne above all things to dwell within the heart of all things in accordance with his super-essential and ecstatic power whereby he nonetheless does not leave himself behind.
>
> For this reason, those who know about God call him zealous, because he is vehement in his manifold and beneficent *eros* towards all beings, and he spurs them on to search for him zealously with a yearning *eros*, thus showing himself zealous for love inasmuch as the things that are desired are considered worthy of zeal and inasmuch as he allows himself to be affected by the zeal of all beings for which he cares.[98]

The self-diffusiveness of the divine goodness and the ecstatic power of divine love, Thomas argues, are particularly visible in the Incarnation. "God so loved the world that he gave his only Son" (John 3:16). The first article of the *Tertia pars* asks whether the Incarnation is fitting for God.

> Fitting for each thing is what belongs to it according to the account of its own nature. For example, it is fitting for man to reason, because this fits him inasmuch as he is rational according to his nature.
>
> God's very nature is goodness, as is clear from Dionysius, *De divinis nominibus* 1. Therefore, whatever belongs to the account of goodness is fitting for God. It belongs to the account of goodness that it communicates itself to others, as is clear from Dionysius, *De divinis nominibus* 4. Therefore it belongs

97. *Super ad Ephesios* 1, lect. 1.
98. Dionysius, *De divinis nominibus* 4.13.

> to the account of the highest good that it communicates itself to creatures in the highest way. This happens through joining a created nature to himself so that one person results from these three, the Word, the soul and the flesh, as Augustine says. Therefore, it is clear that it was fitting for God to become incarnate.[99]

Is the self-diffusiveness of the good and the ecstatic self-gift of love also present in the Trinity? In an argument *sed contra* of the Scriptum on the *Sentences*, Thomas seems to apply *bonum diffusivum sui* positively to the Trinity. The question of the article is whether there is a plurality of persons in God. It does not specifically focus on the procession of the Son or of the Holy Spirit.

> As Dionysius says, the good is self-communicative. But God is supremely good. Therefore, he will communicate himself supremely. But in creatures he does not communicate himself supremely because they do not receive his whole goodness. Therefore, there must be a perfect communication, such that he communicates his whole goodness to another. This, however, cannot be in the diversity of essence. Therefore, there must be many who are distinct in the unity of the divine essence.[100]

Thomas usually agrees with his arguments *sed contra*. When he finds a problem in them, he tends to call attention to it, which is not the case here. Clearly, the argument should not be understood as a philosophical demonstration of the Trinity but as a way of approaching the Trinity that makes clearer for us what is grasped by faith.[101]

The Aristotelian axiom of the self-communication of the perfect and the Platonic axiom of the self-diffusiveness of the good are close to each other, because *perfect* and *good* are close.

> That which has the account of cause is, first and universally, the good. This is clear ... because an agent acts [to bring forth] what is like itself, not inasmuch as it is a being in just any way but inasmuch as it is perfect. For the perfect, as is said in *Meteorology* 4, is what can make something like itself. The perfect, however, has the account of the good.[102]

Both axioms are rooted in being. The Aristotelian axiom is rooted immediately in *being* or *act* itself, and, at least in created beings, it implies efficient cau-

99. Thomas, *Summa* III, q. 1, a. 1, corp.

100. Thomas, *Super I sent.*, 2.1.4 sed contra 1.

101. Thomas addresses the approach to the Trinity through *bonum diffusivum sui* in *Summa* I, q. 32, a. 1, ad 2. He only points out the limits of this approach—it is not a philosophical proof of the Trinity—but he does not address its usefulness as a philosophical manifestation appropriate for human capacities.

102. Thomas, *Super De divinis nominibus* 3, lect. unica, no. 227.

sality. The Platonic axiom is rooted in the good, and, again at least in this world, it implies final causality. In God's interior life, in the Trinitarian relations, such forms of causality do not exist. Analogy and the *via negativa* must therefore be applied with care when one uses the axioms to reflect about the Trinity. Still, Aristotle's understanding of nature glimpses that in the very depths of being one finds the coincidence of perfection or goodness and self-communication.[103]

103. For a more detailed discussion, see the chapter on the Trinity in part II, chap. 7, of this volume.

CHAPTER 7

The Common Good as the *Logos* of Reason

Sexual love between man and woman is authentic, Wojtyła argues, if its inner order flows from the two essential goods of marriage, union and procreation, *inasmuch as they are common goods.* His argument begins with the negative principle that man and woman must not use each other as mere means for sexual gratification.

> The whole previous reflection on the first meaning of the verb "to use" gives us only a negative solution to the problem of the proper relation to the person. The person may not be either exclusively or first and foremost an object of use, because the role of a blind tool or a means to an end intended by another subject is contrary to the nature of the person.[1]

Love for each other in shared pursuit of a common good is the only way in which man and woman can realize a just relation to each other. A common good has the power to create a unique bond of union between two persons.

> Then, between myself and this other person a particular bond is born: the bond of a common good and a common end, which binds us. This particular bond is not limited to the fact that we strive together for a common good, but it unites the acting persons "from within"—and then *it constitutes the essential core of every love.* In any case, love between persons is unthinkable without some common good that binds them....
>
> The capacity to love is determined by the fact that man is ready to seek the

1. Karol Wojtyła, *Love and Responsibility*, trans. Grzegorz Ignatik (Boston: Pauline, 2013), 12.

> good consciously with others, to subordinate himself to this good because of others, or to subordinate himself to others because of this good.[2]

In his *Letter to Families*, John Paul deepens this line of reflection.

> "Good is diffusive of itself." Bonum est diffusivum sui. The more common the good, the more properly one's own it will also be: mine, yours, ours. This is the logic behind living according to the good, living in truth and charity. If man is able to accept and follow this logic, his life truly becomes a "sincere gift." . . .
>
> When a man and woman in marriage mutually give and receive each other in the unity of one flesh, the logic of the sincere gift of self becomes a part of their life. Without this, marriage would be empty; whereas a communion of persons, built on this logic, becomes a communion of parents. When they transmit life to the child, a new human "you" becomes a part of the horizon of the "we" of the spouses, a person whom they will call by a new name: "our son"; "our daughter." . . .
>
> The child becomes a gift to its brothers, sisters, parents and entire family. Its life becomes a gift for the very people who were givers of life and who cannot help but feel its presence, its sharing in their life and its contribution to their common good and to that of the community of the family. This truth is obvious in its simplicity and profundity. . . .
>
> The common good of the whole of society dwells in man; he is, as we recalled, "the way of the Church." Man is first of all the "glory of God": "Gloria Dei vivens homo," in the celebrated words of St. Irenaeus, which might also be translated: "The glory of God is for man to be alive." It could be said that here we encounter the loftiest definition of man: The glory of God is the common good of all that exists; the common good of the human race. (John Paul, *Letter to Families* 10–11)

What is a common good? How is its commonness related to the axiom of self-communication, the good is diffusive of itself? How is this diffusiveness related to glory? What does John Paul mean when he says, "The glory of God is the common good of all"? These are the questions pursued in the present chapter.

1. The Greek Fathers

The primacy of the common good as the good that shapes the very nature of reason plays a key role in the Western philosophical and theological tradition, in part because of the influx of Aristotelian philosophy into the Latin West in

2. Wojtyła, *Love and Responsibility*, 12–13.

the high Middle Ages. It is less widely known that a similar emphasis is found much earlier in the Greek Fathers. Here are a few examples of the many texts that could be quoted.

Apostolic Fathers

Clement of Rome sees devotion to the common good as a necessary aspect of Christian humility. "The more he seems to be superior to others, the more humble-minded ought he to be, and to seek the common good (τὸ κοινωφελὲς) for all, and not his own" (1 Clement 48:6). In this text, leadership is understood not as domination over others for the sake of increase in one's own power (a private good) but as humility, becoming small and close to the earth (*humus*). Leadership aims at the common good, which is both greater than the individual person and the greater good for the individual person.

Ignatius of Antioch makes the same point when he describes the office of the bishop as defined essentially by "devotion to the common good" τὸ κοινὸν (Philadelphians 1:1).

The *Letter of Barnabas* warns against withdrawing into oneself under the illusion that one's own knowledge is sufficient. Being spiritual and a temple of God is only possible together with others in search for the common good.

> Do not live alone, withdrawing into yourselves, as if you had already been made just, but coming together for the same thing seek together for the common good (περὶ τοῦ κοινῇ συμφέροντος). For Scripture says, Woe to those who think themselves intelligent by themselves and knowledgeable before themselves (Is 5:21). Let us become spiritual, let us become a complete temple for God (Barnabas 4:10).

In its incommensurable greatness in comparison with the individual person, the common good remains the good of persons, provided they open their minds and hearts to it and do not obstinately limit themselves to what they see and understand of themselves.

Early Alexandrians

Clement of Alexandria quotes Clement of Rome as an authoritative text and draws the conclusion that the right love of God and neighbor is love for the common good.

> The holy and pure conduct of our love of human beings, according to Clement, "seeks the common good," whether by suffering martyrdom, or by teaching

> by deed and word—the latter being twofold, unwritten and written. This is love, to love God and our neighbor. This leads up to the unutterable height. (*Stromata* 4.18)

To act for the common good, Clement explains elsewhere, is part of conforming to the image and likeness of God, because God's gifts are for the common good. We become like him by a similar devotion to the common good (again κοινωφελής).

> This is the one "after the image and likeness," the gnostic, who imitates God as far as possible, leaving aside none of the things for possible likeness, practicing self-restraint and endurance, living justly, reigning over the passions, giving a share in what he has as far as possible, and doing good both by word and deed. "He is the greatest," it is said, "in the kingdom who shall act and teach" by imitating God in conferring like benefits, because God's gifts are for the common good. (*Stromata* 2.19)

Accordingly, *Origen* understands the saving death of Jesus as establishing a great common good. "He died for the common good of mankind" (*Contra Celsum* 2.44). As a good deriving from Christ's death, the Church's spiritual treasury is "for the common good."[3]

Commenting on the Lamb of God that takes away the sins of the world, Origen sees a preunderstanding of this gift of self for the common good among Greeks and Barbarians. He does not judge the adequacy of their understanding but sees it as a preparation for the Gospel, in which the Lamb gives itself in its atoning death, bearing the sin of all for the common good.

> Now, there are many Greek and barbarian stories in circulation concerning the solution of certain grievous things that frequently prevail among the human race, such as plagues, or harmful cessations of the winds, or famines. Such things are solved when the evil spirit that causes them is rendered impotent, as it were, *because someone gives himself for the common good*. The Greeks and barbarians do not disown or reject the concept of such a person. This is not the time to examine whether such things are true or not.
>
> But never yet has a story been told of one who was able to take responsibility for purification on behalf of the whole universe, that the whole universe might be cleansed, since it would perish had he not taken responsibility to die for it. Nor can such a story be told, since Jesus alone has been able to *take up into himself on the cross the burden of the sin of all on behalf of the whole universe* apart from God, and to bear it in his great strength.[4]

3. Origen, *Commentary on John*, 19:44.
4. Origen, *Commentary on John*, 28:162–63; emphasis added.

The Cappadocian Fathers

St. Basil considers devotion to the common good an essential feature of belonging to the body of Christ under Christ as head. The good that Christ gives to the whole Church is greater than the gift given to each individually, but the good given to the whole Church becomes the good of each member.

> If all we who are united in the one hope of our calling are one body with Christ as our Head, we are also members, one of another. If we are not joined together by union in the Holy Spirit in the harmony of one body, but each of us should choose to live in solitude, we would not serve the common good in the ministry according to God's good pleasure but would be satisfying our own passion for self-gratification.
>
> How could we, divided and separated, preserve the status and the mutual service of members or our subordinate relationship to our Head which is Christ? ... Since no one has the capacity to receive all spiritual gifts, but the grace of the Spirit is given proportionately to the faith of each, when one is living in association with others, the grace privately bestowed on each individual becomes the common possession of his fellows.... He who receives any of these gifts does not possess it for his own sake but rather for the sake of others, so that, in the life passed in community, the operation of the Holy Spirit in the individual is at the same time necessarily transmitted to all.[5]

St. Gregory of Nazianzus tells of two conflicting desires in his heart. One is to withdraw alone into contemplation to hold communion with God, and the other is to step into the midst of the Church as bishop to bring the sacred light to many as their common good (here simply "that which is common," or τὸ κοινὸν). He compares the two and finds that the second is better, even for himself individually as a person.

> The one suggests flights, mountains and deserts, and calm of soul and body, and that the mind should retire into itself, and recall its powers from sensible things, in order to hold pure communion with God, and be clearly illumined by the flashing rays of the Spirit, *with no admixture or disturbance of the divine light by anything earthly or clouded*, until we come to the source of the effulgence which we enjoy here, and regret and desire are alike stayed, when our mirrors pass away in the light of truth.
>
> The other wills that I should come forward, and *bear fruit for the common good, and be helped by helping others*; and publish the Divine light, and bring to God a people for His own possession, a holy nation, a royal priesthood, and His image cleansed in many souls. And this, because, *as a park is better*

5. Basil, *Longer Rule*, Question 7.

> *than and preferable to a tree, the whole heaven with its ornaments to a single star, and the body to a limb, so also, in the sight of God, is the reformation of a whole church preferable to the progress of a single soul:* and therefore, I ought not to look only on my own interest but also on that of others. For Christ also likewise, when it was possible for him to abide in His own honor and deity, not only so far emptied Himself as to take the form of a slave but also endured the cross, despising the shame, that he might by His own sufferings destroy sin, and by death slay death. The former are the imaginings of desire, the latter the teachings of the Spirit.[6]

The phrase "I ought not to regard only my own interest" might give the impression that, in seeking the common good, Gregory is seeking the good of others as others as opposed to his own. His image of the garden and the tree shows that such an understanding would be mistaken. The ordering of the whole Church is the greater good of each member, Gregory included.

St. Gregory of Nyssa: "The word of salvation is indeed given as a common good for all mankind."[7]

St. John Chrysostom

St. John Chrysostom is the great teacher of the common good among the Greek Fathers. He returns often to the absolute primacy of the common good. He interprets Jesus's words "You are the salt of the earth" as implying the commandment of devotion to the common good (here τὸ κοινῇ συμφέρον, from κοινός, "common," and the verb συμφέρω, "to bring together, gather, confer a benefit").

> When he says "You are the salt of the earth," he shows that he commands all this [i.e., the teaching of the beatitudes] of necessity. "For not for your private life," he says, "but for the whole world, shall [you have to give] an account of yourselves." For not to two cities, nor to ten or twenty, nor to a single nation am I sending you, as I sent the prophets but to earth, and sea, and the whole world, and that in a bad condition."
>
> For by saying, "You are the salt of the earth," he signified that all human nature became foolish and was corrupted by sin. Hence, he requires of them the virtues that are most necessary and useful for the care of the many.
>
> For in the first place, the meek, friendly, merciful, and just, does not shut up his good deeds in himself alone but also provides that these good fountains run over for the good of others. And he again who is pure in heart, and a

6. Gregory of Nazianzus, *Oration* 12.4.
7. Gregory of Nyssa, *On the Beatitudes* 4.

> peacemaker, and is persecuted for the truth's sake, he again orders his way of life to the common good.
>
> "Think not then," he says, "that you are drawn to ordinary conflicts, or that for some small matters you are to give account. You are the salt of the earth."[8]

Concern for the common good, Chrysostom argues, is particularly important in the realm of spiritual goods. Our salvation depends on such concern for the common good (τὸ κοινῇ συμφέρον).

> If in matters of daily life no man lives for himself, but artisan, and soldier, and farmer, and merchant, all of them contribute to the common good and to their neighbor's advantage, much more ought we to do this in things spiritual.
>
> For this is most properly to live, since the one who lives for himself alone and overlooks all others is certainly superfluous and not a human being, nor of our race....
>
> Since we are persuaded by all these things that *it is not possible for a person to be saved who has not looked to the common good*, and since we see the man who was cut to pieces (Matthew 24:51) and the one who buried his talent (Matthew 25:24–25), let us choose this way, that we may also reach eternal life.[9]

Against the background of this teaching, it is not surprising that Chrysostom uses a superlative: nothing is as pleasing to God as living for the common good. He points to the example of the poor widow who gave her last coin and of the Apostles who were uneducated men and yet lived for the common good (τὸ κοινῇ συμφέρον and τὸ κοινωφελῶς ζῆν).

> You are not poorer than that widow, you are not more rustic than Peter and John, who were both unlearned and ignorant men; but nevertheless, since they showed zeal and did all things for the common good, they reached heaven. For nothing is as pleasing to God as living for the common good.[10]

In the same way, Paul lived for the common good (here τὸ κοινὸν κέρδος, "the common advantage or gain"). Chrysostom places the following words on Paul's lips.

> I look only to the common good, and whether it be done by me, or by another, it makes no difference to me. This ought to be the disposition of the one who presides, not to seek his own honor but the common good.[11]

8. John Chrysostom, *Homilies on Matthew* 15.10.
9. John Chrysostom, *Homilies on Matthew* 77.6; emphasis added.
10. John Chrysostom, *Homilies on Matthew* 78.2.
11. John Chrysostom, *Homilies on Titus* 2.

In his Homilies on John, Chrysostom unfolds the underlying theological vision of human life more fully in his comments on John 1:18, "No one has ever seen God. The only-begotten Son, who is in the bosom of the Father, he has made him known." The proper content of the only begotten Son's teaching, Chrysostom goes on to argue, lies in a vision of one body united by the common good (τὸ κοινωφελὲς).

> It was for this that he brought his teaching from heaven above, that he might place our thoughts there, that we might be imitators of the teacher according to our power.
>
> But how can we become imitators of Christ? By acting in everything for the common good, and not seeking our own. "For even Christ," Paul says, "did not please himself, but as it is written, The reproaches of those who reproach you fell on me" (Romans 15:3).
>
> Let no one therefore seek his own. For one seeks one's own good when one looks to that of one's neighbor, for what is their good is ours. We are one body, and parts and limbs of one another. Let us not then be as though we were torn apart. Let no one say, "Such a one is no friend of mine, or relative, or neighbor, nor do I have anything to do with him. How shall I approach, how address him?"
>
> Even if he is neither a relative nor a friend, he still is a human being, who shares the same nature with you, has the same Lord, and is your fellow-servant and fellow-sojourner, for he is born in the same world.
>
> And if besides he shares the same faith, then look, he has also become a member of yours. For what friendship could work such union, as the kinship of faith?
>
> And our familiarity with one another like people who live in the same house must not merely be such nearness as friends ought to show to friends but as exists between limb and limb. For nobody can possibly discover any familiarity greater than this sort of friendship and communion. As no limb could say, "Where does my familiarity and closeness with this limb come from?" (that would be ridiculous) so neither can you say so in the case of your brother. "We are all baptized into one body" (1 Corinthians 12:13), Paul says. "Why into one body?" So that we may not be torn apart but preserve the coherence of that one body by our coming together and friendship with one another.[12]

12. John Chrysostom, *Homilies on John* 15.3.

2. De Koninck against the Personalists

In 1943, Charles De Koninck published *The Primacy of the Common Good: Against the Personalists*, in which he presents the account of the common good found in Plato, Aristotle, the Greek Fathers, and Thomas with clarity and emphasis. An intense controversy followed. Many readers understood the book as an attack on Jacques Maritain. More recently, some Thomists who have a justifiably high regard for De Koninck have seen his book as ammunition against St. John Paul. De Koninck, they suppose, has published the definitive refutation of personalism. John Paul is by his own admission a personalist, particularly in TOB.

This judgment is based on mistaking opposite forms of personalism for each other. For De Koninck, personalists are those who hold that the individual person in his or her liberty is an end that stands ultimately above the common good.

> The sin of the angels was practically a personalist error: they preferred the dignity of their own person to the dignity which they would receive through their subordination to a good which was superior but common in its very superiority. The Pelagian heresy, according to John of St. Thomas, can be considered as somewhat like the sin of the angels. It is only somewhat like it, because whereas the angels committed a purely practical sin, the error of the Pelagians was at the same time speculative.
>
> We believe that modern personalism is but a reflection of the Pelagian heresy, speculatively still more feeble. It raises to the level of a speculative doctrine an error which was at the beginning only practical.[13]

Personalism, as De Koninck understands the term, is the theoretical equivalent of Satanic rebellion. Like the Pelagian heresy, it implies a denial of the creaturely status of human beings, exalts human freedom as an end in itself, and denies the radical dependence creatures on God, who alone is the supreme common good to which all creatures are ordered.

> According to Kant, man is an end unto himself. The ultimate end ... is the persons themselves in their proper dignity. This dignity does not come from the person by himself being able to attain to the ultimate end of the universe, that is, to an end other than the person; the person receives his dignity from himself because he is his own end and accomplishes in himself the freedom of autonomy.[14]

13. De Koninck, "Primacy of the Common Good against the Personalists," *Aquinas Review* 4 (1997): 1–71, at 22.

14. De Koninck, "Primacy of the Common Good," 68n72.

Wojtyła resists Kant's personalism at the same point. He rejects Kant's thesis that the human person *is* an end and replaces it with the thesis that the person *has* or should *have* ends. He also resists Scheler's personalism at the same point. The final and most radical objection in his book on Scheler is directed against Scheler's thesis that each person draws ultimate happiness or misery out of himself or herself. A reward conceived as attaining an end distinct from the human person, Scheler claims, could not add to this happiness. Scheler's person, like Kant's, has ultimate dignity in itself. It does not receive its full dignity through participation in a common good.

The true principle of unity of communities, John Paul argues in agreement with De Koninck, is the common good. He uses one of Scheler's favorite terms, *solidarity*, to express his point.

> When interdependence becomes recognized ... the correlative response as a moral and social attitude, as a "virtue," is solidarity. This then is not a feeling of vague compassion or shallow distress at the misfortunes of so many people, both near and far. On the contrary, it is *a firm and persevering determination to commit oneself to the common good*; that is to say to the good of all and of each individual, because we are all really responsible for all [Latin: because we truly receive everyone in us]....
>
> Solidarity helps us to see the "other"—whether a person, people or nation—not just as some kind of instrument, with a work capacity and physical strength to be exploited at low cost and then discarded when no longer useful but as our "neighbor," a "helper" (cf. Genesis 2:18–20), to be made a sharer, on a par with ourselves, in the banquet of life to which all are equally invited by God. (John Paul, *Sollicitudo rei socialis* 38–39)

According to this text, solidarity is a firm commitment to the common good. It grows out of the commonness of the common good. To love a common good as common is to love it in its communicability to many. It is to will it for all and for each individual, and it is to will all individuals to share in it.

Participation expresses this precise place of the human person as taking part and being a part in a larger whole. In *Person and Act*, Wojtyła uses the term "participation" more frequently than the Husserlian term "intersubjectivity," which has a narrower cognitive emphasis. "In this way the term *intersubjectivity* is replaced by that of *participation*."[15] The word *participation* immediately highlights that by its very nature every created person exists as a part ordered to the good of the whole.

15. Karol Wojtyła, *Persona e atto*, Polish text with facing Italian translation, ed. Giovanni Reale and Tadeusz Styczeń (Milan: Bompiani, 2001), 613n13; *The Acting Person*, trans. Andrzej Potocki (Dordrecht: D. Reidel, 1979), 261n75, printed at 315.

3. Defining Common Good

A common good is a good in which many can share at the same time without reducing or dividing it. A private good, by contrast, is a good that excludes such sharing.

Wine is reduced if many share in it. If I drink it, someone else cannot. We might have enough wine to go around, and in a real sense the wine will then be common. Yet it is only imperfectly common, enough to go around. The wine is divided up when many share in it. It can run out.

The peace of a state or a family is a common good in the full sense. When one shares in this peace, one does not take anything away from someone else's share in it. On the contrary, in the degree to which one embraces peace as one's own good, it becomes more available for others. To love peace, to work for peace, is inseparable from willing that peace for the whole, for all members. It is impossible to want peace for oneself alone. It would be absurd to say, "It isn't fair. You are taking a bigger piece of peace. We will run out of peace." Competition and scarcity cannot be present in a true common good.

The streets of a city are shared by many. Are they a common good? Nobody can take them as a private possession. Yet when anybody drives on a street, nobody else can drive in that exact place at that particular time. Traffic jams show that a street cannot be a common good in the strict sense. There is scarcity and competition. A street is not divided into pieces like a cake. Parts of it are occupied for a limited time. Conversely, one only needs a small part of the street at any given time. One does not need to make all of it one's own for an extended time.

A geometrical proof can be shared by many. Is it a common good? If some understand it well, they do not take anything away from others. On the contrary, they can help others understand it better. By sharing it with others, one comes to possess it more completely. Conversely, one does not take only part of the theorem. The more one understands it, the more it becomes one's own as a whole. All who understand it possess it as a whole. Yet, to be truly common, a good must remain one in its reality when it is shared by many. In what sense is a proof the same when many people understand it? In the respect in which geometry is interested in it, the proof is one. Yet the acts and the inner words by which persons understand it are distinct. These acts are in each case a private or personal good. They cannot be directly shared with others.

The happiness of the citizens in a state, is it a common good? It is common in some manner, but if one merely considers the happiness of each rather than a common order and whole, then it is not common in the manner of a common good. It lacks an essential condition for being a common good; namely, being *one* good. The happiness of each citizen is distinct; it is in each case the personal good of the citizen. Conversely, it would be strange if the common good of a state had nothing to do with the individual happiness of its citizens. The state's good could hardly be a true and great common good if it would leave some in misery. One needs to distinguish between happiness as the activity in which a person reaches the end and the end itself, the object of happiness. It is only the object of happiness that can be a common good. Justice and peace in the state are constituents of its happiness in the sense of being objects of the happiness of each. The end in the sense of object is the same for one individual and for the city.

Children are a common good of their parents. One can see an imperfect kind of commonness already on the physical level. The one flesh of mother and father together is the child's origin. Parents and children live physically together. It would be absurd for husband and wife to quarrel about whose child it is. Custody battles, of course, privatize the child. A more perfect common good is at stake in the education of children. Husband and wife communicate not only their physical life but also their cultural, intellectual, and spiritual life. Both can take joy in the growth of their children. They do not divide the object of their joy like bread.

God is the Common Good par excellence, in which all the features of common goods are realized most perfectly. The reason St. Thomas gives for this thesis is at first sight surprising. "The highest good, which is God, is a common good since the good of all depends on him."[16] De Koninck unfolds this reason in helpful ways.

> When we say that the creature participates in God's perfection, we do not mean that it is part of God the way a slice of bread is part of the whole loaf. It means simply that the fullness of God's perfection is such that, no matter how perfect the creature or even the ensemble of all creation, it will never compare to God except in the way in which what is only partial compares to the whole.
>
> Hence, had God created only one single person, he would still have the nature of common good in the latter sense; so that this person would have to love God as a good that far exceeds the measure of any created person. And this is the basis of charity towards neighbor, whom we must love inasmuch as he is "*capax Dei.*"
>
> This is so true that one cannot love God without love of neighbor. Had God produced but one person, this person would still have to love God in his super-abundant communicability to others.[17]

16. Thomas, *Contra gentiles* III, cap. 17.
17. Charles De Koninck, Letter to Sister Margaret Ann, December 22, 1961.

Analogical senses: This survey of examples shows that *common good* is not a univocal term but analogous in different orders. Various kinds of common good are common in different ways and degrees, depending on their nature and the mode of participation in them. A different sort of common good is found in marriage (the child), in the academy (truth), in the state (justice and peace), and in life as a whole (God). It would be pointless to look for *the* common good without distinguishing these different orders.[18] All orders point to one supreme common good. If anything deserves the name *the* common good, it is the infinite common good, God himself.

Two senses of *common:* The phrase *the common good* (with the article) is used in two senses that should be clearly distinguished to avoid a confusion that often plagues arguments about the common good. *The common good* can refer either to a specific common good, such as justice and peace in the political order, or to the nature of the common good in general. The same two meanings can be seen more easily in the phrase *the city.* Romans call Rome *the city*, people in New York use *the city* for Manhattan, and in London the financial district is *the city.* When *the city* appears in a general description such as, "The city is a place for many people to live together," it is applicable to any city. *Gaudium et spes* defines *the common good* in the first of these two senses. "The common good, that is, the sum of those conditions of social life which allow social groups and individual members fuller and readier access to their own perfection" (*Gaudium et spes* 26). In this definition, *the common good* is like *the city* as a name for Rome. It signifies one common good among others—the social or political common good. It would be a mistake to read *Gaudium et spes* 26 as a definition of the common good in general that can be applied analogously to common goods in various orders. God is not a sum of conditions of social life, but the good in all its fullness and thus the separate common good of the universe.

Intrinsic and separate common good: In a text already quoted above, Aristotle distinguishes between intrinsic and separate common goods.

> One must also examine in which way the nature of the universe has the good or the highest good, as something separate and itself by itself (κεχωρισμένον τι καὶ αὐτὸ καθ› αὐτό) or as the order (τάξις). In both ways, it seems, as an army does. For the good is found both in the order and the leader, and more the latter; for he is not through the order, but it is through him.[19]

The two inseparable meanings of the conjugal act in *Humanae vitae* are the intrinsic and the separate common good of the spouses. The union of spouses

18. See Gregory Froelich, "The Equivocal Status of *Bonum Commune*," *New Scholasticism* 63 (1989): 38–57.

19. See Aristotle, *Metaphysics* 12.10.1075a11–1075a24.

is intrinsic to marriage while children are separate from the united spouses, though parents and children are parts of the same family. The separate common good of a community is in most cases the primary good in the sense that it specifies the nature of that community and its intrinsic common good. This primacy implies that, in another sense of intrinsic—namely, being the source of a nature—the separate common good is most intrinsic, more so than the intrinsic common good.

4. Clarifying the Definition

The reason why a good is common is not that it happens to be shared by many but that it is eminently communicable. It pours itself out more fully than a private good. If the fact of being shared were the reason, it would follow that the same good is private when it is possessed by only one person. Whether a good is private or common depends rather on the very nature of that good and the mode of participation in it. It can be shared by many without being reduced.

In many cases, a more material good is more private, a more spiritual more common. A similar proportion holds for modes of participation in a good. Eating an apple is a more material mode of participation than looking at it. Only one person can eat an apple. Many can look at it. A painting, a piece of music, these are material but still more truly common goods than food. It would be false, however, to claim that a good is common in the measure in which it is spiritual. A person's act of knowing is spiritual, but it is exclusively that person's good. As an act performed, it can only belong to one human person. It cannot be the act of other persons besides. It can be communicated to another person by being expressed in words, but the other person's act of knowing will be a distinct act belonging to that person.

Money can be electronically transferred, in which case it is less material than a bag of potatoes or a bar of gold, without being in the least degree more common. For a state to have a monetary system is an important common good that implies many other common goods, such as mutual trust among citizens, justice in the administration of the central bank, and the like. Yet money is inevitably private.

Four Constitutive Features of the Common Good

1. *Eminent Communicability.* The common good is more diffusive of itself than a private good.[20] For this reason, the common good is a more personal

20. For this and the other three points, see De Koninck, "Primacy of the Common Good," 16–17.

good than the private good. "The more common the good, the more properly one's own it will also be: mine, yours, ours" (John Paul, *Letter to Families* 10). Since it is more communicable, it can be more deeply possessed by each person than a private good. One can have and treasure the peace of one's family in a more intimate sense than wine. Wine does become one's own when one drinks it, but it is still in some way outside when it enters the stomach. Once it is assimilated into the body, it is no longer wine. To enjoy it is to destroy it. By contrast, the peace of the family does not remain outside. It is drawn into each mind and heart and remains itself in pouring itself out. *Bonum est diffusivum sui.* The good pours itself out. It is diffusive by giving itself as the good of a person. Eminent communicability is closely connected with commonness. Because it pours itself out more effectively, the common good can be given not only to one but to many. It can more fully and truly become each one's own without for all that being less someone else's. If good is diffusive, the common good is most diffusive.

2. *Superabundance.* A common good is greater than any one person's share in it. Although one can possess the peace of one's family more intimately than most private goods, one's grasp of it cannot close on it, as it closes on a piece of bread. Nevertheless, each person possesses in some sense the whole of it, not a mere part like one slice of bread.

3. *Incommensurability.* A common good escapes the attempt to measure it with the measure of one's individual person. One cannot order it to oneself but must order oneself to it, give oneself to it, not in the sense of serving an alien good or an arbitrary master. It is one's own greater good precisely because it is greater than simply being for oneself.

4. *Part-Whole.* Whenever a common good is shared by many persons, they form a whole to which they are related as parts. The constitution of such a whole is clear already in the imperfectly common goods, for example, friends eating and drinking together, travelers using a common road. It is even clearer in the perfectly common goods. On a much deeper level, truth gives rise to a society of its lovers, and peace and justice in a state give rise to a society of citizens.

Plutarch describes an exchange between Alexander the Great and Aristotle in which one can observe these four characteristics of the common good in their violation.

> Alexander, it seems, received from him [Aristotle] not only the account (*logos*) of ethics and politics but also something of those hidden and deep teachings which these men, by the very names they gave them, professed to reserve for oral communication to the initiated, and did not allow many to share in. For when he had already gone to Asia and heard that Aristotle had published some

> lectures about these matters, he sent him the following letter, addressing him with very plain language about philosophy.
>
> Alexander to Aristotle, greeting. You have not done well to publish your books of oral teaching; for what is there now for us to be different from others, if those accounts which we were taught are common? For my part, I assure you, I want to be different from others more in these experiences about the best (ταῖς περὶ τὰ ἄριστα ἐμπειρίαις), than in the powers [of my conquests]. Farewell.
>
> Aristotle, reassuring his love of honor, defends himself by answering that these lectures are both published and not published. It is true that the treatise *Metaphysics* is not useful for teaching and learning but written as a reminder for those instructed from the beginning.[21]

Aristotle humors his powerful student. Perhaps he knew that the attempt to correct him would be fruitless. By loving metaphysical learning for the distinction it gave him over others, Alexander did not love it as a common good, which means he did not love it itself. If he loved it itself, he would have loved it in its communicability to all, in its superabundance and incommensurability with any private person. He would have understood that knowing such truth makes him part of the community of all lovers of truth. He would therefore have been glad about its publication. Given Alexander's disposition, one can hardly suppose that he made serious progress in studying because his primary interest was something else.

When one pursues a common good for the sake of a private good, one stops loving that common good itself and loves something else instead. St. Augustine describes the logic of this displacement in the *Confessions*. He has little patience for interpreters of Genesis who tenaciously hold on to their own personal interpretation of the text, even when someone shows that other interpretations are possible and reasonable.

> They don't know Moses's meaning but love their own view—not because it is true but because it is theirs. Otherwise they could equally love another true view, as I love what they say when what they say is true—not because it is theirs but because it is true, and immediately not theirs, because it is true. And if they love it because it is true, it is already both theirs and mine, since as common it belongs to all lovers of the truth. . . .
>
> And therefore, O Lord, your judgments should be feared, because *your truth is neither mine nor his nor anyone else's, but it belongs to all of us* whom you publicly call to its communion (*communionem*), warning us terribly not to want to possess it as private, so as not to be deprived of it. For anyone who

21. Plutarch, *Life of Alexander* 7.5–7.7. Plato's Seventh Letter draws a similar portrait of Dionysius, the ruler of Sicily.

> claims as belonging to himself what you have given to all to enjoy and wants to be his own what belongs to all is driven away from the common to his own—that is, from truth to the lie. For the one who "speaks the lie speaks out of his own" (John 8:44).[22]

In the last sentence, Augustine quotes John 8:44: "When he [the devil] speaks the lie, he speaks out of his own, because he is a liar and the father of it." One can translate a little more closely, "He speaks from within what belongs to himself alone," ἐκ τῶν ἰδίων λαλεῖ. Augustine's Vetus Latina has *de suo loquitur*, the Vulgate the more forceful *ex propriis loquitur.* The reason why he speaks from his own is that he is a liar and the father of lying. In this respect, there is a direct contrast with Jesus. "The one who speaks from himself (ἀφ' ἑαυτοῦ) seeks his own glory, but the one who seeks the glory of him who sent him, this one is true and there is no injustice in him" (John 7:18).

Common as Cause and as Predicate

The distinction between the universal in predication and in causality discussed in the chapter on Plato's *Republic* (part I, chap. 5, sections 5 and 6, in this volume) is relevant here as well, as the following difficulty shows.

> The more common a good, the more divine it is, as is clear in *Ethics* I. But bodily good is more common than spiritual good, because *bodily* extends to plants and brute animals while *spiritual* does not. Therefore, bodily good is preeminent over spiritual good; and so happiness must be sought more in bodily goods.[23]

The text from Aristotle's *Nicomachean Ethics* to which Thomas refers is the following.

> Even if [the end] is the same for a single man and for a city, that of the city seems at all events something greater and more complete both to attain and to preserve; for though it is lovable even for one person, it is more splendid and more godlike for a nation or for cities.[24]

A good that extends itself to more persons "is prior and more powerful" *prior est et potior.*[25] Hence to have concern for the more common good is more divine because it is more like God, who is the cause of all goods.

22. Augustine, *Confessions* 12.25.34; emphasis added.
23. Thomas, *Super IV sent.*, d. 49, q. 1, a. 1A, obj. 3.
24. Aristotle, *Nicomachean Ethics* 1.1.1094b.7–10.
25. Thomas, *Sententia libri ethicorum* 1, lect. 2, no. 30.

In his response to the argument, Thomas does not deny Aristotle's principle that it is more divine to pursue the common good. He points out an equivocation.

> Something can be called common in two ways. In one way by predication, but this kind of common is not something one in number found in many. In this way the good of the body has commonness.
>
> In another way something is common according to the sharing of something one and the same in number. This commonness can be found most in things that have to do with the soul because it is by the soul that one can reach the common good for all things, namely, God.[26]

A true common good must be one in number. It must be a reality that remains one when many persons share in it. God remains one and the same while many can share in him. This point is put even more clearly in a later text that responds to a similar objection.

> Something can be called common in two ways. In one way by following after or predication, when something is found in many according to one account; and in this way something that is more common is not more noble but more imperfect, as animal is compared with man....
>
> In another way in the manner of a cause, such as a cause which, remaining one in number, extends itself to many effects; and in this way what is more common is more noble, as preserving the city than preserving the family.[27]

This text helps to focus on the commonness of the common good more clearly. Three points are particularly important. First, something can be common—that is, one in many—by following after (*per consecutionem*) the many, as when we form one account that follows after observing many individual beings. My human nature is numerically distinct from yours, but when they are considered according to their account, they are one—one as something after the many, not one as something before. Plato conceives the Ideas in an opposite way. They are before the individuals because they are not only predicable universals but also universal causes in which individuals participate (see part I, chap. 5, sections 5 and 6, in this volume). It is as a universal cause that the common good is common, not as a predicable universal. As a true cause, it must be in some way before the many of which it is the cause, not after them.

Second, because what is at stake is the good, the cause in question is that for the sake of which. To call an end a common good is to say that it extends its causality as end to many, all of whom can reach one and the same end, numerically one, not merely one by predication.

26. Thomas, *Super IV sent.*, d. 49, q. 1, a. 1A, ad 3.

27. Thomas, *De veritate*, q. 7, a. 6, ad 7.

Third, the more general an account, the less perfect it is as an account. When one knows that justice is a specific kind of virtue without recognizing what makes it unmistakably and specifically justice, justice itself and justice alone, one has not yet come to know it as justice. Knowing the specific and irreducible nature of a thing is the goal of knowledge. The more universal, the less perfect; the less universal, the more perfect.

It is the other way around when one is dealing with a good that is common to many as an actual reality rather than as a general account. Saving a city is more noble and perfect than saving a family within it, because saving the city is something one in number that extends to all persons in the city and thus to all families, while saving a family extends only to that one part. In the destruction of a whole city, all families in it are destroyed.

5. The Person as Part and Whole

Part and Whole

The superiority and primacy of the common good is often explained by appeal to the self-evident axiom that the whole is greater than the part, that the part exists for the sake of the whole, that the good of the part is ordered to the good of the whole, and so on.

Aristotle sees *communion* (κοινωνία) in a common good as a consequence of rationality.

> It belongs to man as his own in comparison with other living beings that he alone has any perception of good and evil, of just and unjust, and the like. Now, the communion (κοινωνία) of living beings who have this perception makes a house and a city.
>
> And the city is *by nature prior to the house and to every one of us*, since the whole is of necessity prior to the part; for example, if the whole body is destroyed, there will be no foot or hand, except equivocally, as we might speak of a stone hand; for when destroyed, the hand will be like that. But all things are defined by their function and power; and we ought not to say that they are the same when they no longer have their proper quality but only that they have the same name.
>
> The proof that the city exists by nature and prior to the individual is that the individual, when isolated, is not self-sufficing; therefore, *he is like a part in relation to the whole*. But he who is unable to be in communion, or who has no need because he is sufficient for himself, is no part of a city: he must either be a beast or a god.[28]

28. Aristotle, *Politics* 1.2.1253a15–29; emphasis added.

If the individual person is fully relativized in function of the city, as fully as the hand is relativized in function of the whole body, can the rational dignity and freedom of each individual person still be preserved? Is Aristotle's not a sub-personal vision of the state, a beehive or anthill, rather than a communion of persons? And is modern personalism with its emphasis on individual dignity and personal rights not a decisive advance in comparison with Aristotle's sub-personal understanding?

One can respond that Aristotle sees the reason for the primacy of the state over the individual and the family in the rational nature of human beings, not in their sentient or vegetative nature. Granted, he uses a subrational organic image: each person is like an organ that is part of a living body. He is clear, however, on this difference between the whole formed by an organism and a family or a state: it is because human beings have a perception of good and evil, and a rational capacity for communion (κοινωνία) in the common good, that they are naturally part of and subordinate to the state. Organs in a body are not rational beings. The good of the whole body is not their common good because only persons can be beneficiaries of a good in the full sense.

Maritain on Part and Whole

The various parts of a human body form a single substantial whole. It is impossible for an individual person to be in this same way part of a whole, because an individual person is the one final subsisting subject. Boethius's classical definition of the person is built upon this truth.

> If, then, the person exists only among substances and only among those that are rational, and every substance is a nature and exists not in universals but in individuals, the definition of the person has been found: an individual substance of rational nature.[29]

Because a person is an individual substance complete in its own rational nature, it cannot be a substantial part of any substantial whole: "The account of part is opposed to the account of person." Ratio partis contrariatur rationi personae.[30] St. Thomas makes this point in his *Scriptum* on the *Sentences* in the context of discussing the question whether the soul after death is the person. Maritain and others have taken this text to imply that the person should not be considered part of the state, because being part would contradict the great value and dignity of the person. The person is primarily a whole.

29. Boethius, *Liber contra Eutychen et Nestorium* cap. 3, first sentence.
30. Thomas, *Super III sent.*, d. 5, q. 3, a. 2.

For St. Thomas, the intelligible value of "whole," "totality," is indissolubly bound to that of person. It is a fundamental thesis of Thomism that the person as such is a whole. The concept of part is opposed to that of person. To say, then, that society is a whole composed of persons is to say that society is a whole composed of wholes.[31]

In a footnote to the sentence "The concept of part is opposed to that of person," Maritain claims that this principle applies analogically to many orders, including the common good.

St. Thomas, in this text, refers to the human composite, *unum per se* [through itself one], and shows that, because it is only a part of the human being, the separated soul cannot be a person. To anyone whose knowledge of Thomism is sufficiently deep, it is clear that the principle—the ratio of part is repugnant to that of personality—is an entirely general principle and is applied analogically depending on the case.[32]

To evaluate Maritain's argument, one should take a close look at the text he quotes. The question of the article is whether the soul separated from the body is the person. The two opening objections of the article seem persuasive. (1) The soul after death is an individual subsisting in a rational nature. Therefore Boethius's definition of the person applies to it. (2) Because the soul is that by which the whole composite human being, body and soul, is a person, the soul by itself must be person in a prior and higher way.[33]

One of the arguments *sed contra* makes the most important point: *person* refers to the complete being, not to a part. "Person has the *ratio* of something complete and whole. The soul, however, is a part. Therefore, the soul does not have the account of person."[34]

Because the person and personal pronouns are closely connected, one can examine this argument by a pronominal test. When I say *I*, I am referring to myself as a person. Which is closer to the truth? *I am a soul*, or *I have a soul*? Clearly the second, because the human body also belongs to human nature, to *what* I am. The body is not another being to which I, being a soul, am joined. The one who strikes my body strikes *me*. When I *sit*, *I* sit.

This substantial unity of human beings is the concern of the Aristotelian account of the soul as the first entelechy, the first act or actuality of a physical body, Thomas argues in the body of the article.

31. Jacques Maritain, *The Person and the Common Good*, trans. John J. Fitzgerald (Notre Dame, IN: University of Notre Dame Press, 1947), 56–57.

32. Maritain, *Person and the Common Good*, 28n29, printed at 42.

33. See Thomas, *Super III sent.*, d. 5, q. 3, a. 2 obj. 1 and 2.

34. Thomas, *Super III sent.*, dist. 5, q. 3, a. 2, sec contra 2.

> About the union of the soul to the body, there were two opinions among the ancients. One was that the soul is united to the body as a complete being to a complete being, so that the soul is in the body like a captain in a ship. Hence Gregory of Nyssa says, Plato held that man is not something constituted out of body and soul but is a soul clothed with a body.
>
> This view is tantamount to saying, the whole personality of man (*tota personalitas hominis*) consists in the soul, so much so that the separated soul can be called a true man, as Hugh of Victor says. The Teacher [Peter Lombard] says for this reason that it would be true to say, when the soul is separated, that it is the person.
>
> But this opinion cannot stand, because in this way the body would come accidentally to the soul, so that this term *man*, the understanding of which implies both body and soul, would not signify something one through itself but by accident, and thus man would not be in the genus of substance.
>
> Another opinion is that of Aristotle, whom all moderns follow, that the soul is united to the body as the form to material, from which it follows that the soul is a part of human nature and not a certain nature through itself. And since the account of part is opposed to the account of person, as was said above [*sed contra* 2], the separated soul cannot be called the person, for although as separated it is not a part in act, it has the nature of being a part.[35]

In this light, Thomas responds to the two opening arguments:

> To the first: The separated soul, properly speaking, is not a substance of some nature but is a part of a nature. To the second: It is not from the soul alone that man has being a person but from it and the body, since he subsists from both.

As pointed out above, Maritain extends the principle Thomas formulates in the *sed contra* in a manner that runs counter to Aristotle's claim that the person is naturally part of the state. Yet in the text under discussion, Thomas focuses on only one kind of part-whole relation; namely, the relation between a substantial whole and its parts. A part of a substantial whole cannot be a person, and a person cannot be part of a substantial whole. An organ of the body is part of a substantial whole; a person cannot be.

The way in which a person can be part of a whole is fundamentally different. Persons can be part of a whole, such as the family or the state, because they are the beneficiaries of the common good. This is a part-whole relation unique in its kind. It must not be confused with the part-whole relation of parts of a substance. To say that being a part in one sense is contrary to being a person is in no way to say that being a part in the other sense is likewise contrary.

35. Thomas, *Super III sent.*, d. 5, q. 3, a. 2, corp.

Crosby on Part and Whole

John Crosby develops a more general and radical objection, building on Maritain's thesis that the account of *part* is opposed to the account of *person*. He argues that there is something ultimately depersonalizing about being a part.

> Only by understanding each partial social function as a kind of mask, as something that does not contain without residue the depths of one's personal being; only by understanding it as something which, however important, even for a person's development as person, can never provide the person with his whole reason for being, absorbing him or her as a part of the community; only by understanding a society or community as a "whole composed of wholes": only then can a person remain intact as person in performing the function.
>
> If one aspect of personal selfhood is thrown into relief by saying that the person is not an instrumental means, then another aspect of the same selfhood is thrown into relief by saying that the person is never a mere part.
>
> This inability to be a part seems to have the same metaphysical ultimacy that we noticed above. For our moral consciousness, it seems to matter little whether one tries to make human beings parts of society or parts of God; the depersonalization inflicted on them is no less grievous in the latter than in the former case. Whatever the larger whole, even if it is God himself, persons can never function as mere parts in it. Pantheistic religion not only exalts but also degrades human beings: by making them parts of *God* it makes them divine, but by making them *parts* of God it abolishes them as persons.[36]

To see in what way Crosby's argument is true, one needs to distinguish.

One sense of part-whole is being a substantial part of a substantial whole. A person can never be a part in this way, as a limb is part of a person. It makes no difference, Crosby is right to insist, whether the whole is God himself or something else. Human persons would gain a merely apparent dignity by being part of God in this substantial way. Being a part in this way is the destruction of the person's own being. Even in the Trinity, the persons are not parts in this sense because each of them is the one God, not a part of God.

A second sense of part-whole is present when persons are ordered to a good alien to them. A slaveholder, for example, constructs a social whole in which the slaves function as mere means for achieving ends that are not theirs but his.

36. John F. Crosby, *The Selfhood of the Person* (Washington, DC: Catholic University of America Press, 1996),18–19. Crosby's position on person and part appears to be strongly influenced by Scheler. "Only the person is never part." Max Scheler, *Der Formalismus in der Ethik und die materiale Wertethik: Neuer Versuch der Grundlegung eines ethischen Personalismus*, 7th ed. (Bonn: Bouvier, 2000), 392. The ultimate reason Scheler holds this position is the divine plenitude of the person. Crosby does not share Scheler's view on this plenitude.

Such subservience is contrary to the dignity of rational nature. Rational nature enables persons to intend and pursue their own good. The human person is a whole in the sense of being ordered to an end that is truly the end of that person. To be rational is to stand vis-à-vis the entire world and God. "The soul is in a certain way all beings."[37] The person grasps this whole and is thus a whole vis-à-vis the whole, a microcosm that mirrors the macrocosm. It is directly and immediately ordered to the good of the whole.

A third sense of part-whole is present in the legitimate claims that common goods can make on persons. These claims differ according to the rank of the social whole. While the family and the state can legitimately claim the person as part, no person can be entirely absorbed as part in these communities because the common goods that define them in their specific nature are not the person's ultimate end, the definitive common good. It would be a mistake, however, to conceive of human dignity primarily as consisting in a private sphere that goes beyond such limited wholes. The person has a dignity greater than being a part of the family or the state because the person is ordered to a higher common good.

The community defined by the highest common good *does* claim created persons in their entirety as parts. Attainment of this common good *does* absorb without residue the depths of their personal being. It *does* provide them with the whole reason for being. In this precise sense of part-whole, the human person is *in no way* a whole in relation to the ultimate common good but *only a part*. God alone is a whole in this sense not because he is personal, but because he is God, infinite and comprehensive in his goodness.

Of course, even if no created person can be a whole in this third sense, each person must remain a whole in the first two senses. All persons must remain substantial wholes and a whole by being "in a certain way all beings," even all of God, at least in the sense of being able to know and love God himself. The person is directly ordered to this good in all its fullness. The person does not merely have a social *function*, as Crosby puts it, but the person's greatest *personal* good is a common good, a good that is greater in the whole than in the part—a greater good for each person.

The High Stakes in the Debate

The stakes in this debate are high. What would follow if one maintained—Crosby, of course, does not maintain this view—that even on the supposition of the

37. Aristotle, *De anima* 431b.21.

third sense of *part-whole* the human person is a whole and not a part? It would be a claim by human beings to the dignity of *being* the final end. One can understand why De Koninck felt he had to attack certain forms of personalism as diabolical. One can also understand the outrage of those among Maritain's friends who thought De Koninck had accused Maritain of a theoretical stance equivalent to the Satanic practical stance. A moving letter by Yves Simon to Maritain reports a discussion with Jacques de Monléon, who was a beloved friend of all three, De Koninck, Simon, and Maritain.

> Finally, we [Simon and de Monléon] talked about the common good: well understood, you don't know anything about it. But here I finally asked some precise questions. I summarized the theory of the common good in five clear propositions, and Jacques [de Monléon] had nothing more to say when I said that on these five essential points there was perfect agreement between you, myself, De Koninck and himself. These five propositions are:
>
> 1. Any good of a higher order is greater than any good of a lower order.
> 2. Within each order there is an absolute priority of the common good over the private.
> 3. When a person is an absolute person (in God), there is an absolute coincidence between the common good and the personal good.
> 4. Insofar as a (created) person is a person, there is a tendency toward the coincidence of the personal good and the common good.
> 5. The primacy of the common good is not subject to any restriction in the same order, for when this primacy disappears (3 and 4) this is not because the primacy belongs to the private good, it is because the problem of primacy has disappeared.
>
> Jacques [de Monléon] had difficulty understanding the fourth proposition and tried to see the fall of the angels in it (naturally) but ended up agreeing. The result of all this for me is that I have lost a friend who is infinitely dear to me....
>
> All of this has tried me enormously. Intensely religious people like Jacques [de Monléon] have the power to hit and shake me in the heart of conscience, in the solar plexus of moral and religious life. I understood better what you have suffered when you were struggling with these theological possessed (énergumènes) who have such holy intentions. I am having the greatest trouble finding my equilibrium again.[38]

De Monléon is right to hesitate about the fourth proposition. He is not an énergumène, possessed or deranged. He should have peacefully insisted on fur-

38. Letter from Simon to Maritain, December 11, 1945, Maritain Archives, University of Notre Dame.

ther clarification. It is the crucial point in the debate. The "coincidence between the common good and the personal good" in the case of the divine persons means that each person *is* that good. The three divine persons are not "participants of the divine nature" θείας κοινωνοὶ φύσεως (2 Peter 1:4) but *are* that nature. It is *common* to them in the sense of *consubstantial*.

When the fourth proposition speaks about a *tendency* toward the coincidence of the personal good and the common good even in the case of created persons, it cannot have *consubstantial* in mind. If it did, de Monléon's suspicion would be justified. It can only mean that the common good is the created person's good, truly reached and possessed. Since being the person's good is what it means for a good to be common, one must conclude that the law of the primacy of the common good does not end but still holds, simply speaking.

Maritain himself came to agree with de Monléon's misgivings about the fourth proposition and with De Koninck's thesis about the absolute primacy of the common good. It is curious that he does not express his agreement in the main text of his book on the common good but in a footnote. If one reads only the main text, one could have the impression that the primacy of the common good no longer holds. Here is the main text and the footnote.

> Here [in the beatific vision], in the intentional identification of each soul with the divine essence, the law of the primacy of the common good over the personal good comes to an end in a certain sense.
>
> [Footnote:] In another sense, this law always holds; in the sense that the infinite communicability of the incomprehensible Essence forever transcends the communication which, through its vision, the creature receives of it.[39]

6. The Person as Beneficiary

Only persons can be *beneficiaries* by possessing a good in the full sense of possession because only persons can know and love the good as good. A tree can be healthy, but it cannot possess this good as its own in the full sense because it has no appreciation of it as good.

In the human body the good of health is primarily the good of the whole. The whole is the true beneficiary because the whole is a person. Health is not in the first place the good of the parts, although it is to their benefit as well. When I am healthy, health is *my* good, not that of my hand, though my hand's health is sustained by the health of the whole. Health is not a common good of my body parts because they are not persons. The part-whole relation is different in a

39. Maritain, *Person and the Common Good*, 88–89 and 89n48.

family or city, when one looks at it from the point of view of the common good. The primary beneficiaries of that good are the individual persons, not the city as a whole as a quasi-individual in its own right. This is the point at which the comparison of persons with members of a body breaks down.

There is a fundamental difference between imperfect and perfect commonness. When the state collects income tax, it acts as a quasi-individual. It takes money that was the private good of one of its citizens. It places that money in a bank account identified as belonging to the state, just as private citizens place their money in their own private bank accounts. When the state has taken my money, the money is no longer mine. It therefore fails to fulfill an essential requirement for a common good; namely, being common. It is a good of the totality, a good of the whole and therefore in some sense common but still not a true common good.

As a quasi-individual, the state can compete against the individual persons who are part of it. One can define a totalitarian regime in these terms: a regime is totalitarian when it makes citizens as parts subservient to the good of the whole state considered as a quasi-individual with its own bank account.

> The common good does not have the character of an alien good—*bonum alienum*—as in the case of the good of another considered as such. Is it not this which, in the social order, distinguishes our position profoundly from collectivism, which latter errs by abstraction, by demanding an alienation from the proper good as such and consequently from the common good since the latter is the greatest of proper goods?
>
> Those who defend the primacy of the singular good of the singular person are themselves supposing this false notion of the common good.[40]

In this text, *proper good* refers to a good that is truly possessed by the persons of whom the state is composed. A good is common in the full sense only if it is the *proper good* or *personal good* of the persons. If one takes the state as a quasi-individual and claims that goods belonging to it as such an individual must have primacy over the good of citizens, one has alienated the citizens from their good and sacrificed them to the state by making them subservient to purposes that are not their own but those of another as other. By contrast, when it is viewed from the perspective of a genuine common good, such as peace or justice, the state is a whole that does not stand as a competing individual over against its citizens but as a whole built up by a good that is common in the sense of being genuinely possessed by each.

Does the individual person exist for the sake of the state, or the state for the sake of the individual person? One should not answer this question without first

40. De Koninck, "Primacy of the Common Good," 18.

asking another question. Do you mean the state as a quasi-individual that can compete against its citizens? Or do you mean the state as a whole composed of persons as parts inasmuch as all these persons share in a true common good as its beneficiaries?

If the persons live for the sake of the state's good in the first alternative, they are reduced to a slavery in which they must serve the good of another, an alien good.[41] What they end up serving is not really the state but a person or group of persons in the state, for example, the dictator or the oligarchs. These are the beneficiaries in a totalitarian state. If there were no such beneficiaries with their private interests, there could be no totalitarian state. In such a condition of slavery, persons exist for the sake of the private good of the rulers, not for the sake of the state. The state functions as a mask of commonness that hides private interests.

If the members of the state live for the sake of the state's good in the second sense—that is, a state inasmuch as it is united by a genuine common good—no such slavery follows. By living for a truly common good—for example, a genuine peace—citizens live for the sake of a good that is truly theirs as persons. It is not the state's good as opposed to theirs, common as opposed to personal but theirs personally exactly because it is genuinely common.

> Thus the common good is not a good other than the good of the particulars, a good which is merely the good of the collectivity looked upon as a kind of singular. In that case it would be common only accidentally; properly speaking it would be singular, or if you wish, it would differ from the singular by being *nullius* [belonging to nobody]. But when we distinguish the common good from the particular good we do not mean thereby that it is not the good of the particulars; if it were not, then it would not be truly common.[42]

De Koninck's point that the common good is not the good of another as other is capital. The impression that the common good is an alien good is suggested by the image of the body and its parts, and the sacrifice of the part for the whole, even to the point of destruction and death.

> We see that every part works by a certain natural inclination for the good of the whole, even with danger or damage to its own good, as is clear when someone exposes his hand to a sword to defend his head, on which the good of the whole depends. And so it is natural that every part loves the good of the whole more than itself. It is in accord with this natural inclination and with political virtue that a citizen exposes himself to the danger of death for the common good.[43]

41. De Koninck, "Primacy of the Common Good," 16–17.
42. De Koninck, "Primacy of the Common Good," 17.
43. Thomas, *Quodlibetum* 1, q. 4, a. 3, corp.

The traditional image of the body and its organs can easily slip into confusion between common and alien. Life is not a common good of the hand and the head in the human body. Life is the private good of the whole person. The hand is entirely subservient to the whole because it is not a true beneficiary of the good of the whole. This is not slavery for the hand because the hand is not a person. The common good of a state, by contrast, is the good of each of its citizens. All persons who are part of the state are the primary beneficiaries of that good, not in the sense of deriving some private gain from it but in the sense of truly possessing it together with others.

One could object, *What about death, which is a supreme gift of oneself for the common good? Does it not show a conflict between part and whole, because a part is destroyed for the sake of the whole?* Suppose there is a famine that threatens the life of a whole family, and the father saves himself by eating the available food, knowing that the others will die. He would lose what is dearer to him personally. His own life will be left to him but as a life deprived of what he loves more. If he risks death and dies, he affirms what is dearer to him and has it as truly his, though his for a shorter while.

Protestant moral discourse tends to focus on the alternative between altruism and selfishness (see the discussion of Luther's condemnation of sexual pleasure in part I, chap. 2, sect. 5, in this volume). To use the concepts of altruism and selfishness to understand the sacrifice of one's life for the common good is to misconceive that sacrifice from the roots up. If altruism means serving an alien good, and if selfishness means serving one's private good, then both are equally opposed to love and sacrifice for the common good. Egoism denies the common good in practice by pursuing only the private good. Altruism denies the common good more radically in theory by misconceiving it as alien. From this perspective, one can see the importance of Aristotle's claim that "the same end seems to belong to human beings both in common and individually."[44] The sameness of these two is precisely what it means for a good to be common.

"Love does not seek its own" (1 Corinthians 13:6). This text is fundamental in Luther's rejection of a theology of glory in favor of a theology of the cross. Following the mainstream of the tradition, Thomas reads this text as speaking about common and private good. He raises the question whether prudence is concerned not only with the private good of a person but also with the common good. The second objection leads straight to the heart of the matter. "The prudent person seems to be the one who seeks and does the good for himself. Often, however, those who seek common goods neglect their own. Therefore, they are not prudent."[45]

44. Aristotle, *Politics* 7.15.1334a.11–12.

45. Thomas, *Summa* II-II, q. 47, a. 10, obj. 2.

In his response, Thomas argues that prudence *does* bear directly on the common good. The knot of the issue lies in the precise meaning of *one's own good* (*bonum proprium*).

> As Aristotle says in *Ethics* 6, some held that prudence does not extend to the common good but only to the private good. The reason is that they thought that one should only seek one's own good.
>
> But this judgment is opposed to love, which does not seek its own (1 Corinthians 13:6). This is why Paul says about himself, "not seeking what is useful for me but for many, that they may be saved" (1 Corinthians 10:33).
>
> It is also opposed to right reason which judges that the common good is better than the good of one. Since it belongs to prudence to hold counsel, to judge and to command rightly about things by which one reaches the due end, it is clear that prudence is related, not only to the private good of one man but also to the common good of the multitude.[46]

This argument is incomplete because it does not clarify in what sense the common good is also one's own good (*bonum proprium*). The clarification can be found in the response to the second objection.

> The one who seeks the common good of the many also seeks his own good, for two reasons.
>
> First, because one's own good cannot be without the common good of the family or city or kingdom. Hence Maximus Valerius says about the ancient Romans that they preferred to be poor in a rich empire rather than rich in a poor empire.
>
> Second, since a man is a part of the house and of the city, it is necessary for him to consider what is good for himself on the basis of being prudent about the good of the many. For the good disposition of the part derives from its relation to the whole since, as Augustine says, "Every part that does not fit its whole is ugly."[47]

What is at issue in the first of these points is a private good, wealth. For one's own private good, it is better to be poor in a rich state that takes care of its poor than rich in a poor state. The poor state is likely to be unstable, which can lead to ruin in one's private possessions. What is at issue in the second point is the common good itself. Since individual persons are as parts in relation to the common good, prudence about themselves implies prudence about themselves as parts and therefore prudence about the common good.

46. Thomas, *Summa* II-II, q. 47, a. 10, corp.
47. Thomas, *Summa* II-II, q. 47, a. 10, ad 2.

7. Happiness and Glorification

Gloria Dei vivens homo

Happiness or glorification of God—which of these two is the end of human life?[48] Happiness is a good of the individual person, a personal good. What sense does it make to speak of the person being ordered to a common good if one holds that *happiness* is the final end of human life?

Peter Lombard formulates the purpose of creation in a sentence that has found wide acceptance in the Christian tradition, particularly in catechisms. "If the question is asked for what the rational creature has been created, the response is to praise God, to serve him, to enjoy him."[49] In this classical statement, the *Magister* echoes a text in the tractate *On Loving God* (*De diligendo Deo*), attributed by some medieval authors to St. Augustine.

> For what, then, has the rational creature been created? To praise God, to serve him, to enjoy him. In these things the creature profits, not God. For God is perfect, full of the highest goodness, and can neither be increased nor diminished. That the rational creature is made by God must be referred to the goodness of the Creator and the benefit of the creature.[50]

The first two of these three purposes—praising God in his glory and serving him by doing his will—are closely related. In both, the primary point of reference lies in God, not in us. Enjoyment seems to shift the focus of attention to us. What is the relation between these two purposes? Do they simply stand next to each other, or is there an inner connection between them?

St. Irenaeus gives a striking answer. "The glory of God is man alive, but the life of man is the vision of God." Gloria enim Dei vivens homo, vita autem hominis visio Dei.[51] A second statement complements the first. "This is the glory of man, to persevere and remain in the service of God." Haec enim gloria hominis, perseverare ac permanere in Dei servitute.[52] John Paul echoes these texts of Irenaeus in the main thesis of TOB formulated in the experiential terms of purity as the right order of sexual love described by *Humanae vitae*.

> Purity is the glory of the human body before God. It is the glory of God in the human body, through which masculinity and femininity are shown. From

48. This question is formulated in penetrating fashion by Balthasar in the thematic essay "Homo creatus est," in *Skizzen zur Theologie V: Homo creatus est* (Einsiedeln: Johannes, 1986); *Explorations in Theology V: Man Is Created*, trans. Adrian Walker (San Francisco: Ignatius Press, 2014), 11–30.

49. Peter Lombard, *Sentences* 2.1.4.4.

50. Ps.-Augustine, *De diligendo Deo* 2.

51. Irenaeus, *Adversus haereses* 4.20.7.

52. Irenaeus, *Adversus haereses* 4.14.1.

> purity springs that singular beauty that permeates every sphere of reciprocal common life between people and allows them to express in it the simplicity and depth, the cordiality and unrepeatable authenticity of personal trust. (TOB 57:3)

Irenaeus speaks about happiness and about service. The happiness of the human person in the vision of God is the glory of God, and the service of God is the glory or happiness of the human person. How can both be true at the same time? Do the two ends remain isolated, connected only by an exterior order? If one tells a child, "Don't be so selfish! Don't insist only on your momentary sense pleasures" and then gives the child a piece of candy for following this maxim, the message is confusing. Immanent self-interest is first forbidden and then satisfied by the reward. Is this the relation between glorifying God and enjoying God?

God's Glory as the End

Thomas affirms the primacy of God's glory as the end of creation. The entire creation is *ad gloriam Dei*, to the glory of God. In the top corner of almost all manuscript pages of TOB, John Paul wrote *amdg*, *ad maiorem dei gloriam*, to the greater glory of God.

> The whole universe with its single parts is ordained to God as an end, inasmuch as by a certain imitation the divine goodness is represented in them to the glory of God. Still, rational creatures have God as the final end in a special way above this [imitation] since they can attain him by their operation, by knowing and loving.[53]

When human persons reach God as their end, the glory of God remains the ultimate end.

> The other cause [of predestination] is the final cause which is that we might praise and know the goodness of God. This cause is noted in the words, "In praise of the glory of his grace" (Ephesians 1:6).[54]

What is this "glory of his grace"? What is Thomas's account of glory? How does he coordinate happiness as the final end with the glorification of God as the final end?

53. Thomas, *Summa* I, q. 65, a. 2, corp.
54. Thomas, *Super ad Ephesios*, 1.1.

> Augustine says in his Tractates on John that glory refers to a certain brightness (*claritatem*). Hence *glorified* and *made to be bright* mean the same thing in this Gospel. Brightness involves a certain evidence according to which something becomes conspicuous and manifest in its splendor (*splendore*). For this reason, glory implies the manifestation of something in its goodness. If news of someone's evil spreads, it is not called glory but rather shame. And so, Ambrose says in his *Commentary on Romans*, that glory is bright renown with praise.[55]

The close connection between glory and splendor explains why Thomas formulates the end of creation also in terms of beauty.

> The multitude and distinction of things has been planned by the divine mind and has been set in things, so that created things would represent the divine goodness in different ways and manifold beings would participate in it in different degrees, in order that out of the order of manifold beings a certain beauty would arise in things, a beauty which commends the divine wisdom.[56]

If the end of creation is to glorify God, then this end must determine the fundamental orientation of the human person in the very act of reaching God as the final end. Happiness must be measured by this criterion. At this point, Josef Seifert, following Dietrich von Hildebrand, sees an insurmountable difficulty in Thomas's thesis that happiness is the final end.

> Especially in St. Thomas and the Thomists we find happiness as the final end of man and as the inescapably pre-given final motive (*Beweggrund*) of human action. According to this view, man has no freedom whatsoever to choose the final end of his striving, but his freedom is limited to the choice of means. . . .
>
> On the other hand, the same thinkers claim that the final purpose of creation (not only the objective purpose but also the subjective purpose, that is, considered in relation to the motivation of the human will) is the *glorificatio dei externa* (the glorification of God that must be achieved by creatures). The Catholic Church has raised this teaching to the status of a dogma. . . . According to this theological teaching, the human person is clearly obliged in his or her moral action not to choose (*wählen*) happiness as the final motive (since this is a secondary and subordinate end of creation) but to subordinate it entirely to the first motive, namely, the glorification of God. In other words, the eudemonistic ethics which St. Thomas adopted from Aristotle stands in flagrant contradiction against the theological doctrine of the final end of creation, a contradiction that can never be resolved within Thomism.[57]

55. Thomas, *De malo*, 9.1, corp.; see Augustine, *In Ioannis evangelium tractatus* 100.1.

56. Thomas, *Compendium*, 1.102 end.

57. Josef Seifert, *Was ist und was motiviert eine sittliche Handlung* (Salzburg: Pustet, 1976), 32–33n19.

Seifert understands the word *happiness* (*eudaimonia, felicitas, beatitudo*) in the texts of Plato, Aristotle, Augustine, and Thomas differently than they do. They understand *happiness* as signifying a life about which one can say absolutely and without any further qualification, *It is good*. Following Hildebrand, Seifert understands the word *happiness* as signifying an affective state of joy or delight. This is the most common understanding of the word *happiness* after Kant's critique of utilitarianism.

Thomas argues that joy is a consequence of a life that is good, not identical with it.[58] If one sets this misunderstanding aside, Seifert still brings an important question into focus. What is the relationship between the glory of God and a human life about which one can say, *It is good?*

Hans Blumenberg, echoing Nietzsche, charges that the Christian faith subjected the human person to an external self-glorifying power. The legitimacy of the modern age, he argues, lies in the justice of the person's self-assertion against such a God, who destroys human freedom and dignity.[59] Nietzsche uses an eloquent image for this destruction.

> You will never pray again, never adore again, never again rest in endless trust .... You live without a view of the mountain summits with snow on their head and red glow in their heart.... There is no longer any love in what will happen to you.... You man of self-denial, you want to deny yourself all that? Who will give you the strength for it? No one has yet had this strength.
>
> There is a lake that one day denied itself to flow away from itself and cast up a dam where it had flowed away until then. Since then, the lake has been rising.... Perhaps man will rise higher and higher from then on, when he no longer flows away into a God.[60]

"God seeks his glory, not for his sake, but for ours," Thomas comments.[61] Still, the primacy of God's glory remains, contrary to the claim of Kant and Scheler that all things are to the greater glory of the human person (see part II, chaps. 2 and 3, in this volume).

58. See Thomas, *Summa* I-II, q. 4, a. 1–2; for a detailed discussion of this controversy, see Michael Waldstein, "Dietrich von Hildebrand and St. Thomas on Goodness and Happiness," *Nova et Vetera* 1 (2003): 403–63.

59. See Hans Blumenberg, *Die Legitimität der Neuzeit* (Frankfurt: Suhrkamp, 1966), Part II; *The Legitimacy of the Modern Age* (Cambridge: Massachusetts Institute of Technology Press, 1983), Part II.

60. Friedrich Nietzsche, *Sämtliche Werke: Kritische Studienausgabe*, 2nd ed. 15 vols., ed. Giorgio Colli and Mazzino Montinari (Berlin: Walter de Gruyter, 1988); KSA 3:527–28.

61. Thomas, *Summa* II-II, q. 132, a. 1, ad 1.

Private Love and Social Love

"You have made us toward yourself and our heart is restless until it rests in you." This famous quote is a subordinate clause. The first part of the sentence, the main clause, is not quoted as often. "You stir us so that praising you delights us because you have made us toward yourself and our heart is restless until it rests in you."[62] The main clause makes the main point, and the subordinate clause explains it. It is by creating us toward himself as restless creatures who long for him as the object of happiness that God stirs us to praise him. Because he stirs us in this way, praising him delights us. The glory of God is the main orientation of the restless heart.

The same point emerges even more clearly in Augustine's explanation of the two loves in the *City of God*, in which the term *glory* functions as one of the main concepts, together with the terms *domination* and *power*, to explain two opposite forms of love.

> Two loves have built the two cities.
> Love of self to the contempt of God built the earthly city;
> love of God to the contempt of self the heavenly.
> One *glories* in itself,
> the other in God.
> One seeks *glory* from men;
> for the other its greatest *glory* is God as the witness of conscience.
> One raises its head in its *glory*;
> the other says to its God, "You are my *glory* and the one who raises my head."
> In one, the lust for *domination dominates* its princes as well as the nations it enslaves;
> in the other, those placed in authority and those subject to them serve each other in love, the rulers by their counsel, the subjects by their obedience.
> One loves its own *power* in its *powerful* men;
> the other says to its God, I will love you, God my strength.[63]

Augustine uses the distinction between God's glory and human self-glory, expressed in domination and power over others, as the main means to illumine and clarify the contrast between the two loves. The right love is a love in which God's glory is the norm and measure. In a less famous parallel text, Augustine formulates the same contrast in terms of common good and private good, an aspect implicit in the political effect of the two loves as origins of two cities.

62. Augustine, *Confessiones* 1.1.
63. Augustine, *De civitate dei* 14.28; emphasis added.

> These two loves,
> one of them holy,
>   the other impure;
> one *social*,
>   the other *private*;
> one looking after the *common* good for the sake of the society on high,
>   the other because of its *arrogant domination*
>   reducing even what is *common* to its own *power* . . .
> have existed already in the angels, one in the good angels, the other in the bad,
> and have distinguished the two cities founded in the human race.[64]

The difference between the two loves, according to Augustine, is that one is a love for the private good and the other a love for the common good. Rome orders its vast dominion to itself as an individual empire, that is, to itself as a quasi-individual that subjugates peoples for its own private good, common though it may be for the Romans or at least their leaders, and in some measure for the states that are subjugated as they share in the *pax Romana* and rule by law. The genuine common good, by contrast, constitutes "the society on high." To love this common good as a common good is to be part of the city of God. Love of God to the glory of God is the love of God as a common good. Augustine's understanding of the fall confirms this point: at its very core, the fall is a fall from love for a common good to love for a private good.

> It is not possible to doubt that the contrary appetites among angels did not arise from different natures and beginnings, since God, the good author and Creator, created both but from their wills and desires, when some remained constant in the good that is common to all, which is God himself, and in his eternity, truth and love, while others, delighted *by their own power as if they were their own good to themselves*, slipped from the superior common good of all, which is the blessedness of all, to their own good. . . . [65]
>
> That carnal or animal sense brings a tempting suggestion for self-enjoyment, that is, for enjoying something as one's very own private good and not as a public and common good which is what the unchangeable good is; then it speaks as the serpent addressed the woman.[66]
>
> Once he has contempt for the divine will, man cannot even use himself except destructively, and in this way he learns the difference between clinging to the good that is common to all and delighting in his own.[67]

64. Augustine, *De Genesi ad litteram* 11.15; emphasis added.
65. Augustine, *De civitate dei* 12.1; emphasis added.
66. Augustine, *De trinitate* 12.12.17.
67. Augustine, *De civitate dei* 13.21.

This explanation of the two loves is often repeated by Thomas, as in the following argument for the vow of poverty in the religious state.

> Concern for one's own wealth belongs to private love, by which someone loves himself temporally; but concern for the common things belongs to love (*caritas*), which does not seek its own (1 Corinthians 13:6). Since the religious state is ordered to the perfection of love, which is completed by "love of God to the contempt of self," it is repugnant to the perfection of the religious state to have something of one's own.[68]

Love receives its nature from its specifying object, which is most of all the common good. To be perfect in love is to love the object of love in its commonness. The road offered by religious life is clear. It removes disordered love of self by removing private goods, above all by removing private property. Contrary to Luther, Augustine interprets the statement "Love does not seek its own" (1 Corinthians 13:6) in these terms. "Love, about which it is written that it does not seek its own" (1 Corinthians 13:6), is understood in this way: it places the common before the private, not the private before the common.[69] Thomas takes up this line of reasoning.

> As Augustine says in his rule, "love does not seek its own" (1 Corinthians 13:6) is understood in this way: it places the common before the private. For the common good is always more lovable to everyone than the good that is [exclusively] his own, just as to a part the good of the whole is more lovable than its own partial good.[70]

The moral and political norm "Don't seek your own good! Place the common good first!" can easily have the appearance of prescribing a bitter medicine that must be taken for some sweet result to be attained after it, distinct from it. In fact, the common good itself is more lovable for the person than the private good. Thomas shows the reason why this is so. In comparison with the common good, each person who shares in it is like a part. Every part loves the good of the whole more than its partial good.

When one sets Augustine's two explanations of the two loves (the glorification of God and love for the common good) side by side, a question arises. What is the connection between love for God's glory and love for the common good in its commonness? That there must be a connection is clear. According to one text, the love that builds the heavenly city is love of God's glory; according to the other, that same city-building love is love of the common good as common.

68. Thomas, *Summa* II-II, q. 188, a. 7, corp.
69. Augustine, *Epistola* 211.
70. Thomas, *Summa* I, q. 26, a. 4, ad 3.

There must be an element of glorification deeply inscribed in the attainment of a happiness that consists in a common good as opposed to a private good.

The commonness of the common good deeply shapes the lived experience of personal subjectivity. At the high point of his account of the common good, De Koninck begins a discussion on the primacy of the common good in the beatific vision by raising the question why God created many persons to share in this vision.[71] God wants to communicate his goodness more richly, he argues. His self-communication to only one person would not meet the greatness of his design. God's primary intention, therefore, is his self-manifestation to the entire city composed of many persons. This does not mean that the city becomes a quasi-individual that has its own act of vision or an individual conceived as a conglomerate of the personal good of each. God is the end of each person but of each person as the common good. He does not become a common good by the mere fact that there are many persons who share in him. He is the common good because of the infinite communicability, superabundance, and incommensurability of his goodness. Even if there were only one created person, God would remain a common good, infinitely more communicable, superabundant, and incommensurable with this one created person.

To unfold this truth, De Koninck turns to an image of the common good in Thomas's commentary on the words of Jesus about the many dwelling places in Father's house (John 14:2).

> [The Lord] says, "In my Father's house are many dwelling places" (14:2). The house of any one is that in which he dwells, and so the house of God is that in which God dwells. Now God dwells in his saints, "You, Lord, are in us" (Jer 14:9).[72]

Each created person, as Thomas goes on to say, is only one chamber. The Father's house is not a private residence. It is the city of God. The whole house is greater than the individual chambers. The greatness of God can be manifested more fully, if it is manifested to the many persons who make up the city. All persons who are parts of this house know that it is better that God is present in the whole house, in all the saints, than only in one.

The commonness of the good in the beatific vision imprints its mark on the very nature of the happiness reached by each person. Created persons cannot be united with this common good without loving it in its commonness. They cannot will it *for themselves* as *their own happiness* in a limited, self-referential

71. See Charles De Koninck, "In Defense of St. Thomas: A Reply to Fr. Eschmann's Attack on the Primacy of the Common Good," *Aquinas Review* 4 (1997): 170–348, at 303–8.

72. Thomas, *Super Ioannem* 14, lect. 1, no. 1853.

fashion but can only love it and rejoice in it according to itself, that is, in its superabundance and incommensurability beyond the entire city and secondarily according to its communicability to that city.

Love for the whole city of God—and, within it, of each neighbor—necessarily springs from the love of God as a common good. It cannot come as a surprise, therefore, that Thomas describes love as a political virtue, the virtue of a citizen of the heavenly Jerusalem, echoing Augustine's *social love* (*amor socialis*).

> The philosopher says in Book 8 of the Politics that to be a good political [person] one must love the good of the city. Now when someone is admitted to participation in the good of some city and becomes a citizen of that city, he must have certain virtues to do what a citizen must do and to love the good of the city.
>
> In the same way, when a man is admitted by divine grace to participating in heavenly beatitude, which consists in the vision and enjoyment of God, he becomes, as it were, a citizen and member of that blessed society which is called the heavenly Jerusalem, according to Ephesians 2:19: "You are citizens with the saints and members of the household of God." A person who is in this way counted as part of the heavenly city must have certain freely given virtues which are the infused virtues.
>
> The right exercise of these virtues requires a love of the common good that belongs to the whole society, which is the divine good as the object of beatitude.[73]

Happiness as Glorification

Thomas sees two ways of understanding, "In my Father's house there are many dwelling places."

> The Father's house is not only the one in which he dwells but also he himself, because he is in Himself. And in this house he gathers us.
>
> That God is the house is clear in 2 Corinthians 5:1: "We have a house from God, not made by hands, eternal in the heavens." And this is the house of glory, which is God himself. "A throne of the height of your glory from the beginning is the place of our sanctification" (Jeremiah 17:12).
>
> One dwells in this place, that is, in God, by will and affection through the enjoyment of love, "He who remains in love remains in God and God in him" (1 John 4:16); and by understanding through the knowledge of truth, "Sanctify them in the truth" (John 17:17).
>
> In this house, therefore, that is, in the glory which is God himself, there

73. Thomas, *De virtutibus*, q. 2, a. 2, corp.

> are many dwelling places, that is, diverse participations of his blessedness, because the one who will know more will have a greater place. The diverse participations of divine knowledge and enjoyment are the diverse dwelling places.[74]

In this house, he gathers us. In hac domo nos colligit. This gathering of many into the unity of one house, of one true city, is not horizontal, rooted in the immediate relation of created persons with each other. It is a gathering into the unity of the house in which all dwell, "in this house, that is, the glory which is God himself" *in hac ergo domo, idest in gloria, quae deus est*. The unity of the city arises because the happiness of all persons lies in attaining one and the same good as a common good.[75]

An important word in Thomas's description of the Father's house in the second sense is *glory*. Thomas uses it three times: this is the house of glory; a throne of the height of your glory from the beginning; this house, that is, the glory that is God himself. The choice of *glory* as a keyword is justified in a commentary on John. The manifestation of glory is the effect of the incarnation to which John draws attention already in the prologue. "And the Word became flesh and pitched his tent among us and we have seen his glory" (John 1:14). If by pitching his tent (ἐσκήνωσεν) among us the *Logos* shows his face in the form of glory, the same must be true in the fulfillment when we see him where he dwells in his Father's house. The house is a house filled with glory. God as he dwells within himself is the glory that fills the house.

Glory, particularly in the phrase "the throne of the height of your glory from the beginning," seems to be connected with the fullness of the divine goodness that remains superabundantly and incommensurably greater above every individual person and the entire city that participates in it. In this perspective, one can understand how the two accounts Augustine gives of the two loves are connected: "One glories in itself, the other in God." Illa in se ipsa, haec in domino gloriatur.[76] "One is social, the other private." Alter socialis, alter privatus.[77] The happiness that consists in union with the common good necessarily carries within itself an element of glorification. It contains the recognition of God in his infinitely communicable, superabundant, and incommensurable glory. In the heavenly Jerusalem, "the twenty-four elders fall before the one who is seated on the throne and worship the one who lives forever and ever; they cast their crowns before the throne, singing, You are worthy, our Lord and God, to receive

74. Thomas, *Super Ioannem* 14, lect. 1, no. 1853.
75. See De Koninck, "Defense of St. Thomas," 308.
76. Augustine, *De civitate dei* 14.28.
77. Augustine, *De Genesi ad litteram* 11.15.

glory and honor and power" (Revelation 4:10–11). This liturgical act of glorification is the immediate response to the superabundance of the divine goodness.

Such glorification is not merely a separate activity carried out in specific liturgical acts, but it is an essential aspect of happiness in the city of God. The commonness of the common good reached in the beatific vision gives its own form to happiness also in its subjective, experiential aspect in each person. The blessed, De Koninck argues, would not see God if they did not see his goodness as incomprehensible and infinite. They see that God's dwelling in the house that is the heavenly Jerusalem is greater than his dwelling in each person individually. They make the divine perspective their own, and it forms their love accordingly. One can call the following text *personalistic* as Wojtyła uses that word because it pays attention to the way the commonness of the common good is reflected in the conscious experience of the person.

> In seeing God, Peter sees what is greater than anything which could be his proper good for he knows that he is only Peter; he sees that God is infinitely more communicable than He is to Peter himself, and it is this infinity of goodness Peter loves, because he loves God in Himself and in that bounty which, of its very nature is diffusive of itself.... And if there be also John to share the vision, Peter cannot fail to rejoice, because the superabundance of the divine good is his joy. And if the share of John be greater than his own, Peter will again rejoice, for the prime measure of their happiness is neither Peter nor John but the immeasurable liberality of the divine good.[78]

The essential ordering of human reason (*logos*) to the common good offers at least one explanation of the principle formulated by St. Irenaeus. "The glory of God is man alive and the life of man is the vision of God." Gloria enim Dei vivens homo, vita autem hominis visio Dei.[79] "This is the glory of man, to persevere and stay in the service of God." Haec enim gloria hominis, perseverare ac permanere in Dei servitute.[80] The happiness of the person in the heavenly Jerusalem contains glorification as one of its essential ingredients. It is a happiness achieved only in self-transcendence into a glory that is infinitely communicable, superabundant, and incommensurable—a common good. Even if there were only one created person in the universe, the object of happiness would remain a common good. In the gift of happiness, the person would be brought into a house that exceeds any creature. "A throne of the height of your glory from the beginning."

Because God is the common good par excellence, my happiness cannot be

78. De Koninck, "Defense of Thomas," 305–6.

79. Irenaeus, *Adversus haereses* 4.20.7.

80. Irenaeus, *Adversus haereses* 4.14.1.

my happiness in a self-referential manner that reduces all the goodness that motivates me to something merely good for me. Granted, happiness, in the sense of the attainment of God as the supreme good by knowledge and love, is a supremely personal activity, a supremely personal good. Each person's acts of knowing and loving belong to that person alone and cannot be the acts of any other person. The life of vision and loving union is the happiness of each person personally, each eternally distinct from all others. Each person is eternally loved by God in his or her unrepeatable individuality; each is ordered as an unrepeatable person to the personal end of blessedness. The persons who make up the new city of Jerusalem are not dissolved into a corporate subject that then becomes the true subject of happiness, a subject that can no longer be personal—an impossible idea. Each person personally sees and loves God. "Each person is made for Him; no person is made for the other persons. He is not the good of a collectivist community."[81]

Nevertheless, God, considered as the object of happiness, transcends all human measures. He is essentially and necessarily a common good that can never become the personal or private good of any creature. Happiness, understood as the life of which one can say simply and definitively "It is lived well, it is good," is deeply marked by the commonness of this common good. It is a happiness in which human beings do not order God to themselves but themselves to God. Blessedness does not have the character of ultimate self-affirmation out of oneself alone but of serving God's glory. It is a gift of self in answer to God's gift of himself as the common good. Thomas continues after the text quoted above on love as a political virtue:

> Now one can love the good of a city in two ways: in one way to possess it, in another that it might be preserved. If someone loves the good of a city to have and own it, he is not a good political [person], because in this way even a tyrant loves the good of a city, to dominate it, which is to love oneself more than the city. He wants this good for himself, not for the city.
>
> But to love the good of the city that it might be kept and defended, this is truly to love the city and this makes a person a good political person, so much so that some expose themselves to the danger of death and neglect their private good to preserve or increase the good of the city.
>
> In the same way, to love the good that is participated by the blessed, to love it so as to have or possess it, does not establish the right relation between a person and blessedness, because even evil people want this good.
>
> But to love that good according to itself, that it may remain and be shared out and that nothing be done against this good, this gives to a person the right

81. De Koninck, "Defense of St. Thomas," 303.

> relation to that society of the blessed. And this is love (*caritas*) which loves God for his sake and the neighbors, who are capable of blessedness, as oneself.[82]

Rational nature (*logos*), as Thomas understands it, reaches its own perfection in the radical self-gift of the created person for the sake of the common good par excellence, God himself. Its moral perfection consists in loving God according to his own superabundant goodness and communicability, which exceeds all participation by creatures. It consists of devotion to the intention that God may remain and be shared, and that nothing may be done against his will. It has, for this reason, the character of a service performed to the glory of God. A creature can receive the gift of God himself only in such a disposition. Glorification of God is the inner form of happiness. On this basis one can understand Irenaeus's two theses as deeply connected. "The glory of God is man alive and the life of man is the vision of God."[83] "This is the glory of man, to keep on and remain in the service of God."[84]

82. Thomas, *De virtutibus*, 2.2, corp.
83. Irenaeus, *Adversus haereses* 4.20.7.
84. Irenaeus, *Adversus haereses* 4.14.1.

PART II

The Breadth of Reason in John Paul

CHAPTER 1

Wojtyła's Trinitarian Personalism of Self-Gift

1. The Conciliar Event

While St. John of the Cross stands at the beginning of Wojtyła's theological and philosophical thought, Vatican II is the center around which this thought came to revolve.[1] Wojtyła sees Vatican II as an event, not only as a series of texts.[2] According to Rocco Buttiglione, Wojtyła saw the heart of the event in the recognition of religious liberty in *Dignitatis humanae.*

> The heart of the conciliar event is the acknowledgment of freedom of conscience as a natural and inalienable right of the human person.... The question of freedom of conscience is not at all a limited or special question, even one endowed with a very high importance. What is at stake here is the whole relationship between Christianity and modernity and between the philosophy of being and the philosophy of consciousness....
>
> The integration of the philosophy of being and the philosophy of consciousness into a complete anthropology of the person seems to be ... the only way to recognize in depth the novelty of the conciliar teaching and at the same time its solid anchor hold in the tradition (which is not the same as traditionalism).... By bringing these two strands of philosophy together, Wojtyła

1. Citations of Wojtyła's book on Vatican II in this chapter, given in the text rather than the footnotes, refer to SR = *Sources of Renewal.* Karol Wojtyła, *Sources of Renewal: The Implementation of the Second Vatican Council* (San Francisco: Harper & Row, 1980).

2. In this respect, his understanding of Vatican II resembles that of the Bologna School as presented in Giuseppe Alberigo and Joseph A. Komonchak, eds., *History of Vatican II,* 5 vols. (Maryknoll, NY: Orbis, 1995). What precisely the event was and how it is related to the texts—on these questions there are different judgments.

> produces a new synthesis in which modern elements and traditional elements are harmoniously fused.... At the same time, the contrast between modernity and Christianity disappears.[3]

Wojtyła's interest in the question of the freedom of religion was undoubtedly strong. The Nazi and Soviet occupying forces violated Poland's freedom with overwhelming power, as did the Soviet-installed Polish government. Five of Wojtyła's twenty-three contributions to the Council deal with this subject. Buttiglione states his thesis under the heading "Philosophical Significance of the Council." He would probably agree that the heart of the conciliar event as Wojtyła experienced it must be connected with the central mysteries of faith. Locating it in the natural right to the freedom of conscience would be a narrow philosophical focus, focused even more narrowly on political philosophy, and again more narrowly on a politically liberal vision (in the European sense of *liberal* epitomized by Kant), that is, a conservative political vision in the American sense of *conservative*.

Wojtyła did study the philosophers of consciousness (Descartes, Kant, Scheler). His writings show an intense interest in understanding consciously lived experience. Without a doubt, reading Scheler was helpful for him. Yet the philosophers of consciousness are not his primary source. The primary source is John of the Cross's spousal poetry and theology. Wojtyła immersed himself in the *Doctor Mysticus* before he studied the philosophers of consciousness. Descartes was born in 1596, John of the Cross half a century earlier, in 1544. Balthasar points out that, already a generation before Descartes, John of the Cross takes "the modern turn toward the personal, the experiential the psychological" suited to the renewal of Catholic religious life after the Reformation.[4] In the philosophers of consciousness, by contrast, the turn to the subject is rooted in the Baconian-Cartesian program of power over nature, as Kenneth Schmitz points out.

> Around the sixteenth century, nature came to be viewed more and more externally as an object set over against the mind, and scientific inquiry posited the ideal of a neutered objectivity. There can be no doubt that the nominalism of the late medieval period helped to shape the background to this shift, while the shift itself occurred under the hegemony of the science of mechanics, or rather of the philosophy of mechanics extrapolated from mechanics....
>
> The interiority of being, already recognized and present in traditional metaphysics, came to be excluded from the external world, which was then

3. Rocco Buttiglione, *Karol Wojtyla: The Thought of the Man Who Became Pope John Paul II* (Grand Rapids, MI: Eerdmans, 1997), 177–84.

4. Balthasar, *Herrlichkeit*, 2/2:466; *Glory*, 3:106.

> handed over to the ideal of neutered objectivity. The short gain was in precision. But the human interiority, the human subject now understood as subjectivity, was turned back upon itself.[5]

The program of power led to a dualism between extended things, which make up the machine of the material cosmos, and thinking things, the inner world of conscious experience.

> This, then, is the genesis of the modern sense of subject as subjectivity. We might say that subjectivity is the self-defense by which consciousness fends off a world either hostile to its inhabitation or at least without companionate room for it, even while consciousness subverts the integrity of that world by its imperious demands. The modern shift gave to the human subject an absolute status precisely in its character qua consciousness; for human consciousness not only sets its own terms but the terms for reality itself.[6]

The absolute status of consciousness is characteristic of Descartes, Kant, and Scheler, not of John of the Cross or Wojtyła. In his turn toward the subject, Wojtyła draws on a source that sprang up authentically from within the Catholic Tradition. He reads Vatican II as concerned with the lived experience of personal subjectivity shaped by faith and love.

What, then, is the heart of the conciliar event according to Wojtyła? He sees it expressed in *Dei verbum* 5.

> "The obedience of faith" (Romans 13:26; cf. Romans 1:5, 1:2; Corinthians 10:5–6) is to be given to God who reveals, an obedience by which man commits himself as a whole (*se totum*) freely to God, offering the full submission of intellect and will to God who reveals.

In a reflection on the implementation of Vatican II three decades after the publication of *Sources of Renewal*, St. John Paul II explains how he sees *Dei verbum* 5 as related to the heart of the conciliar event.

> With the Council, the Church first had an experience of faith, as she abandoned herself to God without reserve, as one who trusts and is certain of being loved. It is precisely this act of abandonment to God which stands out from an objective examination of the Acts. Anyone who wished to approach the Council without considering this interpretive key would be unable to penetrate its depths. Only from the perspective of faith can we see the Council event as a gift whose still hidden wealth we must know how to mine.[7]

5. Kenneth L. Schmitz, *At the Center of the Human Drama: The Philosophical Anthropology of Karol Wojtyla/Pope John Paul II* (Washington, DC: Catholic University of America Press, 1993), 131–32.

6. Schmitz, *Center of the Human Drama*, 135–36.

7. John Paul II, *Address to the Conference on the Implementation of Vatican II*, Vatican City, February 27, 2000.

2. Part I: Conciliar Initiation

Wojtyła's book *Sources of Renewal* sketches an implementation of Vatican II that follows the original guiding question of Vatican II, *Ecclesia, quid dicis de te ipsa*? "Church, what do you say about yourself?" (SR 420) "The people of God" is the Council's answer, Wojtyła claims (SR 112–54). It is "an ecclesiological Council, which was concerned especially with the truth concerning the Church" (SR 39).

The way both the question and the answer, "people of God," must be understood, Wojtyła adds, is pastoral. How can the Church grow in her awareness and life as the people of God? Although the question is in the first place a question about the Church, the growth of the Church's awareness takes place in the lives of its members, in their personal lived experience. For this reason, the question, "Church, what do you say about yourself?" is closely linked to the question, "What does it *mean* to be a believer, a Catholic and a member of the Church?" (SR 17 and 420). The word *mean* pinpoints the aspect of personal awareness, interiority, and subjectivity, the focus of attention in St. John of the Cross.

Wojtyła uses the concept of "enriching faith" to express a growth in the awareness of faith. The early ecumenical councils *enriched* the Church's faith in large measure by doctrinal definitions that unfold the implicit content of baptismal faith or sharpen its contours. The addition of "*homoousios* with the Father" to the creed at Nicaea in AD 325 is an is example of this form of enrichment. Although he sees this form also in Vatican II, Wojtyła focuses primarily on another form of enrichment; namely, *receiving that faith more richly in consciously lived experience so as to be transformed by it* (see SR 420).

The structure of *Sources of Renewal* directly serves to unfold this meaning of *enrichment*. Part I of the book discusses two concepts, *consciousness of faith* and *attitude of faith*, to reach a clearer grasp of the *enrichment of faith. Consciousness* highlights the theoretical or cognitive side of faith. *Attitude* focuses on the existential or moral side of faith, especially its close relation to love (see SR 205). Part II of the book discusses the formation of the believer's *consciousness* of faith, part III the *attitude* of faith, the living relationship with God.

Part I has four chapters.

Chapter 1: The Council addresses the question, "Church what do you say about yourself?" understood in a pastoral manner as, "What does it mean to be a member of the Church?," by calling for an enrichment of faith. Enrichment means receiving the faith in the depth of one's lived experience of personal interiority.

Chapter 2: Faith is a supernatural gift, but it implies human cooperation.

What the Council calls for is a conscious, responsible, and courageous faith. *Dignitatis humanae* is to be understood as part of this call.

Chapter 3: Dialogue with those whose convictions differ from the Catholic faith promotes the enrichment of faith, provided the dialogue is truthful and faithful; truthful in not glossing over the opposition between different points of view, and faithful in holding on to God's revelation.

Chapter 4: The Church is the subject of this enrichment of faith. Its subjective consciousness of itself unfolds in two dialogues, vertical and horizontal, which together constitute the dialogue of salvation. The Church is also an object of faith. Integration is the key element of enrichment in relation to the object of faith, both in seeing the Church in the context of all the mysteries of faith and in reading the Council in the light of the Tradition and vice versa.

Let us look at these four chapters in more detail.

Chapter 1: Faith has its origin in God. It is "the fruit of a unique encounter" with God as he reveals himself (SR 19). Benedict XVI writes in continuity with his predecessor, "Being Christian is not the result of an ethical choice or a lofty idea but the encounter with an event, a person, which gives life a new horizon and a decisive direction."[8] Wojtyła quotes *Dei verbum* to document this understanding of faith.

> "The obedience of faith" (Romans 13:26; cf. Romans 1:5, 1:2; 2 Corinthians 10:5–6) is to be given to God who reveals, an obedience by which man commits his whole self (*se totum*) freely to God, offering the full submission of intellect and will to God who reveals. (*Dei verbum* 5)

Chapter 2: This response to God who reveals himself, Wojtyła adds, is an act of "self-abandonment" to God. In this self-abandonment, one not only accepts the truth of particular propositions but also becomes aware of one's own *vocation* and the "meaning of [one's] existence." The enrichment of faith consists in this self-abandonment to God. As such a self-abandonment, faith "relates to man's whole personal structure and spiritual dynamism" (SR 20).

To highlight the person's participation in the enrichment of faith by such complete self-abandonment, Wojtyła quotes *Dignitatis humanae*. The declaration, he claims, shows above all that the encounter with God is a personal encounter that takes place in the interior depth of the person.

8. Benedict XVI, *Deus caritas est* 1.

> Man's participation in this encounter with God, which is what faith consists in, is a fully personal one. The Declaration on Religious Freedom points this out, while developing the ideas of the Constitution on Divine Revelation concerning the subject of faith, that is, man as the subject of an encounter with God who reveals himself. These ideas point to the human depth which distinguishes man as a person and which is implied by faith; they thus concern the dimension of the human person which, in conscious faith, is manifested in all its fullness. It is from this point of view of the personal subject that the possibility and need for an enrichment of faith must also be considered. (SR 22)

One can recognize in this reading of *Dignitatis humanae* Wojtyła's characteristic emphasis, on the lived experience of the person, on interiority and subjectivity, beginning with his dissertation on John of the Cross. What he places in the foreground is not the right to religious freedom but the full personal responsibility of faith as a free self-abandonment in obedience to God who reveals. He sees the declaration as a call for a more "conscious Catholicism" that must be developed "with greater courage and also greater responsibility" (SR 22).

The right to religious freedom springs from the duty to seek the truth and from the consequent call to abandon oneself in the obedience of faith to God's revelation. "Everybody has the duty and consequently the right to seek the truth in religious matters." This right can be considered *ad extra*, or "in relation to secular authorities," and *ad intra*, that is, "in relation to believers and to the Church" (*Dignitatis humanae* 3). When it is considered *ad intra*, it is above all a call for the enrichment of faith, for a more fully conscious and responsible self-abandonment in obedience to God.

It is instructive to compare Wojtyła with Kant. According to Kant, rights and freedoms are rooted in the personal dignity of man as an autonomous moral agent. Human dignity consists in the autonomous power of the person to legislate for himself and all rational beings in accord with the universal form of the imperative "Do this," without regard to any good or evil encountered in experience. According to Wojtyła, the right to the freedom of religion is also connected with the dignity of the person, but a dignity understood as rooted in the obligation of seeking the truth and the consequent obligation of abandoning oneself consciously and responsibly in the obedience of faith to God who reveals.

From Kant's point of view, to affirm human dignity in Wojtyła's sense is to deny human dignity altogether because it implies an extreme form of heteronomy, of sonship in relation to the Father. From Wojtyła's point of view, Kant's understanding of human dignity as autonomy denies the true basis of human dignity.

Chapter 3: At the beginning of chapter 3, Wojtyła returns to what he takes to be the main question of Vatican II: "What does it mean to be a believing member of the Church?" He shows that because it means having faith and striving for the enrichment of faith, it also means a respectful dialogue with those whose views differ from that faith, including atheists. Again, he quotes *Dignitatis humanae*.

> The search for truth ... must be carried out in a manner that is appropriate to the dignity of the person and his social nature, namely, by free inquiry with the help of teaching and instruction, communication and dialogue. (*Dignitatis humanae* 3)

In the perspective from which Wojtyła discusses it in chapter 3, dialogue primarily serves the enrichment of faith in the believer.

> Here ... it is shown what a "dialogue" can and should mean as a way of enriching faith. It creates a mature faith which keeps extreme contrasts before its eyes and requires of itself the fullest consistency [i.e., faithfulness to the truth] (SR 33).

Chapter 4: "Church, what do you say about yourself?" (SR 36). This question is addressed to the Church as a subject, not only as an object of faith. It is addressed to the Church as composed of individual personal subjects who together give the response of faith to the word of God.

This common response of faith, which is "the mind of the Church," is tied to two dialogues, the vertical dialogue with God and the horizontal dialogue with human beings. These two dialogues are related "inasmuch as the spiritual link and the possibility of dialogue are instituted by a ray of that 'light which enlightens every man' [John 1:9]" (SR 36). The Church is a sign and safeguard of this light of the Word, of the transcendent dimension of every human person. For this reason, dialogue in the horizontal dimension "is not a departure from the vertical dimension, as it is sometimes thought to be: it is an effort which accompanies the profession and witness of the whole Church and every Catholic" (SR 37). Both dialogues, which in their unity constitute "the dialogue of salvation" (St. Paul VI), are essential aspects of the Church's consciousness of herself.

The Church, which is in this way a subject of faith, is also an object of faith. In the Creed, the profession of faith in the Church comes after the profession of the mysteries of the Trinity and Incarnation and must continually be integrated with these mysteries (see SR 37–38). Integration also concerns the Magisterium of the past and of the present. Wojtyła proposes a hermeneutics of continuity.

> Integration ... expresses itself ... in such a way that on the one hand we can rediscover and, as it were, re-read the Magisterium of the last Council in the whole previous Magisterium of the Church, while on the other we can rediscover and re-read the whole preceding Magisterium in that of the last Council. (SR 40)

3. Part II: Consciousness

Wojtyła presents the formation of the believer's consciousness proposed by the Council in five steps. They correspond to the five chapters of part II (chapter titles abbreviated):

1. Creation
2. Trinity and Salvation
3. Christ and Redemption
4. The People of God
5. History and the End

Chapter 1 attends to the order of creation by unfolding the first article of the Creed, which expresses faith in the Creator; the other four chapters turn to the order of redemption and salvation.

Chapter 2 lays down the theological basis of the order of salvation and redemption, God's own Trinitarian life made accessible as definitive salvation to human beings.

Chapter 3 speaks about how God shares this life with human beings through Christ, the Redeemer.

Chapters 4 and 5 draw the consequences for the Church's self-understanding in her essential nature (chap. 4) and her life in history (chap. 5).

Chapter 1: Creation

"Church, what do you say about yourself?" The Church's self-consciousness is conditioned by faith in creation. "In what way does Vatican II enrich our faith in this respect?" (SR 45). It does so by reaffirming faith in creation, including the capacity of reason to arrive by its own powers at a knowledge of God from creation. It does so more extensively in *Gaudium et spes* by reflecting about the presence of the Church in the world (SR 49–51).

> Due to the work of creation, the consciousness of the Church is in a sense also consciousness of the world, and conversely awareness of the world, being permeated by the truth concerning creation and the Creator, becomes awareness of the Church at its very foundation, on which we shall continue to build.
>
> It seems, indeed, that the enrichment of faith that is the gift of Vatican II does not so much proceed from awareness of the creation to the truths subsequently proclaimed in the Creed but rather begins with those truths and proceeds to awareness of the creation, which it thus provides with a richer context of faith. (SR 52)

Chapter 2: Trinity and Salvation

The Council, as Wojtyła reads it, does not see awareness of creation only as a philosophical truth, only as a preamble of faith. It sees it in the context of the whole creed primarily in light of the Trinity and the communication of Trinitarian life by Christ. It connects the Church's consciousness of herself with awareness of the inner life of God as the Trinity. Salvation consists in coming to share in the life of the divine persons.

> Through the Son, the Word of God made flesh, they [i.e., human beings] have access in the Holy Spirit to the Father and become sharers in the divine nature, that is in the Godhead itself. The work of salvation signifies a particular union with God, or rather a communion which is mysterious and at the same time profoundly real. (SR 54)

The consciousness of the Church is closely bound up with consciousness of this salvation, which in turn flows from faith in the Trinity. "Awareness of salvation is … the true response to the mystery of the most holy Trinity. This truth of faith … constitutes, we may say, the acme of the Church's consciousness" (SR 55).

If the main question of the Council is, "Church, what do you say about yourself?" understood in a pastoral manner as equivalent to the question, "What does it mean to be a member of the Church?—if its main question is thus the question of the enrichment of faith, of a fuller reception of faith in the interiority and subjectivity of the person—the Council's answer is that the high point of the Church's consciousness consists in awareness of the saving truth of the Trinity. "God wishes to save man by means of Himself, offering him a share in his own divine being" (SR 58).

Vatican II expresses this Trinitarian self-awareness of the Church in the *definition* of the Church given at the beginning of *Lumen gentium*. "The Church in Christ is as a sacrament, that is, a sign and instrument of union with God and of the unity of the whole human race" (SR 59). This definition, Wojtyła adds immediately after quoting it, is "the starting-point of the main road towards the enrichment of faith." The Church is a sacrament of union in the degree to which the missions of the Son and the Holy Spirit allow human beings to share in the union of divine persons.

At this point in the argument, Wojtyła asks a fundamental question: "Why are the missions of the divine persons addressed to him [man], and why do these in particular constitute the profoundest divine mystery of the Church?" (SR 60) The centrality of this question can hardly be overestimated. There is nothing deeper and more form giving for the whole of Christian life, and therefore for the whole of theology, than this: "the profoundest divine mystery of the Church." The question goes to the very heart of the Council's teaching.

Vatican II, Wojtyła claims, answers this question with "a new emphasis" in *Gaudium et spes* 24. The Church compares the revealed truth concerning God and the revealed truth concerning man, and finds in this comparison her own mission and consciousness. The comparison brings to light a link between the exemplar in which the fullness of life is found and our imitation or participation in this exemplar, the image of the Trinity.

> Indeed, the Lord Jesus,
> when he prays to the Father,
> "that all may be one . . . as we are one" (John 17:21–22),
> thus offering vistas closed to human reason,
> indicates a certain likeness between the union of the divine Persons
> and the union of God's sons in Truth and Love.
> This likeness shows that man,
> who is the only creature on earth God willed for itself,
> cannot fully find himself except through a sincere gift of self. (cf. Luke 17:33)

Wojtyła brings out the new emphasis on the Trinitarian exemplar of communion contained in *Gaudium et spes* 22 and 24 as follows.

> Man's resemblance to God finds its basis, as it were, in the mystery of the most holy Trinity. Man resembles God not only because of the spiritual nature of his immortal soul but also by reason of his social nature, if by this we understand the fact that he "cannot fully realize himself except in an act of pure self-giving." In this way, "union in Truth and Love" is the ultimate expression of the community of individuals. This union merits the name of communion (*communio*), which signifies more than community (*communitas*). The Latin word *communio* denotes a relationship between persons that is proper to them alone; and it indicates the good that they do to one another, giving and receiving within that mutual relationship. (SR 61)

Here lies the heart of the Council, the starting point of the road toward the enrichment of faith. The communion of persons in the Trinity is the source in which Christian life participates. It is therefore also the exemplar that Christian life imitates. This is what a maturing faith must increasingly become aware of. The core of the enrichment of faith is expressed in *Gaudium et spes* 22 and 24 in conformity with Sanjuanist personalism.

In concluding the chapter, Wojtyła points out that the Council's new emphasis on Trinitarian exemplarity is deeply rooted in the Tradition.

> Against this broad background we may perhaps more easily grasp the meaning of the sentence [a quote from Cyprian] in which Vatican II summed up its view of the vital link between the Church and the Trinity. "The Church is a people brought into unity from the unity of the Father, the Son and the Holy Spirit" (*Lumen gentium* 4). This thought was expressed by Fathers of the Church such as Cyprian, Augustine and John Damascene, and is now endorsed and corroborated by the Council. In the light of our analysis, we can see more clearly how to understand the "unification" of the people of God through the Trinitarian unity of God himself. (SR 64–65)

This emphasis on the Trinitarian understanding of Vatican II's teaching on the "people of God" is confirmed by the retreat Cardinal Wojtyła preached for St. Paul VI in 1976, two years before his own election as pope. At a high point of the retreat, the beginning of the seventh talk, he says,

> Let us turn our thoughts to God who is gift and the source of all giving. The Fathers of the second Vatican Council were convinced that the complex reality of the Church cannot be adequately expressed in societal terms alone, even when the society constituted by the Church is called the "people of God."
>
> In order properly to describe this reality and appreciate its underlying significance it is necessary to return to the dimension of mystery, that is to the dimension of the most Holy Trinity. That is why the Constitution *Lumen gentium* starts with an introductory account of the divine economy of salvation, which ultimately is a Trinitarian economy (cf. *Lumen gentium*, nn. 2–4)....
>
> Love, an uncreated gift, is part of the inner mystery of God and is the very nucleus of Theology.[9]

The understanding of the inner mystery of God as "Love, an uncreated gift" is only implicit in the Trinitarian theology of Vatican II. It can be unfolded from *Gaudium et spes* 22, the revelation of the mystery of the Father reveals man to himself, and *Gaudium et spes* 24, the likeness between the union of divine persons and the union of human persons shows that man can only find himself through a sincere gift of self. Gift must be found in the Trinity itself if the likeness is to hold. It is found in the Father, from whom the first uncreated gift proceeds in the generation of the Son.

Chapter 3: Christ and Redemption

If the high point of the Church's self-consciousness is its awareness of the Trinity as the exemplar of communion and the source of salvation, the "pivot"

9. Karol Wojtyla, *Sign of Contradiction: Retreat Preached for Paul VI* (New York: Seabury, 1979), 53 and 55.

> around which this consciousness turns is Christ, the Redeemer. Christ is the way on which faith is enriched. (SR 66–67)

The Council expresses the Church's consciousness of redemption in two complementary ways in its two principal documents. *Gaudium et spes* discusses redemption as a reality constantly directed *to the world. Lumen gentium* discusses redemption as a reality permanently at work *in the Church.* Wojtyła dedicates a section of chapter 3 to each of these perspectives.

The section on *Gaudium et spes* places a special emphasis on paragraph 22, particularly on the sentence "Christ, the final Adam, in the very revelation of the mystery of the Father and his love, fully shows man to man himself and makes his highest calling clear."

> Here Vatican II offers a great contribution to the enrichment of faith from the point of view of consciousness of redemption. This central Christian reality is presented to man in such a way that, following the expression of *Gaudium et spes*, we can perceive a specific kind of anthropocentrism emerging through the Christocentrism which the Constitution reflects so clearly....
>
> We seem here to have reached a key point of the Council's thought. The revelation of the mystery of the Father and his love in Jesus Christ reveals man to man, and gives the ultimate answer to the question, "What is man?" (*Gaudium et spes* 22). This answer cannot be separated from the problem of man's vocation: man accepts his identity by accepting that vocation and making it a reality. (SR 75)

If *Gaudium et spes* 24 points to the core of the enrichment of faith, *Gaudium et spes* 22 unfolds this core in an anthropological direction. The enrichment of faith proposed by Vatican II is anthropocentric, centered on man, because it is Christocentric, centered on Christ ("Christ, the final Adam, shows man to man himself"), because it is theocentric, centered on the Trinity ("by the revelation of the Father and his love").

Kant also took an anthropocentric turn, completing the beginning of such a turn in Descartes, by reducing the three pillars of religion and morality (the freedom of the will, the immortality of the soul, and the existence of God) to mere data of human consciousness in the form of practical reason. The anthropocentric direction of Vatican II, as Wojtyła reads it, is the opposite. The absolute center of all meaning lies in the inner life of the Trinity. This inner life is made accessible in Christ, God made man. For this reason, the man Jesus Christ stands at the center of the Council's attention.

Chapter 4: People of God

Wojtyła follows the Council in placing a special emphasis on the concept "people of God." He is careful to guard this concept against one-sided reduction to sociological categories. He turns to two other concepts to avoid this reduction: *bride of Christ* and *body of Christ*. "The two analogies complement each other and are in a sense intertwined. They both indicate the supreme degree of union between Christ and the Church" (SR 88). Both analogies are important for the Church's self-consciousness as a consciousness of redemption.

> Meditating in the spirit of Vatican II on redemption as a reality continuously present in the Church and maintaining it in being, we must also have in mind the link between the Mystical Body of Christ and the people of God. The Church is at the same time both one and the other.
>
> In *Lumen gentium* the picture of the Church as the people of God is perhaps the more prominent. But in the Council's teaching as a whole we find sufficient reason to affirm that the people of God is also the Mystical Body of Christ and to throw light on this identity.
>
> It is the reality of redemption that helps us to do so. The consciousness of redemption is logically prior to the consciousness of the people of God: this will appear more clearly when we come to talk of the latter. (SR 91)

At the beginning of chapter 4, Wojtyła returns to Cyprian's definition of the Church as "a people brought into unity from the unity of the Father, the Son, and the Holy Spirit" (*Lumen gentium* 4) and calls it "the keystone of the whole construction of *Lumen gentium*" (SR 112). He then points out that the communal and the personal element are "profoundly intertwined" in the consciousness of the Church as the people of God.

> In the teaching of Vatican II we must therefore perceive the clear connection between the reality of the people of God and man's vocation as a person, which is at the same time a vocation to communal life. For, "man, who is the only creature on earth God willed for itself, cannot fully find himself except through a sincere gift of self" (*Gaudium et spes* 24). This statement indicates the nature of man's person and the uniqueness of his relationship to God. (SR 114)

Gaudium et spes 24 appears thus once again at an important point of Wojtyła's reading of Vatican II. It explains how the communal and the personal element are intertwined in the enrichment of faith proposed by Vatican II.

On the basis laid in these opening paragraphs, Wojtyła proceeds in four sections to unfold the self-awareness of the Church as the people of God: (1) the individual person's vocation in the community; (2) the consciousness of the

Church as the people of God *ad intra* and *ad extra*; (3) *communio* as the link that unites the Church as the people of God; and (4) *koinonia* and *diakonia* (communion and service), the hierarchical order of the Church.

Section 1 argues that the basis of the self-awareness of the Church as the people of God is the dignity of the person, understood as flowing from man's rational nature and from the supernatural vocation of each person to a life of communion with God, a vocation addressed to man by virtue of redemption.

> The reality of redemption thus constitutes the Church, as we tried to show in the previous Chapter. This reality unites individuals in a community in such a way that "members render one another mutual service in the measure of the different gifts bestowed on each" (*Gaudium et spes* 32).... The Church is more than a community (*communitas*)—it possesses the nature of a communion (*communio*) in which, by means of mutual services, in different ways and in various relationships, that "sincere giving of himself" takes place in which "man fully finds himself" (*Gaudium et spes* 24). Thus conceived, *communio* constitutes their common and reciprocal membership in the Mystical Body of Christ....
>
> The reality of the Mystical Body indicates and announces to all men, each of whom is called to his own proper dignity, the discovery and fulfillment of themselves by means of the sincere gift of self to others. Since this gift is made to a multitude, it imparts a character of "communion" to it. (SR 120)

Wojtyła sees the concept of *communio* as central in the Church's self-awareness as the people of God. Genuine *communio* involves a *gift of self* to the community, service *for the sake of the common good*. This recourse to *Gaudium et spes* 24 implies the Trinitarian exemplar, the likeness between the union of divine persons and the union of human persons. Wojtyła makes the connection explicit.

> As faith advances, it [i.e., the self-awareness of the Church as the people of God] will always have in view, as its ultimate reality, the *communio personarum* of God himself in the Trinity of persons. As *Gaudium et spes* 24 suggests, it is Jesus who has shown us that there is "a certain likeness between the union of the divine Persons and the union of God's sons in Truth and Love." (SR 121)

In Section 3, which discusses *communio* as the link uniting the people of God, Wojtyła defines *communio* in more detail.

> If we want to follow the main thread of the Council's thought, all that it says concerning the hierarchy, the laity and the religious orders in the Church should be re-read in the light of the reality of *communio* for the community of the people of God. "For the members of the people of God are called upon

> to share their goods, and the words of the apostle apply also to each of the Churches, 'according to the gift that each has received, administer it to one another as good stewards of the manifold grace of God' (1 Pt 5:10)" (*Lumen gentium* 13).
>
> Thus we have the *communio ecclesiarum* [communion of churches] and the *communio munerum* [the communion of gifts, tasks or offices] and, through these, the *communio personarum* [communion of persons]. Such is the image of the Church presented by the Council. The type of union and unity that is proper to the community of the Church as people of God essentially determines the nature of that community. The Church as people of God, by reason of its most basic premises and its communal nature, is oriented towards the likeness there ought to be between "the union of the sons of God in Truth and Love" [*Gaudium et spes* 24] and the essentially divine unity of the divine persons, in *communione Sanctissimae Trinitatis*. (SR 137–38)

The point could not be clearer or more lapidary. "Church, what do you say about yourself?" Increased awareness of the mystery of Trinitarian communion in accord with *Gaudium et spes* 24—this is what allows a correct growth of the believer's consciousness of the Church as the people of God.

> The Council devotes much attention to making the faithful conscious of *communio* as the link binding together the community of the people of God. Thus it appears that the internal development and renewal of the Church in the spirit of Vatican II depends to a very great extent on the authentic deepening of faith in the Church as a community whose essential bond is that of *communio*. (SR 144)

4. Part III: Attitude

The Concept of Attitude

At the beginning of part III, Wojtyła returns to *Dei verbum* 5, which he had quoted in part I to focus on the enrichment of faith proposed by Vatican II.

> The obedience of faith is to be given to God who reveals, an obedience by which man commits himself as a whole (*se totum ... committit*) freely to God, offering the full submission of intellect and will to God who reveals. (*Dei verbum* 5)

The phrase "commits himself as a whole" is suggestive for Wojtyła. It echoes the spirituality of self-gift characteristic of St. John of the Cross. Wojtyła underlines this self-commitment as "the most vital and vivifying point" in the enrichment of faith intended by Vatican II.

> [Faith] ... cannot consist merely of knowledge or the content of consciousness. Essential to faith is an attitude of self-commitment to God—a continual readiness to perform the fundamental "action" which corresponds to the reality of revelation, and all other acts which spring from it and to which it gives their proper character. In speaking of the attitude of self-commitment to God, Vatican II touches on the most vital and vivifying point relating to the whole process of the enrichment of faith. (SR 206)

It is not difficult to see in this reading of *Dei verbum* 5 Wojtyła's familiar emphasis on faith as a means of union with God in agreement with John of the Cross, and on love as a total gift of self, *totus tuus* (*Gaudium et spes* 24). Twenty-eight years later, in 2000, St. John Paul expressed the same understanding of the nucleus of the conciliar event in a text already quoted above.

> With the Council, the Church first had an experience of faith, as she abandoned herself to God without reserve, as one who trusts and is certain of being loved. It is precisely this act of abandonment to God which stands out from an objective examination of the Acts. Anyone who wished to approach the Council without considering this interpretive key would be unable to penetrate its depths. Only from the perspective of faith can we see the Council event as a gift whose still hidden wealth we must know how to mine.[10]

What Wojtyła calls the *attitude* of the believer lies precisely in this self-gift to God.

> The word ["attitude"] is usually applied analogically and denotes various relationships which are endorsed as a whole by the individual consciousness. In simple terms we may say that an attitude is an active relationship but is not yet action. It follows upon cognition and increased awareness but is something new and different from these. It involves "taking up a position" and being ready to act in accordance with it. In a sense it represents what Thomistic psychology would call habitus and even habitus operativus, but the two are not identical. (SR 205)

The main difference between attitude and virtue is that virtue is a lasting disposition for action. It is present even when the person is asleep. Attitude, by contrast, implies acts of knowing and loving. Scheler's concept of *ethos* is similar to Wojtyła's concept of attitude, but one can also hear an echo of St. John of the Cross and his understanding of a living faith that provides a deep source for Christian experience.

An example may clarify this concept of attitude. The conjugal attitude of hus-

10. John Paul II, *Address to the Conference on the Implementation of Vatican II*, Vatican City, February 27, 2000.

band and wife is their conscious belonging to each other in love. It is a position taken up by both and endorsed by both as the permanent fruit of their receiving or taking each other ("I take you ... to be my husband/wife") and therefore giving themselves in the marriage vow and its consummation in sexual union. This conscious position of the two in relation to each other is expressed in the acts of daily life that spring from it. It is "the most vital and vivifying point" in a marriage from which alone an enrichment of married life can spring. In a similar way, the enrichment of faith proposed by Vatican II flows from "the most vital and vivifying point" that is the permanent fruit of the believer's "obedience of faith in which he freely commits himself as a whole to God" (*Dei verbum* 5).

The Order of the Argument

The order of the argument in part III is complex. Wojtyła focuses on the conscious attitude a Christian takes in relation to God, to himself, to the Church, and to the world. It consists in committing oneself as a whole to God by the obedience of faith. The root of this commitment is the gift of sonship. "You did not receive a spirit of slavery to fall back into fear, but you have received a spirit of adoption, by which we cry, 'Abba! Father!'" (Romans 8:15). "Because you are sons, God has sent the Spirit of his Son into our hearts, crying, 'Abba! Father!'" (Galatians 4:6).

In chapters 1 and 2, Wojtyła discusses the root, the gift of sonship and mission. In chapter 3, he shows how the root unfolds itself in the three offices of Christ, priest, prophet, and king. In chapters 4 and 5, he shows that living out the three offices implies two complementary attitudes, the ecumenical and the apostolic attitude. In the concluding chapter 6, he points to the common goal of all attitudes, building up the Church.

Chapter 1: Mission and Testimony as the Basis of the Enrichment of Faith. The first way in which this grace of sonship expresses itself is the attitude of mission and testimony in accord with the identity of the Son of God as the Word of God sent into the world. Mission and testimony are not simply moral demands but expressions of the very being of a Christian.

Chapter 2: Analysis of the Attitude of Participation. The participation of Christians in the being of the Son by the power of the Spirit implies a participation in the three *munera* (gifts, offices, missions, tasks, duties) of Christ: priest, prophet, and king. The most fundamental of these is the *munus* of priest, which consists in relating all things to God. This fundamental *munus* finds expression in the theoretical order as the *munus* of prophet and in the practical order as the *munus* of king.

Chapter 3: The Attitude of Human Identity and Christian Responsibility. In the grace of adoptive sonship exercised in the three *munera* of Christ, Christians do not alienate themselves (as the Marxist critique of religion would have it) but grasp their own deepest identity in solidarity with other human beings and responsibility for human life.

Chapter 4: The Ecumenical Attitude. The grace of adopted sonship, which is consciously grasped in the attitude of human identity and responsibility, expresses itself in a pair of mutually complementary attitudes. The first member of the pair is the ecumenical attitude, in which Christians affirm the dignity of every human being and affirm all that is good and true in the positions of those who are not Catholics.

Chapter 5: The Apostolic Attitude. The second member of the pair is the apostolic attitude. Affirming the dignity and freedom of all human beings as well as the good that lies in their positions does not imply indifference but is necessarily connected with the apostolate. The apostolate is rooted in Jesus's identity as the Son and Word of God sent into the world.

Chapter 6: Building Up the Church as a Community. The final chapter points to the goal of all attitudes; namely, building up the Church as a true *communio* of persons that participates in the Trinitarian communion of persons. Among the requirements for achieving this goal, Wojtyła mentions two attitudes, both rooted in the missionary mandate given by Christ to the Church. One of them is the Church's missionary spirit, which is the direct object of this mandate; the other, in accord with the Council's Declaration on Religious Freedom, is the Church's right to freedom in carrying out the missionary mandate.

There is a helpful passage in which Wojtyła speaks about the link between all six chapters in light of *Dei verbum* 5.

> In the Constitution on Divine Revelation (*Dei verbum*) the Council indicates the basic character of the attitude with which man expresses his response to God's self-revelation, namely a "free commitment of his entire self" (*Dei verbum* 5). This we shall therefore take as fundamental to the rest of our study. Although we shall not attempt to analyze it in detail, it will always be present to our minds in our consideration of particular attitudes to be discovered in the teaching of Vatican II, even if it is expressed and realized in different ways. The process of the enrichment of faith, which is part of the Council's plan and towards which the implementation of the Council should be directed, is in the last analysis comprised in the development and strengthening of that attitude. (SR 205)

According to this statement, the whole of part III with all its six chapters, including the concluding section on *Dignitatis humanae* and its teaching on religious freedom, must be understood in terms of the one "most vital and vivifying point relating to the whole process of the enrichment of faith"; namely, the complete self-commitment of the believer to God (SR 206). Again, this is the heart of the conciliar event.

Chapter 1: Mission and Testimony

Wojtyła begins his argument in a Johannine key with the *mission of the divine persons*. God reveals himself, saves the world, and constitutes his people by sending his Son and Spirit. "Thus in the Council's teaching, awareness of salvation is closely linked with the revelation of the Holy Trinity" (SR 206). Because the missions of the Son and the Spirit are the origin of the Church as the people of God, they impart to them a Trinitarian form.

> The Church originated and continues to originate from that divine mission: this gives a "missionary" character to its whole existence, and at the same time basically determines the attitude of every Christian. (SR 206)

The movement of the argument is clear. The saving act in which God constitutes the Church as the people of God is the sending of the Son and the Holy Spirit. When these saving missions constitute the Church, they impart to her their own Trinitarian form; namely, mission. "As you have sent me into the world, so also have I sent them into the world" (John 17:18). "As the Father has sent me, so also am I sending you [plural]" (John 20:21). Because the Church has a Trinitarian form, the individual person must also have that same form as his or her fundamental *attitude*. Immediately, at the beginning of the argument of part III of *Sources of Renewal*, we find ourselves deeply inside the Trinitarian teaching on which Wojtyła reflected already in his doctoral dissertation on John of the Cross. By giving himself to the self-revealing God in the obedience of faith (*Dei verbum* 5), the believer grasps his own identity as a person who has come to share in the person of the Son in relation to the Father. Mission is thus not in the first place an attitude of moral commitment in response to a moral duty but a way of being, rooted in the person of Jesus as the Son of God.

> This [mission] does not initially imply a function or institution but defines the nature of the Church and indicates its close link with the mystery of the divine Trinity through the mission of the Persons: the Son who comes to us from the Father in the Holy Spirit and the Spirit who proceeds from the Father and the Son. In this sense and on the basis of this reality, we can and should define the attitude of every human being in the Church. (SR 207)

The priority of the Church over the individual person is important to Wojtyła. He emphasizes it several times. The believer "takes part in the 'state of mission' in which all the Church continually finds itself; and each individual is a unique, unrepeatable embodiment of the salvific 'state'" (SR 207).

Mission, Wojtyła argues, is closely linked to witness or testimony. The mission of the Son corresponds to his testimony to the Father. In his trial before Pilate, the Johannine Jesus says, "For this was I begotten [or born] and for this have I come into the world, that I might bear witness to the truth" (John 18:37). Because he is born or begotten as the Father's Word, Jesus is in person the word of witness to the Father. Witnessing to the Father is not a task he assumes as imposed on him from the outside or chosen freely by him from among several possibilities. It is identical with his person as the eternal Word. Those who participate in the life of Jesus participate by necessity also in his being as the one who bears witness to the Father (see SR 207–8). In the remainder of chapter 2, Wojtyła rereads many passages of Vatican II on mission and witness as pointers toward an enrichment of faith through these Trinitarian attitudes.

Chapter 2: The Threefold Office of Christ

The mission of Jesus, and its saving power, expresses itself in his threefold *munus*. *Munus* can be translated as gift, offering, task, duty, office, or power. Those who become part of the body of Christ share in his three *munera*. Wojtyła ties them closely to mission and testimony.

> The Christian bears witness to Christ not "from outside" but on the basis of participation, in him, in his mission. In this way the reality of faith takes shape, as does the Christian testimony in which it is expressed. Faith, in all the wealth of its personal and communal characteristics, is essentially and basically a participation in the testimony of Christ. This is the testimony of God himself, to which Christ has given expression and human dimensions by his threefold office as priest, prophet and king. (SR 219)

The attitude of participation in Christ's *priestly office*—that is, his power of relating all things in this world to the Father—Wojtyła argues, is the most fundamental of the three. It is the source of the attitudes of participation in Jesus's *Munera* as prophet and as king. Within the one Eucharistic sacrifice, the Church offers itself and the world to the Father. It can do so because it shares in Jesus's priestly power to relate himself and all things as the Son to the Father. Wojtyła appeals to *Gaudium et spes* 24 to explain this point.

> This attitude in which man, through and with Christ—together with the sacrifice of the Lord's body—offers himself and the world to the Father expresses in a particularly intimate but fundamental way the existential essence of faith. For it is in faith, as the Council teaches, that man, responding to God's self-revelation, "commits his entire self to God." This commitment, contained in the very essence of faith, is realized most fully in the attitude which derives from sharing in the priesthood of Christ. This attitude, in fact, seems to endow the acts of Christian faith with their fullest existential dimension.
>
> There is thus good reason to consider participation in the priesthood of Christ and the attitude that derives therefrom, before turning to the prophetic and kingly aspects. While all these aspects indicate the orientation of the Conciliar enrichment of faith in respect of the attitudes of every Christian, it is participation in the priesthood of Christ which denotes the simplest and the most complete attitude. This contains within itself the authentic Christian relationship with God and the mystery of creation and redemption, seen in the way in which the consciousness of these mysteries is presupposed and also deepened by the Council. This attitude also expresses the vocation of the person in its existential nucleus—a vocation referred to by *Gaudium et spes* 24 in *the words to which we must constantly return, from various points of view and in different contexts:* "This likeness shows that man, who is the only creature on earth God willed for itself, cannot fully find himself except through a sincere gift of self." When man gives himself to God in this way, he rediscovers himself most fully.... It can in a sense be said that the doctrine concerning Christ's priesthood and man's share in it is at the very center of the teaching of Vatican II and contains in a certain manner all that the Council wished to say about the Church, mankind and the world. (SR 224–25)

The strength of Wojtyła's argument is clear in this text. He allows the reader to grasp what he sees as the center of the Council's thought, a center that holds in itself all that the Council has to say. If one is looking for the heart of the conciliar event, here it is. In full agreement with *Redemptor hominis* and John of the Cross, the center is the personal life of the Son in relation to the Father, opened up for human beings to participate in. The Son himself is the origin of the life of faith in us, enabling us to give ourselves to God and thereby to find ourselves. The life of faith with all its enrichment is a share in this fountain of life, a fountain opened in the Eucharist (see SR 231–43).

> Every liturgical celebration, because it is an action of Christ the Priest and of his Body, which is the Church, is a sacred action surpassing all others. No other action of the Church can equal its efficacy by the same title and to the same degree. The liturgy is the summit toward which the activity of the Church is directed; it is also the fount from which all her power flows. (*Sacrosanctum concilium* 7 and 10, quoted in SR 232–33)

Wojtyła sees the two other *munera* as springing from this source, distinguished according to *truth* and *goodness*, that is, the theoretical and the practical order. The *prophetic munus* is rooted in the person and mission of Jesus as the one who expresses the Father's truth in human language. The *sensus fidei* of the whole people of God belongs here, as does the Magisterium together with the gift of infallibility and assent to it by the whole Church (see SR 245–59).

> The Church, as the people of God, participates in that mission, and the fact that it does so is of enormous importance for the enrichment of faith, not only as regards content but also as regards attitude ... First and foremost, here comes responsibility towards the word of God entrusted to the Church. (SR 244)

The whole of Christian morality, Wojtyła goes on to argue, has a close link to the *royal munus* of Christ. The attitude of participation in the kingship of Jesus allows human beings to conquer evil and rule over themselves.

> Every Christian who conquers sin by imitating Christ achieves the royal self-dominion that is proper to human beings; by so doing he shares in the *munus regale* of Christ and helps to bring about Christ's kingdom. (SR 263)

To summarize the argument of chapters 1 and 2, the most vital and vivifying point from which an implementation of Vatican II must proceed is the total self-commitment of the believer to God. This self-commitment has the form of mission and testimony as a participation in the life of the eternal Son. It unfolds in the three *munera* of Christ. The grace of adoptive sonship, of becoming sons in the Son, stands at the root of all these attitudes.

> Christ and the Christian encounter each other intimately in the priestly, prophetic and kingly mission, and it is this participation which forms the essential characteristics of the Christian. The features in which the Christian resembles Christ are interior ones but also "missionary," since it is thanks to them that the mission of Christ lives on in mankind and in human individuals. These features constitute the reality of the people of God in and through every man and woman. They do not constitute this reality in its profoundest ontological depth, however, since this is effected solely by the grace of "adoption as sons of God." This grace is the most essential, interior and mysterious feature of resemblance to the incarnate Son of God, but after it come the features which reflect the mission of Christ. (SR 270)

Chapter 3: Identity, Solidarity, and Responsibility

Wojtyła begins chapter 3 with a critical discussion of the Marxist argument that religion leads to an alienation of human beings from themselves.

> These divine realities in their essence do not lead man away from himself: they rather enable him to enter into himself more profoundly, to discover the whole truth of his own humanity and personality, which is the opposite of "alienation." (SR 273)

The attitude of human identity consists in this discovery of the whole truth of our humanity through entering into Christ. *Gaudium et spes* 24 is present: the human person discovers itself through the sincere gift of self. Finding oneself is closely tied to solidarity with all human beings and therefore to responsibility for human life (see SR 274–309). The affirmation of all that is genuinely human is the path on which conscious identity grows. The source of all three of these attitudes is the grace of adoptive sonship.

Here we find another brief discussion of *Dignitatis humanae*. The attitudes of human identity, solidarity, and responsibility imply that one respects other persons in the exercise of their own responsibility.

> The Council's teaching sets down the fundamental postulate of responsibility for every human being. This postulate, which applies to every human being and especially to every Christian, emphasizes the dignity and vocation of the human person. This is seen particularly in the conception of man's relationship with God that is presented by the Constitution on Divine Revelation and the Declaration on Religious Freedom. (SR 293)

Wojtyła looks at *Dignitatis humanae* through the lens of *Dei verbum* 5. Respecting the religious freedom of the person is part of an attitude of identity, solidarity, and responsibility that flows from committing oneself as a whole to God.

Chapter 4: Ecumenism

Vatican II's teaching on the ecumenical attitude is rooted, Wojtyła claims, in its teaching on the attitudes of human identity, solidarity, and responsibility. A love for all that is human, heightened by awareness of the saving power of the one sent by the Father, stands behind the ecumenical attitude. Here one finds another brief discussion of *Dignitatis humanae*, documented by five quotes from the document itself.

> Thus, the ecumenical attitude is rooted in faith in the fatherhood of God embracing the universe and in the redemption of Christ, which is offered to all men without exception. The true ecumenical attitude is an expression of that faith: it springs from it and testifies to its enrichment. At the same time, it is the expression of a profound love for man and respect for his inner freedom—that "responsible freedom" which corresponds to an inward conviction concerning truth, "especially in the religious sphere," as the Council states in its Declaration on Religious Freedom. "The Vatican Council declares that the human person has a right to religious freedom.... The Council further declares that the right to religious freedom is based on the very dignity of the human person as known through the revealed word of God and by reason itself." (SR 313, quoting *Dignitatis humanae* 2)

The dignity of the human person can be known both "through the revealed word of God and by reason itself," as *Dignitatis humanae* says in the text just quoted. In the context of chapter 4, Wojtyła views it in the perspective of the revealed word of God as a dignity that flows from the call to communion with God.

Chapter 5: Apostolate

Wojtyła returns to the points he made in chapter 1 about mission and unfolds them in more detail.

> If, following the teaching of Vatican II, we agree that faith, as man's response to the God who reveals himself, is expressed as readiness to accept and assume the salvific mission, then in so doing we point to the apostolic attitude and the very root of apostolicity in the life of the Christian as it is formed by faith. (SR 330)

The chapter goes into much detail about the apostolic character of the Church as a whole, the apostolic office of bishops, and the apostolate of the laity. The governing perspective throughout is that of enriching the faith by growth in the attitude of mission as a participation in the mission of the Son (SR 330–66).

Chapter 6: Building Communion

Wojtyła's discussion of building communion is the high point of the whole book. The guiding question of Vatican II is, "Church, what do you say about yourself?" The answer is "people of God"—understood in the pastoral perspective of increasing the Church's self-consciousness and her share in the life of Jesus through the entire set of attitudes implied in a complete self-commitment to God. The natural point of arrival of the answer is building up the Church as *communio*. Here lies the goal of all attitudes. Wojtyła points to the "Eucharistic first principle" formulated by Vatican II. "No Christian community is built up which does not grow from and hinge on the celebration of the most holy Eucharist. From this, all education for community spirit must begin" (SR 369).

John Paul was to unfold this claim thirty-one years later in the encyclical *Ecclesia de Eucharistia*. The attitudes needed for building up the Church are fruits of "the most vital and vivifying point" of Christian life, a living faith in which one commits one's entire self to God, returning Christ's gift of himself in the Eucharist. Wojtyła elaborates these attitudes in much detail, with attention to the relations between bishop and priests as well as between clergy and laity (see SR 374–97).

5. The Heart of the Conciliar Event

To fill out his discussion of building communion, Wojtyła adds "two supplementary aspects of this theme"; namely, the Church's missionary character and religious freedom (SR 397). The aspect of mission is discussed already in chapters 1 and 5, but Wojtyła returns to it once more, this time paying attention to the role it plays in building up the Church. Building up the Church is a continuation of the Incarnation, which has a missionary character rooted in the sending of the Son from the Father. Mission is not an accidental appendage to the Church's life but part of the Trinitarian form of that life (see SR 408).

The second supplementary aspect of the attitudes needed for building up the Church as a community is bound up with religious freedom. The right to religious freedom, Wojtyła observes at the beginning of his argument, is a right not only of individuals but also of communities (see 408–9). In particular, it is as a right of the Church. An essential part of building up the community of the Church with a missionary impulse is the attitude of freedom in proclaiming the Gospel.

> Clearly, we are concerned here with every aspect of public life which affects the building up of the community and encourages it to develop a sense of its own mission. All we said so far about the building-up of the Church as a community presupposes this freedom. (SR 411)
>
> This community, whether on a world-wide scale or locally, needs religious freedom to carry out its proper mission. (SR 415)

Here, then, is the context of the second major discussion of *Dignitatis humanae*. Religious freedom comes into view as a right that belongs to the Church because of the missionary mandate given by Christ as a reflection of his relation to the Father. It is an integral part of the missionary attitude of Christians that completes the set of attitudes required for building up the Church as a community.

This second discussion of *Dignitatis humanae* counterbalances the first, which was concerned with individual freedom. No doubt, the text of *Dignitatis humanae* affirms the right to religious freedom as a right of individual persons owing to their rational nature. This focus on the right of the individual is clear in the document's first two paragraphs. A discussion of the freedom of the Church is found obliquely in paragraph 4 and more formally toward the end of the document, in paragraph 13.

> [*Paragraph 2: A Right of Individual Persons.*] This Vatican Council declares that the human person has a right to religious freedom. This freedom means that all men are to be immune from coercion on the part of individuals or of social groups and of any human power, in such wise that no one is to be forced to act in a manner contrary to his own beliefs, whether privately or publicly, whether alone or in association with others, within due limits. The Council further declares that the right to religious freedom has its foundation in the very dignity of the human person, as this dignity is known through the revealed Word of God and by reason itself. This right of the human person to religious freedom is to be recognized in the constitutional law whereby society is governed, and thus it is to become a civil right.
>
> [*Paragraph 4: A Right of Individual Persons When They Act in Community.*] The freedom or immunity from coercion in matters religious, which is the endowment of persons as individuals, is *also to be recognized as their right when they act in community.* Religious communities are a requirement of the social nature both of man and of religion itself. Provided the just demands of public order are observed, religious communities rightfully claim freedom in order that they may govern themselves according to their own norms.
>
> [*Paragraph 13: A Right of the Community.*] Among the things that concern the good of the Church … this certainly is preeminent, namely, *that the Church should enjoy that full measure of freedom which her care for the salvation of men requires.* This is a sacred freedom, because the only-begotten Son endowed with it the Church which he purchased with his blood. Indeed, it is so much the property of the Church that to act against it is to act against the will of God. The freedom of the Church is the fundamental principle in what concerns the relations between the Church and governments and the whole civil order.[11]

11. Emphasis added.

Wojtyła fully affirms freedom of religion as a right of individual persons (see SR 313–14). Those who limit this individual right to Christians "because error has no rights"[12] cannot appeal to Wojtyła. Yet at the end of his argument about the implementation of Vatican II, at its high point, the freedom he focuses on is the freedom of the Church, not that of the individual. It is the freedom of the Church implied by Christ's sending. "As you have sent me into the world, so I have sent them into the world" (John 17:18). It is a freedom that flows from Christ's initiative, not simply from individual human dignity.

Let us return to Buttiglione's claim that, for Wojtyła, "The heart of the conciliar event is the acknowledgment of freedom of conscience as a natural and inalienable right of the human person."[13] In *Person and Act*, according to this reading, Wojtyła builds the philosophical foundation for the heart of the Council by integrating the philosophy of being and the philosophy of consciousness into a complete anthropology "in which modern elements and traditional elements are harmoniously fused.... At the same time, the contrast between modernity and Christianity disappears."[14]

Buttiglione's interpretation has no foundation in the text. In *Sources of Renewal*, Wojtyła points to Trinitarian communion as the true heart of the Council. Individual autonomy is not the final end of human life. The final end is communion with the Triune God. Kant's anti-Trinitarian personalism of autonomy stands in extreme contrast with Wojtyła's Trinitarian personalism of self-gift summarized in *Gaudium et spes* 24.

Although one cannot deny that Kant is an authentic representative of the philosophy of consciousness, one should deny that his philosophy of consciousness, which presupposes the Baconian-Cartesian program, is the only authentic representative of modernity. "I am with you always, to the end of the age" (Matthew 28:20). In this light, one can understand Wojtyła's words about St. John of the Cross.

> In it [i.e., the dissertation on John of the Cross], I devoted special attention to an analytical discussion of the central affirmation of the *Doctor Mysticus*: Faith is the only proximate and proportionate means for communion with God.
>
> The *Doctor Mysticus* ... through his example and doctrine, helps Christians to make their faith strong with the very basic qualities of an adult faith which the Second Vatican Council asks of us. This faith is to be personal, free and convinced, embraced with one's entire being, an ecclesial faith, confessed

12. Marcel Lefebvre, *They Have Uncrowned Him: From Liberalism to Apostasy. The Conciliar Tragedy* (Kansas City, MO: Angelus Press, 1988), 172.

13. Buttiglione, *Wojtyła*, 178.

14. Buttiglione, *Wojtyła*, 184.

and celebrated in communion with the Church, a praying and adoring faith, matured through the experience of communion with God.

The presence of God and of Christ, a renewing purification under the guidance of the Spirit, and the living of an informed and adult faith—is this not in reality the heart of the teaching of John of the Cross and his message for the Church and for men and women of today? . . .

Only faith enables us to experience the salvific presence of God in Christ in the very center of life and of history. Faith alone reveals to us the meaning of the human condition and our supreme dignity as sons and daughters of God who are called to communion with Him. (John Paul, *Maestro en la fe* 2, 7, and 3)

CHAPTER 2

Kant's Anti-Trinitarian Personalism of Autonomy

1. Glory and the Critical Turn

Glory is an important theme for Kant both before and after his critical turn.[1]

Glory Before the Critical Turn

In the concluding passage of a precritical work on natural history, Kant cherishes the hope of immortality as he meditates on the glory of the stars.

> [After death] the immortal spirit will rise quickly above everything that is finite and will continue its existence in a new relation to nature as a whole that will spring from a closer union with the highest being....
>
> Indeed, when one fills one's mind with such contemplations ... gazing at the starry sky in a clear night gives a joy experienced only by noble souls. In the universal silence of nature and the rest of the senses the hidden cognitive power of the immortal spirit speaks an unnamable language and gives rise to implicit concepts which can be felt but not described....
>
> How happy is this [planet earth] that under the worthiest circumstances a way stands open to it to reach a happiness and nobility which is infinitely greater in dignity than the advantages which the most propitious arrangement

1. Citations of Kant by AK (Akademieausgabe) refer to *Kant's gesammelte Schriften*, 29 vols. (Berlin: Georg Reimer, Walter de Gruyter, 1902–2009). The *Critique of Pure Reason* is cited as B (2nd ed.) with the original pagination. Translations are based with modifications on Immanuel Kant, *Critique of Pure Reason, Critique of Practical Reason, Critique of Judgment*, trans. Werner S. Pluhar (Indianapolis: Hackett, 2002).

> of nature can reach in all corporeal beings of the world. (*Universal Natural History and Theory of the Heavens,* AK 1:367–68)

The happiness Kant speaks about in this text flows, as he puts it, from closer union with the highest being. The joy experienced by the mind in gazing at the star-studded sky is a dim anticipation of this definitive happiness. Indeed, the beauty of the sky is part of the general "glorification of the divine attributes" in nature (*UnivNatHist*, AK 1:333). When the dense fog surrounding the mysteries of nature is lifted, "the glory of the highest being breaks forth with the most living radiance" (*UnivNatHist*, AK 1:221, cf. 1:336, 1:360, 1:365). The harmony between the human person and subrational nature, which is strikingly concentrated in the beauty of the starry sky, is ensured by the divine origin of the cosmos, by the presence of God's glory in it. By its own innermost orientation, human rationality (*logos*) is ordered to the act of seeing the glory of the divine attributes.

Already at this early point in Kant's development, it is a glory that differs essentially from the glory of self-giving love revealed in the *Logos* made flesh. The God who is Love (1 John 4:8.16) has already been transformed into the deistic rational mind eulogized in Halley's Ode to Newton. It is the glory of reason in its Cartesian form, a mathematical clarity. It is light emitted by the mind of a divine mechanic who can keep his distance.

> According to the Enlightenment mentality, the world does not need God's love. The world is self-sufficient. And God, in turn, is not, above all, Love. If anything, he is Intellect, an intellect that eternally knows. No one needs his intervention in the world that exists, that is self-sufficient, that is transparent to human knowledge, that is ever freer of mysteries thanks to scientific research, that is ever more an inexhaustible mine of raw materials for man—the demigod of modern technology. This is the world that must make man happy.[2]

Kant's vision in his *Natural History* has not yet taken the full form of self-sufficiency, in which autonomy is the one true good. The divine glory itself is the object of happiness. The demigod technology, holding out the promise of a receding and ever more problematic improvement of the human condition, has not yet replaced it.

2. John Paul II, *Crossing the Threshold of Hope*, ed. Vittorio Messori (New York: A. A. Knopf, 1994), 55.

Glory after the Critical Turn

As Balthasar points out, Kant's critical turn changed his understanding of glory from divine glory to the dignity of practical reason.[3] In the concluding passage of the *Critique of Practical Reason*, the starry sky returns to serve once more as a condensed symbol of the meaning of life. Yet the message could hardly be more different. Kant sees its light no longer as the expression of a divine creative power. The true focus of glory is now the moral law, an autonomous law imposed by the human will on itself. Subrational nature is not in harmony with human aspirations. As animals, human beings are virtually nothing; as moral persons, they are of infinite value.

> Two things fill the mind with ever new and increasing admiration and reverence, the more frequently and persistently one's meditation deals with them: the starry sky above me and the moral law within me. . . . The first sight, of a countless multitude of worlds, annihilates, as it were, my importance as an animal creature that, after having for a short time been provided (one does not know how) with vital force, must give back again to the planet (a mere dot in the universe) the matter from which it came. The second sight, on the contrary, elevates infinitely my worth as that of an intelligence by my personhood, in which the moral law reveals to me a life independent of animality and even of the entire world of sense. (*Critique of Practical Reason*, AK 5:161–62)

The moral perfection of the person "independent of animality and even of the entire world of sense"—this is now the supreme value beyond which there is no other. All true glory is absorbed into virtue, into the individual moral dignity of the person. Kant follows the meaning of the term *happiness* in utilitarian ethics. Happiness is a state of pleasure experienced in the appeasement of inclinations. Happiness utterly pales in comparison with the moral dignity of the person. Even worse, the desire for happiness is the main threat to moral goodness. To desire happiness as the goal of life is to abandon oneself to irrational appetites. One must continually overcome the desire for happiness in order to fulfill one's duty. An ultimate harmony between happiness and the fulfillment brought about by God as judge is a practical postulate without theoretical value. It is a decent thought, rather than a true one.

What was the reason for this dramatic shift from the pre-critical glory of the Creator in the natural world to the postcritical glory of the dignity of the human person alienated from the natural world? As a decision of Kant's heart, the choice remains mysterious in its motives. Paul's account of paganism in its pre-Christian polytheistic form seems surprisingly applicable. "They exchanged

3. See Balthasar, *Herrlichkeit*, 3/1/2:827; *Glory*, 5:493.

the glory of the immortal God for images resembling a mortal man" (Romans 1:23). One key factor for the revolutionary change in Kant's thinking was the encounter with Hume's sensualist account of experience as irrational.

> I freely admit that it was precisely the memory of David Hume many years ago that first interrupted my dogmatic slumbers and gave an entirely different direction to my investigations in the field of speculative philosophy. (*Prolegomena to Any Future Metaphysics*, AK 4:260)

The progress of mechanistic thought seems to have played a decisive role as well. Kant was convinced that with Bacon, Descartes, and especially Newton, natural science had found the road of definitive progress that established Cartesian mechanistic determinism beyond any shadow of doubt as the valid way of understanding nature. He defends this progress against the sensualist irrationalism of Hume (*Critique of Pure Reason*, B VII-XIV). The motto of the *Critique of Pure Reason* is a passage from the preface to Bacon's *Instauratio magna*, in which Bacon formulates the program of the technological reformation of knowledge (see *Critique of Pure Reason*, B II).

The success of a mechanistic natural science has disturbing consequences, in Kant's judgment, especially for morality and religion. If the universe is a self-contained material mechanism explained entirely by deterministic laws of nature without recourse to a divine being, the three main pillars of morality and religion are called into question: the freedom of the will, the immortality of the soul, and the existence of God (see *Critique of Pure Reason*, B XXIX-XXXI). While Kant is deeply committed to defending natural science, he is even more deeply committed to the preservation of morality and religion on these three pillars. He is particularly concerned about the defects of the ethical system that arose from the Baconian-Cartesian program; namely, utilitarianism. Utilitarianism, he argues, abandons the holiness of the law in favor of mere calculation of an outcome that serves irrational inclinations, that is, the desire for happiness. It destroys persons precisely as persons by turning them into mere means in the great machine.

The problem arises necessarily from the very root of the Baconian-Cartesian program, the primacy of will and power over *logos*. Wojtyła experienced this primacy of power in its Marxist form, in which the Baconian-Cartesian program is worked out to a radical conclusion. In a letter to Henri de Lubac, Wojtyła writes,

> I devote my very rare free moments to a work that is close to my heart and devoted to the metaphysical sense and mystery of the PERSON. It seems to me that the debate today is being played on that level. *The evil of our times*

> consists in the first place in a kind of degradation, indeed in a pulverization of the fundamental uniqueness of each human person. This evil is even much more of the metaphysical order than of the moral order. To this disintegration, planned at times by atheistic ideologies, we must oppose, rather than sterile polemics, a kind of "recapitulation" of the inviolable mystery of the person. I firmly believe that the truths attacked compel with more urgency the recognition of those who are often the involuntary victims of it.[4]

Wojtyła's way of addressing the problem of mechanism and utilitarianism differs from Kant's. Kant addresses it by a critique of knowledge. "I had to do away with knowledge to make room for faith" (*Critique of Pure Reason* B XXX). This solution is only possible on the premise explicitly laid down in the *Critique of Practical Reason* that practical reason has absolute priority over theoretical reason.

> One cannot in any way demand that pure practical reason be subjected to speculative reason ... because all interest is in the end practical and even the interest of speculative reason is only conditional, complete only in practical use. (*Critique of Practical Reason*, AK 5:121)

Kant's means for doing away with knowledge to make room for faith is the critical turn spelled out in the *Critique of Pure Reason*. He compares this critical turn to the Copernican revolution. Just as Copernicus resolved problems in astronomy by abandoning the rotation of the sun around the earth and substituting for it the daily rotation of the earth on its own axis and its annual rotation around the sun, so Kant reaches his goal of saving morality and faith by abandoning the notion of truth as the conformity of the mind to things and substituting for it the conformity of things to the mind (see *Critique of Pure Reason*, B XVI-XVII).

The Critical Turn

It is difficult to conceive Kant's critical turn clearly in all its radicalism. At its core, the turn consists in a reduction of *being* to *object of consciousness*. Things in themselves are an exception, but Kant insists that we cannot know them, though he has much to say about them nevertheless. A view that asserts the primacy of the human mind and simultaneously avoids the reduction of being to consciousness would involve attributing full creative power to the human mind. The conformity of things to the human mind in this view would be a conformi-

4. The letter is published in Henri de Lubac, *At the Service of the Church: Henri de Lubac Reflects on the Circumstances That Occasioned His Writings* (San Francisco: Ignatius, 1989), 171–72.

ty with human *creative art* rather than theoretical reason. Kant holds that the objects of sense experience are in conformity with our *theoretical or speculative reason*. Thomas offers a helpful metaphysical map to clarify Kant's meaning.

> A thing is related differently to the practical intellect and to the speculative intellect. The practical intellect causes things, which is why it is the measure of the things that come to be through it. But the speculative intellect, which receives from things, is in some way moved by things themselves and so things measure it . . . but they are measured by the divine intellect, in which all things exist, just as all artifacts exist in the artisan's mind.
>
> In this way the divine intellect measures without being measured.
>
> Natural things measure and are measured.
>
> Our intellect is measured and does not measure natural things, only artifacts.
>
> A natural thing is thus set between two intellects.[5]

The metaphysical map Thomas offers in this text helps to clarify where the decisive point of Kant's critical turn lies. It lies in the thesis that natural beings are measured by the human *speculative intellect*, not by a divine practical intellect. This thesis is equivalent to the thesis that (apart from "things in themselves") being is reducible to an object of consciousness, that is, reducible to an appearance, a *phenomenon* in the strict sense of a given for consciousness (see *Critique of Pure Reason*, B 294–315).

In the *Critique of Pure Reason*, Kant often repeats a formula drawn from common human experience and distinctly worked out on the level of philosophical reflection by Socrates, Plato, and Aristotle. Truth is the correspondence or agreement of cognition with its object (see *Critique of Pure Reason*, B 82, 115, 236, 296, 350, 670, 848). Yet the measure in this correspondence, according to Kant, lies ultimately in the mind. This is not to say that the human mind can constitute at whim and will whatever it pleases. If this were the case, there could be no false statements because objects would infallibly be measured by our thought and correspond to our statements. Kant does have a certain limited place for the account of truth as a correspondence in which objects measure the human mind. Yet objects measure the mind only as phenomena in the mind. For example, "Matter is extended" is a true statement inasmuch as it corresponds to the manner in which all material objects appear or are given; namely, as existing in space. Yet these material objects do not have being apart from being objects of consciousness. They are constituted according to fixed laws that lie in our reason before all particular experience.

In this light it becomes clearer what Kant means by saying, "I had to do away

5. Thomas, *De veritate*, q. 1, a. 2, corp.

with knowledge to make room for faith" (*Critique of Pure Reason*, B XXX). Kant does away with knowledge in two ways: first, the material cosmos as studied by Newton is only an object of consciousness; second, theoretical reason is limited to physics and has no competence whatsoever to address the questions of freedom, immortality, and God. Practical reason with its practical faith has room to settle peacefully in the protected area. Newton's mechanistic and deterministic natural science is the one and only competent rational account of the world of "external" nature, but as a theoretical science it is completely limited to the realm of appearances based on received sense data. Practical reason can unfold in the sphere of pure thought, the sphere of the person as such.

Again, it is difficult to conceive Kant's account of morality and religion in all its radicalism. That the will is free, that the soul is destined for a future life, and that a God exists and will judge and reward those who do good—these three statements cannot be considered true (or false) on a theoretical level, that is, in the sense of corresponding or not corresponding to what is actually the case. In Kant's rational faith, we must not acknowledge the actual existence of God. It is only "as if" God existed.

> To believe in him [God] morally and practically means ... acting in a manner *as if* such a rule of the world *were* real. (*On a Recently Assumed Noble Tone in Philosophy*, AK 8:396; emphasis added)
>
> [The proof of the postulates] is not a proof of the truth of these statements seen as theoretical statements, and thus not a proof of the objective existence of the objects corresponding to them ... but one that has only subjective and practical validity, one whose instruction is sufficient to produce the effect of our acting *as if we knew* that these objects *were* real. (*Real Advances Made by Metaphysics*, AK 20:298; emphasis added)

One can compare these texts to the Lutheran doctrine of justification. Luther's God regards us *as if* we *were* just, while we remain sinners. It is perhaps an act of revenge that Kant, the secularized Lutheran, regards God *as if* he existed. Faith in God only comes into play in *praxis*, when morally good persons regulate their own conduct. Freedom, immortality, and God are morally decent thoughts.

> I shall unfailingly have faith in the existence of God and in a future life and I am sure that nothing can shake this faith, for that would overturn my moral principles themselves, which I cannot renounce without being detestable in my own eyes....
>
> No, the conviction is not a logical but a moral certainty; and because it rests on subjective bases (of the moral attitude [*Gesinnung*]), I must not even say, It is morally certain that there is a God, and so on, but I must say, I am

> morally certain, and so on. In other words, the faith in a God and in another world is so interwoven with my moral attitude that, as little as I am in danger of losing my moral attitude, so little am I worried that my faith could ever be torn from me. (*Critique of Pure Reason*, B 856–57)

Kant's faith in God (together with freedom of the will and the prospect of reward in an afterlife) can preserve its certainty without fear because it is perfectly insulated against any assault from theoretical reason. A deterministic natural science dominates the theoretical sphere and excludes God by excluding any causal influence other than the matter of the mechanical universe. This exclusion cannot in any way damage faith in God. Particularly revealing is the contrast between "It is certain" and "I am certain." "It is certain that God exists" could be understood as asserting the being of God as a theoretical conclusion based on a moral argument, for example, an argument for the existence of God from conscience as Newman develops it in his *Grammar of Assent*.

A theoretical affirmation of the being of God, however, even if based on a moral foundation, could fail to correspond to the facts. It could be refuted by science. Kant's faith is absolutely secured against such failure because it can neither correspond to being nor fail to correspond to it. Kant's God is a God without being, a God who is an object of human consciousness alone, and of human consciousness only in its practical form. The thought of God has no object. Using a term coined by analytic philosophers, one might say that, for Kant, *God* is a performative utterance, like the word *please*, which can neither correspond nor fail to correspond to some real being.

Schmitz's characterization of the form of personal subjectivity to which Wojtyła responds is most fully and radically justified at this key point of Kant's system. "The modern shift gave to the human subject an absolute status precisely in its character qua consciousness; for human consciousness not only sets its own terms but the terms for reality itself."[6] It sets the terms for freedom, immortality, and God.

2. Practical Reason

Kant's starting point in the transition from common ethical experience to his own philosophical account of practical reason is the proposition "Nothing can possibly be conceived anywhere in the world, or even out of it, which can be called good without qualification, except a good will" (*Groundwork for a Metaphysics of Morals*, AK 4:393). There is much truth in this starting point.

6. Schmitz, *Center of the Human Drama*, 135–36.

> Any [being] that has a will is called good inasmuch as it has a good will, because it is by the will that we use everything in us. This is why one does not call people good when they have a good intellect but when they have a good will.[7]

The Problem of Happiness

Goodness of the will, Kant goes on to argue, must be presupposed if any other human good is to be worth pursuing. Happiness is an unjust possession unless one is worthy of it by having a good will. One must therefore value the goodness of one's will more than the fulfillment of any inclination, and more than the fulfillment of the entire sum of inclinations, which is happiness (*Groundwork*, AK 4:393). The main competitor of good will in human action is therefore *inclination* (*Neigung*). A morally good will is clearest and most certain when there is a clash between duty and inclination, when devotion to duty overcomes a contrary inclination (*Critique of Practical Reason*, AK 5:87).

Will is defined by reason as opposed to sensation. "The will is a form of causality of living beings inasmuch as they are rational" (*Groundwork*, AK 4:446). Inclination, by contrast, is defined by sensation as opposed to reason. "Habitual sensitive desire is called inclination *Neigung*" (*Anthropology from a Pragmatic Point of View*, AK 7:251). Inclination is the form of *appetitio* proper to the realm of empirical experience. Empirical experience, however, is irrational, individual, accidental, and chaotic. Kant's agreement with Hume's view of experience turns out to be decisive in his moral philosophy. Wojtyła explains.

> The conception of ethical experience that we find in the works of Immanuel Kant . . . is a consequence of his position on experience. Experience, both inner and outer, supplies us with presentations that only represent phenomena of reality. For this reason, the object of our empirical knowledge has only individual and accidental character. Since science can only concern itself with universal and necessary objects, one must not seek its basis in experience but in the thinking subject.[8]

The goal of inclination is invariably pleasure, *Lust* (see *Metaphysics of Morals*, AK 6:212). The sum of all inclinations aims at the sum of all pleasures. "All human beings have already of themselves the most powerful and most deep-seated inclination to happiness, because precisely in this idea all inclinations are united as in their sum" (*Groundwork*, AK 4:399).

7. Thomas, *Summa*, I, q. 5, a. 4, ad 3.

8. Karol Wojtyła, "Akt und Erlebnis [Act and Experience]," in *Lubliner Vorlesungen*, ed. Juliusz Stroynowski (Stuttgart-Degerloch: Seewald, 1981), 27–104, at 54.

What may happen to give pleasure to one individual at a given time varies, however, because pleasure belongs to the empirical order. "About no object presented to us, whatever it may be, can one know *a priori* whether it will be connected with pleasure or pain or whether it will be indifferent" (*Critique of Practical Reason*, AK 5:21). The utterly irrational character of inclination and pleasure is the reason why happiness, the aggregate sum of pleasures, cannot be defined. The pursuit of happiness has no definite end (*Critique of Practical Reason*, AK 5:25). There is, objectively speaking, nothing good or bad in the Newtonian cosmos of matter. It is a purely neutral, mathematical cosmos. There is nothing in it that explains pleasure as an effect of the goodness of being.

Take sexual pleasure as an example. If the act of generating new life were good in itself, then it would be intelligible that we take pleasure in it. On its objective side, however, sex is simply the movement of atoms following mathematical laws of motion. The pleasure we take in it is a mere empirical fact of irrational inner experience without any objective foundation.

Given what he thinks about inclination, it is not surprising that Kant is no friend of happiness. The desire for happiness is an orientation of irrational self-love.

> A rational being's consciousness of the agreeableness of life uninterruptedly accompanying his whole existence is happiness, and the principle of making this the supreme determining ground of choice is the principle of self-love. (*Critique of Practical Reason*, AK 5:22)
>
> All inclinations together—they may be brought into a tolerable system in which case their satisfaction is called "one's own happiness"—are self-seeking (*solipsismus*). This self-seeking is either that of self-love, of a benevolence towards oneself that surpasses everything (*philautia*) or that of delight in oneself (*arrogantia*). (*Critique of Practical Reason*, AK 5:73)
>
> The principle of one's own happiness, which some set up as the highest principle of morality, forms a curious contrast with the commandment ["Love God above all and your neighbor as yourself"]. The commandment would have to be rephrased: Love yourself above all, and God as well as your neighbor for the sake of yourself. (*Critique of Practical Reason*, AK 5:83)

Since pleasure is irrational, a life of happiness is not worth living. Its value sinks below zero.

> The value (*Werth*) which life has for us when that value is judged only according to what one enjoys (*genießt*) (only according to the natural purpose of the sum of all inclinations, namely, happiness) is easy to determine. *It sinks below zero.* For who would want to enter life anew under the same conditions or according to some other plan designed by himself in accord with the course of

> nature, which would mean, again, merely based on enjoyment? (*Noble Tone*, AK 5.434; emphasis added)

Particularly noteworthy is the word *enjoyment* (*Genuß*), a key term in Wojtyła's sexual ethics, as it is in Kant's. The course of nature, which aims at happiness, is a course of life that sinks below zero. One should pause to ponder this claim. The absence of a natural cosmos connatural to the person could not be clearer. Nature is below zero.

What is it, then, that makes life worth living? Kant's ranking is clear: the greatest good is a morally good will; the second highest, closely joined to the first, is being worthy of happiness; the lowest, not worth living for in itself, is happiness. There is a parallel with the military city in Plato's *Republic:* for the military class, the greatest good is a moral virtue, justice.

The Goodness of the Will

What is it that constitutes a good will? A will is good when it springs from respect or reverence (*Achtung*) for duty rather than from inclination (*Neigung*) toward some good.

> I understand at least this much about it [i.e., about reverence]: that it is an act of esteeming the value which by far exceeds everything recommended by inclination; and that the necessity of my acts out of pure respect for the practical law is what constitutes duty, to which every other motive must give way, because it is the condition of a will that is good in itself, the value of which surpasses everything. (*Groundwork*, AK 4:403)

As already the word *reverence* shows, Kant has a clear and powerful sense of the beauty and dignity of the moral law. The most famous passage was already quoted above, "Two things fill the mind with ever new and increasing admiration and reverence, the more frequently and persistently one's meditation deals with them: the starry sky above me and the moral law within me" (*Critique of Practical Reason*, AK 5:161). All other goods have their external use and price. "Character has inner value and is far beyond all price" (*Anthropology*, AK 7:292). Kant's language in praise of the moral law often has biblical overtones, including the divine attributes holiness, majesty, and glory.

> The moral law is holy and inviolable. (*Critique of Practical Reason*, AK 5:87)
>
> The moral law itself in its solemn majesty: . . . when one has once laid aside pride and has allowed reverence to have a practical influence, one cannot get enough of gazing at the glory of this law and the soul seems to raise itself in

> the measure in which it sees the holy law lofty above itself and its own fragility. (*Critique of Practical Reason*, AK 5:77)

The nobility of acting in accord with the law lies in inner conformity to the law. For this reason, if one acts in external conformity with the law but out of inclination, not out reverence for the law, one's act does not have "truly moral value" (*Groundwork*, AK 4:390 and 4:399). If one does what is right merely to be happy, not because it is right, one does not achieve moral goodness.

> The principle that we act for the sake of our own happiness is most reprehensible ... because it gives motives to morality that undermine it and annihilate its entire nobility by putting the motives for virtue together with the motives for vice in a single class [i.e., enjoyment] and simply teaches one to calculate the outcome more cleverly, thereby erasing the specific difference between virtue and vice altogether.
>
> Moral feeling ... remains closer to morality and its dignity because it at least gives virtue the honor of considering her the cause of delight and esteem and does not tell her to her face that it is not her beauty but only advantage, that binds us to her. (*Groundwork*, AK 4:442–43)

When the moral law confronts us in particular situations as the voice of duty, it has the form of a categorical imperative—"Do this!"—rather than the form of a merely hypothetical or conditional imperative—"If you wish to be happy, do this" (*Groundwork*, AK 4:414) The moral law does not suggest or propose a good; it demands *obedience* (see *Groundwork*, AK 4:432).

3. Origin of the Moral Law

How does the moral law arise? What is its claim on our obedience? Why does it bind us? In answering these questions, Kant excludes any pre-given good that motivates the will. For example, if one helps a friend in need because one loves him and is interested in his good, one acts out of inclination and interest, not out of respect for duty. Such behavior is immoral.

Self-Determination by a Universal Law

An explanation of duty in terms of a pre-given good contradicts the very nature of the will. It is the nature of the human will to be a completely self-determined power. The will does not have a natural object that moves it, as inclinations are moved by their object, pleasure. It is entirely self-moved without reference to any object.

When one compares Kant's and Thomas's accounts of the act of will, one notices an important difference. According to Kant, *causing* is the first and fundamental act of the will.

> The will is a form of *causality* of living beings inasmuch as they are rational. (*Groundwork*, AK 4:446; emphasis added)
>
> Desire (*appetitio*) is the self-determination of the power of a subject through the presentation of something future *as its effect.* (Anthrop, 7.251; emphasis added)

According to Thomas, by contrast, *love* is the first and fundamental act of the will from which every other act—for example, joy and sadness—flows. Love, in turn, has a definite object; namely, the good.[9] The difference is significant. The will, according to Kant, is an absolutely original source that does not derive its self-caused movement from anything other than itself, not only in the order of efficient cause but also in the order of final cause. It is a self-movement without good or end.

> The power of desire according to concepts, inasmuch as the ground determining it to act is found in itself, and not in an object, is called a power of doing or not doing at will. Inasmuch as it is connected with the consciousness of the power of its action to produce the object, it is called free choice (*Willkür*); when it is not so connected its act is called wish. The power of desire, whose inner grounds of determination and thus determination at will are found in the subject's reason, is called will.
>
> Will is the power of desire considered not in relation to the action (such as free choice) but rather to the ground determining choice to an action, and *it has truly no determining ground prior to itself*, but it is practical reason itself inasmuch as [practical reason] can determine free choice. (*Metaphysics of Morals*, AK 6:213; emphasis added)

According to this text, the will has two essential features. It is, first, a power of self-caused movement without any external ground or reason *as a freedom of pure indifference*, and it is, second, a rational power that works with universal concepts. Both aspects are important for understanding what is required for a good will. First, since the will is an ultimately self-moving power, its goodness must lie in the absoluteness with which it moves itself apart from anything other than itself and, most important, apart from any good or end encountered

9. Thomas, *Summa* I, q. 20, a. 1.

in experience that might move it by inclination. Second, because the will is a rational power, its goodness must lie in the universality of the imperatives by which it directs itself. Practical reason, as reason, is a power that forms universal imperatives.

When universal imperatives have validity only for oneself, they are called maxims; when they are addressed to all rational beings including oneself, they are called law. It is by legislating to itself and all rational beings in this most universal form that the will achieves self-caused movement in the fullest sense. It posits for itself and for all rational selves a universal law according to which it must act.

All appetitive movements that have a good as their motive are inclinations. They are merely empirical and therefore irrational as well as tied to the principle of self-love. What is required for the goodness of the will is a law that determines the will *a priori*, *from before* any determination by a particular inclination or good. Kant expresses these theses in concentrated form in the first three of his theorems of practical reason.

> Theorem I: All practical principles that presuppose an object (matter) of the power of desire as the grounds of determination of the will are altogether empirical and cannot provide practical laws.
>
> Theorem II: All material practical principles are as such altogether of one and the same sort and belong under the principle of self-love or one's own happiness.
>
> Theorem III: If a rational being is to think its maxims as practical universal laws, it can only think them as principles that include the determining ground of the will, not according to the matter but only according to the form. (*Critique of Practical Reason*, AK 5:21, 5:22, 5:27)

The terms *matter* and *form* as Kant uses them in these axioms should be clarified. Take the practical principle "I shall now eat." Eating is the desired good in this principle. It is the matter. The form of the principle "I shall" is its singularity, its applicability to me alone here and now. "Everyone shall eat" has the same matter but is universal in form. The goodness of the will must lie in its self-determination according to universal laws, without any other motive, that is, without good or evil. This self-determination must have the form of universal legislation without any material content, that is, without any good or evil that might motivate the will. Kant accordingly arrives at what he calls "the categorical imperative" par excellence, which must inform any act if it is to be a morally good act. He formulates it slightly differently in his *Groundwork* and in his *Critique of Practical Reason*.

> Act only according to the maxim by which you can will at the same time that it becomes a universal law. (*Groundwork*, AK 4:421)
>
> Act in such a way that at any time the maxim of your will can at the same time be valid as a principle of a universal legislation. (*Critique of Practical Reason*, AK 5:30)

This imperative fulfills the two requirements for the first principle of willing. The imperative is one of self-determination ("Act!") according to the most universal form of any imperative; namely, universal law. It has no material content, no motivation by any good such as the good expressed in the maxim "Do good and avoid evil!" It prescribes only the form of willing. Good and evil, the matter of willing, belong to the unintelligible flux of Hume's world of sensation as opposed to reason. Only moral good—that is, conformity with the categorical imperative—belongs to the order of reason. All other modes of goodness lie outside it.

How does this imperative work in the concrete? Kant gives the example of someone who is rich and enjoys all the pleasures of his wealth but is completely indifferent to the sufferings of a poor neighbor whom he could help. The rich man's maxim (i.e., the practical principle formulated, at least implicitly, by himself for himself) is: Out of self-love, I shall be indifferent to my neighbor. Now apply the categorical imperative by which this maxim is transformed into a universal law binding all rational beings (in accord with the rational nature of the will). Out of self-love, everyone shall be indifferent to his neighbor. Kant argues that a person who legislates this universal law contradicts himself, because he could easily suffer some misfortune in which he needs the sympathy and love of his neighbors. The law laid down by his will would be contrary to his own will when he needs help. Therefore the maxim cannot be converted into a universal law. Therefore it is immoral to be indifferent to a neighbor's sufferings (see *Groundwork*, AK 4:423).

In his explanation of this example, Kant focuses on the self-consistency of the will that legislates universal laws. His argument is not that one should help one's neighbor to gain the potential advantage of receiving help. This reasoning would be utilitarian and result only in a hypothetical imperative: If you want the advantage of your neighbor helping you when you need him, help him when he needs you! That would mean that one is primarily thinking about one's own happiness, which is immoral. Kant's argument focuses instead on the self-consistency of the will when it legislates a universal law. Maximal self-rule in complete independence from all other motives of action and in the most universal form of law is possible only if one does not contradict one's own will. Self-contradiction destroys complete self-rule.

> The moral and thus categorical imperative … must abstract from any object to such an extent that the object has no influence at all on the will, in order not to reduce practical reason to merely administering an interest foreign to it. [The moral imperative] must prove its own imperious dignity [*Ansehen*] as the highest legislation. For example, I must seek to make others happy not because their happiness is of concern to me (whether on the basis of inclination or some delight that influences me indirectly through my reason) but only because the maxim which excludes this happiness cannot be understood as a universal law within one and the same willing. (*Groundwork*, AK 4:441)

Autonomy as Self-Legislation

Kant clarifies a presupposition of this argument; namely, that the autonomous will is itself the author of the law.

> According to this principle, all maxims are rejected that cannot exist together with the will's own universal legislation. The will is thus not simply subjected to the law but subjected in such a way that it must also be considered as self-legislative and for this reason in the first place subjected to the law, whose author it can consider itself to be. (*Groundwork*, AK 4:431)

Kant's understanding of autonomy and heteronomy is rooted in this self-legislating character of the will. Autonomy can be defined negatively as the complete independence of the will from any motive of good or evil, that is, from any matter of desire. It can be defined positively as the absolute self-determination of the will according to the form of universal law. Heteronomy, by contrast, is the condition of a will when it is motivated by some good or evil encountered in experience (*Critique of Practical Reason*, AK 5:33–34).

It is important to have a clear grasp of these definitions. They are so radically contrary to common experience that one is tempted to dilute them, contrary to Kant's intentions. In classical Greek, a city is called heteronomous when it is dependent and lives under the law (*nomos*) of another (*heteros*) city; it is autonomous when it is independent and can live under a law that it promulgates for itself (*autos*).

For Kant, the distinction between autonomy and heteronomy does not hinge on a distinction of persons or political bodies that impose a law. It hinges instead on the two spheres found within each human person: the ultimately unintelligible sphere of sensory and emotional experience that confronts us with various goods and evils, and the sphere of pure reason prior to all experience, prior to all good and evil. I am autonomous when I will what I will without being motivated by any good or evil; that is, when I move myself according to the categorical imperative. I fall into heteronomy when I will something because it is good. In heteronomy, I degrade my will and make it a servant of my irrational desires. I reach autonomy and freedom only when my will is completely independent from the whole sphere of appearances based on received sense data.

> For, independence of the determining causes of the world of sense (an independence which reason must always claim for itself) is freedom. (*Groundwork*, AK 4:452)
>
> One can never consider a practical precept part of the practical law if it carries with it a material, and therefore empirical, condition. For the law of the pure will, [of the will] that is free, sets that will into a sphere that is wholly other than the empirical, and the necessity which it expresses can only consist in the formal conditions for the possibility of law as such. All matter of practical rules rests always on subjective conditions which provide them with no universality for rational beings, except conditional universality (in case I desire this or that, what I must then do to realize it) and they revolve entirely around the principle of one's own happiness. (*Critique of Practical Reason*, AK 5:34)

The point that autonomy is freedom from empirical conditions becomes clearer when one applies the law of autonomy in the concrete, for example, in the love of neighbor. In a text quoted above, Kant says,

> I must seek to make others happy not because their happiness is of concern to me (whether on the basis of inclination or some delight that influences me indirectly through my reason) but only because the maxim which excludes this happiness cannot be understood as a universal law within one and the same willing. (*Groundwork*, AK 4:441)

In the end, the one and only criterion of virtue for Kant is that the will determines itself universally as absolute origin of its self-rule prior to good and evil.

4. Dignity of the Person

Kant's understanding of the dignity of the person derives from autonomy in the strongest sense; namely, self-imposition of the law by each human person as true legislator. He proposes "the idea of the dignity of a rational being that obeys no law except the law that, at the same time, it gives to itself" (*Groundwork*, AK 4:434). The goodness of a will that obeys the law does not derive from its conformity to the law as a law that is wise and good but from the power of practical reason as a true and universal legislator. To be an absolute causative beginning in the form of universal self-legislation, this is the heart of human dignity. The direct opposite of human dignity therefore lies in heteronomy, that is, in doing something because it is good.

The dignity or "inner value of the person" (*Groundwork*, AK 4:394 and 454) depends strictly on autonomy, that is, on the rule of reason according to universal law. It is not, however, the person as such who is the true bearer of this inner value but its self-caused movement in the form of law. "All respect for a person is really only respect for the law (justice, and so on) of which the person offers us an example" (*Metaphysics of Morals*, AK 4:401). It is highly significant for the whole of Kant's program of defending the person against the threat of utilitarianism that the person ultimately disappears from the picture. Scheler is correct in anchoring his critique of Kant at this point. The true focus of dignity is the principle of self-caused movement. Kant pushes the voluntarism of Scotus and Ockham to a radical extreme.

Persons as Ends

In the degree to which persons have the dignity of autonomy, they are ends in themselves. "The only condition under which something can be an end (*Zweck*) in itself is when it has a value that is not merely relative, that is, a price but an inner value, that is dignity, *Würde*" (*Groundwork*, AK 4:435). Every good in the sphere of empirical experience has a merely relative value, a price, because good and evil in the sphere of experience depend on what happens to be the inclination of the subject. There is no *true* good or evil. The one truly precious thing to which everything else must be ordered, which alone has the character of an end, is the autonomy of the person.

> Concerning man (and thus every rational being in the world) as a moral being one cannot ask further, For what (*quem in finem*) does he exist? His existence has the highest purpose (*Zweck*) in itself, to which he can, as far as possible, subject the whole of nature, at least contrary to which he must not submit himself to any influence of nature.
>
> Now if the beings of the world as beings that are contingent in their existence need a highest cause that acts according to purposes (*Zwecken*), then man is the final purpose (*Endzweck*) of creation. For, without man the chain of purposes subordinate to each other would not be explained in its entirety. It is only in man, and in man only as the subject of morality, that an unconditioned legislation concerning purposes can be found, which thus enables him alone to be a final purpose to which the whole of nature is teleologically subordinated. (*Noble Tone*, AK 5:435–36)

The cosmic grandeur of Kant's vision in this text should not obscure a simple arithmetic fact. Every person is the final end of the cosmos. There are as many final ends as there are persons. Each person is truly a whole, a universe unto itself in the strongest possible sense; namely, as the final end of the entire universe. Maritain's reading of Thomas's principle "the account of part is opposed to the account of the person" ratio partis contrariatur rationi personae[10] is absolutely and completely true for Kant. The many persons, who are each of them the final end, do not come together as parts of a greater whole that has a higher end. Each is in a final and definitive sense the whole because he or she is the final end of the whole. This view can rightly be called *personalism* of the most radical kind.

Because each person is the final end of the universe, it is contrary to the dignity of human beings if one uses them as mere means.

> While man is unholy enough, the humanity in his person must be holy to him. In all of creation, everything one might want, and over which one has power can be used as a mere means. Only man himself and with him every rational creature is end in itself. For, in virtue of the autonomy of his freedom, he is the subject of the moral law, which is holy. (*Critique of Practical Reason*, AK 5:87, cf. 5:131; *Metaphysics of Morals*, AK 6:434)
>
> The practical imperative is thus the following. Act in such a way that at all times you treat human nature in your own person as well as in the person of every other human being simultaneously as a purpose, never as a mere means. (*Groundwork*, AK 4:429)

The rule that we must not use human beings as mere means is another way of formulating the categorical imperative. The categorical imperative demands that I act as the universal lawgiver in autonomy. In acting according to this imperative, I affirm my dignity as a person. I can only be consistent with myself if I also affirm the dignity of other persons.

Human Dignity and the State

If the autonomy of each person is the ultimate end of the whole universe, then, all the more so, it must be the end of the state, a mere part of the universe. Although the person is an end in itself, the state is not. It is subordinate to the individual person, to each individual person.

Civil society is constituted by a contract that Kant calls *pactum unionis civilis:* "the contract of civil union ... the contract by which a civil constitution is instituted" (*On the Common Saying, This May Be True in Theory, but It Does Not*

10. Thomas, *Super III sent.*, d. 5, q. 3, a. 2, corp.

Work in Practice, AK 8:289). The goal of this contract is to overcome the condition of nature in which every person is subject to potential violence from others. The contract creates the political condition that protects the rights of each person against the violence of others.

A possible misunderstanding must be excluded from the very beginning. Kant emphatically protests that the state must intend only the protection of the rights of its citizens against violence from others. It must not get involved in the question of their happiness. Given what Kant thinks about happiness, this restriction is readily understandable. Because happiness is a purely subjective and chaotic matter, there can be no universal law for it.

> [Law is based on] the pure *a priori* legislating reason that does not take into account any empirical aims (all of which are contained under the common name happiness), because human beings think quite differently about this aim, and that in which each wants to place his happiness differs, so that their will cannot be brought under a common principle, nor consequently under an external law that harmonizes with the freedom of each. (*True in Theory*, AK 8:290)

The Refusal of Sonship

There is a further reason why Kant excludes happiness as an end of the state, a reason connected with the dignity of autonomy.

> If a government is built on the principle of benevolence similar to that of a father towards his children, that is, a paternal government (*imperium paternale*), in which subjects are treated like children who have not yet come of age and who cannot distinguish what is truly beneficial from what is harmful for them [a government], furthermore, in which subjects are forced to be passive, to await the judgment of the head of state, how they should be happy, and his sheer benevolence, whether he actually wills them to be so: this is the greatest despotism imaginable (that is, a constitution that annuls the entire freedom of subjects and leaves them without any rights). Not a paternal, but a patriotic government (*imperium non paternale, sed patrioticum*) is the only government conceivable for human beings who are capable of rights. (*True in Theory*, AK 8:290–91)

The superlative in this text is astounding and deserves close attention. What is the *greatest* despotism imaginable? Is it a slave state in which the head of state does not intend the good of citizens but rules them as mere instruments for his private ends without any concern for their good? No! A state under the benevolence of a father who *does* intend the good of the citizens, this is *superlative* despotism. Fatherhood is the supreme form of despotism; sonship the supreme form of slavery.

This astounding superlative can be understood as implied in Kant's view about autonomy. If the state were ordered to the happiness of its citizens, it would cast its citizens in a role of dependence, that is, of sonship under a benevolent father. Because sonship implies dependence, it is incompatible with human dignity as a dignity that resides in autonomy. Filial submission to a benevolent father destroys autonomy even more radically than slavish submission to a violent master because it implies an interior submission, not only external conformity in actions as in the case of slavery. Sonship and slavery are both contrary to human dignity, but sonship is worse because it destroys the very heart of dignity, the autonomy of the will. A slave's heart can be his own; a true son's heart belongs to his father. The direct clash between this aspect of Kant's philosophy and the Lord's Prayer is remarkable. If the Our Father is the paradigmatic prayer of Christians, then the destruction of human dignity—that is, the heteronomy of sonship—lies at the very heart of Christianity. One can see in this light why Kant's personalism is governed by an anti-Trinitarian thrust.

Civil Law and the Common Good

It follows quite logically, according to Kant, that the laws of a state must not be concerned in any way with the happiness of citizens.

> The concept of an external law as such proceeds entirely from the concept of freedom in the external relation among human beings and has nothing at all to do with the aim which all human beings naturally have (namely, the desire for happiness) nor does it have anything to do with proposing the means by which happiness is to be attained. The goal of happiness simply must not mix itself in with that law as a determining factor. (*True in Theory*, AK 8:289)

How does civil law proceed from the freedom of human beings in their external relations to others? The point of departure is freedom. Freedom is the first and most fundamental right of every individual. It is closely related to autonomy. "Everyone [clings] to his own right to do what seems right and good to him and not to depend on the opinions of another" (*Metaphysics of Morals*, AK 6:312). When this primeval right is the only basis for a common life, one can never be sure, as Hobbes argues, that one will be safe from attack. People must join to establish public coercive laws.

Kant explicitly excludes one possible understanding of this argument. One might reason as follows: Experience teaches that people do attack each other. Therefore safeguards with coercive power must be built into their common life because survival and freedom from violence are good. In this way of understanding the argument, the human will's motive is a good found in experience. If the will acts on the basis of this motive, it loses its autonomous legislative power. At the same time, the law loses its categorical character and become conditional: If you want security, you must provide for coercive laws that protect you (see *Metaphysics of Morals*, AK 6:312).

The true origin of the civil law lies completely outside such concerns with good and bad. It lies in the *a priori* legislative power of reason. My will can only be self-consistent as a universal legislative will if my legislation forbids attacks against me. Suppose that I lived according to the maxim "I am free to attack others." Then I apply the categorical imperative. The result is "Everyone is free to attack everyone." This is contrary to my own will, because I do not want to be attacked. Therefore my reason must decree the externally coercive universal law protecting everyone from attack. Civil law is thus purely a function of the autonomy of the person.

Three principles are implied in this *a priori* origin of civil law.

> 1. The freedom of each member of society as human being.
> 2. The equality of each member with every other as subject.
> 3. The self-standing (*Selbstständigkeit*, often translated as "independence") of each member of the commonwealth as citizen. (*True in Theory*, AK 8:290)

Kant's comments on the first of these three principles are particularly illuminating.

> Freedom as a human being: I express its principle for the constitution of a commonwealth as follows: No one can force me to be happy in his way (according to his judgment about the well-being of other human beings), but everyone is permitted to seek his happiness on the path that seems best to him, as long as he does not infringe on the freedom of others, that is, on the right of others to pursue a similar goal, provided that freedom can co-exist with the freedom of everyone according to a possible universal law. (*True in Theory*, AK 8:290)

Given Kant's premises—(1) that autonomy is the only intrinsic value and (2) that happiness is a matter of irrational inclinations—this understanding of political freedom is unavoidable.

On the basis of his account of the origins of civil law, Kant defines civil law as follows.

> [Civil] law (*Recht*) is the limitation of the freedom of each to the condition of its harmony with the freedom of everyone, as far as this is possible in accord with a general law. (*True in Theory*, AK 8:289)

Kant's definition can be understood more clearly when one compares it with Thomas's definition of law: (1) an ordinance of reason (2) for the common good, (3) made by the one who has care of the community, (4) promulgated.[11] Agreement is limited to the first and the last of these four points. Law is an ordinance or imperative of reason and promulgated. There is absolute difference on the decisive second and third points. If the common good is the purpose of law, and if law proceeds from the one who has responsibility for the community, then, according to Kant, the resulting regime will be paternal, not patriotic. A paternal regime is *the greatest despotism imaginable*. From Kant's perspective, Thomas includes despotism in the very essence of law because he sees the common good as its purpose, a purpose that guides the ruler's reason in caring for the community. According to Kant, any pre-given good, any rule guided by it, is opposed to law because law is the autonomous self-legislation of each individual person. The law proceeds from the universal legislative reason of every individual. Its rationality consists in being an expression of the autonomy of each person.

Kant *does* integrate the common good into his system, at least verbally but in a way that goes most directly against the understanding of the common good in Plato, Aristotle, and the Christian tradition.

> The proposition, salus publica suprema civitatis lex est [the public good is the supreme law of the state] remains in its undiminished value and recognition, but the public good which must be considered first is precisely the lawful constitution which assures everyone his freedom through laws. It remains at his own discretion to seek his happiness in any way that seems best to him, as long as he does not do violence to that general lawful freedom, that is, to the rights of other fellow-subjects. (*True in Theory*, AK 8:298)

What exactly is *salus publica*, the common good of the state, according to this text? A first point to note is that this common good is not connected with happiness. The pursuit of happiness is radically individual because it takes place in the irrational and chaotic world of sense experience. The law that enforces harmony among all wills, by contrast, proceeds from pure reason as a necessary implication of the autonomous self-movement of rational beings that interact with each other. This harmony is not sought because it is good. Family harmony as a particular good, for example, is a part of happiness and belongs to the sphere of empirical experience and individual pursuit, not of reason and law.

Kant applies the title *salus publica* directly to the lawful constitution of the state. This constitution exists "to assure everyone his freedom through laws." The common good of the state is a means for securing the autonomy of each

11. Thomas, *Summa* I-II, q. 90, a. 4.

person. This conclusion fits with Kant's main thesis that, in virtue of autonomy, the person is the only thing that can be called an end in an unqualified manner.

One can call this understanding of the state *personalistic* in a radical sense. The state is ordered to the person, not in the sense of allowing persons to reach a life that is good but in the sense of making sure that each person is recognized as the supreme good, which consists in autonomy.

5. Kingdom of God

The Antinomy of Practical Reason

Although the value of a merely happy life "sinks below zero" in comparison with the fulfillment of duty (*Noble Tone*, AK 5:434), a virtuous will is oriented not only toward duty but also toward happiness. Moral virtue—that is, complete and utter autonomy of the will—is the *supreme* (*supremum*) value to which everything else, including happiness, must be subordinated, but it is not by itself the *complete* (*perfectissimum*) human good unless happiness is added. By being virtuous, one becomes worthy of happiness. A morally perfect will, supposing it had all the necessary power, would necessarily desire to unite the value of virtue with the good of happiness in a greater whole that Kant calls "the highest (*höchste*) good" as opposed to "the uppermost (*oberste*) good" (*Critique of Practical Reason*, AK 5:11).

Kant is careful to guard this thesis against any inclusion of happiness in the understanding of morality. The one and only measure of the goodness of the will remains the full autonomy of the person. If happiness were allowed to play a determining role, heteronomy would replace the moral principle (see *Critique of Practical Reason*, AK 5:112–13).

This contrariety between happiness and duty as motives of the will leads to what Kant calls the antinomy of practical reason. Happiness and duty can be linked in one of two, and only two, ways: either desire for happiness is the cause of moral behavior, or moral behavior is the cause of happiness. The first is impossible because desire for happiness cannot be a motive of a morally good will. The second is also impossible because the moral law does not by itself give the power over nature required to ensure happiness. Such power can only be gained through empirical knowledge. Nevertheless, it remains a duty to work for the highest good. This antinomy threatens the moral law itself.

> If the highest Good is impossible according to practical rules, the moral law, which commands us to realize this good, must be mere fantasy and based on empty imaginary purposes, hence in itself false. (*Critique of Practical Reason*, AK 5:114)

Kant's resolution of this antinomy of practical reason differs from his resolution of the antinomies of pure reason. The antinomies of pure reason show that theoretical reason must not even raise the question of freedom, immortality, and God. Practical reason is free of these limits, despite the antinomy, because its interest is supreme. Let us return to a key text already quoted above.

> One cannot in any way demand that pure practical reason be subjected to speculative reason ... because all interest is in the end practical and even the interest of speculative reason is only conditional, complete only in practical use. (*Critique of Practical Reason*, AK 5:121)

What is forbidden to speculative reason, practical reason is allowed to do: it can postulate freedom, immortality, and God. The duty to pursue both virtue and happiness combined in the highest good is (1) a free self-determination of the autonomous will, which leads to the postulates of (2) immortality and (3) the existence of God. The postulate of immortality derives from the first part of the highest good; namely, virtue. Because we cannot realize complete virtue in a finite life, we can only express our absolute commitment to virtue through faith in an eternal life of continuous moral progress (see *Critique of Practical Reason*, AK 5:122–23).

The postulate of the existence of God derives from the second part of the highest good; namely, happiness. If we dutifully pursue the highest good, we necessarily postulate a cause of nature that distributes happiness to those who have made themselves worthy of it by their virtue (see *Critique of Practical Reason*, AK 5:124–32). In these two postulates Kant finds the heart of what he calls "Christian moral doctrine."

> Christian moral doctrine compensates for this lack (of the second indispensable component of the highest good [i.e., of happiness]) by depicting the world in which rational beings consecrate themselves with all their soul to the moral law as a kingdom of God, in which through a divine first cause, who makes the derivative highest good possible, Nature and Morality come into a harmony alien to each by itself.
>
> Holiness of morals is assigned to them as a standard already in this life while the well-being proportionate [to such holiness], namely blessedness (*Seligkeit*), is proposed as attainable only in an eternity. (*Critique of Practical Reason*, AK 5:128–29)

The role of God is clearly circumscribed in these postulates: God gives happiness in proportion to deserved virtue. God is not free to issue any positive commands or enter into a covenant. Nor is God free to give the gift of grace. Nor is God himself the supreme good that moves human love as the final end. Most important, as a mere product of human practical reason, the idea of God does not have any theoretical bearing on the question of whether there is a God (see *Critique of Practical Reason*, AK 5:132–41). Nor can one hold theoretically that there will be an actual eternity of life in heaven in which an actual God will give an actual happiness. The kingdom of God is wholly and exclusively moral and practical.

Kant testifies to the desire for happiness, the third major aspect of Greek *logos* mentioned above, but he cuts off the wings of *eros*. By desiring the reward of virtue, one acts rightly, and by thinking that such a reward will be given, one demonstrates one's moral uprightness, and yet it is only "as if" one desired blessedness and "as if" blessedness were to come.

The People of God

On the basis of this kingdom of God in heaven, Kant constructs the program of a kingdom of God on earth, which he also calls "people of God" *Volk Gottes* (see *Religion in the Boundaries of Bare Reason*, AK 6:98). This people of God in its imperfect form is concretely instantiated in churches (see *Religion in the Boundaries*, AK 6:100–102). The purpose of this kingdom is the victory of virtue, that is, the victory of the autonomy of the individual person.

Much evil, Kant argues, arises in us through interaction with other human beings. By the same token, decisive progress toward virtue can be achieved with the help of others (*Religion in the Boundaries*, AK 6:93–94). The political community emerges from the juridical state of nature, which is the state of being bound in external actions only by one's own free self-rule and thus of being subject to the violence of others. The ethical community or kingdom of God on earth emerges from the moral or ethical state of nature, that is, from the condition of being bound only by one's own moral commitment and thus of being subject to all attacks on moral virtue without support from a community (see *Religion in the Boundaries*, AK 6:96–97).

There is an absolute separation between the political and the ethical community, between state and church. In the political community, every person has the right to remain in the ethical state of nature and cannot be compelled by law to become moral. The compulsion of law, which is the principle of the political order, applies only to external actions. The ethical community, by contrast, is based exclusively on free consent and cannot be subject to political laws. The kingdom of God on earth is radically apolitical.

> In an already established commonwealth all political citizens as such are still in the ethical state of nature and also have the right to remain in it. For, if

> the [political] commonwealth were to force its citizens to enter into an ethical commonwealth, this would be a contradiction in terms, because the latter includes freedom from coercion in its very concept....
>
> But woe to the legislator who wants to use force to realize a constitution directed toward ethical ends! For he would thereby not only produce the exact opposite of an ethical [constitution] but also undermine his political [constitution] and make it insecure. (*Religion in the Boundaries*, AK 6:95–96)

In one respect, however, church and state are similar: their purpose is the individual person in his or her autonomy. Kant's kingdom of God on earth has no common good but is ordered to the autonomy of each person taken individually.

In their imperfect form as they develop toward the perfect kingdom of God, churches make use of an ecclesiastical faith rather than a pure rational faith. Ecclesiastical faith is as a rule formulated in the form of a historical revelation rather than a philosophical account. The revelation is suitably set forth in a holy book (*Religion in the Boundaries*, AK 6:102–10). Pure rational faith, however, is the supreme interpreter of such ecclesiastical faith.[12]

6. Shipwreck of Reason

The Disastrous Return of Theoretical Reason

Philosophy, in Kant's view, aspires to be a "doctrine of wisdom," *Weisheitslehre* (*Critique of Practical Reason*, AK 108–9). Aristotle argues in conformity with the Greek notion of *logos* that wisdom is primarily theoretical.

> It is right also that philosophy should be called knowledge of the truth. For the end of theoretical knowledge is truth, while that of practical knowledge is action, for even if they consider how things are, practical men do not study what is eternal but what stands in some relation at some time.[13]

Kant, by contrast, proposes an absolute priority of practical over theoretical wisdom. It is in practical wisdom that the highest aspirations of the human mind are fulfilled (see *Critique of Practical Reason*, AK 5:108). The final purpose of the three problems of pure reason lies in the fundamental question of practical reason: "What is to be done, if the will is free, if there is a God, and if there is a future world?" (*Critique of Pure Reason*, B 828).

12. Kant thus prepares the essential framework of Bultmann's reading of Scripture, even though Bultmann sees himself in some respects as a radical opponent of Kant. See Michael Waldstein, "The Foundations of Bultmann's Work," *Communio* 14 (1987): 115–45.

13. Aristotle, *Metaphysics* 2.1.993b20; see also 1.2.982b11–28.

In declaring the absolute primacy of *praxis*, Kant rejects the Greek understanding of *logos* even more radically than Descartes. In Kant, theoretical reason is not the power to apprehend being. It is not even such a power in servile subordination to technology, as in Descartes. It is a mere shadow of *logos*, limited to constituting the universe of Newtonian physics as a world of mere appearances, unable even to raise the most burning questions of human beings.

Kant is famous for being critical. His three main works are all called *Critiques*. His intellectual acumen is astonishing. It is surprising that he does not reflect critically about critical reflection. He chases Greek *logos* out by the front door and in that very act readmits it by the back door, apparently invisible to him.

He could not proceed one single step in his critiques without this reentry of Greek *logos*. He writes books. He expects them to be printed in many copies, to be taken in hand by other human beings, to be studied, considered, and assented to. In these books, he finally unfolds the theoretical truth about things in themselves and phenomena, about the limits of theoretical reason and the primacy of practical reason, about science, religion, and morality. He cannot, and does not want to, avoid claiming that his words apply to the minds of all human beings. He says what these minds are, objectively, as they are in themselves. He tells the truth even about mere phenomena and does so under the formality of being, as they *are* in themselves precisely as phenomena. According to his *Critiques*, theoretical reason cannot affirm such truths, and yet it inevitably does.

The root of this breakdown of critical self-reflection seems to be Kant's submission to the prestige of Newtonian science and the philosophical worldview associated with it. Having granted Newtonian science complete sway in the *objective* material world, he finds himself compelled to demote theoretical reason from its ruling position as ordered to truth and wisdom. He assigns it the humble task of ordering phenomena in the Newtonian cosmos. And yet, unnoticed by Kant, theoretical reason ignores the imposition of Kant's will and slips back into the house of philosophy as the master, overseeing and governing all of it. Kant could hardly have offered a stronger confirmation of Greek *logos*. He offers it inescapably and without critical reflection. He effectively displays Greek *logos* as the nature of human reason.

The Shipwreck of Practical Reason

While theoretical reason reenters intact, practical reason suffers complete shipwreck precisely because Kant considers it a doctrine of wisdom. Why is the autonomous rule of reason binding, if it is a rule in which good and evil as the matter of willing are dismissed as irrelevant and even harmful to autonomy? Can being autonomous as a universal legislator be good if the laws are not shaped by any theoretical wisdom about the good? Kant understands the dignity of the human person as a function of the person's practical rationality. Yet he cannot hold that this rationality has any intrinsic worth prior to the autonomous legislation of the will.

> For nothing has any value except the one which is determined by the law. Legislation itself, on the other hand, which determines all value, must for this reason have dignity, that is, an unconditioned, incomparable value. Only the word "respect" is suited to express the esteem which a rational being must have for it. Autonomy is, therefore, the reason for the dignity of human nature and of every rational nature. (*Groundwork*, AK 4:436)

One might read this text as affirming that legislation itself is good and for this reason an end. Everything has value only as decreed by legislation, but legislation itself has value because of its intrinsic dignity, prior to any legislation. This reading is incorrect. It implies that there exists a good prior to legislation, the goodness of which is not a result of legislation. That good would act as an end or final cause of the will. The will would be receptive vis-à-vis that good and would therefore lose its autonomy. It would no longer be a universal legislator. According to Kant, there is nothing prior to the legislation of the will. Therefore the value of legislation itself is decreed by legislation.

Why should such a decree interest anyone? Why does it impose itself as a duty? Kant testifies to the lived experience of the beauty and holiness of the law, but in the end his formalism—that is, his complete disregard for good and evil—compels him to abandon these attributes. They cannot be prior to the self-movement of the will. They are imposed by decree and not received. The question of why we would have any interest in following the universality of reason can be raised, Kant concludes, but not answered.

> The question how pure reason without any other motives that are taken from elsewhere can be practical of itself—that is, how the mere principle of the universal validity of all its maxims as laws (which would indeed be the form of a pure practical reason) without any matter (object) of the will, in which one could take an antecedent interest, can constitute a spring that causes movement (*Triebfeder*) and an interest which would be called purely moral—that

> is, how pure reason can be practical—this is a question which human reason is entirely and altogether incapable of answering and all effort and labor in seeking an explanation is wasted. (*Groundwork*, AK 4:461)

Kant's honesty with himself and the reader is astonishing. All effort and labor in seeking an explanation for morality are wasted. Kant abandons rationality at the very center of his philosophy. The categorical imperative has the outward appearance of rationality, but all effort and labor in seeking its *logos* are wasted.

Just as Kant is famous for being critical, so he is famous for upholding rational morality. Rationality is the very bedrock of the Enlightenment. And yet, at the decisive moment, all light disappears to give way to impenetrable darkness. Kant clings to the universality of Greek *logos*, but this universality has turned into a mere external shell that offers the outward impression of light and clarity. Inside the shell there is nothing.

7. Kant on Sex and Marriage

Kant's anti-Trinitarian personalism comes into clear focus in his account of sex and marriage. The *first* principle of Kant's sexual ethics is related to what Wojtyła calls "the personalistic norm." According to this principle, one must not merely *enjoy* a person as a sexual object and means for pleasure.[14] Mere enjoyment reduces a person to a means, a mere object or thing, and this is contrary to the dignity of the person. The *second* principle of Kant's sexual ethics is that sexual union involves giving oneself to another person.

These two principles are also the two pillars of St. John Paul's sexual ethics.[15] They correspond to the two principles of the life of persons in *Gaudium et spes* 24. Despite these points of close contact—or, rather, precisely in these points of close contact—Kant's view of sex and marriage could hardly be more opposed to John Paul's, not even if Kant were an advocate of indiscriminately promiscuous sex, which he is not.

Sex as a Human Rights Violation

According to Kant, since sexual intercourse is a gift of self, it is contrary to the dignity of the person. In all sexual relations, whether in marriage or outside it,

14. See Wojtyła, *Love and Responsibility*, 40–44.
15. Wojtyła, *Love and Responsibility*, 28–44, 95–100.

both persons turn themselves into mere things by giving their sexual organs, and therefore themselves, to each other to be possessed and used for pleasure. Being possessed and used in this manner, Kant holds, is contrary to the right each person has to itself. The only remedy for this loss of autonomy is marriage. By marriage, each takes possession in a lasting manner of the other as a thing. Each thereby offsets the loss of self in sex. By a permanent contract, each owns the one who episodically uses them for pleasure and by that ownership regains autonomy. The key text in Kant's *Metaphysics of Morals* is worth pondering.

> Sexual intercourse (*commercium sexuale*) is the mutual use which one human being makes of the sexual organs and faculty of another (*usus membrorum et facultatum sexualium alterius*). It is either a natural use, by which a being of the same nature can be conceived, or an unnatural use either with a person of the same sex or with an animal that does not belong to the human species. These transgressions of the law, called unnatural vices (*crimina carnis contra naturam*) and unmentionable vices, must be rejected entirely, without any qualifications or exceptions, because they do injury to human nature in our own person.
>
> Now, the natural union of the sexes occurs either only according to animal nature (*vaga libido, venus volgivaga, fornicatio*) or according to law.—The latter is marriage (*matrimonium*), that is, the union of two persons for the lifelong mutual possession of their sexual characteristics.—The purpose of begetting and educating children may be a reason for which nature implanted a mutual inclination toward each other in the sexes, but for the legality of this bond it is not required that the one who marries must intend this goal for himself, for otherwise marriage would dissolve of itself when the begetting of children ends.
>
> For, although it is *based on pleasure for the mutual use of their sexual characteristics*, the marriage contract is not accidental, but it is necessary in accord with legal principles of pure reason. That is, when man and woman want to enjoy each other in their sexual characteristics, they must necessarily marry. This necessity follows from legal principles of pure reason.
>
> For, the natural use that one sex makes of the sexual organs of the other is *an enjoyment for which one partner gives himself to the other. In this act, a human being makes himself into a thing, which is contrary to the right of human nature to one's own person*. This is possible only under one single condition: when a person is acquired by another in a manner equal to a thing, correspondingly the former acquires the latter, for in this way *the person gains himself back again and reconstitutes his personhood*. Now, the acquisition of one bodily member of a human being is at the same time an acquisition of the whole person, because the person is an absolute unity. For this reason, *the gift and the acceptance of one sex for enjoyment by the other* is not merely permis-

> sible only on the single condition of marriage, but it is only possible on this same condition. That this personal right is nevertheless at the same time also a right in the manner of a right to a thing, is clear, for when one of the spouses has run away or has given himself or herself into the possession of another, the other spouse has the right at any time and without any condition to take him or her back into his or her power like a thing.
>
> For the same reason, the relation of the married persons is a relation of equality of possession, equality both in their possession of each other (hence only in monogamy, for in polygamy the person who gives herself away gains back only part of the man whose possession she has become in her entirety and therefore reduces herself to a mere thing) and of external goods. (*Metaphysics of Morals*, AK 6:277–78; emphasis added)

Sex is a human rights violation. How exactly is it that man and woman can neutralize this human rights violation? How can they regain themselves in their autonomy and reconstitute themselves as persons despite the loss of autonomy in sexual union? It seems to be like the case of a man addicted to gambling who is afraid of losing money—and so he buys the casino.

The nature of money is not violated by this strategy. The money the man owned before he lost it is returned to him after his loss. His former wealth is reestablished without any negative side effect, except for the loss of drama in making large bets. When the wife takes depersonalizing possession of her husband by enjoying him in sexual intercourse, does the husband really regain his autonomy by having permanent possession of her as a thing through the marriage contract? Money in the casino example works by simple subtraction and addition. Subtraction and addition do not work in the loss of dignity as a person. Even if the spouses give permanent possession of each other to each other through the marriage contract, they cannot regain their personal dignity in the concrete act of taking depersonalizing sexual possession of each other. The two possessions do not cancel each other. If anything, they reinforce each other.

If one introduces spousal love, which is central for John Paul, the situation is totally different. "Everybody without exception will agree that it is only love, love alone, that transforms sexual drive into a typically human experience."[16] Evidently, Wojtyła must have common human experience in mind. Kant is a counterexample. John Paul sees the conjugal act as a "natural word" *naturale verbum* (*Familiaris consortio* 32) that is connected with "the spousal meaning of the body." By its very nature as created by God, independent from any choice or determination made by us human beings, the human body has the power to

16. Karol Wojtyła, "Instinkt, Liebe und Ehe [Instinct, Love, and Marriage]," in *Erziehung zur Liebe: Mit einer ethischen Fibel* (Stuttgart-Degerloch: Seewald, 1980), 19–42, at 30.

express love, to speak love through its own "natural word." In accord with this nature, the conjugal act is not depersonalizing but a deep fulfillment of the person through the gift of self. Wojtyła finds sharply anti-Kantian formulations in describing this gift of self.

> For love makes the person want precisely to give himself to another person—to the one he loves. He wants, so to speak, to stop being his own exclusive possession and to become the possession of the other. It signifies a certain relinquishing of that *sui iuris* and of that *alteri incommunicabilis*. Love goes through such relinquishing, being guided, however, by the profound belief that this relinquishment leads not to diminishing and impoverishing the existence of the person but on the contrary to its expansion and enrichment. This is, so to speak, the law of "ecstasy," of going out of oneself in order to exist more fully in the other. In no other form of love is this law realized so clearly as in spousal love.[17]

The sexual speech of the body is a great good, according to John Paul, when it is truthful. What man and woman speak through the body in sexual union is inevitably a gift of self. They cannot take away the spousal meaning of the body, though they can speak that meaning in a manner contrary to itself; that is, they can speak it as a sexual lie.[18] In some cases it may be a thrilling and even beautiful lie, but only for the moment. It is bound to be followed by regret. There is a way of treating other persons in sexual intercourse that corresponds somewhat to Kant's way of understanding it: a gift contrary to the dignity of the person.

> [There is a] persistent mentality which considers the human being not as a person but as a thing, as an object of trade, at the service of what is agreeable to oneself and mere pleasure: the first victims of this mentality are women. (*Familaris consortio* 24)

When Wojtyła describes this depersonalizing sexual use of one person by another, he chooses the term that is the key term of Kant's understanding of sex in general: "to enjoy" *genießen*. In mere enjoyment, the sexual speech is overlaid by a contrary speech.

> Man, since he possesses reason, can in his action not only clearly distinguish pleasure or pain but also in a sense separate them and treat them as a distinct end of action. Then his acts are formed with regard to pleasure alone, which he wants to acquire, or exclusively with regard to pain, which he wants to avoid. Since acts related to the person of the other sex will be formed exclusively or even first and foremost because of that, then that person will become in

17. Wojtyła, *Love and Responsibility*, 108.
18. See John Paul II, *Familiaris consortio* 11.

> a particular way only a means to an end—hence, as we can see, the second meaning of the verb "to use" [= to enjoy] constitutes a particular case of the first meaning.[19]

The difference between Kant and John Paul is clear in their arguments against polygamy. According to Kant, polygamy is immoral because my second wife cannot retrieve the whole of her person, which she loses to me whenever I take depersonalizing sexual possession of her. The reason is that I do not belong to her alone by a marriage contract but also to my first wife. I divide myself, being permanently possessed by both my wives. Each owns only a fifty percent share in the casino. When they lose money on a bet, they can retrieve only half of it.

John Paul's argument against polygamy is also a personalistic argument. It is close to Kant's but at the same time quite the opposite. Polygamy is wrong because it is contrary to the logic of the communion that arises in the gift of love.

> Such a communion is radically contradicted by polygamy: this, in fact, directly negates the plan of God which was revealed from the beginning, because it is contrary to the equal personal dignity of men and women who in matrimony give themselves with a love that is total and therefore unique and exclusive. As the Second Vatican Council writes: "Firmly established by the Lord, the unity of marriage will radiate from the equal personal dignity of husband and wife, a dignity acknowledged by mutual and total love."[20]

Kant's account of the role of children in marriage is helpful because it shows his understanding of the relation between person and body in the procreative meaning of the conjugal act.

> The purpose of begetting and educating children may be a reason for which nature implanted in the sexes a mutual inclination toward each other, but for the legality of this bond it is not required that the one who marries must intend this goal for himself. Otherwise matrimony would end of itself when the begetting of children ends. (*Metaphysics of Morals*, AK 6:277)

Nature may have purposes of her own in linking sexual pleasure with procreation, but these purposes do not touch the order of the person that derives *a*

19. Wojtyła, *Love and Responsibility*, 17. This meaning of *use* and *enjoy* in Wojtyła differs from the meaning in Augustine, *De doctrina Christiana* 1.4. In Augustine, *uti* (to use) is the right relation to a partial good, *frui* (to enjoy) the right relation to the total good of the final end. Wojtyła is mistaken when he claims (*Love and Responsibility*, 28) that Augustine's *frui* signifies the right relation to a finite good according to its true goodness. Ignatik's note on this text (28n29, at 305) seems to sidestep the difference.

20. John Paul II, *Familiaris consortio* 19, citing *Gaudium et spes* 49.

priori from reason, not from nature. Just as the person is violated in the sexual act, precisely inasmuch as that act involves a unitive gift of self, so the person stands outside the procreative purpose of nature.

The ease with which Kant dismisses nature's purpose of procreation as essential to marriage raises the question why he is so emphatic in his condemnation of homosexual acts.

> It [i.e., sexual intercourse] is either a natural use, by which a being of the same nature can be conceived, or an unnatural use either with a person of the same sex or with an animal that does not belong to the human species. These transgressions of the law, called unnatural vices (*crimina carnis contra naturam* [crimes of the flesh against nature]) and unmentionable vices, must be rejected entirely, without any qualifications or exceptions, because they do injury to human nature in our own person. (*Metaphysics of Morals*, AK 6:277)

Kant does not explain in greater detail what he means by "injury to human nature in our person," but ultimately the nature in question must be the autonomous rational nature, not the natural connection between sexuality and procreation. This reading is supported by Kant's explanation of the immorality of masturbation. Masturbation, Kant argues first, is contrary to the natural connection between sexual pleasure and procreation. He then moves on to the decisive argument. In masturbation, one uses one's own person for pleasure, which is contrary to human dignity. The absence of procreative meaning in masturbation does play a role but only a subordinate one.

> Of course, the proof [of the immorality of masturbation] is that man abandons his personhood, throwing it away, by making himself a mere means of satisfying animal drives. Yet, this does not explain the high degree of injury which such a vice in its unnaturalness does to human nature, for in its form, in attitude, it seems to exceed even the crime of suicide.
>
> The explanation of the difference is this: throwing oneself away defiantly to rid oneself of the burden of life in suicide is at least not an indulgent abandonment to animal attractions but demands courage. Some respect for the humanity in one's person always finds room in such courage. [Throwing oneself away in lust], by contrast, is a complete self-abandonment to animal inclination and turns a human being into a consumable thing . . . and deprives man of all respect for himself. (*Metaphysics of Morals*, AK 6:425)

Respect for oneself as an autonomous being is the central point in both masturbation and homosexual acts. Both acts are immoral, not primarily because they are contrary to the natural ordination of sexual acts to procreation but because they are an abandonment of the autonomous person to animal inclination. Why, then, does Kant not condemn all sex as immoral, even in marriage? The necessity of procreation is certainly part of the answer but not the whole. It is clear that Kant would much rather do without sexual inclination. In fact, he would much rather do without any inclinations at all.

> Inclinations are so far from having an absolute value making them desirable in themselves that it must rather be the universal wish of every rational being to be completely free from them. (*Groundwork*, AK 4:428)

Person and Nature

To sum up, one fundamental reason for the divergence between Kant and John Paul is the absence of truly personal conjugal love in Kant. Kant's personalism is not personalistic enough. Human sexuality is not formed and penetrated by personal love but is cut loose as a natural process, foreign to the person and even opposed to personal dignity.

Kant's view of sex is an expression of a deeply disturbed relation between the person and subrational nature. The person is not at home in that nature but stands outside it, carrying a rational order within itself *a priori*, which it must impose on nature from the outside. The external natural world is ruled entirely by mechanistic laws grasped mathematically, a reduced form of rationality incapable of grounding ethics. Nature in its second aspect—namely, sense experience and inclinations—is subjective, chaotic, and irrational. Person and subrational nature are pitted against each other in a strict dualism.

Behind this negative view of inclinations in general and sexual passion in particular one can see Luther's condemnation of all self-seeking love. One can also see Descartes's dualistic separation of the human person into animal nature, which, as Kant puts it, is worth less than money, and personhood, which is of a value beyond price.

> In the system of nature, man (*homo phaenomenon*, animal rationale) is a being of little importance and has a common value (*pretium vulgare*) together with other animals as products of the soil. Even the fact that he exceeds them by having reason and by being able to set goals for himself, even this fact gives him only an external value of usefulness (*pretium usus*), it gives one human being more [value] than another, that is, a price as a commodity in the commercial exchange of these animals as things, in which he has a lower value than money, the universal means of exchange—which is why the value of money is called eminent (*pretium eminens*).
>
> But man being regarded as a person, that is, as the subject of moral-practical reason, is exalted above all price, for as such (*homo noumenon*) he is to be regarded as a purpose in himself, that is, he possesses a dignity (an absolute

> inner value) by which he can compel all other rational beings to have respect for him, can measure himself against all other rational beings of the world and evaluate himself as standing on a footing of equality with every other being of this kind. (*Metaphysics of Morals*, AK 6:434)

Leon Kass, in agreement with Schmitz, points out that the image of the world created by the exclusive pursuit of natural science in the Baconian-Cartesian program decisively conditions Kant's personalism at this point.

> At the bottom of the trouble ... is the hegemony of modern natural science, to whose view of nature even the partisans of personhood and subjectivity adhere, given that their attempt to locate human dignity in consciousness and mind presupposes that the subconscious living body, not to speak of nature in general, is utterly without meaning and dignity of its own.[21]

John Paul is convinced, on the contrary, of the unity of nature and person. One can see this conviction in his account of procreation as the natural end of marriage. In *Familiaris consortio* 14, he repeats the traditional Catholic view in a formulation close to *Gaudium et spes* 50.

> According to the plan of God, marriage is the foundation of the wider community of the family, since the very institution of marriage and conjugal love are ordained to the procreation and education of children, in whom they find their crowning.

Immediately after this traditional paragraph, founded on the Catholic understanding of nature, one finds a paragraph in which John Paul extends this understanding of nature along the lines of his hermeneutics of the gift.

> In its most profound reality, love is essentially a gift; and conjugal love, while leading the spouses to the reciprocal "knowledge" which makes them "one flesh," does not end with the couple, because it makes them capable of the greatest possible gift, the gift by which they become cooperators with God for giving life to a new human person. Thus, the couple, while giving themselves to one another, give not just themselves but also the reality of children, who are a living reflection of their love, a permanent sign of conjugal unity and a living and inseparable synthesis of their being a father and a mother.[22]

21. Leon Kass, *Toward a More Natural Science: Biology of Human Affairs* (New York: Free Press, 1985), 277.

22. John Paul II, *Familiaris consortio* 14.

John Paul does not locate procreation outside the personal love between husband and wife but most immediately and directly in it. The defense of nature's procreative purpose in marriage is at the same time a personalistic defense of interpersonal love.

Anti-Trinitarian Personalism

Kant uses Trinitarian language to express the central teaching of Christianity as understood by his rational faith.

> That which alone can make a world the object of divine decree and the end of creation is Humanity (rational being in general in the world) in its full moral perfection, from which happiness [i.e., humanity's happiness] follows in the will of the Highest Being directly as from its supreme condition.—This human being, which is alone pleasing to God ["This is my beloved Son in whom I am well pleased," Matthew 3:17], "is in him from all eternity" [John 1:1]; the idea of the human being proceeds from God's being; he [i.e., the human being] is not, therefore, a created thing but God's only-begotten Son [John 1:18, 3:16–18], "the Word (the Fiat!) through which all other things are, and without whom nothing that is made would exist" [John 1:1–3], since for him, that is, for a rational being in the world, as it can be thought according to its moral determination, everything was made ["All things were created through him and for him," Colossians 1:16].—"He is the reflection of his glory" [Heb 1:3].—"In him God loved the world" [John 3:16], and only in him and through the adoption of his dispositions can we hope "to become children of God" [John 1:12]. (*Religion in the Boundaries*, AK 6:60–61)

Kant's virtuoso command of Scripture can easily obscure the central point of his rational faith. He calls the human person Son. This Son is equal to the Father but not born from the Father. The Son's self-movement without the Father is the highest value. "He speaks from his own" (John 8:44).

It is with good justification that De Koninck identifies Kant as a representative of personalism in his work *Against the Personalists* and that Wojtyła speaks of "Kantian personalism."[23] Kant focuses all light and glory on the human person's autonomy. Human glory is not a reflection of glory (*Abglanz*) but stands absolutely in the autonomous self. Kant undercuts the relational character of Trinitarian language (Father-Son, glory-reflection, and so on) in favor of an autonomous self, of each and every autonomous self, a series of juxtaposed and unrelated selves.

Anti-Trinitarian is not a philosophical category. One might therefore object

23. De Koninck, "Primacy of the Common Good," 68n72. Wojtyła, *Acting Person*, 22n8, 302.

to its use in an account of Kant's philosophy. Yet *anti-Trinitarian* is necessary to do justice to Kant's own understanding of his philosophy. He develops it in conscious encounter with Christian revelation and in fully conscious rejection of its Trinitarian basis. He remarks tersely, "From the doctrine of the Trinity, taken literally, one can derive nothing at all for the practical sphere" (*Controversy between University Departments*, AK 7:38). Yet he himself derives everything for the practical sphere from his anti-Trinitarian personalism. The ultimate glory rests in the individual person, in each individual person considered in isolation.

The Challenge

The famous text quoted at the beginning of this presentation of Kant can serve as a condensed overview.

> Two things fill the mind with ever new and increasing admiration and reverence, the more frequently and persistently one's meditation dwells on them: the starry sky above me and the moral law within me....
>
> The first sight, of a countless multitude of worlds, annihilates, as it were, my importance as an animal creature....
>
> The second sight, on the contrary, infinitely elevates my worth as that of an intelligence by my personhood, in which the moral law reveals to me a life independent of animality and even of the entire world of sense. (*Practical Reason*, AK 1:61–62)

The dichotomy between *personhood* and *animality* encapsulates the challenge addressed by TOB. There is much that Wojtyła considers positive in Kant, particularly the critique of utilitarianism and the consistent application of this critique to the understanding of sex. In the end, however, Wojtyła stands Kant on his head by his Trinitarian personalism and his richer understanding of nature, which does not uncritically submit to the reductionism of the Baconian-Cartesian empire of man over things.

CHAPTER 3

Scheler's Theomorphic Personalism of Solidarity

1. De-Hellenizing Philosophy

Like Kant, Scheler has a glory of the human person to tell of.[1]

> The value of the person remains the highest value of values; the glorification of the person, ultimately of the person of persons, that is, God, remains the moral meaning of all moral "order." The ultimate measure of community and history is therefore the idea above them; namely, to what extent they provide the basis of existence and life for the pure ontological value [*Seinswert*] of the maximum of most valuable persons (both individual and encompassing persons, as we shall see).[2] (FormEng 504, FormGer 495)

1. Citations of Scheler by FormEng (= *Formalism* English) and FormGer (= *Formalism* German) refer to Max Scheler, *Formalism in Ethics and Non-Formal Ethics of Values: A New Attempt toward the Foundation of an Ethical Personalism*, 5th ed., trans. Manfred Frings (Evanston, IL: Northwestern University Press, 1973); *Der Formalismus in der Ethik und die materiale Wertethik: Neuer Versuch der Grundlegung eines ethischen Personalismus*, 7th ed. (Bonn: Bouvier, 2000). Citations by GW (= *Gesammelte Werke*) refer to Scheler's collected works, *Gesammelte Werke*, ed. Maria Scheler and Manfred Frings, 15 vols. (Bern: Francke Verlag, 1954–86; Munich: Bouvier Verlag, 1986–97). Translations of *Formalism* are by Frings, occasionally modified; translations of other texts are my own.

2. "Encompassing person" following the translation of Scheler's *Gesamtperson* in Frings's monograph on Scheler rather than the rendering "collective person" in Frings's earlier translation of *Formalism*; see Manfred Frings, *The Mind of Max Scheler: The First Comprehensive Guide Based on the Complete Works*, 2nd ed. (Marquette: Marquette University Press, 2001), 114–15. Encompassing persons like the state are for Scheler more than a personified collective; namely, persons properly speaking with their own consciousness distinct from that of individual persons. See the chapter on "Individual Person and Collective Person" (FormEng 519–60; FormGer 509–48). Instead of "person of persons," the English translation reads "persons or persons," probably a typo. The German has *Person der Personen*.

Scheler sees this glory of the person as directly opposed to Greek philosophical *logos*, which places the need-love of *eros* at the center of human life. The authentic glory of the person lies instead in the trans-logical movement of self-gift called *agape*, which is the center of the moral revolution introduced by Jesus. Christian philosophy must be radically de-Hellenized to conform to this authentically Christian understanding of love.

Balthasar's extensive monograph on Scheler shows that the glory of the person, according to Scheler, lies in love. The highest and most perfect form of love is God's self-giving love as revealed by Jesus. Jesus brought a radical reversal in the movement of love. In Plato and Aristotle, love has an ascending movement of longing for fulfillment, fulfillment at the very end by an infinite impersonal good that constitutes the goal or object of human striving. In Christianity, by contrast, all attention is focused on the descending personal love of God in which fullness stands at the beginning, and self-gift is a natural overflow.[3] Balthasar summarizes this core of Scheler's de-Hellenized understanding of Christian philosophy.

> Only the one who has understood that the *Logos* himself is person and love, that the highest value, therefore, "is not the value of a thing (*Sachwert*) but the value of an act (*Aktwert*), the value of love itself as love," can truly embrace philosophy and personalism at the same time. This possibility, however, was disclosed to the world only in God's free self-revelation in Christianity when the entire movement characteristic of *eros*, the ascent to the trans-erotic absolute object, was completely reversed to become the free movement of descent characteristic of God's love for the world. It was only in this lavish self-gift in freedom that the self-glory and highest sovereignty of this love—bound to nothing and obliged to nothing—was revealed.
>
> Once this "reversal in the movement of love" has been initiated by Christ, it becomes the true access to the supreme [value]: it is only "in performing this act of 'bending down,' in letting himself glide down, in 'losing himself,'" that man can "gain the supreme [value]—becoming like God."
>
> Scheler is all the more surprised that "the intellectual and philosophical expression of this singular revolution of the human spirit failed in an almost incomprehensible manner." It was exactly "the Platonic definition of love as striving," that "passed over into Scholastic philosophy, contrary to the innermost intentions of Christianity" so that "there never was, or at best there were only weak beginnings of, a philosophical understanding of the world and of life that sprang originally and spontaneously from Christian experience."[4]

3. See Hans Urs von Balthasar, *Apokalypse der deutschen Seele: Studien zu einer Lehre von letzten Haltungen*, 3 vols. (Einsiedeln: Johannes, 1998), 3:84–192, esp. chap. 4, "Personalism," 152–92.

4. Balthasar, *Apokalypse der deutschen Seele*, 3:153. Balthasar refers to "Das Ressentiment im Aufbau der Moralen," GW 3:70–75; "Liebe und Erkenntnis," GW 6:87–89.

Impersonal Greek *logos* and *eros*, which dominated Catholic philosophy and theology, must be replaced by *person* and *agape*. "*Logos*, form, and ratio stand for him [Aristotle] above the idea of person." To subject the person to a general *logos* is *logonomy*, which is "the most extreme heteronomy" (FormEng 372, FormGer 372). The person is unique in its value essence and cannot be governed by impersonal, universal laws. Only when one rejects the impersonal Greek *logos* can one understand the true glory of God's love as manifested in the human person. It is by losing themselves in solidarity with others that human beings can radiate the glory of this love.

Manfred Frings, the editor of Scheler's collected works, summarizes Scheler's judgment about Aristotle and Catholic Scholasticism in a seven-point syllabus of errors. The first error is the root; the other six grow from it.

> [Scheler] rejected the Aristotelian bases of Catholic theology.
>
> [1.] Aristotelianism does not do justice to *the eminent role of love in Christian religion*. Aristotle lived three centuries before Christ lived. Christ had no interest in Aristotle or Greek philosophy.
>
> [2.] The Greek influence on theological Christianity, especially that found in the Middle Ages, is deplorable because it *tarnished both the essence of the love of the person and the pure exemplarity of the holy and of Christ with rationality*. According to St. Thomas one must first know something in order to love it. According to Scheler, however, one can only know something by first having been drawn to the value of what is to be known. . . .
>
> [3.] The ancient Greek orientation of Christian theology also had deplorable sociological effects on the structure of the church. Popes, bishops, priests and public servants are portrayed like "Roman rulers." They even hold an "office" and observe "legal" stipulations *in contrast to the essence of love*.
>
> [4.] Redemption must be believed in according to "dogma."
>
> [5.] The essence of the human person is supposed to be a "substance" (Aristotle) rather than *the bearer of love*.
>
> [6.] Charity and love tend to be observed as part of a Divine will, rather than in a free, selfless Samaritan way.
>
> [7.] In all of this there is a confusion, says Scheler, of *Christian love and Aristotle's teleological system*, culminating in a theological confusion of Aristotle's god as the "thought of thoughts" or "unmoving mover," on the one hand, and *God as seat of love*, on the other.[5]

According to Frings, Scheler sees the Greek understanding of rationality (*logos*) as the source of the problem. Aristotelian reason and its desire for happiness *tarnished* both the essence of love and the imitation of Christ with *logos*.

5. Frings, *Mind of Max Scheler*, 116; emphasis and numbering added.

In the title of his book on Scheler, Wojtyła raises the question, "Can we, or to what degree can we, attempt to interpret Christian ethics with the help of Scheler's system?"[6] In raising this question, he examines the deepest point of Scheler's intentions. He addresses the question by focusing on Scheler's understanding of the imitation of Christ (see part I, chap. 4, in this volume).

2. Scheler and Kant

Scheler's Critique of Kant

Aristotle, Thomas, and Catholic Scholastics are dim figures on the margins of Scheler's knowledge. It is clear that he has not studied them closely or widely but relies on Kant's post-Lutheran reading of them. Still, he makes some penetrating observations.[7] With Kant, by contrast, he is thoroughly familiar and continuously engaged. Kant is his favorite opponent.

The heart of Kant's system, according to Scheler, lies in the self-initiated activity or spontaneity of the subject, which imposes its own form both in the theoretical and practical sphere (see Scheler FormEng 65–68, FormGer 84–86).[8] In the theoretical sphere, every synthesis in appearances is produced by the mind, which imposes an order on the chaos of sensation. In the practical sphere, moral acts are formed by laws that arise *a priori* from practical reason. It is only through the active imposition of these laws that moral values can arise.

This spontaneity of the subject, Scheler argues, is purely constructed. Con-

6. Wojtyła, *Scheler*, 65. Citations by Wojtyła, *Scheler*, refer to the German translation of Wojtyła's book on Scheler. Karol Wojtyła, Über die Möglichkeit eine christliche Ethik in Anlehnung an Max Scheler zu schaffen [Evaluation of the possibility of constructing a Christian ethics on the assumptions of Max Scheler's system of philosophy], in *Primat des Geistes: Philosophische Schriften*, ed. Juliusz Stroynowski (Stuttgart-Degerloch: Seewald, 1980).

7. An example: "One could call it an irony of history that the Franciscan tradition stimulated the development of natural science on all points, even though it ranks *good* above *true* while, by contrast, the Dominican tradition hindered the development of the new science precisely by placing *true* above *good*." (GW 1:18). One would need to add to Scheler's account that the primacy of the practical order has an opposite meaning for Bonaventure and for Ockham owing to Ockham's voluntarist premises. In Bonaventure, God's wisdom and love interpenetrate.

Another example: "Christian philosophy kept its distance from the *dualism* of body and soul. For Thomas Aquinas, the *soul* is inseparably the body's principle of life and a spiritual power. It was only in modern thought (Descartes and those who followed), prepared by certain Franciscan teachings, that we find this new point of view, in which *the thinking self*, detached from all substrates of life, looks down upon the body as it regards any body, in the same distance from the object as all external bodies." (GW 3:114)

8. In this context, *spontaneous* does not mean *impulsive, uncalculated, unplanned*. The Latin *spons* can mean *free will*, and the adjective *spontaneus* can mean *of one's own will, voluntary*, or *coming straight away* from an agent or patient, as in *spontaneous combustion*.

structing is the mortal sin par excellence in the phenomenological canon of philosophical sins. Phenomenology attempts to give an attentive account (*logos*) of what is evident (*phainomena*). Construction contradicts what is evident and replaces it with some supposition. Kant has no evidence for his construction in anything truly given to him, that is, in any true *phenomena*. He does not offer an account of the given but builds up an account for reasons other than evidence.

The reasons that moved Kant to construct this account, Scheler continues, are closely bound up with his uncritical acceptance of British empiricism, particularly Hume and Hobbes. Once the world is pulverized into a chaos of unconnected sensations and the human heart into a flux of irrational inclinations, there is a need for a synthesizing power that produces the more unified world of experience.

> In short, Hume's notion of nature required a Kantian understanding, and Hobbes's notion of man required a Kantian practical reason, insofar as these theories were to be brought back to the facts of natural experience. But without this erroneous presupposition of a Humean nature and a Hobbesian man there is no need for such a hypothesis and hence no need for an interpretation of the *a priori* as a "law of functions" of such organizing activities. (FormEng 66, FormGer 85)

The roots of these views among the British empiricists, Scheler argues, lie in "the mind-set of Puritan Protestantism" (FormEng 67n23, FormGer 86n1). It is a mindset of distrust in principle for all that is *natural*, all that has not passed through systematic-rational self-control, distrust in principle for all relations between persons that have not been secured in contractual form. As Bouyer points out, what stands behind this image of the chaotically natural is nominalism.

> What, in fact, is the essential characteristic of Ockham's thought, and of Nominalism in general but a radical empiricism, reducing all being to what is perceived, which empties out, with the idea of substance, all possibility of real relations between beings, as well as the stable subsistence of any of them, and ends by denying to the real any intelligibility, conceiving God himself only as a Protean figure impossible to apprehend.[9]

The mindset of Puritan Protestantism, Scheler argues, found expression in Bacon's program of a reformation of the whole of human knowledge for the sake of power over nature and its supreme expression in classical Newtonian mechanics. These historical roots, Scheler argues, are consummated in the mindset that shapes Kant's philosophical system.

9. Louis Bouyer, *The Spirit and Forms of Protestantism* (Princeton, NJ: Scepter, 2004), 153.

> This mind-set I can only describe as a basic "hostility" toward or distrust of the given as such, a fear of the given as "chaos," an anxiety—an attitude that can be expressed as "that world there outside me, that nature there within me." "Nature" is what is to be formed, to be organized, to be "controlled"; it is the "hostile," the "chaos," and so on. Hence this attitude is the opposite of love of the world, of trust in and loving devotion to the world.
>
> Strictly speaking, this attitude belongs only to modern times, which are permeated by hatred for the world, hostility toward the world, and a distrust of it, and by the consequence of this hatred: namely, the limitless need for activity to "organize" and "control" the world.... And all this has culminated in the mind of a philosophical genius. (FormEng 67, FormGer 86)

In Kant, the *homo technicus* heralded by Bacon and Descartes has entered the inner sanctuary of the mind, both the principles of theoretical philosophy and the foundations of ethics. He imposes his controlling power not only over the external world of nature, as in Bacon and Descartes. He imports it also into the very formation of the inner objects of knowledge. The mind imposes space, time, and the categories on the chaotic matter of sensation. In its role as lawgiver, it imposes duty on the chaos of irrational inclinations.

The opposition between Kant and Scheler is radical. For Scheler, the central animating principle of philosophy is the desire to dwell with love and devotion in a receptive, contemplative gaze to grasp what is truly evident. In this respect, he stands in continuity with Greek *logos*, specifically with its understanding of *theoria* as a receptive contemplative gaze. Against the brilliant constructions of Kant, he insists that philosophy must have a supple and obedient regard for the given. Philosophy must be an account (*logos*) of what is truly evident (*phainomenon*). It must be phenomenological.[10]

Phenomenology, Scheler insists, is not reducible to a mere method of thought or observation. It is at root a mindset of the human spirit determined by love. Scheler defines it as "a love-determined movement of the inmost personal self of a finite being toward participation in the essential reality of all possibles."[11] St. John Paul sees the positive aspirations of phenomenology in a similar way.

> Phenomenology is primarily a style of thought, a relationship of the mind with reality, whose essential and constitutive features it aims to grasp, avoiding prejudice and schematisms. I mean that it is, as it were, an attitude of intellec-

10. On this basic level, there seems to be agreement between Husserl and Scheler. There are also far reaching differences in their understanding of Phenomenology; see Frings, *Mind of Max Scheler*, 181–92. Frings (182) places Scheler in the "loose circle" of phenomenologists together with Dietrich von Hildebrand, Alexander Pfänder, Adolph Reinach, and Edith Stein, among others.

11. Max Scheler, *On the Eternal in Man*, trans. Bernard Noble (New York: Harper and Brothers, 1960), 74.

> tual charity to the human being and the world, and for the believer, to God, the beginning and end of all things.[12]

Beyond Realism and Idealism

Scheler's relation to Kant is more complex than his profound critique and counterproposal would suggest. He seems at times to be swept along by the genius of his favorite enemy, in the form of both uncritical acceptance and exaggerated opposition.

Uncritical acceptance of some of Kant's theses is evident when Scheler claims to have achieved "a definitive overthrow of the Idealism-Realism antithesis" (GW 9:185). Idealism and realism, Scheler argues, share one and the same fundamental error; namely, the assumption that "there-being" (*Dasein*) or existence is inseparable from "such-being" (*Sosein*) or essence.[13]

Both idealists and realists, according to Scheler, falsely assume that essence and existence are inseparable. They are either both in the mind or both outside the mind. Idealists combine this false assumption with the correct thesis that essences or natures are in our mind. They infer the false conclusion that existence must be in the mind as well. They conclude that there is nothing outside the mind. Realists combine the false assumption with the true thesis that the existence of things cannot be in the mind. They infer the false conclusion that essences cannot be in the mind either. They suppose that "nothing can ever be given 'in consciousness' except an 'image' or a 'symbol' (perception, idea, thought) which refers to the character of the object." The object itself, its essence or nature, is not a given. They thereby destroy the foundation of philosophy, which is, in Scheler's mind, the preconceptual, presuppositionless, immediate, and intuitive givenness of essences in phenomenological experience (see GW 9:186–87).

How, then, does Scheler propose to overcome both idealism and realism on a higher plane? His key principle is the separability of existence and essence. *Existence* is utterly transcendent with respect to the mind while essences can be immediately given in it.

> One of my principal theses is that in every case the nature of a being (contingent as well as essential nature) can, in principle, be immanent to and truly

12. John Paul II, *Address to a Delegation of the World Institute of Phenomenology*, March 22, 2003.

13. As Scheler uses the word *essence* (Wesen), it is often not limited to the object of the question "What is it?" but includes all such-being (*Sosein*) as opposed to existence (*Dasein*). In this more general sense of essence, *blond* is just as much an essence as *human.*

inherent in knowledge and, further, to reflexive knowledge.... Existence, however, can never be immanent to consciousness. Rather, existence necessarily transcends knowledge and consciousness and is alien to them. Existence is essentially transcendent and remains independent of them.... Existence can never be *in mente* [in the mind]. I shall speak later of how existence can be "given" despite this. (FormEng 289–90, FormGer 185–86)

When he explains how existence can be given even though it is utterly alien to the mind, Scheler appeals to the experience of resistance: the various beings we encounter offer resistance against our efforts. This experience does not take place on the level of reason but on that of our biological instincts and our efforts to overcome resistance. "Reality is not given to us in perceptual acts but in our drives and attempts vis-à-vis the world, or, more broadly, in our dynamic-practical behavior" (FormEng 318, FormGer 209). In contrast to the level of *spirit*, it is the center of *life* and its drives that is at stake here. "Resistance is thus centrally experienced at that level of my 'self' which may be provisionally defined as the drive-like center of life, *triebhaftes Lebenszentrum*" (FormEng 321, FormGer 211).

Does Scheler truly escape from Kantian idealism and reach real being in this line of argument? It seems promising to focus on resistance. If something can offer resistance, it does seem to exist in its own right. Samuel Johnson refuted Berkeley's idealism by kicking a stone. A problem arises, however, because Scheler wants to avoid at all costs the conclusion that the real is "in the mind," since—he appears to think—if something is in the mind, it cannot be real. This assumption is the reason why he assigns the givenness of the real to a nonrational and ultimately noncognitive power, the drive-like center of life.

Once the givenness of real being is located outside the mind, can real being ultimately be known? To resolve this dilemma, one must concede that an existing being cannot be "in the mind" in the sense of being a mere object of consciousness. It must be transcendent in the sense of having its own being independent from the knowledge of those who know it. Yet in a different sense of the word *in*, real being is *in* my consciousness when I know it. It is *inside* in the sense of being apprehended by me in an interior act that makes use of concepts and statements. The real being is represented in me. I possess a likeness of it.

The exact sense of *representation* and *likeness* needs to be clarified to avoid the trap into which realists fall according to Scheler, the trap of having only representations and likenesses of the objects of knowledge, never the objects of knowledge themselves. By its first presence, a real being is present in the world as something real, independent from my mind. By a second presence, a re-presence, that same real being becomes present also to me as the object of my knowledge. This kind of representation and likeness is not a copy, an internal photograph, as it were, which is then the true object of knowledge, while that of which it is the photograph remains outside and unknown. If one understands knowledge in this way, one can never account for the knowledge of real being because one gets involved in an infinite regress. How do I know that the photograph truly reflects that of which it is the photograph? Evidently, I need to compare it with the original. If I know the likeness of the original by producing another photograph, a representation that is a likeness of the correspondence between the first photograph and the original, the same question arises again. How do I know that this second photograph is truly a representation and likeness? I evidently need another photograph and so on, *ad infinitum*.

To grasp the true meaning of *representation* and *likeness*, one must see these as more immediately attached to the object of knowledge. The being itself becomes present in a second way; namely, to me. The being is expressed in a likeness that I possess, a likeness in the sense that as the thing itself is, so also it is in my concepts and statements about it but according to the mode of the recipient. The object of my knowledge is not these concepts and statements as distinct from the being as a photograph is distinct from what it represents but the being itself through or in these concepts and statements.[14] (See part I, chap. 5, sect. 5, in this volume.)

Scheler does not envisage this possibility, and so he situates the givenness of real being in a self-contradictory way: somehow within human experience but not "in the mind." He places it as far away as possible from rational knowledge, so far away that, in the end, real being still remains utterly foreign to the mind and cannot play an architectonic role in Phenomenology. It seems difficult to avoid the impression that, after all, Scheler's real being is Kant's unknowable thing in itself, and that Scheler's intuitively given essences are citizens in the Kantian realm of phenomena.

Essentialism in the Phenomenological Method

Kantian echoes seem to be present in Scheler's description of the phenomenological method in a posthumously published essay written already in 1913 or 1914.

> In a genuine phenomenological investigation, we abstract from two things when we execute the so-called phenomenological reduction (Husserl): First, the actual performance of the act (*realen Aktvollzug*) and all the accompanying phenomena which do not come within the sense and direction of the act

14. See Thomas, *Summa*, I, q. 85, a. 2.

> itself, along with all the characteristics of its bearer (*Träger*) (animal, man, god). Second, we disregard any positing (belief or unbelief) of the particular coefficient of reality with which the content of the act is "given" in natural perception and in science (for example, actuality, appearance, imagination, illusion). (GW 10:394)

Already the first exclusion is highly problematic. We do not know essences immediately but through an inner word, a *verbum mentis* that is formed in the mind, by which certain aspects of things and natures are known, sometimes vaguely and universally, sometimes more distinctly and specifically.[15] Some characteristics of the objects of knowledge—for example, the universality of the predicable universal—stem from their mode of presence in the knower who grasps them through an imperfect *verbum mentis*. Nevertheless, what Scheler fears as a necessary implication of realism does not follow: "nothing can ever be given 'in consciousness' except an 'image' or a 'symbol' (perception, idea, thought) which refers to the character of the object" ("Idealismus-Realismus," 186–87). Scheler is too quick to assume that essences are immediately given in phenomenological experience without any presuppositions. He seems to ignore the fundamental principle "All that is received in something is in it according to the mode of the recipient."[16]

The second exclusion is even more problematic. Phenomenology, Scheler holds, does not occupy itself with real being. It excludes "the coefficient of reality." Scheler immediately qualifies this exclusion. The coefficient is excluded only inasmuch as we refrain from asserting reality. In its essence, it is not bracketed but remains an object of phenomenological insight. "This coefficient of reality and its essence remain the object of investigation" (GW 10:394). It seems to be, in the end, the essence of the coefficient of reality that is still considered. Existence itself is banished outside the mind as something utterly transcendent and alien. One wonders, then, how its essence can be known.

This banishment of real being from the mind has a profound impact on what is left in the mind. What is left is a realm of immediately given essences detached from real being. A radical and pervasive *essentialism*, Wojtyła observes, is the unavoidable result of these principles.[17] This essentialism affects the whole of Scheler's philosophy. Balthasar makes the same observation. "The almost naïve way Scheler drew an absolute line of separation between *factum* [existence] and *eidos* [essence] has disastrous consequences across the whole range of his thought."[18]

15. See Thomas, *Summa* I, q. 27, a. 1, q. 85.
16. *Summa* I, q. 76, a. 2, obj. 3; cf. *Summa* I, q. 89, a. 4, corp.; see Aristotle, *De anima* 2.12, 424a18–23.
17. For the charge of essentialism, see Wojtyła, *Scheler*, 188–89.
18. Balthasar, *Apokalypse der deutschen Seele*, 3:125.

Essentialism in the Understanding of Value

Scheler's essentialism can be seen in his understanding of value. Value, according to Scheler, is manifest or given in a certain kind of feeling. The German word that Scheler uses for *feeling* is *Fühlen* rather than *Gefühl* or *Empfindung*. The latter two words, he points out, can refer to unintentional states of feeling—for example, a toothache—while *Fühlen* understood in the sense of "to feel something" in a transitive sense is an intentional act, that is, an act that *tends into* something by being *about* something.[19] When I feel the roughness of a surface with my hand, my feeling is *about* the roughness. It is intentionally related to the roughness. A toothache, by contrast, is not *about* some object. The feelings Scheler has in mind in his account of value are emotions that have an *intentional* character in the sense that they are about a value.

Scheler partly agrees with Kant in considering love, even the most spiritual love, a feeling rather than an act of will. According to Kant,

> Love is a matter of feeling (*Empfindung*), not of willing, and I cannot love because I will to, even less because I ought to (being necessitated to love). A duty to love is thus nonsense. (MetaphMorals AK 6:401)
>
> [Love] for human beings is possible, but it cannot be commanded, because it is in no man's power to love another simply by command. (*Practical Reason,* AK 5:83)

Scheler agrees with Kant that love is a feeling and rejects the commandment of love for the same reason (see FormEng 220–26, FormGer 226–32). Yet he resists Kant's reduction of all love to sense-desire and the object of all love to sense-pleasure. Love is a spiritual intentional act in which one feels a value.

Feelings—and here one can see one of the clearest examples of Scheler's exaggerated opposition to Kant—are the primary acts of the human person, more fundamental than willing and knowing. For Kant, all feelings (with the single exception of the reverence for duty) are at home in the empirical and irrational realm of sense-desire, far from the rational core of the person. For Scheler, love constitutes the innermost core of the person. The human person can be defined as *ens amans.*[20] Feelings are not chaotic, but they imply a definite order of love connected with a definite objective hierarchy of values.

19. The word *intentional* in this context is used in the technical sense current in phenomenology. It does not refer to an action done *intentionally* as opposed to, for example, seeing a bird fly by without intending to. In the sense at stake here, this act of seeing is still called *intentional* inasmuch as it is *about* the color and movement of the bird and in this way *tends into* something.

20. Frings, *Mind of Max Scheler*, 68.

Value and feeling are correlative. One can speak of values only as objective correlates of acts of feeling.

> He [Scheler] claims there is a primacy of the givenness of contents of values over any other acts of consciousness. Feeling values is basic to the mind's acts; emotive experiences are not internal chaos (Kant) but are suffused with an order of contents of values very different from the laws of logic pertaining to reasoning and thinking. Scheler's argument is like this: just as colors can only be given to us "in" seeing them, so also values are given to us only "in" the feeling of them. Without "seeing" there are no colors. Without "feeling" there are no values.[21]

Frings understands the statement "Without feeling there are no values," in all its metaphysical strictness. Values are inextricably linked with feelings. They are always and only the objects of acts of feeling.

To illustrate the distinction between being and value, Scheler gives the example of fruits that have different kinds of pleasant tastes. Each of these pleasant tastes, as an object of enjoyment, is a value, and each is qualitatively distinct from the others. What determines this qualitative difference is not a particular configuration of objective properties of the fruit's being, which become apparent in sensation, nor is it simply a particular configuration of states of feeling in the one who eats the fruits. The objective value qualities that we feel in our delight in the fruit are "authentic qualities of a value itself" as distinct from being (FormEng 13, FormGer 35). In fact, we can experience values at times in their specific quality before we experience the being of their bearer, such as when we find a person repulsive without being able to name anything in the person's being that would account for this perception. In this case, Scheler claims, we experience the value first and attach it secondarily to a being (see FormEng 17, FormGer 40).

> Value qualities constitute a special essence-domain of objects with its own inherent intelligibility distinct from being. "Values are as a matter of principle given as indifferent with respect to being and non-being" (FormEng 206, FormGer 214). They do not themselves exist but are given only as essences. "As to the question: What is a value? I submit the following answer: Insofar as in the question the word *is* refers to existence (and not only to being as mere copula), a value *is* not at all" (GW 1:98)

Scheler does speak at times of *the being of values*, but this being does not belong to them as values (FormEng 206–8, FormGer 214–15). When we say *This*

21. Frings, *Mind of Max Scheler*, 25. Frings's summary is based on Scheler, FormEng 9–23, FormGer 32–45.

is good, existence does not properly belong to the value but only, in a technical term of Phenomenology, to the *state of affairs* that carries the value, that is, to the fact that this is good. "The statement *It is so* refers not to the value of the being in question but only to the state of affairs that carries this value" (208, FormGer 215). Value is an essence distinct and independent from being.

Essentialism in the Understanding of the Person

One can observe a similar eclipse of real being in Scheler's understanding of the person. The Western theological tradition follows Boethius in defining the person as an individual substance of rational nature. Scheler denies that the person is a substance. The person, he holds, is a certain co-experienced unity of conscious life, an essence given in consciousness. It is a unity of experiencing, a unity experienced within every experience; namely, the presence of all experiences in one and the same consciousness (FormEng 371, FormGer 371).

What the Aristotelian tradition calls *substance* is simply not experienced, Scheler holds. It is a construct of the mind, a supposition that is not needed to understand the person. Scheler offers the following argument by *reductio ad absurdum*. If the person were a substance in itself beyond our conscious experience, there could only be one person "since every kind of manifold, for example, time, space, number, plurality, would be missing" (FormEng 384, FormGer 384).

This argument shows that one of the reasons why Scheler rejects the term *substance* as part of the definition of *person* is that he believes this notion implies a naive picture of an unknown object under or behind attributes that is, in itself and simply speaking, free of these attributes. And thus, because extension and number are conceived as accidents distinct from substantial being, substances are not subject to extension and number (FormEng 384–85, FormGer 384–85).

Thomas, following Aristotle, does not have such a picture of substance. He understands substance as *that which exists*, taking this phrase absolutely or without any further qualification such as *here* or *warm* or the like. Accidents, by contrast, do not exist, but something that exists possesses them as further ways of being that do not constitute it as something that exists in the world in the first place. When I am in various places, first here and then there, my being in a given place is not that in virtue of which I exist at all. Being in a place does not make me *be* without any further qualification, but it makes me *be here or there*. (See part I, chap. 6, sect. 3, in this volume.[22])

22. See Thomas, *Summa* I, q. 5, a. 1, ad 1; I, q. 11, a. 2, ad 1; II-II, q. 17, a. 4, corp.; *De veritate*, q. 21, a. 5, corp.; *Quaestiones disputatae de anima*, a. 9, corp.; a. 11, corp.; *De unione verbi*, a. 3, corp.; 4, corp.; *Principia naturae*, 1.

In a realist metaphysics the notion of substance as that which exists without further qualification is a central and indispensable notion. A realist metaphysics cannot be articulated without a notion of "that which exists, simply speaking." The very fact that such a notion is superfluous in Scheler's account of the person is an indication of his reduction of the person's being to an essence in consciousness. "The person exercises (*vollzieht*) his existence in the lived experience of its possible lived experiences" (FormEng 386, FormGer 385). This loss of the person's being, similar to the loss of the person's being in Kant, is one of the main objects of Wojtyła's critique of Scheler.

> Scheler made use of the epistemological premises of Phenomenology in such a way that his values, particularly moral values, turn out to be mere contents of intentional feeling. Since this content, according to Scheler, is indifferent with respect to existence, one can speak of an essentialism sui generis in his understanding of value. This essentialism goes hand in hand with Scheler's failure to see the person's responsible causal relation to moral values. On the side of the bearer of values, that is, the person, Scheler's essentialism results in actualism, for he denies the existence of the person as a substantial acting being and replaces that being by a series of acts, that is, experiences that are co-experienced in the experience of personal unity.[23]

The Person as a Theomorphic Event

How does Scheler answer the question "What is man?" Does he hold that it must be answered differently in each case, since each person has a unique and unrepeatable value-essence? A horse and a man do not have the same essence. It is only in a certain respect that the two natures are the same; namely, as animal. One can grasp the common genus animal, but human nature is, simply speaking, another nature than the nature of a horse. Is this how distinct human persons differ from each other, according to Scheler? Do human beings not have a common nature?

As pointed about above, Scheler's term *essence* (*Wesen*) does not refer only to the object of the question "What is it?" He often uses it in a more general sense required by the exhaustive distinction between "such-being" (*So-Sein*) and "there-being" (*Dasein*) or existence. *Essence* covers the whole realm of such-being. Essence in this broad sense includes all accidents, considered in their "such-being" rather than their existence. It would thus be in principle possible for Scheler to maintain that human beings share the same nature (in the sense of *what* this person is) and that there is a qualitatively unique "thus-being" (*So-*

23. Wojtyła, *Scheler*, 188–89.

sein) of each person. This qualitatively unique value would not correspond to the question "What?" but to the question "Who?"

Scheler does not take this path. He denies that there is a stable human nature at all. Balthasar argues that the primary reason for Scheler's denial of human nature is theological. Personhood is inseparable from God's glorious descent in the gift of his love. Personhood is an unidentifiable transition between this divine descent and the human search for God.

Scheler sees himself as breaking new ground by this teaching. All accounts of the human person before him were mistaken, because they posited a human nature.

> The error of all accounts of man up until now has been the desire to insert a fixed station between "life" and "God," something that could be defined as an essence, namely, man. But this station does not exist, and it belongs precisely to the essence of man to be indefinable. Man is only a "between," a "limit," an "appearing of God" in the stream of life, an eternal "beyond" of life transcending itself . . . a "theomorphism."[24]

Here we approach the heart of Scheler's personalism as it attempts to shake off the chains of Greek *logos* and break through to an understanding of the person that derives authentically from Christian experience. The reason why human persons do not have a fixed nature is that they cannot be clearly located either on the side of God in a simple identification with God, or on the side of the world in simple distinction from God. Human persons are not individual subjects with a definite rational essence; they are quasi-divine flashes of spirit that enter the stream of life here and there and color it in unique ways. The person is this theomorphic coloring of animal life by spirit.

In this context, Scheler seems to use the term *essence* more in the traditional sense of *what* a being is as opposed to other attributes. If one asks "What is a human person?" the answer is "One cannot answer the question in a determinate way." Human persons have no common *what*.

Scheler attempts to support the denial of human nature by biological arguments. Modern biology, he claims, shows that human beings could have descended independently from several branches of the evolutionary tree. He quotes a biologist's judgment with approval. "If Negroes and Caucasians were snails, zoologists would consider them two species" (FormEng 289n59, FormGer 294n1). The possibility of polygenism and the actual differences between races show that there is no single human nature identifiable by biological descent or biological characteristics. There are only differences of degree among various

24. See Balthasar, *Apokalypse der deutschen Seele*, 3:163.

levels of evolution among primates. Human *life* as opposed to the personal level of *spirit* stands in full evolutionary continuity with animal life. There is, Scheler claims, only a difference of degree between human reason in its more technical aspect corresponding to *homo faber* and the cognitive power of higher animals.

> We conclude that because there is no biological concept of the essence of man, the only boundary with respect to essence and the only relevant boundary with respect to value among earthly beings that have life, does not lie between man and animal at all—rather, man and animal, from the systematic and genetic point of view, represent a continuous transition. The boundary lies between person and organism, between spiritual being (*Geistwesen*) and living being (*Lebewesen*). . . .
>
> In opposition to a certain philosophy that attempts to tell false tales about man as a natural species and that attributes to that species certain "powers" of language, morality, reason, and even a so-called immortal soul-substance, and so on, we expressly deny that these attempts have any *meaning* at all. We assert that within the continuous evolution from animal to man, here and there (that is, not necessarily "everywhere"), acts of a certain essence and laws of acts and values of a certain essence and their connections come to appearance, which we shall first display in their essential contents to show subsequently that they belong in principle to an order above the biological order, and which are nevertheless of sufficient number to allow us a glimpse of the being (*Sein*) of a world of values and persons, which here and there flashes into the human environment but which is not of biological origin. (Scheler FormEng 289–90, FormGer 294)

This explanation of personhood is helpful for understanding Scheler's view about love. At first sight, his claim that we love persons because of what is qualitatively unique in them seems difficult to understand. It seems to dismiss as inferior all attributes one can refer to by general notions, including rationality, goodness, beauty, and virtue, and to raise up as superior what is utterly unique, belonging only to this and no other person, without being able to say what it is and how it is distinct from these common features. Once one sees that what is unique in each person, according to Scheler, is a quasi-divine indefinable flash of spiritual consciousness from above, his view of love becomes a little more transparent. So precious are these flashes of spirit, so transcendent in relation to the inferior biological life of the human animal, including the life of reason, that one can somewhat understand why he would say we love persons because of their qualitatively unique spirit that individuates all such shared attributes.

At the same time, a deeper question arises. Are human persons, according to Scheler, still creatures that stand in need of a good, the infinite good of the divine life? Are they ordered to a common good in which they come to share as parts of a community? Or do they possess definitive fullness of life already within themselves, simply in virtue of being persons? This is the question that stands at the core of Wojtyła's critique of Scheler.

3. Solidarity

For Kant, the one and only absolute value is autonomy. Community can only play a secondary role; it is a means for achieving and living personal autonomy. Scheler, by contrast, strongly emphasizes community, above all by the principle of solidarity, according to which we are responsible not only for ourselves but also for everyone and everything. Scheler mentions Scheeben as a source.

> Mutual solidarity of all for all. [Footnote: Theologically, I find it most deeply portrayed in *The Mysteries of Christianity* by M. Scheeben (Freiburg 1912), especially where he shows how Christ stands at the center of the whole universe.] (GW 6:264n4)

Scheler's main source, however, is Dostoevsky. "In The Brothers Karamazov, Dostoevsky wonderfully expressed the genuine Christian idea of solidarity in guilt and merit in the actions and words of the old starets" (GW 3:120n10).

Solidarity in the Brothers Karamazov

"Everyone is really responsible to all men for all men and for everything."[25] The exchange of place between Christ and sinners seems to be the root of Dostoevsky's understanding of solidarity. The elder Zosima, bearer of Dostoevsky's teaching, says, "On earth, indeed, we are as it were astray, and if it were not for the precious image of Christ before us, we should be undone and altogether lost" (*Brothers Karamazov*, 276). Mark 10:45 comes to mind. "The Son of Man did not come to be served but to serve, and to give his life as a ransom for many."

> If you are penitent, you love. And if you love you are of God. With love all things are bought, all things are saved. If I, a sinner, even as you are, am tender with you and have pity on you, how much more will God. Love is such a priceless treasure that you can buy the whole world by it and redeem not only your own but the sins of others. Go, and be not afraid. (*Brothers Karamazov*, 50)

25. Fyodor Dostoevsky, *The Brothers Karamazov*, 2nd ed., ed. Susan McReynolds, Norton Critical Editions (New York: W. W. Norton, 2011), 268.

The image of Christ was first shown to Zosima when he was only nine years old. His brother Markel became ill and eventually died. Soon after finding out that he would die, a change came over Markel. Until then, he had irritably rejected all religious practices.

> The old nurse would come in and say, "Let me light the lamp before the icon, my dear." And formerly he would not have allowed it and would have even blown it out.
>
> "Light it, light it, dear, I was a wretch to have prevented your doing it. You are praying when you light the lamp, and I am praying when I rejoice seeing you. So we are praying to the same God."
>
> Those words seemed strange to us, and mother would go to her room and weep, but when she went in to him she wiped her eyes and looked cheerful. "Mother, don't weep, darling," he would say, "I've long to live yet, long to rejoice with you, and life is glad and joyful."
>
> "Ah, dear boy, how can you talk of joy when you lie feverish at night, coughing as though you would tear yourself to pieces."
>
> "Don't cry, mother," he would answer, "life is paradise, and we are all in paradise, but we won't see it, if we would, we should have heaven on earth the next day." (*Brothers Karamazov*, 249)

The path toward seeing that life is paradise leads through becoming a servant of all and ascribing all sin to oneself.

> "Mother, my joy," he would say, "there must be servants and masters, but if so I will be the servant of my servants, the same as they are to me. And another thing, mother, every one of us has sinned against all men, and I more than any."
>
> Mother positively smiled at that, smiled through her tears. "Why, how could you have sinned against all men, more than all? Robbers and murderers have done that, but what sin have you committed yet, that you hold yourself guiltier than all?"
>
> "Mother, little heart of mine," he said (he had begun using such strange caressing words at that time), "little heart of mine, my joy, believe me, everyone is really responsible to all men for all men and for everything. I don't know how to explain it to you, but I feel it is so, painfully even. And how is it we went on then living, getting angry and not knowing?"
>
> So he would get up every day, more and more sweet and joyous and full of love. (*Brothers Karamazov*, 250)

Dostoevsky makes clear that Markel's attribution of all sin to himself is not a final excess of depressed reflection on his own sinfulness but a fruit of the intensity of his joyful love for God and his creation. Glory and beauty are the causes of his solidarity with all.

> The first birds of spring were flitting in the branches, chirruping and singing at the windows. And looking at them and admiring them, he began suddenly begging their forgiveness too, "Birds of heaven, happy birds, forgive me, for I have sinned against you too." None of us could understand that at the time, but he shed tears of joy. "Yes," he said, "there was such a glory of God all about me; birds, trees, meadows, sky, only I lived in shame and dishonored it all and did not notice the beauty and glory." (*Brothers Karamazov*, 250)

The memory of Markel's illness and death stayed secretly in Zosima's heart. It reemerged at a decisive moment of crisis. Zosima, now a military officer given to a life of drinking and brawling, challenges someone to a duel. On the evening before the duel, drunk and in a savage mood, he strikes his servant in the face with full force over and over again. He awakes at dawn, haunted by the memory of the event.

> It all arose suddenly before my mind, it all was as it were repeated over again; he stood before me and I was beating him straight on the face and he was holding his arms stiffly down, his head erect, his eyes fixed upon me as though on parade. He staggered at each blow and did not even dare to raise his hands to protect himself. That is what a man has been brought to and that was a man beating a fellow man! What a crime! It was as though a sharp needle had pierced me right through. I stood as if I were struck dumb, while the sun was shining, the leaves were rejoicing and sparkling and the birds were trilling the praise of God....
>
> I hid my face in my hands, fell on my bed and broke into a storm of tears. And then I remembered my brother Markel and what he said on his deathbed to his servants: "My dear ones, why do you wait on me, why do you love me, am I worth your waiting on me?" Yes, am I worth it? Flashed through my mind. After all what am I worth, that another man, a fellow creature, made in the likeness and image of God, should serve me? For the first time in my life this question forced itself upon me.
>
> He had said, "Mother, my little heart, in truth we are each responsible to all for all, it's only that men don't know this. If they knew it, the world would be a paradise at once." (*Brothers Karamazov*, 257)

In Zosima's later teaching as told by Alyosha Karamazov, the same theme comes out as the main point.

> There is only one means of salvation, then take yourself and make yourself responsible for all men's sins, that is the truth ... for as soon as you sincerely make yourself responsible for everything and for all men, you will see at once that it is really so, and that you are to blame for everyone and for all things. (*Brothers Karamazov*, 267)
>
> Remember particularly that you cannot be a judge of anyone. For no one

can judge a criminal, until he recognizes that he is just such a criminal as the man standing before him, and that he perhaps is more than all men to blame for that crime. When he understands that, he will be able to be a judge. Though that sounds absurd, it is true. If I had been righteous myself, perhaps there would have been no criminal standing before me. If you can take upon yourself the crime of the criminal your heart is judging, take it at once, suffer for him yourself, and let him go without reproach. ...

If the evildoing of men fills you with indignation and overwhelming distress, even to a desire for vengeance on the evildoers, shun above all things that feeling. Go at once and seek suffering for yourself, as though you were yourself guilty of that wrong. Accept that suffering and bear it and your heart will find comfort, and you will understand that you too are guilty, for you might have been a light to the evildoers, even as the one man sinless, and you were not a light to them. (*Brothers Karamazov*, 276–77)

Solidarity in John Paul II

John Paul formulates the principle in lapidary form close to Dostoevsky and Scheler. "We are all really responsible for all" (*Sollicitudo Rei Socialis* 38). For Scheler, the principle of solidarity is the fundamental principle of social life.

The principle of solidarity is for us an eternal component and, as it were, a fundamental article of the cosmos of finite moral persons. It is only in virtue of the validity of this principle that the entire moral world ... becomes one great whole that rises and falls as a whole with even the slightest change within it, and as a whole possesses at every moment of its being a unique moral comprehensive value (*Gesamtwert*) (a comprehensive good [*Gesamtgut*] and a comprehensive evil [*Gesamtböses*], a comprehensive guilt [*Gesamtschuld*] and comprehensive merit [*Gesamtverdienst*]) that can never be regarded as a possible sum of individuals' evil and good or as the sum of their guilt and merit. But every person, both the individual person and the comprehensive person, participates in this according to his or her special unique membership.

If we imagine something like a final judgment of the whole world, no one would be examined alone by the supreme judge; all would have to answer him in the unity of one act, and the ear of the supreme judge would have to listen to them in one act. He would not judge anyone until he has co-heard, co-understood, and co-evaluated all others with this one. In each he would co-judge the whole no less than the whole in each. (FormEng 534–35, FormGer 523)

In his writings on World War I, Scheler applies this analysis of solidarity to the moral task Europe was facing in the wake of the war. Without denying that particular individuals and nations had a burden of responsibility for beginning and continuing the war, Scheler argues that cultural reconstruction after the war could take place only if more and more persons ascribed guilt for the war to themselves.

> A cultural reconstruction is only possible if an increasingly large proportion of the European peoples learns to look upon this cataclysm as resulting from a comprehensive guilt (*Gesamtschuld*) of European peoples mutually influencing each other.... First, therefore, must come the recognition that in the final analysis there is only one answer to the question, Who or what nation is responsible for this war? The answer is You, the one who asks the question—by what you have done or left undone. (GW 5:446–47)

An objection could be raised. It seems out of proportion for every person to ascribe the comprehensive sin of the war to himself or herself. One might attempt to calculate the actual impact of each individual person by dividing the comprehensive guilt by the number of persons involved. With millions of persons in Europe, the share of each, leaving aside the key political and military leaders in the war, is so minute as to be negligible. Yet Scheler seems to be in contact with a profound Christian truth when, following Dostoevsky, he urges all to ascribe the comprehensive guilt for the war to themselves in truly substantial measure. Dostoevsky's formulation of the principle of solidarity clearly goes in this direction: "There is only one means of salvation, then take yourself and make yourself responsible for all men's sins ... you are to blame for everyone and for all things" (*Brothers Karamazov*, 267).

What made it possible for a war to take place with such hatred and destructive ferocity was a comprehensive guilt. Europe can only purify itself from this guilt if persons assume serious and substantial responsibility for it. Only a shared act of repentance can achieve the purification required for cultural reconstruction. So long as individuals and nations only point to others and exempt themselves from responsibility, purification is impossible. John Paul speaks in a remarkably similar manner about "social sin."

> To speak of social sin means in the first place to recognize that, by virtue of a human solidarity which is as mysterious and intangible as it is real and concrete, each individual's sin in some way affects others. This is the other aspect of that solidarity which on the religious level is developed in the profound and magnificent mystery of the Communion of Saints, thanks to which it has been possible to say that "every soul that rises above itself, raises up the world." To this law of ascent there unfortunately corresponds the law of descent.
>
> Consequently, one can speak of a communion of sin, whereby a soul that lowers itself through sin drags with itself the Church and, in some way, the whole world. In other words, there is no sin, not even the most intimate and

> secret one, the most strictly individual one, that exclusively concerns the person committing it. With greater or lesser violence, with greater or lesser harm, every sin has repercussions on the entire ecclesial body and the whole human body. (*Reconciliatio et Paenitentia* 16)[26]

This text shows that John Paul understands solidarity in a manner remarkably similar to Dostoevsky and Scheler. Every act, for evil or good, influences the whole world and therefore brings with it a responsibility for the whole and for each member in that whole.

Another objection could be raised. By making everyone responsible for all, universal solidarity makes no one responsible for anything. If I am just as responsible for millions of unknown persons as I am for persons in my home, I am likely to overlook that closer responsibility.[27] As Crosby shows, however, Scheler sees various levels of responsibility though he does not always distinguish them clearly: our responsibility for our own acts over which we have most direct power; our share in the responsibility of others for their acts owing to a mutual influence that establishes a comprehensive moral condition; our *innocent* share in guilt owing to our unity with other persons, among them persons who lived long before us. In the third case, we *innocently* contract guilt because we cannot be directly responsible for the sins of our ancestors. Nevertheless, we do inherit such guilt and can rightly atone for it.[28]

Solidarity and the Mystery of Christ

Toward the end of his extensive discussion of solidarity in *Sollicitudo Rei Socialis*, John Paul considers solidarity in light of the mystery of Christ. He touches the deepest point of Scheler's attempt to develop an understanding of the world that springs from the Christian experience of love.

> Solidarity is undoubtedly a Christian virtue. In what has been said so far it has been possible to identify many points of contact between solidarity and charity, which is the distinguishing mark of Christ's disciples (cf. John 13:35).
>
> In the light of faith, solidarity seeks to go beyond itself, to take on the specifically Christian dimension of total gratuity, forgiveness, and reconciliation. One's neighbor is then not only a human being with his or her own rights and a fundamental equality with everyone else but becomes the living image of God the Father, redeemed by the blood of Jesus Christ and placed under the

26. See John F. Crosby, *Personalist Papers* (Washington, DC: Catholic University of America Press, 2004), 178.

27. See Crosby, *Personalist Papers*, 177n8.

28. Crosby, *Personalist Papers*, 181–84.

> permanent action of the Holy Spirit. One's neighbor must therefore be loved, even if an enemy, with the same love with which the Lord loves him or her; and for that person's sake one must be ready for sacrifice, even the ultimate one: to lay down one's life for the brethren (cf. 1 John 3:16). (*Sollicitudo Rei Socialis* 40)

This deeper level of solidarity seems to be present from the beginning in Dostoevsky's and Scheler's formulation of the principle of solidarity. One can see it in the apparent excess pointed out above. "There is only one means of salvation, then take yourself and make yourself responsible for all men's sins.... You are to blame for everyone and for all things" (*Brothers Karamazov*, 299). "We are all really responsible for all" (*Sollicitudo Rei Socialis* 38). The extent of responsibility goes far beyond what can be reasonably attributed to the causal power of individual human beings. In the end, this excess can only be understood as the mystery of Christ and as sharing in this same mystery. The fourth song of the Suffering Servant, the mysterious solidarity of the Servant, is a key text for the Christian faith.

> Surely, he bore our infirmities
>   and carried our diseases,
> yet we accounted him punished,
>   struck by God, and afflicted.
> But he was wounded for our transgressions,
>   crushed for our iniquities;
> the punishment for our peace was upon him,
>   and by his bruises we are healed.
> All of us have gone astray like sheep.
>   We all turned away to our own way.
> And the Lord has laid on him the sin of us all (Isaiah 53:4–6; cf. 1 Pet 2:22–25).

In Isaiah, the Suffering Servant is identified as the people of Israel. In Isaiah 44:21, the Servant is called Jacob and Israel. An individual Servant seems to be implied as well. In Isaiah 42:6, the Servant is given to the people and is thus distinct from it. For Christian faith, the Suffering Servant is Jesus, though Israel and the Church as a corporate servant are not excluded, nor are individuals within it. In Colossians 1:24, Paul speaks of his own suffering as "filling up" that of Christ. The mystery announced in the last song of the Suffering Servant (Isaiah 52:13–53:12) consists in this, that which apparently belongs most personally to individual persons—namely, their own sins—is shared by another who suffers through them. "This is the lamb of God who bears away the sin [singular] of the world" (John 1:29). "God made him who knew no sin to be sin [singular]" (2 Corinthians 5:21).

In the context of a discussion of the sufferings of Jesus in his passion, St. Thomas speaks about the interior suffering caused by the sins of the whole human race inasmuch as Jesus makes these sins in some way his own and *ascribes* them to himself, as it were, *quasi*. The manner in which Thomas expresses this mystery is close to the principle of solidarity.

> The cause of interior pain was, first of all, all the sins of the human race, for which he satisfied by suffering, which is why he ascribed them to himself, as it were (*quasi*), by saying according to the Psalm, "The words of my crimes."[29]

The phrase "The words of my crimes" is found at the beginning of Psalm 21 (Vulgate) immediately after "My God, why have you forsaken me? Thomas interprets "My God, why have you forsaken me?" as an allusion to the whole psalm, including the phrase "my crimes."[30] "O God, my God, look upon me: Why have you forsaken me? Far from my salvation are the words of my crimes" (Ps 21:2, Vulgate).[31] All these words should be heard as spoken by Jesus on the Cross, according to Thomas. Satisfaction for sin—this is the foundation of Thomas's argument—requires that sinners remember their sin, that they ascribe it to themselves as their own, and that they suffer through it from the perspective of love. This suffering of love is transforming and restores the broken relation of unity. It reverses the sinner's position in relation to sin. Here lies the inescapable key role of suffering in atonement. "The pain of penitence is the greatest among all pains" *maximus est inter omnes dolores.*[32]

When he satisfies for us, taking as his own what belongs to us, Christ attributes our sins to himself "as it were" (*quasi*), to suffer through them. The word *quasi* is important. Christ did not sin, and yet in the mystery of the cross, in the amazing exchange, *admirabile commercium*), he takes what is ours to give what is his.

John Paul understands the principle of solidarity in a similar way. On Sunday, March 12, 2000, he led the Church in a corporate and personal act of repentance for past and present sins for the sake of a "purification of memory." This public act corresponds in a remarkable degree to the purification Scheler called for after World War I. Objections were raised against the act, but the theological foundations are solid. John Paul explains them in his sermon for the occasion.

29. Thomas, *Summa* III, q. 46, a. 6, corp.

30. Thomas, *Super Psalmos*, on Psalm 21. Numbering of Psalm 21 according to the Vulgate, 22, in the Masoretic text.

31. "The words of my crimes" is the translation adopted by the Septuagint and Vulgate. Most modern translations understand the Hebrew as "the words of my groaning."

32. Thomas, *Super Psalmos*, on Psalm 45.

> "He made him who did not know sin to be sin" (2 Corinthians 5:21). A few moments ago, in the second reading, we heard this surprising assertion made by the Apostle. What do these words mean? They seem, and in effect are, a paradox. How could God, who is holiness itself, "make" his Only-begotten Son, sent into the world, "to be sin"? ...
>
> Already in the Old Testament, the Book of Isaiah speaks of it with inspired foresight in the fourth song of the Servant of Yahweh: "We had all gone astray like sheep, each following his own way; but the Lord laid upon him the guilt of us all" (Is 53:6).
>
> Although Christ, the Holy One, was absolutely sinless, he agreed to take our sins upon himself. He agreed to redeem us; he agreed to bear our sins to fulfill the mission he had received from the Father....
>
> Before Christ who, out of love, took our guilt upon himself, we are all invited to make a profound examination of conscience. One of the characteristic elements of the Great Jubilee is what I described as the "purification of memory" (Bull *Incarnationis Mysterium* 11). As the Successor of Peter, I asked that "in this year of mercy the Church, strong in the holiness which she receives from her Lord, should kneel before God and implore forgiveness for the past and present sins of her sons and daughters" (ibid.). Today, the First Sunday of Lent, seemed to me the right occasion for the Church, gathered spiritually round the Successor of Peter, to implore divine forgiveness for the sins of all believers. Let us forgive and ask forgiveness! ...
>
> Indeed, "because of the bond which unites us to one another in the Mystical Body, all of us, though not personally responsible and without encroaching on the judgment of God who alone knows every heart, bear the burden of the errors and faults of those who have gone before us" (*Incarnationis Mysterium*, n. 11). The recognition of past wrongs serves to reawaken our consciences to the compromises of the present, opening the way to conversion for everyone....
>
> Let us confess, even more, our responsibilities as Christians for the evils of today. We must ask ourselves what our responsibilities are regarding atheism, religious indifference, secularism, ethical relativism, the violations of the right to life, disregard for the poor in many countries.
>
> We humbly ask forgiveness for the part which each of us has had in these evils by our own actions, thus helping to disfigure the face of the Church.[33]

The principle of solidarity is clearly visible in these words. Solidarity is first realized in Jesus when God "laid upon him the guilt of us all" and thereby "made him to be sin." It is in the face of his mystery, as a participation in this mystery, that the purification of memory can and must take place.

In comparison with Zosima, John Paul is careful and circumspect in preserving the uniqueness of Christ. He alone gathers up the whole sin of the world

33. John Paul II, *Sermon for the Day of Pardon*, March 12, 2000.

to bear it. He is the only one whose redeeming love enables him to become, as it were (*quasi*, as Thomas is careful to add), the one "responsible for all men's sins," the one "to blame for everyone and for all things."[34]

Scheler's Response to Nietzsche

The principle of solidarity has an important apologetic function in Scheler's response to Nietzsche. Christian love, Nietzsche argues, is the final fruit of the Jewish slave revolt in morals, driven by the resentment of a weak priestly nation against all that is strong, beautiful, and full of vitality.

> The chivalrous-aristocratic judgments of value have as their premise a powerful bodily nature, a blooming, rich, even overflowing health, together with what is required to maintain them—war, adventure, hunting, dancing, tournaments, and generally all that involves strong, free, happy action....
>
> It was the Jews who, in opposition to the aristocratic value equation (good equals noble, powerful, beautiful, happy, beloved by the divine), dared with fearsome consistency to bring about its inversion and to cling to it with the teeth of the most bottomless hatred (the hatred of impotence): "only the miserable are the good; the poor, the impotent, the low are the only good; the suffering, the needy, the sick, the ugly are also the only pious, the only ones blessed by God; for them alone is there blessedness. You, on the other side, you, the noble and powerful, you are for all eternity the evil, the cruel, the lecherous, the insatiable, the godless; you will also for all eternity be the nefarious, the accursed, and the damned!" ...
>
> With the Jews begins the slave revolt in morals, the revolt that has two-thousand years of history behind it and which we no longer notice today because—it has been victorious....
>
> Out of the trunk of that tree of revenge and hatred, Jewish hatred—the deepest and most sublime hatred, that is, a hatred which creates ideals and transforms values, the like of which has never been seen on earth—grew something just as incomparable, a new love, the deepest and most sublime of all the kinds of love. From what other trunk could it have grown?
>
> Whatever else, do not believe that this love arose as the true denial of that thirst for revenge, as the contrary of Jewish hatred. No. Quite the opposite! This love grew out of hatred, as its crown, as the triumphant crown extending wider and wider in the purest brightness and sunshine, entering the realm of light and height to seek for the aims of this hatred, for prey, for seduction, with the same urge with which the roots of that hatred had been sinking down ever more thoroughly and more greedily into everything deep and evil.

34. Dostoevsky, *Brothers Karamazov*, 299.

> This Jesus of Nazareth, the Gospel of love in person, the "Redeemer," who brought blessedness and victory to the poor, to the sick, to the sinners—was not precisely he the seduction in its most terrible and irresistible form, the seduction and detour to exactly those Jewish values and revolutions of the ideal? Did not Israel . . . through this apparent enemy and dissolver of Israel attain the final goal of its sublime thirst for revenge? Does it not belong to the secret black art of a truly great politics of revenge, a far-sighted, underground, slowly gripping and pre-calculating revenge, that Israel itself had to disown and nail to the cross, like some mortal enemy, the true tool of its revenge before all the world, so that "all the world," that is, all of Israel's enemies, could then swallow this bait without any misgivings?
>
> And is it possible with all subtlety of mind to imagine a more dangerous bait? Something to match the enticing, intoxicating, stupefying, corrupting power of that symbol of the "Holy Cross," that ghastly paradox of a "God on the Cross," that mystery of an unimaginable and final most extreme cruelty and self-crucifixion of God for the salvation of man? At least it is certain that *sub hoc signo*[35] Israel, with its revenge and revaluation of all values, has until now triumphed again and again over all other ideals, over all nobler ideals.[36]

Scheler responds that Christian love is not born from the resentment of the weak. It is a movement of free giving out of fullness, a descent from the heights of vital power to the depths of solidarity.

> What does the bourgeois man, who "wants to become something," and who secretly measures himself by his lords and kings even when he rebels against them—what could he know of voluntary self-abasement, of the sweet urge of pouring oneself out felt by those who are something (the ἐσθλοί, the noble), who do not see themselves as standing on the heights precisely because they do, as a matter of course, stand on the heights?
>
> Humility, this is precisely the movement of self-abasement, the movement of coming down from above, of coming from the height, of God letting himself glide down to humanity, of the holy one to the sinner—this free, daring, fearless movement of a spirit whose fullness, a fullness possessed as a matter of course, makes it impossible for him even to understand the concept of lavishly giving oneself away and squandering oneself (*Selbstverschwendung*). (GW 3:25)

35. According to Eusebius of Caesarea, the Cross appeared in the sky to the Emperor Constantine before the decisive battle at the Milvian Bridge. It bore the inscription τούτῳ νίκα, or "Win victory by this!" Eusebius, *Vita Constantini* 1.28. This Greek phrase is usually translated into Latin as *in hoc signo vinces*, or "in this sign you will conquer." Nietzsche's Latin *sub hoc signo* "under this sign" is another way of translating the Greek. It expresses the subordination of Constantine and his legions to the Cross.

36. Nietzsche, *Genealogy of Morals* 1.7–8; KSA 5:268–69; see also the aphorisms about the Jews in *Cheerful Science* 135–41; KSA 3:486–89.

The weak man wants to rule, Scheler goes on to argue. The desire to rule stands at the center of the weak man's being. He only serves his master because he is too weak to dominate his dominator. For the strong, for the natural lord, who has power by sheer vitality, the desire to rule lies on the periphery of his being because he does not need to strive for rule. He achieves it naturally. At the core of his being stands humility before God and the willingness to serve, because he knows he stands on the heights of excellence and is not afraid to let go.[37]

Scheler's response to Nietzsche may be one of the reasons for the increasing distance that, according to Wojtyła, separates Scheler's theomorphic personalism of solidarity from the Gospel. Zosima sees himself as a sinner, as being at the bottom, not as standing on the heights. He does not glide fearlessly down from the heights of divinity but follows his master to the Cross. Balthasar's notes the same problem pointed out by Wojtyła.

> In all these arguments that are supposed to protect Christianity against the accusation of resentment (*Ressentiment*), Scheler radically overlooks the concrete form (*Gestalt*) of God's self-emptying in Christ, which, in its decisive form (*Gestalt*) on the Cross, is not "fearless fullness" but "fearful emptiness," not a sacrifice as "natural overflow" but being sacrificed in the form of being unnaturally squeezed out in the winepress of the Garden of Olives, and finally not "heroic" bending down but simple and obedient being sent down. This defense of the "heroic elements" in Christianity is the sign of a confusion that is no less pernicious than the opposite reduction of Christianity to bourgeois values.... This is nothing but the reflection of the exaltation of the essential core of the spiritual man into heaven.[38]

4. The Uniqueness of the Person

Scheler spells out his understanding of the person most fully in *Formalism in Ethics*. In what follows, I summarize the most important part of the book, closely following Scheler's own outline and using his own headings.

Scheler divides his main treatment into "A. On the Theoretical Understanding of the Person as Such" and "B. The Person in Ethical Contexts".

The first of these has three sections: "1. Person and Reason," "2. Person and the 'I' of Transcendental Appeception," and "3. Person and Act."

37. See Scheler, "Zur Rehabilitierung der Tugend," GW 25–26.
38. Balthasar, *Apokalypse der deutschen Seele*, 3:167.

"Person and Reason"

Kant conceives the person as a logical subject, Scheler argues, as an "X" that exhausts its entire identity in being the point from which practical reason and a rational will in accord with universal law proceeds. The person as person is the subject of morality. In his evaluation of this thesis, Scheler first mentions a point of agreement with Kant.

> As what follows will show, one thing in this definition is entirely correct: namely, that the person must never be considered a thing or a substance with faculties and powers, one of which is the "faculty" or "power" of reason and so on. The person is, rather, the immediately co-experienced unity of experiencing; the person is not a merely thought thing behind and outside what is immediately experienced. (FormEng 371, FormGer 371)

Wojtyła argues in *Person and Act* that the person does not consist of the unity of consciousness. The person is a *suppositum* and substance with definite faculties. On this point, he is opposed to Scheler, though the opposition is not easy to sort out, because what Wojtyła means by *substance* differs from what Scheler means.

After this agreement with Kant, Scheler comes to his main disagreement. If the person's identity consists only in being the subject of practical reason and of a rational will in accord with universal law, then nothing distinguishes individual human beings in their personhood. The idea of an individual person becomes a contradiction in terms. All that accounts for individuality is accidental and subpersonal. This view, Scheler claims, contradicts the essential connection (*Wesenszusammenhang*) given to immediate phenomenological intuition between finite personhood and qualitatively unique individuality. The person does not become an individual only through an accidental configuration of background and experience, or an individual body, or *materia prima*. Each person is individual precisely as a person (see the discussion of individuation in part I, chap. 6, sect. 5, in this volume).

Kant is faced with an inescapable dilemma, Scheler continues. On the one hand, if he rigorously maintains that the person is a mere *X* that is the subject of morality, he cannot maintain that the person possesses autonomy. He condemns the person to *logonomy*, that is, to a condition of subjection under an impersonal general law and therefore (from Scheler's point of view) to "the most extreme heteronomy" (FormEng 372, FormGer 372).

Kant's understanding of autonomy rests on the idea of the person as the absolutely first causal origin of acts without the influence of any prior given. A pre-given good that influences free choice destroys autonomy. A prior father to whom the person relates as son destroys it most radically. Autonomy is thus qualitatively the same in all human beings. It is quite logical, Scheler observes, that some post-Kantian philosophers (esp. Fichte and Hegel) concluded that the person is simply "an indifferent point of passage" for an impersonal activity of reason, as Averroes and Spinoza already held. Rigorously maintained, he concludes, Kant's view of the person destroys the dignity of the person. Kant remains imprisoned in Greek universal *logos*. He does not do justice to the personalist revolution brought by Christianity, which shows the unique glory of the person in opposition to Greek *logos*.

Scheler's understanding of autonomy and heteronomy rests on his understanding of personal uniqueness. To be subject to a general law, a law that applies equally to each person, would be *logonomy* and therefore heteronomy. The underlying premise is that the person is guided by its unique and unrepeatable value-essence. Only in this way can its selfhood and therefore its autonomy be affirmed. Here one can observe Scheler's program of de-Hellenizing Christian thought from another angle: the rejection of the universality of Greek *logos*.

If Kant does not rigorously maintain that the person exhausts its being as the subject of morality but includes other realities and attributes in the foundation of ethics, he opens the floodgates of irrationality. Even the most accidental facts, such as blinking an eye or undergoing a random change of mood, will co-constitute the moral subject. The result will be an ethics in which the person simply lives out what happens to be the desire of the moment (see FormEng 373, FormGer 372). Also in this second option, therefore, Kant would destroy the dignity of the person.

The only way in which one can escape the dilemma, Scheler claims, is to acknowledge spiritual personhood and qualitatively unique individuality as belonging together (FormEng 373, FormGer 372–73). The dignity of the person rests ultimately on the person's unique and unrepeatable value-essence.

The importance of personal uniqueness for Scheler is difficult to overestimate. It is, in his own mind, the distinguishing mark of his own personalism in contrast with Kant's personalism. In *Person and Act*, Wojtyła speaks much about the person as "unique und unrepeatable." We should return to his important letter to Henri de Lubac discussed above (see part II, chap. 2, sect. 1, in this volume).

> I devote my very rare free moments to a work that is close to my heart and devoted to the metaphysical sense and mystery of the PERSON. It seems to me that the debate today is being played on that level. The evil of our times consists in the first place in a kind of degradation, indeed in a pulverization of the fundamental uniqueness of each human person. This evil is even much more of the metaphysical order than of the moral order. To this disintegration,

> planned at times by atheistic ideologies, we must oppose, rather than sterile polemics, a kind of "recapitulation" of the inviolable mystery of the person.[39]

Wojtyła shares the concern for personal uniqueness with Scheler. Nowhere in *Person and Act*, however, nor in any of his other writings, does he affirm the form of qualitative or *essential* uniqueness (in the broad sense of *essential* corresponding to "such-being," *Sosein*) that is Scheler's concern. Instead, he focuses on personal subjectivity, self-awareness, self-determination, and the ordination of each person to the good, which is closely connected with the first principle in *Gaudium et spes* 24, "Man is the only creature on earth which God wills for itself." On this level, the uniqueness of the person is qualitatively the same in every human being, a point affirmed by Boethius's definition of *person* as "individual substance of rational nature." Qualitative differences are not unimportant, but they enter on another level in the course of a person's life.

"Person and the 'I' of Transcendental Apperception"

Kant's view of the person is closely connected with the foundation of his account of reason. He articulates this foundation in the famous transcendental deduction. The act of consciousness, "I think (the *cogito*)," he claims in that pivotal argument of the *Critique of Pure Reason*, is the fundamental act that grounds all thought. The unity of consciousness, of "I think," is the ground of the objective unity of the manifold objects of my thought. The *cogito* supplies the "original synthetic unity of apperception." It places together into unity (*syn* = together; *thetic* = placed) what it looks toward (*ad-perceptio* or *apperceptio* = looking toward).[40] When Kant calls this apperception *transcendental*, he signifies that it is the condition for the possibility of all knowledge. With particular attention to the *object* of knowledge, Scheler summarizes Kant's view as follows.

> Kant holds that the primordial condition of every objective unity given in experience, and thus of the very idea of an object as such . . . is an "I think" which must accompany every act of perception, representation, and so on. That is, the "I" that is meant here is not a correlate after the fact of the unity of the object, but its unity and identity is the condition of the unity and identity of the object. "Object" accordingly means only something identifiable by an I.

39. Henri de Lubac, *At the Service of the Church: Henri de Lubac Reflects on the Circumstances That Occasioned His Writings* (San Francisco: Ignatius, 1989), 171–72.

40. See Kant, *Critique of Pure Reason*, B 131–36. The *Critique of Pure Reason* is cited as B (2nd ed.) with the original pagination. Translations are based with modifications on Immanuel Kant, *Critique of Pure Reason, Critique of Practical Reason, Critique of Judgment*, trans. Werner S. Pluhar (Indianapolis: Hackett, 2002).

> Identity is here (in contrast to our own view) not a characteristic of the essence of the object, a characteristic that would be intuitable as such in any object.... Rather, the meaning of the word "object" supposedly coincides with the identifiability of something by an I. Accordingly, identity would belong more originally to the I than to the object and the object would carry identity as something borrowed from the I. (FormEng 374, FormGer 373–74)

Scheler objects that the *I* is itself an object of thought. It would be circular to make its unity depend on that of the "I think." This objection does not imply that, according to Scheler, the person is an existing subject that can be regarded as an object. As in section 1, Scheler rejects the idea that the *I* is a "soul-thing" or substance. Such a substance, conceived as the true subject and origin of acts, is simply not given in phenomenological experience. It is a mere construct (see FormEng 376–77, FormGer 376).

This discussion of the *I* does not yet bring us to the question of the *person*, according to Scheler. The concept of *person*, he claims, emerges only when one takes two further steps beyond the "I." The first is to focus on the essence of intentional acts such as judging, loving, hating, by excluding everything that is accidentally attached to them, such as real existence and the merely factual dispositions of the subject. Scheler calls this first step phenomenological *reduction*.

The second step is to ask how acts of different nature are one in the agent (*Vollzieher*) of these acts. "It is precisely here—and not 'earlier' within the order of problems involved—that the problem of personhood confronts us" (FormEng 381, FormGer 380).

In *Person and Act*, Wojtyła argues in a similar manner; he formulates the question of the person in terms of the person's acts: the acts throw light on the person. Yet the conclusion he reaches is the opposite of Scheler's. The acts of the person display the person as a concrete substance, a *suppositum*.

Together with the question of the person, Scheler argues, a second question arises; namely, the question of the objective correlate of the person, the *world* as a whole. The body and the *I* have only an environment, but the person stands face-to-face with the world (see FormEng 381, FormGer 381). Because the *world* contains both psychic and bodily phenomena, "the essence of the person is psychophysically indifferent" (FormEng, FormGer 381). Neither the body, nor the soul, nor both together constitute the person. The person is something third; namely, spirit. Wojtyła, by contrast, holds the Thomistic account of the person as a composite of body and soul.

5. "Person and Act"

"a. Person and Act"

Having clarified his agreement and disagreement with Kant in the first two sections, Scheler presents his own theoretical understanding of the person in the third section under the heading *Person and Act.* He divides the argument into seven steps, the first of which also has the heading *Person and Act.* It seems likely that Wojtyła chose the title of his own book, *Person and Act*, as an echo of Scheler's repeated title.

The first of the seven steps, *Person and Act*, is the fundamental step on which all others depend. Scheler offers the following "essential definition" (*Wesensdefinition*) of the person. "The person is the concrete and itself essence-like (*wesenhaft*) unity in being of acts of different essence.... The being of the person 'grounds' (*fundiert*) all essentially different acts" (FormEng 383, FormGer 382–83). The manner in which the person grounds acts of different essence is connected with consciousness. The person is the co-experienced unity of experiencing. According to this definition, the person belongs to the order of consciously experienced essences rather than to the order of real being. It grounds particular acts, not as a really existing being that is the subject or *suppositum* of these acts but as the one consciousness, or rather as a unique qualitative character of one consciousness, in which many acts take place. The real existence of any person "outside the mind" is not a phenomenological given for Scheler.

After offering his definition, Scheler returns to the topic of substance to argue in greater detail that the person cannot be a substance.

> The person is not a "thing" or a "substance" which executes acts in the sense of a substance-causality. For such "things" could in fact be randomly obliterated or exchanged, if there is a multiplicity (one thinks of Kant's picture of electric spheres, which are dynamically unified), with no change at all in immediate experience. In addition, everyone would carry the same "substance" with him, which—since every kind of manifold, for example, time, space, number, plurality, would be missing—could not yield differences between one and the other. (FormEng 384, FormGer 384)

If the person were a substance, as in Boethius's definition, "individual substance of a rational nature," the substance, as Scheler understands it, could not be given in phenomenological intuition because it would be a hidden X behind or beneath all its perceptible accidents. As substance, it would be free of all accidents, simply speaking. He concludes that the person is not a substance but "an act-performing essence" *aktvollziehendes Wesen* (FormEng 385, FormGer 384). The German *Wesen* can also be translated as "being." Frings translates: "a being that executes acts." It seems probable, however, that Scheler means specifically *essence* as opposed to an individual being. He does not seem to be aware of the notion of person as developed in the Christian tradition, particularly at the Council of Chalcedon. Noteworthy in the text of Chalcedon is its cautious use of philosophically elaborated terms such as *hypostasis* on a broad base of ordinary, common conceptions such as personal names, personal pronouns, and the qualifier *one and the same.*

> One and the same Christ, Son, only-begotten, acknowledged to be unconfusedly, unalterably, undividedly, inseparably in two natures, since the difference of the natures is not destroyed because of the union, but, on the contrary, the character of each nature is preserved and comes together in one person (*prosopon*) and one hypostasis, not divided or torn into two persons but one and the same Son and only begotten God, *Logos*, Lord Jesus Christ.[41]

The whole person, Scheler continues, is present in every act. The person varies in and through its acts. In explaining this *variation*, Scheler takes a step that is very important for him but also very difficult to understand. He himself remarks that it is an attempt "to bring the most hidden of all phenomena to givenness" (FormEng 385, FormGer 385). Although the person is nothing but an act-performing essence that provides the point of unity of acts of different essence, the person is not absorbed in its acts but retains its own identity. This is not to say that the person changes in time like a thing. From beyond time, the person lives into time by its acts.

> And for this very reason, no enduring being is needed that maintains itself in this succession to safeguard the "identity of the individual person." Here the identity lies only in the qualitative direction of this pure alteration itself. (FormEng 385, FormGer 385)

To understand what Scheler means by "qualitative direction" and "pure alteration," one needs to recall what he says about the person's unique and unrepeatable value-essence. It is this qualitatively unique value-essence that supplies the ultimate core of the person, a qualitative rather than subsistent core. The person's unique value-essence *varies* in a timeless manner and lives from beyond time into time because it is a quasi-divine flash of spirit. It is, simply speaking, not part of the world but breaks into the world from beyond. Although he considers this value-essence the most hidden of all phenomena, Scheler nevertheless believes he can bring it to givenness by pointing the reader to look in the right direction to see the qualitatively unique value essence.

41. Council of Chalcedon; Denzinger 301. The English translation is taken from Brian Daley, *God Visible: Patristic Christology Reconsidered* (Oxford: Oxford University Press, 2018), 14–15.

"b. The Person Is Never an Object"

In contrast to the *I*, which can be an object of knowledge, an act can never be such an object, even when we know about the act by reflection. The same point holds *a fortiori* for the person.

> If already an act can never be an object, then the person, who lives in its performance of the act, can never be an object. The only and exclusive kind of its givenness is rather its very performance of the act (including the performance of its acts of reflection about its acts). By living in this performance of the act, the person at the same time has lived experience (*erlebt*) of itself. (FormEng 387, FormGer 386)

Lived experience is a key notion for Wojtyła. Scheler distinguishes between acts (such as "remembering and expecting, feeling and preferring, willing and refusing, loving, hating, judging, and so on"; FormEng 390, FormGer 390) and functions (such as "seeing, hearing, tasting, smelling, all forms of attention, noticing and noting, not only sensory noticing, vital feeling, and so on"). Acts are performed (*werden vollzogen*) by the person; functions take place (literally "perform themselves," *vollziehen sich*); that is, they happen of themselves. This distinction closely resembles Wojtyła's distinction between "man acts" and "something happens in man,"[42] which lies at the heart of his account of human acts in *Person and Act*. In contrast to Scheler, however, Wojtyła emphasizes choice, in which the person can be an object for itself through self-knowledge and self-determination.

Functions take place in time. Acts spring from the person from beyond time into time, Scheler holds. Functions belong to the sphere of the *I* and are therefore to be called *psychic*. They necessarily presuppose a body. By contrast, acts are neither psychic nor bodily. "With the person and acts we do not yet imply a lived body (*Leib*)" (FormEng 388, FormGer 387). Acts and persons belong to a third realm, that of *spirit*, *Geist* (FormEng 388, FormGer 388). In chapters 4 and 5 of *Person and Act*, Wojtyła deals with the integration of the *lived body* and the *psyche*, through acts. He also deals with the spiritual principle of the person. As noted above, he does not hold that the person is composed of three principles—body, soul, and spirit—but of body and soul.

The essence of *spirit* becomes clearer in Scheler's account of the relationship between the person and "consciousness of something."

42. See Karol Wojtyła, *Persona e atto*, Polish text with facing Italian translation, ed. Giovanni Reale and Tadeusz Styczeń (Milan: Bompiani, 2001), 171–75; *The Acting Person*, trans. Andrzej Potocki (Dordrecht: D. Reidel, 1979), 61–62.

> If one understands by "consciousness of" … all intentionally directed and meaningful acts (also feeling something, for example, values, willing something, projects, judgments about something, about states of affairs), one can also call the person the concrete "consciousness of." (FormEng 392, FormGer 391–92)

The realm of the *spirit* consists thus of the realm of intentionally directed, meaningful acts, that is, acts that involve *consciousness about something.* The person is spirit, that is, *intentional consciousness* or *consciousness about.* The person is the qualitatively unique direction in which intentional acts take place. The relation between the person and consciousness is discussed in chapter 1 of Wojtyła's *Person and Act.* Wojtyła does not identify the person with consciousness but, in direct opposition to Scheler, claims that the personal *suppositum* (hypostasis) is grasped in our reflexive self-consciousness. In addition, he argues that consciousness is, at root, not intentional. If it were intentional, it could not result in the lived experience of oneself as "I."

"c. Person and World"

The objective correlate of intentional consciousness is the world. As the correlate of world, the person is not part of the world but stands face-to-face with it. "Only the person is never 'part,' but always the correlate of a 'world,' of the world in which it has lived experience of itself, *erlebt*" (FormEng 393, FormGer 392). This thesis is reminiscent of Maritain's reading of the Thomistic principle that the account of part is opposed to the account of the person (see part I, chap. 7, sections 5–6, in this volume).[43] Maritain marshals this reading against the thesis of the primacy of the common good, a primacy clearly affirmed by Wojtyła.

Because each person has a unique value-essence, the objective correlate of each person, each personal world is qualitatively distinct as well.

> Metaphysical truth, or "the" truth itself must thus have a different content … for each person because the content of the world's very being is, in every case, different for each person.… The reason lies in the essence of being, not in the essence of truth. (FormEng 394–95, FormGer 394)

For Wojtyła, the highest dignity of the created person consists in being a part, participating in the acts of others for the sake of a common good. Being is not relative to each person, but there is one single world for all.

43. See Thomas, *Super III sent.*, d. 5, q. 3, a. 2, corp.

"d. Micro- and Macrocosm and the Idea of God"

If the world that corresponds to each person is a qualitatively unique microcosm, is there a common world, a macrocosm, that in some way binds the multitude of distinct worlds? Because Phenomenology can intuitively isolate given essences and discover essential connections that must apply to all worlds, there must be such a macrocosm. The personal correlate of this macrocosm is the idea of an infinite and perfect spirit-person (*Geistesperson*), that is, God (FormEng 396, FormGer 395). Scheler consistently speaks of God as one person in the singular, not plural, of three divine persons. It is by intuiting this macrocosm that finite persons can enter into community with each other.

> Thus, all essence-community (*Wesensgemeinschaft*) between individual persons is not grounded in some "rationality according to law" or in an abstract idea of reason but only in the possible communion (*Gemeinschaft*) of these persons with the person of persons, that is, in communion with God. All other communions that have a moral or legal character have this communion as their foundation. All *amare, contemplare, cogitare, velle* [loving, contemplating, thinking and willing], is thus intentionally tied to the one concrete world, the macrocosm, only inasmuch as it is *amare, contemplare, cogitare, velle* "*in deo*" [loving, contemplating, thinking and willing "in God"]. (FormEng 397–98, FormGer 396)

"e. Lived Body (*Leib*) and the Surrounding World"

How is the body related to the person and to the "I," according to Scheler?

> First, there can be no doubt that the body does not belong to the sphere of the person or the sphere of acts. It belongs to the object sphere of any "consciousness of something" and its kinds and ways of being. The lived body's phenomenal mode of givenness with its foundation is essentially different from that of the "I," with its states and experiences. (FormEng 398, FormGer 397)

Scheler's separation between the body and the person is in many ways close to the body-soul dualism in Descartes. Nevertheless, he is at pains to argue that the body does not lie simply *outside* as one of the objects of the perception of our environment. The person has a sensation of the body "from within" that is irreducible to perceptions from the outside (see FormEng 399, FormGer 397–98). In this respect, the human body is a "lived body" (*Leib*) rather than a "mere body" *Körper*" (FormEng 399, FormGer 397). The German *Leib* refers only to the human body, while *Körper* is applicable to all bodily beings, living and nonliving alike. We are immediately aware that the body we perceive from the outside is identical to the one we sense from within. Still, Scheler would not subscribe to St. John Paul's Aristotelian and Thomistic affirmation "Man is a body," understanding *body* as a true genus in the answer to the question "What is man?" Of course, the genus *body* needs to be specified by three specific differences to arrive at man's specific nature: living (shared with plants and animals), sentient (shared only with animals), and rational (specific). In addition, *rational* implies a subsistent spiritual soul that is irreducible to body. Nevertheless, *body* is a true genus predicable of each human person. The thesis that the human person is a body, rather than merely having a body, is repeated many times in TOB.[44]

In the Cartesian understanding of the human person, there is no unitary "What?" of the human person that includes *body* as a genus. The *res extensa* and the *res cogitans* each have their own "What?" irreducible to the other. In this respect, Scheler's position is close to Descartes's and the opposite of Wojtyła's.

"f. The "I" and the Lived Body: Association or Dissociation"

In discussing the relation between the *I* and the lived body, Scheler mentions the metaphysical distinction between body and soul but dismisses it as irrelevant because it is not given in phenomenological experience (FormEng 417, FormGer 414). Wojtyła takes up the issue of body and soul in *Person and Act* and discusses it in detail at the ends of chapters 4 and 5, both times affirming his agreement with Aristotle's account of body and soul, including the doctrine of first material (*materia prima*).

Scheler's point of departure is the manifold of lived experiences in a single "I." How is the body related to this manifold? There are in principle two options, he argues. In one option, the *I* possesses an original unity that is split or dissociated by the body into the manifold of lived experiences given in inner perception. In the other option, psychic experiences are initially separate and associated with each other as experiences belonging to one body (FormEng 417–18, FormGer 414–15).

Scheler opts for the first of these accounts and illustrates it by the phenomena of self-possession in collectedness and its opposite, the loss of self-possession in being scattered on the periphery of one's being. In deep collectedness, for example, in coming to an important decision, it is as if our whole psychic life, including that of the past, were gathered into one and experienced as efficacious (*wirksam*). We feel full and rich and truly with ourselves. Lived experiences of

44. See TOB 2:4, 5:5–6, 6:3, 8:1, 10:1, 10:4, 19:4, 21:3, 29:4, 44:6, 45:1, 55:2, 60:1–2, 69:2, 69:4, 72:5, 85:9, 86:4, 99:4, 102:5, 119:4.

efficacy (*Wirksamkeitserlebnisse*) speak to us from many points in the past and present. We experience our whole *I* as entering into a single act (FormEng 420, FormGer 417).

This state of collectedness goes hand in hand with a way in which the phenomenon of the body is given to us. "One's own bodiliness is given as something that 'belongs' (*gehört*) to that concentrated totality and over which it can exercise 'power' and dominion" (FormEng 420, FormGer 417).

The opposite phenomenal relation between *I* and the givenness of the body can be observed, for example, when one is overwhelmed by tiredness or weakness, when one is absorbed in empty pleasures and distractions. In this case, one lives in the manifold dissociated periphery of one's being. One lives in the body, and the body comes to occupy the place of the "I" (FormEng 420–21, FormGer 417–18).

In this discussion of the relation between the person and the body, Scheler partly makes up for his denial of the person's causal efficacy and self-rule in the sphere of the will itself, which seems to be driven by his objections against Kant's ethics of duty and choice. Here one can observe one of the most positive points of contact between Scheler and Wojtyła. Scheler's discussion of collectedness, of power and dominion over the body, is closely related to Wojtyła's account of self-possession and self-dominion in chapters 3 and 4 and his discussion of the integration of bodily and psychic phenomena in chapters 5 and 6 of *Person and Act*. Self-possession and self-dominion are also key concepts in TOB.

"g. A Priori Material Principles of Explanatory Psychology"

In the final subsection of "Person and Act," by far the longest, Scheler wrestles with what he considers to be the main competitor of his account of the person; namely, the then-dominant form of psychology, which attempts to explain psychic life in mechanical terms with the help of the principle of association first formulated by Hume. In presenting his alternative to this view of the person, Scheler returns to two doctrines developed earlier.

The first is his doctrine of the qualitatively unique and unrepeatable value-essence proper to each person. This unique value-essence, which is the very core of the person, lies beyond time. From beyond time, it lives into time. For this reason, it cannot be subsumed into the temporal mechanical system posited by the psychology of association (FormEng 424–25, FormGer 421–22).

Second, human acts belong to larger "units of meaning" (see FormEng 433, FormGer 429). These units of meaning cannot be reduced to external connections established between distinct impressions by association. Their meaning must be gathered from themselves. The concept of the unity of *meaning* plays a key role in Wojtyła's *Person and Act* as well as in TOB.

6. Person in Ethical Contexts

Having given his theoretical account of the person, Scheler turns to the person from the point of view of ethics.

"The Essence of the Moral Person"

Wholly Sound Mind

The word *person*, Scheler claims, cannot be used for all beings that have an "I," not even for all those that have the consciousness of the permanence and value of their own "I." Animals have an *I* of some sort but are not persons (see FormEng 476, FormGer 469). Conversely, not every human being can be called a *person*.

> "Man" qua man has never determined the limits within which beings are to be taken as persons. The concept of the person is applicable only to a specific level of human existence. Even if, after we have come to see the phenomenological essence of the person, we broaden the concept of the person and grant that there are seeds (as it were) of personhood in still undeveloped levels of human being (for example, in children or imbeciles), there remains the fact that the place, as it were, in which the nature of the person first flashes up before us is to be sought only in a certain kind of man, not in man in general (FormEng 476, FormGer 470).

This limited use of the term *person*, which excludes many human beings from personhood, is consistent with Scheler's view that there is no stable human nature and that personhood is not an aspect of man's rational nature but a theomorphic flash of spirit that breaks forth here and there into animal life. One of the first conditions of personhood, Scheler explains, is "a wholly sound mind (*Vollsinnigkeit*) in contrast to madness" (FormEng 476, FormGer 470). When we hear someone speak in a manner that is difficult to understand, we make the effort of grasping the meaning of what he or she says. If someone then whispers into our ear, "This man is insane," we switch to another paradigm of understanding.

> Our attitude changes at once in a characteristic manner. An empty spot replaces the previously given spiritual center out of which we relived his acts with him. Only his body and life-center as well as his I-ness remain in the givenness of intuition. We cease to see meaningfully directed intentions that end in his life-expressions. What remains given are movements of expression and other movements behind which we begin to look for psychic processes as causes. A bond of "causality" or of environmental stimuli that cause his expressions replace the "bond of meaning" of his former expressions. "Objects" that we saw with him in understanding now become "stimuli"; intentions become "processes"; the "nexus of meaning" becomes a nexus of causes; the personal act-center becomes an objective unity of body and I; "understanding" becomes "explaining"; and the "person" becomes a piece of nature....
>
> Two things follow from what has been said: 1. Every psychological objectification is identical with depersonalization. 2. The person is given as one who performs intentional acts that are bound together by a unity of meaning. (FormEng 477–78, FormGer 471)

One can recognize a number of key concerns of Wojtyła's *Person and Act* and TOB in this text, especially the contrast between person and nature and the need to resist any depersonalizing objectification of the person. At the same time, it goes without saying that Wojtyła considers every human being a person. The reason why he does so is that he sees the person as a being of a certain nature—namely, a rational nature—which is present no matter whether the person is able or unable to perform personal acts.

Being of Age

A second essential condition of personhood is a sufficient degree of maturity that is expressed in the concept "being of age."

> A second factor involved in the application of the word person is this: it is ascribed only to a certain level of development in man. A child manifests I-ness, possession of a soul, and consciousness of self, but this does not make him a person in the moral sense. Only a child who has "come of age" (*mündig*) is a person in the full sense. (FormEng 478, FormGer 471)

The essential mark of being of age is the capacity to judge and understand one's own intentional acts as distinct from those of others. So long as the child simply follows the judgment and will of its parents and others—that is, so long as it does not *act* in the most proper sense of the word—it cannot be considered a person (see FormEng 478–79, FormGer 471–72).

Dominion over the Body

Personhood is restricted not only to human beings who have a wholly sound mind and who have come of age but also to those who have dominion over their bodies.

> It is further restricted to those men in whom dominion over the lived body appears immediately, who feel, know, and live as masters of the lived body. Of greatest importance in this regard is the phenomenal relation of man to his lived body. One who lives predominantly in his lived body and, as a result, identifies himself with its contents is not a person. Only he who has a lived experience (*erlebt*) of his lived body, identifiable in outer and inner perception as "belonging" to himself through the bond "my lived body" (a phenomenon that forms a condition of the idea of property) is permitted to bear this name.... Not only willing but also the immediate consciousness of the power of willing belong to the person. (FormEng 479–80, FormGer 472–73)

Here we find the main mother lode of insights that Wojtyła shares positively with Scheler: self-dominion, particularly dominion over the body; the lived experience (*Erleben*, *Erlebnis*) of the body as subject to one's power to will certain acts—that is, the lived experience of efficacy—and the lived experience of bodily self-possession. Wojtyła, of course, does not follow Scheler in restricting the concept of *person* to human beings who have this efficacy in relation to their bodies. To illustrate what power and dominion over one's own body means, Scheler describes the nature of a slave in partial agreement with Aristotle.

> One who does not, de facto, have this power [over the body] and the immediate consciousness of it is not a person. Thus, he cannot own his lived body, but he can be the property of someone else; that is, he can be given as a thing (*Sache*). In this way, the "slave" was not a social person, and a true slave (not merely a slave according to positive law) would be given both to himself and to others as a thing. Nevertheless, the slave had an "I," a soul, and a consciousness of self, which proves that these have nothing to do with person.... One can "care for" a slave in any number of ways: the slave can be showered with kind deeds. But he cannot be "loved"—only enjoyed and used. Nor can he "obey," "promise," "take an oath," and so on. He cannot "obey," for, as Aristotle aptly says, "his will is in the master"; the master is the person who owns the slave's lived body and his I. (FormEng 480–81, FormGer 473)

It would not be fair to Scheler to see him as a proponent of slavery. He considers the essence of the slave in its phenomenological givenness without any claim to real existence. Scheler's point that a slave cannot be loved, only enjoyed and used, implies that a true person is to be loved in a manner that excludes mere enjoyment and use. The continuity with Kant and John Paul is evident. In sexual relations, John Paul teaches in TOB, man and woman must not merely enjoy and use each other for pleasure—they do not own each other as things—but must respect each other as persons.

In partial agreement with Kant, Scheler gives the example of polygamy to illustrate this point. In polygamy, women are not considered persons. They are used, not respected.

> When polygamy was dominant in Turkey, for example, the institution was essentially interrelated with the teachings of the Koran, according to which women do not possess a "soul," which obviously means "person" here.... In the Muslim afterlife a woman remains only an impersonal houri.... Even for Kant the married woman is legally (not morally) a "thing" (*Sache*), so that he includes matrimonial law in his discussion of laws pertaining to things *Sachenrecht*. (FormEng 481–82, FormGer 474)

In partial defense of Kant, contrary to Scheler's attack on him, one should highlight that Kant affirms the equality of man and woman, for better or for worse. Before the question of marriage law arises, it is an unavoidable feature of sexual activity that both man and woman treat each other as things to be used and enjoyed rather than as possessing the dignity of autonomy. In this respect, they are equal precisely in their sexual use of each other. This use is unavoidably an abuse, a human rights violation, rooted as in the case of Luther in the very nature of sexual passion and activity. Marriage law is a demand of practical reason to *save* the personal dignity of both man and woman by making them equally the thing-like possession of each other in marriage. The deeper dignity of the person affirmed in the gift of self is invisible to Kant.

Substance and Character

In the final subsection, Scheler argues against two positions that fail to take the essences given in phenomenological insight as their point of departure and rely instead on "concepts of the real and concepts of things" (*Real- und Dingbegriffe*): the definition of the person as a *substance* (Boethius) and the view of the mechanist psychology of association that personhood coincides with character, that is, with hereditary disposition and formation by external stimuli.

> If we completely set aside the question of the justification of the assumption of a soul-substance, we can at any rate say that the soul substance is thought to be a real and thing-like object that is placed by supposition beneath (*supponiert*) the individual lived experience of the I given in inner intuition and to which attributes, powers, faculties, dispositions, and so on, are hypothetically ascribed so that one can causally explain the course of the individual contents of lived experience under the changing conditions of real effects by stimuli on

> the "soul." But all of this lies in a direction completely different from that in which the essence of person is to be found. (FormEng 482, FormGer 475)

This text is helpful for understanding why Scheler rejects the definition of the person as a substance. He sees substance as a mere supposition. The reason for this supposition is the attempt to give a causal explanation of the person's experiences and acts in terms of the effects of certain stimuli on the soul-substance. In other words, the understanding of the person as a substance belongs to the same pattern of misunderstanding that, according to Scheler, characterizes the mechanist psychology of association. *Substance* undercuts the meaning of personal acts. This meaning must be understood, as in the case of a person "of wholly sound mind," and not merely explained, as in the case of an insane man.

Once one rejects the doctrine of substance, Scheler goes on to argue, one can see that the problem of the causal interaction between body and soul discussed by Descartes and later philosophers is a purely *fabricated* problem. To understand how the person exercises dominion over the psyche and the body, it is sufficient to examine "the lived experience of efficacy" (FormEng 483, FormGer 475). The contact with Wojtyła is evident. In chapter 2 of *Person and Act*, he too analyzes the lived experience of efficacy but in a manner quite different from Scheler.

Scheler also rejects the reduction of the person to character. The concept of character he has in mind is the one developed by the contemporary mechanist psychology of association, which sees a deterministic relationship between character and action. Scheler argues that we must understand the acts of persons; we only need to explain them in the case of those who are not of sound mind.

In this context, Scheler appeals to the unrepeatably unique value- essence of each person. When we judge the acts of persons, we do not compare them to what psychology says about character; we compare them with the intuitively given personal value-essence.

> Every moral assessment of another consists in the fact that we measure his actions neither exclusively by universal norms nor by an ideal picture that hovers above us through our own doing but only by the ideal picture we form by drawing out to their end, as it were, the basic intentions of the other person which have been obtained through a central understanding of his individual essence and which we unite in the concrete ideal value picture of the person given only in intuition. And it is by this picture that we measure his empirical actions.
>
> What mediates the intuition of the person's ideal and individual value-essence is, first of all, the understanding of the most central fountain (*Springquell*), which is itself mediated through love of the person. This intelligent

> love is the great master workman and (as Michelangelo says so profoundly and beautifully in his well-known sonnet) the great sculptor who, working from the masses of empirical particulars can intuitively seize, sometimes from only one action or only one expressive gesture, the lines of the person's value-essence.... It is only when I know to which person the experiencing of an experience belongs that I can have a full understanding of this experience. (FormEng 488, FormGer 480–81)

"Person and Individual"

In the immediately following section, Scheler explains in more detail what he means by "individual-personal value-essence." His point of departure is the experience of a moral *ought* addressed to the individual person: do this specific thing here and now! It is here, in what is most personal and individual, Scheler argues, that one finds the core of the moral order, not in the universal laws posited by Kant. This is not to say that morality is subjective, relative to the accidental individual disposition of the person. Quite on the contrary, the experience of the individual *ought* flows from insight into the individual value-essence of the person. Scheler describes it in religious terms as *salvation*.

> There are essences that are given only in one particular individual. And for this reason, it makes good sense to speak of an individual essence and also the individual value-essence. It is this value-essence of a personal and individual kind that I also designate "personal salvation" (*Heil*). It would be a complete mistake to identify this salvation with a personal-individual ought, or to say that it is given in the experience of such an ought.... [The] experience of my obligation ... is already based on the experience of my individual value-essence. (FormEng 489, FormGer 481)

What ultimately stands behind the individual value-essence, at least in Scheler's Catholic period, is "the love of God," which draws a particular value-picture for each person and bears it before that person as the exemplar to be followed. The value-essence thus has the character of a divine call directed toward this and no other person.

> In the domain of the infinite fullness of the good spread out before the eyes of God, there is in one special "place" a good that is a good "for me," my own individual value-essence that, empirically, I *ought* to become. Or this individual value-essence becomes an "ideal image" for me because it lies not only in the direction of divine love as such but also in the direction of the divine love directed toward me.... All empirical life happens and is formed under the

> influence of this value-ideal of the individual person, which provides the goal and fixes the unique place of the person in the realm of the in itself good. And founded on this is the place that the ideal of the person occupies in the divine plan of salvation. (FormEng 491n122, FormGer 483n1)

To understand correctly what Scheler says, one needs to recall that his phenomenological method brackets the reality of God, just as it brackets all real being. "At no point in this book is there ever any question of positing the 'reality' of the essence of God" (FormEng 396n34, FormGer 395n1). The divine love directed toward me personally as a call that gives me a concrete place in the plan of salvation is grasped in immediate and presuppositionless phenomenological intuition of the divine value-essence in complete neutrality as to whether this love really exists or not.

For Kant, the universality of human reason is the true wellspring of the moral law as a law imposed in the form of self-legislation by each person on itself and on all other persons. For Scheler, the individuality of the loving divine call is the true wellspring of morality. Universal laws, he argues, only express the minimum required of each person, not the heart of the moral life, which consists in the person's salvation.

> All universally valid values (universally valid for persons) represent, in relation to the highest value, namely, the holiness of the person, and in relation to the highest good, namely, "the salvation of an individual person," only a minimum of values; if these values are not recognized and realized, the person cannot attain his salvation. But these values do not in themselves incorporate all possible moral values through whose realization the person attains salvation. (FormEng 492, FormGer 484)

This text clarifies what Scheler considers "the highest value" and "the highest good," which gives ultimate order to his personalism as a whole. In close conformity to Kant's moralism, he sees the highest good of the person as a moral good; namely, salvation (*Heil*) and holiness (*Heiligkeit*) as the realization of the person's moral value-essence. Here one finds the deepest point of disagreement between Scheler and Wojtyła: for Wojtyła, God himself, not our own moral goodness, is the final end of the human person.

"The Autonomy of the Person"

Scheler criticizes Kant for his failure to distinguish two aspects of autonomy: the autonomy of personal insight into the good and the autonomy of personally willing what is good. The opposite of the first aspect is the heteronomy of blind willing; the opposite of the second is the heteronomy of externally induced or imposed willing. Kant fails to make this distinction, Scheler argues, because he equates moral goodness with the autonomy of self-movement by universal self-imposed legislation prior to the distinction between good and evil. What is decisive for moral goodness, Scheler responds, is not simply autonomy but the insight into the goodness or evil of the acts performed and the willing of these acts motivated by this insight (see FormEng 494–95, FormGer 486–87).

With his concept of autonomy, Kant proposes a radically individualistic ethics. The dignity of autonomous individual personal liberty is the highest value. In opposition to such individualism, Scheler attempts to safeguard two essential aspects of moral life by arguing that they are compatible with a correct understanding of autonomy; namely, solidarity and obedience or following other persons.

Moral solidarity, and thus a moral community of persons, is impossible in Kant's moral theory because he limits moral responsibility to each person's self-moved acts. He denies the moral community of persons at its roots by reducing respect for one's neighbor to respect for oneself. The affirmation of one's neighbor's dignity, he holds, is necessary only because without it one cannot affirm one's own. Scheler argues on the contrary that love of self and love of neighbor are not reducible to each other. Each love has its own foundation. Ultimately, both are founded on the love of God. It is in loving God that one co-loves (*Mitlieben*) all finite persons (see FormEng 495–98, FormGer 487–90).

Obedience and following other persons are also excluded by Kant's understanding of autonomy, and yet they play a key role in moral life. Obedience in particular can be freely chosen on the basis of one's insight into the moral legitimacy and goodness of an authority (FormEng 498–501, FormGer 490–92).

"Our Concept of Person in Relation to Other Forms of Personalist Ethics"

In the fourth and final section, Scheler distinguishes his own form of personalism from "the very different forms of ethical personalism developed from the nineteenth century to the present" (FormEng 501, FormGer 492). He considers the contrasting forms of personalism under six headings.

The Self-Value of the Person

Scheler contrasts the personalism of Kant and Nietzsche with that of Fichte and Hegel.

> Kant and Nietzsche, however different their concepts of the person may be, assess the value of a community or society, and the value of a historical process as well, according to the degree to which these are able to provide the being of persons with the most appropriate foundation for his existence and action.... The goal of human history is, for Nietzsche, the "greatest exemplars" of men and, for Kant, a community that makes rational persons of free will possible. Neither Kant nor Nietzsche recognizes a supra-personal highest bearer of value (be it the community, culture or its development, the moral world-order, the state, and so on).... Both theories are therefore sharply opposed to all theories of post-Kantian German idealism, especially to Fichte's and Hegel's, which impose devotion to a supra-personal and supra-individual "moral world order" or to a state of this kind and a cultural revolution of this kind, as the highest bearer of value on the value-being of the person and make this devotion the latter's condition. (Scheler FormEng 503, FormGer 494)

Although Scheler considers Fichte and Hegel proponents of some form of personalism, he does not explain in detail what it consists of and why they should not rather be classified as anti-personalists. Having posed the alternative in this way, Scheler sides with the personalism of Kant and Nietzsche against Fichte and Hegel.

> Ethics must stick to value personalism, for which the ultimate meaning and value of community and history lie precisely in their providing conditions within which the most valuable persons can come to the fore and freely bring about their effects. For value personalism, all history has its aim (*Ziel*) in the being and activity of persons. (FormEng 505, FormGer 496)

Scheler formulates the alternatives in terms of the person's value: the highest value is seen either as residing primarily in the person itself or as coming to the person from the person's contribution to the state or to historical progress. That the person should attain a fullness of life by sharing in a common good, supremely by reaching God himself as the most encompassing common good, this possibility affirmed by Wojtyła in agreement with Aristotle and Thomas does not enter even as an option into Scheler's argument. The valuable person has its value within itself. It is its own end.

The Intention of One's Own Value

Many philosophers, Scheler points out, hold that the highest value lies in the ethical person. Yet they conceive of this value as an object that can and should be intended and realized by the person. Scheler argues by contrast that intending one's own perfection as an object is the surest way of not reaching it. "Love for the [moral] good as good is itself bad, because it is necessarily Pharisaism"

(Scheler, *Sympathie*, GW 7:164). Moral goodness cannot be intended because the person can never be an object of knowledge and intention for itself or for other persons (FormEng 505, FormGer 496). In this context, Scheler quotes the saying of Jesus, "Only the one who loses himself will find himself" (FormEng 501, FormGer 493).

Person and Individual

The most distinctive feature of his specific form of personalism in comparison with others, Scheler asserts, is the central place it gives to the individual and unrepeatable value-essence of each person.

> At no point does the ethical personalism to which our investigation had led us reveal its distinctiveness from other present ethical currents to a greater degree than in the position it gives to the becoming and being of the spiritual individuality of the person as the bearer of moral value.... Every man is, as we saw, an individual, and therefore a unique being, distinct from all others, to the same degree that he is a pure person. And, similarly, his value is a unique value. (FormEng 508, FormGer 499)

On this basis, Scheler argues that persons are unequal precisely as persons. In opposition to Kant, for whom what is highest in the person is the same in all, Scheler argues that what is highest in the person is precisely what is in each case unique and unrepeatable.

Individual and Comprehensive Person

This emphasis on individuality does not imply that Scheler is an individualist. His thesis that persons are flashes of divinity that descend in the gesture of *agape* from their inner fullness does not commit him to the Kantian thesis according to which all forms of community are subordinated to the individual person. Scheler sides decidedly with Christian love as a social love. He goes far in emphasizing that individual persons essentially belong to communities, not merely by choice and contract, as Kant holds.

Scheler conceives the various forms of community as persons in their own right, as "centers of lived experience" (*Zentren des Erlebens*), endowed with a consciousness and sovereign will of their own (see FormEng 519–22, FormGer 509–12). If one sees the person as a substance, he points out, one cannot accept this doctrine of comprehensive persons.

> No doubt the comprehensive person does possess a "consciousness-of" that is different from and independent of the consciousness-of the individual person. This proposition will appear paradoxical only to someone who would base the differentiation of consciousness in general on the separation of lived bodies

> or to someone who would base the concept of the person on the concept of a soul-substance. [Footnote:] A comprehensive soul-substance is, of course, nonsense. (FormEng 522–23n170, FormGer 512n3)

Although he affirms the primacy of communities and resists the contract theory of political life, Scheler does not agree with Aristotle about this primacy.

> It would appear that in making these statements [about the importance of community] we should simply side with Aristotle in the old philosophical dispute between Aristotle's doctrine, according to which man as a rational being is by nature a political animal and the doctrine first formulated by the Epicureans, according to which community is first constituted by some form of contract....
>
> Our views do not confirm Aristotle's. For Aristotle, the individual person is not in the same measure original as the whole. He is rather derived from the whole—essentially, not historically. The person is completely absorbed in being a member of a community (first of all, the state) and does not have an independent value of his own apart from his value as member. In our view, however, all persons are with equal originality individual persons and (essentially) members of a comprehensive person; and their own value as individual persons is independent of their value as a member-persons.
>
> Second, Aristotle does not recognize the concept of a comprehensive person. In the manner characteristic of the ancients (even in their theories about God), *logos*, form, and ratio stand for him above the idea of person. Consequently, the state, too, is for him not a sovereign personal will but only the form and rational order of a people's community based on laws. For us, by contrast, all community has its ultimate foundation in the idea of person. It is not communitarian values but personal values that are the highest values. Among communitarian values, therefore, the highest are those belonging to the comprehensive person.... The comprehensive person ... is as much a spiritual individual as the individual person, for example, the Prussian state.
>
> From an ethical point of view, there is for us no relation of subordination between the individual person and the collective person. (FormEng 524–25, FormGer 513–14)

In his Christian personalism, Scheler attempts to overcome the naturalism of Greek *logos*, which fails to see the great dignity of the uniqueness and unrepeatability of the person and subordinates the person to the state. "All 'ancient' conceptions of the state were abolished once and for all by Jesus" (FormEng 512n153, FormGer 503n2). Only Christianity recognizes "the infinite value of each 'soul'" (FormEng 525n173, FormGer 514n1).

Scheler thus criticizes Aristotle on two main points: the value of persons and comprehensive persons. Regarding the value of persons, according to Scheler,

Aristotle sees the community as original or primary and the individual as derived. One can point to Aristotelian texts like the following in support of this reading.

> The city is by nature prior to the house and to every one of us, since the whole is of necessity prior to the part; for example, if the whole body is destroyed, there will be no foot or hand, except equivocally, as we might speak of a stone hand; for when destroyed, the hand will be like that. But all things are defined by their function and power; and we ought not to say that they are the same when they no longer have their proper quality but only that they have the same name.
>
> The proof that the city exists by nature and prior to the individual is that the individual, when isolated, is not self-sufficing; and therefore, he is like a part in relation to the whole. But he who is unable to be in communion (κοινωνία), or who has no need because he is sufficient for himself, is no part of a city: he must either be a beast or a god.[45]

This text indicates that, according to Aristotle, the priority of the community over the individual is due to the final cause, to the good as the first of all causes. Because individuals can only reach the good proportionate to their nature if they are not alone but in community, the good of the community is prior in the order of causality to the good of the individual as individual. If one asks, "Why does this person live and do what she does?" then according to Aristotle the answer is ultimately "because of the common good of the community" (see part I, chap. 7, in this volume).[46]

Scheler reads Aristotle as addressing the question of the value of the person rather than that of the common good. In this reading, he shows his Kantian horizon. The question of the person's value is the main question for Kant. This is probably the reason why he reads Aristotle as denying that the individual has value in itself and as affirming that it derives its value from being a member of the community. It is difficult to escape from one's favorite enemies.

For Aristotle, however, the question is not the value of the person but the good or end reached by the person, the good that allows the person to say: my life is a good life. The priority of the state over the person is a priority of the common good over the private good. Inasmuch as the common good is common, it is the good of those individuals. Aristotle and John Paul agree on this point. According to Aristotle, "The same end seems to belong to human beings

45. Aristotle, *Politics*, 1.2, 1253a.18–29.

46. Thomas, *Summa* I, q. 65, a. 2, argues that every being exists: (1) for the sake of its own activity, (2) for the sake of the intrinsic common good of the whole to which it belongs, and (3) for the sake of the separated common good, which is ultimately God himself.

both in common and individually."[47] According to John Paul, "The more common the good, the more properly one's own it will also be: mine, yours, ours."[48]

The second main point on which Scheler criticizes Aristotle is Aristotle's failure to acknowledge the existence of "comprehensive persons" (*Gesamtpersonen*). Aristotle does not see communities as persons but as impersonal wholes. The only way to acknowledge the absolute superiority of the personal order over the impersonal is to acknowledge that communities are persons in their own right who have their own consciousness (at least "consciousness of" rather than reflexive consciousness) and their own "sovereign personal will" (FormEng 522–23, FormGer 512–13).

What allows Scheler even to entertain such a doctrine of comprehensive persons is his essentialism. If the person is a bundle of act-essences united by a unique value-essence, rather than an ultimately real *suppositum* or hypostasis that is the bearer of all attributes, then to say that communities are persons in their own right is at least not an immediate contradiction.

It is not clear why comprehensive persons (on Scheler's own terms) should be principles of the unity of communities and not rather principles of division and of strife, at least in some instances. The Prussian state, which is Scheler's first example, should give one pause. Is it not conceivable that the sovereign will of a state is corrupt, intent on military prowess? If it is corrupt, the comprehensive person cannot be a principle of unity. The true unity of a community must therefore arise from elsewhere.[49]

Although Scheler seems to be unaware of Aristotle's account of the common good, he develops a notion quite close to it when he explains the nature of comprehensive persons in more detail.

> The highest essential type of social unity ... is the unity of independent, spiritual and individual single persons "in" an independent, spiritual, and individual comprehensive person. We assert that this unity, and it alone, is the nucleus and total novelty of the true and ancient Christian idea of community, and that this Christian idea represents, so to speak, the historical discovery of this unity. In an utterly unique manner, on the basis of the Christian idea of love, this idea of community unites the being and indestructible self-value of the individual "soul" and person ... with the idea of the solidarity in salvation of all in the *corpus christianum*. (FormEng 533, FormGer 522)

When he explains this comprehensive nature of salvation, Scheler uses the concepts of "comprehensive value" and "comprehensive good." A comprehen-

47. Aristotle, *Politics*, 7.15, 1334a.11*ff*.
48. John Paul II, *Letter to Families* 10.
49. For further critical discussion, see Crosby, *Personalist Papers*, 189–90.

sive good—a good that exceeds the individual persons but is nevertheless truly their own good in virtue of their membership in the whole—comes close to the concept of the common good. Scheler unfolds what he means by "comprehensive good" in a detailed discussion of the Church and its specific mode of unity.

> The highest modality in the order of ranks of values—the holy as a personal value and "salvation" as the value of the comprehensive person, that is, solidary comprehensive salvation—is the most indivisible (*unteilbar*) of value-modalities and, for this reason, the most communicable (*mitteilbar*). The comprehensive person to which comprehensive salvation is directed can therefore only be one according to its nature. The unity of the Church ... is an *a priori* principle. (FormEng 554, FormGer 541–42)

This text seems to bring out clearly the two essential features of a common good: its indivisible unity as one good and its eminent communicability to many.

Intimate and Social Person

After strongly insisting on community, Scheler counterbalances his argument by turning to ways in which the person is not absorbed in community but remains alone. John Paul's analysis of original solitude (TOB 5–7) is stimulated, at least in part, by this part of Scheler's argument.

> No matter how rich and diverse the memberships through which each person is enmeshed in the whole of the moral cosmos, and no matter how diverse the directions of the various kinds of co-responsibility by which the person is tied to this whole and its direction and meaning, the person is never exhausted by these kinds of membership, nor is his self-responsibility reduced to various co-responsibilities, nor his duties and rights to those duties and rights which derive from such memberships (duties of family, office, vocation, citizenship, class, and so on). For behind all lived experience (*Erleben*) that enters into these memberships and obstructs or furthers the person as a whole by realizing these memberships, everyone feels (in some measure)—if he attempts to have a clear view of the whole of these kinds of membership and of his own being—a peculiar self-being (similarly, a self-value and a self-disvalue) which towers above this whole and in which he knows himself (descriptively speaking) as alone. And what comes to givenness in this essential form of possible lived self-experiencing (*Selbsterleben*) is what I call the intimate person. I wish to distinguish this sharply from the contents of lived experience (*Erlebnisgehalt*) of all forms of lived self-experiencing that occurs with an explicit or somehow co-given reference to the mere fact of being a bearer of some personal membership, that is, the social person. (FormEng 561, FormGer 548)

Being alone, as Scheler describes it, is not simply the objective condition of not having anyone near. It is a lived experience of oneself as "towering above" membership in a social whole. Such solitude can be experienced even when one is near others, at times especially when one is near to them, for example, in a full bus (FormEng 562n246, FormGer 549n2).

Yet Scheler does not assert an ultimate detachment of persons from all forms of community. He excepts the relation with God and with the Church.

> However, solitude does not exclude one communal relation, namely, the relation to God, who by definition is neither an individual nor a comprehensive person but one in whom both individual and comprehensive person are solidary. Thus, it is in God alone that the intimate person may know himself to be judged as well as sheltered. But he cannot know this without becoming indirectly aware of his solidarity (at least "in God") with the comprehensive person in general and, in the first place, with the Church. And without this certitude there would be no God but merely a deceptive object of the highest nature, that is, an illusory God. (FormEng 563, FormGer 550)

Can one read a full concept of the common good in this text? Such a reading might run as follows: on the level of the Church and of God, there is an ultimate primacy of the common good over the private good. One cannot stand in communion with God, both judged and sheltered by God, without realizing that God communicates himself to many. Just as it is impossible to want peace for oneself alone in detachment from others, so it is impossible to want God for oneself alone without assenting to the communicability of his goodness to many, to his greater communication to the whole than to oneself as part of that whole. If one wants God for oneself alone, one does not want God.

In favor of such a reading, one can point out that teleology does play an important role on at least three levels of Scheler's personalism. Yet on each level there are difficulties. The person's individual value-essence is an ideal essence. It needs to be realized in the person's actual life. Real existence is the ideal essence's intended goal. The obstacle against such a reading is Scheler's thesis that real being is as such outside the mind and thus unknowable, like Kant's thing in itself. The realization of the person's ideal essence should be unintelligible.

In realizing its own value-essence, the person acts "in God" (*velle in deo, amare in deo*). Although the acts of God and the acts of human persons remain distinct, the spiritual life principle is the same in both. It is more than participation in God. This thesis differs from the thesis of the theological tradition that God is goodness itself, the whole plenitude of goodness, participation in which is the final end. As Wojtyła points out, Scheler does not hold that the human person attains an end distinct from itself. There is a quasi-identity of the human spirit with God.

The maximum of maximally valuable persons is the end of history and society. These persons are to live in solidarity with each other in a comprehensive person characterized by a comprehensive good. Nevertheless, Scheler does not describe this good as an end that is to be reached by each individual person.

The main difficulty that prevents Scheler from reaching a full concept of the common good is his rejection of *eros* and his exclusive adoption of Christian *agape*. God is for him not the final end. The final end lies in each person, including comprehensive persons such as the Church; it lies in the unique and unrepeatable personal value-essence of each person.

Model Persons

To conclude his account of what distinguishes his form of personalism from others, Scheler turns to the topic of following model persons. It is the capstone of his account of the person. Wojtyła chose well in selecting it as the topic of his habilitation thesis. The presentation of this capstone is part of the immediately following chapter, which presents Wojtyła's critique of Scheler.

7. Conclusion: Scheler's Theomorphic Personalism of Solidarity

Scheler's philosophy is personalistic in as radical a sense as Kant's. Everything is ordered to the glory of the person. We can return with fuller understanding to the text quoted at the beginning of this chapter.

> The glorification of the person, ultimately of the person of persons, that is, God, remains the moral meaning of all moral "order." The ultimate measure of community and history is therefore … to what extent they provide the basis of existence and life for the pure ontological value of the maximum of most valuable persons. (FormEng 504, FormGer 495)

The personalist glory proclaimed by Scheler in his Catholic period is in some ways the direct opposite of the personalist glory of the autonomous subject in Kant. Scheler conceives it as theomorphic descending *agape* expressed in solidarity. The Greeks, Plato and Aristotle in particular, did not know the *person* and preferred the impersonal universal *logos*. They saw love as a human ascent to an impersonal good that was the end of all longing. Christianity reverses this movement and embraces the glorious downward movement of divine self-giving love. *Agape* and its glory replaces Greek *logos*. Scheler attempts to develop a philosophy that springs originally and spontaneously from this reversal of the striving of *eros* to the self-gift of *agape*.

> I have called it the reversal in the movement of love. No longer valid is the Greek axiom that love is a movement of the lower to the higher, of non-being to true being, of man to a God who does not love, of the bad to the better. Rather, the loving condescension of the higher to the low, of the holy to the sinner, and so on, is taken up into the very essence of the higher, even of the highest, of God.
>
> Precisely this reversal of the movement of love contains at its roots a new kind of foundation for love and knowledge, for value and being. In religious terms, this new foundation shows itself in religious knowledge no longer being primarily a spontaneous act of the individual. The first impetus of movement for this knowledge is transferred into God, that is, into the loving redemptive will of God and his self-revelation as such in Christ....
>
> In place of Indian-Greek self-redemption through knowledge we have the idea of being redeemed by divine love.[50]

Scheler claims that this revolutionary change of the human spirit failed because Greek *logos* was accepted in the Catholic tradition. He sees himself as the first to supply a philosophical understanding of the world and of life that springs originally and spontaneously from the Christian experience. One can call this self-understanding quasi-messianic.

Scheler is intensely engaged with Kant. He rejects Kant's hatred and distrust for the given inherited from Hume, Hobbes, and the Baconian-Cartesian reformation of knowledge. In sharp contrast to Kant, he develops a philosophy based on loving devotion to the world. He understands Phenomenology in an anti-Kantian sense as openness to receive whatever is given. John Paul clearly appreciates this aspect of his work. Phenomenology is "an attitude of intellectual charity to the human being and the world."[51]

At the same time, Scheler follows Kant's separation between essences given in consciousness and real existence. Real existence is alien to consciousness; only essences are given. This Kantian essentialism has disastrous effects on Scheler's account of value. He conceives value as an essence in the consciousness of love, a felt essence belonging to a self-contained order of values distinct from the similarly self-contained order of being.

One result of this value-essentialism, as Wojtyła points out, is the loss of a teleological account of human nature. The absence of the end in Scheler, particularly the absence of the common good, follows from the absence of real being.

50. Scheler, "Liebe und Erkenntnis," GW 8:88–89.

51. John Paul II, *Address to a Delegation of the World Institute of Phenomenology*, March 22, 2003.

For an end, the all-decisive question is whether it is real or can be realized. A radically essentialist philosophy like Scheler's is unable to understand teleology.

The loss of teleology in Scheler is reinforced by his tendency to blur the distinction between God and creatures. This tendency is also due, at least in part, to his essentialism. Creation accounts for the difference between an essence that is merely thought and a being that is truly real. That one *receives* real being is a clear sign that one is not God.

On a related but deeper level, the loss of teleology is due to the rejection of Greek *eros* and the exclusive adoption of self-giving Christian *agape*, not unlike Luther. Human persons are needless descending flashes of the divine *agape* that appears here and there in animal life.

The relation of the person to nature is more positive than in Kant but still deeply touched by the dread of being *outside*.

> Once man—and this belongs to his essence, it is the very act of becoming human—has placed himself outside of the whole of nature and made it into his "object," he must turn around shivering, as it were, and ask, "But where do I stand? What is the place in which I stand?" He can no longer truly say, "I am a part of the world, I am included in it," for the actual being of his spirit and his person is superior even to the forms of the being of this "world" in space and time. In this act of turning around he gazes into nothingness, as it were. He discovers in this gaze the possibility of "absolute nothingness" and this drives him on to the question, "Why is there a world at all? Why and for what reason am I at all?" ...
>
> In the very moment in which human beings placed themselves outside of "nature" and made it the object of their dominion and of the new principle of art and the sign—in that very moment they had to anchor their center in some way outside the world. They could not understand themselves as a simple "part" or as a simple "member" of the world, over which they placed themselves with such audacity. (GW 9:67–69)

One can understand much of what Scheler says here in light of the first aspect of Greek *logos*, "The soul is in a certain way all beings."[52] To be rational means to face being as a whole, to ask questions about the meaning of the whole, to apprehend the whole, even if only imperfectly, in the form of wonder.

Yet Scheler means more. He connects this *more* with *dominion*, that is, with the technological reformation of knowledge. As a flash of divinity—whether descending from God in Scheler's Catholic period or produced by human drives after he left the Catholic Church—the human person cannot be part, not even part of a created universe that includes all created beings.

52. Aristotle, *De anima* 431b.21.

Scheler's insistence that the person is not part of a world does not imply the individualistic personalism of Kant. God's descending *agape* as revealed by Christ enables the person to live in communion with all other persons. In the mystery of Christ, who takes upon himself the sin of the world, each enters into solidarity with each. Scheler understands the truly personal form of community on the basis of the descending movement of *agape* alone, without *eros*. It is not clear what married life would be like on these premises.

Scheler's thought seems to walk along a razor's edge. In his Catholic period, he leans toward the side of reverence for the glory of God's love. After his apostasy in 1922, he chooses the side of self-deification.

> The human being is the being that has lifted itself above and stands lofty above all life and its values, the being in which the psychic level purifies itself and liberates itself from service to life to rise up towards "spirit," a spirit in whose service life now stands in the objective as well as subjective-psychic sense.
>
> An ever new and increasing process of "becoming man" in this precise sense, of humanizing, which is at the same time self-deification and a share in the realization of the idea of the godhead—not waiting for a redeemer from the outside, not reception of capitalized graces of redemption through a Church that turns its founder into a divine thing, always at the price of failing to follow him in his acts but self-deification, and this means co-realization of the idea of spiritual deity that eternally "is" only as an essence (*west*) on the substratum of drive, which remains one and the same drive as it gives rise to all living forms of nature and the genesis of each species, which drives in every drive, manifests itself in the dead and the living in various forms of laws in those "images" that we call "body"—this is where I see the core of all education as well as the final philosophical justification of its meaning and value. (GW 9:101)

In this late text, Scheler develops an understanding of the human person that is akin to some Gnostic speculations. On the background of a tripartite anthropology of body, soul, and spirit (see 1 Corinthians 15:44; 1 Thessalonians 5:23),[53] these gnostic speculations propose a journey of redemption in which the divine spirit in man purifies and frees itself from the material and psychic level (from Scheler's *life*) to enter into the divine sphere. An alienated fragment of divine spirit trapped in matter is saved through knowledge (*gnosis*) of its own divinity.[54] The path of salvation in Scheler is more historical and developmental than in gnosticism. Still, Scheler after his turn away from the faith in 1922 agrees

53. See TOB 50:5–51:4.

54. See Kurt Rudolph, *Gnosis: The Nature and History of Gnosticism* (Edinburgh: T&T Clark, 1985), 88–113.

that the person is "self-deity" or "self-glory" and has no need for redemption.

Scheler thus embraces a personalism of the absolute human subject akin to Kantian personalism, in which each person contains already, as a person, the ultimate and unsurpassable value, the final glory. He rejects gift, dependence, and sonship as radically as Kant does. His personalism, while being theomorphic, is anti-Trinitarian, despite solidarity with others.

The Platonic and Aristotelian understanding of human love as a striving love is part of the Christian understanding of the created person. Balthasar's critique of Scheler focuses on this point.

> Not the (Pseudo-) Augustinian concept alien to the Ancient World of a love that is pure and free from all striving but the concept of a striving love which Thomas adopted from Greek *eros* and which Scheler combated so vigorously—this is the more deeply Christian concept. Granted, according to John "God is love," and certainly there is in God no striving *eros* but resting and self-giving *agape*. Still, although all human love must be a participation in that divine love, it can be so only as a trembling longing of a world that must remain world in an approach that can never leave behind being an approach, never in a usurpation of the divine center itself. For the desire to be like God, even in love, is the ambition of Lucifer.[55]

55. Balthasar, *Apokalypse der deutschen Seele*, 3.182–83.

CHAPTER 4

Wojtyła's Critique of Scheler

1. Reading Scheler

The title of Wojtyła's book on Scheler (completed 1953, published 1960) states its purpose: *Evaluation of the Possibility of Building Christian Ethics on the Foundations of Max Scheler's System.*[1] Although Scheler is usually classified as a philosopher, Wojtyła reads him in a theological perspective.[2] The book is a habilitation thesis in moral theology (not philosophy) for the Faculty of Theology at the Jagiellonian University.[3] Theological themes and arguments play an

1. No English translation has been published yet, which may account for many of the misperceptions about the relation between Scheler and Wojtyła in the English-speaking world. Citations by WojScheler (Wojtyła Scheler) refer to the German translation: *Über die Möglichkeit eine christliche Ethik in Anlehnung an Max Scheler zu schaffen*, in Karol Wojtyła, *Primat des Geistes: Philosophische Schriften*, ed. Juliusz Stroynowski (Stuttgart-Degerloch: Seewald, 1980). Translations are my own, relying on the German as well as the Italian translation: *Valutazioni sulla possibilità di costruire l'etica Cristiana sulle basi del sistema di Max Scheler*, in Karol Wojtyła, *Metafisica della persona: Tuttel le opere filosofiche e saggi integrativi*, ed. Giovanni Reale and Tadeusz Styczeń (Milan: Bompiani, 2003). The German has the advantage of working with Scheler's difficult texts in the original language, which at times clarifies the meaning of Wojtyła's discussion. The Italian has the advantage of collaboration by Tadeusz Styczeń, Wojtyła's student, assistant, and eventual successor in Lublin. Spanish translation: *Max Scheler y la ética cristiana* (Madrid: Biblioteca de Autores Cristianos, 1982). Polish Original: *Ocena możliwości zbudowania etyki chrześcijańskiej przy założeniach systemu Maksa Schelera* (Lublin: Naukowe Katolickiego Uniwersytetu Lubelskiego, 1960).

2. See George Weigel, *The End and the Beginning: Pope John Paul II—The Victory of Freedom, the Last Years, the Legacy* (New York: Doubleday, 2010), 46. Scheler discusses the relation between philosophy, religion, and theology, criticizing Thomas's account of theology in "Probleme der Religion," GW 5:127.

3. In the German university system, which was adopted in Poland, the habilitation thesis corresponds somewhat to the "second book" that assistant professors in the United States are expected to write after their doctoral thesis in order to earn tenure. Passage of the habilitation thesis promotes an *Assistent* (who does not yet have primary responsibility for teaching) to *Privatdozent* (authorized to

important role throughout Scheler's writings. Yet, as Wojtyła points out, Scheler does not understand himself as making theological arguments based on revelation in Scripture. He understands himself as simply looking at given essences without any presuppositions and without affirming the real existence of beings corresponding to these essences (see WojScheler 64–66).

Topic and Perspective

As the theological topic for his evaluation of Scheler, Wojtyła chooses the biblical teaching about following and imitating Jesus, which is a central topic in the Gospels and also in Scheler's personalism. When one compares Wojtyła's book on Scheler with the topic of his doctoral thesis on faith as a means of union with God, one can see a strong link between them. Both approach the mystery of union or communion of human beings with God, but from different angles. There is also a certain kinship between St. John of the Cross and Scheler. Like John of the Cross, Scheler pays close attention to the conscious experience of the person and finds effective ways of expressing it. Like John of the Cross, he has a powerful sense for beauty. Again like John of the Cross, he reflects deeply about love. The understanding of love as *gift of self* is not as prominent in Scheler as it is in John of the Cross, but it is often implicit in other terms used by Scheler. The following text can serve as an example in its use of *Hingabe*, radical giving or surrender, and the phrase *being lost into the other, Verlorensein in den anderen*.

> It is a complete misunderstanding of shame to think that a bride strips off her sense of shame together with her wedding dress. The genuine sense of shame proves itself as genuine precisely by continuing in marriage, not only in relation to other men ... but also in relation to one's beloved spouse. [Shame arises] whenever a stirring of *libido* falls outside of an intensified stirring of love. It is the inner law of shame that each act of *surrender* (*Hingabe*) *without actual love, without being lost into the other,* even in relation to the person one loves decidedly, falls on one's conscience as "guilt."[4]

The understanding of shame as due to a lack of integration of sexual passion into personal love is strikingly similar to John Paul's understanding of shame (TOB 26:4–30:5).

Wojtyła evaluates Scheler from an Aristotelian-Thomist perspective, which is evident already in the structuring of his book by Aristotle's distinction be-

bear such responsibility as an unpaid lecturer), who thereby becomes eligible for appointment as an ordinary professor with tenure.

4. Scheler, "Scham und Schamgefühl," GW 10:123–24; emphasis added.

tween types of causes (see below). His perspective reflects his formation. In 1942, after his encounter with John of the Cross's writings, he entered the clandestine seminary set up by Cardinal Sapieha. His intellectual formation at the seminary was in substance Aristotelian-Thomistic, not unlike the formation John of the Cross received four centuries earlier in Salamanca. After his ordination (November 1, 1946), he continued his studies at the Angelicum and completed the dissertation in 1948.[5] In a letter from Rome he describes his impression of St. Thomas Aquinas.

> There would be much to discuss ... regarding Thomistic studies. This entire system is something beautiful, delightful, and still it bespeaks simplicity. It appears that thought and profoundness do not require many words. Perhaps even the more profound the thought, the fewer words are required.[6]

His later studies of Scheler and Kant enriched this formation.

> My previous Aristotelian-Thomistic formation was enriched by the phenomenological method, and this made it possible for me to undertake a number of creative studies. I am thinking above all of my book *Person and Act*. In this way I was able to take part in the contemporary movement of philosophical Personalism, and my studies were able to bear fruit in my pastoral work. I have often noticed how many of the ideas developed in these studies have helped me in my meetings with individuals and with great numbers of the faithful during my apostolic visits. My formation within the cultural horizon of Personalism also gave me a deeper awareness of how each individual is a unique person. I think that this awareness is very important for every priest.[7]

In this text, John Paul clearly distinguishes his intellectual *formation* from an *enrichment*. The distinction leaves open a range of possible weights for the two sides, but the main point remains. Wojtyła is a Thomist *by formation* whose thinking was *enriched* by a close study of Kant and Scheler. As he explains in *Person and Act*, he uses a form of the phenomenological method that differs in essential respects from Scheler and Husserl (see part II, chap. 5, in this volume).

In the introduction to his book on Scheler, Wojtyła explains why Scheler's ideas attracted the attention of Catholic theologians. Moral theology had always focused on the objects of human acts, that is, on the good or value. Scheler crit-

5. Details about Wojtyła's theological studies from October 1942 (entry into the seminary) to December 1948 (awarding of the doctoral degree at the Jagiellonian University) are presented in Adam Boniecki, *The Making of the Pope of the Millennium: Kalendarium of the Life of Karol Wojtyła* (Stockbridge, MA: Marian Press, 2000), 87–121.

6. Letter to H. Szkocka, March 1947, in Boniecki, *Kalendarium*, 112.

7. John Paul II, *Gift and Mystery: On the Fiftieth Anniversary of My Priestly Ordination* (New York: Doubleday, 1996), 93–94.

icizes Kant for his failure to do justice to these objects of acts. Scheler calls his own ethics a "material ethics of values" in contrast to Kant's formalism, in which moral goodness is due to the universal *form* of the categorical imperative rather than to the *material content* of the act, the good or evil willed by the person (see the presentation of Kant's formalism in part II, chap. 2, sect. 2, in this volume).

A further reason why Scheler attracted the attention of theologians is more specific.

> There were also more particular theses that caused immediate associations with Christian ethics, especially with the ethical teaching of the Gospels. In his system Scheler underlines that love for the person and following an exemplary person have great importance and play a central role in ethical life as a whole. (WojScheler 34)

Scheler and the Gospel's teaching on following and imitating Christ, Wojtyła says, "have points of contact on the level of personalism" (WojScheler 302).

> The personalist foundation of Scheler's system is built in a manner quite similar to the Gospel. The principle of imitation is based on the ideal of the perfection of the person, which is set before us in all its evidence, and it is supposed to help in reaching this ideal. (WojScheler 75–76)

What Wojtyła calls *personalism* in these texts is not a developed philosophical theory but an emphasis on the person visible in concern for the moral perfection of the person, love for the person, and following Jesus as the exemplary person.

The Word Value

Wojtyła follows Scheler in the systematic use of the word *value* rather than *good*. This systematic use goes back to Kant, who was the first to give such a prominent place to *value* (*Wert*). For some readers, *value* is a subjectivist red flag. This impression is mistaken.

Value came into English from Latin *valor*, derived from the verb *valeo*, to have strength, be healthy, be well, fare well. It has two main meanings that correspond roughly to the two English words derived from the Latin; namely, *valor* and *value*. Thomas uses *valor* about forty times in his writings. He uses it in the sense of English *valor* to express God's power. He also uses it in the sense of *value* to refer to the worth of a good as judged in a just judgment. Closely related to both of these meanings is a frequent use closer to Wojtyła's in the context of discussions of the merit of works. In these texts, Thomas connects *value* with words such as dignity, being judged worthy, and so on.

> Christ poured out his blood for his Church and did many other things whose estimation is of infinite value (*infiniti valoris*) because of the dignity of the person. Hence Wisdom 7:14 says, "In it (wisdom) there is an infinite treasure for human beings."[8]
>
> Even a single act of contrition has a certain infinity, both from the power (*ex virtute*) of grace which gives to works an infinite value (*infinitum valorem*), so that through them human beings merit an infinite good, and from the merit of Christ, which is at work in all sacraments and all merits.[9]
>
> [The passion of Jesus] is in some way of infinite value (*infiniti valoris*) inasmuch as it was the suffering of God and man.[10]
>
> *The value of merit* (*valor meriti*) depends on the power of the Holy Spirit moving us into eternal life.[11]
>
> No *value* of our works *is counted worthy* (*nullus valor reputatus dignus*) of eternal glory, except through presupposed acceptance by God.[12]

In each of these uses, *value* refers to a great objective good, but with the added note of a judgment about its greatness. The note of judgment does not subjectivize the good but underlines its objectivity.

The Franciscan Ramon Llull (1232–1315) uses *valor* with similar metaphysical weight, far from Kantian subjectivism. *Valor* is the same in subject as *good*, but it adds the note of appreciation of the good by praise and honor.

> If there are many gods, no value (*valor*) will be worthy of great praise. For, no value (*valor*) will be infinite in goodness, greatness, power, and so on, if there are many gods, since none of them will be infinite but finite. Since it is the nature and property of God to have infinite value (*valorem infinitum*) and to be praised and honored as much as he can be praised and honored, it follows that there is one God, who has infinite *value* (*valorem*) by essence and by operation.[13]

Dante uses *value* (*valore*) much like Llull, close to *good* (*bene*). He often needs it at the end of a line of poetry for a rhyme, but he evidently uses it for more substantive reasons as well.

8. Thomas, *Quodlibetum* 2, q. 8, a. 2, corp.
9. Thomas, *Super IV sent.*, d. 14, q. 1, a. 1, ad 1.
10. Thomas, *Super IV sent.*, d. 14, q. 2, a. 1A, ad 4; emphasis added.
11. Thomas, *Summa* I-II, q. 114, a. 2, corp.; emphasis added.
12. Thomas, *De veritate*, q. 27, a. 5, ad 5; emphasis added.
13. Raymond Lull, *Compendiosus tractatus de articulis fidei catholicae* 91.

Looking into his Son with the Love
which the one and the other eternally breathes,
the first and ineffable value (*valore*),
    whatever moves itself around through mind or place
he made with such order, there can be none
who sees this without enjoying him.
(Dante, *Paradiso* 10.1–6)

In this text, God creates all things according to the paradigm of the primal value seen in the Son and loved in the Spirit. As a result, everyone who sees the order of the world as it reflects the primal value is led back to that value to taste and enjoy its goodness. A use of similar metaphysical dignity is present in the following passage that culminates in a text from Exodus.

The good (*il bene*), inasmuch as it is good, as understood,
so kindles love and all the more
the more goodness it holds within itself. . . .
    The voice of the true author shows this
which says to Moses, speaking about itself
"I will let you see all value (*ogne valore*)."
(Dante, *Paradiso* 26.28–42)

The words which Dante quotes at the very end are taken from the self-revelation of God to Moses, "I will make all my goodness pass before you" (Exodus 33,19). It is not surprising, therefore, that the word *value* returns in Dante's description of the beatific vision.

Now, finally, you see the height and the breadth,
of the eternal value (*valore*): It has made for itself
so many mirrors, in which it divides itself
    remaining one in itself as before.
(Dante, *Paradiso* 29.142–45)

Shakespeare's use of the word is not far from Dante. Again, *value* is closely associated with estimating or appreciating the inner worth of something. It underlines the reality of that worth.

But value dwells not in particular will,
It holds his estimate and dignity
As well wherein 'tis precious of itself
As in the prizer.
(Shakespeare, *Troilus and Cressida*, Act II, Scene 1)

These examples (they could be multiplied) suggest that one should not dismiss the word *value* as a Kantian code word for the subjectivist reduction of goodness to what is decreed by practical reason detached from being. It is an old word often used to refer to the good. In these uses, it does not subtract from good but underlines it.

In Wojtyła, *value* refers to the same reality expressed by *good* and adds the note of conscious appreciation by the person. In this respect, it is like the concept of *bonum honestum, honorable good*, which adds a similar note of appreciation to *good* by the honor given to it. One can readily see how the use of *value* fits with Wojtyła's concern to understand and express not only the objective features of being, truth, goodness, and beauty but also their presence and impact in the awareness of the person. When the subjectivity of the person and the realm of lived experience is seen in this manner, it highlights the objectivity of the good instead of reducing it.

2. Imitation in Kant and Scheler

While Kant argues that imitation cannot play any role in the moral life, Scheler goes directly to the opposite extreme. According to Kant,

> Imitation does not take place in the moral life at all and examples serve only as encouragement. They make the feasibility of the law clear beyond all doubt. They illustrate what the practical rule expresses in more general terms. Yet they never allow us to set aside the true original which lies in reason and to orient ourselves by examples. (Kant, *Groundwork* AK 4:441)

Kant rejects imitation because of his formalism, in which autonomy is the supreme value. The goodness of the will lies in one thing only, in its completely self-caused movement in accord with the universal form of legislation independent of good and evil. When I deliberate whether I should help my friend in need, no example can be relevant because I must move myself by myself according to a universal law. In addition, my friend's good (in Kant's terminology, the *matter* of my will) must not have any influence on my will, because this influence would reduce my will to the status of serving an interest foreign to it, an interest of my irrational appetites, whose ultimate object is happiness. The reason for helping my friend in need must be that my autonomous self-movement according to universal law requires that I do not exclude my friend's good (see Kant, *Groundwork* AK 4:441).

In opposition against Kant, Scheler goes to the opposite extreme. Imitating an exemplar, he claims, plays *the* central role in moral life.

> Moral effectiveness infinitely superior to all these kinds of effectiveness [i.e., the effectiveness of laws and norms] lies in the pure and immediate vision of the pure value and pure being of the person, which invites free "following." There is only one ideal content of the ought (there is no normative ought) that helps us to bring the phenomenon of Jesus to the fore: he himself. (Scheler, FormEng 222n50, FormGer 229n2)
>
> From a genetic point of view, model persons are essentially more original than norms.... The experienced relation that a person has to the content of the personality of his model is following, based on love.... Nothing on earth allows a person to become good so originally and immediately and necessarily as the evidential and adequate intuition of a good person in his goodness. This relation is absolutely superior to any other relation that might be considered the reason for becoming good. (Scheler, FormEng 575, FormGer 560)

Modeling and following, according to Scheler, take place on many different levels and in many different forms. For children, parents are model persons; for a tribe, its ancestors or leaders; for society, its lionized prominent persons and arbiters of elegance; for a nation, its national heroes; for a church, its saints and founders. Some influences of model persons are deep and comprehensive, others transitory and peripheral. There are also negative models and antimodels (see Scheler, FormEng 575, FormGer 560).

Following a truly exemplary person is connected with insight into that person's unique value-essence.

> There can be an evidential insight into a good whose objective essence and value-content contains a reference to an individual person, and whose ought, therefore, comes to this person and to him alone as a "call," no matter if this "call" is addressed to others or not. This, therefore, is to catch sight of the value-essence of my person—in religious terms the value-picture, so to speak, which God's love has of me and which God's love draws and bears before me insofar as this love is directed to me. (Scheler, FormEng 490, FormGer 482)

What the disciple intuits by loving a master is, in the best circumstances, this individual and ideal value-essence of the model person (see part II, chap. 3, sect. 5, in this volume). Again, one can see the sharp edge against Kant. The disciple is formed precisely by what is most unique in his master, not by the most universal principles of practical reason.

The influence of the model occurs primarily on the level of the person's being and moral attitude or *ethos* rather than individual actions. It is not a matter of willing to become like another through certain actions but of a "free giving" of oneself to the influence of the model person by feeling his or her value-essence (see Scheler, FormEng 579–80, FormGer 565–66).

3. Overview

Wojtyła's book on Scheler has seven chapters, divided into a set of three (part I) and a set of four (part II). Part I presents Scheler's value ethics (chap. 1), discusses the relation between philosophy and theology in his thought (chap. 2), and describes the method to be followed in the book (chap. 3). Chapter 1 of part II sketches the teaching of Jesus about following and shows that it implies three truths about the moral life connected with the three Aristotelian causes: form, agent, and end. The remaining three chapters compare these three truths with Scheler's account of the moral life: the formal cause of moral goodness (chap. 2), the efficient cause (chap. 3), and the final cause (chap. 4).

The presentation can begin with part II, chap. 1, because the main points of part I have already been taken up in the chapter on Scheler's theomorphic personalism of solidarity.

In part II, chap. 1, Wojtyła presents the teaching of Jesus (WojScheler 70–74): "If anyone wants to come after me, let him deny himself, take up his cross and follow me" (Matthew 16:24). "If I, your Lord and teacher, have washed your feet, you also must wash one another's feet" (John 13:14). To some, Jesus offers a path of particular closeness in following. "If you want to be perfect … come, follow me" (Matthew 19:21). A condition for walking on the path of following is that one loves Jesus more than father or mother, son or daughter (see Matthew 10:37–38). The ultimate exemplar to be followed is the Father himself. "Be perfect as your heavenly Father is perfect" (Matthew 5:48).

The Gospel's ideal of moral perfection in following Jesus, Wojtyła argues on the basis of these and other texts, has three main characteristics (WojScheler 74–75). (1) It is a religious ideal, both because the perfection to be realized is that of the Father and the Son and because following establishes the right personal relation with God as the final end. (2) It is a real ideal, because it aims at a real perfection of the person that is a likeness of the real perfection already found in Jesus. (3) It is a practical ideal, because it is realized by acts that the person can perform in following the exemplar, acts by which the person becomes really good.

In the second main part of chapter 1, Wojtyła gives a preliminary overview of his evaluation of Scheler's ethics and anthropology, which he then unfolds in the remainder of his book. He returns to the three points which he had derived from the Gospel, not in the order of their first appearance as end, form, and agent but in the order of form, agent, and end.

1. *Form* (WojScheler 80–81): The ideal proposed by the Gospel for following is a real ideal, because it aims at a real perfection of the person in imitation of

a real perfection already found in Jesus. According to Scheler, by contrast, the ideal is an ideal value-essence, which has the character of a call more than a reality. According to Scheler's definition of the person and his understanding of value, this ideal value-essence is something felt rather than a real property of the person. It is exclusively given in the intentional consciousness of certain acts of feeling.

2. *Agent* (WojScheler 81–82): The ideal proposed by the Gospel is a practical ideal because it is realized by acts that the person can perform in following the exemplar, acts by which the person becomes good. Scheler, by contrast, sees following as taking place in the intentional or cognitive aspect of feeling. Love feels the ideal value-essence. As a result, the self-feeling of the person who follows is affected. Deliberate acts of the person, he holds, are secondary. In addition, Scheler excludes moral goodness as a possible motive of any act of will. It is Pharisaical to intend one's own moral goodness. If one cannot intend a perfection, Wojtyła argues, it is certainly not a practical ideal.

3. *End* (WojScheler 82–83): The ideal proposed by Jesus in the call to follow is a religious ideal, both because the perfection to be followed or imitated is that of the Father and the Son and because following establishes the right relation with God and has the fruit of reaching God himself as the end, as the object of supernatural blessedness. Scheler, by contrast, understands the ideal value-essence of a person as a call. It is "the value-picture, so to speak, which God's love has of me and which God's love draws and bears before me insofar as this love is directed toward me" (Scheler FormEng 490, FormGer 482). The Gospel goes further in seeing the perfection we must reach as the content of the will of God. In addition, "the person becomes worthy of real participation in the supernatural divine good" (WojScheler 83). These truths cannot be expressed in the phenomenological method as Scheler understands it.

4. Formal Cause

In part II, chap. 2, Wojtyła asks whether Scheler's philosophy can do justice to the Gospel's teaching that the ideal to be followed is a real moral value in the person.

The chapter has two sections. The first (WojScheler 85–98) argues that Scheler's phenomenological method does not allow him to give an account *of moral value as a real attribute of the person*. The second (WojScheler 99–110) argues that the phenomenological method does not allow Scheler to give an account *of the objective nature of moral acts*.

Phenomenology and the Reality of Moral Values

Wojtyła identifies the phenomenological method as the main reason for the failure of Scheler's ethical system. "It is, therefore, due to its phenomenological principles that Scheler's system is unsuitable for the interpretation of Christian ethics" (WojScheler 97).

Wojtyła's argument for this conclusion begins with the influence of phenomenological principles on Scheler's definition of value. Scheler considers values precisely inasmuch as they are phenomena. Wojtyła emphasizes that this does not mean Scheler's values are purely subjective. Values and their hierarchy, according to Scheler, are objectively given (WojScheler 85–86; cf. the discussion of this point in Scheler, FormEng 265–66, FormGer 270–71). Still, Scheler considers them only inasmuch as they are phenomena, inasmuch as they are given in intentional acts of feeling. This limitation of method to phenomena blocks the recognition of truly real good and evil.

Because he considers values precisely in their intentional position as phenomena, Scheler pays special attention to the conditions under which the value of moral goodness is given. Wojtyła quotes the following text from Scheler's *Formalism*.

> The value "good"—in an absolute sense—is the value that appears, by way of essential necessity, on the act of realizing the value which (with respect to the measure of cognition of that being which realizes it) is the highest. The value "evil"—in an absolute sense—is the value that appears on the act of realizing the lowest value. The value that appears on the act of realizing a higher or lower value, as viewed from the initial value-experience in every case, is relatively good or evil. (FormEng 25, FormGer 47)

The hierarchy of values, Scheler holds, is given in acts of love called *preferring*, not in the sense of a choice of one good over another but as the inclination of love to a value given as higher in comparison with a lower one. The moral goodness of the agent, therefore, is given in an experience that arises as a consequence of feeling the hierarchy of values and at the same time consciously realizing the higher value. Scheler calls this felt value of moral goodness, taken as a whole in a person's life, the *ethos* of that person. *Ethos* is a person's characteristic way of feeling values. It is "a structure of preferring, of loving and hating" (FormEng 299, FormGer 303). It is such a structure as a value, part of whose very essence it is to be felt *on* or *on the back of* moral acts. "Without any difficulty we grasp a strict correlation between *ethos* and the 'ideal value-essence' of the person" (WojScheler 88–89). Scheler's concept of *ethos* tends more toward the factual disposition of the person in feeling values, the ideal value-essence more toward a call, but they overlap in large measure.

Decisive steps in the growth of an *ethos*, Scheler claims, can be achieved by religious-moral geniuses like Jesus.

> The most radical form of renewal and growth of *ethos* occurs in the movement of love and its power, in which "higher" values (with regard to existing ones) are discovered and disclosed.... Thus, it is to the moral-religious genius that the realm of values opens up. In such a variation the rules of preferring among old and new values are automatically altered. Although the rules of preferring among the old values and their mutual objectivity are not necessarily affected, the old realm of values as a whole is nevertheless relativized. [Footnote:] I know of no more grandiose evidence for such a discovery of a whole realm of values which relativizes an older *ethos* than the Sermon on the Mount, whose very form repeatedly announces evidence of the relativizing of the old values of the "law": "But I say to you." (FormEng 305n83, FormGer 309n1, quoted at WojScheler 90n6, chapter endnote 6 printed at 111)

Scheler's characteristic way of viewing Jesus becomes clear in this text. The *ethos* of Jesus, the felt value-essence of his way of loving, stands in the center of attention as an experienced value that can be followed.

> If we took our stand on Scheler's presuppositions, we would have to reduce the whole ethical teaching of the Gospel to the personal value-experience of Jesus Christ as well as his followers and imitators. (WojScheler 93)

Following Jesus would consist in feeling his value-essence and abandoning oneself to its formative power. Wojtyła argues that the Gospel's ethical teaching includes much more. It does not limit itself to speaking about ethical values as they are experienced by Jesus or his followers. It names them in objective terms.

> The personal example of Jesus's life was indeed such a model for the persons around him. Yet, even they needed at times an objective naming of the values toward which the particular actions of Jesus were directed. Otherwise they would not have understood the particular moral meaning of many of his actions, for example, his poverty, his sacrifice, that were the objects of his actions. For this reason, Jesus defined their meaning to them in his teaching. (WojScheler 93–94)

Jesus not only explained objective good and evil. He also spoke as the divinely authorized lawgiver. He announced to the whole human race the will of God in the form of universal norms valid for all. Wojtyła concludes:

> If we reduced Christian ethics as a whole to following the personal model, which is Jesus Christ himself, we would fail to draw out the full ethical content of the sources of revelation. For, Christian ethics contains many teachings of great universal human importance that do not appear immediately in the experiences of the Christ-model. It is indubitably clear that the attempt to build up a Christian ethics on the principle of Jesus's value-essence and following of his example does not cover the ethical teaching of revelation as a whole. The principle turns out to be too narrow. (WojScheler 94)

Already in the Gospel, then also later in Christian tradition, the explanation of these universal norms did not appeal mainly to the *ethos* or individual ideal value-essence of Jesus but to the objective order of natural and supernatural goods. This point is particularly clear in the Beatitudes (Matthew 5:1–12). Each Beatitude names a moral perfection that must characterize the disciples of Jesus and then adds a good, a reward, with which this moral perfection is linked.

> They are called blessed (μακάριοι), because to the good of their persons and their deeds there corresponds the good that comes from God. It is thus supernatural, for example, the good of being children of God, of seeing God, the good of the heavenly kingdom. Jesus Christ reveals to humanity the material world of supernatural goods and defines the relation between the moral goodness of human acts and that world of goods. (WojScheler 95–96)

By limiting himself to the phenomenological method—that is, to value as something given—as felt by emotion, Scheler is unable to give an account of these objective goods. For this reason, one finds in his ethics an excessive dominance of *ethos*.

> According to the epistemological principles of Phenomenology we come to know the world only to the extent in which it is "given" in experience. Only to this extent do we grasp the relations and connections between values and goods.... We see in Scheler's system a hypertrophy of *ethos*. This is a direct result of the fact that ethical values are given a purely emotional position. This, however, is the inescapable consequence of the phenomenological epistemological premises. (WojScheler 97–98)

Phenomenology and the Objective Nature of Morality

In the Gospel and the Christian tradition the moral goodness of an act is determined by the objective nature of the act. For example, in the Sermon on the Mount, Jesus teaches that we should avoid swearing. "Why? Because the nature of the act of swearing is such that one should not perform it for trivial reasons or ordinary concerns" (WojScheler 104). Jesus examines the various forms of oaths in use among his fellow Jews to substantiate this claim. Jesus also gives the commandment "Love your enemies" (Matthew 5:43–48). Why? Because the objective content or nature of this act has a certain similarity with the perfection of God. The nature of the act is the foundation of its moral goodness (WojScheler 104–5).

According to Christian ethics, it is in many cases sufficient to describe the being of an act, what is actually done in it, to understand its goodness. In Scheler, by contrast, it is not sufficient to consider the being of an act, because values are quite separate from being. *Being* and *value* determine two different orders that are fundamentally distinct from each other and cannot be reduced to each other. According to Scheler, we cannot attribute moral goodness or evil to acts like "giving alms" and *fasting*, so long as we consider the objective being of these acts (WojScheler 106).

For Scheler, value necessarily implies a certain relation to the subject. It is never a value "in itself," but only "for somebody." The subjective experience of feeling a value is essential. Value and feeling are correlative. By contrast, in Christian sources, moral goodness is an objective characteristic of some acts. The subjective experience of feeling a value does not need to be included (WojScheler 108). Wojtyła concludes,

> Despite its objectivist tendencies, Scheler's ethical system is not suitable for interpreting an ethics that has an objective character as Christian ethics does.
>
> There is no doubt that Scheler's insufficient objectivism springs from his phenomenological principles. Because of these principles the ethical value always remains in an intentional and—despite everything—subjective position. To grasp ethical value in its real and objective position, one would have to proceed from different epistemological premises, namely, meta-phenomenological and even meta-physical premises. (WojScheler 109)

5. Efficient Cause

In chapter 3, Wojtyła examines whether Scheler's philosophy can do justice to the Gospel's teaching that the ideal to be followed is practical, to be realized by the person as a responsible agent. The chapter has four sections that build on one another. In the first (WojScheler 113–27), Wojtyła examines the innermost point from which moral acts proceed; namely, the person as responsible causal origin of moral acts. In the second (WojScheler 128–34), he turns to conscience as the subjective measure of moral acts. In the third (WojScheler 134–49), he discusses the norms or imperatives that conscience applies; namely, duty and commandments. In the fourth (WojScheler 149–57, he analyzes the "greatest commandment," the commandment of love.

Responsible Agency

The ideal of moral perfection to be reached in following Jesus, Wojtyła argues, is practical in the sense that the person can and does realize it by actions. The core of the practical character of the ideal lies in the person as the responsible causal origin of moral acts (WojScheler 114). Scheler's Phenomenology cannot do justice to this core because it rejects the understanding of the person as a subsistent being with a certain nature and certain powers that can responsibly cause certain acts.

> Due to its phenomenological principles, Scheler's system cannot directly grasp and express that the human person in its acts is the origin of moral good and evil. The whole difficulty is the result of the phenomenological premises of the system and we must assign the blame to these principles. (WojScheler 115)

There are also more specific reasons for which Scheler denies that the person is the responsible causal origin of moral good and evil. We can never intend our own moral good and evil, he claims. If we attempt to will our goodness directly, we lose it and become pharisaical. We must not even love our own moral goodness. According to Scheler, "Love for the good as good is itself bad, because it is necessarily Pharisaism" (GW 7:164, quoted at WojScheler 116n4, note 4 printed at WojScheler 157).

Scheler holds this surprising position, it appears, in reaction against Kant's claim that in our morally good actions we must not be motivated by any good outside of us but only by the will to be morally good, by the will to do our duty because it is our duty. Scheler comments.

> Being-good and being-evil would be wholly independent of all material values. And, indeed, this is Kant's assertion. It is for him a matter of complete indifference with respect to being good and being evil whether we seek to realize the noble or the vulgar, the weal or the woe, the useful or the harmful. For the meaning of the words good and evil is wholly exhausted in lawful or unlawful form. . . .
>
> Let us not further consider *the monstrosity of this claim*, which ignores that the purposes of the devil are no less "systematic" than those of God. It is Kant's first error to deny that [moral] good and evil are *material* values. But they are—avoiding all construction—specific material values that can clearly be felt. (Scheler, FormEng 24–25, FormGer 46–47; emphasis added)

The case of friendship clarifies Scheler's main point. It is impossible for a person who acts according to the Kantian categorical imperative to be a good friend. Schiller's caricature of Kant is not unfounded.

Pangs of Conscience:
Gladly would I serve my friends,
but sadly, I do it from inclination,
and so, it often distresses me that I am not virtuous.
Decision:
There is no other way: You must seek to despise them,
and then do with disgust what duty demands.[14]

Yet, in fleeing from Kant's absurd position, Scheler runs far in the opposite direction. He demands that a moral act must not intend the agent's moral goodness at all.

> The one who does not want to do good to his fellowman—in such a way that he becomes concerned to bring about his fellow man's well-being—but who merely seizes the opportunity "to be good" or "to do good" in this act, neither is good nor does "good"; he is truly an example of a Pharisee, who wishes to appear "good" to himself. The value "good" . . . can never be the content of an act of willing. It is located, so to speak, on the back of this act and this by way of essential necessity; it can therefore never be intended in this act. (Scheler FormEng 27, FormGer 48)

Scheler's claim that moral goodness cannot be intended by the agent would, if true, condemn moral action to a strange condition of unconsciousness. The good that is to be done for my friend and my own moral goodness, he thinks, would compete against each other if both were intended. On the contrary, they necessarily imply each other. I cannot intend my own moral goodness without willing the good for my friend for my friend's sake, because this is exactly what my moral goodness consists of in this case. Conversely, I cannot consciously will to do good to my friend without consciously conforming myself to the true order of reason—and this is again what moral goodness consists of. One could turn Schiller's lines on their head to show the defects of Scheler's view:

Pangs of Conscience:
Gladly would I do what is good,
but sadly, I do it to be good,
and so, it often distresses me that I am a Pharisee.
Decision:
There is no other way: You must seek to forget being good,
and then do good without wanting to be good.

An important factor in Scheler's denial that we can intend our own moral goodness lies in his account of value as something felt. If in helping my friend

14. Friedrich Schiller and Johann Wolfgang von Goethe, *Xenien* 388–89.

I intend to realize my own moral goodness, I am in fact instrumentalizing my friend's need to feel the value "morally good" in myself. I want to feel or look good in my own eyes. Hence the charge of Pharisaism. If what I will is the moral good of the act, Wojtyła responds, one can hardly speak of Pharisaism (WojScheler 116). He sees Scheler's *emotionalism* at work here, that is, his thesis that values are given only in emotions (WojScheler 117).

> Scheler sees Pharisaism in willing one's own moral goodness, because he has subordinated this willing—or, more exactly, its content—to feeling. He has submerged it in the emotional experiences. As a result, *in the very center of his personalist system we find his characteristic denial of moral value in its entirety*, his denial of the practical fruitfulness of the act of will that is directed toward the realization of the ideal of personal perfection. (WojScheler 118; emphasis added)

One can hardly bring a more devastating charge against an account of morality than the one brought by Wojtyła in this text. At the center of his personalist system, Scheler denies moral good and evil in its entirety. The reason is his denial that the person is the responsible, self-directed origin of acts (WojScheler 122). This causal self-direction escapes Scheler because he separates love as a mere emotion from willing as a striving for realization. Love belongs to the heart, the will to the mind. Love feels a value; the will causes external action. The direction toward a felt value is set by love, but love does not direct itself to a particular good. It does not itself, according to Scheler, contain an element of deliberate willing but simply feels given values. Willing follows the direction of love and does not involve any self-direction either. The will does initiate the act of realizing a value. It is in some way the causal origin but not in the sense of directing itself to its act. The direction is set by love, not by the will (WojScheler 123–24).

> Scheler connected values so radically and exclusively with the emotional sphere of the person's life and separated this sphere so thoroughly from the will's efficacy that the person cannot, in fact, be the origin of these [moral values]. On what basis, then, are they values of the person? They are not values of the person in a real and practical sense, because this would demand that they carry within themselves the efficacy of the person. They merely "appear" in the person—they are values of the person only in an intentional and "theoretical" sense. (WojScheler 126)

Wojtyła continued his reflection on moral agency and efficacy in his main philosophical work, *Person and Act* (1969). In *Person and Act*, he focuses in large measure on the person as the responsible causal origin of its own acts. He thereby supplies a key truth he found lacking in Scheler thirteen years earlier. "The role of the person as efficacious origin of ethical values is the basis of personalism in Christian ethics" (WojScheler 128). In the end, according to this judgment, Scheler fails to achieve a truly personalist understanding of ethics. His personalism is less personalistic than the personalism of the Gospel's teaching about following Christ.

Conscience

Conscience is "a subjective norm (measure) of the morality of human acts" (WojScheler 132). Morally good acts are always in agreement with conscience; morally bad acts are always contrary to conscience. Yet, Wojtyła argues, this does not mean that all acts in agreement with conscience are good, because conscience is not an infallible oracle. An erroneous conscience is binding, but it does not excuse evil acts.[15]

Wojtyła uses Paul's discussion of meat sacrificed to idols as an example to explain this understanding of conscience (see Romans 14:21–23; 1 Corinthians 8:7–13, 10:25–30). Eating meat sacrificed to idols is objectively not wrong, but the erring conscience of some persons judged that it was wrong. For a person with such an erring conscience, it would be wrong to eat such meat.

> According to the sources of Christian ethics, the essential meaning of conscience is evident in this: it is binding even when it is false. Precisely this fact shows best that the moral goodness and evil of an act comes from the person who performs this act. (WojScheler 133)

According to the Pauline texts, conscience has two aspects. It is a subjective conviction of the person, and it is a binding norm that involves an obligation. In its first aspect, subjective conviction, conscience shows the practical character of moral good and evil as something done by the person through the person's own inner principles of action; in its second aspect, obligation, conscience immediately attests to the responsible efficacy of the person. When I see that I ought to do something, I am called upon as a responsible cause to cause myself to act here and now (WojScheler 132–33).

In this context, one finds a clear instance of Wojtyła explicitly adopting a phenomenological approach.

> The act of conscience as the sources of revelation of Christian ethics portray it illustrates this direct efficacy of the person in relation to moral good and evil.

15. See Thomas, *Summa*, I-II, q. 19, aa. 5–6.

> For we find this [efficacy] in the very experience of this act, concretely when our insight into the good imposes on us the obligation of really doing the good, and when our insight into evil imposes the obligation not to do it. Since this [efficacy] is immediately given in the content of the experience, we could use the phenomenological method to help us find efficacy in relation to moral good and evil. We draw the conclusion that the phenomenological method alone should not have made it impossible for Scheler to uncover efficacy and thus establish contact with Christian ethics. (WojScheler 133–34)

This passage anticipates Wojtyła's approach in *Person and Act* where he uses a modified phenomenological method, though still only "in a secondary assisting role" (WojScheler 196), subordinate to a comprehensive metaphysical account based on ordinary human experience.

The Problem of Duty and the Commandments

In the third section, Wojtyła turns to a problem closely related to the obligations or duties formulated by conscience. While Kant's ethics is entirely an ethics of the categorical imperative, an ethics of duty for duty's sake, without any positive role of love and the good as the object of love, Scheler's ethics is entirely an ethics of good and evil, an ethics of love, without any positive role of imperatives and duty. The emphasis on duty and law in Kant, Scheler argues, results from the negative mindset that pervades his philosophy (see part II, chap. 3, sect. 2, in this volume).

Any *ought* has a negative thrust. "Justice ought to be done!" implies that justice has *not* been done, and that this state of injustice should be removed. If justice had already been done, there would be no *ought*. Scheler calls a free-floating *ought*—an *ought* that is not addressed to anyone in particular—*ideal ought*. He takes it as an axiom that any ideal *ought* presupposes the nonbeing of some value. A positive value may lie at the root of the "ideal ought," but the *ought* itself is always directed toward the removal of some evil. "Hence every proposition of the *ought* 'rests' on a positive value that it cannot contain. For what 'ought to be' is originally never the being of good but the non-being of evil" (Scheler FormEng 209, FormGer 217).

Imperatives, Scheler's argument continues, are based on such an ideal *ought* and have the same negative thrust. The imperative "You ought to do justice here!" presupposes that justice has not been done by you and, further, that you are in some way unwilling to do it. The only purpose of the imperative is to overcome this double evil. On this basis, Scheler states his case against duty and imperatives as follows.

> According to the nature of the ideal ought, one can speak of an ought only when a value is given in its non-being; so, according to its nature, an imperative pertains to a positive value inasmuch as a person's striving is not yet directed [to that value] in the person's original intention. When, on the other hand, it is directed to the value, it is meaningless it to speak of "duty," "norm," or "imperative." This implies that an (ideal) ought-not-to-be of a striving is the foundation of every imperative proposition. Throughout history, therefore, proscriptions have always come before prescriptions (for example, the Decalogue). Commandments oppose a perceived possible countermovement of striving against the realization of the commandment because such a countermovement is bad.
>
> From this we can see that any ethics based on imperatives—for example, one which takes its point of departure from duty as the ultimate moral phenomenon and attempts to derive the ideas of the good and the bad, of virtue and vice, only from it—has a merely negative, critical and repressive character from the outset. A constitutive distrust not only of human nature but also of the essence of moral acts in general is the very presupposition of all its tenets. (Scheler FormEng 211–12, FormGer 219)

Because a command is only justified when the person who receives it is unwilling to do what is commanded, it is unjust to command a person who is already willing to do the good. A false accusation is necessarily implicit in the command. "You are not really willing and therefore I am commanding you!" This false accusation rightly causes a movement of "moral defiance" in the one who receives it. The defiance is directed primarily against the injustice of the accusation, but it leads to further negative consequences.

> The good person, who would have done the good "of his own accord" because he had insight, is now put on the defensive against the imperative form of the posited content in question and this gives rise to a tendency toward the bad. The autonomy of insight thus comes into conflict with the very idea of "duty." In this sense, every commandment or prohibition that is unnecessary and, hence, unjustified necessarily brings about a tendency to produce the bad and is itself a bad volitional act in that it implies an offense.... If something that lies in the direction of our love is commanded, such a commandment is itself experienced as a grave offense. (FormEng 214, FormGer 221)

Needless to say, God never commits this grave offense. Any appearance to the contrary is due to interference, first by ruling classes of the Jewish people, then by the Church's Magisterium. It is these human institutions that commit the offense. They attempt to cover it up by attributing their own commandments to God.

> Strictly speaking, only church authority can "command," and if it presents God as himself giving commandments, it only conceals under the idea of God its own responsibility for the moral value of its acts of commanding. (FormEng 213, FormGer 220)

Wojtyła shows without much difficulty that Scheler's complete opposition to law, his exclusion of all duty and commandments from Christian ethics, cannot be reconciled with the teaching of Jesus and the Christian tradition (WojScheler 143–49). It is hard to see what force Scheler sees in his own arguments. Wojtyła states the counterargument in all its plainness.

> When I will to avoid evil, I thereby will the good, and when I will the good I am by no means only avoiding evil. Let us assume that I will the good that I ought to will and do not will the evil that I ought not to will: the acts of will follow the direction of the *ought*—we cannot discover any negative significance of *ought* in them. The will, directed by *ought*, turns to the good. (WojScheler 137)

There are, it seems, deeper reasons why Scheler finds his own arguments so persuasive. The deepest reason seems to lie in a mirror image of Kant's radical understanding of personal autonomy, a mirror image contained in Scheler's thesis that the human person is quasi divine. According to Kant, it is contrary to the dignity of the person to be subject to any law that the person does not autonomously impose on itself. The mirror image of the Kantian absolute subject can be seen particularly in Scheler's understanding of the person's individual value essence and its relation to blessedness, which Wojtyła discusses in the last chapter of his book.

A further reason for Scheler's rejection of law lies in his reduction of moral life to the experience of feeling value and his failure to do justice to the genuine efficacy of the person in relation to moral good and evil. Imperatives show their most positive sense when one sees them as directing that efficacy.

> In view of these facts [i.e., the evident weakness of Scheler's arguments] we can only assume that the negative character which Scheler always ascribes to the *ought* is a consequence of the emotivist premises of his system, concretely of the thesis that the person's inner life reduces itself to emotion as its essential content. . . . The place in ethics in which one finds a positive and morally creative role of the *ought* is in the acts of will on which the person's efficacy in relation to values is based. Scheler did not take this efficacy as a point of departure but reduced the person to emotion. This is the reason why the *ought* took on a negative and morally destructive role. (WojScheler 137–38)

There is a certain similarity between Scheler and Kant that arises paradoxically from Scheler's complete rejection of Kant's ethics of duty. Both break the unity of the moral act that is expressed by "the good is to be done and pursued." Kant only allows the imperative, "To be done." Scheler only allows the good or value. Both split the first precept of practical reason.

Ought and *commandments*, Wojtyła argues, are inseparable from the full responsible efficacy of the person in moral acts. A denial of imperatives is possible only together with a denial of this efficacy. This denial seems to lie at the heart of Scheler's system. According to Scheler, the will to realize a value is directed by the love that feels that value, but the will is never truly self-directed in a causally efficacious manner. It is a mere volitional tendency swept up by the emotion of love. The person as responsible origin of acts disappears without leaving a trace (see WojScheler 141).

Behind the elimination of the *ought* and the reduction of the person's moral life to emotion stands ultimately the loss of real being in Scheler's phenomenological method. Values are, as such, indifferent to existence because they constitute a realm of essences separate from the realm of being.

> According to the premises of Scheler's system, value is by its nature indifferent with respect to existence. This means that it is a value regardless of whether it exists or not. [Wojtyła's footnote: It is quite different, for example, in the system of Thomas Aquinas, where the good is the true object of will, of striving (*appetitus*). When we will the good, when we strive for it, our concern is that it exists. The issue is the being of the good; cf. *Summa* I, 1.5.] This indifference in relation to existence is explained quite simply, because values are given as the proper objects of emotional perception. Precisely because they are indifferent with respect to existence they do not give rise to an "ought." (WojScheler 139n29)

Scheler's account of the first principles of moral acts thus has the same root as Kant's; namely, the loss of real being. Contrary to Scheler's protestation that by his rejection of duty he can overcome Kant most decisively, he agrees with Kant on two important points: human acts are not acts in which the person is causally responsible for moral good and evil, and the moral life consists of a certain emotion, that of reverence for the law in Kant's case, and that of love in Scheler's.

> In Scheler's system the main point is that man experiences the good. This is the basis of the fundamental difference between the essence of Christian ethics and the main tendency of Scheler's system. In Christian ethics the good is a certain personal, objective value, and the same is true of evil. This is why the good leads to the realization of the ideal of the person's perfection; evil

> impedes it and prevents it. In Scheler's system, by contrast, good and evil are of interest as content of experiences.
>
> Without a doubt, he adopted this position from Kant. While Kant connected the morality of human acts with the experience of duty and taught that a given human act is moral inasmuch as in it duty is done out of duty—thus morality rests on a single emotion, reverence for the law and for duty—Scheler connects morality with the experience of mere values. In the one system as in the other the morality of acts is connected with the specific character of the experience, while Christian ethics connects the moral character of man's experiences with the efficacy of the human person in relation to objective moral values, to good and evil. (WojScheler 149)

The Commandment of Love

In light of Scheler's general rejection of norms and commandments, it comes as no surprise that he rejects "the greatest commandment" (Matthew 22:36–40, cf. Mark 12:31), the commandment to love God and neighbor. It is immoral for anyone to issue a general commandment of love, because the commandment indiscriminately and unjustly accuses everyone of a failure to love. There is an additional difficulty specific to love: love cannot be commanded because it arises spontaneously as an emotion in contact with a value and cannot be deliberately willed. On this point, Scheler agrees with Kant. "As Kant correctly observed, the acts of faith and love cannot be commanded" (WojScheler 149).

> Ecclesiastical-Catholic writers like to speak of the "law of love." They hold, for example, that Jesus has replaced the old "law" with a new one, that this "law of love" is higher than the old law (of Moses) but still contains it. If they understand by this that love is nothing arbitrary … this manner of speaking is fully justified. If, however, it means that there is a "norm of law" which commands love, a law Jesus established, joined to existing norms, and raised above all other norms in such a way that there is no law "of" love (subjective genitive) but only the law to love (= ought to love), then this manner of speaking is nonsense. (FormEng 220n48, FormGer 227n2)
>
> But in fact, this principle cannot be considered a "norm" that "gives an order," for it does not make any sense, as Kant himself subsequently says, to want to "order" or "command" love. Still, this principle says that he who so acts (that is, he who loves his neighbor as himself) realizes the highest moral value, and that such behavior is of ideal oughtness. Insofar as this proposition is directed toward a subjective will, it is not meant as a norm that commands but as an invitation to follow. (FormEng 222, FormGer 229)

Wojtyła points out that the sources of revelation show that love is indeed the object of a commandment, not only of a recommendation or invitation (see WojScheler 150–51).

> I give you a new commandment, that you love one another, as I loved you, that you too may love one another (John 13:34). This is my commandment, that you love one another as I have loved you (John 15:12). This I command you, that you love one another (John 15:17).

Wojtyła also points to the passages in John that link loving Jesus with keeping his commandments.

> If you love me, you will keep my commandments (John 14:15). The one who has my commandments and keeps them, he is the one who loves me (John 14:21). If you keep my commandments, you remain in my love, as I have kept my Father's commandments and remain in his love (John 15:10).

What is commanded, Wojtyła specifies, is not only the external activity of doing good but also "the internal and formal act of love" (WojScheler 151n43).

Wojtyła draws three conclusions from this thesis (see WojScheler 153–54). (1) Because love is commanded, love must be a voluntary activity of the will and not simply an emotional experience. (2) The one who keeps the commandments expresses his love for God by keeping them. (3) Love must contain in itself the full causal responsibility of the person for the moral good and evil of that person's acts.

In the last two paragraphs of his discussion of the commandment of love, Wojtyła again adopts a phenomenological approach.

> If we want to transfer the entire problem we are investigating to the level of phenomenology, we must ask ourselves this question: Does love, which, according to the sources of revelation, is the object of the greatest commandment, rest more on the experience of value or on the experience of duty? (WojScheler 156)

Wojtyła answers that neither side should be emphasized at the exclusion of the other. What is at stake in the commandment of love is not merely reverence for the law, as Kant would have it in his ethics of imperatives. The object of love is the good or value. Yet love does not exhaust itself in its relation to value, as Scheler would have it in his emotive ethics of values.

> In the experience of these acts [of love] the experience of value must be connected with the experience of duty. Indeed, only the union of these two elements in experience can constitute the moral experience of the act of love which is the object of the greatest commandment.... The thorough experience

> of value makes duty decisively and effectively active, and on its part such a decisive and effective experience of duty determines the actual power of realizing the value in experience. (WojScheler 156–57)

In this application of a phenomenological method, Wojtyła is concerned to hold together in the lived experience of the person the first principle of the practical order, "The good is to be done or pursued" as it undergirds the particular and definitive practical judgment in particular circumstances, "Do this!" What is experientially evident to the acting person is that the good is to be done, because it is good. The intelligibility of the imperative depends entirely on the goodness of the good. Without the good, the imperative would have no reason; it would hang in the air as an irrational self-movement, as it does in Kant.

One can note Wojtyła's interest in *lived experience* in this account of the commandment of love. His way of speaking seems strange to some who habitually focus on the objective factors involved in the first principle of practical reason. In a highly characteristic manner, Wojtyła is interested in how this principle arises and becomes operative in the person's lived experience.

6. Final Cause

In chapter 4, Wojtyła asks whether Scheler's philosophy can do justice to the Gospel's teaching that the ideal to be followed is religious. In the first section (WojScheler 160–66), he examines the relation to God, which is necessarily present in all moral acts. In the second (WojScheler 167–76), he turns to merit, which is one particularly important element in that relation to God. In the last (WojScheler 176–86), he examines the final end of merit, the reward of blessedness and its true object, the goodness of the divine nature.

The Religious Structure of the Moral Act

According to Scheler, man does not have a specific nature. He cannot be defined as a living being endowed with powers such as sensation and reason. Rather, personal consciousness flashes up in certain conscious acts in organisms that have developed gradually and continuously on the evolutionary path from subhuman to human specimens.

Among all human experiences, Scheler asserts, the most characteristic of the human being are acts of transcendence toward God.

> "Man" as the being of "highest value" among earthly beings and as a moral being becomes comprehensible and open to phenomenological intuition only on the presupposition of the idea of God and "in the light" of this idea! We can even say that, correctly viewed, *he is only this movement, the tendency and transition to the divine*.... How nonsensical to look at the idea of God as an "anthropomorphism," when, on the contrary, *the unique value of man's "humanity" lies in the theomorphism of his most noble exemplars*! (FormEng 288–89, FormGer 293; emphasis added)

The theomorphism of the human person does not, however, imply a relation of transcendence to the living God but rather to a certain isolated essence given in phenomenological intuition; namely, *the divine* or *the holy*. This distinction between *God* and *the divine* is important to Scheler.

> In trying to intuit the essence of man, it is not the idea of God in the sense of an extant and positively determined reality that is presupposed; rather, it is only the quality of the divine, or the quality of the holy, that is given in an infinite fullness of being. On the other hand, whatever takes the place of this essence (*Wesenheit*) in the historical time of earthly man and in the changing beliefs of positive religions cannot be presupposed in any sense. Yet, this idea of God is not an empirical abstraction from diverse positive representations of gods that in different positive religions are the objects of worship and cults. The ultimate, that is, the highest value-quality in the order of ranks of values originally guides the formation of all positive representations, ideas, and concepts of "God." (FormEng 292, FormGer 296–97)

As Scheler goes on to explain, the case of the *essence* of the holy is only one case of the general principle that values can be given independently from beings and before them (FormEng 294–95, FormGer 299). The divine value-quality *holy* can be given independently from and before the divine being.

Accordingly, what defines the human being is not a relation to the living God but to the isolated essence of the holy.

> For the Phenomenologist, man is a theomorphic being only and exclusively by virtue of experiencing the idea of God. Scheler is not concerned with the real relation to God as an existing, positive and defined reality. He is concerned with experiencing the idea of God. (WojScheler 161)

Scheler's more specific account of moral life does not alter the picture. The ethical sphere and the religious sphere are each defined by their own set of value-essences that are irreducible to each other. The value *holy* does not belong to the inner constitution of the value "morally good" (WojScheler 163).

In the Gospel, Wojtyła argues, the connection between the moral agent and the living God is close. Human acts establish or damage the relation with the living God (WojScheler 164–65). God is the aim or end of moral acts. "Jesus always stresses the goal-directed character of these acts" (WojScheler 165).

> Although, from the point of view of ethics, the true object of human acts is not God but the moral value of these acts, man nevertheless experiences his relation to God in these acts in view of their moral value. For if moral good is decisive for a good relationship with God and evil for a negative one, and if man is the responsible causal origin of good and evil acts, then it follows that by the moral value of his acts he shapes his relationship with God into a positive or negative relationship. In this way moral values take on a religious character. (WojScheler 165)

Moral values bear this religious character only inasmuch as they are genuinely practical, that is, inasmuch as the person is causally responsible for the moral good or evil of acts (WojScheler 166). Because for him moral acts are not practical in this way, Scheler cannot offer an account of their religious structure.

> If Scheler's system cannot account for this immanent link between ethics and religion, then despite all its theomorphic conception of the person, who is a person, and particularly an ethical person, only "in the light of the idea of God," this system cannot help us in the interpretation of the most elementary principles of revealed Christian ethics. (WojScheler 166)

Merit

In order to reach a purified understanding of God, Scheler excludes any idea of justice in distributing reward and punishment according to merit.

> The idea of a so-called divine justice of reward and punishment: this idea in no way corresponds, either in terms of its essence or its meaning (apart from its existence), to a purified (*geläutert*) idea of God. (FormEng 368, FormGer 368)

Wojtyła nevertheless takes up the question of merit to examine whether it is at least in principle compatible with Scheler's Phenomenology. He outlines the Catholic doctrine of merit in some of its complexity. Without the supernatural grace of justification prior to all good works, no good act can be meritorious. Even after the justification of the sinner, supernatural grace is necessary for any act to be meritorious. Moral acts are at the same time truly God's gifts and truly meritorious (WojScheler 172). "By the law of works, God says to us: Do what I command! By the law of faith, we say to God: Give what you command!"[16]

Wojtyła compares Scheler's principles and the Catholic understanding of

16. Augustine, *De spiritu et littera* 22.

merit on two main points implied in merit, full causal responsibility and the supernatural character of grace. Merit presupposes, first, that the moral agent has full causal responsibility for the moral good or evil of acts. Scheler's ethics does not posit such responsibility and therefore cannot offer an account of merit.

> In the course of our investigations we have seen that Scheler's system does not allow us to grasp the person's responsible efficacy in relation to moral good and evil. For, in this system, the person appears only as the phenomenological "subject" of these values that are given in that subject's intentional feeling.
>
> According to revealed Christian ethics, by contrast, reward and punishment are not given for a "good" and "evil" that are the content of the person's intentional feeling but for the objective good and evil of the acts themselves that are clearly marked by the person's responsible efficacy. (WojScheler 173)

Wojtyła's second main point of comparison is the supernatural character of the grace necessary for any merit. Because Scheler limits himself to the phenomenological method and therefore does not give an account of real being, his philosophy offers no basis for the distinction between the natural and the supernatural. Wojtyła offers two main arguments for this conclusion. In the first, he argues by analogy between the objective moral value of an act and its objective supernatural value.

> According to the teaching of the sources of Christian revelation, a human act must possess two goods in itself to merit eternal life: a moral good and a heavenly good. Due to its phenomenological premises, Scheler's system does not allow us to grasp the objective ethical value of human acts. We must conclude that due to the same premises it does not allow us to grasp the objective supernatural values of human acts. (WojScheler 174)

Wojtyła's second argument goes deeper. Scheler's phenomenological method focuses on the experience of feeling a value. It excludes an account of real being.

> According to Scheler, values are only given as the content of experience. We would therefore have to prove their essentially supernatural character in the content of the experience itself.... Since the experience gains its essentially supernatural character from the relation to essentially supernatural being, it is impossible in the framework of Scheler's system to grasp and explain the essentially supernatural character of the experience....
>
> If we confess our allegiance to the principle of Phenomenology, as Scheler confesses it in his epistemological and methodological premises, we are unable to give an account of the reality contained in the concept "nature." In consequence, also the noun "the supernatural" or the adjective "supernatural" have no counterpart in the reality given as phenomena. (WojScheler 174–75)

Scheler draws many mysteries of Christian faith into his essentialist philosophy as essences given immediately in presuppositionless phenomenological intuition: grace, revelation, the Church, and the like. Wojtyła finds that Scheler says much about these mysteries that is true. What gets lost in Scheler's essentialism is the real drama of redemption, "redemption as an essentially supernatural union of the human person with God as the highest good" (WojScheler 176).

Reward and Punishment

Wojtyła's final and most radical critique of Scheler concerns this loss of God as the highest good. Scheler agrees with Kant that happiness or blessedness cannot be the goal of moral goodness. Yet while Kant locates happiness far from the core of the person as the irrational object of sensual inclinations, Scheler gives it the most central possible place in the human spirit as the source of all morally good acts. Dependence on Kant by exaggerated opposition is particularly clear in this doctrine.

> Deepest happiness and complete bliss are dependent in their being on a consciousness of one's own moral goodness. Only the good person is blissful. This does not preclude the possibility that this very blissfulness is the root and source of all willing and acting. But happiness can never be a goal or even a "purpose" of willing and acting. Only the happy person acts in a morally good way.
>
> Happiness is therefore in no way a "reward for virtue,"[17] nor is virtue the means to reach bliss. Rather, happiness is the root and source of virtue, a fountainhead, although it is only a consequence of the inner goodness of the person. (FormEng 359, FormGer 359–60)

The dependence of bliss on moral goodness should not be understood in the sense that bliss follows the real moral goodness of real acts, that is, in the sense that it is a rejoicing about having really acted well. Bliss is absolutely prior to all such motivations.

> Bliss in its pregnant sense is present whenever there is no particular state of affairs or values outside or inside us that could motivate us feelingly to this fulfillment in bliss, and whenever the being and enduring of bliss appears—phenomenally—unconditioned and unalterable by any performable acts of will, by any deed, or by any way of life. For it is the being and the self-value

17. Scheler seems to have Aristotle in mind. "[Happiness is] ... the reward and end of virtue." Aristotle, *Nicomachean Ethics* 1.9.1099b.16–17.

> of the person himself that is the "foundation" of bliss and despair. (FormEng 343–44, FormGer 345)

The innermost source of bliss, according to Scheler, is thus the person's individual value-essence, which is quasi-identical with the divine nature when one acts "in God." Such a quasi-identity with the divine nature is an unsurpassable source of bliss. No reward could equal it. There is no need to reward good deeds because they flow from unsurpassable bliss.

> In his existence and his acts, the "good" person directly takes part in the nature of God, in the sense of *velle in deo* (willing in God) or *amare in deo* (loving in God), and he is blissful in this participation. A "reward" from God could only put a smaller and lower good in place of a higher one, and a superficial feeling in the place of a deeper pleasure. (FormEng 368, FormGer 368)

In another text, Scheler states more explicitly what such willing in God and loving in God consists of. He criticizes Kant for focusing only on loving God and not on the much deeper and much more characteristically Christian phenomenon of "loving in God." The acts of God are and remain distinct from the acts of human beings, but the spiritual life principle from which the acts flow is identical in the two. The awareness of this identity is deepest bliss.

> Kant has in mind only the phenomenon of the love of God, not *the highest Christian phenomenon* of "loving in God" (*amare in Deo*). In the latter, *man rises above all laws, even the laws of God* (if God can be thought of as a "legislator" at all), by virtue of the fact that man knows himself to have the immediate power of an essential identity of the spiritual principle of life with simultaneously differentiated real acts. (FormEng 223, FormGer 230; emphasis added)

In this text one can see some of the deeper roots of Scheler's arguments about the negativity of all commandments and laws. The human person ultimately rises above all laws, "even the laws of God," because he feels in himself the immediate power of the first spiritual principle of life. This is "the highest Christian phenomenon."

The highest Christian phenomenon is also, according to Scheler, the most distinctive new element of the Christian *ethos*. It is "the tremendous innovation of the Christian theory of life." While other religions and philosophical systems seek to reduce pain by reducing human sensitivity to pain, Christianity affirms a blissful core of the person, which is superior to all disastrous events of life. It is in this superiority of bliss over anything that might happen to the person, superiority over any loss the person might sustain, any unfulfilled longing the person might have, that one can find the novelty of Christianity.

> A blissful man can suffer misery and unhappiness with joy and can do so with no need to deaden his sensing of pain and pleasure on more peripheral levels. No *ethos* has assimilated the sense of the above as deeply as the Christian. The tremendous innovation of the Christian theory of life was its presentation of a way in which one can suffer pain and unhappiness while remaining blissful.... In the Christian theory of life, the essential moment of what it calls the salvation of the soul is positive bliss in the center of the person. (FormEng 346–47, FormGer 348)

Wojtyła does not recognize the Gospel in this Phenomenology of bliss. One element is missing, an all-decisive element. We are not an end to ourselves. We lack the fullness of being and goodness.

> We see that in the teaching of revelation, *all emphasis* in the doctrine of eternal blessedness *falls on the object of blessedness*, namely, the divine nature, which is this object. *In Scheler's phenomenological system, of course, this doctrine cannot be grasped and expressed....* No good that comes from outside the person can be a greater good than the good which the person finds in himself when he experiences himself as the source of a morally good act.... The greatest happiness and the greatest suffering—man draws these from within himself, he himself is its source for himself.
>
> This point of view seems to separate us completely from the Christian teaching. Given such a point of view, can we establish any point of contact with the revealed truth according to which the object of man's final blessedness is the divine nature? (WojScheler 183–84)

At this point, the chasm between Scheler and the Gospel seems unbridgeable. Wojtyła nevertheless looks for a bridge. According to Scheler, he points out, there is a core of the person in which all social relations are left behind (FormEng 561–72, FormGer 548–58). Yet this "intimate person"—and, more deeply, this "absolutely intimate person"—is not completely alone. It still allows for the relationship with God. This relationship includes, in turn, a relationship to the community of the Church.

> However, solitude does not exclude one communal relation, namely, the relation to God, who by definition is neither an individual nor a comprehensive person but one in whom both individual and comprehensive person are solidary. Thus, it is in God alone that the intimate person may know himself to be judged as well as sheltered. But he cannot know this without becoming indirectly aware of his solidarity (at least "in God") with the comprehensive person in general and, in the first place, with the Church. And without this certitude there would be no God but merely a deceptive object of the highest nature, that is, an illusory God. (FormEng 563, FormGer 550)

Wojtyła remarks that there is "a profound connection between these ideas of Scheler and the teaching of revelation" (WojScheler 184). The specter of the solitary human person drawing bliss out of his own theomorphic self in needless fullness of life seems to be overcome by Scheler's vision of solidarity. Wojtyła finds this aspect of Scheler's teaching in conformity with Christian faith.

> If in this most profound experience of oneself, which Scheler calls absolutely intimate person, the person does not stop being in relation to God, then it experiences its happiness in the good and its despair in the evil of its own essence in relation to God. Does such a formulation help us to grasp and express eternal happiness in God and eternal rejection by God. Most certainly, Yes! (WojScheler 185)

Wojtyła does not stop with this positive conclusion but probes further. Scheler speaks about this relation to God only on the level of experience lived by the person in his or her subjectivity without any truly transcendent object, the really existing living God. The person experiences a detached divine value-essence as an object of feeling. In the sources of revelation, the real goodness of God is the reason why he is the end. When Scheler says that the person shares in the divine being, his phenomenological premises reduce this participation to an intentional feeling of the self-value of the person who experiences a God-idea cut off from all real being (WojScheler 184–85). Wojtyła concludes:

> A participation in God understood in this way has nothing in common with the real, essentially supernatural participation in God's nature and God's inner life. Only participation in God understood in this latter way constitutes the basis of final blessedness in God according to the teaching of revelation. The withdrawal of this participation is the basis of the definitive unhappiness of the human person as a consequence of its rejection by God. In Scheler's conception, by contrast, what the person feels as the real object of emotional bliss and despair—despite "participation in God"—is "good" or "evil" as self-values of the person that become perceptible at the source of the acts experienced by the person. (WojScheler 185–86)

This criticism of Scheler's personalism converges with Balthasar's main objection against Scheler (see the end of part II, chap, 3, in this volume). Greek thought with its concept of a striving love, as expressed in the philosophy of Plato and Aristotle, is closer to Christianity than Scheler's theomorphic personalism of solidarity. It is closer to authentic Christian personalism.

7. Conclusions

Can one build Christian ethics on the foundations of Scheler's Phenomenology? Wojtyła concludes his book with two theses:

> Thesis 1:
>
> The ethical system developed by Max Scheler is in principle unsuited for the scientific formulation of Christian ethics. For, although it establishes a relationship with the ethical content of the sources of revelation by defining ethical values as personal values, its phenomenological and emotivist premises do not allow it to grasp this content completely and to understand it scientifically. In particular, Scheler's system is unsuited for grasping these sources theologically, which is absolutely necessary, given that they are sources of revelation and constitute an object of supernatural faith. (WojScheler 187)
>
> Thesis 2:
>
> Although the ethical system developed by Max Scheler is in principle unsuited for the scientific formulation of Christian ethics, it can help us indirectly in our scientific work on Christian ethics. It facilitates the analysis of ethical facts on the phenomenological and empirical plane. (WojScheler 193)

Phenomenology can thus play an assisting role, but a Christian thinker cannot be a Phenomenologist in Scheler's sense.

> [The theologian] should not forego the great advantages which the phenomenological method offers his work. It impresses the stamp of experience on works of ethics and nourishes them with the life-knowledge of concrete man by allowing an investigation of moral life from the side of its appearance. Yet, in all this, the phenomenological method plays only a secondary assisting role.... At the same time, these investigations convince us that *the Christian thinker, especially the theologian, who makes use of phenomenological experience in his work, cannot be a Phenomenologist.* (WojScheler 196)

Wojtyła's judgment "cannot be a Phenomenologist" should be understood with precision. It applies to Phenomenology as understood by Husserl and Scheler in the degree to which they develop a philosophy of essences detached from real being. It does not apply to realist phenomenology as developed, for example, by Edith Stein, Adolph Reinach, and Dietrich von Hildebrand.

Despite his profound critique of Kant, Scheler follows him in the subjectivist shift of the philosophy of consciousness. As Schmitz puts it, "The modern shift gave to the human subject an absolute status precisely in its character qua consciousness; for human consciousness not only sets its own terms but the terms for reality itself."[18] By giving such an absolute status to human consciousness, Scheler's philosophy cannot sustain the causality of goodness.

> The analysis of the systems of Kant and Scheler shows the conclusion that a consistent teleology and perfectiorism has no room in the philosophy of consciousness. Of course, the end is something contained in consciousness, and the end is always some good or value but as a [mere] content of consciousness, the end loses its perfective character. It possesses such a character only in connection with being, on the premises of a philosophy of the real. Only on this basis can one speak of a consistent teleology.[19]

The failure of Scheler's system is not due to particular problems here or there. It is systemic. "The whole difficulty is the result of the phenomenological premises of the system and we must assign the blame to these principles" (Woj-Scheler 115).

Wojtyła's habilitation thesis is primarily a theological work with a point of departure in the teaching of Jesus. Yet, in its evaluation of the possibility of building moral theology on the principles of Scheler's Phenomenology, it develops many philosophical arguments. It resists Scheler's attempt to de-Hellenize Christian thought. In an essay published four years after his book on Scheler, Wojtyła focuses on happiness.

> An attribute of this [that is, human nature] is above all the desire for happiness. It is something natural and necessary. Man is unable not to desire happiness. He wills it always and in everything although he does not always name the object of his desires. And precisely for this reason it can seem as if he did not desire happiness but only strove for the various values with which he is concerned, because he desires happiness in all and through all.
>
> The desire for happiness does not lie on the uppermost surface of willing and even less so on the surface of human acts. It is not difficult, however, to discover it in them and grasp it objectively—nobody will deny that this desire is always alive in the depth of willing.
>
> Ethics can neither reject this fact, not occupy itself with it to the exclusion of all else. According to its nature, Ethics is not the doctrine of happiness, because it is a normative science, while happiness stands outside and above every norm. Happiness is the goal of nature and cannot be an object of choice, while

18. Kenneth L. Schmitz, *At the Center of the Human Drama: The Philosophical Anthropology of Karol Wojtyla/Pope John Paul II* (Washington, DC: Catholic University of America Press, 1993), 135–36.

19. Karol Wojtyła, *Lubliner Vorlesungen*, ed. Juliusz Stroynowski (Stuttgart-Degerloch: Seewald, 1981), 244. In this passage, Wojtyła does not use the term "perfectionism," but the unusual term "perfectiorism" derived from the Latin comparative *perfectior*, "more perfect," an account based on a greater degree of perfection.

the norm concerns only that which is an object of choice. The object of choice is always a way on which a particular person must walk.

Happiness, by contrast, is not a way but the goal of all the ways of human beings. It is, therefore, not difficult to agree that in a mediate way Ethics shows human beings the way toward happiness. Aristotle understood the role of happiness in this way, and so does the Gospel.[20]

20. Karol Wojtyła, "Die ethische Fibel," in *Erziehung zur Liebe: Mit einer ethischen Fibel* (Stuttgart-Degerloch: Seewald, 1980), 110–11.

CHAPTER 5

Wojtyła's *Person and Act*

Introduction

Wojtyła's main philosophical work, *Person and Act*, was written during the Second Vatican Council and published in 1969, ten years after his book on Scheler.[1] Its purpose is to throw light on the person by examining the person's voluntary acts, which display the structure of self-possession and self-dominion.

Person and Act has seven chapters divided into four parts. *The first part* focuses on the person's conscious experience (chap. 1) as the responsible efficacious origin of its own acts (chap. 2). *The second part* presents the core of the argument, which lies in the *vertical transcendence* of the person, that is, the person's standing *vertically above* itself in self-possession and self-dominion (chap. 3) and the person's self-fulfillment by acting (chap. 4). What displays the person as person, Wojtyła argues, is above all this vertical transcendence. *The third part* uses this understanding of self-possession and self-dominion to show how acts integrate the person on the level of bodily (chap. 5) and psychological (chap. 6) experience. *The fourth part* consists of only one chapter (chap. 7), which examines the person acting together with others to participate in the common good.

In accord with the focus on the breadth of reason in John Paul, the present chapter does not analyze and present *Person and Act* as a whole but limits itself to relevant arguments in the first, second, and fourth parts. The third part is

1. Citations of *Person and Act* by P&A (= *Persona e atto, Person and Act*) and TymAP (= *The Acting Person* Tymieniecka redaction) refer to Karol Wojtyła, *Persona e atto*, Polish text with facing Italian translation, ed. Giovanni Reale and Tadeusz Styczeń (Milan: Bompiani, 2001); *The Acting Person*, trans. Andrzej Potocki, This definitive text of the work established in collaboration with the author by Anna-Teresa Tymieniecka for publication in the Reidel book series *Analecta Husserliana* (Dordrecht: D. Reidel, 1979); and the German version, *Person und Tat* (Freiburg: Herder, 1981).

important for TOB because of its rich and subtle discussion of the integration of the body and of emotions in voluntary acts. This discussion also contributes, in the end, to an understanding of the glory of the Logos in the flesh, but from a different angle. The perspective of the present chapter is Wojtyła's relation to Kant, Scheler, and Thomas Aquinas on the breadth of reason.

The Problem of the English Edition

The English translation of *Person and Act* (*The Acting Person*, 1979), carefully prepared by Count Pototski, was substantially redacted by Anna Teresa Tymieniecka in such a way that its usefulness for scholarly purposes was deeply compromised. I have used the Italian and German versions as a basis instead. Quotes of the text are translations from these versions, always with references to the Tymieniecka redaction to allow readers to compare. The tendency of the redaction becomes clear when one collects the changes and observes their pattern.[2] The redaction eliminates many terms and passages that connect Wojtyła's thought with the Catholic intellectual tradition. For example, it changes all instances of *suppositum* (the Latin equivalent of Greek *hypostasis*, a central term in the development of the notion of "person" in the early Church) into phrases such as "ontological support." It omits many passages in which Wojtyła explicitly agrees with Aristotle or Thomas Aquinas. It adds terms and theses distinctive of Tymieniecka's own views as documented by her writings.[3]

The purpose of the redaction, if one gives it maximum benefit of the doubt, seems to be to make the text more accessible and palatable to its original intended readership; namely, philosophers associated with Tymieniecka's World Phenomenological Institute. Even so, the redaction violates norms of academic conduct by the inverse of plagiarism: not publishing someone else's work as one's own, but one's own as someone else's. Wojtyła gave Tymieniecka generous authorization, but the nature of the case remains.

When Wojtyła was elected Pope, the readership changed. From the narrow circle of the World Institute of Phenomenology, it expanded to become worldwide. The need of building a bridge between *Person and Act* and the readership

2. George Kalinowski was one of the first to point out the pattern. See Georges Kalinowski, "Karol Wojtyła face a Max Scheler ou l'origine de Osoba i Czyn," *Revue Thomiste* 80 (1980): 456–65; "Autour de *The Acting Person:* I. En réponse à Jean-Yves Lacoste," *Revue Thomiste* 84 (1984): 626–33; *Autour de Personne et acte de Karol Cardinal Wojtyła: Articles et conférences sur une recontre du thomisme avec la phénoménologie*, ed. Georges Kalinowski (Aix-en-Provence: Presses universitaires d'Aix-Marseille, 1987).

3. See Anna Teresa Tymieniecka, *Phenomenology of Life and the Human Creative Condition* (Dordrecht: Kluwer, 1998).

of the World Phenomenological Institute was replaced by the need for complete accuracy in presenting Wojtyła's own thought without subtractions or additions. When John Paul's close collaborators in Rome became worried about the discrepancy between the original Polish and the English page proofs and asked Tymieniecka to reverse them, she insisted and threatened to sue, ready to prove in court that Wojtyła had discussed changes with her and fully authorized her. When the book appeared and John Paul did not support her publicly against these criticisms, it led to a break in their relation that lasted some years.[4]

The preface to *The Acting Person* is a good example of Tymieniecka's work as a redactor. It states that the conception of the person developed in *The Acting Person* rests on the Schelerian foundation studied in Wojtyła's habilitation thesis.

> Granted the author's acquaintance with traditional Aristotelian thought, it is however the work of Max Scheler that has been a major influence upon his reflection. In my overall conception of the person envisaged through the mechanisms of his operative systems and their variations, as presented here, *may indeed be seen the Schelerian foundation* studied in my previous work. (TymAP viii; emphasis added)

This text is often quoted to prove that Wojtyła moved away from his Aristotelian and Thomistic formation and adopted the Schelerian foundation of philosophy instead, however critical he may have been of Scheler in his habilitation thesis. George Weigel's judgment in his carefully researched biography appears justified by this passage.

> That [Wojtyła] looked to Scheler as a possible guide, and that he put himself through the backbreaking work of translation so that he could analyze Scheler in his own language, suggests that Wojtyła had become convinced that the answers [to the question "Why ought I be good?"] were not to be found in the Neo-Scholasticism of Father Réginald Garrigou-Lagrange.[5]

How can one reconcile the author's preface with Wojtyła's habilitation thesis, which offers a radical critique of Scheler and a vigorous defense of the Aristotelian-Thomistic principles rejected by Scheler? In the decade between the two books, did Wojtyła abandon his earlier critique of Scheler and come to agree with him? Having said that the Christian thinker, especially the theologian, *cannot* be a Phenomenologist, did he become a Phenomenologist after all?

4. A series of letters between Tymieniecka and Wojtyła sold by the Tymieniecka estate to the Polish National Library after her death in 2004 reflects a strong mutual love between Tymieniecka and Wojtyła. See Edward Stourton, *John Paul II: Man of History* (London: Hodder & Stoughton, 2007).

5. George Weigel, *Witness to Hope: The Biography of Pope John Paul II* (New York: Harper Perennial, 2005), 128.

In an editorial note signed by her initials, Tymieniecka distinguishes the original draft of the preface written by Wojtyła himself from the definitive version of the author's preface.

> The definitive version of the author's preface given on p. vii was written and sent to the publisher together with the first half of the manuscript of the book in March 1977. The author might have given to it in the proofreading those *additional personal touches* which *only he could make*; but since these touches are of necessity *missing now*, we are giving on p. xiii an English translation of the original draft of the preface and are reproducing in facsimile the first and last pages of that handwritten draft. A.-T. T. (TymAP x; emphasis added).

John Paul's own handwritten preface has little in common with the definitive version. It contains no statement about the Schelerian foundation. One searches in vain for texts in Wojtyła's own writings that agree with the definitive version of the preface. Tymieniecka admits that Wojtyła ("of necessity" imposed by his duties as Pope) did not go over the proofs of the definitive version to add his "personal touches" at that point. She does not claim that Wojtyła had any part in the definitive version before the final proofs. He could obviously have added personal touches already before the final proofs, but Tymieniecka clearly says that they were to be added in the final proofs.

Aude Suramy is right to conclude that one should question Wojtyła's authorship of the preface, despite Tymieniecka's claim that it is *the definitive version of the author's preface*.[6] The preface is not printed in the authoritative 1985 Polish edition nor in the Italian translation produced with great care by John Paul's close collaborators. The strongest argument against Wojtyła's authorship is that even in its heavily redacted form *The Acting Person* contradicts the preface's statement about the Schelerian foundation. Although he rarely mentions Scheler by name, Wojtyła contradicts many of Scheler's theses, particularly his theses about the foundations of philosophy in phenomenological experience.

Person and Act supplies what Scheler felt forced to deny in order to avoid the Kantian negativity allegedly implied in *ought* and *duty*. It supplies the full causal self-determination of the person. Precisely what Scheler denies is for Wojtyła the main access to the meaning of *person*. It is also the access chosen by Thomas Aquinas in his discussion of the meaning of *person* (see part 1, chap. 6, sect. 5, in this volume). As Jameson Taylor remarks, the main intention of *Person and Act* is to look anew at an old experience and an old question, stimulated by the attention to experience in the phenomenological method. The result is more in harmony with ancient philosophy than with Scheler.

6. See Aude Suramy, "Avertissement," in Karol Wojtyła, *Personne et acte*, trans. Gwendoline Jarczyk, notes by Aude Suramy (Paris: Parole et Silence, 2011), vii–x, at ix.

> Wojtyła wants to look anew at the question of the person—an investigation that requires examining the primary mode by which the person experiences himself. This mode is the experience of personal efficacy. … This elucidation [of experience] is necessary because modern philosophy (and, to a lesser extent, ancient philosophy) failed to see that man's most basic experience of himself is that of a moral actor capable of making himself good or bad by his action. … Indeed, even the original Polish title, *Person and Act* (*Osoba i czyn*), is the title of a subsection of Scheler's primary philosophic work, *Formalism in Ethics and Non-Formal Ethics of Values*.[7]

Taylor's phrase "look anew" is particularly apt. Everybody who seeks knowledge needs to look anew. There is no shortcut.

Wojtyła's Method

At a key point in his analysis of consciousness, at which he diverges from Husserl and Scheler by introducing the personal *suppositum* as the ultimate subject of existence, nature, and acts, Wojtyła writes,

> What has been said so far clearly shows—in accord with the premises about knowledge argued in the introduction—that it is impossible to detach the lived "I" from its ontological bases. The present analysis of consciousness can also serve to place the "I" more solidly on its own bases in being. Every human being, including the one I am, is given *in total or simple experience* as a real, individual being, as a subject of existence and action (and thus as a *suppositum*). (P&A 132–33, TymAP 45; emphasis added)

What is "total or simple experience"? How is it related to "phenomenological experience"? What does it mean that the *suppositum* is given in total or simple experience? It is deeply characteristic of Aristotle's philosophy to take the ordinary experience of the world shared by all human beings as the point of departure and lasting anchor of philosophy (see section 5 of the introduction to this volume). It is likewise characteristic of Descartes's philosophy to set aside this realm of ordinary experience to rebuild knowledge of the natural world on another basis; namely, mathematical physics.

Husserl does not call this Cartesian revolution of knowledge into question. In formulating the motto of Phenomenology, "back to things themselves," he does not advocate a return to things as we encounter them in ordinary experience. His early work was in the philosophy of arithmetic, and mathematics

7. Jameson Taylor, "The Acting Person in Purgatory: A Note for Readers of the English Text," *Logos: A Journal of Catholic Thought and Culture* 13 (2010): 77–104, at 80.

remained a paradigm of certainty for him. His main interest was to construct a scientific philosophy based on absolutely certain knowledge, similar to the kind of knowledge gained in arithmetic. He saw the basis of this knowledge in the phenomena understood as necessary essences (εἴδη) immediately given to the human mind.[8]

Scheler subjects the Cartesian revolution and "the objective world" constructed by it to penetrating criticism (see part I, chap. 4, sect. 1, in this volume) but does not reinstate ordinary experience. He shares Husserl's all-absorbing interest in immediately given essences. What Phenomenology concerns itself with is "the *a priori* structure of essence" (FormEng 396, FormGer 420), that is, the necessary essential connections that can be observed in the phenomena *a priori*, not *after* and *based on* the experience of particular beings. Wojtyła's *total* or *simple* experience is not a norm for his Phenomenology.

> The facts of natural experience and their basic forms are not at all ultimate givens for Phenomenology and philosophy. Phenomenology or phenomeno logical seeing does not dwell in these basic forms. On the contrary, Phenomenology turns these forms into givens of pure intuition. And this pertains to the natural experience of the outer world as well as to the natural experience of the inner world. (FormEng 433, FormGer 429)

One of the most obvious facts of ordinary experience is the real existence of bodies, our own included. Scheler agrees with Husserl that Phenomenology must not simply accept the testimony of the senses about the existence of bodies. It must suspend the question of real being and consider perception and its object as phenomena given to intuition. This process of reduction creates specifically "phenomenological experience."

> In each truly phenomenological investigation we perform the so called phenomenological reduction (Husserl).... We leave out of consideration any positing (belief or unbelief) of the specific character of the coefficient of reality with which the content of the act is "given" in natural perception and in science (for example, actuality, appearance, imagination, illusion).[9]

Phenomenological experience, according to Scheler, has an immediate grasp of the objects of knowledge. The essence itself, and not a mere concept or symbol that points to a reality beyond it, comes to "self-givenness" *Selbstgegebenheit* (FormEng 48, FormGer 67) in phenomenological experience. Wojtyła summarizes,

8. See the first chapter of Edmund Husserl, *Die Idee der Phänomenologie: Fünf Vorlesungen*, 2nd ed., ed. Walter Biemel (The Hague: Nijhoff, 1958); *The Idea of Phenomenology* (The Hague: Nijhoff, 1964).

9. Scheler, "Phenomenology and the Theory of Cognition," GW 10:394.

> For the Phenomenologists, "direct experience" is every act of knowledge in which the object of knowledge is itself given in original form, or as Husserl says, "bodily self-present" (*leibhaft selbstgegeben*). (P&A 47n1, TymAP 9n1 at 301)

It is ironic that in the phrase *bodily self-present* Husserl appeals to the body to express the certainty of phenomenological intuition even though he sets aside the real existence of bodies as uncertain.

Scheler explains "phenomenological experience" in more detail as follows.

> Phenomenological experience … can be distinguished from all other experience, such as that of the natural world-view or of science, by two criteria.
>
> 1. Phenomenological experience alone yields facts "themselves" and, hence, immediately, that is, not mediated by symbols, signs, or instructions of any kind. For example, one can define a specific red in many ways: as the color designated by the word red; as a color in this thing or a certain surface; as a color within an order, such as the order of the colors of the spectrum; as the color that "I am just now seeing"; or as the color of a certain wavelength and form, and so on. This color appears in the above cases as the x of an equation or as the x that fulfills a certain set of conditions. Phenomenological experience, however, is the experience in which the totality of these signs, instructions, and kinds of determination find their basic fulfillment. It alone gives red "itself." It makes a fact of intuition out of this x. It honors, as it were, all the bills of exchange on which the other "experiences" draw. We can also say that all non-phenomenological experience is in principle an experience through or by means of symbols and, hence, a mediated experience that never gives things "themselves." Only phenomenological experience is in principle non-symbolic and, hence, able to fulfill all possible symbols.
>
> 2. Phenomenological experience is at the same time "immanent" experience. For only that which is intuitively present in an act of experiencing … never anything that is meant as a content outside of, or separated from, such an act—can belong to it. In principle all non-phenomenological experience transcends its intuitional contents, as is the case in the natural perception of real things. In this kind of experience, something that is not "given" in it is "meant." Phenomenological experience, in contrast to this, contains no separation between what is "meant" and what is "given." … In phenomenological experience nothing is meant that is not given, and nothing is given that is not meant. It is precisely in this coincidence of the "meant" and the "given" that the content of phenomenological experience alone becomes manifest to us. In this coincidence, in the very meeting point of fulfillment of what is meant and what is given, the phenomenon appears. (FormEng 50–51, FormGer 69–70)

The privileged role of phenomenological experience as the true foundation of philosophy becomes clear in this text. Scheler explicitly contrasts it with "all non-phenomenological experience" such as "the natural perception of real things," which is a constituent part of total or ordinary experience. The insight into "self-present" essences, Scheler claims, is not the fruit of observing many particulars. It is not the result of induction.

> Whenever we have such essences and such interconnections among them ... the truth of the propositions that find their fulfillment in such essences is totally independent of the entire sphere of observation and description, as well as of what is established by inductive experience.... We can also say that essences and their interconnections are "given" "prior" to all experience or given *a priori*. (FormEng 49, FormGer 68)

On these pivotal principles of philosophy, Wojtyła disagrees with Husserl and Scheler. Induction, he holds with Aristotle, is the path to understanding.

> Beginning with this multiplicity and complexity of the facts, to arrive at grasping their substantial identity, previously defined as stabilizing the object of experience, is the work of induction. At any rate, this is how Aristotle seems to have understood the inductive function of the intellect.... It is the intellectual conception of the unity of meaning in the multiplicity and complexity of the phenomena. (P&A 61, TymAP 14)

Both the multiplicity of phenomena and the unity of meaning seen through and in them belong to "total experience" (P&A 57, TymAP 12). Wojtyła does not follow Scheler in drawing an absolute contrast between conceptual knowledge reached by induction and the immediate givenness of essences. He follows the Aristotelian-Thomistic thesis that all intellectual knowledge is conceptual, acquired through the experience of particulars but according to the mode of the recipient, that is, in the form of universal concepts.

Person and Act focuses only on some aspects of the person. It does not enter, for example, a full discussion of the moral good and evil of acts but places this aspect *in brackets*. Yet, Wojtyła points out, such bracketing differs from Husserl's phenomenological method, an essential element of which is the bracketing (*epochē*) of real existence.

> We want to exclude the essentially ethical problems in favor of the anthropological ones. This is not, however, the separation of the essence from actual existence (*epochē*), which is so characteristic of Edmund Husserl's phenomenological method. Thus, this study does not follow the principles of a strictly eidetic method; and yet it is the author's intention through these investigations to grasp man as a person, that is, to define also the *eidos* of the human being. (P&A 59n4, TymAP 13n4, note printed at 301)

Although Wojtyła aligns himself in this manner with Aristotle's account of induction against Husserl and Scheler, he does give a key place to what he himself calls *phenomenological experience* or *phenomenological intuition*, by which he does not mean Husserl's and Scheler's immediate and presuppositionless givenness of essences apart from the whole order of real existence but attention to what is consciously given or manifest (*phainomenon*) to the person, even if this form of knowledge involves a concept formed in induction (P&A 75, TymAP 12).

Wojtyła chooses this modified phenomenological approach because of his interest in the person's lived experience as an agent or subject of acts, as *I*. As a philosopher, he is interested precisely in what held his interest as a theologian in his dissertation on St. John of the Cross; namely, the person's conscious subjectivity in the ordinary experience of acting. A phenomenological method serves him in a modified form and in a subordinate position to explore this subjectivity. Total or simple experience—the ordinary experience of the person in acting—supplies the main framework and remains the main criterion of judgment.

1. Consciousness

Wojtyła's main goal in discussing consciousness in chapter 1 of *Person and Act* is to focus on its role in constituting the lived experience of the person's acts.

Focus on Consciousness

One of the key features of lived experience is that we are conscious of it. In particular, the acts we perform voluntarily are part of our lived experience. From conscious acts, one can go on to focus on the consciousness that accompanies these acts (P&A 90–91, TymAP 9). Wojtyła compares this step to the mathematical operation in which one places a term outside of parentheses. In place of $3x + 3y$, one can consider $3(x + y)$, which allows one to focus on the terms 3 and $x + y$ in themselves. At the same time, one must not lose sight of the close connection between the terms outside and inside the parentheses.

> In reality and human experience, the consciousness of an act is closely connected with the conscious act. Temporarily placing consciousness outside as a distinct aspect is a methodical operation. It is like placing a term outside of parentheses, which also serves to understand better what is found inside the parentheses. For this reason, also the title of this chapter does not point to consciousness alone but to person and act under the aspect of consciousness. (P&A 92–93, TymAP 29–30)

Every act *finds* the person's consciousness already present. In addition, consciousness continues as a unified whole after the act is completed (P&A 96–97, TymAP 31). Everything a person experiences, knows, and does becomes present in consciousness.

"In what way is all this present in consciousness?" (P&A 98–99, TymAP 32). Consciousness has two distinct functions, Wojtyła answers. He describes the first by two metaphors, *mirroring* and *illuminating. Mirroring* expresses a certain doubling. When one stands before a mirror, one's own bodily being, which has a first mode of presence in the world by its own being, becomes present in a second way; namely, as reflected in a mirror, facing one's own being in the opposite direction. Owing to the *mirroring* function of consciousness, acts we perform do not merely take place in the world. In addition to this first mode of presence, they are present to us in our awareness. In the case of a mirror, the second presence of the body is in another place than the original body, though the person who looks into the mirror realizes it is the same body. In the case of acts we are aware of, one and the same act is at stake in both modes of presence.

The metaphor of *illuminating* brings out the same point from another angle. On the level of metaphor, *illuminating* conflicts with *mirroring.* It does not point to a second presence. The metaphor is linked in a different way with the sense of sight. Just as light penetrates the area in which objects are placed and thereby makes them present to us, so consciousness penetrates our acts and makes them present to us. Our acts are not dark objects absent from our awareness. They are penetrated by the light of our awareness. Wojtyła does not deny, of course, that there are aspects of our acts that escape our awareness.

The second function of consciousness, Wojtyła argues, is to allow persons to experience their acts precisely as their own acts. It is in virtue of this self-awareness that persons are able to grasp themselves as personal subjects, as "I." Wojtyła sees the distinctive feature of consciousness above all in this second function.

> While person and act constitute a definite reality which, as the objects of self-knowledge, reveal themselves in their own objectivity, the same person and act also remain "subjectified" thanks to consciousness inasmuch as consciousness conditions the lived experience of the act performed by the person, that is, of the person in its dynamic-efficacious interrelation with the act. (P&A 124–25, TymAP 43)

The seemingly complicated phrase "dynamic-efficacious interrelation with the act" can be understood if one looks at the relation between the person and its act. The person has the power (Greek: *dynamis*) to act and is the efficacious origin of its own acts. Consciousness in its second aspect allows us to experience ourselves as the subject from which the act springs in such a way that the person grasps himself or herself as responsible for the act, that is, as "I am acting."

Grasping ourselves as "I," Wojtyła continues, depends on an activity prior to consciousness (though simultaneous with it in time); namely, self-knowledge. In self-knowledge, we grasp ourselves as beings that exist objectively in the world. "As the name indicates, it is an understanding of oneself, a kind of cognitive penetration of the object that I am for myself"(P&A 108–9, TymAP 36). In self-awareness, by contrast, we grasp ourselves reflexively as subjects, as "I."

Wojtyła emphasizes the priority of self-knowledge over self-consciousness. Consciousness, he argues, is not simply conscious of itself. It is the awareness of ourselves as really existing beings or, in the language developed in the Christological controversies of the early Church, it is the awareness of ourselves as being a *person*, a rational *hypostasis* or *suppositum*.

> Indubitably, man is above all the subject of his own existence and acts; he is the subject insofar as he is a being of determinate nature, and this has its consequences precisely in acting. The subject of existence and acting, which is man, is defined by traditional ontology with the term *suppositum*. We can say that the expression *suppositum* serves to define the subject in a completely objective manner, abstracting from the aspect of lived experience and, in particular, from the lived experience in which the subject is given to itself as "I." In this way, therefore, the expression "*suppositum*" abstracts from the aspect of consciousness, owing to which the concrete man—an object that is a subject—lives himself interiorly as a subject and thus lives his own subjectivity; and this lived experience serves him as the basis for defining himself by means of the pronoun "I."
>
> We know that the personal pronoun "I" always indicates a concrete person. I call attention to the fact that the term "I" contains more than the term *suppositum*, because it adds the moment of lived subjectivity to ontic subjectivity while *suppositum* expresses only the latter: the being as the subjective foundation of existence and acts.
>
> Obviously, such an interpretation of the term "I" presupposes a certain conception of consciousness and of its relation to man as a real subject. One could say that it presupposes precisely the reflexivity of consciousness. In fact, if we separated the lived experience of one's own subjectivity, which provides the basis for defining oneself as "I," from the real subject, which is precisely this "I," then this "I" would not represent anything except the content of consciousness. It is therefore of fundamental importance that consciousness turns reflexively toward the real subject, to constitute it [i.e., the real subject] in its [i.e., consciousness's] own dimension. In this way, the "I" is a real subject that interiorly lives its own subjectivity, that is, that is constituted at the same time in the dimension of consciousness. (P&A 128–33, TymAP 44–45)

In this text, one can clearly see the main thrust of Wojtyła's account of consciousness; namely, the clarification of the role of consciousness in the constitution of the person's lived experience in close union with the person's objective being as a *hypostasis* or *suppositum*. "It is obviously not the goal of these considerations to work out a full and well-defined theory of consciousness" (P&A 102–3, TymAP 33). Their goal is rather to understand the lived experience of personal subjectivity. Lived experience was already Wojtyła's focus of attention in his dissertation on John of the Cross, and it was to become the hallmark of his account of Vatican II and of the male and female body.

Not Intentional

It is axiomatic for Scheler that consciousness is *intentional* in the sense of being *about* some known essence. Kant holds a similar view in his concept of *apperception:* the nature of consciousness is to be related by apperception to the objects of knowledge. It constitutes these objects as one by its own unity as consciousness, *cogito*. Wojtyła denies that consciousness in its reflexive function is intentional.

> Differing from classical Phenomenology, we maintain that in the order of knowing the raison d'être of consciousness and of the acts proper to it does not consist in a deeper understanding of the object, in the objectification that permits understanding and the constitution of the object. (P&A 98–99, TymAP 32)

The proper function of consciousness is to allow one to experience oneself as a subject. To explain the subjectivity implied in calling oneself "I," it is true but not sufficient to point out that one is intentionally related to oneself as the knower to the known. It is not sufficient to know oneself as an object, in the same way one knows other persons. One must have an awareness of oneself as a personal subject from within. If consciousness were intentional in Scheler's sense, it could not establish the person's lived experience of "I." If one understands the word *intentional* to apply generally not only to the conscious relation to an object but also to any consciousness of something, Wojtyła concedes that consciousness can be called intentional (P&A 98–101n15, TymAP 32n16 printed at 303–4).

By arguing that consciousness in its reflective function is not intentional, Wojtyła undercuts the foundation of Kant's and Scheler's subjectivism. According to Kant, consciousness determines being. By its synthetic apperception, it produces the objects of knowledge. According to Scheler, consciousness does not produce being but determines being by providing the necessary correlate of the essences. Schelerian consciousness is always a consciousness of essences, and

Schelerian essences are always that at which the intention of some consciousness aims. They do not have independent being.

According to Wojtyła, by contrast, self-consciousness is not in the first place a Kantian apperception or a Schelerian correlate of immediately given essences. It is a non-intentional aspect of intentional acts of knowing. Acts of knowing, in which we grasp real being, imply self-consciousness as an aspect that arises secondarily within these acts. There is, properly speaking, no distinct act of consciousness. In this respect, Wojtyła sees his analysis of consciousness as standing within the Aristotelian tradition.

> We must adopt a different, dynamic concept of act to grasp the real state of affairs; it must be a concept that is connected with the Aristotelian tradition and consequently presupposes a different concept of intentionality. We thus regard as acts in the strict sense of the word only the actualizations of the real powers of the person.
>
> Thus, when following the manner of speaking widely accepted in Phenomenology we refer to "acts of consciousness," the reader has to remember that we are using the phrase not in its proper but in a transferred sense.
>
> Similarly, we understand "intention" as an active direction toward the object. Thus, in our conception of it, intention in the proper sense does not belong to consciousness, but consciousness has intention only in a transferred and derived sense on the basis of the intentionality of acts of knowledge or self-knowledge as real powers of the person. (P&A 100–101n15, TymAP 304n16 printed at 303–4)

2. Efficacy

In chapter 2, Wojtyła turns to the person's lived experience of efficacy in performing acts. In his habilitation thesis on Scheler, he had argued that Scheler fails to account sufficiently for this efficacy. *Person and Act* unfolds what he had found missing.

The Lived Experience of Acting

Wojtyła's point of departure is the lived experience of performing an act. He brings this experience into focus by contrasting it with something that merely happens in us without our doing it, such as digesting food. We do not perform digestion as a human act. It takes place by nature outside our consciously experienced efficacy in acting.

Inasmuch as we consciously perform acts, we can consider them from the point of view of what Wojtyła (following Scheler) calls "phenomenological experience." The act is given in our self-knowledge and self-consciousness as a phenomenon that is itself present to us (Husserl's *leibhaft selbstgegeben*, bodily self-present), just as the front of a house is given to someone who looks at it, while the back of the house is at this moment not given, though reasonably known to be there. Already at the beginning of his argument, however, Wojtyła emphasizes that, in order not to lead to false conclusions, this phenomenological experience must be placed in the context of "total experience" and a metaphysical analysis of real being based on such experience (P&A 168–69, TymAP 61). In particular, the understanding of the person as a *suppositum* derives from a metaphysical analysis based on ordinary experience. Phenomenological experience, as Wojtyła understands it in contrast to Husserl and Scheler, remains in continuity with ordinary experience, particularly with the real existence of the beings we encounter in ordinary experience.

The Suppositum or Hypostasis

In the Christological debates of the early church, the Greek term *hypostasis* and its Latin equivalent *suppositum* were formed to express the person as the subject of nature, acts, and all attributes. From the point of view of phenomenological experience, "The structure 'man acts' and the structure 'something happens in man' seem to split man into two worlds" (P&A 194–95, TymAP 71). Nevertheless, total experience as metaphysically elaborated in the theological and philosophical tradition shows that one should see them as integrated in one person, one subject, one *suppositum*.

> Man's subjectivity, which is common to both structures—acting and happening—has found expression in the philosophy developed according to the principles of Aristotle and Thomas Aquinas in the concept of *suppositum*. Etymologically, this term indicates something placed underneath (*sub ponere*). In this way man "is under" every action and "under" everything that happens in him. The term *suppositum* indicates being subject or the subject as a being. The subject as a being is present in the foundations of every dynamic structure, of every acting as well as happening, of all efficacy and subjectivity. It is a real being, a human-being that really exists and, as a consequence, also really acts.
>
> There is an intimate relation between existence and acting that is the theme of one of the fundamental human insights. A philosopher has expressed this insight in the terms "*operari sequitur esse*" [operation follows existence], which one could express in this way, "Something must first exist to be able, as a consequence, to act." *Esse* existence is found at the origin of the act; it is also found at the origin of all that happens in man; it is found at the origin of

> the whole dynamism proper to man. *Esse* is not the *suppositum*; it is only its constitutive aspect.... Existence, according to Thomas, is the first act (*actus*) of every being. (P&A 195–97, TymAP 72–73)

Operari sequitur esse is deeply rooted in human experience. "Something works the way it is."[10] Given this order between *esse* and *agere* or *operari*, one can look back from *agere* at the *suppositum* and its *esse* to grasp their specific character. Man is a *suppositum* in a specific manner, in the manner of a person. *Person* thus contains more than the word *individual*. Neither the concept of nature nor of individual is sufficient to grasp "the specific fullness that corresponds to the concept of person" (P&A 198–99, TymAP 74–75). Being *someone* is more than being merely *something*. *Someone* implies a uniqueness and unrepeatability, the uniqueness and unrepeatability expressed in the pronoun "I."

Uniqueness and unrepeatability, as shown above, are central concerns of Scheler's personalism. Partly because there is no *suppositum* in Scheler, he is compelled to understand uniqueness in a qualitative manner as an essence that differs from other personal essences, just as the taste of an apple differs from that of a pear. In Wojtyła, by contrast, uniqueness and unrepeatability are qualitatively the same in every human being. There are, of course, qualitative differences between individual persons, and these differences can be important. It would, however, be strange to say about identical twins that what is most important in them is a qualitative difference. Wojtyła, at any rate, does not mean qualitative distinction when he calls persons unique and unrepeatable. Persons are unique in the sense that each one is *I* or *someone* as opposed to *something*. It is because of their common rational nature that human beings are persons. In this respect, each of them is unique and unrepeatable in the same way.

Nature and Person

Given Wojtyła's concern for the unity of person and nature, which is close to the heart of his philosophical program, his discussion of the integration of acting and happening through the person's nature is particularly important. Nature, he begins his argument, is what is present in a being as a result of its coming to be, its being born (*natus*). It is close to the idea of essence, to *what* a being is (P&A 202–5, TymAP 76–77). Should one conceive nature as lying at the origin of both "what happens in the person" and "the person acting"? Or should one line

10. Eo modo aliquid operatur, quo est. *Summa* I, q. 75, a. 2, corp. Cf. "Everything acts as it is in act." Unumquodque agit secundum quod est actu. *Quaestiones disputatae De anima*, a. 1, corp. "Acting follows actual being." Agere sequitur ad esse actuale. *Contra gentiles* III, cap. 69.

up nature only with what happens in the person? Scheler decidedly opts for the second view. He posits a sharp separation between personal acts and the whole world of nature, including the human body. As a rational animal, according to Scheler, man is not yet personal. Personal acts and personhood enter from beyond time, from beyond the world, from the realm of spirit, into the natural world of the human animal. Wojtyła formulates an argument for such a view without mentioning Scheler.

> [This] understanding of nature appears to result from phenomenological reduction. By phenomenological reduction I mean an operation that leads to the fullest and at the same time the most essential revelation of a given contents. If we conceive man as a specific dynamic whole one may rightly consider the moment of most complete and essential revelation of "nature" to be, not the moment in which "man acts," but rather the one in which "(something) happens in man." . . . Why so?
>
> Because the concept of nature includes that dynamism which is directly and solely the consequence of birth itself, the dynamism that is exclusively inborn or innate, exclusively immanent in the given subject of acting, as if it was determined in advance by its properties. (P&A 206–9, TymAP 78)

This view of nature, Wojtyła goes on to argue, is caused by to too exclusive a reliance on phenomenological experience. It lacks attention to total or ordinary experience as unfolded by metaphysics (P&A 210–11, TymAP 79). Total experience supports a metaphysical reduction (i.e., an account that leads back, *re-ducere*, to beginnings) in which nature is grasped as the comprehensive *what something is*, the essence of the person. In contrast to the lived experience of causal efficacy, the essence—this is Wojtyła's point when he contrasts phenomenological and metaphysical reduction—is not a phenomenon, an immediate datum of self-knowledge and self-consciousness. Our knowledge of our essence is more indirect. It involves *reasoning* from our acts to powers and from powers to the essence (P&A 226–27, TymAP 87). Wojtyła sees a decisive difference between Scheler's Phenomenology and his own approach in this point. His own approach is based on phenomenological experience in the context of ordinary experience and metaphysics.

> In the metaphysical approach nature is in some way the essence, and thus in man it is equivalent to his whole "humanity," . . . humanity as the foundation of the whole dynamism proper to man. In this point lies the substantial difference between the metaphysical and the previous—rather phenomenological—conception of nature. Nature in the metaphysical sense is equivalent to the essence of any being, where essence is regarded as the basis for the dynamism of this being. (P&A 214–15, TymAP 82)

Wojtyła appeals not only to human nature or essence but also to human existence or being (*esse*), as the root of man's dynamism, that is, of the actual working of human powers in both "man acts" and "something happens in man." He sees himself in agreement with Thomas on this point.

> Dynamization through personal *esse* must lie at the root of the integration of humanity by the person. At any rate, in conceiving the experienced cohesion of all acting with *esse*, there is no difficulty in accepting the Thomistic foundation of this cohesion. (P&A 218–19, TymAP 83)

Boethius's Definition of Person

One can see Wojtyła's continuity with Thomas in the manner in which he understands Boethius's definition of *person*. Like Thomas, Wojtyła offers a reading of Boethius's definition that turns on *a particular mode of individual being*. There are higher and lower modes of individuality. The highest mode is that of being a person. It is therefore not sufficient to understand Boethius's term *individual* in a generic manner, but one must focus on the specific mode of individuality proper to the person.

> Boethius's definition: *persona est rationalis naturae individua substantia*. The person is not just "individual humanity." It is rather a mode of individual existence proper to human beings alone (among the visible beings of this world). This mode of existing derives from the fact that the individual existence proper to humanity is personal. (P&A 218–19, TymAP 83)

Nature and person are thus not opposed to each other. On the contrary, it is due to human nature that a human being is a person in the first place. "Humanity, human nature, is furnished with properties that allow a concrete man to be a person, to exist and act as a person. Even more, it does not allow him to exist and act in any other way" (P&A 220–21, TymAP 84). Personal efficacy in acting does not cut human acts away from their anchoring in human nature, but it indicates the specific powers rooted in human nature in virtue of which the human person acts precisely as a person.

These points are fundamental for Wojtyła's thought as a whole and for TOB in particular. Sexuality, which reaches deeply into the vegetative and sentient nature of the human animal, is not an event that takes place in the realm of nature as opposed to person. It is essentially personal. All aspects of human nature—existence as a body, vegetative life, sentient life, and rational life—are united in forming the single nature of a single person with a single *esse*. The person is a personal body, a personal animal. For Scheler, by contrast, the body and animal life are only indirectly personal. The person flashes up in them from the extra-cosmic and nontemporal sphere of spirit. For Kant, the realm of the person is likewise deeply divided from the realm of nature.

Coming to Be and Freedom

Both in the realm of "man acts" and in that of "something happens in man," there is a process of coming to be (Latin: *fieri*). A first and fundamental coming to be of the human person takes place in conception and birth. It is prior to both acting and happening. Still, coming to be is found also in the realms of "man acts" and "something happens in man," though only in a qualified and secondary sense. Wojtyła expresses the difference between these two senses of "coming to be" by appealing to Aristotle's distinction between substance and accident.

> In metaphysical categories, such coming into existence is accidental relatively to that original coming into existence which constitutes the substance itself. Having come substantially into existence, man comes to be more and more "something" and "someone" through all his actions and through all that happens in him—though both these forms of the dynamism proper to him. An analysis of the human dynamism ought to highlight this coming to be, this *fieri*. And it is above all the metaphysical analysis that brings it to light. Precisely this is the case in the Aristotelian and later in the Thomistic understanding of *actus*. It is only secondarily that *actus* as such indicates man's acting or what happens in man; it primarily indicates a certain change, the *fieri* of the subject "man" himself or of his single faculties. (P&A 250–51, TymAP 96–97)

Wojtyła turns to a particular mode of coming to be; namely, coming to be morally good or bad. This coming to be must be understood in terms of being, not of mere consciousness as it is in Scheler. Without mentioning Scheler by name, Wojtyła uses the Thomistic account of *actus* to pass beyond Scheler's reduction of moral goodness to a mere content of consciousness.

> The coming to be, the *fieri* of man from the moral point of view, which is strictly connected with the person, determines the realistic character of good and evil, of the moral values themselves. In no way are they [mere] contents of consciousness itself, but they are part of personal, human coming to be. Man not only lives them interiorly, but because of them he comes to be really good or bad. Morality is a reality that enters into the reality of human acts as a specific *fieri* of the subject, a most profound *fieri* connected in a most essential manner both with his nature, that is, his humanity, and with the fact of his being a person. (P&A 256–57, TymAP 99)

In the final paragraphs of chapter 2, Wojtyła transitions to chapter 3 by focusing on the freedom of the person. Freedom is also more than a mere contents of consciousness. Freedom is given as an aspect of the experience of freely performing acts, "I can but I need not." It is an experience, at one and the same time, of the person's dependence on itself and of its independence from external determinations. The freedom that becomes evident in this experience is a real attribute of the person and of the person's will (P&A 256–59, TymAP 99–101).

3. Self-Determination

Part Two of *Person and Act*, "The Transcendence of the Person in the Act," consists of two chapters. They are the core of the book's argument. The self-determination of the person in acting implies that the person stands in some way vertically above itself as its own master so that it can determine itself in its freely performed acts. Wojtyła calls this self-dominion and self-determination "vertical transcendence."

Chapter 3, "The Personal Structure of Self-Determination," considers the person's vertical transcendence in its root, in the person's power over itself; chapter 4, "Self-Determination and Fulfillment," deepens this account by considering the person's vertical transcendence in its effect, in the performance or fulfillment of acts and the consequent self-fulfillment of the person.

Self-Dominion and Person

Self-dominion plays an important role in St. Thomas's approach to the meaning of the word *person*. To approach the meaning of *person*, Thomas distinguishes less perfect and more perfect ways of being an individual. *Person*, he argues, expresses the most perfect way. To bring to light that most perfect way, he points to self-dominion in human acts (see part I, chap. 6, sect. 5, in this volume).

> In some still more special and perfect way (*adhuc quodam specialiori et perfectiori modo*) particular and individual are found in rational substances, which have dominion (*dominium*) over their acting and are not only acted, as other things are but act through themselves.[11]

The same emphasis on self-dominion returns in the prologue to the *Secunda Pars*, by far the most extensive part of the *Summa*. Thomas quotes the Greek Fathers, according to whom the image of God consists in "having a mind, free

11. Thomas, *Summa* I, q. 29, a. 1, corp.

decision (*liberum arbitrium*), and power through oneself (*per se potestativum*, Greek *autexousion*)." The image of God with respect to mind, free decision, and self-dominion—this is the formal aspect under which the whole *Secunda Pars* is conceived.

> After what we said earlier [i.e., in the *Prima Pars*] about the exemplar, namely about God and what comes from God's power, it remains for us to take up the image, that is, man inasmuch as he too is the beginning of his own works inasmuch as he has free decision and power over his own works (*suorum operum potestatem*).[12]

If one reads the *Secunda Pars* under this formal aspect, one is led to read it in parallel with Wojtyła's argument in *Person and Act*. The whole discussion of morality serves to throw light on the image of God in man, by which he too is the beginning of his own works inasmuch as he has free decision and power over his own works.

Discussions of consciously lived experience are scattered throughout Thomas's works. Teresa Scarpelli Cory has given an excellent philosophical account of them.[13] Especially important on the level of theology are the discussions of the gifts of the Holy Spirit.[14] Common ground with St. John of the Cross is particularly extensive here.

Self-possession, self-dominion, and self-determination play important roles in TOB, but the emphasis clearly differs from *Person and Act*. TOB discusses self-possession as a necessary condition of the gift of self, following the second and more definitive truth about the life of persons expressed by *Gaudium et spes* 24, "cannot fully find himself except through the sincere gift of self." *Person and Act*, by contrast, highlights the first and more elementary truth of *Gaudium et spes* 24 a philosophical truth according to which "man is the only creature on earth which God willed for itself," because he is the only creature on earth able to know the good and pursue it freely by his acts. *Person and Act*, taken in isolation without its sequel TOB, could give a false picture of Wojtyła's personalism as close to Stoic or Kantian personalism with a focus on self-possession and self-determination without an account of the good to which these are ordered; namely, the communion of persons.

In fact, however, Wojtyła skillfully balances two sides. *Somewhat* like Kant, he emphasizes freedom as self-dominion and self-determination. *Somewhat* like

12. Thomas, *Summa* I-II, prologue.

13. See Teresa Scarpelli Cory, *Aquinas on Human Self-Knowledge* (Cambridge: Cambridge University Press, 2014).

14. See Thomas, *Summa* I-II, q. 68–70; II-II, qq. 8–9, 29, 45, 52, 121, 139; John of St. Thomas, *Cursus theologicus: In Iam IIae de donis Spiritus Sancti*, emended text (Quebec: Collectio Lavallensis, 1968).

Scheler, he emphasizes the experience of value or goodness. The qualification "*somewhat*" is needed because Wojtyła sees the unity of the two sides in the first principle of practical reason, "The *good* is *to be done* and pursued," while Kant and Scheler do not. The first phase of the argument (sections 1–6) corresponds somewhat to Kant's insistence on the imperative "is to be done" against Scheler's reduction of the first principle to a felt intuition of the good without any role of the imperative. The second phase (sections 7–9) corresponds somewhat to Scheler's insistence on the felt intuition of value against Kant's reduction of the first principle to the naked imperative "is to be done." What makes self-determination possible is knowledge of the truth about the good as a *good* that is *to be done.*

Self-Determination

The experience of willing an act contains within itself the experience of self-determination, a self-determination by which the person comes to be (*fieri*) morally good or bad. Self-determination implies that the person has power over itself and, more fundamentally, that the person belongs to itself and can exercise this power legitimately. The term *belonging* is related to the key term of Wojtyła's personalism as it appears in TOB; namely, *gift.* A gift is what belongs originally to the giver. It comes to belong to the recipient in virtue of the gift. In this manner, the analysis of self-possession in *Person and Act* prepares the way for the analysis of the gift of self in TOB.

Wojtyła quotes two Scholastic principles to illustrate his thesis about self-possession. The person is *sui iuris*, "of its own right (or law)," and the person is *alteri incommunicabilis*, "incommunicable to another." *Sui iuris* corresponds etymologically to the Greek *auto-nomos* ("self-law"). Following Roman law, Thomas applies *sui iuris* to those who are no longer minors but have come of age and thus direct themselves by their own reason.[15] He also applies it to the soul in contrast to the body: it is in virtue of the soul that we are under our own law.[16] In this individuality and self-possession, the person is incommunicable to any other. *De ratione personae est quod sit incommunicabilis*, "it belongs to the account of the person to be incommunicable."[17] Incommunicability applies in the first place to the order of being. No person can be another person or be predicated of another person. Incommunicability applies in consequence also to the moral order, in which the person is incommunicably *sui iuris* in its self-possession and self-determination.

15. See Thomas, *Summa* II-II, q. 16, a. 2, ad 2.
16. Thomas, *Summa* II-II, q. 104, a. 5, corp.
17. Thomas, *Summa* I, q. 30, a. 4, obj. 4 and ad 4.

From the perspective of TOB, one might object that it belongs more deeply to the person to communicate itself in the manner of gift. Yet the gift of self presupposes the incommunicable self-possession of the person. Without such self-possession, the gift would be impossible, not only at the beginning but also in its continuation in a whole lifetime. If the person were to pass from self-possession to possession by another in the way a mere thing passes from one owner to another, canceling one ownership in favor of another, the communication and communion of distinct persons would collapse into the solitude of a single person. As De Koninck observes, "The incommunicability of personality is a condition of communication. Paradoxically: the more a *suppositum* is incommunicable, the more it is a principle of communication."[18]

By virtue of the self-determination implied in willing, Wojtyła argues directly contrary to Scheler, the person becomes an object for itself, the object of its own self-determination. This objectification does not endanger the person's subjectivity but is one of subjectivity's most essential constituent features. Analyses of human willing, Wojtyła observes, often focus exclusively on the main object of willing; namely, the good that is willed. They sometimes overlook that the person is also its own most proximate object inasmuch as it moves itself to act. Wojtyła quotes Thomas, "Free will is the cause of its movement, because by free will man moves himself to act"[19] (P&A 272–73n38, TymAP 110n39, at 309). By self-movement, Wojtyła argues on this basis, the person is both the subject and the object of its own power to move. An essential feature of personal subjectivity is this correlation of subjectification and objectification.

The manner in which the good is the object of willing corresponds to *intentionality*, while the manner in which the subject itself becomes an object of its self-determination is non-intentional, even though one's own *I* becomes the object of one's own act through self-determination.

> We do not account for the dynamism proper to the will if we refer only to the intentionality of the particular acts of willing. An essential distinction needs to be made here. Willing as a "purely" intentional act, that is, as a lived experience directed toward its proper object (we can define this object as an end and as a value), differs from the lived experience of "I will" in its full content. For the lived experience of "I will" contains also self-determination and not only intentionality. Turning to any external object as an end or a value presupposes the simultaneous fundamental turn toward the "I" as object. (P&A 272–75, TymAP 110)

18. Charles De Koninck, Letter to Mortimer Adler, Quebec, June 15, 1938.
19. Thomas, *Summa* I, q. 83, a. 1, ad 3.

When one compares these two distinct relations to the objects of willing, Wojtyła goes on to argue against Kant's understanding of self-legislation, it becomes clear that what directs the will is not the person's reflexive self-consciousness and its relation to its own *I* as the object of its self-determination but knowledge about the good that is willed. The following passage, which makes this point, is also helpful for understanding how Wojtyła responds to the loss of real being in Kant and Scheler by denying that self-consciousness is intentional.

> It is only in its objectifying function that knowledge guides the will: *nihil volitum nisi praecognitum* (nothing is willed except what known beforehand). In its subjectifying function, as consciousness, on the other hand, knowledge accompanies the will and integrates it within the framework of the specific structure presented by the person, but it does not guide or direct the will. Ignorance of this fundamental difference leads inevitably to solipsism, subjectivism, and idealism, that is, to the subject's loss of itself in its own wholly particular reality, that is, objectivity. (P&A 280–83, TymAP 114)

The guiding function of knowledge plays a key role when Wojtyła goes on, in the second phase of his argument in chapter 3, to argue that the person has the power of self-determination precisely because it is capable of knowing the truth about the good.

Self-determination is closely related to the person's freedom. What provides the basis of freedom is the dependence of willing on the person. In this light, Wojtyła explains in detail what he means by the "vertical transcendence" of the person.

> Crossing the threshold of the subject in the direction of an object, or intentionality, may be defined as "horizontal transcendence." But this is not our main concern when we discuss the transcendence of the person in the act (though, as we shall see later, it will be a concern). The transcendence we have in mind is the one we owe to self-determination; transcendence by the very fact of freedom, of being free in the act ... This kind of transcendence, in contrast to the other kind of transcendence that we have defined as horizontal, could be defined as vertical....
>
> Self-determination brings with itself above all the superiority of the "I." This superiority, which comes from self-determination, forms a vertical structure, as it were.... The act in the strict sense, that is, the deed, cannot take place where there is no capacity of making one's own dynamizations depend on the "I." (P&A 292–95, TymAP 119)

From the perspective of this vertical transcendence of the person, Wojtyła examines the Thomistic definition of the will as *appetitus rationalis*. "The object of the intellectual *appetitus*, which is called will, is the good according to the common [= universal] account of good."[20] "The object of the will, which is the human *appetitus*, is the universal good, just as the object of the intellect is the universal true."[21] The usual Polish translations of *appetitus*, Wojtyła observes, suggest "something that merely happens in the person" as opposed to "the person acts," which makes it difficult to define the will as a kind of *appetitus*. Wojtyła's response to this difficulty is to point out that, in comparison with the usual Polish translation, the Latin *appetitus* is more neutral in meaning.

> The expression "rational appetite" sounds somewhat strange, almost like an internal contradiction, which does not seem to be the case in the Latin *appetitus rationalis*, precisely because of the more neutral meaning of *appetitus*. (P&A 306–7, TymAP 125)

When read in accord with the meaning of the terms in Thomas's Latin, the definition of the will as *appetitus rationalis* is not only acceptable but also classical.

> The great thinkers of the Middle Ages defined this nature [of the will] as rational appetite. This definition is in a certain way classical, due to its conciseness and clarity: it contains, in fact, that organic link between willing and thinking. (P&A 330–31, TymAP 135)

Appetitus rationalis depends entirely on knowledge of the good as good. "The object of the will is the good as known."[22] Transcendence in light of the truth about the good is the most immanent nature of the will in Wojtyła's understanding of it, in agreement with Thomas.

In the paragraphs that immediately follow his discussion of *appetitus rationalis*, Wojtyła provides a transition to the second phase of his argument by situating two aspects of willing in relation to each other, the attraction of the will to the good and self-determination.

When we perform an act, we freely direct ourselves to will a particular good, either in the manner of weighing several alternatives and eventually directing ourselves to one of them or, when we do not need to weigh alternatives, in the manner of a simple decision to will a particular good.

> The will is the origin of acting, of the act. And it is characteristic that this fact is determined precisely by the aspect of decision, properly by the will. In

20. Thomas, *Summa* I-II, q. 59, a. 4, corp.
21. Thomas, *Summa* I-II, q. 2, a. 8, corp.
22. Thomas, *Sententia libri ethicorum* 3, lect. 3, no. 407.

> this aspect the person manifests itself in its causal efficacy and transcendence and, what is more important, it simply shows itself as a person. (P&A 312–13, TymAP 127)

This decision of the will is not, as it is in Kant, a pure self-determination apart from the causality of the good. It presupposes the attractive power of the good and a consequent movement of the will in tending toward the good. Still, decision plays a key role that highlights the dignity of the person as the self-moving cause of its own acts.

> Part of the very essence of every "I will," which is always objective, always "I will something," is a constant disposition to tend toward the good. For the dynamic essence of the will, this disposition is in a certain sense something more primary and more fundamental than the capacity to decide. The capacity to decide, in fact, presupposes the dynamic disposition to tend toward the good. If, however, we were to conceive of the will, of human "I will," solely or even primarily in terms of this disposition, then we would miss in the dynamism of the will that which is most essentially personal, which most strictly unites the dynamism of will with the structure of the person and which allows us to comprehend and interpret the person fully only by means of this structure. (P&A 314–15, TymAP 128)

Truth about the Good

"The good is to be done and pursued."[23] The self-evidence of this first principle of practical reason rests on the intelligibility with which the understanding of *good* gives rise to the imperative "to be done." In the first half of chapter 3, Wojtyła develops the aspect affirmed by Kant: decision as the core of self-determination; in the second half, he develops the aspect denied by Kant but affirmed in some way by Scheler; namely, the ultimate root of self-determination in the truth about the good. The person's ability to know the truth about the good is the root of the person's vertical transcendence in self-dominion and self-determination.

Wojtyła begins his argument by focusing on motivation and on the response of the will to the motive power of the good. "By motivation we mean the influence of motives on the will" (P&A 314–15, TymAP 128). The good has the power of exerting this influence because of its goodness.

> We owe to motivation the motion or movement of the will toward the object that is presented. Not just a turn toward it but the full movement. To will means to tend toward a certain good that for this reason becomes an end.

23. Thomas, *Summa* I-II, q. 94, a. 2, corp.

> When Aristotle identified the good with the end he based himself on what elementary experience shows. (P&A 316–17, TymAP 129)

One would misunderstand motivation, Wojtyła goes on to argue, if one conceived it as a mechanical and deterministic transfer to the will of whatever happens to be presented by the person's mind as the relatively greatest good in a particular situation (P&A 324–27, TymAP 133–34). This deterministic view overlooks the active participation of the will in willing. It overlooks the will's response to the good.

> It is not the objects and values that engage man and his will, but he engages himself in relation to them. Once again, the reflexive pronoun [i.e., I determine *myself*] shows best the essential activity of the will. The specific response to the values presented in motivation seems to indicate the *agere* (acting) that is proper to the will and at the same time also that which determines the *agere* of the person, that which distinguishes *agere* from *pati* (undergoing), which is the term we have been using from the beginning to define all that only happens in the person. (P&A 328–29, TymAP 134–35)

In unfolding the nature of this active response, Wojtyła starts with a Scholastic axiom already quoted in the first part of chapter 3, *Nihil volitum nisi praecognitum*, "Nothing is willed unless it is known beforehand" (P&A 330–31, TymAP 135). This axiom is not found verbatim in Thomas, though he frequently quotes a closely related axiom formulated by St. Augustine, *Nihil amatum nisi cognitum*, "Nothing is loved unless it is known."[24] In either form, the axiom follows from an understanding of the very nature of the will as a power by which we incline to the good on the basis of our knowledge of its goodness.

> Some [beings] incline to the good with a knowledge by which they know the very account [*ratio*] of good, which is proper to the intellect; and these most perfectly incline to the good, not only as directed to the good by another, such as those that lack knowledge, nor only toward the good in the particular, such as those in which there is only sense knowledge but as inclining toward the universal good itself. And this inclination is called will.[25]

The act of choosing reflects this interior and essential relation of the will to the good by way of knowledge. When we choose, we do not merely orient ourselves toward one thing while excluding others. "This would be a merely 'material' conception of choice" (P&A 332–33, TymAP 137). The *formal* conception of choice is that we decide about things in light of the truth about their goodness.

24. See, e.g., *Summa* I, q. 60, a. 1, sed contra; I-II, q. 3, a. 4, ad 4; I-II, q. 27, a. 2, corp.
25. Thomas, *Summa* I, q. 59, a. 1, corp.

> If it did not belong to the dynamic essence of the will to tend to intentional objects on the basis of a certain truth about such objects, then choice as well as decision would no longer be understandable in their own dynamic originality. To understand them, it is not enough to posit that the reference to truth comes only from the outside, from thought.... The reference to truth in all the originality proper to choice and decision derives from the will and belongs to the will's own dynamism....
>
> By this [reference to truth] one can explain the whole originality of choice and in general of decision; that is, one can explain it by coordination with the truth and not only by reference to objects. By this, therefore, one can explain why in choosing and deciding, the will—and thus of course the person—responds to motives instead of being in some way only determined by them. The ability to respond reveals the freedom of the will in the developed sense. (P&A 334–35, TymAP 137–38)

The dependence of the act of willing on the person, which lies at the heart of self-determination, can be understood on this basis. It is a dependence "in the truth." The reference to the truth about the good enables the person to achieve vertical transcendence and become the responsible causal origin of its acts (Wojtyła, P&A 336–37, TymAP 138).

The manner in which this argument develops the axiom *Nihil volitum nisi praecognitum* can be understood more clearly when one contrasts it with Kant. According to Kant, inclinations (*Neigungen*) have a natural object; namely, pleasure. Yet there can be no truth about the *good* pursued by inclinations, except in the completely subjectivist sense of what happens to seem good to me because it happens to please me due to my irrational inclinations at that moment. In contrast to the inclinations, Kant's will does not have a natural object. The will is, rather, an absolutely original source. It is the power of causal self-determination without the causality of the good. Its nature is to have no definite nature. Not even moral goodness can be conceived as a pregiven natural end that moves the will owing to the power of its goodness, because the will legislates in the first place what moral goodness shall be. Precisely for this reason, according to Kant, the will is free.

In response to Kant's radical denial of the causality of the good as the cause of causes in the constitution of the will's nature, Wojtyła unfolds the axiom, *Nihil volitum nisi praecognitum*. He pinpoints the natural relationship of the will to the truth about the good as the inner reason for the freedom of the will and thus as the essential basis of the person's self-determination. Persons are capable of self-determination precisely because they can appeal in their willing to the truth about the good. These conclusions are implicit in Thomas's definition of the will as the power by which we incline to the good by our knowledge of the very account (*ratio, logos*) of good. It seems to have been Wojtyła's engagement with Kant's radically nonteleological understanding of the will that led him to the explicit clarity with which he formulates what is implicit.

Once again, the importance of nature for Wojtyła becomes clear. He differs from Kant precisely on the question of nature in the understanding of the will and its freedom: for Kant, the will is free because it has no nature defined by an end that specifies that nature; for Wojtyła, as for Thomas, the will is free because its nature is defined by a natural object; namely, the good as understood.

4. Fulfillment

While chapter 3 analyzes the root of self-determination, chapter 4 turns to its effect, to the performance of acts. Wojtyła begins, as Aristotle often does, with an observation about a common way of speaking. Common ways of speaking reflect common experience and for this reason often contain a great implicit wealth and depth of truth. In Polish, he points out, one commonly uses the phrase "I fulfill an act." English speakers say, "I perform an act."

> More than once in our study we made use of *common terms or ways of speaking that conceal within themselves particularly deep contents.* Here too, as we continue the considerations of Chapter Three, we *must appeal at the beginning to a way of speaking* that has a set place not only in literary language but also in the spoken word. It is the expression, "I fulfill an act." In the following analyses, the topic of which will be the transcendence of the person in the act, we must occupy ourselves precisely with the fulfillment about which the expression we quoted speaks. The sentence, "I fulfill an act," conceals in itself, as it were, the whole problem of our study.
>
> Indeed, we are here concerned with person and act not as two distinct realities, each by itself but—we have emphasized this from the start—as a single reality that is deeply united. This cohesion exists in reality, and therefore it must exist also in understanding or interpretation. It seems, therefore, that *the classical expression* of this existential and essential cohesion between person and act is the way of speaking, "I fulfill an act." For this reason, one must appeal to it in the philosophical interpretation of person and act. (P&A 358–59, TymAP 149; emphasis added)

Wojtyła comments on the close connection between this way of speaking and the Thomistic understanding of *actus*. To *fulfill* an act, to make it full, to lead it to fullness, is "the most fitting equivalent of the Latin term *actus*, which signifies precisely the fullness that corresponds to a determinate faculty or power" (P&A 360–61, TymAP 149–50). The term *fulfillment*, in fact, has a certain advantage over *actus:* it explicitly points to the person as the fulfiller, as the subject and author of its act, which is not the case in the more general term *actus*.

In a human act that has both an interior and an exterior aspect (such as felling a tree), one can distinguish a transitive aspect of fulfillment (I fell the tree by my act) and an intransitive aspect, a form of fulfillment that remains in the subject (I determine myself as the one who is felling or has felled the tree). The two aspects of fulfillment, intransitive and transitive, do not simply have a one-to-one correlation to the interior act of will and the exterior bodily act. Both the interior and the exterior act can be considered either intransitively in relation to the subject that determines itself (I determine myself both as the one who wills to fell the tree and who actually fells it) or transitively in relation to the object (my act is an objective event in the world and results in the tree's falling).

The intransitive and interior effect of self-determination is a form coming to be (*fieri*) of the person in which the person makes itself morally good or bad. By acting, the person brings itself to fullness.

> In this way, the true meaning of the way of speaking, "to fulfill an act," delineates itself before us. Fulfillment is not the same as efficacy. To fulfill an act does not only mean being its author. Fulfillment is, rather, something coordinated with self-determination. It runs parallel to it but in the opposite direction, as it were. Thus, by being the author of an act, man at the same time fulfills himself in it. He fulfills, that is, he realizes, he in some way brings to its right fullness the structure that is characteristic of him on account of personality, on account of his being someone and not merely something. (P&A 362–65, TymAP 151)

This coming to be (*fieri*) of the person is not simply identical with the level of morality, but it is "a deeper level, the ontological reality, the reality of the self-fulfillment of the person through the act, which is proper only to the person" (P&A 366–67, TymAP 152). In the remainder of chapter 4, Wojtyła unfolds this initial account of fulfillment in four steps: conscience, duty, responsibility, and happiness.

- *Conscience* as the interior subjective principle that governs the fulfillment of an act.
- *Duty* as a call rooted in the goodness of the good as apprehended by conscience and expressed in the practical imperative formed by conscience, a call to the person's self-fulfillment.
- *Responsibility* as the subjective appropriation of this call, answering to one's own authority and, supremely, to that of God.
- *Happiness* as the final subjective fulfillment of this appropriation of the call of the good in the performance of an act.

At the end of chapter 4, immediately after these four steps, Wojtyła uses his analysis of fulfillment as the basis for approaching the spiritual nature of the person and the relation between body and soul.

Thomas, Kant, and Wojtyła on Conscience

Thomas understands *conscience* as an application of our knowledge to our own acts, as the Latin word *con-scientia* suggests (*con* = with; *scientia* = knowledge). By analogical extension, he notes, *conscientia* is also used to signify the power by which we apply our knowledge, or the infused light (the habitus of principles) that lies at the root of our knowledge. He sees three main ways in which conscience is an application of knowledge to acts. Conscience testifies inwardly to past acts as acts truly done by us. It binds our will in the present in the form of commanding or prohibiting the performance of particular acts. It judges the goodness of past acts and thus either approves, excuses, or accuses.[26]

In most discussions of conscience, Thomas has the second mode of application in mind. Understood in this mode, conscience is "a certain dictate of the mind" (*quoddam mentis dictamen*) by which we bind (*ligare*) our will to a particular act.[27] The binding power of this dictate remains in force, whether the judgment of conscience is true or in error.

> If one looks carefully at how conscience binds, one finds that it binds in every case.... For conscience is a certain dictate (*dictamen*) of reason. The will, however, is not moved to desire something, except due to some apprehension. For the will's object is good or bad as imagined or understood. Reason itself shows the intention of good or bad. Since the act of the will has its specific nature from the object, the act of the will must go forward according to the judgment of reason and conscience. This is why we say that conscience binds (*ligare*).
>
> And therefore, whether reason or conscience judges rightly or not, the will is under obligation (*obligatur*) in such a way that the act of will lacks order if it does not follow the judgment or dictate of reason, which is conscience. And this is to impose an obligation (*obligare*), that is, to tie the will to something (*astringere*), such that it cannot tend to something without the harm of deformity.[28]

The insistence that conscience is always binding, whether it is erroneous or not, does not imply, of course, that the question of the truth about the good is incidental to it. Quite on the contrary, it makes an essential difference. The text just quoted continues.

26. See Thomas, *Summa* I, q. 79, a. 13, corp.
27. Thomas, *Summa* I, q. 79, a. 13, ad 1.
28. Thomas, Super *II sent.*, 39.3.3, corp.

> Nevertheless, an erroneous conscience binds differently than a right conscience. A right conscience binds simply and through itself, because what is dictated (*dictatum*) by it is in itself good and appears as such from the judgment of reason. . . . An erroneous conscience, on the other hand, does not bind except by accident and in a certain respect. Since *what conscience dictates does not bind except inasmuch as it is good*, the will is not *per se* under obligation (*obligatur*) but *by accident*, namely, by reason of one's understanding by which it is judged to be good.[29]

The point that an erring conscience binds only *per accidens* makes clear that the dictate of conscience and the obligation it imposes arises from the good. What conscience dictates does not bind except inasmuch as it is good. The dictate of conscience is rooted in the real goodness of the good as apprehended by theoretical reason. The whole effort of forming one's conscience must be directed, in the first place, to finding the truth about the good. This theoretical truth about the good is the necessary point of departure for the practical judgment of conscience.

According to Kant, theoretical reason does not grasp real being. It forms a material universe of mere objects of consciousness from the amorphous material received in sensation. Theoretical reason is completely incompetent to affirm or deny the freedom of the will, the immortality of the soul, and the existence of God. Practical reason alone can affirm these three pillars of religion and morality. Its affirmation of them has no bearing on their real being (or real nonbeing). It is a morally decent and dutiful affirmation, not a theoretically true or false one. Moral duty, therefore, does not rest on theoretical truth, but it arises in complete originality from practical reason alone. Human dignity lies in the autonomous imperative of reason without theoretical knowledge of the good.

Kant's concern in constructing this theory is to resist the utilitarian ethics of the Baconian-Cartesian program by an ethics of personal dignity. He attempts to save the person from being pulverized as a mere means in the great utilitarian machine. Kant focuses on the symptom, utilitarianism, without critically examining its cause; namely, the understanding of matter that followed from the Baconian and Cartesian imposition of the will to power. He uncritically concedes the whole order of theoretical reason to Cartesian-Newtonian physics.

The person is absent from the cosmos of Newtonian physics. It is a cosmos of mere matter and motion, endowed only with mathematical properties, without good or evil, beauty or ugliness, nature or the unnatural. The order of the person, which is the truly important order for Kant, lies outside this impoverished Newtonian cosmos in a completely separate personalist order.

The origin of the Newtonian cosmos is not an act of understanding but the

29. Thomas, Super *II sent.*, 39.3.3, corp.; emphasis added.

imposition of will on what shall count as knowledge; namely, what can give us power over nature. Conceding the whole theoretical order to the Baconian-Cartesian program is therefore a violent destruction of reason as such. This destruction comes first in Kant's argument. Settling the person in what is left—namely, in the practical-religious order of personalism alone—comes second. It is an attempt to avoid the destructive consequences of the choice.

Wojtyła shares Kant's concerns about the Baconian-Cartesian program, particularly the critique of utilitarianism. Like Kant, he emphasizes the dignity of the person, the person's self-mastery and self-determination, to save the person from being pulverized in the great utilitarian machine. He does not follow Kant, however, in simply accepting the Baconian-Cartesian project. He maintains the full breadth of reason by affirming the material cosmos in all its richness, in which there is no such thing as "mere matter," pure externality, with only mathematical properties. It is a cosmos of bodily natures ordered to the good, above all a cosmos that contains persons who "are bodies," bodies filled with goodness and beauty. For this reason, he can see the roots of the practical order in the truth of being and the *truthfulness* of reason.

Wojtyła's account of the transcendental truths—goodness and beauty as well as their convertibility with being—is the core of his response to Kant.

> The concept of the transcendence of the person may be broadened and examined in relation to all the transcendentals: being, truth, goodness and beauty. Man has access to them through knowledge, and in the wake of knowledge, of the mind, through the will and through action. In this approach, action serves also to realize truth, goodness and beauty. It is in this perspective that action was often examined in traditional metaphysics, in one way by Platonic metaphysics, in another by Aristotelian metaphysics.... The transcendence of the person understood metaphysically is not something merely abstract; the evidence of experience tells us that the spiritual life of man is concentrated and pulsates around truth, goodness, and beauty. We may thus certainly speak of a certain experience of the transcendentals that goes hand in hand with the experience of the person's transcendence. (P&A 370–73, TymAP 155–56)

In his three critiques, Kant separates the transcendentals from each other and from being: he separates truth in the *Critique of Pure Reason*, moral goodness in the *Critique of Practical Reason*, and beauty in the *Critique of Judgment*. Truth, goodness, and beauty—each determines its own domain in complete independence from the others. This separation of the transcendentals from each other is the deepest metaphysical consequence of Kant's attempt to "do away with knowledge to make room for faith."[30] The most radically anti-Kantian state-

30. Kant, *Critique of Pure Reason*, B XXX.

ment in *Person and Act* is thus the passage on the transcendentals just quoted. St. John Paul finds the same teaching in Genesis.

> "God saw everything that he had made, and indeed, it was very good" (Genesis 1:31). This is why one can say with certainty that the first chapter of Genesis has formed an incontrovertible point of reference and solid basis of a metaphysics and also for an anthropology and an ethics according to which *ens et bonum convertuntur* (being and good are convertible). Of course, all this has its own significance for Theology as well, and above all for the theology of the body. (TOB 2:5)

Wojtyła unfolds the implications of the convertibility of the transcendentals with being, and thus the nature of conscience, in the concept of *trueness.*

Conscience, Duty, and Trueness

In accord with the purpose of *Person and Act* as a whole and of chapter 4 in particular, Wojtyła considers conscience primarily from the point of view of the person's vertical transcendence, that is, as a key element in the person's efficacious self-determination and self-fulfillment through acts. Conscience is always concerned with the question "What is to be done (or not to be done) *by me* here and now?" My conscience is concerned with myself as the one who comes to be (*fieri*) good or evil through my own acts.

> That the expression "to fulfill an act" indicates not only the action as an external and transitive effect but also as an internal and intransitive effect, has a fundamental significance for the interpretation of the person. At the same time, it opens the road for an adequate interpretation of conscience, which seems possible only by presupposing that the fulfillment of an act constitutes at the same time a fulfillment of the person. Otherwise the specific vitality of conscience, its rigorously personalistic meaning, would not be comprehensible. Conscience is certainly not a more or less abstract dialectic of the moral values of good or evil, but with its roots it reaches down to the ontological fact, which is the self-fulfillment of the person through an act. Man fulfills himself as a person, as someone, and as someone he can become good or evil, that is, he can fulfill himself and can also not fulfill himself. (P&A 366–67, TymAP 153)

What Wojtyła calls "the rigorously personalistic meaning" of conscience is the reflexive bearing of conscience on the person itself. In comparison with Thomas, this emphasis on reflexivity is not new but certainly stronger. It is part of Wojtyła's intense interest in the person's lived experience of subjectivity.

The specific function of conscience in bringing about the person's self-fulfillment, he goes on to argue, lies in binding the person's acts to the theoretical truth about the good, in making acts depend upon that truth. The judgment of conscience, therefore, has two closely related sides: it involves a theoretical judgment, "This is good," and it involves a practical imperative that flows from this theoretical judgment, "I shall do this."

Wojtyła uses the term *duty* (Polish *powinność*, what ought to be) to describe the binding power of conscience. Duty is formed as an imperative in the mind in the manner of con-science, that is, an application of knowledge to acts, when one grasps the theoretical truth about the good and accordingly binds the will to act.

> The function of conscience consists in defining the true good in the act and in forming the duty that corresponds to this good. Duty is the experiential form of dependence on the truth, to which the freedom of the person is subordinate. (P&A 372–73, TymAP 156)

In the first of these two sentences, Wojtyła does not add anything to Thomas's account of conscience. Even the term *duty*, which may sound rather Kantian, is consistent with Thomas's understanding of conscience as *binding* (*ligare*) the will, as imposing an *obligatio* or *debitum*.[31] Still, the prominence of *duty* in Wojtyła appears to be an echo of Kant in opposition to Scheler.

While the first sentence does not go beyond Thomas, the second proposes a characteristic emphasis on something implicit in the first sentence. "Duty is *the experiential form* of dependence on the truth." Wojtyła is interested in *the consciously lived experience* of binding oneself to act in accord with the truth about the good. In the remainder of the section on conscience, Wojtyła unfolds this experience.

His point of departure is the intellect's ordination to truth, which he expresses by the Polish word *prawdziwość*. *Prawdziwość* is an abstract noun formed from the adjective *prawdziwy* = *true*, etymologically parallel to the artificial English word *trueness*. *Trueness* is rarely used, but it is immediately understandable as the abstract noun formed from the adjective *true*. *Truity* would be an alternative, but it is not used at all. In the absence of a better option *trueness* can serve as a placeholder for *prawdziwość*. *The Acting Person* translates *prawdziwość* by the abstract noun *truthfulness* (TymAP 158), which is formed from the adjective *truthful*. *Truthfulness* usually refers to the virtue of telling the truth or to the correspondence of a representation to its original, as in the *truthfulness* of a nar-

31. "It is *debitum* that all our acts be referred to the last end." *Summa* I-II, q. 21, a. 4, corp. The Blackfriars translation renders *debitum* in this text as "duty." In both etymology and meaning, *debitum* is close to "duty."

rative or portrait. This is not what Wojtyła means by *prawdziwość*, although it is one of the possible meanings of the word in Polish. *Prawdziwość* can also mean *genuineness* or *authenticity*.

In *Person and Act*, Wojtyła uses *prawdziwość* in the first place for the radical ordering of the human mind toward truth. He then extends the word by analogy to the power of the good to establish a true apprehension of itself in us in the theoretical order, which is somewhat related to *genuineness*, and finally to the same normative power expressed in the practical judgment, "I should do this now."

> What is essential to [the intellect] is not only to form thought but to gather truth, that is, to distinguish what is true from what is not true. The intellect as a property and faculty of man allows him to remain in potentially complete contact with reality. *Intellectus est quoddammodo omnia* (The intellect is in a certain way all things), as Thomas Aquinas expressed himself. Every being can become a content of the intellect. Essential to the cognitive relation of the intellect with being is trueness (*prawdziwość*).

Wojtyła applies *trueness* (*prawdziwość*) not only to reason's objective nature but also to the conscious activity that flows from this nature, the deliberate striving for truth.

> By *trueness* (*prawdziwość*) we mean man's intellectual effort and activity in its essential point. The understanding of truth is tied to a specific tendency. Truth is therefore an end. Man tends toward truth, and the intellect unites in itself the power to gather it (distinguishing it from non-truth) and the need to search for it. Already in this [unity of power and need], the intellect's dynamic subordination to truth reveals itself, which is at the same time its proper mode, as it were, as human intellect. (P&A 378–81, TymAP 159)

It is here, in the intellect's lived experience of subordination to truth, that Wojtyła sees the root of the person's experience of self-mastery.

> It is precisely this subordination of the intellect to truth that conditions the pre-eminence or transcendence of the person. Man is not only a passive mirror that reflects objects, but he retains in relation to them a specific pre-eminence through truth. What is at issue is "the superiority of the truth," which implies a certain distance from objects and inscribes itself in the spiritual nature of the person. For this reason, the ancient definition of Boethius rightly emphasizes rationality, that is, the intellect, as the distinctive feature of the person: *persona est individua substantia rationalis naturae,* The person is an individual substance of rational nature. (P&A 380–81, TymAP 159)

In this text, Wojtyła forcefully expresses the primacy of theoretical *logos* in his thought in a manner parallel to Benedict XVI's *Regensburg Lecture*. It may seem paradoxical that the lived experience of self-subordination to truth should be, at the same time, the inner reason for the experience of freedom and self-determination. Socrates's argument in the Gorgias explains the apparent paradox (*Gorgias* 469a–c; see part I, chap. 5, in this volume). To be free in one's self-determination is to be able to do what one really wants. To know what one really wants, one needs to know what is good, because only *good* can answer the question, "Is this what I really want?" Self-subordination to the truth about the good coincides with dependence on oneself. One is not first bound passively like a slave to truth and then in a second phase free like a master who depends on himself alone. Dependence on the truth is the essential ingredient in dependence on oneself.

The effort of conscience does not stop with the theoretical truth "X is good." Conscience consists in the end in the practical judgment "X is to be done by me now." What must not be overlooked in this imperative is its reflexivity. By willing an act, I will myself as one who comes to be good or evil by acting. This thesis directly contradicts Scheler's claim that one must not intend one's own moral goodness, because to do so would be Pharisaism. "Love for the moral good as good is itself bad, because it is necessarily Pharisaism" (GW 7:164). This thesis, which is contrary to ordinary experience, is clearly due to Scheler's resistance against Kant's ethics of pure duty. Wojtyła stays close to common human experience.

> No willing as an intentional act can avoid one's own "I," which is in some way the first object of willing. Freedom as independence from the possible objects of willing presupposes freedom as dependence on oneself. The effort of conscience is intimately tied to this reality of the human will and human freedom. In this effort of the intellect, which aims at the truth in the area of values, the point is not only to gather the abstract value of the objects of willing but—with the intransitive aspect of the act—also the fundamental value of the person as the subject of the will and as the author of the act. (P&A 384–85, TymAP 161)

Wojtyła points out that Hume, followed by the tradition of analytic philosophy, builds a wall of separation between *is* and *ought*. Nothing can provide a transition from *is* to *ought*.[32] To move from "is" to "ought" is to be guilty of "the naturalistic fallacy."[33] Wojtyła responds by an appeal to the common human

32. David Hume, *A Treatise of Human Nature: Being an Attempt to Introduce the Experimental Method of Reasoning into Moral Subjects*, ed. L. A. Selby-Bigge (Oxford: Clarendon Press, 1888), book III, part I, sect. 1, last paragraph, 469–70.

33. See George Edward Moore, *Principia Ethica* (Cambridge: Cambridge University Press, 1903), esp. 9–15, 48, 59–63.

understanding that is reflected in the first precept of the natural law. "Good is to be done and pursued and evil to be avoided."[34] This precept is a "dictate of practical reason" *dictamen practicae rationis*.[35] A dictate—that is, an imperative or command—is an act of reason in which a certain power of will is present by which persons efficaciously begin a movement to act, either in themselves or in others.[36] Many of our acts of will are subject to our own command inasmuch as they are voluntary.[37]

The first precept of the natural law contains two main elements: the good and the dictate "to be done and pursued" *faciendum et prosequendum*.[38] The self-evidence of the precept lies in the understanding of good, which of itself gives rise to the understanding of the *ought* expressed in the practical judgment "It is to be done and pursued."

Both Kant and Scheler separate the connection between understanding the good and the imperative of reason. Kant only allows for the imperative *Is to be done*. His first principle of practical reason is *Is to be done* without any good as the reason why it should be done. An act is morally good when it is an exercise of complete autonomy in which one is not motivated by any good but only by the imperative *Is to be done* when this imperative can be promulgated as a universal law. Scheler only allows for knowing a value. He explicitly excludes any imperative derived from this knowledge, because of the alleged Kantian negativity of *ought*.

At the end of the section on conscience, Wojtyła extends the concept of *trueness* (*prawdziwość*) by analogy from the nature of the intellect to the normative power of truth.

> Conscience introduces into self-realization the normative power of truth, which conditions not only the fulfillment of the act by the person but also the person's self-fulfillment in the act. In this fulfillment, the structure of self-possession and self-dominion, which is particular and proper to the person, is confirmed and at the same time actualized. Trueness (*prawdziwość*), the normative power of truth contained in conscience, forms the key stone of this structure. Outside of this normative power, abstracting from it, one cannot understand or rightly interpret conscience. (P&A 384–87, TymAP 161–62)

34. Thomas, *Summa* I-II, q. 94, a. 2, corp.

35. Thomas, *Summa* I-II, q. 91, a. 1, corp.

36. On command (*imperium*), see Thomas, *Summa* I-II, q. 17, a. 1, corp. For an application of imperium and the imperative to law, see Thomas, *Summa* I-II, q. 90, a. 1, obj. 3 with ad 3.

37. See Thomas, *Summa* I-II, q. 17, a. 5.

38. The distinction between *done* and *pursued* follows the distinction between acts and ends. Good acts are to be *done*, and certain other goods—for example, health—are to be *pursued* as ends.

In this text, *prawdziwość* is understood by analogical extension as normative power of truth rather than as the intellect's ordination to the truth. The experience of the objective normative power of truth is deeply connected in the theoretical order with the intellect's natural ordination to the truth, unfolded in the conscious effort of gathering the truth about the good. The experience is completed in the practical order by the self-evident transition from "is good" to "is to be done." In this way, the intellect's submission to the truth in both the theoretical and the practical order explains the experience of duty.

Duty and Self-Fulfillment

In the section on duty, Wojtyła unfolds this second sense of truthfulness by analyzing duty as an expression of the call to self-fulfillment, a call that proceeds from the good. He begins his argument by pointing out that duty, expressed in the statement "I should do X," demands the fulfillment (i.e., performance) of an act and therefore, by its very essence as duty, demands the person's self-fulfillment through that act (P&A 388–89, TymAP 163).

In some circumstances, one might have the impression that duty exists without this essential connection with the person's self-fulfillment. Duty might seem to address the person from the *outside* in the form of a preexisting and, as it were, ready-made moral precept or law that does not arise from within conscience. In this manner, God seems to address human beings as the lawgiver in the *Decalogue*, "You shall not commit adultery" (Exodus 20:14; Deuteronomy 5:18). Nevertheless, even such norms have an essential connection with the person's self-fulfillment. When conscience assimilates the content of a norm, it verifies its normativity in light of the experience of the normative power of the good.

> The power of these norms to generate duty derives from the fact that . . . they objectify a true good that binds the person. The fundamental value of norms lies in *prawdziwość*, the normative power of the good they objectify and not in the generation of duties, even though the normative formulas used in actual practice accentuate the latter by such expressions as *ought*, *must*, *there is the obligation*, and the like. Nevertheless, the essence of the normative statements of morality and law lies in the trueness (= normative power) of the good (*prawdziwość dobra*) that is objectified in them. Through trueness (*prawdziwość*) they come into contact with conscience, which in some way transforms trueness (*prawdziwość*) into the concrete and real duty. (P&A 390–91, TymAP 164)

The main point of this text is the absolute and permanent primacy of the good in the whole order of moral norms. What is truly at stake in every duty is a good. Here are the three levels distinguished by Wojtyła.

The most basic level in conscience is *trueness* in the sense of the ordering of reason to truth, actualized in the effort and search of conscience to find the truth about the good, a truth in the theoretical order measured by the correspondence between thought and reality.

The second level is the encounter with *trueness* (now in the sense of *normative power*) of the good. The person encounters the power of the good, which is the power of being, to bring about a truthful judgment about itself. In the lived experience of contact with this trueness of the good, the person forms a judgment that does not merely hover in midair, as it were, as a mental phenomenon that suddenly appears without any basis, as a mere value preference. The person experiences that the good itself gives rise to the judgment *This is good*. Through this experience, the person knows the truth about the good precisely as truth in the theoretical order; that is, it knows the correspondence between the statement *This is good* and the real good.

This experience of the *trueness* of the good leads to the third level, to the formation of the normative statement *This is to be done or not to be done by me.* On this level, the person experiences the norm itself as true, that is, as flowing from the convincing power of the good and therefore as authoritative in relation to the will. *X is truly to be done by me now, because it is truly good.* The phrase *by me*, which is essential to the normative statement, shows that the norm, in calling for the fulfillment of the act, calls for the self-fulfillment of the person. This third analogous use of *trueness* is like the second, except that it has moved from the theoretical order to the practical order.

In this manner, Wojtyła responds to the attraction of Kant's understanding of autonomy, in which the person is portrayed as the emancipated, creative, legislative origin of moral norms, not as the passive, bound subject to norms imposed on it by authority or mere empirical data from the outside. The response, Wojtyła argues, should not be mere insistence on the authoritative character of moral norms but on the trueness of the good. Conscience itself, by its own energies, transforms the experience of the theoretical truth about the good into the practical judgment.

5. Participation

The Most Personal Good

Wojtyła's discussion of the individual person (chaps. 1–6) is taken one step further in his discussion of the person's acting together with others for the sake of a common good (chap. 7). There is a clear logic in this progression.

> It seems, in fact, that only a rigorous understanding of human acting can lead to a correct understanding of cooperation and not the other way around. The dynamic correlation of the act with the person is itself a fundamental reality that remains also in the sphere of any act "together with others." It is only on the basis of this correlation that all acting "together with others" takes on an adequate human meaning. This is an essential order that cannot be inverted or neglected. Thus, we will arrange our investigation in this order. (P&A 616–17, TymAP 262–63)

Wojtyła further defends this order in the second edition of *Person and Act* in response to a critical question from one of the participants in a symposium about the book.

> The question may arise whether the experience of acting "together with others" is not fundamental, and if it is, whether the conception of community and relation should for this reason not already be presupposed in working out the conception of the person. I think that the interpretation of community and interpersonal relation cannot be presupposed correctly unless it already rests in some way on the conception of person and act, that is, on a conception that in the experience of "man-acts" adequately brings to light the image of the transcendence of the person in the act. Otherwise, in the interpretation of community and of interpersonal acts, one might neglect certain aspects of that which is constitutive of the person and which substantially conditions and at the same time defines community and relation precisely inasmuch as they are a community and relation between persons. Thus, on the level of method as well as of substance the correct solution seems to be the one that—giving priority to the conception of person and act—searches based on this conception for an adequate interpretation of community and interpersonal relation in all their richness and differentiation. (P&A 694–95, TymAP 299–300)

One could respond on behalf of the critical question that what is last in execution is first in intention. The good is absolutely first in the order of causality. In chapter 7 of *Person and Act*, Wojtyła argues that human acts cannot ultimately be understood as personal acts unless one grasps the implications of participation, of acting "with others." It is in this light that he explains the main question to be addressed in chapter 7.

> It seems that to explain the personal nature of human acts it is necessary to grasp what follows from the fact that they are fulfilled [performed] "together with others." By what does this fulfillment distinguish itself in the dynamic correlation between the act and the person? An answer to this question is so necessary because acting "together with others" is so universal, so frequent and so common. We want to answer this question in the considerations of the present chapter. (P&A 618–19, TymAP 263)

Wojtyła's formulation of the question of chapter 7 may seem obscure. "By what does this fulfillment [of acts together with others] distinguish itself in the dynamic correlation between the act and the person?" The question focuses on the performance of acts by the person conceived as a fulfillment. It asks what the distinguishing marks of such a fulfillment are when persons act with others. These distinguishing marks, the question states, can be found "in the dynamic correlation between the act and the person." By "dynamic correlation," Wojtyła means that the act proceeds from the power (*dynamis*, *potentia*) of the person with all the qualifications of that dynamism analyzed in the first six chapters: consciousness, causal efficacy, free self-determination according to the truth about the good, fulfillment, and integration. Conversely, the act realizes, fulfills, and reveals the person.

Let us anticipate the answer so that the movement of the argument is easier to follow. The dynamic interrelation between person and act is realized most deeply through acting with others for the sake of the common good. Participation for the sake of the common good is the ultimate reason for the fully personal value of human acts.

Compare this thesis with De Koninck's understanding of personalism. For De Koninck, personalism is the view that the individual person in his or her liberty is superior to the common good. This definition applies to Kant's personalism. For Wojtyła, personalism is the view that the individual person in its freedom is ordered to the common good as the person's greatest good, through which alone the truly personal character of human acts can be fulfilled. It is in being and acting as part of a whole for the sake of the good of that whole that the person's dignity as a personal agent is most fully realized.

Structure of the Argument

Wojtyła presents the argument in ten sections. Sections 1 through 6 deal directly with participation itself; sections 7 and 8 distinguish authentic and inauthentic attitudes toward participation; sections 9 and 10 turn to the foundation of participation in the concept of *neighbor* and in the commandment of love. Wojtyła's overall focus in *Person and Act* is the interrelation between person and act as a means for understanding the person more deeply. He does not present a comprehensive theory of the common good. Still, what he says about freely performed acts together with others for the common good shows a deep understanding of this ancient notion.

Wojtyła introduces the notion of participation in simple terms as "acting with others." The word *participation*, he states in anticipation of the main thesis of the chapter, contains the answer to the main question: How is the dynamic interrelation between person and act affected by acting with others?

In section 2, Wojtyła sums up the results of the first six chapters of *Person and Act* in the concept of "the personalistic value of the act." The "personalistic value" (he also calls it "personal value") arises from the performance or fulfillment of an act as an act of the person: a conscious act (chap. 1), coming forth from the person's causal efficacy (chap. 2) and free self-determination in accord with the truth about the good (chaps. 3 and 4), an act that for these reasons integrates the person's life both with regard to the experience of the body (chap. 5) and of the psyche (chap. 6). The personalistic value of an act is an expression of the dignity of the person as a being that possesses itself, determines itself, and reaches fulfillment through acting for the good.

On this basis, Wojtyła formulates the main question of chapter 7 more distinctly: "The fact of acting with others: how is it related to the personalistic value of the act?" Once again, for the sake of clarity, let us anticipate the answer: Acting with others for the sake of the common good is that through which the personalistic value of human acts is most fully established.

The philosophical tradition, Wojtyła argues, focused mainly on the rational and social nature of the human person. In *Person and Act*, he attempts to enrich this understanding of the person's nature by analyzing "acting with others" from the side of the person's actual lived experience at the time of acting. Such insistent analysis of lived experience, a hallmark of St. John of the Cross's theology and of Wojtyła's entire thought, is in some respects a fresh contribution to the theory of both person and act. Nevertheless, as Wojtyła notes, the path through the lived experience of acts to human nature is not new but has always been the path. "In fact, at the point of departure of the affirmation of the social nature of man there could be nothing other than precisely the experience that man exists and acts together with others" (P&A 628–29, TymAP 268). The freshness of the contribution lies in the insistence, depth, and clarity with which Wojtyła illumines the lived experience of the person. It is a harmonious development of doctrine in comparison with the tradition.

What is it that is most characteristic of the experience of acting together with others? In answering this question, Wojtyła first lays down three preliminary theses that prepare the ground for his main thesis. (1) Human persons act together with others. (2) By doing so, they reach the good that is involved in these acts. (3) They thereby establish the personalistic value of their acts. Participation encompasses all three of these components and makes it possible for them to be fulfilled (P&A 630–31, TymAP 269). Participation is thus necessary for realizing the personalistic value of human acts; it is necessary for the realization and fulfillment of the person. Participation is not an extrinsic aspect of the person, it is not an alienating ordination of the person to an alien good of the whole that instrumentalizes the person, but it is rooted in the depth of the created person as person (P&A 633–35, TymAP 268–70).

It is at this point in the argument that Wojtyła begins to focus on the good as the main explanatory principle of participation. Participation is achieved when persons act together with others in such a way that they choose what others choose, or even because others choose it, that is, when they choose the good realized or reached by their acts as a good that is shared with others but that is nevertheless truly their own good (P&A 636–37, TymAP 270).

The qualification "their own good" needs to be emphasized. What makes participation possible is the commonness of the common good. When members of a family consciously and freely act together in such a way that they promote the peace of the family as a good that truly belongs to each member, as a good that each member freely and responsibly chooses, enjoys, and cherishes, they act in a fully participatory way. Participation is possible for them because the good of peace is truly common.

Individualism and Totalitarianism

Wojtyła throws his understanding of participation into relief by considering two widespread ways of negating participation.

> Individualism presents the good of the individual as the principal and fundamental good to which every community and society must be subordinated, while objective totalitarianism affirms a diametrically opposite principle inasmuch as it totally subordinates the individual and its good to the community and to the society. (P&A 640–41, TymAP 273)

True as this account may be, Wojtyła adds, it does not yet reach the main point, on which individualism and totalitarianism agree. They share one and the same error; namely, the absence of a true concept of the common good. Both conceive the good of the individual as isolated from, opposed to that of the community, and they conceive the common good as a good alien from the individual. Both, therefore, deny participation. On this common ground, individualism prefers the good of the individual, totalitarianism that of the community, the community (or rather the party) being conceived as an individual in its own right with its own private interests that can conflict with those of the individual person (P&A 642–45, TymAP 273–75).

Wojtyła calls both views "a-personalistic" and "anti-personalistic" because they deny a fundamental characteristic of the person; namely, participation. One can sense Wojtyła's experience with both Nazi and Soviet totalitarianism in the forcefulness with which he writes in this section about the person's right to act in a participatory way, a right that he claims necessarily arises from the truth that participation is a fundamental characteristic of the person (P&A 644–47, TymAP 275–76). This right was systematically trampled underfoot by both the Nazis and the Soviets. At the same time, Wojtyła is clearly aware of the main danger of Western democratic societies; namely, the excessive pursuit of the individual's private good, especially the exaltation of the personal freedom of choice in a utilitarian framework.

Participation and Community

In order to clarify the meaning of participation more fully, Wojtyła makes three points about its relation to community.

1. Neither individualism nor totalitarianism can envisage authentic community because participation is simultaneously an essential feature of the person and of community (P&A 646–49, TymAP 276).

2. Being and acting together with others implies not only a multitude of individual persons but also, as the word *together* indicates, also a single and unitary subject, a community. In sharp contrast to Scheler, however, Wojtyła does not attribute personal subjectivity including consciousness to communities. "It is a 'quasi-subjectivity,' because the human person is the proper (substantial) subject of existing and acting, also when these take place 'together with others'" (P&A 648–49, TymAP 277). This understanding of community is essential to the correct understanding of the common good: it is the persons in the community who are the beneficiaries of the common good, not the community itself as an individual in its own right.

3. Being and acting together with others imply also that persons belong as members to various communities: to a family, a nation, a group of students who take the same courses, and so on. Yet being a member of a community does not yet necessarily mean participating in it. Various communities have various objective goods and ends. From the point of view of person and act, the decisive thing is not only this objective purpose but also the subjective aspect of conscious and freely willed participation to share in this purpose.

> One must see whether man, inasmuch as he is a member of a community ... performs true acts by acting and whether he realizes himself in them. This is determined by participation. While acting "together with others," man can

> still remain outside the community that the participation determines. Here we find ourselves faced with a problem that cannot be resolved without considering [the problem] of the so-called common good.... The moment of participation is situated in choice: man chooses what others choose or chooses it because others choose it, and at the same time it is as his own good and as an end to which he himself tends that he chooses what others choose. (P&A 654–55, TymAP 279–80nm)

The common good (this is the key point of this passage) is truly the person's own good, each person's own good. It is exactly for this reason that it is truly common, and it is exactly in this way that it distinguishes itself from imperfectly common goods, such as taxes collected by the state.

Participation and the Common Good

Section 6 concludes Wojtyła's argument about the role of the common good in establishing the personalistic value of the person's acts. He begins the argument by pointing out that the common good of a community is "the end toward which this community tends" (P&A 656–57, TymAP 281). It is not sufficient, however, to focus on the end in purely objective terms. One must also focus on its impact on the lived experience of personal subjectivity.

> One cannot define the common good without considering the subjective aspect, that is, the moment of acting in relation to the acting persons. If one takes this aspect into account, one must observe that the common good is not only the end, understood in a purely objective way, of the act that is performed in a community, but it is above all that which conditions and in some way reveals participation in the persons who act in common. In this way it forms in them the subjective community of acting. We can understand the common good in an objective and a subjective sense. The subjective sense of the common good is intimately connected with participation as a property of person and act. We can affirm in this approach that the common good corresponds to the social nature of man. (P&A 657–59, TymAP 781)

Wojtyła's point is not that the objective end, the objective common good, should be replaced by a subjective one that is purely relative to the subject's impressions and value choices. His point is that the objective common good gives rise to the lived experience of consciously willed participation. There are passages in De Koninck's work on the common good that go in a similar direction. For example, in the context of discussing the beatific vision as a participation in the ultimate common good, God himself, De Koninck unfolds what such participation implies for the lived experience of the persons involved (see part I, chap. 7, sect. 7, in this volume).

> In seeing God, Peter sees what is greater than anything which could be his proper good for he knows that he is only Peter; he sees that God is infinitely more communicable than He is to Peter himself, and it is this infinity of goodness Peter loves, because he loves God in Himself and in that bounty which, of its very nature is diffusive of itself.... And if there be also John to share the vision, Peter cannot fail to rejoice, because the superabundance of the divine good is his joy. And if the share of John be greater than his own, Peter will again rejoice, for the prime measure of their happiness is neither Peter nor John but the immeasurable liberality of the divine good.[39]

In this passage, De Koninck focuses on how the commonness of the common good forms the lived experience of personal subjectivity as an experience of participation. He does not simply state that in the objective order the beatific vision is a participation in the ultimate common good. He goes on to describe the impact of this participation on the consciously lived experience of the person. In particular, he focuses on the main source of joy in reaching a common good. It is a joy motivated not by the narrow limits of the individual person's capacity to reach God but by the superabundant and incommensurable liberality of God in giving himself as the common good of all.

Wojtyła concludes his argument by bringing out the universal preeminence of the common good in comparison with the private or individual good of the person. Persons *serve* the common good as something that is greater than they are. For this reason, they are ready "to renounce even some individual goods," such as their possessions and even their lives, "sacrificing them for the community" (P&A 660–61, TymAP 282–83). Such a sacrifice, he adds, is not contrary to human nature because it corresponds to participation as a property of the person and allows the person to fulfill himself or herself.

> In this way, the superiority of the common good, its preeminence over private or individual goods, does not stem only from the quantitative aspect of the society.... It is not the number nor the generality in the numerical sense that characterizes the specific character of the common good but its fundamental character (*gruntowność*). (P&A 660–61, TymAP 283)

The key term in this text, the Polish *gruntowność*, is translated differently in the Italian, English, and German editions. The Italian renders it as *fondatezza*, or "foundedness, solidity." Potocki's original English translation has *intrinsicalness* (TymAP 340), which could be read as asserting that the common good

39. De Koninck, "The Primacy of the Common Good," 305–6.

is profoundly intrinsic in the communities founded on it. Tymieniecka changes *intrinsicalness* to the more easily intelligible "intrinsic character" (TymAP 238), which leaves the question unanswered what that intrinsic character is. The German chooses *Fundamentalität*,[40] corresponding grammatically most closely to *gruntowność*.

Wojtyła himself does not explain what he means by *gruntowność*, but the passage immediately preceding his use of this term provides a clue that supports the German translation. In this passage, he speaks about the family, the nation, the church, and the state as "founded (*ugruntowanych*) on the common good." One should probably read *gruntowność* in light of this thesis. The common good is the foundation of these communities, a point most directly expressed by "fundamental character." The title of the whole subsection in which our text is found is "The Common Good as the Foundation of Human Community." A key point needs to be added, once again, to avoid the main misunderstanding that destroys the understanding of "common good" for many people. To say that the common good has absolute primacy, that it is the foundation of communities, is not to say that it is the good of these communities as individual groups in their own right, in contrast to the persons who constitute them. The common good is the preeminently personal good. It is common by being the good of persons. It is the foundational good for persons. It has primacy as the good of persons.

If Wojtyła's main goal in the last chapter of *Person and Act* were to give an account of the common good itself, his argument would be all too sketchy. In fact, his goal is to look closely at the lived experience of acts performed together with others to reach a deeper understanding of person and act. He takes the Aristotelian and Thomistic account of the common good for granted as a point of departure and works out its implications for the person's lived experience of personal subjectivity without unfolding a more detailed account of the common good itself.

Authentic and Inauthentic Attitudes

Because his main interest in *Person and Act* is to explore the subjectivity of the person as displayed in the dynamic interrelation between person and act, Wojtyła completes his sketch of participation by examining the *attitudes* connected with it. The concept of *attitude* (*postawa*) is closely related to Scheler's concept of *ethos*. *Ethos* refers to the consciously lived position a person adopts in relation to goods or values. One of the three parts of Wojtyła's book on Vatican II, the

40. Wojtyła, *Person und Tat*, 327.

most important part, discusses the *attitudes* proposed by the Council (see above, part II, chap. 1, sect. 4, in this volume).

Wojtyła considers two apparently opposite attitudes, solidarity and opposition. John Paul's understanding of solidarity and its relation to the common good has already been discussed. Only the main theses need to be sketched here. Solidarity, Wojtyła claims, is the substantial expression of participation. It is, on the one hand, the attitude that leads one not to overstep one's limits but to act within the limits of one's precise role in a community for the sake of the common good. On the other hand, it also implies taking on more than one's role, if the common good requires it.

> In the attitude of solidarity, the reference to the common good must be constantly alive, it must dominate, so that one knows when it is opportune to take on something that goes beyond one's usual share of acting and responsibility. (P&A 664–67, TymAP 285)

The attitude of opposition does not negate solidarity. If it is truly motivated by commitment to the common good, it is even required by solidarity under some circumstances. Opposition, Wojtyła adds, needs to be shaped by the principle of dialogue, which is another expression of solidarity. Solidarity does not push opponents into the position of antagonists or enemies but regards them as co-beneficiaries of the common good (P&A 666–71, TymAP 286–87).

Wojtyła discusses two attitudes that are the corruption of solidarity and opposition, conformism and withdrawal. Conformism is an external assimilation to the community that looks like genuine solidarity. Yet, because it lacks genuine commitment to the common good, it is not true participation but a kind of escape from the community. Outwardly, the conformist is close to the community, but the heart is far from it, owing to being far from the common good.

> Conformism ... creates a situation of indifference in the face of the common good. One can see in it a specific variant of individualism: flight from the community, which threatens the good of the individual, and at the same time the need to hide from the community through an external appearance. (P&A 674–75, TymAP 290)

In a similar way, withdrawal from the community is only in appearance the opposite of conformism. It is simply another way in which a lack of commitment to the common good can express itself (P&A 676–79, TymAP 290–291).

Love of Neighbor

In the final two sections of his account of participation, Wojtyła explores some of the "deeper strata" on which participation ultimately rests; namely, the notion of *neighbor* and the commandment "Love your neighbor as yourself." *Neighbor,* he argues, introduces a system of reference that is prior to that of "member of a community." To regard someone as *neighbor* is "to participate in that person's humanity" (P&A 682–83, TymAP 294). Such participation is the "nucleus of all participation."

Part of what Wojtyła means by "participating in the other's humanity" seems to be what he expresses in his own Aristotelian transformation of Kant's personalistic norm: one must regard other persons as having and pursuing their own ends; one must will the good for their own sake (cf. the first law of the life of persons in *Gaudium et spes* 24). This is what the commandment of love enjoins.

The focus on the individual person in the commandment of love, on each individual person, is not a shift away from the preeminence of community and the common good. In willing the good for a person, one must will above all the common good for that person, because it is the preeminent good of that person; it is better for that person than the private good. For this reason, the commandment of love has a communitarian character.

> It would be erroneous to understand this [fundamental importance of the commandment of love] as a limitation of the communitarian values of human acting and existing. The commandment "you shall love" has an entirely communitarian character; it expresses that which forms the community, but it highlights above all that which renders the community fully human, that which renders participation particularly living. (P&A 686–87, TymAP 296)

Wojtyła concludes chapter 7 with a section on "the commandment of love as the principle of existing and acting together with others." Without love, both person and community are destroyed.

> If a human community allows this system of reference to be damaged, it condemns itself to losing the fullness of participation, it creates an abyss between the person and the community. It is not only an abyss of indifference but an abyss of destruction that may at first threaten the person more than the community but through the person inevitably endangers also the community. Here one can perhaps see more clearly with what power they [i.e., person and community] are united and what truth is contained in the affirmation of man's "social nature."

CHAPTER 6

John Paul and John of the Cross

1. Wojtyła and St. John of the Cross

The encounter with the writings of St. John of the Cross through Jan Tyranowski early in 1940 was a formative event for Wojtyła.[1] The experience of the violent Nazi and Soviet occupation of Poland heightened the impact of the encounter.[2] After invading Poland on September 1, 1939, Hitler attempted to liquidate the Polish intelligentsia. Stalin took similar measures in the eastern part of Poland. Wojtyła had enrolled in the department of Polish literature and linguistics at Kraków's Jagiellonian University.[3] To avoid execution or deportation as an intellectual, he had to break off his studies and find manual labor. He worked first in a quarry and then in a chemical plant, where his coworkers secretly helped him to keep up his studies.[4]

Hitler removed many Polish priests from their parishes to decapitate Pol-

1. Citations in this chapter given in the text as FSJCEng (= *Faith According to St. John of the Cross*, English) and FSJCLat (= the Latin original) refer to Karol Wojtyła, *Faith According to* St. *John of the Cross* (San Francisco: Ignatius, 1981); *La dottrina della fede in S. Giovanni della Croce* [Doctrina de fide apud S. Joannem a Cruce], Latin text with facing Italian translation, ed. Massimo Bettetini (Milan: Bompiani, 2003). Citations of John of the Cross are given by title of the work (abbreviated after the first citation), version (redaction A or B), and paragraph number according to St. John of the Cross, *The Collected Works*, ed. Kieran Kavanaugh, OCD (Washington, DC: ICS Publications, 2017).

2. See the evidence compiled in the section on "The Challenge of Totalitarianism," in Joseph P. Rice, "Karol Wojtyła on Acting 'Together with Others'" (PhD diss., Catholic University of America, 2007), 28–36.

3. See Adam Boniecki, *The Making of the Pope of the Millennium: Kalendarium of the Life of Karol Wojtyła*, trans. Irena and Thaddeus Mirecki, ed. Kazimierz Chwalek (Stockbridge, MA: Marian Press), 55–62.

4. See George Weigel, *Witness to Hope: The Biography of Pope John Paul II* (New York: HarperCollins, 1999), 57.

ish resistance: "3,646 Polish priests were imprisoned in concentration camps, of whom 2,647 were killed."[5] Lay ministry became a necessity. Early in 1940, Wojtyła came under the pastoral care of Jan Tyranowski, who introduced him to John of the Cross's writings.[6]

> Before entering the seminary [in 1942], I met a layman named Jan Tyranowski, who was a true mystic. This man, whom I consider a saint, introduced me to the great Spanish mystics and in particular to Saint John of the Cross. Even before entering the underground seminary, I read the works of that mystic, especially his poetry. To read it in the original, I studied Spanish. That was a very important stage in my life.[7]

After entering the seminary, Wojtyła continued his studies of the *Doctor Mysticus*. In addition to studying the obligatory Greek and Hebrew, he threw himself into improving his Spanish.

> Karol Wojtyła would not leave the lecture hall and would use every free moment for studying Spanish. He wanted to read St. John of the Cross in the original language. He mastered this language quite quickly, because not long after, the assistant of the Spanish language class asked him for help in translating a Spanish text that was supposed to be read on the Polish radio news a few hours hence.[8]

In 1946, toward the end of his studies in Kraków, Wojtyła wrote a master's thesis, "The Concept of the Means of Uniting the Soul with God in the Teaching of St. John of the Cross," and presented it in a seminar at the Jagiellonian University.[9] From 1946 to 1948, he was enrolled in the *biennium ad doctoratum* at the Angelicum in Rome and wrote a doctoral thesis, "The Teaching of Faith in St. John of the Cross," directed by Réginald Garrigou-Lagrange.[10] The dissertation, written in Latin, quotes John of the Cross's text in Spanish.[11] It was approved by the two readers Garrigou-Lagrange and Philippe, and graded 9 out

5. Weigel, *Witness to Hope*, 52.

6. See Boniecki, *Kalendarium*, 65. He also introduced him to the writings of Louis de Montfort; see Weigel, *Witness to Hope*, 58–62; George Huntston Williams, *The Mind of John Paul II: Origins of His Thought and Action* (New York: Seabury Press, 1981), 77–81.

7. Pope John Paul II, *Crossing the Threshold of Hope*, ed. Vittorio Messori (New York: A. A. Knopf, 1994), 142. See also Pope John Paul II, *Gift and Mystery: On the Fiftieth Anniversary of My Priestly Ordination* (New York: Doubleday, 1996), 23–25.

8. Boniecki, *Kalendarium*, 99.

9. See Boniecki, *Kalendarium*, 106–8, 120.

10. Raimondo Sorgia, "Approcio con l'«opera prima» di K. Wojtlyla," *Angelicum* 57 (1980); Williams, *Mind of John Paul II*, 103–9.

11. According to Huerga, Wojtyła's understanding of the nuances of the Spanish original is excellent. Alvaro Huerga, "Karol Wojtyła, comentador de John of the Cross de la Cruz," *Angelicum* 56 (1979): 252.

of 10 for the written work and 50 out of 50 for the oral defense.[12] Looking back in 1982 at more than forty years of familiarity with John of the Cross, St. John Paul writes about his spiritual master,

> To him I owe so much in my spiritual formation. I came to know him in my youth and I entered into an intimate dialogue with this master of faith, with his language and his thought, culminating in the writing of my doctoral dissertation on "Faith in John of the Cross." Ever since then I have found in him a friend and master who has shown me the light that shines in the darkness for walking always toward God.[13]

John Paul's judgment in this text confirms what the biographical data already suggest; namely, that John of the Cross's writings had a major impact on him at the very beginning of his intellectual and spiritual formation. This impact was continued, sustained, and deepened in the seven years of studies, culminating in the doctoral thesis on the *Doctor Mysticus*. It continued as a friendship and discipleship ("I have found in him a friend and master") throughout John Paul's life. How should one understand the phrase "friend and master"? A friend is one with whom one lives a common life; a master is one from whom one continues to learn. How exactly these two forms of relation were lived out is a mystery of John Paul's interior life.

At the core of John of the Cross's vision of human life stands self-surrender to God, leading to union. Weigel points out the constitutive importance of such self-surrender for Wojtyła.

> It was an approach to the human condition as radically opposed to the Nazi will-to-power as could be imagined. Under the tutelage of the unexpected apostle, Jan Tyranowski, and amid the madness of the Occupation, the imitation of Christ through the complete handing over of every worldly security to the merciful will of God seized Karol Wojtyła's imagination. Over time, it would become the defining characteristic of his own discipleship.[14]

John of the Cross develops the image of bride and bridegroom as the central image for understanding Christian life as a complete self-surrender to God in a union of love. The main concept by which he grasps this image theologically is the *gift of self*, that is, receiving and possessing the gift of other persons and being received and possessed through one's gift in turn. The spousal hermeneutics of the gift, which is the theological method of TOB, has its roots here, in this teaching of the *Doctor Mysticus*.

12. See Boniecki, *Kalendarium*, 116.
13. John Paul II, Homily at Segovia, November 4, 1982, 2.
14. Weigel, *Witness to Hope*, 61–62.

Hitler treated Poles like grains of sand, isolating each person in insignificance without dignity and massing them together in great heaps to shovel them here or there according to grand destructive designs. Wojtyła observed an opposite experience of the person in John of the Cross. On the individual level, persons possess a vast personal interiority, capable of the infinite, of union with God. They have great dignity, supremely because each is uniquely willed by God deeply from within, for their good, an infinite good. On the social level, persons are destined for an unrepeatable relation of spousal union with God, a total mutual gift of self, which takes place in organically differentiated membership in the Church as the bride of Christ. The pattern of this communion lies in the Trinity.

These two principles, personal and social—unique personal subjectivity and the communion of persons rooted in the Trinity—were to become the two pillars of Wojtyła's theological vision. He saw them encapsulated in the two principles of *Gaudium et spes* 24. To see the close relation between John Paul and John of the Cross, it is helpful to begin with these two principles

2. Personalistic Norm

Pascal Ide has shown that St. John Paul came to give a key place in his theology to *Gaudium et spes* 24. He uses this text to work out a comprehensive theology of gift rooted in the Trinity.[15] Let us begin with this point of arrival of Wojtyła's development. When one knows the point of arrival, it is easier to understand the road that leads to it.

Gaudium et spes 24 focuses on a likeness between the union of person in the Trinity and the union of human beings. This likeness, the text argues, shows the universal validity of the law of the gift. Immediately before concluding with the law of the gift, the text focuses on a more elementary principle, God wills the good of each person.

> Indeed, the Lord Jesus,
>   when he prays to the Father,
>   "that all may be one ... as we are one" (John 17:21–22),
>   offering vistas closed to human reason,
> indicates a certain likeness between the union of the divine Persons
>   and the union of God's sons in Truth and Love.
> This likeness shows that man,

15. See Pascal Ide, "Une théologie du don: Les occurrences de *Gaudium et spes*, n. 24, §3 chez Jean-Paul II," *Anthropotes* 17 (2001): 149–78, 313–44.

> who is the only creature on earth God willed for itself,
> cannot fully find himself except through a sincere gift of self (cf. Luke 17:33).

The two principles expressed at the end of this text provide an integral vision of human life, beginning, middle, and end. The first, "God wills man for himself," is equivalent to what Wojtyła calls "the personalistic norm."[16] Persons should not be used as mere means but as having their ends. This norm stands at the beginning of the life of persons. It arises from rational nature, by which persons are persons in the first place. Persons can know and pursue the good. Only for them, therefore, can one truly will the good for their sake. Every person possesses this dignity from the very beginning of existence. It does not need to be acquired. The second principle, "cannot fully find himself except through a sincere gift of self," concerns the end of the life of human beings. It is a matter of "fully finding," of perfection. Perfection is reached only at the end.

Aristotle touches on the personalistic norm in his discussion of friendship.

> Of the love of [beings] without soul we do not use the word "friendship," for it is not mutual love (ἀντιφίλησις), nor is there a wishing of good to the other. It would surely be funny to wish wine well; if one wishes anything for it, it is that it may keep, so that one may have it oneself. For a friend, however, we say we ought to wish what is good for his sake (δεῖν βούλεσθαι τἀγαθὰ ἐκείνου ἕνεκα).[17]

It is with such a love of friendship, St. Thomas writes, that God provides for creatures endowed with reason and will. The following passage stands behind the formulation "willed for itself" in *Gaudium et spes.*

> Divine providence provides for intellectual creatures for their own sake but for other creatures for the sake of these.... Only the intellectual nature is, therefore, sought for itself in the universe (sola igitur intellectualis natura est propter se quaesita in universo) but all other things for its sake (propter ipsam).[18]

Crosby comments on this text,

> The modern reader sees to his amazement that Thomas here has already made his own the Kantian idea that each person in a sense exists for his own sake (is an end in himself).[19]

16. See Karol Wojtyła, *Love and Responsibility,* trans. Grzegorz Ignatik (Boston: Pauline, 2013), 24–28.

17. Aristotle, *Nicomachean Ethics* 8.2.1155b.27–31.

18. Thomas, *Contra gentiles* III, cap. 112, par. 2–3.

19. John F. Crosby, *The Selfhood of the Person* (Washington, DC: Catholic University of America Press, 1996), 20n8.

If one interprets Crosby's phrase "for his own sake" and "end in himself" in the sense of the beneficiary of the good, it is an accurate reading of Thomas. All good, according to Thomas, exists for the sake of persons. In Kant, by contrast, the person is "that for the sake of which" and *end*, not only in the sense of being the beneficiary of the good but also of being the supreme good. For Kant, the personalistic norm is an alternate way of formulating the first principle of ethics, the categorical imperative.

> While man is unholy enough, the humanity in his person must be holy to him. In all of creation, everything one might want, and over which one has power can be used as a mere means. Only man himself and with him every rational creature is end in itself. For, in virtue of the autonomy of his freedom, he is the subject of the moral law, which is holy.[20]
>
> The practical imperative is thus the following. Act in such a way that at all times you treat human nature in your own person as well as in the person of every other human being simultaneously as a purpose, never as a mere means.[21]

The categorical imperative says, "Act in such a way that at any time the maxim of your will can at the same time be valid as a principle of a universal legislation."[22] By acting according to this categorical imperative, Kant holds, one grasps one's own dignity as an autonomous person. Autonomy consists in moving oneself in the most radical sense of *oneself*; namely, as the universal lawgiver for oneself and for all other rational beings. One must consider the dignity of this autonomy the only absolute value, the only final end of the entire cosmos. It immediately follows that one must affirm the same dignity in others as well. One can only be consistent with oneself in affirming one's own dignity on the condition that one grants the same dignity to other persons.

For, so runs Kant's argument, suppose one did not grant this dignity to others but only to oneself. One's maxim—that is, the practical universal principle valid for oneself—would in this case be, I shall affirm only my own dignity but not that of others. Now, apply the categorical imperative by which this maxim is raised to the status of a universal law. The result is: everyone shall affirm only his or her own dignity but not that of others. This universal law is self-contradictory. When others follow it, they will not treat me as an end in myself, while I do treat myself as an end in myself.

This argument is in Kant's mind not an argument from utility. An argument

20. Kant, *Critique of Practical Reason* AK 5.87; cf. 5.131. See also *The Metaphysics of Morals* AK 6.434.

21. Kant, *Groundwork for the Metaphysics of Morals* AK 4.429.

22. Kant, *Critique of Practical Reason* AK 5:30.

from utility might run as follows. If I grant the dignity of others, others will repay me by granting mine. Therefore it is useful for me to grant them their dignity. No, the main issue for Kant is autonomy, which requires the rational self-consistency of my universal legislative will. I can only be and remain autonomous if I do not contradict my own will. And the only way not to contradict my own will is to legislate to other persons that they need to treat me as I treat myself; namely, as having the dignity of autonomy. This is why I must treat others as being an end.

In its actual application, Kant's categorical imperative works much like the Golden Rule in the teaching of Jesus. "Do to others as you would have them do to you" (Luke 6:31). "In everything do to others as you would have them do to you; for this is the law and the prophets" (Matthew 7:12). Yet this similarity goes hand in hand with a profound opposition between Kant and the Gospel. The opposition becomes apparent when one examines Wojtyła's explanation of the personalistic norm. Wojtyła sees the norm as rooted in the rational nature of the person that enables persons to direct their lives consciously and freely to an end.

> For a person should not be merely a means to an end for another person. This is excluded due to the very nature of the person, due to what every person simply is. For the person is a subject that is thinking and capable of self-determination—these are two properties that first of all we discover in the interiority of the person. Accordingly, then, every person is capable by his nature to define his ends himself. When someone else treats a person exclusively as a means to an end, then the person is violated in what belongs to his very essence and at the same time constitutes his natural right.[23]

Noteworthy in this argument is the focus on the rational nature or essence of the person inasmuch as that rational nature allows the person to understand and pursue ends. In Kant, the point is not that the person can *pursue* ends but that the person *is* an ultimate end. The dignity of the person is itself the highest value. It is the one and only true end. Everything in the entire cosmos can and must be subordinated to it. In this respect, the personalistic norm as Kant understands it is the direct contrary of the same norm as Wojtyła understands it.

> Immanuel Kant formulated this elementary principle of the moral order in the following imperative: "Act in such a way that the person is never a mere means of your action but always an end." In light of the previous reflections, this principle should not so much be formulated in the wording Kant gave to it but rather as follows: "Whenever the person is an object of action in your conduct, remember that you may not treat him merely as a means to an end, as

23. Wojtyła, *Love and Responsibility*, 9–10.

a tool, but [you must] take into account that the person himself has or at least should have his end." The principle thus formulated stands at the basis of every properly comprehended freedom of man, especially freedom of conscience.[24]

Wojtyła's understanding of the personalistic norm is radically different from Kant's. Being an end differs from having an end; being the highest good differs from receiving the highest good; being God differs from receiving a share in God. One is compatible with being a creature, the other is not.

One of the most important and far-reaching disagreements between Kant and Wojtyła lies here. It is connected with the question of the common good. According to John Paul, the created person's highest dignity consists in being able to share in the goodness of God, supremely in the beatific vision. In this participation, the created person becomes "a sharer in the divine nature" (2 Peter 1:4). Sharing and participation in the final end are separated by an infinite gulf from *being* the final end. On occasion, John Paul uses more directly Kantian language in speaking of the person as being an end. The context of the following passage makes clear that *end* refers to the beneficiary of the good. The person is an end in the sense of being the one for the sake of whom the good is loved, not in the sense of being the supreme good.

> The person can never be considered a means [Latin: "instrument"] to an end; above all never a means [Latin: "thing"] of "pleasure." The person is and must be nothing other than the end of every act. Only then does the action correspond to the true dignity of the person.[25]

To see the power of the personalistic norm in establishing an integral vision of the human person and an adequate anthropology in which the whole truth about the person comes to light, one must see its close relation to the commandment of love. The personalistic norm has a negative and a positive component. It forbids the use of other persons as means, pure and simple, and commands treating them as having certain ends.

> As a principle formulated negatively, this norm states that the person is a kind of good that is incompatible with using, which may not be treated as an object of use and, in this sense, as a means to an end. Hand in hand with this goes the positive formulation of the personalistic norm: the person is a kind of good to which only love constitutes the proper and fully-mature relation.[26]

24. Wojtyła, *Love and Responsibility*, 11.

25. John Paul II, *Letter to Families*, 12. The contrast in the Latin text is *instrument-end* and *thing-end* rather than *means-end*, though means-end can be properly understood as well.

26. Wojtyła, *Love and Responsibility*, 25.

In its positive component, the norm is thus close to the commandment of love as formulated in Leviticus and in the teaching of Jesus. "You shall love your neighbor as yourself" (Leviticus 19:18; Matthew 19:19 and parallels). Kant's understanding of the personalistic norm does not imply the commandment of love, because the one and only basis of his norm is autonomy, that is, the absolute dignity of one's own moral self. One's neighbor does not come into view as a person to be loved but as a circumstance for the affirmation of humanity, that is, of the affirmation of my autonomy and my recognition of the autonomy of others.

"Your word is a lamp to my feet and a light to my path" (Psalms 119:105). These words in praise of the law apply especially to the commandment of love. This is the law and the prophets (Matthew 7:12).

> The commandments, You shall not commit adultery; You shall not murder; You shall not steal; You shall not covet; and any other commandment, are summed up in this word, Love your neighbor as yourself. Love does no wrong to a neighbor; therefore, love is the fulfilling of the law. (Romans 13:9–10)
>
> For the whole law is summed up in a single commandment, You shall love your neighbor as yourself. (Galatians 5:14)
>
> You do well if you really fulfill the royal law according to the scripture, You shall love your neighbor as yourself. (James 2:8)

These texts show the great illuminating power of the commandment of love. The moral life as a whole becomes intelligible through this one commandment. "Love and then do what you want!" *Dilige et quod vis fac.*[27]

The personalistic norm, understood in light of the commandment of love, stands at the very beginning of the life of persons. It is elementary in the sense of flowing directly from what accounts for a person being a person in the first place; namely, rational nature. It accompanies the person, of course, also into the supernatural order and its final fulfillment.

3. Law of the Gift

The second of the two principles affirmed in *Gaudium et spes* 24, that "man ... cannot fully find himself except through a sincere gift of self," has its roots not immediately in human nature but, as the Council clearly affirms, in the revelation of the Trinity through the teaching and life of Jesus. It is a principle that regards not the beginning but the supernatural perfection of life, which is referred

27. Augustine, *In Ioannis epistulam tractatus* 7.8.

to by the phrase "fully finding oneself." Let us return to the full text of *Gaudium et spes* 24 to see how the Council situates the gift of self.

> Indeed, the Lord Jesus, when he prays to the Father, "that all may be one ... as we are one" (John 17:21–22), offering vistas closed to human reason, indicates a certain likeness between the union of the divine Persons and the union of God's sons in Truth and Love. This likeness shows that man, who is the only creature on earth God willed for itself, cannot fully find himself except through a sincere gift of self (cf. Luke 17:33).

According to the text's first sentence, Jesus shows a similarity between the union of divine persons and the union of human persons ("one as we are one"). According to the second sentence, this similarity shows that human persons can only find themselves in a gift of self. The theological argument is clear. The basis is the union of divine persons. Its similarity to human communion shows the truth of the law of the gift. The law of the gift must therefore apply also to the Trinitarian exemplar.

The Council insists clearly on the radical newness of this revelation brought by Jesus. Jesus opens vistas closed to human reason. He opens the unheard-of heart of God's inner life. The nature of this inner life is briefly alluded to in the phrases "as we are one" and "union of divine Persons." An earlier version of *Gaudium et spes* 24 was more explicit.

> Indeed, Catholic doctrine, opening up vistas closed to human reason, teaches that God, though he is one, subsists in three persons, each of which lives in such a way toward the others that it is constituted by that very relation. One can infer that human persons, since they are created in the image of God one and three and are reformed in his image, show in themselves a certain imitation of him. While, then, man is the only creature on earth which God willed for its own sake, he himself is related out of himself toward others in such a way that he cannot find himself except by giving himself.[28]

This earlier version bases itself less immediately on Scripture but more on "Catholic doctrine," according to which the divine persons are subsistent relations and therefore radically and without any remainder *toward* each other. It is this radical relationality that the draft sees imitated by the divine image in the social life of the human person, specifically in the gift of self. The phrase "he himself is related out of himself toward others" connects "giving himself" with the life of the divine persons as subsistent relations toward each other.

28. See Francisco Gil Hellín, "Concilii Vaticani II synopsis," in *Ordinem redigens schemata cum relationibus necnon Patrum orationes atque animadversiones: Gaudium et spes* (Rome: Libreria Editrice Vaticana, 2003), 171.

The final text of *Gaudium et spes* 24 is more scriptural. The essential point remains, though *relation* does not play an architectonic role any longer on the level of concepts. Relation is implicit, of course, in the concept of gift.[29]

On what grounds do we know that "man cannot fully find himself except through a sincere gift of self"? The final text is clear, clearer than the draft. "This similarity shows." It is the similarity between "the union of the divine persons" and "the union of God's sons in truth and charity" that shows the necessity and efficacy of the gift of self in "finding oneself." It may well be that the law of the gift is reflected also in the natural order, as Thomas argues in his Aristotelian account of love, but *Gaudium et spes* 24 does not draw attention to that order as such.

The Trinity as exemplar is concretely mediated by Christ. The Council expresses this point by adding a reference to Luke 17:33, one of the few sayings of Jesus reported by all four Gospels, twice in Matthew and Luke. The formulation of the saying in Matthew is closest to the formulation chosen by *Gaudium et spes*: *will f*ind his life, will find himself.

> Matthew 10:39: The one who finds his life will lose it,
> and the one who loses his life for my sake will find it.
>
> Matthew 16:25: For whoever would save his life will lose it,
> and whoever loses his life for my sake will find it.
>
> Mark 8:35: For whoever wants to save his life will lose it,
> but whoever loses his life for my sake,
> and for the sake of the Gospel, will save it.
>
> Luke 9:24: For whoever wants to save his life will lose it,
> but whoever loses his life for my sake will save it.
>
> Luke 17:33: Whoever seeks to make his life secure (περιποιήσασθαι)[30] will lose it,
> but whoever loses will make it live (ζῳογονήσει αὐτήν).[31]
>
> John 12:25: The one who loves his life loses it,
> and the one who hates his life in this world will keep it for eternal life.

29. For the objections of some of the Council Fathers against the earlier text, and even against the final version, see Friedrich Bechina, *Die Kirche als «Familie Gottes»: Die Stellung dieses theologischen Konzeptes in Zweiten Vatikanischen Konzil und in den Bischofssynoden von 1974 bis 1994 im Hinblick auf eine «Familia-Dei-Ekklesiologie»* (Rome: Pontificia Università Gregoriana, 1998), 221n129. A complementary account of the objections appears in Pierre d'Ornellas, *Liberté, que dis-tu de toi-même: Une lecture des travaux du Concile Vatican II, 25 janvier 1959 - 8 décembre 1965* (Paris: École Cathédrale, Parole et Silence, 1999), 538–42.

30. Greek περιποιήσασθαι is a compound formed from *around* and *make*, for example, "*make* a defensive wall *around* something, keep it safe."

31. Greek ζῳογονέω means "beget, produce a living being." It can also be used in contexts in which it means "keep alive" as opposed to "kill" (e.g., Exodus 1:17–18, Septuagint).

Immediately before this saying in Matthew, Mark, and the first Lucan text, Jesus speaks about discipleship, denying oneself, taking up one's cross, and following after him. The law of losing and finding, which he formulates as a general law of the life of persons, is an explanation of this discipleship and particularly of the Cross. Luke 17:33 is in several respects unique among the formulations. The versions in Matthew, Mark, and Luke qualify *losing* by the phrase "for my sake" or "for my sake and for the sake of the Gospel." John qualifies the root of losing (viz., hating) by the contrast between "this world" and "eternal life." Luke 17:33 lacks these qualifications. It formulates the principle in the most general way. In addition, "keep safe" and "make it live" are strikingly expressive.

The Council links this saying with the prayer of Jesus in John 17. "Holy Father, preserve them in your name, which you have given me, that they may be one as we … that all may be one as you, Father, are in me and I in you, that they too may be in us … that they may be one as we are one, I in them and you in me, that they may be completed into one" (John 17:11, 17:21–22). The two Scripture passages, John and Luke, point to the deepest mysteries of faith, the Trinity and the Cross. By showing us these two mysteries, Scripture "opens up vistas closed to human reason."

This deep Trinitarian and Christological background must be kept in mind when one reads what St. John Paul says about "the gift of self" in TOB. In particular, it must be kept in mind to see the image of God in the union between man and woman. John Paul considers this union primarily in its sacramental and thus supernatural richness, though the perspective of nature not suppressed.

4. Wojtyła on the Two Laws

Together with Jean Danielou, Wojtyła had the responsibility of producing one of the drafts of *Gaudium et spes*.[32] He may well be in some measure responsible for the paragraph containing the two principles of the life of persons. He formulated and joined the two principles already some years before *Gaudium et spes* in *Love and Responsibility*, first delivered as a series of lectures in 1957–59 and published in 1960. One passage is particularly clear because it speaks about two principles that govern the existence of persons, the personalistic norm and the law of the gift.

> The person can give himself to another person, both to a human person and to God, and through this giving a particular shape of love, which we define as spousal love, is formed. This also testifies to a particular dynamic of the

32. See d'Ornellas, *Liberté*, esp. 22, 447–54, 481–83.

> person and particular laws governing his existence and development. Christ expressed this in the sentence that seems to contain a deep paradox: "Whoever wants to save his soul will lose it, and whoever loses his soul for my sake will find it" (Matthew 10:39).
>
> Indeed, the problem of spousal love contains a deep paradox, not only verbal but utterly real. The words of the Gospel indicate the particular reality and contain the truth that is realized in the life of the person. Now, because of his nature, every person is somebody nontransferable, in-communicable. In the order of nature, the person is disposed to perfecting himself, to attaining an ever greater fullness of his being, the being which, after all, is always some concrete "I." We have already stated that this perfecting of oneself comes through love and together with love. The fullest and so to speak the most radical form of love consists precisely in the fact of giving oneself, of making one's nontransferable and incommunicable "I" someone else's possession. The paradox in this case is twofold and proceeds in two directions: first, that one can go out of one's own "I" in this way, and second, that by doing so, this "I" is not in the least destroyed or devalued but, on the contrary, is developed and enriched—of course in the supra-physical sense, in the moral sense. The Gospel emphasizes this vividly and decidedly: "will lose—will find," "to save—to lose." We evidently discover in it not only the personalistic norm itself but also very detailed and bold instructions that develop this norm in various directions. The world of persons possesses its own laws of existence and laws of development.[33]

With full clarity, this text formulates the two principles of the life of persons found in *Gaudium et spes* 24. It formulates them as a comprehensive pair of principles that throw light on human life as a whole. Wojtyła even appeals to the same saying of Jesus to which *Gaudium et spes* 24 also appeals.

The text is helpful for understanding *Gaudium et spes* 24. It shows that the personalistic principle and the principle of the gift do not stand next to each other without any connection. The principle of the gift "amplifies and elaborates" the personalistic principle. The two principles concern one single reality—the life of the person—first in its beginnings and potential in human nature, then in its full realization in the divinized love of those who have been grasped by Christ.

Wojtyła found a parallel pair of principles in Kant that governs the entire architecture of Kant's understanding of sex and marriage (see part II, chap. 2, sect. 7, in this volume).

> The Personalistic Norm:
>
> In all of creation, everything one might want, and over which one has power can be used as a mere means. Only man himself and with him every

33. Wojtyła, *Love and Responsibility*, 79–80.

> rational creature is end in itself. (*Practical Reason*, AK 5:87, cf. 5.131; see also *Metaphysics of Morals*, AK 6:434)
>
> Sexual Union as a Gift of Self
>
> For, the natural use that one sex makes of the sexual organs of the other is enjoyment (*Genuß*), for which a part gives itself to the other (*sich dem anderen hingibt*). In this act, a human being makes himself into a thing (*Sache*), which is contrary to the right of human nature to one's own person.... Now, the acquisition of one bodily member of a human being is at the same time an acquisition of the whole person, because the person is an absolute unity. (*Metaphysics of Morals*, AK 6:278)

Kant's understanding of sexuality and marriage is built on this pair of principles as on two interlocking and complementary ways of grasping the whole: no person can be a means, but in sexual union persons give themselves to be used as means for pleasure. The only way to preserve human dignity in that depersonalizing sexual gift of self is to acquire the other person as a thing in marriage. One regains one's dignity of autonomy despite the loss of dignity in being sexually enjoyed by the other. The pair of principles in Kant is thus quite contrary in meaning to the parallel pair in Wojtyła.

In Wojtyła's understanding of the pair of principles, the gift of self is positive. It does not consist in letting another person use one's sexual qualities for pleasure but in the gift of the person resulting in the communion of persons, expressed through the body in such a way that sexual pleasure becomes itself a constituent of the expression of love. Still, the pair of principles is evidently so similar that there must be some connection. The hypothesis of a direct line of descent from Kant's *Metaphysics of Morals* through Wojtyła's *Love and Responsibility* to *Gaudium et spes* 24 would be too simple. Wojtyła's immersed himself in the theology of the gift of self in St. John of the Cross long before his reading of Kant. The personalistic norm and the law of the gift were known also to other participants in the Council. Still, Kant's sexual ethics may have been an important catalyst for formulating the pair of principles governing the life of persons.

When Wojtyła began to study Kant, having already been formed by John of the Cross, he must have heard an inverse echo, as it were, of the *Doctor Mysticus* in Kant's account of sexuality and marriage, at least on the terminological level of *gift of self*.

5. Interiority

Wojtyła points to the agreement between St. John of the Cross and St. Thomas but also to distinctive features and emphases in the *Doctor Mysticus*. On the level of theological method and doctrine, he finds a radical conformity.

> In composing his works, the Mystical Doctor could rely on a varied theological preparation. First, the study of Scholastic Theology provided the foundation, for he was a student at the University of Salamanca after the great Thomistic revival that began toward the end of the fifteenth century under the leadership of Francisco de Vitoria....
>
> The study of Scholastic Theology made a lasting impression on John of the Cross, as he testifies in the prologue to *The Spiritual Canticle*. Not only did he learn a sound theological method, but even at that time he was laying the foundation for the mystical doctrine that he would later develop from sound theological principles. This supports the statement of Dom Chevallier concerning the radical conformity between the teaching of John of the Cross and that of Thomas Aquinas. (FSJCEng 18–19)

At the end of the dissertation, Wojtyła summarizes his main findings about faith in John of the Cross and then compares them with the teaching on faith and the gifts of the Spirit in Thomas. He concludes, "there is a fundamental similarity of doctrine in both of these Doctors of the Church" (FSJCEng 269).

John of the Cross's understanding of the human person is marked by a deep sense of subjectivity or interiority, by an acute attention to the lived experience of the person. At root, it is the experience of a receptive or filial inner embrace of God's gifts. Among these gifts, the gift of being is the beginning and the gift that consists in the divine persons themselves is the end. This inner reception grows hand in hand with self-possession and self-dominion, which allow the actively generous response in the form of self-gift to God. This aspect is less pervasive in St. Thomas, although there are important discussions of it. Hans Urs von Balthasar shows that John of the Cross gives a Catholic response to Luther, a specifically modern response in which personal subjectivity and interpersonal relations play a pronounced role, as they do in Luther, yet without any polemical edge against the objective content of faith and its elaboration in monastic and Scholastic theology.

> What was challenging and scandalous in the Carmelite response to Luther was the manner in which it integrated the entire Monastic tradition from the Greeks through the Middle Ages into the new Christian radicalism and gave to that tradition a hitherto unknown radicalism by the modern turn toward the personal, the experiential and the psychological.[34]

34. Balthasar, *Herrlichkeit*, 2/2:466; Glory, 3:106.

Wojtyła sees this turn toward the subject as an essential feature of John of the Cross's theology.

> And here, it seems, we touch a constitutive element of his works. They are not simply speculative treatises on mystical Theology; they are a witness to mystical experience....
>
> The writings of John of the Cross are the fruit of experience. It was a vital experience of the supernatural reality that is communicated to the soul, a dynamic experience of participation in the intimate life of the Blessed Trinity, and, finally, an experience of the unifying power of [faith], which serves as a "means of union" with God....
>
> The doctrine we shall study is a testimony of experience. It is expressed in Scholastico-mystical language, using words and concepts well known in Scholastic Theology, but its primary value and significance is as a witness of personal experience. It is there, in fact, that we can discover the living and dynamic reality of the virtue of faith, its activity in the human intellect, its corollaries and the effects on the movement of the soul toward union with God. For that reason, we take the experiential witness of John of the Cross as the material of our investigations. (FSJCEng 21–23)

Wojtyła connects the literary form of John of the Cross's writings with this attention to the lived experience of personal subjectivity. It is not accidental that the *Doctor Mysticus* wrote poetry and that he composed his theological treatises in the form of commentaries on this poetry. The treatises spring from poetic inspiration, while poetic inspiration is a fruit of the intense personal experience of faith, hope, and love (FSJCEng 24).

This attention to Christian experience, Wojtyła points out, is not absent from Thomas. It is present particularly in his discussion of the gifts of the Holy Spirit (FSJCEng 269–72). The difference between Thomas and John of the Cross is a matter of emphasis and the degree of explicit elaboration, not a matter of divergence or disagreement.

Wojtyła finds a particularly clear expression of John of the Cross's sense for the interiority and subjectivity of the person in stanza 3 of the *Living Flame of Love*, in the image of deep caverns of feeling in the person that are obscured and blinded by sin but that become open and filled with fire and light in a faith that is enriched by the gifts of the Holy Spirit.

> O lamps of fire!
> in whose splendors
> the deep caverns of feeling,
> once obscure and blind,
> now give forth, so rarely, so exquisitely,
> both warmth and light to their Beloved.

Wojtyła quotes a passage from John of the Cross's commentary on the phrase "deep caverns of feeling."

> These caverns are the soul's faculties: memory, intellect, and will. They are as deep as the boundless goods of which they are capable since anything less than the infinite fails to fill them. From what they suffer when they are empty, we can gain some knowledge of their enjoyment and delight when they are filled with God, since one contrary sheds light on the other.... It is noteworthy that when these caverns of the faculties are not emptied, purged, and cleansed of every affection for creatures, they do not feel the vast emptiness of their deep capacity. (B 18)

Wojtyła comments:

> What an insight into the spiritual part of human nature! The infinite capacity of the higher faculties of the soul, their capacity for the infinite, is precisely the metaphysical reason and basis why they are the subjects or faculties of the theological virtues, for it is through the theological virtues that the soul is united with the infinite. (FSJCEng 232)

The understanding of the person expressed in "the deep caverns of feeling" is characteristic of John of the Cross throughout. As Wojtyła describes him in his dissertation, the *Doctor Mysticus* is in a preeminent way the teacher of Christian interiority and subjectivity—without any subjectivism. Many theologians in modernity have given a prominent place to personal experience in their theology, often combined with an exaltation of feeling and a polemical subjectivist edge against the objective content of faith. Schleiermacher is a particularly radical and problematic example of this subjectivist tendency.[35] Roman Catholic school catechesis in the post-Vatican II era has at times followed a similar direction. It is thus important to define St. John Paul's specific understanding of Christian subjective experience.

What is this elementary experience, more precisely? In his philosophical work (esp. *Person and Act* and its intended sequel, *Man on the Field of Responsibility*), Wojtyła focuses on the experience of the person in action, on the acting person in the ordinary and natural experience connected with living a human life both as an individual person and in community. Elementary experience is constituted by a nucleus of evidences and desires by which nature and grace propel human beings to meet reality and to act in it.[36] Experience in this natural,

35. See especially Karl Barth, *The Theology of Schleiermacher: Lectures at Göttingen, Winter Semester of 1923/24*, ed. Dietrich Ritschl, trans. Geoffrey W. Bromiley (Grand Rapids, MI: Eerdmans, 1982).

36. See Karol Wojtyła, *L'uomo nel campo della responsabilità* [Man on the field of responsibility] (Milan: Bompiani, 2002]), 57–67; "Akt und Erlebnis," in *Lubliner Vorlesungen*, ed. Juliusz Stroynowski (Stuttgart-Degerloch: Seewald, 1981).

full, and total sense differs from partial and specialized forms of experience such as merely emotional religious experience, which bypasses the objective content of faith, or "Phenomenological experience," which is the seeing (*Schau*) or intuition of Husserl's and Scheler's immediately given phenomena or essences (*Wesen*), adopted by Wojtyła in modified form.[37]

In his theological writings, John Paul focuses on the experience of the person in acting. The starting point of this elementary experience of Christian life is thus faith. Faith is not left behind to be replaced by experience, but faith remains the comprehensive form of Christian experience. This is the point John Paul emphasizes in his Apostolic Letter on John of the Cross as "the central affirmation of the *Doctor Mysticus.*"

> I myself have been especially attracted by the experience and teachings of the Saint of Fontiveros. From the first years of my priestly formation, I found in him a sure guide in the ways of faith. This aspect of his doctrine seemed to me to be of vital importance to every Christian, especially in a trail-blazing age like our own which is also filled with risks and temptations in the sphere of faith....
>
> I wrote my doctoral thesis in Theology on the subject of Faith according to John of the Cross. In it, I devoted special attention to an analytical discussion of the central affirmation of the *Doctor Mysticus:* Faith is the only proximate and proportionate means for communion with God.
>
> Even then I felt that John had not only marshaled solid theological doctrine but that, above all, he had set forth Christian life in terms of such basic aspects as communion with God, the contemplative dimension of prayer, the strength that apostolic mission derives from life in God, and the creative tension of the Christian life lived in hope.[38]

This is the first point to be made about Christian experience as John Paul understands it in agreement with John of the Cross: its origin and measure lie in faith, not the other way around. Faith must be *enriched*; that is, it must become more mature and conscious, able to form the whole of experience.

> Faith, as well as the enrichment of faith, is a supernatural gift of God and is not subject to human planning or causation; but man, and the Church as a human community, can and must cooperate with the grace of faith and contribute to its enrichment. The Council itself acted in this way, and its action,

37. See Karol Wojtyła, "The Problem of the Separation of Experience from the Act in Ethics in the Philosophy of Immanuel Kant and Max Scheler," in *Person and Community: Selected Essays* (New York: P. Lang, 1993).

38. John Paul II, Apostolic Letter *Maestro en la fe* to Felipe Sáinz de Baranda, Superior General of the Discalced Carmelites on the Occasion of the Fourth Centenary of the Death of John of the Cross, December 14, 1990, 2.

> considering the level on which it took place, may be considered a plan of action for the whole Church. (SR 203–4)

The primacy of faith in Christian experience, even in the most exalted forms of experience characteristic of mysticism, is the main point Wojtyła brings out in his dissertation when he historically situates John of the Cross.

> Against false interpretations of communion with God, the *Doctor Mysticus* calmly taught that faith is the proper means of union—faith in accord with all its implications: in complete nakedness, austerity, and obedience of the intellect.... And now the issue becomes immediately clear.
>
> Against long-standing inclinations, the root of which is perhaps still present in the teaching of Averroes and in Arabian mysticism, inclinations that had recently been revived also by a false interpretation of Flemish authors and the Rhineland mystics, whose works were widely read in the Iberian peninsula, against these the most interior manifestation of the Spirit in the life of the Church proposed faith, whose saving power and ability to unite the soul with God is glorified in Sacred Scripture. (FSJCEng 16–17; translation following FSJCLat 46)

The primacy in Christian experience belongs to faith "in complete nakedness, austerity, and obedience of the intellect." Wojtyła clearly rejects the opposite approach in which experience becomes the measure of faith.

> John of the Cross is consistent in his teaching: all these things [visions, locutions and spiritual feelings] must be rejected in favor of the virtue of faith, which operates in the dark night and, by reason of its intimate proportion to divinity, surpasses any experience in which the natural faculties, however much purified, can find fruition and satisfaction. Faith, as we have seen, is the means of true and proper union with God, who by his essence incomparably transcends every created nature; for that reason, faith surpasses even the loftiest mystical experience. (FSJCEng 123)

The superiority of faith over all experiences does not imply that the whole order of human experience is irrelevant. On the contrary, the importance of experience is a necessary implication of faith inasmuch as a living faith deeply transforms human experience and introduces the person to a path of union with God, which is begun by faith and achieved by love.

> The virtue of faith is subordinated to union as means to the end.... (FSJCEng 48)
>
> [John of the Cross teaches] the definitive power and essential characteristic of love—and therefore of the will—in union.... The power and characteristic of love flows from its very nature insofar as it causes likeness and subjects

> the lover to the beloved. Hence if it is a question of union of likeness, love must necessarily be the unifying factor. This explains what the *Doctor Mysticus* explains time and time again: union consists of the total conformation of the human will with the divine will. (FSJCEng 100)

John of the Cross sees faith as a means within human life as a whole, which is directed toward the union of the human person with God through love. Human experience is not excluded from this process. On the contrary, it is to be formed by love. Nevertheless, faith remains the proximate means of union that cannot be supplanted by feeling or some other surrogate.

In his apostolic letter on John of the Cross, John Paul identifies John of the Cross's understanding of Christian experience with the central concern of Vatican II.[39]

> In it [i.e., the dissertation on John of the Cross], I devoted special attention to an analytical discussion of the central affirmation of the *Doctor Mysticus:* Faith is the only proximate and proportionate means for communion with God.
>
> The *Doctor Mysticus* ... through his example and doctrine, helps Christians to make their faith strong with the very basic qualities of an adult faith which the Second Vatican Council asks of us. This faith is to be personal, free and convinced, embraced with one's entire being, an ecclesial faith, confessed and celebrated in communion with the Church, a praying and adoring faith, matured through the experience of communion with God.
>
> The presence of God and of Christ, a renewing purification under the guidance of the Spirit, and the living of an informed and adult faith—is this not in reality the heart of the teaching of John of the Cross and his message for the Church and for men and women of today? ... Only faith enables us to experience the salvific presence of God in Christ in the very center of life and of history. Faith alone reveals to us the meaning of the human condition and our supreme dignity as sons and daughters of God who are called to communion with Him. (*Maestro en la fe* 2 7, and 3)

These passages highlight not only the formal aspect of Christian experience—that it is a living, conscious, and personal faith—but also the content of this experience, "the salvific presence of God in Christ in the very center of life and of history." These words in which John Paul summarizes John of the Cross's teaching strikingly resemble the opening words of his inaugural encyclical *Redemptor hominis* (1979). "The Redeemer of Man, Jesus Christ, is the center of the

39. See Angelo Scola, *L'esperienza elementare: La vena profonda del magistero di Giovanni Paolo II* (Genova: Marietti, 2003), 47.

universe and of history." Later in the same encyclical, John Paul formulates the program of his pontificate in a similar way.

> While the ways on which the Council of this Century has set the Church going, ways indicated by the late Pope Paul VI in his first encyclical, will continue to be for a long time the ways that all of us must follow, we can at the same time rightly ask at this new stage: How, in what manner should we continue? . . .
>
> To this question, dear brothers, sons and daughters, a fundamental and essential response must be given. Our response must be: Our spirit is set in one direction, the only direction for our intellect, will and heart is—towards Christ our Redeemer, towards Christ, the Redeemer of man. We wish to look towards Him—because there is salvation in no one else but Him, the Son of God—repeating what Peter said: "Lord, to whom shall we go? You have the words of eternal life." (*Redemptor hominis* 7)

It is remarkable that the terms in which John Paul summarizes the core of John of the Cross's teaching are the very terms he uses to define the program of his pontificate: John of the Cross places "the salvific presence of God in Christ in the very center of life and of history," which is exactly what the new pontiff does in setting the direction of his pontificate. "The Redeemer of Man, Jesus Christ, is the center of the universe and of history."

In his dissertation, Wojtyła devotes an entire chapter to the personalist understanding of faith in John of the Cross.

> Revealed truths are given to the intellect, but Christ himself is given as the life of Christians. In him is found the revelation of God to human beings, both in himself and as the exemplar that all should imitate and, through love, reproduce in themselves. In this way, and not in eager scrutiny of revealed truths, the manifestation of God is attained and shared by each one. For John of the Cross the revelation of God consists much more in personal witness than in the purely intellectual knowledge of revealed truths. (FSJCEng 174)

This summary of John of the Cross's teaching, which is free of any opposition against dogma and doctrine, is akin to John Paul's words of profound experience, "Our spirit is set in one direction, the only direction for our intellect, will and heart is—towards Christ our Redeemer." The "eager scrutiny of revealed truths" practiced in academic theology has its proper place within this overarching experience.

There is a great danger that John Paul's words about the direction of his entire pontificate pass by unnoticed. One might imagine a headline proposed by a conscientious reporter for an article on *Redemptor hominis*, the new programmatic encyclical of the new pope that sets the new direction of the new pontificate at its very beginning: "Pope Says Christians Should Look towards Christ." Such a headline would be striking by its tautological flatness. What is new? What else would a pious Pope say?

Yet there is no event more dramatic, more form giving for a person's life, than precisely this: an encounter in which one turns one's entire heart toward Christ and grasps oneself as having been grasped by Christ. A new teaching on personal rights and liberty may command public attention because a modern audience is interested in the growth of the Church from medieval obscurantism to enlightened agreement with the dominant contemporary culture's defense of the rights and freedoms of persons.

When one can point to a reversal—for example, a papal declaration that every person has a right to insurance coverage for contraceptives—this would be news indeed. Any such teaching on rights and freedoms, however novel it may be, pales completely in comparison with the deeply dramatic intensity of John Paul's proposal in *Redemptor hominis*. The only direction for our intellect, will, and heart is toward Christ our Redeemer. To speak like this is not a matter of course. It is the heart of John Paul as a theologian and as a pastor trained in the school of John of the Cross.

When he returns to this heart of his teaching a little later in his programmatic encyclical, John Paul speaks in a manner highly characteristic of his personalist understanding of the lived experience of subjectivity in accord with John of the Cross.

> Man cannot live without love. He remains a being that is incomprehensible for himself, his life is senseless, if love is not revealed to him, if he does not encounter love, if he does not experience it and make it his own, if he does not participate intimately in it. This, as has already been said, is why Christ the Redeemer "fully reveals man to himself." . . .
>
> The man who wishes to understand himself thoroughly—and not just in accordance with immediate, partial, often superficial, and even illusory standards and measures of his being—he must with his unrest, uncertainty and even his weakness and sinfulness, with his life and death, draw near to Christ. He must, so to speak, enter into Him with all his own self, he must "appropriate" and assimilate the whole of the reality of the Incarnation and Redemption to find himself. (*Redemptor hominis* 10)

In this text, which combines the essential points of *Gaudium et spes* 22 and 24, there is a remarkable density of words that express the assimilation of faith in the lived experience of personal subjectivity. Persons receive the revelation of God's love; they encounter it, experience it, make it their own, participate intimately in it, enter into it with all of their own self; they appropriate and assimilate it by bringing their unrest, uncertainty, weakness, and sinfulness to Christ to enter into Christ, and only in this way, to find themselves. This emphasis on personal subjectivity in the gift of self to Christ coincides with what John Paul sees in John of the Cross's core teaching. John Paul's understanding of John of the Cross, his understanding of Vatican II, and the program of his own pontificate as set forth in *Redemptor hominis*—all three of these visions are expressions of one and the same vision, a vision that was first formed in Wojtyła by John of the Cross.

In this reception of John of the Cross, John Paul resolutely takes the side of his thesis advisor Réginald Garrigou-Lagrange. Garrigou-Lagrange argues against those who dismiss John of the Cross as a mystic, that is, as a rare and irrelevant example of Christian life concerned with extraordinary and miraculous mystical phenomena that are not part of the life of ordinary believers. He attempts to establish that much of John of the Cross's teaching concerns the normal development of the supernatural life of faith and love under the action of the gifts of the Holy Spirit as described by Thomas.[40] Wojtyła might have come to the same conclusion by his reading of John of the Cross, but it is likely that Garrigou-Lagrange helped significantly to shape the core of John Paul's understanding of the lived experience of personal subjectivity.[41]

The acute sense for the lived experience of the person, which Wojtyła found in John of the Cross and later (in a different way) in Phenomenology, is one of the main features of TOB in continuity with *Humanae vitae*. Already in 1969, in an important text to which Don Asci draws attention, Wojtyła explains how he understands the concept of *meaning* in *Humanae vitae*, a concept that turns up again in TOB's key concept, "the spousal meaning of the body."[42]

40. See Réginald Garrigou-Lagrange, *Christian Perfection and Contemplation According to Thomas Aquinas and John of the Cross* (St. Louis, MO: Herder, 1949); *The Three Ages of the Interior Life: Prelude of Eternal Life*, 2 vols. (Rockford, IL: Tan, 1989).

41. Wojtyła is not the only one who was formed by Garrigou-Lagrange's understanding of the spiritual life. "If his [Garrigou-Lagrange's] form of dogmatic Theology failed to win the day at the Second Vatican Council, we will see that his most passionately held spiritual propositions were incorporated into official Catholic teaching by the Council Fathers." Richard Peddicord, OP, *The Sacred Monster of Thomism: An Introduction to the Life and Legacy of Réginald Garrigou-Lagrange, O.P.* (South Bend, IN: Augustine, 2005), 179. See also the chapter on Garrigou-Lagrange and Wojtyła, 214–20. Unfortunately, Peddicord focuses only on the philosophical points of contact between Wojtyła and Garrigou-Lagrange. A systematic comparison of their doctrines in spiritual theology and especially Trinitarian theology must still be carried out.

42. See Donald Asci, *The Conjugal Act as Personal Act: A Study of the Catholic Concept of the Conjugal Act in the Light of Christian Anthropology* (San Francisco: Ignatius Press, 2002), 96.

> By appealing to the meaning of the conjugal act, the Pope places the whole discussion *not only and not so much* in the context of the nature of the act but also and even more in the context of human awareness, in the context of the awareness that should correspond to this act on the part of both the man and the woman—the persons performing this act. One can detect in this part of the encyclical a very significant passage from what some might call a "Theology of nature" to a "Theology of person."[43]

What does Wojtyła mean by the passage between these two forms of theology? How are the *nature* and the *meaning* of the act related in the second type? "Not only and not so much in the context of the nature of the conjugal act but also and even more in the context of human awareness." The nature of the conjugal act, determined by the specifying good and end of the act, is the basis of the meaning. The nature does not disappear; otherwise, the meaning would disappear. Yet the focus of attention is on the act's nature as consciously lived. It is the conjugal act as consciously experienced that is brought into focus when one speaks of its *meaning*, as Asci explains.

> While the term "goodness" corresponds to human desire and perfection and while the term "end" expresses the human ability to intend goods deliberately, the term "meaning" relates to the subject's ability to experience his deliberate intentions and to experience himself as the subject of such intentions through consciousness. Thus, meaning includes the human capacity for experience in addition to the human capacity for rational activity that is expressed in the notion of an end. In other words, just as "end" includes and expands upon "good," "meaning" includes and expands upon "end" by viewing procreation and union from the perspective of conscious experience.[44]

The emphasis on consciously lived experience is characteristic of TOB throughout. "Our human lived experience is in some way a legitimate means for theological interpretation and ... it is an indispensable point of reference to which we must appeal in the interpretation of the beginning" (TOB 4:4). The importance of lived experience is visible in the key concept of TOB, "the spousal meaning of the body," and in a cluster of surrounding concepts: awareness, consciousness, sensibility, sensitivity, interiority, subjectivity, attitude, motivation, *ethos*, rereading, and so on.[45] The purpose of TOB is not only to teach what is objectively true about the human body and its sexuality but also to help men and women gain an awareness of the spousal meaning of their bodies.

43. Karol Wojtyła, "The Teaching of the Encyclical *Humanae vitae* on Love: An Analysis of the Text," in *Person and Community: Selected Essays* (New York: P. Lang, 1993), 308; emphasis in the first sentence added.

44. Asci, *Conjugal Act*, 240.

45. See the index in TOB for texts with these terms.

> So many human beings and so many Christians search in marriage for the fulfillment of their vocation. So many want to find in it the way of salvation and holiness. For them, the answer Christ gave to the Pharisees, who were filled with zeal for the Old Testament, is particularly important. Those who seek the fulfillment of their own human and Christian vocation in marriage are called first of all to make of this "theology of the body," whose "beginning" we find in the first chapters of Genesis, the content of their lives and behavior. In fact, on the road of this vocation, how indispensable is a deepened consciousness of the meaning of the body in its masculinity and femininity! How necessary is an accurate consciousness of the spousal meaning of the body, of its generative meaning, given that all that forms the content of the life of the spouses must always find its full and personal dimension in shared life, in behavior, in feelings! And this all the more against the background of a civilization that remains under the pressure of a materialistic and utilitarian way of thinking and evaluating. (TOB 23:5)

In agreement with Thomas and John of the Cross, John Paul sees the opening of "the deep caverns of feeling" in spousal life especially in the gifts of the Holy Spirit. Among these gifts, the gift of reverence (*pietas*) is particularly important.

> Piety as a gift of the Holy Spirit seems to serve purity in a particular way by making the human subject sensitive to the dignity that belongs to the human body in virtue of the mystery of creation and of redemption. Thanks to the gift of piety, Paul's words, "Or do you not know that your body is a temple of the Holy Spirit within you ... and that you do not belong to yourselves?" (1 Corinthians 6:19) take on the convincing power of an experience and become a living and lived truth in actions. (TOB 57:2)

According to this text, the objective truth that the body is a temple of the Holy Spirit enters the sphere of experience through the gift of reverence or piety. The objective truth of the Spirit dwelling in its temple does not disappear. On the contrary, the focus of attention on this truth as consciously lived gives greater weight to the objective indwelling. It is in being consciously lived that this objective indwelling has the persuasive power of an experience.

The effectiveness of TOB lies in large measure in John Paul's penetrating attention to experience in conformity with his roots in John of the Cross. Just as the emphasis on experience played a key role in the renewal of religious life by John of the Cross and Teresa of Avila, so a similar emphasis plays a key role in the renewal of the Church proposed by Vatican II and in the renewal of marriage and family life proposed by John Paul.

6. Gift of Self

While the argument for Wojtyła's dependence on St. John of the Cross in the area of Christian experience and personal interiority rests on extensive and explicit texts in Wojtyła's dissertation, the argument in the area of the gift of self, spousal love, and Trinitarian exemplar has a much smaller textual basis. Had Wojtyła written a dissertation about love rather than faith in John of the Cross, the situation would be different. At several points in the dissertation, when he touches on spousal love and its Trinitarian roots, he draws back. "The manner in which all of this [i.e., the union of love and the mutual gift and possession of lover and beloved] is realized is something that lies outside the scope of our study" (FSJCEng 213). After quoting the most important passages on Trinitarian gift of self and its reflection in the spousal love between God and the soul, he writes,

> These are the peaks whose foundations are firmly established in the doctrine of the *Doctor Mysticus* on participation and the motion of the Holy Spirit. We shall not attempt to explain them here, but we merely mention them to show what is meant by "most enlightened faith." (FSJCEng 231)

About a decade passed between Wojtyła's dissertation and the emergence of the second column of his thought in his published works. St. John of the Cross's characteristic way of speaking about spousal love as a gift of self is not clearly visible in Wojtyła's first published essay about sexuality and marriage (1952).[46] In the foreground of that essay, one finds Scheler's idea of the "rehabilitation of virtue" applied to the virtue of purity. Wojtyła also mentions Scheler's discussion of sexual shame and Scheler's teaching that sexual intercourse implies in a radical sense a *belonging* of man and woman to each other, an idea already developed powerfully by Kant. It is only in the last two pages of this early essay that the notion of *gift* becomes explicit. It fully emerges in Wojtyła's works twelve years after his 1948 dissertation, in *The Jeweler's Shop* and *Love and Responsibility*, both first published in 1960. Wojtyła's Trinitarian theology appears another twelve years later in his book on Vatican II, *Sources of Renewal* (1972). Twenty-four years passed between his dissertation and *Sources of Renewal*, a long period of gestation.

One might suppose, for this reason, that the stimulus for John Paul's mature Trinitarian theology came mainly from Vatican II and from his later study of SS. Augustine and Thomas, rather than from St. John of the Cross. Yet Wojtyła's long silence about the Trinity can be explained by the philosophical focus of

46. Karol Wojtyła, "Instinkt, Liebe und Ehe" [Instinct, love and marriage], in *Erziehung zur Liebe: Mit einer ethischen Fibel* (Stuttgart-Degerloch: Seewald, 1980).

the works he published during these twenty-four years. Even his habilitation thesis about Scheler, which is a theological work with a point of departure in the imitation of Christ, does not offer a broad view of Wojtyła's theology because it focuses on the question whether Scheler's philosophy is a suitable foundation for moral theology. *Sources of Renewal* is Wojtyła's first fully theological work after his dissertation.

John of the Cross's characteristic way of speaking about the Trinity by the analogy of mutual love with emphasis on gift and mutual belonging is not a prominent characteristic of Vatican II. It is implicit but not developed in *Gaudium et spes* 24. John Paul's Trinitarian theology, by contrast, carries this hallmark of John of the Cross.

The similarities between John of the Cross and John Paul in spousal and Trinitarian theology are so substantial and distinctive, and the relevant data of Wojtyła's biography so suggestive, that it is difficult to avoid the conclusion that the roots of TOB lie in these aspects of John of the Cross's works. John Paul's words about the forty years of familiarity with the *Doctor Mysticus* should be recalled. "Ever since then [i.e., the early 1920s] I have found in him a friend and master who has shown me the light that shines in the darkness for walking always toward God."[47] What is striking in this text, as mentioned above, is not only the word *master* but also the word *friend*. *Friendship* refers to a shared life with someone experienced as present.

The main textual basis in the area of spousal and Trinitarian theology is, once again, the third stanza of *Living Flame of Love*. We should reexamine it from the point of view of Trinitarian theology.

> O lamps of fire! in whose splendors
> the deep caverns of feeling,
> once obscure and blind,
> now give forth, so rarely, so exquisitely,
> both warmth and light to their Beloved.

In his commentary on the last two lines, John of the Cross writes,

> Since God gives himself with a free and gracious will (*Dios se le está dando con libre y graciosa voluntad*), so too the soul (possessing a will more generous and freer the more it is united with God) *gives to God, God himself in God*; and this is a true and complete gift of the soul to God.
>
> It is conscious there that God is indeed its own and that it possesses him by inheritance, with the right of ownership, as his adopted child *through the grace of his gift of himself* (*por la gracia que Dios le hizo de dársele a sí mismo*).

47. John Paul II, Homily at Segovia, November 4, 1982, 2.

> Having him for its own, it can give him and communicate him to whomever it wishes. Thus, it gives him to its Beloved, who is the very God who gave himself to it. By this donation it repays God for all it owes him, since it willingly gives as much as it receives from him.
>
> Because the soul in this gift to God *offers him the Holy Spirit*, with voluntary surrender, as something of its own (*so that God loves himself in the Holy Spirit as he deserves*), it enjoys inestimable delight and fruition, seeing that it gives God something of its own that is *suited to him according to his infinite being*. It is true that the soul cannot give God again to himself, since in himself he is ever himself. Nevertheless, it does this truly and perfectly, giving all that was given it by him to repay love, which is to give as much as is given. And God, who could not be considered paid with anything less, is considered paid with that gift of the soul; and he accepts it gratefully as something it gives him of its own. In this very gift he loves it anew; and in this re-surrender of God to the soul, the soul also loves as though again.
>
> A reciprocal love between God and the soul is thus actually formed, *in conformity with the marriage union and surrender* (*en conformidad de la unión y entrega matrimonial*), in which the goods of both (the divine essence that each possesses freely by reason of the voluntary surrender between them) are possessed by both together. *They say to each other what the Son of God spoke to the Father through John* (17:10): *All that is mine is yours and yours is mine.* (B 72–80; emphasis added)

The theological heart of this passage lies in the text from the Gospel of John quoted at the very end, *All that is mine is yours and yours is mine* (John 17:10). In God, there is an eternal relation of complete mutual belonging of distinct persons, *totus tuus*. Other passages in the Gospel of John show that this mutual belonging goes back to the Father's eternal gift of the whole fullness of the divine Life to the Son. "As the Father has Life in himself, so he has given also to the Son to have Life in himself" (John 5:26). Despite the great distance between these two realities, John of the Cross sees a certain likeness or conformity (*conformidad*) between the divine mutual gift and "the marriage union and surrender" in which husband and wife also say, "I am yours and you are mine." The soul's union with God lies between these two unions. It is symbolized by the marriage union and it shares in the union of love between Father and Son by the Holy Spirit.

The indwelling of the Holy Spirit in person allows the soul to respond to God's self-gift with the same radical gift of love. The soul's happiness lies not only in attaining God as the end but also in repaying his love with love, his gift of self with a return of the gift, the gift of the Spirit in person returned to God.

The emphasis of this thesis seems distinctive of John of the Cross in comparison with St. Thomas. When Thomas speaks about the ultimate end of union with God, he usually focuses on the vision of God, on resting in an infinite good. In most texts, he does not focus on the creature's gift of self to God as an essential aspect of happiness.

The creature's gift in answer to God's gift of self to it, this is what it means for the deep caverns of feeling in the soul to give forth warmth and light to their beloved. This, precisely this, is the theological world in which TOB was born.

In his dissertation, Wojtyła quotes key sections of the text quoted above but does not discuss them in detail (FSJCEng 89n89, 227–33, FSJCLat 421–30). His most important comment highlights the Trinitarian aspect of the transforming union between the soul and God.

> This concept of the relationship between God and the soul, at once filial and conjugal, is based on two constant elements: the adoptive communication of grace and the power of love. The soul becomes "God by participation" and therefore by participation it possesses divinity itself and the will gives to the Beloved through love nothing less than that which it had received from him: the gift of participated divinity. Hence the soul gives God to himself and through himself because the motion of the Holy Spirit is continuously transformed.[48]
>
> Nevertheless, the one who gives is in fact the soul, which loves God in return to a supreme degree. Since its will is perfectly united with the divine will, it cannot carry out any other works than those that adhere to the divine will. Consequently, due to the perfection of the transforming union, the soul's will is entirely occupied in the same objectives of the divine will, namely, loving God and giving to him in love that which it has from him by participation—divinity itself, not only through the lover's will but as God loves, by the movement of the Holy Spirit.
>
> With this, we reach the "Trinitarian" mystical teaching that was already mentioned in the Spiritual Canticle. (FSJCEng 230, FSJCLat 424, 426)

What Wojtyła chooses to emphasize in these comments is the intersection in John of the Cross's teaching between the Trinitarian (filial) and the conjugal features of the relationship between God and the soul, both of which are rooted in the soul's divinization, in virtue of which it can give to God a gift that truly corresponds to his divine perfection. He also emphasizes the complete conformity of will that is brought about by the transforming union, so that the soul can love God as God loves; namely, by the movement of the Holy Spirit. He does not draw attention to the concept a reader of TOB would expect him to fasten on; namely, God's gift of self and the closely related theme of spousal self-giving.

48. The Latin *motio* is in the nominative. Perhaps Wojtyła intended the ablative *motione*. With the ablative, the text should be translated, "because by the motion of the Holy Spirit it [i.e., the soul] is continually transformed."

"Self-giving" lies just below the surface of what he does say, but he does not explicitly draw it out.

The text from the Spiritual Canticle that Wojtyła uses to document John of the Cross's Trinitarian teaching is a passage from the commentary on stanzas 38 and 39:

> There you will show me
> what my soul has been seeking,
> and then you will give me,
> you, my life, will give me there
> what you gave me on that other day:
> the breathing of the air,
> the song of the sweet nightingale,
> the grove and its living beauty
> in the serene night,
> with a flame that is consuming
> and painless.

The text Wojtyła quotes is taken from John of the Cross's comments on the first line of stanza 39, "the breathing of the air."

> This breathing of the air is an ability that the soul states God will give her there in the communication of the Holy Spirit. By his divine breath-like spiration, the Holy Spirit elevates the soul sublimely and informs her and makes her capable of breathing in God the same spiration of love that the Father breathes in the Son and the Son in the Father. This spiration of love is the Holy Spirit himself, who in the Father and the Son breathes out to her in this transformation to unite her to himself.[49]

To the reader's disappointment, Wojtyła does not comment on this text but withdraws with the remark that he quotes it merely to illustrate John of the Cross's teaching about truly enlightened faith.

Sample Texts on the Gift of Self

The phrase *give oneself* plays a prominent and architectonic role in John of the Cross. It neither was nor is entirely new in John of the Cross or unique to him. St. Augustine develops it most forcefully and its echoes can be heard in Luther, in Nietzsche, and even in novels, such as Stevenson's *David Balfour.*

49. John of the Cross, *Collected Works*, 622–23.

Augustine (354–430):

God wants to be worshiped for free and loved for free, that is, to be loved *chastely*, to be loved not because he gives something other than himself but *because he gives himself*.[50]

If I said, "God has promised gold!" you would be delighted. He promised himself, and you are sad? If a rich man does not have God, what does he have? Don't seek anything from God except God. Love him without payment. Ask him for him himself. Don't be afraid of poverty. *Let him give himself to us* and let this be enough for us.[51]

He who buys something, at whatever price he may have found it, must acquire it in such a way that *he gives what he has and receives what he does not have*. He from whom the payment departs remains, and that for which he gives the payment comes near. Now, the one who wants to buy this Word, who wants to have it, let him not look outside himself for what he should give in payment. *Let him give himself*. When he does this, he does not lose himself, as he loses a payment when he buys something. ... Therefore, let the one who wants to buy *give himself*. This is the price of the Word, if one may say so in some way, although he who gives does not lose himself but acquires the Word, *for whom he gives himself*, and acquires himself in the Word, *to whom he gives himself*.[52]

Bernard of Clairvaux (1090–1153):

In the first work *he gave me myself*; in the second *himself*. And where *he gave himself*, he *gave me back to myself*. As one given and given back, I owe myself for myself, and owe myself twice. What shall I render to God for himself? Even if I could *give myself* back to him a thousand times, what am I to God?[53]

Thomas Aquinas (1225–74):

Love is twofold, namely, love of friendship and love of concupiscence, but they differ. In the love of concupiscence, we draw to ourselves what is outside of us when by that very love we love things other than ourselves inasmuch as they are useful or delightful to us. In the love of friendship, on the other hand, it is the other way around, because *we draw ourselves to what is outside*. For, to those whom we love in that love we are related as to ourselves, *communicating ourselves to them in some way*.[54]

John of Avila (1499–1569):

If it is great wealth not to possess one's heart because it has been given to God, what will it be to possess God's heart as our own? For God gives his heart to those to whom he gives his love, and after giving his heart, he gives all that

50. Augustine, *Enarrationes in Psalmos* 52.8; emphasis added.
51. Augustine, *Sermo* 331; emphasis added.
52. Augustine, *Sermo* 117; emphasis added.
53. Bernard of Clairvaux, *De diligendo deo* 15; emphasis added.
54. Thomas, *Super Ioannem*, cap. 15, lect. 4, no. 2036; emphasis added.

he is. Without doubt *we belong entirely to the one to whom we give our heart....* When God gives his heart, *he gives himself.*[55]

Teresa of Avila (1515–82):

His majesty is not wont to fail, nor can he fail *to give Himself* to the one who has given him everything.[56]

The sovereign gift [is spiritual marriage] ... Between the spiritual betrothal and the spiritual marriage the difference is as great as that which exists between two who are betrothed and two who can no longer be separated.[57]

Friedrich Nietzsche (1844–1900):

Despite every concession I am willing to make to the monogamous prejudice, I will never admit that men and women have equal rights in love. These do not exist. The reason is that man and woman, each of them, understand something different by love—and it is one of the conditions of love in the two sexes that the one sex does not presuppose in the other sex the same feeling and the same concept *love.*

What a woman means by love is clear enough: *complete gift* (*not mere giving*) *with soul and body, without reserve or reservation,* rather with shame and horror at the thought of a gift that might be subject to special clauses or conditions. In this absence of conditions her love is thus a faith: woman has no other faith.

A man, when he loves a woman, wants precisely this love from her and is, therefore, for his own person as far as one can be from the starting point of feminine love. Supposing, however, that there should also be *men to whom the desire for total gift is not foreign*; well, then they simply are—not men. A man who loves like a woman becomes a slave; while a woman who loves like a woman becomes a more perfect woman. ...

A woman's passion, in its unconditional renunciation of rights of her own, presupposes precisely that on the other side there is no equal pathos, no equal will to renunciation; *for if both renounced themselves out of love,* what would come to be from this—well, I don't know what, *perhaps an empty space?*

Woman wants to be taken, accepted as a possession, wants to dissolve into the concept of "possession," "possessed." Consequently, *she wants one who takes, who does not give himself and give himself away,* one who, quite on the contrary, is supposed to be made richer in "himself" by what the woman gives herself as, namely, for him as an increase in strength, happiness, and faith.

The woman gives herself away; the man takes more to add to himself—I do

55. John of Avila, *Audi filia* 103, trans. Joan Frances Gormley, Classics of Western Spirituality (New York: Paulist Press, 2006), 293; emphasis added.

56. Teresa of Avila, *Meditations on the Song of Songs* 10, *The Collected Works of St. Teresa of Avila,* ed. and trans. Kieran Kavanaugh, OCD, and Otilio Rodriguez, OCD, 3 vols. (Washington, DC: Institute of Carmelite Studies Publications, 1976–85), 2:254; emphasis added.

57. Teresa of Avila, *The Interior Castle* 7.2; *Collected Works,* 2.433; emphasis added.

not see how one can get over this natural contrariety by means of social contracts, not even with the sincerest will for justice, desirable as it may be not to place continually before one's eyes the harshness, terror, enigma, and immorality of this antagonism. For love, thought of whole, great, and full, is nature, and as nature it is in all eternity something "immoral."[58]

Robert Louis Stevenson (1844–1900):

[Note: In Stevenson's *David Balfour*, sequel to *Kidnapped*, David falls in love with Catriona early in the novel. He proposes to her several times. She refuses him because she suspects he has decided to marry her, not because he wants and desires her, but out of charity. At the very end of the novel, in the climax of the plot, she seems to turn away from him once again.]

I stepped before her so as to intercept her walking on.

"Try to put up with me," I was saying, "try and bear with me a little."

Still she had never the word, and a fear began to rise in me like a fear of death.

"Catriona," I cried, gazing on her hard, "is it a mistake again? Am I quite lost?"

She raised her head to me, breathless. "Do you want me, Davie, truly?" said she, and I scarce could hear her say it.

"I do that," said I. "O, sure you know it—I do that."

"I have nothing left to give or to keep back," said she. "I was all yours from the first day, if you would have had a gift of me!" she said.[59]

7. The Sanjuanist Triangle

A triangle of governing theses run like a deeply embedded watermark through TOB. (1) To love is to give oneself. (2) The gift of self is particularly clear to us human beings in spousal love. (3) The Trinity is the exemplar of love and gift.

Love as a Gift

St. John of the Cross describes the soul's relation to God as a cycle of mutual giving. The deep satisfaction and happiness of love lies in union with the beloved, not only in the sense of arrival at the end, but also of *a cycle of giving and receiving.* St. John Paul's discussion of the beatific vision in TOB echoes this Sanjuanist thesis.

58. Nietzsche, *The Cheerful Science* 363, KSA 3:611–12; emphasis added. The keen insight into gift attested to by this text comes perhaps from Luther. Nietzsche's father was a Lutheran pastor. In Luther, however, the gift is mutual between man and woman, not one-sided as in Nietzsche. See part I, chap. 1, section 1, in this volume.

59. Robert Louis Stevenson, *David Balfour* (New York: Charles Scribner's Sons, 1924), 341.

> The *reciprocal gift of oneself to God*—a gift of self in which man will concentrate and express all the energies of his own personal and at the same time psychosomatic subjectivity—will be the response to God's gift of himself to man. In this *reciprocal gift of self* by man, a gift that will become completely and definitively beatifying as the response worthy of a personal subject to God's gift of himself, the "virginity" or rather the virginal state of the body will manifest itself completely as the eschatological fulfillment of the "spousal" meaning of the body, as *the specific sign and authentic expression of personal subjectivity as a whole.* (TOB 68:3; emphasis added)

According to John of the Cross, what the soul gives is not herself but God, who has given himself to her. Self-gift is not explicit but implicit in his phrase *something of its own*. In the *Spiritual Canticle*, he speaks more directly of the bride giving herself.

> There he gave me his breast;
> there he taught me a sweet and living knowledge;
> and *I gave myself to him, keeping nothing back*;
> there I promised to be *his bride.*

In this stanza, the promise to be his bride seems to express in alternate words what the immediately preceding words describe as a total gift. "I gave myself to him, keeping nothing back." John of the Cross comments:

> In this stanza the *bride* tells of *the mutual surrender* made in this spiritual espousal between the soul and God, saying that in the interior wine cellar of love they were joined by *the communication he made of himself to her*....
>
> In that sweet drink of God, in which the soul is imbibed in him, she most willingly and with intense delight *surrenders herself wholly to him in the desire to be totally his* and never to possess in herself anything other than him....
>
> Hence, not only in her will but also in her works she is really and totally *given to God without keeping anything back*, just as God has freely *given himself entirely to her.* This union is so effected that the two wills are mutually paid, surrendered, and satisfied (so that neither fails the other in anything) with the fidelity and stability of an *espousal.* She therefore adds: there *I promised to be his bride.*
>
> Just as one who is *espoused* does not love, care, or work for any other than her *bridegroom*, so the soul in this state has no affections of the will or knowledge in the intellect or care or work or appetite that is not entirely inclined toward God. She is as it were divine and deified, in such a way that in regard to all she can understand she does not even suffer the first movements contrary to God's will. (B 27.5–7)

The characteristic feature of the spousal love between human beings and God, according to this text, is the totality of the gift of self, which is reflected in the totality of the orientation of affections toward the spouse.

> When there is union of love, the image of the Beloved is so sketched in the will, and drawn so intimately and vividly, that it is true to say that the Beloved lives in the lover and the lover in the Beloved. Love produces such likeness in this transformation of lovers that one can say each is the other and both are one.
>
> The reason is that in the union and transformation of love *each gives possession of self to the other and each leaves and exchanges self for the other.* Thus, each one lives in the other and is the other, and both are one in the transformation of love. (B 12.7)

In this text, John of the Cross uses the concept *gift of self* to unfold the more traditional language about the *transformation* and *union* of love, and of one person being the other, that is, of the other as a second self. The key seems to be that each gives entire possession of self to the other. This is the meaning of John Paul II's motto, *Totus tuus.*

Love between Man and Woman

John of the Cross does not thematically discuss love between man and woman. Yet his frequent use of the bride-bridegroom image contains a rich implicit theology of the body inspired above all by the Song of Songs. Wojtyła seems to have developed his own explicit account of spousal love in substantial measure from John of the Cross's implicit theology of the body. Let us look again at some of the key texts.

> A reciprocal love between God and the soul is thus actually formed, *in conformity with the marriage union and surrender un amor recíproco en conformidad de la unión y entrega matrimonial*, in which the goods of both (the divine essence that each possesses freely by reason of the voluntary surrender between them) are possessed by both together. *They say to each other what the Son of God spoke to the Father through John*: All that is mine is yours and yours is mine (John 17:10; *Living Flame*, B 80; emphasis added).
>
> Just as one who is *espoused* does not love, care, or work for any other than her *bridegroom*, so the soul in this state has no affections of the will or knowledge in the intellect or care or work or appetite that is not entirely inclined toward God. (Canticle B 27.7; emphasis added)

The comparison *just as one who is espoused* shows that John of the Cross clearly sees the gift of self in the spousal relation between man and woman. He uses the marriage analogy across the whole breadth of Christian experience, even in its imperfect forms. It is most applicable, however, to what he calls *spiritual marriage*, which follows *spiritual betrothal.*

> This spiritual *marriage* is incomparably greater than the spiritual *betrothal*, for it is a total transformation in the Beloved, in which *each surrenders the entire possession of self to the other with a certain consummation of the union of love.* The soul thereby becomes divine, God through participation, insofar as is possible in this life....
>
> *Just as in the consummation of carnal marriage* there are two in one flesh, as Sacred Scripture points out (Genesis 2:24), so also when the spiritual marriage between God and the soul is consummated, there are two natures in one spirit and love, as Paul says in making this same comparison: Whoever is joined to the Lord becomes one spirit with him (1 Corinthians 6:17; *Canticle*, B 22.3; emphasis added)

The defining element of spiritual marriage, according to this text, is the total surrendering of the self-possession of each to the other, analogous to the consummation of carnal marriage by sexual union, which is also a surrender of self-possession and in this way a consummation of the union of love. John of the Cross uses this analogy to understand spiritual marriage by comparison with carnal marriage, but—with all due regard for the difference between these two—one can turn the comparison around to see what John of the Cross implicitly says about spousal love between man and woman. The conclusion one reaches in such an inversion is Wojtyła's vision of spousal love.

> Spousal love is something else than all the aspects or forms of love analyzed up to this point. It consists in giving one's own person. The essence of spousal love is giving oneself, giving one's "I." It constitutes at once something other and something more than fondness, than desire, and even than benevolence. All these forms of going out toward the other person with regard to the good do not reach as far as spousal love.... The fullest and so to speak the most radical form of love consists precisely in the fact of giving oneself, of making one's nontransferable and incommunicable "I" someone else's possession.[60]

This central text of *Love and Responsibility* can be set next to some of John of the Cross's formulations and John Paul's mature teaching.

> JOHN OF THE CROSS: I *gave myself* to him, *keeping nothing back*; there I promised to be his bride ... The bride tells of the *mutual surrender* made in this spiritual espousal between the soul and God.... She most willingly and with intense delight *surrenders herself wholly* to him in the desire *to be totally his*.... Each *surrenders the entire possession of self* to the other with a certain consummation of the union of love.

60. Wojtyła, *Love and Responsibility*, 79–80.

> JOHN PAUL II: [Sexuality] is realized in a truly human way only if it is an integral part of the love by which a man and a woman commit themselves totally to one another until death. The *total physical self-giving* would be a lie if it were not the sign and fruit of a *total personal self-giving*, in which the whole person, including the temporal dimension, is present: if the person were to withhold something or reserve the possibility of deciding otherwise in the future, by this very fact he or she would not be *giving totally*. (*Familiaris consortio* 11; emphasis added)

The striking similarity between these formulations suggests that Wojtyła's way of thinking about spousal love was deeply formed by the language of *gift* as developed by John of the Cross.

The Trinity as the Exemplar of Gift

The Son of God, according to John of the Cross, is the first to say to the Father, "All that is mine is yours and what is yours is mine" (*Living Flame*, B 80). Both the soul's filial/spousal relation to God and the marriage union and surrender between man and woman are reflections and imitations of the mutual belonging that characterizes the union of love within the Trinity. John of the Cross's focus of attention is the soul's relation to God. He speaks suggestively about the spousal relation in marriage as an analogue and the Trinitarian relations as the divine exemplar of the soul's relation to God, but he does not unfold the analogy and the exemplar.

Neither John of the Cross nor John Paul apply spousal language directly to the Trinity. It is the Father-Son relation, not the bride-bridegroom relation, that normative image for them, in agreement with the teaching of Jesus. Still, they see the spousal relation as a likeness that reflects the Trinity.

According to John of the Cross, the gift the soul gives to God is the Holy Spirit. Evidently, he comments, the soul adds nothing to God and yet it gives the Spirit as a gift to God in order to repay love with love. This return of love to the Father through the Son, John Paul argues, is rooted in the Holy Spirit's personal mode of being as the gift between the Father and the Son (see part II, chap. 7, section 8, in this volume).

To conclude, it was in John of the Cross that Wojtyła saw the triangle of theses about the Trinity and the spousal gift of self that came to define the depth-structure of his vision of the person. The vision grew in clarity, scope, and depth, but its fundamental articulations impressed themselves on Wojtyła when he read John of the Cross.

CHAPTER 7

Man and Woman as an Image of the Trinity

Some theologians reject St. John Paul's thesis that man and woman are an image of the Trinity. An esteemed professor and friend challenged me earnestly. Don't go down that path! It leads nowhere! Stay on the established ground of the analogy of the word developed by SS. Augustine and Thomas. This is the heart of scientific Trinitarian theology.

The present chapter issues a counterchallenge. To claim that the analogy of the word is the heart of Trinitarian theology and to exclude or sideline the analogy of mutual love tends toward collapsing the supernatural mystery of the Trinity into the natural order, replacing the Church's public faith in the Trinity with a private philosophical conviction.

Section 1 shows that Thomas and John Paul agree on the image of the Trinity in man and woman.

Section 2 turns to a shared premise in this agreement. According to the Church's faith, God is not alone. The Trinity is a communion of persons.

Section 3 presents arguments by Karl Rahner and Bernard Lonergan, among others, who call this communion of persons into question.

Section 4 presents Thomas's commentary on John 1:1, "In the beginning was the *Logos*." The commentary explains the analogy of the word as an argument based on the principle, *Wherever there is knowledge there must be an inner word*, and on the proportion, *As the human mind is to the inner word, so is the Father to the person of the Logos.*

Section 5 presents Thomas's teaching that the analogy of the word is not a theological argument but a philosophical one, not a proof but a manifestation, not part of the Church's public faith but privately proposed by theologians, not based on necessity but on fittingness, not held as certain but as a probable conjecture, and not asserted as true but as verisimilar.

Section 6 argues that the analogy of the word nevertheless has an important function in Trinitarian theology.

Section 7, finally, turns to the analogy of mutual love as presented in the Gospel of John. In accord with the purpose of this volume, it focuses on the *glory of the Logos in the flesh* as a glory connected with love and gift.

1. The Image in Man and Woman

An Apparent Disagreement

According to St. John Paul, man and woman are an image of the Trinity in the inseparably unitive and procreative meaning of marriage and of the conjugal act.

> Man became the "image and likeness" of God not only through his own humanity but also through the communion of persons, which man and woman form from the very beginning. The function of the image is that of mirroring the one who is the model, of reproducing its own prototype. Man becomes an image of God not so much in the act of solitude as in the act of communion. He is, in fact, "from the beginning" an image in which not only the solitude of one Person, who rules the world, mirrors itself but also the inscrutable, essentially divine communion of Persons. ... This is obviously not without significance for the theology of the body but constitutes perhaps the deepest theological aspect of everything one can say about man. (TOB 9:3; emphasis original)
>
> The divine "we" constitutes the eternal model of the human "we," which is formed in man and woman, created in the image of God, according to his likeness. (*Letter to Families* 6)

In some texts, John Paul focuses on the procreative meaning as an integral part of the image.

> In his innermost mystery, our God is not solitude but a family, since he has in himself fatherhood, sonship, and the essence of the family, which is love. In the divine family, this love is the Holy Spirit. (Sermon, Puebla, Mexico, January 28, 1979)
>
> The original model of the family must be sought in God himself, in the Trinitarian mystery of his life. (*Familiaris consortio* 6)

John Paul gives a fuller account of the image of God in *Mulieris dignitatem*.

> Every individual is made in the image of God, insofar as he or she is a rational and free creature capable of knowing God and loving him.

> Moreover, we read that man cannot exist "alone" (cf. Genesis 2:18); he can exist only as a "unity of the two," and therefore *in relation to another human person*. It is a question here of a mutual relationship: man to woman and woman to man. Being a person in the image and likeness of God thus also involves existing in a relationship, in relation to the other "I." This is a prelude to the definitive self-revelation of the Triune God: a living unity in the communion of the Father, Son and Holy Spirit....
>
> In the Pastoral Constitution *Gaudium et spes*, we read: "The Lord Jesus, when he prays to the Father 'that all may be one ... as we are one' (John 17: 21-22), thus opening up vistas closed to human reason, indicates *a certain likeness* between the union of the divine Persons and the union of God's children in truth and love. This likeness shows that man ... cannot fully find himself except through a sincere gift of self" (*Gaudium et spes* 24). With these words, the council text presents a summary of the whole truth about man and woman—a truth which is already outlined in the first chapters of the Book of Genesis, and which is the structural basis of biblical and Christian anthropology. Man—whether man or woman—is the only being among the creatures of the visible world that God the Creator "has willed for its own sake"; that creature is thus a person. Being a person means striving toward self-realization (the Council text speaks of self-discovery), which can only be achieved "through a sincere gift of self."
>
> The model for this interpretation of the person is God himself as Trinity, as a communion of Persons. To say that man is created in the image and likeness of God means that man is called to exist "for" others, to become a gift. (*Mulieris dignitatem* 7; emphasis original)

John Paul sees the image of the Trinity not only in marriage but also (and more eminently) in consecrated life (see TOB 77:5–78:5).

> The deepest meaning of the evangelical counsels is revealed when they are viewed in relation to the Holy Trinity, the source of holiness. They are in fact an expression of the love of the Son for the Father in the unity of the Holy Spirit. By practicing the evangelical counsels, the consecrated person lives with particular intensity the Trinitarian and Christological dimension which marks the whole of Christian life.
>
> The chastity of celibates and virgins, as a manifestation of dedication to God with an *undivided heart* (cf. 1 Cor 7:32–34), is a reflection of the *infinite love* which links the three Divine Persons in the mysterious depths of the life of the Trinity, the love to which the Incarnate Word bears witness even to the point of giving his life, the love "poured into our hearts through the Holy Spirit" (Rom 5:5), which evokes a response of total love for God and for brothers and sisters.
>
> *Poverty* proclaims that God is man's only real treasure. When poverty is

> lived according to the example of Christ who, "though he was rich . . . became poor" (2 Cor 8:9), it becomes an expression of that *total gift of self* which the three Divine Persons make to one another. This gift overflows into creation and is fully revealed in the Incarnation of the Word and in his redemptive death.
>
> *Obedience*, practiced in imitation of Christ, whose food was to do the Father's will (cf. Jn 4:34), shows the liberating beauty of a *dependence which is not servile but filial*, marked by a deep sense of responsibility and animated by mutual trust, which is a reflection in history of the loving *harmony* between the three Divine Persons.
>
> The consecrated life is thus called constantly to deepen the gift of the evangelical counsels with a love which grows ever more genuine and strong in the *Trinitarian* dimension: love *for Christ*, which leads to closeness with him; love *for the Holy Spirit*, who opens our hearts to his inspiration; love *for the Father*, the first origin and supreme goal of the consecrated life. The consecrated life thus becomes a confession and a sign of the Trinity, whose mystery is held up to the Church as the model and source of every form of Christian life.
>
> Even *fraternal life*, whereby consecrated persons strive to live in Christ with "one heart and soul" (Acts 4:32), is put forward as an eloquent witness to the Trinity. It proclaims *the Father*, who desires to make all of humanity one family. It proclaims *the Incarnate Son*, who gathers the redeemed into unity, pointing the way by his example, his prayer, his words and above all his death, which is the source of reconciliation for a divided and scattered humanity. It proclaims *the Holy Spirit* as the principle of unity in the Church, wherein he ceaselessly raises up spiritual families and fraternal communities. (*Vita consecrata* 21; emphasis original)

In *Summa* I, q. 93, a. 6, Thomas raises the question whether the image of God is found in man only according to the mind or also according to the body. The second objection appeals to Genesis 1:27.

> It seems that the image of God is in man not only according to the mind. . . . "God created man to his image (*ad imaginem*), to the image of God he created him, male and female he created them" (Genesis 1:27). But the distinction between male and female is according to the body. Therefore, also according to the body the image of God is observed in man, not only according to the mind.[1]

The body of the article argues that the image of God is found in man alone, not in irrational animals. It is therefore first found in what distinguishes man from irrational animals, the rational mind. An image, it continues, must represent its exemplar by a *specific* likeness. Otherwise it is a mere footprint (*vestigi-*

1. Thomas, *Summa* I, q. 93, a. 6, obj. 2.

um) in the sense of an effect that represents its cause without reaching a *specific* likeness. Inanimate substances, plants, and animals are footprints because they can represent God as existing and living. The human person is an image because it represents God more *specifically* as understanding and loving.

> Since the uncreated Trinity is distinguished according to the procession of the Word from the one who speaks and of Love from both ... one can say that in the rational creature, in which one finds the procession of word according to intellect and the procession of love according to will, there is an image of the uncreated Trinity by some representation of the species.[2]

The response to the second objection introduces a new focus, *according to many.* Man and woman enter into the argument as distinct persons.

> According to Augustine, some held that the image of the Trinity is in man, *not according to one individual but according to many,* saying, "The man suggests the person of the Father, while the person who proceeded from the man in the manner of being born from him suggests the person of the Son, and the third person, representing the Holy Spirit, is the woman, who proceeded from the man in such a manner that she was not his son or daughter."[3]

Although the focus on *according to many* becomes important, *according to the body* remains primary. The image resisted by Augustine and Thomas consists in a *specific pattern of bodily relations of origin* between Adam, Eve, and their child. Adam represents the Father in the Trinity. Eve comes from Adam, not as begotten by him but in some other way that has no name. She is therefore an image of the Holy Spirit, who also comes from the Father without being a Son.

> Even at first glance, this is absurd, *prima facie absurdum.*
>
> *First,* since it would follow that the Holy Spirit is the beginning of the Son, as the woman is the beginning of the offspring who is born from the man.
>
> *Second*, one man would be only to the image of one person.
>
> *Third*, according to this, Scripture should not have spoken of the image of God in man until a child had been born.
>
> And so one should say that Scripture, after it says, "to the image of God he created him," adds "male and female he created them," not so that the image of God might be seen according to the distinction of sexes but because the image of God is common to both sexes since it is according to the mind, in which there is no distinction of sexes. Hence the Apostle, after saying, "according to the image of the one who created them," adds, "where there is neither male nor female" (Colossians 3:11).[4]

2. Thomas, *Summa* I, q. 93, a. 6, corp.
3. Thomas, *Summa* I, q. 93, a. 6, ad 2; emphasis added. See Augustine, *De trinitate* 12.2.5–6.
4. Thomas, *Summa* I, q. 93, a. 6, ad 2.

Do the arguments in this text apply to John Paul's understanding of the image?

1. *The Holy Spirit, corresponding to the woman, would be the beginning of the Son.* John Paul does not claim that the triadic pattern of the family (father-mother-child) corresponds one-to-one to the triadic pattern of the Trinity (Father-Son-Spirit). In particular, he does not say that the mother has a place corresponding to the Holy Spirit.

2. *One man would only be to the image of one person.* John Paul does not claim such a one-to-one correspondence. He does not deny the image of the whole Trinity in each human person. He does not deny that we speak an inner word in our acts of knowledge and breathe the presence of the beloved in our acts of love. He does not deny that these are an image of the whole Trinity.[5]

3. *Scripture should not have spoken of the image of the Trinity until after the birth of the first child.* John Paul does not claim that the family image is the only aspect of the divine image. In his list of aspects, he first mentions the image of the one God in each human person (see *Mulieris dignitatem* 7, quoted above).

An important part of Thomas's argument is the appeal to Colossians 3:11, "neither male nor female." The appeal fails because the phrase "neither male nor female" is not part of the genuine text of Colossians. It is found only in a handful of Greek manuscripts of the Western tradition, among them Codex D for the Pauline letters (Claromontanus). It is also present in the Old Latin translation but not in the revision of the Old Latin by St. Jerome, the Vulgate.[6] Augustine still uses the Old Latin to deny that man and woman are an image.[7] Thomas follows him even though his own authoritative text, the Vulgate, does not have "neither male nor female." The phrase was probably added by a copyist who remembered the similar *neither-nor* list in Galatians 3:28 and supplied the added phrase from memory. In Galatians, the context is not the image of God but baptism. Both men and woman are baptized. Even if "neither male nor female" were part of the text, however, Augustine's argument would be doubtful. Colossians highlights a particular aspect of the image; namely, "the knowledge of God" (Colossians 3:10) in which the relation between the sexes is not as relevant as in mutual love and procreation.

A global observation is more important. Augustine and Thomas understand

5. See esp. John Paul II, General Audience, November 14, 1990, which explicitly discusses the analogy of the word and of proceeding love.

6. See Petrus Sabatier, *Bibliorum sacrorum latinae versiones antiquae seu Vetus italica*, 3 vols. (Rheims: Florentain, 1743–49), 3:839–40; *Epistulae ad Philippenses et ad Colossenses*, ed. Hermann Josef Frede, Vetus Latina 24/2 (Freiburg: Herder, 1966–71).

7. See Augustine, *De trinitate* 12.7.12; *De Genesi ad litteram* 11.42.58; *Contra Faustum* 24.1.

the image they refute as an image taken formally according to the body (*secundum corpus*), that is, according to the *genus* body, not *the species* rational animal. On the generic level of body, reproduction is found in animals and plants. John Paul does not claim that reproducing plants and animals are an image of the Trinity. He claims that the image is found in the coming to be of a new person in inseparable connection with the union of love between spouses.

Procreation and Union of Love

As for PROCREATION, Thomas distinguishes between the generation of a living being understood generically and the generation of a human being understood specifically. In a comparison of the image in angels and man, he argues that the image of the Trinity is more perfect in angels because they understand and love more perfectly. Still, there are some respects in which the image is more perfect in man. Procreation is one of them.

> About the image of God we can speak in two ways. In one way with respect to that in which the account of image is first seen, which is the intellectual nature. And in this way the image of God is more in angels than in men, because the intellectual nature is more perfect in them....
>
> In a second way, we can consider the image of God in man with respect to that in which it is secondarily seen, inasmuch as in man one finds a certain imitation of God, for example, *man is from man as God is from God*....
>
> In these and similar [respects] *the image of God is more perfect in man* than in an angel. But in this respect the account of the divine image is not found per se in man, except if the first imitation is presupposed, which is according to the intellectual nature. Otherwise even brute animals would be to the image of God. Therefore, since in its intellectual nature an angel is more to the image of God than man, we must grant simply that an angel is more to the image of God than man but in some respect man is.[8]

The double negative "the image of God *is not found* per se in man, *except if* the first imitation is presupposed" should be converted into the equivalent positive. The image of God *is found* per se in man, *if* the first imitation is presupposed.

The reason for saying *is found per se in man* lies in the unity of human nature. Human nature is not a composite of two natures accidentally joined, the nature of an irrational animal and that of a spiritual soul. Each human person has only one nature. In procreation, a personal body proceeds from personal

8. Thomas, *Summa* I, q. 93, a. 3, corp.; emphasis added. Compare *Super I sent.*, d. 3, q. 3, ad 4; *Super II sent.*, d. 16, a. 3.

bodies. Some-body proceeds from some-bodies. *Person from person* is not a mere footprint. It is an image in the full sense because it has a specific likeness through itself (*per se*), not incidentally (*per accidens*). *Father* and *Son* are not metaphors when speaking about the Trinity.

THE UNION OF LOVE between husband and wife belongs to the same image in inseparable connection with procreation. *Gaudium et spes* 24, to which John Paul returns often to express his Sanjuanist account of love as a gift of self, begins with an emphasis on union and explains it by means of the gift of self.

> The Lord Jesus, when he prays to the Father, "that all may be one ... as we are one" (John 17:11, 17:20–23) ... indicates a certain likeness between the union of the divine Persons and the union of God's sons in Truth and Love. This likeness shows that man ... cannot fully find himself except through a sincere gift of self.

Gaudium et spes is based on John 17:11 and 17:20–23. In his commentary on John, dated several years after the questions on the Trinity in the *Summa*, Thomas explains *one as we are one*.

> "Holy Father, keep them in your name, which you have given me, that they may be one as we [are one]" (17:11). They are kept for this goal, namely, to be one (John 17:9). For, *our whole perfection* (*nostra perfectio tota*) *consists in the unity of the Spirit*, "Take every care to keep the unity of the Spirit by the peace that binds you together" (Ephesians 4:3). "How good and joyful it is when brothers dwell in unity" (Ps 133:1). But he adds, "as we are one" (John 17:11).
>
> *Sed contra:* They are one in essence. Therefore, we will also be one in essence. But this is not true.
>
> *Responsio, dicendum:* The perfection of each being is nothing other than a participation in the divine likeness. For we are good to the degree in which we are made like God. Our unity, therefore, is perfective precisely in the degree to which it participates in the divine unity.
>
> Now, there is *a twofold unity in God*, namely, the unity of nature, "I and the Father are one" (John 10:30) and *the unity of love* in the Father and the Son which is the unity of the Spirit. Both of these are in us, not in equality of rank but by a certain likeness. For the Father and the Son are numerically of one nature, but we are one in nature according to our kind. Again, they are one by a love that is not derived from the gift of someone else but that proceeds from them. For the Father and the Son love each other by the Holy Spirit but we by a love in which we participate as something derived from a higher source.[9]

9. Thomas, *Super Ioannem*, cap. 17, lect. 3, no. 2214; emphasis added.

In John 17:21–23, Jesus returns to the same theme. He speaks twice about the likeness between two unions, first as a future desired result to be realized by the Father (not yet) and then as an accomplished fact realized by himself (already). The two passages follow the same pattern. After an introductory clause, there are three clauses introduced by ἵνα *that*. The first two *that* clauses frame a comparison introduced by *as*. The resulting pattern is *that-as-that-that*. The commandment of love in John 13:34–35 is structured in a similar literary pattern and can be read in parallel with 17:20–23. The three panels give an encompassing view of *being one*: as a *future* desired result, as *already* realized in Jesus's gift of glory to his own, and as the content of the new *commandment*.

> *Future Desired Result*:
> I pray also for those who believe in me through their word,
> that all may be one
> as you, father, are in me and I in you,
> that they too may be in us,
> that the world may believe that you sent me. (John 17:20–21)
>
> *Already Given Gift*:
> And I, the glory you have given to me I have given to them,
> that they may be one
> as we are one, I in them and you in me,
> that they may be completed into one,
> that the world may know that you sent me
> and loved them as you loved me. (John 17:22–23)
>
> *Commandment of Love*:
> I give you a new commandment,
> that you love one another
> as I have loved you,
> that you too love one another.
> In this all will know that you are my disciples,
> if you have love for one another. (John 13:34–35)

Thomas's commentary on the first of these three panels (John 17:20–21) again distinguishes a twofold unity in God, unity of essence and of love. Unity of love must be meant in "one as you Father are in me and I in you."

> Thus, he says, I pray that all may be one. For, as the Platonists say, anything has its unity from that from which it has its goodness. For the good is what keeps a thing, but nothing is kept except by this, that it is one. And thus, when the Lord prays for the perfection of the disciples in goodness, he prays that they may be one, which was fulfilled: "The multitude of believers had one heart

and one soul" (Acts 4:32). "How good and joyful it is when brothers dwell in unity!" (Psalm 133:1).

But he adds the exemplar and cause of unity (*unitatis exemplum et causam*) by saying, "as you, Father, are in me and I in you" (John 17:21).... Arius argued from this that the Son is in the Father and the Father in the Son in the same way that we are in God. We are not in God by the unity of essence but by conformity of will and love. Therefore, the Father is not in the Son by the unity of essence.

One should say, however, that in the Father and the Son, there is *a twofold unity*, namely unity of essence and *of love* (*unitas essentiae et amoris*), and according to both the Father is in the Son and the Son in the Father.

What he says here, "As you, Father, are in me and I in you," can be referred ... to the unity of love, according to Augustine, so that the meaning is: as you, Father, are in me through love, because love makes one be one with God, as if he said, *as the Father loves the Son and conversely, so they love the Father and the Son*. The term as (*sicut*) does not signify the same level but a certain remote likeness (*remotam similitudinem*).[10]

Thomas's commentary on the second of the three Johannine panels (John 17:22–23) focuses on the gift of glory and emphasizes even more clearly that unity of love is the goal of the whole order of grace.

"We are transformed from glory to glory" (2 Corinthians 3:18). "He gave gifts to men" (Psalm 67:19). And this in order that they may be one as we are. For this is the end of the divine gifts that we are united by that unity which conforms to the unity of the Father and the Son.[11]

The *Summa* does not make the distinction between two forms of unity in these terms, although it is implicit, but the distinction is found explicitly in the early Parisian *Scriptum* on the Sentences, the *Summa contra gentiles*, and the late *Lectura Romana*.

Parisian Scriptum: Love has the account (*ratio*) of uniting the lover and the beloved. And since the Holy Spirit proceeds as love, he has it from his way of proceeding that he is the union of the Father and the Son. For, the Father and the Son can be thought of either as they come together in essence, and thus they are *united by essence*, or as they are distinguished in persons, and thus they are *united by the harmony of love* (*per consonantiam amoris*).[12]

Contra gentiles: When the Lord says to the Father about the disciples "that

10. Thomas, *Super Ioannem*, cap. 17, lect. 4, no. 2238–40; emphasis added.

11. Thomas, *Super Ioannem*, cap. 17, lect. 4, no. 2246.

12. Thomas, *Super I sent.*, d. 10, q. 1, a. 3, corp.; emphasis added.

they may be one as we are one," it is shown that the Father and the Son are one *in the way the disciples should be one, namely, by love.* This mode of union does not exclude the unity of essence, but rather shows it. For it says, "The Father loves the Son and has given all things into his hand" (John 3:35), which shows that the fullness of divinity is in the Son.[13]

Lectura Romana: The Father and the Son are one in two ways: by essence, and accordingly he says, "I and the Father are one" (John 10:30); and *by the harmony of love* (*consonantia amoris*) and this union is by the Holy Spirit, and about this union it says in John 17, "that they may be one in us as we are one," namely by the harmony of love, for it is in this way that we are all one in God, and not by essence. For *if there were no other union in God except by essence, the Lord would not have said,* "That they may be one in us as we are one." Therefore, it is understood about the unity which exists through the harmony of love.[14]

When one compares these interpretations of *one as we are one* with *Gaudium et spes* 24 and the texts of John Paul quoted above, one can see points of agreement. All three interpret the Johannine adverb *as* (καθώς, *sicut*) in the phrase *one as we are one* by the term *likeness* (*similitudo*), which is used in Genesis 1:26 in parallel with *image*: "Let us make man according to our image and likeness." The likeness expressed by Jesus in John 17 is a likeness between the divine Persons and human persons with respect to *union* (*Gaudium et spes* 24) or in Thomas with respect to *unity of love* or *harmony of love* such that the unity of love among the divine persons is *the exemplar and cause* of the unity of human persons.

In *De potentia*, Thomas unfolds in greater detail how the role of the Holy Spirit in this unity/harmony of love can be understood.

The Holy Spirit proceeds from the Father into the Son and from the Son into the Father, not as into a recipient but as into the object of love. For one says that the Holy Spirit proceeds from the Father into the Son inasmuch as he is the love (*amor*) by which the Father loves the Son, and for a similar reason one can say that the Holy Spirit is from the Son into the Father, inasmuch as he is the love by which the Son loves the Father.[15]

Like John Paul, Thomas sees the divine communion of persons concentrated in the Person of the Holy Spirit. The unity of love between the Father and the Son is the unity of the Spirit. The Father and the Son express their unity by breathing the Spirit into each other. Our whole perfection consists in sharing

13. Thomas, *Contra gentiles* 4, cap. 8, no. 3438; emphasis added.
14. Thomas, *Lectura Romana*, d. 10, q. 3, ad 3; emphasis added.
15. Thomas, *De potentia*, q. 10, a. 4, ad 10; compare *Summa* I-II, q. 28, a. 2, ad 1.

by likeness in this unity of the Spirit. The warrant of these statements is not only Augustine's account of the inner processions in the human mind but also the more elementary testimony of Scripture that the Spirit is the third person, in some way common to the other two. "God sent the Spirit of his Son into our hearts, crying Abba, Father" (Galatians 4:6). "The love of God has been poured into our hearts through the Holy Spirit who has been given to us" (Romans 5:5).

Reaching our whole perfection (Thomas), understanding our highest calling (*Gaudium et spes* 22), and finding ourselves (*Gaudium et spes* 24)—all of these expressions point in the same direction.

Is the likeness affirmed by *one as we are one* the specific likeness of an image or the less specific likeness of a footprint? The term *likeness*, Thomas argues, has a broad range of meanings. *Likeness* in a more general sense includes the likeness of a mere footprint. In a more specific sense, it expresses the particular excellence of an image.

> Likeness is taken as a preamble to image inasmuch as it is more general than image.... It is taken as following the image when it signifies a certain perfection of the image. For we say that the image of something is like that of which it is the image inasmuch as it represents [the original] itself perfectly or imperfectly.[16]

The latter sense of *likeness*, perfection of the image, is clearly at stake in Thomas's interpretation of *one as we are one* in John 17. The likeness in question is one of rational creatures participating in the unity of the Spirit, a specific likeness, and it is excellent in its specificity. It is, therefore, the likeness of an image. Thomas does not draw this conclusion in the extant writings. However, he does not deny it and, more important, he shows the truth of all the premises from which it follows that it is the likeness of an image.

The Body in a Neo-Manichaean Age

As Scheeben points out, caution about a bodily image of God became a dominant concern in the Arian controversy early in the fourth century. The caution was part of an effort to avoid conceding any ground to Arianism.[17] In the second century, the concern was different. St. Irenaeus describes the *Logos* made flesh as a *visible* image of the invisible Father. This emphasis on the visible body was sharpened by Irenaeus's struggle against gnosticism. According to gnostic accounts (see part I, chap. 2, section 5, in this volume), sexual reproduction is

16. See Thomas, *Summa* I, q. 93, a. 9.
17. See Scheeben, *Dogmatik*, 3:327–29.

the diabolical creator's plan for gaining power over divine spirit by chaining it within a bodily prison. The conception of every child is a tragic captivity of spirit in matter. Salvation sets the imprisoned fragment free so that it can return to its natural condition, separation from body.[18] Against this flight from body into spirit, Irenaeus affirms the teaching of Genesis about man as the image of God. Man as a whole is the image. As a whole, body and soul, he is the visible image of the invisible God.

> God shall be glorified in the shaped being [*plasma*, the corresponding verb is used in the Septuagint of Genesis 2:7, "God shaped *eplasen* the man"] when he conforms it and makes it suited to his Child (*puer*). For by the Father's hands, that is, by the Son and the Holy Spirit, man comes to be in the likeness of God but not only a part of man. The soul and the spirit can be a part of man but certainly not a man. The complete man is the mixing and union of the soul, which receives the spirit of the Father and is mingled with that fleshly nature which was shaped (*plasmata*) according to the image of God.[19]

In this passage and many others, Irenaeus's point of departure is Genesis 2:7. "God shaped (*eplasen*) the man from clay of the earth and blew into his face (*prosopon*) the spirit of life." His point of arrival is the *Logos* of God, who by his incarnation, suffering, and death is the perfect visible image of the invisible Father.

> The shaping (*plasis*) of Adam was from the earth that is ours ... Therefore, we should not look for another Father apart from this one, nor for another substrate of our shaping (*plasis*) ... nor for another hand of God apart from the one that shapes (*plassousa*) us from beginning to end, fits us into life, accompanies the shaped figure (*plasma*), and perfects it according to the image and likeness of God.
>
> This was shown in its truth when the *Logos* of God became man, making himself like man and man like himself, so that by this likeness with the Son, man might be dear to the Father. For the *Logos*, according to whose likeness man was made, was still invisible and so it was easy for [man] to lose the likeness. But when the *Logos* of God became flesh, he made both [image and likeness] firm. For he showed the true image by becoming that which his image was and he made the likeness firm by making man *like the invisible Father through the visible Logos.*
>
> The Lord showed himself and the Father ... also through his very passion. For he dissolved the disobedience that happened in the tree (of knowledge)

18. See the polemical interpretation of Genesis in *Secret John*; Michael Waldstein and Frederik Wisse, *The Apocryphon of John: Synopsis of Nag Hammadi Codices II,1 III,1 and IV,1 with BG 8502,2*, Nag Hammadi Studies 33 (Leiden: Brill, 1995), 115–95.

19. Irenaeus, *Adversus Haereses* 5.6.1.

> from the beginning by "becoming obedient to death, even death on a cross" (Philippians 2:8). He healed the disobedience that took place in the wood by obedience on the wood.[20]

In contrast to Thomas, Irenaeus does not focus primarily on likeness of nature and activity but on the effective expression of God's life in the body, supremely in the invisible Father's visible *Logos*. In virtue of this expression, the body is not merely drawn into an image that resides elsewhere, in the spiritual part of man or the divine sonship of the *Logos*. As that through which the invisible Father expresses himself, the body plays a primary role in the image. Scheeben clarifies the decisive point.

> According to the strict letter and the whole context of Genesis one cannot say that image and likeness merely express an attribute inherent in the nature or a constituent part contained *within* the nature. They rather refer to *man as a whole* or contain man according to his *whole nature*. For, according to Scripture's way of speaking, man does not only *have* an image and likeness of God, he *is* one....
>
> When one places the character of the image as image not in a likeness of *nature* with the represented object but in the sensibly perceptible expressive portrayal or manifestation of the object, one can rightly say that man is the image of God not *secondarily* [Scheeben is referring to the use of "secondarily" in *Summa* I, q. 93, a. 3, corp.] but *in the first place* according to the body. *The body has been fitted for the glory of a soul that bears a likeness with God.* It is a body that allows this glory to appear. In this way the pre-Nicene Fathers saw the image of God in the *plasma* or the flesh.
>
> Even so, it remains true that the body is not *by* and *through itself alone* an image of God.... Only in the soul does it possess the inner enlivening form, the substantial being by which it becomes a living and true image of God. This is why these Fathers did not distinguish a twofold image in man but inasmuch as man is a living *plasma* they saw him as a plasmatic image in which the external form is not merely dead clothing or an organ of the spirit but the product of the spirit enlivening and shaping it from within.[21]

John Paul's concern in his teaching about the bodily image of God is similar to Irenaeus's. He points out that Descartes gave to our age its Neo-Manichaean attitude toward the body as mere matter separated from life and intelligence.

> The philosopher who formulated the principle of "*cogito, ergo sum*"—I think, therefore I am—also gave the modern concept of man its distinctive dualistic character. It is typical of rationalism to make a radical contrast in man

20. Irenaeus, *Adversus Haereses* 5.16.1–3; emphasis added.
21. Scheeben, *Dogmatik*, 3:327–28; emphasis added.

> between spirit and body, between body and spirit. But man is a person in the unity of his body and his spirit. The body can never be reduced to mere matter....
>
> The human family is facing the challenge of a new Manichaeism, in which body and spirit are put in radical opposition; the body does not receive life from the spirit, and the spirit does not give life to the body. Man thus ceases to live as a person and a subject. Regardless of all intentions and declarations to the contrary, he becomes merely an object. This neo-Manichaean culture has led, for example, to human sexuality being regarded more as an area for manipulation and exploitation than as the basis of that primordial wonder which led Adam on the morning of creation to exclaim before Eve: "This at last is bone of my bones and flesh of my flesh" (Genesis 2:23). This same wonder is echoed in the words of the Song of Solomon: "You have ravished my heart, my sister, my bride, you have ravished my heart with a glance of your eyes" (Song of Songs 4:9).[22]
>
> For some, "nature" becomes reduced to raw material for human activity and for its power: thus, nature needs to be profoundly transformed, and indeed overcome by freedom, inasmuch as it represents a limitation and denial of freedom.[23]

In this diagnosis of our age, John Paul converges with the Jewish philosopher Hans Jonas, whose first major works were a study of gnosticism.[24] In his critique of existentialism, Jonas identifies the root of difficulties in the reduction of the cosmos to a mathematical mechanism.

> A change in the vision of nature, that is, of the cosmic environment of man, is at the bottom of that metaphysical situation which has given rise to modern existentialism and to its nihilistic implications.... The essence of existentialism is a certain dualism, an estrangement between man and the world, with the loss of the idea of a kindred cosmos—in short, an anthropological acosmism.[25]

22. John Paul II, *Letter to Families* 13.

23. John Paul II, *Veritatis splendor* 46.

24. Jonas first presented an existentialist reading of texts called Gnostic, a reading based on hermeneutical principles of his teachers Heidegger and Bultmann. See *Gnosis und spätantiker Geist*, 3rd ed., 2 vols. (Göttingen: Vandenhoeck & Ruprecht, 1943, 1993). A more cautious interpretation reflecting Jonas's turn during World War II to a greater appreciation of the material cosmos and organic life can be seen in Jonas's *The Gnostic Religion: The Message of the Alien God and the Beginnings of Christianity*, enlarged ed. (Boston: Beacon Press, 1963). For a discussion of Jonas's understanding of Gnosticism, including his 180-degree turn from existentialism to the traditional Jewish appreciation of creation, see Michael Waldstein, "Hans Jonas' Construct 'Gnosticism': Analysis and Critique," *Journal of Early Christian Studies* 8 (2000): 341–72.

25. Hans Jonas, "Epilogue: Gnosticism, Existentialism and Nihilism," in *The Gnostic Religion: The Message of the Alien God and the Beginnings of Christianity* (Boston: Beacon, 1963), 320–40, at 325.

If anything, Jonas argues, the alienation in modernity is worse than in gnosticism.

> There is no overlooking one cardinal difference between the Gnostic and the existentialist dualism: Gnostic man is thrown into an antagonistic, anti-divine, and therefore anti-human nature, modern man into an indifferent one. Only the latter case represents the absolute vacuum, the really bottomless pit. In the Gnostic conception the hostile, the demonic, is still anthropomorphic, familiar even in its foreignness, and the contrast itself gives direction to existence.... Not even this antagonistic quality is granted to the indifferent nature of modern science, and from that nature no direction at all can be elicited. This makes modern nihilism infinitely more radical and more desperate than Gnostic nihilism could ever be for all its panic terror of the world.[26]

It is in this cultural context that John Paul focuses on a rehabilitation of the body as the expressive and effective sign of the human person and of participation in the life of the Trinity. Hence the main thesis statement of TOB.

> The body, in fact, and only the body, is capable of making visible what is invisible: the spiritual and the divine. It has been created to transfer into the visible reality of the world the mystery hidden from eternity in God, and thus to be a sign of it.
>
> In man, created in the image of God, the very sacramentality of creation, as it were, the sacramentality of the world, was thus in some way revealed. In fact, through his bodily visibility, through his masculine/feminine visibility, man becomes a visible sign of the economy of Truth and Love. (TOB 19:5)

2. God Is Not Alone

The mystery of the Trinity is densely expressed in the words of Jesus, "Go and teach all nations, baptizing them in the name of the Father and of the Son, and of the Holy Spirit" (Matthew 28:19). This formula of baptism points back to a rich body of evidences in the words, deeds, and suffering of Jesus. It also points forward to the early Church's reflection and the teaching of the first seven ecumenical councils.[27] Gilles Emery shows that the center of St. Thomas's Trini-

26. Jonas, "Epilogue," 338–39.

27. *Nicaea* I (AD 325), on the Son as consubstantial with the Father, against Arianism; *Constantinople* I (AD 381), on the divinity of the Holy Spirit; *Ephesus* (AD 431), on the unity of the person of Christ, expressed by the title of Mary as the mother of God, against Nestorius; *Chalcedon* (AD 451), on the one person of Christ in two natures; *Constantinople* II (AD 553), emphasizing the unity of Christ, against Nestorians; *Constantinople* III (AD 680), on the two wills of Christ as a consequence of the distinction of natures; *Nicaea* II (AD 787), more emphasis on the full humanity of Jesus as seen in reverence for icons.

tarian theology in the order of discovery lies in the self-revelation of the Trinity, expressed in the baptismal formula together with its roots in the life of Jesus and its unfolding in the reflection and teaching of the early Church. "Trinitarian faith rests on acceptance of God's revelation in the history of salvation. Before all theological research on the mystery of the Trinity one must therefore consider the Trinity's revelatory action."[28]

In the baptismal formula, Jesus uses the word *name* in the singular. One name for one God. Then he lists three names, Father, Son, and Holy Spirit. The tension between one and many is striking. As St. John Henry Newman points out, *one God* and *three persons* taken separately are plain and exact statements; taken together they rise up before human reason as a mystery beyond its measure.

> This solemn and supernatural ordinance of discipleship was to be administered in the Name—of whom? in the Name (can we doubt it ?) of Him whose disciples the converts forthwith became, of that God whom, from that day forward, they confessed and adored; whom they promised to obey; in whose word they trusted; by whose bounty they were to be rewarded. Yet when Christ would name the Name of God, He does but say, "in the Name of the Father, and of the Son, and of the Holy Ghost." . . .
>
> Christ makes no mystery for the occasion; He uses the plainest and most exact form of speech which human language admits of. And this deserves notice; for it may be extended to the details of this great Catholic doctrine. . . . I mean that, much as is idly and profanely said against the Creed of St. Athanasius as being unintelligible, yet the real objection which misbelievers feel, if they spoke correctly, is, that it is too plain. No sentences can be more simple, nor statements more precise, than those of which it consists. The difficulty is *not in any one singly; but in their combination.*[29]

Neither the baptismal formula nor its gradual expansion in the various forms of the Creed makes any attempt to remove the tension between one and many. The tension is sustained and preserved. It remains the norm of faith and thus also the norm for speculative theology, as Balthasar argues in agreement with Newman.

> [Faith in the Trinity] can never speak otherwise than in two statements that run in opposite directions and cannot be joined into one. . . . That the hypostases really exist vis-à-vis each other is known to faith from the facts of reve-

28. Gilles Emery, OP, *The Trinitarian Theology of Saint Thomas Aquinas*, trans. Francesca Aran Murphy (Oxford: Oxford University Press, 2007), 7; *La théologie trinitaire de saint Thomas d'Aquin* (Paris: Cerf, 2004), 15.

29. John Henry Newman, "The Mystery of the Holy Trinity," Sermon for Trinity Sunday, in *Parochial and Plain Sermons*, 8 vols. (London: Longmans, Green, 1907), 6:343–44 and 6:346–47; emphasis added.

> lation. That Father, Son, and Holy Spirit are one God is likewise known to it from revelation and its ecclesial interpretation.
>
> The speculative challenge presented by the mystery that these two sides are identical can in each case be met adequately only by a converging movement of two propositions that cannot be reduced to one.[30]

The Council of Nicaea (AD 325) responded to two opposite ways of removing the tension, Arian subordinationism and Sabellian modalism. A letter by Arius written five years before the Council eloquently shows that his concern was the defense of the unity of God, following the teaching of Moses and Jesus. "The Lord our God, the Lord is one," understood as setting the deepest orientation of human life. "And you shall love. . ." (Deuteronomy 6:4; Mark 12:29). Arius's unyielding opposition to his bishop has its roots in the commitment to this bedrock of piety.

> The bishop . . . has driven us out of the city as atheists, because we do not agree with what he publicly preaches, namely, that God has always been, and the Son has always been. Father and Son exist together. . . . The Son is from God himself. These are impieties to which we could not listen, even though the heretics threaten us with a thousand deaths.[31]

St. Thomas observes in his explanation of Sabellian modalism. "The fixed mental conception of all who think rightly about God is that there can only be one God."[32] The difference between Arius and Sabellius lies in the means by which they defend this fixed mental conception. Arius defends *one* against *many* by pushing *many* to the extreme and thereby pushing it outside of God. He sees the Son as distinct in his very being from the Father and thus as a creature. Sabellius defends *one* against *many* by pushing *one* to the extreme, reducing *many* to the point of disappearance within God. The Father is born of a woman and as the son (her son) suffers and dies for us.

Although the means used by Arius and Sabellius differ, the result is the same. *One God* is the person of the Father *alone*. The Father is alone. A personal God who is alone is certainly not Father, Son, and Holy Spirit. The most direct way of opposing both ways of destroying the tension is to affirm that God is *one but not alone*.

According to St. Gregory of Nazianzus, Greek philosophers discuss three possible ways of understanding the *arche*, the beginning of all things: none-rule, many-rule, and one-rule. Plato's *Republic* and Aristotle's *Metaphysics* show that

30. Balthasar, *Theologik*, 2:123–24; *Theo-Logic*, 2:132–33.

31. Letter of Arius to Eusebius of Nicomedia; James Stevenson, ed., *A New Eusebius: Documents Illustrating the History of the Church to AD 337* (London: SPCK, 1987), 324–25.

32. Thomas, *Contra gentiles* IV, cap. 5, no. 3374.

this discussion involves both the metaphysical question of the origin (*arche*) of beings and the political question of rule (*arche*).[33]

Gregory presents the Christian option for one-rule (monarchy) but not a monarchy circumscribed by one person. For Christians, he argues, the distinction of persons in God decisively qualifies the understanding of monarchy.

> Three opinions about God have come down to us, none-rule (*anarchia*), many-rule (*polyarchia*), and one-rule (*monarchia*).... None-rule is disorder. Many-rule is conflict, and thus none-rule, and thus disorder. Both, then, are toward the same, toward disorder, which is toward destruction, for disorder is the symptom announcing destruction.
>
> For us, by contrast, one-rule is worthy of honor, not the one-rule which is circumscribed by one person, for if that one is in conflict with itself, it becomes many, but the one which is established by equal honor of nature, breathing together of will, sameness of activity, and leaning together toward the one by those who are from it... so that, even though it differs in number it is not divided in being.[34]

Especially noteworthy are the phrases "breathing together of will, sameness of activity, and leaning together toward the one by those who are from it." A text by Augustine can be set next to Gregory's.

> Whether [the Holy Spirit] is the unity between [Father and Son], or their holiness, or their love, or whether the unity, therefore, because he is the love, it is obvious that he is not one of the two. Through him both are joined together; through him the begotten is loved by the begetter, and in turn loves him who begot him; in him they preserve the unity of spirit through the bond of peace, not by a participation but by their own essence [*non participatione sed essentia sua*], not by the gift of anyone superior to themselves but by their own [*neque dono superioris alicuius sed suo proprio*]... Whatever the Holy Spirit is, therefore, it is something common [*commune aliquid*] between the Father and the Son. But this communion is consubstantial and co-eternal... and this again is a substance, because God is a substance, and "God is Love" [1 John 6:14].[35]

One finds the denial of solitude and the affirmation of communion consistently in Thomas's writings on the Trinity, from his early to his late writings.

33. See Plato, *Republic* 8–9, 543c–576b. The last sentence of book 12 of Aristotle's *Metaphysics* is a quote from Homer, "It is not good to have many-rule (*poly-koiranie*); one ruler let there be." Aristotle, *Metaphysics* 12.10, 1076a4.

34. Gregory of Nazianzus, *Oratio theologica* 3.2.

35. Augustine, *De trinitate* 6.5.7; translation by Lewis Ayres, *Augustine and the Trinity* (Cambridge: Cambridge University Press, 2010), 252, with excellent commentary on the text and its context.

> *Scriptum on the Sentences* (1252–56): One should not speak of … [God] being alone (*solitudo*) in order that the society of persons (*societas personarum*), which is by the unity of love, is not taken away.[36] Alone (*solus*) … can in no way be accepted in divine things, because one person always has the fellowship of the society of another person (*consortium societatis alterius personae*).[37] He [Peter Lombard] posits three persons united by a certain society of love (*societate quadam amoris*) which is the Holy Spirit and therefore he predicates harmony, as is evident from Hilary, and excludes solitude.[38]
>
> *De potentia* (1265–68): Against being alone, we confess the harmony and bond of love (*consonantiam et connexionem amoris*).[39]
>
> *Summa* (1267–68): The word *alone* must be avoided so that one does not take away the fellowship of the three persons (*consortium trium personarum*).[40]
>
> *Commentary on John* (1270–72): Never was the Father alone (*solitarius*) without the Son or Word but always this one, namely the Word, was with God.[41]

The anti-Sabellian arguments in the *Summa contra gentiles* are for the most part simple and obvious. Exactly for this reason they are powerful.

> Where there is one subsistent *suppositum*, the plural is not admitted. But Christ speaks about himself and the Father in the plural when he says, "I and the Father are one" (John 10:30). Therefore the Son is not the Father himself.[42]
>
> "I came down from heaven not to do my own will but the will of him who sent me" (John 6:38). And likewise, "Now glorify me, Father, in your presence" (John 17:5). From these and similar texts it is clear that the Son is other than the Father.[43]

In the second argument, Thomas links the beginning of Jesus's mission, "I came down from heaven" with the end, his glorification on the Cross. A close connection between *love*, *gift*, and *glory* can be seen in Johannine texts about this beginning and end. "The perfection of glory consists in a certain greatness of complete giving which love brings about."[44] The statement "not to do my own will but the will of him who sent me" brings the mutual love between the Father and the Son into sharp focus. "That the world might know that I love the Father and as the Father commanded me, thus I do" (John 14:31). "On account of this

36. Thomas, *Super I sent.*, d. 2, q. 1, a. 5, expositio textus.
37. Thomas, *Super I sent.*, d. 21, q. 1, a. 1, qc. 1, corp.
38. Thomas, *Super I sent.*, d. 24, q. 2, a. 1, corp.
39. Thomas, *De potentia*, q. 9, a. 8, corp.
40. Thomas, *Summa* I, q. 31, a. 2, corp.
41. Thomas, *Super Ioannem*, cap. 1, lect. 2, no. 61.
42. Thomas, *Contra gentiles* 4, cap. 5, no. 3383.
43. Thomas, *Contra gentiles* 4, cap. 5, no. 3380.
44. Thomas, *De potentia*, q. 9, a. 9, sed contra 2.

the Father loves me that I lay down my life to take it up again" (John 10:17). The text on the end focuses on the mutual glorification in which this mutual love expresses itself.

> I glorified you on earth
> by completing the work you have given me to do.
> And now you, Father, glorify me in your presence
> with the glory I had in your presence before the being of the world.
> (John 17:4–5)

The glory manifested in the end is due to a primordial love. "The glory you have given me because you loved me before the foundation of the world" (John 17:24).

In the texts just quoted, the distinction of persons is made clear by the personal pronouns *I, you*, and *we*. These pronouns express an elementary experience that has been present in human life as far as we can look back in history. They are deeply interwoven with personal consciousness. Children use and understand such pronouns. They continue to use and understand them when they have grown up.

Personal pronouns were the starting point from which the Greek-speaking Church developed the notion of *prosopon, person. Prosopon* is a compound of *pros* (toward) and *opon* (object of sight). In classical Greek, it can refer to the surface of a thing that faces the viewer, such as the face of the moon. When it signifies *face* as a specific part of an animal, Aristotle, claims, it is used only for the human face. "What is below the skull is called face (*prosopon*) but only in the case of man among the animals, for the term is not applied to a fish or to an ox."[45] Already at this early stage of development, *prosopon*, understood as the face of a living being, singles out rational beings and thus tends toward *person*.

In a seminal essay, Carl Andresen shows how the development from *face* to *person* took place.[46] Hellenistic scholars of ancient texts systematically raised the question, *Who is speaking in this text?* Is it Agamemnon or Achilles or Homer himself? Is it Callicles or Socrates or Plato himself? They called this analysis *prosopography*, the recording of faces. The question *who* as distinct from *what* is answered by pointing to *this face, prosopon*. A more developed understanding was slowly worked out with the help of terms such as *ousia* (*substantia*), *physis*

45. Aristotle, *History of Animals* 1.8.491b.9–11.

46. See Carl Andresen, "Zur Entstehung und Geschichte des trinitarischen Personbegriffes," *Zeitschrift für die neutestamentliche Wissenschaft* 52 (1961): 1–39, esp. 14–18. See also Alois Grillmeier, SJ, *Christ in Christian Tradition: From the Apostolic Age to Chalcedon* (451), 2nd ed., trans. John Bowden (Atlanta: John Knox Press, 1975), 124–31; *Jesus der Christus im Glauben der Kirche: Band 1. Von der apostolischen Zeit bis zum Konzil von Chalcedon* (451), 3rd ed. (Freiburg: Herder, 1990), 251–57.

(*natura*), and *hypostasis* (*suppositum* or *subsistentia*), but the anchor of *prosopon* remained: *Who*?

The Cappadocian Fathers (Basil, Gregory of Nazianzus, and Gregory of Nyssa) and Hilary of Poitiers formulated a truth distinctly that is implicit in the New Testament, especially in the Gospel of John, and in the early Church's theological reflection on it. To be a father is to be an origin, and to be a son is to be from that origin. Fatherhood and sonship stand in relative opposition to each other: *to* as opposed to *from*. The Father and the Son are one in being, life, and understanding, but they are personally distinct by this relative opposition between fatherhood and sonship.

> *Basil of Caesarea (ca. AD 329–79):* When we hear of the unbegotten light, we think of the Father; of the begotten light, we think of the Son. As regards light and light there is no contrariety between them, but as regards begotten and unbegotten one considers them under the aspect of their opposition (*antithesis*).[47]
>
> *Gregory of Nazianzus* (ca. *AD 329–89):* Father is a name neither of substance nor of activity, but of relationship, of the manner of being, which holds good between Father and Son. Just as with us these names indicate kindred and affinity, so here too they designate the sameness of stock, of parent and offspring.[48]
>
> *Gregory of Nyssa (ca. AD 335–95):* If anyone brings the objection against the account that, since it does not accept the difference according to nature, it leads to the mixing and circular conflation of hypostases, we will say in defense against this charge that by confessing no difference in nature we do not deny the distinction with respect to cause (αἴτιον) and caused (αἰτιατὸν), by which alone we claim that the one is distinct from the other, by believing that one is the cause (αἴτιον), the other from the cause (ἐκ τοῦ αἰτίου).[49]
>
> *Hilary of Poitiers (ca. AD 310–67):* The Son cannot and ought not to be distinguished from the Father except inasmuch as he is born while nevertheless not being different.[50]

47. Basil of Caesarea, *Contra Eunomium* 2.28. Translation following Gilles Emery, *The Trinity: An Introduction to the Catholic Doctrine of the Triune God*, trans. Matthew Levering (Washington, DC: Catholic University of America Press, 2011), 87–88.

48. Gregory of Nazianzus, *Oratio theologica* 3.16; translation following Lewis Ayres, *Nicaea and Its Legacy: An Approach to Fourth-Century Trinitarian Theology* (Oxford: Oxford University Press, 2004), 247.

49. Gregory of Nyssa, *Ad Ablabium, Quod non sint tres dii*; PG 145:133B. For an excellent commentary on this text, see Ayres, *Nicaea and Its Legacy*, 344–58.

50. Hilary, *De trinitate* 7.20.

3. Mutual Love Questioned

Karl Rahner

For us who live in the modern age, Rahner argues, the word *person* has come to mean something quite different than it did for the Fathers and medieval Doctors. When we repeat the old dogmatic formulae and speak of three divine persons, we think of persons as distinct centers of consciousness that can say *you* to each other. The Fathers and medieval theologians were free of this tendency.[51]

To speak of mutual love between the divine persons from the modern perspective, Rahner charges, is "latent tritheism."[52] He states in lapidary fashion what he sees as the essential point, on which he means to defend the heritage of the Fathers and Doctors. "In the Trinity there is no mutual *you*. The Son is the Father's speaking of himself, which must not be conceived in turn as speaking."[53]

> Even with absolute respect for the magisterial and classical formulations and self-evident assent of faith to what is meant in these formulations, one will have to admit that statements about the Trinity in their catechetical formulations are almost unintelligible for a contemporary person and almost unavoidably lead to misunderstandings....
>
> When in our common use of language today we speak of one person as distinct from another person, we can hardly avoid the notion that for them to be persons and to be distinct, each of them has its own free center of conscious and free activity which has mastery over itself and differentiates itself from others, and that it is precisely this which constitutes a person. But this is the very thing which is excluded by the dogmatic teaching on the single and unique essence of God. This unicity of essence implies and includes the unicity of one single consciousness and one single freedom, although of course the unicity of one self-presence in consciousness and freedom in the divine Trinity remains determined by that mysterious threeness which we profess about God when we speak haltingly of the Trinity of persons in God.[54]

51. See Karl Rahner, "Der dreifaltige Gott als transzendenter Ursprung der Heilsgeschichte," in *Mysterium Salutis: Grundriss heilsgeschichtlicher Dogmatik*, ed. Johannes Feiner and Magnus Löhrer, 5 vols. (Einsiedeln: Benziger, 1967), 2:317–401, at 2:388–89.

52. Rahner, "Der dreifaltige Gott," 393.

53. Rahner, "Der dreifaltige Gott," 366n29. See Balthasar's discussion of this thesis in *Theodramatik*, 2/2:481n15; *Theodrama*, 3:526n1.

54. Karl Rahner, *Foundations of Christian Faith: Introduction to the Idea of Christianity* (New York: Crossroad, 1978), 134; *Grundkurs des Glaubens: Einführung in den Begriff des Christentums*, new ed. with different pagination (Freiburg: Herder, 2008), 133.

Rahner seems to overstretch the differences between us and the early Church. The root of the concept person in personal pronouns remains common ground between us and the early Church. The understanding of relative opposition in relations of origin developed by the Cappadocians and Hilary is still available to us, even if we have a sophisticated understanding of centers of consciousness. The one divine center of consciousness is an aspect of the divine being, life, and understanding, to which the principle of relative opposition applies. In the Son, the one divine center of consciousness is from the Father. In the Father, it is toward the Son in the mode of gift. "You are my son. Today have I begotten you" (Psalm 2:7; Hebrews 1:5, 5:5; Acts 13:32–33). "You are my beloved Son. In you I am well pleased" (Mark 1:11).

Bernard Lonergan

The divine persons do not say *you* to each other, Lonergan claims, because the analogy of the word allows for only one speaker in the Trinity, the Father.

> Within God, just as only one person is generating, so only one is speaking. For as the one generating stands to the Son, so the one speaking stands to the Word; and just as the same property is signified by "Word" as by "Son," so the same property is signified by "speaking" as by "generating." Therefore, within God no one speaks except the Father.... All that can be signified through the pronouns "I" and "you" are spoken by the Father through the Word; but within God no material sounds are heard, nor are there many distinct concepts, but one alone who is the Word.
>
> Externally to God, however, nothing prevents the occurrence of an utterance that proceeds from the divine will, whether it be one in which the incarnate Word says, "As you, Father, are in me and I in you" (John 17:21), or one that states that "God has sent the Spirit of his Son into our hearts, crying, Abba! Father!" (Galatians 4:6; Romans 8:15). But within God there is nothing that proceeds from an act of the divine will as from a really distinct principle.[55]

Lonergan is obviously right to point out that *speaking*, in the sense of audible expressions of distinct concepts, cannot be said about God. He is also right to point out that speaking in the sense of begetting belongs to the Father alone. It is not clear whether he means to say more. The analogy of mutual love seems rather muted in his Trinitarian theology. He affirms this analogy with respect to our relations with the divine persons but does not go further.

55. Bernard Lonergan, *The Triune God: Systematics*, ed. Robert M. Doran and H. Daniel Monsour, trans. Michael G. Shields (Toronto: University of Toronto Press, 2007), 397–99.

> Since through the truth revealed by God and accepted by faith we acknowledge three divine persons, we can thereby converse with the Three, addressing each one as "you." But if the only interpersonal relations recognized as such are those that are known to the subject through the experience of his or her own intersubjectivity, there arises a whole new and quite complex series of questions that we think best to omit here.[56]

Hyacinthe Dondaine

Dondaine questions the analogy of mutual love as a specialist in the history of Thomas's Trinitarian theology. Thomas changed his mind about the scientific starting point of Trinitarian theology, he claims. Thomas accepted this interpersonal analogy in his early works but rejected it with convincing arguments in his mature works. In his early writings he understood *mutual love* between the Father and the Son as analogical. By the time he wrote the *Summa*, he came to see it as a metaphor. He chose God's *essential love of himself* instead as the scientific account of the Holy Spirit's procession. Having been attracted to the Trinitarian theology of Richard of St. Victor, he switched sides and from then on remained loyal to Augustine's intrapersonal analogy of the word.[57]

Maurílio Penido

Early in his career, Penido claims, Thomas accepted some of Richard of St. Victor's statements about mutual love between the persons of the Trinity. In his mature years, he freed himself from this interpersonal analogy and embraced the analogy of the word as the only viable way of thinking about the Trinity. He decided the battle between the two analogies and led Augustinianism to triumph.

> These two doctrines represent two irreducible types of Trinitarian Theology.... Since they see the mystery from opposite points of view, the two conceptions cannot be reconciled. If one insists, one condemns oneself to incoherence or one adopts one of them and keeps some elements of the other as erratic blocks. Thomas began with Richard's theory but freed himself from it little by little. In the *Summa*, Augustinianism triumphs.[58]

56. Lonergan, *Triune God*, 397.

57. See Hyacinthe François Dondaine, *Somme théologique: La trinité, 1a, questions 27–*[43], 2 vols. (Paris: Cerf, Desclée, 1943–1946), 2:397–401. Dondaine's work is held in high esteem by Yves Congar, who quotes it with approval. See his *I Believe in the Holy Spirit*, 2 vols. (New York: Seabury Press, 1983), 1:90.

58. Maurílio Teixeira-Leite Penido, "Gloses sur la procession d'amour dans la Trinité," *Ephemerides Theologicae Lovanienses* 14 (1937): 3–68, at 48–49.

What Augustinianism? Augustine writes,

> The Holy Spirit is something common of the Father and the Son, whatever it is, or the consubstantial and eternal communion itself, which, if it is fittingly called friendship (*amicitia*), let it be called that, though it is more fittingly called love (*caritas*).[59]

If the Augustinianism that triumphs is not that of Augustine but that of the mature Thomas, who had a better understanding of Augustine than Augustine himself, what is one to make of the following text by the mature Thomas? "The procession of the intellect is from one alone, but the friendship (*amicitia*) that is mutual love proceeds toward each other from two who love each other."[60] Another mature text shows that the two forms of analogy are not only reconcilable but necessary complements of each other.

> If one focuses on the power of breathing, the Holy Spirit proceeds from the Father and the Son as one in the power of breathing.... But if one considers the supposits of breathing, in this way the Holy Spirit proceeds from the Father and the Sun as many. For it proceeds from them as love unitive of two.[61]

The impression of opposition between the two forms of analogy, at times in a softer and less resolute form than Penido's, lies at the root of influential misgivings about TOB among many Thomists. Thomas, they point out, spends little time and effort on the interpersonal analogy. Most of his writings on the Trinity develop the analogy of the inner word and proceeding love. Interpersonal love, they infer, is speculatively less fruitful for scientific theology of the Trinity, even if it is practically more useful for a pastoral theology of the body. A rigorous theology of the Trinity sets the interpersonal analogy aside and limits itself to the analogy of the word.

Does this judgment agree with Thomas's understanding of the analogy of the word? And, more important, is it true? What are the consequences of holding it?

4. The Analogy of the Word

Commentary on John 1:1

Thomas's commentary on John 1:1 is a good text for observing his understanding of the analogy of the word. The commentary, written after the *Prima pars*

59. Augustine, *De trinitate* 6.5.7.
60. Thomas, *De potentia*, q. 10, a. 2, ad 11.
61. Thomas, *Summa* I, q. 36, a. 4, ad 1.

of the *Summa*, is his most mature and detailed statement of the analogy.[62] It understands the analogy of the word as an argument in two parts. The first part discusses the inner word in the human mind; the second rises from the human word to the divine Word.

Part One: The Word Proceeding in the Human Mind

1. The Latin Verbum and the Greek Logos

Verbum signifies a word spoken out loud. It recalls "*verberatio aeris*, the beating of the air," and "*boatus*, shout, since *verbum* is nothing other than *verum boans*, shouting the true."[63] In this respect, the commentary points out, Greek *logos* differs from Latin *verbum*. *Spoken word* is one of the possible meanings of *logos*, but a more frequent meaning is *ratio*—that is, *account* or *reason*—without the connotation of *spoken*. One might expect, therefore, that the commentary would prefer *ratio* since *ratio* brings the discussion immediately to the inner word without the apparent detour through *verbum*, the audibly spoken word. This expectation is mistaken.

> Augustine raises the following question. In Greek, where we have *verbum*, the text has *logos*. Now, since *logos* means both Latin *ratio* (account) and *verbum*, why did the translators translate it as *verbum* and not as *ratio*, since *ratio* is something within, in the way *verbum* is as well?
>
> I answer. One should say that *ratio* properly names the concept of the mind inasmuch as it is in the mind, even if nothing comes to be through it outside. But *verbum* signifies a reference to what is outside. When the Evangelist said *Logos*, he did not intend to signify only a reference to the Son's existence in the Father, but also his power to produce works, by which all things were made. And so the ancients translated *logos* as *verbum*, which implies a reference to what is outside, rather than *ratio*, which only suggests the concept of the mind (no. 32).

The immediately preceding passage in the commentary points in the same direction. Why does John say *Logos* rather than the more usual *Son*? It fits his presentation of the Son as the audible and visible manifestation of the Father in the economy of salvation.

> The Evangelist is about to present the Word as coming to manifest the Father. Therefore, since the account (*ratio*) of manifestation is expressed more by the word *verbum* than by the word *Son*, he used the word *verbum*. (no. 31)

62. Thomas, *Super Ioannem*, cap. 1, lect. 1, no. 25–29.

63. Thomas, *Super I sent.*, d. 27, q. 2, a. 1, obj. 1 and ad 1; *De veritate*, q. 4, a. 1, obj. 8 and ad 8.

Verbum has a further advantage in comparison with *ratio*. The outer word proceeds as spoken from a speaker. When *verbum* is said of the inner word, it keeps the connotation of being spoken. Speaking and being spoken are opposite relations of origin. Since it includes these relations of origin, *verbum* is the name of a person in God, not a name of the divine essence (n. 29). By contrast, Greek *logos*, as Thomas understands it, can be a name of the essence when it means *ratio* and a personal name when it means *verbum*.

2. Analogical Extension to the Inner Concept

After defining *verbum* as spoken sound, the commentary turns to Aristotle's remark that "spoken sounds are signs of *pathemata,* things undergone, of the soul."[64] One can give the name of the sign by analogy to what it signifies. Scripture exemplifies this way of speaking, the commentary claims, in 1 Corinthians 10:4, "The rock was Christ" petra autem erat Christus. The rock struck by Moses in the desert gave living water to the people dying of thirst. For this reason it can serve as a sign of Christ.

The example is not an ideal fit. The grammatical subject of the statement in 1 Corinthians 10:4 seems to be *rock*. The sign (the rock) receives the name of the signified (Christ). *The dog's fur is healthy* is a well-known example of this form of analogy in which the name of the signified is transferred to the sign. The dog's *health* is the signified and *fur* the sign. In the case of *word*, the order is the opposite. *Word*, the name of the sign, is given to the signified, the inner concept. It would be an unusual analogy to say, *The dog's health is furry.*

"Of necessity, then, what is inside our soul, which is signified by our outer word, must be called *word*." *Must of necessity be called word* evidently does not mean that everyone does call thoughts *words* or should do so but rather that one can give a legitimate reason for it. Noteworthy, however, is the use of language appropriate for strict proof, not only here but also elsewhere in the argument.

The question arises "whether the term *verbum* belongs first (*per prius conveniat*) to the external sound brought forth by the voice or to the conception of the mind." This question, not directly answered by the commentary, concerns the order of before and after in analogy. The *Summa* answers the question. "The inner concept of the mind is first and mainly called *word*."[65] The reason is that the outer word is only called word inasmuch as it signifies an inner word. *Word* as said about the inner concept must therefore be included in the definition of *word* as said about the articulated sound. In the logical order, *word* said about the concept comes before *word* as externally spoken. In the temporal order of the

64. Aristotle, *On Interpretation* 16a3–4.

65. Thomas, *Summa* I, q. 34, a. 1, corp.; emphasis added.

use of *word*, the opposite is true, because *word* is extended by analogy from the outer to the inner word.

3. The Nature of the Inner Word

Since the outer word is a sign of the inner word, one can find the inner word by investigating what the outer word signifies. *Stone* does not signify the power of knowing, nor the *species* that informs or actualizes the power, nor the activity of knowing, because the stone is outside the knower while these three are within.[66] Does this argument also apply to the inner word? Yes and no. Outer words do not signify things immediately. They signify them as we know them, as present to the knower in the inner word.

The human mind forms two kinds of inner words: simple apprehension as in *stone* and statements as in *The stone is heavy*. Only a statement can be true or false. Only a statement, therefore, can be the expression of knowledge in the fullest way.

Since the inner word expresses knowledge, "it compares to the mind, not as that *by which* the mind knows but as that *in which* the mind knows. For in the expressed and formed [word] itself it sees the nature of the thing understood.... And so we have the meaning of *verbum*."

Having shown *what* the inner word is, the commentary focuses on four aspects of its mode of procession.

4. First Aspect of Procession: As Act from Act

Since the inner word expresses knowledge, "it is always something that proceeds from a mind existing in act." It proceeds as act from act, not as actualizing a potency. Without the word, knowledge would not be knowledge. Still, the word does not add a perfection to knowledge but expresses the perfection of knowledge.

5. Second Aspect: As Spoken

The inner word proceeds as spoken. Its procession therefore implies two opposite relations of origin in the *speaker* and the *spoken*.

6. Third Aspect: as a Likeness

The inner word proceeds as a likeness, not the kind of likeness exemplified by a marble statue. The statue is a second real being. To see it as a likeness, one must first know the statue and the person portrayed by it as two real beings and compare them. The inner word is a likeness in a more intimate sense. It is not *that which* one knows, as one must know the statue before comparing it to the person portrayed, but immediately *that in which* one knows something. It is a representation in the sense of a second presence that presents the first presence

66. Cf. Thomas, *Quodlibetum* 5, q. 5, a. 2.

of a being by its own existence. The presence of a being in the world (first presence) becomes itself present to someone who knows it (representation).

7. Fourth Aspect: As a Likeness of the Speaker

When one knows oneself, one speaks an inner word that expresses one's knowledge of oneself in the form of a likeness of oneself.

Part Two: The Word Proceeding in the Divine Mind

1. The Existence of a Word in God

The first step is to argue *that* there is a Word in God. The key principle of the argument is the connection between knowledge and the word that expresses it.

> One must posit a word in any intellectual nature because it belongs to the account (*ratio*) of understanding that the intellect forms something by understanding. This formation is called word. And thus one must posit a word in anything that understands.

There must be a word, therefore, in human, angelic, and divine knowledge. "In the beginning was the Word ... all things were made through him" (John 1:1, 1:3) cannot apply to the first two, but only to the third. Therefore there is a Word in God.

Having answered the question *whether there is* a divine Word, the commentary turns to the question *what it is* or *how it is*. It does so by drawing three contrasts between the human word and the divine Word.

2. First Contrast: Imperfect as Opposed to Perfect

Our words are first formable and then formed gradually as our thought progresses from potency to act. They become words in the most actual sense when they express knowledge in the most actual sense. The divine Word, by contrast, proceeds as pure act from pure act without progression.

3. Second Contrast: Partial as Opposed to Comprehensive

Our words are imperfect while God's Word is most perfect. We must form many words because each of them is incomplete. By contrast, "God speaks once" (Job 3:14) and by this one word expresses all there is to be expressed.

4. Third Contrast: Intelligible Being as Opposed to Real Being

Third, the human inner word is not a real subsistent being. "It has only intelligible being" habet esse intelligibile tantum. "It befalls someone" est accidens ei.[67]

67. The phrase *est accidens ei* is probably not to be taken as *is his accident* in the sense of Aristotle's genera of accidents. The inner word "only has intelligible being." In *Quodlibetum 7*, q. 1, a. 4, Thomas discusses whether the *notitia* which Augustine calls an offspring of the mind is an accident. Since he understands *notitia* as the act of knowledge, he concludes that it is an accident while the

Since all that is in God is God, the Word in God is not merely a thought about God but God. It subsists as God and is therefore a divine person.

From the three contrasts, the commentary draws three corollaries.

5. First Corollary: Word is Always the Name of a Person

A *word* is something expressed or spoken by someone. It therefore implies opposite relations of origin in the speaker and the spoken. *Word* includes the relation of origin expressed by *spoken*. For this reason, *word* is always said personally in God, never essentially, because the divine persons are distinct by relative opposition in relations of origin. As pointed out above, this statement applies to Greek *logos* when it means *verbum*. It does not apply to it when it means *ratio*.

6. Second Corollary: Likeness, Co-Eternal, Equal, and Consubstantial

The Word proceeds as a likeness. It is co-eternal with God because it proceeds without beginning as act from eternal act. It is equal to God because it is perfect and expressive of the Father's whole being. It is consubstantial with the Father because it is his substance.

7. Third Corollary: The Word Can Be Called Son

Since the Word proceeds as a living likeness, the Father's act of speaking can be called *begetting* and the Word itself can be called *Son*.

What Sort of Argument?

The analogy of the word as presented in Thomas's commentary on John 1:1 is not simply an explanation of the meaning of the word *logos* in John. It is an argument for the existence, mode of procession, and characteristics of an inner Word of God based on an analysis of the word in the human mind.

Is it a philosophical or a theological argument? John 1:1 is the text commented on, which seems to settle the question in favor of *theological*. If Scripture did not say, "In the beginning was the Word," the argument would certainly not be given. On the other hand, John 1:1 is not used as a premise. The conclusion follows without the appeal to Scripture from the key principle about knowledge and word. *Wherever there is knowledge, there must be a word that expresses it.* The argument looks like a philosophical proof, similar to one of the five ways. Yet this is exactly what it cannot be. How, then, should one understand its nature and function?

Summa I, q. 32, a. 1, ad 2, addresses this question. It shows how Thomas understands the argument. The opening question of the whole article is whether the Trinity can be known by natural reason. It cannot, the body of the article

relation of knowledge to the thing known is not. The account of the inner word does not yet appear in this text in its developed form.

argues. We can know God through the sensible beings of this world as effects of his creative power. Since this power is common to the divine persons, the effects can lead us to God as one, but not to the distinction of persons.[68]

If arguments from natural reason *cannot* lead us to the Trinity in the form of a proof, what *can* they do? The body of the article leaves this side of the opening question unanswered, but the response to the second objection addresses it. The second objection sketches several ways for natural reason to come to know the Trinity.

> [*The First Way: The Good is Diffusive*] To prove the Trinity of persons some have given an argument from the infinity of divine goodness, which communicates itself infinitely in the procession of the divine persons.
>
> [*The Second Way: The Joy of Communion*] Others through this that there cannot be joyful possession of any good without fellowship.
>
> [*The Third Way: The Analogy of the Word*] But Augustine proceeds to manifest the Trinity of persons by the procession of the word and of love in our mind, which is the way (*via*) we have been following above.
>
> Therefore the Trinity of persons can be known by natural reason.[69]

Augustine's way appears in this objection as one of three ways in which natural reason can come to know the Trinity. The error is not that Augustine's way is a way of natural reason like the others but that it is a way for natural reason to *know* in the sense of *prove* the Trinity.

The response to this objection has two parts. The first distinguishes two ways in which natural reason can give an argument and illustrates each with an example from astronomy. The second part states that in the first way natural reason can give arguments about God in the unity of his essence and in the second way about God in the Trinity of persons. Importantly, the response goes beyond simply denying the possibility of proof. It affirms that an argument for an inner Word of God such as the one in the commentary on John 1:1 is an argument of the second type.

> [Two Ways Natural Reason Can Give an Argument]
>
> One can give an argument about something in two ways.
>
> *In one way*, to prove some root sufficiently, as a sufficient argument is given in natural science to prove that the movement of heaven is always of uniform velocity.
>
> *In another way*, one can give an argument, not one which sufficiently proves a root, but one which shows that the consequent effects fit (*congruere*) the al-

68. See Thomas, *Summa* I, q. 32, a. 1, corp.

69. Thomas, *Summa* I, q. 32, a. 1, obj. 2.

ready posited root, as in astronomy the argument of eccentric circles and epicycles is posited because on this hypothesis the sensible appearances concerning heavenly movements can be saved. Nevertheless, this argument is not sufficient proof, because the appearances can perhaps be saved on another hypothesis.

[It Can Give Arguments for the Trinity in the Second Way, Not the First]

In the first way, an argument can be given to prove that God is one and the like.

In the second way, however, an argument is disposed that is given to manifest the Trinity. For, once the Trinity is posited, such arguments fit (*congruunt*). Not in such a way, however, that by these arguments the Trinity of persons is sufficiently proved.

And this is evident in each case.

[*First Argument:*] Infinite goodness is shown even in bringing forth creatures, because it is of infinite power to bring forth from nothing. If God communicates himself with infinite goodness, it is indeed not necessary for something infinite to proceed from God, but for it to receive the divine goodness in its own way.

[*Second Argument:*] Likewise also the statement that there cannot be joyful possession of any good without fellowship applies when perfect goodness is not found in one person. Hence for the full goodness of joy he needs the good of another associated to himself.

[*Augustine's argument:*] The likeness of our intellect, finally, does not sufficiently prove anything about God, because intellect is not found univocally in God and us. For this reason, Augustine says that one comes to knowledge through faith rather than the other way around.[70]

The example of eccentrics and epicycles serves as an illustration. It is not helpful as an illustration, of course, if one transfers the wrong characteristics to the analogy of the word. It would be a mistake, for example, to see the analogy of the word as *one among many possible equivalent hypotheses*, as if love or power or mercy could in principle work equally well instead of knowledge. Caution is clearly needed.

Conversely, if one shields the analogy of the word against false transfers so completely that only the negation of proof is left, one has done too much of a good thing. The example of eccentrics and epicycles no longer illustrates, which removes the only reason why Thomas would give such a complex example.

The example is not the only basis for interpreting the text. There are direct positive statements about the second way of giving an argument. The analogy of the word is "an argument, not one which sufficiently proves a root, but one

70. Thomas, *Summa* I, q. 32, a. 1, ad 2.

which shows that the consequent effects fit the already posited root . . . Once the Trinity is posited, such arguments fit."

The illustration for the first way of giving an argument is the proof for the uniform velocity of heaven. We are likely to dismiss such a proof without even looking at it. We have been told that the daily movement of heaven is due to the earth's rotation on its axis. We have good reason to believe what we have been told. Still, we continue to use words like *sunrise* and *sunset*. On this spontaneous level, we have understood the sufficient proof of uniform motion and have made it our own. The sun rises every day when it ought and sets when we expect it to. We perform an induction that concludes to uniform velocity.

Aristotle's arguments for uniform velocity in *De caelo* 2.6 touch on many aspects, such as the geometric properties of circles. The root of all the arguments, however, is this induction from daily experience. "Irregularity of this kind [viz., speeding up and slowing down] would be particularly unlikely to pass unobserved since contrast makes observation easy."[71] Although the assumption that the earth is stationary misplaces the motion, the illustration remains clear. The proof of the root is an induction based on observation. It is not the strongest kind of proof, but it is at least close to the senses.

The arguments illustrated by this example—namely, the five ways and the arguments about the divine attributes—are not inductions. This feature of the example must not be transferred but denied. The point of likeness is limited to *sufficient proof* and does not extend to *the specific kind of* sufficient proof.

Such a judgment about points of likeness and unlikeness is even more important in the second example, the hypothetical explanation of how uniform circular motion causes the nonuniform apparent motion of the planets. Alternate hypotheses are possible. In this respect the analogy of the word differs. It is not one among several possible hypotheses. It is concerned with knowledge and the inner word. It does not leave open the possibility of other hypotheses based on other divine attributes.

The hypothesis of eccentrics and epicycles addresses a problem. Seven heavenly bodies visible without a telescope (the Moon, Mercury, Venus, the Sun, Mars, Jupiter, and Saturn) move not only in their daily rotation around the earth. They also travel at varying speeds along the ecliptic. The Greeks called them *planetai*, wanderers gone astray, from the verb *planaomai*, to be led astray, to travel randomly. In his commentary on Aristotle's arguments for uniform circular motion, Thomas explains the problem the ancients saw in these irregularities.

71. Aristotle, *De caelo* 2.6.289a6–7.

> Certain anomalies or irregularities appear in the motion of the planets. The planets sometimes appear to be moving faster, sometimes slower, sometimes to stand still, and sometimes to go back. This does not seem to fit the heavenly movements as is clear from the above. Plato first set this difficulty before Eudoxus, an astronomer of his time [Eudoxus of Cnidus, about 390–337 BC]. Eudoxus then tried to bring these irregularities back into the right order by assigning distinct movements to the planets. Later astronomers also attempted to do this in various ways.[72]

Almost half a millennium after Eudoxus, Ptolemy (about AD 100–170) took up Plato's challenge and proposed hypotheses that endured for a millennium and a half. "We think that the mathematician's task and end should be to show all heavenly appearances as produced by uniform circular motions."[73] Thomas comments on Ptolemy's project as follows.

> Since Plato attributed unfailing circularity and uniformity to the heavenly movements, he laid down mathematical hypotheses by which the appearances of erratic movements could be saved while still maintaining that the movements of the planets are ordered as circular and uniform. To bring back to due order the irregularity that appears in the movements of the planets from stopping and going back, speeding up and slowing down and different appearances of quantity, the Pythagoreans supposed that the movements of planets occurs in eccentric spheres and in small circles called epicycles. Ptolemy pursued this opinion further.[74]

The mathematician's task includes observing and recording the appearances faithfully. This is the first meaning of *saving the appearances*. One needs to explain what one has actually observed and recorded. Saving the appearances might also mean saving the apparent vagabonds from chaos by showing ways in which they could still be subject to the mathematical order observed elsewhere in the cosmos.

To save the appearances of Venus, Ptolemy combines three hypotheses: an eccentric circle, an epicycle, and a more complex kind of eccentric called equant.[75]

72. Thomas, *In librum De caelo* 2, lect. 17, no. 451. See Plato, *Republic* 429a–530c.

73. Ptolemy, *Almagest* 3.1; Gerald J. Toomer, *Ptolemy's Almagest* (London: Duckworth, 1984), 140.

74. Thomas, *Sententia super Metaphysicam* 12, lect. 10, no. 2567. Aristotle disagrees with such deviations from perfect circularity posited by the Pythagoreans and Ptolemy to save the appearances. He championed perfect circularity. "Ptolemy's opinion about epicycles and eccentric circles does not agree with the natural principles which Aristotle laid down, and so this opinion does not please the followers of Aristotle." Thomas, *Super Boetium De trinitate*, pars 2, q. 4, a. 3, ad 8.

75. See Ptolemy, *Almagest* 9.4, 10.1–5, 11.11, 12.5–10, 13.1–11. The discussion of Venus is scattered across several books because Ptolemy does not take up each planet separately but groups them by similar mathematical or observational questions.

The Eccentric Circle: Venus appears to speed up and slow down. If she traveled with uniform velocity on a circle concentric with the universe, the effect for an observer on earth would necessarily be uniform apparent motion. To save the appearance of speeding up and slowing down, Ptolemy constructs the hypothesis that Venus travels with uniform velocity on a circle located off-center in the universe. Motion on this eccentric circle has the consequent effect of variations in apparent velocity. What an observer on earth sees is Venus's *angular* velocity (angles swept in a given time) around the earth, not her *linear* velocity around the center of the eccentric circle. Her velocity is uniform on the eccentric circle. It only looks nonuniform to an observer on earth.

The Epicycle: Venus appears to stop and go back periodically. An eccentric circle alone cannot explain this retrogression. Ptolemy proposes a second circle (the epicycle), the center of which moves uniformly along the circumference of the eccentric circle. Venus's motion around the epicycle looks like motion back and forth on the eccentric circle. Combined with the epicycle's movement on the excentric circle, this hypothesis comes close to saving the appearances—close but not close enough.

The Equant: If Venus's epicycle moves with uniform *linear* velocity (covering equal distances in equal times) on the eccentric circle, the appearances that would be consequent effects do not quite match the observed appearances. Ptolemy posits that the epicycle moves with uniform *angular* velocity (sweeping equal angles in equal times) around a point other than the center of the eccentric circle. This point is called equant. Uniform angular velocity around the equant has the consequent effect of varying linear velocity on the circumference. All three hypotheses combined and adjusted save the appearances remarkably well.[76]

Let us return to Thomas's description of this type of argument.

> In astronomy the argument of eccentric circles and epicycles is posited because on this hypothesis the sensible appearances concerning heavenly movements can be saved. Nevertheless, this argument is not sufficient proof, because the appearances can perhaps be saved on another hypothesis.

Ptolemy does not see himself as proving the exact way in which uniform circular motions produce Venus's irregular apparent motion. He proposes a hy-

76. Ptolemy is often accused of using ad hoc hypotheses to force observations into the preconceived idea of uniform circular motion. His achievement is much greater. He reached a comprehensive mathematical theory of planetary motions that is a close structural equivalent of modern mathematical theories. When one leaves aside mechanical aspects (mass, force, etc.), relative motion is a matter of perspective. See Richard Fitzpatrick, "A Modern Almagest: An Updated Version of Ptolemy's Model of the Solar System," accessed July 25, 2019, http://farside.ph.utexas.edu/Books/Syntaxis/Almagest.pdf.

pothesis that fits the observed motion as well as the root, uniform circular motion. In the absence of proof, he holds the hypothesis as a conjecture. It could be true, but so could other hypotheses. He therefore asserts it as verisimilar, as like the truth, not as true. Thomas underlines this point. One should not say that these hypotheses are true.

> The hypotheses which astronomers devised are not necessarily true. Although on such hypotheses the appearances are saved, nevertheless one should not say that these hypotheses are true, because the appearances of the stars can perhaps be saved in some other way not yet understood by man.[77]

One reason given by Copernicus for proposing his heliocentric hypothesis is that Ptolemy's equant does not fit the root, uniform circular motion. It gives up uniform linear velocity. By placing the sun at the center, Copernicus was able to save the appearances without an equant. In the case of Venus, he uses an eccentric circle and two epicycles.

> The theories proposed by Ptolemy ... are very much in doubt because they are not sufficient unless equant circles are imagined as well, with the result that the planet ... does not move with uniform velocity. A theory of this kind seemed thus neither absolute enough nor sufficiently in accordance with reason.[78]

Copernicus agrees with Ptolemy that the art of astronomy saves the appearances by combining uniform circular motions but does not claim that a particular hypothesis is true.

> This art, it is quite clear, is completely and absolutely ignorant of the causes of the apparent nonuniform motions. And if any causes are devised by the imagination, as indeed very many are, they are not put forward to convince anyone that they are true, but merely to provide a reliable basis for computation.[79]

77. Thomas, *In librum De caelo* 2, lect. 17, no. 451.

78. Nicolaus Copernicus, *Commentariolus*, preface; text quoted according to Swerdlow's English edition of the Commentariolus. Noel M. Swerdlow, "The Derivation and First Draft of Copernicus's Planetary Theory: A Translation of the Commentariolus with Commentary," *Proceedings of the American Philosophical Society* 117 (1973): 423–512, at 434.

79 Nicolaus Copernicus, *De revolutionibus orbium coelestium* (Frankfurt: Johannes Petreius, 1543), preface. *De revolutionibus* was published after Copernicus's death. The preface is not by Copernicus but was added by Osiander for publication. Some scholars suspect that it minimizes Copernicus's truth claims. In fact, however, it fits with the principles of astronomy accepted by Ptolemy and Copernicus.

Applied to the Commentary on John 1:1

Summa I, q. 32, a. 1, ad 2, needs to be applied rigorously to the argument presented in the commentary on John 1:1. Here is a summary of the analogy of the Word in *Super Ioannem*.

The Word in the Human Mind:

1.1 A word is a vocal sound that signifies a conception in the mind.
1.2 By analogy, the conception itself can be called word.
1.3 The inner word is not *that which* one knows but *that in which* one knows something.
1.4 It is an expression of knowledge, proceeding as act from act.
1.5 It proceeds as spoken, which implies opposite relations of origin in the speaker and the spoken.
1.6 It is spoken as a likeness of what is known.
1.7 When one knows oneself, the word is a spoken likeness of oneself.

From the Human Word to the Divine Word:

2.1 Wherever there is knowledge there must be a word that expresses it. Therefore, there is a Word in God. John 1:1 affirms the existence of such a word in God.
2.2 In God, the Word is not formed gradually but spoken eternally as pure act.
2.3 While we speak many partial words, God speaks all things at once.
2.4 Since everything in God is God, God's Word subsists as God, as a person, but as distinct from the speaker due to relative opposition in the relations of origin.
2.5 *Word*, therefore, is always the name of a person in God, not of the divine essence.
2.6 As a perfect likeness of the one who speaks, the Word is consubstantial with the speaker.
2.7 Inasmuch as it proceeds as living from a conjoint living origin, it can be called begotten and Son.

The step from the human word to the divine Word rests on the key principle in 2.1. *There must be a word wherever there is knowledge.* This principle justifies the four-member proportion that undergirds the argument. *As the human mind is to its inner word, so is the divine mind to the divine Word.* Further philosophical steps follow in accord with philosophical proofs about God in the unity of his nature.

The step from one God to the personal distinction between the Word and its Speaker takes place in 2.4. Since everything in God is God, God's Word subsists as God and is therefore a person. Due to relative opposition in the relations of origin, it is a person distinct from the speaker. One of the premises of this argument is the philosophical truth stated in 1.5. The inner word proceeds as spoken, which implies opposite relations of origin in the word and the speaker. The four-member proportion, As the human mind is to the human word, so the divine mind is to the divine Word, is the basis of a transfer of these relations of origin to God. God's Word must subsist as God and as distinct from the speaker.

The argument looks like a proof, but it cannot be a proof. "The likeness of the human intellect does not sufficiently prove anything about God." The key principle of the argument, *Wherever there is knowledge there must be a word that expresses it*, is not evident. It is taken from the human mind and then affirmed by likeness about the divine mind. The reason for holding the key principle is not objective necessity but fittingness. In the absence of objective necessity, it can only be held as a conjecture based on fittingness. It follows that one cannot affirm it as simply true but as verisimilar, as like the truth.

The human mind is fully proportionate to a geometrical arrangement of uniform circular motions. No such proportion to the object is possible in arguments about the Trinity. "He dwells in inaccessible light which no man has seen or can see, to whom be eternal honor and strength. Amen" (1 Timothy 6:16). "No one has ever seen God. The only-begotten God, who is in the bosom of the Father, he has made him known" (John 1:18). Faith, which rests on God's own testimony, is the only proportionate way of coming to know the Trinity. The problem is not that we cannot judge which of several likenesses happens to be sufficient. No likeness is. The reason why the analogy of the word can only be held as a conjecture is not the possibility of other hypotheses but the transcendence of God.

Given this difference, which features of the astronomical illustration correspond to features of the analogy of the word? *Being one hypothesis among others* does not correspond. The corresponding features are at least the following: (1) Both arguments start by positing a root, uniform circular motion in one case, the Trinity in the other. (2) Both develop arguments that fit the already posited root. (3) In both, the arguments are not proofs in the sense of being objectively certain. (4) In the absence of objective certainty, both arguments are subjectively held as conjectures from likeness or fittingness. (5) Both are affirmed as like the truth, not as true.

These points about the analogy of the word do not depend only on the astronomical illustration. They are implied in the very short, direct statements that apply universally, both to the astronomical illustration and the analogy of the word. The analogy of the word is "an argument, not one which sufficiently proves a root, but one which shows that the consequent effects fit the already posited root ... Once the Trinity is posited, such arguments fit."

The Impression of Proof and Certainty

Summa I, q. 32, a. 1, ad 2, does not seem to fit the language with which the argument of the analogy of the word is presented in the commentary on John 1:1. The language gives the impression of objective necessity, of subjective certainty, and of being affirmed as simply true. Arguments involving the analogy of the word in the *Summa* and the *Compendium* give a similar impression.

An instructive exception is *De potentia*, q. 8, a. 1, which addresses the question whether the relations of origin in God are real. The argument of the body closely parallels the argument of *Summa* I, q. 27, but in the order of discovery rather than of teaching.

The argument begins with the truth of faith. "The Catholic faith posits that in God there are three persons of one essence." Remaining within that truth as a truth of faith, the argument points out that *three persons* implies that the distinction between them is real. It then points out that *God* is said absolutely while *Father* and *Son* are said in relation to each other. If there were a real distinction in God with respect to what is said absolutely, there would be three Gods. The real distinction must, then, lie in what is said relatively. If what is said relatively were not real, the divine persons would not be really distinct, which is the Sabellian heresy. Therefore the relations are real.

Up to this point, which coincides with the principle of relative opposition in relations of origin formulated by the Cappadocians and Hilary, the argument moves within the truth of faith, taken formally as a truth of faith. At this exact point, the text marks a boundary and adds a warning. "How this may be is something one should try to investigate by following the sayings of the Saints [the Fathers] even though reason cannot to a full degree arrive at this." It is only after this boundary and warning that the argument introduces the analogy of the word. In the *Summa* and the *Compendium*, there is no corresponding marker and warning.

The *Summa* simplifies and streamlines arguments for beginners in theology. The *Compendium* does the same even more. In a seamless transition from the philosophical arguments about the existence and attributes of the one God, the *Compendium* presents a clear statement of the analogy of the word, rising from the human mind to the Trinity.

> From what was said above it must be agreed that God understands and loves himself and also that in him to understand and to love is nothing other than to be (*esse*).
>
> Since, then, God understands himself and all that is understood is in the one who understands, God must be in himself as the understood is in the one who understands. Now, the understood as it is in the one who understands is a

> word of the intellect. For, we signify by an external word what we understand within. For, according to the Philosopher vocal sounds are signs of understandings.
>
> Therefore, one must posit God's own Word in God ... When the intellect understands itself, the word conceived is compared to the intellect as offspring to father. Since, then, we are speaking about the Word according to which God understands himself, the Word must be compared to God, whose Word it is, as Son to Father.
>
> Hence it is that we are taught in the rule of the Catholic faith to confess the Father and the Son in God.[80]

The explanation "hence it is" *hinc est* sounds as if the rule of faith teaches us to confess the Father and the Son because the analogy of the word, understood as an argument from natural reason, has concluded that there must be a Word in God. *Summa* I, q. 32, a. 1, ad 2, shows that one cannot understand the argument as a proof, contrary to the language used in this simplified and streamlined form of presentation.

How can one reconcile these two contrary indications? "Even where Aquinas clearly sees that he cannot apply this rigorously deductive ideal in its purity, he will nonetheless imitate this ideal as closely as possible and present a sort of substitute process giving at least its aesthetic illusion."[81] This suggestion does not fit. It is clear that Thomas loves beauty, but falling for aesthetic illusion is out of character. This much, however, seems true in the suggestion. The language usually reserved for proofs serves to underline intelligibility. The aim seems to be not to burden arguments meant for beginners. Beginners need a streamlined and catechetical way of teaching. Qualifications can be added later.

It seems, however, that this way of teaching beginners produced an unintended result in the more advanced. Many if not most of the classical Thomistic commentators see the arguments given in the *Compendium* and the *Summa* as completely certain. They are evidently puzzled about *Summa* I, q. 32, a. 1, ad 2. Cajetan's commentary on the whole article runs to less than 20 lines. It summarizes the body of the article and the response to the first objection but says nothing about the response to the second.[82] Diego Ruiz de Montoya, SJ (1562–1632), praised by many as the prime Thomistic commentator on the *Summa*'s Trinity questions, refers to the astronomical example in the response to the second as showing how the three arguments of objection 2, including Augustine's

80. Thomas, *Compendium theologiae*, cap. 37–39.

81. Robert L. Richard, *The Problem of an Apologetical Perspective in the Trinitarian Theology of St. Thomas Aquinas* (Rome: Gregorian University Press, 1963), 18. Richard mentions this way of understanding the tension but rejects it.

82. See Leonine edition, *Opera Omnia*, 4:351.

analogy of the word, should be understood; namely, "in no other way than the way astronomy gives the arguments of eccentrics and epicycles."[83] Yet Ruiz de Montoya does not explain this way in detail or apply it in detail to Augustine's argument. Elsewhere in his commentary, he takes the argument as completely certain. "The processions ... are quidditatively operations of understanding and willing ... because Scripture calls the Son of God *Verbum*."[84] The Trinity volume of the *Cursus Theologicus Salmanticensis*, famous for its acumen and loyalty to Thomas, runs to nearly one thousand pages, but only one of them is spent on q. 32, a. 1, as a whole. There is no comment at all on the response to the second objection.

Garrigou-Lagrange quotes the response to the second objection in full and unfolds its arguments against the three supposed proofs. He does not unfold in more detail what the response says about the nature of the argument. In the immediately following passage, he sketches a view of natural science that is in some respects similar to ancient astronomy, but more radical in cutting the connection with reality.

> Many might perhaps respond as many modern critics say in the ordering of natural science: these theories do not even intend to explain what is probably the case in reality, but they are only representations useful to us for ease in classifying phenomena now known. When other phenomena are found, as in the case of radioactivity, those representations will be changed.
>
> According to the mind of St. Thomas, one should respond that the arguments of fittingness are not only representations useful to us, but they explain with some probability what is, or rather what is not, in God. And they explain this all the more in the degree to which they are based on revelation itself. In fact, it seems that the formal mode of the first procession by intellectual speaking, if it is not formally revealed in the Son of God being called *Verbum*, is at least something certain as a theological conclusion virtually revealed. But the many others remain only probable.[85]

Garrigou-Lagrange does not give any detailed arguments to make his case.

Gilles Emery's brief comment on the question is circumspect and precise.

> Would one, then, have *proved* the personal existence of a divine Word in God, falling for the rationalist temptation of demonstrating an article of the Creed?—No, St. Thomas answers, because "the analogy of our understanding

83. Diego Ruiz de Montoya, *Commentaria ac disputationes in primam partem sancti Thomae de Trinitate* (Lyons: Prost, 1625), 382, par. 18.

84. Ruiz de Montoya, *Commentaria*, 12, par. 5.

85. Réginald Garrigou-Lagrange, *De Deo Uno: Commentarium in Primam Partem Summae S. Thomae* (Turin: Marietti, 1938), 233.

does not constitute sufficient proof for [demonstrating] something about God since understanding is not found univocally in God and us." It is an "argument of congruity," a "verisimilar account," which allows one to grasp what only the acceptance of revelation, that is to say faith, makes known. But one has *manifested* how we can grasp the generation of the word by means of an analogy.[86]

5. The Limits of the Argument

Six Theses on the Analogy of the Word

Several texts should be seen together with *Summa* I, q. 32, a. 1, ad 2, to fill out this account of the analogy of the word.

> Text 1 (the text just analyzed): *Summa* I, q. 32, a. 1, ad 2
>
> One can give an argument, not one which sufficiently proves a root, but one which shows that the consequent effects fit the already posited root....[In this way] an argument is disposed that is given to manifest the Trinity. For, once the Trinity is posited, such arguments fit, not in such a way, however, that by these arguments the Trinity of persons is sufficiently proved.
>
> Text 2: *De veritate*, q. 10, a. 13, ad 2
>
> Since in God the one understanding, the act of understanding, and the power of understanding are the same, natural reason does not compel one to posit that God begets one distinct from himself by understanding.
>
> Text 3: *De veritate*, q. 10, a. 13, ad 10
>
> By natural reason a philosopher would never admit that God speaks in the sense of speaking that brings about a distinction of persons but only in the sense of speaking said essentially.
>
> Text 4: *Super Boetii De trinitate*, pars 1, q. 2, a. 3, corp.
>
> In sacred teaching we can use philosophy in three ways. First, to demonstrate the preambles of faith ... that God exists, that God is one, and others like these that are proved about God or creatures in philosophy.... Second, to make matters of faith known by likenesses, as Augustine uses many likenesses taken from philosophical teachings to manifest the Trinity. Third, to resist what is said against faith, by showing either that it is false or not necessary.
>
> Text 5: *De potentia*, q. 8, a. 1, ad 12
>
> Just as we can know about God that he is but not what he is, so we can know about God that he understands but not how he understands. Conceiving

86. Emery, *Trinitarian Theology of Saint Thomas*, 185; *Théologie trinitaire de saint Thomas*, 223.

a word in understanding belongs to how God understands. Hence this argument [based on wherever there is knowledge there must be a word] cannot sufficiently prove, but from what is in us it can conjecture in some way by likeness, *ex eo quod est in nobis aliqualiter per simile coniecturare.*

Text 6: *Super Boetii De trinitate*, pars 1, q. 1, a. 4, corp.

That God is three and one is only believed and can in no way be proved demonstratively, although one can have some sort of arguments for it, not necessary and not very probable except for one who believes.

Text 7: *Contra gentiles* I, cap. 8, no. 48–49; cap. 9, no. 54

For the truth of faith … reason can gather likenesses of the truth (*verisimilitudines*) that are not sufficient for grasping these truths demonstratively, as it were, or through themselves. Nevertheless it is useful for human reason to exercise itself in such arguments, however weak they may be, as long as the presumption of comprehending or proving is absent, because it is a great joy to be able to see something about the highest, however small and weak it may be.… Verisimilar (*verisimiles*) arguments should be made for the exercise and consolation of those who believe.[87]

From these texts, one can draw six theses about the analogy of the word.

1. *The Science at Stake in the Argument:* The analogy of the word is not a formal statement of the mystery of faith nor a theological argument derived from revelation, but a philosophical argument based on natural reason placed at the service of revelation. (Texts 1 and 4)

2. *The Purpose of the Argument:* The purpose of the analogy is to manifest the Trinity in the sense of bringing the mystery of faith in some way closer to the imperfect human mind by a likeness that is fitting, which is a great joy and consolation despite the weakness of the argument. (Texts 1, 5, 6, and 7)

3. *The Agent Responsible for the Argument:* The analogy is not taught by the Church as part of her faith. It is developed by individual theologians on their own responsibility. This thesis follows from the first two theses.

4. *The Mode of Certainty in the Argument's Object:* The analogy is not based on objective necessity but on a plausible fit with an already posited root. (Texts 1–5)

5. *The Mode of Certainty in Holding the Argument:* The analogy is not held with subjective certainty but as a conjecture by likeness. It is held as probable, even if "not very probable except for those who believe." This thesis follows from thesis 4. (Texts 5 and 6)

6. *The Logical Form of Assertion:* The analogy is not asserted as true but as

87. Thomas, *Summa contra gentiles* I, cap. 8, no. 48–49; cap. 9, no. 54.

verisimilar, that is, as in some way like the truth. This thesis also follows from thesis 4. (Texts 1 and 7)

An objection is likely to arise. "In the beginning was the Word" is revealed in John 1:1. The analogy of the word is not a philosophical argument based on fittingness and held by conjecture as merely like the truth. It is revealed or at least (as Garrigou-Lagrange has it) virtually revealed.

To judge this objection, one needs to distinguish. *Analogy of the word* can refer to the philosophical argument that rises from the word in the human mind to the Word in the divine mind by means of the key principle, *Wherever there is knowledge there must be a word.* Second, *analogy of the word* can refer to any statement in which *word* is said analogously about God, such as John 1:1, "In the beginning was the Word." Third, it can refer to the more distinct understanding of *Word* in John 1:1 that is the fruit of the argument.

The six theses do not apply to John 1:1 as it stands in the context of the Gospel. They apply to the argument based on the principle that a word must be present wherever there is knowledge. Do they apply to the more distinct understanding of John 1:1 that is a fruit of the analogy of the word? They apply in the degree to which the distinct understanding of *Word* in John 1:1 depends on the argument. This question will be taken up in more detail below.

This understanding of the analogy of the word holds with due adjustments also for the intrapersonal analogy of proceeding love, the parallel argument about the Holy Spirit. As the analogy of the word begins with the presence of the known in the mind, so the analogy of proceeding love begins with the presence of the beloved in the will. This presence differs from the presence of the object of knowledge in the inner word. "The Love which is an inner procession of the will is not a likeness of the will or of what is willed but an impression left by what is willed or a union of one with another."[88] The intrapersonal analogy of love is built on a four-member proportion parallel to the four-member proportion in the case of *word.* As the one who loves is to the presence of the beloved in the human will, so are the Father and the Son to the Spirit.

The frequent description of the Holy Spirit as the bond of love between Father and Son does not depend on this analogy of love but rests on the order of processions in which the Son proceeds from only one, while the Spirit proceeds from both, from one through the other or from one and the other (*filioque*).

If the analogy of the word were revealed by John 1:1, one would expect the Church to teach it, at least at some point in the development of her doctrine. She has not taught it. If the analogy, understood in the first and the last of the three

88. Thomas, *De potentia*, q. 10, a. 2, ad 11.

senses distinguished above, is an argument from natural reason, she will never teach it.

Joseph Dalmau quotes the *Catechism of the Council of Trent* 1.1.14 and 1.8.5 as evidence to the contrary. The catechism, he claims, clearly presupposes the analogy of the word as at least proximate to the truth of faith.[89] The two passages Dalmau cites simply repeat the traditional appropriation of wisdom to the Son and of love to the Holy Spirit, which do not depend on the analogy of the word. The distinguishing marks of the analogy, the key principle and the four-member proportion built on it, are missing. Dalmau does not mention the following passage in the *Roman Catechism* that addresses the question more directly.

> Of all the different comparisons made to indicate the mode and account (*ratio*) of this eternal generation, the one taken from the thinking of our mind seems to come nearest to the reality, which is why (*quam ob rem*) St. John calls the Son the Word. For as our mind when it understands itself somehow forms an image which theologians call *word*, so God, as far as we may compare what is human to what is divine, by understanding Himself begets the eternal Word. Yet, to contemplate what faith proposes is more excellent (*praestat*).[90]

"Seems to come nearest" is a strong recommendation. "But to contemplate what faith proposes is more excellent." If one thing is more excellent than another, it is not the same. Contemplating what faith proposes is not the same as comparing the eternal Word to the inner word in the human mind.

In the planning stages of the *Catechism of the Catholic Church*, some theologians argued that the Catechism should include the analogy of the word. The Committee for the Catechism chaired by Cardinal Ratzinger discussed the proposal and rejected it, not because it disagreed with Augustine and Thomas, but because it agreed that the analogy of the word is an account of the Church's faith from natural reason and not itself part of the faith.[91]

89. See Joseph M. Dalmau, SJ, "De deo uno et trino," in *Sacrae Theologiae Summa*, 4 vols., ed. Joachim Salaverri, SJ (Madrid: Biblioteca de Autores Cristianos, 1964), 2:11–438, at 328.

90. *Roman Catechism* 1.2.9. *Catechismus ex decreto concilii Tridentini ad parochos* (Rome: Paolo Manuzio, 1566), 22.

91. Cardinal Schönborn, who was responsible for writing this section of the Catechism and was present as a member of the committee, testified to these deliberations and decisions of the committee in a lecture at the International Theological Institute in Gaming, Austria.

The Analogy of the Word Compared with a Strictly Theological Argument

How does a strictly and formally theological argument differ from the argument given in Thomas's commentary on John 1:1? *De potentia*, q. 10, a. 2, discusses the number of processions in God with special attention to the distinction between the Son and the Holy Spirit. It shows that the theological account of this distinction is the Cappadocian principle of relative opposition in relations of origin, not the distinction between procession according to intellect and according to will.

Gregory of Nyssa's formulation of the principle was quoted above. "We do not deny the distinction with respect to cause and caused, by which alone we claim that the one is distinct from the other." Immediately after this statement, Gregory turns to the distinction between the Son and the Spirit.

> And of that which exists from the cause we recognize another distinction, for one is immediately from the first and another through the one who is immediately from the first, so that only-begotten belongs without doubt to the Son and being from the Father does not cast doubt on the Spirit, because the intermediacy of the Son guards the Son's own status as the only-begotten while not depriving the Spirit of his natural relation to the Father.[92]

De potentia argues that this is the proper theological account. It also considers an alternate account given by the analogy of the word and proceeding love. The *Summa* formulates this alternate account as follows.

> In God there is no procession except according to an activity that does not tend to something outside but remains in the agent itself. In an intellectual nature, activity of this kind is the activity of the intellect and the activity of the will. The procession of the Word takes place according to intelligible activity. But according to the activity of the will another procession is found in us, namely, the procession of love according to which what is loved is in the one who loves, just as by the conception of the word the spoken or understood thing is in the one who understands. And therefore, besides the procession of the Word another procession is posited in God, namely, the procession of love.[93]

De potentia refers to this argument without unfolding it. "Some have said that the processions in God are distinct ... in that one procession is through the mode of nature or understanding, the other through the mode of will." This is not the proper theological account. "If one examines it carefully, one can see

92. Gregory of Nyssa, *Ad Ablabium, Quod non sint tres dii*; PG 145:133B.
93. Thomas, *Summa* I, q. 27, a. 3, corp.

easily that this is not enough for the distinction between the divine processions."

To show the truth of this claim, *De potentia* constructs an argument by reduction to the absurd. Suppose that the analogy of the word and of proceeding love is the scientific theological account of the two processions. If something false follows from this supposition, then the analogy cannot be that account.

> The likeness of that which is the principle must be found in what proceeds, just as in created things the form of the one generating is in the one generated. Therefore, if the processions in God are distinct inasmuch as nature or intellect is the principle of one and will of the other, then in the one who proceeds according to one procession there will be only what belongs to nature or intellect and in the other only what belongs to will. This is clearly false.

Of course, no theologian who holds that the analogy of the word is the proper theological account would hold that the Son of God is *only* Word, *only* Wisdom begotten, at the exclusion of other perfections. Whether one holds it or not, the consequence still follows objectively. *Word* in no way specifies or contracts the Son's mode of procession to the mode of intellect.

> By the one procession, which is that of the Son from the Father, the Father communicates to the Son whatever he has—nature, intellect, power, will, and whatever is said absolutely. Therefore, just as the Son is Word, that is, *Wisdom* begotten, so he can be called *Nature* begotten or *Will* begotten or *Power* begotten, that is, received by generation, or rather receiving these by generation.

After clarifying that the procession of the Son is not specified in the mode of intellect, the text states the conclusion of the refutation. The processions cannot be distinguished according to an essential attribute, such as the activity of intellect and the activity of the will.

> Hence it is clear that since all essential attributes come together in the one procession of the Son, the difference between the processions cannot be found according to diverse accounts of attributes, such that [or: which would have the consequence that] the communication of one attribute takes place by one procession and the communication of another by the other.

Having excluded the immanent activities of intellect and of will as the theological account of the distinction between the processions, *De potentia* sketches the proper theological account.

> Since the term of a procession is having (*habere*), because a divine person proceeds for this, namely, to have what it receives by proceeding, and since the processions are distinct according to their terms, it necessarily follows that proceeding is distinct in God in the way that having is distinct. But having is

> not distinct in God inasmuch as this [person] has these attributes and that one others, but inasmuch as one has the same from the other. For the Son has all that the Father has, but the Son is distinct from the Father because the Son has it from the Father.
>
> In this way, one who proceeds is distinct from another who proceeds, not because by proceeding the one receives this and the other that, but because one of them receives from the other.
>
> Therefore, whatever is found in a divine procession that can be immediately understood in one procession without involving the prior understanding of the other, belongs only to one procession. But when what is received in the first procession is again derived to another, there immediately is another procession.
>
> And thus only the order of processions observed according to the origin of the procession multiplies in God.[94]

The phrase *only the order according to origin* echoes Gregory of Nyssa's phrase *by this alone, that one is the cause, the other from the cause*. The Son and the Spirit are distinct inasmuch as one proceeds only from the Father, while the other proceeds from the Father *through* the Son or as Western theologians say, *and* the Son. This Cappadocian principle is the scientific theological argument. The *Summa* makes the same point.

> If two persons proceed from the one person of the Father, namely the Son and the Holy Spirit, there must be some order between them. And *no other order* can be posited except the order of nature by which one is from the other.[95]
>
> The Holy Spirit is personally distinct from the Son in that the origin of one is distinct from the origin of the other. But the difference of origin is by this that the Son is only from the Father but the Holy Spirit from the Father and the Son. For the processions are not distinct in any other way.[96]

At the very end of the text, *De potentia* returns to the analogy of the word.

> Hence those who posited that one procession is through the mode of nature and intellect and the other through the mode of will have spoken fittingly (*convenienter*) in this respect, namely, that the procession which is according to nature or intellect does not require another procession beforehand, but the procession which is through the mode of will requires another procession beforehand, for the love of something cannot proceed from the will unless one understands that the word that is conceived from the understanding of that thing proceeded beforehand. For the good as understood is the object of the will.

94. Thomas, *De potentia*, q. 10, a. 2, corp.; emphasis added.
95. Thomas, *Summa* I, q. 36, a. 2, corp., third argument; emphasis added.
96. Thomas, *Summa* I, q. 36, a. 2, ad 7.

The analogy of the word fits the already posited order among the processions. It does not explain this order. If the words *must* and *because* signify *proof*, it is simply false to say that the procession of the Holy Spirit *must* come after that of the Son *because* procession according to love presupposes procession according to knowledge.

Another text is sometimes quoted to show that the analogy of the word is a sufficient explanation. "If the procession of the word and of love is not sufficient to insinuate the personal distinction (*ad distinctionem personalem insinuandam*) there cannot be a personal distinction in God."[97] To read this text as asserting that the analogy of the word is a sufficient theological argument would be to overlook the word *insinuate*, which is not the same as *explain*. If one reads it as *explain* or *prove*, it contradicts what is clearly said elsewhere. It is only after the order of processions has been posited as the root that one can see the analogy of the word correctly as in some way fitting the already posited root.

The qualification *not the properly theological explanation* applies to all arguments that invoke the analogy of the word. There are many such arguments in the *Summa*'s questions on the Trinity (qq. 27–43). To select a few of them, the analogy of the word shows:

- how the Son's generation can be understood as immaterial (q. 27, aa. 1–2);
- how the unity of essence and the distinction of persons may be reconciled (q. 27, a. 1; a. 3, ad 1);
- why the procession of the Son is called generation or conception (q. 27, a. 2);
- why there are three divine persons (q. 27, a. 5);
- why the Son is called Image (q. 35);
- how the divine persons are in each other (q. 42, a. 5);
- how appropriations to the Son and to the Holy Spirit differ (q. 43, a. 5, ad2).

The analogy's inability to *explain* these truths does not destroy its ability to *manifest* them in some way. By focusing on the procession of the inner word in the human mind according to the immanent activity of knowing, the analogy *points in the direction of* a purely spiritual procession within God, and it *points in the direction of* understanding how one God exists as three persons. It *points* but cannot *explain*. It is like the truth, not true.

One can conclude that SS. Augustine and Thomas agree about the limits of

97. Thomas, *De potentia*, q. 9, a. 9, ad 7.

the analogy of the word. Toward the end of *De trinitate*, Augustine summarizes what he says at many points in the course of his argument.

> As often as I wanted to show in us creatures something like this [divine] reality . . . I felt that I had more an attempt of understanding than an achievement. In the one person which is man, I found an image of that highest Trinity . . . . But the three of one person could not fit (*convenire*) those three persons in the way human intention asks for.[98]

Penido on the Analogy of the Word

Maurílio Penido argues that the analogy of the word is the proper theological account and the heart of Trinitarian theology. He sees certainty about this claim as established by a syllogism.

> I know. People perpetually refer us to *Summa* I, q. 32, a. 1, ad 2, as if there our Doctor had finally put his own explanation in its true place, mere "philosophical argument of fittingness" (de Régnon). Total error of interpretation.
>
> In reality, what this passage calls into question is any *demonstration of the existence* of the mystery, not an analogical unfolding. It is concerned with Anselm and especially Richard of St. Victor, who seem to believe that God is necessarily triune, not only in himself (*quoad se*) but to us (*quoad nos*), and that as a consequence one can prove the Trinity by "necessary arguments" *rationibus necessariis*. Such a demonstration can be attempted before revelation (*ante revelationem*)—and in that case the arguments are, properly speaking, worth nothing—or after revelation (*post revelationem*) once the fact that there are three persons in God is known—*posita trinitate*, once the Trinity is posited, as St. Thomas puts it—as someone who believes the existence of God then demonstrates it, in which case the proofs have some value, but only as arguments of fittingness (*raisons de convenance*). "Once the Trinity is posited, such arguments fit" posita trinitate congruunt huiusmodi rationes.
>
> The "psychological" theory itself is no exception, for the excellent reason that it would cease being analogy and would change into univocity since it argues from the double spiritual procession in us to conclude to their existence in God, which is the characteristic fault of univocity. "The likeness of our intellect does not sufficiently prove anything about God. The reason is that intellect is not found univocally in God and in us."
>
> But, while it has simple weak value as a proof as long as one claims to establish the *existence* of the processions, the "psychological" analogy can come to have certainty when one wishes to unfold their *nature*. We are not using

98. Augustine, *De trinitate* 15.25.45. The word *fit* (*convenio*) seems to be used in this text in the sense of *truly apply* rather than the weaker sense of *fitting* as opposed to *necessary*.

> sleight of hand here. It is indeed a fact that an analogy of proper proportionality as such can never prove existence (*quod sit*). Its only role is to explore a nature (*quomodo sit*). And this is exactly the meaning of the Augustinian-Thomistic teaching. It does not show, nor can it show, that in God there are two processions, that in God these two processions issue in two substantial terms, and so on. All of this it *presupposes*. It is the major premise given by faith. Our analogy gives the minor premise from reason. The minor *unfolds* (*explique*) the revealed premise. The conclusion is not probability or simple fittingness, but theological certainty.[99]

In the syllogism sketched by Penido, the major premise is the Church's faith about the existence of two processions, one of them the procession of the Word (John 1:1). The minor premise is the philosophical analysis of *word*. Penido does not present the syllogism formally and explicitly. He may have the following in mind. The Son proceeds as the Word of God. Every word proceeds through the mode of knowledge. Therefore the Son proceeds through the mode of knowledge.

This argument can be reduced to a first figure syllogism.[100] The major and minor premises, however, need to be switched to put them in proper logical order.

MAJOR: Every word proceeds through the mode of knowledge.
MINOR: The Son proceeds as Word.
CONCLUSION: Therefore the Son proceeds through the mode of knowledge.

This syllogism cannot establish certainty about the analogy of the word because it presupposes it. The middle term *word* needs to be the same in both premises, not necessarily the same univocally but at least analogically. It presupposes the four-member proportion, *As the human mind is to the human word so is the divine mind to the divine Word.*

Thomas clearly states the reason why the conclusion of the argument cannot be certain. The likeness of the human mind does not prove anything about the divine mind. *Does not prove anything* holds equally for arguments about *what* and *how*. Precisely *what* and *how*, which Penido describes as more knowable by analogy, Thomas describes as less knowable by analogy. A text quoted above is relevant here.

99. Maurílio Teixeira-Leite Penido, "La valeur de la théorie 'psychologique' de la Trinité," *Ephemerides Theologicae Lovanienses* 8 (1931): 5–16, at 11–12; emphasis original.

100. Since one of the premises has an individual subject (the Son), the argument is not a syllogism in the strict sense but only reduces to one. An affirmative proposition with an individual subject functions like a universal affirmative proposition. The argument thus reduces to a first figure syllogism in the mood Barbara.

> Just as we can know about God *that* he is but not *what* he is, so we can know about God *that* he understands but not *how* he understands. Conceiving a word in understanding belongs to *how* God understands. Hence this argument [based on the key principle *There must be a word wherever there is knowledge*] cannot sufficiently prove, but it can conjecture in some way by likeness from what is in us.[101]

Penido does not see that the analogy of the word depends on the key principle *There must be a word wherever there is knowledge.* Human reason cannot grasp this principle as evident because the likeness of the intellect does not prove anything about *how* God understands. Whether one reasons from below, from the word in the human mind, or from above, from the revelation of a *Logos* in God, the key principle is needed in either direction to affirm the four-member proportion, *The human mind is to its inner word as the Father to the eternal Word.*

The Logos in John 1:1

As for the premise of faith supplied by John 1:1, Penido neglects the many options one needs to consider to find the meaning of the word *logos* in John 1:1. He takes it as self-evident that *logos* means *verbum* in the specific sense of spoken inner word.

Logos is a word with an extraordinary breadth of meanings. It is the verbal noun of the verb *lego*, as *eros* is of *erao*, to love. The meanings of *lego* are: (1) to gather, pick up; (2) to pick out, to choose, to count, to calculate, to reason; (3) to say, to mean, to speak. *Logos* reflects mainly the second and the third of these meanings. The *Brill Dictionary of Ancient Greek* lists meanings for *logos* in four groups.

> [From Lego in the Sense of Picking Out, Choosing, Counting]
> 1. Count, calculation; sum, total. Amount of money; bank account, balance in a bank account; tax collection office.
> 2. Account, explanation.
> 3. Assessment, evaluation.
> 4. Value, significance.
> 5. Relationship, relation. Ratio, proportion, analogy; in grammar: rule, norm.

101. Thomas, *De potentia*, q. 8, a. 1, ad 12.

[From Lego in the Sense of Reasoning]
1. Reasoning, argumentation.
2. Faculty of reasoning or reflection, reason, thought, common sense; in philosophy: of practical as opposed to speculative reason. John and the Greek Fathers: divine reason personified; angels.
3. Motive, cause, force, foundation, justification, reason, pretext.
4. Plan, project, design, expectation.

[From Lego in the Sense of Saying, Meaning]
1. Speech. Word, but rarely in the sense of one individual word. Mention.
2. Declaration, affirmation; answer; promise. Saying, proverb, maxim. Decision, resolution; order, command. Proclamation, teaching; doctrine or part of a doctrine. In philosophy: definition; hypothesis. Condition, agreement. Conditioning, limitation.
3. Fame, tradition, legend; renown, reputation (good or bad). Rumor, hearsay, news.
4. Revelation, oracle, response. Jewish and Christian theology: Scripture; revealed teaching; commandment as in the ten commandments, message of Jesus, gospel; creative, vital force: *Logos* in John and the Greek Fathers.
5. Argument, subject, object, question; of a literary work: theme, argument. Fact, matter, thing. Function.
6. Grammatical: discourse, language; phrase; prose.

[From Lego in the Sense of Speaking]
1. Act of Speaking. Faculty of speech, parlance. Use of speech, right to speak.
2. Colloquy, conversation, dialogue, discussion, dispute.
3. Fable; imaginary tale, legend, myth. Historical narrative, history or part of an historical work. Dialogue; oration, discourse. Treatise or part of a treatise, work or part of a work, book. Christian: Scripture. Letters, literature, studies.[102]

Even after one discounts the most obviously irrelevant meanings of *logos*, such as *balance in a bank account* or *tax collection office*, many are left. That *logos* is rarely used in the sense of one individual word makes the translation *verbum* unlikely but not impossible. The *Brill Dictionary* lists two main meanings for *logos* in Christian texts: personified reason and vital creative force. It does not list *interior word*. Whether one agrees with the dictionary or not, one needs to give more thought to the meaning of *logos*.

In John, *logos* appears as a name or title for Jesus only in 1:1 and 1:14. In other

102. Franco Montanari, Madeleine Goh, and Chad Schroeder, eds., *The Brill Dictionary of Ancient Greek* (Leiden: Brill, 2015), s.v. *logos*. Some specific meanings have been added from Liddell-Scott, *A Greek Lexicon*. The sequence of the four main groups has been rearranged in accord with the order of the meanings of *lego*, following the article on *logos* in Liddell-Scott.

passages in John it refers most often to a statement, commandment, or discourse of Jesus. There is some helpful context in the Prologue. The opening words *In the beginning* echo the opening words of Genesis. This context is further strengthened by the statement that the *Logos* is the one through whom all things came to be (John 1:3), parallel to the spoken words of creation in Genesis 1.

Another aspect of the *Logos* can be seen in the one and only parallel in the New Testament, the horseman warrior in the Revelation to John. "I saw heaven open and, behold, a white horse, and one sitting on it . . . whose name was called *the Logos of God*" (Revelation 19:13). He rides into battle with a robe soaked in blood, his own blood, since he rides out with it. A sharp sword comes out of his mouth, symbolizing words to "strike the nations" (Revelation 19:15). A similar warrior appears in the Wisdom of Solomon, sent by God to kill the firstborn of the Egyptians. "Your all-powerful *Logos* leaped from heaven, from the royal throne, into the midst of the doomed land, a stern warrior carrying the sharp sword of your relentless command" (Wisdom 18:15). This warrior shares some features with the "angel of the Lord" who throws Pharaoh's army into confusion Exodus 14:19). It is unclear whether or how the angel of the Lord is distinct from God. "Behold, I am sending my angel before your face to guard you on the way. . . . Pay attention to him for your own sake and listen to him . . . because my own name is in him" (Exodus 23:20–21). In his prayer to the Father in John 17, Jesus speaks about "your name, which you have given me" (John 17:11).

Many parallels are found in the Wisdom of Solomon and other wisdom texts in the Septuagint, especially Proverbs, Baruch, and Sirach. "Their importance for interpreting the Johannine Prologue can hardly be overestimated. All of the elements of the Prologue are paralleled. . . . It is evident that we have here the raw materials from which the Prologue may have taken shape."[103]

The *Logos* in John shares features with *Sophia*, personified Wisdom. References to Wisdom pitching her tent are especially significant in view of John 1:14: "The *Logos* became flesh and pitched his tent among us."

> The Lord created me [wisdom] as the beginning of his ways. (Proverbs 8:22)
>
> When he was strengthening the foundations of the earth, I was beside him, fitting all together. I was what he delighted in, and every day I rejoiced in his presence at all times, when he rejoiced in completing the inhabited earth and rejoiced in the sons of men. (Proverbs 8:22, 8:29–31)
>
> [God] found out every way of knowledge and gave her [Wisdom] to Jacob, his child, and to Israel, his beloved. After this she appeared on earth and lived among men. (Baruch 3:37–38)

103. Craig A. Evans, *Word and Glory: On the Exegetical and Theological Background of John's Prologue* (Sheffield: Sheffield Academic Press, 1993), 92. See esp. 83–93, where Evans presents the evidence in clear and compact form.

> I [wisdom] came forth from the mouth of the Most High and covered the earth like a mist. I pitched my tent in high places, and my throne was in a pillar of cloud.... Then the Creator of all things commanded me, and the one who created me gave rest to my tent and said, "Pitch your tent in Jacob, and in Israel receive your inheritance." (Sirach 24:3, 24:8)
>
> Wisdom glorifies her noble birth, having a shared life with God, and the Master of all loves her. (Wisdom 8:3)
>
> With you is Wisdom, she who knows your works and was present when you made the world; she understands what is pleasing in your sight and what is right according to your commandments. (Wisdom 9:9)

Hellenistic Jewish texts are rich in images and speculations about such intermediary figures.[104] A story appears in 1 Enoch 42 about Wisdom seeking a place to dwell with human beings, which is comparable to the story in Sirach 24 but more pessimistic.

> Wisdom did not find a place where she might dwell, so her dwelling was in the heavens. Wisdom went forth to dwell among the sons of men, but she did not find a dwelling. Wisdom returned to her place, and sat down in the midst of the angels. (1 Enoch 42:1–2)[105]

A heavenly figure called *Logos* appears in the writings of Philo of Alexandria (ca. 20 BC to AD 40).

> Like a shepherd and king, God governs ... the earth ... appointing as the immediate superintendent his own right *Logos* and first-born son, τὸν ὀρθὸν αὐτοῦ λόγον καὶ πρωτόγονον υἱόν, who is to receive the charge of this sacred company, as the lieutenant (ὕπαρχος) of the great king. For it says somewhere, "Behold, I AM! I will send my angel before your face to guard you on the way."[106]
>
> There are, as it seems, two temples belonging to God. One is this world, in which the high priest is the divine *Logos*, his firstborn son, ἀρχιερεὺς ὁ πρωτόγονος αὐτοῦ θεῖος λόγος. The other is the rational soul.[107]

The parallels between John, Revelation, the Wisdom books, and non-biblical Jewish writings suggest that John 1:1 links the person of Jesus with an already known personal or personified figure.

Most important, the *Logos* in John 1:1 is immediately personal. No argument

104. A gold mine of relevant texts and ideas is discussed by Martin Hengel, *The Son of God: The Origin of Christology and the History of Jewish-Hellenistic Religion* (Philadelphia: Fortress Press, 1976).

105. Translation following George Nickelsburg and James VanderKam, *1 Enoch: A Commentary on the Book of 1 Enoch*, Hermeneia Commentary, 2 vols. (Minneapolis: Fortress Press, 2012), 2:138.

106. Philo, *De agricultura* 51; quoting Exodus 23:20 in a Greek version that includes the presence of the divine name I AM in the angel.

107. Philo, *De somniis* 1.215.

is needed to establish that in this particular case *logos* is not only a thought but also a thought that subsists and is therefore personal. Seen from this point of view, John 1:1 is an example of the interpersonal analogy rather than the intra-personal analogy of the word. *Verbum as the expression of God's knowledge of himself* is not the self-evident or immediate meaning of John 1:1.

Nevertheless, a good case can be made that the analogy of the word is a valid explanation of John 1:1. God's creative speech, one can argue, presupposes a more interior speech that expresses God's knowledge as a whole. Explaining the reality to which a text refers is not the same, however, as establishing the immediate meaning of the text. When one finds the word *water* in Plato, does it mean *hydrogen dioxide*? Yes and no. It means *the thing* called *hydrogen dioxide*, but not the explanation of molecular structure signified by the words *hydrogen dioxide*. If the explanation of the molecular structure is true, it may, of course, be helpful for understanding Plato's *water*. In the case of *logos*, it is not as easy to distinguish these levels of meaning in the word because the same word is used in John 1:1 and in the explanation.

When the analogy of the word is used to explain John 1:1, it still presupposes the key principle. *Wherever there is knowledge there must be a word.* It also implies the four-member proportion justified by this principle. *As the human mind is to its inner word so is the divine mind to the divine Word.* The six theses apply to it.

6. The Complementarity of the Two Analogies

If the six theses about the analogy of the word contained in explicit statements by St. Thomas are true—that is, if the analogy of the word is not a theological argument but philosophical, not a proof but a manifestation, not part of the Church's faith but privately proposed by theologians, not based on necessity but on fittingness, not held as certain but as a probable conjecture, not asserted as true but as verisimilar—then the analogy of the word cannot be the heart of Trinitarian theology. The claim that it is that heart, joined with the claim that the analogy of mutual love should be rejected or downplayed, is an error with enormously destructive consequences. It tends toward collapsing the supernatural mystery of the Trinity into the natural order, toward reducing the Church's faith in the Trinity to a private philosophical conviction.

In contrast to the analogy of the word, the analogy of mutual love is not a philosophical argument but directly revealed. One can hold it with certainty as simply true. "The Lord Jesus, when he prays to the Father that all may be one as we are one (John 17:11; 17:20–23) . . . indicates a certain likeness between the union of the divine persons and the union of the sons of God in truth and love" (*Gaudium et spes* 24).

It would be a mistake, however, to turn the tables on Penido and displace the analogy of the word from the heart of Trinitarian theology, settling the analogy of mutual love in that place instead. This would be to repeat one of Penido's errors; namely, the exclusive reliance on only one analogy. No created likeness can be the full and exclusive representation of the transcendent mystery. "One must gather likeness from many ways so that what is lacking in one can in some way be filled in by another."[108] The analogy of the word is a philosophical argument that gives better access to God's unity without denying the plurality of persons. The plurality of persons is part of the Church's faith. The two analogies together are more truly the heart of Trinitarian theology than either of them can be by itself. To rely exclusively on the analogy of mutual love would be to lose the heart of Trinitarian theology. The principle highlighted by Balthasar (see section 2 of this chapter) is critically important.

> [Faith in the Trinity] can never speak otherwise than in two statements that run in opposite directions and cannot be joined into one. . . . That the hypostases really exist vis-à-vis each other is known to faith from the facts of revelation. That Father, Son, and Holy Spirit are one God is likewise known to it from revelation and its ecclesial interpretation.
>
> The speculative challenge presented by the mystery that these two sides are identical can in each case be met adequately only by a converging movement of two propositions that cannot be reduced to one.[109]

Revelation enables faith to be certain of both, that there is one God and that there are three persons, but (as Vatican I teaches) it does not enable human reason to grasp the mystery of the Trinity through itself.

> Even when revelation has been handed on and received by faith, the divine mysteries by their nature surpass the created mind to such an extent that they are still hidden by the veil of faith and enveloped in a kind of mist as long as in this mortal life we "sojourn away from the Lord, for we walk by faith and not by sight" (2 Corinthians 5:6–7).[110]
>
> If anyone says that divine revelation contains no true mysteries in the proper sense, but that reason rightly developed can understand and demonstrate all dogmas of the faith from natural principles, let him be anathema.[111]

108. Thomas, *Summa* I, q. 42, a. 2, ad 1; Augustine, *Sermo* 117, cap 6–10; PL 38:666–76.
109. Balthasar, *Theologik*, 2:123–24; *Theo-Logic*, 2:132–33.
110. Vatican I, *Dei filius* 4; Denzinger 3016.
111. Vatican I, *Dei filius, Canones* 4; Denzinger 3041.

Ptolemy observes that from any place on earth one can see exactly half of the sky. He uses this observation as a premise for an argument about the size of the earth relative to the distance of the stars.

> The earth has, to the senses, the ratio of a point to the distance of the stars.... A clear indication is that the planes drawn through the observer's lines of sight at any point on earth, which we call horizons, always bisect the whole heavenly sphere. This would not happen if the earth were of perceptible size in relation to the distance of the heavenly bodies; in that case only the plane drawn through the center of the earth could bisect the sphere, while a plane through any point on the surface of the earth would always make the section below the earth greater than the section above it.[112]

To say that the earth has, to the senses, the ratio of a point to the distance of the stars is to say that the distance of the stars is huge, beyond all ratios accessible to the senses. In recent times, astronomy has developed instruments and arguments to measure cosmic distances. Still, it seems hardly possible to develop a sense of scale for 46.6 billion light years, the estimate for the radius of the observable universe.

However true and deep human analogical speech may be, it has, to our reason, the ratio of a point to infinity. The length, breadth, and depth of the Trinity exceeds human reason beyond all ratios. Both analogies are to the Trinity as a point to the distance of the stars.

Yet while both analogies, taken separately, are like a point in their insufficiency, they strengthen each other by their opposite directions.

> An abyss separates the soul and its God.
>
> In us the faculties or acts belong only to one person, while in God the generation of the Word and the procession of the Holy Spirit constitute three persons.
>
> On the other hand ... the analogy of friendship between human beings is insufficient, because in our experience there is never an absolute unity among the lovers, while in God the three persons are one substance.
>
> Thus, inter-subjective love fails, because it leaves us many, and intra-subjective love fails, because it leaves us alone. Plurality of *we*; aloneness of *I*.[113]

The two analogies complement each other in accord with the principle that Trinitarian theology must rely on two sets of statements in order to express what is given to us by revelation.

112. Ptolemy, *Almagest* 1.6; Toomer, *Ptolemy's Almagest*, 43.

113. Maurice Nedoncelle, "L'intersubjectivité humaine est-elle pour saint Augustin une image de la Trinité?," in *Augustinus Magister*, 3 vols. (Paris: Études Augustiniennes, 1954), 1:595–602, at 600.

> The image of the Trinity in the spiritual realm of creatures ... can only be unfolded in two series in the order of being and of thought that are related to each other in the manner of an antinomy. One is the inner structure of the created spirit ... [The other is] the encounter in which the *I* becomes truly itself by giving itself to a *you* and both realize themselves in a *we* that overcomes any preoccupation with themselves alone. It is only in such transcendence that the first image, the image interior to the spirit, becomes an event....
>
> It is thus inappropriate to exclude all use of the second schema out of strict adherence to the first, where likeness with God lies above all in the unity of the spirit, or to declare that a divine *you* is impossible. Conversely, a naïve construction of the divine mystery from relationships between human beings ... must not take itself to be absolute, because it overlooks the crude anthropomorphism of a plurality of substances.
>
> The creaturely image must resign itself to look at one and the same time from its two points of departure in the direction of the mystery of God.[114]

Nedoncelle's and Balthasar's case for the complementarity of the two analogies is strong because it rests on the primal and lasting structure of the Church's faith in the Trinity: one God and three persons.

7. John 5:20 and 17:24

The main scriptural basis for the analogy of mutual love in TOB is the Gospel of John.

> The Father loves the Son and has given all things into his hand. (3:35)
> The Father loves the Son and shows him all that he himself is doing. (5:20)
> Because of this the Father loves me, that I lay down my life. (10:17)
> That the world may know that I love the Father. (14:31)
> As the Father has loved me, so I have loved you. (15:9)
> I have kept my Father's commandments and remain in his love. (15:10)
> You loved them as you loved me. (17:23)
> My glory, which you have given me because you loved me. (17:24)
> That the love with which you loved me may be in them. (17:26)

Listing these texts is proof-texting unless one goes on to responsible exegesis. Two passages stand out in their importance as anchors of John Paul's "hermeneutics of the gift" (TOB 13:2), "because the Father loves the Son" (5:20)

114. Balthasar, *Theodramatik*, 2.2.480–82; *Theodrama*, 3:525–26. In note 15, Balthasar quotes Rahner's denial of *you* and the counterarguments by Scheffczyk. For a similar argument, see Balthasar, *Theodramatik*, 4:71–72; *Theodrama*, 5:82–83.

and "because you loved me before the foundation of the world" (17:24).[115] Let us take a closer look at these two texts in their context with special attention to Thomas's interpretation.

John 5:20, Because the Father Loves the Son

The controversy between Jesus and the Judean authorities in 5:1–47 raises the question of the unity of God and his relation to Jesus in a pointed manner. The authorities decide to kill Jesus "because he makes himself equal to God" (5:18). To make oneself equal to God is to rebel (see Isaiah 14:14; Ezekiel 28:2). It is an attack on the first law of piety, "The Lord our God, the Lord is one. You shall love. . . ." (Deuteronomy 6:4).

Analysis of John 5:19–20

In his response to this accusation, Jesus does not take back anything from his claim to equality with God but appeals to his relations of origin to the Father.

A 5:19 The Son cannot do anything of himself
    B but only what he sees the Father doing
    B *because* whatever that one does
A this also the Son does likewise
C 5:20 *because* the Father loves the Son
C and shows him all that he himself is doing. (5:19–20)

The four units of verse 19 are carefully laid out in concentric parallels, A-B-B-A. Parallelism can work with likeness as well as contrast. The first and the last unit (A) speak about the Son's activity. The two units in the middle speak about the Father's activity. In this respect, they form a concentric parallelism based on likeness. At the same time, parallelism by contrast can be seen in the relation between the first two units (AB) and the other two (BA).[116] The first two express the Son's subordination to the Father, the other two his equality. The polyphonic interplay between the two forms of parallel can be seen in this schematic table

Subordination
    Son's activity
    Father's activity

115. For a more detailed exegesis and discussion of scholarly literature, see Michael Waldstein, "The Mission of Jesus in John: Probes into the *Apocryphon of John* and the Gospel of John," doctoral diss. (Harvard University, 1987), 156–93; 235–77.

116. See Thomas, *Super Ioannem*, cap. 5, lect. 3, no. 746–49.

Equality
Father's activity
Son's activity

Jesus answers the charge of rebellion by affirming his subordination to the Father. "The Son cannot do anything of himself / but only what he sees the Father doing." That this subordination cannot be understood in Arian terms as a creature's submission to the creator is made clear in the very next sentence, in which Jesus affirms his equality with the Father. "Whatever that one does / this also the Son does likewise." The prologue makes a similar statement about creation: "All things came to be through him, and without him nothing came to be" (1:3). While the prologue focuses only on the activity of creating, 5:19 embraces all divine activities without exception.

It may seem paradoxical that subordination and equality are linked by *because:* the Son is subordinate *because* he is equal, "*because* whatever that one does, this also the Son does likewise." The logical connection is nevertheless quite clear. If the Son does all that the Father does and nothing else, then it follows that he cannot do anything of himself.

The second *because* clause takes the explanation one step further to the root of the unity and equality of activity. "*Because* the Father loves the Son, / and shows him all that he himself is doing" (5:20). Other texts use the word *giving* instead of *showing.* "The Father loves the Son and has *given* everything into his hand" (3:35). "The works the Father has *given* me" (5:36). "The work which you have *given* me" (17:4). "The glory which you have *given* me because you loved me before the foundation of the world" (17:24).[117] The phrases *show all* and *give all* are close to each other, equivalent to total gift.

Total gift is the one and undivided whole within which both subordination and equality have their own place. Total *gift* implies subordination to the origin, *Total* gift implies equality.

To summarize, Jesus answers the accusation of rebellion in four steps, reasoning back from the most immediate response to the charge of rebellion to the ultimate root of the response.

He is not a rebel against God because he cannot do anything of himself.

He cannot do anything of himself because he is equal in all activities to the Father.

117. See Albert Vanhoye, "L'œvre du Christ, don du Père," *Recherches de Science Religieuse* 48 (1960): 377–419, here 387–91, 404.

He is equal in all activities because the Father shows or gives him everything.

The Father shows or gives him everything because he loves him.

One can invert the order of steps in the argument according to the order of reality.

The Father's love is first.
Because of this love, the Father gives everything to the Son.
Because he gives everything to the Son, the Son is equal in all activities.
Because he is equal in all activities, he cannot do anything of himself.
Because he cannot do anything of himself, he is not a rebel against God.

In this argument, the Father's love is, as Balthasar puts it, *unvordenklich*, that than which nothing prior can be thought.[118]

Hilary and Thomas on Love and Gift

Hilary of Poitiers (AD 310–368) throws light on these connections between love, total gift, and the Father.

> God never knows anything other than to be love (*dilectio*) nor anything other than to be Father. The one who loves does not envy and the one who is Father is not incompletely Father. The name [Father] does not allow portions such that in one respect He would be Father and in another not Father. The Father is Father with respect to everything that is in Him, for he has himself as a whole in the one [the Son] who does not have a mere portion of what the Father is—not that the Father is with respect to himself Father of what he himself has, but that, with respect to what he himself is, he is wholly Father for the one who is from him.[119]

The completeness of the gift from the Father to the Son is clearest in the statement, "Just as the Father has life in himself, so he has given also to the Son to have life in himself" (5:26). The Father does not have life by participation as creatures do but in himself by being life itself. By gift of the Father, the Son also has life in himself so that he can claim to be life itself. "I am way, truth, and life" (14:6). Hilary comments:

118. See Balthasar, *Theologik*, 2:126–28; *Theologic*, 2:135–37. The English translation wrestles with *unvordenklich* and renders it (at least to begin with) by the difficult phrase *cannot be anticipated by thought*. *Unvordenklich* is mainly used in the phrase *unvordenkliche Zeit, time immemorial,* a time so far back that one cannot remember or conceive an earlier time. See the entry *unvordenklich* in Jacob Grimm and Wilhelm Grimm, *Deutsches Wörterbuch*, 32 vols. (Leipzig: S. Hirzel, 1854–1960), 24:2148.

119. Hilary, *De trinitate* 9.61. Benedict XVI quotes this passage as the main text in his *summary* of Hilary's Trinitarian theology. Benedict XVI, *General Audience*, October 10, 2007.

> The only-begotten is from one only. He has life in himself just as the one who begets has life. For he says, "As the Father has life in himself, so he has given to the Son to have life in himself" (5:26). Not a mere part of the Father is in the Son, because the Son testifies, "All that the Father has is mine" (16:15). "All that is mine is yours and yours mine" (17:10). Whatever the Father has he has given to the Son, as the apostle Paul also testifies. "In him dwells all the fullness of the godhead bodily" (Colossians 2:9). That which is a part does not possess being all by nature. But the perfect is from the perfect because the one who has all gave all. One should not think that since he still possesses he has not given or that he no longer possesses since he has given.[120]

Thomas follows Hilary closely in his reading of the same texts.

> He shows the equality of the Son to the Father when he says, "as the Father has life in himself"; and he shows their distinction when he says, "he has given to the Son." For the Father and the Son are equal in life, but they are distinct, because the Father gives, and the Son receives (*distinguuntur, quia Pater dat, Filius accipit*).
>
> We should not understand this to mean, however, that the Son receives life from the Father as if the Son first existed without having life, as in lower things first material (*materia prima*), already existing [in potency], receives a form, and as a subject is subjected to accidents, because in the Son there is nothing that exists prior to the reception of life. For as Hilary says: "the Son has nothing except as born" filius nihil habet nisi natus, that is, nothing except what he receives through his birth.[121]

Instead of *life* one can also say *being* or *essence*. "The divine essence is the gift which the Father gives to the Son, *donum quod pater dat filio*.... The essence is called the Father's gift, *donum patris*."[122]

It is on this basis that Thomas interprets the notorious Arian proof-text, "The Father is greater than I" (14:28) not only in the traditional antisubordinationist way as applying to Jesus in his humanity but also in his divinity. He sees the testimony "greater than I" as the Son's response to the Father's gift, that is, as his filial piety.

120. Hilary, *De trinitate* 2.8.

121. Thomas, *Super Ioannem*, cap. 5, lect. 5, no. 782; emphasis added. Hilary's formulation is slightly different. Nihil enim nisi natum habet filius. Hilary, *De trinitate* 4.10. Hilary's text has the neuter *natum*, agreeing with *nihil*, while Thomas's quote of it has the masculine *natus*, agreeing with *filius*. A slightly different formulation is found in Hilary, *De trinitate* 12.31. nihil aliud de se patitur intelligi et dici posse, nisi natum. "He does not allow anything to be understood and said about him except as born."

122. Thomas, *Summa* I, q. 38, a. 1, obj. 2 and ad 2; see Hilary, *De trinitate* 8.20.

> One could also say, as Hilary does, that even according to the divine nature the Father is greater than the Son, yet the Son is not inferior to the Father but equal. For the Father is not greater than the Son in power, eternity, and greatness but *by the authority of a giver or beginning.* For the Father receives nothing from another but the Son, if I may put it in this way, receives his nature from the Father by an eternal generation. So, the Father is greater because he gives, yet the Son is not inferior but equal because he receives all that the Father has. "God has given him the name that is above every name" (Phil 2:9). No less than the giver is he to whom one and the same being is given.[123]
>
> Following Hilary, the Father is greater by the authority of the giver; but no less is he to whom one and the same being is given; and, "The subjection of the Son of nature is piety (*pietas*), that is, recognition of paternal authority while the subjection of all others is the weakness of creation."[124]

Thomas throws further light on the connection between love and gift in his discussion of *gift* as a name of the Holy Spirit. He begins with Aristotle's remark that a gift is what is given without the expectation or obligation of return. ἡ δωρεὰ δόσις ἐστὶν ἀναπόδοτος.[125]

> According to the Philosopher, *gift* is in its own meaning (*proprie*) what is given without return, that is, what is not given with the intention of repayment, and thus it involves gratuitous giving. The reason for gratuitous giving, however, is love. The reason why we give something to somebody gratuitously (*gratis*) is the love by which we will the good for him. It is clear, therefore, that love has the account of the first gift by which all other gratuitous gifts are given.[126]

In Aristotle's definition, ἀναπόδοτος, *not to be given back, gratuitous* is the specific difference added to the genus *what is given. Gratuitous* therefore characterizes the gift as such rather than the act by which it is given. It signifies *freely* in the sense of *for free*, that is, *free of obligation to return* rather than *freely* in the sense of *by free choice.* Love stands behind the gift, but it need not take the form of free choice. To interpret *because the Father loves the Son* in the sense of a choice by the Father to show the Son everything would imply the Arian understanding of the Son as created without necessity by free choice.

123. Thomas, *Super Ioannem*, cap. 14, lect. 8, no. 1971; emphasis added.
124. Thomas, *Summa* I, q. 42, a. 4, ad 1; see Hilary, *De trinitate* 9.54.
125. Aristotle, *Topics* 4.4.125a18.
126. Thomas, *Summa* I, q. 38, a. 2, corp.

John 17:24, Because You Loved Me

> Father, what you have *given* me,
> I will that where I am, they too may be with me,
> that they may see my *glory*,
> which you have *given* me *because* you *loved* me
> before the foundation of the world. (John 17:24; emphasis added)

The terms *glory*, *gift*, and *love* are the key terms in this text. Thomas comments on their relation to each other. "The perfection of glory consists in a certain greatness of complete giving (*communicatio*) which love (*caritas*) brings about."[127]

The best commentary on John 17:24 is the beginning of Jesus's prayer to the Father, John 17:1–5. Before we turn to this text, some remarks on the word *glory* are in order.

The Word "Glory"

English *glory* (from Latin *gloria*) is the usual translation of Hebrew *kabod* and Greek *doxa*. It is not an ideal translation because the root meanings and further uses of *kabod*, *doxa*, and *glory/gloria* are strikingly different, even if there is some overlap. The verb *kabad* means *to be heavy, weigh heavily*. "Heavily weighs his hand on my groaning" (Job 23:3). The root meaning of the corresponding noun *kabod* is *weight, heaviness*. The sons of Laban complain, "Jacob has gained much weight at the cost of our father Laban" (Genesis 31:1). They mean *weightiness*, *importance*, *wealth*, and perhaps also the effect of these; namely, *honor*.

The Septuagint consistently translates *kabod* as *doxa*. It is a strange decision. The root meaning of doxa is *opinion*, *expectation*, often in the sense of *favorable opinion*, *fame*, *honor*. The choice seems to be based on the one meaning shared by *kabod* and *doxa*; namely, *honor*. This common ground, however, is potentially misleading. While *kabod* signifies mainly the cause of honor, *doxa* focuses on the effect, honor itself. The Septuagint's consistent use of *doxa* for *kabod* added new layers of meaning to *doxa*, so that it came to signify the cause of honor.

The Vulgate is sensitive to the difference between cause and effect in its translation of *doxa*. In contexts that suggest the cause, it uses *claritas*, *brightness*, *radiance*, *beauty*; in contexts that suggest the effect, it uses *gloria*, *being well known and praised*.

English translations, by contrast, tend to use only the word glory for *kabod* and *doxa*. To compensate for the tendency of English *glory* toward *honor*, one

127. Thomas, *De potentia*, q. 9, a. 9, sed contra 2.

needs to remain aware of the causal sense: the intrinsic power of a being to make itself known and acknowledged, its *radiance* and *beauty.*

The causal sense is especially important in the verb *doxazo*: active voice, transitive, *to glorify, give glory, make glorious*; middle voice, intransitive, *to prove oneself glorious, show oneself in one's glory.* John uses *doxazo* occasionally in the sense of *give glory, praise*, but more often, following the Septuagint, in the sense of *make glorious, give the power to cause honor.* An important example of the causal sense of *doxa* and *doxazo* is the beginning of the Song of Moses in the Septuagint. "Let us sing to the Lord, because he has gloriously glorified himself, ἐνδόξως γὰρ δεδόξασται, horse and rider he has cast into the sea" (Exodus 15:1). The need to sing—that is, to give glory in the sense of praise—is explained by the event in which God *gloriously proved himself glorious* or *showed himself in his glory.*

Ezekiel's description of the chariot of divine glory brings out this causal sense. The emphasis on indirection is striking. A light that is not directly visible and accessible nevertheless expresses itself in appearances while remaining deeply hidden within them.

> In the middle of the living beings there was *something that looked like* burning coals of fire, like torches moving to and fro among the living creatures; the fire was bright, and lightning issued from the fire.... and seated above the *likeness* of a throne was *something that seemed like* a human form. Upward from *what appeared like* the loins I saw *something like* gleaming amber, *something that looked like* fire enclosed all around; and downward from *what looked like* the loins I saw *something that looked like* fire, and there was a splendor all around. Like the bow in a cloud on a rainy day, such was *the appearance* of the splendor all around. This was *the appearance of the likeness of the glory* of the Lord. I saw and I fell down on my face. (Ezekiel 1:13–14, 1:26–28; emphasis added)

The references to *fire, lightning,* and *gleaming amber* may seem impersonal, but God's glory is "the light of your face, because you loved them" (Psalm 44:4). Paul identifies this face by name. "It is the God who said, Let light shine out of darkness, who has shone in our hearts to give the light of the knowledge of the glory of God in the face of Jesus Christ" (2 Corinthians 4:6). The great paradox of the Gospel is that God's glory is definitively expressed in the face of the crucified. The Cross brings the hiddenness of glory to its extreme end, but it is also the extreme end of the expressive power of love because it is the event in which God goes to the end in giving himself. "Loving his own in this world, he loved them to the end" (John 13:1). "The perfection of glory consists in a certain greatness of complete giving which love brings about."[128]

128. Thomas, *De potentia*, q. 9, a. 9, sed contra 2.

Mutual Glorification (John 17:1–5)

John 17:24, "the glory you given me because you loved me before the foundation of the world," needs to be understood in the context of Jesus's prayer as a whole. In its overall structure, the prayer mirrors the movement of love. It moves outward from the center like a source of light that communicates itself. Jesus prays for himself (1–8), for the disciples who are with him (9–19), and for all future believers (20–26), following the pattern of the high priest's prayer on the Day of Atonement according to Leviticus 16. The prayer begins with a focus on *glorify* and *glory.*

A 1a Father, the hour has come: glorify your Son,
    B 1b so that the Son may glorify you,
        2 so that, as you have given him power over all flesh,
        he may give eternal life to all you have given him.
            C 3 And eternal life is this: that they know you,
            the only true God, and Jesus Christ whom you have sent.
    B 4 I have glorified you on earth
        by completing the work that you gave me to do.
A 5 Now, Father, glorify me in your presence
    with the glory I had with you before the world existed. (17:1–5)

The opening (17:1a) closely corresponds to the end (17:5): A = A. Both speak about the moment of the passion, *the hour* (17:1), *now* (17:5); in both, Jesus asks the Father to glorify him. The second element (17:1b) closely corresponds to the next to last (17:4): B = B. Both speak about glorifying the Father. The definition of eternal life in 17:3, finally, is framed in the middle like a jewel: A-B-C-B-A.

The two frames (17:1–2 and 17:4–5) interpret the hour of Jesus's suffering and death in opposite directions. The first frame (17:1–2) explains glory in terms of the effect of the hour—namely, the gift of eternal life—while the second frame (17:4–5) goes back to the root, the glory of the preexistent Son.

The beginning of the prayer, "Father, glorify your Son" (17:1), is not a petition for an isolated personal glorification. It is ordered to the glorification of the Father, "so that your Son may glorify you." This glorification of the Father achieved in the gift of life, "so that . . . he may give eternal life." This second *so that* clause explains the first: so that the Son may glorify you, that is, so that he may give eternal life to all." Compare "In this is my Father glorified that you bring much fruit and become my disciples" (15:8). The parenthetical phrase "as you have given him power over all flesh" specifies the extent of the power given to the Son in the hour, the power by which he achieves the glorification of the Father and gives the gift of eternal life. Compare "When I am lifted up from the earth, I will draw everyone to myself. He said this to signify the kind of death he was to die" (12:32–33). A similar point is made in the image of the grain of wheat.

> The hour has come for the Son of Man to be glorified.
> Amen, Amen, I say to you,
> unless the grain of wheat falls into the ground and dies, it remains alone.
> But if it dies, it brings much fruit. (12:23–24)

The image of the grain of wheat interprets the glorification of the Son of Man. As the grain of wheat does not remain alone but becomes fruitful through its death, so the Son of Man does not remain alone but by his death builds the community of his own. The glory of the *Logos* in the flesh lies in the power of his suffering and death to "take away the sin of the world" (1:29–36) and thereby to be with his own. "I will that where I am, they too may be with me" (17:24). The mutual glorification of the Father and the Son is an expression of their mutual love.

> The human career of Jesus is, as it were, a projection of this eternal relation (which is the divine love, ἀγάπη) upon the field of time. It is such, not as a mere reflection or representation of the reality, but in the sense that the love which the Father bore the Son "before the foundation of the world," and which he perpetually returns, is actively at work in the historical life of Jesus.[129]

The second unit interprets Jesus's hour in the opposite direction: not by its effectiveness in giving life, but by its root and goal; namely, Jesus's preexistent glory. "I have glorified you on earth by completing the work you gave me to do. And now, Father, glorify me in your presence with the glory I had with you before the being of the world" (17:4–5). The nature of this preexistent glory is clarified later in John 17.

> And I, the glory you have given to me I have given to them,
> that they may be one
> as we are one, I in them and you in me,
> that they may be completed into one,
> that the world may know that you sent me
> and that you loved them as you loved me. (17:22–23)

The gift of glory has unity as its effect, a particular form of unity; namely the mutual indwelling of the Father and the Son. This unity, perceived as it is communicated to human beings, is not an end point. Its function is to be a sign to show "that you sent me and that you loved them as you loved me." The gift of glory, made visible in the union of disciples, manifests the Father's love.

An even closer link between "glory" and the Father's love is suggested by the

129. C. H. Dodd, *The Interpretation of the Fourth Gospel* (Cambridge: Cambridge University Press, 1953), 262.

parallel between "the glory you have given to me I have given to them, that they may be one as we are one" (17:22) and "I have made your name known to them ... that the love with which you loved me may be in them" (17:26). The parallel suggests that Jesus's glory is the presence of the Father's love in him.

> The Son's glory before the world corresponds to love before the world and can be explained in terms of it, because the eternal love of the Father does not give something foreign from itself to the Son, but itself. The preexistent glory of Jesus is thus not only based on the love of the Father, it is determined by this love not only causally, but in its very contents or nature. We can understand the "glory" of 17:5 and 17:24 as the Son's being filled with the fire and light of the Father's love.[130]

The same connection is evident in 17:24, "My glory which you have given me because you loved me before the foundation of the world" (17:24). Love is the motive of the gift of glory and it shapes the nature of this glory. "The perfection of glory consists in a certain greatness of complete giving which love brings about."[131] On these foundations, Ignace de La Potterie sketches some of the aspects of *glory* as follows.

> The glory the Son received from the Father is, according to the Prologue, the glory he holds from his Father as the only Son (1:14); it is, further, the glory that represents for him the fact of being eternally *loved* by the Father (17:24). The formulation in 17:11, "your name, which you have given me," signifies thus not only that the Father *manifested* himself to the Son. In 17:11 John does not use the verb *manifest* or *make known* but *give*, which he uses elsewhere for the gift of glory (17:22–24), of life (5:26), or of everything (3:35), as a sign of love.... By *giving* his name to the Son, the Father makes himself known to him as Father, but at the same time *gives himself* to him in an eternal love.[132]

Thomas's Reading of "Because You Loved Me"

The Causality of a Sign

A rabbit must have run here *because* there are rabbit tracks. Obviously, what is meant is not that the tracks are the reason why the rabbit ran. Rather, the tracks are the reason why one *knows* that the rabbit ran. In his commentary on John, Thomas reads *because you loved me* in this way as pointing to love as the

130. Wilhelm Thüsing, *Die Erhöhung und Verherrlichung Jesu im Johannesevangelium* (Münster: Aschendorff, 1960), 214.

131. Thomas, *De potentia*, q. 9, a. 9, sed contra 2.

132. Ignace de La Potterie, *La vérité dans saint Jean*, 2nd ed., 2 vols. (Rome: Pontificio Istituto Biblico, 1999), 2:732.

sign by which one can know that the Father has given everything to the Son. In the order of reality, the Father loves the Son because of the Son's goodness, and therefore because of the Father's gift of the whole divine nature to the Son. The gift comes before love.

> "The Father Loves the Son and has Given Everything into his Hand" (John 3:35)
>
> If this text is applied to Christ according to the divine nature, then *loves* does not point to the principle but to the sign. There are two reasons why we cannot say that the Father gives everything to the Son because he loves him.
>
> First, loving is an act of the will, while giving his nature to the Son is begetting him. If the Father gave his nature to the Son by will, the Father's will would be the principle of the Son's begetting. In this way it would follow that the Father begot the Son by will and not by nature, which is the Arian heresy.
>
> Second, the Father's love toward the Son is the Holy Spirit. If, therefore, the Father's love toward the Son were the reason why the Father gave everything into his hand, it would follow that the procession of the Holy Spirit is the principle of the begetting of the Son, which does not fit.
>
> One should therefore say that *loves* only refers to the sign. What it says is that the perfect love by which the Father loves the Son is a sign that the Father gave everything he has into his hand.[133]

> "Because the Father Loves the Son and Shows him Everything" (John 5:20)
>
> To know how the Father's love for the Son accounts for the origin or communication of the Son's power, one should note that something is loved in two ways. Since only the good is lovable, a good can be related to love in two ways, namely, as the cause of love or as caused by love. In us, the good causes love. For the cause of our love of someone is his goodness. For he is not good because we love him, but we love him because he is good.... But in God it is otherwise, because God's love is the cause of the goodness in things that are loved. It is because God loves us that we are good, since to love is nothing other than to will good for someone....
>
> In God, love is taken in two ways, namely, essentially, according to which the Father loves, and the Son loves, and the Holy Spirit loves, and notionally or personally, inasmuch as the Holy Spirit proceeds as love. But in neither of these ways can love be the principle of the origin of the Son.
>
> For, when it is taken essentially, love refers to an act of will. If it were the principle of the Son's origin, it would follow that the Father begot the Son by will and not by nature, which is false.
>
> Nor can love be taken notionally, which pertains to the Holy Spirit, because then it would follow that the Holy Spirit is the principle of the Son, which is false. In fact, no heretic has said this. Although love taken notionally is the

133. Thomas, *Super Ioannem*, cap. 3, lect. 3, no. 545.

principle of all the good that is given to us by God, the Holy Spirit is nevertheless not the principle of the Son, but he proceeds from the Father and the Son.

And thus, one should say that this reason is not taken from love as from a principle but as from a sign. Since likeness is a cause of love, "Every animal loves its like" (Sirach 13:19), where the perfect likeness of God is found, there also the perfect love of God is found. Now, the perfect likeness of the Father is in the Son, "who is the image of the invisible God" (Colossians 1:15), "who is the bright radiance from his glory and the express likeness of his substance" (Heb 1:3). And therefore the Son is perfectly loved by the Father. That the Father perfectly loves him is thus a sign that he has shown him everything and has communicated to him his power and nature. And about this love it says above, "The Father loves the Son and has given all things into his hand" (John 3:35) and "This is my beloved Son" (Matthew 3:17).

"The glory you have given me because you loved me (John 17:24)

If it refers to Christ inasmuch as he is God, the word *because* refers to the sign. He did not give because he loved, because *giving by which the Father gives to the Son* refers to his eternal generation.

If *love* is taken essentially, it points to the divine will; if it is taken notionally, it designates the notion of the Holy Spirit. The Father gave glory to the Son by nature and not by will, because he begot him by nature. Nor did he give it to the Son because he breathed forth the Holy Spirit.[134]

The argument follows a method of division and exclusion. Thomas divides *love* into *essential love* and *notional love* and *because* into *reason in the order of reality* and *reason in the order of knowledge*. He eliminates both essential love and notional love as reasons in the order of reality and settles on love in the order of knowledge. The Father's love for the Son is a reason for knowing that he has given the fullness of the divine nature to the Son.

One should not dismiss this reading. It is grammatically possible. If in general goodness is a cause of love, the reason for the Father's love for the Son is indeed the goodness of the divine nature, at least in our mode of understanding. In addition, Thomas does not claim that this reading is the only possible one. The division of logical possibilities is not exhaustive (see below).

Thomas does not appeal to the analogy of the word in his argument for this reading. Some theologians do appeal to it in the following way. Love cannot be the reason why the Father gives all to the Son, because the first procession must be a procession through the mode of knowledge, not through the mode of love. Knowledge comes before love. The Father loves the Son *because* he knows that the Son is goodness itself. Only the second procession can be through the mode

134. Thomas, *Super Ioannem*, cap. 17, lect. 6, no. 2262; emphasis added.

of love. Further, if the Son proceeded through the mode of love, his mode of procession would be the same as that of the Holy Spirit and there could be no distinction between the Son and the Holy Spirit.

One can respond that *giving out of love* is not the same as *breathing through the mode of love*. Augustine and Thomas never say that the Father and the Son breathe forth the Holy Spirit *because of love* in the sense of *out of love* for the Holy Spirit. *Giving out of love* is not a mode of origination linked with a particular immanent activity. It is therefore not a direct alternative to *speaking the Word through the mode of knowledge*, such that only one of the two alternatives can be true, either *out of love* or *through the mode of knowledge*. The question, *Why does the Father give?* is not the same as the question, *What is the immanent activity through the mode of which he generates the Son?* The principle that love is given as the first of all gifts and as the motive of each further gift seems to be implicit in *because you loved me*. Although there is no distinction in God between the first gift consisting of the Father's love for the Son and the gift of the divine nature out of love, the concepts are distinct in our way of understanding, and they call for one definite order, not another. In that order, love is the first of all gifts, just as in the order of immanent acts love presupposes knowledge.

"Love has the account of the first gift by which all other gratuitous gifts are given."[135] From the point of view of this principle, Thomas's reading of "because you loved me" is at least quite awkward. It is nevertheless true that love follows the good and can be a sign of the presence of the good, in this case of the fact that a good has been given. If a reading is grammatically possible and in itself true, Thomas welcomes it as a legitimate meaning of the letter.

> In Scripture there are many meanings of the letter and every one of them is true. In other writings only one meaning is true, namely, the meaning which the author intends. Since Sacred Scripture is handed to us by the Holy Spirit, and nothing can be thought out in it which the Holy Spirit has not thought out, whatever one says about Sacred Scripture, as long as it does not contradict the faith, truly belongs to it, as Augustine says.[136]

Not an Exhaustive Division

If the argument in the commentary were meant as a strict proof, the alternative *essential love or notional love* would need to be exhaustive. There are, in fact, other options.

Thomas does not mention God's essential love as a necessary love, but only essential love in the form of choice. "Some of God's willing is absolutely neces-

135. Thomas, *Summa* I, q. 38, a. 2, corp.
136. Thomas, *Lectura Romana*, I, a. 4, qc. 1, ad 3.

sary."[137] God's essential love in relation to himself is always necessary, Thomas argues. Also not included in the alternative is essential love in the hypostatic mode of fatherhood. The Father is the one divine nature (essential love included) subsisting in the hypostatic mode of fatherhood. The problem of Arianism does not arise if one understands *because you loved me* in the sense of *because you are love in the mode of fatherhood.*

The Ecstatic Aspect of Love

Love in the mode of fatherhood seems to be Hilary's understanding in a text quoted. "God never knows anything other than to be love (*dilectio*) nor anything other than to be Father. The one who loves does not envy and the one who is Father is not incompletely Father."[138]

Hilary touches on an ecstatic aspect of love as gift to another person when he contrasts fatherhood and envy. One way of seeing the importance of the ecstatic aspect is to consider its radical exclusion by Pierre Rousselot. Rousselot argues that a battle took place in the middle ages between two irreconcilable conceptions of love, the natural and the ecstatic.[139] The ecstatic conception, as he sees it, brings persons face-to-face, naked, stripped of all natural inclinations, reduced to the movement of giving. "This movement itself, ultimately, and precisely because natures have disappeared, becomes absolutely inexplicable."[140] Rousselot himself sides with the natural conception of love, which he attributes to Thomas.

Rousselot highlights four implications of ecstatic love. Ecstatic love requires duality. In accord with this first implication, Abelard posited the necessity of creation because God can only be love if he has another to love. His self-love alone is not true love.[141] Ecstatic love is violent and unnatural. The lover willingly abases and annihilates himself for the beloved.[142] Ecstatic love is irrational and opposed to hierarchical order.[143] And, finally, ecstatic love is its own final end. The essence of beatitude lies in an act of love, not knowledge.[144]

> Love, for the supporters of this school, is all the more perfect, is all the more love, the more thoroughly it places the subject "outside of itself." It follows that a love that is perfect and truly worthy of the name calls for a real *duality* of

137. Thomas, *Summa* I, q. 29, a. 3, corp.

138. See Hilary, *De trinitate* 9.61; Benedict XVI, *General Audience*, October 10, 2007.

139. Pierre Rousselot, *Pour l'histoire du problème de l'amour au moyen âge* (Münster: Aschaffendorff, 1908); *The Problem of Love in the Middle Ages: A Historical Contribution*, trans. Alan Vincelette (Milwaukee: Marquette University, 2001).

140. Rousselot, *Problem of Love*, 194; *Pour l'histoire du problème de l'amour*, 78.

141. See Rousselot, *Problem of Love*, 155–68; *Pour l'histoire du problème de l'amour*, 58–65.

142. Rousselot, *Problem of Love*, 169–88; *Pour l'histoire du problème de l'amour*, 65–76.

143. Rousselot, *Problem of Love*, 189–96; *Pour l'histoire du problème de l'amour*, 76–80.

144. Rousselot, *Problem of Love*, 197–211; *Pour l'histoire du problème de l'amour*, 80–87.

> terms. The paradigm of true love is no longer . . . the one [love] that every natural being necessarily bears for itself. Rather, here love is both extremely violent and extremely free. It is free because no reason can be found for it other than itself, independent as it is from the natural appetites. It is violent because it runs counter to these appetites and tyrannizes them. Indeed it seems it could only be satisfied by the destruction of the loving subject, by its absorption in the object loved. Being such, love has no other aim than itself and everything in the human person is sacrificed for its sake, including happiness and reason.[145]

It is no wonder that Thomas, as Rousselot reads him, rejects this violent and irrational conception of love and affirms the physical or natural conception of love in which self-love is the one and only principle. Whenever one loves something, one subordinates it to oneself as an instrument.

> Through the love of desire, I constitute an object as an instrument in relation to myself—as a part of myself, so to speak. I consider it only in reference to myself (so it is with the water that I drink, the bread that I assimilate, the flower that I inhale and that I discard when it no longer pleases me) . . . When I desire a fruit or a flower, it is myself that I am loving in reality.[146]
>
> In the love of desire, I subordinate the object loved entirely to myself, I destroy its own individual finality and I constitute it as instrument in regard to me: it is no longer for itself, but as a part of my being, subordinated to me entirely. It is in this way that we love the rose we pluck, or the water we drink.[147]

Questions can be raised already about the rose we pluck and the water we drink. They need to be raised all the more about the persons we love and the God we worship. At this point it is obvious that Rousselot misinterprets Thomas. The root of his reading seems to be the projection of his Kantian starting point into the Angelic Doctor.

> What is here called the "problem of love" could be formulated in abstract terms as follows: Is a love that is not egoistic possible? And if it is possible, what is the relation between this pure love of the other and the love of self that seems to be the basis of all natural tendencies? The problem of love is thus analogous to that of knowledge: regarding the latter we ask ourselves whether and how a being can be conscious of that which is not itself; regarding the former we ask ourselves whether and how the appetite of a being can tend toward that which is not its own good. In both cases an affirmative response seems

145. Rousselot, *Problem of Love*, 79; *Pour l'histoire du problème de l'amour*, 3.

146. Rousselot, *Problem of Love*, 92; *Pour l'histoire du problème de l'amour*, 13.

147. Pierre Rousselot, *Intelligence: Sense of Being, Faculty of God*, trans. Andrew Tallon (Milwaukee: Marquette University, 1999), 47.

more and more implausible once the notion of consciousness and the notion of appetite are more thoroughly studied.[148]

That we cannot be conscious of anything other than ourselves and that we subordinate to ourselves whatever we love—this is Kant's view of knowledge and inclination (see part II, chap. 2, sections 2–4, in this volume).

Rousselot's Kantian reading is useful. It vigorously highlights an aspect of love that needs to be considered and integrated. Augustine, Richard of St. Victor, Thomas, John of the Cross, and John Paul II hold these aspects of love together without pitting them against each other.

St. Albert the Great proposes a reading of *because you loved me* that integrates this ecstatic aspect of love without succumbing to the problems pointed out by Thomas's commentary.

> Because the Father Loves the Son (5:20)
>
> He touches on the concomitant cause of both, not a cause that precedes, nor one diverse in being, but a cause that is concomitant according to the mode of understanding. "For the Father loves the Son" (5:20) by essential love. For *love concomitant with generation* is here understood about that love. "The Father loves the Son . . ." (3:35). The Father also loves the Son by the love of the Holy Spirit, but he does not speak about this love here . . .
>
> The love concomitant with generation brings it about (*facit*) that he does not retain anything for himself which he does not communicate to the beloved Son, whom he loves as himself. And for this reason he says, "The Father loves the Son and has given all things into his hand." For natural love brings it about that he retains nothing of the substance that he does not communicate to the Son by generating. "My son, you are always with me, and all that is mine is yours" (Luke 15:31).[149]
>
> Because you loved me (17:24).
>
> "Because you loved me," by essential and personal love "before the foundation of the world," and therefore you poured all glory over into me. "In the splendours of the holy ones from the womb before the dawn I begot you" (Psalms 109:3). Therefore he is here called the brightness of eternal life because he shines back as light from heaven, from the Father, as the one who is the splendor of glory and the figure of his substance. For, all of this he gave by eternal generation to one whom he loved as himself.[150]

148. Rousselot, *Problem of Love*, 76; *Pour l'histoire du problème de l'amour*, 1.

149. Albert, *In evangelium secundum Ioannem*, in Auguste Borgnet, ed., *Alberti Magni Opera Omnia*, 38 vols. (Paris: Vivès, 1890–99), 24:213.

150. Albert, *In evangelium secundum Ioannem*, 24:622.

It is not clear why Thomas does not consider this reading, which touches on the deepest foundation of John Paul's "hermeneutics of the gift" (TOB 13:2). One cannot presume that his silence is due to disagreement.

8. Conclusion

Gaudium et spes 22 and 24 as unfolded by John Paul touch on the mystery of the Trinity. "The revelation of the Father and his love fully shows man to himself and makes his highest calling clear" (*Gaudium et spes* 22). The Trinitarian exemplar of unity "shows that man cannot fully find himself except through a sincere gift of self" (*Gaudium et spes* 24). Taken together, the two Council texts imply that the primordial gift takes place in the generation of the Son by the Father, in which the Father gives the whole fullness of divine nature to the Son, so that the Son can say, "All that is mine is yours and yours mine" (John 17:10). "The mystery of the Father and his love" stands at the origin of all. It is the primal light and glory. This is the glory that appears in the flesh. "The Logos became flesh and pitched his tent among us and we have seen his glory, a glory as of an only-begotten from the Father, full of gift and truth" (John 1:14).

> The analogy of the love of spouses (or spousal love) seems to emphasize above all the aspect of God's gift of himself to man who is chosen "from ages" in Christ (literally, his gift of self to "Israel," to the "Church"); a gift that is in its essential character, or as gift, total (or rather "radical") and irrevocable. This gift is certainly "radical" and therefore "total." One cannot speak here of totality in the metaphysical sense. As a creature, man is in fact not capable of "receiving" the gift of God in the transcendental fullness of his divinity. Such a "total gift" (an uncreated gift) is shared only by God himself in the "trinitarian communion of persons." By contrast, God's gift of himself to man, which is what the analogy of spousal love speaks about, can only have the form of a participation in the divine nature (see 2 Pet 1:4) as theology has made clear with great precision. Nevertheless, according to such a measure, the gift given by God to man in Christ is a "total" or "radical" gift, which is precisely what the analogy of spousal love indicates: it is in some sense "all" that God "could" give of himself to man, considering the limited faculties of man as a creature. In this way the analogy of spousal love indicates the "radical" character of grace: of the whole order of created grace. (TOB 95b:4)

In his encyclical on the Holy Spirit, John Paul focuses on the trinitarian communion of persons.

> It can be said that in the Holy Spirit the intimate life of the Triune God becomes totally gift, an exchange of mutual love between the divine Persons, and that through the Holy Spirit God exists in the mode of gift. It is the Holy Spirit who is the personal expression of this self-giving, of this being-love" (*Dominum et vivificantem*, 10). The third Person—we read in St Augustine—is "the supreme love that unites both the Persons" (*De Trinitate*, n. 7, 3, 6). Indeed, the Father begets the Son *by loving* him (*amandolo*); the Son is begotten by the Father, *letting* himself be loved and *receiving* from him the capacity to love; the Holy Spirit is love *given* in total gratuitousness by the Father, *received* with full gratitude by the Son, and *given back* by them to the Father. (John Paul II, *General Audience*, July 29, 1998, 2)

Particularly important is the statement "The Father begets the Son by loving him (*amandolo*)." This primal gift of love corresponds to the Son's receiving the gift and to the consequent breathing forth of the Holy Spirit as the definitive gift between Father and Son. This divine union of love, rooted in and completely shaped by gift, is the exemplar of the union of human persons. The likeness between these two unions shows the reason why human persons are called to find themselves through a sincere gift of self. The ultimate reason is the mystery of the Father and his love.

From this perspective, one can understand TOB's teaching about glory in the human body. "Purity is the glory of the human body before God. It is the glory of God in the human body" (TOB 57:3). Purity in the relationship between husband and wife, according to TOB, depends on the authenticity of love as a radical reception and corresponding gift of self. The glory of God in the human body is ultimately the Father's glory in his total gift to the Son. "A total gift (an uncreated gift) is shared ... by God himself in the Trinitarian communion of persons" (TOB 95b:4). This, in brief, is the Trinitarian foundation of TOB, and it explains its main thesis.

> The body, in fact, and only the body, is capable of making visible what is invisible: the spiritual and the divine. It has been created to transfer into the visible reality of the world the mystery hidden from eternity in God, and thus to be a sign of it. (TOB 19:3–4)

PART III

Map

Introduction

1. How to Use This Map

Looking at a car's navigation system on a trip through the Alps is no substitute for looking at the road and landscape. The map is a tool. The same applies to the map of TOB presented here. The best way to use it is to look back and forth between the road and map. Only careful reading of TOB will make the map understandable. It is not a text to be read by itself. Its purpose is to help readers reach a clearer and deeper understanding of TOB.

The map uses John Paul's own part, chapter, and section headings to understand the literary and logical structure of the text. It summarizes the main point of each numbered paragraph in a sentence or two. John Paul usually draws attention to this point by italics. An account of the order of his argument is given at the beginning of larger divisions and within the text by headings added in square brackets.

Seeing the order in an argument is a matter of "looking before and after," asking two questions on each level of division: (1) What is the purpose of the whole? (2) What are the parts within that whole, and how do they serve the overall purpose? To read a text well, one needs to pursue these questions from the largest divisions all the way down to the order between individual sentences in a paragraph. John Paul's writing is careful and deliberate in looking before and after. The effort of thinking through why he says what he says exactly when he says it is richly repaid by the wealth of meaning one discovers.

2. Overall Structure

Part One of TOB unfolds the concept "spousal meaning of the body," that is, the body's innate meaning in expressing and realizing a total mutual gift of self between man and woman: "I am yours, you are mine." Part Two turns to "the language (or speech) of the body," that is, to the act in which a particular man and woman speak this spousal meaning to each other at a particular moment in time. They speak it once and for all in their vows and in the consummation of these vows. They renew the same speech in their conjugal acts. John Paul sees *Humanae vitae* in this context. The speech of the body needs to be truthful as speech of the communion of persons. It needs to affirm the procreative and the unitive meaning of the conjugal act as constitutive of its nature, raised to the level of sacrament.

The three chapters of Part One discuss the spousal meaning at three moments: at the beginning, God's intention as portrayed in the first four chapters of Genesis; in the middle, the present time, which is marked by both sin and redemption; and the end, the future definitive fulfillment in the resurrection.

The first two chapters of Part Two belong together as discussions of marriage as a sacrament. "Chapter One: Grace and Covenant" discusses the sacrament under the aspect of what it signifies and effects; namely, grace and the covenant. "Chapter Two: The Sacramental Sign" discusses it under the aspect of sign with particular attention to the maturation of the sign between man and woman. "Chapter Three: He Gave Them the Law of Life as Their Inheritance" turns to *Humanae vitae* and the question of contraception. The structure can be summarized as follows.

- Part One. The spousal meaning of the body
    - Chapter One. In God's original intention
    - Chapter Two. Now, threatened by sin but redeemed
    - Chapter Three. Then, in the resurrection
- Part Two. Speaking the spousal meaning in the sacrament of marriage
    - Chapter One. Grace as union with God in the covenant
    - Chapter Two. The mutual gift of self of man and woman in word and flesh as sign
    - Chapter Three. Speaking the sign according to its full meaning

Once one understands this structure, one can state the argument of TOB in a single sentence. When the spousal meaning of the body (Part One, Chapters One through Three) is brought into play by men and women as an effective sign of grace (Part Two, Chapters One and Two), it needs to be spoken or reread by them according to its full truth, which is inseparably unitive and procreative (Part Two, Chapter Three).

3. Searching for a Map

Modern books (in contrast to ancient texts) are usually divided into chapters with subheadings. A table of contents conveniently assembles all of these headings. It functions as a map that helps readers orient themselves. The first printed editions of TOB (I used the Italian, English, and German) did not contain such help. Each of the audience talks had a heading, but the headings differed in each edition. The talks were grouped under five or six headings, but these also differed in the various languages. No reliable guidance could be expected from these sources.

John Paul, I was sure, must have had a written outline from which he worked. Picking up my courage, I wrote a letter, addressed "To Pope John Paul II, Vatican City," only a few months before he died, as it turned out. Among the questions in the letter, two were particularly important to me: "What is the original language of TOB?" and "Is there a detailed written outline from which you worked, and could you send me a copy of it?"

An answer came back almost immediately, written by the Sostituto at the Vatican Secretariat of State, Archbishop Sandri, at the request of Pope John Paul II. The original text of TOB, the archbishop wrote, was the Italian as delivered at the Wednesday audiences and published in the *Insegnamenti di Giovanni Paolo*. I now understand what I did not understand then. In this context, *original* means *authentic*, not *written first*. The letter said nothing about the second question, the outline.

After John Paul died, the news reported that he had asked for all his papers to be burned. I was bitterly disappointed. The map I was looking for would be burned. A few days later, another news report quoted John Paul's secretary, Archbishop Dziwisz. "I found nothing worth burning." Pope Benedict had decided the papers were to be preserved. I immediately contacted Archbishop Dziwisz, who was living at Dom Polski, the Polish pilgrimage house in Rome. He revived my hopes. "Yes, there is much I can show you. Yes, theology of the body, very important! Very close to the Holy Father's heart." "An outline or map?" I asked. "Yes, of course," he answered, "I can show you. It is very clear. His mind was always very clear, yes. The argument has a detailed structure. Call me in a few months. It is a busy time for me now."

The same conversation took place when I called again some months later. When I called for the third time, Archbishop Dziwisz had been made Archbishop of Kraków. "I am on the way to Kraków," he said. "Don't worry. You can contact the head of the Polish section in the Secretariat of State. He can show you the papers."

I contacted the head of the Polish section and told him what Archbishop Dziwisz had said, authorizing him to show me the papers. His answer was a bitter disappointment. "I am very sorry; Archbishop Dziwisz no longer has control over the papers. I cannot show them to you. They are now in the secret archives and will remain there for the next seventy-five years." He added a consolation, though a heavily qualified one. "Some of the more public papers, particularly from the time before the Pontificate are kept at Dom Polski. You can take a look at those. I doubt you will find much."

Wojtek Janusiewicz, a Polish professor at the International Theological Institute in Austria, where I served as a professor of New Testament and president, traveled with me to Dom Polski. We had reserved rooms for several days. The head of the archives brought us the Italian folders of the audiences, the original text, as he said. The boxes stretched across a long table. We looked and looked but found no trace of an outline or map.

Exhausted and disappointed, we asked the head of the archives if there were any Polish materials. "Yes," he answered, "but if you found nothing in the Italian folders, I doubt you will find anything in the Polish translation. The Italian, after all, is the original."

As we looked through the Polish boxes, we came across a text that had been typed on an old typewriter. The Italian as well as the Polish of the audience talks had all been printed on a laser printer, but this typescript looked definitely older. The text, the same as the Polish audience talks, was not divided into audience talks. It had chapter headings and subheadings. We began to suspect that it might be older than the Italian.

The paradigm shift took us a while because we had the firm impression from Archbishop Sandri's letter and the archivist's words that the Italian was the original text. It did not occur to us that *original* did not necessarily mean older but could mean *authentic*. Some magisterial documents are written in a modern language first. Then they are translated into Latin. The Latin then becomes the *original* text, not in the sense of being older but in the sense of being the *authentic* point of reference.

Our suspicion that the typescript was older changed to certainty when we came across a folder with handwritten notes by John Paul II to his secretary that explained how the typescript was to be used in producing the audience talks. John Paul himself marked the beginning of any given audience talk in the typescript. Each piece had to be about twenty minutes long. We could see the marks clearly in the margin of the typescript, written in John Paul's own characteristic hand. He also consecutively numbered the paragraphs of the typescript within each audience talk. On separate sheets of paper, he wrote an introductory sentence or two, though some audience talks begin immediately as the typescript does. Then he copied the marginal paragraph numbers he had added to the typescript. In some cases, he wrote out a few concluding sentences in Polish. A few longer passages, also written by hand in Polish, are entirely new in comparison with the typescript.

The first of these notes was particularly important. When Father Janusiewicz translated one of its sentences, I knew we had found the map. "The small additions do not in any way extend (nor do they change) the original structure of the text."[1] According to this statement, the structure indicated by the Polish divisions and headings in the typescript was the unchanged structure of TOB.

We asked the head of the archives, "Who was Archbishop Wojtyła's typist?" "Sister Emilia Ehrlich." "Do you have her phone number?" "Yes, here is her number in Poland!" We called, and she picked up the phone right away. "Yes," she said, "Archbishop Wojtyła had completed the manuscript when he was still in Kraków. I typed it. It was ready to go to the printer, but then he was elected."

Our next discovery was as highly ironic. We compared Sister Emilia's typescript with the Polish edition of TOB (Libreria Editrice Vaticana, 1986) and saw that, with only few exceptions, they were exactly the same. The printed edition had the same chapter and section headings as the typescript. It had no division into audience talks. We thought we had discovered a precious secret map that had disappeared from the text and become hidden in the archives. In fact, the map had been in print for years, studied and understood by thousands, provided they could read Polish, which I cannot.

Still, our search had not been completely in vain. It proved beyond doubt that the original (in the sense of oldest) text of TOB was the Polish text, not the Italian. The chapter and section headings of the Polish had not been added by a Polish translator. They were John Paul's own divisions. They were an integral part of the original text as published later by John Paul himself. One can rely on them for understanding the structure of the argument.

4. The Authentic TOB

If the Polish text published by Libreria Editrice Vaticana is the original, why was it not used as the pattern for editions of TOB in other languages? One factor may have been that collections of audience talks had been published before. The Curia and the publishers followed the usual method. They collected the talks,

1. See the facsimile and translation of this note in John Paul II, *Man and Woman He Created Them*, xvi–xviii.

used the headings given to each talk in the various language editions of *L'Osservatore Romano*, and printed the whole between two covers. What prevented the recognition of the importance of the Polish edition was, in part, the widespread mistaken impression that it was a translation from the Italian. The formidable language barrier between Polish and other languages contributed as well.

Some years after this discovery at Dom Polski, Christopher West and I took a trip through Poland to visit the places of John Paul. We also visited Archbishop Dziwisz. "What is the relation between the Polish and the Italian text of TOB?" we asked him. "John Paul himself," the Archbishop answered, "asked me to publish the Polish text when the catecheses were completed. He gave me specific instructions about using the original typescript. Yes, the one at the archives at Dom Polski. The structure is very clear, as I told you years ago," he added. "Only a few passages which John Paul composed as new Polish text for the audience talks were to be added. The introductory and concluding sentences of the talks were to be omitted. *Nevertheless*, the Polish edition explicitly states, as he instructed me, that it is an edition of the talks he delivered during the Wednesday audiences. It is the edition of the talks he himself gave instructions for."

Several years passed until I learned further details of the early literary history of TOB. Andreas Widmer, a Swiss guard at the beginning of John Paul's pontificate, personally witnessed some of the events. "The newly elected pope," he told me, "originally wanted to publish his theology of the body as a book. Members of the Curia objected that popes do not publish books. Later in his pontificate, John Paul set this custom aside and published several books, but in 1978, at the very beginning of his pontificate, he submitted to the Curia. Instead of publishing TOB as a book, he decided to use the text for his weekly catecheses at the Wednesday audiences. It was so close to his heart."

The Wednesday audience talks had been firmly established as regular occasions for papal catechesis. Catechesis and preaching are the two main ways in which a bishop, including the pope, exercises his Ordinary Magisterium. If John Paul had published TOB as a book, it could have become part of his Ordinary Magisterium only if he had taken the additional extraordinary step of explicitly declaring that this was his intention.

The complicated literary history raises a difficult question. Which version is the real TOB? Given that TOB saw the light of day as a text of the Ordinary Magisterium, it is important to answer this question. Members of the Curia usually answer, the Italian text as delivered at the audiences and published in the official *Insegnamenti*—this is the authentic text. The letter I received from Archbishop Sandri had made this very point. The first Italian edition, produced by Carlo Caffarra, then head of the John Paul II Institute, prints not only the talks actually delivered as audience talks but included those prepared by John Paul and included in the Polish edition. It omits the (often misleading) headings given by L'Osservatore Romano to each audience when it appeared shortly after being delivered. It does not contain the original headings but structures the whole by an intelligent guess, which largely hits its target. For several years, members of the John Paul II Institute in Rome worked on an edition that would list all the differences between the Italian and the Polish and include all the original headings. These plans were not carried through to the end by the Polish-speaking editor. He was replaced by an Italian editor who used the position of the curia as a basis for the easiest alternative. The new Italian edition only prints the audiences actually delivered and printed in the *Insegnamenti*. It does not include the headings. In comparison with the first edition, it is an unfortunate regress. The recent retranslations of TOB from Italian into French and German, by contrast, contains the whole text written by John Paul, including the headings.

When I asked Cardinal Dziwisz, "Which is the authentic text, the Polish original or the Italian translation?" his answer was differentiated. "The Italian," he said, "is without doubt an authentic text because it was the text delivered by John Paul at the Wednesday audiences. Yet, according to John Paul's clearly expressed intention, the Polish text is, in a different way, authentic as well. There are two reasons. *First*, just as John Paul himself delivered the audience talks, so he himself ordered the Polish original to be published according to his own detailed instructions. Both the delivery of the Italian and the publication of the Polish were his acts as Pope. The Polish edition makes explicit reference to the audiences. It states that the Polish text *is the text for the audiences*, which applies also to the talks he prepared but did not deliver. *Second*, the Polish text carries John Paul II's meaning with precision as he himself first expressed in his own mother tongue. The Italian translation is, on the whole, quite good, but it was not always possible to check and correct it. When it comes to understanding what John Paul II meant to say, the Polish original is the final measure."

The strength of Cardinal Dziwisz's view in comparison with others is that it looks at all the relevant factors.

5. Italian versus Polish

At the end of his discussion of original nakedness free of shame, John Paul introduces the main concept of Part One, "the spousal meaning of the body." In the Genesis narrative, he argues, man and woman see each other in light of *the mystery of creation*. By "mystery of creation," he understands a chain of three truths: (1) God is love. (2) He created man and woman *out of* love and (3) *for* love. This truth, he goes on to say, allows man and woman to see each other more clearly. Here is the translation of the Italian.

> Seeing each other reciprocally through the very mystery of creation, as it were, the man and the woman see each other still more fully and clearly than through the sense of sight itself, that is, through the eyes of the body. (TOB 13:1)

The word *than* was added by the Italian translator. The Polish original does not have it.[2] Adding *than* makes the passage easier to understand, but it misses an important point that needs to stand at the center of a theology of the body. For comparison, I will keep the overall translation the same, only omitting *than* and adding emphasis.

> Seeing each other reciprocally through the very mystery of creation, as it were, the man and the woman see each other still *more fully and clearly through the sense of sight itself*, that is, through the eyes of the body.

John Paul's point is that the spiritual sight in light of "the mystery of creation" is not simply external to the bodily act of sight. It enters that bodily act and deepens it, so that one sees the other person more clearly through one's bodily eyes. One sees more clearly, not as clearly after getting glasses that correct shortsightedness or astigmatism but in a deepening of "I see you." What one sees in looking at another person is not color and shape alone. One does not merely suppose that there is a person hidden *behind* the iconostas of bodily appearances. In the same way, to see a person through the mystery of creation deepens the unified bodily-spiritual act of sight.

The addition of *than* does not contradict this truth. It states a different truth. Spiritual vision distinguished from bodily vision and taken by itself can be clearer than the bodily vision of color and shape. Yet spiritual vision informs and intensifies the act of bodily vision, and conversely it depends on bodily vision since all knowledge begins with sensation. Seeing begins in the heart and penetrates into the heart of another. The concept *spousal meaning* comes out much more clearly and vividly when one removes *than*. Other differences in this passage are relatively minor. Here is the revised translation of the sentence with the context added.

> Seeing each other reciprocally as if with the sight of the very mystery of creation, the man and the woman see each other more fully and clearly through

2. Many thanks to Grzegorz Ignatik, who helped me to compare my English translation of the Italian text with the Polish text, a two-year project conducted over several hours on Fridays.

the sense of sight itself, that is, through the eyes of the body. They see and embrace each other, in fact, with all the peace of the interior gaze, which creates the fullness of personal intimacy....

Seeing and embracing each other in all the peace of the interior gaze, they "communicate" in the fullness of humanity, which reveals itself in them as reciprocally complementary precisely because it is "male" and "female."

At the same time, they "communicate" based on the communion of persons in which they become a mutual gift for each other, through their femininity and masculinity. In reciprocity, they reach in this way a particular lived experience of the meaning of their own bodies. The original meaning of nakedness corresponds to such a simplicity and fullness of seeing in which the understanding of the meaning of the body is born in the very heart, as it were, of their community-communion.

We will call this meaning "spousal." (TOB 13:1)

PART ONE, CHAPTER ONE

Christ Appeals to the Beginning (TOB 1–23)

Chapter One unfolds the concept *spousal meaning of the body* in light of Christ's appeal to the beginning (Genesis 1–2), in which "the Creator created them male and female."

1. What Is Meant by "Beginning"? (TOB 1–4)
2. Original Solitude (TOB 5–7)
3. Original Unity (TOB 8–10)
4. Original Nakedness (TOB 11–13:1)
5. Man in the Dimension of Gift (TOB 13:2–19)
6. "Knowledge" and Procreation (TOB 20–22)
7. An Integral Vision (TOB 23)

The term *meaning* is the key concept of the encyclical *Humanae vitae*: the conjugal act has two meanings, unitive and procreative. After an introduction (Section 1,) the argument is ordered according to these two meanings. Sections 2-5 discuss primarily the unitive aspect of the spousal meaning, already with a view to the procreative meaning; Section 6 takes up the procreative aspect more fully, yet also with a view to the unitive meaning that is evident in sexual *knowing* (Genesis 4:1).

Sections 2–4 discuss the experience of three original meanings of the body in the second chapter of Genesis: original solitude (Section 2), original unity (Section 3), and original nakedness free of shame (Section 4).

Original solitude is an experience in which the "I," a personal subject, grasps itself precisely as personal. Original solitude therefore corresponds to the first of the two principles expressed in *Gaudium et spes* 24: "Man is the only creature on earth God willed for itself" because of his rational nature, by which he is a person. Original unity corresponds to the second principle: "Man cannot fully find himself except through a sincere gift of self." Original nakedness free of shame is a sign of the purity and authenticity with which these two principles of the life of person are lived according to the Genesis narrative.

Sections 5 and 6 explore the "inseparable connection" between the unitive meaning and the procreative meaning affirmed in *Humanae vitae*, although John Paul takes up this connection more thematically in the last chapter of TOB. They unfold the theological implications of these meanings by means of a hermeneutics of the gift in the concept "spousal meaning of the body." Together with the theological highpoint of Part Two ("sacrament and mystery," TOB 94–99:3), Sections 5 and 6 are the theological heart of TOB.

Section 7 concludes the chapter by reflecting on another concept in *Humanae vitae*, the "integral vision" of the human person, in contrast to the partial perspectives adopted by popular philosophies that tend to limit rationality (*logos*) to the methods of the natural sciences.

1. What Is Meant by "Beginning"? (TOB 1–4)

§1 Approaching Genesis (TOB 1:1–2:1)
§2 First Account of the Creation of Man (TOB 2:2–5)
§3 Second Account of the Creation of Man (TOB 3:1–3)
§4 The Perspective of the Redemption of the Body (TOB 3:4–4:5)

§§1–3 belong together as an introduction to Jesus's moral teaching about the indissolubility of marriage. §1 presents that teaching and its appeal to the Creator's plan as expressed in Genesis. §§2–3 sketch the character of these two creation accounts.

Following the Pauline distinction between law and Gospel, §4 explains that Jesus does not speak as a mere moral teacher who points to God's law about the indissolubility without any concern for the weakness of men and women; he speaks as the Redeemer, whose grace enables men and women to live according to his law. The perspective of redemption dominates TOB as a whole (TOB 86:8). §4 concludes with some reflections on method in interpreting Genesis. Genesis alludes to human experiences and needs to be understood in terms of human experience, particularly the experience of longing for redemption and the present dawn of that redemption.

§1 Approaching Genesis (TOB 1:1–2:1)

1:1–2 Twice Christ uses the phrase "from the beginning." "*From the beginning* the Creator created them male and female. . . . Moses allowed you to divorce your wives, but *from the beginning* it was not so" (Matthew 19:4–8). **1:3** *Beginning* is what Genesis speaks about. **1:4** Christ's insistence on the beginning of the Creator's plan leads one to reflect about the way in which, in the mystery of creation, man was formed precisely as male and female. **1:5** This reflection will accompany the Synod on the Family (1981) by showing the deep roots from which marriage and the family spring. **2:1** The texts to be discussed: Genesis, chapters 1–4.

§2 First Account of the Creation of Man (TOB 2:2–5)

2:2 According to some biblical scholars, the first account (Genesis 1) is more recent than the second (Genesis 2–3). **2:3** It has a cosmological character, inasmuch as it describes the creation of man in objective terms as part of the creation of the visible world. **2:4** It is above all theological, inasmuch as it describes man as created in the image of God. **2:5** It is also metaphysical, inasmuch as it focuses on both creation and procreation and affirms the goodness of all created being: being and good are convertible.

§3 Second Account of the Creation of Man (TOB 3:1–3)

3:1 The second account (Genesis 2–3) has a subjective or psychological depth, inasmuch as it describes man's self-awareness and self-understanding (e.g., shame) and documents human conscience. **3:2** By appealing to it, Christ leads us to the boundary between two situations, original innocence and original sin. **3:3** These two situations imply two states of human nature, the state of integral nature and the state of fallen nature.

§4 The Perspective of the Redemption of the Body (TOB 3:4–4:5)

[*Christ Speaks as Redeemer* (*TOB 3:4–4:3*)] **3:4** While God's plan for human love has not lost its original binding force, man has lost his original innocence. **4:1–2** There is an essential connection between man's hereditary state of sin and the beginning. His roots reach back deeply into original innocence. **4:3** In showing us these roots, Christ does not speak primarily as a teacher of morality who insists on the absolute demands of love, leaving men and women in despair because of their hardness of heart; he speaks as the Redeemer of the body whose Spirit enables them to live that love (for a more detailed discussion of this point, see TOB 50–59).

[*Method of Reading: Experience of Love and Redemption* (*TOB 4:4–5*)] **4:4** The human experience of love is a legitimate means for theological interpretation. **4:5** "We ourselves, who have the first fruits of the Spirit, groan inwardly while we wait for ... the redemption of our bodies" (Romans 8:23). If we place ourselves in this position, in deep harmony with our experience, the beginning speaks with the great wealth of light that comes from revelation.

2. Original Solitude (TOB 5–7)

§1 distinguishes two kinds of solitude, one rooted in human nature (being alone as a person among animals) and the other rooted in the male and female sex (being alone as a man without a woman and vice versa).

§§2–4 belong together as an analysis of the first kind of solitude. §2 shows that the experience of the first kind of solitude contains the discovery of the definition "rational animal." §3 moves to the proper focus of TOB, human consciousness and the meaning of the body. Original solitude as a meaning of the body is a testimony to human subjectivity, which includes an original covenant relationship with God. §4 argues that human subjectivity as expressed in original solitude is inseparably bodily and spiritual. §5 moves from the beginning, from original solitude, to the end, to the final destiny of the body in the alternative between death and immortality. This end was a component of original solitude as the man stood alone before God. "In the day that you eat of it, you will die" (Genesis 2:17).

§1 A Twofold Context (TOB 5:2–3)

5:1 Recap of previous audience talk. **5:2** There are two meanings of being alone. One is the solitude of a rational animal, a person, in the midst of nonrational animals; the other is the solitude of the man without the woman. **5:3** The first of these is prior by nature and presupposed by the second.

§2 Man in Search of His Essence (TOB 5:4–6)

5:4 When God brings the animals to the man to see what he would call them and to test whether they would be the *help* that can overcome his solitude, the man experiences himself as both similar to and different from them. **5:5** Standing before God, he experiences himself as a sentient bodily being like the animals. He thereby grasps his nearest genus *animal.* **5:6** Yet he also experiences himself as superior to the animals by knowing them and himself; he experiences his personal subjectivity and thus the specific difference *rational* in the definition "rational animal."

§3 Solitude and Subjectivity (TOB 6:1–2)

6:1 God's commandment not to eat from the tree in the middle of the garden highlights the second constitutive element of personal subjectivity; namely, self-determination. **6:2** Personal subjectivity (I-ness, subject of responsible acts) as presented in Genesis 2 includes a unique, exclusive, and unrepeatable relationship in a covenant with God.

§4 Solitude and the Meaning of the Body (TOB 6:3–7:2)

6:3 While he experiences himself as being a body among bodies, the man experiences himself as in a bodily sense alone, as being a person among the surrounding animals. **6:4** The personal dignity of the body is evident in the typically human activity of bodily work, of "tilling the ground" (Genesis 2:5), which is closely related to "subduing and ruling the earth" (Genesis 1:28). **7:1** By being aware of himself as being in a bodily sense alone, the man also becomes aware of the distinction between body and soul. The relation between body and soul is the central problem of anthropology. **7:2** Yet in a theology of the body we should speak primarily of the meaning of the body rather than of body and soul. When he is the author of a genuinely human bodily activity (e.g., tilling the ground), the man experiences his body as expressing the person. An integral understanding of the body is a vision of the whole man, body and soul; it is a vision of the sacrament of the person.

§5 The Alternative between Death and Immortality (TOB 7:3–4)

7:3 "When you eat of it you shall certainly die" (Genesis 2:17). Although the man had no direct experience of death, he did understand his dependence in being on the Creator, and therefore he was able to grasp the possibility of non-existence. This awareness is part of the meaning of solitude before God. **7:4** The alternative between death and immortality is a new meaning of the body that goes beyond its "essential meaning." It is its "eschatological meaning," that is, its meaning in reference to man's final (Greek: *eschatos*) end and destiny.

3. Original Unity (TOB 8–10)

§1 The Unity of the Two (TOB 8:1–3)
§2 Dimensions of Homogeneity (TOB 8:4–9:1)
§3 "Communion of Persons" (TOB 9:2–3)
§4 "Flesh from My Flesh" (Genesis 2:23) (TOB 9:4–10:1)
§5 The Unity of Becoming "One Flesh" (TOB 10:2–5)

§1 introduces the discussion of being one. §2 focuses on the most fundamental unity between man and woman, the oneness of nature. §3 turns to the unity that consists in the communion of persons in the image of the Trinity. §§4–5 consider the unity of "one flesh." §4 considers it as unity in humanity, "flesh from my flesh," and §5 speaks about "one flesh" in the sense of sexual union.

§1 The Unity of the Two (TOB 8:1–3)

8:1 Being a body belongs more deeply to man as a personal subject than being male and female. For this reason, the solitude rooted in human nature (the first kind of solitude) is prior to the original unity based on masculinity and femininity. **8:2** One must keep the "image of God" (Genesis 1:26) in mind as the narrative of Genesis 2 unfolds. Attention is also to be paid to the dialogue between God and the man and to the unfolding of human consciousness. **8:3** The man's sleep is a return to the nothingness before creation, so that the one who was alone would reawaken in the unity of the two, male and female.

§2 Dimensions of Homogeneity (TOB 8:4–9:1)

8:4 That the woman is created from the man's rib signifies in the first place the homogeneity of their whole being. The man rejoices in her humanity, in the "second I." **9:1** A second dimension of homogeneity is found in the order of goodness. "God saw everything that he had made, and indeed it was very good" (Genesis 1:31). The man's cry of joy (Genesis 2:23) shows that he experiences this goodness, he lives a value. Genesis 2:23 is the biblical prototype of the Song of Songs.

§3 "Communion of Persons" (TOB 9:2–3)

9:2 Being alone is the way that leads to the communion of persons. *Communion* implies *help*, living with and especially for another person. **9:3** Inasmuch as they form a communion of persons, man and woman are an image of God, an image of the inscrutable divine communion of persons. This Trinitarian concept of the image of God is the deepest theological aspect of everything one can say about man. The blessing of fruitfulness descends on this communion of persons.

§4 "Flesh from My Flesh" (Genesis 2:23) (TOB 9:4–10:1)

9:4 "Flesh from my flesh" expresses the perception that the body reveals man. This perception contains in some way everything that human science can say about man. **9:5** "Flesh from my flesh" also expresses a new consciousness of the meaning of the body, which consists in the mutual enrichment of man and woman by each other (see TOB 17:6). **10:1** Genesis 2:23 indicates that our knowledge of who man is must pass through the communion between man and woman, through two complementary ways of being conscious of the meaning of the body.

§5 The Unity of Becoming "One Flesh" (TOB 10:2–5)

10:2 When they become one flesh in the conjugal act, man and woman rediscover each time the mystery of creation. This means reliving man's original virginal value, which springs from his solitude before God. One must take on oneself the solitude of the body of the second *I* as one's own. **10:3** Taking this solitude on oneself is something chosen. Marriage and the conjugal act have from the beginning the character of a chosen, voluntary union. The body *helps* ("a help similar to himself"; Genesis 2:18–20) the two to find themselves in a communion of persons (*Gaudium et spes* 24). **10:4** The conjugal act carries within itself a particular awareness of the meaning of the body in the reciprocal self-gift of the persons. Each union renews the mystery of creation in its original depth and power. **10:5** This analysis shows how the authentic unity of "one flesh" is a norm and task for men and women at all times.

4. Original Nakedness (TOB 11–13:1)

§1 discusses original experience in general, applicable to all three original experiences: solitude, unity, and nakedness free of shame. §§2–3 offer a preliminary sketch of shame (a fuller discussion of shame is found in TOB 26:4–33:5). The first of these argues that shame is the experience that marks the boundary between innocence and sin. The other sketches the positive meaning of shame, which points to a fullness of meaning of the naked body.

§§4–6 unfold this fullness of meaning. §4 focuses on its exterior aspect, the full visibility of man and woman for each other. §5 focuses on the interior aspect, the fullness of interior vision based on the communion of persons. §6 shows that in this vision man and woman see the spousal meaning of the body.

§1 Introductory Observations about Genesis 2:25 (TOB 11:1–2)

11:1 Revelation focuses on primordial experiences that show what man and woman are "from the beginning." These experiences are always at the root of every human experience. They rest on an ontological depth so great that we do not easily perceive them in daily life even though we presuppose them in all that we do. **11:2** Original nakedness free from shame is not an accidental detail in the narrative but the key for understanding it fully.

§2 Shame: A "Boundary" Experience (TOB 11:3–6)

11:3 The statement "They were naked but did not feel shame" describes the man's and the woman's reciprocal experience of the body with great precision. We must therefore unfold the meaning of this statement in the dimension of personal subjectivity. **11:4** Shame marks the boundary between the states of innocence and sin. It is not just one among other experiences but a boundary experience. **11:5** There is a radical change in the meaning of the nakedness of the woman before the man and vice versa. **11:6** Can we reconstruct the first meaning of this nakedness? This seems possible, if we start with shame as a boundary experience.

§3 Attempted Reconstruction (TOB 12:1–2)

12:1 Shame implies the experience of fear for one's own *I* in the face of the other "I." Shame shows the need to be accepted according to one's true value. In this way, shame expresses the essential rules for the communion of persons, which it seeks to reestablish. It is deeply rooted in the dignity of the person experienced in man's original solitude. **12:2** The absence of shame asserted in Genesis 2:25 is not a defect. It is neither shamelessness nor immaturity. Original nakedness indicates, rather, a particular fullness of consciousness and experience of the body. What is this fullness?

§4 Participation in the Visibility of the World (TOB 12:3)

12:3 Nakedness is a participation in the visibility of the world. The woman is fully visible to the man and vice versa. Her humanity as "flesh from my flesh" is thus fully evident to him. This visibility is closely linked with the meaning of the body.

§5 The Inner Dimension of Vision (TOB 12:4–5)

12:4 For the meaning of original nakedness, the interiority of the person is more decisive than exterior visibility. Communication in the full sense takes place on the basis of the full communion of persons as expressed and reached through the body. Such communication is the basis of a new meaning of the body. The body expresses the person from within, from his or her concrete interiority, which is more than individuality. **12:5** Original nakedness free of shame signifies an original depth in affirming what is interior in the other person. This affirmation establishes the personal intimacy of communication in radical simplicity and purity. A necessary condition of such communication is an inner fullness of seeing the other person in God, according to the measure of "image of God."

§6 Intimacy: The Hidden Meaning of Vision (TOB 13:1)

13:1 Seeing each other naked, the man and the woman see each other through the mystery of creation—that is, the mystery that God is love—creates what is "very good" out of love, and impresses the vocation to love on man and woman. The peace of this interior gaze creates the fullness of intimacy between persons. Seeing each other naked, the man and the woman communicate with each other on the basis of the communion of persons, in which they become a mutual gift for each other; they see the meaning of their bodies as spousal.

5. Man in the Dimension of Gift (TOB 13:2–19)

Section 5 presents the core of "the integral truth about the human person" on the basis of the three original meanings of the body. It is the key theological passage of Part One. In theological weight, it is the counterpart of the main theological passage of Part Two, "Sacrament and Mystery" (TOB 94–99), which explicitly returns to this section and quotes its main theses.

Section A unfolds the spousal meaning of the body in light of the notion of *gift*. Section B shows the roots of this spousal meaning in original innocence.

A. The Spousal Meaning of the Body (TOB 13:2–16:1)

Section A develops the concept *spousal meaning of the body* in a strictly theological manner, moving to the human body from the revelation of God as love. It is divided into seven paragraphs arranged with great literary and logical intelligence.

§1 Creation as Giving (TOB 13:2–3)
§2 Giving and Man (TOB 13:4–14:1)
§3 Gift: Mystery of a Beatifying Beginning (TOB 14:2–4)
§4 Discovery of the "Spousal" Meaning of the Body (TOB 14:5–6)
§5 "Freedom of the Gift": Foundation of the Spousal Meaning of the Body (TOB 15:1–2)
§6 The "Spousal Character" of the Body and the Revelation of the Person (TOB 15:3–4)
§7 The Spousal Meaning of the Body as the Fruit of Rootedness in Love (TOB 15:5–16:1)

§§1–6 explain the spousal meaning in a theological manner, that is, in a downward movement of thought that begins with God and proceeds to the deepest foundation of the spousal meaning in the personhood of the human person as defined by *Gaudium et spes* 24.

§7 ties the end of this downward movement back to the beginning by showing that the irradiation of divine Love stands at the origin of the spousal meaning of the body, "more interior than my innermost" (Augustine).

The seven sections are thus arranged like a Russian doll, where inside each doll one finds another one enclosed, more inside, until one reaches the smallest, most inside.

§1 starts with the most encompassing beginning, God as giver of what is good: by giving the gift of created being, the Creator shows that he is Love.

§2 moves from the Creator as Love to the creature by arguing that the Creator impresses his own character as Love, as the giver of gifts, on man and woman "from the beginning." What comes out of the fire is like its origin, hot.

§3 moves further inside by focusing on the human body as we experience it from within, in the exchange of the gift of self. The body has the power to express and realize love in the gift of self, which leads to happiness (beatifying).

§4 shows that in the moment of happiness the meaning of the body is discovered and revealed as spousal and thus procreative. When one is happy, things make sense, their sense.

§5 moves one level further down or inside, to a necessary quality of the person without which the spousal meaning would collapse; namely, being free to give oneself rather than acting compulsively out of passion. To be able to say *yes*, one needs to be able to say *no*.

§6 moves yet another level deeper and more inside, to the character of the person as person, who can only find herself or himself through a sincere gift of self (*Gaudium et spes* 24).

§7 returns to the divine source and paradigm to show that the spousal meaning of the body is rooted in the radiation of the Holy Spirit.

The seven elements are also arranged symmetrically. The spousal meaning stands in the middle of the seven; God embraces the whole from both ends, and objective and subjective characteristics form two pairs between God and the spousal meaning: the order in the first pair is objective-subjective, and in the second pair it is subjective-objective.

§1. The presence and action of God as Creator, as Giver, surrounding the whole.
§2. *Objective* consequence: creatures, most of all persons, can receive and give.
§3. *Subjective* consequence: original happiness experienced in the body.
§4. Spousal meaning of the body.
§5. *Subjective* requirement: free self-possession.
§6. *Objective* reality of the person revealed by *Gaudium et spes* 24.
§7. The presence and action of the Holy Spirit on the deepest and innermost level.

One can also see the seven elements as a chain that forms a circle. The first element of each link in the chain picks up the last element of the link before it. The first element in the first link picks up the last element of the seventh, so that the circle closes.

§1. God is love/gift.
§2. Love/gift is our call.
§3. Our call, when realized, brings happiness.
§4. Happiness teaches us the true meaning of the body, its spousal meaning.
§5. The spousal meaning requires freedom to give ourselves.
§6. Freedom to give shows what our innermost being, the person, is.
§7. In our innermost being the Spirit dwells, more inside than our innermost.

§1 Creation as Giving (TOB 13:2–3)

[*The Three Meanings as Background*] **13:2** The three original meanings of the body allow us to reach an adequate anthropology. The "image of God" is the key to such an anthropology.

[*The Creator Is Love in Giving a Good Gift*] Christ's words "From the beginning the created them male and female" point to a new criterion of interpretation; namely, *gift* as the key concept of a hermeneutics of the gift. **13:3** Christ's words "the Creator created" point to God as Love and to creation as a gift.

§2 Giving and Man (TOB 13:4–14:1)

[*The Image of God*] **13:4** God's character as giver of good gifts is impressed on every creature. As the image of God, man is able to understand the gift as gift.

[*The Need Arising from This Image*] **14:1** The man is alone because none of the animals make it possible for him to live in a relationship of reciprocal gift.

§3 Gift: Mystery of a Beatifying Beginning (TOB 14:2–4)

[*The Content of the Image of God*] **14:2** The words *alone* and *help* allow us to understand gift as the content of "image of God." Because they are created in the divine image, persons can find fulfillment only by living with and living for another.

[*The Experience of Happiness in Giving*] **14:3** Such fulfillment of the desire implicit in original solitude is a cause of happiness. Emerging from God's creatively giving love, the man finds happiness only with another person in a similarly giving love. In this way, the *beginning* leads us at one and the same time to the person and to sex—to both together and to neither at the exclusion of the other.

[*First Definition of the Human Sexual Body*] **14:4** This is the body: a witness to divine Love from which the original giving springs. This is the meaning with which sex enters into TOB.

§4 Discovery of the "Spousal" Meaning of the Body (TOB 14:5–6)

[*Unitive Meaning*] **14:5** The beginning contains inseparably the revelation and the discovery of the spousal meaning of the body: the *revelation* because God's love is revealed and affects the original consciousness of man and woman; and the *discovery* because the revelation becomes an experience of reciprocal gift between man and woman.

[*Procreative Meaning*] **14:6** "Becoming one flesh" is ordered to the end of procreation. Yet sexuality in human beings is not a mere drive that impels human beings to this end, as in the case of sub-personal animals, but it is raised to the level of the person and the communion of persons. The end of procreation, as the procreation of new persons, is deeply connected with the spousal meaning of the body.

§5 "Freedom of the Gift": Foundation of the Spousal Meaning of the Body (TOB 15:1–2)

15:1 A precondition of the spousal meaning the freedom of the gift. **15:2** Freedom of the gift implies self-mastery, not being swept away by passion. One can truly say *yes* if one can say *no*.

§6 The "Spousal Character" of the Body and the Revelation of the Person (TOB 15:3–4)

15:3 *Gaudium et spes* 24 expresses "the whole truth" about the human person, which gathers in particular the beginning of man and woman in the mystery of creation. Man and woman find each other as persons "willed by God for their own sake," and they welcome each other within themselves as a gift in precisely this way. In this consists the revelation and discovery of the spousal meaning of the body. **15:4** Ordered from within to the mutual gift of self, the human body has a great beauty that goes far beyond the merely physical level. The meaning of the body, which man and woman experience consciously, involves on the one hand the power to express and realize the gift of self, and on the other hand the power and deep availability for living the fact that the other person is willed by God for his or her own sake (*Gaudium et spes* 24).

§7 The Spousal Meaning of the Body as the Fruit of Rootedness in Love (TOB 15:5–16:1)

15:5 The spousal meaning remains the deepest level, the fundamental component of human existence in the world. The body has a spousal meaning because the human person is willed by God for its own sake and can only find itself in a sincere gift of self (*Gaudium et spes* 24). **16:1** The irradiation of Love (the Holy Spirit) is part of the mystery of creation. This irradiation is the reason why consistent giving shapes the deepest levels of their existence as subjects, which is reflected in their reciprocal experience of the body. **16:2** Christ testifies to this beginning in love.

B. The Mystery of Original Innocence (TOB 16:2–19:6)

Having given an account of the spousal meaning of the body in Section A, John Paul turns in Section B to the manner in which original innocence upheld the spousal meaning in its full integrity. Section B is divided into seven sections.

§§1–4 belong together. They unfold the mystery of original innocence in four steps, moving out from the center. §1 explains the center itself: original innocence is a gift given to the human heart that allows participation in God's Trinitarian life. §2 explains that the spousal meaning of the body and the happiness flowing from it are immediate consequences of this gift. §3 moves further out, from the meaning of the body to innocence in the mutuality of the acts of giving and receiving between man and woman. §4 moves out one further step, to the symptom of this innocent mutuality; namely, nakedness free of shame (Genesis 2:25). It uses *Gaudium et spes* 24 to show the depth of meaning that lies in original nakedness.

§5 takes a step back from the argument to clarify once again the method to be used. It distinguishes theological accounts that focus on objective aspects of original innocence (e.g., original justice) from those (including TOB) that focus on the lived experience of personal subjectivity.

§§6–7 present the main findings of the second kind of account, first in the order of morality and then in the order of being. §6 draws out the moral implications of original innocence in the key of lived experience, and §7 sketches the sacramental aspect in the same experiential key. §7 is particularly important because it answers the main question of any theology of the body: Why did God create the body? It contains the thesis statement and theological heart of TOB as a whole. John Paul returns to this thesis statement in the key theological passage of Part Two (TOB 96 in the context of 94–99).

§1 Gift to the Human Heart (TOB 16:3)

16:3 Original nakedness free of shame (Genesis 2:25) is the testimony of the body as *eyewitness* to the grace of original innocence. By grace, the man and the woman shared in the inner life of God himself, in his life as the Trinitarian communion of persons, which enabled them to live in the reciprocal relationship of the disinterested gift of self (*Gaudium et spes* 24).

§2 Original Innocence and the Spousal Meaning of the Body (TOB 16:4–5)

16:4 Original innocence is that which radically excludes the experience of shame in original nakedness. **16:5** It is the true content of the experience of the spousal meaning of the body; it is also the true source of the happiness experienced in this spousal meaning. This happiness depends on the tranquil testimony of conscience that the gift is being given in true faithfulness.

§3 Innocence at the Foundation of the Exchange of the Gift (TOB 17:1–3)

17:1–2 Innocence is that which allows the reciprocity and exchange of the gift of the body as the gift of the person. **17:3** Original innocence in the man consists in an acceptance of the woman in her gift as a person willed by the Creator "for her own sake" (*Gaudium et spes* 24).

§4 Exchange of the Gift: Interpretation of Genesis 2:25 (TOB 17:4–6)

17:4 Original nakedness free of shame is a sign of the innocence of the gift of self and of the acceptance of the other person as a gift. Giving and accepting interpenetrate. Giving oneself becomes accepting the other, and accepting the other becomes giving oneself.

[*The Woman as Active and First Gift*] **17:5** In her gift of self to the man, the woman "finds herself" (*Gaudium et spes* 24); that is, she comes to the innermost depth of her person and to a full possession of herself. Finding herself in this way becomes the source of a new gift of herself to the man.

[*The Man as Receptive and His Consequent Task*] **17:6** God entrusts the woman as a gift to the man. The man, on his part, must ensure the reciprocity of the gift. The specific essence of his masculinity reaches the innermost depth of self-possession through his sincere gift of himself (*Gaudium et spes* 24).

§5 Theology of Original Innocence (TOB 18:1–3)

[*One Method: Analyzing Objective Characteristics*] **18:1** Theology has built up an image of what was "from the beginning" by considering the objective aspects of the human condition before the fall.

[*Another Method: Analyzing Lived Experience*] We are rather pursuing the aspect of subjectivity in accord with Genesis, chapters 2–3 (see Genesis 3:1–3). **18:2** The experience of the body was shaped by a different degree of spiritualization, another degree of sensibility for the gifts of the Holy Spirit. **18:3** Following Christ's words, we are attempting to understand the relation between original innocence and the original meaning of the body.

§6 The Root of the Ethos of the Body (TOB 18:4–19:2)

18:4 The Creator gave man and woman to each other. The understanding of the spousal meaning of the body is thus fundamental for understanding who they are and what they ought to be. **18:5** Man and woman come from the Creator's hand first of all as brother and sister in the same humanity. Owing to original innocence, they are endowed with the freedom of the gift, aware of the spousal meaning of the body, in which procreation is deeply rooted. In this way, original innocence constitutes the perfect *ethos* of the gift. **19:1** The *ethos* of the gift implies a certain subjective or experiential profile of love. Man and woman are united by the consciousness of the spousal meaning of their bodies, in which the freedom of the gift is expressed. They experience each other as subjects, not as mere objects of pleasure. **19:2** Despite the loss of original innocence, the spousal meaning of the body remains a task given to man and woman by the *ethos* of the gift, which is a distant echo of original innocence.

§7 Foundation of the Primordial Sacrament: The Body as Sign (TOB 19:3–6)

19:3 Man appears in the visible world as the highest expression of the divine giving because he bears within himself the inner dimension of gift. In this respect he bears the likeness of God. **19:4** In this dimension, a primordial sacrament is established, a sign that efficaciously transmits in the visible world the invisible mystery of God; namely, the procession of the Son as Truth and the procession of the Holy Spirit as mutual Love. The body was created to transfer this invisible mystery into the visibility of the world. **19:5** With man, holiness has entered the visible world. Holiness permits man to express himself fully with his own body, through the sincere gift of self (*Gaudium et spes* 24). In the body, man and woman sense themselves as subjects of holiness. **19:6** Genesis 2:23–25 speaks about the first feast of humanity in the original fullness of the experience of the spousal meaning of the body. This feast draws its origin from the divine sources of Truth and Love.

6. "Knowledge" and Procreation (TOB 20–22)

Section 6 unfolds the meaning of Genesis 4:1: "Adam knew Eve his wife, who conceived and gave birth to Cain and said, I have acquired a man from the Lord."

- §1 Between Poverty of Expression and Depth of Meaning (TOB 20:1–3)
- §2 Knowledge as Personal Archetype (TOB 20:4–21:1)
- §3 Fatherhood and Motherhood as the Human Meaning of Knowledge (TOB 21:2–6)

§4 Knowledge and Possession (TOB 21:7–22:4)
§5 Knowledge Stronger Than Death (TOB 22:5–7)

§1 points out that the Hebrew word *know* (in the sense of sexual union) has a deep meaning that immediately connects human sexuality with subjectivity and personhood.

§§2–3 belong together. They unfold two meanings of *knowledge* according to the two meanings discussed in *Humanae vitae*, the unitive and the procreative. §2 unfolds the unitive meaning of knowledge, in which man and woman are given to each other as persons in the form of a gift. §3 unfolds the procreative meaning of *knowledge*, of which man and woman become fully conscious by pregnancy and birth.

§§4–5 belong together. They turn to the relation between sexual *knowledge* and two other kinds of knowledge discussed above. §4 turns to the relation between sexual knowledge and the knowledge of the natural world (naming the animals) by which man takes possession of that world. §5 turns to the relation between the same knowledge and God's knowledge: "God saw everything that he had made, and indeed, it was very good" (Genesis 1:31). The overall argument serves to bring out the close connection between the unitive and the procreative aspects of sexual knowing.

§1 Between Poverty of Expression and Depth of Meaning (TOB 20:1–3)

20:1 The continuity between original innocence and hereditary sinfulness (see TOB 4:1–3) justifies an analysis of the statement "Adam knew Eve his wife, and she conceived" (Genesis 4:1) in the context of Christ's teaching about the beginning. **20:2** The use of *knowledge* for sexual intercourse may arise from a lack of specific terms in ancient Hebrew, but it contains a great depth of meaning in which we find all the meanings of the body analyzed up to this point. **20:3** *Knowledge* conceives conjugal relations on the specific level of the person rather than on the level of sexual drive as in the other animals.

§2 Knowledge as Personal Archetype (TOB 20:4–21:1)

20:4 *Knowledge* implies consciousness of the meaning of one's body. When they become *one flesh*, man and woman reveal themselves to one another and "are given" to each other in the mode of knowledge. **20:5** What is given (*datum*) goes hand in hand with *gift* (*donum*). Nevertheless, knowledge stresses above all "being given" (*datum*). By knowing each other, man and woman "are given" to each other in their identity as unique and unrepeatable persons, that is, as "I." **21:1** For this reason, knowledge establishes a "personal archetype" of sexuality. This archetype includes the meaning of original solitude because knowledge implies the personal subjectivity (self-consciousness and self-possession) that stands at the root of original solitude. It also includes the meaning of original unity because the very knowledge that stood at the root of original solitude stands now at the root of the "one flesh" union.

§3 Fatherhood and Motherhood as the Human Meaning of Knowledge (TOB 21:2–6)

21:2 Although man and woman know each other as masculine and feminine when they are one flesh, a fuller knowledge of the meaning of their bodies as father and mother comes only later, through pregnancy and birth. **21:3** Begetting thus lies in some way outside of their knowledge. Nevertheless, begetting does in some way enter into their knowledge because in that knowledge man and woman are given to each other in their objective concreteness, which includes their generative powers. Grasping this objective aspect of the body goes hand in hand with experiencing the subjectivity of the gift of self. **21:4** Man and woman also know each other in the third, in their child. **21:5** Many exterior features of woman's body, particularly those that are sexually attractive, are connected with motherhood. **21:6** Eve's words "I have acquired a man from the Lord" (Genesis 4:1) express awareness of the mystery of creation, of God's involvement as Creator in reproducing the image of God.

§4 Knowledge and Possession (TOB 21:7–22:4)

21:7 By knowing and naming the visible world, the man took possession of it. By knowing each other, man and woman take possession of the divine image in the sense of taking it again from the mystery of creation and transmitting it with the Creator's help. Here lies the great dignity of human generation. **22:1** By knowing his wife, the man not only knows but also realizes humanity in the child to be conceived. **22:2** In this way, the cycle of knowledge and generation closes. In relation to the animals, knowledge and possession signify mastery; in relation to human beings, each other and the child, possession does not have this meaning. **22:3** It is more the other way around. Humanity takes possession of man and woman and carries them away when they take possession of it by drawing it from the mystery of creation. **22:4** Biblical knowledge can thus be explained as "possession." Is this understanding of love similar to the Platonic *eros* that Socrates defines as desire for the possession of the beautiful? The idea of the man taking possession of the woman or vice versa is not made explicit in Christ's teaching about the beginning.

§5 Knowledge Stronger Than Death (TOB 22:5–7)

22:5 The prospect of death arises together with the generative meaning of the body, both after the fall. Life is not taken away completely from the human race but is renewed in the cycle of knowledge and generation, which all generations receive as a task, again and again from the beginning. **22:6** Genesis is silent about the relation between the generative and the spousal meaning of the body. It simply shows man on the threshold between the state of innocence and of sin with the consciousness of the generative meaning of his body. **22:7** The knowledge that man and woman have of each other is the reason for the unyielding strength of life struggling against the prospect of death. Sexual knowledge has this power because it is a participation in God's original knowledge: "God saw everything that he had made, and indeed, it was very good" (Genesis 1:31).

7. An Integral Vision (TOB 23)

23:1 The beginning to which Christ appeals is the first inheritance of every human being, the first witness of human identity, the first source of certainty about one's vocation. **23:2** Christ spoke in a definite historical context in response to questions raised by Pharisees on the basis of their concern for the Law of Moses. In our own time, different questions are raised with different concerns. In responding to these new questions and concerns, Christ would still appeal to the beginning. **23:3** His answer contains an "integral vision of man" (*Humanae vitae* 7).

Our age is characterized by a multitude of partial visions in which the human person is often the passive object of technological power rather than the active subject who makes decisions in light of the integral truth. **23:4** This integral truth concerns the meaning of the body in the structure of the personal subject. It is grasped in a theology of the body based on the revelation of the body contained in the teaching of Christ and the creation accounts of Genesis.

23:5 Those who seek fulfillment in their vocation are called to make this theology of the body the content of their lives and behavior. The purpose of this theology of the body is to allow men and women to gain a deepened consciousness of the spousal and generative meaning of the body. **23:6** Christ's answer to the questions of our time includes not only his appeal to the beginning (Part One, Chapter One) but also his appeal to the human heart in its present condition (Part One, Chapter Two) and to the future fulfillment of the human person in the resurrection (Part One, Chapter Three).

PART ONE, CHAPTER TWO

Christ Appeals to the Human Heart (TOB 24–63)

Chapter Two unfolds the theology of the body implicit in Christ's words about adultery in the heart. It is divided into seven sections, plus an appendix about the right way of portraying the naked human body compared with pornography.

Sections 1–5 analyze Christ's words from the point of view of *ethos* (law). Section 6 analyzes Paul's teaching about purity from the point of view of life according to the power of the Spirit (Gospel).

Sections 1–3 belong together as an account of Christ's words in their direct meaning as a negative judgment: "has already committed adultery with her in his heart." Section 1 presents a preliminary overview of the text. Section 2 presents the anthropological foundation of Christ's words. It returns to Genesis to analyze the experience of shame and thereby to reach a systematic understanding of the man of concupiscence. Section 3 turns from anthropology (order of being) to ethics (order of goodness) and explains the ethical content of Christ's teaching on this anthropological basis. Sections 4–5 belong together as an account of the positive call expressed in Christ's words. Section 4 argues that Christ's positive call, rather than the negative judgment, is the predominant element in his words. Section 5 clarifies the "*ethos* of the redemption of the body" that undergirds this call.

Section 6 takes up a topic complementary to that of adultery in the heart: purity of heart. It begins with a word of Christ about purity of heart but then focuses on the words of Paul about purity as life according to the Spirit. The emphasis on Gospel as opposed to law returns here: the gift of the Holy Spirit enables man and woman to live according to the new *ethos*.

Section 7 concludes the chapter by summarizing its results and explaining the purpose of the theology of the body once again, this time in light of the Gospel of the purity of heart. An excursus appended to the chapter considers the *ethos* of portraying the body in art and the media.

1. In the Light of the Sermon on the Mount (TOB 24–25)

Section 1 introduces the discussion of Matthew 5:27–28: "You have heard that it was said, You shall not commit adultery. But I say to you: Whoever looks at a woman to desire her has already committed adultery with her in his heart." It is divided into four paragraphs.

§1 Matthew 5:27–28: Whoever Looks to Desire (TOB 24:1)
§2 Matthew 5:27–28: Ethical Meaning (TOB 24:2–4)
§3 Matthew 5:27–28: Anthropological Meaning (TOB 24:4–25:2)
§4 Matthew 5:27–28 Indicates a Further Dimension (TOB 25:3–5)

§1 places Matthew 5:27–28 in the larger context of the new understanding of the law brought by Jesus.

§§2–3 form a pair corresponding to the pair "good and being" or "ethics and anthropology." §2 points to the ethical meaning of Christ's words (the order of goodness or the moral order), while §3 points to their anthropological meaning (the order of being).

§4 argues that on the surface of the words "adultery in the heart" one might see only desire for a woman who is not one's wife. Desire for one's own wife thus appears as legitimate. Yet already here John Paul indicates what he unfolds later (TOB 43:2–4); namely, that Christ does not restrict adultery in the heart to desire for a person who is not one's spouse. He points to the defective nature of a certain reductive type of desire, even if its object is one's own spouse.

§1 Matthew 5:27–28: Whoever Looks to Desire (TOB 24:1)

24:1 In Matthew 5:27–28, Jesus proposes a fundamental revision in the way of understanding and carrying out the law: in accord with the true will of the Legislator, so that justice may abound (Matthew 5:20). Following the will of the Legislator and realizing an abundant justice characterize the kingdom of God.

§2 Matthew 5:27–28: Ethical Meaning (TOB 24:2–4)

24:2 The key importance of Matthew 5:27–28 for the theology of the body consists in the clarification of the Legislator's true will in the commandment "You shall not commit adultery" and in the fullness of justice this commandment calls for. **24:3** The text is concerned not only with norms but also with *ethos* [Definition: *Ethos* is the conscious stance of a person, the way of seeing, feeling, and acting. It lies halfway between virtues and acts as the overall form of one's conscious life.] *Ethos* is the inner form, the soul of morality. In *ethos*, the *I* enters deeply into the norm, and the norm enters deeply into the "I." **24:4** In the Old Testament, the commandment against adultery was conceived above all in terms of the external actions of man and woman; Christ shifts the essence of the problem to the dimension of the heart and its *ethos*.

§3 Matthew 5:27–28: Anthropological Meaning (TOB 24:4–25:2)

24:4 Christ appeals to the inner man, which is of anthropological interest. **25:1** He addresses historical man who has from the *beginning* a precise sense of the meaning of his body. **25:2** His words have an explicitly anthropological meaning inasmuch as he appeals to the heart. The heart is the dimension of humanity with which the sense of the meaning of the human body and the order of this sense are linked.

§4 Matthew 5:27–28 Indicates a Further Dimension (TOB 25:3–5)

25:3 Because adultery is a violation of the unity of husband and wife by union with a person who is not one's spouse, "adultery in the heart" must be the desire for such an adulterous union, a desire that expresses itself in a certain look. **25:4** Christ, however, does not specify whether the person one desires is one's spouse. But because it is impossible to commit adultery with one's spouse, it seems impossible to commit adultery in the heart. **25:5** Nevertheless, Christ's words seem to have a further theological dimension, a fuller ethical and anthropological meaning—namely, the difference between concupiscence and authentic love—which applies also to husband and wife.

2. The Man of Concupiscence (TOB 26–33)

Section 2 is an anthropological introduction to the ethical analysis carried out in Section 3.

[*Introduction to Concupiscence from 1 John* (*TOB 26:1–3*)] **26:1** The First Letter of John distinguishes three forms of concupiscence, "the concupiscence of the flesh, the concupiscence of the eyes, and the pride of life" (1 John 2:16). Although this text does not explain the nature of this threefold concupiscence, it indicates its origin: "not from the Father but from the world." **26:2** The world created by God in Genesis became the *world* in the Johannine sense when man and woman broke the first covenant with God. This transition directs us once more to "the beginning" in Genesis, to the threshold between innocence and sin. **26:3** Both the man who looks to desire and the woman who is the object of this desire find themselves in the dimension of the threefold concupiscence that comes from the world, not from the Father. We need to understand this concupiscence and the man of concupiscence.

Section A analyzes the coming to be of concupiscence according to the second creation account (Genesis 2–3).

Section B shows the immediate damage concupiscence inflicts on the unity between man and woman; namely, the insufficiency of the union: sexual union no longer fully satisfies the aspiration to realize the communion of persons.

Section C shows the ultimate consequence of concupiscence in the corruption of the spousal meaning of the body.

A. The Meaning of Original Shame (TOB 26:4–28:6)

The argument of Section A follows the order of dependence from the first cause of concupiscence (the original sin) to its final symptom (sexual shame) with three intermediate steps.

§1 Casting Doubt on the Gift (TOB 26:4–5)
§2 Man Alienated from Original Love (TOB 27:1–2)
§3 Change in the Meaning of Original Nakedness (TOB 27:3–4)
§4 "Immanent" Shame (TOB 28:1–3)
§5 Sexual Shame (TOB 28:4–6)

§1 presents the theological root of concupiscence in the nature of the original sin. §2 shows the first effect of the original sin, the alienation of man and woman from love. §3 shows the change in the meaning of original nakedness as an effect of this alienation. §4 explains the immanent shame that arises from the new meaning of nakedness. §5 turns to sexual shame as the final symptom of the fall.

§1 Casting Doubt on the Gift (TOB 26:4–5)

26:4 The original sin consists in casting doubt on the deepest meaning of the gift, on love as the motive for creation. It consists in turning one's back on God-Love, on the Father. In this light one can explain the Johannine concept of concupiscence. By turning his back on the Father, man cuts himself off from "what comes from the Father," and the only thing left to him is "what comes from the world" (1 John 2:16). **26:5** The first symptom of this fall is shame. Shame shows the beginning of concupiscence in the human heart.

§2 Man Alienated from Original Love (TOB 27:1–2)

27:1 Shame touches the deepest level and shakes the very foundations of human existence. Man and woman attempt to hide from God; in the depth of their shame before each other, a new fear before God has matured. **27:2** What now shows itself through nakedness is man deprived of the Gift, alienated from original Love. In this way, concupiscence is to be explained as a lack.

§3 Change in the Meaning of Original Nakedness (TOB 27:3–4)

27:3 The words "I was afraid because I am naked, and I hid myself" express a new state of consciousness, a radical change in the meaning of original nakedness. In its nakedness, the body expressed original solitude and original unity, supremely in the gift of self. Thus the body carried the imprint of the image of God. The original acceptance of the body also implied the acceptance of the whole visible world. **27:4** In the fall, man loses the certainty of the image of God and his right to participate in the visibility of the world as "very good." The words "I was afraid because I am naked, and I hid myself" thus express the collapse of the acceptance of the body (as a sign of the person) and of the consequent acceptance of the material world. Hostility between man and the visible world arises. This hostility gives rise to a "cosmic shame."§4 "Immanent" Shame (TOB 28:1–3)

28:1 Another type of shame arises from within, from the innermost disorder in that through which man and woman were made in the image of God, both in their personal *I* and in their interpersonal communion. Genesis stresses the sexual character of this shame: "They made themselves loincloths." **28:2** This shame before each other, however, has a deep background in the interiority of man and woman—namely, a difficulty in sensing the human essentiality of one's body, a breakup of the original spiritual-bodily unity—which is humiliating. **28:3** In this way, shame is immanent, connected with the inner threat to self-possession and self-dominion. The man of concupiscence does not rule his own body with the same naturalness as the man of original innocence.

§5 Sexual Shame (TOB 28:4–6)

28:4 Man experiences the breaking of the personal integrity of his body particularly in the sexual sphere. For this reason, shame is always, at least indirectly, relative to other persons. **28:5** Shame of the body is motivated by concupiscence, which indicates the state of the human spirit distanced from original simplicity and from the fullness of values man and woman possess in the dimension of God. **28:6** Shame has a twofold meaning: it reflects the threat to these values and at the same time attempts to preserve them.

B. The Insufficiency of the Union (TOB 29:1–31:4)

Section B argues that concupiscence causes an insufficiency (*insufficiency* is a better translation than *insatiability*) in sexual union, a failure to satisfy the aspiration to a genuine communion of persons.

§§1–2 prepare the account of insufficiency. §1 focuses on the cause of this insufficiency, the corruption of the unitive meaning of the body. §2 shows how this cause is reflected in a deeper sense of shame that arises from domination in the relation between man and woman.

§§3–4 focus on the insufficiency itself. §3 defines the insufficiency of the union. §4 returns to the cause by showing how the insufficiency of sexual union is rooted in the defects of concupiscence.

§1 Corruption of the Consciousness of the Unitive Meaning of the Body (TOB 29:1–3)

29:1 The analysis of shame allows us to examine in what relation concupiscence stands to the communion of persons. The first thing to consider is the failure of sexual union to satisfy the desire for communion. **29:2** Shame shows that the original power of self-communication through the body has been shattered. The body comes under suspicion. **29:3** Shame expresses an imbalance brought into the original meaning of bodily union. It is as if sexuality became an obstacle in the relation between man and woman.

§2 A Deeper Dimension of Shame (TOB 29:4–30:4)

29:4 Concupiscence causes a difficulty in identifying oneself with one's own body, not just in regard to one's own subjectivity but even more so in regard to the subjectivity of the other. **29:5** This difficulty explains the need to hide from the other. Here we discover the deepest dimension of shame. **30:1** We find an explanation of this dimension in God's statement to the woman, "Your desire shall be for your husband, but he will dominate you" (Genesis 3:16). **30:2** Inequality in the form of domination arises between man and woman, which the woman experiences as a lack of full unity with the man. **30:3** What is at stake is not only sexual union but also the communion of conjugal life in a broad sense. This communion was to be a source of happiness for man and woman, both through union and fruitfulness, a union subordinated to fruitfulness. **30:4** Now, however, it is deformed, which causes a deeper echo of shame.

§3 The Meaning of "Insufficiency the Union" (TOB 30:5–6)

30:5 In this deformation, man and woman find themselves estranged from their own bodies. Sexual union is now insufficient to satisfy the aspiration to realize in it the communion of persons. **30:6** This failure is rooted in the threefold concupiscence: "the concupiscence of the flesh, the concupiscence of the eyes, and the pride of life" (1 John 2:16). The man's domination over the woman corresponds to the third form of concupiscence.

§4 Where Does the Insufficiency of the Union Come From? (TOB 31:1–4)

31:1 The explanation of shame is therefore not to be found in the body, in sexuality but in the deepest transformations of the human spirit. This spirit is conscious of concupiscence as the cause of the insufficiency of bodily union to satisfy the aspiration for communion. In relation to this consciousness, shame is a secondary experience. On the one hand, shame contains the consciousness of concupiscence; on the other hand, it contains the consciousness of the spousal meaning of the body. It attempts to protect the spousal meaning from concupiscence. **31:2** If we begin with original union (Genesis 2:24), we can thus understand the deformation of communion (Genesis 3:16). **31:3** The man's concupiscence takes the form of desire for sexual appeasement and of the simultaneous impulse to dominate the woman as an object of possession for his own use. In the woman, the experience of such domination causes an insatiable desire for a union free of domination and possession. The woman's concupiscence in relation to the man, however, can take a form similar to that of the man, for example, domination over the man by arousing his desires. **31:4** Although both man and woman are subject to concupiscence, it takes a partly different form in them.

C. The Corruption of the Spousal Meaning of the Body (TOB 31:5–33:5)

Section C shows the ultimate effect of concupiscence, the corruption of the spousal meaning of the body.

§1 introduces the discussion by deeper reflection about "meaning of the body."

§§2–4 belong together. They discuss three ingredients of the spousal meaning corrupted by concupiscence. §2 shows how concupiscence limits the expression of the spirit in the body. §3 shows how concupiscence leads to the loss of the freedom of the gift. §4 shows how concupiscence deforms belonging.

§1 Meaning: Measure of the Heart (TOB 31:5–6)

31:5 The meaning of the body is decisive for the way one lives the body. Meaning is the measure the heart applies to the body. It is the depth and very root of man's historicity (that is having a story). **31:6** The original spousal meaning of the body, which was the measure the heart of both applied to the body, suffered deformation. What does this deformation consist of?

§2 Threat against the Expression of the Spirit in the Body (TOB 32:1–3)

32:1 The human body has a spousal character; that is, it has the power to express the love by which a human person becomes a gift for another. Concupiscence limits and deforms this original and objective character of the body. The human heart experiences this deformation when the male body and the female body are no longer the expression of love but merely objects of attraction, as happens among animals. **32:2** Human sexuality then becomes an isolated force, a compulsion of the body. **32:3** Nevertheless, the spousal meaning has not been totally suffocated but only habitually threatened. One should not mistrust the human heart but test it.

§3 Loss of the Freedom of the Gift (TOB 32:4–33:2)

32:4 Concupiscence undermines the two principles of *Gaudium et spes* 24. It undermines the second principle (we can find ourselves only in the sincere gift of self) inasmuch as it deprives man and woman of the dignity of the gift, turning them into objects of desire. **32:5** And it undermines the first principle (human beings are willed for their own sake) inasmuch as it does not will the good of other persons but uses them for one's own good. **32:6** Concupiscence causes an inner compulsion and thereby limits self-mastery, without which the freely given gift of self becomes impossible. The relationship of the gift changes to a relationship of appropriation. **33:1** "He will dominate you" means that the man appropriates or *takes* a woman instead of receiving her as a gift. This domination is more at the woman's expense. **33:2** And yet the man was to be especially the guardian of the reciprocity and balance of the gift of self.

§4 The Inner Measure of Belonging (TOB 33:3–5)

33:3 In analogy to the *belonging* of things to persons, there is an authentic *belonging* of man and woman to each other: "My beloved is mine and I am his" (Song of Songs 2:16). Yet there is an essential difference between the two forms of belonging. **33:4** Concupiscence leads to the form of belonging proper to things rather than persons. From possession, concupiscence goes on to the use of the object for enjoyment. **33:5** The concupiscence of the flesh (1 John 2:16) thus shows above all the state of the human spirit. "Another law at war with the law of the mind" (Romans 7:23) enters. This anthropological truth must be kept in mind to understand Christ's appeal to the heart.

3. Commandment and *Ethos* (TOB 34–43)

Section 3 analyzes the ethical content of Christ's teaching about adultery in the heart, on the basis of the anthropological truths laid out in Section 2.

34:1 In his appeal to the beginning, Christ points to "hardness of heart" as the reason why the law allows divorce, contrary to the original intention of the Legislator. **34:2** We now focus on the ethical content of Christ's teaching, which is part of his proclamation of the *ethos* of the Gospel. **34:3** On the one hand, we should place Christ's words in their historical context by presenting the situations and institutions familiar to his first listeners; on the other hand, we should bring out the significance of these words for every human being. They show us the inner experience of historical man in every place and time. **34:4** By appealing to the heart, Christ calls every person in his or her concrete and unrepeatable identity. **34:5** The image of the man of concupiscence lies at the heart of Jesus's words about looking to desire.

A. It Was Said, Do Not Commit Adultery (TOB 35–37)

Section A unfolds what Christ means in the words "It was said, Do not commit adultery."

In order to present the point of view familiar to Christ's first listeners, Section A looks at the understanding of adultery in the history of Israel (§1), the law (§2), and the prophets (§3). The final paragraph (§4) points to the key truth expressed in the Old Testament, particularly in the prophets; namely, the understanding of adultery as a violation of the covenant between man and woman.

§1 The History of a People (TOB 35)

35:1 Christ takes the specific interpretation of the law familiar to his first listeners as the point of departure to recover the Legislator's intention. **35:2** In the history of the patriarchs, we see a systematic defection from monogamy. This defection influenced the Old Testament understanding of adultery. **35:3** The history of David and Solomon shows that effective polygamy established itself for reasons of concupiscence. The necessity of monogamy as an essential implication of the commandment against adultery was not seen. **35:4** The law attempts to eradicate adultery (even by means of the death penalty), but adultery is understood only as a violation of the man's property right to all the women that legally belong to him. The law does not understand adultery from the point of view of the monogamy established by the Creator. **35:5** In the story of the woman caught in adultery (John 8:3–11), Jesus identifies adultery as a sin and appeals to the conscience of his listeners rather than to specific legislation, "Let the one among you who is without sin throw the first stone" (John 8:7).

§2 Legislation (TOB 36:1–4)

36:1 The law combated sin, but it was not able to remove the structures of sin, for example, the institution of concubines and the right of cohabitation with a slave woman. **36:2** While the way the prohibition of adultery was interpreted shows a compromise with concupiscence, other laws (e.g., the law against homosexuality) did not allow exceptions. On the whole, women were judged more harshly than men. **36:3** The language of the law shows a certain objectivism. It is not directly concerned with the order of the heart but with the order of social life as a whole, for which marriage and the family are fundamental. **36:4** There is a close connection between legislation and medicine as well as hygiene.

§3 The Prophets (TOB 36:5–37:2)

36:5 The prophets draw an analogy between idolatry and adultery that is important for the understanding of adultery. **36:6** It helps us to appreciate the renewal of *ethos* in Christ's words. **37:1** Hosea shows that the betrayal of God in idolatry is similar to betrayal in marriage. He also emphasizes the continuing love of the Bridegroom despite all betrayals. **37:2** Ezekiel presents a similar image.

§4 Covenant (TOB 37:3–6)

37:3 The point of likeness in the spousal analogy drawn by the prophets consists in the covenant accompanied by love. **37:4** Adultery is a sin inasmuch as it breaks the personal covenant between a man and a woman. Sexual union is thus seen as the regular sign of the communion of persons in the covenant. Adultery is a radical falsification of the covenantal sign. **37:5** The real reason for the sinfulness of adultery is that it is the antithesis of the covenant understood as a communion of persons. **37:6** The key question is whether a particular act of sexual union is a truthful covenantal sign.

B. Whoever Looks to Desire (TOB 38–41)

Section B unfolds what Christ means by the words "whoever looks to desire."

§1 characterizes Christ's teaching in a preliminary way: the shift in the understanding of adultery from the body to the heart, the theological point of view of experience and redemption, and the appeal to the Wisdom tradition.

§§2–3 turn to the Wisdom tradition to show that this tradition was a point of contact between Jesus and his first listeners.

§§4–6 unfold the teaching on concupiscence implicit in Christ's appeal to the heart. §4 focuses on the look as the threshold between interior desire and exterior action. §5 pinpoints the main defect of this concupiscent look, the reduction of the fullness of the sexual call. On this basis, 6 analyzes the relation between the sexual urge and the communion of persons.

§1 Shift in the Center of Gravity (TOB 38:1–3)

38:1 Christ's words shift the center of gravity of the sin from the body to the heart. **38:2** Christ speaks about concupiscence in a theological, not only psychological, manner by addressing human experience in the context of salvation. The interpenetration of these two contexts (experience and salvation) is part of the *ethos* of redemption. **38:2** Christ appeals to the experience of his first listeners in terms that must have reminded them of the Wisdom books. **38:3** These terms were particularly understandable for Jesus's listeners. They are also understandable for us.

§2 The Wisdom Tradition (TOB 38:4–6)

38:4 The Wisdom books show a particular interest in the morals of Israelite society. Their warnings and counsels are addressed mainly to men. Women appear as occasions of sin, although one also finds passages in praise of the perfect wife. **38:5** The meaning of the Wisdom texts is pedagogical, sharpened by a specific moral psychology. They are close to Christ's appeal to the heart, yet without fundamentally transforming the *ethos* expressed in legislation. **38:6** Just as the prophets prepare a correct understanding of *adultery*, so the wisdom texts prepare an understanding of "adultery in the heart."

§3 The Inner State of the Man of Concupiscence (TOB 39:1–2)

39:1–2 Among the Wisdom books, Sirach 23:16–24 offers a classical description of concupiscence as a fire that flares up and invades all senses, consuming the man in his own desires.

§4 Christ's Call to Halt at the Threshold of the Look (TOB 39:3–5)

39:3 Christ appeals to the interior knowledge of his listeners about the meaning of "looking to desire." **39:4** He does not analyze the experience of desiring. He halts at the threshold between desire and action, at the look that expresses the desire in the heart. **39:5** In such a look, one experiences detachment from the spousal and the procreative meaning of the body. This detachment is adultery in the heart.

§5 Concupiscence: Reduction of a Perennial Call (TOB 40:1–41:1)

40:1 Concupiscence, understood in theological rather than merely psychological terms, is the deception of the human heart with regard to the perennial call of man and woman to communion. **40:2** This perennial call is an invitation mediated by the body, but it is not yet the concupiscent desire Christ speaks about. Concupiscence diminishes the meaning of the call. **40:3** It causes an intentional reduction, a restriction or closure of the horizon of the mind and heart. Instead of being conscious of the whole personal richness of femininity and masculinity, it limits the range and obscures the hierarchy of values. **40:4** For a man, femininity ceases to be a specific speech of the spirit, it ceases to bear the spousal meaning of the body. Concupiscence aims at satisfying only the body's sexual urge. **40:5** This intentional and axiological reduction takes place already in an interior act of desire expressed by looking. Through the intentionality proper to knowledge and desire, one must see the intentionality of the very existence of man and woman. **41:1** This intentionality of existence is bound up with *who* the woman is or becomes for the man. She begins to exist intentionally for him as an object for the satisfaction of his sexual urge.

§6 Concupiscence: "Communion" of Persons versus "Urge" of Nature (TOB 41:2–6)

41:2 This change in the intentionality of existence comes to be in the heart only when it has come to be in the will, only when the man makes the decision for a relation with another human being according to the scale of values of concupiscence. **41:3** Only then can we speak of compulsion of the body, which causes the loss of the freedom of the gift. **41:4** To say that desire transforms the intentionality of the existence of a man or a woman does not call the sexual urge as such into question. Christ is far from Manichaeism. As an objective aspect of human nature, the sexual urge calls man and woman to a way of existing as persons in a reciprocal *for* that builds communion. **41:5** It is contrary to the nature of the sexual urge for the man to exist only as the subject of the satisfaction of this urge and for the woman to exist only as its object. Concupiscence removes man and woman from the personal sphere of communion. **41:6** Christ's statement attributes great importance to man's interiority, to his heart. Here lies the core of the transformation of *ethos* that is the aim of his words.

C. Has Committed Adultery in the Heart (TOB 42–43)

Section C unfolds what Christ means in the words "has committed adultery in the heart."

§1 introduces the key phrase in Christ's teaching, "adultery in the heart," which contains his negative diagnosis of concupiscence.

§§2–3 present two readings of this key phrase. §2 presents a reading that remains on the surface, on the level of psychology, and of marriage as a state of life defined by law. §3 presents a reading that penetrates into the depth, into a theological understanding of concupiscence and of *who* man and woman are for each other.

§4 moves from the negative diagnosis to the positive side of Christ's teaching: the fulfillment of the commandment against adultery by purity of heart.

§1 The "Key" Phrase (TOB 42:1–4)

42:1 Our method has been to separate the three phrases "It was said, Do not commit adultery"; "Whoever looks to desire"; and "Has committed adultery in the heart." Each of them has its own content, but they must be explained in strict relation to each other. **42:2** Christ shows how the commandment against adultery must be understood and practiced so that the justice willed by the Legislator abounds. **42:3** He does not reduce the sixth commandment ("Do not commit adultery") to the ninth ("Do not desire your neighbor's wife") but shows how the sixth must be understood. **42:4** His words are paradoxical. How can adultery occur without committing adultery as an external act?

§2 First Reading: [Defective with False Conclusion] (TOB 42:5–43:1)

42:5 The first of the three phrases, "Do not commit adultery," speaks about an exterior act between a man and a woman who are not spouses in the legal sense. **42:6** Therefore the second phrase, "Whoever looks to desire," should be understood as looking with desire at a woman who is not one's wife. Because one cannot commit the exterior bodily act of adultery with one's wife, one cannot commit adultery in the heart with her, either. **42:7–43:1** This interpretation is not deep enough. Christ knows the interior of every person (John 2:25). He bases the moral evaluation of desire above all on the personal dignity of the man and the woman.

§3 Second Reading: [Better and Fuller with True Conclusion] (TOB 43:2–4)

43:2 What is decisive for adultery in the heart is the nature of concupiscence. A man commits adultery in the heart not only because he looks to desire a woman who is not his wife but also because he looks in this way at a woman. **43:3** Concupiscence changes the intentionality of a woman's existence *for* a man. A deformation takes place in the reciprocal *for*. *For* loses its character as a communion of persons in favor of a use of persons for pleasure. A man can commit such adultery in the heart even with his wife. **43:4** A purely psychological understanding of concupiscence is not enough to understand Christ's teaching. Without undervaluing the psychological interpretation (the first reading), one must consider the theological interpretation (the second reading) more complete.

§4 Purity of the Heart as the Fulfillment of the Commandment (TOB 43:5–7)

43:5 In showing the true meaning of the commandment "Do not commit adultery," Christ goes deep down into the innermost recesses of the heart to teach that one fulfills the commandment by purity of heart. Such purity requires firmness in facing the concupiscence of the flesh and in being consistently demanding in relation to one's heart. **43:6** The true reason for the commandment "Do not commit adultery" is the unity and indissolubility of marriage. Adultery conflicts with this unity as a unity that corresponds to the dignity of persons. The new *ethos* allows man and woman to shine more fully in their hearts in all the inner truth of reciprocal *for.* **43:7** Christ challenges man and woman to regain the lost fullness of their humanity. The dignity of human life depends at all times and in all places on *who* she shall be for him and he for her.

4. The Heart: Accused or Called? (TOB 44–48)

Section 4 argues that a positive call, rather than a negative judgment, is the predominant content of Christ's words in Matthew 5:27–28.

Section A argues against the most extreme negative understanding of Christ's words; namely, the Manichaean view that sexuality is as such evil. Section B argues against a more moderate negative understanding that casts continual suspicion on the heart.

Section C points to the positive content contained in Christ's call by showing the positive impact of the *ethos* of the Sermon on the Mount on sexual *Eros.*

[*Introduction* (*TOB 44:1–4*)] **44:1** In Christ's words about adultery in the heart, is the heart accused or called to the good? How can and should someone act who accepts Christ's words? **44:2** How can he act; that is, on what can he count in his innermost heart as the source of his acts? And how should he act; that is, how do the values revealed by Christ oblige him and constitute a duty? **44:3** Many answers have been given to these questions both in words and, more importantly, in deeds. In this area, *ethos* and praxis interpenetrate. **44:4** Christ's statement about adultery in the heart is stupendously concise, and its power in the history of *ethos* lies perhaps in this conciseness. Yet the history of *ethos* has seen many changes, from puritanical strictness to present-day permissiveness.

A. Condemnation of the Body? (TOB 44:5–45:5)

Section A argues against the most extreme negative interpretation of Christ's words, the Manichaean interpretation.

§1 presents the Manichaean view. §2 highlights the aspects of Christ's teaching that differ from the Manichaean view. §3 focuses on the most radical point of opposition; namely, the Christian thesis that the body and its sex are always a value that is not sufficiently appreciated.

§1 Manichaeism (TOB 44:5–6)

44:5 A meaning was at times given to Christ's words that conflicts with Christ's words. Manichaeism, which sees the source of evil in matter, in the body, also condemned sexuality and marriage. **44:6** Some confused the strictness of Christ's teaching with the strictness of the Manichaean condemnation of sexuality. In fact, Christ does not condemn the body but addresses a demand to the human spirit. This demand springs from an affirmation of sexuality in its full meaning.

§2 The Correct Understanding (TOB 45:1–3)

45:1 Christ's words are not an accusation but rather a call to a critical self-examination. They presuppose the affirmation of the body. Together with the spirit, the body constitutes man's subjectivity and participates in his dignity as a person. **45:2** Christ defends the inviolability of the unity established by man and woman in becoming "one flesh." His ethical teaching is deeply penetrated by what Paul calls "redemption of the body." **45:3** The Christian *ethos* is characterized by a transformation of the heart that enables man and woman to express and realize the value of the body and of sex according to the Creator's plan. For Christianity, the body and sex are not an anti-value but always a value not sufficiently appreciated.

§3 Anti-Value or Value Not Sufficiently Appreciated? (TOB 45:4–5)

45:4 Even if Christ's words contain a certain accusation, all the more do they contain an appeal to detach oneself from the evil of the act. One must never transfer the evil of the man's act to the woman's body, as if her body were at fault. This transfer would accept the Manichaean anti-value and overlook that the evil of concupiscence is not physical but moral and therefore essentially spiritual. In the end, the transfer would justify concupiscence to the detriment of the woman. **45:5** It is a fruit of the evil of concupiscence that the woman's body is devalued, that it becomes a value not sufficiently appreciated. The human heart is called to discover the full meaning of the body.

B. The Heart under Suspicion? (TOB 46)

Section B argues against a more moderate negative reading of Christ's words in continual suspicion against one's heart, similar to the modern masters of suspicion.

§1 "Masters of Suspicion" (TOB 46:1–3)

46:1 Freud, Marx, and Nietzsche, the "masters of suspicion" (Ricoeur), propose a hermeneutics that significantly converges with, but also fundamentally diverges from, the hermeneutics that has its source in the Bible. Like Christ, these thinkers judge and accuse the human heart of its threefold concupiscence. **46:2** Yet the Bible does not turn the threefold concupiscence into the fundamental and absolute way of judging, even if it is an important factor. **46:3** Still, there is valid point: when a man "looks to desire," he leaves his inner acts at the mercy of the forces of nature and falls into concupiscence. Although Christ speaks primarily about the act of concupiscence, his words indirectly refer also to the man of concupiscence.

§2 Essential Divergence (TOB 46:4–6)

46:4 Christ does not stop at the accusation but, in the context of the *ethos* of redemption, appeals to the heart to rediscover and realize the spousal meaning of the body. **46:5** His words, which are addressed to the listener from the outside, correspond to an echo heard deep within the human heart, the echo of the spousal meaning of the body created at the beginning. The original power and grace of creation become in Christ the power and grace of redemption, which is able to confer the supreme value on man and woman; namely, love. **46:6** The hermeneutics of suspicion is thus radically different from the hermeneutics we discover in the words of Christ. Man and woman are not irrevocably accused and given up to concupiscence. They have an inheritance of the heart from the beginning that is deeper than the inheritance of sin, deeper than the threefold concupiscence. Christ's words as the Redeemer of the body reactivate this inheritance and give it real power in human life.

C. Eros and Ethos (TOB 47–48)

Section C unfolds the positive content of Christ's call, the positive impact of *ethos* on *eros*. It is divided into three paragraphs.

§1 focuses on the word *eros*. §2 argues that the *ethos* of the Gospel can become an inner power of *eros*. §3 argues that erotic spontaneity is not destroyed by the *ethos* of the Sermon on the Mount but deepened.

§1 Eros as the Source of the "Erotic" (TOB 47:1–3)

47:1 The words of Christ are above all an appeal linked with the *ethos* of the Gospel. In contemporary discourse, the words *eros* and *erotic* play a significant role. *Eros* has many shades of meaning, including its meaning in Plato as the aspiration for the transcendent and divine. One should evaluate *eros* and the erotic in an equally nuanced way. **47:2** In Plato, *eros* is the inner power that draws man toward all that is good, true, and beautiful. In its common meaning, *eros* refers to an attraction that is above all sensual and aims at the union of bodies. The way we understand concupiscence is decisive for answering the question of whether the meaning of *eros* is the same as the attraction described in Genesis. **47:3** If we used the word *eros* simply in the common psychological or sexological sense, as a subjectively intense attraction of the body that extends its mastery over the sphere of emotions, then Christ's words about adultery in the heart would seem to express a negative judgment about everything that is erotic.

§2 Ethos as an Inner Power of Eros (TOB 47:4–6)

47:4 Given the many nuances of the meaning of *eros*, however, it is possible to find room within *eros* for the *ethos* of the Sermon on the Mount. The many nuances of *eros* can help us to understand the specific and complex richness of the heart to which Christ appealed. **47:5** If *eros* includes the inner power that attracts the person to the good, true, and beautiful, and if the *ethos* of redemption in Christ's appeal to the heart includes the possibility and necessity of a transformation of the heart, then we must conclude that *eros* and *ethos* are called to meet in the human heart and to bear fruit in this meeting. **47:6** We often link a negative meaning with the ethics proclaimed in the Sermon on the Mount because we tend to see only its prohibition in the erotic sphere. We must rather unveil the essential values that the prohibition protects. This is what Christ teaches us.

§3 The Problem of Erotic Spontaneity (TOB 48)

48:1 The *ethos* of the Sermon on the Mount calls us to rediscover the spousal meaning of the body and the true dignity of the gift in the erotic. If we do not assume this task, we will not experience the fullness of *eros*.

[*A Superficial Objection: The Only Path to Erotic Enjoyment* (*TOB 48:2*)] **48:2** People often maintain that *ethos* takes away the spontaneity of the erotic and that therefore one must set aside *ethos* for the benefit of *eros*. This opinion is false but especially superficial.

[*A Deeper Answer: Christ Calls Us to Erotic Spontaneity* (*TOB 48:3–5*)] The Sermon on the Mount calls us to full and mature erotic spontaneity, which is the gradual fruit of the discernment of the impulses of our heart. **48:3** Christ's words are demanding. They demand that we become the authentic masters of our innermost impulses by building with consciousness and consistency the personal sense of the spousal meaning of the body. **48:4** We cannot learn this meaning only by objectifying abstraction and only from books, but we must also reach a deep knowledge of human interiority. The movements of the heart can at times be confused with each other. Christ calls us to distinguish and judge them. Only on this basis can one experience not merely sensual arousal but the deep emotion with which both inner sensibility and sexuality itself react to the integral expression of femininity and masculinity. **48:5** Only on this basis can we reach the deeper and more mature spontaneity in which the heart discovers the spiritual beauty of the sign constituted by the male and female body. *The most important sphere of praxis is the one that traces this road step by step to such spontaneity.*

5. The *Ethos* of the Redemption of the Body (TOB 49)

Section 5 presents the *ethos* of the redemption of the body, which is the foundation of Christ's teaching about adultery in the heart.

§1 brings out the central importance of redemption in the new *ethos*. §2 turns to an effect of redemption that is a key part of the *ethos* of redemption; namely, the fullness of life. Number 4 formulates the main thesis: fullness of life is the goal of Christ's teaching about adultery in the heart. Number 5 turns to this fullness on the side of the object (value), number 6 on the side of the subject. §3 concludes the account of the words of Jesus in Matthew 5:27–28.

§1 The Importance of Redemption in the New Ethos (TOB 49:1–3)

49:1 The words of Christ about adultery in the heart contain an ethical meaning that expresses the *ethos* of the Gospel and a meaning that throws light on the human person. The *ethos* Christ brings is new, not only in relation to the Old Testament but also more generally in relation to historical man. **49:2** This new *ethos* is an *ethos* of the redemption of the body. **49:3** In the Sermon on the Mount, Christ speaks from the perspective of redemption. This is the perspective of the whole Gospel, of the whole teaching, of the whole mission of Christ. His appeal to the beginning can only be justified by the reality of redemption.

§2 The Goal: Fullness of Life (TOB 49:4–6)

49:4 Christ does not invite man and woman to return to original innocence, but he leads the minds and hearts of his listeners toward the fullness of justice willed by the Legislator. This fullness must be discovered with an inner vision of the heart and with a corresponding way of being and acting. Self-mastery and temperance are required to achieve this goal. **49:5** Temperance does not mean being left hanging in the void of values. In genuine temperance, the heart remains bound to the value of the spousal meaning of the body, the value of a transparent sign by which the Creator has written into the hearts of man and woman the gift of communion, his image. **49:6** Temperance likewise does not mean being left hanging in the void of the subject. Through temperance, man and woman experience their dignity as persons and fulfill what is essentially personal in them. Above all, they are able to experience the spousal meaning of the body, in which the deepest layers of human subjectivity acquire a voice.

§3 Conclusion of the Analysis of Christ's Teaching (TOB 49:7)

49:7 Christ's positive call, rather than the negative judgment, is the predominant element in his words. The awareness of sin is nevertheless an indispensable condition for the aspiration to purity of heart. By appealing to the heart, Christ teaches in the most concrete way. The human person is unique and unrepeatable above all by reason of the heart. Christ's call is reminiscent of original solitude, in which man stands alone before God. Still, purity of heart is explained, in the end, by the relation to the other human subject.

6. Purity as Life According to the Spirit (TOB 50–57)

Section 6 presents Paul's teaching on purity as life according to the Spirit, which further unfolds Jesus's teaching.

§§1–4 belong together as a presentation of the anthropological foundation of Paul's teaching. §1 examines Christ's general understanding of moral impurity and purity that flow from the human heart. §2 turns to Paul's similarly general understanding of purity in the context of his account of flesh and Spirit. §3 sketches Paul's teaching about the works of the flesh, which include idolatry and sorcery. §4 analyzes the anthropological roots of the *ethos* of redemption in Paul's teaching about the freedom for which Christ set us free, a freedom for the true gift of self in love.

§§5–7 belong together as an account of Paul's teaching about sexual purity. §5 shows that, in accord with his teaching about life according to the Spirit, Paul sees both the negative side of purity (abstaining from impurity) and the positive side (keeping the body with reverence). §6 complements this discussion by showing that Paul's description of the human body in 1 Corinthians 12 expresses precisely this reverence for the body. §7 is the theological heart of the argument. It presents Paul's teaching that sexual purity is both a virtue and a gift of the Holy Spirit, centered in the gift of reverence. It shows the great beauty, even glory, of the body when it is lived with a purity inspired by the gift of reverence.

§8 appends some parallels between Paul and Wisdom literature and concludes that the anthropology of rebirth in the Holy Spirit is fundamental in Paul's understanding of purity.

§1 "Purity" and "Heart" (TOB 50:1–4)

50:1 The analysis of purity completes Christ's words about adultery in the heart. He calls the heart to purity. **50:2** He uses the term *impure* in another context to describe all evil that comes from the heart and makes a person impure (Matthew 15): evil intentions, murder, adultery, prostitution, theft, false witness, blasphemy. **50:3** He resists the idea of impurity coming from the outside and insists that it comes from inside, from the heart. **50:4** When we use the term *purity* in the moral sense, it is an analogy, moral evil being compared with dirt.

§2 "Body" and "Spirit" According to Paul (TOB 50:5–51:4)

50:5 Paul uses *purity* in a general sense but also in the specific sense of sexual purity. The Johannine distinction between "from the Father" and "from the world" corresponds to his distinction between *Spirit* and *flesh*. **51:1** *Flesh* does not refer simply to the physical body but to a disposition of powers formed in man together with original sin. It indicates not only "the outer man," but also the person interiorly subjected to the Johannine *world* as, for example, in humanistic autarchy, secularism, and sensualism. **51:2** The one who lives according to the flesh lives at the pole opposite the desire of the Spirit. The desire Christ speaks about in "looks to desire" is a manifestation of life according to the flesh. Thus the phrases "according to the flesh" and "according to the Spirit" are a synthesis of two modes of life. They are a program for change. **51:3** The same antithesis is expressed in Romans 8:5–10. **51:4** One can see two horizons in this text. One is the sin committed at the beginning; the other is the final victory over sin and death. Justification by faith is intended for historical man already now, for his heart, as a real power at work in man that reveals itself in his actions.

§3 "Works of the Flesh" and "Fruit of the Spirit" (TOB 51:5–52:3)

51:5 Paul contrasts the works of the flesh with the fruit (singular) of the Spirit (love, joy, and self-mastery). The fruit of the Spirit is closely linked with the nature and structure of the *ethos* of redemption, which is expressed in mastery over the threefold concupiscence. **51:6** Self-mastery as a fruit of the Spirit shows that a specific human choice, an effort of will, is involved. The Spirit works within the human spirit to achieve this fruit. **52:1** The grace of justification bears fruit in man's heart and behavior so that the justice Jesus demands in the Sermon on the Mount may abound (Matthew 5:20). **52:2** For Paul, the "works of the flesh" include not only sins of fleshly enjoyment but also idolatry and sorcery (Galatians 5:20–21), which we would classify as sins of the human spirit rather than the flesh. **52:3** Christ's understanding of the *impurity* that comes from the heart is similar in breadth to Paul's understanding of "the works of the flesh." Sexual sin, which we call impurity and sin of the flesh, is only one of the many kinds of impurity and works of the flesh.

§4 "Flesh" and "the Freedom for Which Christ Set Us Free" (TOB 52:4–53:3)

52:4 Mastery over sin is an indispensable condition of life, according to the Spirit. Paul emphasizes the connection between sin and death, spiritual death and eternal death: "no fornicator . . . has any inheritance in the kingdom of God" (Ephesians 5:5). **52:5** The freedom for which Christ has set us free is closely connected with justification by faith, which works through love. We are to realize purity of heart according to the measure of this freedom. **53:1** Here Paul reveals the anthropological roots of the *ethos* of the Gospel. If the whole law finds its fullness in the commandment of love, then the dimension of the new *ethos* of the Gospel is an appeal to freedom for the fullest realization and use of the powers of the human spirit. **53:2** Christ set us free inasmuch as he showed us the ethical and theological subordination of freedom to love. **53:3** The one who subordinates himself to concupiscence ceases to be capable of this freedom, ceases to be suitable for the true gift of self, which is the fruit and expression of such freedom; he ceases to be suitable for he spousal meaning of the body.

§5 Purity: "Keeping the Body with Holiness and Reverence"? (TOB 53:4–54:4)

53:4 Paul also has a more specifically sexual concept of purity, which he discusses in 1 Thessalonians. **53:5** In Galatians, he mentions self-mastery, which seems to include sexual purity. **53:6** repeated in **54:1** In 1 Thessalonians, he explicitly focuses on sexual purity: "that you abstain from unchastity . . . for God did not call us to impurity" (cf. 1 Thessalonians 4:3–8). **54:2** "That each of you knows how to keep his own body with holiness and reverence, not as the object of lustful passions" (1 Thessalonians 4:4). Purity is a practical ability to act and not to act. It is part of the virtue of temperance (St. Thomas Aquinas). **54:3** Purity as temperance is the ability to hold back lustful passions. In addition to this negative function, however, it also has a more positive one; namely, keeping one's own body and that of the other with holiness and reverence. The positive *keeping* is not possible without abstaining from what is opposed to it. **54:4** The reason why Paul has such a positive understanding of purity is that he considers it as a manifestation of life according to the Spirit. The gift of reverence turns out to be the most essential power for keeping the body with holiness. We will have to enter deeply into the meaning of reverence.

§6 Pauline "Description of the Body" (TOB 54:5–55:7)

54:5 Paul's explanation of his concept of the Church as the body of Christ in 1 Corinthians 12:18–27 helps us to understand his teaching about purity in 1 Thessalonians 4. **54:6** In this explanation, Paul touches on the most essential line of thought of his teaching about purity; namely, the role of reverence. **55:1–2** Paul weaves a thread of evaluation into his description of the body, which is indispensable because the body is not a mere physical object, but man expresses himself through it. **55:3** The truth of creation and the redemption of the body is presupposed in this description. It corresponds to the spiritual attitude of reverence toward the body. **55:4** Paul looks at the body above all as possessing the dignity of the person but also the testimony of shame connected with the "less presentable" and "less honorable" members. **55:5** "The members of the body we think less honorable we clothe with greater reverence" (1 Corinthians 12:23). In this manner, modesty and reverence are born from shame. **55:6** The Creator's intention is the inner unity of the body, which has been disturbed after the fall by disunion, as witnessed by shame for the less presentable and honorable members. **55:7** Victory over this disunity is possible on the way of purity, of keeping the body with holiness and reverence. Paul's description of the body thus has a fundamental significance for his teaching about purity.

§7 Purity as a Virtue and a Gift (TOB 56:1–57:3)

56:1 Purity, according to Paul, is an ability centered on the dignity of the body, the dignity of the person. It has a moral dimension as a virtue and a charismatic dimension as a gift of the Holy Spirit. **56:2** The body is a temple of the Holy Spirit, and sexual sins are, more than any others, sins against the body (1 Corinthians 6:18). **56:3** The indwelling of the Holy Spirit is a further source for the dignity of the body. Sexual sins therefore imply a profanation of the temple, not only a violation of the dignity of the person. **56:4** We have received ourselves and our bodies anew from God as a gift, and so the redemption of the body introduces a new measure of the holiness of the body. **56:5** Because purity, understood as a particular commitment based on ethics, is an aspect of "life according to the Spirit," what bears fruit in it is the redemption of the body. That "we were bought at a great price" makes the commitment spring up to "keep the body with holiness and reverence." **57:1–2** The mystery of redemption works in us in a charismatic way, through the gifts of the Holy Spirit. The gift most congenial to the virtue of purity is the gift of piety (*pietas, eusebeia*). This gift opens the person to an experience of the sacred. It allows Paul's words about the body as a temple of the Holy Spirit to take on the convincing power of an experience and to become a living and lived truth in action. **57:3** Purity causes in the body such a fullness of dignity in interpersonal relations that God himself is thereby glorified. Purity is the glory of the human body before God. It is the glory of God in the human body. From purity springs the singular beauty that permeates the common life of men and woman and allows them to express in it the simplicity, the cordiality, and unrepeatable authenticity of personal trust.

§8 Purity and Wisdom (TOB 57:4–6)

57:4 In the Wisdom books, the virtue of purity is presupposed for wisdom, and wisdom disposes the person to receive the gift of purity. **57:5** Fundamental for Paul's teaching on purity is his anthropology of rebirth in the Holy Spirit. Ultimately, purity must be understood in light of the Resurrection. **57:6** The Wisdom books contain an indirect but real preparation for Paul's teaching about purity as life according to the Spirit. Christ's first listeners were able to draw on the same background.

7. The Gospel of the Purity of Heart: Yesterday and Today (TOB 58–59)

Section 7 serves as an overview and concludes Chapter Two.

§1 summarizes the argument of Chapter Two, going back also to its foundation in Chapter One. §2 concludes the argument by pointing to the intimate connection between theology of the body and pedagogy of the body.

§1 Theology of the Body (TOB 58)

58:1 Christ's appeal to the heart is a synthesis, like the words in which he appealed to the beginning, which allowed us to develop the outlines of an authentic theology of the body. **58:2** The theological basis of man's truth about his vocation lies in the eternal mystery of the person as an image of God. **58:3** Christ reaffirms this same truth in the context of hereditary sinfulness, speaking not only to people of his time but also to every human being. **58:4** It is an ethical truth concerning the evil of concupiscence and the good of purity. **58:5** It is also an anthropological truth that shows that the man of concupiscence is embraced by the redemption of the body.

For this reason, Christ can appeal to the heart to open itself to life according to the Spirit in order to find again and realize the value of the body. **58:6** Purity opens a way to the discovery of the dignity of the body connected with the freedom of the gift. The truth of the spousal meaning of the body must be felt with the heart. Only in this way can relations between man and woman, even looks between them, regain their full spousal meaning. **58:7** Among the gifts of the Holy Spirit, the gift of piety is particularly efficacious in giving to the experience of the body the simplicity, lucid clarity, and inner joy of this spousal meaning.

§2 Theology and Pedagogy (TOB 59)

[*Christ's Call to Find Ourselves through the Sincere Gift of Self* (*TOB 59:1–2*)] **59:1** Christ's appeal to the heart identifies the innermost and most essential theme of human history as a history of good and evil and of redemption. **59:2** The anthropology implicit in this appeal to the heart is also a pedagogy. The Creator entrusted a task to man and woman: the body as a transparent sign of communion and of the realization of the person through the gift of self.

[*The Particular Need for This Call in the Scientific Age* (*TOB 59:3*)] **59:3** The pedagogy of the body, which derives from this theology of the body, is especially needed today. Biology gives us much partial knowledge, but it does not develop the consciousness of the body as a sign of the person. The body tends to be seen as an object of manipulations, and the person no longer identifies himself or herself with the body.

[*Spirituality of the Body* (*TOB 59:4–7*)] **59:4** Pedagogy implies a spirituality of the body. Spiritual maturity is needed to experience the body as a sign of the person and to discover the spousal meaning of the body. Biological knowledge without this spiritual maturity can lead to opposite results. **59:5** According to this key, one should reread recent magisterial texts about marriage and the family, especially *Gaudium et spes* and *Humanae vitae*. **59:6** *Humanae vitae* shows that the demands of Christian morality can be fulfilled. **59:7** The goal of the pedagogy of the body is to ensure that the signs of love between husband and wife conform to the moral order, that is, to the dignity of the person.

[Excursus: Pornography and the True Beauty of the Naked Body (TOB 60–63)]

The Excursus reflects on how a climate favorable to purity can arise. It analyzes the moral implications of representing the naked human body in art and the media.

§1 presents some preliminary distinctions and argues that representations of the naked body should be judged according to the *ethos* of the body taught by Christ. §2 brings out the precise point at which moral questions arise; namely, the transfer of the naked body outside the spousal context. There are no headings. I have added them and enclosed them in square brackets.

On this basis, §3 explains why some representations of the naked body are morally objectionable. §4 explains why other representations of the naked body are morally good and helpful for creating a climate favorable to purity.

[*§1 Ethos of the Body and the Portrayal of the Body* (*TOB 60*)] **60:1** The problems of the *ethos* of the body are linked with the objective fact of the body's being the body of the person (the ontological dimension) and with the content and quality of the subjective experience of living in one's own body (the dimension of personal subjectivity). **60:2** Representations of the body allow these two dimensions to extend beyond living persons. Looking at such representations cannot be isolated in man's consciousness from the look about which Christ speaks. **60:3** Aesthetic experience thus lies within the sphere of the *ethos* of the body. It is legitimate to ask how one can create a climate favorable to purity in art and the media. **60:4** The present question is the representation of the naked human body in art and photography. **60:5** In photography, the body can become an anonymous object spread to many viewers. In painting or sculpture, a transfiguration of the model can occur.

[*§2 Transfer of the Naked Body outside the Spousal Context* (*TOB 61:1–3*)] **61:1** The meaning of the naked human body is spousal. The gift of the body meets the reception of the gift by the other person and an answering gift. Artistic or photographic representation uproots the body from this context. This does not mean that one must not represent the naked body, only that doing so raises delicate moral issues. **61:2** The positive meaning of shame and of covering the body is to protect the intimacy of the gift oriented toward the depth of the other person. **61:3** A person with developed sensibility crosses the boundary of shame into nakedness only with difficulty. In the concentration and extermination camps of the Holocaust, the Nazis used the violation of bodily shame by forced nakedness to trample on the personal dignity of prisoners. Concupiscence implies an analogous abuse of the person.

[§3 The Pornographic Way of Representing the Naked Body (TOB 61:4–62:5)]

61:4–62:1 A representation of the naked body is pornographic when it violates the body's right to intimacy, when it violates the deep order of the gift. **62:2**

Pornography turns into a public object of appropriation and uses what belongs to the sphere of interpersonal relations. **62:3** It is precisely the great value of the naked body in the system of interpersonal communion that makes its pornographic representation objectionable. **62:4** Artists must respect the boundary between legitimate and illegitimate ways of representation. **62:5** To raise the question of pornography is not the effect of a puritanical mentality, of narrow moralism, or of Manichaean hatred of the body. What is at stake is the personal dignity and eloquence of the human body.

[§4 The Right Way of Representing the Naked Body (TOB 63)]

63:1 What is the right relation between the *ethos* of the representation of the naked body and the *ethos* of seeing such a representation? **63:2** The question arises because of the anonymity of representations of the naked body, their objectivity that does not allow the naked person any choice about being seen or not seen. **63:3** The naked body has always been a subject of artistic representation. **63:4** Our earlier reflections did not intend to call the right to such representation into question. They intended to point out that the artist must be aware of the full truth of the naked body and must live that truth. **63:5** In all epochs of art, especially in classical Greece, we find representations of the naked human body that draw us into the whole truth of the person. We do not feel pushed by them to "look to desire." But we also find representations contrary to our personal sensibility. The problem does not lie in the object of these representations, the naked body because the naked human body always has its inalienable dignity. The problem lies in reducing the body to the rank of an object of enjoyment intended for the satisfaction of mere concupiscence. **63:6** *Humanae vitae* calls for a climate favorable to education in purity, a climate that affirms the dignity of the body and its role in the communion of persons. This is why an appendix to the *ethos* of the image and the *ethos* of seeing is included here. **63:7** Creating a favorable climate implies these two components of *ethos* in the sphere of art and the media and a reinforcing cycle between them.

PART ONE, CHAPTER THREE

Christ Appeals to the Resurrection (TOB 64–86)

Part One, Chapter Three, unfolds the theology of the body implicit in Christ's teaching that in the Resurrection there will be no marriage.

1. The Resurrection of the Body (TOB 64–72)

A. The Synoptics

Section A unfolds Christ's teaching about the spousal meaning of the body in the Resurrection, in which there will be no marriage.

§§1–2 present Christ's words. §§3–5 analyze the new meaning of the body on the basis of these words. §3 presents the thesis that there will be a new meaning of the body. §4 explains this new meaning in terms of spiritualization. §5 explains it in terms of divinization. §6 offers a concluding overview in the context of Christ's teaching as a whole, including his appeal to the beginning and his appeal to the heart.

§1 The Third Part of the Triptych (TOB 64)

64:1 Christ's appeal to the Resurrection has a fundamental importance for understanding marriage and the life of consecrated virginity. It is the third panel of a triptych of words that are essential and constitutive for the theology of the body. **64:2** Christ's teaching about marriage in the Resurrection is found in a dialogue with the Sadducees, who use the Levirate law given by Moses to argue against the Resurrection. **64:3** Christ's answer also appeals to Moses, to whom

God reveals himself as "the God of Abraham, the God of Isaac, and the God of Moses." The Patriarchs must therefore be alive. Yet there will be no marriage. **64:4** In Luke, he adds, "they are equal to the angels and, being sons of the resurrection, they are sons of God."

§2 Witness to the Power of the Living God (TOB 65)

65:1–2 Christ's reference to Scripture and the power of God is the basis of his answer. **65:3** God's revelation of himself as the God of Abraham, Isaac, and Jacob is only intelligible if one admits the reality of a life that does not end with death. **65:4** Christ's definitive answer to the Sadducees consists in his own resurrection from the dead, but here he appeals to the testimony of the Old Testament, to which the Sadducees appeal as well. **65:5** When God, who is the inexhaustible fountain of life, enters into a covenant, he continually renews the reality of life as a share in his own life. **65:6** Christ is God's final word about this gift of life, but in the pre-paschal context of the dialogue with the Sadducees, this final word is not made explicit. **65:7** It is implicit, however, in the appeal to the power of God.

§3 The New Meaning of the Body (TOB 66:1–4)

66:1 The words "they take neither wife nor husband" have a key meaning for the theology of the body. **66:2** Marriage belongs exclusively to this world, in which the increase in the number of human beings created in the image of God is necessary. In the world of God, God himself will be "all in all." **66:3** That definitive world is man's true fatherland, reached through the Resurrection, which implies a wholly new state of human life. **66:4** The meaning of being male and female will be constituted differently.

§4 Spiritualization (TOB 66:5–67:2)

66:5 How will this meaning of being male and female be different? The comparison with the angels suggests a new spiritualization of man, though not one that leaves the body behind. Resurrection establishes the true life of human bodiliness, which implies a new submission of the body to the spirit. **66:6** Faith in the Resurrection played a key role in the formation of theological anthropology. It was because of faith in the Resurrection that St. Thomas Aquinas abandoned the Platonic view of the relation between body and soul dominant in the Augustinian tradition he inherited and to draw near to Aristotle. The Resurrection shows that the final state of man is a definitive and perfect integration of body and soul. **67:1** This integration can be called *spiritualization* inasmuch as the powers of the Spirit will fully permeate the energies of the body. **67:2** The possibility of an opposition between body and spirit will be eliminated, not by disincarnation, which would be the destruction of human nature, but by a deep harmony between body and spirit that safeguards the primacy of the Spirit.

§5 Divinization (TOB 67:3–68:4)

67:3 In Luke, Christ speaks not only about spiritualization, "equal to the angels," but also divinization, "sons of God." God will communicate himself to the whole of man's bodily-spiritual subjectivity, which will be formed anew by union with God in his Trinitarian mystery. **67:4** Is the definitive discovery of the spousal meaning of the body the virginal meaning of the body? To answer this question, we must reflect about the essence of the beatific vision. **67:5** This vision will reveal in a living and experiential way God's most personal self-giving in his divinity. The mystery hidden from eternity in the Father—that is, the spousal union of Christ and the Church—will become the *form* of human experience. We see here the same characteristics that mark the spousal meaning of the body. **68:1** The object of the vision will be the Trinitarian communion of persons. **68:2** According to the law of the integral order of the person, the perfection of communion determines the spiritual maturity of the subject. The authentic maturity of the subject's response to God's self-gift explains the absence of marriage. **68:3** In this mature response, the virginal state of the body will reveal itself as the final fulfillment of its spousal meaning. The vision of God gives birth to a love of such depth and power of concentration on God that it completely absorbs the person's whole subjectivity, body and soul. **68:4** The concentration of knowledge and love on God in his Trinitarian communion of persons implies communion also among created persons in the communion of saints. In this way, the Trinitarian order will be established in the created world of persons.

[§6 Overview of Christ's Teaching: Beginning, Present, and Future (TOB 68:5–69:8)]

68:5 repeated in **69:1** The words of Christ about the future resurrection complete the revelation of the body. This revelation not only penetrates to the heart of the present reality we experience but also allows us to pass beyond the present to the very beginning and the very end of God's plan for the person. The theological image of man in these three dimensions is coherent. **69:2** The truth about the beginning and the end cannot be reached by empirical methods alone, but it is open to theological reconstruction. Man carries these two dimensions in the depth of the experience of his being. **69:3** In his appeal to the beginning, the present, and the end, Christ speaks about the same human being, male and female. The meaning of being male and female in the future world lies outside of marriage and procreation but not outside of what derives from the mystery of creation; namely, the spousal meaning of the body. **69:4** The original spousal meaning of being male and female as a body is grounded in human personhood (first experienced as original solitude) and thus with the call to the communion of persons (experienced in original unity). Marriage and procreation express this vocation to communion in the dimensions of history. After the closure of history, the spousal meaning of the body will still be perfectly personal and communitarian. **69:5** The experience of the glorified body in the vision of God contains this same meaning as the fulfillment of man's original inheritance. **69:6** The perennial meaning of the body will be revealed with such simplicity and splendor that everyone will find in the body the fountain of the freedom of the gift. **69:7** Although it is difficult to construct an adequate image of the future world, Christ's words allow a certain approximation. **69:8** Conclusion: Christ's appeal to the Resurrection allows us to reread in a new way the whole revealed meaning of the body.

B. Paul

§1 relates Paul's teaching to Jesus's argument, which is based on seeing God as "God of the living." §2 explains Paul's teaching on the First Adam and the Last Adam as a change of the system of powers in man.

§1 Final Victory over Death (TOB 70:1–4)

70:1 Christ's words about the Resurrection are echoed in Paul's teaching, which is based on his own experience of the Risen Jesus. **70:2** Paul appeals above all to the reality and truth of the Resurrection. **70:3** The Resurrection is the final word of the self-revelation of God as "God of the living." It is the final victory over death. **70:4** First Corinthians 15 can be considered a synthesis of Paul's anthropology of the Resurrection.

§2 The First Adam and the Last Adam (TOB 70:5–72:6)

Past, Present, and Future (*TOB 70:5–71:1*) **70:5** Paul appeals to the beginning (the first Adam), the present (perishable, weak), and the definitive future (the last Adam). **70:6** He thus touches on everything contained in Christ's words about the beginning, the present, and the Resurrection. **70:7** He appeals to creation and redemption in a cosmic perspective: the slavery to corruption and the hope for the redemption of the body affects the whole visible creation. **70:8** The mystery of the redemption of the body is already at work through the gifts of the Spirit. **71:1** It is completed in the Resurrection.

The First Adam and the Last Adam (*TOB 71:2–4*) **71:2** In view of his eternal destiny, man is situated between two poles: the first and the last Adam. **71:3** The humanity of the first Adam contains the potentiality for receiving the incorruptibility of the last Adam. It thus contains the desire for glory. **71:4** The reason for this desire is that, in the earthly image and likeness of God, the human body can also gather and reproduce the heavenly image of the last Adam.

Change in the System of Powers (TOB 71:5–72:6) **71:5** While Christ speaks about the divinizing depth of the vision of God face-to-face, which is the source of both perpetual virginity and intersubjectivity, Paul speaks about the inner structure or system of powers of the human person. **71:6** This system of powers undergoes a radical change in the resurrection. **72:1** The change corresponds to two states of man, earthly and risen. **72:2** Paul formulates the contrast as *weak* and "full of power." The spiritualization of the body will be the source of its power and imperishability. **72:3** This change is not a mere return to the deathless origin in Genesis but an introduction to a new fullness. **72:4** That the body becomes spiritual signifies the perfect sensitivity of the senses, their harmonization with the activity of the human spirit. **72:5** Paul is thus not proposing a Platonic dualism of body and spirit. He considers the psychosomatic subjectivity of the person as a whole as spirit, inasmuch as it is under the influence of the life-giving Spirit, or as flesh, inasmuch as it is under the influence of resistance against the Spirit. **72:6** This anthropology of the Resurrection permeates Paul's entire anthropology.

C. Conclusion (TOB 72:7)

72:7 We return to Christ's words about the Resurrection, "in which they will take neither wife nor husband." These words have a fundamental significance for the whole theology of the body, for understanding both marriage and virginity.

2. The Unmarried State for the Kingdom (TOB 73–85)

Section 2 analyzes the unmarried state for the kingdom as a charismatic sign of the Resurrection, as an even higher realization of the spousal meaning of the body and of fruitfulness than marriage.

Section A explains the teaching of Christ on the unmarried state.

§§1–2 are introductory. §1 points out that celibacy is a counsel, not a commandment. §2 focuses on the particular way Jesus expresses himself; namely, by using the striking expression *eunuchs*.

§§3–5 identify the purpose of the unmarried state "for the kingdom." §3 states that the purpose is twofold: a special likeness with Christ, which includes a special participation in the mystery of redemption, and a new supernatural form of fruitfulness. §4 argues that these purposes must also be the subjective motivation of those who choose the unmarried state. §5 shows that by instituting the unmarried state for these purposes, God preserves his original plan for human love, according to which we find ourselves in a sincere gift of self.

§6 explains in what way the unmarried state is superior to marriage and in what way the two complement each other. §§7–9 belong together as an account of the relation between the unmarried state and the spousal meaning of the body. §7 presents the ultimate motive for the unmarried state: spousal love for Christ. §8 shows that the unmarried state implies a renunciation of the great good of marriage, which is rooted in the spousal meaning of the body. §9 moves from renunciation to affirmation by pointing out that the unmarried state is ultimately an affirmation of that spousal meaning.

A. The Words of Christ (TOB 73–81:7)

§1 Christ's Word and the Rule for Understanding (TOB 73)

73:1 The call to an exclusive gift of self to God in virginity reflects a particular sensibility of the human spirit that anticipates the resurrection in which "they do not take wife or husband." **73:2** Yet the context in which Christ speaks about virginity is not the Resurrection but the indissolubility of marriage. The disciples object that if marriage is indissoluble, then "it is not advantageous to marry." Christ answers them by pointing to those who "made themselves eunuchs for the kingdom of heaven." **73:3** In response to the doubts of the disciples about the value of marriage, he does not answer directly, "It is advantageous to marry," but appeals to another principle. There is a choice against marriage for virginity, but it is not because of a supposedly negative value of marriage but rather a positive value connected with that choice. "Not all can understand it but only those to whom it has been granted." **73:4** These words contain a rule for understanding: the unmarried state is not a commandment binding for all but a counsel that regards only some. It is a charismatic orientation toward the Resurrection "in which they take neither wife nor husband." It is thus an exception to the present state, in which they do take wife and husband. **73:5** The context of Christ's words about the unmarried state is his teaching about the indissolubility of marriage, which is the highest affirmation of the value of marriage in the historical state.

§2 Three Kinds of "Eunuchs": Why? (TOB 74:1–5)

74:1 By comparing the unmarried state for the kingdom to two kinds of eunuchs—those impotent by birth and those impotent by castration—Christ emphasizes that the unmarried state he proposes is voluntary (made themselves eunuchs) and supernatural (for the kingdom). **74:2** For the Old Testament, marriage was so much the rule that only the physical defect of being a eunuch could cause an exception. **74:3** Marriage was a religiously privileged state owing to the promise of numerous descendants given to Abraham. **74:4** For this reason he chooses the comparison with eunuchs as if to say, "I realize that my teaching about the unmarried state will raise difficulties due to your way of understanding the meaning of the body." The unmarried state can be chosen voluntarily for a supernatural motive. **74:5** The expression "eunuchs for the kingdom" signifies a turning point in understanding the meaning of the body. It also signals that the unmarried state is a renunciation and requires spiritual effort.

§3 The Unmarried State and "Fruitfulness from the Spirit" (TOB 74:6–75:4)

74:6 Although Christ himself does not unfold the supernatural goals of the unmarried state, his words are a sufficient basis for discovering them. **75:1** The unmarried state for the kingdom is a charismatic sign of the definitive virginity in the kingdom, in which the absolute and eternal spousal meaning of the body is revealed. It expresses the power of the redemption of the body in the present. Above all, it bears the imprint of likeness to Christ, who did not marry. **75:2** The new meaning of the body is clear already in Christ's birth from a virgin. Joseph and Mary became the first witnesses of a new fruitfulness from the Spirit. "What is begotten in her comes from the Holy Spirit" (Matthew 1:20). **75:3** The marriage of Joseph and Mary was a true communion of persons in the conjugal covenant and at the same time a state of virginity that served this fruitfulness of the Spirit, the most perfect fruitfulness. The same kind of fruitfulness is at work in the unmarried state for the kingdom. **75:4** The main basis of understanding available to the disciples was the example of Jesus, who lived in the unmarried state for the sake of a particular spiritual and supernatural fruitfulness.

§4 The Expression "For the Kingdom of Heaven" Indicates Motivation (TOB 76)

76:1 The privilege given in Christ's words to the unmarried state for the kingdom was an absolute novelty and has a decisive importance for the new *ethos* and theology of the body. **76:2** While marriage has a fundamental, universal, and ordinary value for the kingdom, which is reflected in Christ's teaching about its indissolubility, the unmarried state has a particular and exceptional value. **76:3** Christ insists on the motivation (i.e., on the subjective appreciation of the objective end) "for the kingdom." Those who choose the unmarried state must discover in it the spiritual fruitfulness that comes from the Holy Spirit. They must consciously choose it as a likeness with Christ that allows a particular participation in the redemption of the body. **76:4** The words "Not all can understand it but only those to whom it has been granted" point to a gift or grace that resonates in the mind as understanding and in the will as motivation. This motivation—and the choice based on it—subsists by continually renewing itself. **76:5** "Making oneself a eunuch" signifies that this choice is not without travail for the normal and noble inclinations of nature. Christ's proposal of the unmarried state in the context of his teaching about the indissolubility of marriage, in which he appeals to the beginning of God's plan for man and woman, stands in some way in contrast to that beginning. **76:6** The fact that these two teachings are found in the same context of Christ's words indicates not only that marriage throws light on the unmarried state but also that the unmarried state throws light on marriage viewed in the mystery of creation and redemption.

§5 The Unmarried State and Marriage: Vocation of "Historical Man" (TOB 77:1–4)

77:1 The radically new idea of the unmarried state proposed by Christ fully preserves God's original plan for the person, both in the dimension of solitude and of communion with others. **77:2** Those who are called to the unmarried state discover in their solitude before God a new and even fuller form of personal communion with other human beings in which the image and likeness of God are developed in their Trinitarian meanings by the person becoming "a sincere gift" for others (*Gaudium et spes* 24). **77:3** The choice of the unmarried state contains a renunciation of marriage and of all the good that lies in it. It is a certain self-sacrifice. **77:4** The call to the unmarried state reflects the same *ethos* as Christ's words about adultery in the heart, although it widens the perspectives of this *ethos* toward the kingdom and the Resurrection. It is one and the same historical man who lives in marriage or the unmarried state and who must submit his sinfulness to the powers that flow from the redemption of the body.

§6 The "Superiority" of the Unmarried State (TOB 77:5–78:5)

77:5 Christ only implicitly affirms the superiority of the unmarried state to marriage, but Paul does so explicitly. **77:6** The whole doctrinal and pastoral tradition of the Church follows this judgment. It is dictated by the motive "for the kingdom" without any disparagement of marriage. **78:1** It does not contain any Manichaean tendency. Nor does it imply a negative judgment about sexual union in the flesh, but it emphasizes the motive "for the kingdom." **78:2** Superiority and inferiority are held within the complementarity of the unmarried state and marriage. The whole Christian community is ordered to the resurrected state signified by the unmarried state. **78:3** Although the unmarried state is called "the state of perfection," the perfection of Christian life is measured exclusively by love. The evangelical counsels of chastity, poverty, and obedience help in reaching a deeper love. Conversely, those who are married reach the perfection of love through faithfulness to the spirit of these counsels. **78:4** The two states of life thus complete each other and interpenetrate. Conjugal love must be marked by the faithful gift of self to the one Bridegroom on which the unmarried state for the kingdom is based. **78:5** The unmarried state for the kingdom must in turn be marked by spiritual fatherhood or motherhood analogous to physical fatherhood and motherhood, in which conjugal love matures and is confirmed.

§7 Between Renunciation and Love (TOB 79:1–80:1)

79:1 The kingdom of heaven, *for* which the unmarried state is chosen, is an objective reality defined in a particular way. **79:2** The unmarried state "for the kingdom" refers to a unique participation in the establishment of the kingdom of God on earth, which prepares the definitive realization of this kingdom. **79:3** The unmarried state thus bears within itself the power of the redemption of the body. It implies denying oneself and following Christ. Christ does not explain in what way the unmarried state contributes *more* to this kingdom. **79:4** He does not explain the specific and exceptional relation between this kingdom and those who choose the unmarried state. **79:5** Nevertheless, it is clear from his words that they must choose it because of its particular value in itself, not because "it is not advantageous to marry." **79:6** Those who choose marriage must choose it for the value placed in it by the Creator; those who choose the unmarried state must seek in it the values proper to such a vocation and thus act in conformity with this vocation.

79:7 Ephesians 5:25–33 is the key text for understanding the value of the unmarried state inasmuch as it shows the spousal relationship between Christ and the Church. In this text we find concretized what Christ meant by the phrase "for the kingdom of heaven." **79:8** Christ's words are demanding, and they show the depth and seriousness of the decision for the unmarried state. Yet what above all shines through the depth and seriousness of the decision is love as the readiness to make an exclusive gift of self to Christ. **79:9** repeated in **80:1** The human heart accepts even difficult demands in the name of love. The main content of the unmarried state for the kingdom is love for Christ himself as the Bridegroom. It is a particular response to Christ's spousal gift of self.

§8 The Spousal Meaning of the Body as the Foundation (TOB 80:2–81:2)

80:2 The meaning of Christ's words in Matthew 19:11–12 for the theology of the body can be seen when one connects them with his teaching about the beginning of God's plan for the person, about the spousal meaning of the body. **80:3** Contemporary mentality speaks about sexual drives and thus transfers a category suited to animals (drive) to the human person. Genesis 1–2 show a clear boundary between man and animals connected with the image of God. **80:4** The boundary becomes clear in the discovery of the spousal meaning of the body. **80:5** Christ's words about the unmarried state must thus be understood in light of the consciousness of the freedom of the gift (rather than the compulsion of drives) in the spousal meaning of the body, which is inscribed by nature in all human subjectivity. **80:6** In their personal communion, man and woman are *for* each other. The same *for* is present in the unmarried state *for* the kingdom as a total gift of self to Christ. What stands behind both is the fundamental nature of the personal subject, which only finds itself in a sincere gift of self (*Gaudium et spes* 24). **80:7** It follows that the choice of the unmarried state must be made on the basis of the full awareness of the spousal meaning of the body in its masculinity and femininity. **81:1** Quote of Matthew 19:10–12. **81:2** One must be fully aware of the value of the spousal meaning of the body when one renounces marriage. Yet renunciation is not enough.

§9 Renunciation That Is an Affirmation (TOB 81:3–7)

81:3 The renunciation of marriage affirms the value and beauty of the spousal meaning of the body in its masculinity and femininity. It is needed in the Christian community for the clearer recognition of the spousal meaning of the body in conjugal life. **81:4** In this way the exceptional vocation to the unmarried state is needed for the evangelical authenticity of the ordinary vocation to marriage. **81:5** How is the call to the unmarried state formed? **81:6** While the unmarried state renounces marriage, it is based on the discovery of the gift and thus affirms that persons only realize themselves through a gift of self. While it renounces marriage, it does not negate the essential value of marriage but highlights what is most lasting and personal in marriage, what corresponds in the temporal order to the dignity of the gift. **81:7** In this perspective, Christ's words about the unmarried state are correctly associated with the Resurrection, in which "they will take neither wife nor husband."

B. Paul on the Unmarried State (TOB 82–85)

§1 Christ's Statement and the Teaching of the Apostles (TOB 82)

82:1 We encounter the question of celibacy in Paul as a question that troubled the minds of the first generation of Christians, in particular of those who converted from Hellenism. **82:2** Paul speaks in a magisterial and pastoral way by entering into a dialogue with the Corinthians. The basis of his teaching should be sought in the life and teaching of Christ. **82:3** Paul underlines the rule for understanding found also in the teaching of Christ (see TOB 73:4); namely, that the unmarried state is not a commandment binding for all but a counsel that regards only some.

82:4 If anyone thinks that he is not behaving properly toward his virgin, if she is past her prime, and it is fitting that it happens in this way, let him do as he wishes; it is no sin. Let them even marry. But if someone stands firm in his heart, being under no necessity, but being the arbiter of his own will, and has determined in his own mind to keep his virgin, he will do well. So, then, he who marries his virgin does well, and he who refrains from marrying her does better (1 Corinthians 7:36–38).

82:5 It is not clear whether Paul addresses a young man who needs to decide whether to marry, or a newly married man influenced by the view reported earlier in the letter, "It is better for a man not to touch a woman" (1 Corinthians 7:1), or a father or guardian who needs to decide whether to let his daughter or ward marry. What is clear is that only the voluntary unmarried state is *better* than marriage. **82:6** Paul may be responding to a dualistic view according to which marriage is a sin. It is not a question of good and evil but a question of good and better.

§2 Paul's Argumentation (TOB 83:1–84:7)

83:1 "The stage of this world is passing away. Let those who have wives live as though they had none.... I want you to be free from anxieties" (1 Corinthians 7:29–32). **83:2** "Those who marry will have troubles in the flesh" (1 Corinthians 7:28). **83:3** What are these troubles? True conjugal love is a difficult love. **83:4** Christ does not attempt to direct his listeners to the unmarried state by pointing to the troubles of marriage. "Making oneself a eunuch" points to the greatness and exceptional nature of the choice of the unmarried state as a renunciation. **83:5** Paul points to the transitory character of the temporal world. "The stage of this world is passing away." **83:6** He explains what "for the kingdom" means. "The unmarried person is anxious about what is the Lord's, how to please the Lord" (1 Corinthians 7:32). **83:7** Here one can see the field of anxiousness to which the unmarried man can dedicate himself. **83:8** "What belongs to the

Lord" refers to the whole objective reality of the kingdom. **83:9** "How to please the Lord" expresses the subjective reality of the kingdom. **83:10** "Being anxious" and "how to please the Lord" overlap. **84:1** One tries to please the person one loves with spousal love. **84:2** The married man "finds himself divided" (1 Corinthians 7:34) by his family duties. The unmarried man integrates and unifies his life by completely devoting himself to the kingdom. **84:3** The goal is to keep oneself united with the Lord without distraction. **84:4** Paul explains the statement "being anxious about what is the Lord's" by adding, "to be holy in body and spirit" (1 Corinthians 7:34). **84:5** Holiness implies being separated from the profane in order to belong only to God. **84:6** Corinthian Christians understood marriage as a way of "using the world." **84:7** In reference to such a "use of the world," Paul writes, "It is better to marry than to be aflame" (1 Corinthians 7:9).

§3 "Concupiscence" and "Gift from God" (TOB 84:8–85:8)

84:8 It is clear that Paul does not see marriage only as a remedy for concupiscence because he also says, "Each has his own gift from God" (1 Corinthians 7:7). Both those who marry and those who do not marry receive a gift of grace suited to their vocation. **84:9** In accord with the reputation of Corinth, Paul emphasizes the concupiscence of the flesh; at the same time, he underlines the sacramental and charismatic character of marriage. **85:1** In connection with marriage, he underlines the transitory nature of the world, which is the fruit of the great expectation of the return of Christ. **85:2** In agreement with the teaching of Christ about the absence of marriage after the Resurrection, he holds that marriage implies a certain closure in the transitory world. Still, among the reasons for the unmarried state he gives first place to "pleasing the Lord" and "being anxious about what is the Lord's." **85:3** These points also apply to Paul's counsel to widows not to remarry.

85:4 His teaching shows his realism about concupiscence. This realism does not eclipse for him the reality of the gift from God, in virtue of which the body is a temple of the Holy Spirit both in marriage and in the unmarried state. **85:5** We do not find any premise for a Manichaean view of marriage in Paul. The "one flesh" union of husband and wife is subject to the power of their own gift from God. **85:6** The marriage debt (1 Corinthians 7:3–4) must be understood in the context of the sacramentality of marriage. **85:7** Both conjugal relations and periodic abstinence from them (1 Corinthians 7:5–7) must be a fruit of "the gift from God" given to the spouses as "their own." **85:8** The whole sexually differentiated subjectivity of man and woman must remain under the influence of this gift.

§4 Conclusion (TOB 85:9–10)

85:9 What does it mean to be a body, to be a man or a woman? In Paul's view, one can find the basis for answering this question both about the present life (marriage and the unmarried state) and about life after the Resurrection (in which there is no marriage). **85:10** The theology of the body is fundamental for interpreting man and for understanding human *ethos*. In both of these fields we must listen to Christ's appeal to the beginning, his appeal to the heart, and his appeal to the Resurrection.

3. Redemption of the Body (TOB 86)

86:1 The redemption of the body has an anthropological dimension—"We groan inwardly while we wait for . . . the redemption of our bodies" (Romans 8:20)—and a cosmic dimension—"The whole creation groans" (Romans 8:22). **86:2** In both dimensions, it is an object of hope. **86:3** Christ, who "came to reveal man to himself" (*Gaudium et spes* 22:1), speaks about the divine depth of the mystery of redemption. This redemption fulfills the hope of the proto-Gospel (see Genesis 3:15), confirms the hope "in which we were saved," and reopens the hope of final fulfillment.

86:4 To understand the redemption of the body, an authentic theology of the body is needed. We attempted to build one on the basis of Christ's threefold appeal: to the beginning, to the heart, and to the Resurrection. **86:5** We hope for the final victory over death through the Resurrection (see Chapter Three, "Christ Appeals to the Resurrection"). Both Christ and Paul understand the unmarried state for the kingdom in light of this hope. **86:6** The redemption of the body is present not only in the Resurrection but also in Christ's teaching about indissolubility (see Chapter One, "Christ Appeals to the Beginning") and in his invitation to overcome concupiscence (see Chapter Two, "Christ Appeals to the Human Heart"). In these ethical teachings, the redemption of the body is the basis of the hope of victory over sin, which is the hope of everyday. **86:7** In their everyday lives, whether in marriage or the unmarried state, man and woman must draw from the redemption of the body the inspiration to overcome the threefold concupiscence.

86:8 On the basis of the redemption of the body, man and woman discover the good that is the object of the hope of everyday; namely, the strengthening of the bond between the dignity of the person and the spousal meaning of the body. On this basis, they can understand and realize the freedom of the gift in marriage and the unmarried state. In these ways, "Christ fully reveals man to himself and makes his supreme vocation clear" (*Gaudium et spes* 22:1). This vocation is inscribed in man's body and soul by the redemption of the body. The redemption of the body is the definitive foundation of everything we have said about Christ's teaching.

PART TWO, CHAPTER ONE

The Dimension of Covenant and of Grace (TOB 87–102)

Part Two of TOB is called "The Sacrament." The phrase is strikingly encompassing in meaning. It unites in "a single great sign" (TOB 95b:7) marriage as the primordial sacrament in Paradise, Christ's redemptive and spousal gift of self, and marriage reinstituted by him as a sacrament of the New Covenant.

A sacrament is a sign of grace that effectively gives grace. Chapter One of Part Two focuses on the dimension of grace, Chapter Two on the dimension of sign. Chapter Three looks at the practical moral implications of the sign by taking a close look at the encyclical *Humanae vitae.*

1. Reading of Ephesians 5:21–33 (TOB 87–93)

§1 The Text of Ephesians 5:21–33 (TOB 87:1)
§2 Christ's Words (TOB 87:2)
§3 Two Meanings of "Body" (TOB 87:3)
§4 Does It Speak about the Sacramentality of Marriage? (TOB 87:4)
§5 Sacrament and Body (TOB 87:5)
§6 Direction of the Following Analyses (TOB 87:6)

§1 quotes the text to be interpreted. §2 makes the main point about method in reading Ephesians 5:21–33. It should be read in light of Christ's three words, as their crowning and synthesis.

§§3–5 raise two questions to be addressed: First, what is the relation between the body of Christ and the male/female sexual body? Further, does Ephesians address the sacramentality of marriage? The second of these questions has been controversial since the Reformation. Luther and Calvin denied that Ephesians affirms the full sacramentality of marriage; theologians of the Catholic reform tended to affirm it. John Paul takes a mediating position. On this basis, §6 sets the direction and structure of the discussion.

A. Ephesians 5:21–33

§1 The Text of Ephesians 5:21–33 (TOB 87:1)
87:1 Quote of the text.

§2 Ephesians 5:21–33 and Christ's Words (TOB 87:2)

87:2 Ephesians 5:21–33 is the crowning of Christ's three key words about the body. We must read this text in light of what Christ has told us about the human body, all in the theological perspective of the redemption of the body.

§3 Ephesians 5:21–33—Two Meanings of "Body" (TOB 87:3)

87:3 In a metaphorical sense, the Church is the body of Christ; in the proper sense, the term refers to the human body in its masculinity and femininity. In what way do these two meanings converge in Ephesians? One must answer this question in the broad, biblical context of the theology of the body.

§4 Does Ephesians 5:21–33 Speak about the Sacramentality of Marriage? (TOB 87:4)

87:4 We can only answer this question by observing how the sacramentality of marriage comes to light; namely, in the analogy of spousal love between God and his people. The answer must pass through the whole theology of the body.

§5 Sacrament and Body (TOB 87:5)

87:5 Sacramentality intersects with the body. A sacrament is a visible—that is, bodily—sign of grace. It is an efficacious sign: it does not merely indicate grace but produces it.

§6 Direction of the Following Analyses (TOB 87:6)

87:6 After reaching a preliminary understanding of Ephesians 5:21–33, we must proceed to understanding the depth of truth revealed in its Section 2, "Sacrament and Mystery." In a particular way, the passage from Ephesians "reveals man to man himself and makes his supreme vocation clear" (*Gaudium et spes* 22:1).

B. Detailed Analysis (TOB 88–93)

§1 In the Context of Ephesians as a Whole (TOB 88:1)
§2 The Mystery of Christ and the Vocation of the Christian (TOB 88:2)
§3 The Atmosphere of the Christian Community's Life (TOB 88:3)
§4 Indications for the Community of the Family (TOB 88:4–5)
§5 The Spouses: "Reciprocally Subject in the Fear of Christ" (TOB 89:1–6)
§6 Analogy and Mystery (TOB 89:7–90:4)
§7 An Additional Aspect of the Analogy: Head and Body (TOB 90:5–91:4)
§8 Two Subjects or One? (TOB 91:5–92:3)
§9 "As Their Own Body" (TOB 92:4–8)
§10 "This Mystery Is Great" (TOB 93)

Section B discusses Ephesians 5:21–33 step by step, beginning with the context, then unfolding the text in four units.

§§1–4 belong together as descriptions of the context of Ephesians 5:21–33 and of its general character. §§5–10 discuss Ephesians 5:21–33 in detail, divided into four units. John Paul reserves Ephesians 5:31–32 for the very end, as the high point of the discussion.

§1 In the Context of Ephesians as a Whole (TOB 88:1)

88:1 The first part of Ephesians outlines the eternal plan of salvation.

§2 The Mystery of Christ and the Vocation of the Christian (TOB 88:2)

88:2 The second part passes to more detailed instructions to define Christian life as a vocation that flows from the divine plan.

§3 The Atmosphere of the Christian Community's Life (TOB 88:3)

88:3 Ephesians 5 gives instructions for the climate of spiritual life in the community in general and then goes on to the family in particular.

§4 Indications for the Community of the Family (TOB 88:4–5)

88:4 The immediate context of Ephesians 5:21–33 shows how the Christian vocation is to be lived in the family as a whole, including children and slaves (Ephesians 5:21–6:11). **88:5** The literary form of the whole passage on the family is that of a domestic code (Luther used the term *Haustafeln* for "house tables," that is, tables of law for the household), which details the moral obligations of the society of the family.

[*Text of Ephesians 5:21–25*] 5:21 Be subject to one another in the fear of Christ. 5:22 Wives, be subject to your husbands as you are to the Lord. 5:23 For the husband is the head of the wife as Christ is the head of the Church, he who is the Savior of his body. 5:24 And as the Church is subject to Christ, so also wives ought to be subject to their husbands in everything. 5:25 And you, husbands, love your wives, as Christ loved the Church and gave himself for her.

§5 The Spouses: "Reciprocally Subject in the Fear of Christ" (TOB 89:1–6)

89:1 The relationship between husband and wife must be formed by their reverence (pietas) for Christ. **89:2** The specific directives are drawn from the mystery of Christ. **89:3** Mutual submission explains the submission of the wife to the husband. It shows that the conjugal covenant is not a contract of one-sided domination of the wife by the husband. The source of mutual submission lies in pietas, and its expression is love. **89:4** Particularly, husbands must love their wives. Love makes the husband also subject to the wife and subject in this to the Lord. The reciprocal gift of self implies such a mutual submission. **89:5** The author of Ephesians is not afraid to accept the concept of one-sided subordination characteristic of his time, because this submission finds its just balance in the mutual submission of husband and wife in the fear of Christ. **89:6** In our time, the relation between husband and wife has the same foundation in the fear of Christ.

§6 Analogy and Mystery (TOB 89:7–90:4)

89:7 Ephesians 5:22–25 inserts its moral teaching into the mystery of Christ. We witness an encounter between this mystery and the very essence of marriage. **89:8** The encounter has first of all the form of an analogy: "as X, so Y." **90:1** The mystery of Christ includes the particular feature of spousal love in the relationship between Christ and the Church. The marriage analogy clarifies the mystery. **90:2** The mystery also clarifies the marriage analogy and thus reveals the essential truth about marriage; namely, that it must mirror the relationship between Christ and the Church. **90:3** This norm can be valid only if marriage contains a particle of the mystery of Christ. **90:4** We can therefore read the analogy not only beginning with marriage to understand the mystery of Christ but also in the opposite direction, beginning with the mystery of Christ to understand marriage. We will first follow the direction from the mystery of Christ to marriage by showing how marriage becomes a visible sign of the eternal divine mystery. Here we discover the foundations of the sacramentality of marriage.

§7 An Additional Aspect of the Analogy: Head and Body (TOB 90:5–91:4)

90:5 Christ formed his body through a total gift of self. **90:6** His redeeming love thus becomes a spousal love. **91:1** The head-body analogy supplements the husband-wife analogy. **91:2** Yet it does not lie outside the husband-wife analogy.

Both show the nature of the union between Christ and the Church. **91:3** Two distinct subjects become in some way one subject: the body, head and members, one flesh. **91:4** Yet "one subject" does not blur the individuality of the subjects.

[*Text of Ephesians 5:25–27*] 5:25 And you, husbands, love your wives, as Christ loved the Church and gave himself for her, 5:26 in order to make her holy by cleansing her with the washing of water accompanied by the word, 5:27 so as to present his Church before himself all glorious, without spot or wrinkle or anything of the kind but holy and immaculate.

§8 Two Subjects or One? (TOB 91:5–92:3)

91:5 Quote of Ephesians 5:25–27. **91:6** In this passage, bi-subjectivity predominates, although the image of one body remains. The essential goal of Christ's love for the Church is her sanctification, the beginning of which is baptism. **91:7** Baptism prepares the bride for the bridegroom. **91:8** His ultimate (eschatological) goal is to present the Church before himself "all glorious," beautiful with the beauty of grace. **92:1** Another quote of Ephesians 5:25–27. **92:2** The Church is presented as a bride all beautiful in her body, which shows the deep importance of the body in the analogy of spousal love. **92:3** The beautiful body refers metaphorically to the moral, spiritual, and supernatural order. It is significant, however, that Paul explains the supernatural order through the body and through the love by which man and woman become "one flesh."

[*Text of Ephesians 5:28–30, 5:33*] 5:28 In the same way, husbands have the duty to love their wives as their own body, for the one who loves his wife loves himself. 5:29 No one, in fact, ever hates his own flesh, but he nourishes and cares for it, as Christ does with the Church, 5:30 because we are members of his body. . . . 5:33 Therefore also you, each one on his part, should love his wife as himself, and the woman should have reverence toward her husband.

§9 "As Their Own Body" (TOB 92:4–8)

92:4 In Ephesians 5:28, too, bi-subjectivity predominates. Love binds the bridegroom to be concerned for the good of the bride, to desire her beauty, to sense this beauty and care for it. **92:5** "As their own body" returns to "one flesh," which is built on the basis of bi-subjectivity. It is a unity produced by love. **92:6** The husband is above all the one who loves, and the wife the one who is loved. The wife's submission consists in her experiencing her husband's love, as the parallel with the relation between Christ and the Church shows. **92:7** "Each one on his part should love his wife as himself" (Ephesians 5:33) refers to the moral unity conditioned and constituted by love. In union through love, the body of the other person becomes one's own inasmuch as one is concerned for the good of the other as one is concerned for the good of one's own body. **92:8** "Nourishing and caring for the body" (Ephesians 5:29) probably refers to the Eucharist. This reference helps us to understand the dignity of the body.

[*Text of Ephesians 5:31–32*] 5:31 For this reason a man will leave his father and his mother and unite with his wife, and the two will form one flesh. 5:32 This mystery is great; I say this with reference to Christ and the Church.

§10 "This Mystery Is Great" (TOB 93)

93:1 Ephesians 5:31 quotes Genesis 2:24 to present the mystery of Christ with the Church, from which the author deduces the truth of the unity of the spouses. This is the most important point of the whole text. The foundation of the husband-wife and Christ-Church analogy lies in the unity of God's plan. Marriage is the most ancient revelation of this plan, while its definitive revelation is Christ's spousal love for the Church. **93:2** As God's salvific plan for humanity, the mystery is the central theme and reality of revelation. It is what God wishes above all to transmit through his Word. **93:3** In Christ, God not only transmits the good news but also begins the work of salvation as a fruit of grace. Paul indicates the continuity of God's saving initiative from the ancient covenant to the definitive covenant, even the sameness of "the great mystery." **93:4** Ephesians does not speak directly about the sacrament of marriage but about the foundations of the sacramentality of Christian life and thus indirectly about the sacramentality of marriage. **93:5** *Sacrament* and *mystery* are not synonyms. As a visible and efficacious sign of grace, a *sacrament* implies both the manifestation of the mystery and its accomplishment in man and woman. **93:6** The mystery is not only God's plan hidden from eternity but also above all its realization in Christ, who united himself with the Church in an act of spousal love. The statement "This mystery is great" explains one of the key statements of Vatican II: "The Church is in Christ like a sacrament or a sign and instrument of intimate union with God and of the unity of the whole human race" (*Lumen gentium* 1). **93:7** The sacramentality of the Church remains in a particular relationship with marriage, the most ancient sacrament.

2. Sacrament and Mystery (TOB 94–99:3)

Section 2 draws systematic conclusions from the reading of Ephesians. It has great theological weight, similar to the theological weight of the reading of Genesis in TOB 13:2–19:6, "Man in the Dimension of Gift." It explicitly returns to this earlier section, quoting key passages of it, in order to develop the sacramental nature of marriage implicit in the reading of Genesis.

The section shows the deep roots of the sacramentality of marriage, that is, of the nature of marriage as an efficacious sign of grace. Its division into eight paragraphs rather than seven (as in the two sections about creation) may be deliberate, symbolizing the new creation (which includes marriage) on the eighth day, the day of the Resurrection.

The first paragraph stands by itself over against the remaining seven. It speaks about Christ. The others speak about marriage. The purpose of the argument is to lay down the foundation of the sacramentality of marriage: it is by his spousal gift of self that Christ reveals (sign) and accomplishes (efficacious) the mystery hidden from ages.

The remaining seven sections can be divided into two. The first three (§§2–4) focus on the analogy of spousal love as the basis on which the sacramentality of marriage is to be understood. It is in virtue of this analogy that marriage can be a sign. §§2–3 present the analogy as expressed in Ephesians and Isaiah 54. §4 presents the two functions of the analogy: a deeper understanding of the essence of grace and the covenant as a gift of self, and a deeper understanding of marriage in light of the covenant. Ephesians brings the visible sign of marriage at the beginning together with the visible sign of Christ into a single great sign.

On this basis, §§5–8 explain the sacramentality of marriage. §5 presents marriage in the beginning as the primordial sacrament, rooted in the sacrament of Creation. §§6–8 present marriage after Christ as the sacrament of the Church rooted in the sacrament of Redemption. §6 explains how marriage is rooted in the sacrament of Redemption. §7 distinguishes two aspects of marriage: it is a figure or prototype according to which the sacramental order is built, and it is in its own reality a sacrament, part of the new sacramental order. §8 explains on this basis that marriage is a sacrament of the New Covenant inasmuch as it is a new realization of the primordial sacrament.

§1 The Mystery Hidden from Ages Revealed and Active in Christ (TOB 94:1–5)

94:1 Ephesians 1 presents the mystery "hidden from ages in God" as a gift (cf. "hermeneutics of the gift"; TOB 13:2, 16:1), as a grace eternally destined for man. **94:2** The grace becomes a real part of man through Christ, through redemption in his blood. **94:3** Christ reveals the mystery (sign) and accomplishes it (efficacious). **94:4** The moral instruction in the remainder of the letter is always linked, not only with the revelation of the gift but also with the sacramental order, especially baptism. **94:5** Christ himself is the center of the mystery. The gift of redemption is above all a spousal gift in which he gives himself to the Church as Bride.

§2 The Analogy of Spousal Love (TOB 94:6–95:3)

94:6 The analogy of spousal love allows us to penetrate into the essential content of the mystery. **94:7** The prophets often focus on idolatry and injustice as *adultery* in the spousal relation with God. The love of God for his people can and must be compared to the love that unites bride and bridegroom. The Song of Songs outlines the image of spousal love without any reference to adultery. **94:8–95:1** Quote of Isaiah 54. **95:2** Isaiah 54 does not contain any reproaches, which allows the essential content of the analogy of the conjugal covenant to come to light. The prophet leads us back to the mystery of God's heart, to his spousal love, in the same direction in which the author of Ephesians leads. **95:3** Isaiah 54 reflects the specific mentality of the people of the Old Testament and also reveals the true character of God's gift as grace, as a gratuitous self-initiated declaration of love.

§3 Isaiah and Ephesians (TOB 95:4–7)

95:4 The analogy of God's spousal love and of marriage is linked with the "covenant of peace" (Isiah 54:10) and with God's role as the Redeemer. **95:5** In Ephesians, the first dimension of love is fatherly, not conjugal. **95:6** The analogy of spousal love appears only when the Creator becomes the Redeemer. Being the Redeemer is proper to the Son, beloved from eternity, "in whom we have redemption through his blood according to the riches of his grace." It is as the Redeemer that he gives his spousal gift of self. **95:7** His redeeming love is thus a spousal love by which he marries the Church. This Christological and ecclesiological dimension is only foreshadowed in Isaiah.

§4 Interpretation: The Reality of the Gift, the Meaning of Grace (TOB 95b)

95b:1 The analogy of spousal love has two functions in the revelation of the Old and New Covenant. First, it allows us to penetrate into the essence of the mystery. **95b:2** It allows us to understand the mystery as a love expressed in a total and irrevocable gift of self to the Church. **95b:3** The mystery of the God of the covenant is a mystery of spousal love. **95b:4** The analogy of spousal love emphasizes above all the aspect of God's gift of self, which is a total gift not in the manner of the complete gift that takes place in the Trinity but in the form of a participation in the divine nature. It emphasizes the character of grace as a radical gift. **95b:5** The analogy helps us to understand the mystery of grace as an eternal reality in God and as a historical fruit of redemption.

Second, the analogy allows us to understand marriage itself as an "image and likeness" of the divine mystery the Trinity. **95b:6** It is in this perspective that we approach the sacramentality of marriage. Marriage is connected with the expression of the mystery of divine life in the visible order, with its entry into the sphere of the sign. **95b:7** The visible sign of marriage in the beginning, linked with the visible sign of Christ and the Church, transposes the eternal plan into history and makes it the foundation of the whole sacramental order. Ephesians thus brings the sign of marriage in the beginning together with the sign of Christ and the Church and makes of these two signs the single *great* sign.

§5 Marriage as the Primordial Sacrament (TOB 96:1–97:1)

[*Return to the Analysis of Genesis 19:3–5* (*TOB 96:1*)] **96:1** Man appears in the visible world as the highest expression of the divine giving because he bears within himself the inner dimension of gift. For this reason, he bears the likeness of God. In this dimension, a primordial sacrament is established, a sign that efficaciously transmits in the visible world the invisible mystery of God; namely, the procession of the Son as Truth and the procession of the Holy Spirit as mutual Love. The body was created to transfer this invisible mystery into the visibility of the world.

[*Rereading of These Conclusions* (*TOB 96:2–5*)] **96:2** Ephesians leads us to approach the original state of man from the point of view of the mystery hidden from eternity in God. **96:3** From the beginning, man and woman were chosen in Christ "to be holy and immaculate before him" (Ephesians 1:4). **96:4** They were called to holiness through the grace of adoption as sons in Christ. **96:5** Although this grace preceded the Incarnation, God gave it out of regard for his beloved Son.

[*Rereading the Main Thesis Statement of TOB* (*96:6–97:1*)] **96:6** The body was created to transfer into the visible reality of the world the mystery hidden from eternity in God and thus to be an efficacious sign of it (see TOB 19:4). The divine words of institution ("the man will . . . unite with his wife, and the two shall be one flesh"; Genesis 2:24) thus constitute marriage as the central part of the sacrament of creation, as the primordial sacrament. **96:7** The institution of marriage flows from the Creator's saving initiative in Christ, which gives its efficacy to the original sacrament of creation even though in time the sacrament of creation comes before God's saving initiative in Christ. Marriage was instituted to spread the same sacrament of creation to further generations of human beings. **97:1** This heritage of grace was driven out when man and woman broke the first covenant. Instead of being illuminated by grace, the perspective of procreation was darkened by original sin. Nevertheless, marriage never ceases to be the figure of "the great sacrament." It has remained the platform for the realization of God's plan, which is to bring the sacrament of creation near to human beings and thereby prepare them for the sacrament of Redemption.

§6 "The Sacrament of Redemption" (TOB 97:2–5)

[*The Marital Form of Redemption* (*TOB 97:2–3*)] **97:2** The sacrament of Redemption, which is Christ's spousal gift of self, is the fundamental *great* sign of grace. It clothes itself in the figure and form of the primordial sacrament of marriage in order to renew the grace of the original covenant. **97:3** It is a new realization of the mystery hidden from eternity in God. While the sacrament of creation realized the mystery in the grace of innocence, the sacrament of Redemption realizes the mystery in the grace of forgiveness.

[*Unitive and Procreative Meanings* (*TOB 97:4*)] **97:4** By the power of Christ's spousal gift of self, the sacrament of Redemption becomes a permanent dimension of the life of the Church. It has a unitive meaning inasmuch as it realizes the union of love between Christ and the Church; it also has a procreative meaning inasmuch as it is the origin of the Church's spiritual fruitfulness and motherhood.

[*Visibility of the Mystery* (*TOB 97:5*)] The mystery initially became visible through the marriage of the first man and woman and then in the indissoluble union of Christ with the Church. **97:5** When it becomes visible, the mystery does not cease to be mysterious. The realization of the mystery in Christ's spousal gift of self gives a sacramental stamp to the whole heritage of the covenant in reference to creation as well as redemption. It also gives a sacramental stamp to the conjugal covenant.

§7 Figure and Sacrament of the New Covenant (TOB 98:1–5)

[*Figure and Sacrament* (*TOB 98:1*)] **98:1** On the one hand, the primordial sacrament of marriage is a model and figure of the sacrament of Christ and the Church. On the other hand, when Christ appeals to the original institution of marriage by the Creator, he makes this primordial sacrament an essential part of the new order of redemption. Marriage thus has a twofold relation to the sacramental order in the New Covenant.

[*Figure* (*TOB 98:2*)] **98:2** As the primordial sacrament, marriage is the figure according to which the order of redemption is built. It is assumed and inserted into the sacramental order as the pattern of that order. All the sacraments of the New Covenant have their pattern in marriage.

[*Sacrament* (*TOB 98:3*)] **98:3** When Christ confirms the Creator's plan for marriage, he declares that marriage is an integral part of the new sacramental order.

[*For the Man of Concupiscence* (*TOB 98:4–5*)] **98:4** The new sacramental order differs from the original order in addressing not the man of innocence but the man of concupiscence. **98:5** When we see these points on the background of Christ's teaching about "adultery in the heart," they prepare us in two ways to understand marriage as a sacrament of the New Covenant. First, they prepare us to understand marriage as an integral part of the new sacramental order of being. Second, they prepare us to understand that it bears fruit in the *ethos* of redemption.

§8 The Sacraments of the Church (TOB 98:6–99:3)

[*The Basis of the Sacraments: Christ's Spousal Love* (*TOB 98:6–8*)] **98:6** We turn to the seven sacraments of the Church. **98:7** We have been using *sacrament* in a wider sense than the sacraments that express and confer grace. **98:8** The sacrament of creation (understood in this wider sense) is the basis for understanding the original sacramentality of marriage. The sacrament of Redemption is the basis for understanding the sacramentality of Christ's union with the Church. What is at stake is not only a comparison of this union with marriage but also a renewal of the content of the primordial sacrament. It is in this light that we can understand the sacramentality of marriage as one of the seven sacraments.

[*Baptism, Eucharist but Not Developed* (*TOB 99:1–2*)] **99:1** The manner in which Ephesians alludes to baptism and the Eucharist shows that these sacraments derive their essential significance and sacramental power from the Redeemer's spousal love. **99:2** Yet Ephesians does not present a developed sacramental theology, not even in its teaching about marriage. Nevertheless, it provides the basis for understanding marriage as a sacrament of the New Covenant.

[*Argument for the Sacramentality of Marriage in the Order of Being* (*TOB 99:2*)] The Church herself as the great sacrament, as the new sign of the covenant and of grace, comes forth from the sacrament of Redemption, from Christ's spousal gift of self. Similarly, marriage as the primordial sacrament, as the primordial sign of the covenant and of grace, came forth from the sacrament of creation. This primordial sacrament is realized in a new way—that is, as a sacrament of the New Covenant—in the sacrament of Christ and the Church.

[*Conclusion for the Moral Order* (*TOB 99:2–3*)] In conclusion for the moral order, then, it is for this reason that Ephesians 5:21 asks husband and wife to be "subject to one another in the fear of Christ" and to model their lives on the spousal covenant of grace between Christ and the Church. **99:3** Although Ephesians does not speak directly about marriage as one of the sacraments of the Church, it explains why marriage is sacramental.

3. Sacrament and Redemption of the Body (TOB 99:4–102)

Section 3 brings together the main theological theme of Part One (the redemption of the body) and the main theological theme of Part Two (the sacrament). In this manner it completes the analysis of Ephesians.

Section A brings *redemption* together with *sacrament* by focusing on the words of Jesus discussed in Part One. Section B does the same by focusing on the text of Ephesians discussed in Part Two.

A. The Gospel (TOB 99:4–101:11)

§1 The Words of Christ and the Mystery of Redemption (TOB 99:4–5)

§2 The Sacrament of Redemption and the Indissolubility of Marriage (TOB 99:6–100:4)

§3 Sacrament Given as Grace and Entrusted as an Ethos (TOB 100:5–101:3)

§4 Sacrament as Call to "Life According to the Spirit" (TOB 101:4–6)

§5 Sacrament and the Eschatological Hope of the "Redemption of the Body" (TOB 101:7–11)

Section A brings *sacrament* to bear on *redemption* by focusing on the words of Christ in light of the text of Ephesians. §1 introduces the argument following the sequence of Christ's three words. §2 discusses indissolubility and redemption; §3 and §4 concupiscence and redemption; §5 resurrection and definitive redemption.

§1 The Words of Christ and the Mystery of Redemption (TOB 99:4–5)

99:4 We return to Christ's three words, which he speaks from the divine depth of the redemption of the body. **99:5** These words are a permanent source of hope: of eschatological hope, of everyday hope, and of cosmic hope.

§2 The Sacrament of Redemption and the Indissolubility of Marriage (TOB 99:6–100:4)

99:6 Quote of Christ's word about divorce. **99:7** When he appeals to the primordial sacrament as normative for fallen man, Christ speaks from the depth of the mystery of redemption (see TOB 4:3). Redemption is a new creation that takes up all that is created to express the fullness of justice and holiness. **100:1** Christ's word about indissolubility speaks about the primordial sacrament in which man and woman unite "in Truth and Love" according to "likeness with the union of divine Persons" (*Gaudium et spes* 24). **100:2** The order of being or of the sacrament: when Christ confirms the primordial sacrament instituted by the Creator, he opens it at the same time to the redemption of the body. **100:3** The moral order: on the basis of the mystery of redemption, his word about the indissolubility of the conjugal covenant indicates the new *ethos* of the redemption of the body. The dignity of the human body stands at the root of this indissolubility. **100:4** Redemption is thus given to man in the order of being as the grace of the New Covenant and assigned in the moral order as an *ethos*.

§3 Sacrament Given as Grace and Entrusted as an Ethos (TOB 100:5–101:3)

[*The Teaching of Jesus* (*TOB 100:5–101:1*)] **100:5** The moral dimension is particularly clear in Christ's word about adultery in the heart. This word cannot be separated from the whole sacramental substratum of the conjugal covenant. **100:6** It entrusts the dignity of every woman—the sacrum of her body, to every man, and vice versa—and it entrusts each person's own dignity to him or herself. Although Christ does not directly speak about the sacrament, his word about adultery reaches its full meaning only in relation to the sacrament in both its primordial and historical forms. **100:7** It is a word that penetrates into the depths of the human mystery. In marriage, the sacrament of Redemption is given precisely to the man of concupiscence in the order of being as a grace and sign of the covenant and in the moral order as a task. **101:1** As a sacrament reborn from the spousal love of Christ and the Church, marriage in the order of being is an expression of Christ's saving power and in the moral order an exhortation to gain mastery over concupiscence.

[*The Teaching of Paul* (*TOB 101:2–3*)] **101:2** Paul expresses this twofold—that is, ontological and moral—truth in 1 Corinthians 7, where he says, "each has his own gift from God." A particular grace corresponds to marriage. Paul's moral teaching is built on this foundation. **101:3** The statement "It is better to marry than to be aflame" (1 Corinthians 7:9) has been taken to imply that marriage is a specific remedy of concupiscence. It is true that *aflame* signifies the disorder of the passions and that *marriage* signifies the ethical order in which *eros* and *ethos* meet.

§4 Sacrament as Call to "Life According to the Spirit" (TOB 101:4–6)

101:4 As a sacrament of the Church, *marriage* is a word of the Spirit exhorting man and woman to shape their lives according to the redemption of the body. This redemption gives rise to the hope of every day on the basis of which one can master the concupiscence of the flesh. **101:5** Those who become "one flesh" are called by the sacrament to a "life according to the Spirit." The unitive meaning: in virtue of their *gift*, man and woman can find the true freedom of the gift together with the awareness of the spousal meaning of the body. **101:6** The procreative meaning: Life according to the spirit also expresses itself in mutual *knowledge* (Genesis 4:1), by which the spouses submit their masculinity and femininity to the blessing of fruitfulness. It expresses itself in the deep awareness of the holiness of the new life to which both give rise.

§5 Sacrament and the Eschatological Hope of the "Redemption of the Body" (TOB 101:7–11)

101:7 As the primordial sacrament and as a sacrament of the New Covenant, marriage "comes from the Father . . . and the one who does the will of God will remain in eternity" (1 John 2:16–17). The new life to which husband and wife give rise is destined for eternity. **101:8** This eternal destiny is described in Christ's appeal to the Resurrection. **101:9** Christ affirms that marriage does not belong to the future world. Yet the human beings who will rise originate in marriage. Even more, they are called to the Resurrection because they have their origin in the marriage of their parents. Here lies the meaning of this sacrament for their participation in the future resurrection. **101:10** Marriage contains an eschatological hope. As a sacrament, it immutably serves the purpose that man and woman master their concupiscence and do the will of the Father. The one who "does the will of God will remain in eternity" (1 John 2:17). **101:11** As a sacrament of the temporality of historical man, marriage thus serves man's extratemporal future.

B. Ephesians (TOB 102)

Section B brings *redemption* to bear on *sacrament* by focusing on the text of Ephesians in light of the words of Christ.

§1 shows how Ephesians unites the spousal and the redemptive meaning of love. §2 points to the universality of Christ's spousal and redemptive love as a love that encompasses human life and the cosmos as a whole.

§1 The Spousal and Redemptive Meaning of Love (TOB 102:1–4)

102:1 Ephesians speaks about a "great mystery" of the union of Christ and the Church linked with the primordial sacrament "at the beginning" through the continuity of God's plan of redemption. In this great analogy, marriage as a sacrament is both presupposed as the primordial sacrament and rediscovered as a fruit of redemption. **102:2** Ephesians exhorts man and woman to learn this sacrament anew from the spousal relationship of Christ and the Church. In virtue of its participation in the Christ's saving love, marriage is confirmed and simultaneously renewed as the sacrament of the human beginning, that is, as the sacrament in which man and woman share in the creative love of God both in the unitive and in the procreative meaning of their union. **102:3** The primordial sacrament of marriage is renewed when the spouses receive it as the sacrament of the Church, drawing on the grace that flows from the mystery of redemption. **102:4** Ephesians unites the redemptive and the spousal dimension of Christ's love. Both of these dimensions penetrate together with the grace of the sacrament into the life of the spouses.

§2 Redemption of the Body and "The Sacrament of Man" (TOB 102:5–8)

102:5 The link between the spousal and the redemptive meaning of the body is valid for the hermeneutics of man in general. In this link, the spouses find the answer to the question, "What does it mean to be a body?" **102:6** The spousal and redemptive love of Christ is also the fullest incarnation of the ideal of the unmarried state for the kingdom. **102:7** This love thus passes beyond Christian spouses, who are immediately addressed in the letter, to embrace all human beings and the whole world. In this way "the great sacrament" is a new sacrament; it is the sacrament of man and of the world. **102:8** Man must seek the meaning of his humanity by reaching back to the mystery of creation through the reality of redemption. The union between Christ and the Church allows us to understand how the spousal meaning of the body is completed by its redemptive meaning on all the roads of life: marriage, virginity, suffering, birth, and death.

PART TWO, CHAPTER TWO

The Dimension of Sign (TOB 103–117)

A sacrament is an efficacious sign of grace. Chapter One of Part Two focused on the grace; Chapter Two focuses on the sign.

The Polish *mowa*, translated as "language" in the 2006 edition of TOB, refers to language in the concrete sense of particular words or speech rather than in the abstract sense of a symbol system such as the English language. In this concrete sense, one can tell someone not to use "bad language," and one can "add language" to a contract or "delete language" from it, and so on. What John Paul II has in mind when he speaks about "the language of the body" is thus not "body language" as a system of signs analogous to the English language but the concrete expression of the gift of self in the words of the vow ("I take you" together with the implicit "I give myself to you"). This gift of self in words is fully realized in the consummation of marriage and renewed as an actual gift in each subsequent act that expresses and realizes the total gift of self.

Section 1 develops the concept "speech of the body" in order to outline the full reality of the sacramental sign of marriage (TOB 103–107). Section 2 turns to the Song of Songs to illuminate and unfold this sacramental sign (TOB 108–113). Section 3 takes the prayer of Tobias and Sarah as a point of departure to explain the relation between the speech of the liturgy and the speech of the body in the sacramental sign (TOB 114–117).

1. The Sign of Marriage: Speech of the Body (TOB 103–107)

Section 1 develops the concept of "rereading the speech of the body in the truth" by analyzing the full reality of the sacramental sign. §§1–3 focus on the sacramental sign in itself, and §§4–5 focus on the same sign inasmuch as it must be built by historical man, who is subject to concupiscence.

§1 sketches what is implied in the full reality of the sacramental sign. §§2–4 develop this sketch by the concept of "speech of the body. §2 argues that this speech is prophetic and thus measured by truth. §3 unfolds what rereading this prophetic speech in the truth implies. §4 shows that the task of building the sacramental sign must be accomplished by historical man, who is the man of concupiscence and at the same time the man of the call.

§5 concludes that the hermeneutics of the sacrament confirms the hermeneutics of man presented in Part One, especially the analysis of Christ's teaching about adultery in the heart.

§1 The Marital Promise (TOB 103)

[*The Full Reality of the Sacramental Sign* (*TOB 103:1–4*)] **103:1** With the words "I take you ... as my husband/wife," the man and the woman administer and receive the sacrament. **103:2** These words only signify and realize the coming to be of marriage, however, not its full reality, which is constituted by conjugal intercourse. **103:3** From the words one must therefore pass to the reality. Both are important for the structure or nature of the sacramental sign. The words constitute the sacramental sign not only by what they signify but also together with what they signify. **103:4** The man and the woman themselves, aware of the spousal meaning of their bodies, are part of the reality of the sign when they give themselves to each other. The speech of the body consists of the words of the vow "I take you," together with the fulfillment of this speech in conjugal acts, in which man and woman give themselves to each other afresh.

[*Rereading* (*TOB 103:5–7*)] **103:5** Man and woman take up again the same speech of the body as at the beginning ("one flesh"; Genesis 2:24) as the constitutive content of their communion of persons. **103:6** At the moment of contracting marriage, they thus reread the perennial speech of the body and thereby form the visible and efficacious sign of grace. **103:7** In socio-juridical terms, marriage is a contract. Yet, in theological terms, the key for understanding it is the reality of the sign.

§2 "Prophetism of the Body" (TOB 104)

104:1 That the speech of the body is part of *what* marriage is as a sacramental sign is confirmed by a long biblical tradition. The speech of the body is prophetic, both in the sense that it is present above all in the prophets and in the sense that its content is prophetic. **104:2** The analogy between spousal love and the covenant has two levels.

First, the covenant as the prophets portray it is a marriage: "Your Creator is your husband, Lord of hosts is his name" (Isaiah 54:5). **104:3** The absolute of lordship thus turns out to be the absolute of love. **104:4** Second, the covenant is expressed and realized in the speech of the body, both in the objective and in the subjective or experiential sense. The prophets let the body speak with the mysterious speech of the personal gift and of faithfulness or its opposite. **104:5** Hosea is in a particular way the prophet of Israel's adultery. **104:6** Ezekiel is similar. **104:7** The author of the speech is not the body but the bridegroom and the bride. Yet they would be unable to express this speech without the body. The deepest words of the spirit (love, gift, faithfulness) call for an appropriate speech of the body. **104:8** The prophets use this speech not just with an ethical meaning; *truth* is essential for it. **104:9** The speech of the body is true when it corresponds to the spousal meaning of the body.

§3 "Speech of the Body" Reread in the Truth (TOB 105)

[*Prophetic Speech* (*TOB 105:1–5*)] **105:1** The words of conjugal consent, "I take you," constitute the sacramental sign because they express the spousal meaning of the body. They confirm the truth of the speech of the body and exclude all untruth. **105:2** When man and woman reread the spousal meaning as integrally inscribed in the body, they reread the speech of the body in the truth. When they proclaim this speech, they act prophetically. A prophet is one who expresses the truth that comes from God and does so in the name and with the authority of God. **105:3** In speaking the speech of the body, man and woman thus perform an act of prophetic speech because they proclaim the truth that comes from God and do so in the name and with the authority of God. **105:4** The speech of the body contains the whole richness of the mystery. It draws its prophetic power and sacramental strength from the mystery of creation and redemption. Before being spoken by the spouses, this speech was spoken by God himself in his written word from Genesis through the prophets to Ephesians. **105:5** This is why rereading the speech of the body is an act of prophetic speech.

[*Moral Implications* (*TOB 105:6*)] The words of consent, "I take you," also contain a decision of the spouses to act in conformity with this speech. **105:6** In virtue of this decision, man and woman are the authors of the speech of the body. Their words have a lasting effect, the conjugal bond. This bond gives rise to the ethical task of filling the sign of the sacrament with the contents of conjugal life. Part of the truth of the sign, and consequently part of the *ethos* of conjugal life, is the procreative meaning of the body.

§4 "Speech of the Body" and the Concupiscence of the Flesh (TOB 106:1–107:2)

106:1 The expression "speech of the body" is an example of the analogy of attribution because the one who speaks is not the body as such but man. Yet he speaks on the basis of what can be expressed only through the body. **106:2** In this sense the body speaks like a prophet; that is, it speaks for the person and with the authority of the person. The speech of the body is rich in meanings. Man and woman are called to form their common life in accord with these meanings. **106:3** These meanings are initiated in conjugal consent for the sake of building the same sacramental sign in life as a whole. If man and woman behave in a manner that corresponds to the truth of the speech of the body, then they are in the truth. **106:4** They are called to a testimony worthy of true prophets. **106:5** The sacramental sign must be built by historical man, who is also the man of concupiscence. **107:1** Yet the human heart is not primarily accused and condemned but first of all called. **107:2** The man of concupiscence is at the same time the man of the call. He is called through the mystery of redemption, which implies the *ethos* of redemption.

§5 "Speech of the Body" and "Hermeneutics of the Sacrament" (TOB 107:3–6)

107:3 Concupiscence does not destroy the capacity to reread the speech of the body in the truth. **107:4** Historical man is able to constitute the sacramental sign of conjugal love as an enduring sign because he is redeemed. **107:5** In this way, the hermeneutics of the sacrament confirms the hermeneutics of man presented above. As a conscious subject with the ability of self-determination, man can be the author of marriage as the sacramental sign, as a sign of the divine creation and redemption of the body. **107:6** The hermeneutics of the sacrament allows us to conclude that he is always essentially called and not merely accused.

2. The Maturing of the Sacramental Sign in the Song of Songs (TOB 108–113)

§1 Resuming Genesis: Wonder (TOB 108:1–109:2)
§2 "My Sister, My Bride" (TOB 109:3–110:4)
§3 "A Garden Closed, a Fountain Sealed" (TOB 110:5–111:6)
§4 Eros or Agape? (TOB 112:1–113:6)

Section 2 analyzes the coming to be and maturing of the sacramental sign, according to the Song of Songs.

§1 focuses on the root of the speech of the body: wonder, fascination, desire, and enchantment unfolded by the Song of Songs in continuity with the first man's words of wonder, "This one finally is bone of my bones and flesh of my flesh" (Genesis 2:24). The remaining paragraphs describe the maturing of the sacramental sign on the basis of this primal wonder in two steps, according to the two principles of *Gaudium et spes* 24.

§2 focuses on the first principle, willing the good for the person for his or her own sake. It specifies fascination, desire, and enchantment by arguing that the image of the woman as both sister and bride rereads the speech of the body so as to avoid the woman's reduction to a mere object of sexual desire and expresses the man's disinterested tenderness for her, *disinterested* not in the sense of a lack of interest but of *sincere* gift.

§§3–4 focus on the second principle of *Gaudium et spes* 24, the law of the gift, although it begins with an alternate expression of the first principle. By calling the woman a garden closed and a fountain sealed, the man recognizes her as the master of her own mystery (first principle). This recognition of her freedom of the gift enables the woman to speak the words of definitive gift to the man, "Set me as a seal upon your heart, as a seal upon your arm," which express the maturation of the sacramental sign (second principle). §4 shows that this definitive gift is not simply concluded once and for all but that *eros* remains restless, always in search for a fuller gift. In its jealousy, limitation by death and restlessness, *eros* calls for its own fulfillment and purification in *agape*.

§1 Resuming Genesis: Wonder (TOB 108:1–109:2)

[*Introduction* (*TOB 108:1–3*)] **108:1** The Song of Songs tells us much about the sacramental sign even though it does not explicitly draw the analogy we find in Ephesians. It illumines what rereading the speech of the body in the truth implies. **108:2** It was the source of inspiration of the greatest mystical writers—for example, John of the Cross—and was inserted into the Church's liturgy. **108:3** Although it does not explicitly mention the great analogy, it cannot be separated from the primordial sacrament.

[*Wonder, Fascination, Desire, Enchantment* (*TOB 108:4–109:2*)] **108:4** The Song of Songs unfolds the wonder of discovery experienced by the first man: "This one finally." **108:5** A similar fascination runs in fuller form through its verses. It is a duet that shows how the sign of spousal union is formed. **108:6** In this reciprocal fascination, one can hear the speech of the body. The attraction toward the other person lingers over the body in an enchantment that springs from the experience of beauty. **108:7** The image created by the words of man and woman is at one and the same time an image of experience and an image of the beloved person. **108:8** The metaphors, unfamiliar to us today, show how the speech of the body seeks support and confirmation in the whole visible world. The words "You are all-beautiful, my friend" leave behind all metaphors to focus on the person as a whole. **109:1** The speech of the body is a speech without words, but as a speech of the heart it is the source of inspiration for the poetic words. These words express wonder, not only about the other's *I* but also about love itself. **109:2** The words of both express an experience of values that sheds its rays on everything connected with the other person.

§2 "My Sister, My Bride" (TOB 109:3–110:4)

109:3 Of essential importance in a theology of the body is the question, "Who is she for him, and vice versa?" She is not only *bride but* also *friend* and *sister.* **109:4** *Friend* indicates that love places the second *I* next to one's own. *Sister* is even more deeply rooted in the poem. It expresses both unity in humanity and diversity in sex. It expresses the subjectivity of the feminine *I* in its openness toward the man understood as *brother.* **109:5** It signifies a particular rereading of the speech of the body. **109:6** *Sister* and *bride* do not diverge. They converge in that *sister* overcomes any determination of the speech of the body by libido alone, which is essential for the right understanding of *bride.* **110:1** Love leads the two to a sense of belonging, as if they had a common past and were united by common memories. Feeling like brother and sister allows them to live their closeness in security. **110:2** By expressing the history of the femininity of the bride, *sister* embraces her with a disinterested tenderness that is a necessary foundation of peace. It is the peace of an encounter in humanity as the image of God on the basis of a disinterested gift (*Gaudium et spes* 24). **110:3** *Sister* recalls Genesis 2:23–25, where union in the same humanity as brother and sister under God's fatherhood is the first foundation of the communion of persons. *Sister* expresses a dimension of the experience of femininity that must be present in every experience of love to preserve the richness of the primordial sacrament. **110:4** In this way, the Song of Songs presents a fully authentic understanding of *eros*, authentic with the authenticity of Scripture.

§3 "A Garden Closed, a Fountain Sealed" (TOB 110:5–111:6)

110:5 These images reveal another deep layer of content in the Song of Songs. **110:6** Their beauty is a beauty of the truth: they confirm and surpass what is expressed in *sister* by revealing another vision of the feminine "I." **110:7** They should be read in relation to the conjugal act, in which the woman opens to the man what is most profoundly hidden in herself. She presents herself as the master of her own mystery, which underlines the personal dignity of her gift of self. **110:8** The images reflect the discovery of the inner inviolability of the person and at the same time the consciousness of belonging to the other. "My beloved is mine and I am his" (Song of Songs 2:16). **110:9** In response to her recognition by the man as the master of her own mystery, the woman expresses her gift of self, "I am his," in a depth of trust that corresponds to the inner truth of the person and to the freedom of the gift. **111:1** This inner truth allows man and woman to reread the speech of the body in the truth. Both things grow at the same time: the closeness of the persons to each other and the deepened mystery of the person. **111:2** In the image "Sweet is his fruit apples to my taste" (Song of Songs 2:3), the woman speaks about the discovery of her beloved within herself, in the dimension of the heart. Closeness expressed by the body is a source for the growth of the intimate speech of the heart. The man's words, by contrast, focus more on the visible expression of femininity in her body. **111:3** Quote of Song of Songs 6:13–7:7. **111:4** The "garden closed" opens up before the eyes of the man's soul and body. His words speak about her beauty but above all about gift and self-gift. In all its poverty, Genesis 2:23 ("This one finally") expresses the same experience of union even more powerfully. One must read the wealth of the Song of Songs in light of this poverty of Genesis and vice versa. **111:5** The woman knows that "his desire is for me," and she goes to meet him with the readiness of the gift of self. In this gift, she asks him, "Set me as a seal upon your heart." **111:6** In this way, the visible sign of the sacrament matures as a definitive gift.

§4 Eros or Agape? (TOB 112:1–113:6)

112:1 The Song of Songs shows us the human face of *eros* with authenticity free from defects. In reaching each other, the man and the woman continue to tend toward something further. **112:2** The poem expresses a continual process of tension and search. **112:3** In the words "my perfect one," the man expresses a search for integral beauty, just as Christ desires to see his bride "holy and immaculate" (Ephesians 5:27). **112:4** Love is restless; it is in search and never satisfied. **112:5** In this restlessness, love shows itself as greater than what the body is able to express. From the depth of the union the words come forth, "Love is strong as death" (Song of Songs 8:6). Yet love is definitively limited by death. **113:1** A more interior limitation of *eros* lies in its jealousy. The exclusive and indivisible belonging of man and woman to each other flows from desire, which is not able to surpass the limits of jealousy. **113:2** The restlessness of *eros* shows the continual need for *eros* to surpass itself. The mutual belonging of man and woman to each other is a fruit of the search, and yet a new search springs from this mutual belonging. **113:3** The continuing search shows that a person cannot be appropriated and possessed in a conclusive manner. The truth of the mutual gift continually calls both to reach the very nucleus of the gift of person to person. **113:4** In this manner, *eros* seeks fulfillment by a further truth of love, which Paul expresses in 1 Corinthians 13. **113:5** Do Paul's words confirm the truth of love expressed in the Song of Songs? What is the relation between these two expressions of love? These questions will not be discussed here. Paul seems to point to a love that emerges from another dimension of the person, a love called *agape*. *Agape* brings *eros* to fulfillment while purifying it. **113:6** Presented here is not a commentary on the Song of Songs but a fragment of reflection about the sacrament of marriage, whose visible sign is constituted by rereading the speech of the body in the truth.

3. When the Language of the Body Becomes the Language of the Liturgy (Reflections on Tobit) (TOB 114–117)

Section 3 considers another side of the sacramental sign, its liturgical enactment in the wedding. §§1–3 belong together as reflections on the text of Tobit. §§4–5 belong together as concluding reflections on Ephesians in the dimension of the sacramental sign. §1 argues that the prayer of Tobias and Sarah outlines the liturgical dimension of the sacrament. §2 focuses on life and death as words of the speech of the body taken up into the liturgy. §3 rereads the prayer in detail to show how the speech of the body is taken up into the liturgy.

§4 returns to Ephesians and reverses the argument. The speech of the liturgy must become speech of the body. §5 concludes in this light that the integral meaning of the sacramental sign lies in the spiritual maturity of the mutual fascination of man and woman as portrayed in the Song of Songs.

§1 The Marriage of Tobias and Sarah (TOB 114)

114:1 Quote of the night prayer of Tobias and Sarah. **114:2** The Book of Tobit portrays husband and wife as brother and sister. **114:3** It does so not only because Tobias and Sarah are cousins but also because, "from now on," a relation is to be formed between them similar to that between brother and sister. **114:4** According to the Song of Songs, "love is strong as death." In Tobit, the threat of death hangs over Tobias. **114:5** A demon killed all seven of Sarah's husbands before they could consummate the marriage. **114:6** From the first moment, Tobias's love has to face this threat, this test of life or death. **114:7** Life wins the victory through prayer. **114:8** In this prayer, the dimension of the liturgy proper to the sacrament is outlined against the background of the speech of the body.

§2 Love as a Test (TOB 115)

[*The Words of Life and Death* (*TOB 115:1–3*)] **115:1** In comparison with the rich speech of the body expressed in the Song of Songs, Tobit is spare and sober. What stands in the foreground is Tobias's readiness to share in Sarah's lot, even to the point of death. Love is validated by *ethos*. **115:2** The truth and strength of love are shown in the ability of love to enter the battle between good and evil, confident in the victory of the good. **115:3** In these circumstances, the rich dialogue of love falls silent, and the speech of the body is spoken with the words of choices and acts. The body expresses itself through the mystery of life and death.

[*The Words of the Liturgy* (*TOB 115:4–6*)] **115:4** The dimension of the liturgy takes up into itself the speech of the body reread in the truth of human hearts. The duet of love is replaced by the unison of prayer. **115:5** Prayer becomes the one and only way to repel the threat of evil by preventing the evil spirit from having access to the soul. **115:6** Tobias and Sarah open themselves totally in the unity of the two to the living God. Their prayer is a model of the liturgy, whose word is a word of power drawn from the sources of the covenant and of grace.

§3 The Prayer of the New Spouses (TOB 116)

116:1 The prayer is above all praise and thanksgiving on the cosmic background of the praise and blessing sung by the whole of creation. The spouses recall the creation of Eve as "a help similar to himself." **116:2** These words are the core of their conjugal creed. They reread the speech of the body in its divine source. In this way, the speech of the body becomes the speech of the liturgy. **116:3** This speech includes a moment of purification: not out of lust. **116:4** In the prayer, the speech of the body is an objectivized speech filled with the truth of existence. When the spouses profess this truth before God, the speech of the body becomes the speech of the liturgy spoken by the ministers of the sacrament as a sign of the covenant of God with man. They respond to God's call contained in the mystery of the beginning. **116:5** Both the ardent words of love in the Song of Songs and the words of prayer in Tobit share in forming the sacramental sign. Through one as well as the other, the speech of the body becomes the speech of the liturgy.

§4 When the Speech of the Liturgy Becomes the "Speech of the Body" (TOB 117)

117:1 We return to Ephesians to reread this text under the aspect of the sacramental sign. Ephesians reveals the eternal sources of the covenant in the love of the Father and its definitive institution in Christ. This connection explains the sacramentality of marriage also in the dimension of sign. **117:2** Husbands must love their wives "as their own bodies" and "as themselves." **117:3** These words do not contain the speech of the body in the whole richness of its subjective meaning as presented in the Song of Songs, but they objectively confirm it. In this way, Ephesians offers a personalistic commentary on "they shall be one flesh." The speech of the liturgy is equally personalistic. **117:4** "As their own bodies" and "as themselves" indicate a moral unity that is a fruit of love. Love makes the other *I* in a certain way one's own. **117:5** In this way, the speech of the body, seen in light of the personalistic commentary of Ephesians, becomes the speech of the liturgy. Ephesians thus shows how, through the speech of the body reread in the truth, the sacramental sign of marriage is built up in the speech of the liturgy. **117:6** Conversely, the speech of the liturgy ought to form the speech of the body, the absolute meaning of which can be reached only in the analogy of the love of Christ and the Church.

§5 The Sacramental Sign: "Mysterium and Ethos" (TOB 117b)

117b:1 Ephesians extends the mystical analogy of Christ and the Church to the speech of the body. **117b:2** It thereby brings the speech of the body closer to real holiness. The liturgy elevates the conjugal covenant to "the mystery" and entrusts the sacred character of the person and the communion of persons as a task to man and woman. **117b:3** It is in this sense that the speech of the liturgy becomes speech of the body, giving rise to a series of acts and tasks that form the spirituality of marriage. "Be subject to one another in the fear of Christ." "The woman should have reverence toward her husband." According to these texts, the speech of the body expresses itself both in the deep mutual fascination and pleasure expressed in the Song of Songs, and also in the experience of the sacred infused into the sign by the *mystery*. **117b:4** The "fear of Christ" and *reverence* demanded by Ephesians is nothing other than a spiritually mature form of the mutual fascination of man and woman. The spiritual maturity of this fascination is a fruit of the gift of fear or reverence. **117b:5** Mutual fascination matures spiritually through the virtue of temperance and the gift of fear. In this way, the speech of the sacrament becomes speech of the body in a depth, simplicity, and beauty hitherto unknown. **117b:6** This is the integral meaning of the sacramental sign.

PART TWO, CHAPTER THREE

He Gave Them the Law of Life as Their Inheritance (TOB 118–133)

1. The Ethical Problem (TOB 118–125)

§§1–3 set the context for discussing the ethical problem of contraception and natural family planning. §§4–6 focus on the ethical problem, first negatively and then positively.

In setting the context, §1 connects the teaching of *Humanae vitae* with the discussion of the sacramental sign: what is at stake in the moral norm about contraception is simply rereading the speech of the body in the truth. Decisive for this truth is the nature of the conjugal act and of the acting persons. §2 shows that Paul VI not only proposed the norm but also had an effective pastoral concern for its practicability. §3 argues through an analysis of the relevant passages of *Gaudium et spes* and *Humanae vitae* that "responsible parenthood" is an ethical concept that includes respect for the norm proposed by *Humanae vitae*.

§4 focuses on the moral defect of contraception; §5 on the moral good that can be present in the natural regulation of fertility. §6 shows how person, nature, and method are related in this moral good.

§1 The Moral Norm and the Truth of the "Speech of the Body" (TOB 118:1–119:2)

118:1 Our reflections on human love in the divine plan must be completed by a look at their concrete application in conjugal morality as proposed by the encyclical *Humanae vitae*. **118:2** The teaching of the encyclical is built on the inseparable connection between the unitive and the procreative meaning of the conjugal act. **118:3** This teaching is closely related to our reflections about the sacramental sign of marriage. **118:4** The sign is based on the speech of the body reread in the truth. Precisely in the conjugal act, which is so full of meaning, it is important to reread the speech of the body in the truth. This is a condition for acting in the truth, for conformity with the moral norm. **118:5** The basis of this norm is the innermost structure or nature of the conjugal act and of the acting subjects. **118:6** Because the act is both unitive and procreative by nature, man and woman must, with the necessity proper to reason (logical necessity), read the two meanings and their inseparable connection. Nothing else is at stake here but rereading the speech of the body in the truth, first in the ontological dimension (innermost structure), then in the subjective and psychological dimension (meaning). The encyclical underlines this norm of the natural law. **119:1** At the same time, it underlines the subjective and psychological dimension when it speaks about meaning. Meaning is born in consciousness with the rereading of the ontological truth of the object. **119:2** The norm and the corresponding ordering of sexual acts consist in the adequate rereading of the meanings and their inseparable connection.

§2 The Rightness of the Norm and Its "Practicability" (TOB 119:3–120:6)

[*Rightness* (*TOB 119:3–120:2*)] **119:3** The norm is not just part of the natural law, in conformity with reason as such; it also corresponds to revealed teaching as a whole as contained in the biblical sources. **119:4** The theology of the body is the ultimate foundation of the norm. **119:5** The norm thus concerns all human beings, and in a special way all believers, because it is supported by the *ethos* of the redemption of the body. **120:1** The encyclical develops the teaching of *Gaudium et spes*, in particular its teaching that there cannot be a contradiction between divine laws pertaining to the transmission of life and those pertaining to fostering conjugal love. **120:2** While *Gaudium et spes* excludes the contradiction between these two, *Humanae vitae* affirms an inseparable connection.

[*Practicability* (*TOB 120:3–6*)] **120:3** Like *Gaudium et spes*, *Humanae vitae* is a pastoral document that responds to the questions of contemporary men and women, particularly to the concern that observing the norm against contraception requires heroic sacrifices. **120:4** *Humanae vitae* engages this question in all its weight. It argues that the efforts to observe the norm ennoble man and benefit the human community. **120:5** The encyclical speaks about both noncontradiction on the level of norms and the possibility of observing the divine law. This possibility belongs to the very nature of divine law. **120:6** The theology of the body confirms the norm and prepares us to consider the practical and pastoral question at greater depth. The true good of the person consists in putting the divine plan into practice.

§3 Responsible Parenthood (TOB 120:6–122:3)

120:6 (continued) *Humanae vitae* not only recalls the moral norm but also is concerned with the possibility of observing it. On this basis we can approach the topic of responsible parenthood.

[*Gaudium et spes* (*TOB 121:1–3*)] **121:1** The Council speaks about "responsible transmission of life" by pointing to objective standards: husband and wife may not use methods of birth control found blameworthy by the Magisterium. **121:2** It enumerates factors that must be considered to reach a responsible judgment and then insists, "The parents themselves and no one else should ultimately make this judgment in the sight of God." **121:3** The judgment of conscience must be measured by the divine law authentically interpreted by the Magisterium.

[*Humanae vitae* (*TOB 121:4–122:3*)] **121:4** The encyclical defines responsible parenthood in light of an integral conception of man and thus avoids limiting this concept to birth control. **121:5** Responsible parenthood is exercised not only in limiting but also in increasing the number of children, both in accord with the objective moral order. **121:6** Man and woman cannot proceed at will but must be faithful to God's creative intention. **122:1** Responsible parenthood thus includes observing the distinction between morally licit and morally illicit methods. Recourse to the infertile period is morally licit. **122:2** There is an essential ethical difference between this recourse and contraception. **122:3** Nevertheless, those who have recourse to the infertile period can lack valid reasons for avoiding another child. Still, the fact remains that such recourse and contraception have their own intrinsic moral qualification, positive and negative.

§4 The Truth of the "Speech of the Body" and the Evil of Contraception (TOB 122:4–123:8)

[*Introductory Points* (*TOB 122:4–5*)] **122:4** In the normative dimension, *Humanae vitae* specifies and clarifies the principles of action; in the pastoral dimension, it shows the possibility of acting according to these principles. We must see this normative-pastoral whole in light of the theology of the body. **122:5** The theology of the body is both a theory and pedagogy of the body because it is based on the Gospel, which is God's salvific message about man's true good.

[*The Essence of the Question* (*TOB 123:1*)] **123:1** The essence of the Church's teaching about the transmission of life is to maintain the right relationship between man's power over nature and his self-mastery. The extension of power over nature to every sphere of life threatens the person, for whom self-mastery is the natural method. The extension of power into the area that should be shaped by self-mastery breaks the constitutive dimension of the person, deprives man of the subjectivity proper to him, and turns him into an object of manipulation.

[*The Moral Argument* (*TOB 123:2–8*)] **123:2** The human body expresses the person, which reveals itself through the speech of the body. This is the personalistic aspect of the question. The speech of the body should express the truth of the sacrament. This is the sacramental or theological aspect. *Humanae vitae* carries both aspects to their final consequences. **123:3** The unity of the personalistic and the sacramental dimension corresponds to the revelation of the body. Man and woman are called by God to become witnesses and interpreters of the eternal plan of love by becoming the ministers of the sacrament. **123:4** As ministers of the sacrament, they are called to express the speech of their bodies in all the truth that properly belongs to it. In the conjugal act, through its tension and enjoyment, the person speaks. As a speech of the person, the speech of the body is subject to the demand for truth. **123:5** Inasmuch as man possesses himself, he can give himself in the freedom of the gift through the conjugal act. Because the union achieved in this act is a communion of persons, the speech of the body must be judged by the criterion of truth. **123:6** According to this criterion, the conjugal act means not only the union of love but also potential fruitfulness. One cannot separate these two because both belong to the innermost truth of the conjugal act. The one is realized with and through the other. When one deprives the conjugal act of its inner truth because one artificially deprives it of its procreative capacity, it also ceases to be an act of love. **123:7** A real bodily union is brought about, but it violates the inner order of conjugal communion. This constitutes the essential evil of the contraceptive act. **123:8** The reflections on the sacramental sign of marriage are especially important for understanding this argument. The essence of the violation of the conjugal act by contraception cannot be understood without reflections on the concupiscence of the flesh.

§5 Ethical Regulation of Fertility: Primacy of Virtue (TOB 124)

124:1 *Humanae vitae* approves the natural regulation of fertility and responsible parenthood based on it. **124:2** This honorable practice demands that husband and wife have solid convictions about the true values of life and of the family and self-mastery in the practice of periodic abstaining. **124:3** These convictions are the basis of the pedagogy of the body outlined by the 1980 Synod of Bishops and the post-synodal exhortation *Familiaris consortio*. **124:4** Purity as life according to the Spirit is the true basis on which Paul VI defines responsible parenthood. Periodic abstaining is not a matter of mere technique but of the virtue of purity. **124:5** In reverence, husband and wife understand themselves as ministers rather than arbiters of the Creator's plan. There must be serious reasons for periodic abstaining. **124:6** Periodic abstaining is an exercise of conjugal purity. It is a natural method inasmuch as it is in conformity with natural law, with the order of nature as understood by right reason. The virtue is determined by faithfulness to the personal Creator, who is the source and Lord of the order shown in the natural law.

§6 Ethical Regulation of Fertility: Person, Nature, and Method (TOB 125)

125:1 The ethical regulation of fertility is natural inasmuch as it corresponds to the dignity of the person, which belongs by nature to the person. Ethical regulation of fertility is nothing other than rereading the speech of the body in the truth. The natural rhythms of the body belong to the objective truth of this speech. **125:2** This teaching does not reduce ethics and the speech of the body to biology, as some mistakenly hold, but it ensures the integral truth of that speech. What is the true good of the human person? What corresponds to the dignity of the person? **125:3** The use of infertile periods can be an abuse if husband and wife fall short of the just number of children, which must be determined not only in light of the good of one's own family, health, and means but also in light of the common good of the Church and of humanity. Responsible parenthood is not one-sidedly a matter of limiting the number of children but can include the readiness to welcome a greater number of children. **125:4** *Humanae vitae* gives primacy to ethics. It is a common way of thinking to detach the natural method from ethics and give primacy to merely functional or even utilitarian aspects. In this way of thinking, the natural method appears as just another form of contraception. **125:5** For this reason, we must have a deep grasp of the ethical dimension, especially temperance. **125:6** We must also understand the moral values that are close to temperance. **125:7** In this way, the encyclical completes the picture. It proposes an attitude that builds on the moral maturity of the persons and that completes this maturity.

2. Conjugal Spirituality (TOB 126–132)

Section 2 outlines the spirituality of conjugal life based on *Humanae vitae*.

§1 argues that the love poured out in the heart by the Holy Spirit is the main power that forms conjugal spirituality. The task of this love is to coordinate the ends of marriage according to the hierarchy of these ends, in which procreation is primary.

§§2–4 discuss the virtue of temperance, first in itself as a virtue (§§2–3). §2 discusses the nature and effects of temperance. §3 discusses the task of temperance in relation to sexual arousal and erotic emotion. §4 discusses the same virtue of temperance in its relation to the gift of reverence. The gift of the Holy Spirit that stands at the heart of conjugal spirituality is reverence, the living and conscious sense for the presence of what is holy.

§1 The Powers That Flow from Sacramental "Consecration" (TOB 126:1–127:3)

[*Introduction* (*TOB 126:1–4*)] **126:1** Quote of *Humanae vitae* 25. Husband and wife receive from the sacrament of marriage the consecration and strength to carry out their vocation. **126:2** *Humanae vitae* lays down the premises for a spirituality of conjugal life. The theology of the body understood also as pedagogy of the body is the essential core of conjugal spirituality. **126:3** Responsible parenthood understood integrally is a component of conjugal spirituality as a whole. **126:4** Also in marriage, "the gate is narrow, and the way is hard that leads to life." The hope of future life opens the horizons of powers that guide husband and wife along this way.

[*The Power of Love and Its Task* (*TOB 126:5–127:3*)] **126:5** The essential and fundamental power that flows from sacramental consecration is love, poured out in the heart by the Holy Spirit. Love allows the spouses to build up their life together according to the truth of the sign. **127:1** Love is a power given to the human person to participate in the love with which God loves. The powers of concupiscence detach the speech of the body from the truth while the power of love strengthens this speech in the truth. **127:2** Love safeguards the inseparable unity of the two meanings of the conjugal act. **127:3** The task of love is to coordinate the ends of marriage, according to which the moral order of conjugal life is constituted. Although *Gaudium et spes* and *Humanae vitae* do not use the terms "primary end" and "secondary end," they confirm the traditional teaching of the ends of marriage and their hierarchy: procreation, mutual aid, and remedy of concupiscence.

§2 Analysis of the Virtue of Temperance (TOB 127:4–129:1)

[*Introduction* (*TOB 127:4–5*)] **127:4** The most common objection against *Humanae vitae* is that the need for periodic abstinence contradicts the need for husband and wife to express their love in the conjugal act. Love excludes this contradiction, in theory and above all in practice. One should not speak about contradiction, only about a difficulty that arises from the concupiscence of the flesh. **127:5** Love is by nature linked with purity, which implies self-mastery and temperance. Ephesians alludes to this understanding of temperance when it says, "be subject to one another in the fear of Christ." A deeper analysis of temperance is necessary to understand this point.

[*The Nature and Effects of Temperance* (*TOB 128:1–129:1*)] **128:1** Education in self-control requires a clear perception of the values expressed in the norm accompanied by the corresponding disposition of the will. "Mutual submission" signifies the shared concern of husband and wife for the truth of the speech of the body, while "in the fear of Christ" signifies the gift of the fear of God as a gift of the Holy Spirit. **128:2** To say that temperance opposes the concupiscence of the flesh is true but not enough. What is more important in temperance is opening oneself to the deeper and more mature values that are part of the spousal meaning of the body. **128:3** Here we see the organic link between purity and the power of love poured out in the heart by the Holy Spirit, by which husband and wife become more sensitive to the deeper and more mature values connected with the spousal meaning of the body. The ascesis of temperance does not impoverish the expressions of love but makes them spiritually more intense and richer. **128:4** In this light one can see that there is no contradiction between the unitive and the procreative meaning of the conjugal act when conception needs to be avoided, only a difficulty for the man of concupiscence. Precisely because of this difficulty, the ascetical commitment of man and woman is necessary to realize the true order of conjugal life. **128:5** This order implies a subjective harmony between parenthood and union created by purity. Both the conjugal act and other expressions of love thereby acquire the dignity proper to them. **128:6** The conjugal act is a specific kind of expression of love because it is procreative. Chastity reveals many other kinds of expression of love. It does not do harm to the communion of the spouses. **129:1** Some think that temperance causes inner tensions from which the spouses must free themselves. On the contrary, temperance is the only way to free oneself from such tensions. It is a spiritual effort to express the speech of the body in the truth and authentic richness of an expression of love.

§3 Temperance between "Arousal" and "Emotion" (TOB 129:2–130:5)

[*Introduction* (*TOB 129:2–4*)] **129:2** Parenthood is responsible when it corresponds to the personal dignity of man and woman, to the truth of their person and their conjugal act. What is at stake is an authentically humanistic meaning of the development and progress of human civilization. **129:3** The question of *Humanae vitae* is not reducible to biology but goes back to the subjectivity of the human person. **129:4** Within that subjectivity, there is a distinction between arousal and emotion. Arousal is in the first place bodily and sexual, while emotion refers to the other person as a whole.

[*The Task of Temperance, the Ordering of Arousal and Emotion* (*TOB 129:5–130:2*)] **129:5** Temperance is not mainly the ability to abstain but to order both arousal and emotion in their content and character. **129:6** It has the task of maintaining the equilibrium between arousal, which tends toward the conjugal act, and emotion, which can limit itself to other expressions of the spousal meaning of the body that do not include the procreative meaning. **130:1** Temperance is able to direct arousal toward its correct development and to orient emotion toward the intensification of its pure and disinterested character. **130:2** Arousal and emotion are not opposites, but arousal does and ought to imply a deep emotional stirring by the other person. Letting oneself be stirred in this way by the other person is part of what it means to be "subject to one another in the fear of Christ."

[*The Effects of Temperance* (*TOB 130:3–5*)] **130:3** *Humanae vitae* gives due attention to the regularity of the woman's cycle, but the question of responsible parenthood, which has such a deeply personalistic and sacramental meaning, cannot be resolved on the level of biology alone. **130:4** The naturalness of the natural method is not a mechanical application of biological laws. It is naturalness on the level of the person, of the freedom of the gift. **130:5** The human body is oriented from within to the communion of persons. In this consists its spousal meaning. Concupiscence deforms this meaning almost at its roots. In its mature form, temperance reveals the purity of that meaning and thus develops the personal communion between man and woman. This is precisely what *Humanae vitae* affirms in showing the two aspects of this truth: the personalistic and the theological.

§4 The Gift of Reverence (TOB 131:1–132:5)

[*The Place of Reverence in Conjugal Spirituality* (*TOB 131:1–3*)] **131:1** According to *Humanae vitae*, love poured out in the heart by the Holy Spirit is the fundamental power of conjugal spirituality. This love is connected with conjugal purity, which allows the development of the many expressions of love in the meaning proper to them. **131:2** At the center of conjugal spirituality stands purity, as a virtue connected with the gift of reverence for everything that comes from God. This is part of the meaning of "be subject to one another in the fear of Christ." **131:3** The spouses cannot realize their union as a communion of persons except through the powers of the Holy Spirit. Conjugal spirituality is thus open to the gifts of the Holy Spirit.

[*The Functions of Reverence* (*TOB 131:4–132:5*)] **131:4** The gift of reverence gives spouses a singular sensibility for everything that comes from the mystery of creation and redemption, including the two inseparable meanings of the conjugal act. **131:5** In its negative function, reverence implies a fear of violating what bears the sign of the mystery of creation and redemption. In its positive function, it is a sensibility full of veneration for the essential values of conjugal union. It harmonizes union with responsible parenthood by eliminating the appearance of contradiction between them. **131:6** The regulation of fertility in accord with the natural rhythms is thus part of Christian conjugal spirituality. Only if one lives "according to the Spirit" does this regulation become interiorly true and authentic. **132:1–2** The gift of reverence united with love and purity helps one to understand, among the many acts that express love, the exceptional meaning of the act that is both unitive and procreative. It thereby protects the dignity of this expression of love. **132:3** It helps one to ensure that this act does not lose its interior content, that it does not become routine. **132:4** The fundamental fruit of the gift of the Holy Spirit is a deep understanding of the personal dignity of both the masculine and the feminine *I* in conjugal life. It is from here that all the expressions of love draw true spousal meaning. **132:5** This fruit is decisive for the spiritual identification of what is bodily and personal. From this spiritual identification arises the awareness of what it means to become one flesh. Only this deep and all-encompassing attention to the person creates the climate in which responsible parenthood can mature.

[§5 Conclusion of the Discussion of Conjugal Spirituality (TOB 132:6)]

132:6 *Humanae vitae* allows us to draw an outline of conjugal spirituality. This spirituality is the human and supernatural climate in which the inner harmony of marriage is formed in relation to the two meanings of the conjugal act. On its basis, spouses can live together in the inner truth of the speech of the body. *Humanae vitae* proclaims the inseparability of the connection between this truth and love.

3. Conclusion (TOB 133)

133:1 One can grasp the catecheses under the title "Human Love in the Divine Plan" or, to reflect the two parts of the work, "The Redemption of the Body and the Sacramentality of Marriage." The first part was devoted to an analysis of Christ's words, the second to an analysis of the sacrament. We developed a theology of the body by focusing on the moment in which the light of revelation first touches the human body. The words "and the two shall be one flesh" stand at the basis of our argument. **133:2** All the reflections about "The Redemption of the Body and the Sacramentality of Marriage" were an extensive commentary on *Humanae vitae*. **133:3** The analysis of the biblical aspects of this encyclical is important for the development of theology. The intense development of philosophical anthropology helped us in unfolding the text of Scripture. The analysis of the personalistic aspects shows that the fundamental problem is the authentic development of the human person. **133:4** The questions raised by *Humanae vitae* run through the whole of our reflections. Although the chapter on the encyclical is the last, it stands at the beginning of the whole. This is important from the point of view of structure and method. To face the questions raised by the encyclical, one must find the biblical theological sphere, which we called "the redemption of the body and the sacramentality of marriage."

SELECT BIBLIOGRAPHY

The authors whose work has been especially helpful are marked with an asterisk.

Aguas, Jove Jim S. "Aquinas and Wojtyla on the Human Person and Human Dignity." *Budhi* 13 (2009).

———. "Karol Wojtyla: On Person and Subjectivity." *Ad Veritatem* 8 (2009): 413–53.

———. *Person, Action and Love: The Philosophical Thoughts of Karol Wojtyla (John Paul II).* Manila: University of Santo Tomas, 2014.

*Allen, Prudence. *The Concept of Woman I: The Aristotelian Revolution, 750 B.C.–A. D. 1250.* Grand Rapids, MI: Eerdmans, 1997.

———. "Philosophy and Relation in John Paul II's New Feminism." In *Women in Christ: Toward a New Feminism*, ed. Michele M. Schumacher, 67–104. Grand Rapids, MI: Eerdmans, 2004.

———. *The Concept of Woman II: The Early Humanist Reformation, 1250–1500.* Grand Rapids, MI: Eerdmans, 2005.

———. "Four Principles of Complementary: A Philosophical Perspective." In *Pope Francis, Not Just Good, but Beautiful: The Complementary Relationship between Man and Woman*, ed. Helen Alvaré and Stevan Lopes, 49–60. Walden, NY: Plough, 2015.

———. *The Concept of Woman III: The Search for the Communion of Persons.* Grand Rapids, MI: Eerdmans, 2016.

Anderson, Carl A., and José Granados, eds. *Called to Love: Approaching John Paul II's Theology of the Body.* Garden City, NY: Doubleday, 2012.

———. *Llamados al amor: Teología del cuerpo en Juan Pablo II.* Burgos: Monte Carmelo, 2011.

Anderson, Carl A., and William J. Gribbin, eds. *The Family in the Modern World: A Symposium on Pope John Paul II's Familiaris Consortio.* Washington, DC: American Family Institute, 1982.

*Anscombe, Elizabeth. "Contraception and Chastity." In *Faith in a Hard Ground: Essays on Religion, Philosophy, and Ethics by G. E. M. Anscombe*, ed. Mary Geach and Luke Gormally, 170–91. Charlottesville, VA: Imprint Academic, 2008.

———. "On *Humanae Vitae*." In *Faith in a Hard Ground: Essays on Religion, Philosophy, and Ethics by G. E. M. Anscombe*, ed. Mary Geach and Luke Gormally, 192–98. Charlottesville, VA: Imprint Academic, 2008.

———. "Address to the Clergy: On Contraception and Natural Family Planning." In *Faith in a Hard Ground: Essays on Religion, Philosophy, and Ethics by G. E. M. Anscombe*, ed. Mary Geach and Luke Gormally, 199–205. Charlottesville, VA: Imprint Academic, 2008.

———. "Contraception, Chastity, and the Vocation of Marriage." In *Faith in a Hard Ground: Essays on Religion, Philosophy, and Ethics by G. E. M. Anscombe*, ed. Mary Geach and Luke Gormally, 206–13. Charlottesville, VA: Imprint Academic, 2008.

Aranda, Antonio, ed. *Trinidad y salvación: Estudios sobre la trilogía trinitaria de Juan Pablo II*. Pamplona: Ediciones Universidad de Navarra, 1990.

Arjonillo, Rolando B. *Conjugal Love and the Ends of Marriage: A Study of Dietrich von Hildebrand and Herbert Doms in the Light of the Pastoral Constitution Gaudium et Spes*. New York: P. Lang, 1998.

*Asci, Donald P. *The Conjugal Act as Personal Act: A Study of the Catholic Concept of the Conjugal Act in the Light of Christian Anthropology*. San Francisco: Ignatius Press, 2002.

———. "Conjugal Chastity and the Procreative Personalism of Pope John Paul II." *Josephinum Journal of Theology* 14 (2007): 182–206.

———. "Integration in Action: The Conjugal Act and the Sincere Practice of Conjugal Chastity." In *Una caro: Il linguaggio del corpo e l'unione coniugale*, ed. José Granados, 75–100. Siena: Cantagalli, 2014.

Ashley, Benedict. *Theologies of the Body: Humanist and Christian*. Braintree, MA: Pope John Center, 1995.

Atkinson, Joseph C. "Nuptiality as a Paradigmatic Structure of Biblical Revelation." In *Dialoghi sul mistero nuziale: Studi offerti al Cardinale Angelo Scola*, ed. Gilfredo Marengo and Bruno Ognibeni, 15–34. Rome: Lateran University Press, 2003.

———. "The Revelation of Love in the Song of Songs." In *The Way of Love: Reflections of Pope Benedict XVI's Encyclical Deus Caritas Est*, ed. Livio Melina and Carl A. Anderson, 123–36. San Francisco: Ignatius Press, 2006.

Balmaseda, María Fernanda. "'Metafísica del pudor': Un aspecto central de la filosofía del cuerpo en 'Amor y responsabilidad' de Karol Wojtyla." *Espiritu: Cuadernos del Instituto Filosófico de Balmesiana* 59 (2010): 517–37.

Barron, Robert. "The Christian Humanism of Karol Wojtyła and Thomas Aquinas." *Nova et Vetera* 3 (2005): 529–42.

Beattie, Tina. "Deforming God: Why Nothing Really Matters. A Lacanian Reading of Thomas Aquinas." *New Blackfriars* 95 (2014): 218–33.

———. "Dignity, Difference and Rights: A Gendered Theological Analysis." *Louvain Studies* 40 (2017): 58–81.

Bellusci, David. "Others as Gift in the Personalism of Karol Wojtyla." *Maritain Studies/Etudes Maritainiennes* 31 (2015): 34–46.

Böckle, Franz. "Birth Control: A Survey of German, French and Dutch Literature on the Question of Birth Control." *Concilium* 5 (1965): 97–129.

———. "Möglichkeiten einer dynamischen Sexualmoral." In *Menschliche Sexualität und kirchliche Sexualmoral: Ein Dauerkonflikt*, ed. Franz Böckle, 123–38. Düsseldorf: Patmos Verlag, 1977.

———. "'*Humanae Vitae*' und die philosophische Anthropologie Karol Wojtylas: Zur päpstlichen Lehrposition zur künstlichen Befruchtung und ihrer Begründung." *Herder-Korrespondenz* 43 (1989): 374–80.

———. "*Humanae vitae* Als Prüfstein des wahren Glaubens: Zur kirchenpolitischen Dimension moraltheologischer Fragen." *Stimmen der Zeit* 208 (1990): 3–16.

Böckle, Franz, and Carl Holenstein, eds. *Die Enzyklika in der Diskussion: Eine orientierende Dokumentation zu "Humanae vitae."* Zürich: Benziger, 1968.

Bonino, Serge-Thomas. "Thomisme et personnalisme selon Jean-Paul II." *Recherches Philosophiques* 5 (2009): 219–32.

———. "Saint Thomas d'Aquin dans l'exhortation apostolique *Amoris laetitia.*" In *San Tommaso il matrimono e la famiglia*, ed. Serge-Thomas Bonino and Guido Mazzotta, 25–42. Rome: Urbaniana University Press, 2019.

Bonino, Serge-Thomas, and Guido Mazzotta, eds. *San Tommaso il matrimono e la famiglia.* Rome: Urbaniana University Press, 2019.

Boone, N. S. "D. H. Lawrence's Theology of the Body: Intersections with John Paul II's Man and Woman He Created Them." *Religion and the Arts* 18 (2014): 498–520.

Bouyer, Louis. "*Humanae Vitae* Ten Years After: Toward a Positive Theology of Marriage." *American Journal of Jurisprudence* 25 (1980): 133–45.

Boyle, John, ed. *Creative Love: The Ethics of Human Reproduction.* Front Royal, VA: Christendom Press, 1989.

Boyle, Joseph, John Finnis, and Germain Grisez. "Every Marital Act Ought to Be Open to New Life." *Thomist* 52 (1988): 365–426.

Bransfield, Brian J. *The Human Person According to John Paul II.* Boston: Pauline Books and Media, 2010.

Brock, Stephen Louis. "Is Uniqueness at the Root of Personal Dignity? John Crosby and Thomas Aquinas." *Thomist* 69 (2005): 173–201.

Brown, Susan Mader. "*Mulieris dignitatem:* A New Perspective on the Image of God." *Journal of Dharma* 23 (1998): 501–16.

Budziszewski, J. *On the Meaning of Sex.* Wilmington, DE: Intercollegiate Studies Institute, 2014.

*Burke, Cormac. "Marriage and Contraception." In *Creative Love: The Ethics of Human Reproduction*, ed. John Boyle, 151–67. Front Royal, VA: Christendom Press, 1989.

———. "Personalism and the Bona of Marriage." *Studia Canonica* 27 (1993): 401–12.

———. "The Object of the Marital Self-Gift as Presented in Canon 1057, para 2." *Studia Canonica* 31 (1997): 403–21.

———. *Covenanted Happiness.* San Francisco: Scepter, 1999.

———. "A Postscript to the 'Remedium concupiscentiae.'" *Thomist* 70 (2006): 481–536.

———. *The Theology of Marriage: Personalism, Doctrine, and Canon Law.* Washington, DC: Catholic University of America Press, 2015.

Butler, Sara. "Personhood, Sexuality and Complementarity in the Teachings of Pope John Paul II." *Chicago Studies* 32 (1993): 43–53.

Buttiglione, Rocco. *Karol Wojtyla: The Thought of the Man Who Became Pope John Paul II.* Grand Rapids, MI: Eerdmans, 1997.

*Caffarra, Carlo. "L'uomo immagine di Dio Amore." In *La "Familiaris Consortio,"* ed. Dionigi Tettamanzi, 89–93. Rome: Libreria Editrice Vaticana, 1982.

———. "La trasmissione della vita nella *Familiaris consortio.*" *Mater et Magistra* 4 (1983): 391–99.

———. "Conscience, Truth and Magisterium in Conjugal Morality." *Anthropo[te]s* 2 (1986): 79–88.

———. *Creati per amare: Non è bene che l'uomo sia solo. L'amore, il matrimonio, la famiglia nella prospettiva cristiana.* Siena: Cantagalli, 2006.

———. "La verità e fecondità del dono." In *Amare l'amore umano*, ed. Livio Melina and Stanisław Grygiel, 187–93. Siena: Cantagalli, 2007.

———. “Natura, ragione pratica, matrimonio secondo san Tommaso.” In *San Tommaso, il matrimonio e la famiglia*, ed. Serge-Thomas Bonino and Guido Mazzotta, 209–18. Rome: Urbaniana University Press, 2019.

Cahall, Perry J. “Preaching, Teaching, and Living the Theology of the Body.” *Linacre Quarterly* (2007): 213–29.

———. *The Mystery of Marriage: A Theology of the Body and the Sacrament.* Chicago: Hillenbrand Books, 2016.

Cahill, Lisa Sowle. “Current Teaching on Sexual Ethics.” *Irish Quarterly Review* 76 (1987): 20–28.

———. “Catholic Sexual Ethics and the Dignity of the Person: A Double Message.” *Theological Studies* 50 (1989): 120–50.

———. Accent on the Masculine.” In *John Paul II and Moral Theology*, ed. Charles Curran and Richard McCormick, 85–91. New York: Paulist Press, 1998.

Cahill, Lisa Sowle, John H. Garvey, and Thomas Frank Kennedy. *Sexuality and the U.S. Catholic Church: Crisis and Renewal.* New York: Crossroad, 2006.

Caldecott, Léonie. “Sincere Gift: The Pope’s ‘New Feminism.’” In *John Paul II and Moral Theology*, ed. Charles Curran and Richard McCormick, 216–34. New York: Paulist Press, 1998.

Caldera, Rafael Tomás. “El don de sí.” In *Trinidad y salvacion: Estudios sobre la trilogia trinitaria de Juan Pablo II*, ed. Antonio Aranda, 275–87. Pamplona: Ediciones Universidad de Navarra, 1990.

Cannon, Andrew. “Development from *Humanae Vitae* to Theology of the Body: Saint John Paul’s Theology of the Body as a Development of the Doctrine of *Humanae Vitae*.” PhD diss., Catholic University of America, 2020.

Carelli, Roberto. *L’uomo e la donna nella teologia di H. U. von Balthasar.* Lugano: EUPRESS, 2007.

Castán Vásquez, José María. “Influencia de San Juan de la Cruz en la poesia de Juan Pablo II.” In *Giovanni Paolo II: Le vie della giustizia. Itinerari per il terzo millennio*, ed. Aldo Loiodice and Massimo Vari, 1002–3. Rome: Bardi Editore, 2003.

Chorpenning, Joseph F. “John Paul II’s Theology of the Mystery of the Holy Family.” *Communio* 28 (2001): 140–66.

Ciccone, Lino. “Per una corretta comprensione della Catechesi di Giovanni Paolo II nelle udienze generali del mercoledì.” *Divus Thomas* 84 (1980): 356–80.

———. *Uomo-Donna: L’amore umano nel piano divino: La grande Catechesi del mercoledí di Giovanni Paolo II.* Turin: Elle Di Ci, 1986.

Cloutier, David M. “Heaven Is a Place on Earth? Analyzing the Popularity of Pope John Paul II’s Theology of the Body.” In *Sexuality and the US Catholic Church*, ed. Lisa Sowle Cahill, John H. Garvey, and Thomas Frank Kennedy. New York: Crossroad, 2006.

———. “Aquinas’ Charity and Catholic Sexual Ethics.” *Josephinum* 14 (2007): 240–68.

Cloutier, David M., and William C. Mattison III. “Bodies Poured Out in Christ: Marriage beyond the Theology of the Body.” In *Leaving and Coming Home: New Wineskins for Catholic Sexual Ethics*, ed. David Cloutier, 206–25. Eugene, OR: Cascade, 2010.

Cokeley, Meghan K. “Shame, Lust and the Human Body after the Fall: A Comparison of St. Augustine and Pope John Paul II.” *Nova et Vetera* 2 (2004): 249–56.

Colton, Randall G. “Two Rival Versions of Sexual Virtue: Simon Blackburn and John Paul II on Lust and Chastity.” *Thomist* 70 (2006): 71–101.

Connell, Richard. “A Defense of *Humanae Vitae*.” *Laval Théologique et Philosophique* 26 (1970): 57–87.

Connor, Robert A. "The One Truth of Freedom: Gift of Self." *Communio* 21 (1994): 367–71.

Cooke, Bernard. "*Casti Connubii* to *Gaudium et Spes:* The Shifting Views of Christian Marriage." In *Marriage in the Catholic Tradition: Scripture, Tradition, and Experience*, ed. Todd A. Salzman, Thomas M. Kelly, and John J. O'Keefe, 109–14. New York: Crossroad, 2004.

*Cory, Therese Scarpelli. *Aquinas on Human Self-Knowledge.* New York: Cambridge University Press, 2014.

Cottier, Georges, OP. "Reflections on Marriage and the Family." *Nova et Vetera* 1 (2003): 11–25.

Coughlin, John J. "Family Law: Natural Law, Marriage, and the Thought of Karol Wojtyla." In *Recovering Self-Evident Truths: Catholic Perspectives on American Law*, ed. Michael A. Scaperlanda and Teresa Stanton Collett, 275–91. Washington, DC: Catholic University of America Press, 2007.

*Crawford, David S. "*Humanae Vitae* and the Perfection of Love." *Communio* 25 (1998): 414–38.

———. "Discerning the Signs of Our Times: *Gaudium et Spes*, Contraception, and Some Cultural Implications for Marriage and the Family as Natural Communities." In *Enlightening the Mystery of Man: Gaudium et Spes Fifty Years Later*, ed. Antonio Lopez. Washington, DC: Humanum Academic Press, 2018.

———, ed. *The Body as Anticipatory Sign: Commemorating the Anniversaries of Humanae Vitae and Veritatis Splendor.* Washington, DC: Humanum Academic Press, 2020.

Crosby, John F. "The Personalism of John Paul II as the Basis of His Approach to the Teaching of *Humanae vitae.*" In *Why Humanae Vitae Was Right: A Reader*, ed. Janet Smith, 195–226. San Francisco: Ignatius Press, 1993.

———. "John Paul II's Vision of Sexuality and Marriage: The Mystery of 'Fair Love.'" In *The Legacy of Pope John Paul II: His Contribution to Catholic Thought*, ed. Geoffrey Gneuhs, 52–70. New York: Crossroad, 2000.

Cuison, Paul Antiga. "The Mystery and Sign of Marriage: The Magisterium of John Paul II." PhD diss., Universidad de Navarra, 1998.

Cullen, Christopher M. "Between God and Nothingness: Matter in John Paul II's Theology of the Body." In *Pope John Paul II on the Body: Human, Eucharistic, Ecclesial. Festschrift Avery Cardinal Dulles, SJ*, 65–75. Philadelphia: Saint Joseph's University Press, 2007.

Curran, Charles E. *Contraception: Authority and Dissent.* New York: Herder and Herder, 1969.

———. "Personal Reflections on Birth Control." In *The Catholic Case for Contraception*, ed. Daniel Callahan, 19–29. London: Arlington Books, 1969.

———. *The Moral Theology of Pope John Paul II.* Washington, DC: Georgetown University Press, 2005.

———. *Loyal Dissent: Memoir of a Catholic Theologian.* Washington, DC: Georgetown University Press, 2006.

———. "*Humanae Vitae:* Fifty Years Later." *Theological Studies* 79 (2018): 520–42.

Curran, Charles E., and Richard A. McCormick, eds. *John Paul II and Moral Theology.* New York: Paulist, 1998.

Dauphinais, Michael. "Married Sexuality within the Drama of Creation and Redemption: *Humanae Vitae* through the Lens of *Gaudium et Spes.*" *Nova et Vetera* 16 (2018): 113–40.

De Broglie, Guy. "La conception thomiste des deux finalités du mariage." *Doctor Communis* 27 (1974): 3–41.

DeFord, R. Bradley. "Gabriel Marcel and a Christian Theology of the Body." PhD diss., University of Chicago, 1986.

deLadurantaye, Paul F. "Irreconcilable Concepts of the Human Person and the Moral Issue of Contraception: An Examination of the Personalism of Louis Janssens and the Personalism of Pope John Paul II." *Anthropotes* 13 (1997): 433–55.

———. "From *Humanae Vitae* to Donum Vitae: Symmetry and Consistency in Catholic Biomedical Teaching." *Linacre Quarterly* 66 (1999): 7–20.

DeMarco, Donald. "The Body as Supernatural, Personalistic and Nuptial." *National Catholic Bioethics Quarterly* 3 (2003): 81–93.

DeVille, Adam A. "The Trinity and Contraception." *Homiletic and Pastoral Review* 100 (2000): 30–43.

"Documentum syntheticum de moralitate regulationis nativitatum." In *Contrôle des naissances et théologie: Le dossier de Rome. Traduction, présentation et notes de Jean-Marie Paupert*, ed. Jean-Marie Paupert, 156–62. Paris: Seuil, 1967.

Durkin, Mary G. *Feast of Love: Pope John Paul II on Human Intimacy.* Chicago: Loyola University Press, 1983.

Eberstadt, Mary. "The Vindication of *Humanae Vitae.*" *First Things* 185 (2008): 35–42.

———. *Adam and Eve after the Pill: Paradoxes of the Sexual Revolution.* San Francisco: Ignatius Press, 2012.

Echeverria, Eduardo J. *In the Beginning: A Theology of the Body.* Eugene, OR: Pickwick Publications, 2011.

Elliott, Peter J. *What God Has Joined . . . : The Sacramentality of Marriage.* New York: Alba House, 1990.

* Endriß, Stefan. *Ehe als Schule der Heiligkeit: Die Mittwochskatechesen Johannes Pauls II. (1979–1984) und ihr Beitrag zur Sexualethik.* Sankt Ottlilien: Eos Verlag, 2019.

Engel, Randy. *John Paul and the Theology of the Body: A Study in Modernism.* Export, PA: New Engel Publishing, n.d.

Evert, Jason. *Theology of the Body in One Hour.* Scottsdale, AZ: Totus Tuus Press, 2017.

*Faraone, Mario. *La inhabitación trinitaria según san Juan de la Cruz.* Rome: Gregorian University Press, 2002.

*Finley, John. "The Metaphysics of Gender: A Thomistic Approach." *Thomist* 79 (2015): 585–614.

Finnis, John. "Personal Integrity, Sexual Morality, and Responsible Parenthood." *Anthropotes* 1 (1985): 43–55.

———. "The Good of Marriage and the Morality of Sexual Relations: Some Philosophical and Historical Observations." *American Journal of Jurisprudence* 42 (1998): 97–134.

Flannery, Kevin L. "'In This Regard, the Teaching of the Magisterium Is Already Explicit': On *Dignitatis Personae* §12." In *Fertility and Gender: Issues in Reproductive Ethics*, ed. Helen Watt, 184–200. Oxford: Anscombe Bioethics Center, 2011.

Ford, John C. *The Teaching of Humanae Vitae: A Defense.* San Francisco: Ignatius Press, 1988.

Ford, John C., and Germain Grisez. "Contraception and the Infallibility of the Ordinary Magisterium." *Theological Studies* 39 (1978): 258–312.

*Franks, Angela. *Margaret Sanger's Eugenic Legacy: The Control of Female Fertility.* Jefferson, NC: McFarland, 2005.

———. "The Gift of Female Fertility: Church Teaching on Contraception." In *Woman, Sex, and the Church: A Case for Catholic Social Teaching*, ed. Erika Bachiochi, 97–119. Boston: Pauline Books and Media, 2010.

———. *Contraception and Catholicism: What the Church Teaches and Why*. Boston: Pauline Books and Media, 2013.

———. "The Body, Alienation, and Gift in Marx and Wojtyła." In *Pensando il lavoro: Contributi a carattere prevalentemente filosofico*, ed. Giorgio Faro, 223–37. Rome: Edizioni Università Santa Croce, 2018.

———. "End-less and Self-Referential Desire: Toward an Understanding of Contemporary Sexuality." *National Catholic Bioethics Quarterly* 18 (2018): 629–46.

———. "Thinking the Embodied Person with Karol Wojtyła." *Nova et Vetera* 16 (2018): 141–71.

———. "Review of Thomas Petri, Aquinas and the Theology of the Body: The Thomistic Foundations of John Paul II's Anthropology." *Nova et Vetera* 17 (2019): 603–7.

———. "A Body of Work: Labor and Culture in Karol Wojtyła and Karl Marx." In *Leisure and Labor: Essays on the Liberal Arts in Catholic Higher Education*, ed. Anthony P. Coleman. Lanham, MD: Lexington Books, 2019.

———. "Fluidity: Man, the Triune God, and the Eucharistic Christ." *Communio* 46 (2019): 585–619.

———. "Deleuze on Desire." *First Things* (April 2020): 37–42.

———. www.angelafranks.com. Accessed August 15, 2020.

Galvin, John. "*Humanae Vitae*: Heroic, Deficient—Or Both?" *Latin Mass* 11 (2002): 7–17.

Gałuszka, Paweł Stanisław. *Karol Wojtyła e Humanae vitae Il contributo dell'Arcivescovo di Cracovia e del gruppo di teologi polacchi all'enciclica di Paolo VI*. Siena: Edizioni Cantagalli, 2017.

Gams, Corbin. "Amor—Der Leib und seine Sprache." *Theologie des Leibes Jahrbuch* 1 (2019).

Gams, Corbin, and Birgit Gams. *Eine Vision von Liebe: Die Theologie des Leibes nach Johannes Paul II*. Kisslegg: fe-Medienverlag, 2014.

Garcia de Haro, Ramon. "El matrimonio, comunidad de amor al servicio de la vida: Estudio sobre la noción de matrimonio en la Ex. *Familiaris Consortio*." *Divinitas* 26 (1982): 332–49.

George, Francis E. "Education in Love: The Interior Culture of the Person." *Anthropotes* 14 (1998): 179–83.

Gerardi, Renzo. *L'ultima enciclica di Paolo VI: Una rilettura di Humanae vitae. Nuova traduzione con testo Latino a fronte*. Bologna: Edizioni Dehonianae, 2018.

Giertych, Wojciech. "The Virtue of Chastity in Marriage: Its Reality and Difficulties." In *San Tommaso, il matrimonio e la famiglia*, ed. Serge-Thomas Bonino and Guido Mazzotta, 219–36. Rome: Urbaniana University Press, 2019.

Glick, Daryl J. "Recovering Morality: Personalism and Theology of the Body in John Paul II." *Faith and Reason* 12 (1986): 7–25.

González Alió, José Luis. "La Santisima Trinidad Comunion de Personas." *Scripta Theologica* 18 (1986): 11–115.

Gonzalo, María. "'There I Will Give You My Love': Revisiting Bernard's Four Degrees of Love alongside John Paul II." *Cistercian Studies Quarterly* 52 (2017): 347–64.

Good, James. "A Theology of the Body: The Legacy of Augustine." *Doctrine and Life* 53 (2003): 358–61.

Gotcher, Robert F. "The Theology of the Body: Some Reflections on the Significance for Medical Professionals." *Linacre Quarterly* 73 (2006): 115–31.

Gotia, Oana. *L'amore e il suo fascino: Bellezza e castità nella prospettiva di san Tommaso d'Aquino*. Siena: Cantagalli, 2011.

———. "Educazione delle emozioni e sessualità in Martha Craven Nussbaum." In *La*

soggettività morale del corpo, ed. Livio Melina and Juan José Pérez-Soba, 245–60. Siena: Cantagalli, 2012.
*Grabowski, John S. "Theological Anthropology and Gender since Vatican II: A Critical Appraisal of Recent Trends in Catholic Theology." PhD diss., Marquette University Press, 1991.
———. "The Status of the Sexual Good as a Direction for Moral Theology." *Heythrop Journal* 35 (1994): 15–34.
———. "Person or Nature? Rival Personalisms in 20th Century Catholic Sexual Ethics." *Studia Moralia* 35 (1997): 283–312.
———. *Sex and Virtue: An Introduction to Sexual Ethics*. Washington, DC: Catholic University of America Press, 2003.
———. "'And So He Revealed His Glory': Cana and the Sacramentality of Marriage." *Thomist* 78 (2014): 37–63.
———. *Transformed in Christ*. Ave Maria, FL: Sapientia Press, 2017.
*Granados, José. "Toward a Theology of the Suffering Body." *Communio* 33 (2006): 540–63.
———. *La carne si fa amore: Il corpo, cardine della storia della salvezza*. Siena: Cantagalli, 2010.
———. *I segni della carne: Il matrimonio nell'economia sacramentaria*. Siena: Cantagalli, 2011.
———, ed. *Una caro: Il linguaggio del corpo e l'unione coniugale*. Siena: Cantagalli, 2014.
———. *Una sola carne en un solo Espiritu: Teología del matrimonio*. Madrid: Palabra, 2014.
———. "'The Flesh Is of No Avail': Theology of the Body as Necessary to Understanding Life in the Spirit." *Communio* 43 (2016): 175–93.
Grecco, Richard. "La teologia del corpo di Giovanni Paolo II." *Concilium* 20 (1984): 135–47.
Grisez, Germain, Joseph Boyle, John Finnis, and William May. "'Every Marital Act Ought to Be Open to New Life': Toward a Clearer Understanding." *Thomist* 52 (1988): 365–426.
Grondelski, John. *Fruitfulness as an Essential Dimension of Acts of Conjugal Love: An Interpretive Study of the Pre-Pontifical Thought of John Paul II*. New York: Fordham University Press, 1985.
Groos, Maria, Teresa Loichen, and Manfred Gerwing. *Liebe, Leib, und Leidenschaft: Zur Theologie des Leibes von Johannes Paul II*. Kisslegg: fe-Medienverlag, 2013.
Groos, Maria, and Janusz Surzykiewicz. *Kann man so lieben? Beiträge der 3. Internationalen Tagung zur Theologie des Leibes in Eichstätt*. Sankt Ottilien: EOS Editions, 2018.
Grootaers, Jan, and Joseph A. Selling. *The 1980 Synod of Bishops "On the Role of the Family."* Louvain: Leuven University, 1983.
Grygiel, Ludmiła, Stanisław Grygiel, and Przemisław Kwiatkowski. *Bellezza e spiritualità dell'amore coniugale: Con un inedito di Karol Wojtyla*. Siena: Cantagalli, 2009.
Grygiel, Stanisław, and Przemisław Kwiatkowski, eds. *L'amore e la sua regola: Karol Wojtyła e l'esperienza dell' "Ambiente" di Cracovia*. Siena: Cantagalli, 2009.
Guerra López, Rodrigo. *Volver a la persona: El método filosófico de Karol Wojtyla*. Madrid: Caparrós, 2002.
———. *Afirmar a la persona por sí misma: La dignidad como fundamento de los derechos de la persona*. Mexico City: Comisión Nacional de los Derechos Humanos, 2003.
———. "Entender a Wojtyla para comprender a Bergoglio: El carácter personalista de 'Amoris laetitia.'" *Metafísica y Persona* 11 (2019): 37–50.
Haas, John, ed. "The Theology of the Body [Monographic Issue]." *National Catholic Bioethics Quarterly* 3 (2003): 164–76.

*Hadjadj, Fabrice. *La profondeur des sexes: Pour une mystique de la chair.* Paris: Éditions du Seuil, 2008.

———. *La profundidad de los sexos: Por una mística de la carne.* Granada: nuevoinicio, 2010.

———. "Sexuality as Transcendence: An Interview with Fabrice Hadjadj." Translated by Artur Sebastian Rosman. *Ethika Politika*, April 14, 2015. https://ethikapolitika.org/2015/04/14/sexuality-as-transcendence-an-interview-with-fabrice-hadjadj.

———. *Dernières nouvelles de l'homme (et de la femme aussi): Chroniques d'une disparition annoncée.* Paris: Éditions Tallandier, 2017.

———. Últimas noticias del hombre (y de la mujer) [*Crónicas de una desaparición anunciada*]. Madrid: Homo Legens, 2018.

Haggerty, Donald. "Contraception outside Marriage: Prudence or Sin?" *Nova et Vetera* 12 (2014): 123–45.

*Hahn, David P. *Mystical Theology of the Body: Love According to St. John Paul II and St. John of the Cross.* Sewanee, GA: St. Polycarp, 2019.

*Hahn, Scott. *First Comes Love: Finding Your Family in the Church and the Trinity.* New York: Image Books, 2006.

———. *The First Society: The Sacrament of Matrimony and the Restoration of the Social Order.* Steubenville, OH: Emmaus Road, 2018.

Handren, Walter J. *No Longer Two: A Commentary on the Encyclical Casti Connubii of Pius XI.* Westminster, MD: Newman Press, 1995.

Harper McCarthy, Margaret. "The Body, 'Sacrament of the Person.'" In *Dialoghi sul mistero nuziale: Studi offerti al Cardinale Angelo Scola*, ed. Gilfredo Marengo and Bruno Ognibeni, 97–113. Rome: Lateran University Press, 2003.

Harris, Alana, ed. *The Schism of '68: Catholicism, Contraception and Humanae Vitae in Europe, 1945–1975.* London: Palgrave Macmillan, 2018.

Healy, Mary. *Men and Women Are from Eden: A Study Guide to John Paul II's Theology of the Body.* Cincinnati, OH: Servant Books, 2005.

Healy, Nicholas J., Jr. "The World as Gift." *Communio* 32 (2005): 395–406.

———. "Christian Personalism and the Debate over the Nature and Ends of Marriage." *Communio* 39 (2012): 186–200.

———. "The Merciful Gift of Indissolubility and the Question of Pastoral Care for Civilly Divorced and Remarried Catholics." *Communio* 41 (2014): 306–30.

———. "The Indissoluble Nexus of Nature, Body, and Person: Fifty Years after *Humanae Vitae*." *Communio* 45 (2018): 553–66.

Heller, Karin. "The Interpersonal Communion of Trinity, Origin and Aim of Communion between Man and Woman." In *Dialoghi sul mistero nuziale: Studi offerti al Cardinale Angelo Scola*, ed. Gilfredo Marengo and Bruno Ognibeni, 115–29. Rome: Lateran University Press, 2003.

Hilpert, Konrad, and Sigrid Müller, eds. *Humanae vitae: Die anstößige Enzyklika.* Freiburg: Herder, 2018.

Hittinger, Russell. "Human Nature and States of Nature in John Paul II's Theological Anthropology." In *Human Nature in Its Wholeness: A Roman Catholic Perspective*, ed. Daniel N. Robinson, Gladys M. Sweeney, and Richard Gill, 9–33. Washington, DC: Catholic University of America Press, 2006.

Hogan, Margaret Monahan. *Finality and Marriage.* Milwaukee: Marquette University Press, 1993.

Hogan, Richard M. *The Theology of the Body in John Paul II: What It Means, Why It Matters.* Frederick, MD: The Word among Us, 2006.

Hogan, Richard M., and John M. LeVoir. *Covenant of Love: Pope John Paul II on Sexuality, Marriage, and Family in the Modern World.* Garden City, NY: Doubleday, 1985.

Hołub, Grzegorz. "Wojtyła on Persons and Consciousness." *Forum Philosophicum* 19 (2014): 43–60.

Hurtado Domínguez, Rafael. *La paternidad en el pensamiento de Karol Wojtyla.* Pamplona: Ediciones Universidad de Navarra, 2011.

Hütter, Reinhard. "Christliche Freiheit und die Wahrheit des Gesetzes: Das Anliegen der römisch-katholischen Moralenzyklika *Veritatis Splendor* in der Perspektive reformatorischer Theologie." *Kerygma und Dogma* 42 (1996): 246–71.

———. "(Re-)Forming Freedom: Reflections 'after Veritas Splendor' on Freedom's Fate in Modernity and Protestantism's Antinomian Captivity." *Modern Theology* 17 (2001): 117–61.

———. "Empfang und Gestalt: Überlegungen zum Verhältnis von Freiheit und Gesetz." *Kerygma und Dogma* 49 (2003): 210–35.

———. "Pornography and Acedia." *Nova et Vetera* 10 (2012): 901–7.

———. "The Virtue of Chastity and the Scourge of Pornography: A Twofold Crisis Considered in Light of Thomas Aquinas's Moral Theology." *Thomist* 77 (2013): 1–39.

———. "Human Sexuality in a Fallen World: An Economy of Mercy and Grace." In *San Tommaso, il matrimonio e la famiglia*, ed. Serge-Thomas Bonino and Guido Mazzotta, 71–100. Rome: Urbaniana University Press, 2019.

Hütter, Reinhard, and Theodor Dieter, eds. *Ecumenical Ventures in Ethics: Protestants Engage Pope John Paul II's Moral Encyclicals.* Grand Rapids, MI: Eerdmans, 1998.

*Ide, Pascal. *Le don du corps: Une lecture des catéchèses de Jean-Paul II sur le corps humain.* [Unpublished manuscript.]

———. "Une théologie du don: Les occurrences de *Gaudium et spes*, n. 24, §3 chez Jean-Paul II." *Anthropotes* 17 (2001): 149–78, 313–44.

———. "Don et théologie du corps dans les catéchèses sur l'amour dans le plan divin." In *Jean-Paul II face a la question de l'homme: Actes du 6ème Colloque International de la Fondation Guilé*, ed. Yves Semen, 159–212. Boncourt: Guilé Foundation Press, 2004.

———. *Le Christ donne tout: Benoît XVI, une théologie de l'amour.* Paris: Éditions de l'Emmanuel, 2007.

———. "La philosophie de la nature de Charles De Koninck." *Laval Théologique et Philosophique* 66 (2010): 459–501.

———. *Une théologie de l'amour: L'amour, centre de la Trilogie de Hans Urs von Balthasar.* Brussels: Lessius, 2012.

———. *Une théo-logique du don: Le don dans la Trilogie de Hans Urs von Balthasar.* Louvain: Peeters, 2013.

———. "John Paull II's 'Meditation on Givenness.'" *Communio* 43 (2016): 123–38.

Institute for Theological Encounter with Science and Technology. *Christianity and the Human Body: A Theology of the Human Body. Proceedings of the Itest Workshop, October, 2000.* St. Louis, MO: ITEST Faith / Science Press, 2001.

Jacobson, Heather L., M. Elizabeth Lewis Hall, and Tamara L. Anderson. "Theology and the Body: Sanctification and Bodily Experiences." *Psychology of Religion and Spirituality* 5 (2013): 41–50.

Jason, Joel O. *Free Love, True Love: Rediscovering Love and Intimacy in John Paul II's Theology of the Body.* Quezon City, Philippines: Shepherd's Voice, 2007.

Johnson, Luke Timothy. "A Disembodied 'Theology of the Body': John Paul II on Love, Sex and Pleasure." *Commonweal*, January 26, 2001.

———. *The Revelatory Body: Theology as Inductive Art.* Grand Rapids, MI: Eerdmans, 2015.

Kalbian, Aline H. *Sex, Violence, and Justice: Contraception and the Catholic Church.* Washington, DC: Georgetown University Press, 2014.

Kalinowski, Georges. "Humanisme théocentrique: L'enseignement de Jean Paul II sûr l'homme." *Seminarium* 32 (1980): 130–44.

———. "La pensée de Jean Paul II sur l'homme et la famille." *Divinitas* 26 (1982): 3–18.

Kampowski, Stephan. "Riceversi donarsi: L'affetto, il desiderio, l'incontro." In *La soggettività morale del corpo*, ed. Livio Melina and Juan José Pérez-Soba, 93–107. Siena: Cantagalli, 2012.

———. "Die Theologie des Leibes und die Theologie der Liebe—Johannes Paul II. und Benedikt XVI. über die menschliche Bestimmung." In *Liebe, Leib und Leidenschaft: Zur Theologie des Leibes von Johannes Paul II. Reflexionen und examplarische Einblicke*, ed. Maria Groos, Teresa Loichen, and Manfred Gerwing, 121–41. Kisslegg: fe-Medienverlag, 2013.

Kellmeyer, Steven L. *Sex and the Sacred City: Meditations on the Theology of the Body.* Peoria, IL: Bridegroom Press, 2003.

Kelly, Timothy. "Christ and the Church: Duo in carne una. A Study of the Union of Christ and the Members of His Mystical Body from the Vantage Point of its Bodiliness." STD diss., University of Fribourg, 2010.

Knapp, James G. "Purity in the Adequate Anthropology of John Paul II." In *Pope John Paul II on the Body: Human, Eucharistic, Ecclesial: Festschrift Avery Cardinal Dulles, SJ*, 255–75. Philadelphia: Saint Joseph's University Press, 2007.

Knieps-Port le Roi, Thomas. "Innovation or Impasse? The Contribution of *Familiaris consortio* to a Contemporary Theology of Marriage." *Bijdragen* 70 (2009): 67–86.

Koterski, Joseph W., and John J. Conley, eds. *Creed and Culture: Jesuit Studies of Pope John Paul II.* Philadelphia: Saint Joseph's University Press, 2004.

Krapiec, Mieczyslaw. "Towards an Integral Anthropology." *Doctor Communis* 54 (2001): 175–90.

Kube, Constanze. "Die philosophischen Grundlagen und die politische Zielstellung der personalistischen Grundkonzeption von Karol Wojtyla." PhD diss., Humboldt-Universität, 1990.

*Kupczak, Jaroslaw. *Destined for Liberty: The Human Person in the Philosophy of Karol Wojtyla/John Paul II.* Washington, DC: Catholic University of America Press, 2000.

———. *Gift and Communion: John Paul II's Theology of the Body.* Washington, DC: Catholic University of America Press, 2014.

Kurz, William S. "The Scriptural Foundations of the Theology of the Body." In *Pope John Paul II on the Body: Human, Eucharistic, Ecclesial. Festschrift Avery Cardinal Dulles, SJ*, ed. John M. McDermott and John Gavin, 27–46. Philadelphia: Saint Joseph's University Press, 2007.

Lacroix, Xavier. "L'homme et la femme selon Karol Wojtyla." *Recherches Philosophiques* 5 (2009): 137–46.

Laffitte, Jean. "Mystère de l'amour, symbolique du coeur." In *Dialoghi sul mistero nuziale: Studi offerti al Cardinale Angelo Scola*, ed. Gilfredo Marengo and Bruno Ognibeni, 131–47. Rome: Lateran University Press, 2003.

———. "The Sacramental Reality of Human Love: A Catholic Perspective." In *Not Just Good, but Beautiful: The Complementary Relationship between Man and Woman*, ed. Stevan Lopes and Helen Alvaré, 69–84. Walden, NY: Plough, 2015.

Laffitte, Jean, and Livio Melina. *Amour conjugal et vocation à la sainteté*. Paris: Éditions de l'Emmanuel, 2001.

Langan, Janine. "John Paul II's Letter to Families: Dead Letter or Good News?" *Communio* 22 (1995): 65–76.

Larchet, Jean-Claude. *Theology of the Body*. Yonkers, NY: St. Vladimir's Seminary Press, 2017.

Larrú, Juan de Dios. "John Paul II's Theology of the Body and His Roman Triptych." *Communio* 36 (2009): 374–86.

———, ed. *El misterio de la acción conyugal: Perspectivas abiertas a 50 años de Humanae vitae*. Madrid: Ediciones Universidad San Dámaso, 2019.

Latkovic, Mark S. "John Paul II on the Phenomenon of Sexual Shame." *National Catholic Bioethics Quarterly* 3 (2003): 45–51.

Lawler, Michael G. *Marriage and Sacrament: A Theology of Christian Marriage*. Collegeville, MN: Liturgical Press, 1993.

———. *Marriage and the Catholic Church: Disputed Questions*. Collegeville, MN: Michael Glazier, 2002.

Lawler, Ronald D., ed. *The Christian Personalism of Pope John Paul II*. Chicago: Franciscan Herald, 1982.

Lawler, Ronald D. "Personalism in the Thought of John Paul II." In *Catholic Social Thought and the Teaching of John Paul II: Proceedings of the Convention of the Fellowship of Catholic Scholars*, ed. Paul L. Williams, 2–18. Scranton, PA: Northeast Books, 1983.

———. "Experience as the Foundation of Karol Wojtyla's Personalist Ethics." *Proceedings of the American Catholic Philosophical Association* 60 (1986): 148–55.

Lee, Patrick, and Robert P. George. *Conjugal Union: What Marriage Is and Why It Matters*. Cambridge: Cambridge University Press, 2014.

Lee, Su Li. "Persons as Gifts: Understanding Interdependence through Pope John Paul II's Anthropology." *Catholic Social Science Review* 14 (2009): 321–37.

Leies, John A., ed. *Human Sexuality and Personhood*. Braintree, MA: Pope John Center, 1990.

LeJeune, Marcel. *Set Free to Love: Lives Changed by the Theology of the Body*. Cincinnati, OH: Servant Books, 2010.

Lemmons, R. Mary Hayden. "The 'Feminism' of Aquinas' Natural Law: Relationships, Love and New Life." In *Abortion: A New Generation of Catholic Responses*, ed. Stephen Heaney, 237–42. Braintree, MA: Pope John Center, 1992.

———. "Equality, Gender and John Paul II." *Logos* 5 (2002): 111–30.

———. "The Feminine Genius: Personalist Feminism, and the Call for Women to Prophecy According to John Paul II." In *Woman as Prophet in the Home and in the World*, ed. R. Mary Hayden Lemmons, 31–44. Lanham, MD: Lexington Books, 2016.

———. "Prophetic Femininity in the Bible, the Church and Nature: Reflection on John Paul II's Prophetism of Femininity and Marian Ecclesiology." In *Woman as Prophet in the Home and in the World*, ed. R. Mary Hayden Lemmons, 79–108. Lanham, MD: Lexington Books, 2016.

Lestapis, Joseph de. "A Summary of Karol Wojtyla's Love and Responsibility." In *Christian Married Love*, ed. Raymond Dennehy. San Francisco: Ignatius, 1981.

Levinas, Emmanuel. "Notes sur la pensée philosophique du cardinal Wojtyla." *Communio* 5 (1980): 88.

Lio, Ermenegildo. *Humanae vitae e coscienza: L'insegnamento del Card. Wojtyla teologo e Papa*. Rome: Libreria Editrice Vaticana, 1980.
———. *Humanae vitae e infallibilità: Paolo VI, il Concilio e Giovanni Paolo II*. Rome: Libreria Editrice Vaticana, 1986.
Lofgren, Mary Elizabeth Zagrobelny. "John Paul II's Theological Anthropology and the Intersexual Body." PhD diss., Catholic University of America, 2020.
*López, Antonio. "Eternal Happening: God as an Event of Love." *Communio* 32 (2005): 214–45.
———. *Spirit's Gift: The Metaphysical Insight of Claude Bruaire*. Washington, DC: Catholic University of America Press, 2006.
———. "Toward an Understanding of Fruitfulness." *Nova et Vetera* 6 (2008): 801–27.
———. "God the Father: A Beginning without Beginning." *Communio* 36 (2009): 219–58.
———. "Donum Doni: An Approach to a Theology of Gift." In *Being Holy in the World: Theology and Culture in the Thought of David L. Schindler*, 252–80. Grand Rapids, MI: Eerdmans, 2011.
———. "Marriage's Indissolubility: An Untenable Promise?" *Communio* 41 (2014): 269–305.
———. "Fruitfulness and the Rediscovery of Finitude." *Communio* 41 (2014): 774–803.
———. "Vides Trinitatem si caritatem vides: Persons in Communion." *Communio* 42 (2015): 394–429.
———. "Affirming Childhood: The Form of Familiar Relations." *Communio* 44 (2017): 606–36.
———. "Receiving the Gift of Being: Ferdinand Ulrich and the Work of the John Paul Ii Institute." *Communio* 46 (2019): 7–10.
Loughlin, Gerard. "Sexing the Trinity." *New Blackfriars* 79 (1998): 18–25.
———. *Queer Theology: Rethinking the Western Body*. Oxford: Blackwell, 2007.
Maddox, Brenda. *The Pope and Contraception: The Diabolical Doctrine*. Chatto Counterblasts. London: Chatto and Windus, 1991.
Mankowski, Paul. "Fertility, Celibacy, and the Biblical Vindication." In *Fertility and Gender: Issues in Reproductive Ethics*, ed. Helen Watt, 10–16. Oxford: Anscombe Bioethics Center, 2011.
Marczewski, Robert. *A Legacy of Saint John Paul II: The Reception of John Paul II's Theology of the Body in the Catholic Church in the United States of America (1984–2012)*. Plymouth, MI: SqOne, 2015.
Mardas Billias, Nancy, Agnes B. Curry, and George F. McLean, eds. *Karol Wojtyla's Philosophical Legacy*. Washington, DC: Council for Research in Values and Philosophy, 2007.
Marengo, Gilfredo. "L'antropologia adeguata nella catechesi sull'amore umano." In *Amare l'amore umano*, ed. Livio Melina and Stanisław Grygiel, 149–72. Siena: Cantagalli, 2007.
———. *La nascita di un'enciclica: Humanae vitae alle luce degli Archivi Vaticani*. Vatican City: Liberia Editrice Vaticana, 2018.
Marengo, Gilfredo, and Bruno Ognibeni, eds. *Dialoghi sul mistero nuziale: Studi offerti al Cardinale Angelo Scola*. Rome: Lateran University Press, 2003.
*Martelet, Gustave. "Morale conjugale et vie chrétienne." *Nouvelle Revue Théologique* 87 (1965): 245–66.
———. *Amour conjugale et renouveaux conciliaire*. Lyons: Xavier Mappus, 1967.
———. "Pour mieux comprendre l'encyclique Humanæ Vitæ." *Nouvelle Revue Théologique* 90 (1968): 897–917, 1009–63.
———. *L'Existence humaine et l'amour: Pour mieux comprendre l'encyclique Humanae vitae*. Paris: Desclée, 1969.

———. "Essai sur la signification de l'encyclique Humanæ Vitæ." In *Paul VI et la modernité dans l'Eglise*, 399–415. Rome: Studium, 1984.

———. "Sixteen Christological Theses on the Sacrament of Marriage." In *Contemporary Perspectives on Christian Marriage*, ed. Richard Malone, 275–83. Chicago: Loyola University Press, 1984.

Marti, Kevin. "Dante's 'Baptism' and the Theology of the Body in 'Purgatorio' 1–2." *Traditio* 45 (1989–90): 167–90.

Martin, Francis. "Male and Female He Created Them: A Summary of the Teaching of Genesis Chapter One." *Communio* 20 (1993): 240–65.

———. "Radiation of Fatherhood: Some Biblical Reflections." *Josephinum Journal of Theology* 9 (2002): 22–41.

*Mattheeuws, Alain. *Union et procréation: Développements de la doctrine des fins du mariage*. Paris: Cerf, 1989.

———. "De la Bible à *Humanae Vitae:* Les catéchèses de Jean-Paul II." *Nouvelle Revue Théologique* 111 (1989): 228–48.

———. *Les "dons" du Mariage: Recherche de théologie morale et sacramentelle*. Brussels: Culture et Vérité, 1996.

May, William E. *Contraception, Humanae Vitae, and Catholic Moral Thought*. Chicago: Franciscan Herald, 1984.

———. *Theology of the Body in Context: Genesis and Growth*. Boston: Pauline Books and Media, 2010.

*McAleer, Graham J. "The Politics of the Flesh: Rahner and Aquinas on Concupiscentia." *Modern Theology* 15 (1999): 355–65.

———. *Ecstatic Morality and Sexual Politics: A Catholic and Antitotalitarian Theory of the Body*. New York: Fordham University, 2005.

McCarthy, Margaret Harper. "'Husbands, Love Your Wives as Your Own Bodies': Is Nuptial Love a Case of Love or Its Paradigm?" *Communio* 32 (2005): 260–94.

———. "*Agápē*, the Revelation of Love and Its Appeal to the Heart: A Comment on *Deus Caritas Est* in Light of John Paul II's Category of 'Elementary Experience.'" In *The Way of Love: Reflections of Pope Benedict XVI's Encyclical Deus Caritas Est*, ed. Livio Melina and Carl A. Anderson, 107–22. San Francisco: Ignatius Press, 2006.

McDermott, John M. "Science, Sexual Morality, and Church Teaching: Another Look at '*Humanae vitae.*'" *Irish Theological Quarterly* 70 (2005): 237–61.

McDermott, John M., and John Gavin, eds. *Pope John Paul II on the Body: Human, Eucharistic, Ecclesial: Festschrift Avery Cardinal Dulles, SJ*. Philadelphia: Saint Joseph's University Press, 2007.

Meiring, Jacob. "Theology in the Flesh: A Model for Theological Anthropology as Embodied Sensing: Original Research." *Theological Studies* 71 (2015): 1–8.

*Melina, Livio. "La responsabilità procreativa nella visione cattolica." *Anthropotes* 19 (2003): 249–64.

———. "Dimensioni etiche del mistero nuziale: Per una cultura della famiglia." In *Dialoghi sul mistero nuziale: Studi offerti al Cardinale Angelo Scola*, ed. Gilfredo Marengo and Bruno Ognibeni, 175–84. Rome: Lateran University Press, 2003.

———. "Love: The Encounter with an Event." In *The Way of Love: Reflections of Pope Benedict XVI's Encyclical Deus Caritas Est*, ed. Livio Melina and Carl A. Anderson, 16–28. San Francisco: Ignatius Press, 2006.

———. "La verità dell'amore: *Veritatis splendor.*" In *Amare l'amore umano*, ed. Livio Melina and Stanisław Grygiel, 233–44. Siena: Cantagalli, 2007.

———. "Il nesso tra sessualitá e generazione, condizione di una procreaszione responsiblile." In *Feconditá nell'infertilitá*, ed. José Noriega and Di Pietro Maria Luisa, 113–27. Rome: Lateran University Press, 2007.

———. "From *Humanae Vitae* to Deus Caritas Est: Developments in the Theological Thought on Human Love." *Josephinum Journal of Theology* 18 (2011): 368–76.

———. "Prefazione. Natura e famiglia: Un nesso da esplorare." In *Il criterio della natura e il futuro della famiglia*, ed. Livio Melina, 5–11. Siena: Cantagalli, 2011.

———. "*Veritatis splendor*: Verità sul bene e dignità dell'uomo." *Anthropotes* 34 (2018): 521–32.

Melina, Livio, and Carl A. A. Anderson, eds. *The Way of Love: Reflections on Pope Benedict XVI's Encyclical, Deus caritas est.* English ed. San Francisco: Ignatius Press, 2006.

Merecki, Jaroslaw. "Corpo, sacramento della persona." In *Amare l'amore umano*, ed. Livio Melina and Stanisław Grygiel, 173–85. Siena: Cantagalli, 2007.

Millare, Roland. "Towards a Common Communion: The Relational Anthropologies of John Zizioulas and Karol Wojtyla." *New Blackfriars* 98 (2017): 599–614.

———. "The Wedding Feast of the Lamb Has Begun: The Relationship between Eschatology and the Liturgy in the Logoscentric Theology of Joseph Ratzinger." STD diss., University of St. Mary of the Lake, 2018.

Miller, Paula Jean. "The Body: Science, Theology, and *Humanae Vitae.*" *Logos* 3 (2000): 154–65.

———. "The Theology of the Body: A New Look at *Humanae vitae.*" *Theology Today* 57 (2001): 501–8.

Miller-McLemore, Bonnie J. "Embodied Knowing, Embodied Theology: What Happened to the Body?" *Pastoral Psychology* 62 (2013): 743–58.

Mitchell, Louise M. "A Bibliography for the Theology of the Body." *National Catholic Bioethics Quarterly* 3 (2003): 69–77.

Modras, Ronald E. "The Moral Philosophy of Pope John Paul II." *Theological Studies* 41 (1980): 683–97.

———. "Birth Control, Personalism, and the Pope." *Currents in Theology and Mission* 8 (1981): 283–90.

———. "The Thomistic Personalism of Pope John Paul II." *Modern Schoolman* 59 (1982): 117–27.

———. "Pope John Paul II, St. Maximilian Kolbe, and Antisemitism. Some Current Problems and Perceptions Affecting Catholic-Jewish Relations." *Journal of Ecumenical Studies* 20 (1983): 630–39.

———. "Implications of Rahner's Anthropology for Fundamental Moral Theology." *Horizons* 12 (1985): 70–90.

———. "A Man of Contradictions? The Early Writings of Karol Wojtyla." In *The Church in Anguish: Has the Vatican Betrayed Vatican II?*, ed. Hans Küng and Leonard J. Swidler, 39–51. San Francisco: Harper and Row, 1987.

———. "Karl Rahner and John Paul II: Anthropological Implications for Economics and the Social Order." In *Religion and Economic Ethics*, 123–50. Lanham, MD: Lexington Books, 1990.

———. "Pope John Paul II's Theology of the Body." In *John Paul II and Moral Theology*, ed. Charles E. Curran and Richard A. McCormick, 149–56. New York: Paulist, 1998.

———. "Karol Wojtyla the Philosopher." In *The Vision of John Paul II*, ed. Gerard Mannion, 29–44. Collegeville, MN: Liturgical Press, 2008.

Moleski, Martin X. "The Prophetic Mission of Marriage: John Paul II's Vision of Human Sexuality." In *Prophecy and Diplomacy: The Moral Doctrine of John Paul II. A Jesuit Symposium*, ed. John J. Conley and Joseph W. Koterski, 247–69. New York: Fordham University Press, 1999.

Mortensen, Beth. "The Relation of the Juridical and Sacramental in Matrimony According to Thomas Aquinas." STD diss., University of Fribourg, 2012.

Mullady, Brian. "The Person in the Theology of the Body of Pope John Paul II." In *Man's Desire for God*. Bloomington, IN: First Books Library, 2003.

Muller, Earl C. "The Nuptial Meaning of the Body." In *Pope John Paul II on the Body: Human, Eucharistic, Ecclesial. Festschrift Avery Cardinal Dulles, SJ*, 87–120. Philadelphia: Saint Joseph's University Press, 2007.

Murphy, William F. "Revisiting the Biblical Renewal of Moral Theology." *Nova et Vetera* 2 (2004): 403–44.

———. "Forty Years Later: Arguments in Support of *Humanae Vitae* in Light of *Veritatis Splendor*." *Josephinum Journal of Theology* 14 (2007): 122–67.

———. "A Reading of Aquinas in Support of '*Veritatis Splendor*' on the Moral Object." *Logos* 11 (2008): 100–126.

———. "Revisiting Contraception: An Integrated Approach in Light of the Renewal of Thomistic Virtue Ethics." *Theological Studies* 72 (2011): 812–47.

Nachef, Anthony E. *The Mystery of the Trinity in the Theological Thought of Pope John Paul II*. New York: Peter Lang, 1999.

Napier, Malachy Joseph. "The Theology of Whose Body? St. John Paul II's Anthropology and Gender Theory." *Dunwoodie Review* 40 (2018): 198–207.

Newton, William. "John Paul II and '*Gaudium et Spes*' 22: His Use of the Text and His Involvement in Its Authorship." *Josephinum Journal of Theology* 17 (2010): 168–93.

———. "Condoms and HIV: The State of the Debate." *Linacre Quarterly* 78 (2011): 29–44.

———. "The Link between Life Issues and Social Justice: Insights into Pope Benedict XVI's Social Encyclical *Caritas in Veritate*." *National Catholic Bioethics Quarterly* 12 (2012): 449–60.

———. "Contraception and Abortion: Fruits of the Same Rotten Tree?" *Linacre Quarterly* 82 (2015): 135–48.

———. "Aquinas and the 'Genius of Woman.'" *Downside Review* 135 (2017): 173–85.

———. "Why Aquinas's Metaphysics of Gender Is Fundamentally Correct: A Response to John Finley." *Linacre Quarterly* 87 (2020): 198–205.

Noonan, John T. *Contraception: A History of Its Treatment by the Catholic Theologians and Canonists*. Cambridge, MA: Harvard University, 1966. [Enlarged ed., 1986.]

———. *The Church and Contraception: The Issues at Stake*. New York: Paulist Press, 1967.

———. "Contraception and the Council." In *The Catholic Case for Contraception*, ed. Daniel Callahan, 3–18. London: Arlington Books, 1969.

*Noriega, José. "Lo Spirito Santo e l'universalità della morale cristiana." In *Quale dimora per l'agire? Dimensioni ecclesiologiche della morale*, ed. Livio Melina and Pablo Zanor, 57–70. Rome: Lateran University Press, 2000.

———. *Il destino dell'eros: Prospettive di morale sessuale*. Bologna: EDB, 2006.

———. "The Spark of Sentiment and the Fullness of Love." In *The Way of Love: Reflections of Pope Benedict XVI's Encyclical Deus Caritas Est*, ed. Livio Melina and Carl A. Anderson, 287–99. San Francisco: Ignatius Press, 2006.

———. "La vocazione al dono di sé." In *Amare l'amore umano*, ed. Livio Melina and Stanisław Grygiel, 195–203. Siena: Cantagalli, 2007.

———. "Fantasia e virtù: La conformazione dei desideri corporali." In *La soggettività morale del corpo*, ed. Livio Melina and Juan José Pérez-Soba, 173–85. Siena: Cantagalli, 2012.

Notare, Theresa. "A Revolution of Morals: Resolution #15 of Lambeth 1930." *Revue d'Histoire Ecclésiastique* 94 (1999): 54–75, 471–501.

———. "A Revolution of Morals: Resolution #15 of Lambeth 1930." *Revue d'Histoire Ecclésiastique* 94 (1999): 471–501.

Notare, Theresa, and Charles J. Chaput, eds. *Humanae Vitae, 50 Years Later: Embracing God's Vision for Marriage, Love, and Life. A Compendium*. Washington, DC: Catholic University of America Press, 2019.

Nycz, Kazimierz. "Redemptor hominis et homo redemptor: Zum personalistischen Menschenbild in der Lehre Johannes Pauls II." In *Europa und die Anthropologie seiner Politik: Der Mensch als Weg der Geschichte—Zur Philosophie Karol Wojtylas*, ed. Christoph Böhr and Christian Schmitz, 177–88. Berlin: Berliner Wissenschaftsverlag, 2016.

Obach, Robert. *The Catholic Church on Marital Intercourse: From St. Paul to Pope John Paul II*. Lanham, MD: Lexington Books, 2008.

Ocáriz, Fernando. "La nota teologica dell'insegnamento dell' *Humanae vitae* sulla contraccezione." *Anthropotes* 4 (1988): 25–43.

O'Donnell, John Joseph. "Man and Woman as Imago Dei in the Theology of Hans Urs von Balthasar." *Clergy Review* 68 (1983): 117–28.

Ognibeni, Bruno. *Dominare la moglie? A proposito di Gn 3,16: Lezione inaugurale Cattedra di Teologia biblica del matrimonio e della famiglia. Istituto "Giovanni Paolo II." Anno accademico 2001–2002*. Rome: Lateran University Press, 2002.

———. "Caroselli femminili: A proposito de Ger 31,22." In *Dialoghi sul mistero nuziale: Studi offerti al Cardinale Angelo Scola*, ed. Gilfredo Marengo and Bruno Ognibeni, 217–28. Rome: Lateran University Press, 2003.

———. *Il matrimonio alla luce del Nuovo Testamento*. Rome: Lateran University Press, 2007.

Okonkwo, Bartholomew. *The Mystery of Human Personhood: A Renewal of The Theology of the Body. Karol Wojtyla*. Palo Alto, CA: Academica Press, 2011.

O'Reilly, Ailbe. *Conjugal Chastity in Pope Wojtyla*. New York: Peter Lang, 2010.

O'Sullivan, Alan. *Self-Giving, Self-Mastery: St John Paul II on Men, Women and Conjugal Chastity*. Oxford: Peter Lang, 2017.

*Ouellet, Marc. "Theological Perspectives on Marriage." *Communio* 31 (2004): 419–34.

———. *Divine Likeness: Toward a Trinitarian Anthropology of the Family*. Grand Rapids, MI: Eerdmans, 2006.

———. "Marriage and the Family within the Sacramentality of the Church: Challenges and Perspectives." *Communio* 41 (2014): 226–44.

———. *Mystery and Sacrament of Love: A Theology of Marriage and the Family for the New Evangelization*. Grand Rapids, MI: Eerdmans, 2015.

Page, Jean-Guy. "La Pensée de Karol Wojtyla (Jean-Paul II) sur la relation homme-femme." *Laval Théologique et Philosophique* 40 (1984): 3–30.

Palladino, Emilia, and Humberto Miguel Yáñez, eds. *La famiglia a cinquant'anni da Humanae vitae: Attualità e riflessione etica*. Roma: Studium Edizioni, 2019.

Papal Commission for the Study of Population, Family, and Birth Rate. "Majority Papal Commission Report." In *The Catholic Case for Contraception*, ed. Daniel Callahan, 149–73. London: Arlington Books, 1969.

———. "Minority Papal Commission Report." In *The Catholic Case for Contraception*, ed. Daniel Callahan, 174–211. Latin text, "Status Quaestionis." In *Contrôle des naissances et théologie*, 163–78. London: Arlington Books, 1969.

Patterson, Colin, and Conor Sweeney. *God and Eros: The Ethos of the Nuptial Mystery*. Eugene, OR: Cascade Books, 2015.

Paul VI et la modernité dans l'Église: Actes du colloque organisé par l'École française de Rome (Rome 2–4 juin 1983). Rome: École française de Rome, 1984.

Paupert, Jean-Marie. *Contrôle des naissances et théologie: Le dossier de Rome. Traduction, présentation et notes de Jean-Marie Paupert*. Paris: Éditions du Seuil, 1967.

Prader, Helmut, ed. *50 Jahre Enzyklika Humanae vitae: Referate der Internationalen Theologischen Sommerakademie 2018 des Linzer Priesterkreises in Aigen/M*. Kisslegg-Immenried: Christiana-Verlag, 2019.

Percy, Anthony. *Theology of the Body Made Simple*. Boston: Pauline Books and Media, 2006.

Pérez, Adán José, and Vicente Villar Amigó. *Sexo: Razón y pasión. La racionalidad social de la sexualidad en Juan Pablo II*. Pamplona: Ediciones Universidad de Navarra, 1997.

Pérez-López, Angel. "Karol Wojtyła's Thomistic Understanding of Consciousness." *Thomist* 79 (2015): 407–37.

———. *Procreation and the Spousal Meaning of the Body: A Thomistic Argument Grounded in Vatican II*. Eugene, OR: Pickwick Publications, 2017.

*Pérez-Soba, Juan José. *"Amor es nombre de persona" (I, q. 37, a.1): Estudio de la interpersonalidad en el amor en Santo Tomás de Aquino*. Rome: Lateran University Press, 2001.

———. *La pregunta por la persona: La respuesta de la interpersonalidad*. Madrid: Ediciones San Dámaso, 2004.

———. "Status quaestionis: Lo splendore del corpo, guida dell'azione." In *La soggettività morale del corpo*, ed. Livio Melina and Juan José Pérez-Soba, 21–62. Siena: Cantagalli, 2012.

———. "Con suavidad y firmeza: Un camino eclesial a recorrer, la *Veritatis splendor* vista tras Amoris laetitia. Una respuesta a un libro reciente de Alain Thomasset y Jean-Miguel Garrigues." *Anthropotes* 33 (2017): 565–614.

———. "¿Existe en verdad un sujeto cristiano? La pregunta moral básica a partir de la *Veritatis splendor*." In *Ricostruire il soggetto morale cristiano: Una sfida a 25 anni Veritatis splendor*, 393–419. Siena: Cantagalli, 2019.

———. "La questione del soggetto e la proposta morale della *Veritatis splendor:* Status quaestionis." In *Ricostruire il soggetto morale cristiano: Una sfida a 25 anni Veritatis splendor*, 25–76. Siena: Cantagalli, 2019.

Pesarchick, Robert A. *The Trinitarian Foundation of Human Sexuality as Revealed by Christ According to Hans Urs von Balthasar: The Revelatory Significance of the Male Christ and the Male Ministerial Priesthood*. Rome: Gregorian University Press, 2000.

*Petri, Thomas. *Aquinas and the Theology of the Body: The Thomistic Foundations of John Paul II's Anthropology*. Washington, DC: Catholic University of America Press, 2016.

Pinto, Matthew. *Freedom: 12 Lives Transformed by the Theology of the Body*. West Chester, PA: Ascension Press, 2009.

Place, Michael D. "*Familiaris Consortio:* A Review of Its Theology." In *The Changing Family:*

Views from Theology and the Social Sciences in the Light of the Apostolic Exhortation Familiaris Consortio, 23–46. Chicago: Loyola University Press, 1984.

Prokes, Mary Timothy. "The Nuptial Meaning of the Body in Light of Mary's Assumption." *Communio* 11 (1984): 157.

———. *Toward a Theology of the Body*. Edinburgh: T&T Clark, 1996.

———. "The Body: Precious Sacramental or Processed Artifact." *National Catholic Bioethics Quarterly* 3 (2003): 139–62.

Quinn, John R. "Birth Control and the Relevant Church." In *The Debate on Birth Control*, ed. Andrew Bauer, 109–18. New York: Hawthorn Books, 1969.

Raedy, Kevin. "Marriage, Sacramental Grace, and Contraception." *Nova et Vetera* 16 (2018): 1051–65.

Rakoczy, Susan. "Mixed Messages: John Paul II's Writings on Women." In *The Vision of John Paul II*, ed. Gerard Mannion, 159–83. Collegeville, MN: Liturgical Press, 2008.

Reimer-Barry, Emily. "On Women's Health and Women's Power: A Feminist Appraisal of *Humanae Vitae*." *Theological Studies* 79 (2018): 818–40.

*Reimers, Adrian. "The Thomistic Personalism of Karol Wojtyla (Pope John Paul II)." In *Atti del IX Congresso tomistico internazionale*. Rome: Libreria Editrice Vaticana, 1992.

———. *An Analysis of the Concepts of Self-Fulfillment and Self-Realization in the Thought of Karol Wojtyla, Pope John Paul II*. Lewiston, NY: Edwin Mellen, 2001.

———. "Human Suffering and John Paul II's Theology of the Body." *Nova et Vetera* 2 (2004): 445–60.

———. "Karol Wojtyla on the Natural Moral Order." *National Catholic Bioethics Quarterly* 4 (2004): 317–34.

———. *The Truth about the Good: Moral Norms in the Thought of John Paul II*. Ave Maria: Sapientia Press, 2011.

———. *The Good Is Love: The Body and Human Acts in Humanae Vitae and John Paul II*. South Bend, IN: St. Augustine's Press, 2020.

Rhea, Rob, and Rick Langer. "A Theology of the Body for a Pornographic Age." *Journal of Spiritual Formation and Soul Care* 8 (2015): 90–103.

Rhonheimer, Martin. "Intrinsically Evil Acts and the Moral Viewpoint: Clarifying a Central Teaching of *Veritatis Splendor*." *Thomist* 58 (1994): 1–39.

———. "The Perspective of the Acting Person and the Nature of Practical Reason: The 'Object of the Human Act' in Thomistic Anthropology of Action." *Nova et Vetera* (2004): 461–516.

———. "The Use of Contraceptives under Threat of Rape: An Exception?" *Josephinum* 14 (2007): 168–81.

———. *Ethics of Procreation and the Defense of Human Life: Contraception, Artificial Fertilization, and Abortion*. Edited by William F. Murphy. Washington, DC: Catholic University of America Press, 2010.

Rhonheimer, Martin, Nicoletta Lateri, and Francesca Giglio. "La Creación y la ley natural como fundamento de la moral de la vida en Juan Pablo II." *Medicina y Etica: Revista Internacional de Bioetica, Deontologia y Etica Medica* 19 (2008): 307–39.

Rice, Joseph. "Karol Wojtyla on Acting 'Together with Others.'" PhD diss., Catholic University of America, 2007.

———. "On the 'Proper Weight of a Man': Re-Examining the Poetic Foundations of

Wojtyła's Theory of Participation." In *Karol Wojtyla's Philosophical Legacy*, ed. Nancy Mardas Billias, Agnes B. Curry, and George F. McLeon, 297–324. Washington, DC: Council For Research in Values and Philosophy, 2008.

Rickert, Kevin G. "Wojtlya's Personalistic Norm: A Thomistic Analysis." *Nova et Vetera* 7 (2009): 653–78.

Rieser, Doris M. "The Female Body in Catholic Theology: Menstruation, Reproduction, and Autonomy." *Horizons* 44 (2017): 1–27.

*Rimmel, Marc. *Die Theologie des Leibes von Papst Johannes Paul II.* St. Ottilien: Eos Verlag, 2014.

Roberts, Augustine. "Spousal Meaning: John Paul II's Anthropology for Monks and Nuns." *Cistercian Studies Quarterly* 44 (2009): 191–227.

Ross, Susan A. "'Then Honor God in Your Body' (1 Cor 6:20): Feminist and Sacramental Theology on the Body." *Horizons* 16 (1989): 7–27.

Rousseau, Mary F. "Deriving Bioethical Norms from the Theology of the Body." *National Catholic Bioethics Quarterly* 3 (2003): 59–67.

———. "John Paul II and Theology of the Body." *Chicago Studies* 39 (2000): 162–75.

Rubio, Julie Hanlon. "Beyond the Liberal/Conservative Divide on Contraception: The Wisdom of Practitioners of Natural Family Planning and Artificial Birth Control." *Horizons* 32 (2005): 270–94.

Ryan, Robert. "Pope Francis, Theology of the Body, Ecology, and Encounter." *Journal of Moral Theology* 6 (2017): 56–73.

Ryłko, Stanisław. "La pedagogia dell'amore di Karol Wojtyła e il suo 'Ambiente.'" In *Amore e la sua regola: Karol Wojtyła e l'esperienza dell' 'Ambiente' di Cracovia*, ed. Stanisław Grygiel and Przemisław Kwiatkowski, 17–20. Siena: Cantagalli, 2009.

Salas, Elizabeth. "Person and Gift According to Karol Wojtyla / John Paul II." *American Catholic Philosophical Quarterly* 84 (2010): 99–124.

Salas, Victor M. "The Analogical Structure of Self-Giving and Receiving According to John Paul II." *Gregorianum* 90 (2009): 473–84.

———. "Thomas Aquinas's Metaphysics of the Person and Phenomenological Personalism: The Case of Incommunicability." *Gregorianum* 94 (2013): 573–92.

Salzman, Todd A., and Michael G. Lawler. *The Sexual Person: Toward a Renewed Catholic Anthropology*. Washington, DC: Georgetown University Press, 2008.

———. "Theology, Science, and Sexual Anthropology: A Methodological Investigation." *Journal of Religion and Society, Supplement Series* 11 (2015): 46–72.

Savage, Deborah. *The Subjective Dimension of Human Work: The Conversion of the Acting Person According to Karol Wojtyla / John Paul II and Bernard Lonergan*. New York: Peter Lang, 2008.

———. "The Centrality of Lived Experience in Wojtyla's Account of the Person." *Annals of Philosophy* 61 (2013).

———. "Woman as Knower." *Lonergan Review* 5 (2014): 109–38.

———. "The Nature of Woman in Relation to Man: Genesis 1 and 2 through the Lens of the Metaphysical Anthropology of Aquinas." *Logos* 18 (2015): 71–93.

———. "Woman as Prophet: A Feminism for the Twenty-First Century." In *Woman as Prophet in the Home and in the World*, ed. Mary Hayden R. Lemmons, 45–64. Lanham, MD: Lexington Books, 2016.

Schall, James V. "Person and Society: John Paul II on Substance and Relation." In *Prophecy and Diplomacy: The Moral Doctrine of John Paul II. A Jesuit Symposium*, ed. John J.

Conley and Joseph W. Koterski, 3–20. New York: Fordham University Press, 1999.
Schemenauer, Kevin. *Conjugal Love and Procreation: Dietrich von Hildebrand's Superabundant Integration*. Lanham, MD: Lexington Books, 2011.
*Schindler, David L. "Catholic Theology, Gender, and the Future of Western Civilization." *Communio* 20 (1993): 200–239.
———. *Heart of the World, Center of the Church: Communio Ecclesiology, Liberalism, and Liberation*. Grand Rapids, MI: Eerdmans, 1996.
———. "The 'Nuptial-Sacramental' Body and the Significance of World and Culture for Moral Theology." *Anthropotes* 21 (2005): 35–55.
———. *John Paul II and the 'Nuptial Attribute' of the Body: The Family and the Future of Humanity*. The Church, Marriage, and the Family. South Bend, IN: St Augustine, 2007.
———. "The Embodied Person as Gift and the Cultural Task in America: Status Quaestionis." *Communio* 35 (2008): 397–431.
———. *Ordering Love: Liberal Societies and the Memory of God*. Grand Rapids, MI: Eerdmans, 2011.
———. "Being, Gift, Self-Gift: A Reply to Waldstein on Relationality and John Paul II's Theology of the Body (Part One)." *Communio* 42 (2015): 221–51.
———. "Being, Gift, Self-Gift (Part Two)." *Communio* 43 (2016): 409–83.
Schlueter, Nathan W. "Healing the Hidden Wound: The Theology of the Body in Wendell Berry's 'Remembering.'" *Communio* 36 (2009): 510–33.
*Schmitz, Kenneth L. *The Gift: Creation. Aquinas Lecture, 1982*. Milwaukee: Marquette University Press, 1982.
———. *At the Center of the Human Drama: The Philosophical Anthropology of Karol Wojtyla/Pope John Paul II*. Washington, DC: Catholic University of America Press, 1993.
———. "The Passage of Love: Wojtyla's Radiation of Fatherhood." *Communio* 22 (1995): 99–106.
———. "Jacques Maritain and Karol Wojtyla: Approaches to Modernity." In *The Bases of Ethics*, ed. William Sweet. Milwaukee: Marquette University Press, 2000.
———. "A Contemporary Philosophy of Action." In *Person and the Polis*, 17–37. Arlington, VA: Institute for the Psychological Sciences Press, 2006.
———. *The Texture of Being*. Washington, DC: Catholic University of America Press, 2007.
Schockenhoff, Eberhard. "Der Glaubenssinn des Volkes Gottes als ethisches Erkenntniskriterium? Zur Nicht-Rezeption kirchlicher Lehraussagen über die Sexualmoral durch die Gläubigen." *Theologie und Philosophie* 91 (2016): 321–62.
———. "Die Zukunft der Familie: Anthropologische Grundlagen und ethische Herausforderungen." Ökumenische Rundschau 67 (2018): 6–19.
Schu, Walter J. *The Splendor of Love: John Paul II's Vision for Marriage and Family*. New Hope, KY: New Hope Publications, 2003.
*Schumacher, Michele M. "An Inseparable Connection: The Fruitfulness of Conjugal Love and the Divine Norm." *Nova et Vetera* 1 (2003): 381–402.
———. "The Unity of the Two: Toward a New Feminist Sacramentality of the Body." In *Women in Christ: Toward a New Feminism*, ed. Michele M. Schumacher, 201–30. Grand Rapids, MI: Eerdmans, 2004.
———. "A Speyrian Theology of the Body." In *The Virgin Mary and Theology of the Body*, ed. Donald Calloway, 243–78. Grand Rapids, MI: Eerdmans, 2005.
———. "John Paul II's Theology of the Body on Trial: Responding to the Accusation of the Biological Reduction of Women." *Nova et Vetera* 10 (2012): 463–84.

———. "A Woman in Stone or in the Heart of Man? Navigating between Naturalism and Idealism in the Spirit of *Veritatis Splendor*." *Nova et Vetera* 11 (2013): 1249–86.

———. *A Trinitarian Anthropology: Adrienne von Speyr and Hans Urs von Balthasar in Dialogue with Thomas Aquinas*. Washington, DC: Catholic University of America Press, 2014.

———. "Human Ecology and the Prophetic Value of *Humanae Vitae*." *Nova et Vetera* 16 (2018): 1227–60.

*Schwaderlapp, Dominik. *Erfüllung durch Hingabe: Die Ehe in ihrer personalistischen, sakramentalen und ethischen Dimension nach Lehre und Verkündigung Karol Wojtylas/Johannes Pauls II*. St. Ottilien: Eos, 2002.

*Scola, Angelo. "Claim of Christ, Claim of the World: On the Trinitarian Encyclicals of John Paul II." *Communio* 18 (1991): 322–31.

———. "L'imago Dei e la sessulalità umana: A proposito di una tesi originale della *Mulieris dignitatem*." *Anthropotes* 8 (1992): 61–73.

———. "The Nuptial Mystery at the Heart of the Church." *Communio* 25 (1998): 630–62.

———. "*Familiaris consortio* e mistero nuziale." *Anthropotes* 17 (2001): 203–5.

———. *L'esperienza elementare: La vena profonda del magistero di Giovanni Paolo II*. Genova: Marietti, 2003.

———. *The Nuptial Mystery*. Grand Rapids, MI: Eerdmans, 2005.

———. "Il mistero divino dell'amore nell'insegnamento di Giovanni Paolo II." In *Amare l'amore umano*, ed. Livio Melina and Stanisław Grygiel, 23–34. Siena: Cantagalli, 2007.

Sealey, Margaret. "The Meaning of Human Sexuality According to Karol Wojtyla and Sigmund Freud." *Ethics and Medicine* 23 (2007): 159–68.

Sedgwick, Peter H. "The Lambeth Conferences on Contraception, 1908–68." *Theology* 123 (2020): 95–103.

Séguin, Michel. "The Biblical Foundations of the Thought of John Paul II on Human Sexuality." *Communio* 20 (1993): 266–89.

Seidl, Horst. "Sul duplice fine del matrimonio secondo la dottrina tomista." *Sapientia* 51 (1996): 505–15.

Selling, Joseph A. "Moral Teaching, Traditional Teaching and *Humanae vitae*." *Louvain Studies* 7 (1978): 24–44.

———. "Re-Reading *Gaudium et spes* on Marriage and the Family." *Louvain Studies* 8 (1980): 82–94.

———. "A Closer Look at the Text of *Gaudium et Spes* on Marriage and the Family." *Bijdragen* 43 (1982): 30–48.

———. "The Development of Proportionalist Thinking." *Chicago Studies* 25 (1986): 165–75.

———. "The Context and the Arguments of *Veritatis Splendor*." In *Splendor of Accuracy: An Examination of the Assertions Made by Veritatis Splendor*, ed. Joseph A. Selling and Jan Jans, 11–70. Grand Rapids, MI: Eerdmans, 1995.

———. "The 'Meanings' of Human Sexuality." *Louvain Studies* 23 (1998): 22–37.

———. "Sexual Ethics and the New Testament: Behavior and Belief." *Ephemerides Theologicae Lovanienses* 77 (2001): 482–84.

———. "The Recovery of Aquinas's Action Theory: A Reply to William Murphy." *Theological Studies* 73 (2012): 139–50.

———. "Regulating Fertility and Clarifying Moral Language." *Heythrop Journal* 55 (2014): 1033–43.

Selner-Wright, Susan C. "John Paul II on the Genius of Women." In *Woman as Prophet in the Home and in the World*, ed. Mary Hayden R. Lemmons, 3–14. Lanham, MD: Lexington Books, 2016.

*Semen, Yves. *La Sexualité selon Jean-Paul II*. Paris: Presses de la Renaissance, 2003.

———. "Jean-Paul II et l'anthropologie chrétienne." In *Jean-Paul II face à la question de l homme: Actes du 6e Colloque International de la Fondation Guilé*, ed. Yves Semen, 17–22. Zürich: Thesis Verlag, 2004.

———. "Mariage: La révolution de la Théologie du corps." In *Jean-Paul II, héritage et fécondité*, ed. Michel Boyancé, 109-53. Paris: Parole et Silence, 2007.

———. "La théologie du corps de Jean-Paul II." *Le Corps, Sources vives* 44 (2009): 65–81.

———. "Qu'est-ce que l'humanisme chrétien?" In *Qu'est-ce que l'homme?*, ed. D. François-Xavier de Guibert, 187–220. Paris: Académie d'Education et d'Etudes Sociales, 2010.

———. *La spiritualité conjugale selon Jean-Paul II*. Paris: Éditions Plon, 2010.

———. "La personne sexuée: Homme et femme, il les créa." In *La théorie du Gender: Vers une nouvelle identité sexuelle? Actes du colloque de l'Observatoire sociopolitique du diocèse de Fréjus-Toulon*, 115–30. Paris: Parole et Silence, 2012.

———. "La pédagogie de la sexualité à la lumière de la Théologie du corps de Jean-Paul II." In *La teologia del corpo di Giovanni Paolo II: Atti del Convegno Internazionale, Ateneo Pontificio Regina Apostolorum*, ed. Pedro Barrajon, 281–93. Rome: D. APRA, 2012.

———. *La préparation au mariage selon Jean-Paul II et la théologie du corps*. Paris: Presses de la Renaissance, 2013.

———, ed. *Jean Paul II. La théologie du corps: L'amour humain dans le plan divin*. Paris: Cerf, 2014.

———. "Cooperatori dell'amore di Dio creatore (cf. GS 50): Genitorialità dei coniugi e paternità del presbitero." In *Presbiteri e sposi, sorgente di fecondità educativa per la comunità cristiana*, ed. Paolo Gentili and Tommaso e Giulia Cioncolini. Siena: Cantagalli 2014.

———, ed. *Amour humain, amour divin: Actualité de la théologie du corps. Actes du Colloque inaugural de l'Institut de théologie du corps (Domaine Lyon St-Joseph, 27 et 28 nov. 2014)*. Paris: Cerf, 2015.

———. *La Famille selon Jean-Paul II*. Paris: Presses de la Renaissance, 2016.

———. *Abrégé de la théologie du corps*. Paris: Cerf, 2016.

———. "L'imago Dei chez Thomas d'Aquin et Jean-Paul II: Contradiction ou prolongement?" *Cahiers de l'IPC* 83 (2016): 63–85.

———. *Compendio della teologia del corpo*. Milan: Edizioni Ares, 2017.

———. *Amour, sexualité . . . mariage: Lumières sur le mariage d'amour*. Paris: Mame, 2018.

———. *Un corps pour se donner: Aimer en vérité selon saint Jean-Paul II*. Paris: Mame, 2018.

———. "Le mystere de l'engendrement du langage du corps a la surabondance du don." *Anthropotes* 34 (2018): 199–210.

Serrano Ruiz, José María. "La rilevanza giuridica dell'amore coniugale nel Magistero di Giovanni Paolo II." In *Giovanni Paolo II: Le vie della giustizia. Itinerari per il terzo millennio*, ed. Aldo Loiodice and Massimo Vari, 441–42. Rome: Bardi Editore, 2003.

Seyfer, Tara L., and John M. Travaline. "'The Theology of the Body' and Modern Medicine: Informing the Practice of Healing." *Linacre Quarterly* 75 (2008): 16–30.

Sharkley, Sarah Borden. "Edith Stein and John Paul II on Women." In *Karol Wojtyla's Philosophical Legacy*, ed. Nancy Mardas Billias, Agnes B. Curry, and George F. McLeon, 265–76. Washington, DC: Council for Research in Values and Philosophy, 2008.

Shivanandan, Mary. *Crossing the Threshold of Love: A New Vision of Marriage in the Light of John Paul II's Anthropology*. Washington, DC: Catholic University of America Press, 1999.

———. "Body-Soul Unity in Light of the Nuptial Relation." In *Dialoghi sul mistero nuziale: Studi offerti al Cardinale Angelo Scola*, ed. Gilfredo Marengo and Bruno Ognibeni, 369–81. Rome: Lateran University Press, 2003.

———. "Natural Family Planning and the Theology of the Body: A New Discourse for Married Couples." *National Catholic Bioethics Quarterly* 3 (2003): 23–32.

———. "John Paul II: The Redemption of the Body and the Call to Holiness." *Faith and Reason* 31 (2006): 109–32.

Shivanandan, Mary, and Joseph C. Atkinson. "Person as Substantive Relation and Reproductive Technologies: Biblical and Philosophical Foundations." *Logos* 7 (2004): 124–56.

Sikorski, John. "Towards a Conjugal Spirituality: Karol Wojtyła's Vision of Marriage before, during, and after Vatican II." *Journal of Moral Theology* 6 (2017): 103–29.

Słomka, Marek. *Who Is Man? The Anthropology of Karol Wojtyła*. Lublin: John Paul II Catholic University of Lublin Press, 2017.

*Smith, Janet E. "The Importance of the Concept of Munus to Understanding *Humanae Vitae*." In *Humanae Vitae: 20 Anni Dopo. Atti del II Congresso Internazionale di Teologia Morale*, 671–90. Milan: Edizioni Ares, 1989.

———. "The Vocation of Marriage: An Approach to the Vatican Instruction on Respect for Human Life." In *Creative Love: The Ethics of Human Reproduction*, ed. John Boyle, 117–35. Front Royal, VA: Christendom Press, 1989.

———. *Humanae Vitae, a Generation Later*. Washington, DC: Catholic University of America Press, 1991.

———, ed. *Why Humanae Vitae Was Right: A Reader*. San Francisco: Ignatius Press, 1993.

———. "Pope John Paul II and *Humanae Vitae*." In *Why Humanae Vitae Was Right: A Reader*, ed. Janet E. Smith, 229–50. San Francisco: Ignatius Press, 1993.

———. "Natural Law and Personalism in *Veritatis Splendor*." In *John Paul II and Moral Theology*, ed. Charles Curran and Richard McCormick, 67–84. New York: Paulist Press, 1998.

———. "Reclaiming or Rewriting the Tradition? Discussion Article of Jean Porter's *Natural and Divine Law*." *American Catholic Philosophical Quarterly* 76 (2001): 601–11.

———. "The *sensus fidelium* and *Humanae vitae*." In *Called to Holiness and Communion: Vatican II on the Church*, 291–319. Scranton, PA: University of Scranton Press, 2009.

———. "Conscience, Contraception, and Catholic Health-Care Professionals." *Linacre Quarterly* 77 (2010): 204–28.

———, ed. *Why Humanae Vitae Is Still Right*. San Francisco: Ignatius Press, 2018.

———, ed. "Law as Gift at the Basis of *Humanae vitae* and *Veritatis splendor*." *Scripta Theologica* 50 (2018): 729–45.

———. *Self-Gift: Essays on Humanae Vitae and the Thought of John Paul II*. Steubenville, OH: Emmaus Academic, 2018.

*Smith, Janet E., John S. Grabowski, J. Budziszewski, and Maria Fedoryka. "Self-Gift: The Heart of *Humanae vitae*." *National Catholic Bioethics Quarterly* 16 (2016): 449–74.

Smith, Russell E., ed. *Trust the Truth: A Symposium on the Twentieth Anniversary of the Encyclical Humanae Vitae*. Braintree, MA: Pope John Center, 1991.

———. *Communicating the Catholic Vision of Life: Proceedings of the Twelfth Bishops' Workshop, Dallas, Texas*. Braintree, MA: Pope John Center, 1993.

Snyder, Patrick. *La femme selon Jean-Paul II: Lectures des fondements anthropologiques et théologiques et des applications pratiques de son enseignement*. Montréal: Fides, 1999.
Solenni, Pia Francesca de. "Bibliography on Feminist Philosophy." *Acta Philosophica* 11 (2002): 335–37.
———. "Created Complementarity [and Cognitive Transcendence] in His Divine Image." In *San Tommaso, il matrimonio e la famiglia*, ed. Serge-Thomas Bonino and Guido Mazzotta, 45–58. Rome: Urbaniana University Press, 2019.
Solignac, Laure, ed. *La figure d'Adam: Saint Paul, Origène, Saint Grégoire de Nysse, Saint Bernard, Saint Bonaventure, Blaise Pascal, Emmanuel Kant, Soren Kierkegaard, Charles Péguy, Karl Barth, Gaston Fessard, Karol Wojtyla, Jean-Louis Chrétien*. Paris: Hermann, 2015.
Spencer, Mark K. "Aristotelian Substance and Personalistic Subjectivity." *International Philosophical Quarterly* 55 (2015): 145–64.
Spindelböck, Josef. *Theologie des Leibes kurzgefasst: Eine Lesehilfe zu "Liebe und Verantwortung" von Karol Wojtyla sowie zu den Katechesen Johannes Paul II. über die menschliche Liebe*. Kleinhain: St. Josef, 2015.
Spinello, Richard A. *Understanding Love and Responsibility: A Companion to Karol Wojtyła's Classic Work*. Boston: Pauline Books and Media, 2014.
———. "The Logic of Gift: Spousal Love and Marriage in the Thought of Karol Wojtyla / St. John Paul II." In *Woman as Prophet in the Home and in the World*, ed. R. Mary Hayden Lemmons, 177–96. Lanham, MD: Lexington Books, 2016.
Sri, Edward P. *Men, Women, and the Mystery of Love*. Cincinnati, OH: St. Anthony Messenger Press, 2007.
Stegman, Thomas D. "'Actualization': How John Paul II Utilizes Scripture in the Theology of the Body: A Response to William S. Kurz, S.J." In *Pope John Paul II on the Body: Human, Eucharistic, Ecclesial: Festschrift Avery Cardinal Dulles, SJ*, 47–64. Philadelphia: Saint Joseph's University Press, 2007.
Styczeń, Tadeusz. "L'antropologia della *Familiaris Consortio*." *Anthropotes* 9 (1993): 7–42.
———. *Comprendere l'uomo: La visione antropologica di Karol Wojtyla*. Rome: Lateran University Press, 2005.
Sullivan, Clayton. *Rescuing Sex from the Christians*. New York: Continuum, 2006.
*Suramy, Aude. "L'apport de la pensée thomiste dans la formation intellectuelle de Karol Wojtyla." *Recherches Philosophiques* 5 (2009): 21–46.
———. *La voie d'amour: Une interprétation de Personne et acte de Karol Wojtyla, lecteur de Thomas d'Aquin*. Rome: Cattedra Karol Wojtyła, Istituto Giovanni Paolo II per Studi su Matrimonio e Famiglia, 2014.
Sutton, Agneta. "Facing the Sexual Revolution: John Paul II's Language of the Body." In *John Paul the Great: Maker of the Post-Conciliar Church*, ed. William Oddie, 131–50. London: Catholic Truth Society and the Catholic Herald, 2003.
———. "The Complementarity and Symbolism of the Two Sexes: Karl Barth, Hans Urs von Balthasar and John Paul II." *New Blackfriars* 87 (2006): 418–33.
Sutton, Philip M. "Chastity as the Fruit of 'Genuine Affirmation': Reflections on the Work of Anna Terruwe, Conrad Baars, and John Paul II." In *The Church, Marriage, and the Family*. South Bend, IN: St. Augustine's Press, 2007.
Swafford, Andrew Dean. *John Paul II to Aristotle and Back Again: A Christian Philosophy of Life*. Eugene, OR: Wipf and Stock, 2015.
Swierzawski, Waclaw. "Die Würde des Menschen: Über die theologisch-anthropologischen

Grundlagen der Lehre Papst Johannes Pauls II." In *Die Würde des Menschen: Die theologisch-anthropologischen Grundlagen der Lehre Papst Johannes Pauls II*, ed. Gerhard Höver, Rainer Öhlschläger, Heinz Theo Risse, and Heinz Tiefenbacher, 77–91. Mainz: Grünewald, 1986.

Tarasiewicz, Pawel. "The Common Sense Personalism of St. John Paul II (Karol Wojtyla)." *Studia Gilsoniana* 3 (2014): 619–34.

Taylor, Jameson. "Beyond Nature: Karol Wojtyla's Development of the Traditional Definition of Personhood." *Review of Metaphysics* 63 (2009): 415–54.

———. "The Acting Person in Purgatory: A Note for Readers of the English Text." *Logos* 13 (2010): 77–104.

Tentler, Leslie Woodcock. *Catholics and Contraception: An American History*. Ithaca, NY: Cornell University Press, 2004.

Tettamanzi, Dionigi. *La risposta dei vescovi all'Humanae vitae*. Milan: Àncora, 1969.

———. *La verginità per il regno: Dalle catechesi di Giovanni Paolo II*. Milan: O.R., 1982.

———. *L'esortazione sulla famiglia: Familiaris consortio. Introduzione alla lettura*. Milan: Massimo, 1982.

———. *Alle sorgenti della vita: Humanae vitae attualità di un'enciclica*. Casale Monferrato: Piemme, 1993.

Thompson, Walter J. "Aristotle and John Paul II on the Family and Society: A Reply to John Hittinger." *Saint Anselm Journal* 8 (2013) 1–7.

Tosato, Angelo. "Magistero pontificio e sacra scrittura." *Anthropotes* 8 (1992): 239–72.

Tóth, Beáta. "Love between Embodiment and Spirituality: Jean-Luc Marion and John Paul II on Erotic Love." *Modern Theology* 29 (2013): 18–47.

Trainor, Brian T., and Conor Sweeney. *The Politics of Conjugal Love: A Baptismal and Trinitarian Approach to Headship and Submission*. Eugene, OR: Pickwick Publications, 2019.

Tranzillo, Jeffrey. *John Paul II on the Vulnerable*. Washington, DC: Catholic University of America Press, 2013.

Vacek, Edward. "Review of *The Acting Person*." *Theological Studies* 41 (1980): 228–29.

———. "Scheler's Phenomenology of Love." *Journal of Religion* 62 (1982): 156–77.

———. "Vatican Instruction on Reproductive Technology." *Theological Studies* 49 (1988): 110–31.

———. "Contemporary Ethics and Scheler's Phenomenology of Community." *Philosophy Today* 35 (1991): 161–74.

Valković, Mariano. *L'uomo, la donna e il matrimonio nella teologia di Matthias Joseph Scheeben*. Rome: Gregorian University Press, 1965.

Valsecchi, Ambrogio. *Controversy: The Birth Control Debate, 1958–1968*. Washington, DC: Corpus Publications, 1968.

Vanier, Jean. *Man and Woman He Made Them*. Toronto: Anglican Book Centre, 1985.

Villarejo Garaizar, Antonio. *El matrimonio y la familia en la "Familiaris Consortio."* Madrid: Ediciones Paulinas, 1984.

Waldstein, Michael Maria. "John Paul II and St. Thomas on Love and the Trinity." *Anthropotes* 18 (2002): 113–38, 269–86.

———. "Famiglia e comunione: La concezione cattolica del matrimonio." *Anthropotes* 19 (2003): 229–46.

———. "Il matrimonio nell'antropologia di Giovanni Paolo II." *Nuovo Areopago* 22 (2003): 132–44.

———. "John Paul II: A Thomist Rooted in St. John of the Cross." *Faith and Reason* 30 (2005): 195–218.

———. "The Common Good in St. Thomas and John Paul II." *Nova et Vetera* 3 (2005): 569–78.

———. "Introduction." In John Paul II, *Man and Woman He Created Them: A Theology of the Body*, trans. Michael Waldstein, 1–128. Boston: Pauline Books and Media, 2006.

———. "Johannine Foundations of the Church as the Family of God." In *The Way of Love: Reflections of Pope Benedict XVI's Encyclical Deus Caritas Est*, ed. Livio Melina and Carl A. Anderson, 250–65. San Francisco: Ignatius Press, 2006.

———. "La dignità della persona e il bene comune: La loro reciproca implicazione nella procreazione umana." In Pontifical Council for the Family, *Famiglia e procreazione umana: Commenti sul documento*, 125–50. Rome: Libreria Editrice Vaticana, 2007.

———. "Covenant and Union of Love in M. J. Scheeben's Theology of Marriage." *Letter and Spirit* 3 (2007): 139–52.

———. "Review of Marc Ouellet, *Divine Likeness: Toward a Trinitarian Anthropology of the Family*." *Nova et Vetera* 5 (2007): 931–35.

———. "Three Kinds of Personalism: Kant, Scheler and John Paul II." *Forum Teologiczne* 10 (2009): 151–71.

———. "Children as the Common Good of Marriage." *Nova et Vetera* 7 (2009): 697–709.

———. "Constitutive Relations: A Response to David L. Schindler." *Communio* 37 (2010): 495–518.

———. "The Gift of Self as Preamble of Faith and Trinitarian Mystery in John Paul II and Thomas Aquinas." *Doctor Communis* (2013): 331–36.

———. "Die Sprache des Körpers: Was sagt der menschliche Körper in der Liebe?" In *Liebe, Leib und Leidenschaft: Zur Theologie des Leibes von Johannes Paul II. Reflexionen und exemplarische Einblicke*, ed. Maria Groos, Teresa Loichen, and Manfred Gerwing, 63–94. Kisslegg: fe-Medienverlag, 2013.

———. "John Paul II / Karol Wojtyła." In *Key Theological Thinkers: From Modern to Post-Modern*, ed. Staale Johannes Kristiansen and Svein Rise, 291–300. Burlington, VT: Ashgate, 2013.

———. "The Argument about Contraception in the Theology of the Body." In *Why Humanae Vitae Is Still Right*, ed. Janet Smith, 111–26. San Francisco: Ignatius Press, 2018.

———. "A Thomistic Appreciation of John Paul II's *Theology of the Body*." In *San Tommaso, il matrimonio e la famiglia*, ed. Serge-Thomas Bonino and Guido Mazzotta, 59–70. Rome: Urbaniana University Press, 2019.

———. "Einführung zur Theologie des Leibes." In *Amor: Als Abbild Gottes schuf er ihn*, ed. Corbin Gams, 53–213. Jahrbuch zur Theologie des Leibes 2. Heiligenkreuz: Be&Be Verlag, 2020.

———. "Leitfaden für die Theologie des Leibes." In *Amor: Als Abbild Gottes schuf er ihn*, ed. Corbin Gams, 214–351. Jahrbuch zur Theologie des Leibes 2. Heiligenkreuz: Be&Be Verlag, 2020.

Walker, Adrian. "'Sown Psychic, Raised Spiritual': The Lived Body as the Organ of Theology." *Communio* 33 (2006): 203–15.

———. "The Original Best: The 'Coextensiveness' of Being and Love in Light of *Gaudium et Spes*, 22." *Communio* 39 (2012): 49–65.

———. "'What God Has Conjoined, Let No Man Put Asunder': A Meditation on Fruitfulness, Fidelity, and the Conjugal Embrace." *Communio* 41 (2014): 372–79.

Walsh, Vincent M. *Love and Responsibility, Pope John Paul II: A Simplified Version*. Wynnewood, PA: Key of David Publications, 2001.

Weigel, George. "The Soul of John Paul II." In *Occasional Papers*, vol. 3. *The Achievements of John Paul II*, 36–45. Oxford: Oxford University Catholic Chaplaincy, 2001.

*West, Christopher. *Theology of the Body Explained: A Commentary on John Paul II's Man and Woman He Created Them*. Revised ed. Boston: Pauline Books and Media, 2007.

———. *Heaven's Song: Sexual Love as It Was Meant to Be*. West Chester, PA: Ascension Press, 2008.

———. *At the Heart of the Gospel: Reclaiming the Body for the New Evangelization*. New York: Image, 2012.

———. *Fill These Hearts: God, Sex, and the Universal Longing*. New York: Image, 2013.

———. *Theology of the Body for Beginners: Rediscovering the Meaning of Life, Love, Sex, and Gender*. North Palm Beach, FL: Beacon Publishing, 2018.

———. *Our Bodies Tell God's Story*. Grand Rapids, MI: Brazos, 2020.

Wierzbicki, Alfred. "La barca interiore: Affinità spirituale del pensiero di Karol Wojtyla con il pensiero di San Giovanni della Croce." In *Karol Wojtyla: Metafisica della persona. Tutte le opere filosofiche e saggi integrativi*, ed. Giovanni Reale and Tadeusz Styczen, 3–20. Milan: Bompiani, 2003.

Wilk, Rafał Kazimierz. "Personalistic and Utilitarian View of Marriage According to Early Wojtyła." *Forum Philosophicum* 14 (2009): 145–58.

Wilkin, Vincent. *The Image of God in Sex*. New York: Sheed and Ward, 1954.

Williams, Thomas D. "Theology of the Body and *Humanae Vitae*." *Alpha Omega* 11 (2008): 365–86.

Windley-Daoust, Susan. *Theology of the Body, Extended: The Spiritual Signs of Birth, Impairment, and Dying*. Hobe Sound, FL: Lectio, 2014.

Woznicki, Andrew N. "On the Meaning of Marriage." In *The Dignity of Man as a Person: Essays on the Christian Humanism of His Holiness John Paul II*, ed. Andrew N. Woznicki, 29–46. San Francisco: Society of Christ, 1987.

Wrenn, Michael J., ed. *Pope John Paul II and the Family: The Text with a Theological and Catechetical Commentary with Discussion Questions on the Apostolic Exhortation of Pope John Paul II on the Role of the Christian Family in the Modern World* (*Familiaris Consortio*). Chicago: Franciscan Herald Press, 1983.

Wright, N. T. "From Genesis to Revelation: An Anglican Perspective." In *Not Just Good, but Beautiful: The Complementary Relationship between Man and Woman*, ed. Stevan Lopes and Helen Alvaré, 85–96. Walden, NY: Plough Publishing House, 2015.

Zeno, Katrina J. *The Body Reveals God*. Tempe, AZ: Women of the Third Millennium, 2008.

———. *Discovering the Feminine Genius: Every Woman's Journey*. Boston: Pauline Books and Media, 2010.

Zimmermann, Nigel. *Facing the Other: John Paul II, Levinas, and the Body*. Eugene, OR: Cascade Books, 2015.

Zoffoli, Enrico. *Ecumenismo ed umanesimo di Giovanni Paolo II: Assoluta ortodossia del Papa alla luce del tomismo*. Rome: Libreria Editrice Vaticana, 1995.

INDEX OF NAMES

INDEX OF SUBJECTS

main discussions set in bold italics
TOB references to the map in parentheses

JOHN PAUL II, *THEOLOGY OF THE BODY*, TABLE OF CONTENTS

PART ONE: THE WORDS OF CHRIST

Chapter 1. Christ Appeals to the Beginning

A. The Spousal Meaning of the Body

B. The Mystery of Original Innocence

Chapter 2. Christ Appeals to the Human Heart

Chapter 3. Christ Appeals to the Resurrection

PART TWO: THE SACRAMENT

Chapter 1. The Dimension of Covenant and of Grace